Praise for *The Ultimate Guide to America's B*

"Finally...one college book that does it all by providing relevant statistics in an easy-to-read format and helpful text to better understand the nuances of each university."

— **Dr. Robin Boren**
The College Doctor LLC
Former Director of Guidance
Dakota Ridge High School

"I was mesmerized by the attention to detail in this book! The descriptive nature of the book gave me the impression I was strolling across a campus in the middle of a typical day in the life of a college student. I loved the straightforward nature of the book and believe it will become a classic amidst the host of material dedicated to the college selection process."

— **John Beischel**
College/Career Counselor and Department Chair
Princeton High School

"Choosing the right college can be a daunting task. Academics, student life, and financial considerations have an impact on the decision making process. This comprehensive guide will be a valuable tool for students and parents."

— **Christine Bland**
Gifted Resource Teacher
West Chester East High School

"The most honest guide to colleges that I have come across. Not only does this book present the positive aspects of each school, it also discusses potential drawbacks. Throughout the guide, you hear from various students on the campuses who maintain the same degree of honesty. You really get a feel for what it may be like to walk onto each campus."

— **Peggy Espada**
Director
Wilkes University Upward Bound

"If you are exploring colleges, *The Ultimate Guide to America's Best Colleges* should be your first purchase! Up-to-date information both positive and negative that you may not find elsewhere."

— **Linda Kimmel**
College/Career Specialist and AP and California Partnership Academies Coordinator
Irvington High School

"In an age where a college education is a major commitment of family resources including money, time, and emotion, and high school juniors and seniors are inundated with information, this book should be a 'must-read!' The details and insights provided are so timely and unique that they're not found in other guides and students may not even think to ask about them!"

— **Sue Beattie**
College & Career Center
Rush-Henrietta Sr. High School

"The layout of this book and the information included sets it apart from many of the college guides on the market. Students can quickly look at the highlights listed for each college and decide if they want to read more about the school.

"The detailed description of each school is well written, easy to read and includes information that other books don't have. I love the You May Not Know sections because they bring to life some of the history and/or traditions of the schools, creating a more personal connection for the reader. In addition, the information listed in financial aid and scholarships is invaluable because it identifies various scholarships and aid available to families.

"I will definitely use this book with my college bound students and their families and recommend it to anyone who's looking for a must have college book."

— **Chris Ward**
School Counselor
Lake Park High School

Praise for *The Ultimate Guide to America's Best Colleges*

"Finally, a book that has it all! Students need to see the hard data about colleges but will really get invested in the selection process when they read about the uniqueness of the institution. *The Ultimate Guide to America's Best Colleges* brings both perspectives to the reader and much more. A godsend for savvy students."

— Lana Klene
Counselor
Lawrence North High School

"*The Ultimate Guide to America's Best Colleges* is incredibly detailed, and yet the important information about the college statistics are concise and to the point. Potential college applicants will find step-by-step information on the process of understanding the features of a school and the questions to ask to narrow down the choices."

— Holly Craw
Phoenix Homeschooling Examiner
Homeschool Consultant

"*The Ultimate Guide to America's Best Colleges* has unique features to consider. For the reader looking for a quick summary, the sidebars in the college profiles contain distinctive information, such as the percentages of classes of various sizes instead of just the average and information about wait lists. When it's time to read in detail, each profile is written for students in clear, friendly language. If you can only afford one book, this is the one!"

— Lynda McGee
College Counselor
Downtown Magnets High School

"There are many guidebooks that give facts and figures but do little to distinguish between the character of various schools. This book resonates with my students because it paints a picture for them as if they were there. It serves as a quick reference when I am working with my students. In particular, sections like Distinguished Alumni, Graduate School and Employment Rates, and the Merit Based Aid provide quick talking points I can use when trying to convince a student to explore a school that is new to them. It has become a part of my counseling tool kit."

— Tricia Bryan
College Counselor
John Marshall High School

"*The Ultimate Guide to America's Best Colleges* provides a balanced approach to learning about various colleges and universities across the country. It not only supplies useful data and statistics, it gives the reader a sense of being right there on the campus learning firsthand about the individuality of each institution, how current students perceive their school, what opportunities that they can take advantage of over their four years, and how these experiences would prepare students for their future endeavors."

— Dr. Mary O'Reilly, NCC, NCSC
College Counselor
Josephinum Academy

"An essential must have for any student considering a post-secondary education. The guide is written in a format that is easy to read and understand, while focusing on the many points that professionals like myself try to emphasize to my students and their parents."

— Marcia Duffy
Counselor
Bishop Timon - St. Jude High School

THE ULTIMATE GUIDE TO

America's Best Colleges

2015

DETAILED PROFILES on academics, student life, campus vibe, athletics, admissions, scholarships, and financial aid

GEN AND KELLY TANABE

AUTHORS OF *THE ULTIMATE SCHOLARSHIP BOOK*

The Ultimate Guide to America's Best Colleges 2015
By Gen and Kelly Tanabe

Published by SuperCollege, LLC
2713 Newlands Avenue
Belmont, CA 94002
www.supercollege.com

Credits: Cover design TLC Graphics, www.TLCGraphics.com. Design: Monica Thomas. Cover photo © istockphoto.com/Uschools University Images. Author photo by Alvin Gee, www.alvingee.com.

Directory Data is copyrighted material which is reproduced in this publication by permission of Wintergreen Orchard House, a division of Alloy Education. Copyright © 2014 by Wintergreen Orchard House. All rights reserved.

Trademarks: All brand names, product names and services used in this book are trademarks, registered trademarks or tradenames of their respective holders. SuperCollege is not associated with any college, university, product or vendor.

Disclaimers: The author and publisher have used their best efforts in preparing this book. It is intended to provide helpful and informative material on the subject matter. Some narratives and names have been modified for illustrative purposes. SuperCollege and the author make no representations or warranties with respect to the accuracy or completeness of the contents of the book and specifically disclaim any implied warranties or merchantability or fitness for a particular purpose. There are no warranties which extend beyond the descriptions contained in this paragraph. The accuracy and completeness of the information provided herein and the opinions stated herein are not guaranteed or warranted to produce any particular results. SuperCollege and the author specifically disclaim any responsibility for any liability, loss or risk, personal or otherwise, which is incurred as a consequence, directly or indirectly, of the use and application of any of the contents of this book.

ISBN-13: 978-1-61760-044-9

Manufactured in the United States of America
10 9 8 7 6 5 4 3 2 1

Please send comments and corrections to:
The Ultimate Guide to America's Best Colleges
2713 Newlands Avenue
Belmont, CA 94002
Email: ugabc@supercollege.com

CONTENTS

SECTION ONE
INTRODUCTION   1

   CHAPTER ONE: The Most Honest Guide to Helping
You Choose the Right College   3

   CHAPTER TWO: How This Book Came to Be   5

   CHAPTER THREE: About the Profiles and Data   7

SECTION TWO
HOW TO GUIDES   13

   CHAPTER FOUR: How to Pick the Perfect College   15

   CHAPTER FIVE: 18 Tips and Tricks to Getting into College   21

   CHAPTER SIX: Five Steps to Getting the Most Financial
Aid You Deserve   25

SECTION THREE
THE RANKINGS   31

   Colleges with Popular Programs in Specific Majors   32

   The Top 100 Best College Values   38

   Public Colleges by Price   39

   Private Colleges by Price   40

SECTION FOUR
COLLEGES PROFILES   43

SECTION FIVE
INDEXES   974

   Colleges by Name   974

   Colleges by Location   979

SECTION SIX
WORKSHEETS   982

ACKNOWLEDGMENTS

This book would not have been possible without the contributions of so many dedicated people. We would like to express our sincere thanks for their writing and researching assistance to Colin Adamo, Maya Amoils, Nikki Anderson, Andrea Ayala, Emily Chapman, Caroline Chen, Morgan Duffy, Chanda Feldman, Becky Fradkin, Cora Frazier, Mary Glen Fredrick, Emma Hantoot, Laura Horton, Jaslyn Law, Laura Lilly, Aida Luu, Jessica Moore, Christa Morris, Devin Nambiar, Jeff Norman, Tierney O'Rourke, Blake Parkinson, Katy Peaslee, Georgia Schaubroeck, Erin Schwabe-Fry, Quincy Tanner, Gregory Yee and Mercedes Zapata.

We would also like to specially thank Chenxing Han, Alice Hu, and Elizabeth Soltan for their tireless writing and researching contributions.

SECTION ONE
INTRODUCTION

CHAPTER ONE

THE MOST HONEST GUIDE TO HELPING YOU CHOOSE THE RIGHT COLLEGE

If you're looking for honest insights instead of college marketing speak... If you need more than superficial sound bites or raw numbers and stats... If you want to learn more about schools you know and discover new ones... If you want to know how to get into and pay for the colleges you find...

This is the college guide for you.

Our college guide gives you detailed profiles of 300 top colleges—plus essential statistics and admissions information—that will help you select and get into the school that is right for you. We believe it is critical to provide full-length, detailed essays on each college that give the most complete profile of what it's really like at the school. Our essays include information from actual students and graduates as well as experts in the field such as college and career counselors. And since statistics also matter, we've selected the most important data points so you can quickly compare colleges.

What's Inside

- In-depth coverage of the colleges' academics, student life, campus vibe, athletics, admissions, scholarships, and financial aid

- Insider views and insights into what makes each college unique, plus honest appraisals of each college's strengths and weaknesses

- Vital information on the admissions and financial aid process for each college

- Strategies to help you determine your best college match

- The top 18 tips and tricks to get into your dream college

- The strongest majors for each college

- Descriptions of special academic opportunities, study-abroad programs, and career services

- Admissions tips, deadlines, requirements, and the importance of each criteria in each college's admissions decision

- Specific details on financial aid and merit-based scholarship programs and the five steps to getting the most financial aid

- Indexed rankings of colleges by majors and cost

- Exclusive rankings of the 100 Best College Values

In short, we feel that this is the only guide you'll need to discover, evaluate, and ultimately choose the best college for you.

CHAPTER TWO

HOW THIS BOOK CAME TO BE

We have spent the past 11 years researching and writing books (13 so far) on college admissions and financial aid. We've travelled across the country and spoken at more than 1,000 high schools to tell students how to get into college. During this time, we realized there was something missing in college guides. When students or parents asked us how to learn more about a college, we could never recommend just one source. There were books that contained a lot of statistical information on schools but were weak with descriptive profiles. There were books that assembled quotes from students but these always seemed too superficial and never really revealed what a school was really like. Then there was a motley collection of websites that posted a ton of user reviews, but it was almost too much and you never knew what hidden agenda the reviewer might have had. What students really needed was a guide that provided both stats and data and critical essays that took into account actual student experiences and reviews but served as an editorial filter. That's when the idea for *The Ultimate Guide to America's Best Colleges* was born.

We began to gather data and information during our national speaking tours since this allowed us to visit colleges as well as speak to the local high school counselors. After getting input from these counselors, college representatives, students, and parents and conducting additional research, we developed the list of 300 colleges. We based our decision on factors such as academic reputation, special academic programs, richness of student life, and financial aid provided to students. We sought diverse geographic locations and a mix of public and private institutions.

We realize that we are inviting some controversy by selecting and naming these 300 colleges as America's Best Colleges. But choosing a college has always been a personal and subjective practice. There is no objective standard for what makes a great school. There never has been. So we accept (even embrace) our subjectivity and fully recognize that we are making editorial choices. But with few exceptions, we think you'll agree with our choices.

Once we had our list, the hard work began. In addition to our own research, we conducted an exhaustive national survey of students. We felt it was

5

absolutely necessary to include input from students to give the real story on each college. The students weren't afraid to let us know what they liked—and didn't like—about their schools. One of the most difficult tasks was distilling all of this information—data, insights on the schools, and feedback from students and experts—into a unified narrative that exposed as much as possible the true nature and atmosphere of each unique college.

CHAPTER THREE

ABOUT THE PROFILES & DATA

The heart of this book is the college profiles. Each profile is divided into topical sections designed to help you evaluate the pros and cons of the school and get a feel for what it is like to be on campus. Sidebars feature the crucial data and stats for each college making it quick to compare and contrast the schools. What follows is a description of how each profile is organized and what you can expect to learn.

Overview

Each profile starts with highlights of the key differentiating factors about the college. It's what makes the college special or unique. It is meant to be a high-level overview of the college's major attributes, one of which is its location and a description of the campus itself. It's amazing how important the campus' physical environment is in the ultimate happiness that students feel.

Academics

One of the most important factors in selecting a college is its academic offerings. We've spent some time trying to capture the major strengths of the school's educational choices. These often include:

General education requirements. Your first year in college will be largely influenced by these requirements. In fact, some students report that the hardest academic year was their first, due to the required courses they needed to take. The colleges vary in their requirements with some only having a handful and others having more than a dozen required classes.

Majors offered and strong majors. In selecting a college, it's important to know what your options for study will be. While most students don't know which specific major they will choose (and often change within their college career), you should have a general idea of what areas you like or don't like. Science or humanities. Art or writing, for example. The colleges vary from having more than 300 majors to just one. If you know what you want to major in, it's crucial to know which colleges are strong in that subject.

Academic opportunities. Colleges offer more than classroom instruction. There are special programs that range from research opportunities to honors programs. Some have museums with nationally renowned collections. Others offer programs in spying and national security; while still others provide seed money to start a business and become an entrepreneur.

Study abroad. Colleges may offer a handful of in-house programs or even require that every student participate in a funded program abroad. These programs range from a couple of weeks to an entire year and may be led by faculty, in partnership with other colleges, or by affiliate programs. If you want to study in a foreign country—especially if you have a country of choice—then you need to pay attention to your college's offerings.

Career/internships/alumni relations. While a college education accomplishes many things, a key benefit should be how well it prepares you for a future career or graduate school. Some colleges provide one major career fair a year while others provide more than a dozen, including specialized ones such as for government, science, or art-related fields. The schools also vary in their availability of internships. Those located in major cities often offer opportunities to work at multiple Fortune 500 companies while those in state capitals may offer political internships. Alumni relations may be pivotal for a college, providing undergraduates with mentors and a source of career and graduate school advice, or they may be less significant. Some schools are even known as "feeder" schools for specific career fields and/or graduate programs.

Student Life

The truth is that you will spend a lot more time in college outside the classroom than in it. So all the other aspects from housing to socializing are extremely important to your overall success and happiness.

Student organizations. Colleges typically have between 50 and 350 student organizations ranging from service to the arts to cultural to political interests. But there are also groups that stand out, such as secret societies and knitting clubs that give you a clue to the vibe of the campus.

Events. Some colleges have small events every week while others host blowout celebrations once or twice a year. Knowing which special events are important to a campus community will help you understand if the environment is a fit for you.

Greek organizations. Greek organizations vary in their prevalence on campus. Some colleges are the self-proclaimed epitomes of the movie *Animal House* while others have organizations centered on public service. Some don't have Greek organizations at all.

Athletics. At some colleges, sports are the main source of school spirit and the central activity around which weekends revolve. At others, it is mostly enjoyed by the athletes themselves. Colleges with notable club or intramural programs or outdoor recreational opportunities are noted.

Off-campus activities. The surrounding areas of colleges can be hotspots with numerous offerings for students or can be pretty much the doldrums.

Housing. Housing options are described with details that include amenities, dorm conditions, and possible overcrowding as well as any special housing options.

Student Body

The ethnic makeup and geographic background of the student body is outlined to indicate how diverse the student body is. In addition, student input describes the political, religious, and other attitudes that are common. The LGBT atmosphere and resources are also detailed.

You May Not Know

These are fun, lesser known facts about the college. While these are entertaining, they often indicate the unique personality of the college.

Distinguished Alumni

Knowing some of the graduates of the college points to certain academic strengths that the college may have.

Admissions and Financial Aid

In this section we have tips for admissions. For example, does not having an interview harm your chances, or what are the admissions officers looking for in candidates? There is helpful information about the financial aid programs available as well. There are specific merit-scholarship programs described for each college that should help you determine how you will pay for your education.

The College Data

How do you like your data? We serve the most important and useful data points and stats that will help you understand the college and compare it to other choices. The following is a breakdown of the numbers that we give for each school.

Students

- Total enrollment: The total number of full-time and part-time graduate and undergraduate students.

- Undergrads: The total number of full-time and part-time undergraduate students.

- Freshmen: The number of freshmen students.

- Part-time students: The percentage of students who attend part-time.

- From out-of-state: The percentage of students whose permanent residences are outside the state where the college is located.

- From public schools: The percentage of students who graduated from public high schools.

- Male/Female: The percentage of males and females.

- Live on campus: The percentage of students who live on campus or in college-affiliated housing.

- In fraternities/In sororities: The percentage of students who participate in fraternities/sororities.

- Off-campus employment rating: A rating of the opportunities for working off campus.

- Ethnic breakdowns: Percentages of students by ethnic group as self-reported.

Academics

- Calendar: Academic calendar used such as semester or quarter. The term "4-1-4" means that there is a four-month period, a one-month period, and then a four-month period.

- Student/faculty ratio: The ratio of the number of students to the number of faculty members.

- Class sizes: The percentage of classes by size.

- Returning freshmen: The percentage of freshmen who return for their sophomore years.

- Six-year graduation rate: The percentage of students who graduate from the college within six years.

- Graduates who immediately enter careers related to the majors: The percentage of students who enter the workforce who are employed in jobs related to their majors within 12 months of graduating.

- Graduates who immediately go to graduate school: The percentage of students who attend graduate school within 12 months of graduating.

Most Popular Majors

- The three majors with the most number of students as identified by the college.

Admissions

- Applicants: The number of students who applied to the college during the most recent application period.

- Accepted: The number of students accepted by the college.

- Acceptance rate: The percentage of students accepted.

- Placed on wait list: The number of students placed on the wait list.

- Enrolled from wait list: The number of students from the wait list that eventually enrolled at the college.

- Average GPA: The average GPA of students accepted to the college using a 4.0 scale.

- ACT range: The middle 50 percent of ACT scores of students accepted.

- SAT Math range: The middle 50 percent of scores on the Math section of the SAT of students accepted.

- SAT Reading range: The middle 50 percent of scores on the Reading section of the SAT of students accepted.

- SAT Writing range: The middle 50 percent of scores on the Writing section of the SAT of students accepted.

- Top 10% of class: The percentage of students who graduated in the top 10 percent of their high school classes.

- Top 25% of class: The percentage of students who graduated in the top 25 percent of their high school classes.

- Top 50% of class: The percentage of students who graduated in the top 50 percent of their high school classes.

Note that for the average GPA, test score ranges, and percentages in high school graduating classes, these are meant to provide insight into the selectivity of the colleges. If your grades, test scores, or class ranking are below the numbers stated, this does not mean that you shouldn't apply to the college. Remember that 25 percent of students accepted have scores below the test score ranges and that most colleges consider factors other than these three criteria.

Admissions Criteria

- Academic criteria: These show the level of importance of the academic criteria that the colleges use in their admissions decisions:

  ☆ = Academic criterion is considered.
  ☆ ☆ = Important academic criterion.
  ☆ ☆ ☆ = Very important academic criterion.

- Non-academic criteria considered: The other criteria that the colleges use in their admissions decisions.

Deadlines

- Early Action: Deadline for early action admissions.

- Early Decision: Deadline for early decision admissions.

- Regular Action: Deadline for regular admissions. Rolling admissions means that the college accepts students on a first-come, first-served basis. The priority deadline is typically the deadline to submit your admissions application if you want to be considered for merit-based scholarships, priority housing, or priority admission. The final deadline is the last date the application may be submitted.

Note that all deadlines are typically determined by postmarks for paper applications and date submitted for online applications.

- Notification of admission by: The last date in which the college notifies applicants of its decision.

- Common Application: Whether the Common Application, a single application used to apply to many colleges, is accepted. For more details, please visit www.commonapp.org.

Financial Aid

- In-state tuition: Tuition price for students who are residents of the state in which the college is located.

- Out-of-state tuition: Tuition price for students who are not residents of the state.

- Room: Price of on-campus housing as reported by the college.

- Board: Price of campus meal program.

- Books: Average price of textbooks.

Note that all prices are annual unless otherwise noted.

- Freshmen receiving need-based aid: Percentage of first-year students who are awarded need-based financial aid such as student loans, work-study, and grants.

- Undergrads rec. need-based aid: Percentage of all undergraduate students who are awarded need-based financial aid.

- Avg. % of need met by financial aid: Average percentage of a family's demonstrated financial need that is met by financial aid offered by the college.

- Avg. aid package (freshmen): Average amount of financial aid awarded to first-year students.

- Avg. aid package (undergrads): Average amount of financial aid awarded to undergraduate students.

- Freshmen receiving merit-based aid: Percentage of first-year students who receive merit-based aid such as scholarships.

- Undergrads rec. merit-based aid: Percentage of undergraduate students who receive merit-based aid.

- Avg. debt upon graduation: Average amount of debt per student upon graduation.

SECTION TWO
HOW TO GUIDES

CHAPTER FOUR

HOW TO PICK THE PERFECT COLLEGE

We've heard almost every reason imaginable for why a student would pick a college. For example, we know one student who decided to apply to a college because during the campus tour he noticed that there was a Krispy Kreme donut shop right in the center of campus. We even know of another student who wanted to get so far away from home that she took out a compass and a map and drew a 400 mile circle around her house. She vowed never to apply to a college within that circle. Depending on your personal priorities, these may or may not be good reasons to pick a college. But since we all have our own personal preferences, it's important to remember that the same factors that make one school a student's dream college may make it a nightmare choice for you. Following are some of the top tips for picking the right college.

Researching the Colleges

College brochures. Besides this book, one of the first places to look for more information about a college is in those beautiful full-color brochures that come in the mail. These brochures are filled with lots of useful information, but you must remember that they are biased and will tout only the positive aspects of the school. Always view the college's brochure with a healthy dose of caution.

College fairs. Don't just settle for pictures and printed words. Go to college fairs and speak with the college representatives. For a schedule of national fairs, visit the website of the National Association for College Admission Counseling (www.nacacnet.org). When you go, don't be shy about asking the representatives all of your questions about the college—that's why they are there. Rather than trying to meet with every college, focus on a handful with which to spend quality time. Ask for the representatives' business cards, and follow up with email reiterating your interest and sharing more information about yourself.

Campus visits. The single best way to learn about colleges is to visit, but don't just settle for the official tour. Take time to do your own investigation by walking the campus, sitting in a class, eating in the cafeteria, and talking with some students who are not tour guides. If you can, arrange ahead of time to meet with an admissions officer and contact the department of your major. The best time to visit is when school is in session. It's hard to get a feel for a college when it's empty! Also, if you don't have the budget to travel to all the schools or the more distant ones, visit those closest to you—even if you aren't interested in applying. The more campuses you visit, including those that are not on your list, the better idea you'll have for what you really want in your dream college.

College rep visits. When college reps visit your high school, attend the meetings. It's worth giving up your lunch time for an opportunity to get more in-depth information about the college and to form a more personal connection with the reps. Be sure to ask questions, and speak with the reps one-on-one afterward. Again, ask for business cards, and follow up. The relationships that you build with the reps are taken into account by some colleges when they make their admissions decisions.

College students. Speak to recent graduates of your high school and ask them what they think of their school. If the school is close to you, visit the campus, take a tour, and ask to be put in touch with a current student who can answer your questions. If you call the office of admissions they might be able to put you in touch with a "student ambassador"—a current student who can answer your questions by phone or email.

Counselors and teachers. There's help close to home too. Your teachers and school counselors have helped thousands of students get into college and can share what they've learned over the years. If you haven't already, make an appointment to meet with your counselor.

Websites. Visit colleges' websites to learn about their admissions and financial aid policies, academic offerings, student life, and campus surroundings. To get a preview of student life, take a look at the websites that tell about the campus newspaper, student organizations, and even the individual homepages of students. These student sections are where you'll find the true portrait of the college beyond the marketing hype.

Besides researching the colleges, it's important to make an evaluation of yourself, too. The best way to do this is to ask questions about what you want from your education.

What Are Your Academic Goals?

Do you want to be trained for a specific line of work or do you want a more general liberal arts education? A pre-professional education prepares you for a specific job and includes areas such as engineering and premed. Some schools like MIT have very strong programs for those interested in the sciences but might not be right for someone interested in literature. A liberal arts education, on the other hand, aims to equip you with general knowledge and reasoning skills suitable for many jobs.

What might you major in? Most universities are stronger in some areas and weaker in others. While it may be too early for you to know whether you want to major in English or history, check out how strong the programs and professors are in the various fields you are considering. Investigate the courses offered and required, how many students are majoring in your area(s) of interest, the professors' areas of research, whether you need to apply to enter the major, and whether a thesis is required. In addition to speaking with a professor or administrator in the department, ask to speak with a student currently in the major.

How many years does it take to graduate? Most schools graduate their students in four years, but some fields of study may take longer. Even the same majors—but in different schools—have varying requirements for the number and difficulty level of courses. Laboratory work, research, senior theses, tutorials, or seminars may be requirements for your field. All of this can affect how long it takes to finish.

Do you prefer a small college or large university setting? Most students find smaller classes that allow more active participation to be more rewarding than large, impersonal lectures. But larger institutions also have advantages, such as more resources and often (but not always) more acclaimed faculty.

What do you plan to do with your degree after graduating? Whether you want to go directly to graduate school or work for a non-profit organization after graduation affects what you look for in a college. Investigate what recent students have done post-graduation, and learn about what those who work in your future career studied in college.

Do You Want to Attend Party Central?

Do you want to have three Greek letters emblazoned on your chest everywhere you go? Does the school have a Greek system? Some students are inclined to join a fraternity or sorority, while others feel that their existence on campus is overbearing for those who choose not to go Greek.

Does the school offer extracurricular activities that you would enjoy? If you join the Hasty Pudding Club at Harvard, you'll have the chance to cross-dress and sing on stage at its famous annual performance. It's important that your future college offers activities you'd enjoy.

What Type of Digs Do You Want?

Do most students live on campus or commute? Whether students spend most of their lives on campus or off makes a big difference in the social atmosphere of the college.

Can you live with strangers? Can you bathe near strangers? If you lived in the dorm, would you have roommates? How modern or ancient are the dorms? Does each room have its own bathroom or do you use a shared facility? These are questions you'll want to explore.

What Kind of Campus Environment Do You Want?

What size student body fits you? Some students like the intimate feeling of a small school where they know the names of all their classmates, while others prefer the diversity of a large student body.

Is the campus in the inner city, countryside, or somewhere in between? Is it a college town where the college is the social center of the city? Is it in the middle of nowhere, where you have to drive 40 miles just to see a movie? If locality matters to you, then you'll want those facts to consider.

What is the weather like? If you've never endured a minus-20 degree winter or a 90 percent humidity summer, you might want to think twice about how the weather will affect your life (e.g., being able to sunbathe between classes vs. literally not seeing the sun for months at a time).

How far is the college from home? Do you want to remain geographically close to your family and friends, or do you want to venture into the world of collegedom solo? What are the chances of your parents dropping in for a surprise visit? Is this a good thing? (It can be if they are willing to do your laundry!)

Is the school known for attracting students of a particular political view? Most schools have a surprisingly even balance of conservative and liberal students. However a few have a noticeable imbalance. While you should keep this in mind, don't let it be an overriding factor since you will always find others who share (and oppose) your views.

Now What?

You will not be able to find answers to all these questions, but asking them should help you narrow down your list of prospective colleges. Also, some of these questions may not be important to you and recognizing that is also helpful in your college search.

Your goal when choosing colleges is to find schools that offer what is important to you. The only way to do this is to first ask yourself questions like those posed above and then do some detective work to find schools that match your needs. Refer to the appendices for a College Search Worksheet that will help you summarize your research on the colleges.

Decide if you want to apply Early Action or Early Decision

There are three types of early application. With all three you apply early and receive a decision early.

- **Early Action:** You are not bound to attend the college.

- **Restrictive Early Action:** While you are not bound to attend the college, you are often not allowed to apply to another college Early Action or Early Decision. When you are restricted from applying to another college early, this is known as "Single Choice Early Action."

- **Early Decision:** You are bound to attend the college.

There are three major advantages to applying for Early Action or Early Decision: 1) you demonstrate to the college that it is your top choice; 2) you will find out sooner if you are accepted and thus may not have to apply elsewhere; and most importantly, 3) many colleges have higher acceptance rates for Early Action or Decision applicants than for regular admissions applicants. Keep in mind, however, that the applicant pool for Early Action or Decision is usually very competitive.

The disadvantages are that: 1) for Early Decision, you are committed to attending that school if you are accepted and must withdraw your applications to all other schools (for Early Action, you don't have to make this commitment); and 2) you will not be able to compare financial aid packages since you have to make your decision early. If you apply during the regular action cycle, you can compare financial aid from different colleges. Since this may differ significantly, it could influence your final decision in selecting which college to attend.

Don't Worry About Money (Yet)

Until now, we have not discussed perhaps the biggest factor in determining where you will go to college—money. Yes, it is true that college costs a bundle, with private colleges being especially guilty of exorbitant prices. It is not uncommon for parents to take out a second mortgage on their homes or for students to have loans for years after they graduate. And unfortunately, costs are only rising.

However, at this point, do not let costs dictate your goals. Even if money is tight, don't make it your primary concern just yet. (If you have trouble paying for the application fee, ask your counselor about a fee waiver.) The reason that money should not be an issue now is that while tuition is expensive, there is also a ton of financial aid available. Just last year over $238 billion in financial aid was given to students to help them pay for college. The real question is not how much a college costs, but how much you'll have to pay out of pocket after taking into account scholarships and financial aid.

Once you get accepted, you can work with the college to put together a financial aid package that will make the school affordable for you. This is why you need to wait until you are accepted by the college and they determine what kind of financial aid package they can offer before making cost a limiting factor. Be sure to check out Chapter Six, Five Steps to Getting the Most Financial Aid You Deserve, to see what kind of support is available and how you can maximize your aid package.

Your college education is one of the most important investments in your future, and you need to know all of the information that pertains to it before making the right decision.

CHAPTER FIVE

18 TIPS AND TRICKS TO GETTING INTO COLLEGE

Each year more than three million students apply to college. Given this large number, you might be tempted to throw up your hands and resign yourself to the fact that there is nothing that you can do to make your application stand out from this awesome pile. While it is true that a record number of students will apply to college, it is a huge mistake to assume that there isn't anything you can do to gain an advantage when it comes to getting into college. With a little bit of preparation and some extra effort, you can create an application that highlights your strengths, makes a strong impression on the college admissions officers, and results in a mailbox filled with sought-after acceptance letters.

1. Think before you write. Before you open an application, take the time to do a little self-reflection. What strengths do you want to convey to the college? What are your goals for the future? How will this college help you meet these goals? This kind of self-reflection will help guide you in choosing what information you provide to the college, how you do so, and how much you emphasize each of your accomplishments. A lot of students simply dive into filling out the application and skip this important step. What typically happens to these students is they waste a lot of time writing about things that aren't important to them or that don't fully explain who they are to the colleges.

2. Academics are king. Your parents may not be right about whom you should date or what time your curfew should be, but they are right about one thing: you need to hit the books. When evaluating your application, an important question that college admissions officers ask is this: Can you handle the academic coursework? You can be the most brilliant musician, talented artist, or philanthropic volunteer, but if you can't handle college-level academics, you won't be admitted. Challenge yourself with as many Advanced Placement, honors, or International Baccalaureate classes as you can.

3. Follow your passions. Because colleges want the type of students that are involved in athletics, the arts, and other activities on campus, they consider what you do outside the classroom as extremely important. Some students think that there is a secret formula for activities that they should participate in that will be impressive to colleges. The real secret is that you should do what you enjoy. You will dedicate yourself to (and excel in) those activities that you like. Don't participate in athletics if you are inept with balls and bats. Don't volunteer at a homeless shelter if you really don't want to. Find something that you do care about, and dedicate yourself to it. Admissions officers can detect when you do something just to impress them. They really want to see that you do what you are passionate about.

4. Make a cheat sheet. With anywhere from six to 12 applications to complete, you may feel overwhelmed by the work ahead of you. It will help if you make a cheat sheet or resume of your accomplishments, awards or honors, work experience, volunteer work, and summer activities. This is information for which nearly all colleges ask. If you have a handy list you can refer to, it will save time and will help you make sure not to miss anything or leave something out.

5. Get feedback from others on the admissions essay. Students often think that they just need to pound out a few hundred words for the essay and hit submit to send it off to the college. The truth is that you need time to develop your essay. And even more importantly, you need feedback. Useful feedback can come from teachers, friends and, yes, even your parents. Hearing how other people respond to your essays is the only way you will know if what you are trying to say is actually being communicated to the reader. It will also give you invaluable information about which parts of the essay are working and which need to be improved. It also doesn't hurt to have someone point out any careless spelling or grammatical errors.

6. Don't be afraid to be revealing. In other words, as you are writing the essay, convey something about who you are to the college. What makes you unique? What special strengths do you have to offer the college? In the essay, countless students recount the information that is easily found in their applications or write about shallow topics that don't reveal who they are or how they feel. It's not just recommended to get personal in the essay, it's required.

7. Razzle, dazzle, and captivate your audience. When you begin writing, keep in mind that you need to write a truly memorable essay. To do this, you need to draw the admissions officers into your essay with a quick, catchy, and creative introduction. You want to pique their curiosity by posing questions they will want the answers to and dilemmas they too have faced. Most important, you want the admissions officers to be able to relate to your essay (not necessarily to the actual events but to the feelings involved).

8. How you write is just as important as what you write. You should constantly ask yourself if you would be interested in your essay if you were the reader. Imagine yourself as an admissions officer. Read the first few paragraphs and ask yourself what makes you want to finish it? Do not just rely on your own judgment. Seek the opinions of others. If your essay does not captivate the reader, you will need to rework it.

9. Use original language. Try to describe people, places, and events in a unique—but not awkward—style. Appeal to the different senses. What can the reader see from your essay? Hear? Smell? By adding rich detail, you can often turn an ordinary topic into a one-of-a-kind masterpiece. The more you can bring the reader into your essay by using description, the better. Try to think of language as a toy, and play with it. Just make sure that if you use unfamiliar words, you use them in the right way. It is better to use ordinary language correctly than to use roller coaster-exciting language incorrectly.

10. Ask teachers early for recommendations to avoid the rush. Teachers typically have anywhere from 20 to more than 50 requests to write recommendations each year. You can get a jump on your classmates and perhaps receive greater attention from your teachers if you ask early. Remember that "early" means several weeks or even a couple of months before the recommendations are due.

11. Help teachers write the recommendations. While you may have a mental catalogue of every award that you have won, you can't expect your teachers will have the same extensive knowledge. Help jog their memories and receive better evaluations by providing a cover letter and resume. The cover letter should explain which recommendations you need, the deadlines, and any relevant information that the teacher may use to write the recommendation. For example, if you did well on a specific class project, you can mention this in the cover letter. The resume should include a brief description of some of your most important accomplishments.

12. Practice, practice, practice for interviews. If you were performing a piano concert, you would never go on stage without practicing. In a similar way, you should not go to a college interview without first rehearsing. Practice answering the most common questions: Why do you want to attend our college? What do you plan to study and why? What do you plan to do after graduating? What meaningful academic experience have you had? What do you do outside class? By practicing interviewing, you will be less nervous and better equipped when it comes time for the real thing.

13. Go beyond the brochures. In essays and interviews, colleges commonly ask students why they want to attend the school to get a sense of how well they would fit in. Most students just repeat information directly from the school's brochures or websites. This is a big mistake. To show that you have a better understanding of what the school has to offer and how it fits what you are looking for, go a step further. If you can, do some additional research by speaking with students, calling the department you wish to enter, or visiting the campus. Mention something you have learned that is not described on the college's website or in the brochures. Then, explain how it relates to your goals.

14. Time test-taking. Most colleges require that you take the SAT or ACT Test and three SAT Subject Tests. It is also highly recommended that you take some Advanced Placement (AP) tests as well.

The general rule for when you should take the ACT or SAT is once or twice during the spring of your junior year. If you are not satisfied with your scores, test again in the fall of your senior year.

For the SAT Subject Tests, ideally you should take the subject tests soon after you have completed courses covering the subject. The exception is when you are planning to take another course in the same subject area. If you are, you may want to take the test once, take the next course, and take the test again.

If you plan to take any of the exams again in the fall of your senior year, you should spend the summer studying. Try to take the exams as early in the fall as you can because later in the fall you will be busy completing your actual applications and will not want to have to worry about taking more tests.

Here is a quick summary of when to take the tests:

PSAT: Definitely your junior year and maybe even earlier.

SAT Test: Spring of junior year and fall of senior year.

ACT Test: Spring of junior year and fall of senior year.

SAT Subject Tests: As soon as possible after you have taken the related courses, unless you will take a more advanced related course.

APs: As soon as possible after you have taken the related courses.

Remember that if you plan to apply Early Action or Early Decision, you will need to take your exams as early as possible.

15. Make personal connections. The old saying, "It's not what you know but who you know," rings true for college admissions. However, don't think that you have to be from a well known politician's family, have a cousin who's a philanthropist, or parents that are alumni donors to make the kinds of connections that you need. Try to start a personal relationship with someone at the college. You can do this when you meet a representative who visits the school, when you visit the college, or by contacting the admissions office. You should request additional information and ask questions. Many colleges keep records of these kinds of contacts. If they are deciding between a student who has not made any personal contact and one who has attended an information night, they will choose the student that has shown greater interest.

16. Assume everyone is important. In other words, many students don't think much of meeting a college representative at a college fair or at an informational meeting at school. The truth is that oftentimes these college representatives are the ones who will review your application. It helps to make a good impression on them. You can do this by asking lots of questions and by spending time to speak about why you want to attend the school and telling what your interests are. It's better to assume that everyone you meet or speak with during the admissions process can be influential.

17. Look at the whole enchilada. As you wrap up the applications, look at all of the pieces and make sure that you have conveyed the most important things about yourself. You should imagine that you are an admissions officer and what impression you would leave.

18. Proofread. Proofreading may not seem like an admissions trick, but considering how many students don't do it, it really is. Take the time to make sure that all the pieces of the application are included and complete, and that they are as flawless as possible. Silly errors show a lack of attention to detail, which is the last impression you would like to leave.

You might be surprised to learn that despite the fact that colleges receive thousands or even tens of thousands of applications, admissions officers at these schools read every single piece of paper in your application. We've spoken to hundreds of admissions officers at colleges across the country, and we are always impressed at the dedication that these professionals show, giving applicants a complete and fair chance to show them why they should be admitted. College admissions officers truly want to admit you. It's now your responsibility to give these admissions officers a reason to do so.

CHAPTER SIX

FIVE STEPS TO GETTING THE MOST FINANCIAL AID YOU DESERVE

We are going to break down the financial aid process into five easy steps. We will also give you a little inside information on how each step of the process works so that you can see what factors will affect your outcome. In many ways applying for financial aid is like doing your federal taxes. There are forms to fill out and rules (even loopholes) that can help or hurt your bottom line. Now, we know that no one enjoys filling out a 1040 tax return, but at least in this case there is a good possibility that you will be getting a nice chunk of change back from the government to help you pay for college, so it's certainly worth your time to tackle it.

Step 1: Fill Out the FAFSA

As with anything from the government, you need to fill out a form. In this case, to be considered for federal financial aid, you will need to complete the Free Application for Federal Student Aid or FAFSA. Most states and many public universities also require this form to be eligible for their aid programs. If you are applying to a private college, you may also have to submit the CSS/PROFILE form, which is similar to the FAFSA. The main difference between the CSS/PROFILE and FAFSA is not in the data it collects but the formula that is used to determine how much financial aid you deserve. Unfortunately, you don't have a choice in which form the colleges use since they will require either one or both. Some colleges have additional forms that you need to fill out as well.

Since all families should complete the FAFSA (similar to the CSS/PROFILE), let's take a look at it in detail. The FAFSA is a multi-page form that asks for detailed financial information including items from your previous federal income tax return. It's not a difficult form to complete. What is difficult is that you need to collect a lot of information about your income and assets. In fact, the information that you include in your FAFSA should match the numbers on your federal tax return. But here's the kicker: While you have until April 15 to do your taxes, you must turn in the FAFSA to the Department of Education as soon as possible after January 1 of the year you will be starting or continuing school. If you are a high school student applying to college, this means that after January 1 of your senior year, you must submit the FAFSA form. If you are already in college, you must submit the FAFSA each year to continue to receive financial aid.

It's also important that you don't miss the colleges' deadlines—and each school sets its own. Most want you to submit the FAFSA no later than February or March.

Don't let the fact that you haven't completed your taxes prevent you from missing the deadline. It's better to bite the bullet and do your taxes early, or if this is impossible, you should use estimates and update the information later. Whether you use actual numbers or estimates, it is vital that you submit the FAFSA as soon as possible. Financial aid is awarded on a first-come, first-served basis. If you wait until April, it is possible that funds may already be depleted even if you do deserve the help.

There is a big push by the Department of Education, which administers the FAFSA, to get you to fill out the application online. This is not a bad idea since the online form is designed to help prevent errors and give you faster results. You can begin the process by going to the Department of Education's website at www.fafsa.ed.gov. Be sure to download the pre-application worksheets. These will help you collect the information you will need to complete the FAFSA. If you prefer to fill out the FAFSA on paper, get a copy by calling 800-4-FED-AID.

At first glance, the FAFSA may intimidate you, as is the case with many government forms. However, if you spend some time working on it, you'll find that the information is relatively straightforward. To help, here are some tips for completing the form:

File the FAFSA as soon as possible after January 1. This is an important form. Don't procrastinate. Notice how many times we repeat this!

Complete your income taxes early. Unless you're an accountant, there are more enjoyable things you'd probably rather do, but information from your income tax forms will be very helpful for completing the FAFSA. Plus, while others are stressed and panic-stricken around April 15, you'll already be done with your taxes. If you can't finish your taxes, don't be afraid to use estimates.

Follow directions. The Department of Education reports that delays are caused most often because students or parents don't follow directions when completing the FAFSA. Spend the time to read the directions and follow them completely. If you have questions, don't guess, but contact the Federal Student Aid Information Center at 1-800-4-FED-AID.

Be thorough. Answer questions completely. Take the time to find the answers to all the information requested.

Realize that the FAFSA takes time. Set aside half a day to gather the information and complete the form. Don't think that you can complete it during the commercials between episodes of *American Idol*.

Save time with the Renewal FAFSA. If you've applied for federal financial aid before, you can usually use the Renewal FAFSA. This form saves you time because many of the blanks are pre-filled with data from the prior year. Ask your school counselor or an employee of the financial aid office for more information.

If you transfer schools, check with your new school to see what forms you should complete. Your financial aid package does not automatically transfer with you.

Don't think you're on your own. Use the help provided by your school and by the government. The Department of Education has an entire staff of people to assist you with completing the necessary forms and answering your questions about financial aid. Visit their website at www.fafsa.ed.gov and don't hesitate to contact them by phone or email with your questions.

Step 2: Review Your Student Aid Report

After you submit the FAFSA, you will need to wait patiently as the Department of Education computers crunch the numbers to determine your Expected Family Contribution. If you submitted the CSS/PROFILE, the computers at the College Board are also furiously working using a slightly different formula. At this stage, the process is completely computational. The same calculations are applied to every student. For example, if you and your friend submitted FAFSAs with identical numbers, the results would be the same for both of you.

The magic number that the computers spit out is your Expected Family Contribution or EFC. This number represents what your family (you and your parents) are expected to contribute toward one year of your education. Whether or not your EFC is accurate is another topic that we will discuss later. But for now, let's look at how your EFC is determined:

Parent income X up to 47% +
Parent assets X up to 5.65% +
Student income X 50% +
Student assets X 20% =
Expected Family Contribution

Now don't have a heart attack. Not all your income or assets are subject to the 47 percent and 5.65 percent assessment rate. There are both income and asset protections that effectively shelter some of your money. Plus, depending on your income, the assessment rate may not be the full 47 percent or 5.65 percent. In fact, the lower your income and assets, the lower your assessment rate.

The best way to get an estimate of what your Expected Family Contribution will be is to use a free online EFC calculator. These calculators let you enter some numbers and quickly get an estimate of your Expected Family Contribution. The College Board's website has a free calculator at http://www.collegeboard.com. You can also adjust the numbers to see how changes in your income and assets affect your EFC.

Two to three weeks after you submit the FAFSA, you will receive the Student Aid Report (SAR) from the Department of Education. The SAR includes a summary of the information that you submitted in the FAFSA and shows your Estimated Family Contribution (EFC). Carefully review your SAR. If there are any mistakes, you need to correct them immediately.

Step 3: Make the College Aware of Special Circumstances, if Necessary

You are not the only one who receives the information in the SAR. Each college that you apply to will also receive this information along with your Expected Family Contribution. The financial aid officer takes this information and uses it to determine your financial need.

Determining financial need is fairly easy. All the financial aid officer does is subtract the Cost Of Attendance (COA) from your Expected Family Contribution (EFC).

> Cost Of Attendance –
> Expected Family Contribution =
> **Financial Need**

The Cost Of Attendance (COA) is the total price tag for attending your college or university for one year. These costs include the following: tuition and other fees, room and board, transportation between your home and the college, books and other supplies, and estimated personal expenses.

Let's take a look at an example:

You have completed the FAFSA. You have also received your SAR that reports an EFC of $8,000. This means that you and your parents are expected to contribute $8,000 to pay for next year's college expenses. If the college costs $7,000 per year, then you would not receive any financial aid since it's assumed that you can afford it. However, if another college costs $20,000 then you would expect to receive an aid package of $12,000. In other words, at the first college you are not considered to have financial need but at the second college you have a financial need of $12,000.

Now it's at this point in the process when the computers stop and the humans take over, so that any special circumstances may be considered. Financial aid officers at the colleges have the ability to raise or lower the EFC for a variety of reasons. Therefore, it is crucial that you are open about your family's true financial situation to the financial aid officer.

Remember too that all financial aid is based on the previous year's taxes. A lot may have happened this year that is not reflected by last year's tax return. If you want to share additional information, send a letter to the college financial aid office to explain any unusual circumstances that may affect your family's finances. Most colleges include a space on their financial aid forms for you to describe any relevant information such as this. When you are thinking about writing this letter, consider these three points:

Don't hide the financial dirty laundry. Many parents feel compelled to hide embarrassing circumstances when filling out financial forms. After all, you are revealing financial strengths and weaknesses to a total stranger. However, if there are special circumstances such as large medical bills, current or impending unemployment, recent or ongoing divorce, siblings attending private elementary or high schools, or any additional expenses that may not be reflected in the FAFSA or CSS/PROFILE, tell the financial aid officer. Don't be embarrassed. It could cost you big time.

Give the college a reason to give more money. Financial aid officers are numbers people. However, they have wide latitude for interpreting numbers and can apply a variety of standards. They can make exceptions, which can help or hurt your case. To get the most support from these professionals, make a case with numbers. Don't just say that you don't have enough money–show it. Document with numbers why your tax forms don't accurately reflect your true income or expenses.

Don't ever try to trick the college. The human being in the financial aid process is also what keeps it safe from trickery. You could, for example, take all the money in your savings account and plunk it down to buy an around-the-world vacation. On paper you'd have no savings. Yet, when the financial aid officer looks at your income, he or she will think it is very odd that someone who earns a decent living and owns a nice house is so cash poor. Not only would the financial aid officer not give you more financial aid, but you would also have depleted your savings.

Step 4: Compare Award Letters

Every college does try to create a financial aid package that meets your needs using a combination of grants, loans, and work-study. However, not every school is able to do this. Some colleges with limited resources may only be able to offer a financial aid package that covers a portion of your entire financial need.

If you are a high school senior, you will receive financial aid award letters several weeks after receiving college acceptance letters. Each one details how much and what type of financial aid you are being offered. It's not necessary to accept or reject the whole package. You are free to pick and choose. For example, definitely accept any grants or scholarships, but carefully consider loans or work-study.

You should also compare award letters. While one college may cost twice as much as another, you may find that it is also willing to give twice the financial aid. In that case, the actual costs of the two colleges may be the same.

What's most important is what you'll pay out of pocket and how much you'll need to borrow. Compare this among the colleges rather than their sticker prices.

If you feel that the amount of financial aid you are offered by a college is simply not enough, ask for a re-evaluation. To be effective, provide the financial aid office with concrete reasons why their initial assessment was wrong. Start with a letter or call to the financial aid office. Be sure to have all your documents ready, and remember that the squeaky wheel often gets the grease. If you don't say anything about the package, the college will assume that you are happy with it.

If you do ask for a reassessment, don't make the mistake of approaching it like you would buying a car where you haggle with a salesperson over the cost of floor mats and how much below the sticker price you will pay. Financial aid officers are really on your side and they do want to give you every penny that you deserve. However, to make it feasible for them to do so, you need to make a strong (and documented) case for why their initial evaluation was flawed.

Good reasons to ask for a reassessment include the following:

- Unusual medical expenses
- Tuition for a sibling including private secondary or elementary school
- Unemployment of a spouse or parent
- Ongoing divorce or separation
- Care for an aging relative

There is one other situation that may warrant a reassessment. If one college offers you significantly more than your first choice college, it may be possible to use that to get a better package. For example, if you are accepted to College A and College B, but College B offers a more generous financial aid package, you could try to work with College A to raise or match College B's package. First, write a letter to College A, stating that you would like very much to attend the college but that you may not be able to because of the financial aid package offered. Outline in quick bullet points the financial aid package offered by College B. Provide brief reasons why you need a package like that to be offered by College A. Reiterate that you would prefer to attend College A and would like to know if there is anything the financial aid office can do to increase the package. Follow up with a phone call. This does not always work, and some colleges have a strict policy of not matching award offers of other colleges. However, some colleges have the means to be more flexible and just might raise their initial offer.

It's always important to be proactive when it comes to financial aid. If at any point during your time in college your financial circumstances change significantly, contact your school's financial aid office. We recommend first writing a letter that outlines your special circumstances in quick, easy-to-understand bullet points. The financial aid officer will then have all the information he or she needs to reassess your financial situation. Follow up with a telephone call to check on any additional information and on the status of your inquiry.

SECTION THREE
THE RANKINGS

Who wants to be the only student in a major? When choosing a college you want one that not only offers your major but also has a lot of other students in the major since popular majors usually mean a wide variety of professors and resources.

Agriculture / Aquaculture / Animal Sciences

Clemson University
Colorado State University
Cornell University
Iowa State University
Kansas State University
Louisiana State University -- Baton Rouge
North Carolina State University -- Raleigh
Oregon State University
Purdue University -- West Lafayette
Texas A&M University -- College Station
Texas Tech University
University of Arkansas
University of California, Davis
University of Florida
University of Idaho
University of Illinois at Urbana-Champaign
University of Kentucky
University of Maine
University of Nebraska -- Lincoln
University of Wyoming

Architecture

Carnegie Mellon University
Catholic University of America
Cornell University
Georgia Institute of Technology
Hobart and William Smith Colleges
Illinois Institute of Technology
New Jersey Institute of Technology
Rhode Island School of Design
The Cooper Union

Area / Ethnic / Gender Studies

Amherst College
Barnard College
Bowdoin College
Brandeis University
Brown University
Carleton College
Colby College
Connecticut College
Dartmouth College
Dickinson College
Earlham College
Hampshire College
Hobart and William Smith Colleges
Kalamazoo College
Marlboro College
Middlebury College
Mills College
Mount Holyoke College
Oberlin College
Pomona College
Scripps College
Smith College
St. Olaf College
Trinity College
University of California, Santa Cruz
University of North Carolina at Chapel Hill
Washington University in St. Louis
Wellesley College
Wesleyan University
Wheaton College
Willamette University
Williams College
Yale University

Biological / Life Sciences

Agnes Scott College
Albion College
Allegheny College
Alma College
Baylor University

Birmingham-Southern College
Bowdoin College
Brigham Young University -- Provo
Brown University
Case Western Reserve University
Colgate University
College of Wooster
Colorado College
Connecticut College
Cornell University
Denison University
DePauw University
Dickinson College
Drew University
Duke University
Earlham College
Eckerd College
Florida Institute of Technology
Franklin & Marshall College
Gettysburg College
Grinnell College
Gustavus Adolphus College
Hamilton College
Harvard University
Haverford College
Hendrix College
Hiram College
Johns Hopkins University
Juniata College
Kalamazoo College
Knox College
Lawrence University
Loyola University Chicago
Macalester College
McGill University
Middlebury College
Millsaps College
Mount Holyoke College
Muhlenberg College
North Carolina State University -- Raleigh
Oberlin College
Occidental College

32

Ohio Wesleyan University
Randolph College
Reed College
Rhodes College
Spelman College
St. Lawrence University
St. Olaf College
State University of New York -- Albany
State University of New York -- Stony Brook
Swarthmore College
Sweet Briar College
Union College
United States Coast Guard Academy
University of California -- Los Angeles
University of California, Berkeley
University of California, Davis
University of California, Irvine
University of California, Riverside
University of California, San Diego
University of California, Santa Barbara
University of California, Santa Cruz
University of Colorado, Boulder
University of Maryland -- Baltimore County
University of Miami
University of Puget Sound
University of Rochester
University of South Carolina -- Columbia
University of the Pacific
University of Wisconsin -- Madison
Ursinus College
Vassar College
Wabash College
Washington and Lee University
Whitman College
Wofford College
Xavier University of Louisiana
Yeshiva University

Business / Marketing

Alma College
Auburn University
Babson College
Baylor University
Bentley University
Birmingham-Southern College
Boston College
Boston University

Chapman University
City University of New York -- Queens College
Clemson University
College of Charleston
College of New Jersey
DePaul University
Drexel University
Elon University
Fairfield University
Florida Southern College
Florida State University
Fordham University
George Mason University
Georgetown University
Guilford College
Hiram College
Hofstra University
Illinois Wesleyan University
Indiana University Bloomington
Iowa State University
Lehigh University
Loyola Marymount University
Loyola University Chicago
Loyola University New Orleans
Manhattanville College
Marquette University
Miami University -- Oxford
Michigan State University
Millsaps College
Morehouse College
Muhlenberg College
Northeastern University
Oglethorpe University
Pepperdine University
Quinnipiac University
Ripon College
Santa Clara University
Seattle University
Southern Methodist University
State University of New York -- University at Buffalo
Susquehanna University
Texas Christian University
Texas Tech University
Trinity University
Tulane University
University of Alabama
University of Arizona

University of Arkansas
University of California, Riverside
University of Dayton
University of Delaware
University of Denver
University of Georgia
University of Hawaii at Manoa
University of Iowa
University of Miami
University of Mississippi
University of Montana
University of Nebraska -- Lincoln
University of Notre Dame
University of Pennsylvania
University of Redlands
University of Richmond
University of San Diego
University of San Francisco
University of Southern California
University of Tennessee at Knoxville
University of the Pacific
University of Tulsa
Villanova University
Virginia Polytechnic Institute and State University
Wake Forest University
Washington & Jefferson College
Washington and Lee University
Wofford College
Yeshiva University

Communications / Journalism / Advertising

American University
Baylor University
Boston College
Boston University
Chapman University
College of Charleston
Denison University
DePaul University
DePauw University
Elon University

Emerson College

Fordham University

Goucher College

Hofstra University

Indiana University Bloomington

Ithaca College

James Madison University

Loyola Marymount University

Loyola University Chicago

Marquette University

Michigan State University

Ohio University

Pennsylvania State University -- University Park

Pepperdine University

Quinnipiac University

Rollins College

Rutgers, the State University of New Jersey -- New Brunswick

Santa Clara University

State University of New York -- Purchase College

Susquehanna University

Syracuse University

Texas Christian University

Trinity University

University of Alabama

University of Georgia

University of Kansas

University of Miami

University of Missouri -- Columbia

University of Montana

University of North Carolina at Chapel Hill

University of Oregon

University of Rhode Island

University of San Diego

University of Southern California

University of Tennessee at Knoxville

University of Texas at Austin

Villanova University

Wake Forest University

Computer / Information Sciences

California Institute of Technology

Carnegie Mellon University

DePaul University

Drexel University

George Mason University

Georgia Institute of Technology

Guilford College

Harvey Mudd College

Illinois Institute of Technology

Massachusetts Institute of Technology

Montana Tech of the University of Montana

New Jersey Institute of Technology

New Mexico Institute of Mining and Technology

Pennsylvania State University -- University Park

Rensselaer Polytechnic Institute

Rochester Institute of Technology

Rose-Hulman Institute of Technology

Stanford University

State University of New York -- Stony Brook

Stevens Institute of Technology

Syracuse University

United States Naval Academy

University of Maryland -- Baltimore County

University of North Carolina at Asheville

Worcester Polytechnic Institute

Education

Arizona State University

Auburn University

Brigham Young University -- Provo

Calvin College

College of Charleston

College of New Jersey

Florida Southern College

Hope College

Indiana University Bloomington

Juniata College

Kansas State University

Knox College

Louisiana State University -- Baton Rouge

Miami University -- Oxford

Ohio University

Randolph College

Ripon College

State University of New York -- Geneseo

University of Alabama

University of Cincinnati

University of Dayton

University of Delaware

University of Idaho

University of Kentucky

University of Maine

University of Mississippi

University of Nebraska -- Lincoln

University of New Mexico

University of North Carolina at Greensboro

University of Wyoming

Wittenberg University

Engineering

Alfred University

Auburn University

Bucknell University

California Institute of Technology

Carnegie Mellon University

Case Western Reserve University

Clarkson University

Clemson University

Colorado School of Mines

Colorado State University

Columbia University

Cornell University

Drexel University

Duke University

Florida Institute of Technology

Georgia Institute of Technology

Harvey Mudd College

Illinois Institute of Technology

Iowa State University

Johns Hopkins University

Kansas State University

Lafayette College

Lehigh University

Louisiana State University -- Baton Rouge

Massachusetts Institute of Technology

Montana Tech of the University of Montana

New Jersey Institute of Technology

New Mexico Institute of Mining and Technology

North Carolina State University -- Raleigh

Northeastern University

Ohio State University -- Columbus

Oregon State University

Pennsylvania State University -- University Park

Princeton University

Purdue University -- West Lafayette

Rensselaer Polytechnic Institute

Rice University

Rochester Institute of Technology

Rose-Hulman Institute of Technology

Santa Clara University

Stanford University

State University of New York -- University at Buffalo

Stevens Institute of Technology

Texas A&M University -- College Station

Texas Tech University

The Cooper Union

Tufts University

United States Air Force Academy

United States Coast Guard Academy

United States Military Academy

United States Naval Academy

University of California, Berkeley

University of Cincinnati

University of Dayton

University of Florida

University of Illinois at Urbana-Champaign

University of Maine

University of Michigan -- Ann Arbor

University of Minnesota -- Twin Cities

University of Nebraska -- Lincoln

University of Texas at Austin

University of Tulsa

University of Virginia

Vanderbilt University

Virginia Polytechnic Institute and State University

Washington University in St. Louis

West Virginia University

Worcester Polytechnic Institute

English and Literature

Agnes Scott College

Alma College

Bard College

Barnard College

Beloit College

Bennington College

Bryn Mawr College

College of the Holy Cross

Davidson College

DePauw University

Emerson College

Eugene Lang College The New School for Liberal Arts

Hampshire College

Haverford College

Hollins University

Kenyon College

Knox College

Mills College

Oberlin College

Oglethorpe University

Randolph College

Reed College

Rhodes College

Ripon College

Sewanee: The University of the South

Spelman College

State University of New York -- Albany

Sweet Briar College

University of Dallas

University of Mary Washington

University of Pittsburgh

Vassar College

Wells College

Wheaton College

Willamette University

Health Professions / Medical

Adelphi University

Baylor University

Calvin College

Catholic University of America

Clark University

Creighton University

Drexel University

Fairfield University

Florida Southern College

Ithaca College

James Madison University

Johns Hopkins University

Marquette University

Montana Tech of the University of Montana

New York University

Northeastern University

Ohio University

Quinnipiac University

Seattle University

State University of New York -- Stony Brook

Texas Christian University

University of Alabama

University of Cincinnati

University of Connecticut

University of Delaware

University of Kansas

University of Miami

University of Missouri -- Columbia

University of New Hampshire

University of North Carolina at Greensboro

University of Oklahoma

University of Pennsylvania

University of Pittsburgh

University of Rhode Island

University of Rochester

University of San Francisco

University of Wyoming

Villanova University

Law / Legal Studies

Amherst College

Dickinson College

Drew University

Hampshire College

James Madison University

McGill University

United States Air Force Academy

United States Military Academy

University of California, Santa Cruz

University of Massachusetts Amherst

35

Liberal Arts / General Studies

DePaul University
Eugene Lang College The New School for Liberal Arts
Evergreen State College
George Mason University
Hobart and William Smith Colleges
James Madison University
Louisiana State University -- Baton Rouge
New College of Florida
New York University
Oglethorpe University
Oregon State University
Pitzer College
Rochester Institute of Technology
Sarah Lawrence College
Seattle University
St. John's College
St. John's College
State University of New York -- Purchase College
Susquehanna University
Union College
University of Connecticut
University of Iowa
University of Mary Washington
University of New Mexico
University of Oklahoma
University of Virginia
West Virginia University

Mathematics

Agnes Scott College
California Institute of Technology
Colorado School of Mines
Hamilton College
Harvey Mudd College
Pomona College
St. Olaf College
United States Coast Guard Academy
University of Chicago
Williams College

Environmental Science / Natural Resources

Allegheny College
Bates College
Birmingham-Southern College
Bowdoin College
Colorado College
Eckerd College
Hobart and William Smith Colleges
Juniata College
Knox College
Middlebury College
Oberlin College
Oregon State University
Pitzer College
Pomona College
Rollins College
Sewanee: The University of the South
University of California, Berkeley
University of California, Santa Cruz
University of Idaho
University of Montana
University of North Carolina at Asheville
University of Redlands
University of Vermont
Warren Wilson College

Fitness / Recreation Studies

Brigham Young University -- Provo
Colorado State University
Cornell College
Creighton University
Elon University
Indiana University Bloomington
James Madison University
Ohio Wesleyan University
Rice University
Truman State University
University of Delaware
University of Iowa
University of the Pacific
University of Utah
Ursinus College
Whittier College

Philosophy / Religion / Theology

Colgate University
College of Wooster

Colorado College
Cornell College
Gettysburg College
Haverford College
Hendrix College
Lawrence University
Marlboro College
Randolph College
Reed College
Rhodes College
Sewanee: The University of the South
St. Olaf College
University of Dallas
Vassar College
Wabash College
Wheaton College
Wheaton College
Whitman College

Physical Sciences / Chemistry / Physics / Astronomy

Albion College
Beloit College
Bryn Mawr College
California Institute of Technology
Carleton College
Carnegie Mellon University
Case Western Reserve University
College of the Holy Cross
College of Wooster
Colorado College
Earlham College
Florida Institute of Technology
Furman University
Grinnell College
Gustavus Adolphus College
Harvard University
Harvey Mudd College
Haverford College
Hendrix College
Hope College
Juniata College
Kalamazoo College
Macalester College
Massachusetts Institute of Technology
Millsaps College
New Mexico Institute of Mining and Technology
Pomona College

Princeton University
Reed College
Rhodes College
St. Olaf College
Stanford University
Union College
United States Naval Academy
University of California, Santa Barbara
University of Chicago
University of Mary Washington
University of San Francisco
Wabash College
Wesleyan University
Whitman College
Williams College
Wofford College
Xavier University of Louisiana

Protective Services / Criminal Justice

American University
Arizona State University
Brandeis University
College of New Jersey
Duke University
Elon University
Florida State University
George Mason University
Guilford College
Indiana University Bloomington
Loyola University Chicago
Northeastern University
Pennsylvania State University -- University Park
Princeton University
Rutgers, the State University of New Jersey -- New Brunswick
University of Chicago
University of Cincinnati
University of Maryland -- Baltimore County
University of Mississippi
University of San Francisco
University of Wyoming
Warren Wilson College

Psychology

Allegheny College
Barnard College

Birmingham-Southern College
Carleton College
Centre College
City University of New York -- Queens College
Clark University
College of the Holy Cross
Davidson College
Goucher College
Guilford College
Hendrix College
Hollins University
Lewis and Clark College
Loyola University Chicago
Loyola University New Orleans
Manhattanville College
Mills College
Muhlenberg College
Oglethorpe University
Ripon College
Scripps College
Spelman College
State University of New York -- Albany
State University of New York -- Stony Brook
State University of New York -- University at Buffalo
University of California, Irvine
University of California, Riverside
University of California, Santa Barbara
University of California, Santa Cruz
University of Maryland -- Baltimore County
University of North Carolina at Asheville
University of Rochester
Wells College
Wesleyan University
Wheaton College
Xavier University of Louisiana
Yeshiva University

Trade / Construction / Vocational Education

Florida Institute of Technology
Kansas State University
Ohio University
Purdue University -- West Lafayette
Rhode Island School of Design
University of Chicago

University of Massachusetts Amherst
University of Oklahoma

Visual / Performing Arts

Alfred University
Bard College
Barnard College
Bennington College
Birmingham-Southern College
Carleton College
Carnegie Mellon University
Chapman University
Drew University
Emerson College
Eugene Lang College The New School for Liberal Arts
Hampshire College
Hollins University
Illinois Wesleyan University
Ithaca College
Lawrence University
Loyola Marymount University
Loyola University New Orleans
Manhattanville College
Marlboro College
Mills College
Muhlenberg College
New York University
Oberlin College
Randolph College
Rhode Island School of Design
Rochester Institute of Technology
Scripps College
Skidmore College
State University of New York -- Purchase College
Syracuse University
The Cooper Union
University of Southern California
Vassar College
Wells College
Wesleyan University

Rankings

THE TOP 100 BEST COLLEGE VALUES

A list of 104 schools that offer the most bang for the buck based on academic quality and offerings and financial aid programs.

Adelphi University
Amherst College
Arizona State University
Auburn University
Baylor University
Boston College
Brigham Young University
Bryn Mawr College
California Institute of Technology
Claremont McKenna College
Clemson University
Colgate University
College of Charleston
College of New Jersey
College of William and Mary
Colorado School of Mines
Colorado State University
Dartmouth College
Davidson College
Duke University
Elon University
Emerson College
Emory University
Evergreen State College
Florida State University
George Mason University
Georgetown University
Georgia Institute of Technology
Grinnell College
Harvard University
Howard University
Illinois Institute of Technology
Indiana University - Bloomington
Iowa State University
James Madison University

Louisiana State University
Marquette University
Massachusetts Institute of Technology
Miami University - Oxford
Millsaps College
Morehouse College
New College of Florida
North Carolina State University - Raleigh
Ohio State University - Columbus
Oregon State University
Princeton University
Rice University
Rollins College
Scripps College
Stanford University
SUNY - Binghamton University
SUNY - Geneseo
SUNY - Stony Brook University
SUNY - University at Buffalo
Swarthmore College
Texas A&M University
Trinity University
Truman State University
Tufts University
United States Air Force Academy
United States Coast Guard Academy
United States Military Academy
United States Naval Academy
University of Alabama
University of Arizona
University of Arkansas (Fayetteville)
University of California - Berkeley
University of California - Davis
University of California - Irvine
University of California - Los Angeles

University of California - San Diego
University of California - Santa Barbara
University of California - Santa Cruz
University of Chicago
University of Colorado - Boulder
University of Connecticut
University of Delaware
University of Florida
University of Georgia
University of Illinois - Urbana-Champaign
University of Iowa
University of Mary Washington
University of Maryland - College Park
University of Michigan - Ann Arbor
University of Missouri - Columbia
University of Nebraska - Lincoln
University of North Carolina - Asheville
University of North Carolina - Chapel Hill
University of Oklahoma
University of Oregon
University of Richmond
University of South Carolina (Columbia)
University of Tennessee - Knoxville
University of Texas - Austin
University of Virginia
University of Washington
University of Wisconsin - Madison
Vanderbilt University
Virginia Polytechnic Institute
Wabash College
Washington State University
Washington University in St. Louis
Wheaton College (IL)
Yale University

The Ultimate Guide to
America's Best Colleges

PUBLIC COLLEGES BY PRICE

All tuition rates are for in-state tuition only. Excludes room and board, books, and fees.

Less than $6,000

City University of New York -- Queens College

James Madison University

Louisiana State University -- Baton Rouge

McGill University

Montana Tech of the University of Montana

New Mexico Institute of Mining and Technology

State University of New York -- Albany

State University of New York -- Binghamton

State University of New York -- Geneseo

State University of New York -- Purchase College

State University of New York -- Stony Brook

State University of New York -- University at Buffalo

Texas A&M University -- College Station

United States Air Force Academy (tuition free)

United States Coast Guard Academy (tuition free)

United States Military Academy (tuition free)

United States Naval Academy (tuition free)

University of Idaho

University of North Carolina at Greensboro

University of Oklahoma

University of Toronto

University of Wyoming

$6,000 - $9,000

Colorado State University

Evergreen State College

Florida State University

Georgia Institute of Technology

Iowa State University

Kansas State University

New College of Florida

North Carolina State University -- Raleigh

Oregon State University

Texas Tech University

Truman State University

University of Arkansas

University of Colorado, Boulder

University of Florida

University of Georgia

University of Iowa

University of Mary Washington

University of Maryland -- Baltimore County

University of Mississippi

University of Montana

University of Nebraska -- Lincoln

University of New Mexico

University of North Carolina at Asheville

University of North Carolina at Chapel Hill

University of Oregon

University of Utah

West Virginia University

$9,000 - $12,000

Arizona State University

Auburn University

College of Charleston

College of William and Mary

George Mason University

Indiana University Bloomington

Ohio State University -- Columbus

Ohio University

Purdue University -- West Lafayette

Rutgers, the State University of New Jersey -- New Brunswick

University of Alabama

University of Arizona

University of California, Irvine

University of California, Riverside

University of Cincinnati

University of Connecticut

University of Hawaii at Manoa

University of Illinois at Urbana-Champaign

University of Kansas

University of Kentucky

University of Maine

University of Maryland, College Park

University of Missouri -- Columbia

University of Rhode Island

University of South Carolina -- Columbia

University of Tennessee at Knoxville

University of Texas at Austin

University of Virginia

University of Washington, Seattle

University of Wisconsin -- Madison

Virginia Polytechnic Institute and State University

Washington State University

More than $12,000

Clemson University

College of New Jersey

Colorado School of Mines

Miami University -- Oxford

Michigan State University

New Jersey Institute of Technology

Pennsylvania State University -- University Park

University of California -- Los Angeles

University of California, Berkeley

University of California, Davis

University of California, San Diego

University of California, Santa Barbara

University of California, Santa Cruz

University of Massachusetts Amherst

University of Michigan -- Ann Arbor

University of Minnesota -- Twin Cities

University of New Hampshire

University of Pittsburgh

University of Vermont

Rankings

Less than $20,000

Brigham Young University -- Provo
Xavier University of Louisiana

$20,000 - $30,000

Adelphi University
Alfred University
Birmingham-Southern College
Calvin College
Elon University
Florida Southern College
Hiram College
Hope College
Howard University
Morehouse College
Spelman College
Warren Wilson College

$30,000 - $40,000

Agnes Scott College
Albion College
Allegheny College
Alma College
Austin College
Baylor University
Bentley University
California Institute of Technology
Catholic University of America
Centre College
Clark University
Clarkson University
College of the Atlantic
Cornell College
Creighton University
DePaul University
Drexel University
Eckerd College
Emerson College

Eugene Lang College The New School
for Liberal Arts
Florida Institute of Technology
Goucher College
Guilford College
Gustavus Adolphus College
Hampden-Sydney College
Harvard University
Hendrix College
Hofstra University
Hollins University
Illinois Institute of Technology
Illinois Wesleyan University
Ithaca College
Juniata College
Kalamazoo College
Knox College
Lake Forest College
Loyola Marymount University
Loyola University Chicago
Loyola University New Orleans
Manhattanville College
Marlboro College
Marquette University
Millsaps College
Oglethorpe University
Quinnipiac University
Randolph College
Rhodes College
Rice University
Ripon College
Rochester Institute of Technology
Rose-Hulman Institute of Technology
Seattle University
Sewanee: The University of the South
Southern Methodist University
Susquehanna University
Sweet Briar College
Syracuse University
Texas Christian University
The Cooper Union (every student re-
ceives a scholarship of about $20,000)
Trinity University
University of Dallas

University of Dayton
University of Denver
University of San Francisco
University of the Pacific
University of Tulsa
Wabash College
Washington & Jefferson College
Wells College
Wheaton College
Whittier College
Wittenberg University
Wofford College
Yeshiva University

More than $40,000

American University
Amherst College (comprehensive fee
includes tuition, room, and board)
Babson College
Bard College
Barnard College
Bates College
Beloit College
Bennington College
Boston College
Boston University
Bowdoin College
Brandeis University
Brown University
Bryn Mawr College
Bucknell University
Carleton College
Carnegie Mellon University
Case Western Reserve University
Chapman University
Claremont McKenna College
Colby College
Colgate University
College of the Holy Cross
College of Wooster
Colorado College
Columbia University
Connecticut College

The Ultimate Guide to
America's Best Colleges

Cornell University
Dartmouth College
Davidson College
Denison University
DePauw University
Dickinson College
Drew University
Duke University
Earlham College
Emory University
Fairfield University
Fordham University
Franklin & Marshall College
Furman University
George Washington University
Georgetown University
Gettysburg College
Grinnell College
Hamilton College
Hampshire College
Harvey Mudd College
Haverford College
Hobart and William Smith Colleges
Johns Hopkins University
Kenyon College
Lafayette College
Lawrence University
Lehigh University
Lewis and Clark College
Macalester College
Massachusetts Institute of Technology
Middlebury College
Mills College
Mount Holyoke College
Muhlenberg College
New York University
Northeastern University
Northwestern University
Oberlin College
Occidental College
Ohio Wesleyan University
Pepperdine University
Pitzer College
Pomona College
Princeton University
Reed College
Rensselaer Polytechnic Institute

Rhode Island School of Design
Rollins College
Santa Clara University
Sarah Lawrence College
Scripps College
Skidmore College
Smith College
St. John's College
St. John's College
St. Lawrence University
St. Olaf College
Stanford University
Stevens Institute of Technology
Swarthmore College
Trinity College
Tufts University
Tulane University
Union College
University of Chicago
University of Miami
University of Notre Dame
University of Pennsylvania
University of Puget Sound
University of Redlands
University of Richmond
University of Rochester
University of San Diego
University of Southern California
Ursinus College
Vanderbilt University
Vassar College
Villanova University
Wake Forest University
Washington and Lee University
Washington University in St. Louis
Wellesley College
Wesleyan University
Wheaton College
Whitman College
Willamette University
Williams College
Worcester Polytechnic Institute
Yale University

SECTION FOUR

COLLEGE PROFILES

ADELPHI UNIVERSITY

Overview

In the summer, brown-eyed susans representing the school colors of Adelphi University (AU) bloom across the main campus. Located in a wealthy, quiet suburb of Long Island, AU's 75-acre main campus is lush and beautiful, not surprising given its status as a registered arboretum and its name, the "Garden City" campus. A liberal arts school with notable pre-professional programs, Adelphi may feel small to some, with about 5,000 undergrads. Many students are commuters so student life, especially on the weekends, may not be as vibrant as other schools where more students live on campus. However, those seeking fun and adventure at the end of a studious week always have the option of taking a 45-minute train ride to New York City. It's that close.

Academic and social activities will always be more limited at a smaller school compared to a large university, but Adelphi has made notable efforts in recent years to expand opportunities for its students. In 2006, AU built the Adele and Herbert J. Klapper Center for Fine Arts, offering 18,000 square feet of studios and exhibit areas. An ambitious, recently completed campus expansion project also added a new recreation center, the Alice Brown Early Learning Center, and parking.

Academics

Classes at Adelphi are rigorous but not overwhelming. Eighty-three percent of classes have fewer than 30 students, and the most common class size is 10 to 19 students. Classes may be difficult to get into due to Adelphi's small size and limited offerings; however, faculty are accessible with an 12:1 student/faculty ratio. The Society of Mentors matches every freshman and sophomore with a faculty adviser. "There's no shortage of attention from professors," says a student.

Of the university's more than 100 majors, Adelphi's pre-professional programs are particularly strong, including the BS in nursing and the various degree programs in the undergraduate School of Business (including BBA degrees and a five-year combined Bachelor/MBA program). Other notable undergrad programs at Adelphi include communications in the College of Arts and Sciences, various options in the Ruth S. Ammon School of Education, and psychology in the Gordon F. Derner Institute of Advanced Psychological Studies.

Students can earn a bachelor's and master's degree in five years in the Scholars Teacher Education Program (STEP), including the fields of Adolescent Education and Childhood Education, as well as in social work.

In keeping with its goal of offering a liberal arts and sciences education, Adelphi has a General Education program consisting of 34 credits that all students must take. For freshmen, required courses include First-year Orientation Experience, English Composition, and a First-year Seminar. Sections and topics vary, with titles like "Daring the Nightmare: Examining Horror in Literature and Film" and "Coming to America: Golden Promises or Broken Dreams." One student sums it up as she explains, "The first-year seminars are hit and miss, but probably more hits than misses."

Honors College students at Adelphi enjoy special student research and travel opportunities, including on-campus independent and supervised research in nationally-funded labs as well as off-campus placements and special opportunities in Greece and Crete during the summer. Honors students take about half their courses in the Honors College freshman year, and all write a thesis that is the culmination of a year's worth of original research.

For those wanting to expand their horizons beyond Long Island, The Adelphi Study Abroad Program offers short-term and long-term opportunities in more than 90 approved destinations in 40 countries around the world.

Adelphi's proximity to New York City allows for many internship opportunities. AU Connect offers an online portal for the alumni community, and there are

ADELPHI UNIVERSITY

Four-year private
Founded: 1896
Garden City, NY
Large town
Pop. 22,450

Address:
1 South Avenue
Garden City, NY
11530

Admissions:
516-877-3050

Financial Aid:
516-877-3365

admissions@adelphi.edu

www.adelphi.edu

ADELPHI UNIVERSITY

Students

Total enrollment: 7,859
Undergrads: 5,103
Freshmen: 999
Part-time students: 11%
From out-of-state: 14%
From public schools: 74%
Male/Female: 30%/70%
Live-on campus: Not reported
In fraternities: 12%
In sororities: 9%
Off-campus employment rating: Good
Caucasian: 54%
African American: 10%
Hispanic: 13%
Asian / Pacific Islander: 7%
Native American: 0%
Mixed (2+ ethnicities): 3%
International: 3%

Academics

Calendar: Semester
Student/faculty ratio: 12:1
Class size 9 or fewer: 12%
Class size 10-29: 71%
Class size 30-49: 15%
Class size 50-99: 2%
Class size 100 or more: -
Returning freshmen: 81%
Six-year graduation rate: 66%
Graduates who immediately enter career
   related to major: 88%

Most Popular Majors

Nursing
Education
Business administration/management

Admissions

Applicants: 9,184
Accepted: 6,104
Acceptance rate: 66.5%
Average GPA: 3.5
ACT range: 22-28
SAT Math range: 510-620
SAT Reading range: 500-600
SAT Writing range: 5-29
Top 10% of class: 23%
Top 25% of class: 55%
Top 50% of class: 85%

networking and info sessions for students seeking career guidance. Among recent graduates, 44 percent pursued a degree one year after graduation (with the most popular areas of study being business and medicine), and 82 percent were employed within one year of graduation.

Student Life

Adelphi has more than 80 student clubs and organizations, including the Student Government Association, *The Delphian* student newspaper, religious organizations, and community service (especially in community health) clubs. There are also nearly two-dozen academic honors societies and 13 Greek sororities and fraternities.

The university is officially a dry campus but of course there are still parties, most of which occur on Thursday and Friday nights because many students go home for the weekends. Participation in activities is somewhat hampered by the college being a commuter school. "There's some activity on campus during weekends, but it's not the typical weekend college experience," comments a student.

For undergrads, the Center for Student Involvement helps coordinate on-campus social events and sponsors trips to New York City theaters. Adelphi has a vibrant arts, music and theater scene, especially with the opening the state-of-the-art venue provided by the new Adelphi University Performing Arts Center.

Other community spaces on campus include the Ruth S. Harley University Center (UC), which has a full bookstore, a cafeteria and several lounges, including a lounge designated for commuter students. The newly renovated 60,000-square-foot Center for Recreation and Sports, which opened in the summer of 2008, houses the Adelphi Panthers' athletic department, as well as facilities for all students: a 5,000 square foot fitness center, swimming pool, indoor track, three court gymnasiums, and others. A dozen intramural sports are offered throughout the year along with group fitness classes.

At such a small school, one might not expect much in the way of athletics. However, the women's lacrosse team became the first NCAA Division II women's lacrosse program to win three championships in 2008, and the women's soccer team were national runners-up in 2004. The popularly of basketball is seen in the annual tradition of Midnight Madness, which kicks off the men and women's basketball season and Homecoming Week.

More than 70 percent of students live off campus. Freshmen and sophomores have priority in selecting housing, and 43 percent of freshmen live in residence halls. It can be very competitive to get on-campus housing in the six residence halls or housing near campus. New Hall, the most recently constructed dorm, is a handsome brick building completed in fall 2003 that features private bathrooms and individual climate control—including air conditioning—in each room. A new $20 million residence hall was completed in fall 2011.

Student Body

There are almost 8,000 full-time and part-time students at Adelphi from 37 states and almost 50 countries. Over half of these students are full time undergrads. Eighty-eight percent of students are from New York, and nearly 70 percent are female. "It's not the best environment for meeting men," laughs a female student. "But there are plenty of opportunities off campus."

A diversity of ages is represented among the students with 17 percent of undergrads over 25 and 40 percent of graduate students over 30. "There are more adult students here than your average college," explains one student. "And this affects everything from the social scene to classroom dynamics." Adelphi is also racially diverse, with 33 percent students of color, more than one third of whom identify as Hispanic.

You May Not Know

- The university's Learning Disabilities Program was one of the first established in the country.
- It started the first dance department in the U.S. in 1938.
- The university's Garden City campus is a registered arboretum.

Distinguished Alumni

Thomas J Donohue, U.S. Chamber of Commerce President and CEO; Marjorie J. Hill, Gay Men's Health Crisis CEO; Alice Hoffman, *New York Times* best-selling author; Jonathan Larson, author of Pulitzer Prize-winning musical *RENT*; Gregory Meeks, New York Congressman, 6th District, representing Queens.

Admissions and Financial Aid

Admission to Adelphi is among the most selective for the Long Island private institutions, with more than 65 percent of freshman applicants accepted. Applications include a letter of recommendation along with other materials. An admissions interview is "strongly recommended" for all applicants and required for Honors College applicants (those who cannot visit the campus are interviewed by phone).

The university offers rolling admissions and usually notifies candidates of the admissions decision three weeks after receiving a completed application. Students should apply by March 1 for the fall semester and November 30 for the spring semester. Early Action (non-binding) applicants should submit completed applications by December 1, and are notified by December 31. Prospective students have until May 1 to decide whether to attend.

The university awards a number of merit-based scholarships including Trustee Scholarships up to $24,000, Presidential Scholarships up to $16,000, and Provost Scholarships up to $14,500. There are also scholarships for transfer students, part-time students, students in the arts, business majors, and children of alumni.

ADELPHI UNIVERSITY

Highlights

Admissions Criteria
Academic criteria:
Grades: ☆ ☆ ☆
Difficulty of class schedule: ☆ ☆ ☆
Class rank: ☆ ☆
Standardized test scores: ☆ ☆
Teacher recommendations: ☆ ☆
Personal statement: ☆ ☆
Non-academic criteria considered:
Interview
Extracurricular activities
Special talents, interests, abilities
Character/personal qualities
Volunteer work
Work experience
State of residency
Alumni relationship

Deadlines
Early Action: December 1
Early Decision: No
Regular Action: Rolling admissions
Common Application: Accepted

Financial Aid
In-state tuition: $29,300
Out-of-state tuition: $29,300
Room: Varies
Board: Varies
Books: $1,400
Freshmen receiving need-based aid: 73%
Undergrads rec. need-based aid: 63%
Avg. % of need met by financial aid: 32%
Avg. aid package (freshmen): $19,000
Avg. aid package (undergrads): $19,000
Avg. debt upon graduation: $35,429

School Spirit
Mascot: Panther
Colors: Brown and gold

AGNES SCOTT COLLEGE

AGNES SCOTT COLLEGE

Four-year private
women's college
Founded: 1889
Decatur, GA
Major city
Pop. 19,555

Address:
141 East College
Avenue
Decatur, GA
30030

Admissions:
800-868-8602, extension 6285

Financial Aid:
404-471-6285

admission@agnes-scott.edu

www.agnesscott.edu

Overview

With Gothic and red brick and stone Victorian buildings stretching across its 100-acre campus, Agnes Scott College is a tree-filled vision of what a college campus can be. Plus, the all women's college is only six miles north of downtown Atlanta, a source of culture, entertainment, and internship opportunities.

The college itself offers a rigorous academic curriculum, a renowned liberal arts education and an individualized experience that includes enviable interaction with professors and cooperation among students. While affiliated with the Presbyterian Church, students of all faiths are welcome and represented. Agnes Scott College offers a small-college feel with the added benefit of being a next-door neighbor to a welcoming major metropolitan center.

Academics

Academics at Agnes Scott are rigorous. For more than 90 years, the college has ranked in the top 10 percent of colleges whose graduates receive PhD degrees. As one student reports, "There are really no classes that you can coast through." But while the courses may be difficult, the helpfulness of the professors and even other students makes classes doable. The professors "always welcome drop-ins from students," and with the average class size of 13 students, they also know their students on a first-name basis. Scotties describe their classmates as "collaborative" and "not very competitive." Because of the school's more than 100-year-old honor code, students "basically don't cheat," says a junior.

There are 35 majors and 31 minors; pre-law and pre-medicine programs; and dual-degree programs in architecture, engineering, and nursing. The college is known for its biology, English literature, pre-medicine, and psychology programs.

In addition to the requirements for their majors, students are required to take a course in English composition and reading, foreign language, physical education (two courses), literature, religious and philosophical thought, historical studies or classical civilization, fine arts, math, natural science (two courses), social science and social and cultural analysis, and a first-year seminar.

While one student stated that there are "limited" options for courses, there are many opportunities for independent study and to cross-register at affiliate colleges including Emory University, Georgia Tech, and Georgia State.

More than half of students study abroad at some point. There are two programs offered that are short-term (two to three weeks abroad) and faculty-led. The Global Awareness Program allows students to study the history, culture, arts, economics, and politics of a country on campus and then participate in a seminar abroad. Through Global Connections, students draw parallels between an on-campus course and study abroad.

There are plentiful opportunities for internships with 13 Fortune 500 companies headquartered in Atlanta. The college offers internship programs specifically for learning about women and leadership (Atlanta Semester Program), business (Kemper Scholars Program), humanitarian service (Hubert Scholars Program), and public leadership (Public Leadership Education Network). "There's no shortage of being able to learn on the job," says one student. Almost one third of students attend graduate school within one year of graduating.

Student Life

On campus, Scotties participate in the many dorm activities and more than 85 clubs and organizations. Community service is popular, with five recognized service clubs as well as service days and a spring break service week organized by the college. A highlight of the year is Black Cat, a week of decorating in class colors, class parties, a class dance performance, and the Black Cat Formal. Diversifest is a week of "dinners, discussions and dancing" to celebrate diversity including a fashion show and artist showcase. Spring Fest and the Spring Fling formal top off the year with an annual theme such as Casino Night, Fire and Ice Ball, or House Party. There are no sororities on campus.

With Atlanta a short MARTA trip away, many students go off campus, especially on weekends. Atlanta offers bars, clubs, restaurants, shopping, and cultural events that are convenient to campus. "When we want to have fun, we head to Atlanta. It's cheesy, but there's a reason why they call it Hot-lanta," says a student. To meet guys, students often head to close by Georgia Tech. A student notes, "Despite that we're an all-women's college, there's no shortage of guys if you make the effort."

The Scotties have six NCAA Division III teams for basketball, lacrosse, soccer, softball, tennis, and volleyball; club sports in cross country, cycling, swimming, and the triathlon and intramural sports in yoga, tennis, aikido, and Tai Ji.

Students praise the housing at Agnes Scott. "I've seen other dorms, and I'd have to say compared to them, ours are almost luxurious," comments a student. First-year students live in the top two floors of Walters Hall and Winship Hall, resulting in a friendly rivalry between the two groups. Upper-class students have their choice of six halls, the Avery Glen Apartments, or theme houses that center on academic or extracurricular interests which can change annually. Almost 90 percent of students live on campus. "I know my hallmates better than my own family members," says one student.

Student Body

Many students cite that the school, as might be expected, has a southern slant with the majority hailing from the South. "Sometimes I feel left out because I didn't grow up eating grits for breakfast," laments a student. Still, with 45 states and territories and 27 countries represented and more than 50 percent of its students from minority groups, Agnes Scott does offer diversity.

The majority of students also identified themselves as liberal. "At a college that's about empowering women, it makes sense that we'd be forward thinking," explains one student.

You May Not Know

- It's free to apply to Agnes Scott if you do it online.
- If you are a Scotty and get engaged, it's a tradition for your friends to throw you in the alumnae pool.
- Decatur has wireless Internet that envelopes the entire city and Agnes Scott campus.

Distinguished Alumnae

Katherine Krill, CEO of Ann Taylor Stores Corporation; Jennifer Nettles, Grammy Award winner; Marsha Norman, Pulitzer Prize- and Tony-winning playwright; Jean Toal, Chief Justice of the South Carolina Supreme Court.

AGNES SCOTT COLLEGE

Highlights

Students
Total enrollment: 885
Undergrads: 885
Freshmen: 232
Part-time students: 2%
From out-of-state: 55%
From public schools: 70%
Male/Female: 1%/99%
Live on-campus: 86%
Off-campus employment rating: Excellent
Caucasian: 35%
African American: 33%
Hispanic: 8%
Asian / Pacific Islander: 3%
Mixed (2+ ethnicities): 5%
International: 11%

Academics
Calendar: Semester
Student/faculty ratio: 11:1
Class size 9 or fewer: 19%
Class size 10-29: 69%
Class size 30-49: 13%
Class size 50-99: -
Class size 100 or more: -
Returning freshmen: 82%
Six-year graduation rate: 64%
Graduates who immediately go to graduate school: 25%
Graduates who immediately enter career related to major: 45%

Most Popular Majors
Psychology
Social science
English language/literature

Admissions
Applicants: 1,554
Accepted: 963
Acceptance rate: 62.0%
Average GPA: 3.6
ACT range: 22-29
SAT Math range: 510-620
SAT Reading range: 520-670
SAT Writing range: 9-38
Top 10% of class: 39%
Top 25% of class: 69%
Top 50% of class: 92%

AGNES SCOTT COLLEGE

Admissions Criteria
Academic criteria:
Grades: ☆ ☆ ☆
Difficulty of class schedule: ☆ ☆ ☆
Class rank: ☆ ☆ ☆
Standardized test scores: ☆
Teacher recommendations: ☆ ☆ ☆
Personal statement: ☆ ☆ ☆
Non-academic criteria considered:
Interview
Extracurricular activities
Special talents, interests, abilities
Character/personal qualities
Volunteer work
Work experience
Geographical location
Minority affiliation
Alumni relationship

Deadlines
Early Action: November 15
Early Decision: No
Regular Action: March 1 (priority)
Common Application: Accepted

Financial Aid
In-state tuition: $34,548
Out-of-state tuition: $34,548
Room: Varies
Board: Varies
Books: $1,000
Freshmen receiving need-based aid: 85%
Undergrads rec. need-based aid: 78%
Avg. % of need met by financial aid: 89%
Avg. aid package (freshmen): $32,686
Avg. aid package (undergrads): $32,209
Avg. debt upon graduation: $27,462

School Spirit
Mascot: Scotties
Colors: Purple and white

Admissions and Financial Aid

The college seeks students who have "proven academic capabilities" and who have "dedicated themselves" to extracurricular activities. According to the admissions office, the college also takes into consideration how challenging students' academic course loads have been. An on-campus interview is not required but recommended, which means that if you have the opportunity to visit the campus you should arrange for an interview with an admissions counselor.

The college provides a number of merit-based scholarships including Presidential Scholarships, which cover tuition, room, and board for all four years; Deans Scholarships, which provide $80,000 over four years, and the Agnes Scott Scholars program, which provides $20,000 over four years. The Agnes Solution provides $63,000 in merit scholarships over four years, including $3,000 which may be used for study abroad, an internship, or mentored research.

ALBION COLLEGE

Overview

Albion College is a private college associated with the United Methodist Church. With a scant 1,400 undergrads, the college is located in a small town in Michigan whose population isn't much greater than the college's (less than 10,000).

Proud of its "pioneering heritage" in the liberal arts of Michigan, Albion College's original Quad is still intact and a popular place for study and play on warm days. The school is quite homogeneous, which may turn off students who are seeking greater diversity. This certainly is not a place to disappear anonymously into a crowd: you'll get to know students, faculty, and plenty of people around town intimately. As a four-year residential college, some students may find the college to be insular, though a number of study-abroad opportunities do exist.

As an exclusively undergraduate institute, the liberal arts and pre-professional programs and social opportunities, including a strong Greek culture, are focused on undergrads. New facilities include a $41.3 million science complex and 340-acre equestrian center. The college's 2015 Strategic Plan aims to increase diversity, enhance sustainability, and improve facilities for athletics and the arts.

Academics

Albion offers 30 academic majors and eight interdisciplinary concentrations. To graduate, students must pass a writing competence exam and complete courses in the humanities, sciences, social sciences, and fine arts, as well as one unit each in environmental studies, ethnicity studies, gender studies, and global studies. Academics are strong, and the college promises that all classes are taught by professors. Of the college's 101 tenured or tenure-track faculty members, 85 percent have PhDs or the relevant professional degree in their field. There are plenty of opportunities to get to know these qualified professors, since 88 percent of Albion classes have fewer than 30 students.

Strong majors include biology, English, economics and management, mathematics, and political science. The Pre-Medical pre-professional program is also highly regarded. While students can choose any major, biology and chemistry are most popular. Similarly, pre-law students may also choose any major. Of note is the recently designed Law, Justice, and Society concentration, which offers a way to study law at an undergraduate level.

The William Atwell Brown, Jr., and Mary Brown Vacin First-year Experience (FYE) program at Albion is designed to support high schoolers' academic and social transition to Albion. Major academic components of FYE include First-year Seminars and the Common Reading Experience. Social programming and activities take place through the FYE residential Program Learning Strategies, which addresses "issues such as study skills, time management, wellness, diversity, sustainability, and communication."

The Foundation for Undergraduate Research, Scholarship, and Creative Activity (FURSCA) supports research with academic grants, travel grants, and summer research grants. There are no standardized senior year requirements, though a capstone experience might include directed study, an honors thesis, or internship. Another popular program is the Gerald R. Ford Institute for Public Policy, which has more than 175 student members from a wide range of majors and minors. The program aims to develop leaders for public service and administration through a curriculum that incorporates seminars and coursework, visiting scholars and lecturers, service hours, and internships.

Albion's Center for International Education (CIE) offers study-abroad opportunities divided into three categories: research, programs with an internship, and study only. There are more than 50 programs of varying lengths: Japan, Senegal, India, Chile, and Germany are a sampling of the countries represented.

ALBION COLLEGE

Four-year private
Founded: 1835
Albion, MI
Large town
Pop. 8,581

Address:
611 East Porter Street
Albion, MI
49224

Admissions:
800-858-6770

Financial Aid:
517-629-0440

admission@albion.edu

www.albion.edu

ALBION COLLEGE

Students

Total enrollment: 1,382
Undergrads: 1,382
Freshmen: 373
Part-time students: 2%
From out-of-state: 8%
Male/Female: 51%/49%
Live on-campus: 90%
In fraternities: 51%
In sororities: 44%
Caucasian: 80%
African American: 4%
Hispanic: 3%
Asian / Pacific Islander: 1%
Native American: 0%
Mixed (2+ ethnicities): 4%
International: 4%

Academics

Calendar: Semester
Student/faculty ratio: 11:1
Class size 9 or fewer: 26%
Class size 10-29: 65%
Class size 30-49: 9%
Class size 50-99: -
Class size 100 or more: -
Returning freshmen: 73%
Six-year graduation rate: 72%
Graduates who immediately go to graduate school: 48%
Graduates who immediately enter career related to major: 52%

Most Popular Majors

Economics/management
Psychology
Biology

Admissions

Applicants: 2,383
Accepted: 1,673
Acceptance rate: 70.2%
Average GPA: 3.4
ACT range: 22-27
SAT Math range: 480-640
SAT Reading range: 460-620
SAT Writing range: Not reported

The Office of Career Development helps students choose majors, connect with internships, prepare for graduate school, and seek jobs after graduation. The Office of Alumni Engagement provides opportunities for alumni to stay involved with Albion after graduation and beyond.

Student Life

On campus, the four-story Kellogg Hall provides a hub for social life with a bookstore, "campus living room," eateries, pool table/video game area, and the Office of Campus Programs and Organizations. Despite its small size, Albion has more than 100 student organizations that help bring in keynote lecturers, put on musical performances, organize political rallies, and more. Recent lecturers have included former first lady Barbara Bush, feminist Gloria Steinem, Nobel Peace Prize winner Desmond Tutu, and author Kurt Vonnegut.

From astronomy club to Habit for Humanity, Euphonics (a cappella) to WLBN (college radio), and College Democrats to College Republicans, a variety of interest areas are available, including some that are competing and others that are service oriented. Project 250 is a student program that in 1971 raised $250,000 in endowment funds to honor former Albion College President Bernard T. Lomas and now offers $2,000 annual awards to upperclassmen.

Distinctive annual events include the drive-in (or sit-in with blankets, as many students do) movie on the Quad every fall, and Day of the Woden, a huge picnic with games that celebrates the last day of classes. The Quad is a popular place to play Frisbee and football and to have outdoor classes on warm days. Another famous tradition at Albion is the Rock, a graduation gift from the class of 1899 that sits at the northeast corner of the Quad and gets painted almost daily.

Albion's Greek community is over 130 years old and is a major part of campus culture, with one third of students joining the 13 sororities and fraternities. "We have a reputation for being a party school, and it's pretty much deserved," says a Greek student.

There are 14 intramural sports, from basketball to wallyball, and five club sports, including the popular equestrian team. The Nancy G. Held Equestrian Center, opened in 2004, offers programs for everyone from beginners to experienced competitors. There are three varsity equestrian teams that compete in the Intercollegiate Horse Show Association (IHSA), and the Held Center has three arenas, including the Randi C. Heathman Indoor Arena, one of the largest indoors arenas owned by a U.S. college.

Albion's sports teams, the Britons, compete in Division III athletics. Football and basketball games are the most popular for students to watch. The football team earned Michigan's first NCAA football national title in 1994. Track and field, cross-country, swimming, and women's soccer have performed well in their divisions as well.

Albion, Michigan is far from the most "happening" college town, though students do like to take advantage of the local movie theatre's offer of free movies for students. The annual Festival of the Forks in the fall is a popular historic event to attend, and Albion's largest festival. The Whitehouse Nature Center, a 135-acre nature preserve, is adjacent to campus and offers outdoor recreation.

Albion College is truly residential: more than 90 percent of students live in the dorms. Indeed, the college's policy requires "all students, except married students or those residing with their parents, to live and board within the College residence system." Wesley Hall, the largest residence hall on campus, houses 460 first-year students. Upperclassmen choose from a number of residence halls, apartments and annexes, and special interest and themed housing.

Student Body

With such a small student body, students really get to know each other. "We're kind of like one big family, which can be good and bad," explains a student. The student body is fairly homogeneous, with 92 percent from Michigan and only 12 percent minority students. A consortium of student groups called Umbrella aims to highlight and increase diversity. The college's 2015 Strategic Plan aims to increase "geographic (national and international), spiritual, racial/ethnic, socio-economic, political, and cultural" diversity.

You May Not Know

- Albion College was the first private college in the state to have a chapter of Phi Beta Kappa, which was established in 1940.
- Albion, Michigan is located in an area known as *The Forks*, because it is situated at the junction of the north and south branches of the Kalamazoo River. The river provided power for mills, explaining why Albion became a mill town in the mid-19th century.
- In 1835, Methodist Episcopal settlers established Albion College, just two years after the first European immigrant arrived.

Distinguished Alumni

Doug Parker, chairman and CEO of US Airways; Anna Howard Shaw, leader in American women's suffrage movement, physician, and first ordained female Methodist minister in the U.S.; Richard M. Smith, *Newsweek* Chairman and Editor-in-chief.

Admissions and Financial Aid

Albion College accepts both the Common Application and the Albion Application. Albion considers high school GPA and coursework (including AP and honors), standardized test scores, interest in Albion, extracurricular activities, the personal essay, and a letter of recommendation when assessing student qualifications. There is no minimum GPA or ACT/SAT score; rather, the admissions panel looks for "consistency in academic performance."

Early Action is recommended for students who want to be in the initial round of consideration for academic scholarships. Applications received after December 1 are reviewed on a rolling basis. Students who apply after March 1 are only considered on a space-available basis.

For first-time freshmen there is no application fee when applying online. Academic scholarships range from $11,500 to full tuition, and departmental scholarships are also available.

ALBION COLLEGE

Highlights

Admissions Criteria
Academic criteria:
Grades: ☆ ☆ ☆
Difficulty of class schedule: ☆ ☆ ☆
Class rank: ☆
Standardized test scores: ☆ ☆
Teacher recommendations: ☆
Personal statement: ☆ ☆
Non-academic criteria considered:
Interview
Extracurricular activities
Special talents, interests, abilities
Character/personal qualities
Volunteer work
Work experience
State of residency
Alumni relationship

Deadlines
Early Action: December 1
Early Decision: No
Regular Action: Rolling admissions
Common Application: Accepted

Financial Aid
In-state tuition: $35,454
Out-of-state tuition: $35,454
Room: $4,962
Board: $5,182
Books: $900
Freshmen receiving need-based aid: 74%
Undergrads rec. need-based aid: 70%
Avg. % of need met by financial aid: 79%
Avg. aid package (freshmen): $26,742
Avg. aid package (undergrads): $26,466
Avg. debt upon graduation: $36,029

School Spirit
Mascot: Britons
Colors: Purple and gold
Song: *Fyte Onne*

ALFRED UNIVERSITY

ALFRED UNIVERSITY

Four-year private
Founded: 1836
Alfred, NY
Rural
Pop. 5,237

Address:
1 Saxon Drive
Alfred, NY
14802-1205

Admissions:
800-541-9229

Financial Aid:
607-871-2159

admissions@alfred.
edu

www.alfred.edu

Overview

An aerial view of Alfred University (AU) reveals neatly trimmed lawns and about 50 buildings; it is a small campus situated between the Allegheny Mountains foothills and the Finger Lakes region in western New York. Upon closer inspection, one might notice the white cupola of Alumni Hall, listed in the National Register of Historic Places. The distinctive stone castle on campus also catches the eye, and seems apropos for the second oldest co-ed institution in the United States (Alfred was founded in 1836), a university whose mascot, a Saxon, conjures images of medieval knights in shining armor.

The 1,900 undergrads who attend Alfred University certainly don't wear chain mail armor, but they do courageously brave bitter winters on their hamlet-like campus. Alfred, New York is technically a "village," fitting for a university located in what could fairly be called the middle of nowhere. Rochester is an hour away, and Buffalo is two hours away, so the campus can feel secluded, with very limited public transportation. As a dry campus without Greek organizations, Alfred University is not exactly party central either.

Don't be fooled into seeing AU as a place of frozen isolation, though. The university has roots in demanding equal rights, and students are known to be a liberal bunch. A large portion of students are drawn to AU for its engineering and art programs, making for an interesting mix of mostly New York techies and artists.

Academics

Alfred offers more than 60 majors or "areas of concentration" and about as many minors in four schools: College of Business, Kazuo Inamori School of Engineering, School of Art and Design, and College of Liberal Arts and Sciences. The most popular—and most competitive—majors include ceramic engineering and the various fine/studio arts programs that lead to a Bachelor of Fine Arts in the School of Art and Design. Students can earn a minor in astronomy, with the benefit of the Stull Observatory on campus, which houses the largest telescope in the state.

Classes in the School of Engineering, which offers six majors including Glass Engineering Science, are especially rigorous. In fact, ceramic engineering is known to be particularly tough. Most classes have 20 or fewer students, with an average class size of 18 students.

Students in the College of Liberal Arts and Sciences, as part of their General Education requirement, enroll in the First-Year Experience Program. Taught by a professor who is comfortable with a wide range of topics, the make-up and setting of these classes provide newcomers the chance to be part of a small seminar of 18 or fewer students.

The School of Art and Design's program is extensive and interdisciplinary, providing "opportunities to combine studies in ceramic art, art history, drawing, painting, photography, expanded media, and sculpture/dimensional studies." The fine/studio arts programs are "top-notch" according to students.

The Honors Program offers a range of discussion oriented seminars, capped at 15 students, and there are about 120 Alfred students in the program. Other academic opportunities include Alfred Research Grants for Undergraduate Students (ARGUS) and service learning activities through The Gary Horowitz Center for Service Learning.

Alfred's Office of International Programs offers study-abroad programs, typically a semester during junior year. There are exchange programs with universities in China, Europe, Japan, and the UK, with several programs earmarked especially for art students. Approved programs endorsed by Alfred tend to be more costly but expand the choices.

The McComsey Career Development Center at the Allen Steinheim Museum—aka the castle—offers a number of services for students from career counseling to a resume development workshop to an annual Career Fair.

Student Life

The Center for Student Involvement (CSI) at Alfred organizes a broad range of programming and activities, from new student orientation to more than 90 student clubs and organizations that cover a range of interests. Whether it's anime or swing dance, slam poetry or robots, the chances are high that some group will draw you in. The Student Activities Board organizes on-campus movies, music performances, lectures, and comic acts, usually hosted at the 60,000 square-foot Powell Campus Center with its "Knight Club," modern theater, Cybercafe, and more. Theater, dance, and music performances are hosted in the Miller Performing Arts Center.

There isn't a big party scene on campus since Alfred has no Greek organizations (Greek life closed in 2002) and is a dry campus. Alfred State College is also located in Alfred, New York and students sometimes go there to party. One student opines, "If you're looking for parties, this school is probably not what you're looking for."

Perhaps the most memorably named tradition at Alfred is Hot Dog Day, an event in April that raises money for local charities in conjunction with Alfred State College. Hot Dog Day marks the arrival of spring with a parade, Mud Olympics, and, of course, consumption of hot dogs. Each year over 5,000 hot dogs are served. Another popular event is Glam Slam, a campus-wide dance sponsored by Spectrum, Alfred's LGBT group. The Alfie Awards in spring is AU's version of the Academy Awards, where "the dress ranges from extremely formal to extremely outrageous." The Large Act Concert, put on by the Student Activities Board, brings rising acts to campus; past acts have included Vanessa Carlton, Black Eyed Peas, and Alanis Morissette.

Alfred is not known for excelling in intercollegiate sports, and the school offers no athletic scholarships. However, intramural sports, co-recreational sports, and non-competitive general recreation are popular—fifty percent of students participate in one or more of these. The McLane Physical Education Center provides a hub for sports on campus, with courts for basketball and other sports, a pool, and a 4,000-foot fitness center. Club sports, which are initiated and directed by AU students, are extremely popular. They include Ultimate Frisbee, Equestrian Club, and rugby. The state-of-the-art Bromeley-Daggett Equestrian Center opened in 2005. There are over 40 university-owned horses, 40 acres of turnout fields, and five miles of trails.

Alfred is a residential campus, and students are only allowed to live off-campus during their senior year. All residence halls are co-ed. Freshmen halls and upperclassmen halls are available, with options varying from traditional dorms to suites and apartments to special interest housing such as International House, Hillel House, and the newest residence hall Ann's House, an energy-efficient building. Among freshmen, Barresi is one of the more sought-after dorms, though it has a reputation for being quiet. Openhym is popular among those looking for a more social residence.

ALFRED UNIVERSITY

Highlights

Students
Total enrollment: 2,362
Undergrads: 1,935
Part-time students: 3%
From out-of-state: 20%
Male/Female: 49%/51%
Live on-campus: 76%
Off-campus employment rating: Poor
Caucasian: 68%
African American: 7%
Hispanic: 6%
Asian / Pacific Islander: 2%
Native American: 0%
Mixed (2+ ethnicities): 2%
International: 3%

Academics
Calendar: Semester
Student/faculty ratio: 13:1
Class size 9 or fewer: 19%
Class size 10-29: 66%
Class size 30-49: 11%
Class size 50-99: 3%
Class size 100 or more: 1%
Returning freshmen: 68%
Six-year graduation rate: 64%

Most Popular Majors
Art/design
Mechanical engineering
Business administration

Admissions
Applicants: 3,332
Accepted: 2,342
Acceptance rate: 70.3%
Placed on wait list: 49
Enrolled from wait list: 3
Average GPA: 3.2
ACT range: 21-27
SAT Math range: 500-600
SAT Reading range: 480-580
SAT Writing range: 2-14
Top 10% of class: 17%
Top 25% of class: 51%
Top 50% of class: 80%

ALFRED UNIVERSITY

Admissions Criteria
Academic criteria:
Grades: ☆ ☆ ☆
Difficulty of class schedule: ☆ ☆ ☆
Class rank: ☆ ☆ ☆
Standardized test scores: ☆ ☆
Teacher recommendations: ☆ ☆
Personal statement: ☆ ☆
Non-academic criteria considered:
Interview
Extracurricular activities
Special talents, interests, abilities
Character/personal qualities
Volunteer work
Work experience
State of residency
Minority affiliation

Deadlines
Early Action: No
Early Decision: December 1
Regular Action: Rolling admissions
Common Application: Accepted

Financial Aid
In-state tuition: $27,824
Out-of-state tuition: $27,824
Room: $6,020
Board: $5,598
Books: $1,150
Freshmen receiving need-based aid: 85%
Undergrads rec. need-based aid: 81%
Avg. % of need met by financial aid: 83%
Avg. aid package (freshmen): $25,728
Avg. aid package (undergrads): $23,774
Avg. debt upon graduation: $34,494

School Spirit
Mascot: Saxons
Colors: Purple and gold
Song: *Hail to Thee Alfred*

Student Body

Students at Alfred tend to be liberal. "I know of only one student who is a conservative, and even he seems to be coming around," laughs one student. Almost two out of every five students are engineering or art majors, making for an eclectic mix within the student body. With 17 percent minority students, and 80 percent in-state, the school may not be as racially or geographically diverse as some would like. However the arts are multi-cultural, as many student groups attest, and Alfred's unique Drawn to Diversity program uses popular art and media forms to promote diversity.

You May Not Know

- King Alfred the Great became the King of Wessex and Mercia in 871. This explains why the first three digits of all Alfred University numbers are 871, respectively.
- Ella Eaton Kellogg, who graduated from Alfred University in 1872, invented corn flakes along with her husband John Harvey Kellogg.
- Alfred University offers one of the nation's only classes in gay and lesbian history.

Distinguished Alumni

Mary Newton Bruder, better known as "The Grammar Lady" newspaper columnist; Robert Klein, stand-up comedian, singer and actor; Robert Littell, spy novelist; Arnold Zimmerman, award-winning American ceramic artist.

Admissions and Financial Aid

Alfred University is part of the Common Application system, though applicants may also fill out Alfred University's own application form. If a student is able to visit campus and interview with an admissions counselor, the application fee can be waived. Requirements for admission are fairly straightforward and include letter(s) of recommendation, test scores, and an art portfolio for those applicants to the School of Art and Design. Incoming freshman whose first choice is Alfred University may apply through Early Decision.

More than 95 percent of students receive need- or merit-based financial aid, making Alfred a good college buy. Alfred University gives out more than $37 million in financial assistance each year. Scholarships awarding academic and artistic merit are available, including state-sponsored and private college programs. The Presidential Scholarship provides up to $14,000 per year.

ALLEGHENY COLLEGE

Overview

A small liberal arts college tucked away in northwest Pennsylvania, 90 minutes away from Pittsburgh, Allegheny College's rural and beautiful campus is home to many of the 2,100 undergrads. The 77-acre central campus is supplemented by an outdoor recreational complex and nature preserve that add another 465 acres. Students brave harsh winters in this remote part of the state, though this doesn't seem to put a damper on their academic resolve or commitment to service.

One of the nation's oldest liberal arts colleges, Allegheny prides itself on a rigorous liberal arts education that requires students to excel academically and also diversify their courses through having both a major and a minor. According to the college, "With more than 40 programs of study and a capstone comprehensive senior project, the College's rigorous education results in benefits that include acceptance to medical and law schools at rates that are twice the national averages." However, students will probably find more academic diversity among these future doctors, lawyers, and leaders than racial or geographic diversity. There are plenty of service initiatives within the local community that students can become a part of, but the campus itself is not one that is bustling with a dynamic social life.

Academics

About 70 percent of Allegheny students graduated in the top 25 percent of their high school class, making academics at Allegheny fairly competitive. The college also prides itself on students who don't just excel in one area. According to the college, "We feel so strongly about unusual combinations that they are built right into our curriculum: We're one of the few liberal arts colleges nationally that will ask you to choose a minor as well as a major." Students appreciate this requirement because they are forced to specialize outside their major by selecting a minor in a different area. An Allegheny education is very "well-rounded," say students.

Allegheny takes its vision of a liberal arts education further with the Distribution Requirement, which states that all students must take at least two courses in the division least represented in their major and minor. For students not in the natural sciences, this includes at least one laboratory course.

All students take three First-year/Sophomore (FS) courses in order to hone communication and research skills and prepare for a Junior Seminar and Senior Project in their major. Since Allegheny is such a small college, students have close relationships with professors and grad students do not teach classes. The average class size for freshmen is 21 (more for intro science courses), and the average laboratory just 15 students. There are about 500 courses offered, in addition to Independent Studies, internships, and senior projects.

Strong programs include the sciences—biology, chemistry, and physics—pre-health professions, and international studies, an interdisciplinary major.

Allegheny's communication arts and theatre programs are housed in the 40,000-square-foot Vukovich Center for Communication Arts built in 2009. The building is hard to miss with its "garden roof" covered in grass, ground cover, and trees. The Allegheny Center for Experiential Learning (ACCEL) offers diverse academic opportunities for students, including service learning, a leadership program, three-week summer internships as well as shadowing experiences in pre-law and pre-health.

Allegheny sponsors semester- and year-long study-abroad opportunities—there are currently 22 options in 16 countries besides the United States. It is also possible to apply to study off campus independently. Several scholarships are available for studying abroad. "My best semester was studying abroad in Paris," reminisces a student. A blog (studyabroad.allegheny.edu) captures perspectives from the various overseas journeys on which students may embark.

ALLEGHENY COLLEGE

Four-year private
Founded: 1815
Meadville, PA
Small town
Pop. 13,616

Address:
520 North Main Street
Meadville, PA
16335

Admissions:
800-521-5293

Financial Aid:
800-835-7780

admissions@allegheny.edu

www.allegheny.edu

ALLEGHENY COLLEGE

Students
Total enrollment: 2,140
Undergrads: 2,140
Freshmen: 612
Part-time students: 2%
From out-of-state: 47%
From public schools: 84%
Male/Female: 46%/54%
Live on-campus: 90%
In fraternities: 28%
In sororities: 34%
Off-campus employment rating: Excellent
Caucasian: 81%
African American: 5%
Hispanic: 5%
Asian / Pacific Islander: 3%
Native American: 0%
Mixed (2+ ethnicities): 3%
International: 0%

Academics
Calendar: Semester
Student/faculty ratio: 12:1
Class size 9 or fewer: 20%
Class size 10-29: 67%
Class size 30-49: 13%
Class size 50-99: 1%
Class size 100 or more: -
Returning freshmen: 89%
Six-year graduation rate: 78%
Graduates who immediately go to graduate school: 37%

Most Popular Majors
Biology
Economics
Psychology

Admissions
Applicants: 4,795
Accepted: 3,034
Acceptance rate: 63.3%
Placed on wait list: 216
Enrolled from wait list: 26
Average GPA: 3.7
ACT range: 24-29
SAT Math range: 560-650
SAT Reading range: 540-650
SAT Writing range: 8-35
Top 10% of class: 40%
Top 25% of class: 70%
Top 50% of class: 93%

58

The Office of Career Services at Allegheny provides resources for finding jobs, internships, and other career-related opportunities. Alumni enjoy free individual career counseling, resume and cover letter critiques, and more. Allegheny shines in the pre-health professions. In fact, over the past 10 years, Allegheny students' acceptance to medical schools has averaged 77 percent compared to the national average of 35 percent over the same period. Acceptance rates to dental, veterinary, optometry, and podiatry schools are similarly impressive. About 34 percent of students pursue a graduate degree immediately after graduation.

Student Life

There are more than 100 student organizations at Allegheny. Popular ones include Orchesis Dance Company, Gator Activities Programming, Outing Club, and Student Government. The school has an outdoor recreational area of more than 120 acres. The Henderson Campus Center, renovated in 2004, is another campus hotspot—you'll find students playing Wii, pool, and ping pong in the Game Room.

Campus social traditions include Homecoming and Winter Carnival during the colder months. The warming weather signals the season for Springfest (fireworks recently kicked off the weekend) and Wing Fest, when students enjoy live music and free wings on the lawn. An annual Hut-A-Thon has a social change agenda which focuses on raising awareness for homelessness during a 48-hour event associated with Habitat for Humanity. Activities for Hut-A-Thon include fundraising, of course, but also a rather unique experience where students are offered the opportunity to live temporarily in a basic hut to get a taste of what it is like to be physically homeless.

Greek organizations have a strong presence on campus, not surprising given the limited activities off campus. Twenty-eight percent of men and 34 percent of women are active members of the 11 fraternities and sororities on campus. The party scene is "heavy but not mandatory for a good time" says a student.

Allegheny College offers no athletic scholarships. The college is a member of the North Coast Athletic Conference (Division III), and intramurals and club sports are popular. Many students participate in over a dozen sports, from basketball to a 100-mile club for runners. The new Wise Center Athletic Facility has a gym, racquetball courts, dance studios, indoor track, and more. The Mellon Pool offers scuba classes and the outdoor Robertson Complex provides fields and tennis courts.

Meadville, where Allegheny College is located, offers a limited city life with some bars and restaurants, but with less than 14,000 residents, it's not a particularly lively social scene. Farther afield, Conneaut Lake is about 20 minutes away and Lake Erie is less than an hour away—two places that offer boating, waterskiing, and skiing.

Almost 90 percent of students live on campus and housing is guaranteed for four years. Only seniors are allowed to live off campus. There are a variety of housing options, including single-sex and co-ed. Floors in certain halls are designated wellness, community service, and quiet study. Apartment, special interest houses, and frat houses are also available. Students enjoy being able to personalize their rooms by painting the walls, as long as they paint them back to white at the end of the school year.

Student Body

The 2,100 undergraduates at Allegheny hail from 46 states and 40 countries. However, it is not highly geographically diverse, since more than 50 percent of students call Pennsylvania home. The college is moderately racially/ethnically diverse, with 16 percent of the student population minority students.

Service is popular among Allegheny students, who initiated the Service-Learning Challenge program in 2000 to integrate service learning into their curriculum, and who can be found volunteering at day-long service events throughout the year. "Make a Difference Day" in October brings together over 700 students and 700 community members to complete over 125 projects. On "Service Saturdays," students gather for breakfast before going out to meet the needs of the Meadville community. Even the name of the campus coffee shop, Grounds for Change, attests to the emphasis on service.

You May Not Know

- Founded in 1815, Allegheny College is the 32nd oldest college in the U.S., making it among the oldest 1 percent of colleges and universities in America.
- Alumnus Ida Tarbell, the only woman in her graduating class of 1880, was an investigative journalist who was inducted into the National Women's Hall of Fame in 2000 and commemorated on a U.S. postage stamp in 2002.
- The Wrecking Ball Café at Allegheny is named after a 2007 accident in Meadville where a 1,500-pound wrecking ball came loose and hit nine parked cars.

Distinguished Alumni

Benjamin P. Burtt, Jr., Academy Award winner for sound design and effects; Jane Earll, Pennsylvania State Senator; Ida Tarbell, journalist.

Admissions and Financial Aid

Allegheny accepts more than 63 percent of applicants, most of whom are the most competitive of their high schools. The admissions process at Allegheny focuses on "academic promise," so difficulty of high school classes, class rank, and standardized test scores are all important criteria for getting admitted. An admissions interview is recommended though not required. Prospective students can arrange overnight stays with advance notice. Allegheny accepts the Common Application or its own application, and there is an application fee that can be waived for financial hardship and for all campus visitors. Students may apply Early Decision.

Financial aid is quite generous: more than 70 percent of undergrads receive need-based aid, and more than one-quarter receive merit-based aid. The financial aid office website is updated periodically with news about scholarships, many of which reflect Allegheny's location and Methodist ties such as Pittsburgh Foundation and United Methodist Higher Education Foundation scholarships.

ALLEGHENY COLLEGE

Highlights

Admissions Criteria
Academic criteria:
Grades: ☆ ☆ ☆
Difficulty of class schedule: ☆ ☆ ☆
Class rank: ☆ ☆ ☆
Standardized test scores: ☆ ☆
Teacher recommendations: ☆ ☆
Personal statement: ☆
Non-academic criteria considered:
Interview
Extracurricular activities
Special talents, interests, abilities
Character/personal qualities
Volunteer work
Work experience
State of residency
Geographical location
Minority affiliation
Alumni relationship

Deadlines
Early Action: No
Early Decision: November 15
Regular Action: February 15 (final)
Notification of admission by: April 1
Common Application: Accepted

Financial Aid
In-state tuition: $38,710
Out-of-state tuition: $38,710
Room: $5,220
Board: $4,700
Books: $1,000
Freshmen receiving need-based aid: 75%
Undergrads rec. need-based aid: 72%
Avg. % of need met by financial aid: 88%
Avg. aid package (freshmen): $31,387
Avg. aid package (undergrads): $30,739

School Spirit
Mascot: Alligator
Colors: Blue and gold

ALMA COLLEGE

Four-year private
Founded: 1886
Alma, MI
Small town
Pop. 9,312

Address:
614 West Superior
Street
Alma, MI
48801-1599

Admissions:
800-321-2562

Financial Aid:
800-321-2562

admissions@alma.edu

www.alma.edu

ALMA COLLEGE

Overview

A small liberal arts college with less than 1,500 undergrads in the small town of Alma, Michigan (population about 9,000), Alma College covers a modest 125 acres plus a 200-acre ecological tract. Visitors are greeted by a scenic central mall surrounded by 26 major buildings, with the tall white pillars and steeple of The Dunning Memorial Chapel commemorating the college's founding in 1886 by Presbyterians. Alma College maintains a close relationship with the Presbyterian Church while welcoming all religious backgrounds. Visitors will probably note the college's Scottish roots—the marching band's kilts are made of the college's own patented tartan.

Despite its small size, Alma offers plenty of opportunities for student growth. Though academics are far from overwhelmingly rigorous, students tend to excel in their fields of study. In fact, 27 Alma students have won prestigious national fellowships such as Fulbright, Truman, Udall, and Gates-Cambridge since 2003. Alumni have high job and graduate school placement rates, and the school continues to expand, with an arena and convocation center building project underway, the Eddy Music Center renovation and building addition planned, and its largest fundraising campaign in history for more than $35 million completed nine months ahead of schedule, paving the way for enhanced classroom learning. A small residential college in Michigan obviously can't offer all the excitement of a large college or a big city, and some may find ethnic and geographic diversity lacking, with the vast majority of students hailing from Michigan. However, students will also find a community of friendly, engaged students ready to explore the possibilities ahead of them.

Academics

The small class sizes—92 percent of classes have 29 or fewer enrolled—plus the lack of teaching assistants, guarantee plenty of interaction with professors. Students describe the workload as "manageable" and the professors as "very accessible."

The college offers 31 majors in 21 departments, plus 31 minors and programs, including nine pre-professional programs. Students may earn Bachelor of Arts, Bachelor of Science, Bachelor of Fine Arts, and Bachelor of Music degrees. For students who can't find the perfect major, the Program of Emphasis (POE) allows students to work with a faculty committee to create an individually tailored concentration. Previous examples include arts management, personnel administration, and pre-gerontology.

For those who take a more traditional route, strong established programs at Alma include business administration; elementary, secondary, and early childhood education; numerous pre-professional programs in health fields; political science; and psychology.

The college's general education distributive requirements mandate a first-year seminar, a writing course, a second language course, and courses in the arts and humanities, social sciences, and natural sciences.

The academic year follows a "4-4-1" calendar: two 14-week semesters then a one-month intensive Spring Term in May. Spring Term enables students to focus intensively on a single academic topic and offers the opportunity to venture off campus to study in the U.S. or abroad. Students are required to have two Spring Terms before graduation. "I love the Spring Term," comments one student, "because I can study abroad without missing out on the regular school year."

Freshmen become acquainted with the campus through the week-long Preterm Orientation. Freshmen who want to pursue departmental honors and gain membership in Phi Beta Kappa enroll in First-Year Honors Seminars and participate in Honors Scholars events. They conduct independent study with a faculty member and participate in a Senior Capstone Course.

The Center of Responsible Leadership, "an emerging hallmark program at Alma," prepares ethical leaders through a Leadership Fellows program, speaker series (past speakers have included former President of Mexico Vicente Fox and former Secretary of State Madeleine Albright), service opportunities, and more. The Posey Global Leadership Initiative develops leadership skills through international internships. The new PRISM project—funded by a $5 million grant from the National Science Foundation—increases research opportunities in the sciences.

Studying abroad provides students the opportunity to study beyond the scope of what Alma has to offer, with a dozen choices of countries. All language majors are required to spend a semester abroad in order to hone their language skills. An impressive 41 percent of students study abroad at some point during their Alma College experience.

Over the past five years, Alma has a 90 percent acceptance rate in medical school (compared to the national average of less than 50 percent) and an 87 percent acceptance rate in law school. Historically, over 90 percent of students are employed or enter graduate or professional school within six months of graduation. The Academic and Career Planning office offers a plethora of career resources.

Student Life

There are 79 student organizations at Alma, from the performing arts to honor societies to faith-based fellowships. The Alma College choirs are popular, not to mention numerous music ensembles and theater and dance opportunities. The fact that more than a third of all Alma students take part in at least one cultural performance each year attests to the college's vibrant art scene, housed at Remick Heritage Center, the region's premiere performing arts facility. Additionally, the Model UN group is very successful; Alma has won 24 outstanding delegation awards in the last 15 years at the National Model UN Conference—more than any other school. Community service is particularly popular at Alma, as seen by its place on the President's Higher Education Community Service Honor roll.

There are 11 sororities and fraternities on campus, including two dedicated to music. The Student Handbook outlines a detailed alcohol policy—kegs are not allowed on campus. Despite limitations on serving alcohol, Greek parties are central to the partying scene at Alma. "If you want alcohol, you can find it," a student admits.

Alma's most famous tradition is undoubtedly the Highland Festival and Games, when students revel in traditional Scottish games, music, and sports. The president might even be seen sporting a kilt and blazer during this Memorial Day weekend celebration.

More than one third of students are members of intercollegiate athletic teams. There are 18 Division III sports. Intramural sports are also popular, with half of all students participating. Sports at Alma are characterized more by engagement than excellence, which is to be expected for a small school with no athletic scholarships. The Alan J. Stone Recreation Center houses a fitness room, suspended running track, and even a 600-square-foot climbing wall.

The city of Alma is small and doesn't provide much excitement for students. Mt. Pleasant is about 15 minutes away and has some restaurants. Some students venture to Michigan State University and Central Michigan for parties.

Students must live on campus during their freshman and sophomore years, and 90 percent of all students choose to do so. In addition to nine residence halls, there is also an international house and

ALMA COLLEGE

Highlights

Students
Total enrollment: 1,464
Undergrads: 1,464
Part-time students: 3%
From out-of-state: 9%
From public schools: 90%
Male/Female: 46%/54%
Live on-campus: 90%
In fraternities: 21%
In sororities: 27%
Off-campus employment rating: Good
Caucasian: 86%
African American: 3%
Hispanic: 2%
Asian / Pacific Islander: 1%
Native American: 1%
Mixed (2+ ethnicities): 2%
International: 1%

Academics
Calendar: 4-4-1 system
Student/faculty ratio: 12:1
Class size 9 or fewer: 29%
Class size 10-29: 63%
Class size 30-49: 7%
Class size 50-99: 1%
Class size 100 or more: -
Returning freshmen: 80%
Six-year graduation rate: 66%

Most Popular Majors
Business administration
Biology
English

Admissions
Applicants: 2,232
Accepted: 1,604
Acceptance rate: 71.9%
Average GPA: 3.5
ACT range: 21-26
SAT Math range: 450-620
SAT Reading range: Not reported
SAT Writing range: 10-14
Top 10% of class: 23%
Top 25% of class: 54%
Top 50% of class: 84%

61

ALMA COLLEGE

Women's Resource Center. Wright Hall is the newest residence, opened in 2005. Known as Alma's "green" dormitory facility, the 60-bed apartment-style hall includes rooftop solar heating panels and geothermal heating and cooling. There is a swimming pool in the Hogan Center, which underwent a $10.2 million renovation.

Student Body

An exclusively undergraduate institution, Alma's more than 1,400 students represent 24 states and 15 foreign countries. However, an overall account of the student population shows that they are not very ethnically or geographically diverse. Only 9 percent are minority students, and only 9 percent come from out of state. "We may not be the most diverse school, but everyone feels welcome, and what we lack in ethnic diversity, we have in diversity of interests," explains a student.

You May Not Know

- Alma is the only American college with its own patented tartan fabric, used to make the kilts that marching band members wear.
- There are more than 100 tree species on Alma's campus and a student group is actively trying to increase this number to make Alma "the tree capital among the nation's college campuses."
- In Alma's popular Percussion Ensemble, you won't just find drum sets and marimbas. Packing crates, pickle buckets, fire truck sirens, and conch shells are all considered fair game.

Distinguished Alumni

George Allen, Pro Football Hall of Fame NFL coach; Kristen Dubenion-Smith, opera soloist for the American Opera Theater company; Gary Peters, Michigan politician.

Admissions and Financial Aid

Alma's online application is free and fairly straightforward. Unlike many other applications, the personal essay is optional, though recommended. Required supplemental materials include a counselor recommendation, high school transcript, and ACT or SAT scores. Admissions decisions are rolling, and notification is given two weeks after all materials are received. Most regular applicants apply during fall of senior year. Applications sent by December 1 have priority consideration for scholarships.

Campus Close-ups offers an intimate view of the Alma College experience and includes a Saturday morning presentation, tour with Alma students, and complimentary lunch at a dining hall. Out-of-state students can contact an admissions representative to ask about financial assistance with lodging, food, and travel expenses.

Virtually 100 percent of students receive need- or merit-based financial aid. Merit-based scholarships include the Distinguished Scholar Award (full tuition), Trustee Honors Scholarship ($14,000), Presidential Scholarship ($13,000), and Dean's Scholarship ($12,000).

AMERICAN UNIVERSITY

Overview

American University is a medium-sized, private university located in Washington, DC. The school's crown jewel is its well-respected School of International Service. AU is located on "Embassy Row," a suburban, residential area near various foreign embassies, while bustling downtown DC is just a metro ride away. As a result of its desirable address, the university draws famous guest lecturers, and students have access to a smorgasbord of internships. The restaurants, museums, bars, and performance venues of DC keep weekends hopping.

When it comes to academics, students will find the strongest programs are in the fields of politics and international relations. Special programs like the Honors Program and the Global Scholars Program help high-achieving students find their niche in such a large school. The diverse student body and high study-abroad participation rates underscore the university's globally-aware atmosphere.

Students with a penchant for politics and a desire to acquire a more international perspective can't go wrong in choosing AU.

Academics

American University offers undergraduates 122 degree programs in five schools. The strongest areas are political science, business administration, and international studies. In fact, AU is home to the largest undergraduate international studies program in the U.S., with over 1,500 students in the major. AU boasts many well known professors, but nonetheless students report that the quality of teaching can be hit-or-miss. "A handful of professors seem to be more concerned about their own careers than teaching, but most are outstanding," one student says. Class sizes are small, averaging about 22 students.

The general education requirements at AU consist of 10 courses. Students must take an introductory-level and a secondary-level course in each of these named areas: The Creative Arts, Traditions That Shape The Western World, Global and Multicultural Perspectives, Social Institutions and Behavior, and The Natural Sciences.

The School of International Service, which embraces eight different areas of study, is highly renowned. There are several special programs for undergraduates. The most prestigious is the Global Scholars Program. Twenty-five freshmen get the chance to begin a 3-year BA with the option of completing an MA their fourth year. Students take International Service courses together and have the opportunity to study abroad the summer after freshmen year. They also participate in special academic advising, organize community service and other activities together, and spend their freshman year in a living/learning program. The School of International Service has its own Alumni-Student Mentoring Program that matches students with successful alums. "There is no better place to go if you want to work abroad," one student remarks.

Each year, around 15 percent of incoming freshmen are invited to join the Honors Program, with benefits that are much more extensive than at many other schools. Honors students can take special courses, which foster active participation and contact with professors, including multi-disciplinary Honors Colloquia. They can live together on an Honors floor, snag great research opportunities, attend special events with prestigious guests, enjoy free lunches with professors, and register for classes before everyone else. They also have the opportunity to take a week-long, professor-led trip over an academic break to destinations like Macchu Picchu and the Great Pyramids—but trips are not funded. Lastly, there is the Capstone project with faculty mentors that is clearly the cherry on top of the honors program sundae.

Through Learning Communities, first-year students get to extend their classroom education to include trips and events in DC. Learning Communities also help

AMERICAN UNIVERSITY

Four-year private
Founded: 1893
Washington, DC
Major city
Pop. 617,996

Address:
4400 Massachusetts
Avenue, NW
Washington, DC
20016

Admissions:
202-885-6000

Financial Aid:
202-885-6100

admissions@american.edu

www.american.edu

AMERICAN UNIVERSITY

Highlights

Students
Total enrollment: 12,904
Undergrads: 7,299
Freshmen: 1,541
Part-time students: 5%
From out-of-state: 86%
Male/Female: 41%/59%
Live-on campus: Not reported
In fraternities: 20%
In sororities: 18%
Off-campus employment rating: Excellent
Caucasian: 56%
African American: 6%
Hispanic: 9%
Asian / Pacific Islander: 7%
Native American: 0%
Mixed (2+ ethnicities): 4%
International: 7%

Academics
Calendar: Semester
Student/faculty ratio: 12:1
Class size 9 or fewer: 5%
Class size 10-29: 74%
Class size 30-49: 19%
Class size 50-99: 2%
Class size 100 or more: 1%
Returning freshmen: 90%
Six-year graduation rate: 77%

Most Popular Majors
International studies
Business administration
Political science

Admissions
Applicants: 17,039
Accepted: 7,531
Acceptance rate: 44.2%
Placed on wait list: 1,379
Enrolled from wait list: Not reported
Average GPA: 3.7
ACT range: 26-30
SAT Math range: 570-670
SAT Reading range: 590-690
SAT Writing range: 18-50
Top 10% of class: 45%
Top 25% of class: 80%
Top 50% of class: 97%

64

students get to know a small group of peers with similar interests. Activities often include cultural excursions, service projects, and creative pieces.

Study abroad is a big part of AU life. There are 100 programs in 41 different countries. Fifty-five percent of students take part in study abroad, earning AU the eighth highest percentage of study-abroad participation in the country.

Since Washington, DC is a veritable internship Mecca, AU students have no trouble getting a head start on career preparation. Eighty percent participate in an internship or co-op. The Career Center offers a helpful school-specific listing of internship organizations.

Student Life

There are 220 student organizations at AU. Some of the most popular are *The Eagle*, the campus newspaper, and WVAU, the student radio station. Greek life is fairly prominent on campus, with 12 sororities and 16 fraternities.

Students dress up every February and dance the night away to live bands and DJs at the black-tie Founder's Day Ball. Then in April, they pull out their ratty T-shirts and gardening gloves to help out at Campus Beautification Day, an event with a barbecue and raffle that keep things from being all work and no play. Nerdy as it may be, the lectures and speakers' series that are always going on are a huge draw for students. It's no wonder, considering the big names that grace the campus. Senators, ex-presidents, and assorted world leaders are the norm. "I heard Bob Schieffer speak about the role of the media and politics," says a student.

AU is in NCAA Division I and has 16 teams. Students feel that the lack of a football team just makes for more attention on the basketball team. Volleyball games and wrestling matches are also popular with student spectators, but the variety of intramurals is rather lackluster with only 15 offerings to choose from. "Most of us are too busy to play sports," one student remarks.

Off campus, the possible activities are never-ending. Students hang out at Georgetown, frequent the bars in DuPont Circle, take in some culture at DC's many museums (especially the Smithsonian Museums, which are free), check out the national monuments, enjoy top-notch performances at the Kennedy Center, and fill up at the huge variety of restaurants in town. "You'll never lack something to do," one student comments.

The majority of students live on campus, having the choice between single sex and co-ed floors. Housing is divided between "Northside" and "Southside." Northside is quieter, with no Greek houses, and it hosts more international students. Northside halls include Hughes (home to the honors program), Leonard (for upperclassmen), and McDowell (a hub that includes a study lounge, recreation center, and computer room). Southside has a reputation for being more social. Southside dorms include Anderson (freshmen and sophomores, home to a professor-in-residence who often hosts get-togethers), Centennial (upperclassmen suites), and Letts (freshman-only, with great views from the Sky Lounge).

Student Body

The student body is highly geographically diverse, with 144 different countries and all states represented. Students share an international outlook; 80 percent report that "improving their understanding of other countries and cultures" is important to them. Students also tend to be politically involved. Seventy-two percent report that "keeping up-to-date with political affairs" is a priority, and there are more liberals than conservatives in the student body. Ethnic diversity is moderate, with one quarter minority students.

You May Not Know

- AU is a Methodist-affiliated school; its founder, John Hurst, was a well-traveled Methodist bishop and author of a cultural history of Sri Lanka.
- President John F. Kennedy delivered AU's 1963 commencement speech.
- The heroine of the TV series *Bones* is modeled after AU alum Kathy Reichs.

Distinguished Alumni

Robert Byrd, longest-serving U.S. Senator; David Gregory, Moderator of NBC's *Meet the Press*; Goldie Hawn, actress; Judith Sheindlin, "Judge Judy."

Admissions and Financial Aid

Prospective students may apply using the Common Application or the AU-specific online application. No separate application is required for the Honors Program or for merit-based scholarships. The university offers Preview Days for interested students (either before or after they are accepted) to visit campus and participate in programmed events.

AU has three main merit scholarship programs: Presidential Scholarship, Dean's Scholarship, and Leadership Scholarship. The Frederick Douglass Scholars Program provides four years of full tuition (including room and board) to a small number of high-achieving students "dedicated to careers in social justice and improving under-resourced, underserved communities around the world." First-generation students and "those from diverse ethnic, cultural, and socioeconomic backgrounds" receive preference for this award.

Other awards include one-time endowed scholarships that can range from $100 to $10,000. In addition, scholarships are available to students whose parents work at one of 160 Tuition Exchange colleges and to children of Methodist ministers. Finally, athletes should consult the athletic department about possible scholarships.

AMERICAN UNIVERSITY

Highlights

Admissions Criteria
Academic criteria:
Grades: ☆ ☆ ☆
Difficulty of class schedule: ☆ ☆ ☆
Class rank: N/A
Standardized test scores: ☆ ☆
Teacher recommendations: ☆ ☆
Personal statement: ☆ ☆
Non-academic criteria considered:
Extracurricular activities
Special talents, interests, abilities
Character/personal qualities
Volunteer work
Work experience
State of residency
Geographical location
Minority affiliation
Alumni relationship

Deadlines
Early Action: No
Early Decision: November 15
Regular Action: January 15 (final)
Notification of admission by: April 1
Common Application: Accepted

Financial Aid
In-state tuition: $40,132
Out-of-state tuition: $40,132
Room: $9,466
Board: $4,714
Books: $800
Freshmen receiving need-based aid: 53%
Undergrads rec. need-based aid: 52%
Avg. % of need met by financial aid: 72%
Avg. aid package (freshmen): $30,402
Avg. aid package (undergrads): $27,138

School Spirit
Mascot: Clawed
Colors: Red, white, and blue
Song: *American University Fight Song*

Four-year private
Founded: 1821
Amherst, MA
Rural
Pop. 34,874

Address:
P.O. Box 5000
Amherst, MA
01002-5000

Admissions:
413-542-2328

Financial Aid:
413-542-2296

admission@amherst.
edu

www.amherst.edu

AMHERST COLLEGE

Overview

Amherst College, not to be confused with the nearby University of Massachusetts Amherst, may sound small with its enrollment of about 1,800 undergrads. However, a stroll through the college's 1,000-acre campus, which includes a number of museums, a planetarium, and a wildlife sanctuary, will attest to the college's extensive physical resources, thanks to an endowment of more than $1 billion. The western Massachusetts town of Amherst—population 35,000—is nearby though you're more likely to find students trekking to the other four colleges in the Five College Consortium as well as UMass Amherst for classes and parties. Amherst isn't a college for students who want a one-stop shop for all their academic and social needs: students escape four years of studying and living on campus by going to nearby higher ed institutes, making the occasional trip to Boston, and studying abroad.

Amherst has outgrown its reputation as a white preppy school. In fact, Amherst's progressive financial aid policies underscore a commitment to ethnic and socioeconomic diversity, and in past years about 40 percent of students have been minorities. Academics at the competitive college are rigorous, but students don't forget to have fun either: during winter, it's not uncommon to see students sledding down Memorial Hill on makeshift sleds—aka dining hall trays!

Academics

With 83 percent of students graduating in the top 10 percent of their high school classes, academics at Amherst are demanding. The 2014 *U.S. News* ranking of Amherst as the second highest liberal arts college attests to the college's intellectual rigor. However, students report that they aren't studying 24/7. "We work hard but we also know how to have fun, at least when we're not buried in the library," says a student. Amherst offers BA degrees in 34 different majors and more than 800 courses. Strong programs include the majors of American studies, biology, chemistry, economics, and political science along with pre-law, a pre-professional program.

Amherst is a member of the Five Colleges, an educational consortium that includes Hampshire, Mount Holyoke, and Smith Colleges along with the University of Massachusetts at Amherst (UMass Amherst). Students may take courses at the member colleges, and the schools' close proximities add to Amherst's student life. There are no core requirements, so students have plenty of flexibility in choosing their classes. Faculty advisors help steer students in charting their courses. Not surprising for the high-achieving student body, nearly half the graduating class in recent years has conducted honors work.

Since Amherst is an exclusively undergraduate school, teaching assistants never teach classes. Students appreciate their professors' attention and accessibility—with an impressively small student/faculty ratio of 8:1, allowing for plenty of individualized focus from profs. There is even the TYPO (Take Your Professor Out) program where students receive funds to take their professors out to dinner in small groups.

For the past 10 years, about 35-40 percent of Amherst's junior class studied abroad. Most students spend a semester abroad with a program or through direct enrollment with an overseas university. Some spend a full year out of country.

Amherst boasts more than 18,000 graduates. According to the college, almost 70 percent of alumni make a gift to Amherst each year, the "highest alumni participation rate in the country." The career center offers a plethora of workshops and programs as well as individual advising for students planning their career paths.

Student Life

There are more than 100 student organizations, from "AAAAAAAA" (a CD compilation of original musical works by Amherst students) to the Zumbyes, an all-male a cappella group that has been singing since 1950. Student government representatives allocated about $250,000 among student organizations, which cover a broad spectrum of interests: service and activism, religion and cultural affinity, arts, debate, and more. Student organizations at the colleges in the Five College consortium are also open to students.

With 99 percent of students living on campus, there's always something to do on the weekends at Amherst, though there is no Greek life (fraternities were abolished in 1984). School-sponsored "theme parties," or TAPs, are social events that, as staff writer for *The Amherst Student* magazine wrote, "herald the coming of each new holiday or season, and, more generally...mark the passage of time on campus." From the Luau TAP that marks the beginning of the school year to Endless Summer TAP, these are popular events. Homecoming TAP and Screw your Roommate TAP are also popular. Another party of note is Casino Night, which combines food, casino games, and live music with a good cause.

At Amherst 32 percent of students participate in varsity sports—there are 27 NCAA Division III varsity teams—and an astonishing 80 percent are active in club and intramural sports. The school mascot is Lord Jeff, named after Lord Jeffery Amherst. In recent years, the women's tennis, women's lacrosse, men's basketball, women's cross-country, and women's ice hockey teams have all won NCAA team or national championships.

It's a moderate trek to Boston—about 90 minutes—so Amherst students don't typically go to Beantown every weekend. And they generally don't make the trip to the other colleges in the Five College Consortium or to UMass Amherst for parties since there are plenty on campus. However, Amherst's close proximity to these colleges means that bigger music and theater acts make an effort to come to the area. Closer to campus is downtown Amherst, a small town that has some bars and restaurants that students can get to by free bus service. "Amherst is small but has enough to do," says a student.

Housing is guaranteed for four years. Freshmen live together in new or newly renovated residences on the Main Quad, while sophomores and above have several theme houses to choose from. Students like the dorms for their spaciousness. "Of course the dorms aren't palaces, but they're pretty nice," says a student.

Student Body

More than 1,800 undergraduates attend Amherst. While the old stereotype of Amherst students could be summarized in two words—white and preppy—the current student population is actually very diverse. As the college emphasizes, "Diversity, in its broadest sense, is fundamental to Amherst's mission. The college enrolls students from every state and more than 40 countries, and for the past several years about 40 percent of Amherst's students have been students of color." The generous financial aid options increase socioeconomic diversity among students.

While Amherst students tend to be liberal, they aren't known to be particularly politically active. Many students participate in athletics, either varsity or intramural. "We're known both for being brainy and athletic," one student explains.

AMHERST COLLEGE

Highlights

Students
Total enrollment: 1,817
Undergrads: 1,817
Freshmen: 463
From out-of-state: 86%
Male/Female: 51%/49%
Live on-campus: 99%
Off-campus employment rating: Fair
Caucasian: 40%
African American: 11%
Hispanic: 12%
Asian / Pacific Islander: 12%
Native American: 0%
Mixed (2+ ethnicities): 6%
International: 10%

Academics
Calendar: Semester
Student/faculty ratio: 8:1
Class size 9 or fewer: 27%
Class size 10-29: 61%
Class size 30-49: 9%
Class size 50-99: 3%
Class size 100 or more: -
Returning freshmen: 98%
Six-year graduation rate: 95%
Graduates who immediately go to graduate school: 28%

Most Popular Majors
English
Political science
Economics

Admissions
Applicants: 8,565
Accepted: 1,110
Acceptance rate: 13.0%
Placed on wait list: 1,430
Enrolled from wait list: 80
Average GPA: Not reported
ACT range: 30-34
SAT Math range: 670-760
SAT Reading range: 670-770
SAT Writing range: 61-35
Top 10% of class: 83%
Top 25% of class: 95%
Top 50% of class: 100%

67

College Profiles

AMHERST COLLEGE

Admissions Criteria

Academic criteria:
Grades: ☆ ☆ ☆
Difficulty of class schedule: ☆ ☆ ☆
Class rank: ☆ ☆
Standardized test scores: ☆ ☆ ☆
Teacher recommendations: ☆ ☆ ☆
Personal statement: ☆ ☆ ☆
Non-academic criteria considered:
Extracurricular activities
Special talents, interests, abilities
Character/personal qualities
Volunteer work
Work experience
Geographical location
Minority affiliation
Alumni relationship

Deadlines

Early Action: No
Early Decision: November 15
Regular Action: January 1 (final)
Notification of admission by: April 1
Common Application: Accepted

Financial Aid

In-state tuition: $57,970 (comprehensive
    fee includes tuition, room, and board)
Out-of-state tuition: $57,970
Room: Varies
Board: Varies
Books: $1,000
Freshmen receiving need-based aid: 56%
Undergrads rec. need-based aid: 55%
Avg. % of need met by financial aid:
    100%
Avg. aid package (freshmen): $45,438
Avg. aid package (undergrads): $44,888
Avg. debt upon graduation: $14,566

School Spirit

Mascot: Lord Jeffs

You May Not Know

- Robert Frost taught on and off at Amherst for over forty years, beginning in 1916.
- To demonstrate class spirit, the freshman class of 1874 burned or buried the textbooks of their hardest courses—especially mathematics—in an elaborate mock funeral.
- Amherst's athletic program is the oldest in the nation.

Distinguished Alumni

Debby Applegate, Pulitzer Prize-winning history and biographer; Dan Brown, author of *The Da Vinci Code* and other books; Calvin Coolidge, 13th U.S. President; Caroline Thompson, screenwriter, film director, and producer (*Edward Scissorhands*, *The Nightmare before Christmas*); Scott Turow, author and lawyer.

Admissions and Financial Aid

Admission to Amherst is extremely selective, with 13 percent of applicants accepted. According to the college, "No one aspect will make or break our decision; instead, we look at the sum total of your experiences." The academic transcript and the rigor of the classes taken in high school weigh the heaviest in admission decisions. The college offers student blogs to provide more insight, and there are special requirements for students in the arts.

Amherst College has long been progressive in its financial aid policy. It was one of the initial schools to offer need blind admission, giving admitted students—including international students—financial aid to meet their full financial requirement. Amherst was the nation's first college to eliminate loans for low-income students, and loans in financial aid packages were replaced with scholarships for *all* students. More than half of Amherst students receive need- or merit-based financial aid. According to the college, "The college's financial aid packages are consistently among the most generous in the U.S., and among its peer universities and colleges Amherst has the greatest economic diversity."

Although Amherst does not give merit, athletic, or academic scholarships, other special scholarship opportunities abound. The college recently created a permanently endowed scholarship fund for veterans of the U.S. armed forces. Other programs help talented students transfer from community colleges and QuestBridge is a nonprofit scholar's fund that serves low-income youth.

ARIZONA STATE UNIVERSITY

Overview

Everything about Arizona State University (ASU) screams big: the buildings where over 70,000 students reside or take classes; the four distinct campuses that make ASU "one university in many places;" the school's location in metropolitan Phoenix, the nation's fifth largest city; the school's reputation for partying and drinking. At the largest public university in the country, students find they must forge their own experiences. There are a seemingly infinite number of opportunities—for research, sports, social activities, and the like. But students must be determined to seek them out to take advantage of them. It takes initiative not to feel lost at such a big place.

ASU's year-round warm weather is definitely a draw for prospective students. The skies are sunny most of the time, with hot summers (average temperatures ranging from the upper 60s to low 100s) and mild winters (average temperatures from the low 40s to upper 60s). This gorgeous weather supports some memorable greenery: Palm Walk is a famous walkway lined with 70-foot palm trees, and the main campus in Tempe has a nationally recognized arboretum. Many of ASU's buildings, such as the Walter Cronkite School of Journalism and Mass Communication, are "sustainability points of pride," in keeping with the university's initiative to be a "living laboratory" for environmental stewardship.

Academics

With more than 59,000 undergraduates, some classes may be attended by several hundred students, though more than half of all undergraduate classes contain fewer than 30. Class sizes get smaller for upperclassmen. The average student/faculty ratio is 23:1.

Professors are available to students during their set office hours, and the teacher assistants are very accessible. Both professors and TAs vary in their teaching abilities and the strengths of their backgrounds. Notable standouts include economics professor and 2004 Nobel Laureate Ed Prescott and 21 other professors who have been inducted into the National Academy of Engineering and the National Academy of Sciences.

To serve its large student body, ASU offers more than 300 majors and programs. Strong areas of study include art, architectural studies, business, communication, drama, journalism and mass communication, and psychology. The university's general studies requirements include five core areas of literacy and critical inquiry; mathematical studies; humanities, fine arts, and design; social and behavioral sciences; and natural sciences. Classes must also be taken in the three awareness areas of cultural diversity in the U.S., global awareness, and historical awareness.

ASU's high admissions rate suggests that the school is not as academically rigorous as other colleges. Most students are "not 100 percent focused on their studies," says a student. For academically accomplished students who want a smaller-school feel while still benefiting from the resources of a large university, the Barrett Honors College offers an intellectually rigorous environment as ASU's selective residential college. Barrett boasts more than 250 National Merit and National Hispanic Scholars, a $10 million endowment to support its 2,700 honors students, and a 15:1 faculty/student ratio. Those interested in "finding real-world solutions to environmental, economic, and social challenges" will be interested in the School of Sustainability, the first of its kind in the country.

Students may participate in more than 300 study-abroad programs covering 60 countries. These may range in duration for a term, semester, or a full academic year. The study-abroad office offers Study Abroad 101 sessions and they have personnel who are equipped to help students select the program that is right for them.

To assist students in preparing for life after college, the career services office provides the Sun Devil CareerLink, an online database of jobs and internships; career

ARIZONA STATE UNIVERSITY

Four-year public
Founded: 1885
Tempe, AZ
Major city
Pop. 1,469,471

Address:
P.O. Box 870112
Tempe, AZ
85287-0112

Admissions:
480-965-7788

Financial Aid:
855-278-5080
admissons@asu.edu

www.asu.edu

ARIZONA STATE UNIVERSITY

Highlights

Students
Total enrollment: 73,376
Undergrads: 59,382
Freshmen: 9,652
Part-time students: 16%
From out-of-state: 33%
From public schools: 93%
Male/Female: 50%/50%
Live on-campus: 20%
In fraternities: 6%
In sororities: 7%
Off-campus employment rating: Excellent
Caucasian: 60%
African American: 5%
Hispanic: 19%
Asian / Pacific Islander: 6%
Native American: 2%
Mixed (2+ ethnicities): 3%
International: 4%

Academics
Calendar: Other
Student/faculty ratio: 23:1
Class size 9 or fewer: 11%
Class size 10-29: 56%
Class size 30-49: 16%
Class size 50-99: 12%
Class size 100 or more: 5%
Returning freshmen: 80%
Six-year graduation rate: 57%
Graduates who immediately go to graduate school: 17%
Graduates who immediately enter career related to major: 70%

Most Popular Majors
Business
Biological/biomedical sciences
Education

Admissions
Applicants: 30,686
Accepted: 26,986
Acceptance rate: 87.9%
Average GPA: 3.4
ACT range: 21-27
SAT Math range: 500-630
SAT Reading range: 480-610
SAT Writing range: Not reported
Top 10% of class: 30%
Top 25% of class: 59%
Top 50% of class: 86%

70

advising; and job- and career-related workshops on practically every day of the week.

Student Life

Despite the university's recent efforts to curb under-age drinking, ASU has a reputation as a party school. Of course, there are still opportunities for sober fun, since ASU has more than 850 clubs, as well as volunteer, study-abroad, research, and entrepreneurship opportunities. Though the absolute number of students participating in ASU's more than 50 fraternities and sororities is not high, Greek life is still a big part of the campus culture. "The Greek parties are huge, especially among freshmen and sophomores," says a student.

Besides offerings on campus, those of age may participate in pub crawls, some giving drink discounts and costumes and that take advantage of the city's light rail. Arizona Fall Frenzy is a three-day musical festival that has recently featured the Stone Temple Pilots, Weezer, and Primus. There's also the ASU Undie Run in May. As the name suggests, tens of thousands of students run throughout the ASU campus and downtown Tempe in their underwear, after donating their outer clothes to charity.

ASU's Division I Athletic teams are called the Sun Devils, a nickname that also refers to students and alumni. Football is arguably the biggest sport on campus; the football team Pac-10 conference champions in 2007. The team plays home games at Sun Devil Stadium, which seats over 70,000. The stadium is usually filled to capacity for the big game against University of Arizona, known as "The Duel in the Desert."

Baseball, softball, golf, women's basketball, and track are also popular sports. For recreational athletes or those who want to compete with other ASU teams, indoor and outdoor intramural sports options abound, from flag football to soccer to volleyball.

ASU's main campus is located in Tempe, which is in the greater Phoenix area. As with any large city, Phoenix has everything you'd expect in a major metropolitan area. Right next to campus is Mills Avenue, where students like to go for the bars and clubs, restaurants, and shopping. Nature lovers will find fun at nearby Town Lake for watersports, and Papago Park for hiking.

There is a large range in the quality of dorms. Entering students should turn in their housing application early for the best options. Freshmen are expected to live on campus. Additionally, they are encouraged to live on the campus of their major to get the most out of their first year. Programs like the First Year Residential Experience (FYRE) offer a residential community to help freshmen transition from college, and 4,700 students are part of this. The majority of upperclassmen and graduate students typically live off campus since most residence halls are set aside for freshmen.

Student Body

With more than 70,000 undergraduate and graduate students, you'll find almost every type of person on campus. However, the vast majority of undergraduates still hail from Arizona—66 percent—though there are students from all 50 states and more than 100 countries. ASU offers high cultural diversity, with 35 percent of the student body identifying as minority students.

Despite a reputation as any easy school to get into, many of ASU's population are high-achieving students. The Barrett Honors College hosts 197 National Hispanic Scholars and 410 National Merit Scholars.

You May Not Know

- The university has its own air field, a boon for aviation management students.
- For its Last Lecture Series, faculty respond to the prompt, "If you were to give your last lecture ever, what would it be?" Recent topics include "Lessons I Have Learned from Music of the 1970s and 1980s" and "Heroism Past and Future, or Why Hobbits Will Save the World."
- When ASU was first established in Tempe in 1885, its core campus was a 20-acre cow pasture designed to educate public school teachers and instruct the teachers' children in agriculture and mechanical arts.

Distinguished Alumni

Barbara McConnell Barrett, attorney and former U.S. Ambassador to Finland; Barry Bonds, professional baseball player; Susan Falk, President of clothing retailer Express; David Spade, actor, comedian and writer.

Admissions and Financial Aid

ASU accepts freshman, transfer, international, and non-degree applicants. Prospective students must be high school graduates and meet basic aptitude and competency requirements outlined on ASU's website. These requirements are not particularly rigorous, as reflected by ASU's acceptance rate of approximately 88 percent. However, some majors have higher requirements, and getting into Barrett Honors College is significantly more competitive than getting into ASU itself. The Honors College "welcomes applications from motivated, high achieving, academically strong" students. Prospective candidates submit the Barrett application after they have sent their ASU Application. Freshmen are encouraged to apply early to take advantage of automatic review for merit-based scholarships and to have early choice in housing requests and the orientation schedule.

ASU has "one of the lowest tuitions in the nation" according to the college, and offers nearly half a billion dollars in financial aid each year. As with all state schools, tuition is a particularly good deal for in-state residents, which undoubtedly contributes to the high percentage of students from Arizona. The university has a New American University Scholarship program, which provides awards of up to $9,000 a year for residents and up to $15,000 for non-residents. There are more than 50 other merit-based scholarship programs.

ARIZONA STATE UNIVERSITY

Highlights

Admissions Criteria
Academic criteria:
Grades: ☆ ☆
Difficulty of class schedule: ☆ ☆
Class rank: ☆ ☆ ☆
Standardized test scores: ☆ ☆ ☆
Teacher recommendations: N/A
Personal statement: N/A

Deadlines
Early Action: No
Early Decision: No
Regular Action: Rolling admissions
Common Application: Not accepted

Financial Aid
In-state tuition: $9,484
Out-of-state tuition: $23,136
Room: $6,150
Board: $3,190
Books: $1,100
Freshmen receiving need-based aid: 65%
Undergrads rec. need-based aid: 64%
Avg. % of need met by financial aid: 56%
Avg. aid package (freshmen): $12,756
Avg. aid package (undergrads): $12,011
Avg. debt upon graduation: $18,615

School Spirit
Mascot: Sparky
Colors: Maroon and gold
Song: *Fight Devils*

AUBURN
UNIVERSITY

Four-year public
Founded: 1856
Auburn, AL
Large town
Pop. 54,566

Address:
108 Mary Martin Hall
Auburn, AL
36849

Admissions:
800-282-8769

Financial Aid:
334-844-4634

admissions@auburn.
edu

www.auburn.edu

AUBURN UNIVERSITY

Overview

Calling all fans of football, southern belles, and gentlemen, or the conservative Southern way of life: Auburn might just be the college for you. In a city self-described as "The Loveliest Village on the Plains," Auburn University comprises 13 schools and colleges, with more than 25,000 students and about 1,200 faculty on its main campus. Established in 1856, it is based in the small city of Auburn, Alabama, home to over 54,000 residents. With nearly 50 percent of the city being students, there is an abundance of activity even if the town might be a sleeper. Although it is not the most metropolitan environment, the city is 50 miles east of Alabama's capital, Montgomery, and 115 miles southwest of Atlanta, Georgia. In 2012, CNNMoney. com ranked the city as one of the 100 best places to live in the nation.

Since the university drives the city's economy, it offers a genuine college town experience where football Saturdays attract massive audiences, featuring the Tigers and their mascot Aubie the Tiger. However, the eagle is also associated with the school. During a "losing" game, a disgruntled crowd looked upward to see an eagle circling the stadium. Fans began to shout "War Eagle," Auburn came from behind to win, and the "War Eagle" chant stuck. These and other such stories pepper Auburn's reputation, and with a variety of educational and cultural opportunities, a youthful presence, and numerous major sporting events that captivate national audiences, this institution offers a multifaceted university experience.

Academics

With the motto, "For The Advancement of Science and Arts," Auburn encourages strengths in the sciences, engineering, and liberal arts. The university is also designated as a land-grant, sea-grant, and space-grant research center. The academic offering is extensive—271 majors are available—but varies by department in terms of rigor, with nationally renowned programs in a number of fields. These include architecture and engineering, pre-veterinary medicine, mathematics, agricultural business, journalism, forestry, and business economics. Many of the technical fields provided are directly influenced by the school's earlier history as Alabama Polytechnic.

A number of projects have been launched to ensure that a modern and innovative approach to education is provided for Auburn students. Completed in 2006, the four-floor $9.3 million M. Miller Gorrie Center functions as a teaching tool with various mechanical systems exposed to reveal their inner workings for investigation. Furthermore, the university recently began offering Bachelor of Wireless Engineering degrees, the first such degrees in the nation.

Supplementing these areas, Auburn offers a rigorous Honors College, selecting 200 entering freshmen each year and offering small sections with in-depth dialogue. Additionally, Auburn's Office of International Education provides access to a wide selection of study-abroad programs, a range of faculty-led and exchange programs, and numerous affiliates with whom students have previously traveled.

To prepare for these and other opportunities, freshmen can take advantage of the summer orientation program, Camp War Eagle. It provides early exposure to faculty, academic advisors, and opportunities to register for fall semester classes. Approximately 3,800 incoming freshmen participate in one of eight three-day, two-night sessions. A separate program for parents is also provided.

Upon graduation, students can expect to remain in touch with peers through a thriving Auburn Alumni Association and an active Office of Alumni Affairs. Resources include access to a quarterly alumni magazine, career services, scholarship opportunities, and links to an extensive list of groups and clubs.

Student Life

With more than 300 student organizations, it's no surprise that students often take advantage of everything from the nationally recognized Auburn University Band to the award-winning *Auburn Plainsman* student newspaper to the Art of Living Yoga Club. If for some reason students still end up without a niche, they can easily jump online and launch their own organization.

Depending on your outlook, you will either jump for joy or run for cover given the thriving Greek community, with 34 Interfraternity Council fraternities, eight National Pan-Hellenic Council fraternities and sororities, 16 Panhellenic sororities, and two Greek honor societies. Students note that Greek life is "huge," and although many do go Greek, parties are often open to non-members.

Auburn provides extensive extracurricular activity space, allowing students to partake in intramural sports, fitness classes and weight training, club sports, and lifetime wellness initiatives. A new recreation and wellness center completed in 2013 offers eight basketball courts, a one-third mile indoor track, a rock climbing wall, and a golf simulator room.

Auburn University has 19 Division I teams. The university has recently won championships in football, men's swimming and diving, and equestrian. Auburn's burnt orange and navy blue colors provide a sea of excitement at football events. With over 85,000 fans filling the Jordan-Hare stadium, and festive tailgating events preceding games, it is no wonder that football enhances the college experience at this university. One of the biggest games of the year is the Iron Bowl versus rival University of Alabama.

Additional notable student groups include the Auburn University Student Space Program (AUSSP), which the university describes as a "student-led, faculty-mentored program to design, build, launch, and operate spacecraft;" The Sol of Auburn, Auburn University's Solar Car Team; and The War Eagle Flying Team (WEFT), a group that participates in flying competitions.

Auburn has four on-campus housing areas throughout the campus, comprising "The Quad," "The Village," "The Hill," and "The Extension." The oldest of these, "The Quad," is located in Central Campus and dates back to the Great Depression. Regular renovations have ensured that all housing includes cable TV, wireless Internet access, and laundry facilities. On-campus dorms are competitive to get into, and students must sign up as early as possible for on-campus housing. Even then, it is not guaranteed. Students seem to prefer "The Quad" and "The Hill," while many students also explore off-campus living arrangements. Be warned, students do note that finding parking can be an uphill battle.

Regarding off-campus activities, keep in mind that although Auburn can be limited in scope, you can access bars and restaurants as options. If you're looking for even more fun, Atlanta is roughly a 90-minute drive away.

Student Body

With 60 percent of students from within Alabama, the school maintains a strong Southern influence and presence. Given these dynamics, students have noted that the school leaves much to be desired in terms of diversity of ethnicity, mindset, and engagement with global affairs. However, students describe themselves

AUBURN UNIVERSITY

Highlights

Students
Total enrollment: 25,134
Undergrads: 20,175
Freshmen: 4,803
Part-time students: 9%
From out-of-state: 40%
From public schools: 88%
Male/Female: 51%/49%
Live on-campus: 17%
In fraternities: 21%
In sororities: 31%
Off-campus employment rating: Excellent
Caucasian: 85%
African American: 7%
Hispanic: 3%
Asian / Pacific Islander: 2%
Native American: 1%
International: 1%

Academics
Calendar: Semester
Student/faculty ratio: 18:1
Class size 9 or fewer: 8%
Class size 10-29: 55%
Class size 30-49: 22%
Class size 50-99: 9%
Class size 100 or more: 6%
Returning freshmen: 90%
Six-year graduation rate: 68%
Graduates who immediately enter career related to major: 75%

Most Popular Majors
Biomedical sciences
Psychology
Accounting

Admissions
Applicants: 17,463
Accepted: 13,486
Acceptance rate: 77.2%
Average GPA: 3.8
ACT range: 24-30
SAT Math range: 550-650
SAT Reading range: 530-630
SAT Writing range: 5-29
Top 10% of class: 32%
Top 25% of class: 63%
Top 50% of class: 90%

AUBURN UNIVERSITY

Admissions Criteria
Academic criteria:
Grades: ☆ ☆
Difficulty of class schedule: ☆ ☆
Class rank: N/A
Standardized test scores: ☆ ☆ ☆
Teacher recommendations: ☆
Personal statement: ☆ ☆ ☆
Non-academic criteria considered:
Extracurricular activities
Special talents, interests, abilities
Character/personal qualities
Volunteer work
Work experience
Geographical location
Alumni relationship

Deadlines
Early Action: On a rolling basis beginning
    October 1
Early Decision: No
Regular Action: Rolling admissions
Common Application: Not accepted

Financial Aid
In-state tuition: $9,852
Out-of-state tuition: $26,364
Room: $6,364
Board: $5,188
Books: $1,200
Freshmen receiving need-based aid: 38%
Undergrads rec. need-based aid: 38%
Avg. % of need met by financial aid: 48%
Avg. aid package (freshmen): $12,352
Avg. aid package (undergrads): $10,502
Avg. debt upon graduation: $24,903

School Spirit
Mascot: Tigers
Colors: Orange and blue
Song: *War Eagle*

as "friendly" and with "Southern hospitality," and the apples are staying close to trees, as legacies are quite common among incoming students and alumni. Politically, the campus tends to lean toward the conservative side of the spectrum.

You May Not Know

- Six astronauts have graduated from Auburn University.
- Auburn University owns the Auburn-Opelika Robert G. Pitts Airport, and its flight program is the second oldest in the country.
- Auburn started the oldest Southern rivalry when it first played football against the University of Georgia in 1892.

Distinguished Alumni

Charles Barkley, former professional basketball player; Jimmy Buffett, singer and songwriter; Bo Jackson, former professional football and baseball player; Jimmy Wales, Internet entrepreneur and co-founder of Wikipedia.

Admissions and Financial Aid

Auburn admissions are rolling, and students can begin applying as early as August 1. If students submit an application by October 1, Early Action decisions will be made by October 15. These Early Action decisions are based solely on a combination of high school GPA and the ACT or SAT scores, and the school states that other factors are not considered. Non-Early Action decisions are made in three rounds beginning November 15. These decisions are based on academic achievement and "other factors" included in the application. Getting your application in early seems to be the name of the game.

For incoming freshmen and transfer students, the admissions application is submitted entirely online. For international students, applications can be submitted online or using a paper application and sending it to the university via U.S. mail. In addition to the application for admission, international students will also need to include an affidavit for financial support and a bank letter.

You should also keep a lookout for one the 6,000 university scholarships awarded annually, supporting current and incoming freshmen and transfer students. As an example, the Spirit of Auburn Scholarships provide up to full tuition, a $1,500 technology allowance, and a $4,000 enrichment stipend for resident students. The Presidential Scholarship provides two-thirds non-resident tuition, a $1,500 technology allowance, and a $4,000 enrichment stipend for non-resident students.

AUSTIN COLLEGE

Overview

Austin College (AC to students and faculty) was named after the school founder, not the state capitol, which is more than four hours away. The 60-acre liberal arts college's green lawns and neatly organized buildings are actually located in Sherman, Texas, 60 miles north of Dallas and close to the Oklahoma state line. The school also has 300 acres of nature preserve for science and environmental research.

The small town of Sherman feels apropos for a college with 1,300 undergraduates, who each have professor mentors and get to know all their classmates. The students are known to be friendly, personable, and often religious, since AC is affiliated with the Presbyterian Church. Students at Austin College don't get to hide in anonymity like their counterparts on larger campuses, but the small school atmosphere has a lot to offer as well. *U.S. News & World Report* ranked AC in the top 100 among liberal arts colleges, and many are drawn to its excellent pre-professional programs.

Another major drawing point may seem ironic for a school comprised mostly of students from a very small part of the world: three-quarters of Austin College students go overseas for at least a semester. Sports may not be big for the Austin College—though Greek life is—but if the Kangaroos can't brag about their football team, they can certainly boast about spotting wild 'roos in Australia in one of more than a dozen Australian cities available through their extensive study-abroad programs.

Academics

Austin College offers 35 majors and pre-professional programs. The five-year Masters of Arts in Teaching program terminates in a masters of arts in teaching (MAT) degree and aims to develop dedicated and creative teachers. Other strong programs include business administration and education along with the pre-professional programs for pre-law and the health sciences (particularly medicine and dentistry).

All freshmen are required to take Communication/Inquiry, a seminar course, in the fall. Eight courses in the humanities, sciences, and social sciences as well as a course in quantitative reasoning and writing are also mandated.

Due to AC's small class sizes—99 percent of classes have an enrollment under 50—students are able to have a personalized experience and professors invariably know their students' names. Professors also mentor students in groups of 20, strengthening relationships even outside the classroom. Access to professors doesn't mean lenient courses, though: classes can be very rigorous, especially in pre-med. Students describe classes as "challenging but manageable" and "thought-provoking."

Special academic opportunities include Early Decision/Acceptance to the Texas Tech School of Medicine. Incoming students must demonstrate excellence through high GPAs and SAT/ACT scores; in return, they're able to get into med school without taking the MCAT. For students with exceptional leadership potential, the Posey Leadership Institute gives 20 students an opportunity to hone their skills through a number of courses, an internship, and a conference that spans all four years as an undergrad.

Students look forward to four-week courses taught in January Term, Austin College's mini-semester. Off-campus Jan Terms offer opportunities to go abroad, with different options each year. Recent offerings include China, Germany, and Guatemala.

An astounding three-quarters of graduating seniors have studied abroad for at least one academic term, many for more than one. The Institute of International Education ranked AC number one in the United States among baccalaureate institutions in 2008. The college's innovative Jordan Family Language House, completed in 2008, encourages the study of foreign languages in a residential setting that incorporates a multimedia language laboratory.

AUSTIN COLLEGE

Four-year private
Founded: 1849
Sherman, TX
Medium city
Pop. 38,690

Address:
900 North Grand Avenue
Sherman, TX
75090-4400

Admissions:
800-526-4276

Financial Aid:
800-526-4276

admission@austincollege.edu

www.austincollege.edu

AUSTIN COLLEGE

Highlights

Students

Total enrollment: 1,260
Undergrads: 1,242
Freshmen: 359
Part-time students: 1%
From out-of-state: 9%
From public schools: 84%
Male/Female: 48%/52%
Live on-campus: 77%
In fraternities: 27%
In sororities: 27%
Off-campus employment rating: Fair
Caucasian: 63%
African American: 4%
Hispanic: 12%
Asian / Pacific Islander: 13%
Native American: 0%
Mixed (2+ ethnicities): 4%
International: 2%

Academics

Calendar: 4-1-4 system
Student/faculty ratio: 12:1
Class size 9 or fewer: 29%
Class size 10-29: 60%
Class size 30-49: 10%
Class size 50-99: 1%
Class size 100 or more: -
Returning freshmen: 75%
Six-year graduation rate: 77%
Graduates who immediately go to graduate school: 36%
Graduates who immediately enter career related to major: 36%

Most Popular Majors

Business administration
Psychology
Biology

Admissions

Applicants: 3,003
Accepted: 1,774
Acceptance rate: 59.1%
Placed on wait list: 13
Enrolled from wait list: 1
Average GPA: 3.6
ACT range: 23-29
SAT Math range: 570-670
SAT Reading range: 560-660
SAT Writing range: 6-40
Top 10% of class: 36%
Top 25% of class: 70%
Top 50% of class: 96%

Career services at AC include experiential learning and internship opportunities. Roo Connect is the college's online career management system. The College tracks its graduates; for example, one year after graduating, 83 percent of the class of 2012 were working or attending graduate or professional school; most others were preparing for further education or actively seeking a job.

Student Life

There are more than 60 registered student organizations at Austin College and more than 400 leadership opportunities. A large number are religious-affiliated registered organizations. InterVarsity Christian is a particularly popular group that is an evangelical and interdenominational campus ministry on over 500 college and university campuses. The Service Station group aims to cultivate a culture of service and provides a hub for students to find service opportunities.

The annual Austin College Great Day of Service reflects the popularity of service on campus. Recently over 400 Austin College students volunteered at more than 500 local sites. Another popular annual event is Asia Week, which promotes Asian culture through demonstrations and lectures. A decidedly less serious tradition is the pre-Christmas-break "Baker Bun Run." Facebook fans have described it as an eagerly anticipated event where "guys dart through the bitter chill of the night sporting their boxers and their tighty-whiteys."

There are six sororities and six fraternities at AC, all of which are local, without national affiliations. Students rush in February and can do so as soon as they have completed one semester. Twenty-seven percent of men and women belong to a fraternity or sorority, making the Greek organizations central organizers for parties and social life on campus. "For the best parties, you should pledge," says a student.

More than 225 student athletes participate on the Kangaroo Division III teams. Lacrosse is a club sport and there is also a dance team, the Aussies.

Because of its small size, Sherman might be described as a sleepy town with a limited selection of restaurants, bars, and clubs. Students insist that the college's location is relatively isolated and that having a car—or a generous friend with a car—is required. Dallas is an hour away and students occasionally go there for big city entertainment.

Freshmen choose from five residence halls, only two of which are co-ed. One of the residences divides freshmen men and freshmen women into separate wings, though upperclassmen and women may reside in the rooms between these two wings. The Jordan Family Language House offers 48 women and men an immersive language experience for students of German, Spanish, French, and Japanese. Two additional residence halls, Bryan Apartments and the new Johnson 'Roo Suites, are only available to upperclassmen and graduate students.

Student Body

Although most Austin College students venture out into the world during their four years at the college, global diversity isn't widely reflected in the student demographic. Indeed, most of the United States is not even represented, as 91 percent of students are from

Texas and many of the remaining nine percent hail from neighboring Oklahoma. There is, however, a high level of ethnic diversity, with 33 percent students of color.

Many students are religious, not surprising given the college's proud affiliation with the Presbyterian Church. Religious offerings include weekly Bible study and worship; the *Acolyte*, a "journal of faith, doubt, and other things at Austin College;"a group called Austin College Students Considering Church Vocations, and more.

You May Not Know

- According to the college, it is the "oldest institution of higher education in Texas operating under its original name and charter."
- Twice a year the college hosts an Etiquette Dinner to help students prepare for business meals covering topics such as the "appropriate way to pass items around the table … or respond to offers of alcoholic beverages."
- The college has a Lake Campus, 30 acres dedicated to camping and recreation.

Distinguished Alumni

Ron Kirk, former Mayor of Dallas, Texas; Candace Kita, actress; Ray Morehart, former professional baseball player.

Admissions and Financial Aid

Admission to Austin College is quite competitive: three to four applications are received for every available spot in the incoming class. The admissions office emphasizes a challenging high school course load, noting that acceptable grades in tougher classes are more impressive than easy A's. While the numbers certainly matter, they aren't everything: Austin College also considers extracurriculars, recommendations, personal essay, and the optional admissions interview in reviewing applications.

In accordance with NCAA guidelines, Austin College does not award athletic scholarships. The college does offer merit-based scholarships, which 23 percent of students receive. A large number of renewable general academic scholarships are available to all students. These awards are not dependent on financial need and range from $8,000 to $18,000 annually; students who apply by the Early Action II deadline receive priority. There are also more specific scholarships that look for not only academic potential but also leadership ability, excellent in service to others, or exceptional talents in the performing arts.

AUSTIN COLLEGE

Highlights

Admissions Criteria
Academic criteria:
Grades: ☆ ☆ ☆
Difficulty of class schedule: ☆ ☆ ☆
Class rank: ☆ ☆
Standardized test scores: ☆ ☆
Teacher recommendations: ☆ ☆
Personal statement: ☆ ☆
Non-academic criteria considered:
Interview
Extracurricular activities
Special talents, interests, abilities
Character/personal qualities
Volunteer work
Geographical location
Religious affiliation/commitment
Minority affiliation
Alumni relationship

Deadlines
Early Action: January 15
Early Decision: No
Regular Action: Rolling admissions
Common Application: Accepted

Financial Aid
In-state tuition: $33,645
Out-of-state tuition: $33,645
Room: $5,205
Board: $5,510
Books: $1,250
Freshmen receiving need-based aid: 67%
Undergrads rec. need-based aid: 66%
Avg. % of need met by financial aid: 99%
Avg. aid package (freshmen): $34,793
Avg. aid package (undergrads): $33,603

School Spirit
Mascot: Kangaroo
Colors: Crimson and gold
Song: *The Crimson and Gold*

BABSON COLLEGE

Four-year private
Founded: 1919
Babson Park, MA
Large town
Pop. 26,613

Address:
231 Forest Street
Babson Park, MA
02457-0310

Admissions:
781-239-5522

Financial Aid:
781-239-4219

ugradadmission@
babson.edu

www.babson.edu

The Ultimate
Guide to America's
Best Colleges

BABSON COLLEGE

Overview

Located 14 miles from Boston in Wellesley, Massachusetts, Babson College's campus is situated on 370 acres of woods with rolling hills and meticulously landscaped grounds. Many of the building interiors shine pristinely, as befits a college with one undergraduate major (a BS in business). The college's prime location affords easy access to plentiful internship opportunities, as well as to the nearby partner schools of Wellesley College and the Olin College of Engineering.

Babson is renowned for its first-year Foundations in Management and Entrepreneurship program, where student teams show off their academic and professional acumen—as well as their generosity and ethical decision-making skills—by creating businesses that are ultimately liquidated so that the proceeds can go to charity. Though there is room for flexibility and creativity in pursuing business ventures and selecting from the 25 concentrations on offer, Babson's structured curriculum may feel constraining to some students. Its rigor provides little opportunity to think outside the business bubble.

Students have to be prepared to live and breathe business management, administration, and leadership, whether learning from faculty who are accomplished business leaders or competing for jobs with their fellow classmates. Highly-driven students who want to immerse themselves into the world of business will thrive at Babson; those looking for a culture that isn't strictly defined by business formal attire and marketing pitches may find its offerings constraining.

Academics

Babson has a reputation for difficult grading and challenging courses, but professors are supportive and students don't have classes on Fridays. Babson emphasizes its faculty's academic expertise along with their corporate connections, boasting "the largest dedicated entrepreneurial faculty in the world." Adjunct "entrepreneurs" teach alongside faculty members. There are no teaching assistants at Babson, and over 92 percent of the faculty hold doctoral degrees or equivalents. Case studies, mostly seen in graduate schools of business, are often employed as a teaching method in undergrad classes.

All undergraduates receive BS degrees in business but can choose from 25 concentrations that include entrepreneurship and leadership as well as more liberal-arts focuses such as gender studies and historical and political studies. Strong concentrations include finance and entrepreneurship. Students can cross-register at Brandeis University, Wellesley College, and the Olin College of Engineering.

Freshmen participate in the Foundations of Management and Entrepreneurship, a "year-long immersion into the world of business" according to the college. This flagship program includes weekly first-year seminars; courses in diverse topics ranging from quantitative methods, science, business law, accounting, and rhetoric; and a spring semester Coaching for Leadership and Teamwork program that enhances communication and ethical decision-making. "I learned more in one year of the Foundations program than others learn in five years on the job," asserts a student.

A key part of the Foundations Program is the year-long project of developing a business model by a team of 30 students. These teams plan, launch, and ultimately liquidate their own for-profit ventures, with the proceeds from the business going to charity. Past students have raised thousands of dollars, and businesses in spring 2010 included Germstoppers, an enterprise selling hand sanitizer dispensers to small offices and restaurants and Totes2Promote, which provided an eco-friendly alternative to disposable plastic bags.

The Intermediate and Advanced Programs guide Babson students through their sophomore, junior, and senior years. Upperclassmen can participate in Management

Consulting Field Experience (MCFE), a program in which students perform consulting work with an international perspective. Previous companies have included AOL and Boston Properties.

Babson's study-abroad program offers students the opportunity to study at 47 institutions in more than 27 countries. The college encourages students to take a semester abroad in order to become global business leaders.

More than 100 on-campus recruiting opportunities give Babson students plenty of opportunities to job-search. Ninety-six percent of respondents were employed or in graduate school within six months of graduation. For those who found jobs, the average starting salary was $48,000.

Student Life

There are more than 90 clubs, organizations, and teams at Babson. Popular ones include the Babson Dance Ensemble and the Babson Entrepreneurial Teaching Alliance, which teaches business skills to middle school students. You'll find Babson students listening to local live bands at the Reynolds Student Center or bigger acts at the PepsiCo Pavilion, watching a game at Roger's Pub, taking in a performance at the Sorenson Center, and attending the many concerts and speaker events organized by the student government. Past guests have included Nobel Peace Prize winner John Hume, entrepreneur Steve Forbes, and comedian Jimmy Fallon.

Greek parties are also popular social activities. There are four fraternities and three sororities on campus, and 15 percent of male students and 25 percent of female students are part of the Greek system. The Undergraduate Honor Code, which aims to create a campus culture of integrity, requires students to help other students who have had too much to drink rather than report them to the authorities.

Throughout the year, students look forward to the monthly Knight Parties—dance parties held in the Knight Auditorium. Autumn brings a festive Homecoming weekend, while spring promises the excitement of the Mr. and Mrs. Babson pageant competition along with Founder's Day, a daylong tribute to Babson College founder Roger Babson and an annual tradition dating back to 1947. Other recent events included business plan competitions and a business fair, a community-wide lunch, and panelists.

Babson College offers 22 varsity athletic programs in Division III, with 16 club sports and a number of intramurals to choose from, including ballroom dancing and yoga. The Webster Center houses a majority of Babson's indoor athletic and recreational facilities, including the 750-seat Staake Gymnasium, a six-lane pool, PepsiCo Pavilion with 15,000 square feet of playing space, and more.

A weekend shuttle to Boston takes Babson students to the clubs, professional sporting events, and shopping facilities of Beantown. Most students prefer Boston to nearby Wellesley, whose upscale restaurants and shopping are not particularly student-budget-friendly. "There's not much for us in Wellesley," says a student.

Housing is guaranteed for all four years, but students' choices of dorms improve as they progress through college. There are 15 residence halls, one of which is Forest Hall, a large building with a lively and social first-floor lounge. The college offers housing for students based on their area of academic concentration; for example,

BABSON COLLEGE

Highlights

Students
Total enrollment: 3,250
Undergrads: 2,015
From out-of-state: 57%
Male/Female: 56%/44%
Live on-campus: 85%
In fraternities: 15%
In sororities: 25%
Off-campus employment rating: Excellent
Caucasian: 36%
African American: 4%
Hispanic: 10%
Asian / Pacific Islander: 12%
Native American: 0%
Mixed (2+ ethnicities): 2%
International: 27%

Academics
Calendar: Semester
Student/faculty ratio: 15:1
Class size 9 or fewer: 5%
Class size 10-29: 41%
Class size 30-49: 51%
Class size 50-99: 3%
Class size 100 or more: -
Returning freshmen: 94%
Six-year graduation rate: 90%

Admissions
Applicants: 5,512
Accepted: 1,648
Acceptance rate: 29.9%
Placed on wait list: 1,190
Enrolled from wait list: 25
Average GPA: 3.6
ACT range: 26-29
SAT Math range: 610-700
SAT Reading range: 550-640
SAT Writing range: 13-52
Top 10% of class: 53%
Top 25% of class: 84%
Top 50% of class: 98%

BABSON COLLEGE

Admissions Criteria

Academic criteria:
Grades: ☆ ☆ ☆
Difficulty of class schedule: ☆ ☆ ☆
Class rank: ☆ ☆ ☆
Standardized test scores: ☆ ☆ ☆
Teacher recommendations: ☆ ☆ ☆
Personal statement: ☆ ☆ ☆
Non-academic criteria considered:
Interview
Extracurricular activities
Special talents, interests, abilities
Character/personal qualities
Volunteer work
Work experience
Geographical location
Minority affiliation
Alumni relationship

Deadlines

Early Action: November 1
Early Decision: November 1
Regular Action: November 1 (priority)
January 1 (final)
Notification of admission by: April 1
Common Application: Accepted

Financial Aid

In-state tuition: $43,520
Out-of-state tuition: $43,520
Room: $9,126
Board: $5,016
Books: $1,020
Freshmen receiving need-based aid: 43%
Undergrads rec. need-based aid: 44%
Avg. % of need met by financial aid: 95%
Avg. aid package (freshmen): $37,261
Avg. aid package (undergrads): $34,782
Avg. debt upon graduation: $31,918

School Spirit

Mascot: Beaver
Colors: Green and white

E-Tower is reserved for students in the entrepreneurism concentration. Other options include the I-Tower (for students with interest in investment), Health Living Tower (substance-free), the Liberal Arts Tower, The Green Tower (interest in green business), and the ONE tower (diversity housing).

Student Body

More than half of Babson's approximately 3,300 students are undergraduates, about one half of whom hail from out of state. There is a unilateral interest in business among the student body, which can be a double-edged sword. On the plus side, students develop strong networks based on similar interests. However, this means many students with overlapping interests end up competing for the same types of jobs and internships. "It's not cutthroat, but there's more competition here than at other colleges," one student explains.

There are more male than female students, though this gender imbalance is gradually shifting towards greater equality. The Center for Women's Leadership supports female entrepreneurs on campus.

Students are known for being well off financially, especially the large contingent of international students that comprise 27 percent of the student body.

You May Not Know

- The 28-foot diameter Babson Globe was for many years the world's largest free standing globe.
- Roger Babson, a strong believer in experiential education, founded the Babson Institute in 1919. The Institute was renamed Babson College in 1969, a year after the college became co-ed.
- On Course, the 17-foot stainless steel sculpture by Frances Pratt sits atop Glavin Family Chapel, a sacred space designed to meet the spiritual needs of Babson's interfaith community.

Distinguished Alumni

Arthur M. Blank, co-founder of The Home Depot, Inc; Roger Enrico, Dreamworks CEO; Martha D. Vorlicek, COO of HarbourVest partners, private equity investment manager.

Admissions and Financial Aid

Babson's first-year curriculum requires that all first-year students enroll in the fall semester. Prospective students fill out the Common Application, including a teacher recommendation and counselor recommendation, as well as the Babson College Supplement.

About 45 percent of undergrads receive financial aid each year, $22 million of which is Babson grants and scholarships. In recent years, the college has met 95 percent of undergraduate financial need. The admissions website notes that "awards are made primarily on the basis of financial need, but consideration is also given to students' academic and personal accomplishments." Babson is one of 28 schools that partner with the Posse Foundation, which offers a scholarship that covers full tuition for four years to exceptional urban student leaders from diverse backgrounds.

BARD COLLEGE

Overview

Ninety miles north of New York City, Bard College's 600-acre campus is a sleepy slice of nature that even has its own waterfall. The park-like Annandale campus, where undergraduates and students in six of the nine graduate programs study, borders the Hudson River and covers fields and forests. Gorgeous views of the Catskill Mountains can be seen from many student dorms. The buildings on campus are varied in architectural styles, including what the college describes as "19th-century stone houses and riverfront mansions." World-renowned architect Frank Gehry designed the distinctive Richard B. Fisher Center for the Performing Arts.

Bard offers a unique liberal arts experience with a very liberal student population and flexibility for students to form their own curriculum without traditional majors. Students who had a reputation in high school for being "weird" or "following the beat of their own drummer" may find themselves very at home on a campus full of motivated and independent thinkers. Conservatives might find themselves ill at ease here unless it is their plan to at last break out of the box. At such a small college, everyone knows everyone, which can create a nice sense of familiarity and a comfortable place for the exchange of ideas. Students at Bard appreciate a sense of adventure. Perhaps this is why 50 percent of students go abroad at some point.

Academics

The absence of teaching assistants enables students to form a strong connection with professors. With small classes averaging 18 in size, professors don't just know students' names, but strive to get to know something about each of them. Ample discussion increases the sense of camaraderie; lectures are less common.

Many of Bard's faculty are distinguished, with five MacArthur fellows and notable faculty such as soprano Dawn Upshaw and novelist Chinua Achebe. Over the years, four Nobel Prize winners in literature have taught at Bard.

Bard offers almost 70 majors. A BS in economics and finance, added in 2007, is a five-year dual degree (BS-BA) program. A dual degree program in music and another field is also offered.

Strong concentrations include written arts, film and electronic arts, and photography. There is also an interdivisional program in human rights spanning the arts, social sciences, and literature. It encourages students to "treat human rights as an intellectual question, challenge the new human rights orthodoxy, and think critically about human rights as a discourse rather than merely training for it as a profession."

Bard's liberal arts education offers breadth through the two-semester First Year Seminar, where students read and discuss core texts; along with distribution requirements. Students undergo "moderation," the process where students establish a major in their program in the second semester of sophomore year. The mandated Moderation papers enable students to assess their prior studies and propose future goals, while the capstone requirement is fulfilled through a Senior Project.

Nearly 50 percent of Bard students participate in an international or study abroad program. Bard's own programs have attracted students from over 100 institutions in the past five years. Bard's International Human Rights Exchange (IHRE) program in Johannesburg, South Africa is the "world's only multidisciplinary, semester long program in human rights."

Bard's Career Development office provides career planning assistance for students and alumni. According to the school, graduates have a 78 percent placement rate to medical school (as compared to the national average of 50 percent).

Student Life

There are hang-out spots aplenty on Bard campus, from the Kline Commons (the main dining facility) to the Root Cellar (organic and vegan café with poetry readings

BARD COLLEGE

Four-year private
Founded: 1860
Annandale on Hudson, NY
Rural
Pop. 2,400

Address:
P.O. Box 5000
Annandale on Hudson, NY
12504

Admissions:
845-758-7472

Financial Aid:
845-758-7525

admission@bard.edu

www.bard.edu

BARD COLLEGE

Students

Total enrollment: 2,322
Undergrads: 2,051
Part-time students: 5%
From out-of-state: 66%
From public schools: 64%
Male/Female: 44%/56%
Live on-campus: 73%
Off-campus employment rating: Fair
Caucasian: 59%
African American: 5%
Hispanic: 3%
Asian / Pacific Islander: 3%
Native American: 1%
International: 13%

Academics

Calendar: Semester
Student/faculty ratio: 10:1
Class size 9 or fewer: 38%
Class size 10-29: 59%
Class size 30-49: 2%
Class size 50-99: 1%
Class size 100 or more: -
Returning freshmen: 86%
Six-year graduation rate: 79%

Most Popular Majors

Political science
English
Psychology

Admissions

Applicants: 5,410
Accepted: 1,902
Acceptance rate: 35.2%
Placed on wait list: 313
Enrolled from wait list: 10
Average GPA: 3.5
ACT range: Not reported
SAT Math range: 600-670
SAT Reading range: 650-710
SAT Writing range: Not reported
Top 10% of class: 60%
Top 25% of class: 95%
Top 50% of class: 97%

and music) and the SMOG (Bard's student-run venue that hosts concerts and dances).

There are more than 150 student-run organizations. Prominent groups include the student newspaper *Bard Free Press*, cultural organizations, the student-run bike co-op, and college radio station WXBC. Other clubs range from the serious (Students Stop Trafficking of Persons) to the relaxing (High Tea club) to the irreverent (People Eating Tasty Animals, committed to providing community roasts and no small dose of irony in the club's acronym). With so many creative student organizations, it's no surprise that students find no need for Greek life.

Another distinctively quirky club is the Surrealist Training Circus, whose members "train for the surreal apocalypse through an ongoing study of puppetry, costuming, stilt-walking, acrobatics, and theater." Other popular annual events include the seven days of Coming Out Week along with Urban Cowboy Night, whose tagline is, "A mechanical bull, live music, an entire roasted pig, vegan chili and hay bales - need we say more?" To celebrate the end of senior projects, Spring Fling is an outdoor festival with dozens of musical acts, outdoor vendors, and even an astrojump.

Despite having a fierce mascot (a Raptor), Bard is not particularly strong in intercollegiate athletics, a Division III participant. Rugby is one of the more popular sports. The Stevenson Gymnasium offers sports courts, a swimming pool, and classes. Intramurals range from badminton to volley-pong (played on a ping-pong table with an oversized tennis ball and bare hands). Club sports include equestrian, fencing, and rugby.

New York City is about a two-hour train ride, and skiing at the Catskills Mountains is a two-hour car drive. Prospective students should be aware that Bard encourages students to use biking and other alternate transportation forms, charging an annual registration fee for cars.

Hiking trails wrap around the Hudson River and Blithewood, while rock climbing is available in the nearby artsy town of Tivoli. Besides opportunities for outdoor enthusiasts, Bard is a "center for spiritual life," with "churches, temples, mosques, Zen and Tibetan Buddhist monasteries, and meditation centers."

Freshmen are required to live on campus, and along with sophomores, are guaranteed on-campus housing. Seventy-three percent of all undergrads live on campus in over 40 student residences that vary in architecture, social style, and size. Most residence halls are co-ed, and almost half of the rooms are singles. Themed housing includes smoke- and alcohol-free residence halls and co-op living. Upperclassmen may live in The Village, which contains nine environmentally friendly student residence halls that use timber from non-virgin sources and a geothermal heat exchange system.

Student Body

Among the approximately 2,000 undergrads, there is large geographic diversity, with two-thirds of the student population from out of state and all 50 states represented. The 13 percent of international students represent over 50 countries. However, there is less racial/ethnic diversity, with 12 percent of the student population identifying as minority students. Women outnumber men by a significant amount.

Students at Bard describe themselves as being unique, the "odd one out" in high school. The Bard reputation for attracting independent students is readily apparent in its student body. "We're not afraid to say that we're weird," says a student.

Students are known to be very liberal and politically involved. This reputation is epitomized by the fictitious left-wing website mentioned by Jon Stewart on *The Daily Show*, whose web address ended in "bardcollege.edu."

You May Not Know

- From 1928 until 1944, Bard was a school of Columbia University.
- The Bard Prison Initiative provides a college education to 200 prisoners at five prisons.
- The university hosted 300 Hungarian Freedom Fighters for "an intensive language and cultural orientation designed to prepare them for life in the United States" in 1956.

Distinguished Alumni

Blythe Danner, actress; Lola Glaudini, actress in *The Sopranos*; Zeena Parkins, avant-garde harpist; Nick Zinner, guitarist in the *Yeah Yeah Yeahs*.

Admissions and Financial Aid

As the admissions office states, getting into Bard is hard: each year the college receives 10 times the number of applicants than it can accept. According to the college, "Bard expects applicants to be proven, motivated students with an average GPA of 3.5 or above, who have taken Honors or AP courses where appropriate in a curriculum."

Lest all these requirements feel too restrictive, Bard also emphasizes that admission isn't just about the numbers, though high achievement and motivation are important. In line with the college's individualistic approach, SAT/ACT scores are not required, and each application is carefully reviewed in search of the independent thinkers who will take full advantage of Bard's offerings.

The admissions process has many options, including the Bard Application, Common Application, or Universal College Application. They also offer not only early action but also the "Immediate Decision Plan," a day-long session where candidates participate in a seminar and meet with an admissions counselor. The Bard admissions committee mails decisions the following day.

Sixty-eight percent of Bard students receive financial aid, including international students. The college notes that "financial aid is need-based and competitive," so more competitive applicants are more likely to receive financial aid. There are five different kinds of full-tuition awards. Of note is the Excellence and Equal Cost Program, where public high school seniors who are ranked in the top 10 percent of their classes receive funds that would make the cost of Bard the same as attending an in-state four-year public university.

BARD COLLEGE

Highlights

Admissions Criteria
Academic criteria:
Grades: ☆ ☆ ☆
Difficulty of class schedule: ☆ ☆ ☆
Class rank: ☆
Standardized test scores: ☆
Teacher recommendations: ☆ ☆ ☆
Personal statement: ☆ ☆ ☆
Non-academic criteria considered:
Interview
Extracurricular activities
Special talents, interests, abilities
Character/personal qualities
Volunteer work
Work experience
Geographical location
Religious affiliation/commitment
Minority affiliation
Alumni relationship

Deadlines
Early Action: November 1
Early Decision: No
Regular Action: Rolling admissions
Common Application: Accepted

Financial Aid
In-state tuition: $45,730
Out-of-state tuition: $45,730
Room: Varies
Board: $6,920
Books: $950
Freshmen receiving need-based aid: 71%
Undergrads rec. need-based aid: 68%
Avg. % of need met by financial aid: 88%
Avg. aid package (freshmen): $39,829
Avg. aid package (undergrads): $36,279
Avg. debt upon graduation: $24,913

School Spirit
Colors: Black and white

**BARNARD
COLLEGE**

Four-year private wom-
en's college
Founded: 1889
New York, NY
Major city
Pop. 8,244,910

Address:
3009 Broadway
New York, NY
10027

Admissions:
212-854-2014

Financial Aid:
212-854-2154

admissions@barnard.
edu

www.barnard.edu

84

BARNARD COLLEGE

Overview

Barnard College is a member of the Seven Sisters, a group of prestigious liberal arts colleges founded between 1837 and 1889 that have historically been women's colleges. Barnard distinguishes itself from her fellow "Sisters" by being located in the heart of Manhattan and, through the Barnard-Columbia partnership, enables its women undergraduates to take classes, use academic resources, join student groups, live in dorms, and receive degrees from neighboring Columbia University. This makes Barnard the only all-women's college that offers the intimacy of a small college environment where classes are taught by professors rather than teaching assistants, while also being able to take advantage of all the resources of a large Ivy League university. The relationship between the two colleges is not without some friction, though. Barnard students dislike phrases like "Barnard to bed. Columbia to wed."

Barnard's four-acre campus houses the renowned Center for Research on Women and even manages to fit in a greenhouse and the Minor Latham Playhouse theater. However, visitors are likely to find themselves wowed by the luminous terra-cotta glass panels of the Diana Center, just opened in 2010. The Center's transparent and fluid design offers stunning views of campus and the vibrant city.

Academics at Barnard are very rigorous, so women who are prepared to excel in academics and leadership will feel most at home at Barnard. The liberal politics on campus may be uncomfortable for more conservative students, and Barnard isn't the ideal place for students looking for a one-stop shop for their education. Learning at Barnard means not only taking advantage of the college's resources but also those of Columbia, neighboring colleges and universities, and New York City as a whole.

Academics

Barnard students' classes are very rigorous and competitive, not surprising considering that more than three-quarters of those admitted were students in the top 10 percent of their graduating high school class. There are more than 300 full- and part-time faculty members, yielding a low faculty-to-student ratio of 10:1. An impressive 64 percent of faculty members are women, compared with 37 percent nationally, and 90 percent hold a PhD or highest appropriate degree in their field.

Barnard offers 57 majors, and strong programs include biological sciences, dance, economics, English, history, and political science. Dance majors will be especially proud to note that famed choreographer Twyla Tharp is a Barnard alum, while English majors may celebrate famous alum writers Zora Neale Hurston, Erica Jong, and Jhumpa Lahiri. A 2007 *New York Times* article noted, "Barnard has helped an exceptionally large group of women become distinguished contemporary writers."

To ground their liberal arts education, all Barnard students take an interdisciplinary First-Year Seminar, First-Year English, and general education requirement called "The Nine Ways of Knowing," which provides intellectual breadth through courses from literature to the social sciences, language, and the arts, to lab sciences and the quantitative areas.

Educational opportunities include special degree programs in cooperation with Columbia, Juilliard, The Jewish Theological Seminary, and the Manhattan School of Music. The highly selective Juilliard Exchange Program enables students to take music lessons at Juilliard while earning their BA at Barnard. "There are just so many opportunities at Barnard," explains a student.

Students who want to study abroad at Barnard can choose from over 50 countries. Two programs, Semester at Sea and International Honors Program, enable students to visit multiple countries. There is a language requirement for studying abroad.

The college reminds alumnae: "We are friends, sisters, mentors, and partners. We are students, graduates, professionals, and leaders. The Barnard Alumnae Network is here to strengthen the bonds between us." Graduates benefit from this network as well as the Career Development Office in their education, leadership, and work-life planning. The recently launched (2009) Athena Center for Leadership Studies promotes women's leadership through internships and a mentoring program. About one fifth of students attend graduate school within one year of graduating.

Student Life

Barnard students may join 100 official cultural, performance, pre-professional, and special interest clubs, all funded by the Student Government Association. Some groups are based out of Barnard while others are based out of Columbia. Popular ones include Bacchante, Barnard's only a cappella group; The Bach Society orchestra and choir; the fusion dance group Raw Elementz; and Nightline, a group of student counselors providing confidential support to their peers. Additionally, the Ferris Reel Film Society screens films most Thursday nights.

Barnard's McIntosh Activities Council (McAC) organizes various community events on campus. These include fall semester's Big Sub, in which students make—and consume—a mile-long sandwich. Before finals, another food-themed event is eagerly attended by students: Midnight Breakfast. Each year the college deans, trustees, and president serve standard breakfast fare—as well as "themed" foods—to about a thousand students. Past foods have included "I YUMM the 90s," "Grease," and "Take me out to the ballgame." Barnard's Spirit Day involved a large BBQ and ice cream, plus plenty of activities, Barnard freebies, and "I Love BC" T-shirts for sale. As one student explains, "We have a lot of school spirit."

All these events foster a sense of on-campus community, but students still tend to spend more of their free time off campus—and who wouldn't with all the excitement of New York City at their fingertips? The city's bars, clubs, restaurants, museums, Broadway shows, and art galleries are frequent hangouts for students. Barnard's campus is a short walk to Central Park and to the Hudson River, where students can jog and bike.

Barnard's impressive new building, The Diana Center (2010), provides a 70,000-square-foot hub for cultural, social, and intellectual life. The multi-level building offers a "layering of functions, including a black box theater, a 500-seat performance/multiuse space, a cafe, a dining room, a library, classrooms, and exhibition galleries," according to the building's architects.

Greek life is present but minimal. There are four sororities on campus. "Most partying takes place off campus," says a student.

Barnard athletes compete in 15 Division I sports with Columbia as well as more than 30 club sports. Barnard's extensive intramurals feature basketball, indoor soccer, tennis, lacrosse, and volleyball and are open to Columbia undergrads as well.

All freshmen live in the Quad, four residence halls that face an enclosed courtyard on the southern end of campus. Upperclass students choose from 11 Barnard residences and four Columbia residences. Ninety percent of students opt for on-campus housing since it is so expensive to live off campus. Most students dine at Barnard's Hewitt Cafeteria or Columbia's John Jay Cafeteria.

BARNARD COLLEGE

Highlights

Students
Total enrollment: 2,504
Undergrads: 2,504
Part-time students: 2%
From out-of-state: 74%
Male/Female: 0%/100%
Live on-campus: 90%
Off-campus employment rating: Excellent
Caucasian: 61%
African American: 5%
Hispanic: 10%
Asian / Pacific Islander: 17%
Native American: 0%
Mixed (2+ ethnicities): 0%
International: 7%

Academics
Calendar: Semester
Student/faculty ratio: 10:1
Class size 9 or fewer: 21%
Class size 10-29: 61%
Class size 30-49: 10%
Class size 50-99: 6%
Class size 100 or more: 2%
Returning freshmen: 97%
Six-year graduation rate: 90%
Graduates who immediately go to graduate school: 21%

Most Popular Majors
Psychology
English
Political science

Admissions
Applicants: 5,440
Accepted: 1,228
Acceptance rate: 22.6%
Placed on wait list: 1,142
Enrolled from wait list: 64
Average GPA: 3.8
ACT range: 28-31
SAT Math range: 620-710
SAT Reading range: 630-730
SAT Writing range: 56-35
Top 10% of class: 79%
Top 25% of class: 98%
Top 50% of class: 100%

BARNARD COLLEGE

Admissions Criteria

Academic criteria:
Grades: ☆ ☆ ☆
Difficulty of class schedule: ☆ ☆ ☆
Class rank: ☆ ☆
Standardized test scores: ☆ ☆
Teacher recommendations: ☆ ☆ ☆
Personal statement: ☆ ☆ ☆
Non-academic criteria considered:
Interview
Extracurricular activities
Special talents, interests, abilities
Character/personal qualities
Volunteer work
Work experience
State of residency
Geographical location
Minority affiliation
Alumni relationship

Deadlines

Early Action: No
Early Decision: November 15
Regular Action: January 1 (final)
Notification of admission by: April 1
Common Application: Accepted

Financial Aid

In-state tuition: $43,100
Out-of-state tuition: $43,100
Room: $8,450
Board: $600
Books: $1,146
Freshmen receiving need-based aid: 40%
Undergrads rec. need-based aid: 39%
Avg. % of need met by financial aid:
    100%
Avg. aid package (freshmen): $40,899
Avg. aid package (undergrads): $41,408
Avg. debt upon graduation: $19,931

School Spirit

Mascot: Millie the Dancing Bear
Colors: Blue and white

Student Body

The women at Barnard come from a wide range of locales: 74 percent are from out of state and 7 percent have been educated abroad. The student body is also ethnically diverse with 32 percent students of color.

A sampling of some of Barnard's popular student groups shows that Barnard students tend to be politically active and liberal. Every year, over 1,000 Barnard and Columbia students march in Take Back the Night, a national movement against sexual assault and domestic violence.

You May Not Know

- Barnard's mascot is Milly, the dancing Barnard Bear.
- Founded in 1889, Barnard was named for Frederick Augustus Porter Barnard, then-President of Columbia. However, student and writer Annie Nathan Meyer was a huge force behind the college's founding: she was dissatisfied with Columbia's education of women.
- Barnard has an impressive collection of over 1,700 zine issues, including rare zines. The website notes, "Barnard's zines are written by women with an emphasis on zines by women of color."

Distinguished Alumnae

Judith Kaye, first female Chief Judge of New York; Margaret Mead, anthropologist; Anna Quindlen, author, journalist, and onion columnist; Martha Stewart, entrepreneur.

Admissions and Financial Aid

Admission and financial aid at Barnard both reflect the college's "priorities of quality, access, and diversity," according to the college. Admissions is highly selective, though also personalized, so that the school looks at academic records, recommendations, writing, and standardized test scores as well as talents, interests, and "the context of [each applicant's] school, community, and personal story" when seeking out applicants. On the financial aid side, admission is need-blind, and there are no merit-based scholarships to Barnard.

BATES COLLEGE

Overview

"Bates is a small college with a big reach," notes the college of the 109-acre highly rated liberal arts college in the quiet town of Lewiston, Maine. "Small" translates to a tight-knit community and lively campus atmosphere: since there's not much to do in Lewiston, undergrads form strong bonds with each other and with their exceptionally accessible professors. "Small" doesn't mean obscure, though: Bates College was recently ranked 22nd on the list of liberal arts colleges by *U.S. News & World Report*.

A tour of campus features beautiful views from Mount David, a wooded hill, and buildings ranging from the historic Hathorn Hall (built in 1857), the college's first building; to Pettengill Hall, the 91,000-square-feet social science building erected in 1999 that features a distinctive 8,000-square-foot three-story glass atrium. Newer buildings highlight Bates' emphasis on going green, including the New Dining Commons and a new student residence.

"Small" does mean that the social scene can get repetitive though, so it's helpful that the college maintains a "big reach," with one of the highest study-abroad participation rates in the country. Bates' big reach is also exemplified by its emphasis on a "truly equal-opportunity education." From the college's inception in 1855, men and women from different racial, ethnic, religious, and socio-economic backgrounds were all welcome. The college was founded by Maine abolitionists and to this day Bates emphasizes inclusivity, which explains its lack of Greek organizations. Students searching for rigorous academics in an unpretentious environment within an extremely close-knit community will be drawn Bates. Being able to endure the cold winters helps too.

Academics

Bates operates on a 4-4-1 schedule, with two semesters that are four months long and a month-long "Short Term." There are over 30 department and interdisciplinary program majors and 25 secondary concentrations (minors). It's also possible for students to design their own majors. Recently, 11 percent of graduating students double-majored and 32 percent had a secondary concentration. Strong programs include chemistry, history, psychology, and the pre-professional tracks for pre-law and pre-med.

Students must complete writing, scientific, and quantitative literacy requirements as well as two general education concentrations. All students are required to produce a senior thesis or capstone project. This emphasis on student-led research is reflected by a biology professor's comment that Bates students "are the ones driving the bus in terms of getting research done."

The college highlights the "uncommonly high collegiality between faculty and students [that] often results in lifelong professional relationships and friendships." These relationships begin in the first-year seminar, which is capped at 15 students and continues with opportunities for college-funded summer research, co-publication, and conference presentations, as well as internships, all the way to the one-on-one relationship cultivated during the senior thesis. All classes are taught by professors whose energy seems focused on teaching rather than being diverted by research and graduate students. Because of the small class sizes, many courses are discussion-based rather than lecture classes. "I plan to keep in touch with my professors long after graduating," says a student. "They've become friends to me."

The one-month Spring term allows many students to study abroad, and about 2/3 of students participate in off-campus study. There are nearly 80 countries to choose from, with Italy, the UK, China, Austria, and Spain being the most popular.

In 2003, a *Wall Street Journal* article ranked Bates as one of the top 50 colleges for sending the "most students to elite grad schools" in business, law, and medicine,

BATES COLLEGE

Four-year private
Founded: 1855
Lewiston, ME
Large town
Pop. 36,491

Address:
2 Andrews Road
Lewiston, ME
04240

Admissions:
855-228-3755

Financial Aid:
207-786-6096

admission@bates.edu

www.bates.edu

BATES COLLEGE

Students

Total enrollment: 1,753
Undergrads: 1,753
Freshmen: 503
From out-of-state: 89%
From public schools: 52%
Male/Female: 47%/53%
Live on-campus: 92%
Off-campus employment rating: Good
Caucasian: 74%
African American: 4%
Hispanic: 5%
Asian / Pacific Islander: 4%
Native American: 0%
Mixed (2+ ethnicities): 4%
International: 6%

Academics

Calendar: 4-4-1 system
Student/faculty ratio: 10:1
Class size 9 or fewer: 34%
Class size 10-29: 49%
Class size 30-49: 14%
Class size 50-99: 3%
Class size 100 or more: -
Returning freshmen: 95%
Six-year graduation rate: 88%
Graduates who immediately go to gradu-
    ate school: 10%
Graduates who immediately enter career
    related to major: 82%

Most Popular Majors

Politics
Psychology
History

Admissions

Applicants: 4,906
Accepted: 1,304
Acceptance rate: 26.6%
Placed on wait list: 1,599
Enrolled from wait list: 72
Average GPA: Not reported
ACT range: 30-32
SAT Math range: 630-710
SAT Reading range: 630-718
SAT Writing range: 44-49
Top 10% of class: 45%
Top 25% of class: 71%
Top 50% of class: 94%

to which Bates President Elaine Tuttle Hansen raised some objections. True to Bates' liberal arts vision, she noted that "the nature of a college education ought to consist not in doing 'what looks good on med-school applications,' but in nurturing the skills of precise thinking, rigorous discipline, and intense compassion that make good doctors and good human beings."

Student Life

With 92 percent of students living on campus, the social scene at Bates is vibrant. Cultural events such as contradances and films are well attended. Popular student hang-outs include Pettengill Hall, the social sciences academic building with its large atrium, and The New Commons, which, as the only dining hall, makes social life even more tight-knit.

There are more than 100 student organizations. WRBC is Bates' fully licensed radio station, which hosts concerts and events such as the much-celebrated Trivia Night. Other student groups provide popular entertainment, including The Strange Bedfellows (comedy), the Robinson Players (theater), and the Bates Musicians' Union. Brooks Quimby Debate Council is internationally ranked: its description declares, "Debate and Bates are practically synonymous." Another popular group is Outing Club, which every Bates student is technically a member of. The organization offers year-round outdoor trips in New England and hosts events including Clambakes, a Winter Carnival, and a hike up Katahdin.

There is no Greek system at Bates as a matter of firm principle from Bates' inception. Bates also has a detailed alcohol policy that includes a three-strikes policy for alcohol and drugs. This doesn't mean that students don't drink though. Indeed, a popular annual celebration is Newman Day, in which students imbibe 24 beers in 24 hours. A more sobering—or shivering—tradition is the Winter Carnival Puddle Jump in January. Several Batesies began the tradition in 1975, when they cut a hole in the ice on Lake Andrews and braced themselves for a freezing cold dip.

There are 31 Division III varsity teams and nine club teams at Bates. Men's and women's rugby are particularly popular to watch. Another intercollegiate club team, men's ice hockey, has also enjoyed championship wins. The college notes that most of its students take part in intramural sports program, although it is not particularly competitive.

Housing is guaranteed to students for four years. The majority of freshmen live in the all-freshmen dorms Clason House (which is chemical free), Smith Hall, and Milliken House. There are a large number of dorms and Victorian houses to choose from, including low-chemical, quiet/study, and themed houses which focus on decors like local living and Irish and Celtic culture.

Student Body

Bates' 1,700+ students are a geographically diverse lot representing 46 states and districts as well as 65 countries. Almost 90 percent of students are from outside the state, though many students are from the New England area, with 40 percent hailing from Massachusetts and New York. Six percent of the student body is international students, and the campus is moderately ethnically diverse with 17 percent underrepresented minorities.

The college describes students as friendly and unpretentious, noting that "students are stimulated by good talk, great books and artistic expression, and they welcome the hard academic work that is the price of discovery." Students describe themselves as "incredibly tight-knit" and the "friendliest group you'll ever meet."

You May Not Know

- According to the college, its Outing Club is the "oldest collegiate coeducational outing club in the country."
- Bates is the first co-ed institution in New England.
- Six of the first nine African American students at the college were former slaves.

Distinguished Alumni

Bryant Gumbel, television host; Benjamin Mays, mentor to Martin Luther King Jr.; Edmund Muskie, former U.S. Secretary of State; Constance Berry Newman, former U.S. Assistant Secretary of State.

Admissions and Financial Aid

Admissions to Bates has grown increasingly selective in recent years, with acceptances rates of 27 percent and a 30 percent increase in the number of early applicants for fall 2013 over fall 2012. The admissions office describes the "ideal Bates student" as exhibiting the traits of "motivation, imagination, initiative, strong personality, and character." Intelligence obviously matters too, as shown by grades, essays, and recommendations. Admissions interviews are strongly recommended—indeed, lacking an interview is likely to hurt one's application. Inconvenience is not an excuse for foregoing an interview: students can interview with deans and alumni both on campus and off.

What students won't be required to submit are SAT/ACT scores. Bates was one of the first schools to join the SAT optional movement in 1984 and remains a leader in the movement with research that shows how this policy helped increase diversity and did not negatively affect the quality of students' performance.

All financial aid at Bates is awarded on the basis of demonstrated financial need, so there are no merit or athletic scholarships. There are awards that meet students' full calculated need, however, and about 42 percent of enrolled students receive need-based financial aid. Individual grants can range from a few hundred dollars to more than $48,000.

BATES COLLEGE

Highlights

Admissions Criteria
Academic criteria:
Grades: ☆ ☆ ☆
Difficulty of class schedule: ☆ ☆ ☆
Class rank: ☆ ☆ ☆
Standardized test scores: ☆
Teacher recommendations: ☆ ☆ ☆
Personal statement: ☆ ☆ ☆
Non-academic criteria considered:
Interview
Extracurricular activities
Special talents, interests, abilities
Character/personal qualities
Volunteer work
Work experience
Geographical location
Minority affiliation
Alumni relationship

Deadlines
Early Action: No
Early Decision: November 15
Regular Action: January 1 (final)
Notification of admission by: April 1
Common Application: Accepted

Financial Aid
In-state tuition: $45,380
Out-of-state tuition: $45,380
Room: Varies
Board: Varies
Books: $1,750
Freshmen receiving need-based aid: 42%
Undergrads rec. need-based aid: 42%
Avg. % of need met by financial aid: 100%
Avg. aid package (freshmen): $38,185
Avg. aid package (undergrads): $38,887
Avg. debt upon graduation: $24,515

School Spirit
Mascot: Bobcats
Colors: Garnet

BAYLOR UNIVERSITY

Overview

Baylor University (BU), a private research university and the largest Baptist university in the world, "integrates faith and learning" on its 735-acre campus near downtown Waco, Texas. Founded in 1845, BU holds strong to many one-of-a-kind traditions—but also has ambitious goals for growth and improvement in its near future, as captured by the President's Scholarship Initiative, a three-year fundraising effort to raise $100 million.

Waco might not be as appealing as other college towns, but the large Baylor campus, aka the "Baylor bubble," has a lot to offer. Baylor's affiliation with the Baptist Church and strong Christian influence are seen in requirements for religion courses and Chapel group worship attendance, strict alcohol policies, and single sex dorms. Obviously this strong religious emphasis isn't for everyone, though you shouldn't let these strict policies put a dour face on the university. Indeed, Baylor has many quirky traditions, from an annual spring festival honoring the school's mascot to the nation's largest Homecoming.

Academics

Academics are fairly rigorous at Baylor, but students aren't lost in a sea of cutthroat competition among hundreds of students, finding great support from faculty. With an average undergraduate class size of 28 students, it's likely that professors will know you by name when you stop by during their office hours. Over 92 percent of classes at Baylor are taught by faculty members; the remaining courses are taught by doctoral students. The 2014 *U.S. News* ranking attests to Baylor's academic strength: the university was ranked 75th out of 262 national universities.

Baylor has 144 undergraduate degree programs spread across eight colleges and schools, including the George W. Truett Theological Seminary and the Honors College. Baylor's strongest programs include the many degrees in the Hankamer School of Business (including entrepreneurship and management), chemistry, engineering, mathematics, and religion.

All students are required to take two religion classes and two semesters of Chapel. On Mondays and Wednesdays, the student body gathers "to worship, to engage important issues, and to experience wonderful presentations on the Waco Hall stage" as part of their spiritual education. The worship services draw from "the expansive traditions of the Christian church."

As part of its 2012 initiative, the university expanded their facilities to strengthen research on campus. The recently constructed Baylor Sciences Building—completed in 2004 to the tune of over $103 million—has over half a million square feet of space for the science departments, including more than 150 labs. Almost all students are likely to benefit from the building, as 97 percent of all undergraduate students take one or more science courses at Baylor. Students say that the science facilities at the college are "top-notch."

Baylor's Honors College, established in 2002, consists of four interdisciplinary programs/majors. Honors students can take advantage of on-campus housing opportunities and are privy to high levels of interaction with faculty.

For those who want to venture away from the Waco area, there are over 60 study-abroad programs, with especially strong representation in Europe. Students may study abroad after freshman year for a summer session or spring/fall semester. The university hopes to increase student participation in study-abroad programs to 30 percent.

The Paul L. Foster Success Center offers career services for students and alumni, including a career library, workshops, employment services such as help with resumes, and job fairs.

Student Life

The most memorable of on-campus activities at Baylor are long-standing traditions unique to the school that may sound strange to outsiders' ears. Dr. Pepper Hour is a weekly hospitality time and opportunity to relax and casually socialize. Inaugurated in 1953, the event always features plenty of beverages—including soft drinks mixed with ice cream (hence the name).

Diadeloso, Spanish for "The Day of the Bear," is the university's spring holiday festival, a tradition since 1931. No classes are held on this day so students can enjoy the annual entertainment, from Ultimate Frisbee to gospel choirs. An even older tradition is home-coming, an event designed in 1909 to "catch the Baylor spirit" that has grown to be the largest collegiate Homecoming celebration in the entire United States. Students say that there is a "ton of school spirit" and that the "traditions make Baylor *Baylor*."

For more run-of-the-mill everyday activities, there are over 275 clubs and organizations to choose from, including 41 national and local sorority and fraternity chapters. Baylor also has a Phi Beta Kappa chapter. Most drinking occurs off campus since the no drinking policies are strictly enforced on campus.

Extracurriculars cover academic and professional clubs, honors societies, music groups, and religious and service organizations. The university places a strong emphasis on service, with Baylor students, faculty, and staff volunteering more than 150,000 hours annually. Indeed, Baylor was the site of the first Habit for Humanity chapter.

For the athletically inclined, the Student Life Center offers opportunities for pool parties and rock climbing. The Baylor Marina presents students with the chance to canoe, kayak, or sail. Intramurals are popular, especially dodgeball. There are also 22 club sports. The $34 million Highers Athletic Complex, a "green" building that opened in 2008, includes three football practice fields. Football is a popular sport to watch, even if Baylor's team is not the strongest—The Bears are the only Big 12 team *not* to have played in a bowl game since the conference's start. By contrast, Baylor's tennis, baseball, track and field, and women's basketball have done well in Division I Big 12 championships.

Almost all housing is single sex. Freshmen are required to live on campus, but most upperclass students choose to live off campus due to the on-campus dorms' strict policies regarding visitors and alcohol. Nearly 40 percent of students live on campus in 12 residence halls, a number the university hopes to raise to 50 percent. As part of this expansion effort, the university built Brooks Village in 2007, a $42.8 million project.

Student Body

Almost three-quarters of Baylor students were in the top 25 percent of their high school graduating class. The almost 13,000 undergraduates and approximately 2,500 grad students at Baylor hail from every state and more than 70 countries, though 75 percent of them come from Texas. Over 50 percent of undergrads pursue post-graduate degrees.

The majority of students identify themselves as religious, and most students tend to be conservative. However, it would be a mistake to assume that the college is not very diverse due to its religious affiliation: indeed, 32 percent of students are minorities,

BAYLOR UNIVERSITY

Highlights

Students
Total enrollment: 15,364
Undergrads: 12,918
Part-time students: 2%
From out-of-state: 25%
Male/Female: 41%/59%
Live on-campus: 39%
In fraternities: 13%
In sororities: 21%
Off-campus employment rating: Good
Caucasian: 64%
African American: 7%
Hispanic: 14%
Asian / Pacific Islander: 6%
Native American: 0%
Mixed (2+ ethnicities): 5%
International: 3%

Academics
Calendar: Semester
Student/faculty ratio: 15:1
Class size 9 or fewer: 13%
Class size 10-29: 61%
Class size 30-49: 17%
Class size 50-99: 7%
Class size 100 or more: 3%
Returning freshmen: 87%
Six-year graduation rate: 75%

Most Popular Majors
Biology
Nursing
Psychology

Admissions
Applicants: 27,828
Accepted: 16,879
Acceptance rate: 60.7%
Placed on wait list: 3,145
Enrolled from wait list: 32
Average GPA: Not reported
ACT range: 24-29
SAT Math range: 570-670
SAT Reading range: 550-660
SAT Writing range: 11-34
Top 10% of class: 39%
Top 25% of class: 73%
Top 50% of class: 97%

BAYLOR UNIVERSITY

Admissions Criteria
Academic criteria:
Grades: ☆ ☆ ☆
Difficulty of class schedule: ☆ ☆ ☆
Class rank: ☆ ☆ ☆
Standardized test scores: ☆ ☆ ☆
Teacher recommendations: ☆
Personal statement: ☆
Non-academic criteria considered:
Interview
Extracurricular activities
Special talents, interests, abilities
Character/personal qualities
Volunteer work
State of residency
Religious affiliation/commitment
Alumni relationship

Deadlines
Early Action: November 1
Early Decision: No
Regular Action: November 1 (priority)
Common Application: Accepted

Financial Aid
In-state tuition: $32,574
Out-of-state tuition: $32,574
Room: $5,312
Board: $4,022
Books: $1,370
Freshmen receiving need-based aid: 61%
Undergrads rec. need-based aid: 58%
Avg. % of need met by financial aid: 62%
Avg. aid package (freshmen): $23,498
Avg. aid package (undergrads): $23,851

School Spirit
Mascot: Bears
Colors: Green and gold
Song: *That Good Old Baylor Line*

with Hispanics comprising the largest group, and dozens of religions are represented within Christianity as well as other religious traditions (Buddhist, Judaism, Islam—albeit in much smaller numbers). In 2006, over 40 percent of students identified as Baptist. "You'll be most comfortable here if religion plays some kind of role in your life," confides a student.

You May Not Know

- The Baylor Bear Program provides for the university's live bear mascots named "Judge." In addition to having an individual care taker, the bears also meet with a professional movie industry bear trainer.
- Baylor has partnered with the City of Waco to manage the Waco Mammoth Site, the "nation's first and only recorded discovery of a nursery herd of Pleistocene mammoths."
- The NoZe Brotherhood is an unofficial fraternity whose members wear special glasses during graduation and pull pranks.

Distinguished Alumni

Robert Lee Fulghum, author of many collections, including *All I Really Need to Know I Learned in Kindergarten*; Mark Hurd, CEO and President of Hewlett-Packard; Michael Johnson, sprinter, four-time Olympic gold medalist; Angela Kinsey, actress, *The Office*; Ann Richards, politician, second female Governor of Texas.

Admissions and Financial Aid

Baylor admits about half of all applicants, making the college fairly selective. As part of the Baylor 2012 initiative, the school hopes to attract more competitive applicants. For example, the average SAT score for incoming freshmen has risen 50 points in the past decade; the median SAT score for accepted first-year students is 1130-1300.

Supplemental materials to the general admissions forms are optional, though some schools do have special requirements; for example, the Baylor School of Music and the Department of Theatre Arts mandate auditions. Applications received by November 1 are reviewed under the first round. A consequence of first-round selection includes certain benefits such as first priority in housing. Applications received after February 1 are only considered on a space-available basis.

More than 80 percent of Baylor students receive some form of merit- or need-based financial assistance. Priority for on-campus jobs during fall term is given to students eligible for Federal Work Study. Merit-based scholarships are awarded on the basis of ACT/SAT scores and class rank. The largest scholarship, the Regents' Gold Scholarship, provides for the cost of tuition, fees, and room and board. There are also scholarships for National Merit finalists for full tuition and awards for students based on their academic department.

BELOIT COLLEGE

Overview

Most of the nearly 1,400 students at Beloit College live in the Wisconsin city by the same name, making campus a hub for social and intellectual life. The college campus, a scant four blocks long and half as wide, is regarded as safe, but some parts of Beloit have had higher levels of crime than other cities in Wisconsin. Modern science and arts facilities complement Colonial and Victorian architecture. The new Science Center, completed in 2008, is LEED certified and houses 10 academic departments and programs in its 117,000 square feet of space. However, the highlight of Beloit's natural grounds is more ancient than all of these buildings: 23 ancient Native American effigy mounds.

Students enjoy a strong liberal arts education with a stand-out anthropology program whose strength is evidenced by its accomplished graduates and also the Logan Museum of Anthropology on campus. Beloit students can also reach beyond the small campus and town by taking advantage of the college's focus on global understanding and study-abroad programs that about 56 percent of students participate in.

Beloit is a beautiful campus, though students must be courageous enough to endure harsh winters. Though not located in a particularly lively college town, Beloit has much to offer in its laid-back atmosphere and liberal arts program that includes special initiatives to fight the sophomore slump. The nearest big cities are Madison (an hour's drive) and Chicago (two hours). However, on-campus social events and other activities are abundant.

Academics

Beloit offers BA and BS degrees in more than 50 fields of study, as well as preprofessional programs in environmental management and forestry, engineering, law, and medicine. Strong programs include anthropology, international relations, modern languages and literature, and sociology. Anthropology is particularly renowned. The department notes: "Anthropology at Beloit College is almost as old as the study of anthropology in the United States. The College's Logan Museum of Anthropology began in 1894, just two years after the first degree in anthropology was awarded in this country." The Logan Museum now houses over 300,000 ethnographic and archeological objects.

Students say the learning atmosphere isn't really cutthroat and that they generally aren't competitive with one another. Professors are close to students and often ask to be called by their first name. Beloit's First-Year Initiatives (FYI) program offers all freshmen an introduction to Beloit and the skills needed for succeeding in the liberal arts. Professors lead FYI seminars, mentor, and advise students. The advising relationship continues through the end of the sophomore year, when students declare a major. The Venture Grant program offers competitive awards to first-year students who have ambitious, self-directed project ideas.

Students must take at least two courses in each of the three academic divisions: natural sciences and mathematics, social sciences, and arts and humanities. There are also required classes in writing and interdisciplinary studies. Students say the required courses are "manageable" and "mostly interesting."

The Sophomore-Year Initiatives was one of the nation's earliest programs for sophomores. The program aims to fight the sophomore slump. Early in September, FYI seminars reunite for a welcome back dinner. Students may also attend the two-day Sophomore Retreat at a Wisconsin resort, which focuses on investigating academic opportunities, internships, and field experiences in a social setting. The retreat also helps students work on their MAP, "My Academic Plan," required of all sophomores.

In 2010 the college celebrated its 50th anniversary of its excellent study-abroad program, in which more than half of students participate. There are 15 Beloit Col-

BELOIT COLLEGE

Highlights

Students

Total enrollment: 1,359
Undergrads: 1,359
Freshmen: 360
Part-time students: 5%
From out-of-state: 81%
From public schools: 76%
Male/Female: 41%/59%
Live on-campus: 94%
In fraternities: 8%
In sororities: 6%
Off-campus employment rating: Fair
Caucasian: 68%
African American: 4%
Hispanic: 8%
Asian / Pacific Islander: 2%
Native American: 1%
Mixed (2+ ethnicities): 4%
International: 10%

Academics

Calendar: Semester
Student/faculty ratio: 11:1
Class size 9 or fewer: 21%
Class size 10-29: 76%
Class size 30-49: 2%
Class size 50-99: -
Class size 100 or more: -
Returning freshmen: 91%
Six-year graduation rate: 78%
Graduates who immediately go to graduate school: 15%

Most Popular Majors

Anthropology
Psychology
English/creative writing

Admissions

Applicants: 2,205
Accepted: 1,479
Acceptance rate: 67.1%
Placed on wait list: 74
Enrolled from wait list: 2
Average GPA: 3.5
ACT range: 24-30
SAT Math range: 560-690
SAT Reading range: 550-710
SAT Writing range: Not reported
Top 10% of class: 34%
Top 25% of class: 74%
Top 50% of class: 97%

lege programs, including a cross-cultural psychology program in Morocco and Estonia and an environmental studies program in the Galapagos. Students may also study abroad through non-Beloit programs.

Beloit ranks 20th in the country for producing future PhDs. More anthropology PhDs earned their undergraduate degrees at Beloit than at any other four-year liberal arts college not connected to a university.

Student Life

The 94 percent of students living on campus support a lively social scene with a laid-back attitude. Students are creatively involved in developing activities and events. Beloit has almost 100 student organizations, clubs, and societies, including three sororities and three fraternities. About 8 percent of men and 6 percent of women are part of the Greek system. The Women's Center, Beloit Student Congress, special interest groups, and athletics are also popular, as well as influential, on campus. WBCR, the college's radio station, has been broadcasting since 1907.

Beloit students tend to party Thursday, Friday, and Saturday nights, and social life is centered around campus. Aldrich, one of the largest residence halls, has a reputation for being a party dorm. The alcohol policy is fairly lenient. Coughy Haus, the student pub, is open Wednesday through Saturday. "If you're looking for alcohol, there's plenty," says a student. For those seeking caffeine over alcohol, the Java Joint serves up coffee and pastries, and hosts open mics on occasion.

New Student Days welcome Beloit students during their weeklong orientation. Not long after, students look forward to the Folk 'n' Blues Fall Music Festival. The event is free of charge and open to the public, and students have been producing it since its inception in 1972. Throughout the school year, Beloit's International Performing Arts and Lecture Series offer musical entertainment and present speakers from around the world. The annual three-day International Film Festival is part of the series. Spring Day is a festival in April that provides a welcome respite from classes.

Beloit offers 17 Division III varsity sports and extensive intramural and club sports. Its biggest rival is Ripon College. The popularity of Ultimate Frisbee at Beloit is attested by the presence of a Frisbee golf course on campus.

Students are required to live on campus for three years as part of a residential liberal arts education. Luckily, they have plenty of options: 35, to be exact. Housing is pretty posh as far as college dorms go; many of the traditional residences, which house mostly freshman and sophomores, have been recently renovated. Special interest housing allows student clubs and organizations the chance to obtain group housing. More than a dozen are available, including Art House, Interfaith House, Substance Free House, and the Women's Center. Many of these host social gatherings.

Student Body

Beloit's nearly 1,400 students come from 48 states, with a strong Midwestern representation, particularly for the states of Wisconsin and Illinois, though 81 percent of students are from out of state. International students make up 10 percent of the student body and come from 40 foreign countries. This geographic diversity is matched by ethnic diversity, with about 19 percent minority students on campus.

Students are left-leaning, which is not surprising given the college's alternative history in the 60s and 70s. You'll still find many hippies on campus. "We're a liberal haven in the conservative Midwest," laughs a student.

On the whole, Beloit students don't consider themselves particularly religious, though spiritual choice is supported by the tolerant atmosphere of the campus in general. The school website hints at this as a part of the description for the school's Spiritual Life Program: "Some of us see life as spiritual. Some of us practice a religion. Many of us do neither one." A minority of students identify themselves as pagans. The Yoga and Meditation Club is also categorized under the Spiritual Life program.

You May Not Know

- Indiana Jones is based on Roy Chapman Andrews, a graduate of Beloit who was the director of the American Museum of Natural History.
- In 2006, 30 Beloit students played 72 hours to set a new world record for the longest game of Ultimate Frisbee.
- Beloit's official mascot is a swashbuckling buccaneer, but its unofficial mascot is the much gentler turtle. Campus is built around several Native American mounds, the largest of which is called Turtle Mound—hence the unofficial mascot.

Distinguished Alumni

Roy Chapman Andrews, former director of the American Museum of Natural History; Clarence "Ginger" Beaumont, the first player to bat in the World Series; Suzzane K. Hale, former American ambassador.

Admissions and Financial Aid

Applying for admissions to Beloit is fairly standard: applicants submit the Common Application, Beloit supplement, recommendations, high school transcripts, and standardized test scores. Interviews, additional letters of recommendation, and samples of creative work are all optional.

Admission to Beloit is need-blind. Merit awards at Beloit College look for academic achievement, talent, and leadership. Students who apply Early Action have priority for merit scholarships, which include the prestigious Presidential Scholarship ranging from $13,000 to $17,000 a year for four years; the Charles Winter Wood Scholarship for underrepresented students that offers full tuition each year, renewable for four years; a music scholarship valued at $5,000 a year for four years; and several others.

BELOIT COLLEGE

Highlights

Admissions Criteria
Academic criteria:
Grades: ☆ ☆ ☆
Difficulty of class schedule: ☆ ☆ ☆
Class rank: ☆ ☆
Standardized test scores: ☆ ☆
Teacher recommendations: ☆ ☆ ☆
Personal statement: ☆ ☆ ☆
Non-academic criteria considered:
Interview
Extracurricular activities
Special talents, interests, abilities
Character/personal qualities
Volunteer work
Work experience
State of residency
Alumni relationship

Deadlines
Early Action: December 1
Early Decision: November 1
Regular Action: Rolling admissions
Common Application: Accepted

Financial Aid
In-state tuition: $40,970
Out-of-state tuition: $40,970
Room: $4,256
Board: $3,000
Books: $600
Freshmen receiving need-based aid: 72%
Undergrads rec. need-based aid: 67%
Avg. % of need met by financial aid: 87%
Avg. aid package (freshmen): $28,742
Avg. aid package (undergrads): $28,562
Avg. debt upon graduation: $27,981

School Spirit
Mascot: Buccaneers
Colors: Blue and gold

BENNINGTON COLLEGE

Overview

Bennington College, located in the Vermont town of the same name, has almost as many acres of forest, ponds, wetlands, and scenic beauty (470) as it does undergraduate students (670). Central campus is comprised on 10 acres situated in a natural wonderland that boasts 80 species of trees and more than 120 species of birds. The college is next to the Green Mountains, part of the Appalachians.

The small campus size will be a boon to some—student-professor relationships are very tight-knit, for instance—and a burden to others who might prefer a more active social scene or simply want to get away from their fellow classmates, who are generally known to be very liberal. The arts are strong at Bennington, so cultural offerings are quite vibrant, but men will find themselves outnumbered by women and students of color are only a small percent of the student body.

Academics

The core of Bennington's academic structure is the "Plan Process," which requires that students integrate different areas of the curriculum around central ideas or questions to create areas of concentration. As a result, Bennington doesn't have traditional majors but rather individualized, student-developed programs. These different concentrations make the academic environment less competitive, and the pressure to do well compared to one's fellow students is further alleviated by the fact that grades are optional—students can get written evaluations instead.

Bennington requires a seven-week internship during what they call a "Field Work Term." Many students take advantage of this winter term to escape their rather remote campus and connect to the world. According to the college, the FWT has offerings of 500 to 1,000 jobs a year, and 40 percent of students create their own jobs. Singer and actress Carol Channing was discovered during her Field Work Term. One student sums it up by commenting, "FWT is an unbelievable way to get hands-on work experience and do something you really love."

The small size of the student body lends itself to close student-professor relationships. Professors, rather than teaching assistants, teach all classes and help students select their concentrations. Strong programs include dance, visual arts, science, and writing. The dance program was founded by legendary choreographer and Bennington alumnus Martha Graham.

The Democracy Project is a new curricular initiative at Bennington that aims to deepen students' study of democracy and understanding of mediating conflict. This project has benefitted from conversations with highly regarded people such as former Secretary of State Madeleine Albright and Economics Nobel Laureate Amartya Sen. Besides academic and fieldwork opportunities, there are also featured speakers and conferences.

Those who want to study abroad can choose from programs that Bennington already has in place, or students may propose their own ideas. Anyone interested in studying at another school must plan a year in advance and discuss it with his or her Plan Process committee.

Field Work Term is bundled up with Bennington's Career Development office. While many Bennington students enter the work force, approximately nine percent pursue a graduate degree immediately after graduation, and another 54 percent enter graduate school within two years. Bennington has the highest rate of students participating in internships in the country, with 100 percent of its class of 2012 having had an internship.

Student Life

Most social activities are concentrated on campus since the town of Bennington is small and has only a few student-friendly restaurants or entertainment possibilities. Students are often found congregated at the new Student Center, which opened in fall of 2006, taking advantage of the café/snack bar/pub. The lofty building is made of cedar and glass and has an enclave for studying and having conversations, as well as a performance space for a number of activities such as rock concerts, poetry readings, open-mic nights, dance parties, and more. The living rooms of students' houses also provide cozy alternatives for hanging out.

As can be expected at a school known for its visual and performing arts, theatrical and musical performances are very popular. There are over 30 student groups on campus, many with quirky, fun, and/or artsy missions. All Sorts of Stuff "organizes happenings, situation art, and flash mobs across campus;" Bennington Association of the Fantastic brings together fantasy literature/film fanatics; Cupcakes for a Cause raises money through baking; and Shimmy Shimmy! is for students interested in belly dancing. There is no Greek life at Bennington. However, students describe the student organizations at Bennington as "out there" and "very creative."

Students on the Program Activity Council (PAC) plan dance parties, guest performers, and bands. Major annual events include Rollerama in November, when Greenwall, a huge auditorium space in the art building, gets converted into a skating rink. Skates, student DJs, and disco balls make for a fantastic time. SunFest, a 24-hour music festival, takes place in the spring: as the college describes it, "It's part outdoor concert, part campus tradition, and part holiday." The student-run Campus Activities Board ensures a steady stream of social events, including many that have the word "Night" as a part of their titles: Karaoke Night, Transvestite Night, Motown Night, and Jazz Night, to name a few.

Art trumps athletics at Bennington College. There are no varsity teams, so students tend to participate in sports on a recreational, noncompetitive level. There are a dozen intramurals, including bocce ball and laser tag, and the Meyer Recreation Barn houses the school's fitness center, which is highlighted by its rock-climbing wall. Students might opt for outdoor rock climbing, one of the many trips offered by the Outdoor Recreation Program.

For off-campus activities, students sometimes head north to the Massachusetts Museum of Contemporary Art and the Sterling and Francine Clark Art Institute. Within Vermont, Killington, Stratton, and Mount Snow are about an hour's drive and provide some of the best skiing on the East Coast.

Bennington offers 20 units of housing that accommodate about 30 students each. Juniors and seniors are guaranteed sought-after singles, and the houses have weekly Coffee Hours in the living room for their residents to gather around the fireplace and socialize. Welling Town House is the only off-campus house with organic co-op living. Another house has a porch and porch swing that became the centerpiece of this residence's Porch Party.

Student Body

There are more female than male students at Bennington, which affects the social scene quite dramatically. "If you're looking for a

BENNINGTON COLLEGE

Highlights

Students
Total enrollment: 826
Undergrads: 688
Freshmen: 204
Part-time students: 1%
From out-of-state: 98%
From public schools: 57%
Male/Female: 36%/64%
Live on-campus: 95%
Off-campus employment rating: Excellent
Caucasian: 77%
African American: 2%
Hispanic: 5%
Asian / Pacific Islander: 2%
Native American: 0%
Mixed (2+ ethnicities): 3%
International: 7%

Academics
Calendar: Other
Student/faculty ratio: 9:1
Class size 9 or fewer: 25%
Class size 10-29: 74%
Class size 30-49: 1%
Class size 50-99: -
Class size 100 or more: -
Returning freshmen: 83%
Six-year graduation rate: 64%

Most Popular Majors
Visual/performing arts
Social sciences
English

Admissions
Applicants: 1,236
Accepted: 779
Acceptance rate: 63.0%
Placed on wait list: 175
Enrolled from wait list: 27
Average GPA: 3.5
ACT range: 26-30
SAT Math range: 560-660
SAT Reading range: 620-720
SAT Writing range: 27-51
Top 10% of class: 35%
Top 25% of class: 67%
Top 50% of class: 93%

97

BENNINGTON COLLEGE

Admissions Criteria

Academic criteria:
Grades: ☆ ☆ ☆
Difficulty of class schedule: ☆ ☆ ☆
Class rank: ☆ ☆ ☆
Standardized test scores: ☆
Teacher recommendations: ☆ ☆ ☆
Personal statement: ☆ ☆ ☆
Non-academic criteria considered:
Interview
Extracurricular activities
Special talents, interests, abilities
Character/personal qualities
Volunteer work
Work experience
State of residency
Geographical location
Minority affiliation
Alumni relationship

Deadlines

Early Action: December 1
Early Decision: November 15
Regular Action: January 3 (final)
Notification of admission by: April 1
Common Application: Accepted

Financial Aid

In-state tuition: $44,490
Out-of-state tuition: $44,490
Room: $7,080
Board: $6,110
Books: $1,000
Freshmen receiving need-based aid: 60%
Undergrads rec. need-based aid: 64%
Avg. % of need met by financial aid: 80%
Avg. aid package (freshmen): $36,238
Avg. aid package (undergrads): $35,822
Avg. debt upon graduation: $25,716

School Spirit

Mascot: The Pioneer
Colors: Blue, white, and green

boyfriend, you may want to go somewhere else," says a student. Students of color are in an even smaller minority than men, making up only 12 percent of the student population.

Bennington students are known to be very liberal and have even made headlines acting out their political beliefs: in 2004, for example, students protested a campus ban on nudity. As the Reuters article put it, "Students occasionally parading buck naked around Vermont's Bennington College campus has been a tolerated, if peculiar, part of the university's student culture here since the 1960s. Now...Bennington's dean of students, has embarked on a crusade against public nudity—one that has run afoul of the school's free-spirited students."

This is not to suggest that students spend all their time sunbathing topless or running naked at the annual bonfire. Many have a genuine passion for learning rather than just caring about their grades, since grades are optional and students design their own academic concentration.

You May Not Know

- Bennington became formally co-ed in 1969 but began admitting men into the Bennington Theater Studio program in 1935 since males were needed for performances. Academy Award winner Alan Arkin was one of these men.
- In 1994, Bennington made news in the field of higher education when it abolished tenure for professors.
- Kelly Muzzi, a dance student at Bennington, died tragically on campus in 2005. A memorial garden was planted on campus in her honor.

Distinguished Alumni

Andrea Dworkin, radical feminist and writer; Helen Frankenthaler, pioneering Color Field painter; Michael Pollan, environmentalist and journalist; Jonathan Lethem, bestselling author and MacArthur 'genius' grant recipient.

Admissions and Financial Aid

In addition to the Common Application and Bennington Supplement, the college also requires a graded analytical paper and two teacher recommendations in different subject areas. The analytical paper should be an original analysis rather than a creative writing sample or research paper. SAT/ACT scores are optional, and tours and interviews are recommended but not required.

Sixty-four percent of Bennington students receive need-based financial aid—though the college is not always able to meet a student's full need. There are need-based and merit-based scholarships, but no athletic scholarships. Merit awards are assessed based on the strength of a student's application; no separate application is required. Scholarships range up to the cost of full tuition and include The Richard Holme Global Citizen Scholarship for students committed to public action ($2,500 to $25,000 annually), minority student and international student scholarships ($2,500 to $25,000 annually), and the Brockway Scholarship ($2,500 to $30,000 annually) for exceptional students.

BENTLEY UNIVERSITY

Overview

In the suburbs 10 miles west of Boston, Bentley University is ranked in the top 25 undergraduate business schools by *Bloomberg/Business Week*. While the university's core focus is definitely business education, it also integrates a liberal arts curriculum and cutting-edge technology in its specialized learning labs. Real-world, applied learning occurs through internships, which almost all undergrads pursue, as well as excellent service-learning programs. The prime location near Boston makes for even more career-oriented opportunities, not to mention plenty of social offerings. You'll find students lined up at the four subway stops on campus to take advantage of their proximity to Boston.

Bentley's red brick buildings, neatly manicured trees, and concrete paths are orderly and dignified, matching the business-like demeanor of many of its students. Buildings like the Smith Technology Center capture the spirit of the campus. Full of high-tech interactive classrooms, the center features the financial Trading Room, the largest facility of its kind in higher education. From the top of the stairs at the Smith Center, students can enjoy a great view of campus and city lights at sunset.

Students at Bentley may find the programs more conservative than the average liberal arts college. However, diversification of curriculum spans the gap between opposing world views and offers all majors the opportunity to be immersed in the corporate world. Overall, students are likely to be *participating* in capitalism rather than critiquing it.

Academics

Bentley's curriculum combines business programs with liberal arts and sciences. As the college puts it, students can "learn about management and moral behavior, about accounting and art, about technology and trust, about real estate and religion, about profits and prophets."

Undergrads can receive BS degrees in 11 business disciplines and BA degrees in six arts and sciences fields. There are over 40 majors and minors to choose from. The strongest programs are finance, corporate finance and accounting, and marketing.

Many professors work in their fields in addition to teaching, which brings workplace experience into the classroom. No courses enroll more than 40 students. Freshmen have an opportunity to get to know Bentley University during a three-day summer orientation as well as First Week, which gives students a chance to acclimate before upperclassmen arrive. The required First-Year Seminars are taught by a faculty member who also acts as an academic advisor. "All of the support offered makes the transition to college very smooth," says a student.

In addition to the required First-Year Seminar, students fulfill a core curriculum with courses in information technology, writing, literature, humanities/social science, philosophy, history, microeconomics, macroeconomics, government, behavioral science, science lab, and math.

Students in the top 10 percent of the entering class are invited to participate in the four-year honors program. A Five-Year Master's Candidate Program provides an accelerated way to earn an undergraduate degree and MBA or MS.

Information technology is integrated into this business education cum liberal arts curriculum, as exemplified by several specialty learning labs. The Bentley Trading Room, described by the college as "a virtual laboratory of world financial markets," is popular among finance and global finance students as well as the corporate community, which uses the room for employee training. According to one student, "The trading room is the best in the country." The Design and Usability Center provides hands-on experience in information design and IT. The Center for Languages and International Collaboration offers technological solutions for communicating abroad.

BENTLEY UNIVERSITY

Four-year private
Founded: 1917
Waltham, MA
Major city
Pop. 61,181

Address:
175 Forest Street
Waltham, MA
02452-4705

Admissions:
800-523-2354

Financial Aid:
877-362-2216

ugadmission@bentley.edu

www.bentley.edu

BENTLEY UNIVERSITY

Students

Total enrollment: 5,643
Undergrads: 4,237
Freshmen: 1,138
Part-time students: 3%
From out-of-state: 55%
From public schools: 71%
Male/Female: 59%/41%
Live on-campus: 78%
In fraternities: 11%
In sororities: 11%
Off-campus employment rating: Good
Caucasian: 61%
African American: 3%
Hispanic: 7%
Asian / Pacific Islander: 7%
Native American: 0%
Mixed (2+ ethnicities): 2%
International: 14%

Academics

Calendar: Semester
Student/faculty ratio: 14:1
Class size 9 or fewer: 7%
Class size 10-29: 54%
Class size 30-49: 40%
Class size 50-99: -
Class size 100 or more: -
Returning freshmen: 95%
Six-year graduation rate: 87%
Graduates who immediately go to graduate school: 17%
Graduates who immediately enter career related to major: 98%

Most Popular Majors

Economics/finance
Finance
Marketing

Admissions

Applicants: 7,040
Accepted: 3,172
Acceptance rate: 45.1%
Placed on wait list: 1,400
Enrolled from wait list: 59
Average GPA: Not reported
ACT range: 25-29
SAT Math range: 593-670
SAT Reading range: 530-620
SAT Writing range: 5-44
Top 10% of class: 45%
Top 25% of class: 83%
Top 50% of class: 98%

The Service-Learning Center at Bentley provides extensive programs to facilitate students' engagement in community service. The fourth credit option offers students the ability to earn one more credit for a three-credit course by serving at least 20 hours at a local nonprofit.

Service isn't just confined to the Boston area: the Bentley International Service-Learning program offers opportunities to combine service with study abroad; for example, economic development in Ghana. Each year, several hundred Bentley students go to Europe, Latin America, Asia, and Australia for a semester at one of Bentley's international partner universities.

According to Bentley, "more than 95 percent of (its) students find professional employment or enroll in graduate school" within six months of graduation. The university's recruiting programs feature "more than 1,200 job opportunities" each year. Part of students' success in finding jobs is likely due to the fact that 93 percent of their students complete an internship. The more than 44,000 alumni are also a rich resource.

Student Life

With more than 100 organizations and popular on-campus events, there's always something going on. Cultural organizations and the Campus Activities Board—the largest education, recreational, and social event programming organization on campus—are popular student groups. Greek life also has a strong presence, with 12 fraternities and sororities.

The Student Center is a major social hub on campus. "At one point in the day, everyone passes through the Student Center," says a student. There is a rec room with weekly pool tournaments, Wii, and flat-screen TVs; Blue Line, the campus pub (students with valid IDs can be served alcohol); and the Sacred Space for religious ceremonies and spiritual reflection.

Some unique traditions at Bentley include Greedy Bingo, where the giveaways include DVD players, TVs, and iPods; the Festival of Colors, which showcases international dance and food; and Breakfast by Moonlight, an evening before finals when students get breakfast at midnight served by Bentley faculty. Spring Week includes BBQs, prizes, and giveaways before a concert featuring a major musical act, recently Third Eye Blind.

Bentley's Division II varsity programs offer 23 sports, and the men's ice hockey program is a Division I program. The rugby team has won two national titles, and the men's basketball team set the record for the most regular season wins in a row in Division II in 2008. "Basketball games are where we show our school spirit," explains a fan. Bentley's rival is Babson College—the athletic competition is matched by an academic rivalry, since Babson also focuses on business. Intramurals are offered for a fee, and all students can use the 86,000 square foot Dana Athletic Center.

Waltham has shopping, bars, and restaurants, but in addition, this suburb is near the biggest college town in the country, Boston, which is just a 20-minute drive away. A free daily shuttle takes students to Harvard Square in Cambridge. Access to Cambridge and Boston not only provides social activities but also a venue for internships. "Our location is the best—not too crazy in Waltham but totally accessible to Boston," comments a Bentley student.

Housing is guaranteed for four years, and students generally rave about the dorms, which have air conditioning and high speed Internet and come in the form of residence halls, suites, and apartments. Specialty housing includes the Wellness House, Global Living Center, and Stratton Green House whose residents are interested in sustainability as a lifestyle and a business.

Student Body

Business is the natural common link among Bentley's 4,000 undergrads. As a result, many students are highly motivated and career focused. "Everyone is always thinking, 'How will this person I'm meeting help me in my career in the future?'" explains a local.

While there may seem to be a lack of variation in what students study, work at, and want careers in, there is a fair amount of ethnic diversity, with 19 percent students of color. There is also above average geographic diversity, with 55 percent of the student population hailing from out of state. International students are well represented at 14 percent of undergrads.

Politically, Bentley is a mix of liberals and conservatives. There are more conservatives than at other liberal arts colleges, perhaps due to the capitalistic nature of the business world.

You May Not Know

- Bentley University only recently got the University moniker in 2008. Previously, it was Bentley College, and before that, Bentley School of Accounting and Finance.
- Jay Leno attended for a semester but dropped out.
- Bentley's mascot is "Flex the Falcon."

Distinguished Alumni

Elkin B. McCallum, former chairman and CEO of Jo-Ann Fabrics Corporation; Daniel Welbeck, chief operation officer of Radio Shack; Tanya Hairston Whitner, Esq., partner at Kilpatrick Stockton LLP.

Admissions and Financial Aid

Bentley accepts the Common Application and Bentley supplement and the admissions committee takes a holistic look at each application, which also requires two letters of recommendation, a personal essay, a transcript, and SAT/ACT scores.

Scholarships and grants are based on financial need, academic promise, special skills, or some combination of these. Bentley also offers alternative financing programs such as the flexible financing program that spreads out tuition payments over five months.

The Bentley-City Year "give a year" Scholarship Program offers scholarships for spending one year serving as a City Year Corps Member to selected Bentley students. The scholarship offers a $20,000 credit toward senior year tuition. There is an addition $5,350 education award from AmeriCorps for completing the year of service.

BENTLEY UNIVERSITY

Highlights

Admissions Criteria
Academic criteria:
Grades: ☆ ☆ ☆
Difficulty of class schedule: ☆ ☆ ☆
Class rank: ☆
Standardized test scores: ☆ ☆ ☆
Teacher recommendations: ☆ ☆
Personal statement: ☆ ☆
Non-academic criteria considered:
Interview
Extracurricular activities
Special talents, interests, abilities
Character/personal qualities
Volunteer work
Work experience
Geographical location
Minority affiliation
Alumni relationship

Deadlines
Early Action: November 1
Early Decision: November 1
Regular Action: January 7 (final)
Notification of admission by: April 1
Common Application: Accepted

Financial Aid
In-state tuition: $39,600
Out-of-state tuition: $39,600
Room: $8,085
Board: $5,170
Books: $1,200
Freshmen receiving need-based aid: 46%
Undergrads rec. need-based aid: 47%
Avg. % of need met by financial aid: 95%
Avg. aid package (freshmen): $31,077
Avg. aid package (undergrads): $31,152
Avg. debt upon graduation: $30,375

School Spirit
Mascot: Falcons
Colors: Blue and gold

Four-year private
Founded: 1856
Birmingham, AL
Medium city
Pop. 212,413

Address:
900 Arkadelphia Road
Birmingham, AL
35254

Admissions:
800-523-5793, exten-
sion 4696

Financial Aid:
800-523-5793, exten-
sion 4688

admission@bsc.edu

www.bsc.edu

BIRMINGHAM-SOUTHERN COLLEGE

Overview

Birmingham-Southern College (BSC) is nicknamed the Hilltop due to its location on the top of a large hill on a wooded campus three miles from Birmingham. Academically, the school is also at the top among liberal arts schools in Alabama. According to the college, it has the best academic profile in the state for the incoming freshman class each fall.

Of the 45 buildings on campus, 25 have been renovated since 1976, and a number of new facilities have been built since 1998. The handsome $24.1 million 100,000 square foot Elton B. Stephens Science Center with its three-story atrium and numerous laboratories is "among the largest and most extensive such facilities on a college campus of this size in the country," according to the college. The new Fraternity Row hints at the very strong Greek scene on campus. The United Methodist Center houses the offices of the North Alabama Conference of the United Methodist Church and reveals the college's official affiliation.

BSC's Unique January Interim Term allows students a one-month period for an internship, study abroad, or a special project. While these opportunities foster creativity, some students may feel constrained by the requirements of the College's Foundations Curriculum, and others may wish for a more diverse and less conservative campus—or at least wish they could live in co-ed housing.

Academics

Birmingham Southern College offers five bachelor's degrees in 50 fields of study, plus interdisciplinary and specially individualized programs. There are dual degree programs in engineering, environmental studies, and nursing. Strong degree plans include biology, business administration, education, English, and pre-law. Students are required to take four classes during fall semester, one class during the January Interim Term, and four classes in the spring.

BSC's "Foundations Curriculum" outlines a general education plan that includes two required First-Year Foundation courses. Other requirements throughout the four years include Disciplinary Foundations courses in the arts and sciences; Skills Foundations courses in creative art, foreign language or culture, math, and writing; an Intercultural Foundations course; and a Scholarship Foundations requirement for scholarly research or inquiry appropriate to one's discipline.

With 61 percent of students graduating in the top 25 percent of their high school class, students accepted to BSC are focused on academics. They have close relationships with their professors, as each student is assigned a faculty mentor. Most class sizes are 10 to 19 participants, which fosters discussion and interaction. This translates into accountability, as one student explains, "Classes are so small you can't just go to class and fall asleep in the corner."

Over 70 percent of BSC students participate in the service learning program through the Bunting Center for Engaged Study and Community Action. The Center offers local and global programs. Major partner organizations include Habitat for Humanity and Urban Ministries. "I spent my spring break building a house for a family. There's nothing more gratifying than that," relates one student.

The January Interim term provides four weeks for students to pursue internships, study or research, and other projects on campus and off. The term is designed to stimulate creativity and independent study. First-year students pick from a list of Interim projects, but upperclassmen may contract their own individualized Interim projects. The four-week term provides an excellent opportunity for study abroad. Students can also go abroad for as long as a year through BSC's Sklenar Center for International Programs.

Almost half of Birmingham-Southern students go on to graduate or professional schools. The Alumni Office provides services for the 14,500 alumni of the College, and the online portal BSC AlumNet helps alumni stay connected on the web.

Student Life

Popular campus events include football games, art exhibits, theatre productions, dance performances, basketball games, on-campus concerts, and Greek-sponsored events. With almost 45 percent of students pledged into the 13 fraternities and sororities at BSC, Greek organizations are the dominant players in the social scene at the College. Interfraternity Block Party is an all-day event for the purpose of welcoming new members. Members frequently meet in "fraternity houses" and "sororities townhouses" to plan social events and service projects. The Panhellenic Association sponsors the annual Halloween on the Hilltop, a safe and fun Halloween event for more than 1,000 kids and parents in the community. "We are definitely about more than just parties. Getting involved in the community is a major activity," says a participant.

There are more than 80 student organizations at BSC, from honor societies to service groups to a wide range of other interest groups. Religious organizations are popular, as is the Student Government Association and its campus programming board, Quest II, "responsible for much of the entertainment on campus" according to the group. Quest II sponsors the college's two major weekend band parties each year: E Fest in the fall and SOCO in the spring. Another annual tradition is Summer Splash, a fun day under the sun on the dorm quad. Other events include Game Night in the Attic (the Attic is the on-campus Coffeehouse) and Movie Night Out, where free tickets are available to see new film releases in local theaters.

BSC students enjoy watching football, basketball, and baseball games. The new Panther stadium, opened in 2008, seats 1,600 fans and has an eight-lane regulation track. The varsity sports teams compete at the Division III level, and intramurals are popular as well, varying in the types of sports played during fall, interim, and spring terms. Additionally, there is a rifle range for the varsity rifle team, and the Ultimate Frisbee Club sport has gained popularity in recent years.

Off campus, the bars, clubs, and restaurants of Birmingham are popular and easily accessible. "The Nick and Blue Monkey are the best places to go on a Saturday night," one student acknowledges, "and there are plenty of options for going out." Quieter attractions include Birmingham's zoo, botanical gardens, and Cahaba River.

Consistent with the conservative posture of the college, BSC offers only single-sex housing. There are six residence halls and the new Hilltop Village Apartments, 16 buildings with their own pool that also provide a home for themed housing such as Spanish, wellness, or recycling. When selecting housing after the first year, students with higher GPAs are given priority. It is mandatory to live on campus until junior year, or until a student turns 21.

Student Body

The approximately 1,200 students at BSC hail from 30 states and a dozen foreign countries. There is moderate ethnic diversity with

BIRMINGHAM-SOUTHERN COLLEGE

Highlights

Students
Total enrollment: 1,231
Undergrads: 1,231
Freshmen: 327
From out-of-state: 44%
Male/Female: 53%/47%
Live on-campus: 80%
In fraternities: 35%
In sororities: 53%
Off-campus employment rating: Good
Caucasian: 83%
African American: 8%
Hispanic: 3%
Asian / Pacific Islander: 4%
Native American: 1%
Mixed (2+ ethnicities): 1%

Academics
Calendar: 4-1-4 system
Student/faculty ratio: 13:1
Class size 9 or fewer: 26%
Class size 10-29: 67%
Class size 30-49: 7%
Class size 50-99: 1%
Class size 100 or more: -
Returning freshmen: 81%
Six-year graduation rate: 65%
Graduates who immediately go to graduate school: 45%
Graduates who immediately enter career related to major: 20%

Most Popular Majors
Business administration
Biology
Psychology

Admissions
Applicants: 1,846
Accepted: 1,202
Acceptance rate: 65.1%
Average GPA: 3.5
ACT range: 24-29
SAT Math range: 520-640
SAT Reading range: 530-650
SAT Writing range: 7-14
Top 10% of class: 29%
Top 25% of class: 61%
Top 50% of class: 82%

BIRMINGHAM-SOUTHERN COLLEGE

Admissions Criteria
Academic criteria:
Grades: ☆ ☆
Difficulty of class schedule: ☆ ☆
Class rank: ☆ ☆
Standardized test scores: ☆ ☆ ☆
Teacher recommendations: ☆ ☆ ☆
Personal statement: ☆ ☆ ☆
Non-academic criteria considered:
Interview
Extracurricular activities
Special talents, interests, abilities
Character/personal qualities
Volunteer work
State of residency

Deadlines
Early Action: November 15
Early Decision: No
Regular Action: Rolling admissions
Common Application: Accepted

Financial Aid
In-state tuition: $29,600
Out-of-state tuition: $29,600
Room: $3,590
Board: $5,900
Books: $1,300
Freshmen receiving need-based aid: 63%
Undergrads rec. need-based aid: 57%
Avg. % of need met by financial aid: 83%
Avg. aid package (freshmen): $26,675
Avg. aid package (undergrads): $26,596
Avg. debt upon graduation: $27,629

School Spirit
Mascot: Panthers
Colors: Black and gold

17 percent students of color, as well as out-of-state diversity with more than 44 percent of students from outside Alabama. However, many students are from nearby states.

Politically, the student body skews towards the conservative side, perhaps due to BSC's United Methodist affiliation. As one BSU representative put it, "There are liberal students here; but if you ask around, you'll find that most of us are more conservative."

You May Not Know

- Birmingham-Southern College resulted from the 1918 merger of Southern University and Birmingham College.
- BSC has a Phi Beta Kappa chapter and 20 other honorary or professional societies, including the business honorary Beta Gamma Sigma.
- There is a false rumor that BSC has a secret elevator that leads to an underground system of tunnels that encompass much of the campus.

Distinguished Alumni

Rebecca Gilman, playwright; Dr. Donald Harrison, former president of the American Heart Association; Howell Raines, former *New York Times* executive editor.

Admissions and Financial Aid

According to the admissions office, the college admits students "whose ability, training, motivation, and interests indicate that they will do successful college work" as determined by their coursework, SAT/ACT scores, personal statement, and references. The high school coursework requirement includes four units of English and twelve academic credits spread out over other fields. Early admissions applicants must have at least a 3.0 GPA and must also interview with the dean of enrollment management.

The BSC financial aid office notes that the vast majority of students graduate in four years, eliminating the costs of a fifth or sixth year.

There are a number of merit-based scholarships. All students are automatically considered for the three Guaranteed Achievement Scholarships, partial tuition awards that look for scholarly achievement and extracurricular involvement. These renewable awards range from $12,000 to $16,000 and require that students apply for admission by January 1. The numerous Distinguished Scholars Awards, which cannot be combined with Guaranteed Achievement Scholarships, are competitive and valued up to full tuition. There are also scholarships for the fine and performing arts, and for United Methodist students, clergy families, and those called to ministry.

BOSTON COLLEGE

Overview

There is much to be commended about Boston College (BC): its prime location, active student community, fervent school spirit, and reputation for academic excellence as well as being among the oldest Jesuit, Catholic institutions in the nation. The college's handsome buildings, many of which are seminal examples of the Collegiate Gothic style, are spread across three lushly landscaped campuses.

The largest campus is located in Chestnut Hill, six miles from downtown Boston and conveniently near the T's (subway) green line. With just over 9,000 undergrads, BC is large enough to offer diverse experiences but small enough to feel tight-knit rather than overwhelming. The college's $1.4 billion endowment is among the largest in the country. BC's 10-year Institutional Master Plan ensures that the campus will be beautified and upgraded as part of a larger 30- to 50-year Campus Vision Plan.

While students need not be Catholic to attend the school, the college's strong Jesuit and Catholic influence may make the school more inviting for students of a similar faith background. Some students may be turned off by the "preppy" feel of the school. BC has a reputation as a party school, though this reputation is counter-balanced by a heavy focus on academics and community service. Social opportunities abound on campus and off, though Greek life isn't one of them.

Academics

Statistics support BC's reputation for academic excellence. The *U.S. News & World Report* ranked the school 31st. They are 10th among the nation's research universities in producing Fulbright Fellowship winners. Courses are demanding, and there are over 1,400 to choose from, with over 75 majors and concentrations, interdisciplinary programs, and pre-professional programs in nine schools and colleges. Strong areas of study include management and leadership, communication, history, nursing, political science, and theology.

All undergrads must satisfy the Core Requirements, 15 classes spread across a variety of categories, including two courses in theology and one course in cultural diversity. Freshmen are required to take the First-Year Writing Seminar (FWS), which emphasizes composition and rhetoric in a small group setting. First Year Experience (FYE) offers academic programs such as Conversations in the First Year, which brings students together through a common book; and the Cornerstone Program, a collection of elective academic classes. The similarly named Capstone program is for second-semester juniors or seniors who want to "review their educations and to preview their upcoming long-term commitments in life."

Other unique academic opportunities include the honors programs in all four schools, each of which has different curriculum and admissions requirements. The honors program in the College of Arts and Sciences offers classes with no more than 15 students and close interaction with professors who also serve as academic advisors. "If you can get into the honors program, you should," a student advises. "The small classes make it worth it." Of note is the Perspectives in Western Culture program, which is a two-semester, 12-credit course that fulfills all the Core requirements in Philosophy and Theology.

Besides a plethora of classes, there is also an abundance of research opportunities. The Undergraduate Faculty Research Fellows program provides grants for students to assist a faculty member's search project. The recently completed $85 million expansion of the Higgins Biology and Physics Center is a great boon to science research.

BC provides extensive study-abroad opportunities that almost 40 percent of students take advantage of. With 60 academic partnerships in over 30 countries on six continents, Boston College offers semester and summer programs for virtually every

BOSTON COLLEGE

Four-year private
Founded: 1863
Chestnut Hill, MA
Large town
Pop. 84,600

Address:
140 Commonwealth Avenue
Chestnut Hill, MA 02467

Admissions:
800-360-2522

Financial Aid:
617-552-3320

www.bc.edu

BOSTON COLLEGE

Highlights

Students
Total enrollment: 13,783
Undergrads: 9,110
Freshmen: 2,405
From out-of-state: 78%
From public schools: 48%
Male/Female: 47%/53%
Live on-campus: 85%
Off-campus employment rating: Good
Caucasian: 60%
African American: 4%
Hispanic: 11%
Asian / Pacific Islander: 10%
Native American: 0%
Mixed (2+ ethnicities): 3%
International: 4%

Academics
Calendar: Semester
Student/faculty ratio: 14:1
Class size 9 or fewer: 13%
Class size 10-29: 56%
Class size 30-49: 24%
Class size 50-99: 4%
Class size 100 or more: 3%
Returning freshmen: 95%
Six-year graduation rate: 92%
Graduates who immediately enter career related to major: 70%

Most Popular Majors
Communications
Finance
Economics

Admissions
Applicants: 34,061
Accepted: 9,813
Acceptance rate: 28.8%
Placed on wait list: 6,220
Enrolled from wait list: 71
Average GPA: Not reported
ACT range: 29-32
SAT Math range: 640-740
SAT Reading range: 620-710
SAT Writing range: 43-46
Top 10% of class: 81%
Top 25% of class: 96%
Top 50% of class: 99%

field of study. Some are through the college itself, while others are approved external programs. Travel grants are available.

There are 152,000 living undergraduate and graduate alumni. Recently, 26 percent of students directly entered graduate school, and 89 percent planned to attend graduate school. The Boston College Career Center offers extensive career resources, including internships and jobs. With the help of the University Fellowships Committee, many students are awarded prestigious fellowships and scholarships, such as the Rhodes, Fulbright, Marshall, Churchill, and Truman.

Student Life

The Student Programs Office is an official portal for on-campus activities, providing information about more than 200 educational, cultural, and social student organizations. Campus-wide organizations include the Undergraduate Government of Boston College, which serves as the official representative voice for students, as well as WZBC, which provides a college radio voice for the greater Boston area. The Jesuit influence makes volunteer groups such as the Appalachia Volunteers Program popular.

BC's alcohol policy does not allow kegs, punch bowls, and other central alcohol sources, though there are still ample parties. About half of seniors live off campus, and there are parties at the on-campus Mods (modular apartments that hold about 450 students). The Boston College Police Department is strict about cracking down on underage drinking. "No matter what the rules are, if you want to find a party, you will," says a student.

The 32,000 square foot O'Connell House provides a central location for many campus events. Nights on the Heights provide opportunities to socialize on Thursday to Saturday nights. The nationally-renowned, student-run, 37-year-and-counting tradition of the Middlemarch Ball is one of the premier social events of the year, made all the more exciting for its exclusivity. The ball has had a "20 foot chocolate fountain from Willy Wonka" and the "tilted floors of the sinking Titanic," based on previous years' themes.

Boston College has 27 Division I sports. Students love tailgating for football games. Hockey is also a popular sport for this school. There are 59 intramural, recreational, and club sports, which more than 7,300 undergrads participate in annually. Many of these are housed in the Silvio O. Conte Forum, which seats about 8,600 people for basketball and hockey.

Off-campus activities are almost too numerous to list: bars, clubs, Fenway Park, the historical sites, and museums of Boston... "There's a reason why Boston is the premier college city in the country," explains a student.

Though the city is close by, most students end up living on, or within one mile of, campus. All admitted freshmen are guaranteed to be able to live on campus for at least three years. Distinctively, almost all juniors live off campus for a year but return to live on campus during senior year. A BC bus shuttle service makes living off campus more convenient. There is a lottery for housing assignments, and upper-class students tend to have nicer accommodations with private kitchens and bathrooms. BC dining has won industry awards and has a strong emphasis on sustainability.

Student Body

Though the college notes that "you do not have to be Catholic to feel accepted on campus," it also emphasizes its Jesuit and Catholic heritage and "religious commitment." One student says, "Of course there are many Catholics here, but you won't feel out of place if you aren't Catholic or even religious at all." About 70 percent of the student body is Catholic; correspondingly, religion does exert a strong influence on campus culture and student life.

In 1979, two BC students coined the term AHANA to describe students of African American, Hispanic, Asian, and Native-American descent. About a quarter of students are AHANA, and Asian Americans make up the largest minority group.

In contrast to the racial/ethnic diversity, some students say there isn't much socioeconomic diversity. Some complain that all other students are well-heeled and preppy. "There's a guy who's driven by a chauffeur," comments a student, adding, "that's not typical, but there are a lot of very wealthy people."

Only 22 percent of students are from Massachusetts, so there is a strong representation of out of state and international students. All 50 states and nearly 100 nations are represented.

You May Not Know

- In the first seven decades after its founding, BC remained offered a strictly liberal arts education with courses in Greek, Latin, English, philosophy, and religion.
- BC's main campus is listed on the National Register of Historic Places with historical college gothic architecture.
- The bald eagle that represents BC at athletic events is named Baldwin from the "bald" head of the bird and the word "win."

Distinguished Alumni

Doug Flutie, star quarterback; Margaret Heckler, former Secretary of Health and Human Services; John Kerry, Massachusetts senator and former Presidential nominee; Amy Poehler, comedian, *Saturday Night Live*.

Admissions and Financial Aid

In the past decade, the college has seen an impressive 75 percent increase in undergrad applications. Because admission is so competitive, students for whom BC is their first choice may want to apply Early Action. Early Action is non-binding.

According to the college, there are very limited merit scholarships offered because it is "committed to need-based financial aid." Admission to the university is need-blind. The only merit-based scholarship awarded by the college is the full-tuition Presidential Scholars Program given to 15 students each year. There are a handful of merit-based scholarships for minority students such as the Archbishop Oscar A. Romero Scholarship and Martin Luther King, Jr. Scholarship.

BOSTON COLLEGE

Highlights

Admissions Criteria
Academic criteria:
Grades: ☆ ☆ ☆
Difficulty of class schedule: ☆ ☆ ☆
Class rank: ☆ ☆
Standardized test scores: ☆ ☆ ☆
Teacher recommendations: ☆ ☆
Personal statement: ☆ ☆
Non-academic criteria considered:
Extracurricular activities
Special talents, interests, abilities
Character/personal qualities
Volunteer work
Work experience
State of residency
Religious affiliation/commitment
Minority affiliation
Alumni relationship

Deadlines
Early Action: November 1
Early Decision: No
Regular Action: January 1 (final)
Notification of admission by: April 15
Common Application: Accepted

Financial Aid
In-state tuition: $44,870
Out-of-state tuition: $44,870
Room: $7,790
Board: $4,818
Books: $1,000
Freshmen receiving need-based aid: 42%
Undergrads rec. need-based aid: 43%
Avg. % of need met by financial aid: 100%
Avg. aid package (freshmen): $34,302
Avg. aid package (undergrads): $34,578
Avg. debt upon graduation: $20,975

School Spirit
Mascot: Eagles
Colors: Maroon and gold
Song: *For Boston*

**BOSTON
UNIVERSITY**

Four-year private
Founded: 1839
Boston, MA
Major city
Pop. 625,087

Address:
1 Silber Way
Boston, MA
02215

Admissions:
617-353-2300

Financial Aid:
617-353-2965

admissions@bu.edu

www.bu.edu

BOSTON UNIVERSITY

Overview

As the fourth-largest private, nonprofit university in the United States, Boston University's huge numbers of academic, research, and social offerings can be overwhelming. Add that to the seemingly infinite variety of opportunities that the city of Boston has to offer, and the possibilities are truly dazzling. Though BU is increasingly a residential campus, because of its location in the heart of Boston and integration into the city, the university hardly feels like the typical college campus.

It's best not to get too distracted by all the sights and thrills of the city, though, and concentrate on academics. Indeed, courses are difficult and require investments of time and energy. BU is a good fit for vibrant, ambitious students looking to be part of a diverse and driven student body.

Academics

BU has an impressive 17 Schools and Colleges in undergraduate, graduate, and professional programs—10 for undergrads alone. The largest is the College of Arts and Sciences, with over 70 majors, which is still just a sample of BU's more than 250 fields of studies. There is certainly no shortage of options, and it's possible to double-major or even design one's own major. Students in the College of Arts and Sciences must complete courses in writing, foreign, language, mathematics, and general education.

Courses are very rigorous. Indeed, in 2006, an article in the *New York Times* addressed BU students' feelings that the university "deflated" grades in order to enhance the university's prestige by a display of "academic rigor built on rigid curve grading." However, an article in the *BU Today* noted that there were no official caps or quotas around grade distribution and went on to defend the rigor of classes. "Students still feel that there's grade deflation now," says a student.

Introductory classes are large, though classes get smaller as students become upperclassmen. "You have to take the initiative to get to know your professors," says a student. Faculty members are carefully chosen for their credentials. Of note is Elie Wiesel, Nobel Laureate, Holocaust survivor, and writer; and there are two other Nobel Laureates on the faculty, as well as many winners of other major awards.

Strong programs include anthropology, biology, business administration, and management (with a large number of concentrations available), communication (with three specializations to choose from), economics, history, music, pre-law, pre-med, and theatre arts. Some departments allow a joint BA/MA course of study, such as seven-year liberal arts/medical and liberal arts/dental programs.

New facilities include the elegant, high-profile 33,000 square foot School of Hospitality Administration building on Commonwealth Avenue (2006), and the $83 million Life Sciences and Engineering Building with more than 40 research labs to support expansions in the fields of biology and chemistry (2005).

BU was one of the initial universities to send students abroad and today offers one of the most comprehensive study-abroad programs in the country with 75 programs on six continents. Students choose from internships, fieldwork/research, or languages and liberal arts programs. BU's International Programs attract 2,100 students from more than 200 colleges and universities each year.

BU's Career Services Center offers current students and alumni a wealth of resources such as career counseling, workshops, a resource library, on-campus recruiting, and the Career Advisory Network (CAN), which allows current students to speak to BU alumni for informational purposes.

Student Life

Since Boston is the quintessential American college town, BU students enjoy a wide range of activities both on campus and off. There are more than 500 student organizations, including 55 cultural organizations and 31 that are religious. The most popular student group is broomball, played on a hockey rink without ice skates. If the list of clubs, from Alpine Ski Team to the Zen Society, doesn't capture your interests, it's possible to start your own organization. The university also hosts several hundred events each year: arts shows, famous lecturers, and the like.

BU has a strict alcohol policy; however, students of age can find local bars for recreation. "You'll never lack for options," says a student. Greek life is not a strong presence on campus, since about 11 percent of undergrads join fraternities or sororities.

The First-Year Student Outreach Project (FYSOP) offers BU freshman a chance to get to know their classmates and surrounding community by performing a week of service before the first week of classes in nine Issue Areas, including Environment, HIV/AIDS Awareness, and Human Rights. For all students, the academic year kicks off with Splash following the President's Convocation Ceremony on Labor Day. Students enjoy music, games, food, and freebies as they interact with representatives from university departments and student organizations. In March, BU's cultural groups put on a number of performances, activities, and events during Culture Fest.

Boston is a sports-rabid city, and though most of BU's students aren't from the city, they get plenty of opportunities to participate and watch sports. There are 23 varsity sports teams, 33 club sports, and 15 intramural sports, as well as over 400 fitness classes. Hockey is very popular, and BU is rightfully proud of its players: the men's team were the 2009 national champions in NCAA Division I and have won five National Championships, *and* there are 18 alumni playing in the NHL. According to the college BU has "sent more students to professional hockey teams than any other college or university." Beanpot, the annual hockey tournament between BU, Boston College (their biggest rival), Harvard, and Northeastern, brings out the true competitiveness of hockey players and fans alike. "Hockey is a religion," says a student. Basketball, lacrosse, and crew are also popular sports.

The T (greater Boston's subway system) cuts right through campus, making it easy to travel throughout Boston. Students frequent the bars and clubs of Boston, shop on Newbury Street, and cheer their favorite team at Fenway Park.

More than three-quarters of all undergrads live in dorms, and virtually all freshmen live on campus. Students are guaranteed four years of housing through a lottery system. Many freshmen are assigned to the 18-story Warren Towers, the second largest dorm in the nation outside of the military, which is reportedly not one of the more sought-after dorms on campus, such as the Commonwealth Avenue dorms and the Student Village apartments. The latter are part of the 10-acre John Hancock Student Village residential and recreational center. The 843,000 Agganis Arena and Fitness and Recreation Center is part of this complex as well.

Student Body

There are more than 32,000 students at BU, and more than18,000 undergrads. Seventy-six percent of undergrads are from out of state, representing all 50 states and over 100 countries. The student body is racially/ethnically diverse with more than one-quarter made up of

BOSTON UNIVERSITY

Highlights

Students
Total enrollment: 32,603
Undergrads: 18,306
Freshmen: 3,897
From out-of-state: 76%
From public schools: 68%
Male/Female: 40%/60%
Live on-campus: 77%
In fraternities: 8%
In sororities: 14%
Off-campus employment rating: Excellent
Caucasian: 48%
African American: 3%
Hispanic: 9%
Asian / Pacific Islander: 13%
Native American: 0%
Mixed (2+ ethnicities): 3%
International: 14%

Academics
Calendar: Semester
Student/faculty ratio: 13:1
Class size 9 or fewer: 18%
Class size 10-29: 60%
Class size 30-49: 11%
Class size 50-99: 6%
Class size 100 or more: 4%
Returning freshmen: 92%
Six-year graduation rate: 84%
Graduates who immediately go to graduate school: 22%

Most Popular Majors
Communications
Business administration/management
Engineering

Admissions
Applicants: 44,006
Accepted: 20,071
Acceptance rate: 45.6%
Placed on wait list: 2,649
Average GPA: 3.6
ACT range: 26-30
SAT Math range: 610-720
SAT Reading range: 570-670
SAT Writing range: 21-54
Top 10% of class: 57%
Top 25% of class: 87%
Top 50% of class: 99%

109

BOSTON UNIVERSITY

Admissions Criteria

Academic criteria:
Grades: ☆ ☆ ☆
Difficulty of class schedule: ☆ ☆ ☆
Class rank: ☆ ☆
Standardized test scores: ☆ ☆
Teacher recommendations: ☆ ☆
Personal statement: ☆ ☆
Non-academic criteria considered:
Interview
Extracurricular activities
Special talents, interests, abilities
Character/personal qualities
Volunteer work
Work experience
Geographical location
Minority affiliation
Alumni relationship

Deadlines

Early Action: No
Early Decision: November 1
Regular Action: January 1 (final)
Notification of admission by: mid-April
Common Application: Accepted

Financial Aid

In-state tuition: $43,970
Out-of-state tuition: $43,970
Room: Varies
Board: Varies
Books: $1,000
Freshmen receiving need-based aid: 46%
Undergrads rec. need-based aid: 44%
Avg. % of need met by financial aid: 89%
Avg. aid package (freshmen): $37,655
Avg. aid package (undergrads): $37,038
Avg. debt upon graduation: $36,150

School Spirit

Mascot: Terriers

minority populations. There are also a large number of international students: 14 percent of the student body.

The university emphasizes the school's diversity, noting that "there *is* no BU type." According to one student, "The thing we all share is a passion for life. It's rare to meet someone you know who doesn't greet you with a smile." Most students agree that, "You have to be the kind of person who is independent and can take care of things yourself. No one is going to hold your hand here."

You May Not Know

- BU was the first university to open all its academic divisions to women in 1872, and BU was the first American university to award a doctorate degree to a woman in 1877.
- Alexander Graham Bell invented the telephone in a BU lab.
- According to the college, the BU Bridge is the only location in the country where "a plane can fly over a car driving over a train going over a boat, all at the same time."

Distinguished Alumni

Martha Coakley, attorney general of Massachusetts; William Cohen, former U.S. Secretary of Defense under Bill Clinton; Tipper Gore, former second lady; Martin Luther King, Jr., clergyman, activist, and Nobel Peace Prize winner; Julianne Moore, actress; Bill O'Reilly, Jr, TV host and political commentator.

Admissions and Financial Aid

The acceptance rate is 45 percent, which is very competitive when considering the high-achieving applicant pool BU chooses from. Academic factors are most important, especially the rigor of one's high school course load.

BU requires the Common Application in addition to the Boston University supplement. Application deadlines vary based on program; most are due January 1 for regular decision regarding September enrollment.

BU offers a number of merit scholarships; some even cover full tuition. Most are based on academic merit, but athletics and artistic scholarships are also offered—last year this total reached $13 million for incoming freshman. The most prestigious merit-based award is the Trustee Scholarship, which is a four-year, full-tuition award. On the other hand, "need-based grants are awarded based on a combination of calculated financial eligibility and academic merit."

BOWDOIN COLLEGE

Overview

Many people may not know where the town of Brunswick is located (hint: Maine coast, 25 miles northeast of Portland), or how to pronounce the name of the 205-acre pine-tree lined college campus there, "Bowdoin" (hint: "bow" as in "bow-tie", and "din" rhymes with "tin"). But don't let the geographic or pronunciation obscurity fool you: this small liberal arts college, with almost 1,800 undergrads, boasts excellent athletics, dining, housing, and a highly selective admissions rate.

Bowdoin prides itself on its tight-knit community of students, faculty, and staff. The warmth of these relationships must balance the very cold winters (the average minimum temperature in January is 11 degrees) and energize the Polar Bear mascot, a fitting choice for the college. Most students who select Bowdoin as their college love the outdoors and don white for sports games, which are a huge part of the campus culture.

The cold weather does not seem to have made Bowdoin students bitter or withdrawn. In absolute contrast, students on campus are known for their friendly "Bowdoin hello," a tradition which involves two students greeting one another as they pass. Unlike actual polar bears, whose Arctic habitat is increasingly threatened, Bowdoin Polar Bears have enjoyed expanding facilities on their campus, from 26,000 square foot academic building Kanbar Hall completed in 2004, to "green" residence halls built in 2005, to a $15.2 million dollar athletic center, completed in 2009.

Academics

Bowdoin students enjoy close relationships with professors due to the small size of the college and professors' exclusive focus on undergrads. Class size limits vary depending on the course: first-year seminars are capped at 16, 200-level and higher classes are limited to 35, and the maximum class size is 50.

Bowdoin offers BA degrees in over 40 departmental and interdisciplinary majors. Strong programs include art history, biology, chemistry, economics, education, English, environmental studies, government and legal studies, and neuroscience.

There is a Distribution Requirement that requires one course in each of six areas, including visual and performing arts. However, since over half of a student's non-major credits are up to the student, there is the flexibility to delve into a concentration or branch out into new fields. More than 60 percent of students engage one-on-one with faculty for independent studies. "I chose Bowdoin because of the choice we have in determining which classes to take. I didn't want to be forced to take classes I wasn't interested in," comments one student.

Bowdoin's hub for service learning is The Joseph McKeen Center for the Common Good, which works with over 100 organizations to offer experiences for students in community-based teaching, learning, research, and service. Bowdoin students are active volunteers and leaders, representing interests from recycling to human rights to global service projects.

Over half of Bowdoin students have studied abroad by graduation. Students elect to study for a semester or full academic year and are expected to use the time "to deepen and bring fresh perspectives to [their] understanding of an academic field," according to the college. Bowdoin has over 100 programs to choose from, including English-speaking university enrollment, non-English-speaking university enrollment, and field study programs. One student says about his experience, "Walking through the city streets and university campus evoked a strange sense of time travel."

Bowdoin's Career Planning website offers a catchy reminder about the close-knit feeling of Bowdoin's alumni community: "A polar bear never leaves a polar bear out in the cold." Bowdoin staff and the Career Advisory Network of 1,500 alumni pro-

---

BOWDOIN COLLEGE

Four-year private
Founded: 1794
Brunswick, ME
Small town
Pop. 21,849

Address:
5700 College Station
Brunswick, ME
04011-8448

Admissions:
207-725-3100

Financial Aid:
207-725-3273

admissions@bowdoin.edu

www.bowdoin.edu

BOWDOIN COLLEGE

Highlights

Students
Total enrollment: 1,839
Undergrads: 1,839
Freshmen: 492
From out-of-state: 89%
From public schools: 53%
Male/Female: 50%/50%
Live on-campus: 92%
Off-campus employment rating: Good
Caucasian: 64%
African American: 5%
Hispanic: 13%
Asian / Pacific Islander: 7%
Native American: 0%
Mixed (2+ ethnicities): 6%
International: 4%

Academics
Calendar: Semester
Student/faculty ratio: 9:1
Class size 9 or fewer: 27%
Class size 10-29: 55%
Class size 30-49: 15%
Class size 50-99: 3%
Class size 100 or more: -
Returning freshmen: 97%
Six-year graduation rate: 95%
Graduates who immediately go to graduate school: 11%
Graduates who immediately enter career related to major: 60%

Most Popular Majors
Government
Economics
History

Admissions
Applicants: 6,716
Accepted: 1,060
Acceptance rate: 15.8%
Average GPA: Not reported
ACT range: 31-33
SAT Math range: 670-760
SAT Reading range: 670-760
SAT Writing range: 62-34
Top 10% of class: 86%
Top 25% of class: 98%
Top 50% of class: 100%

vide networking assistance. There is special advising for students pursuing health professions.

Student Life

Bowdoin has over 100 student-run organizations, including *Bowdoin Orient*, one of the country's oldest newspapers. However, the most popular is undoubtedly Outing Club, with over 300 members who can be part of more than 100 excursions per year. Outing Club members venture out on bikes, hikes, canoes, sea kayaks, white-water rafts, and even participate in ecology-related service projects. "Outdoor sports and Bowdoin are synonymous," says a student.

About 20 years ago, Bowdoin eliminated fraternities and established college-owned "College Houses." Each first-year student is assigned to live in a traditional residence hall, which is partnered with one of the eight College Houses. About 25 upperclassmen live in each House, and these upperclassmen become "buddies" to freshmen. Each house sponsors a full schedule of activities, making College Houses a focal point of social life. The college describes the various social offerings, some limited to house members and others open to the entire community: "pizza parties, poetry readings, community service activities, faculty dinners, concerts, dances, and field trips to Portland and Boston."

Two of the most popular college-wide events are held in the spring: Junior/Senior Ball and the Ivies, a long-standing tradition and a "campus-wide party of monumental proportions spanning two days" according to a *Bowdoin Orient* article.

The importance of athletics at Bowdoin is hard to miss: more than one third of students play intercollegiate sports, and the college's state-of-the-art athletic facilities are extensive. There are 30 varsity teams and six club teams, as well as a number of intramurals. The Bowdoin Polar Bears' biggest rivals are Colby and Middlebury in their Division III conference. Men's ice hockey is very popular, and women's field hockey has won three national titles (in 2007, 2008, and 2010). The Sidney J. Watson Arena seats 2,300 for hockey games, which one student describes as "screaming until you go hoarse." The $15.2 million Buck Center for Health and Fitness, completed in September 2009, is LEED-certified and features a 40-foot climbing wall among the many other offerings in the impressive, glass-encased three-story building.

Off-campus activities include skiing; shopping at Freeport, a coastal Maine village with over 200 shops; and visiting Boston, which is three hours away.

More than 90 percent of the student body live on campus, and freshmen dorms were recently renovated. Students generally offer positive reviews of campus housing and food. Bowdoin dining is nationally recognized for its sustainability—and deliciousness—to the delight of students. Freshmen halls are situated at the heart of campus, within close walking distance of dining halls and classes. Hyde Hall, a four-story brick residence for freshmen, offers a chemical and substance-free environment.

Student Body

Of the more than 1,800 undergraduates at Bowdoin, almost 90 percent are from out of state. New Englanders make up the bulk of the student body at more than 40 percent. Most of the student body is from the United States.

Many describe students as "preppy," though you're more likely to find students in athletic gear than polo shirts. Bowdoin students bond over a passion for the outdoors and athletics, which explains the popularity of Pre-Orientation Trips ("Pre-O Trips") organized by Bowdoin's outing club, where incoming freshmen hike, canoe, or kayak with a small ground of new friends, exploring the outdoor offerings of Maine. According to the students themselves, most have liberal political views.

Despite a reputation in the past for homogeneity, diversity initiatives have paid off. Over a quarter of the students enrolled at Bowdoin are students of color, making Bowdoin a diverse campus. Fifteen student groups, from Africa Alliance to the Native American Student Association, promote multicultural life on campus.

You May Not Know

- Founded in 1794, Bowdoin was not co-ed until 1971.
- Massachusetts Hall, which currently houses Bowdoin's English department, is a Registered Historical Landmark that was built in 1802, making it the oldest college building in Maine.
- The polar bear became Bowdoin's mascot in 1913 to honor the discovery of the North Pole in 1909 by Admiral Robert E. Peary, Bowdoin Class of 1877.

Distinguished Alumni

Nathaniel Hawthorne; Henry Wadsworth Longfellow.

Admissions and Financial Aid

With a 16 percent admission rate, Bowdoin is highly selective. According to the college, "Academic, athletic, and personal traits weigh heavily in Bowdoin's decision to admit students, but they play no part in the determination of how much grant aid students receive." SAT and ACT scores are optional, a policy that has been in place since 1970.

Bowdoin has need-blind admission, and eligibility for grants is need-based. In January 2008, Bowdoin replaced all loans with grants. Over 40 percent of students receive grants. Bowdoin does not offer merit-based scholarships.

BOWDOIN COLLEGE

Highlights

Admissions Criteria
Academic criteria:
Grades: ☆ ☆ ☆
Difficulty of class schedule: ☆ ☆ ☆
Class rank: ☆ ☆ ☆
Standardized test scores: ☆ ☆
Teacher recommendations: ☆ ☆ ☆
Personal statement: ☆ ☆ ☆
Non-academic criteria considered:
Interview
Extracurricular activities
Special talents, interests, abilities
Character/personal qualities
Geographical location
Minority affiliation
Alumni relationship

Deadlines
Early Action: No
Early Decision: November 15
Regular Action: January 1 (final)
Notification of admission by: April 5
Common Application: Accepted

Financial Aid
In-state tuition: $45,004
Out-of-state tuition: $45,004
Room: $5,790
Board: $6,598
Books: $816
Freshmen receiving need-based aid: 48%
Undergrads rec. need-based aid: 47%
Avg. % of need met by financial aid: 100%
Avg. aid package (freshmen): $40,879
Avg. aid package (undergrads): $38,283
Avg. debt upon graduation: $22,755

School Spirit
Mascot: Polar Bears
Colors: Black and white
Song: *Raise Songs to Bowdoin*

BRANDEIS UNIVERSITY

Four-year private
Founded: 1948
Waltham, MA
Large town
Pop. 61,181

Address:
415 South Street
Waltham, MA
02454-9110

Admissions:
781-736-3500
800-622-0622 (out-of-state)

Financial Aid:
781-736-3700

admissions@brandeis.edu

www.brandeis.edu

Overview

Brandeis University boasts a "vibrant, freethinking intellectual atmosphere that reflects the values of the first Jewish Supreme Court Justice Louis Brandeis," according to the college. Founded in 1948, this private research university maintains a liberal arts focus and has been ranked among the top 35 national universities by *U.S. News & World Report* every year since the rankings began. Based in Waltham, Massachusetts, Brandeis spans 235 acres and comprises over 100 academic and residential buildings, many of which provide stunning views of the Boston skyline.

There is no official religious affiliation, but an estimated one half of the student population is Jewish. The school also maintains a politically active history, with a thriving student government. Overall, it offers the experience commonly associated with the typical close-knit liberal arts college setting, in a quaint low-key area just nine miles from Boston.

Academics

The school maintains an academically rigorous environment, with more than 65 percent of freshmen entering from the top 10 percent of their high school classes. Almost 80 percent of classes have 29 students or fewer, and students often compliment the availability of university faculty members to mentor and guide them.

The sciences account for some of the most rigorous offerings, with extensive access to research opportunities. In 2009, Brandeis completed its more than $150 million science complex "designed to further enhance the university's leadership in the natural sciences and interdisciplinary research." The 175,000 square foot facility has laboratories, classrooms, and a café. "Everything is state-of-the art," states one student.

As a tribute to the school's creative pulse, the music building resembles a grand piano, and the campus theater is shaped as a top hat. Students can purchase both Brandeis Theater Company Season Passes and Flex Passes to stay apprised of current performances.

Strong programs include Islamic and Middle Eastern studies, Near Eastern and Judaic studies, Hebrew language and literature, chemistry, neuroscience, physics, economics, and creative writing. There is also a wealth of academic advising services available for students pursuing pre-medical and pre-law tracks.

The Brandeis curriculum includes General Education Requirements which include the University Seminar (USEM), a seminar-style class for first-year students, and classes in composition, foreign language, physical education, quantitative reasoning, non-Western and comparative studies, and writing. Another mandate is the University Writing Seminar for all first-year students, which is a full-credit course treating writing as a "multifaceted art." One Brandeis freshman comments, "Having two classes that are just for freshmen is helpful because we're all just getting used to the college experience."

Brandeis students may participate in over 250 approved study-abroad programs in roughly 70 countries around the world. Over one third of the junior class at Brandeis studies abroad during the academic year while other students secure international opportunities during the summer. Notable programs include opportunities in Mongolia, Australia, and at Oxford University.

On campus, the Hiatt Career Center offers a number of experiential programs including leadership training, volunteering, the Hiatt Shadowing Experience and Alumni Networking, part-time on-campus jobs, internships, and international opportunities. Typically, over 250 alumni volunteer their time and expertise during the Shadowing Experience program. Given the close proximity to Boston, Brandeis also has a history of placing students into a range of internships in the city in fields including the fine arts, journalism, and education. "Whatever your field, you can find an internship in Boston. I interned at a small travel magazine and actually wrote some articles that were printed," comments a student. About 65 percent of students enter a career related to their major within one year of graduating.

Student Life

Brandeis is home to over 250 clubs and organizations involved in arts, culture, and political activism. Some of the more popular include the Argentine Tango Society, Bellydance Ensemble, Comic Book Club, Culinary Arts Club, and Students Organized Against Racism. The Shapiro Campus Center is a meeting place for students with a theater, a bookstore, a café, and lounges for gatherings. Student media groups include the newspaper, *The Justice*, and the small college radio station, WBRS, with the apropos slogan "Something for Everyone."

Often touting the school colors of blue and white, Brandeis has over 20 Division III teams but no football team. Brandeis has won national titles in men's soccer and men's cross country. Brandeis has 20 club sports, including martial arts, archery, and cheerleading, while intramural sports include indoor and outdoor soccer, tennis, volleyball, squash, basketball, and dodgeball. At most of the sporting events, you can keep an eye out for the school mascot, Ollie the Owl, whose namesake is Justice Oliver Wendell Holmes, Jr.

As the university aims to maintain an all-inclusive environment, there are no official Brandeis-sanctioned fraternities and sororities. However, there exist an estimated five fraternities and two sororities on campus, with students often organizing for greater presence. "Greek life really isn't big on campus," says a student. However, it is clear that no matter the interest, there is an outlet for its expression. These might include the Topics Night dance, Bronstein Weekend Festival, Modfest, and Naked dance (don't worry, it's with underwear).

Students note that Brandeis' small size fosters close-knit relationships, whether it's socializing in dorms for underclassmen, or partying in on-campus apartment suites known as "Mods" for seniors. One dorm is affectionately described as "The Castle" and offers an "eclectic" living arrangement as a residence hall for approximately 120 upperclassmen. It provides "breathtaking views of the Boston Skyline" according to the college, and it is home to Cholmondeley's—or Chum's—Brandeis's coffeehouse and late night snack bar. The Castle, listed on the National Register of Historic Places, is the oldest building on campus, and was featured on a 1998 U.S. Postal Service stamp. In 2009, the new Ridgewood Residence Halls, primarily for upperclassmen, became available. Given this dynamic environment, more than three-quarters of students live on campus, especially since first-year students are guaranteed housing for their first four consecutive semesters.

Off campus, students note that Waltham offers surprisingly little aside from a selection of restaurants and bars on Moody Street. "Moody Street can get old really quick," says a student. However, Boston is nearby, one of the greatest college cities in the nation, with restaurants, bars, clubs, shopping, cultural activities, and professional athletic events. Brandeis maintains a regular shuttle bus to Boston, the "BranVan," which includes late-night stops.

BRANDEIS UNIVERSITY

Highlights

Students
Total enrollment: 5,808
Undergrads: 3,588
Freshmen: 878
Part-time students: 1%
From out-of-state: 71%
From public schools: 71%
Male/Female: 43%/57%
Live on-campus: 82%
Off-campus employment rating: Fair
Caucasian: 50%
African American: 4%
Hispanic: 6%
Asian / Pacific Islander: 13%
Native American: 0%
Mixed (2+ ethnicities): 3%
International: 14%

Academics
Calendar: Semester
Student/faculty ratio: 10:1
Class size 9 or fewer: 16%
Class size 10-29: 63%
Class size 30-49: 12%
Class size 50-99: 7%
Class size 100 or more: 3%
Returning freshmen: 95%
Six-year graduation rate: 90%

Most Popular Majors
Economics
Psychology
Biology

Admissions
Applicants: 8,380
Accepted: 3,277
Acceptance rate: 39.1%
Placed on wait list: 1,347
Enrolled from wait list: 117
Average GPA: 3.8
ACT range: 28-32
SAT Math range: 620-740
SAT Reading range: 610-710
SAT Writing range: 34-50
Top 10% of class: 66%
Top 25% of class: 93%
Top 50% of class: 98%

115

College Profiles

BRANDEIS UNIVERSITY

Admissions Criteria
Academic criteria:
Grades: ☆ ☆ ☆
Difficulty of class schedule: ☆ ☆ ☆
Class rank: ☆ ☆ ☆
Standardized test scores: ☆ ☆ ☆
Teacher recommendations: ☆ ☆
Personal statement: ☆ ☆
Non-academic criteria considered:
Interview
Extracurricular activities
Special talents, interests, abilities
Character/personal qualities
Volunteer work
Work experience
State of residency
Geographical location
Minority affiliation
Alumni relationship

Deadlines
Early Action: No
Early Decision: November 15
Regular Action: January 1 (final)
Notification of admission by: April 1
Common Application: Accepted

Financial Aid
In-state tuition: $44,380
Out-of-state tuition: $44,380
Room: $6,230
Board: $5,510
Books: $1,000
Freshmen receiving need-based aid: 54%
Undergrads rec. need-based aid: 52%
Avg. % of need met by financial aid: 90%
Avg. aid package (freshmen): $37,687
Avg. aid package (undergrads): $35,208
Avg. debt upon graduation: $27,906

School Spirit
Mascot: Judges
Colors: Navy and white

Student Body

Based on a campus-wide philosophy of non-exclusion, students note that all groups tend to feel welcome. "It's the school's philosophy, and now our philosophy, to include everyone," explains a student. The college has high geographic diversity with more than 70 percent of students from out of state and high ethnic diversity with 26 percent of students identifying as minority. Over the past several years, the administration has announced steps to improve Brandeis' diversity. However, students note that, for the most part, it remains predominantly white and Jewish.

Politically, the campus leans toward the liberal side. A 2007 visit by former President Jimmy Carter resulted in a mix of both applause and protest. In 1969, there was a memorable takeover of what was Ford and Sydeman Hall during the civil rights movement. An estimated 70 students took control of the halls to demand increased minority representation.

You May Not Know

- Former first lady Eleanor Roosevelt served on the university's board of trustees.
- Alumni include Pulitzer Prize winners, a Nobel Laureate, and Emmy Award winners.
- The U.S. Postal Service awarded Louis Dembitz Brandeis with his own stamp in 2009.

Distinguished Alumni

David Crane and Marta Kauffman, co-creators of *Friends*; Thomas Friedman, world-renowned author and columnist with *The New York Times*; Ha Jin, novelist; Debra Messing, Emmy Award-winning actress; Tim Morehouse, Olympic fencer; Shen Tong, student leader in the 1989 Tiananmen Square uprising.

Admissions and Financial Aid

The admissions office seeks to "understand how you will fit into the Brandeis community." As is typical, applicant reviews include academic record, extracurricular activities, essays and recommendations, and standardized tests. It's notable that interviews are "casual by nature" but still evaluative according to the college.

The university does not guarantee to meet students' demonstrated financial need. However, there is approximately $40 million in funded grants and scholarships to undergraduates. One of the most prestigious is the Annenberg Scholarship, a full-tuition award. Brandeis also awards the Wien International Scholarship for international students with scholarships for up to full tuition.

BRIGHAM YOUNG UNIVERSITY

Overview

Established in 1875, Brigham Young University (BYU) is a private co-educational university that aims to "develop students of faith, intellect, and character," through a strong connection to its sponsor, The Church of Jesus Christ of Latter-Day Saints (LDS). This university is proud of its history rooted in the dynamic heritage of Utah, and strives to maintain academic excellence in tandem with a code of honor in line with LDS teachings. This does however give way to a highly conservative college experience. The code stresses dress, hair, and grooming standards, chastity, and abstinence from use of drugs and alcohol. Men, in particular, are required to remain clean-shaven.

Based in Provo, Utah, an urban city of roughly 115,000 people, BYU is 45 miles south of Salt Lake City, at the base of the Wasatch Mountain range and just east of Utah Lake. The mountain range, along with Mount Timpanogos, is clearly visible from campus, no doubt influencing the campus' appreciation for the outdoors. The university maintains 560 acres of grounds with 311 buildings, all of which reflect architectural styles of distinct periods.

BYU maintains the second-largest private university enrollment in the U.S. An estimated 98.5 percent of the 34,000 students are Mormon, and a significant number of students take a hiatus from studies to serve as Mormon missionaries. Through such activities, in addition to on-campus language courses, over 75 percent of students obtain some level of foreign language proficiency. In Laie, Hawaii, the small BYU-Hawaii campus has 2,500 students, while in Rexburg, Idaho, the BYU-Idaho campus has an enrollment of 13,000.

Academics

With more than 200 majors, BYU offers nationally recognized academic options ranging from business to music. Strong undergraduate programs include accounting, business and management, chemistry, English, and multiple focuses in the fields of education, engineering, and pre-law course offerings. Additionally, BYU regularly teaches more than 55 languages on campus, and 30 more are available pending student demand. Each semester at BYU, 31 percent of the student body is enrolled in language courses. Despite the relaxing surroundings, students claim that BYU is "academically rigorous."

The university provides unique academic opportunities. Freshmen participate in "Freshman Mentoring," a university-wide initiative that provides students with priority registration in University Core classes, a peer mentor, and guidance during critical periods. Students can partake of the honors program, which aims to bestow the "benefits of a smaller liberal arts community" through smaller classes, a "spirit of ongoing inquiry," and undergraduate research in a "mentored environment."

To graduate, students must complete 14 credit hours that fulfill BYU General Religion Requirements including Book of Mormon courses, a Doctrine and Covenants course, a New Testament course, and other elective courses. At the same time, students have access to an impressive range of study-abroad options through the Kennedy Center for International Studies and its Office of International Study Programs. Choices include programs in Africa, Asia, Europe, Latin America, the Middle East, North America, and the Pacific. The Office of International Study Programs also provides access to rewarding internship opportunities in its various locations.

On campus, the BYU Counseling and Career Center (CCC) has a staff of 80 to help students with academic advising, career advising and development, graduate school preparation, and study skill improvement. The CCC also holds regular recruiting fairs and maintains a database of job opportunities from a number of employers. "Networking at BYU helps out while you're in school and after graduation too," a student reveals. "BYU alums look out for each other."

BRIGHAM YOUNG UNIVERSITY

Four-year private
Founded: 1875
Provo, UT
Medium city
Pop. 115,321

Address:
1 University Hill
Provo, UT
84602

Admissions:
801-422-2507

Financial Aid:
801-422-4104

admissions@byu.edu

www.byu.edu

BRIGHAM YOUNG UNIVERSITY

Students

Total enrollment: 34,409
Undergrads: 31,060
Part-time students: 9%
From out-of-state: 64%
Male/Female: 51%/49%
Live on-campus: 19%
Off-campus employment rating: Good
Caucasian: 69%
African American: 0%
Hispanic: 4%
Asian / Pacific Islander: 2%
Native American: 0%
Mixed (2+ ethnicities): 2%
International: 3%

Academics

Calendar: Semester
Student/faculty ratio: 23:1
Class size 9 or fewer: 23%
Class size 10-29: 51%
Class size 30-49: 13%
Class size 50-99: 6%
Class size 100 or more: 8%
Returning freshmen: 89%
Six-year graduation rate: 77%

Most Popular Majors

Business/management/marketing/related
    support services
Education
Public administration/social service pro-
    fessions

Admissions

Applicants: 12,557
Accepted: 6,895
Acceptance rate: 54.9%
Average GPA: 3.8
ACT range: 26-31
SAT Math range: 590-690
SAT Reading range: 580-690
SAT Writing range: 12-41
Top 10% of class: 53%
Top 25% of class: 84%
Top 50% of class: 98%

Student Life

Student life at Brigham Young University is heavily influenced by the religious focus. However, with 390 clubs, BYU is a hotbed for events and social activities. There are 18 unique music and dance theatre groups; and since 1971, BYU groups have given more than 12,000 performances throughout the world. For instance, BYU's ballroom dance team performs nationally and internationally. In addition to these groups, students note that service groups are also "some of the most popular," for example, the Service Squad.

It should be noted that there is no Greek presence on campus. Students say that church organizations and alternative activities take up the greater part of student life. Every Tuesday, a campus devotional is held at the Marriott Center, where students, employees, and the public are encouraged to attend and enjoy talks from LDS Church Leadership and faculty. "The talks round out our whole BYU experience," says a student.

The intramural program dates back to the early 1900s, and has grown to include over 25,000 members who participate each year. BYU has 21 Division I athletic teams. BYU Cougar football games are well attended, especially against main rival, the University of Utah.

BYU's location near the Wasatch Mountains offers opportunities for skiing, hiking, and rock climbing. On campus, students enjoy a bowling alley and movie theater. Despite the urban setting, nightlife in Provo is virtually nonexistent and restaurants are notorious for closing early. Salt Lake City, 45 miles to the north, also provides student with theatres, shopping centers, and restaurants within close proximity.

Almost one fifth of the student body resides on campus, mostly freshmen. All single BYU undergraduates must live on campus or in contracted off-campus housing. Of note are the foreign-language student residences (FLSR), which are apartments that promote native English speaker connections with ESL students.

Each residence hall has a unique gender mapping system and no co-ed or gender-neutral rooms are available. Housing services also encourage students to form and maintain gospel-centered communities, which foster additional forums within residence halls consistent with university guidelines. There are limited visiting hours, including "lobby hours" and "TV room hours," and visitors of opposite genders may not be in bedrooms or bathrooms outside of residence hall common areas.

Student Body

Given the university's religious ties, many students are admittedly conservative. A particularly strong focus on hard work and serving the community is a common characteristic among students. An estimated 36 percent of students are from within Utah, while 3 percent are international students. One-quarter of all students are married. Students do commonly note that there is a prevalent focus on students seeking a spouse rather than just casual dating or relationships. "We know that this is going to be our best opportunity to meet people of the same faith so we're into serious relationships," one student explains.

A relatively small 8 percent of the student population is of minority background. Hispanics comprise the largest minority group with 4 percent.

You May Not Know

- Lighting the Y during Homecoming week and ringing in the victory bell after athletic events are two unique traditions on campus.
- BYU has several supercomputers allowing students to model languages, compare DNA sequences, and study the collapse of stars.
- BYU has its own bowling alley, food court, police station, and power plant.

Distinguished Alumni

Paul D. Boyer, Nobel Prize winner in Chemistry; Stephenie Meyer, author of the *Twilight* series; Mitt Romney, businessman and politician; Steve Young, Super Bowl MVP.

Admissions and Financial Aid

BYU has a particularly low tuition at $2,500 per semester for LDS church members and $5,000 for non-members. The operating costs of the college are supplemented by the gifts of LDS members who make contributions. Additionally, the church financially supports the school through tithes.

BYU's various freshman scholarships include academic scholarships, talent awards, ROTC military awards, Y service awards, the Thomas S. Monson Presidential Scholarship, and need-based awards. Be aware that many of the awards require separate applications.

BRIGHAM YOUNG UNIVERSITY

Highlights

Admissions Criteria
Academic criteria:
Grades: ☆ ☆ ☆
Difficulty of class schedule: ☆ ☆ ☆
Class rank: N/A
Standardized test scores: ☆ ☆ ☆
Teacher recommendations: ☆ ☆
Personal statement: ☆ ☆
Non-academic criteria considered:
Interview
Extracurricular activities
Special talents, interests, abilities
Character/personal qualities
Volunteer work
Work experience
Geographical location
Religious affiliation/commitment
Minority affiliation

Deadlines
Early Action: No
Early Decision: No
Regular Action: December 1 (priority)
February 1 (final)
Notification of admission by: February 28
Common Application: Not accepted

Financial Aid
In-state tuition: $5,000
Out-of-state tuition: $5,000
Room: Varies
Board: Varies
Books: $992
Freshmen receiving need-based aid: 30%
Undergrads rec. need-based aid: 44%
Avg. % of need met by financial aid: 34%
Avg. aid package (freshmen): $6,486
Avg. aid package (undergrads): $7,178
Avg. debt upon graduation: $14,377

School Spirit
Mascot: Cougars
Colors: Blue, white, and tan

BROWN UNIVERSITY

BROWN UNIVERSITY

Four-year private
Founded: 1764
Providence, RI
Medium city
Pop. 178,053

Address:
Box 1920
Providence, RI
02912

Admissions:
401-863-2378

Financial Aid:
401-863-2721

admission_undergrad-
uate@brown.edu

www.brown.edu

Overview

Brown University offers one of the most unique and well-balanced academic and social experiences in the country. Students can choose from over 175 majors and even design their own major while studying abroad and participating in a number of student groups and events on campus.

Located in Providence, Rhode Island, Brown's campus sprawls into surrounding neighborhoods, thereby making it difficult to distinguish where the grounds begin or end. However, most of the school can be divided into Main Campus, Pembroke Campus, and East Campus. Main Campus is home to many of Brown's academic departments that are themselves housed in Victorian-style houses. Pembroke Campus is home to most of the university's dormitories.

Some say that Brown students are more laid back than their other Ivy League counterparts, but Brown students emphasize their independence. Rather than ask students to complete a general education curriculum before diving into their majors, the university allows students to choose the classes that best fit their majors, interests, and abilities. In addition, students are encouraged to seek mentorship from faculty advisors and to take part in the school's activities, organizations, and traditions.

Academics

Brown offers a comprehensive academic environment with 180 majors, ranging from the standard biology and economics fields of study to the more specialized self-designed majors, independent studies, and honors programs. Brown students are held to a high standard with minimum GPAs required to remain in good academic standing and to graduate.

Though considered one of the less competitive Ivy League schools, Brown students are in no way slackers; they are instead offered broader education opportunities. There are no required courses except for those necessary to fulfill one's major, classes may be taken for Satisfactory/No Credit, and a two-week shopping period at the beginning of each semester allows students to test run courses. These policies enhance students' abilities to choose the classes that are best suited to their abilities and interests. "Our reputation is of being the most relaxed Ivy; but from my experience, it's still academically intense," says a student.

Some of Brown's strongest disciplines include: biological and life sciences; business, finance, sales and marketing; area, ethnic, and gender studies; and architecture.

Notable professors include: Chinua Achebe, author of *Things Fall Apart*, the most widely-read novel in modern African Literature; Fernando Cardoso, former Brazilian president; and Leon Neil Cooper, recipient of the Nobel Prize in Physics.

To ensure that students make the most of their first year at Brown, incoming freshmen are assigned two advisors—a Brown faculty member who serves as an academic advisor and a peer student advisor. The academic advisor provides information on Brown's educational opportunities and institutional rules, while the student advisor provides information regarding the nitty gritty aspects of course and faculty reputations. Freshman can also choose to take part in two unique advising opportunities: the Curricular Advising Program, which allows students to take classes with their academic advisors, or the University Community Academic Advising Program, which connects students and their academic advisors with service opportunities in the community. After freshman year, students may receive advice through Advising Central, a physical space on campus where students and faculty members discuss academics over weekday afternoon coffee and tea. There are also opportunities for students to dine with faculty advisors and deans at various faculty homes. One student explains, "The faculty and staff pretty much hold your hand throughout your experience here."

Special academic opportunities at Brown include group independent study projects and the ability to take up to four courses at the Rhode Island School of Design, in addition to double majors, dual degrees, honors programs, and internship assignments.

Over 500 Brown students study abroad each year in 14 different countries including Barbados, Brazil, Cuba, the Czech Republic, India, and Japan. For those students who are interested in visiting other countries, alternative programs are available, including Brown's Global Independent Study Initiative and some that are offered by other universities.

The Career Development Center at Brown provides a multitude of options for current and graduating students. Those looking for a summer or temporary job can work through the UCAN Internship Exchange Database, whereas those looking for full-time employment can enjoy the benefits of the Brown Career Connection. Advisors at the CDC can also help student decide on gap-year/one-year plans, apply for fellowships, and explore graduate programs. About 30 percent of students attend graduate school within one year of graduating.

Student Life

Almost 80 percent of Brown students live on campus. Fourteen dorms offer housing to freshmen, supplying a variety of dorm and room sizes. Incoming freshmen are assigned roommates; upperclassmen may enter a lottery for the next year's housing. Upperclassmen may choose from a diverse range of housing options, such as sorority and fraternity housing, student apartments, and cooperative housing. Additionally, Brown offers special housing for disabled students.

Brown boasts over 350 student organizations, the most popular being those that are musically, theatrically, politically, and service oriented. The Swearer Center for Public Service at Brown provides a wide range of opportunities, including community partnerships and programs, courses, research, fellowships, and social entrepreneurship. "Service is the 'in' thing to do," says a student. There are 13 fraternities and five sororities, but only about 10 percent of students participate in Greek organizations.

Throughout the year, Brown students can take part in several different events. In the fall, students can partake in the Queer Alliance's SexPowerGod party or in the Brown Association for Cooperative Housing's Naked Party. The former soiree aims to unite Brown's and neighbor school Rhode Island School of Design's heterosexual and homosexual populations, while the latter aims to celebrate all body shapes and sizes.

Students enjoy Spring Weekend, Brown's annual end-of-year celebration. The weekend includes individual events such as a carnival, foam party, and concerts. In past years, performers have included OK Go, Lupe Fiasco, and Snoop Dogg.

And to ring in the end of each semester, students can choose to take part in the Naked Donut run, in which various student groups run unclothed through various student libraries and offer free donuts to their more studious counterparts. "We're an outgoing crowd," laughs one student.

For those who are athletically inclined, intramural sports are a large part of student life at Brown. Students can choose to participate in basketball, flag football, ice hockey, Ultimate Frisbee, and

BROWN UNIVERSITY

Highlights

Students
Total enrollment: 8,885
Undergrads: 6,435
Part-time students: 5%
From out-of-state: 97%
Male/Female: 47%/53%
Live on-campus: 79%
In fraternities: 15%
In sororities: 5%
Off-campus employment rating: Excellent
Caucasian: 45%
African American: 6%
Hispanic: 10%
Asian / Pacific Islander: 13%
Native American: 0%
Mixed (2+ ethnicities): 5%
International: 12%

Academics
Calendar: Semester
Student/faculty ratio: 8:1
Class size 9 or fewer: 32%
Class size 10-29: 49%
Class size 30-49: 9%
Class size 50-99: 6%
Class size 100 or more: 3%
Returning freshmen: 97%
Six-year graduation rate: 95%

Most Popular Majors
Economics
Biological sciences
International relations

Admissions
Applicants: 28,742
Accepted: 2,759
Acceptance rate: 9.6%
Average GPA: Not reported
ACT range: 29-34
SAT Math range: 660-770
SAT Reading range: 660-760
SAT Writing range: 66-27
Top 10% of class: 94%
Top 25% of class: 99%
Top 50% of class: 100%

121

BROWN UNIVERSITY

Admissions Criteria

Academic criteria:
Grades: ☆ ☆ ☆
Difficulty of class schedule: ☆ ☆ ☆
Class rank: ☆ ☆
Standardized test scores: ☆ ☆
Teacher recommendations: ☆ ☆
Personal statement: ☆ ☆
Non-academic criteria considered:
Interview
Extracurricular activities
Special talents, interests, abilities
Character/personal qualities
Volunteer work
Work experience
Geographical location
Minority affiliation
Alumni relationship

Deadlines

Early Action: No
Early Decision: November 1
Regular Action: January 1 (final)
Notification of admission by: April 1
Common Application: Accepted

Financial Aid

In-state tuition: $44,608
Out-of-state tuition: $44,608
Room: $7,200
Board: $4,420
Books: $1,404
Freshmen receiving need-based aid: 49%
Undergrads rec. need-based aid: 44%
Avg. % of need met by financial aid: 100%
Avg. aid package (freshmen): $40,523
Avg. aid package (undergrads): $39,526
Avg. debt upon graduation: $23,521

School Spirit

Mascot: Brown Bear
Colors: Brown and red
Song: *Ever True to Brown*

volleyball. The university has 37 Division I sports teams. Standout programs include the men's and women's rowing teams, men's soccer, football, and equestrian.

For special evenings and weekends, Brown students can dine and shop on Thayer Street or go to downtown Providence for additional shops, restaurants, and cultural institutes. For short trips away, students may opt to travel an hour to Boston or just a bit further to New York City. Rhode Island and Massachusetts have some lovely beaches to enjoy in the summer.

Student Body

Brown's student body is extremely diverse. Only 3 percent of students hail from Rhode Island and 34 percent identify themselves as minority. "You will eat, learn, and live with people from not only across the country but around the world," says one student. With more than 90 percent of applicants having graduated in the top 10 percent of their high school class, it is not surprising that students are academically focused. "This is one of the most intelligent and creative collections of students in the world," explains a Brown scholar. "I learn not only from lectures but from discussions over meals and in my dorm room."

Most students consider themselves liberal; in fact, Brown College Democrats is one of the most popular student organizations. Several programs on campus are dedicated to students with personal, psychological, religious, and learning needs.

You May Not Know

- Brown University was ranked third in the Princeton Review's list of America's Happiest College Students in 2012.
- WBRU 95.5 FM is an alternative rock radio station transmitted from Providence, Rhode Island. When it began as the Brown Network at Brown University in 1936, it was the first student-owned and operated college radio station in the United States.
- Brown is a university steeped in superstition. The Van Wickle Gates open inward each fall to welcome students to the new academic year, and open outward each spring to congratulate graduates. But if any student passes through the gates a second time before the gates open outward for his/her graduation, rumor has it that student will not graduate.

Distinguished Alumni

John F. Kennedy Jr., former President of the United States; John Krasinski, actor; Laura Linney, actress; Randy Pausch, inspirational professor; John D. Rockefeller Jr., American philanthropist; Ted Turner, founder of CNN; Thomas J. Watson Jr., CEO of IBM.

Admissions and Financial Aid

Brown University admits applicants based on academic achievement, extracurricular activities, special talents and interests, character, and volunteer and work experience. According to the college, "The transcript showing your courses and your performance in them is a key source of information, but no single part of the application can tell a complete story." With an acceptance rate of just under 9 percent, applicants must be outstanding both inside and outside of the classroom to receive a coveted letter of acceptance.

Admissions is need-blind and meets students' full demonstrated financial need. No athletic or merit-based scholarships are available.

Students whose families make $100,000 or less do not have a loan component in their financial aid awards. Students whose families make $60,000 or less do not have to pay tuition.

BRYN MAWR COLLEGE

Four-year private women's college
Founded: 1885
Bryn Mawr, PA
Major city
Pop. 4,382

Address:
101 North Merion Avenue
Bryn Mawr, PA 19010

Admissions:
800-262-1885

Financial Aid:
610-526-5245

admissions@bryn-mawr.edu

www.brynmawr.edu

Overview

Enter Bryn Mawr's historic and beautifully landscaped 135-acre campus to admire the Collegiate Gothic architecture style of the buildings and stroll through the arboretum campus with its 75 varieties of trees and scenic trails. This peaceful suburban campus is home to 1,300 undergraduate women and 450 graduate students, though students hardly have a reputation for being quaint on this left-leaning, politically active campus.

Though diverse, student population is small. For some, this intimate intellectual and social environment may feel too constrictive or limiting, as this is certainly not a place where one can be invisible. On the other hand, a smaller student body creates a sense of community—in this case, a conscientiously cultivated small community, supported by a unique student-ratified and student-enforced Honor Code.

The college is located in the upscale and suburban Main Line region of Philadelphia. Luckily, downtown Philadelphia is a 20-minute train ride away, and students can tap into academic and social opportunities at Haverford College, Swarthmore College, and the University of Pennsylvania.

Academics

The women undergraduates accepted to Bryn Mawr are an academically accomplished lot: Almost seventy percent graduated in the top 10 percent of their high school class. "There is some competition among students," admits one student. "We all pretty much want to be future doctors and CEOs," she adds. Indeed, the *U.S. News* ranked Bryn Mawr in the top 30 national liberal arts college corroborates.

As a part of their curriculum, students are required to take an Emily Batch Seminar that encourages "focused discussion and cogent writing" and to fulfill a quantitative skills and foreign language requirement. Students must also take two units each in the social sciences, natural sciences, math, and humanities.

A unique feature of academics at Bryn Mawr is the Honor Code, "a set of principles that stresses mutual respect and integrity." The college is proud of this tradition. The provisions are not only ratified by students, but they are enforced by them as well. Students are not allowed to discuss grades among themselves, but the Honor Code also bestows privileges such as the ability to take self-scheduled final exams and non-proctored take-home tests through the semester.

The small classes at Bryn Mawr enable students to get to know their high-caliber professors. "I still talk to professors I had two years ago because we actually became friends when we worked so closely together," says a student. Half of the 158 professors are women, and 15 percent are professors of color. Bryn Mawr's empowerment of women is also clear in the percentage of its undergraduates who pursue majors in the natural sciences or mathematics—30 percent compared to the national average among female undergrads of 7 percent.

Bryn Mawr offers 36 academic majors and 38 minors, along with eight interdepartmental concentrations. Realistically, the actual selection from which students choose is much larger, due to the college's special partnerships with Haverford College, Swarthmore College, and the University of Pennsylvania. These partnerships give Bryn Mawr students access to over 5,000 courses and more than 2.5 million library books. Haverford is just one mile from Bryn Mawr; Swarthmore is 20 minutes away. A regular shuttle service runs between the colleges to facilitate this academic exchange. Penn is 25 minutes away by car or less than an hour by commuter rail. Strong programs include the arts, classics, a number of foreign languages, and the natural sciences (biology, chemistry), as well as psychology and sociology.

Special academic opportunities at Bryn Mawr abound. The Praxis Program is an experiential, community-based learning program that combines classroom study and fieldwork, thereby integrating the theoretical and the practical. The Katharine

Houghton Hepburn Center "challenges women to lead publicly engaged lives and to take on important and timely issues affecting women," with a focus on film and theater, civic engagement, and women's health. The three interdisciplinary Centers for 21st Century Inquiry encourage collaboration and innovation in natural sciences, social sciences, arts, and humanities.

More than one third of Bryn Mawr's students study abroad for one semester during their junior year. The program encompasses about 30 countries, including several programs in the UK and Europe.

The Bryn Mawr-Haverford Career Development Office focuses on career opportunities; for example, the Career Network offers individual counseling and other help with the job search. Bryn Mawr is among the top 10 of all colleges and universities in the percentage of graduates who go on to earn a PhD. The admission rate to medical school is more than 75 percent, and the admission rate to law school is almost 80 percent.

Student Life

First-year students are introduced to Bryn Mawr through a heady mix of activities during Customs Week. Each dorm is divided into groups, which are led by sophomore "customs people." The groups remain together during the school year. "It's easy to make friends with this instant social group," says a student.

There are plenty of traditions to learn at Bryn Mawr. Parade Night celebrates the completion of the first day of classes and introduces first-year students "to their sister class, the juniors, as well as to their adversarial class, the sophomores, and the apathetic seniors." Lantern Night in mid-November passes the light of knowledge from the sophomores to the first-year class. The mysteriously named "Hell Week" offers "the true welcoming of the first-year class" in mid-February. May Day gathers the college community for a day of medieval-themed fun, including a parade, Scottish dancing, and a traditional King Arthur Play. A tradition less steeped in medieval times (and less formal) is skinny dipping in the Cloisters fountain outside M. Carey Thomas Library, following the tradition of alumna Katharine Hepburn. "Traditions are our thing," laughs a student.

There are more than 100 student-run clubs and organizations at Bryn Mawr, funded by the nation's oldest Self-Government Association (founded in 1892). Advocacy, service, and political clubs are some of the most popular. The newly renovated Marjorie Walter Goodhart Theater offers a vaulted auditorium for the performing arts.

The Bryn Mawr College Party Policy outlines fairly strict details for hosting parties. However, students often trek to nearby campuses to check out their social venues as well. There are no sororities at Bryn Mawr. "You can always find a party if you want to," explains one student, "but there's not a lot of pressure to drink."

There are 12 Division III varsity athletic teams. The badminton team won national titles in 1996 and 2008. Club sports include equestrian, Ultimate Frisbee, and rugby, all co-sponsored by Haverford College. Recreation facilities include a 50,000-square-foot gym and outdoor tennis courts and fields.

Road tripping to NYC makes for a popular off-campus excursion, although closer to campus are Haverford and Swarthmore.

BRYN MAWR COLLEGE

Highlights

Students
Total enrollment: 1,774
Undergrads: 1,322
Freshmen: 365
Part-time students: 1%
From out-of-state: 88%
From public schools: 63%
Male/Female: 0%/100%
Live on-campus: 93%
Off-campus employment rating: Good
Caucasian: 35%
African American: 5%
Hispanic: 9%
Asian / Pacific Islander: 13%
Native American: 0%
Mixed (2+ ethnicities): 4%
International: 20%

Academics
Calendar: Semester
Student/faculty ratio: 8:1
Class size 9 or fewer: 29%
Class size 10-29: 59%
Class size 30-49: 9%
Class size 50-99: 4%
Class size 100 or more: -
Returning freshmen: 90%
Six-year graduation rate: 82%

Most Popular Majors
English
Anthropology
Biology

Admissions
Applicants: 2,626
Accepted: 1,086
Acceptance rate: 41.4%
Placed on wait list: 846
Enrolled from wait list: 5
Average GPA: Not reported
ACT range: 26-30
SAT Math range: 590-720
SAT Reading range: 600-710
SAT Writing range: 37-45
Top 10% of class: 68%
Top 25% of class: 93%
Top 50% of class: 100%

125

BRYN MAWR COLLEGE

Admissions Criteria

Academic criteria:
Grades: ☆ ☆ ☆
Difficulty of class schedule: ☆ ☆ ☆
Class rank: ☆
Standardized test scores: ☆
Teacher recommendations: ☆ ☆ ☆
Personal statement: ☆ ☆
Non-academic criteria considered:
Interview
Extracurricular activities
Special talents, interests, abilities
Character/personal qualities
Volunteer work
Work experience
State of residency
Geographical location
Minority affiliation
Alumni relationship

Deadlines

Early Action: No
Early Decision: November 15
Regular Action: January 15 (final)
Notification of admission by: April 1
Common Application: Accepted

Financial Aid

In-state tuition: $42,870
Out-of-state tuition: $42,870
Room: Varies
Board: Varies
Books: $1,000
Freshmen receiving need-based aid: 51%
Undergrads rec. need-based aid: 55%
Avg. % of need met by financial aid: 100%
Avg. aid package (freshmen): $41,074
Avg. aid package (undergrads): $40,897
Avg. debt upon graduation: $23,579

School Spirit

Mascot: Owls

A quick train ride takes students to Philadelphia. With its many museums like the Philadelphia Museum of Art, cultural experiences like the Philadelphia Orchestra, and historic sites, the city has much to offer. "Everything is accessible to us," says a student.

Undergraduates are guaranteed four years of housing, and 93 percent of students choose to live on campus. Housing is very nice, with 14 dormitories, houses, and apartments to choose from. Each residential space is unique: Batten House offers upperclass students environmentally focused co-operative living; Brecon House's spacious rooms have large windows, high ceilings and hardwood floors; some rooms in the castle-like Pembroke Hall still contain the original fireplaces.

Student Body

The approximately 1,300 undergraduates on campus are a diverse group: 31 percent are students of color, and in the class of 2013, 19 percent were first generation college students. These women undergrads hail from 47 states and 58 countries.

Students are known to be free, independent thinkers, and the school leans politically left. "You can be conservative here and you won't be harassed, but you will be in the minority," says a student. A studious bunch, the women place a strong emphasis on academics.

You May Not Know

- The name "Bryn Mawr" means "large hill" in Welsh.
- There are many mentions of Bryn Mawr in popular culture: for instance, one of Toni Morrison's characters in *Song of Solomon* is a Bryn Mawr alumna, as is the philosophy professor in the Woody Allen film *Another Woman*.
- Ten of Bryn Mawr's buildings are listed in the National Register of Historic Places.

Distinguished Alumnae

Emily Green Balch, Noble Peace Prize winner; Drew Gilpin Faust, Harvard University's first female president; Katharine Hepburn, Academy Award-winning actress; Marianne Moore, modernist poet; Nettie Stevens, geneticist.

Admissions and Financial Aid

Bryn Mawr offers Early Decision I and II options. Both are binding and for students whose clear first-choice college is Bryn Mawr. The deadlines for early decisions are November 15 and January 1. The "Test Flexible" standard that Bryn Mawr has recently implemented allows a spectrum of standardized testing options, including AP exams in lieu of SATs or ACTs. Interviews are recommended but not required.

There are no merit-based scholarships offered by the college. However, the college does meet 100 percent of students' demonstrated financial need.

BUCKNELL UNIVERSITY

BUCKNELL UNIVERSITY

Four-year private
Founded: 1846
Lewisburg, PA
Small town
Pop. 6,500

Address:
1 Dent Drive
Lewisburg, PA
17837

Admissions:
570-577-3000

Financial Aid:
570-577-1331

admissions@bucknell.
edu

www.bucknell.edu

Overview

The 450-acre campus of Bucknell University features elegantly manicured lawns and handsome historic buildings. Summer offers up vast blue skies and autumn brings colorful leaves that are rich red and match many of these buildings. This beautiful scene provides a backdrop for 3,500 undergrads who are known to be sports fans and partiers who enjoy a rich social life without neglecting their studies. Students describe Bucknell as offering a strong academic program but also a great party scene, especially through the Greek organizations.

Some students say the university leans a little to the preppy side, and the campus is charming but might feel somewhat insular since its closest town is historic Lewisburg. However, the area is full of old-fashioned charm which the college describes as "gingerbread architecture, carved wooden doors, and three-globed streetlights." Bucknell is about three hours away from New York City, Philadelphia, and Washington, DC, so most students find themselves staying in the "Bucknell Bubble." Nearly half the student body does manage to get away at some point during their undergraduate careers, taking advantage of the many study-abroad opportunities.

Bucknell prides itself on its academic caliber, and "The Plan for Bucknell" shows the university's commitment to strengthening the academic core curriculum, among other initiatives. The university is not particularly ethnically diverse, a fact that Bucknell hopes to change as part of its plan.

Academics

A small college atmosphere facilitates close student ties with professors. Ninety-eight percent of classes have 50 students or fewer, and all classes are taught by professors. "Classes vary in how difficult they are depending on your major and even which professor you get," says a student. Bucknell offers 71 majors. Strong programs include education, management, international relations, and the many options of the College of Engineering,

The university has a College Core Curriculum (previously the Common Learning Agenda), which is required of all students in the College of Arts and Sciences. Mandated classes include a foundation seminar, lab science, foreign language, quantitative reasoning, arts and humanities, natural sciences and math, and social sciences. Students must also complete a culminating experience or senior project.

The Institute for Leadership in Technology and Management (ILTM) consists of a two-summer sequence of programs that includes an intensive six-week training before junior year and an internship before senior year. ILTM is designed to bridge the disciplines of engineering and management. As one student attests, "The hands-on experience you get is invaluable."

The Justice and Social Change Program is a community for students interested in "issues of justice, social problems, and social change." Students in the program take classes together, often live together, and complete a culminating experience such as a thesis or project.

Bucknell's study-abroad program encompasses almost 60 countries, and recently 40 percent of students have studied off campus. Juniors and first-semester seniors are eligible for off-campus study; however, seniors must spend their last semester on campus to earn their degree.

Bucknell's Career Development Center aids students in exploring majors, preparing for the job search, and finding internships and jobs or graduate schools. According to the class of 2012 statistics, 92 percent of the senior class was employed or in graduate/professional school within nine months of graduation. The Bucknell Professional Network includes 49,000 alumni across the world, mostly centralized in Pennsylvania, New Jersey, New York, Maryland, and California.

BUCKNELL UNIVERSITY

Highlights

Students
Total enrollment: 3,618
Undergrads: 3,536
Freshmen: 928
Part-time students: 1%
From out-of-state: 82%
From public schools: 62%
Male/Female: 48%/52%
Live on-campus: 86%
In fraternities: 39%
In sororities: 43%
Off-campus employment rating: Poor
Caucasian: 80%
African American: 3%
Hispanic: 4%
Asian / Pacific Islander: 3%
Native American: 0%
Mixed (2+ ethnicities): 3%
International: 5%

Academics
Calendar: Semester
Student/faculty ratio: 10:1
Class size 9 or fewer: 21%
Class size 10-29: 63%
Class size 30-49: 13%
Class size 50-99: 2%
Class size 100 or more: 1%
Returning freshmen: 95%
Six-year graduation rate: 90%
Graduates who immediately go to graduate school: 21%
Graduates who immediately enter career related to major: 71%

Most Popular Majors
Economics
Management
Biology

Admissions
Applicants: 8,291
Accepted: 2,238
Acceptance rate: 27.0%
Placed on wait list: 2,348
Enrolled from wait list: 3
Average GPA: 3.5
ACT range: 27-31
SAT Math range: 620-710
SAT Reading range: 580-680
SAT Writing range: 21-51
Top 10% of class: 66%
Top 25% of class: 89%
Top 50% of class: 99%

128

Student Life

The Campus Activities and Program (CAP) Center on campus is home to over 150 clubs and organizations, provides shuttle services and other useful resources for students, and even has a Craft Center with weaving looms, potter's wheels, and glass grinders. The many student groups offer varied leadership opportunities and include something for everyone, whether a student wants to act in a theater group, give to the community, intellectually engage in an academic society, or start his or her own club. Common Ground is a student-led diversity immersion retreat program that is part of the leadership development program, Building on Foundations.

Music lovers will be grateful for the Bucknell Concert Committee, a selective student group that invites big-name bands and artists to campus. Bucknell even has its very own venue for both national touring and student bands, the Uptown on-campus night club. With pub nights, pool tournaments, and Texas Hold 'em, Uptown provides the type of entertainment that makes it a popular hangout for students.

Bucknell's clear and detailed alcohol policy encourages moderation for students. Violations earn "points" for students that can result in a required leave. The university asks for students to "apply a conscious and intelligent attitude to one's personal life as well as to one's academic undertakings"—in short, to "Work Hard and Play Smart."

Popular events on campus include First Night, a ceremony honoring freshmen for completing their first semester; and Chrysalis Ball, an annual tradition that brings together students, faculty, and staff for an evening of celebration. "The Chrysalis Ball is the time to get all prettied up and party," laughs a student.

There is a strong Greek presence, with more than 40 percent of students involved and many of the parties hosted by the 19 fraternities and sororities. The Greek system is not just about parties: service also plays a strong role, with 85 percent of seniors participating in community service or volunteer work.

Sports are a major part of campus culture, perhaps because over 70 percent of Bucknell students played varsity sports in high school. About one third of students are involved in the extensive intramural sports program. Built in 2003, the Kenneth Langone Athletics and Recreation Center houses a natatorium, basketball pavilion, and fitness center. Division I sports are popular to watch among students, especially men's basketball, which is often sold out. "You must attend at least one if not all of the basketball games to get the true Bucknell experience," comments a student. The intercollegiate program includes 27 men's and women's sports, and Bucknell was the winner of its league's all-sports trophy, 15 of the past 19 years.

Students tend not to venture too far off campus or outside Lewisburg, and many seem happy to remain in the "Bucknell Bubble." Indeed, 86 percent of students live on campus, with first-year students being required to live on campus, often in Smith or McDonnell Hall. Upperclassmen have a housing lottery. As one student explains, "Dorms get better and roomier as you move up."

Student Body

Many students are politically conservative and many are of upper-middle and upper class economically. "We have a not-totally undeserved reputation as being rich and preppy," says a student.

There are 13 percent minority students, a number Bucknell hopes to increase as part of its Plan for Bucknell. Though racial/ethnic diversity is moderate, geographic diversity among students is high, with only 18 percent of students hailing from Pennsylvania. The class of 2016 includes students from 36 states and 48 countries.

In spite of the large party scene fueled by the Greek organizations on campus, students are generally academically focused. This is perhaps to be expected since 66 percent of students graduated in the top 10 percent of their high school class.

You May Not Know

- When the university was in dire financial straits in 1881, William Bucknell gave generously to what was then the University of Lewisburg. In 1886 the trustees voted unanimously to change the name to honor Bucknell.
- Maung Shaw Loo of Burma (Myanmar) was the university's first international student and the country's first student from Burma in 1864.
- The bison mascot was suggested in 1923 and was likely inspired by Bucknell's location in the Buffalo Valley.

Distinguished Alumni

Sunil Gulati, United States Soccer Federation President; Jessica Flannery, co-founder of microlending website Kiva.org; Leslie Moonves, President and CEO of CBS corporation; Philip Roth, Pulitzer Prize-winning novelist.

Admissions and Financial Aid

Bucknell is in the top 4 percent of the most selective colleges in the nation. A teacher recommendation is required with the application along with coursework including two years of a foreign language. Bucknell only accepts applications for students enrolling in the fall semester. Early Decision I applications are intended for those students who have Bucknell as their first choice and are due on November 15. If accepted, these students are automatically committed to attend. Early Decision II applications are also binding, but have a later deadline of January 15. Applications are reviewed according to first-choice major; students who are undecided must explain their choice. Certain programs are very competitive, so the major listed may affect a student's chances of admissions.

Students do not need to complete a separate application to apply for merit-based scholarships. There awards are given based on academic achievement, cultural and intellectual diversity, performing arts, and athletics. The Presidential Fellows Program provides 25 awards of $20,000 per year. Dean's Scholarships are given up to 125 students and provide renewable awards of $10,000 a year.

BUCKNELL UNIVERSITY

Highlights

Admissions Criteria
Academic criteria:
Grades: ☆ ☆ ☆
Difficulty of class schedule: ☆ ☆ ☆
Class rank: ☆ ☆ ☆
Standardized test scores: ☆ ☆ ☆
Teacher recommendations: ☆ ☆
Personal statement: ☆ ☆ ☆
Non-academic criteria considered:
Extracurricular activities
Special talents, interests, abilities
Character/personal qualities
Volunteer work
Work experience
State of residency
Geographical location
Religious affiliation/commitment
Minority affiliation
Alumni relationship

Deadlines
Early Action: No
Early Decision: November 15
Regular Action: January 15 (final)
Notification of admission by: April 1
Common Application: Accepted

Financial Aid
In-state tuition: $46,646
Out-of-state tuition: $46,646
Room: $6,622
Board: $4,636
Books: $900
Freshmen receiving need-based aid: 44%
Undergrads rec. need-based aid: 45%
Avg. % of need met by financial aid: 95%
Avg. aid package (freshmen): $28,500
Avg. aid package (undergrads): $27,000
Avg. debt upon graduation: $21,163

School Spirit
Mascot: Bison
Colors: Orange and blue
Song: *Ray Bucknell*

CALIFORNIA INSTITUTE OF TECHNOLOGY

Overview

Referred to as "Caltech," the California Institute of Technology is internationally recognized for rigorous academics in the sciences, math, and engineering. Founded in September 1891 as "Throop University," Caltech was firmly set on its course toward becoming a first-class engineering and scientific research institution by astronomer, George Ellery Hale, who became a member of the University's Board of Trustees in 1907. Thirty-two Nobel Prizes won by Caltech faculty or alumni (physics, physicology or medicine, chemistry, economics, and peace) speak to the college's indisputable reputation as a premier science and engineering institution.

The campus itself sits on 124 acres of property soaking up the Southern California sun in suburban Pasadena. The San Gabriel Mountains are an hour's drive from campus and offer skiing, hiking, canyoneering, and camping. The average "Techer" doesn't very often venture off campus or, for that matter, out of the lab or library. But for the more adventurous types, the cultural powerhouse that is the Greater Los Angeles metropolitan area is right outside the door, with downtown Pasadena within walking distance and Los Angeles a 20-minute drive away.

Students who lean more toward social science, humanities, or the arts might be better served elsewhere. But if you daydream about speeding atoms crashing into each other, or have Sir Isaac Newton on the short list of people from the past you would have loved to have met, then you may just be a Techer.

Academics

At this renowned university, the student-to-faculty ratio is a remarkable 3:1, and more than 70 percent of undergraduate classes have fewer than 20 students. Caltech is home to many nationally and internationally known engineers, mathematicians, and scientists who are passionate about their fields of study and demand the same dedication from their students. "While not all professors are the best teachers, the incredible research they do makes up for it," says a student.

Students who find themselves confused in lectures, or having to work a little harder than their classmates to understand the proofs in textbooks, should be prepared to honestly assess their situation. One student explains, "It's up to you to seek help from the professors, and you will need help."

As an indication of the academic rigor, students are able to take classes pass/fail for the first two trimesters. "Trust me, even if you have an 800 on the math SAT, it's so challenging here that you'll need the pass/fail," says a student. Students also say collaboration on homework and other assignments is strongly encouraged for success at Caltech. There is a lot of trust between professors and students, with most tests given out as take-home assignments, rather than proctored exams. Students are often given 24-hour access to labs, workshops, and other campus facilities.

Caltech offers 61 majors, and the school's general education core requires all students to take 12 terms of humanities courses, which includes two terms each of writing, introductory social-science, advanced humanities, and advanced social-science. "We all suffer through the humanities classes together," a student laughs. Study-abroad opportunities are limited, and most students don't take advantage of the five opportunities offered in Denmark, France, and the United Kingdom.

The Summer Undergraduate Research Fellowships program, or SURF, is modeled on the grant-seeking process. Students who are accepted are able to conduct their own research under the guidance of seasoned research mentors. Applicants write research proposals outlining their projects. Students conduct research over a 10-week period and then submit a technical paper.

Also notable are the Jet Propulsion Laboratory (JPL) and Palomar and the Keck Observatory. JPL was established by Caltech in the 1930s and is a key laboratory in NASA's program of exploration of Earth, our solar system, and the universe. Explorer 1, the United States' first satellite launched in 1958, was created at JPL. More recently, JPL launched Kepler, a space-borne telescope that will look for Earth-like planets, and Dawn, a robotic spacecraft, which is orbiting the asteroid Vesta and the dwarf planet Ceres.

Keck Observatory was jointly built and is operated by CARA, an organization formed by Caltech and the University of California system. The observatory itself, which sits on the 13,800-foot summit of an extinct volcano, consists of two 10-meter (or about 30-foot) telescopes on top of Mauna Kea on the Big Island in Hawaii.

Caltech alumni enjoy an active alumni association, which primarily uses LinkedIn, as well as its own Alumni Job Connection site. Campus-wide career fairs are held twice a year with 150-200 companies attending to recruit for internships, research, and career opportunities. "With a Caltech diploma, you pretty much have a ticket into a solid, if not amazing, career path," says a student.

Student Life

While living on campus is only required for freshmen, 93 percent of all undergrads choose to do so, with housing being guaranteed for all four years. Caltech has eight undergraduate houses. Unique to Caltech is the rotation system in which freshmen get to choose where they want to live after learning about each of the undergraduate houses. Techers are also able to choose their roommates all four years.

A distinctive feature of the house system at Caltech is the dining. Sit-down dinner with table service is provided on weeknights, with meals served "family style." One student explains, "You really get to know classmates intimately." As with the family style meals, many of the social aspects of Caltech revolve around the fact that most students live on-campus. Some students say this has a down side since they "don't get out of the Caltech bubble much."

There are plenty of things for future Techers to look forward to on campus. Popular spots include the Coffeehouse, Espresso Bar, and Pie 'n Burger. Caltech offers 150 official student organizations, among them, the student newspaper, Caltech/MIT Enterprise Forum, Computer Science Cluster, and *Caltech Undergraduate Research Journal*. The more lighthearted clubs include the Cooking Club, Folk Music Society, and Vegetarian Club. There are no fraternities or sororities.

Techers celebrate every Halloween with the infamous, "Millikan pumpkin-drop experiment", which, in short, involves dropping pumpkins frozen in liquid nitrogen from the top of Millikan Library. Those who happen to be around to see this incredible geeky—albeit very cool—spectacle should be sure to keep their eyes peeled for the elusive triboluminescent spark that this event is said to produce.

Caltech students are also infamous for their pranks. Two of the most famous include altering the Hollywood sign to say, "Caltech," and altering the spectator cards at the 1961 Rose Bowl game between Washington and Minnesota to read, "Caltech." More recently in 2007 students gave out fake copies of MIT's newspaper to pro-

CALIFORNIA INSTITUTE OF TECHNOLOGY

Highlights

Students
Total enrollment: 2,243
Undergrads: 997
Freshmen: 264
From out-of-state: 65%
Male/Female: 62%/38%
Live on-campus: 93%
Off-campus employment rating: Good
Caucasian: 31%
African American: 2%
Hispanic: 10%
Asian / Pacific Islander: 40%
Native American: 0%
Mixed (2+ ethnicities): 5%
International: 11%

Academics
Calendar: Trimester
Student/faculty ratio: 3:1
Class size 9 or fewer: 35%
Class size 10-29: 44%
Class size 30-49: 11%
Class size 50-99: 7%
Class size 100 or more: 3%
Returning freshmen: 96%
Six-year graduation rate: 92%
Graduates who immediately go to graduate school: 55%

Most Popular Majors
Engineering/applied science
Physical sciences
Mathematics and statistics

Admissions
Applicants: 5,225
Accepted: 651
Acceptance rate: 13%
Placed on wait list: 651
Enrolled from wait list: Not reported
Average GPA: Not reported
ACT range: 34-35
SAT Math range: 770-800
SAT Reading range: 720-780
SAT Writing range: 85-14
Top 10% of class: 94%
Top 25% of class: 99%
Top 50% of class: 100%

131

College Profiles

CALIFORNIA INSTITUTE OF TECHNOLOGY

Admissions Criteria
Academic criteria:
Grades: ☆ ☆ ☆
Difficulty of class schedule: ☆ ☆ ☆
Class rank: ☆ ☆
Standardized test scores: ☆ ☆
Teacher recommendations: ☆ ☆
Personal statement: ☆ ☆
Non-academic criteria considered:
Extracurricular activities
Special talents, interests, abilities
Character/personal qualities
Volunteer work
Work experience
State of residency
Minority affiliation

Deadlines
Early Action: November 1
Early Decision: No
Regular Action: January 3 (final)
Notification of admission by: April 1
Common Application: Accepted

Financial Aid
In-state tuition: $39,990
Out-of-state tuition: $39,990
Room: Varies
Board: Varies
Books: Varies
Freshmen receiving need-based aid: 62%
Undergrads rec. need-based aid: 52%
Avg. % of need met by financial aid: 100%
Avg. aid package (freshmen): $37,984
Avg. aid package (undergrads): $38,756
Avg. debt upon graduation: $13,095

School Spirit
Mascot: Beaver
Colors: Black and orange

spective students. Headlines read, "Infinite Corridor Not Actually Infinite" and "MIT Invents the Interweb."

It is imperative to describe some of the originality of Caltech's Senior Ditch Day in order to have a complete overview of student life. Toward the end of each academic school year, Senior Techers must leave their labs and textbooks behind and get off campus or risk being kidnapped by rogue undergrads. In an effort to protect their rooms from being ransacked, seniors assemble elaborate "locks and obstacles" for their rooms, with many planning scavenger hunts, quests, and red-herring searches for their younger counterparts.

Not surprisingly, "athletics are not our strong suit," says a student. The university has 17 teams that mostly compete at the Division III level. Caltech doesn't have a football team, and even in athletics, students are most recognized for how they perform outside their sport: "Beaver Student-Athletes Win Robotics Contest" was a recent headline. The men's basketball team recently broke its 207-game losing streak and the women's basketball a 50-game losing streak. Still, the university is strong in club sports such as table tennis and Ultimate Frisbee.

Student Body

The student body is on the geeky side at Caltech. "We embrace our geekiness. Imagine the geekiest kid at your school and then multiply that twentyfold. Then multiply that kid by 1,000 and you'll get our student body," says a student. The main interest for most, if not all students, is their academic field. Academics come above all else for the average Techer. In the words of the student newspaper, *The California Tech*: "Social life is close to nil."

Men outnumber women on a pretty significant scale, and while Caltech will claim they're ethnically diverse, what this really translates into is a 40 percent Asian and Pacific Islander population.

You May Not Know

- Caltech alumni may apply to be a member of the Athenaeum, a private membership club that has over 3,500 members, which include Caltech faculty, trustees, alumni, and senior administrators. The lounge and courtyards of the Athenaeum are popular among film makers.
- George Ellery was a Caltech trustee known for his discoveries of solar vortices and the magnetic fields of sun spots through his invention of the spectroheliograph.
- So what happens when a Techer has a great idea? They turn to Caltech's Office of Technology Transfer (OTT). OTT helps researchers, scientists, and engineers protect their intellectual property by patenting and licensing inventions for industry.

Distinguished Alumni

David Ho, director of Aaron Diamons AIDS Research Center; Gordon E. Moore, former chairman and co-founder of Intel Corp; Linus Pauling, American chemist and Nobel Laureate; Benjamin M. Rosen, former chairman of Compaq Computer Corp; Harrison

Schmitt, astronaut; Henry C. Yuen, President and CEO of Gemstar Development Corp.

Admissions and Financial Aid

There are several things to take into consideration before applying to Caltech. Aside from SAT scores and GPA, students should give a great deal of thought to their recommendation letters and whether they will submit supplemental materials. Caltech requires that prospective students submit two letters of recommendations: one from a humanities or social sciences teacher, and one from a math or science teacher. Supplementary recommendation letters from a mentor who is not also a student's school teacher are strongly encouraged. Caltech also allows prospective students to submit supplementary materials such as research papers or reports that may have been written as part of a research internship or project in high school.

Caltech will meet a family's demonstrated financial need, but there are no merit scholarships offered by the university. Need-based scholarships are awarded by the university and through named scholarships given by donors. Students only need to complete a financial aid application to be considered for these awards.

Four-year private
Founded: 1876
Grand Rapids, MI
Medium city
Pop. 189,815

Address:
3201 Burton Street, SE
Grand Rapids, MI
49546

Admissions:
800-688-0122

Financial Aid:
800-688-0122

admissions@calvin.
edu

www.calvin.edu

134

CALVIN COLLEGE

Overview

At first glance, Calvin College might appear to be your standard Midwestern mid-sized private liberal arts school, with a leafy 390-acre campus in Grand Rapids, Michigan, just 30 miles to the east of Lake Michigan. The campus boasts the architecture of Frank Lloyd Wright's prairie style and a few ponds. But if you peek at the college's official website, you'll see that Calvin augments its educational mission with a religious "calling," in which it says, "Christ the warrior has come...to equip a people—informed, devout, educated, pious, determined people—to follow him in righting what's wrong... That's what Christian higher education is for." Put more simply, Calvin College is a Christian Reform Church school (yes, *that* John Calvin), so whatever other appealing aspects Calvin offers—including strong academics, extensive study abroad, and a lively campus cultural scene—keep in mind the very strong influence of religion that you'll find on this campus. Religion plays a central role in academics at Calvin. According to the college, "100 percent of Calvin's faculty are committed Christians who actively integrate their faith with learning, teaching, and scholarship."

But if Calvin's Christian mission resonates with you, then you'll find that at Calvin, it's not all fire and brimstone. Calvin offers extensive core curricula and strives for a holistic, "big-picture" education with an emphasis on service learning, contributing positively to the local and global community, and updating and reformulating the Christian message to adapt to modern times. The environment that Calvin fosters, both academically and in extracurriculars, is one of a strong liberal arts school where in-class dialogues continue outside of class as part of lectures, concerts, and events and where Christian faith is, very visibly, at the heart of everything.

Academics

Calvin offers 92 majors, of which the humanities and education are the strongest. All students will get a healthy dose of the humanities as part of the core curriculum, beginning with a first-year "Gateway" that consists of the courses entitled "Prelude" and "Developing a Christian Mind." Beyond that, students must take basic "Core Competencies," which include written rhetoric, information technology, health and fitness, and foreign language.

"Core Studies" require classes in history, philosophy, the *Bible* and theology, literature, arts, mathematics, and natural and physical sciences, among others. Finally students must participate in a "Core Capstone" class in "Integrative Studies." This load, while comprehensive, is exactly as burdensome as it sounds; academics at Calvin are demanding, but lack of grad students, a beneficial student-to-faculty ratio, and the comfortable size of Calvin make it a supportive learning environment—Calvin was previously ranked in *U.S. News & World Report's* top 25 "schools committed to undergraduate teaching." One student says, "There's support everywhere you look, from the students, the faculty, the administration."

Undergraduate research opportunities and chances to work one-on-one with professors abound, particularly in Calvin's strong engineering offerings (chemical, civil and environmental, electrical and computer, and mechanical) and the sciences. The new and well-equipped DeVries Hall houses biochemistry and biotechnology classroom and research facilities, and the campus also boasts an 85-acre ecosystem preserve for hands-on research and teaching. "The labs are cutting edge," says a student.

Whatever discipline students pursue, Calvin offers an Honors program. Honors classes offer students more individualized attention from faculty as well as the opportunities to participate in the Honors Student Research Conference, Honors Dinner, conversations with speakers in Calvin's award-winning January Series of lectures, and to live in the Honors Living Learning Community. "To be able to have a meal with speakers like Cal Ripken, Jr. and a famous professor with autism is mind-blowing," says a student. Students with qualifying test scores are automatically invited to participate.

To 12 juniors interested in going into the ministry who demonstrate academic achievement and commitment to service and leadership in the Christian community, Calvin's Jubilee Fellows program offers a year-long program that includes a seminar course, 10-week summer internship with travel and living expenses covered, and service learning opportunities along with a $4,000 stipend.

Students not in pre-professional majors (i.e., not nursing, medical, or dental) who wish to gain experience working with non-profit organizations can apply to the Comenius Scholars Program, which the college describes as: "Paid internship with a non-profit + credit seminar course = Comenius Scholars." Students participate in a seminar on non-profit leadership in tandem with paid work (minimum wage) through a local non-profit organization.

Many of Calvin's study-abroad programs take place in the Interim Session in January: these smaller-group, faculty-led trips include destinations within the U.S. as well as countries such as Jamaica, Mexico, Germany, UK, Switzerland, Greece, the Czech Republic, Kenya, Liberia, Israel, and China. Programs that travel to the UK and Japan are also offered after the Spring Semester. Other countries with programs include Britain, China, France, Ghana, Honduras, Hungary, New Mexico, the Netherlands, Spain, and Thailand. Calvin financial aid, or a portion thereof, may be applied to certain non-Calvin study-abroad programs.

Calvin graduates enjoy higher-than-average success: in 2007, 93 percent of its engineering graduates had found jobs by graduation, while 90 percent and 100 percent of applicants from Calvin were accepted to professional and graduate school, respectively.

Student Life

More than 60 student groups operate on campus, including the Calvin Theatre Company, Rock Climbing Club, and Mu Kappa, the group for children of missionaries. As you might expect, "the religious groups are some of the most popular," says a student. Concerts may happen as often as twice a week, featuring mostly contemporary Christian music as well as hip-hop and jazz, among others. The lectures and speakers that are a part of Calvin's January Series are major draws, including speakers such as Temple Grandin and Cal Ripken, Jr.

As Calvin's international student population is the sixth largest of liberal arts colleges in the U.S., much of campus life is devoted to celebrating and promoting understanding of diversity. Rangeela, the annual international student variety show, featuring music and drama performances, is one of the school's most popular events both with students and the local community.

But not all events are serious: in the so-called "pseudo-athletic" competition Chaos Day, residence halls compete against one another in silly activities. Teams come up with their own themes and mascots, and frequently go above and beyond with their props, which have included horses, fire trucks, and helicopters in the past. Its counterpart, Mud Bowl, features a muddy tug-of-war between teams from apartment-style residences. "You will be covered in icky, gooey mud," predicts a student.

CALVIN COLLEGE

Highlights

Students
Total enrollment: 4,008
Undergrads: 3,930
Freshmen: 1,031
Part-time students: 4%
From out-of-state: 45%
From public schools: 45%
Male/Female: 47%/53%
Live on-campus: 61%
Off-campus employment rating: Good
Caucasian: 76%
African American: 3%
Hispanic: 3%
Asian / Pacific Islander: 4%
Native American: 0%
Mixed (2+ ethnicities): 2%
International: 10%

Academics
Calendar: 4-1-4 system
Student/faculty ratio: 12:1
Class size 9 or fewer: 8%
Class size 10-29: 72%
Class size 30-49: 19%
Class size 50-99: 1%
Class size 100 or more: -
Returning freshmen: 86%
Six-year graduation rate: 77%
Graduates who immediately go to graduate school: 20%

Most Popular Majors
Business
Elementary education
Nursing

Admissions
Applicants: 3,284
Accepted: 2,478
Acceptance rate: 75.5%
Average GPA: 3.7
ACT range: 24-30
SAT Math range: 540-690
SAT Reading range: 520-670
SAT Writing range: Not reported
Top 10% of class: 34%
Top 25% of class: 60%
Top 50% of class: 85%

135

CALVIN COLLEGE

Admissions Criteria

Academic criteria:
Grades: ☆ ☆ ☆
Difficulty of class schedule: ☆ ☆ ☆
Class rank: ☆
Standardized test scores: ☆ ☆ ☆
Teacher recommendations: ☆ ☆
Personal statement: ☆ ☆
Non-academic criteria considered:
Extracurricular activities
Character/personal qualities
Volunteer work
Work experience
State of residency
Religious affiliation/commitment

Deadlines

Early Action: No
Early Decision: No
Regular Action: Rolling admissions
Common Application: Accepted

Financial Aid

In-state tuition: $28,025
Out-of-state tuition: $28,025
Room: Varies
Board: Varies
Books: $1,050
Freshmen receiving need-based aid: 65%
Undergrads rec. need-based aid: 65%
Avg. % of need met by financial aid: 70%
Avg. aid package (freshmen): $21,083
Avg. aid package (undergrads): $19,642
Avg. debt upon graduation: $32,957

School Spirit

Mascot: Knights
Colors: Maroon and gold
Song: *The Calvin Fight Song*

For more serious athletes, Calvin has 18 NCAA Division III varsity athletic teams. Women's cross country and volleyball, and both soccer and basketball teams, are competitive. Intramurals at Calvin are offered at three levels depending on ability.

There is a jogging/biking track on campus as well as a new cross country course; nearby Lake Michigan is also a popular destination for outdoor activities. "When the weather isn't freezing, there are a ton of outdoor activities," says a student. For those desiring a more urban destination, Grand Rapids is a major local hub, while Chicago is just a road trip away.

Students generally live on campus during their first two years in traditional, single residence halls with two-room suites or in "Living Learning Communities" organized around themes such as environmental stewardship. Juniors and seniors can live in on-campus apartment-style residences or campus-operated off-campus housing. There are no fraternity or sorority houses as Calvin has no Greek system.

Student Body

The Calvin student body is nearly evenly split between an in- and out-of-state population. Unsurprisingly, a large portion of the student body comes from the Christian Reformed Church. Generally this translates into a conservative student body, both politically and socially. Calvin stands by the CRC's stance condemning "homosexual behavior." It forbids its faculty to engage in homosexual relations.

You May Not Know

- When Calvin College first opened in 1876, it was housed on the second floor of an elementary school.
- Calvin's Hekman Library is the second largest academic library in Michigan.
- The Science Building is shaped like a hexagon, supposedly built to resemble a benzene ring.

Distinguished Alumni

Richard DeVos, President of Amway Corporation; Jeannie Claudia Oppewal, Oscar-nominated art director; Robert Ottenhoff, COO of Public Broadcasting System.

Admissions and Financial Aid

Applicants whose test scores are under those Calvin requires will be evaluated on an individual basis, and if admitted, may be required to participate in the Access Program during summer Passport sessions to meet certain academic goals and learn strategies for success.

Applicants with outstanding academic records are automatically considered for a range of academic merit awards, ranging from $1,000 to $10,000 annually, including National Merit and Trustee Scholarships, awarded to the top 3 percent of the entering class.

CARLETON COLLEGE

Overview

The average low temperature in Northfield, Minnesota is a brutal four degrees in January—not including wind chill. But it's not the sub-zero weather that draws students from across the country to Carleton. Carleton College is known for its top-notch academics. According to the college, Carleton enrolls more National Merit Scholars than any other small liberal arts college in the country and has had 18 Rhodes Scholars.

Carleton is a 10-minute walk from downtown historic Northfield, 35 miles south of Minneapolis. The proximity to Minneapolis—and its big-city hustle and bustle—doesn't spill over into the small town of Northfield or the Carlton campus. It isn't an urban environment, but rather, a small, closely bonded community. The college is set on 1,040 acres, which includes the 880-acre Cowling Arboretum, nicknamed "the Arb."

In the autumn, the leaves turn orange, red, and yellow, and it's the kind of atmosphere that inspires scenes of scarves, mittens, and hot chocolate. The student community is also devoted to its myriad traditions. Perhaps the best word to describe Carleton is "quirky." Like most small communities, Carleton has a very distinct personality.

Academics

Because of its small, tight-knit environment, Carleton is able to provide a rigorous academic curriculum with a lot of support for its students. The college offers 38 majors. Standouts are biology, chemistry, English, geology, history, math, and physics. Carleton is on a trimester system and students take only three classes per trimester. "Three classes per semester isn't easy," remarks a student. "There's more work per class, and midterms and finals are here before you know it."

Classes are small and they are always taught by professors who are generally regarded as accessible. Carleton makes a point of distinguishing their professors as "leading scholars in their fields, but...teachers first." Students can take advantage of self-designed majors, pass/fail grading for some classes, and independent study programs.

Many colleges believe that the strength of a liberal arts education lies in its core curriculum, and Carleton is certainly no different. By the end of their undergraduate career, Carleton students will have learned a new language, taken an Argument and Inquiry Seminar (where the basics to critical thinking and intellectual independence will be learned), and happily (hopefully) completed three terms of required physical education. "I was a little hesitant about the physical education requirement, but it's pretty easy to get out of the way and not at all like high school gym class," says a student. Students are also required during sophomore year to complete a writing portfolio, which is evaluated by faculty.

Science and math students may participate in summer research through the Carleton Interdisciplinary Science and Math Initiative (CISMI). About 40-50 students are mentored by faculty and able to conduct hands-on research.

Carleton also has a 3-2 engineering, 3-2 nursing, and 3-3 law programs in which students spend three years at Carleton and then two to three years at a partner university to receive their bachelor's and master's degrees.

Study-abroad programs, or Off-Campus Studies, are divided into three areas: Carleton Programs led by faculty, Affiliated Programs hosted by outside providers, and Unaffiliated Programs. Students who are interested in a program that falls within the Unaffiliated Programs category must submit a petition for review and approval. With this kind of flexible structure, the possibilities are endless.

Most Carleton graduates go straight into the workforce, but about 26 percent go on to graduate school directly following undergrad and more than 65 percent

CARLETON COLLEGE

Four-year private
Founded: 1866
Northfield, MN
Small town
Pop. 20,084

Address:
1 North College Street
Northfield, MN
55057

Admissions:
800-222-2275

Financial Aid:
800-995-2275

admissions@carleton.edu

www.carleton.edu

CARLETON COLLEGE

Students

Total enrollment: 2,053
Undergrads: 2,053
Freshmen: 528
Part-time students: 1%
From out-of-state: 79%
From public schools: 60%
Male/Female: 47%/53%
Live on-campus: 94%
Off-campus employment rating: Good
Caucasian: 67%
African American: 3%
Hispanic: 6%
Asian / Pacific Islander: 8%
Native American: 0%
Mixed (2+ ethnicities): 5%
International: 8%

Academics

Calendar: Trimester
Student/faculty ratio: 9:1
Class size 9 or fewer: 16%
Class size 10-29: 73%
Class size 30-49: 11%
Class size 50-99: -
Class size 100 or more: -
Returning freshmen: 98%
Six-year graduation rate: 94%
Graduates who immediately go to graduate school: 26%

Most Popular Majors

Biology
Political science/international relations
Economics

Admissions

Applicants: 5,856
Accepted: 1,496
Acceptance rate: 25.5%
Placed on wait list: 1,618
Enrolled from wait list: Not reported
Average GPA: Not reported
ACT range: 29-33
SAT Math range: 670-760
SAT Reading range: 670-760
SAT Writing range: 54-39
Top 10% of class: 80%
Top 25% of class: 98%
Top 50% of class: 100%

of students attend graduate and professional schools within five years of graduating. The Carleton Career Center is available as a resource both for current students and alumni. "There aren't a ton of Carleton alums so when you encounter one, you really go the extra mile to help them out," says a recent alumnus.

Student Life

Even though Carleton offers buses to the Twin Cities on weekends, access to a varied selection of bars and nightclubs is limited. Northfield is a little town that offers a passable list of restaurants that fall within a college student's budget, but it's really more of a strolling-and-antique-shopping type of place—translation: pricey. But for the creative student, there is always something to do.

There are 132 official student organizations. Almost one third of Carleton students participate in Acting in the Community Together (ACT), a student-run community service organization. Other popular groups include Experimental Theater Board, Mustache Club, the Wellstone House of Activism, and the Association of Nature and Outdoor Enthusiasts.

The fitness-conscious student has plenty of options at Carleton. The Cowling Arboretum offers a network of walking, running, and cross-country skiing trails adjacent to the Cannon River. In fact, the Arb was ranked as one of the top 10 places to run in the country by *Runner's World Magazine*. There are also sports and recreation facilities that include a skating rink, a fitness center, a climbing wall, a bouldering wall, a swimming pool, and batting cages.

For those who enjoy more of a team atmosphere, intramural sports abound. Ultimate Frisbee is especially popular with students. "If you're going to do one thing outside of classes, it has to be Ultimate. It's huge!" says a student. Carleton offers 19 Division III varsity athletic teams. Strong teams include basketball, women's golf, and men's and women's soccer.

Rotblatt is an annual marathon intramural softball game that begins at sunrise and lasts one inning for each year of Carleton's existence since its founding in 1866. As if that weren't crazy enough, it is Rotblatt tradition for students to both bat and field with their favorite beverage in one hand.

Other Carleton traditions include sledding down Bell Field on dining hall trays, the 24-Hour Show (which is a series of plays written, rehearsed, and performed in 24-hours), and baking cookies to share at a former employee's home, Dacie's House.

Finally, it's worth mentioning the Hunt for Schiller. A plaster bust of the German poet, Friedrich Schiller, is periodically stolen and creatively displayed around campus and during events. The bust has had its share of tumbles, having shattered and been glued back together on several occasions, but the tradition remains fast. "We really get into all of it," says a student.

There are no fraternities or sororities at Carleton. Naturally there are parties but students say that there isn't a lot of peer pressure to drink in order to be socially active. With 94 percent of students living on campus, the dorms are at the center of the social scene. Most residences are co-ed, four-class dorms. All residence halls feature a student lounge area and laundry facilities. There are also shared-interest living communities, which offer like-minded students an opportunity to live closely and engage daily with one another. Other communities include those that are ethnically themed and Canoe House for students who like outdoor adventures.

Student Body

Carleton's student body is socioeconomically fairly diverse. More than half of all students receive some sort of need-based financial aid and 80 percent hold jobs on campus. Students represent all 50 states and 30 countries. For a small liberal arts college in Minnesota, the racial diversity is also pretty impressive. Twenty-three percent of the student body is minority.

The political lean at Carleton is left. Because the college is so highly regarded and selective, the campus community is comprised of students with talents in many areas. "I am always impressed to find out something amazing that someone here has done," says a student. Students also take community service seriously, serving more than 12,000 hours per school year.

You May Not Know

- Though now non-denominational with no official religious affiliation, Carleton was founded by the General Conference of the Congregational Churches of Minnesota.
- Carleton was the first higher education institute in Minnesota to implement a single-stream recycling program.
- Students first attended classes in the former American House hotel, which is described by the college, "the building's plumbing was disgraceful, its heating meager, and its mice legion."

Distinguished Alumni

Peter Basquin, concert pianist and music educator; Mary-Clair King, professor of genetics at University of Washington; Christopher Kratt, producer of educational television; Glen Sizemore, physician, scholar, and researcher in the field of endocrinology; Ann Parson Wallin, expert in the area of persistent toxic substances and sustainability.

Admissions and Financial Aid

In making admissions decisions, the transcript is "most important" according to the admissions office. Activities outside of the classroom, recommendations, and the essay are given "a great amount of weight" while the ACT or SAT scores are "the last thing" considered. Interviews are not required but strongly recommended. Students who are unable to travel to Carleton's campus for an interview may schedule an interview with an alum in their geographic area.

Finalists in the National Merit Scholarship Program, the National Achievement Scholarship Program, and the National Hispanic Recognition Program are eligible for Carleton scholarships of $2,000 per academic year. Carleton does not offer athletic scholarships.

CARLETON COLLEGE

Highlights

Admissions Criteria
Academic criteria:
Grades: ☆ ☆ ☆
Difficulty of class schedule: ☆ ☆ ☆
Class rank: ☆ ☆ ☆
Standardized test scores: ☆ ☆
Teacher recommendations: ☆ ☆
Personal statement: ☆ ☆
Non-academic criteria considered:
Interview
Extracurricular activities
Special talents, interests, abilities
Character/personal qualities
Volunteer work
Work experience
Geographical location
Minority affiliation
Alumni relationship

Deadlines
Early Action: No
Early Decision: November 15
Regular Action: January 15 (final)
Notification of admission by: April 1
Common Application: Accepted

Financial Aid
In-state tuition: $45,900
Out-of-state tuition: $45,900
Room: $6,279
Board: $5,703
Books: $751
Freshmen receiving need-based aid: 56%
Undergrads rec. need-based aid: 56%
Avg. % of need met by financial aid: 100%
Avg. aid package (freshmen): $35,113
Avg. aid package (undergrads): $37,454
Avg. debt upon graduation: $17,289

School Spirit
Mascot: Knights
Colors: Maize and blue
Song: *Carleton Our Alma Mater*

CARNEGIE MELLON UNIVERSITY

CARNEGIE MELLON UNIVERSITY

Four-year private
Founded: 1900
Pittsburgh, PA
Major city
Pop. 307,484

Address:
5000 Forbes Avenue
Pittsburgh, PA
15213

Admissions:
412-268-2082

Financial Aid:
412-268-2082

undergraduate-admissions@andrew.cmu.edu

www.cmu.edu

Overview

Renowned for its computer science and engineering programs as well as the arts, Carnegie Mellon University is heavy on the workload, males, and nerds while light on social life since students are so busy studying. CMU is actually comprised of seven separate colleges, with students accepted for admission by each individual school.

Carnegie Mellon's campus is three miles from the center of Pittsburgh, Pennsylvania. A panoramic view of the campus from the College of Fine Arts lawn offers a grassy spread punctuated by handsome buildings, including the Cathedral of Learning of neighboring University of Pittsburgh. The campus is near the Carnegie Museums, which, like the university, are part of Andrew Carnegie's legacy.

When not engrossed in their studies, you'll find students building, racing, and cheering Buggies (aerodynamic torpedo-shaped vehicles) and Mobots (mobile robots) as well as the less technologically-complicated cafeteria trays that serve as sleds in the winter. If you celebrate the fact that chess is an intramural sport, this university may be a good fit for you.

Academics

Carnegie Mellon offers more than 200 majors in seven colleges. One student says that despite the university's emphasis on interdisciplinary learning, "It can be difficult to get into classes outside your college." General education requirements vary by college, but typical requirements include courses on communicating, reflecting (societies and cultures), math, social sciences, and design. Students must also take a computing course and freshman seminar.

Difficulty of coursework depends on a student's major, though all students work hard on weekdays and weekends. "The workload is phenomenal," says a student. Carnegie Institute of Technology (CIT) courses are among the most challenging, and students report no grade inflation. Nearly all undergraduate courses are taught by faculty, who are known to be very accessible both in person and by email.

Strong programs include undergraduate business, the computer science department, drama, CIT's various engineering programs, English, and music. CMU offers degree programs in 10 countries and has campuses in Doha, Qatar and Silicon Valley, California. The Fifth-Year Scholars Program allows a handful of exceptional students to stay an extra year at CMU after completing their degree without paying tuition and with a $7,000 fellowship.

Study-abroad opportunities vary by major, financial situation, and semester of study. Many students choose to study abroad during the summer. Those who want to use Carnegie funding must choose from university-sponsored programs or exchange programs, while the option of external programs and direct enrollment offers virtually unlimited study-abroad opportunities.

CMU has more than 70,000 alumni worldwide, making for a strong alumni network. IBM, Lockheed Martin, Google, and Microsoft frequently hire graduates, and 85 percent of CMU students who enter the work force find employment in a field related to their major within a year of graduation. "Our college is widely recognized among some of the biggest employers," comments a student. One third of students attend graduate school within one year of graduating.

Student Life

CMU boasts more than 275 student organizations—in short, something for everyone. The alphabetical listings from A to (almost) Z range from AB Coffeehouse, a committee that brings musical performances to campus, to Young African Leaders Alliance. Arts, music, and drama enjoy several forums on campus: The Frame for student art, the Carnegie Mellon Philharmonic, and the Carnegie Mellon School of Drama. The theater group Scotch'n'Soda is among the oldest in the nation.

The University Center (UC), a mixed-use space, offers plenty of places to hang out. Cheap $1 movies on the weekends at the UC's 450-seat theater are popular to watch, and the athletic facilities there include a swimming pool, and facilities for non-aquatic sports.

A distinct Carnegie Mellon tradition is buggy racing, so don't be surprised if you find students pushing aerodynamic cylinders over a three-quarter mile course at up to 35 mph. "The races are exciting not only for the builders but for spectators too," says a student. The tradition began in 1920, and student groups build the buggies every year to race them at the Spring Carnival. This event—CMU's oldest tradition—features carnival rides, food, and plenty of reminders of Andrew Carnegie's Scottish heritage, from bagpipe players to the university's mascot, a Scottish terrier. If Buggy Races mark the onset of spring, cafeteria trays are the competitive vehicle of choice in the winter, when you'll find students speeding down slopes on these makeshift sleds. As if buggies and sleds weren't enough, there is also the Mobot races, an annual competition where mobile robots must autonomously pass through gates to reach the finish line.

The CMU tradition with year-round visibility is The Fence, the university's billboard for announcements on the Cut, the campus' central grassy lawn. The Fence must be painted between midnight and sunrise, and students even guard their artistic announcements through the night. Greek events are often advertised, as CMU has a fairly active Greek scene, with 15 percent of men and 14 percent of women pledging to the 24 fraternities and sororities. As for athletics, students are more enthused about intramural sports—of which there are over 30—than the Division III intercollegiate sports. "It's sad that our teams are not very well supported, but most of us are too busy to get into school spirit," explains a student.

Off campus, the bars and restaurants of nearby Oakland and Squirrel Hill are popular. Students also enjoy the museums, cultural performances, and professional athletics of Pittsburgh. The city's waterfront offers shopping and a movie theater. "Pittsburgh is not known for it, but the city has a great music scene," attests a student.

Freshmen are required to live on campus, and housing is guaranteed for all four years. Most first-year students live in Mudge House, a mansion donated by the Mudge family. The top two floors were converted into student housing, and first floor living, dining, and parlor rooms were remodeled to create a spacious lounge, study area, and TV room. Some dorms are for men only, and there is also gender neutral housing.

Student Body

Carnegie Mellon's undergraduate student body has very high ethnic diversity, with 38 percent minority students, as well as remarkable geographic diversity with 85 percent of students coming from out of state. There is also a sizeable international student population at 18 percent.

With 57 percent of the student population male, the dating odds are curved in favor of women. Additionally, some female students complain that a large number of the men are socially awkward. "The guys seem to be more into building buggies or problem sets

CARNEGIE MELLON UNIVERSITY

Highlights

Students
Total enrollment: 12,569
Undergrads: 6,279
Freshmen: 1,408
From out-of-state: 85%
Male/Female: 57%/43%
Live on-campus: 64%
In fraternities: 15%
In sororities: 14%
Off-campus employment rating: Excellent
Caucasian: 39%
African American: 5%
Hispanic: 7%
Asian / Pacific Islander: 22%
Native American: 0%
Mixed (2+ ethnicities): 4%
International: 18%

Academics
Calendar: Semester
Student/faculty ratio: 13:1
Class size 9 or fewer: 35%
Class size 10-29: 46%
Class size 30-49: 9%
Class size 50-99: 6%
Class size 100 or more: 4%
Returning freshmen: 95%
Six-year graduation rate: 87%
Graduates who immediately go to graduate school: 30%

Most Popular Majors
Computer science
Electrical/computer engineering
Business administration

Admissions
Applicants: 17,313
Accepted: 4,807
Acceptance rate: 27.8%
Placed on wait list: 3,664
Average GPA: 3.7
ACT range: 29-33
SAT Math range: 690-790
SAT Reading range: 630-730
SAT Writing range: 50-41
Top 10% of class: 76%
Top 25% of class: 93%
Top 50% of class: 99%

141

College Profiles

CARNEGIE MELLON UNIVERSITY

Admissions Criteria

Academic criteria:
Grades: ☆ ☆ ☆
Difficulty of class schedule: ☆ ☆ ☆
Class rank: ☆ ☆ ☆
Standardized test scores: ☆ ☆ ☆
Teacher recommendations: ☆ ☆
Personal statement: ☆ ☆
Non-academic criteria considered:
Interview
Extracurricular activities
Special talents, interests, abilities
Character/personal qualities
Volunteer work
Work experience
State of residency
Minority affiliation
Alumni relationship

Deadlines

Early Action: No
Early Decision: November 1
Regular Action: January 1 (December 1
   for fine arts applicants) (final)
Notification of admission by: April 15
Common Application: Accepted

Financial Aid

In-state tuition: $46,670
Out-of-state tuition: $46,670
Room: $7,070
Board: $4,920
Books: $2,400
Freshmen receiving need-based aid: 53%
Undergrads rec. need-based aid: 46%
Avg. % of need met by financial aid: 83%
Avg. aid package (freshmen): $31,612
Avg. aid package (undergrads): $32,077
Avg. debt upon graduation: $31,747

School Spirit

Mascot: Tartan
Colors: Cardinal, grey, and white
Song: *Fight for the Glory of Carnegie*

than dating," says a student. The vast majority of students, male or female, are career-driven and therefore focused on doing well in classes. That means CMU students aren't afraid to work hard, spending weekends on schoolwork and summers on internships.

While Carnegie Mellon may have a reputation as a techie school, there are also many students in the arts, making for a dichotomy of computer/engineering nerds and artsy students. "There is a definite divide between the two groups," laughs a student.

You May Not Know

- Carnegie Mellon's Internet domain, cmu.edu, was among the first six .edu URLs when it launched on April 24, 1984.
- The School of Computer Science held the first Internet-enabled Coke machine, which allowed students to check the supply of sodas from their computers.
- CMU is affiliated with 18 Nobel Laureates, seven Emmy Award recipients, and three Academy Award winners.

Distinguished Alumni

James Gosling, software developer who created the Java programming language; Stephanie Kwolek, National Medal of Technology recipient and inventor of Kevlar; John Forbes Nash, Nobel Prize winner in Economic Sciences; Andy Warhol, pop artist.

Admissions and Financial Aid

Admission to CMU is competitive, particularly for the School of Computer Science, which admitted only about 8 percent of applicants for fall 2012. Applicants must fill out the Common Application, send *all* standardized test scores, and arrange for an audition or portfolio review if necessary—for example, if applying for certain schools in the College of Fine Arts. Academic requirements vary by college.

The college cannot guarantee meeting each family's financial aid, though admission to Carnegie Mellon is need blind. CMU reviews financial awards to compete with certain private institutions a student is admitted to under the regular decision plan, and early decision students' full demonstrated need is met by the university. CMU proudly notes their "use of statistical modeling as an aid in the distribution of limited financial aid dollars." The model "takes into account students' intended majors, academic and artistic talents, non-academic talents and abilities, as well as financial need."

CMU offers limited scholarship options that include the Carnegie Scholarships for "academically and artistically talented middle income students who qualify for little to no need-based financial aid." There are also ROTC scholarships and need-based corporation and foundation scholarships.

CASE WESTERN RESERVE UNIVERSITY

Overview

Based in Cleveland, Ohio, Case Western Reserve University is a private university renowned for its unique history of innovative alumni, strengths in independent research, and strong academic programs. Known also as CWRU or "crew," the university focuses heavily on experiential learning and was ranked 37th in the nation by *U.S. News & World Report*.

The 155-acre university is roughly five miles east of bustling downtown Cleveland in University Circle, which features a wide range of educational, medical, and cultural institutions. Within this urban setting, the campus architecture ranges from the traditional splendor of Adelbert Hall, and the regal Hadyn Hall, to the modern chic of the Peter B. Lewis building designed by renowned architect Frank Gehry.

Notably, this university takes pride in giving back to its surrounding community, with campus-wide events such as Case for Community Day. Service-oriented groups, like the Center for Civic Engagement and Learning, also keep students engaged in service throughout the school year. Given all of these strengths, this is likely to be a good match for the student who has a passion for the sciences and engineering, a sharp interest in cultural offerings, and a need for an accepting environment. It is also worth noting that though many students fit the stereotype of engineering and science nerds, (with the Sci–Fi marathon being a huge draw), there is an active student social life with a vibrant Greek system, parties, and creative outlets. However, being able to take the notorious Cleveland winters is a must.

Academics

Even though it has an undergraduate population of only 4,400 students, students note that Case Western still manages to provide the resources of a larger university. CWRU faculty members tend to bring their subjects to life through "lively discussions" and "involved lectures." The academic experience is often described as one that provides students with small seminars, accessible faculty mentoring, and hands-on learning. The university has a reputation for being academically challenging. In fact, students have adapted to the rigors of CWRU by creating unique traditions that serve as de-stressors. One such event is the traditional Midnight Scream, a campus-wide scream by students at midnight before the start of finals.

CWRU also offers innovative general education curricula through its Seminar Approach to General Education and Scholarship (SAGES). Students first complete three interdisciplinary seminars during their freshman and sophomore years. Junior year requires a departmental seminar in the student's major, and senior year requires a capstone project.

There are 75 majors and minors offered. Strong academic programs include unique offerings and resources in biomedical engineering, health law, nonprofit management, nursing, premed studies, and social work. Case Western also provides combined undergraduate and graduate studies. These include access to BS/MS degrees, Integrated Graduate Studies, Accounting, BS in Engineering/Master of Engineering and Management, Senior Year in Professional Studies at CWRU, and Senior Year in Absentia. Additionally, exceptional students are accepted both to the undergraduate college and graduate school through the Pre-Professional Scholars Program (PPSP) for dental medicine, law, medicine, and social work. The medical positions are "highly sought after," explains a student. The Emerging Leaders Program gives first year students an "opportunity to develop a foundation of leadership skills by providing knowledge and experiences essential for lifelong leadership engagement."

Case Western's Study Abroad Program recognizes programs from over 40 countries. Students can also opt to remain within the U.S. and take advantage of a unique

CASE WESTERN RESERVE UNIVERSITY

Highlights

Students
Total enrollment: 10,026
Undergrads: 4,386
Freshmen: 1,429
From out-of-state: 66%
From public schools: 70%
Male/Female: 56%/44%
Live on-campus: 77%
In fraternities: 39%
In sororities: 33%
Off-campus employment rating: Excellent
Caucasian: 54%
African American: 5%
Hispanic: 5%
Asian / Pacific Islander: 18%
Native American: 0%
Mixed (2+ ethnicities): 3%
International: 8%

Academics
Calendar: Semester
Student/faculty ratio: 9:1
Class size 9 or fewer: 21%
Class size 10-29: 54%
Class size 30-49: 15%
Class size 50-99: 7%
Class size 100 or more: 3%
Returning freshmen: 92%
Six-year graduation rate: 78%
Graduates who immediately go to graduate school: 38%
Graduates who immediately enter career related to major: 48%

Most Popular Majors
Engineering
Nursing
Biology

Admissions
Applicants: 14,778
Accepted: 8,027
Acceptance rate: 54.3%
Placed on wait list: 3,480
Enrolled from wait list: 39
Average GPA: Not reported
ACT range: 29-33
SAT Math range: 660-760
SAT Reading range: 600-720
SAT Writing range: 29-49
Top 10% of class: 74%
Top 25% of class: 94%
Top 50% of class: 100%

exchange program with Fisk University, enabling students to spend a semester at the university.

Upon graduation, students join over 100,000 alumni in the university's alumni association. When it comes to internships and careers, students and alumni draw upon resources through the CWRU Career Center. The Center provides access to career workshops, career fairs, career searching resources, and means of gaining experience or securing advanced studies. Forty-four percent of students attend graduate school within one year of graduating.

Student Life

Students note the popularity of on-campus events, including traditions such as the 26-mile Hudson Relays, which draw teams from each class year to run within the University Circle area. Another popular event is the Sci-Fi Marathon, held by the Film Society since 1974. Described as the oldest of its type, the film festival features over 30 hours of movies. The Drag Ball is hosted by Spectrum, one of many student organizations aiming to increase positive awareness of LGBT life on campus. Contestants take the stage, dancing, modeling, and lip-syncing for the crowd, while the audience selects winners and submits donations to charity. The Drag Ball is "wildly entertaining," says a student.

Greek organizations are highly active with more than one third of students pledging. There are 15 fraternities and eight active sororities on campus, including the nine historically Black Greek fraternities and sororities. Greek Week is a time to "show chapter pride with the entire Case fraternal community." Events include a food drive, rope pull, and obstacle course.

CWRU supports 19 Division III sports. The school mascot is the Spartan, often found sporting the university colors of Case blue, white, and Case grey, getting crowds riled up against the university's main rival, Carnegie Mellon. Over half the undergraduates participate in the 40+ intramural competitions.

Students can also access a number of on-campus and off-campus entertainment options within walking distance, or via a short bus ride. University Circle surrounds campus with a rich offering of the arts, music, and history, while neighborhoods all over Cleveland provide a wide range of cultural institutions. For instance, the Cleveland Orchestra performs at Severance Hall, which abuts the campus. Students praise the accessibility of the Cleveland Museum of Art, the Cleveland Play House, the Rock and Roll Hall of Fame, and the Squire Valleevue Farm and Cleveland Metroparks.

Though Cleveland is not known as a college town, it has a fair number of restaurants, bars, shopping, and professional athletic teams associated with it. Students often frequent The Coffee House on campus, which has become a Cleveland institution, but also visit Little Italy, said to have the "best pizza in Cleveland." Students also visit Coventry, an eclectic village, featuring restaurants and shopping. Though there are both nice and less nice parts of the surrounding town, one student says, "We know where we're safe and where to avoid."

CWRU residential villages are all recently renovated, and first-year students reside within one of nine residence halls, spread among three residential colleges, namely Cedar (focusing on "Growth through the Arts"), Juniper ("Knowledge through Multiculturalism"), or Mistletoe ("Leadership through Service"). CWRU has a two-year residency requirement. The South Residential Village is particularly popular among second-year students, located within walking distance of historic Little Italy, Coventry Road, and the Cedar-Fairmont areas. The Village at 115 is "popular among upperclassmen." This new Village incorporates seven apartment-style residential complexes with accommodations for approximately 740 students.

Student Body

CWRU maintains a strong level of ethnic diversity with more than one-quarter of its student population representative of minorities. The school is also geographically diverse with two-thirds of its students hailing from out of state, representing 41 states and 9 countries.

Students complain about the male-to-female ratio. "The guys moan that there aren't enough girls on campus, and the girls say that there are a lot of guys, but the pool of desirable ones is low," says a student.

You May Not Know

- University professors Albert Michelson and Edward Morley conducted interferometer experiments to support Einstein's Special Theory of Relativity, and Morley determined the atomic weights of oxygen and hydrogen.
- In 1896, Professor Dayton C. Miller took the first full-body x-ray—his own.
- In 1930, alumnus Al Gross invented the walkie-talkie, and in 1949 he invented the pager.

Distinguished Alumni

Herbert Henry Dow, founder of Dow Chemical; John J.R. Macleod, discoverer of insulin; Dennis Kucinich, U.S. Representative; Craig Newmark, founder of Craigslist.

Admissions and Financial Aid

The admissions office urges students to make their essay "genuine" and to "personalize it." About one fifth of students are selected for on-campus interviews.

There are 11 merit-based scholarships, including full-tuition awards such as the Adelbert Alumnus Scholarship, Warren E. Rupp Engineering Scholarship, and Andrew and Eleanor Squire Scholarship. Additional scholarships may be available via Cleveland Scholarships Programs, which recently awarded $2.7 million to 2,156 students.

CASE WESTERN RESERVE UNIVERSITY

Highlights

Admissions Criteria
Academic criteria:
Grades: ☆ ☆ ☆
Difficulty of class schedule: ☆ ☆ ☆
Class rank: ☆ ☆ ☆
Standardized test scores: ☆ ☆ ☆
Teacher recommendations: ☆ ☆
Personal statement: ☆ ☆
Non-academic criteria considered:
Interview
Extracurricular activities
Special talents, interests, abilities
Character/personal qualities
Volunteer work
Work experience
State of residency
Minority affiliation
Alumni relationship

Deadlines
Early Action: November 1
Early Decision: No
Regular Action: January 15 (final)
Notification of admission by: March 20
Common Application: Accepted

Financial Aid
In-state tuition: $41,420
Out-of-state tuition: $41,420
Room: $7,140
Board: $5,296
Books: $1,200
Freshmen receiving need-based aid: 62%
Undergrads rec. need-based aid: 65%
Avg. % of need met by financial aid: 82%
Avg. aid package (freshmen): $33,989
Avg. aid package (undergrads): $33,214
Avg. debt upon graduation: $37,640

School Spirit
Mascot: Spartan
Colors: Blue, gray, and white
Song: *Fight on Case Reserve*

CATHOLIC UNIVERSITY OF AMERICA

CATHOLIC
UNIVERSITY OF
AMERICA

Four-year private
Founded: 1887
Washington, DC
Major city
Pop. 617,996

Address:
620 Michigan Avenue,
NE
Washington, DC
20064

Admissions:
800-673-2772

Financial Aid:
888-635-7788

cua-admissions@cua.
edu

www.cua.edu

Overview

Founded in 1887, the Catholic University of America is the only official university of the Catholic Church in the United States. Located just a few blocks from downtown Washington DC, Catholic University students enjoy convenient access to the unique internship opportunities and vibrant cultural activities that characterize America's capitol.

While Catholic University is in the middle of a bustling metropolis, the campus itself is enclosed, serene, and filled with large green common areas. The university's distinct architecture includes a mixture of historic Gothic buildings and contemporary designs. Next door to the university is the largest Catholic church in the United States—the Basilica of the National Shrine of the Immaculate Conception. Many Catholic University students attend regular masses at the Basilica. Although students are not required to be Catholic to attend the university, a large majority of the student body are practicing Catholics.

Academics

The university's Catholic underpinnings support its mission as a rigorous academic institution "dedicated to advancing the dialogue between faith and reason" and seeking to "discover and impart the truth through excellence in teaching and research." Catholic University offers 80 majors, with some of the strongest being architecture, drama, engineering, music, nursing, and religious studies. While all students are held to high academic expectations, the science and engineering courses at Catholic University are particularly rigorous. Class sizes normally range from 10 to 19 students, facilitating the development of close ties between students and faculty. "I feel like I can always reach out to my professors," one student confides.

The freshmen core liberal arts curriculum is required of all students and consists of philosophy, writing, and other humanities courses. Freshmen are able to complement these core studies with some classes in other fields of interest. Many majors, especially in the sciences, require that students declare their major by the end of sophomore year. However, *all* majors require electives outside a student's immediate field of study to be added to the freshmen liberal arts core curriculum.

The Honors Program at Catholic University entitles its students to a host of privileges, including honors seminar classes, priority class registration, honors housing options, honors research opportunities, and unique study-abroad programs, such as a 10-day European Honors Seminar. Students who are not in the Honors program may also study abroad for either short-term (spring break or summer) or long-term (semester or academic year). There are study-abroad opportunities in over 18 countries on every continent, with curriculum varying depending on the program. A number of the study-abroad offerings include internships, such as parliamentary internship in England and Ireland. Many—but not all—of the affiliated universities in the Catholic University study-abroad network are also Catholic.

Due its location in central Washington DC, Catholic University stands out as having first-rate internship opportunities. Many students work or intern for both government and non-government organizations, such as the Pentagon, National Institute of Health, and the Smithsonian. "Our location is the best in the country," remarks a student, "especially if you want to do anything related to politics or policy." There are bountiful research options on campus; Catholic University recently received the designation of "doctoral-research extensive" by the Carnegie Foundation.

Catholic University students also have research and academic opportunities beyond the school's purview and the DC vicinity. Catholic University is a member of the Consortium of Universities, which allows its students to register for classes in any of the 14 universities in the Consortium. Additionally, Catholic University is a member of Oak Ridge Associated Universities, which gives students access to federal research facilities across the country.

Catholic University alumni have enjoyed great success in the workforce, with 87 percent of graduates entering a field related to their major within six months of graduation.

Student Life

Students at Catholic University participate in a variety of student groups, the most prominent being Campus Ministry, the hub for Catholic spiritual activities. Like many other student groups, Campus Ministry provides community service opportunities within the city, such as homeless outreach, visits to nursing homes, and tutoring services. "Everyone I know is involved in community service in some way," shares a student. Political organizations and performing arts groups are also popular.

There are a number of annual events and traditions that Catholic University students look forward to every year. Metro Madness, a massive scavenger hunt through Washington DC, kicks off the start of the school year in September. In early spring, the formal Beaux Arts Ball takes place in one of DC's most famous museums. Luaupalooza is a lively celebration on the last day of classes, where students enjoy free food, games, music, and Luau events.

Catholic University has 21 Division III teams, although intercollegiate sports do not play a large role in campus life. One student explains, "There's too much else going on to be that supportive of team sports." Students have the opportunity to participate in a number of club sports as well as intramural ones, such as flag football, tennis, and badminton. For casual sports, students often take advantage of the green spaces on sunny fall and spring days to play Frisbee or football.

There are no housed Greek organizations on campus, but students have a good time without fraternities and sororities. They throw small-scale parties and attend gatherings at other universities. With a Metro station located conveniently on campus, students are able to take advantage of the numerous museums, national monuments, bars and clubs, restaurants, and cultural events throughout the Washington DC area. Due to the college's location in the heart of the city, students learn to take extra safety precautions, such as traveling in groups after dark. "I never feel unsafe, but I also never walk around at night by myself," confides a student.

Almost 60 percent of Catholic University students live on campus. There are two major sets of residences. The first is Centennial Village, which is located near the Pryzbyia student center. The second housing option is the newly constructed Millennium complex, which offers state-of-the-art suites and apartment-style rooms. Due to the university's Catholic affiliation, students are not allowed to have guests stay overnight in their rooms.

Outside of the residences, students utilize the Kane Student Health and Fitness Center's weight training circuits, treadmills, ellipticals, and stationary bikes. At the DuFour Athletics Center, students can use the pool, basketball court, racquetball court, indoor and outdoor track.

CATHOLIC UNIVERSITY OF AMERICA

Highlights

Students
Total enrollment: 6,838
Undergrads: 3,694
Freshmen: 1,095
Part-time students: 7%
From out-of-state: 99%
From public schools: 54%
Male/Female: 45%/55%
Live on-campus: 59%
In fraternities: 1%
In sororities: 1%
Off-campus employment rating: Good
Caucasian: 61%
African American: 5%
Hispanic: 9%
Asian / Pacific Islander: 3%
Native American: 0%
Mixed (2+ ethnicities): 3%
International: 4%

Academics
Calendar: Semester
Student/faculty ratio: 9:1
Class size 9 or fewer: 16%
Class size 10-29: 65%
Class size 30-49: 15%
Class size 50-99: 4%
Class size 100 or more: -
Returning freshmen: 84%
Six-year graduation rate: 67%

Most Popular Majors
Architecture
Politics
Nursing

Admissions
Applicants: 6,361
Accepted: 4,017
Acceptance rate: 63.2%
Average GPA: 3.4
ACT range: 22-27
SAT Math range: 500-610
SAT Reading range: 510-610
SAT Writing range: Not reported

CATHOLIC UNIVERSITY OF AMERICA

Admissions Criteria
Academic criteria:
Grades: ☆ ☆ ☆
Difficulty of class schedule: ☆ ☆ ☆
Class rank: ☆
Standardized test scores: ☆ ☆ ☆
Teacher recommendations: ☆ ☆ ☆
Personal statement: ☆ ☆
Non-academic criteria considered:
Interview
Extracurricular activities
Special talents, interests, abilities
Character/personal qualities
Volunteer work
Work experience
State of residency
Geographical location
Alumni relationship

Deadlines
Early Action: November 15
Early Decision: No
Regular Action: February 15 (final)
Notification of admission by: March 15
Common Application: Accepted

Financial Aid
In-state tuition: $38,000
Out-of-state tuition: $38,000
Room: $7,112
Board: $3,020
Books: $1,440
Freshmen receiving need-based aid: 65%
Undergrads rec. need-based aid: 61%
Avg. % of need met by financial aid: 77%
Avg. aid package (freshmen): $25,293
Avg. aid package (undergrads): $22,879

School Spirit
Mascot: Cardinals
Colors: Red and black

Student Body

A large majority of students at the university are practicing Catholics who attend daily masses, night prayers, and religious retreats. "You won't feel unwelcome if you're not Catholic," says a student, "but you'll definitely be in the minority." The student body has high ethnic diversity, with 20 percent of the students being non-white. The university also has extremely high geographic diversity, with 99 percent of its student body coming from out of state.

Catholic University's beginnings placed significance on its graduate school, and the university today still has about the same number of graduate students as undergraduates. "You'll interact some with graduate students," explains one student, "but you'll definitely interact more with undergrads."

As one might expect, the university's location in Washington DC does facilitate a politically active student body. On the whole, students tend to lean conservative given their Catholic background. In particular, Catholic University is known for its pro-life activism, hosting participants in "March for Life" on Washington each year.

Because Catholic University supports the Vatican in its oppositional views toward homosexuality, there are no official LBGT student groups or services on campus.

You May Not Know

- The Basilica of the National Shrine of the Immaculate Conception is the largest Catholic church in the U.S. and the seventh largest Catholic church in the world.
- Washington DC is home to 400,000+ university students.
- Catholic University does not allow public figures whose views are known to conflict with those of the Vatican—particularly on the issue of abortion—to speak at the university.

Distinguished Alumni

Robert P. Casey, U.S. Senator, Pennsylvania; Brian M. Cashman, General Manager, New York Yankees; Maureen David, columnist, *The New York Times*.

Admissions and Financial Aid

The university looks at the "whole person" for admission decisions and seeks "well-rounded" students. According to the admissions office, a student who "can boast a strong grade point average and standardized test scores as well as one who is actively involved in school, church, and/or community" is a strong candidate.

Catholic University has a need-blind admission policy. While the university does not promise to meet all of a student's demonstrated financial need, on average, 77 percent of the student body's demonstrated need is met. The most prestigious scholarships are Archdiocesan Scholarships; these are four year, full-tuition scholarships offered to five students who have outstanding academic merit. There are a number of other smaller scholarships available based on various qualifications, which are outlined in detail on the Catholic University of America Financial Aid website.

CENTRE COLLEGE

Overview

The "centre" in Centre College refers to the small private liberal arts college location in the *center* of Kentucky. When it comes to national rankings, Centre is often far above the center: *Forbes* recently ranked the college first in the nation among religiously affiliated colleges, while *Consumers Digest* rated Centre as the number one "educational value" in the nation.

City-dwellers may not be enthused by the college's location in historic Danville, with its restrictions on the sale of alcohol and lack of activities, but students can make a trek to Lexington, just 30 miles away. For what the town of Danville might lack in social events, the college makes up for it. With almost all of the 1,300 students living on the 152-acre campus, social interactions abound. Students all eat in the same place and even the president of the college addresses students by first name.

The campus can feel homogeneous due to the lack of ethnic diversity, the largely Christian student body, and the fact that virtually all students participate in Greek life and/or athletics. Luckily, those who want to get away are backed by the "Centre Commitment," which guarantees students 1) an internship 2) a study-abroad experience and 3) that all students will graduate within four years. To back up this promise, Centre offers a free passport to incoming first-year students and offers to pay for up to one year of additional study if students don't graduate in four years.

Academics

Centre offers 27 majors, 28 minors, the option to create a self-designed major, and dual-degree engineering programs with four universities. Double majors are common. Centre requires all students demonstrate basic skill requirements in expository writing, foreign language, and mathematics, as well as general education requirements such humanities, social studies, and science courses, along with two religion or philosophy courses in "fundamental questions." The Convocation Requirement is co-curricular—convocations are designated events that bring the Centre Community together.

Undergrads appreciate that professors are not dividing their time among grad students. Small class sizes—virtually all classes have fewer than 50 students—help foster this level of closeness. "There's a lot of work, but there's also a lot of help from the truly dedicated professors," says a student. Strong majors include art (art history and studio art), English, government, and history; the pre-med program is also well-regarded.

Centre's 4-1-4 schedule includes a three-week term called CentreTerm in January, where students can study abroad; for example, visit volcanoes, geysers, and hot springs in New Zealand while skydiving during their free time. CentreTerm also includes unusual course offerings. Previous topics have included Duke Ellington, the psychology of Alfred Hitchcock films, and "Snakes on a Plane" (examining the biological, cultural and social aspects of snakes). Steve Powell, a famous hot glass artist, often teaches a course in one of the country's few collegiate glass studios.

More than four-fifths of students study abroad, the highest rate in any Kentucky college or university and among the highest rates in the nation. Centre operates its own study-abroad sites in England, France, and Latin America. Short-term study programs have recently included China, New Zealand, and Costa Rica as destinations.

Internships are guaranteed at the college, and the Career Services Office helps students during their time at Centre and also offers lifetime career counseling. According to the college, 97 percent of Centre students are employed or engaged in advanced study within 10 months of graduation, and about 40 percent earn advanced degrees within 10 years.

CENTRE COLLEGE

Four-year private
Founded: 1819
Danville, KY
Small town
Pop. 16,273

Address:
600 West Walnut
Street
Danville, KY
40422

Admissions:
800-423-6236

Financial Aid:
800-423-6236

admission@centre.edu

www.centre.edu

CENTRE COLLEGE

Students
Total enrollment: 1,344
Undergrads: 1,344
From out-of-state: 47%
Male/Female: 47%/53%
Live on-campus: 99%
In fraternities: 41%
In sororities: 38%
Off-campus employment rating: Fair
Caucasian: 84%
African American: 5%
Hispanic: 2%
Asian / Pacific Islander: 3%
Native American: 0%
Mixed (2+ ethnicities): 3%
International: 3%

Academics
Calendar: 4-1-4 system
Student/faculty ratio: 11:1
Class size 9 or fewer: 19%
Class size 10-29: 69%
Class size 30-49: 12%
Class size 50-99: -
Class size 100 or more: -
Returning freshmen: 91%
Six-year graduation rate: 87%
Graduates who immediately go to graduate school: 30%
Graduates who immediately enter career related to major: 46%

Most Popular Majors
Economics/financial economics
History
English, psychology

Admissions
Applicants: 2,539
Accepted: 1,768
Acceptance rate: 69.6%
Placed on wait list: 141
Enrolled from wait list: 9
Average GPA: 3.7
ACT range: 26-31
SAT Math range: 580-700
SAT Reading range: 560-690
SAT Writing range: 16-47
Top 10% of class: 49%
Top 25% of class: 79%
Top 50% of class: 95%

150

Student Life

There are restrictions on when students are allowed to go into the dorm rooms of members of the opposite sex. This doesn't seem to deter the long-term matchmaking that occurs for Centre students: according to a recent study of alumni, about one out of five Centre alums marry another student from the college. While dating prospects may be easy to find, alcohol is another matter: students often make 60-mile round-trip beer runs because of restrictions on the sale of alcohol in Danville. "It seems extreme, but you have to do what you have to do," says a student.

Social life is—pardon the pun—centered on campus, where virtually all students live, many of whom participate in the 80 student organizations. The popularity of the Centre Christian Fellowship attests to students' strong religious faith, while the Bonner Program demonstrates students' commitment to service. The Bonner Scholars and Bonner Leaders programs not only include opportunities to serve but also offer scholarships and loan forgiveness.

There is a very strong Greek system with more than one third of men and women pledging to one of the 10 fraternities and sororities. Almost all parties are held in the fraternities, though these frat parties are open to nonmembers.

The Student Activities Council (SAC) offers at least one campus-wide event each week. Some of these include Capture the Flag game, Dive-in Movies held at the college's indoor pool, and the enormously popular Midnight Movies with free showings of current films. SAC puts on the annual Spring Carnival, which first began in 1903 and has now become a well established institution. The front lawn of Old Centre is transformed by inflatable games, free food, and music.

Two of Centre's traditions are a bit quirky: Running the Flame and Kissing on the Seal. Running the Flame is a popular event where unclothed students race from frat houses to a large metal sculpture called "The Flame," which they must then run around. Kissing on the Seal is an act which is obviously mclore private. Two students who kiss while standing on the college's seal at the stroke of midnight are destined to get married.

While running around campus unclothed may not appeal to everywhere, sports certainly do: 40 percent of the student body participates in one or more of the 19 Division III sports on campus, and 80 percent of students participate in intramurals, which offer 15 sports. "Unless you're a hermit, you participate in sports of some kind," says a student. The Centre Colonels also hold a place in athletic lore: in 1921, Centre's football team upset Harvard 6-0: this is what the C6H0 painted on the side of one of Centre's historical buildings refers to.

Virtually all students live on campus. Many of the residence halls are single-sex dorms or separate gender by floor. Students of the opposite sex are not allowed to sleep over. The newest residence, Pearl Hall, was built in 2008 and is "where everyone wants to live," remarks a student. The building is the first in all of Kentucky to be certified LEED GOLD for its environmentally friendly design and construction.

Student Body

Forty-seven percent of the 1,300 undergrads who attend Centre come from out of state. Though this signifies geographic diversity, ethnic diversity is much lower with only 13 percent minority students. Christianity is strong among students: a recent study of alumni found that 75 percent called themselves Christians. "Everyone is friendly, but there's sometimes a line drawn between Christians and non-Christians," says a student.

An extensive alumni survey of the classes of 1969 to 1994 by sociologist Beau Weston provides a profile of Centre alumni. Weston found that most Centre College alumni participated in Greek life, played sports at least recreationally, and went to parties. Alumni pursued graduate degrees, most commonly in law, married, and had at least two kids. The majority are very religious Christians who lived in suburbs, with 43 percent of all alumni living in Kentucky. Most are Democrats, though closer to the political middle than extreme.

You May Not Know

- Centre College faced six wars after its founding in 1819, including the occupation of Old Centre, the first building on campus. Both the Confederate and Union troops used the building as a hospital during the Civil War.
- Even after he died in 1953, former U.S. Supreme Court Justice Fred Vinson is able to attend football games. The Phi Delta Theta fraternity members take a portrait of him to every home game and even some away games.
- Centre alumni include two vice presidents, two U.S. Supreme Court Justices, and 10 governors.

Distinguished Alumni

Stephen Powell, internationally acclaimed glass blower; Adlai Stevenson, Vice President of the United States; Mary Hall Surface, playwright and producer; Isaac Tigrett, founder of the Hard Rock Café and the House of Blues.

Admissions and Financial Aid

The college gives "most weight to quality of high school coursework, achievement in those courses, and teacher evaluations." Standardized test scores are required, and there is no online application fee.

Centre College proudly cites its rating by the *U.S. News & World Report* as the "most affordable of any top-50 liberal arts colleges in the nation." The need-based aid system at Centre meets students' demonstrated need.

Centre also offers a number of scholarships based on academics, extracurricular activities, or leadership—though there are no athletic scholarships. The Brown Fellows Program offers a "full-ride-plus" with tuition, room and board covered for four years, plus four summer enrichment programs that have included a trip to Panama, while the Centre Fellows Scholarship Program guarantees a minimum scholarship level of $12,500 per year for students nominated by their high school counselors.

CENTRE COLLEGE

Highlights

Admissions Criteria
Academic criteria:
Grades: ☆ ☆ ☆
Difficulty of class schedule: ☆ ☆ ☆
Class rank: ☆ ☆
Standardized test scores: ☆ ☆
Teacher recommendations: ☆
Personal statement: ☆ ☆
Non-academic criteria considered:
Interview
Extracurricular activities
Special talents, interests, abilities
Character/personal qualities
Volunteer work
Work experience
Geographical location
Minority affiliation
Alumni relationship

Deadlines
Early Action: December 1
Early Decision: No
Regular Action: January 15 (final)
Notification of admission by: March 15
Common Application: Accepted

Financial Aid
In-state tuition: $36,000
Out-of-state tuition: $36,000
Room: Varies
Board: Varies
Books: $1,400
Freshmen receiving need-based aid: 64%
Undergrads rec. need-based aid: 63%
Avg. % of need met by financial aid: 84%
Avg. aid package (freshmen): $27,404
Avg. aid package (undergrads): $26,961
Avg. debt upon graduation: $21,800

School Spirit
Mascot: Colonels
Colors: Gold and white
Song: *Centre Dear*

**CHAPMAN
UNIVERSITY**

Four-year private
Founded: 1861
Orange, CA
Major city
Pop. 138,409

Address:
1 University Drive
Orange, CA
92866

Admissions:
888-CU-APPLY

Financial Aid:
714-997-6741

admit@chapman.edu

www.chapman.edu

CHAPMAN UNIVERSITY

Overview

Chapman is a church-affiliated, non-profit university renowned for its strong combination of liberal arts and professional programs. Located in Orange County, California, Chapman is a wonderful place to study film and media, as Hollywood is only 30 miles away and the school encourages internships in the industry. Experiential learning in all areas is supported through research mentorships and study-abroad programs. But perhaps what is most notable is the 14:1 faculty-to-student ratio, especially meaningful because of the effort that professors make to engage with and get to know students. More than 5,600 students call the palm-lined campus their home—or at least the place where they take classes, as 34 percent of students live on campus. Nevertheless, Chapman students create community through constant arts events, athletics, and service projects.

Academics

A Chapman education begins with general education mandates, which aim to help students lead "inquiring, ethical, and productive lives as global citizens." All students are required to take one Freshman Foundations Course, which is an introduction to university-level work in a wide array of subjects, from globalization, citizenship, and consumption to expeditions: leadership lessons from Shackleton and the Polar Explorers. Next are the Shared Inquiry Courses, where students must complete units in different dimensions of scholarship, including artistic, written, quantitative, and ethical. Finally, students must take 12 units outside their major area for a Multidisciplinary Cluster, and 12 units in the Global Citizen Cluster.

For incoming freshman, Chapman offers four first-year programs: the Associates Program, which holds seminars on how to be academically successful in college; the Leadership Academy, which is a twice-a-year weekend retreat where students develop their personal leadership abilities; First Nights, which are fun monthly events providing an alternative to drunken partying; and finally, the Peer Mentoring program. "Adjusting to freshman year was easy. There was always someone available or somewhere to turn to for help," says a student.

Chapman offers 45 majors with more than 60 areas of study, with the most popular being business administration, film and production, communication studies, psychology, and public relations and advertising. The quality of faculty in these programs is matched by the facilities; for instance, the Dodge College of Film and Media Arts offers a 76,000 square foot studio where faculty has worked on more than 150 feature films. Chapman's location only 30 miles away from Hollywood gives students a close-up experience with the industry, facilitating "internships with studios and production companies as well as on-campus visits from major Hollywood directors, cinematographers, editors, screenwriters, digital artists, PR and ad execs, and others."

Professors, not teaching assistants, teach all classes and students develop close relationships with their professors. Chapman prides itself on its small class size, with only 1 percent of classes having 50 or more students. "Every professor I've had really cares about his or her students," comments a student. Additional support comes from the Tutoring, Learning, and Testing Center, which provides Math and Computer Science Clinics, weekly study sessions for particularly difficult classes, writing and editing mentorship, and tutoring in almost every subject.

Chapman encourages experiential learning with many different initiatives, including domestic and international internships, individually designed projects, student-faculty mentored research, and study-abroad programs. The abroad programs are located in a sweeping array of cities and countries, from The Alliance for Global Education, International Business in China, to SIT Study Abroad Tanzania: Wildlife Conservation and Political Ecology.

The Career Development Center helps students put their Chapman education and experiences to use by providing career counseling, off-campus jobs and internships, résumé critiques, and mock interviews.

Student Life

Chapman's events calendar always seems full of film screenings and faculty forums, as well as larger, livelier events. Students look forward to Spring Sizzle, an all-campus festival with free food and music, and Reel Justice, the student-run socially conscious film festival. Another big social occasion is Greek week, where the 15 sororities and fraternities compete against each other in jump rope, eating contests, mystery events, and more. "You really see the school spirit during Greek week," comments a student.

The prominence of Greek life in general depends on who you ask; those in a sorority or fraternity (one third of the students) say that it is the dominant social scene. Clearly, the other two-thirds find things to do as well, with 180 official student organizations, the most popular being music, theatre, political, and service groups. There are also nine honor societies; the official school newspaper, *Panther*, published weekly; and countless student films, plays, and other creative performances.

Chapman has an impressive NCAA Division III athletics program. The university has won national titles in baseball, men's tennis, and softball. Currently, the men's and women's water polo and women's tennis teams are also strong. Students who are not at the varsity level can compete on club teams in men's and women's lacrosse, men's swimming and crew, sailing, or cheerleading. Intramural sports and open recreation hours are available.

For good-old-fashioned swimming and beach lounging, there is no better place than Orange County. Nearby Disneyland, Knott's Berry Farm, and Los Angeles (about 30 miles away) are also popular destinations for undergrads during their free time. Old Towne Orange provides a nice hometown atmosphere to chill with a coffee or venture into a bar or a movie.

Almost 90 percent of freshmen live on campus, mostly in triples, which facilitates friendships and school spirit. Only 34 percent of undergraduates continue to live in university housing, which detracts a bit from the community of the school. "A lot of activities happen off campus," explains a student.

Student Body

Less academically focused than some, only about half of Chapman students are in the top 10 percent of their high school classes. That doesn't mean that they aren't a bright bunch, with an average freshman year GPA of 3.2. The stereotypical Chapman student is wealthy, white, and from Orange County, though overall there is high ethnic diversity with 29 percent minority students. As for geographic diversity, 32 percent of students are from out of state and international students hail from 60 different countries. "Don't believe the stereotypes about us," implores a student. The college and student groups such as Nadi-as-Salaam and the Black Student Union frequently host film series, speakers, and other diversity events.

CHAPMAN UNIVERSITY

Highlights

Students
Total enrollment: 7,566
Undergrads: 5,677
Freshmen: 1,523
Part-time students: 4%
From out-of-state: 32%
Male/Female: 43%/57%
Live on-campus: 34%
In fraternities: 26%
In sororities: 30%
Off-campus employment rating: Good
Caucasian: 59%
African American: 2%
Hispanic: 13%
Asian / Pacific Islander: 9%
Native American: 0%
Mixed (2+ ethnicities): 5%
International: 4%

Academics
Calendar: 4-1-4 system
Student/faculty ratio: 14:1
Class size 9 or fewer: 4%
Class size 10-29: 71%
Class size 30-49: 24%
Class size 50-99: 1%
Class size 100 or more: -
Returning freshmen: 91%
Six-year graduation rate: 72%

Most Popular Majors
Business administration
Film production
Communications

Admissions
Applicants: 10,489
Accepted: 4,578
Acceptance rate: 43.6%
Placed on wait list: 1,200
Enrolled from wait list: 45
Average GPA: 3.7
ACT range: 25-29
SAT Math range: 560-660
SAT Reading range: 550-650
SAT Writing range: 13-49
Top 10% of class: 53%
Top 25% of class: 90%
Top 50% of class: 98%

153

CHAPMAN UNIVERSITY

Admissions Criteria
Academic criteria:
Grades: ☆ ☆ ☆
Difficulty of class schedule: ☆ ☆ ☆
Class rank: ☆ ☆ ☆
Standardized test scores: ☆ ☆ ☆
Teacher recommendations: ☆
Personal statement: ☆ ☆ ☆
Non-academic criteria considered:
Interview
Extracurricular activities
Special talents, interests, abilities
Character/personal qualities
Volunteer work
Work experience
Geographical location
Minority affiliation
Alumni relationship

Deadlines
Early Action: November 1
Early Decision: No
Regular Action: Rolling admissions
Common Application: Accepted

Financial Aid
In-state tuition: $42,890
Out-of-state tuition: $42,890
Room: $8,238
Board: $3,966
Books: $1,450
Freshmen receiving need-based aid: 65%
Undergrads rec. need-based aid: 63%
Avg. aid package (freshmen): $31,324
Avg. aid package (undergrads): $30,611
Avg. debt upon graduation: $20,441

School Spirit
Mascot: Panthers
Colors: Cardinal and gray

You May Not Know

- The University is famous for the unique Rodger's Center for Holocaust Education, which, through lecture series, writing contests, and courses, brings survivors and scholars to the Chapman community.
- Classes at Chapman (then Hesperian College) began on March 4, 1861, the day and precise hour of the inauguration of Abraham Lincoln. The progressive initial goal of the college was to provide equal education for all.
- The faculty at Chapman was recently joined by Yakir Aharonov, Ph.D., Nobel nominee and co-discoverer of the Aharonov-Bohm Effect, a member of the impressive new physics and computational sciences team.

Distinguished Alumni

David Bonior, Former U.S. Congressman from Michigan, Former House Majority Whip; Djay Brawner, film and music video director; Jeff Lewis, real estate agent on *Flipping Out*.

Admissions and Financial Aid

Chapman admits almost 44 percent of all applicants, though the number of applicants is growing dramatically every year. You can submit the Common Application as well as an artistic portfolio to demonstrate special talents, interests, and abilities. Students applying to the Dodge College of Film and Media Arts, the Conservatory of Music, or the Departments of Theatre, Dance, or Art must submit separate departmental application materials. While the college doesn't conduct interviews, they offer daily information sessions with admission counselors, and the "Discover Chapman" day program invites prospective students and their families to campus for academic sessions, tours, and presentations.

Almost one fifth of all undergraduates receive merit aid, mostly through academic and talent scholarships, which are determined upon admission based on grade point averages and portfolios/auditions, respectively. Chapman attempts to reward "eminent talent in music, theater, dance, art, film, creative writing, science, and mathematics." More than 60 percent of students receive need-based aid, though the school does not guarantee to meet demonstrated need.

CITY UNIVERSITY OF NEW YORK – QUEENS COLLEGE

CUNY – QUEENS COLLEGE

Four-year public
Founded: 1937
Flushing, NY
Major city
Pop. 2,272,771

Address:
65-30 Kissena Boulevard
Flushing, NY
11367

Admissions:
718-997-5600

Financial Aid:
718-997-5101

www.qc.cuny.edu

Overview

CUNY Queens College in Flushing, New York—often referred to as the jewel of the CUNY system—offers the culture and excitement of an urban area, and the tranquil beauty of a more rustic setting. As a commuter school, students can enjoy both the fast-paced life of New York City and the 77 acres of open space that is the main campus.

CUNY Queens College not only provides a diverse setting; it is also full of diverse people. Flushing, Queens is one of the most ethnically diverse places in the country, drawing from a local Asian, Jewish, Greek, and Italian culture. The student population itself is also incredibly varied, comprised of young people from around the world.

While affordable, CUNY Queens is by no means lacking in quality facilities. The college boasts a traditional quad, plus up-to-date computer and science buildings. The Kupferberg Center for the Visual and Performing Arts provides a space for the Music, Art, Drama, and Media Studies programs. In 2009, a new residential hall, the Summit, was built to welcome students to on-campus living.

Academics

Graduation requirements include core courses in writing, mathematics, abstract and quantitative reasoning, foreign language, and general education. These general education requirements fall into two categories. The first is Core Areas of Knowledge and Inquiry, a study program that includes courses in reading literature, appreciating and participating in the arts, cultures and values, analyzing social structures, and natural science. The second facet of the general education requirement is Global Contexts. This includes courses on the United States, European traditions, world cultures, and pre-industrial society. Students must also fulfill requirements for a major.

There are 135 majors offered, with standout programs in economics and psychology. Students report that the degree of academic rigor of courses can vary, largely depending on the dedication of the professors. "Some are really into teaching, and others are less enthusiastic," says a student. It can also be difficult to get into all of the classes one wants to take. "Registration can be frustrating," remarks a student.

In some areas, CUNY Queens does not provide a program for certain fields of study, but does, however, offer preparation studies. For example, CUNY Queens does not offer an engineering program, but provides the specialized courses for first and second year engineering, preparing students should they choose to switch to an engineering program in the their third or fourth semester.

Seven of the colleges in the CUNY system participate in the smaller Macaulay Honors College, which offers full tuition for four years of study, a laptop, and a grant of up to $7,500 to be used for global research, service, and internships. In addition to the obvious financial benefits of such a program, the Macaulay Honors Program provides its members with four seminars focused on New York City, advising, and networking opportunities. "Being accepted into the Macaulay Program is like attending a private college—for free," says a participant.

CUNY also provides special support programs. One such example is the SEEK program, which is designed for students who would not otherwise attend college. The program begins over the summer and aids members into passing CUNY assessment exams. Once the undergraduate year begins, students are assigned into study groups with whom they will take at least three classes, receiving consistent peer support throughout the year.

The Freshman Year Initiative Program provides resources that are designed to help new students adjust to college life. Students meet together and get to know one another. The Freshman Year Initiative also allows students additional access to classes

CUNY – QUEENS COLLEGE

Students

Total enrollment: 20,100
Undergrads: 16,187
Freshmen: 1,449
Part-time students: 30%
From out-of-state: 1%
From public schools: 70%
Male/Female: 42%/58%
Live-on campus: Not reported
In fraternities: 1%
In sororities: 1%
Off-campus employment rating: Good
Caucasian: 45%
African American: 8%
Hispanic: 17%
Asian / Pacific Islander: 25%
Native American: 0%
International: 5%

Academics

Calendar: 4-1-4 system
Student/faculty ratio: 15:1
Class size 9 or fewer: 13%
Class size 10-29: 60%
Class size 30-49: 19%
Class size 50-99: 6%
Class size 100 or more: 2%
Returning freshmen: 88%
Six-year graduation rate: 54%

Most Popular Majors

Accounting
Psychology
Economics

Admissions

Applicants: 19,032
Accepted: 7,045
Acceptance rate: 37.0%
Average GPA: 3.6
ACT range: Not reported
SAT Math range: 540-610
SAT Reading range: 477-570
SAT Writing range: 4-13

156

and special attention from professors. "The program helps make everything more accessible," remarks a student.

Advising at CUNY Queens is a four-year experience. The Academic Advising Center provides a setting in which students may create their academic plans of study and make the best use of the resources various departments have to offer. "If you seek it out, the advising center has a lot of helpful guidance," says a student. The center puts an emphasis on freshman students, acquainting them with the CUNY requirements with one-on-one meetings and larger workshop settings.

CUNY Queens offers a variety of study-abroad programs, which are available for lengths of time ranging from short summer/winter trips to two-semester prolonged stays. The college does not require that students have mastery of a foreign language to study abroad, as many courses are taught in English. Exchange programs have been established with universities in France, Italy, Japan, and Canada.

Students graduating from CUNY Queens do so with a range of contacts as diverse as their student body, going on to achieve success in a variety of fields. The college provides resources for career seeking while students are still undergraduates. The Academic Advising Center, for example, aids students in crafting pre-professional plans of study. The Division of Student Affairs is also active in helping undergraduates find jobs.

Student Life

Queens College has 140 student organizations which offer a range of interests, from serious to recreational. Students interested in communication might find an outlet in the WQMC radio station, which has been broadcasting since the 1960s. Others might seek out the International Students Club, which hosts trips, cultural events, and panel discussions for international undergraduates. There is also a New York Public Interest Research Group chapter that promotes issues such as voter registration, higher education funding, and environmental protection.

Because the great majority of students commute to CUNY Queens, the social scene isn't as active as at residential schools. "We are focused on learning. The social aspects are secondary," remarks a student. One popular pastime, however, is to watch performances at the Kupferberg Center for the Visual and Performing Arts. There are five Greek organizations, including the Phi Iota Alpha Fraternity, Inc., the oldest Latino Greek Letter club. Only about 1 percent of men and women choose to join fraternities or sororities. "To be honest, I didn't even know we had fraternities and sororities," notes a student.

CUNY Queens College has 20 Division II athletic teams, distinguishing it from the other colleges in the CUNY system. CUNY Queens does not have a football team, and students report that school spirit is "almost non-existent." The college does have intramural sports, and there are a few student organizations devoted to athletics, such as the soccer club.

CUNY Queens College is connected to the New York City subway system and the Long Island Railroad, so travel to Manhattan or outer city areas is easy. "There's something to do in the City at all hours of the day and night, every day of the week," says one student. The Queens Museum of Art and Shea Stadium, where the New York Mets play, are also in the vicinity.

The college is only able to house about 500 students on campus in the new residential facility, the Summit. This architectural structure built in 2009 is modern and conforms to the city's energy efficiency standards. "Living on campus makes it feel more like a typical college experience, and the students who live in the Summit are a tight-knit group," says a student. Most students, however, commute to CUNY Queens.

Student Body

The student body is incredibly diverse in terms of culture, race, and ethnicity with half identifying as minority, but not necessarily in terms of geography; only about 1 percent of students come to CUNY Queens from out of state. There are more adult and part-time students as compared to many other colleges. One student comments, "As an 18-year-old freshman, I feel really young at times." Students say that there is also diversity in interests. "No matter what you're into, you'll find someone else who's into it too," notes a student.

You May Not Know

- The Chaney-Schwerner-Goodman Clocktower is named after three civil rights workers who were lynched in Mississippi.
- The college operates the Louis Armstrong House, a National Historic Landmark and Armstrong's former home.
- Queens County was named the most diverse county in the country with 46 percent of residents born in foreign countries.

Distinguished Alumni

Jerry Seinfeld, comedian; Paul Simon, singer-songwriter and musician; Charles B. Wang, owner of the New York Islanders ice hockey team.

Admissions and Financial Aid

CUNY Queens College evaluates students on academic performance by factors such as their combined SAT or ACT score as well as the number and rigor of academic courses taken. The college provides aid packages to incoming freshmen based on need, but merit scholarships are also available.

Admission into the Macaulay Honors Program will guarantee full tuition to CUNY Queens for four years. For CUNY Queens undergraduates, there are merit-based scholarships based on college academic performance. One example is the Belle Zeller Scholarship Award, which is given to students with a GPA of 3.75 or higher and a dedication to community service. The college also offers scholarships to students who need financial aid to study abroad, such as the Eleanor Diekmann Picken Scholarship Award.

CUNY – QUEENS COLLEGE

Highlights

Admissions Criteria
Academic criteria:
Grades: ☆ ☆ ☆
Difficulty of class schedule: ☆ ☆ ☆
Class rank: N/A
Standardized test scores: ☆ ☆ ☆
Teacher recommendations: N/A
Personal statement: Required for some programs
Non-academic criteria considered:
State of residency

Deadlines
Early Action: No
Early Decision: No
Regular Action: February 1 (priority)
Notification of admission by: May 30
Common Application: Not accepted

Financial Aid
In-state tuition: $5,730
Out-of-state tuition: $14,550
Room: Varies
Board: Varies
Books: $1,179
Avg. aid package (freshmen): $7,566 for grants or scholarship aid, $4,857 for student loans
Avg. aid package (undergrads): $6,025 for grants or scholarship aid, $6,357 for federal student loans
Avg. debt upon graduation: $20,000

School Spirit
Mascot: Knights
Colors: Royal blue and silver
Song: *Blue and Silver*

CLAREMONT MCKENNA COLLEGE

Overview

Claremont McKenna might be considered a "little" college by some, but it manages to have a *little bit* of everything. Located 30 miles east of Los Angeles, California, and just over 10 miles south of the tallest peak in the San Bernardino Range, students at Claremont McKenna have easy access (traffic permitting) both to urban nightlife and rustic wildlife.

The campus is also a mix. As part of the Claremont Colleges Consortium, Claremont McKenna combines an intimate college feel with the appeal of a larger university. Even the architecture combines Californian and Spanish styles; the beautiful Kravis Center was just built in 2008, and construction is set to begin on a new athletic facility in 2014, doubling the size of the current gym.

If you're interested in government or international relations, are looking for a strong, private, liberal arts school ranked ninth among national liberal arts colleges by *U.S. News & World Report*, and like sunny, Southern Californian weather, you might consider Claremont McKenna College.

Academics

"It varies," explains one student, when asked about the academic rigor of classes. "Some were extremely easy. Others—in my experience, the courses in the science and economics departments—were often very challenging." Students are diligent and receive attention from faculty. In fact, the small teacher-to-student ratio fosters a highly collaborative environment. Claremont McKenna offers 50 listed majors, with strengths in government, international relations, business, economics, and psychology.

The Robert A. Day 4+1 MBA program, which allows students to complete a bachelor's and MBA in five years, is only one of the special programs Claremont McKenna has to offer. If you want recognition for your academic achievement, apply junior year to be a Robert A. Day Scholar, and get connected with a network of selected leaders in business and government. Instead of minors, Claremont McKenna offers interdisciplinary sequences which are shown on students' transcripts. An example of such a sequence is the Leadership Studies Sequence, for those who wish to pursuit a career in the study or practice of leadership.

All freshmen must enroll in a basic Composition class, Lit 10, and a Humanities Seminar, FHS 10, by the end of their first year. By graduation, students must also complete courses in foreign language, math or computer science, biological lab, physical lab, and physical education as well as write a senior thesis. Students must also take courses in the humanities and social sciences. "The GERs [general education requirements] can be a pain because there are just so many of them, but somehow everyone manages to get them in," says a student. GERs may be waived, for instance through AP placement or transfer credit, but all waiver requests must be brought before the Academic Standards Committee.

Claremont McKenna features study-abroad programs in 47 countries throughout the world, as well as domestic travel, like the U.S. exchange program. The Washington program is especially noteworthy, as students have the chance to work and study on Capitol Hill.

The college also offers a strong career counseling center, which hosts many recruiting events in a variety of different fields, especially in finance and consulting. "They offer services tailored to the individual student," comments a student. One fifth of students attend graduate school within one year of graduating.

Student Life

At Claremont McKenna, students can choose between a number of activities and events to keep their extracurricular lives full and satisfying. Claremont McKenna fields

19 Division III teams (eight men's, nine women's, and two mixed) jointly with Harvey Mudd and Scripps College. Cross country, water polo, and tennis are the most competitive. If you're more into club sports, which can be just as intense, Claremont McKenna offers that as well. Both the men's lacrosse team and rugby team are five-college club sports, meaning you could end up playing with students from anywhere in the Consortium. If team sports aren't so much your thing, look at Claremont's outdoor program. The Wilderness Outdoor Adventure, known affectionately as W.O.A., helps build relationships between incoming freshmen by introducing them to the surrounding California wilderness.

Organizational Meetings at the beginning of each year introduce students to and help them choose between over 40 different student-run groups, including the Cycling Club, Model United Nations, and the Claremont Colleges' radio station KSPC.

When not in class or on the field, students at Claremont McKenna are still enjoying life on campus, keeping up with at least a couple of celebratory traditions on campus. The most common is getting dunked in the fountain on your birthday. The less frequent, but admittedly larger event is called the Thesis Party, where, as one student describes it, "after you hand in your senior thesis (a graduation requirement for all seniors), the administration throws us a party *in* the fountain topped off with personal bottles of the finest Andre Champagne."

Off campus also has much to offer. Claremont is only 30 miles from Los Angeles, two hours from San Diego, and 10 miles from the Angeles National Forest. Claremont itself provides a haven for students who feel constrained by the boundaries of the college campus. Claremont Village, only walking distance from campus, offers many places to eat and shop. "Claremont Village is great for dates," says one student. "It has a sophisticated atmosphere."

Dorm housing, which is co-ed, comes with maid service. Freshmen are guaranteed housing. Most students live all four years on campus. It's very rare for students, even seniors, to live off campus, but appears to be growing more prevalent. Still, the best place to live as a senior is the sought after senior apartments on the east end of campus. There is no Greek life on campus, but instead, there is what students call "a lively on-campus party scene." Two to three in-dorm events per week is normal.

Student Body

"Claremont McKenna students are social, academically interested, athletic people," says one student. In general, the college's students are typically academically and career focused. Politically, the student body tends to be conservative in its leaning. There's a high percentage of minority students (29 percent), the largest number being Hispanic or Asian/Pacific Islander. A moderate percentage of students are from out of state (52 percent).

You May Not Know

- For good eating, check out The Hub Grill; students have access to cafeterias on every college campus in the consortium, and brunch at Collins.

CLAREMONT MCKENNA COLLEGE

Highlights

Students
Total enrollment: 1,295
Undergrads: 1,264
Freshmen: 291
From out-of-state: 52%
Male/Female: 52%/48%
Live on-campus: 94%
Off-campus employment rating: Fair
Caucasian: 45%
African American: 3%
Hispanic: 9%
Asian / Pacific Islander: 11%
Native American: 0%
Mixed (2+ ethnicities): 6%
International: 13%

Academics
Calendar: Semester
Student/faculty ratio: 8:1
Class size 9 or fewer: 6%
Class size 10-29: 88%
Class size 30-49: 5%
Class size 50-99: 1%
Class size 100 or more: -
Returning freshmen: 95%
Six-year graduation rate: 92%

Most Popular Majors
Economics
Government
Psychology

Admissions
Applicants: 5,058
Accepted: 688
Acceptance rate: 13.6%
Placed on wait list: 549
Enrolled from wait list: 54
Average GPA: Not reported
ACT range: 29-32
SAT Math range: 660-760
SAT Reading range: 650-750
SAT Writing range: 57-36
Top 10% of class: 63%
Top 25% of class: 93%
Top 50% of class: 100%

CLAREMONT MCKENNA COLLEGE

Admissions Criteria
Academic criteria:
Grades: ☆ ☆ ☆
Difficulty of class schedule: ☆ ☆ ☆
Class rank: ☆ ☆ ☆
Standardized test scores: ☆ ☆ ☆
Teacher recommendations: ☆ ☆ ☆
Personal statement: ☆ ☆
Non-academic criteria considered:
Interview
Extracurricular activities
Special talents, interests, abilities
Character/personal qualities
Volunteer work
Work experience
State of residency
Geographical location
Minority affiliation
Alumni relationship

Deadlines
Early Action: No
Early Decision: November 1
Regular Action: January 1 (final)
Notification of admission by: April 1
Common Application: Accepted

Financial Aid
In-state tuition: $45,380
Out-of-state tuition: $45,380
Room: $6,730
Board: $5,710
Books: $900
Freshmen receiving need-based aid: 46%
Undergrads rec. need-based aid: 41%
Avg. % of need met by financial aid: 100%
Avg. aid package (freshmen): $39,953
Avg. aid package (undergrads): $39,332
Avg. debt upon graduation: $23,179

School Spirit
Mascot: Stags (men)/Athenas (women)
Colors: Maroon and gold

- The Reading Room on campus is a great place to study if you don't need access to a library.
- Claremont McKenna is one of the only schools to have recently instituted a shared bike program.

Distinguished Alumni
Paul Brickman, filmmaker and director of *Risky Business*; Michael S. Jeffries, chairman and CEO of Abercrombie & Fitch; Ron Ridenhour, My Lai massacre whistleblower.

Admissions and Financial Aid
Claremont McKenna is a competitive school, but you won't have to be perfect in every way to get in. According to the college, students with A's and high B's in challenging classes are considered. Accomplishments outside of class are also important. "Generally, students who have committed themselves to meaningful extracurricular activities in high school are more likely to be considered than those who haven't." Interviews are informational, not evaluative, and the Admissions Department emphasizes their usefulness as a way for the potential applicants to evaluate the school, not to sell themselves. Alumni interviews are also available in some areas.

Claremont McKenna uses the Common Application. No additional essays are required, and neither are SAT Subject Tests, unless your high school experience was non-traditional (e.g. homeschooling).

Claremont McKenna has three merit-based scholarships, one of which totals $10,000 per year, while the other two are full-tuition scholarships. Recently funded by the Bill and Melinda Gates Foundation, the Interdisciplinary Science Scholarship (ISS) gives full-ride scholarships to 10 or so incoming freshman who are committed to majoring both in a science and non-science.

CLARK UNIVERSITY

Overview

Clark University opened in 1889 as the "first all-graduate university in the United States" as described by the university. Today, Clark University is a private liberal arts institution for both graduate and undergraduate students, with especially renowned programs in psychology and geography. Although Clark is a small university, it offers unique, top-quality academic opportunities and many generous merit scholarships. The "Fifth-Year Free" program is particularly popular, as it allows Clark undergraduates to earn a BA and master's degree in five years while only paying tuition for four years.

Located 40 miles west of Boston in Worcester, Massachusetts, the Clark campus has a large Campus Green and is adjacent to the quaint Victorian-era Woodland Street neighborhood. While the historic industrial city of Worcester does not boast a lively nightlife scene, students enjoy plenty of social events and activities on campus.

Academics

Clark University offers 32 majors, with an option that allows students to design their own major with faculty approval. Students do not need to declare their major until the spring of their sophomore year, leaving plenty of time for exploring a wide range of interests. All Clark students are required to complete eight courses in the Liberal Studies Program during their first year, with classes in verbal expression, formal analysis, aesthetics, global comparisons, history, language and culture, natural sciences, and values (ethics). Students can select their own courses within the Liberal Studies Programs, or specialize in an International-Studies-themed Liberal Studies curriculum. In addition to the Liberal Studies Program, engineering, pre-med, and other science students must take core classes for their major during their first year. Freshmen may also choose to take first-year in-depth seminar courses in a particular field of interest.

With the average class size being 21 students and an abundance of seminar style courses, students say they have the opportunity to interact closely with professors. Academic difficultly varies with each major, with engineering, pre-med, and the sciences having the most requirements. Perhaps because of its historic roots as one of America's first graduate institutions, Clark has some renowned academic departments, especially psychology, international relations, physics, and geography. Clark University also has an extensive pre-health career advising program.

Clark students have a number of unique academic opportunities, including the opportunity to earn an accelerated BA/Master's Degree in five years, with the fifth year being tuition-free. Engineering students at Clark can enroll in a special 3/2 program with Columbia University, in which students earn a BA in three years at Clark and a BS in two years at Columbia. Clark also has an arrangement with the Massachusetts College of Pharmacy and Health Sciences, allowing students to earn a BS in nursing, a master's of physician assistant studies, or doctor of pharmacy. Clark University is a member of the College of Worcester Consortium, allowing Clark students to cross-register in courses at any of the 12 other consortium colleges as well.

Clark has 57 study-abroad programs in 34 countries in both foreign languages and in English. Study abroad is popular; in fact, one third of students do so. "I love that so many of us study abroad. It makes you feel like you aren't missing out when you're away," comments a student.

Forty-nine percent of Clark graduates attend graduate school, with six percent earning doctoral degrees. Twenty-five percent of graduates return to Clark to complete master's degrees through the "Fifth-Year Free" program. "Where else can you go where you get a master's degree for free?" asks a student. Thirty-eight percent of Clark graduates immediately enter the work force.

CLARK UNIVERSITY

Four-year private
Founded: 1887
Worcester, MA
Medium city
Pop. 181,631

Address:
950 Main Street
Worcester, MA
01610-1477

Admissions:
800-462-5275 (out-of-state)

Financial Aid:
508-793-7478

admissions@clarku.edu

www.clarku.edu

CLARK UNIVERSITY

Students

Total enrollment: 3,503
Undergrads: 2,352
Freshmen: 630
Part-time students: 4%
From out-of-state: 65%
From public schools: 70%
Male/Female: 42%/58%
Live on-campus: 71%
Off-campus employment rating: Excellent
Caucasian: 65%
African American: 4%
Hispanic: 6%
Asian / Pacific Islander: 5%
Native American: 0%
Mixed (2+ ethnicities): 2%
International: 11%

Academics

Calendar: Semester
Student/faculty ratio: 10:1
Class size 9 or fewer: 19%
Class size 10-29: 61%
Class size 30-49: 14%
Class size 50-99: 4%
Class size 100 or more: -
Returning freshmen: 92%
Six-year graduation rate: 80%
Graduates who immediately go to graduate school: 50%

Most Popular Majors

Psychology
Political science
Biology/biochemistry

Admissions

Applicants: 4,297
Accepted: 3,010
Acceptance rate: 70.0%
Placed on wait list: 228
Enrolled from wait list: 4
Average GPA: 3.5
ACT range: 24-29
SAT Math range: 530-640
SAT Reading range: 530-640
SAT Writing range: 7-38
Top 10% of class: 36%
Top 25% of class: 73%
Top 50% of class: 94%

162

Student Life

Clark University prohibits sororities and fraternities, so there are no Greek parties on the weekends. However, there are many other student events on campus, many of which are hosted by the over 120 active student organizations. For those craving a city excursion, Boston and Providence are within driving distance. Many students also take advantage of Clark's transportation service into Worcester to eat at restaurants and go shopping. For enhanced safety, Clark has police security, an escort service, and blue-light emergency phones located across campus. "If you use common sense, you'll be fine," says a student.

The university hosts some popular events, such as Clark Trek, the outdoors program held for freshmen before orientation. The university cancels classes and transforms the Campus Green into a Carnival on Spree Day each spring (the date is kept a secret until the morning of the event). Students say Spree Day is "the highlight of the year" and a "day when everyone lets loose." Another popular event is the International Gala, which showcases international entertainment, fashion, and cuisine. During finals week each semester, students turn out in droves for the free Midnight Breakfasts of waffles and pancakes.

Despite their busy academic and social schedules, a large number of Clark students find time to give back to their community, with 53 percent of students volunteering in community service groups. Thirty-nine percent of students participate in student internships in the city of Worcester.

Clark has 17 Division III varsity teams, with basketball being the most popular since Clark has no football team. Non-varsity athletes can participate in a number of club sports, including snowboarding, horse riding, salsa dancing, and tae kwon do. Intramural sports are very popular at Clark, with 40 percent of the student body participating in sports such as Ultimate Frisbee, floor hockey, volleyball, and soccer. Clark students can keep fit by taking recreation classes or using gym equipment at the Bickman Fitness Center. The Kneller Athletic Center also has a swimming pool, courts for basketball, volleyball, badminton, tennis, racquetball and squash, an indoor track, and an indoor soccer field.

Housing is guaranteed for all four years at Clark University, but students are only required to live on campus during their freshman and sophomore years. Overall, 71 percent of students live on campus, and those not living on campus generally live in apartments close to the university. Freshmen live in three freshmen dorms: Bullock, Wright, and Sanford. Upperclassmen can choose between suite-style apartments and theme houses, ranging from the Art Activism and Human Rights houses to Gaming House and "Captain Planets Headquarters" house. Clark University offers gender-neutral housing options for upperclassmen as well.

Student Body

Clark University describes itself as a "cultural melting pot," as it attracts students from well beyond Massachusetts, with 63 percent of its students being from out of state. Nine percent of Clark students are international. The student body has moderate ethnic diversity, with 17 percent of students identifying as minorities. Religious diversity is split fairly evenly between Catholics (16 percent), Protestants (16 percent), and Jewish (13 percent). Forty-two percent of students state that they have no religious preference. A common complaint among Clark women is that there are many more women on campus than men, with women comprising nearly 60 percent of student body. Clark students lean liberal politically, but students say that all backgrounds and interests are represented at Clark.

You May Not Know

- Clark University has the oldest geography program in the United States.
- G. Stanley Hall, Clark University's first president, founded the American Psychological Association.
- George H. Blakeslee created the academic field of international relations as a professor at Clark.

Distinguished Alumni

Albert A. Michelson, the first American to win a Nobel Prize in Science; Hugh Panero, CEO and president, XM Satellite Radio; Ronald Shaich, CEO and chairman, Panera.

Admissions and Financial Aid

The college considers typical factors such as academics, course load, recommendations, essays, interviews, and activities as part of admission standards. However, the college also values social commitment and encourages applicants, "if you are interested in making a difference in the community or beyond, tell us."

While Clark University does not guarantee to meet demonstrated financial aid for students, the university states that "welcoming students of all income levels is at the very heart of who we are. When financial aid is factored in, many students are surprised to find that the cost of attending Clark is comparable to or less than that of a state school." Clark offers a large number of generous merit-based scholarships, including Presidential Scholarships, Traina Scholarships, Achievement Awards, Make a Difference Awards, and Global Scholar Awards, ranging from $12,000 to $17,000 per year for four years.

CLARK UNIVERSITY

Highlights

Admissions Criteria
Academic criteria:
Grades: ☆ ☆ ☆
Difficulty of class schedule: ☆ ☆ ☆
Class rank: ☆
Standardized test scores: ☆
Teacher recommendations: ☆ ☆ ☆
Personal statement: ☆ ☆
Non-academic criteria considered:
Interview
Extracurricular activities
Special talents, interests, abilities
Character/personal qualities
Volunteer work
Work experience
State of residency
Geographical location
Minority affiliation
Alumni relationship

Deadlines
Early Action: November 15
Early Decision: No
Regular Action: January 15 (final)
Notification of admission by: April 1
Common Application: Accepted

Financial Aid
In-state tuition: $39,200
Out-of-state tuition: $39,200
Room: $4,170
Board: $3,300
Books: $800
Freshmen receiving need-based aid: 57%
Undergrads rec. need-based aid: 57%
Avg. % of need met by financial aid: 95%
Avg. aid package (freshmen): $32,364
Avg. aid package (undergrads): $32,364
Avg. debt upon graduation: $25,175

School Spirit
Mascot: Cougar
Colors: Scarlet and white
Song: *Fiat Lux*

CLARKSON UNIVERSITY

CLARKSON UNIVERSITY

Four-year private
Founded: 1896
Potsdam, NY
Small town
Pop. 9,416

Address:
8 Clarkson Ave, Box 5605
Potsdam, NY 13699

Admissions:
800-527-6577

Financial Aid:
800-527-6577

admission@clarkson.edu

www.clarkson.edu

Overview

Clarkson University—located on a beautiful wooded campus in the small college town of Postdam, New York—is more than picturesque. It is a collaborative, innovative school that prepares students for the "real world." What does that really mean? For starters, the fact that one in six alumni becomes a CEO, president, or vice president of a company should give you an idea. As a research institution focusing on engineering and business, Clarkson provides ample career-building experiences in internships, clubs, classes, and collaborative projects.

The student body is as homogenously enterprising as it is homogenous in other ways, with 12 percent minority and 72 percent male students. However, through culture days and theme houses, Clarkson sincerely tries to embrace and support diversity.

While not architecturally exciting, Clarkson buildings house numerous labs and testing centers in which faculty and students conduct world-class research. The Center for Advanced Materials Processing or the D1 hockey rink may well keep you occupied. Additionally, the campus borders the six million acre Adirondack Park, where the Outing Club runs an overwhelming array of outdoor adventures, all starting from the on-campus Adirondack lodge, a cozy place to study or tie your hiking boots.

Clarkson's location in upstate New York means that winters are long and cold and escape to the more "happening" locales of Montreal and Ottawa is difficult. But if spending that brutal winter alternately skiing and designing, building, and marketing a zero-emissions motorcycle is your idea of a good time, Clarkson just may be the school for you.

Academics

Academic life at Clarkson begins with the Clarkson Common Experience (CCE). This required combination of classes and internships is centered on effective communication, diversity appreciation, ethics, and technology for society and sets the tone for all four years of a student's education at the college. Students may add any of 63 majors in the three schools of Arts and Sciences, Business, and Engineering to their CCE. Dual degrees, honors programs, accelerated studies, and self-designed majors are just some of the ways that students can tailor their education to meet their interests.

Clarkson's diverse academic opportunities include the nationally recognized Venture@Moore House, which is a residence for exemplary business majors. Students live together so that they may work on long-term product launch strategies through team, management, and leadership building. "Venture has been the highlight of my college experience," confides one student. "Just make sure that you keep your business and social life separate since you will be living with people you'll be working with," she adds.

Clarkson boasts the Research Experiences for Undergraduates (REU) program, which enables students to earn a stipend and free housing while doing projects in environmental sciences and engineering. The Symposium on Undergraduate Research Experiences (SURE) allows students to present their research experience. Though students say the classes are challenging, especially in engineering, the small-school environment means there is a lot of support from professors and peers; more than four out of five classes have less than 50 students. Business and engineering are considered to be the best overall programs, especially the tracks in advanced materials, biotechnology, environment and energy, entrepreneurship, and global supply chain management. Alongside graduate students and faculty, undergrads have ample opportunities in these disciplines to work on cutting-edge projects with real-world applications.

Clarkson also encourages students—as well as requiring business majors—to take advantage of their 20 study-abroad programs in 14 countries, ranging from Australia to India. "There's a real focus on making sure we understand not only what happens domestically but internationally as well," comments a student.

Career guidance at Clarkson is highly regarded. In fact, they pride themselves on having a 98 percent job placement rate, and more than half of students who enter the workforce are employed in a career related to their major. "Clarkson is incredibly career-focused," says a student. Despite today's tough job market, Clarkson sustains this rate with required internship experiences in their vast network of 35,000 involved alumni and a helpful career center. Twenty-nine percent of students attend graduate school within one year of graduating.

Student Life

Just looking at the list of student activities at Clarkson shows how energetic campus life is. There are about 150 clubs with a gamut of varied interests. Some examples include cricket or broomball, Amnesty International, Autonomous Robotics, and the campus radio show.

For those interested in organized sports, 275 intramural teams range from Alpine Skiing to archery. Hockey is the most popular sport and the only Division I team; all other athletics are Division III. "There's a lot of school spirit at the hockey games," remarks a student. Non-competitive outdoor activities such as kayaking and hiking are also very popular, with the Adirondacks and Raquette River in Clarkson's backyard.

The school itself holds many special events during the year. The World in Postdam Diversity Festival, a joint effort with Village of Postdam and SUNY Postdam, showcases cultural and ethnic diversity through food, dances, and displays. As a celebration of school spirit, Clarkson first year students gather on the lawn in front of Thomas S. Clarkson's old mansion to sing the alma mater and watch a fireworks display during Holcroft Knight. More regular spirit days precede games against the school's athletic rival, St. Lawrence. Student groups also put on events such as Winterfest, organized by the popular Outing Club, which brings students together to revel in the bitter cold and deep snow of February by skiing, snow-biking, sledding, dog sledding, and more. "You'll practically freeze to death, but it's definitely worth it," says a student.

While Potsdam is a quiet place with very few entertainment options, many students say their favorite Friday nights include dinner in town, where there are plenty of restaurants and shops. More notably, the Crane School of Music at SUNY Potsdam offers often-free concerts almost every night. For livelier weekends, students take road trips to Syracuse or Albany or closer to the popular clubbing spots of Ottawa and Montreal. "You'll want to make sure you have your passport because some of the best clubs are in Canada," explains a student. Parties are not allowed in the dorms, so most are held in Greek Houses off campus. About one in eight students joins the 11 fraternities and three sororities.

Except for those living in Greek Houses, all students reside on campus. After living in doubles on the quad as freshmen, students can choose between themed houses, townhouses, co-ed and single sex dorms, suites, and special housing for married, disabled, and international students. Theme housing is becoming more popular;

CLARKSON UNIVERSITY

Highlights

Students
Total enrollment: 3,604
Undergrads: 3,072
Freshmen: 792
From out-of-state: 28%
From public schools: 85%
Male/Female: 72%/28%
Live on-campus: 83%
In fraternities: 12%
In sororities: 14%
Off-campus employment rating: Good
Caucasian: 82%
African American: 3%
Hispanic: 4%
Asian / Pacific Islander: 3%
Native American: 0%
Mixed (2+ ethnicities): 2%
International: 3%

Academics
Calendar: Semester
Student/faculty ratio: 15:1
Class size 9 or fewer: 12%
Class size 10-29: 44%
Class size 30-49: 19%
Class size 50-99: 20%
Class size 100 or more: 6%
Returning freshmen: 86%
Six-year graduation rate: 71%
Graduates who immediately enter career related to major: 91%

Most Popular Majors
Mechanical engineering
Civil engineering
Engineering/management

Admissions
Applicants: 4,199
Accepted: 3,195
Acceptance rate: 76.1%
Placed on wait list: 131
Average GPA: 3.6
ACT range: 23-28
SAT Math range: 560-660
SAT Reading range: 500-610
SAT Writing range: 3-19
Top 10% of class: 38%
Top 25% of class: 74%
Top 50% of class: 93%

165

CLARKSON UNIVERSITY

Admissions Criteria

Academic criteria:
Grades: ☆ ☆ ☆
Difficulty of class schedule: ☆ ☆ ☆
Class rank: ☆ ☆
Standardized test scores: ☆ ☆
Teacher recommendations: ☆ ☆
Personal statement: ☆
Non-academic criteria considered:
Interview
Extracurricular activities
Special talents, interests, abilities
Character/personal qualities
Volunteer work
Work experience
State of residency
Alumni relationship

Deadlines

Early Action: No
Early Decision: December 1
Regular Action: Rolling admissions
Common Application: Accepted

Financial Aid

In-state tuition: $39,770
Out-of-state tuition: $39,770
Room: $6,886
Board: $6,112
Books: $1,416
Freshmen receiving need-based aid: 87%
Undergrads rec. need-based aid: 86%
Avg. % of need met by financial aid: 89%
Avg. aid package (freshmen): $39,187
Avg. aid package (undergrads): $36,967
Avg. debt upon graduation: $27,866

School Spirit

Mascot: Golden Knights
Colors: Green and gold

for example, Women in Science and Engineering (WISE) provides housing, community, mentorship, and networking for ambitious female students.

Student Body

With 82 percent of the students being Caucasian, 72 percent male, and only about three percent each African American, international, and Asian American, diversity is not Clarkson's strong point. That said, the international students testify that they find the school to be very accepting and student organizations offer support and community for those in the minority. One student describes Clarkson students as, "either a business major or close to it, 100 percent focused on our future career, and always ready to network."

You May Not Know

- The most recent graduated student salary averages $50,000.
- The university's namesake Thomas S. Clarkson, a New York entrepreneur who owned a sandstone quarry, buried his horse "Trick" on campus.
- The Student Projects for Engineering Experience and Design (SPEED) program organizes 16 teams of students to compete in design challenges from creating a formula-1 style race car to strategizing hazardous waste treatment processes.

Distinguished Alumni

James Geiger, Chairman/President/CEO of CBeyond Com; David Herrick, Executive Director of wind development for NextEra Energy Resources, builder and owner of the world's two largest wind farms; Paul Horn, Senior Vice President and Director of IBM Research; Kevin Parker, President/CEO of Deltek Systems; Martin Roesch, Chief Technology Officer at Sourcefire.

Admissions and Financial Aid

"Do you have the Clarkson Gene?" the university website asks. Apparently, 76 percent of applicants do, and are accepted. The admissions office recommends a minimum grade average of B and a ranking in the top 25 percent of one's high school class.

Nine out of 10 students receive some amount of financial aid, but Clarkson only averages meeting 89 percent of demonstrated need. In addition to multiple program-specific and regional scholarships, Clarkson offers merit based school scholarships, ranging from the $500 per year Holcroft Alumni Recognition awards to the Clarkson Leadership Awards, which give $11,000 per year to outstanding high school juniors. The only athletic scholarships are provided for both men's and women's Division I hockey players.

CLEMSON UNIVERSITY

CLEMSON UNIVERSITY

Four-year public
Founded: 1889
Clemson, SC
Small town
Pop. 13,946

Address:
105 Sikes Hall
Clemson, SC
29634

Admissions:
864-656-2287

Financial Aid:
864-656-2280

cuadmissions@clemson.edu

www.clemson.edu

Overview

Clemson University, located in upstate South Carolina, attracts more than 4,000 new students each fall. Some say it's the location—less than two hours separate the campus from nearby Atlanta, Charlotte, and Columbia. The university's foothill setting also offers a prime view of the majestic Blue Ridge Mountains. But there's more to Clemson than just scenery. The university ranks in America's top 25 public institutions and prides itself on how well it "combines the best of small-college teaching and big-time science, engineering, and technology." Clemson also stands out for its exceptional dedication to public service; both faculty and students alike busy themselves with sustainability, conservation, and other "green" activities when away from the classroom.

Love the carillon? Clemson boasts its special relationship with the musical instrument. According to the school, "classes were started in 1999, and more than 100 Clemson students from more than 40 different majors have taken carillon lessons and classes."

The Clemson Tigers pride themselves on ardent sports fans from the university and surrounding community, though lately the university's teams haven't been as successful as in the past. Athletics, besides football, do not dominate academics at Clemson. However, "a commitment to service and a love of winning" permeates life on campus, according to the university.

Academics

Clemson University offers undergraduates 80 fields in which to earn a bachelors diploma. Founded as an agricultural college, Clemson continues to flaunt a healthy program of study in the rural sciences. Several other strong offerings have blossomed since the university's inception, the most notable being business and engineering. According to the university, the College of Business and Behavioral Science is the only one in the country to combine the two disciplines. "There's an academic advising center and professional development office aimed only at CBBS students," says a student.

Most courses have between 10 and 19 students, and large lectures comprise a very small percentage of the academic experience. "Most of my professors are 100 percent committed to teaching," remarks a student. Clemson's general education requirements ensure that all students take part in such programs as Creative Inquiry, where team-based projects involve students from various disciplines and begin in the freshman or sophomore year. Other required courses include communication; academic and professional development; mathematical, scientific and technological literacy; arts and humanities; social sciences; cross-cultural awareness, and science and technology in society.

The National Science Foundation listed Clemson among its top 100 research-focused universities, which translates into bountiful opportunities in research for students. The Charles H. Houston Center for the Study of the Black Experience in Education at Clemson, established in 1988, is noted for its insightful scholarship in the field of the African-American educational experience. The university highlights its Communication across the Curriculum program, which showers students with endeavors to strengthen their skills in writing, speech, and media.

Study-abroad programs abound in Europe, and the university encourages students from every major to avail themselves of the opportunity to travel and learn. There are study-abroad fairs and workshops so that students may acquaint themselves with the university's programs. For example, Clemson has a Brussels Center where students may study and research. According to the college, the Brussels Center is "at

CLEMSON UNIVERSITY

Students
Total enrollment: 20,768
Undergrads: 16,562
Part-time students: 6%
From out-of-state: 40%
From public schools: 87%
Male/Female: 54%/46%
Live on-campus: 41%
In fraternities: 20%
In sororities: 33%
Off-campus employment rating: Good
Caucasian: 84%
African American: 6%
Hispanic: 3%
Asian / Pacific Islander: 2%
Native American: 0%
Mixed (2+ ethnicities): 2%
International: 1%

Academics
Calendar: Semester
Student/faculty ratio: 18:1
Class size 9 or fewer: 16%
Class size 10-29: 49%
Class size 30-49: 21%
Class size 50-99: 10%
Class size 100 or more: 4%
Returning freshmen: 91%
Six-year graduation rate: 82%
Graduates who immediately enter career
    related to major: 35%

Most Popular Majors
Business
Management
Engineering

Admissions
Applicants: 18,500
Accepted: 10,706
Acceptance rate: 57.9%
Placed on wait list: 1,820
Enrolled from wait list: 4
Average GPA: 4.2
ACT range: 26-31
SAT Math range: 590-680
SAT Reading range: 560-660
SAT Writing range: Not reported
Top 10% of class: 54%
Top 25% of class: 84%
Top 50% of class: 97%

the very heart of Europe and next door to dozens of international and European Union organizations and international companies."

The Michelin Career Center provides workshops almost every week on subjects dealing with strategies and facts related to jobs, internships, and graduate school. The Center also hosts career fairs, education job fairs, and specialized job fairs. Students may drop in for counseling services or schedule a one-hour appointment with a counselor to discuss graduate school or career plans.

Student Life

According to the college, students participate in activities such as "cheering the Tigers to victory in 'Death Valley' stadium," as well as more adventuresome hobbies such as "sky-diving and water-skiing." No matter the field of interest, "Clemson students are happiest when active." With more than 350 student organizations, there is plenty of opportunity for activity.

Greek life is well represented on campus, with more than one quarter of students belonging to one of the 10 sororities or 19 fraternities. As for the scene after sunset, frat parties seem to be big hits. "The parties are especially popular with freshmen and sophomores," comments a student. Downtown is also teeming with bars, like Esso Club and Backstreets, and pub crawls for those who can legally imbibe.

Many students take part in Clemson's thriving intramural sports scene; classics like basketball and Ultimate Frisbee join such quirky offerings as darts and "quickball." The Fike Recreation Center provides 275,000 square feet of exercise and recreation options. Outdoor activities are popular—there is the 900 mile shoreline of Lake Hartwell for water sports and Blue Ridge Mountains for hiking and other outdoor activities.

The student body rallies around its athletics, i.e. *football*. It's quite common for hordes of people to tailgate during a Clemson Tiger's football game weekend to watch the team hustle down the lush knoll known as "The Hill." First Friday Parades launch the season with a spectacle held during the weekend of the first match. And annually, the school devotes a pep rally with skits dedicated to the pigskin troop, fittingly known as Tigerama. "You see Clemson orange everywhere you look on game days," remarks a student.

A slight majority of Clemson's student body lives away from the campus, and 41 percent choose on-campus housing. Freshmen typically live on campus in residence halls with catchy names like The Suites and The Shoeboxes; four and two occupants per room, respectively, fit cozily in these living facilities. Upperclassmen may reside in the campus' apartment complexes. Lightsey Bridge I, for instance, offers 30 apartments that house strictly two persons—meaning the pair shares a private bathroom! "Most upperclassmen move off campus," notes a student. Housing for those who are without substantial means is a cause that really activates this campus. Habitat for Humanity has vigorously celebrated Clemson's chapter; the university has "greenlit" construction on South Carolina's very first LEED-certified Habitat dwelling.

Student Body

The university caters to the students of its state, and only 40 percent of students hail from outside South Carolina. To be more specific:

students from "out of state" tend to hail from states that are adjunct to South Carolina geographically. No doubt, the university is as southern as mint juleps and verandas. "We're filled with southern hospitality," says a student.

Clemson pales somewhat in terms of diversity, in that the school's population is predominantly white with 13 percent minority students. Most at Clemson are "regular churchgoers." The school tends to lean to the right politically. "There are some very conventional students here who hold conservative beliefs about issues like abortion," notes a student.

You May Not Know

- The university's official fight song is the jazz standard *Tiger Rag* performed by the likes of Louis Armstrong, Billie Holiday, and Frank Sinatra.
- The university's class of 1944 was the smallest class in Clemson history with just 13 graduates.
- Several notable writers called nearby town Greenville home, including the late Poet Laureate Carl Sandburg, who often paid visits to the university.

Distinguished Alumni

David Beasley, Governor of South Carolina from 1995-1999; Robert H. Brooks, founder of Hooters Restaurant; Nancy O'Dell, host of *Access Hollywood*; Gary Parsons, former CEO of XM Radio; Strom Thurmond, the longest serving Senator in American history.

Admissions and Financial Aid

Class rank, grades, academic curriculum, and test scores are some of the most important factors in admission to Clemson. According to the admissions office, "the school record is more important than test scores." Other factors may play a role in assessment, such as the student's chosen major, residency, community service, involvement in school activities, and work experience.

Clemson outclasses many colleges with its manifold scholarship plans. Community service diehards can earn Restricted University Grants for their efforts, and whiz kids need no financial aid application to be evaluated for Academic Recruiting Scholarships. The invitation-only Bridge to Clemson University program privileges particularly promising freshmen to a more rigorous academic collegiate experience. The few students chosen attend nearby Tri-Country Technical College in their first year before returning to Clemson to complete their degree. The Calhoun Honors College proves to be similar in rigor and expectation. Applicants boasting SAT scores of 1400 or higher, and who graduate among the top three percent of their class, stand a chance of being one of the 250 freshmen who enjoy perks like smaller class sizes, study abroad in Brussels, and fellowship application support. Should these programs not seem a fit for you, look no further than the university's National Scholars Program, which provides full four-year scholarships.

CLEMSON UNIVERSITY

Highlights

Admissions Criteria
Academic criteria:
Grades: ☆ ☆ ☆
Difficulty of class schedule: ☆ ☆ ☆
Class rank: ☆ ☆ ☆
Standardized test scores: ☆ ☆ ☆
Teacher recommendations: ☆
Personal statement: ☆
Non-academic criteria considered:
Extracurricular activities
Special talents, interests, abilities
Alumni relationship

Deadlines
Early Action: No
Early Decision: No
Regular Action: Rolling admissions
Common Application: Not accepted

Financial Aid
In-state tuition: $13,382
Out-of-state tuition: $30,826
Room: Varies
Board: Varies
Books: $1,112
Freshmen receiving need-based aid: 52%
Undergrads rec. need-based aid: 55%
Avg. % of need met by financial aid: 50%
Avg. aid package (freshmen): $12,173
Avg. aid package (undergrads): $9,578
Avg. debt upon graduation: $31,172

School Spirit
Mascot: The Tiger
Colors: Orange and purple
Song: *Tiger Rag*

COLBY
COLLEGE

Four-year private
Founded: 1813
Waterville, ME
Small town
Pop. 15,697

Address:
4000 Mayflower Hill
Waterville, ME
04901-8840

Admissions:
800-723-3032

Financial Aid:
207-859-4800

admissions@colby.edu

www.colby.edu

COLBY COLLEGE

Overview

Rated in the top 25 of liberal arts colleges in the country by *U.S. News & World Report*, Colby College is often referred to as the most beautiful college campus in America. The Georgian "Colby brick" and copper roofed campus buildings sit above the small town of Waterville, Maine, and amidst forested rolling hills where the nearest airport is 90 minutes away. Challenging academics, organized and outdoor sports, and active student groups make up the bulk of college life at Colby. The unique January Program, known as the "Jan Plan" allows students to take diverse classes and study or research domestically or abroad.

Winter is a chilly reality at Colby College and requires enduring average lows in the single digits and temperatures with subzero wind chills, plus an average 58 inches of snow each year. However, skiing and snowboarding at nearby Sugarloaf Mountain can prevent cabin fever.

Notable facilities include the new Harold Alfond Stadium for lacrosse, hockey, and football. The student Center, Cotter Union, recently underwent an 18,000 square foot expansion with additions of Pulver Pavilion and a new bookstore.

Academics

There are 56 majors to choose from with biology, English, and government being particularly strong programs. As a liberal arts college, Colby encourages interdisciplinary and independent study. Also, academic requirements for all majors provide a broad foundation in the liberal arts. Areas mandated include English composition, foreign language, arts, historical studies, literature, quantitative reasoning, natural sciences, social sciences, and diversity.

First Year Supper Seminars are also a graduation requirement. All new students must attend dinners, lectures, and the AlcoholEdu program. The purpose is to "encourage and assist in the development of responsibility for one's own lifestyle through programs centered on mental, emotional, social, physical, and spiritual fitness," according to the college. "I think the alcohol program is a little patronizing; but I suppose for some students, they need to hear the message," comments one student.

Class sizes are small—85 percent of classes have fewer than 30 students—and it's common for professors to invite students to their homes for dinner and get to know them personally in the classroom and at campus social events. "My professors are so open. One says it's fine to call her until 2 a.m.," says a student.

The unique Jan Plan is an intensive four-week study period between the fall and spring semesters where students explore interests and passions. Considered a defining element of the Colby experience, Jan Plan offers courses on campus, off campus, non-credit courses, internships, and research opportunities.

Experimentation and curiosity are encouraged in courses on Sustainable Agriculture and Food Systems, Reading and Writing of Graphic Memoirs, Blacksmithing, and Emergency Medical Technician Training. Students can also pursue Jan Plan domestic and international internships in places such as Arkansas, India, New York, and South Africa; or, conduct research with faculty.

Partly because of the time afforded through the Jan Plan, more than two-thirds of students study abroad during their time at Colby. The major semester-abroad programs include University of Salamanca in Spain, University of Burgundy in Dijon, France, and St. Petersburg, Russia.

Preparing students for their time post-college, the Career Center offers help and resources for Colby graduates from internships, job shadowing, resume workshops, and fellowship information. The alumni network is 25,000 strong. One quarter of students attend graduate school within one year of graduating.

Student Life

Colby culture includes several rites of passage: every Colby student knows about the Champagne Toast that takes place on the last day of classes when seniors toast their many bottles—not petite glasses—of champagne on the Miller Steps. The Miller Steps themselves mark the beginning and ending of the Colby experience as incoming students and parents walk up those famous steps to hear the College's welcome speech and again for graduation. Another tradition is the Mr. Colby beauty pageant for men only. The men strut their stuff and showcase humorous talent. "It's a nice reversal of the gender roles," laughs a student.

There are some off-campus bars and restaurants in nearby Waterville, but most of student life revolves around campus activities and popular student spots. In Cotter Union, the pub is a campus hangout for students 21+. The Pavilion, the Spa (dining and coffee shop), and the athletic center are major student draws as well. There's no movie theatre on campus, but films are shown in the various residence halls. Student dance, music, and theatre are also performed regularly on campus. "Because there's not much to do in Waterville, we create our own entertainment on campus," comments a student.

Colby no longer has Greek organizations, but students are more than social. They tend to find friends through student clubs and organizations. In fact, there are over 100 active clubs on campus that attract students to share their love of quilting, rugby, human rights activism, Asian culture, and much more.

COOT, the Colby Outdoor Orientation Trips organization, sponsors wellness and outdoor adventures at all levels. Backpacking, Improv Theater, Whitewater Rafting, and Yoga are popular COOT excursions. But there's no need to leave campus to get a fresh-air fix. Ice skating on Johnson pond and hiking over eight miles of trails on campus are popular activities as well.

Off-campus there are even more outdoor activities. Skiing, snowboarding, hiking, and water sports are abundant. Those seeking bright lights and the big city will need to travel to Portland, Maine, 78 miles away, or Boston, 180 miles. "This is a remote area," notes one student. "You have to love the outdoors or get involved in school activities to keep yourself occupied."

Even though there are 32 Division III varsity teams, of which 30 percent of students play in over the course of the year, it's the intramural sports that draw 74 percent of the student body. These range from competitive to recreational and include broomball, field hockey, and other sports. Athletic rivals with Bowdoin and Bates Colleges are historical and part of the sports and non-sports culture. "Even if you're terrible at sports, pretty much everyone plays intramurals," remarks a student.

More than 90 percent of students live in campus housing, and all the dorms are completely coed and mixed. The exception is a small residence for seniors only, Alfond Senior Apartments and Dialog Housing (Green House and Music-and-Arts House). "Chem-free" housing is available for those students who are looking to live in a substance-free environment, as students at Colby apply the same rigor to their educations as they do to their party lives. Quiet halls are available too.

COLBY COLLEGE

Highlights

Students
Total enrollment: 1,863
Undergrads: 1,863
Freshmen: 493
From out-of-state: 88%
From public schools: 50%
Male/Female: 45%/55%
Live on-campus: 94%
Off-campus employment rating: Fair
Caucasian: 60%
African American: 3%
Hispanic: 5%
Asian / Pacific Islander: 6%
Native American: 0%
Mixed (2+ ethnicities): 4%
International: 7%

Academics
Calendar: 4-1-4 system
Student/faculty ratio: 10:1
Class size 9 or fewer: 26%
Class size 10-29: 59%
Class size 30-49: 12%
Class size 50-99: 3%
Class size 100 or more: -
Six-year graduation rate: 90%
Graduates who immediately go to graduate school: 26%
Graduates who immediately enter career related to major: 60%

Most Popular Majors
Economics
English
Global studies

Admissions
Applicants: 5,241
Accepted: 1,518
Acceptance rate: 29.0%
Placed on wait list: 1,161
Enrolled from wait list: 11
Average GPA: Not reported
ACT range: 29-32
SAT Math range: 630-720
SAT Reading range: 610-710
SAT Writing range: 32-49
Top 10% of class: 65%
Top 25% of class: 88%
Top 50% of class: 99%

COLBY COLLEGE

Admissions Criteria
Academic criteria:
Grades: ☆ ☆ ☆
Difficulty of class schedule: ☆ ☆ ☆
Class rank: ☆ ☆
Standardized test scores: ☆ ☆
Teacher recommendations: ☆ ☆
Personal statement: ☆ ☆
Non-academic criteria considered:
Interview
Extracurricular activities
Special talents, interests, abilities
Character/personal qualities
Volunteer work
Work experience
Geographical location
Minority affiliation
Alumni relationship

Deadlines
Early Action: No
Early Decision: November 15
Regular Action: January 1 (final)
Notification of admission by: April 1
Common Application: Accepted

Financial Aid
In-state tuition: $43,840
Out-of-state tuition: $43,840
Room: $6,080
Board: $5,670
Books: $700
Freshmen receiving need-based aid: 39%
Undergrads rec. need-based aid: 37%
Avg. % of need met by financial aid: 100%
Avg. aid package (freshmen): $40,178
Avg. aid package (undergrads): $38,613
Avg. debt upon graduation: $24,453

School Spirit
Mascot: Mules
Colors: Blue and grey

Student Body

Students are known for their friendly attitudes. Due to the college's small size—approximately 1,900 undergrads—it's easy to get to know people and form strong friendships. There's an outdoorsy aesthetic and hippy vibe to the campus and students tend to be politically liberal.

The student body is diverse: 18 percent ethnic minority; and, while 88 percent of students come from out of state, a majority are from the New England area. Seven percent of students are international.

Students seem to enjoy learning for the sake of learning at Colby: "… Colby is full of kids who make it their mission to follow their hearts and do the things they love." says one student.

You May Not Know

- Colby College admitted its first female student, Mary Low, in 1871, becoming the first coed college in New England. Mary Low graduated as the 1875 Valedictorian.
- Colby College uses 100 percent green energy with 90 percent bought from completely renewable resources and 10 percent produced by the college itself.
- Colby's mascot, the White Mule, made its debut in 1923 at the Armistice Day football game against rival Bates College. It was suggested that a new mascot was in order to redeem Colby's erroneous "dark horse" reputation. In the 1923 game, a white mule from a local farm was dressed in the school colors of grey and blue. The mule actually led the way onto the field. Colby defeated Bates that day, and the mascot was permanently adopted.

Distinguished Alumni

David Bodine, Chief of Genetics and Molecular Biology, National Institutes of Health; Doris Kearns Goodwin, historian and frequent guest on the *Daily Show*; Dan Harris, Sunday anchor for *ABC World News*; Annie Proulx, Pulitzer Prize winning fiction writer.

Admissions and Financial Aid

A highly competitive college, Colby accepts 29 percent of applicants. The college offers Early decision I (Fall), Early Decision II (Winter), and Regular Decision admissions. Prospective students can apply using the Common Application Form. There is no application fee.

One remarkable facet of Colby's financial aid package is need-based grants that don't require repayment, allowing eligible students to graduate with no student loan debt. It's typical for at least $24.7 million in grants awarded to students to come from the college's own resources. There are no athletic or merit-based scholarships.

COLGATE UNIVERSITY

Overview

Named after the same family that brought the world brighter smiles with Colgate toothpaste, Colgate University was founded in 1819 as a private liberal arts college. Nineteenth and twentieth century architecture characterizes the campus, which is set on 550 acres in Hamilton, New York, 38 miles southeast of Syracuse. Hamilton is a small town, but the surrounding area offers plenty of running and biking trails. The nearby Adirondack Mountains are also ideal for hiking and skiing. The university even maintains a camp on Upper Saranac Lake for use by students and faculty.

Colgate University strives to teach students how to reduce their ecological footprint and preserve nature's resources. They promote sustainability initiatives relating to energy conservation and efficiency, alternative transportation, waste minimization and recycling, and a sustainable food program that serves locally produced food in the dining halls.

Colgate is big on tradition. The Torchlight Ceremony is a tradition that began in 1930 and bookends a Colgate student's experience at the university. Incoming freshmen are led up a hill by faculty in full academic regalia. The procession continues into the academic quad, and then in the Chapel for Convocation. The night before commencement, seniors process in their gowns and with lit torches from Memorial Chapel to Taylor Lake. Students circle the lake and sing the Alma Mater, then spend the night hanging out as a class before commencement ceremonies the next day.

Academics

Chances are good that a student will never see a class size of over 30 students, with the most common class size being 10 to 20 students. All classes are taught by faculty rather than teaching assistants. In addition, 85 percent of faculty live within 10 minutes of campus, making coffee or dinner invitations common. Such significant faculty support could be why Colgate students engage in full-time, grant-funded research opportunities each year. Professor-student relationships are "tight" and "easy to form," say students.

The university offers 53 majors. Of these, standouts are economics, English, and political science. A core curriculum of four general education courses—Legacies of the Ancient World, Challenges of Modernity, Communities and Identities, and Scientific Perspectives on the World—builds a foundation for critical thinking and exposes students to Western and non-Western thought and culture. All students must take a "Global Engagements" course, and an Areas of Inquiry requirement has students further explore a range of disciplines in three areas: Human Thought and Expression; Social Relations, Institutions, and Agents; and Natural Sciences and Mathematics. In addition to the general education requirements, all students must complete two units of physical education.

Colgate has a strong, if not expansive, study-abroad program. More than 20 semester-long courses are available in countries such as Australia, China, the Dominican Republic, France, Italy, Japan, and Spain. More than 50 percent of undergraduates study abroad during their time at Colgate.

More than 200 employers visit the university each year for recruitment. About two-thirds of Colgate graduates eventually pursue graduate study. The most popular career fields for graduating seniors who do not immediately pursue graduate school are communications, education, financial services, law, nonprofit, research, and science. To find out more about what recent Colgate graduates are doing, you can access a Google map that pinpoints students and their whereabouts: http://www.colgate.edu/success. "It's really easy to see what Colgate grads are up to and to get in touch with them when it comes time to find a job," explains a student.

COLGATE UNIVERSITY

Four-year private
Founded: 1819
Hamilton, NY
Rural
Pop. 4,236

Address:
13 Oak Drive
Hamilton, NY
13346

Admissions:
315-228-7401

Financial Aid:
315-228-7431

admission@colgate.edu

www.colgate.edu

COLGATE UNIVERSITY

Students

Total enrollment: 2,886
Undergrads: 2,871
Freshmen: 756
Part-time students: 1%
From out-of-state: 76%
From public schools: 55%
Male/Female: 47%/53%
Live on-campus: 92%
In fraternities: 30%
In sororities: 32%
Off-campus employment rating: Excellent
Caucasian: 69%
African American: 4%
Hispanic: 8%
Asian / Pacific Islander: 4%
Native American: 0%
Mixed (2+ ethnicities): 3%
International: 8%

Academics

Calendar: Semester
Student/faculty ratio: 9:1
Class size 9 or fewer: 18%
Class size 10-29: 75%
Class size 30-49: 6%
Class size 50-99: 2%
Class size 100 or more: -
Returning freshmen: 95%
Six-year graduation rate: 90%

Most Popular Majors

English
Political science
Economics

Admissions

Applicants: 7,798
Accepted: 2,289
Acceptance rate: 29.4%
Placed on wait list: 1,422
Enrolled from wait list: 35
Average GPA: 3.6
ACT range: 30-32
SAT Math range: 640-720
SAT Reading range: 630-730
SAT Writing range: Not reported
Top 10% of class: 68%

Student Life

The Jug is a popular bar among Colgate students, but the majority of students stay on campus even on weekends. With 92 percent of students living on campus, students find ways to entertain themselves and keep the social scene interesting. There are 180 official student organizations, including 12 honor societies and the official school newspaper, *Maroon-News*. Popular student hang-outs include the library, co-op, and the Barge Canal Coffee Company.

The Greek scene is very popular, with six fraternities and three sororities on campus. Overall about 30 percent of the male population and 32 percent of the female population pledge with a fraternity or sorority. The "biggest" and "rowdiest" parties on-campus are hosted by fraternities.

Colgate also has a strong athletic program. The university is a Division I school, and the hockey and football teams enjoy a solid fan base among students. For students interested in playing on a team, intramural sports include basketball, bowling, flag football, golf, ice skating, soccer, Ultimate Frisbee, and volleyball.

Colgate recently expanded its on-campus offerings with a new fitness center, the Ho Science Center, the Case Library and Geyer Center for Information Technology, and new student residences. Avid golfers will be happy to know that the Seven Oaks Golf Course is named one of the top five courses on a college campus by *Golf Digest*.

In 2009, the university began hosting an annual Diversity Week, a multicultural celebration that includes intellectual discussions, workshops, lectures, and a community festival. Colgate also participates in the National Coalition Building Institute aimed at eliminating prejudice.

For more than on-campus activities, students are welcome to explore recreational sites if they are willing to drive a bit. The Baseball Hall of Fame and Glimmerglass Opera are less than an hour away in Cooperstown. Syracuse, also about an hour's drive away, has the Syracuse Stage, the Everson Museum, and the Syracuse Symphony. New York City is a five-hour drive away.

All freshmen live together in Andrews Hall, Curtis Hall, East Hall, Gate House, Stillman Hall, or West Hall. Gate House is generally known as the less social dorm. Incoming freshmen are asked to fill out a "First-Year Student Preference" form, which is used to make housing assignments. "The housing office makes matches that turn into both best friends and worst enemies, but most are in between," says a student. Students looking to get off the beaten path can apply to live in one of three special interest residences: Harlem Renaissance Center, Wellness Living, or Leadership Options for Tomorrow.

Student Body

Students report that "many come from upper-class backgrounds," and a common trait among students is a general "love of the outdoors." Sixty-nine percent of the student body is Caucasian, but Colgate is surprisingly ethnically diverse for a small liberal arts school. Additionally, Colgate is geographically diverse, with 76 percent of students hailing from out of state.

The ALANA Cultural Center represents the African, Latin American, Asian, and Native American communities at Colgate.

ALANA is a learning center that serves as an umbrella organization for student organizations that sponsor intellectual, educational, and social programming for students of color. Fourteen student groups are housed under ALANA.

You May Not Know

- The swans on Taylor Lake are named Adam and Eve and are the eighth generation of swans that have lived at the lake.
- The number 13 is a lucky one at Colgate. Colgate was founded by 13 men who, at first, each offered $13 and 13 prayers.
- The *Colgate Maroon-News* is the oldest weekly college newspaper in the country.

Distinguished Alumni

Charles Addams, cartoonist for the *New Yorker* and inspiration for the 1960s television show, *The Addams Family*; Carl Braun, five-time all-star with the NY Knicks; Bennett Cohen, co-founder of Ben & Jerry's Ice Cream; Monica Crowley, Richard Nixon biographer; Andy Rooney, columnist and *60 Minutes* commentator.

Admissions and Financial Aid

Students should know that the most important determining factor for admission is academic achievement. Colgate looks closely at a student's high school transcript, looking for a rigorous and challenging academic program. While class rank is not essential for admission, a student's review does focus on how they measure up compared to their high school peers and other applicants. Colgate does not offer merit-based scholarships but does award athletic scholarships.

The Host Program enables prospective students to spend the night with current Colgate undergraduates and experience campus life first hand. The university encourages interested students to visit the university and make an appointment with an admissions counselor. These informal one-on-ones are not required and are non-evaluative, but it's a good way for students to get their specific questions answered and see if Colgate is a good fit.

COLGATE UNIVERSITY

Highlights

Admissions Criteria
Academic criteria:
Grades: ☆ ☆ ☆
Difficulty of class schedule: ☆ ☆ ☆
Class rank: ☆ ☆ ☆
Standardized test scores: ☆ ☆
Teacher recommendations: ☆ ☆
Personal statement: ☆ ☆
Non-academic criteria considered:
Extracurricular activities
Special talents, interests, abilities
Character/personal qualities
Volunteer work
Work experience
State of residency
Geographical location
Minority affiliation
Alumni relationship

Deadlines
Early Action: No
Early Decision: November 15
Regular Action: January 15 (final)
Notification of admission by: April 1
Common Application: Accepted

Financial Aid
In-state tuition: $46,060
Out-of-state tuition: $46,060
Room: $5,555
Board: $5,955
Books: $1,040
Freshmen receiving need-based aid: 33%
Undergrads rec. need-based aid: 36%
Avg. % of need met by financial aid: 100%
Avg. aid package (freshmen): $42,313
Avg. aid package (undergrads): $42,522
Avg. debt upon graduation: $20,751

School Spirit
Mascot: Raider
Colors: Maroon and white
Song: *Alma Mater*

Four-year public
Founded: 1770
Charleston, SC
Medium city
Pop. 120,083

Address:
66 George Street
Charleston, SC
29424-0001

Admissions:
843-953-5670

Financial Aid:
843-953-5540

admissions@cofc.edu

www.cofc.edu

COLLEGE OF CHARLESTON

Overview

The College of Charleston may have been named an "up and coming" university by *U.S. News & World Report*, but the mid-sized university, which ranks fourth among public universities in the South, has been around for quite a while, as the classical, colonial, and antebellum architecture of the school can attest. The 13th oldest educational institution in the country, the campus features historic buildings draped in Spanish moss with a distinctive Southern flair. Additionally, the College of Charleston boasts an extensive collection of historic archives, including just about every book published in America between 1639 and 1800 and the Avery Research Center for African American History and Culture's source material. Add to that a social life that is governed by long-standing tradition and you have quite an attractive mix.

At the same time that it celebrates its heritage, CofC is instituting major innovations, both in its facilities—such as the Marlene and Nathan Addlestone Library, completed in 2005, and the Grice Marine Laboratory—and its focus on undergraduate education. The four-square-city-block campus is also well-integrated into the city of Charleston. CofC isn't without drawbacks: students complain of the limited number of majors and the relative homogeneity of the students. But CofC is a lively campus with increasingly competitive academics, right in the heart of an unbeatable college town.

Academics

In total, CofC's six schools offer 47 majors, including the nation's only discovery informatics program, and a host of minors. CofC is known for its English and Pre-Health Program, which combines any science major (biology is particularly strong) with a complementary advising, internship, and development program. All students must complete the General Education Requirements, which consist of four courses in the humanities and two courses each in English, history, natural science with lab components, math and logic, foreign language, and social sciences. About two-thirds of classes have fewer than 30 students. This fosters close student/professor relationships, as one student explains, "It's not unusual to have discussions with all of my professors outside of class."

All first-year students get a chance to become acquainted with faculty as part of the required First-Year Experience, which either entails a First-Year Seminar or a Learning Community. First-Year Seminars are faculty-taught, research- and writing-based classes of up to 25 students, augmented by field trips outside of class. "The first-year seminars require you to not just read the material but understand it," notes a student. A Learning Community is a cluster of two or more faculty-taught courses organized around an interdisciplinary theme or subject; the courses are designed to work together, and include cross-course homework and activities. A weekly synthesis seminar led by an upperclassman peer facilitator brings it all together, covering topics both related to the classes and to college and academic life in general. Learning Communities may or may not be residential.

Students in any major may apply to the Honors College, which offers small, faculty-taught Honors seminars as well as special Honors housing, advising, priority registration, and an Honors Semester in Washington, DC. Students must complete the Honors College course requirements in addition to CofC's general education requirements, which can get cumbersome, according to students. Honors College students must also complete an independent study in their junior year and an extensive research-based Bachelor's Essay in their senior year. A special Honors Program in Business and Economics is also offered. Students in this program take on leadership roles in service-learning projects and must spend a semester abroad at a business program at one of CofC's partner universities.

Leadership development programs are accessible through the Higdon Student Leadership Center, which offers Cougar eXcursions. Designed to provide incoming freshmen opportunities to learn about the college and its activities, these programs also offer students the chance to meet upperclassmen and develop their own leadership skills. The Center also holds an annual Leadership Conference and runs the Leadership College of Charleston Program, a year-long chain of events designed with upperclassmen in mind. Through this program, they experience working and networking with local businesses, government agencies, and service organizations.

Student research and creative endeavors are supported through the Undergraduate Research and Creative Activities (URCA) program, which awards the Academic Year Research Award (AYRA), Major Academic Year Support (MAYS), and Summer Undergraduate Research with Faculty (SURF) grants of between $500 and $6,500. Students may find additional opportunities for research at the Grice Marine Laboratory, about 15 minutes from campus on James Island in the Charleston Harbor. Grice collaborates with the two state and two federal partner institutions at Fort Johnson Marine Resources Center.

Students can study abroad through CofC-sponsored semester programs in Spain, Cuba, Dubai, France, Argentina, or Chile; otherwise, faculty-led summer classes or programs in Austria, Germany, Italy, Brazil, the British Virgin Islands, Cambodia, China, Costa Rica, Ecuador, Egypt, France, the UK, India, Morocco, Nicaragua, Panama, Peru, Poland, Russia, and Spain are among students' choices. Exchanges are also available.

CofC's Career Center can help students find jobs and internships, critique résumés, and conduct practice interviews. Current students can also network with alums through the CofC Alumni and Student Network. "Alumni are really helpful in offering advice and even give us leads on jobs," says a student.

Student Life

Over 150 student groups exist at CofC, including Habitat for Humanity, the a cappella group Chucktown Trippintones, and the newspaper, the *George Street Observer*. Much daily socializing takes place at the Cistern, the grassy patch next to Randolph Hall, where students hang out, study, and enjoy the sun. In fact, on their first day of class, students sign "the book" of all matriculating students.

Major events on campus include Homecoming Week—organized around the basketball season because of CofC's lack of a football team—with its concerts, tailgating, and the Spirit Cup Challenge, which pits student groups, residence halls, and Greek organizations against each other in parade float competition as well as the "Chucktown Follies" talent show. Cougarpalooza marks the end of the year with a day-long festival featuring live music, free food, and games. In a break from tradition, students wear white dresses and dinner jackets rather than caps and gowns for Commencement.

Less than a fifth of students belong to one of 27 fraternities and sororities. The Greek system is sometimes quite prominent in Southern colleges, and there are those that feel it's a big part of life at CofC. "Fraternities and sororities matter a lot to members but aren't nearly as important to independents," says a student.

CofC has 20 NCAA Division I varsity teams—basketball replaces football as the most popular sport, but women's sailing and equestrian are the most competitive. CofC students are active types

COLLEGE OF CHARLESTON

Highlights

Students
Total enrollment: 11,649
Undergrads: 10,461
Freshmen: 2,854
From out-of-state: 46%
From public schools: 80%
Male/Female: 38%/62%
Live on-campus: 32%
In fraternities: 14%
In sororities: 21%
Off-campus employment rating: Fair
Caucasian: 84%
African American: 6%
Hispanic: 3%
Asian / Pacific Islander: 2%
Native American: 0%
Mixed (2+ ethnicities): 3%
International: 1%

Academics
Calendar: Semester
Student/faculty ratio: 16:1
Class size 9 or fewer: 8%
Class size 10-29: 55%
Class size 30-49: 31%
Class size 50-99: 5%
Class size 100 or more: 1%
Returning freshmen: 83%
Six-year graduation rate: 63%
Graduates who immediately go to graduate school: 16%

Most Popular Majors
Biology
Communications
Psychology

Admissions
Applicants: 11,086
Accepted: 8,149
Acceptance rate: 73.5%
Average GPA: 3.8
ACT range: 23-27
SAT Math range: 550-640
SAT Reading range: 560-650
SAT Writing range: Not reported
Top 10% of class: 28%
Top 25% of class: 63%
Top 50% of class: 93%

177

College Profiles

COLLEGE OF CHARLESTON

Admissions Criteria

Academic criteria:

Grades: ☆ ☆ ☆

Difficulty of class schedule: ☆ ☆ ☆

Class rank: ☆ ☆

Standardized test scores: ☆ ☆ ☆

Teacher recommendations: ☆

Personal statement: ☆

Non-academic criteria considered:

Extracurricular activities

Special talents, interests, abilities

Character/personal qualities

Volunteer work

Work experience

Geographical location

Minority affiliation

Deadlines

Early Action: November 1

Early Decision: No

Regular Action: February 1 (priority)

April 1 (final)

Common Application: Accepted

Financial Aid

In-state tuition: $10,230

Out-of-state tuition: $26,694

Room: $6,817

Board: $3,039

Books: Varies

Freshmen receiving need-based aid: 47%

Undergrads rec. need-based aid: 46%

Avg. % of need met by financial aid: 58%

Avg. aid package (freshmen): $12,320

Avg. aid package (undergrads): $12,933

Avg. debt upon graduation: $20,541

School Spirit

Mascot: Cougar

Colors: Maroon and white

and are likely to be tossing a Frisbee around campus, participating in one of many club sports, or playing one of the intramurals available (pickleball, HORSE, and chess are offered).

As CofC is "smack dab in the middle" of historic Charleston, the city's restaurants and shops are easily accessible. Charleston is also host to a vibrant artsy scene, but is also only about 20 minutes away from the beach, where students can surf and partake of other outdoor recreational opportunities like rock-climbing and kayaking. "The weather here is amazing year round," comments a student. "Charleston is underrated, but it is one of the *best* college towns."

First-year students are guaranteed housing in traditional residence halls; upperclassmen can live in suites, on-campus apartments, or historic houses on campus. Special housing, like immersive language housing and themed communities, is also available. Living off campus can be a challenge with Charleston's high rents.

Student Body

About half of students come from in state, making CofC low in ethnic diversity but a little more liberal politically than you'd expect from a Southern school. "It would be nice to have more diversity both in ethnic and racial background as well as in opinion," says a student.

The female population is almost twice the male population, although the other colleges in the area provide plenty of males for date life; the Southern sorority girl type is fairly prevalent. "You will see a lot of sorority types even among those who aren't a member of a sorority," notes a student.

You May Not Know

- The historic buildings on campus make it a popular place to film movies and TV shows; *Cold Mountain*, *The Patriot*, *The Notebook*, *Dear John*, and episodes of *General Hospital* have been filmed there.
- The grassy patch known as the Cistern was initially a retention area to help control flooding and provide water for fighting fires.
- Randolph Hall is one of the oldest continuously-used buildings in the United States.

Distinguished Alumni

Nafees Bin Zafar, Academy-Award winning visual effects engineer; Brett Gardner, professional baseball player; Arlinda Locklear, legal expert and first Native American woman to appear before the Supreme Court; Robert Mills, first American-born architect.

Admissions and Financial Aid

Applicants to CofC can be eligible for a number of merit scholarships, mostly for South Carolina residents. CofC itself awards two Colonial Scholarships based on academic merit, community involvement, and personal interviews, as well as Presidential Scholarships of varying amounts. Applications must be submitted by December 1. The State of South Carolina also offers Palmetto Fellow, LIFE, and HOPE Scholarships for academically qualified residents.

COLLEGE OF NEW JERSEY

Overview

The College of New Jersey may sound obscure to those from outside New Jersey, but it might be one of New Jersey's best kept secrets. TCNJ's well-manicured campus and Colonial Georgian buildings occupy 289 suburban acres in Ewing, just outside of the state capital, Trenton. With a midsized student population, TCNJ offers a wealth of resources disproportionate to its size at a cost equivalent to that of a state school. *U.S. News & World Report* has named TCNJ the leading public institution in the region. Research opportunities are readily available and the undergraduate education, particularly a strong liberal arts and service learning foundation, is the school's number one priority; a large new library opened its doors in 2005. While Ewing and the campus environs may be sleepy and quiet, Princeton is just down the road, and the vibrant entertainment opportunities of Philadelphia and New York are both just an hour away.

Admission to TCNJ is competitive, and if you're not from New Jersey, the odds may be stacked against you. The school explicitly states its mission to admit New Jersey's "most talented" students, while allowing "only the most exceptional students from out of state." TCNJ fosters an atmosphere of academic focus and elitism that may be the intellectual paradise full of equally studious peers that some students have fantasized about throughout high school; for others, it might be a pretentious nightmare where a straightforward name will never do when there's a polysyllabic turn of phrase available (distribution requirements, for instance, are called "Broad Sectors of Human Inquiry"). Ultimately, the quality of TCNJ's facilities and liberal arts education are undeniable, and the real question is one of environmental fit.

Academics

TCNJ offers over 50 majors in addition to an extensive "Liberal Learning" core curriculum with a heavy emphasis on civic values. These requirements are divided into three sectors: Intellectual and Scholarly Growth, Civic Responsibility, and Broad Sectors of Human Inquiry. "Intellectual and Scholarly Growth" consists of a writing-intensive First-Year Seminar course and three writing courses over the course of four years; students must also demonstrate computer literacy and proficiency in a foreign language. "Civic Responsibility" requires a class in each of four areas: Community, Global, Gender, Race and Ethnicity. "Broad Sectors of Human Inquiry" is designed to enable "students to be conversant in the broad range of intellectual discourse." This translates roughly to "distribution requirements" and can be satisfied in three ways: Students may either pick a pre-designed course of study, design their own interdisciplinary concentration, or take nine classes in arts and humanities, social sciences, natural science, and quantitative reasoning. Additionally, TCNJ has a Community Engagement requirement that students can meet by taking a service-learning seminar or participating along with their dorm-mates in one of many Community-Engaged Learning days throughout the year. "I can't believe I fulfilled a graduation requirement by reading Dr. Seuss books to children. Seriously, the service requirement is truly eye-opening," says a student.

Academics at TCNJ are demanding, and students tend to be very academically focused and competitive, particularly in TCNJ's flagship programs, which include the majors in biology, business administration, and the School of Education. Many students also choose to pursue some of TCNJ's combined degree offerings, which include a demanding seven-year combined BS/MD degree.

TCNJ students who are particularly devoted to "the life of the mind," as TCNJ puts it, have several options for expansion. The College Honors Program, open to students from all majors, offers small, interactive, faculty-team-taught Honors seminars that meet the Liberal Learning requirements. Students also have the op-

COLLEGE OF NEW JERSEY

Four-year public
Founded: 1855
Ewing, NJ
Large town
Pop. 35,707

Address:
P.O. Box 7718, 2000
Pennington Road
Ewing, NJ
08628-0718

Admissions:
800-624-0967

Financial Aid:
609-771-2211

tcnjinfo@tcnjj.edu

www.tcnj.edu

COLLEGE OF NEW JERSEY

Highlights

Students
Total enrollment: 7,267
Undergrads: 6,545
Freshmen: 1,363
Part-time students: 3%
From out-of-state: 7%
From public schools: 70%
Male/Female: 43%/57%
Live on-campus: 48%
In fraternities: 16%
In sororities: 13%
Off-campus employment rating: Excellent
Caucasian: 66%
African American: 6%
Hispanic: 10%
Asian / Pacific Islander: 9%
Native American: 0%
Mixed (2+ ethnicities): 1%
International: 0%

Academics
Calendar: Semester
Student/faculty ratio: 13:1
Class size 9 or fewer: 8%
Class size 10-29: 76%
Class size 30-49: 16%
Class size 50-99: -
Class size 100 or more: -
Returning freshmen: 94%
Six-year graduation rate: 86%
Graduates who immediately go to graduate school: 31%
Graduates who immediately enter career related to major: 78%

Most Popular Majors
Psychology
Biology
Elementary education

Admissions
Applicants: 10,295
Accepted: 4,750
Acceptance rate: 46.1%
Placed on wait list: 1,437
Enrolled from wait list: 9
Average GPA: Not reported
ACT range: Not reported
SAT Math range: 580-680
SAT Reading range: 550-650
SAT Writing range: 14-45
Top 10% of class: 56%
Top 25% of class: 89%
Top 50% of class: 99%

portunity to travel and present work at regional Honors conferences. The extensively-named Faculty-Student Scholarly and Creative Collaboration program supports students participating in faculty-supervised research or creative projects in all fields. Students may also collaborate with faculty during the eight-week Mentored Undergraduate Summer Experience (MUSE), which provides students conducting faculty-mentored projects in all fields with on-campus housing and stipends.

Under the four-year Bonner Community Scholars Program, students can join one of several issue-based community service teams that cooperate with organizations in the Trenton area, putting in a total of about 300 hours of service. Bonner students also organize Community-Engaged Learning events for the student body at large. Students' service-learning is augmented by seminars, including a special First-Year Seminar, weekly meetings, and workshops. Students may also participate in service trips to places such as New Orleans or Nicaragua. Study abroad, which goes by the name "Global Engagement" at TCNJ, is available directly, through faculty-led, program-specific travel courses to locations in Russia, China, the UK, Italy, Spain, and Australia. TCNJ offers programs and exchange agreements at numerous international institutions.

Of TCNJ graduates who enter the workforce, 78 percent find work in their field within six months of graduation; about a third of students choose to enter graduate school.

Student Life

Of TCNJ's 200 student groups, many are service-oriented, such as Habitat for Humanity, or intellectual or artistic, such as the *Lion's Eye* literary magazine and All-College Theatre. While about 14 percent of the school belongs to the Greek system, TCNJ's 11 fraternities and 13 sororities are largely based off campus.

A few on-campus events bring students out in crowds. Most popular among these is LollaNobooza, whose name, while a stretch, means exactly what you think it does. Called one of the "best events of the year," this alcohol-free party features carnival-style fun, food, games (think "musical chairs"), and dancing, and is open to students, faculty, and staff alike. Mystique of the East is a major dance, music, and martial arts showcase put on by the Asian American Association. Finally, Senior Week features parties of all kinds for graduating seniors, including a dinner and "Soiree" in Atlantic City; it includes trips to the Jersey Shore, Mystery Speakers (who have included Big Bird and Elmo), and a Gala dance. The parties, concerts, and tailgates associated with Homecoming are also popular.

TCNJ's 18 varsity sports, which compete in NCAA Division III, are fairly popular—football and basketball especially, although TCNJ puts a heavy emphasis on its women's athletic program, particularly lacrosse, as well. A fairly standard array of intramural offerings are also available.

For off-campus entertainment, the Greek scene is available; otherwise, Princeton is just 10 miles away, while Philadelphia and New York are only an hour's drive. "Every student must take a weekend trip to the City at least a handful of times before graduating," advises a student.

Freshmen and sophomores are guaranteed on-campus housing in either traditional or suite-style residences. Upperclassmen wishing to live on campus can enter a housing lottery for traditional or suite-style dorms or on-campus townhouses and apartments. As one student explains, "The dorms vary in quality, getting better as you become an upperclassman."

Student Body

While it's hard to pin down a particular "type" of TCNJ student, a few broad generalizations can be made. Most students are academically hard-core and the great majority graduated in the top quarter of their classes; most are upper middle-class. "Pretty much everyone here would have been at the top of my class in high school. The atmosphere is pretty intellectual," says a student. Ethnic diversity is high and very few come from outside of New Jersey.

You Might Not Know

- TCNJ, originally the New Jersey State Normal School, was the first institution to train teachers in New Jersey.
- TCNJ has been named the top institution in Division III for female athletics by *Sports Illustrated for Women*.
- The institution's name change from Trenton State College to the College of New Jersey incited legal action from Princeton, which had traditionally been called the College of New Jersey. The case was dismissed.

Distinguished Alumni

Holly Black, writer; Sheila Callaghan, playwright; Christopher Henry Smith, U.S. Congressman; Tom McCarthy, radio announcer of the New York Mets.

Admissions and Financial Aid

Students can get to know TCNJ through on-campus open houses and visits as well as online chats with admissions officers. TCNJ does not require applicants to submit recommendations but encourages them to do so nonetheless.

Students from New Jersey are eligible for between $3,000 and $6,000 in merit scholarships; these are awarded based on "holistic" evaluation, including GPAs and test scores as well as extracurriculars and leadership. Students must complete a FAFSA. Out-of-state students are subject to the same holistic evaluation and must also fill out the FAFSA, but must complete a separate scholarship application after they have been accepted to TCNJ. These awards range from $2,000 to $10,000.

COLLEGE OF NEW JERSEY

Highlights

Admissions Criteria
Academic criteria:
Grades: ☆ ☆ ☆
Difficulty of class schedule: ☆ ☆ ☆
Class rank: ☆ ☆ ☆
Standardized test scores: ☆ ☆ ☆
Teacher recommendations: ☆ ☆
Personal statement: ☆ ☆
Non-academic criteria considered:
Extracurricular activities
Special talents, interests, abilities
Character/personal qualities
Volunteer work
Work experience
Geographical location
Minority affiliation
Alumni relationship

Deadlines
Early Action: No
Early Decision: November 15
Regular Action: November 15 (priority)
January 15 (final)
Notification of admission by: April 1
Common Application: Accepted

Financial Aid
In-state tuition: $15,780
Out-of-state tuition: $26,184
Room: Varies
Board: Varies
Books: $1,200
Freshmen receiving need-based aid: 55%
Undergrads rec. need-based aid: 52%
Avg. % of need met by financial aid: 46%
Avg. aid package (freshmen): $11,034
Avg. aid package (undergrads): $10,647
Avg. debt upon graduation: $21,032

School Spirit
Mascot: Lion
Colors: Blue and gold
Song: *Alma Mater*

COLLEGE OF
THE ATLANTIC

Four-year private
Founded: 1969
Bar Harbor, ME
Rural
Pop. 5,235

Address:
105 Eden Street
Bar Harbor, ME
04609

Admissions:
800-528-0025

Financial Aid:
207-801-5645

inquiry@ecology.coa.
edu

www.coa.edu

COLLEGE OF THE ATLANTIC

Overview

College of the Atlantic (COA) is the first college to reduce greenhouse gas emissions to zero, and that's just one example of what makes this very small, 300-student college unique. While students are incredibly diverse—hailing from nearly all 50 states and more than 30 countries—they will all graduate with the same degree: human ecology.

Though the college may have only one major, it certainly doesn't encourage conformity. All students design their own interdisciplinary academic program, and the lack of letter grades encourages collaboration over competition. Founded in 1969, COA has already established its own quirky traditions that start with the first day of school and go with students to the very end: entering students may participate in the quarter-mile Bar Island Swim in the icy waters of Frenchman Bay, and graduating seniors deck out in all sorts of clothing and pass a flower to the next graduate in line instead of donning gowns and shifting the tassels on their caps.

Not surprisingly, COA draws environmental students, many of whom are vegetarians and liberal in their political views. The 35-acre campus on the rocky coast of Mount Desert Island, Maine, is a mile away from the seaside town of Bar Harbor, a popular summer tourist destination; but you're more likely to find students on outdoor adventures in nearby Acadia National Park than shopping for lobster paraphernalia in the gift shops.

COA is obviously not for everyone. Students must be prepared for harsh winters where temperatures dip below zero, but having some of the smallest class sizes in the nation makes for a very tight-knit community where everyone knows everyone else. The partying, organized sports, and dating scenes can feel limited, and students must be fans of experiential learning as well as highly self-directed and self-motivated.

Academics

Since the College of the Atlantic has only the Human Ecology major, there are no departments, though courses are loosely divided into three "resource areas"—arts and design, environmental sciences, and human studies—with optional further specialization in nine "focus areas." Students design their own academic programs, though overall course offerings are somewhat limited.

Each class is extremely small. The college boasts "only 10 percent of our classes have more than 20 students, the sixth smallest percentage in the nation, according to *U.S. News & World Report*." One student says, "you get more attention here from professors than from your own parents." Students receive written evaluations rather than grades based on traditional standards, though any student who wishes may also receive a letter grade.

The academic year is divided in three 10-week terms, and most students take three courses each term. Most courses are simply one credit, making it easy to calculate meeting the 36-credit requirement for graduation. There are a number of course requirements, and all students must also complete community service, an internship, a human ecology essay, and a term-long three-credit final project.

Students interested in the natural sciences can take advantage of COA's nearby research stations at Great Duck Island and Mt. Desert Rock. The Idea Network for Biomedical Research Excellence (INBRE) connects COA students to research opportunities at nearby Jackson Laboratory and Mt. Desert Island Biological Laboratory. The college also owns 86-acre Beech Hill Farm, which provides organic produce as well as opportunities to learn about sustainable agriculture. "Where else can you intern to learn about organic farm management at a working farm?" asks a student.

A whopping 55 percent of COA graduates study abroad. International study experiences include programs in Mexico, Guatemala, and Newfoundland.

After graduating, 55 percent of COA alumni eventually pursue advanced degrees. Among those who do not attend graduate school, 23 percent pursue careers in education, 20 percent become scientists, 17 percent work in arts and design, 13 percent go into business, and 12 percent go into social service or government work. One student comments that many graduates "don't just get a job to get a job but want to do something that will make an impact."

Student Life

With more than half of students living off campus and no Greek organizations, social life at COA can feel somewhat circumscribed. There isn't much of a drinking scene on campus, though students certainly seek fun in other venues. The college has nine official student organizations: popular student groups include environmental groups such as SustainUS, as well as the international cultural organization that puts on Fandango, the college's annual showcase of talent that raises funds for an international humanitarian organization. "Generally, we're more doers than joiners," remarks a student.

Tuesday nights at COA feels like a typical college's Friday night because there are no classes on Wednesdays. Wednesdays are devoted to All College Meeting, a weekly student-facilitated open forum that serves as the community-wide decision-making body for COA. This community spirit is also reflected in the student center, Deering Common, which has a fireplace, ocean views, and even a meditation room.

Freshmen all attend on-campus orientation, but many also enjoy a weeklong Outdoor Orientation Program (whimsically named OOPs) beforehand. These student-led wilderness trips are COA's longest standing program. "I sailed off the coast of Maine for a week," reminisces a student.

There are no intercollegiate sports teams, though the school does have intramurals. Not surprisingly, the outdoor-loving students aren't just holed up in their rooms all the time. Recreational equipment—including a fleet of ocean kayaks and lake canoes—is available for free to students, and camping gear is easy to borrow. The sailing class is popular, as is the local YMCA's scuba diving classes. All students have a free membership to the local YMCA.

The local town of Bar Harbor is a mile away, and COA runs a shuttle there several times each evening for easy access to the YMCA, grocery store, and the popular Reel Pizza, where students can sit on comfy couches and munch on real-dough pizza while watching a movie. During the summer, the town teems with tourists and lobster kitsch; winter, by sharp contrast, makes for sparsely populated streets. COA students are also close to Acadia National Park, which provides opportunities for hiking, cross-country-skiing, and snowshoeing.

First-year students are guaranteed housing in one of the five on-campus residences, each with its own character and, more importantly, a kitchen! COA's newest housing addition, the Kathryn W. Davis Student Residence Village, is a "green" dorm with wood pellet heating that boasts a pool room and media center. Blair Dining Hall, affectionately nicknamed "Take-A-Break" or "TAB," offers mouthwatering and eco-friendly items that use local, organic ingredients when possible, as well as humanely raised meat and sustainable seafood. This menu is topped off by baked goods made

COLLEGE OF THE ATLANTIC

Highlights

Students
Total enrollment: 340
Undergrads: 330
Freshmen: 94
From out-of-state: 83%
From public schools: 63%
Male/Female: 28%/72%
Live on-campus: 44%
Off-campus employment rating: Fair
Caucasian: 68%
African American: 2%
Hispanic: 1%
Asian / Pacific Islander: 1%
Native American: 0%
Mixed (2+ ethnicities): 2%
International: 16%

Academics
Calendar: Trimester
Student/faculty ratio: 9:1
Class size 9 or fewer: 29%
Class size 10-29: 71%
Class size 30-49: -
Class size 50-99: -
Class size 100 or more: -
Returning freshmen: 83%
Six-year graduation rate: 64%
Graduates who immediately go to graduate school: 5%
Graduates who immediately enter career related to major: 85%

Most Popular Majors
Human ecology

Admissions
Applicants: 377
Accepted: 266
Acceptance rate: 70.6%
Placed on wait list: 23
Enrolled from wait list: 7
Average GPA: 3.6
ACT range: 25-33
SAT Math range: 540-680
SAT Reading range: 610-690
SAT Writing range: 18-55
Top 10% of class: 52%
Top 25% of class: 70%
Top 50% of class: 93%

183

College Profiles

COLLEGE OF THE ATLANTIC

Admissions Criteria

Academic criteria:
Grades: ☆ ☆ ☆
Difficulty of class schedule: ☆ ☆ ☆
Class rank: ☆ ☆
Standardized test scores: ☆
Teacher recommendations: ☆ ☆ ☆
Personal statement: ☆ ☆ ☆
Non-academic criteria considered:
Interview
Extracurricular activities
Special talents, interests, abilities
Character/personal qualities
Volunteer work
Work experience
Geographical location
Minority affiliation
Alumni relationship

Deadlines

Early Action: No
Early Decision: December 1
Regular Action: February 15 (final)
Notification of admission by: April 1
Common Application: Accepted

Financial Aid

In-state tuition: $38,403
Out-of-state tuition: $38,403
Room: $5,952
Board: $3,306
Books: $600
Freshmen receiving need-based aid: 92%
Undergrads rec. need-based aid: 87%
Avg. % of need met by financial aid: 95%
Avg. aid package (freshmen): $33,696
Avg. aid package (undergrads): $35,359
Avg. debt upon graduation: $22,473

School Spirit

Mascot: Black Flies

from "scratch." One student comments, "this is a place where it's pretty easy to be a vegan." It's not every school that will stock sassafras organic fair trade chocolate truffles in their vending machines!

Student Body

COA students are those who, by their own admission, "guide our own way." The college selects self-motivated and adventurous students since most of their opportunities—internships, independent study, and the like—must be self-crafted. According to the college, it seeks students who have "the ability to question, and the desire to challenge the status quo."

The uneven ratio of female to male students (about two to one) and the few students on campus combine to make for a limited dating scene. In general, the environmental focus draws what some would call "hippy" types, "staunch liberals," and politically active students.

Because of the Davis United World College (UWC) Scholars program, which covers full financial need for its graduates, there is a large population of international students representing many different countries. COA was one of the five schools piloted for the program in 2000 and the college now has the third largest percentage of international students among all private colleges in the United States.

You May Not Know

- COA was founded in 1969 by Mount Desert Island residents who wanted to establish another source of revenue during the seasons when tourism was low.
- According to the college, it was the first founded to have "as its primary focus the relationships between humans and the environment."
- All food and napkins are composted, and recycling bins are available on "every floor of every building on campus."

Distinguished Alumni

Amy Goodman, journalist; Nell Newman, founder of Newman's Own Organics; Chellie Pingree, First District Congresswoman from Maine; Greg Stone, Vice President of Global Marine Programs at the New England Aquarium.

Admissions and Financial Aid

As befits a college with a policy described by the admissions office as "a personal and highly individualized process," standardized test scores are not required. Likewise, a personal interview is recommended but not required. Indeed, the college's admissions office doesn't prescribe the usual checklist of requirements, but rather, it emphasizes four general points that they look for in students: academic achievement, enthusiasm for learning, desire to be part of COA's community, and a hunger for intellectual and personal challenges.

COA offers over a dozen scholarships, from the Presidential Scholarship that every applicant is automatically considered for, to more specific funding such as the Scholarship for Children of Maine Teachers.

COLLEGE OF THE HOLY CROSS

Overview

Holy Cross is a private Roman Catholic college about an hour from Boston, the beach, and skiing. Since it has such a small student body, students form tight relationships with one another and with professors. Students undoubtedly receive preparation for the future, both through strong academics and through unusually comprehensive career services and study-abroad offerings. On an ideological level, an appreciation for the importance of community service permeates life at Holy Cross, from the classroom to extracurricular activities.

Although it's far from a bustling metropolis, Worcester has a surprising amount of opportunities. The school itself is an oasis of green, as the campus is a registered arboretum. In 2010, Holy Cross opened its new Integrated Science Complex, a state-of-the-art, environmentally-friendly conjunction of buildings that house research labs, classrooms, and lecture halls for both the hard sciences and the social sciences.

Those looking for a partying Greek-heavy school may not enjoy Holy Cross since it has no Greek life. However, for service-minded, serious students—especially those who are practicing Catholics—Holy Cross is a highly appealing, supportive environment.

Academics

Holy Cross offers 27 majors. The economics program, which offers one major in economics and another in economics and accounting, is particularly strong. Premed and prelaw students also receive an excellent grounding at Holy Cross. Among students who apply to medical school, 78 percent are admitted. For law school, the admittance rate reaches 84 percent.

Holy Cross is the only Catholic college that serves only undergraduates, so students can expect to receive more of their professors' attention than at most universities. What's more, virtually all classes have fewer than 50 students. "Because classes are small, we actively participate in discussions," explains a student. For classes not offered at Holy Cross, students can cross-register for courses at a dozen other universities in central Massachusetts through the Colleges of Worcester Consortium.

Holy Cross calls its easy-to-understand distribution courses "Common Requirements." Students must take one course in each of the following areas: arts, literature, studies in religion, philosophical studies, historical studies, and cross-cultural studies. In addition, Holy Cross requires two courses each in language studies, social science, and natural and mathematical sciences.

Freshmen get adjusted to Holy Cross life within the even smaller communities of their Montserrat classes where each freshman takes part in a small seminar for the entire year. Montserrat is a much more extensive experience than most other freshman seminars, as it promises to unite "learning, living, and doing." The seminars are grouped into five interdisciplinary "clusters": Core Human Questions, Divine, Global Society, Natural World, and Self. Students share dorms with others from their cluster. Beyond fostering friendships among classmates, Montserrat also makes it easy for students to get to know their professors. "Montserrat is the best introduction to being in college," one student comments.

In addition to honors programs within some departments, Holy Cross also offers an interdisciplinary College Honors Program for students from all majors. Just 36 students are chosen for the program. Once they've proven themselves in this arduous process, honors students enjoy challenging, interdisciplinary seminars, receive great training in independent research, work intensively with professors, and benefit from an honors colloquium, which is a "series of interdisciplinary discussions." In their senior year, they complete an honors thesis.

COLLEGE OF THE HOLY CROSS

Four-year private
Founded: 1843
Worcester, MA
Medium city
Pop. 181,631

Address:
1 College Street
Worcester, MA
01610-2395

Admissions:
800-442-2421

Financial Aid:
508-793-2265

admissions@holy-cross.edu

www.holycross.edu

COLLEGE OF THE HOLY CROSS

Highlights

Students
Total enrollment: 2,926
Undergrads: 2,926
Freshmen: 764
Part-time students: 1%
From out-of-state: 68%
From public schools: 49%
Male/Female: 49%/51%
Live on-campus: 91%
Off-campus employment rating: Fair
Caucasian: 68%
African American: 5%
Hispanic: 10%
Asian / Pacific Islander: 5%
Native American: 0%
Mixed (2+ ethnicities): 2%
International: 1%

Academics
Calendar: Semester
Student/faculty ratio: 10:1
Class size 9 or fewer: 11%
Class size 10-29: 79%
Class size 30-49: 9%
Class size 50-99: 1%
Class size 100 or more: -
Returning freshmen: 95%
Six-year graduation rate: 93%
Graduates who immediately go to graduate school: 20%
Graduates who immediately enter career related to major: 63%

Most Popular Majors
Economics
Psychology
English

Admissions
Applicants: 7,228
Accepted: 2,424
Acceptance rate: 33.5%
Placed on wait list: 1,540
Enrolled from wait list: Not reported
Average GPA: 3.9
ACT range: 27-30
SAT Math range: 620-680
SAT Reading range: 600-700
SAT Writing range: 28-54
Top 10% of class: 60%
Top 25% of class: 95%
Top 50% of class: 100%

186

Holy Cross's course offerings demonstrate the college's dedication to service with over 80 community-based learning courses. Students can undertake real-world projects that range from testing water samples with the Blackstone River Coalition in the Freshwater Ecology course to applying tenets of democratic participation to field projects in Worcester in the History and Traditions course.

Holy Cross students can study abroad in 18 countries. As a part of some programs, students are required to do an "Independent Cultural Immersion Project" in their host country. These projects range from service, internships, or simply becoming involved in a club, sport, or other activity. In conjunction with the American Institute for Roman Culture, Holy Cross offers a new program that allows students with an interest in classics and archaeology to study and participate in excavations in Rome. For those who prefer to stay a bit closer to home base, the Washington Semester Program is a good option. Through this competitive program, students complete internships (often in government and public service), take courses, and do independent research in the nation's capital.

Holy Cross's Career Planning Center is highly active. This office capitalizes on the human resource of the college's more than 33,000 alumni and 27 alumni clubs through its Career Advisor Network. Sophomores and juniors can also benefit directly from the Holy Cross network through paid, project-based internships specifically designed for Holy Cross students in the Summer Internship Program. Past interns have enjoyed jobs like public relations with Starkman and Associates in New York City and human resources with the Avon Foundation.

Student Life

There are over 102 student organizations at Holy Cross. Reflecting the service ethos, volunteer and service organizations are very popular. Among the most influential groups are Pax Christi (a Christian organization devoted to nonviolence), CAB (Campus Activities Board), and Student Government.

Holy Cross embraces several fun traditions. The college celebrates St. Patrick's Day in a big way, with free trips to the Faneuil Hall marketplace in Boston, performances by Irish bands, and an Irish movie marathon. "Everyone gets into the spirit," one student recalls. At the end of April, just before classes end, Spring Weekend brings students out to the college lawn for a carnival, battle of the bands, and lip sync contest. Students can take part in an annual semi-formal cruise in Boston Harbor, complete with dinner and dancing. There's plenty of partying on campus throughout the weekend. To top things off, the winners of the battle of the bands open for a big-name musical performer in a campus concert. Finally, students who have just 100 days left at the college enjoy the tradition of "100 Days Ball," a formal dance.

The school has 27 Division I teams. Holy Cross participates in the Football Championship Subdivision, and the men's hockey team is particularly strong as well. In addition, there are six intramural sports with more than 1,300 participants. "Intramurals are more fun than competitive sports," one student comments.

Off campus, many bars in the area cater to students. Ralph's Diner in Worcester is popular for its dining car atmosphere, delicious burgers, and live music next door at Ralph's Rock Club. Adventurous eaters will find all different types of cuisine to satisfy their appetite. Worcester also has respectable concert venues, theater and opera. To spice up the weekends, road trips to Boston and Providence are also common. "We are in a prime location," notes a student.

Since the great majority of students live on campus and the Greek system is nonexistent, "the best place to make friends is the dorms," one student explains. Freshmen who choose to participate in the Substance-Free Living Program will be matched with roommates with the same preference and housed in the same part of a larger dorm. Upperclassmen have the option of apartment-style housing.

Student Body

Not surprisingly, the majority of students are religious. Most are Catholic. "No matter what your religious background, everyone is accepted," notes a student. A common trait among students is a desire to be involved in service. "It's ingrained," one student says.

Ethnic diversity is high, with 23 percent of students identifying as minorities.

You May Not Know

- Bishop Fenwick, the founder of Holy Cross, wrote that he would take students for $125 per year and "supply them with everything but clothes." Nowadays the college isn't *quite* that sweet a deal.
- School songs include the humorously-titled "Chu! Chu! Ra! Ra!" and "Eat 'em up."
- Holy Cross has twice won top honors in contests for the best-landscaped U.S. college.

Distinguished Alumni

Jonathan Favreau, Chief Speechwriter for President Obama; Christopher Matthews, host of MSNBC's *Hardball*; Clarence Thomas, Associate Justice, U.S. Supreme Court.

Admissions and Financial Aid

The admissions process at Holy Cross is fairly standard, although students with good community service records and a profound commitment to extracurriculars will stand out. Those who would like to showcase their talents can send in supplementary materials like CDs, videos, or artwork demonstrating their skills. Although interviews are not required, they are encouraged.

Holy Cross's admissions process is need-blind, and students are guaranteed that 100 percent of their financial need will be met. Additionally, there are four types of merit scholarships available. Three grant full tuition. These are the Ellis Scholarship for a Worcester resident high school graduate, the Brooks Scholarship for a music major, and the Bean Scholarship for a classics major. Scholarships for male and female basketball players are also available.

COLLEGE OF THE HOLY CROSS

Highlights

Admissions Criteria
Academic criteria:
Grades: ☆ ☆ ☆
Difficulty of class schedule: ☆ ☆ ☆
Class rank: ☆ ☆
Standardized test scores: ☆
Teacher recommendations: ☆ ☆ ☆
Personal statement: ☆ ☆
Non-academic criteria considered:
Interview
Extracurricular activities
Special talents, interests, abilities
Character/personal qualities
Volunteer work
Work experience
State of residency
Geographical location
Minority affiliation
Alumni relationship

Deadlines
Early Action: No
Early Decision: December 15
Regular Action: January 15 (final)
Notification of admission by: April 1
Common Application: Accepted

Financial Aid
In-state tuition: $43,660
Out-of-state tuition: $43,660
Room: $6,450
Board: $2,260
Books: $700
Freshmen receiving need-based aid: 62%
Undergrads rec. need-based aid: 58%
Avg. % of need met by financial aid: 100%
Avg. aid package (freshmen): $33,492
Avg. aid package (undergrads): $33,123
Avg. debt upon graduation: $26,567

School Spirit
Mascot: Crusaders
Colors: Purple and white

Four-year public
Founded: 1693
Williamsburg, VA
Small town
Pop. 14,444

Address:
P.O. Box 8795
Williamsburg, VA
23187-8795

Admissions:
757-221-4223

Financial Aid:
757-221-2420

admission@wm.edu

www.wm.edu

The Ultimate
Guide to America's
Best Colleges

COLLEGE OF WILLIAM AND MARY

Overview

Like its surrounding town of Williamsburg, the College of William and Mary is a curious mix of old and new. The main thoroughfare through town, Duke of Gloucester Street, plays host to horse-drawn carriages and Colonial-life re-enactors in full period dress. It's also the center of entertainment for students at William and Mary. W&M itself is much the same way: it's the second-oldest college in America, and the campus includes a number of Colonial buildings that have been retained or restored to their original appearance. The school's most famous alums include U.S. Presidents Thomas Jefferson, James Monroe, and John Tyler. The 1,200-acre campus features quiet Virginia forests, lakes, and quaint bridges on Crim Dell. On-campus social life is punctuated by traditional events, such as Charter Day, which celebrates the enactment of the Royal Charter that created W&M.

"New campus" features red brick buildings that are modern and energy efficient. And while students may drink at places with names like "Green Leafe" and dance the night away at the "King and Queen Ball," their academic programs feature a liberal arts foundation that is hardly stodgy traditional fare, with unparalleled support for original research not only in science but in the liberal arts. And W&M's commitment to undergraduate education pays off: *U.S. News & World Report* ranks the school as sixth among all public universities (while the name still says "College," W&M is actually a university with grad students and doctoral programs). The school is one of just eight universities that are considered "Public Ivy," but offer superior education at public-school prices.

Academics

The basic tenets of academics at W&M are research, relationships with faculty, programs that are interdisciplinary, and community service—probably in that order. A course of study at W&M begins with basic requirements, which include two years of college-level foreign language, lower-division and in-the-major computing and writing courses, and the General Education Requirements. To satisfy these GERs, students must take classes in mathematics and quantitative reasoning, natural sciences, social sciences, world cultures and history, literature and history of the arts, creative and performing arts, and philosophical, religious, and social thought. All first-year students must also take a Freshmen Seminar, which requires a research project. The seminars include classes such as "Aspects of Film Noir," "Race and Music," and "Astrophotography."

Academics at W&M are "very rigorous," and students are likely to seek the most demanding and diverse courses of study. W&M students started the Phi Beta Kappa academic honor society, and W&M consequently claims to have "invented Greek life." Close work with faculty is encouraged and easy, since the most common course size is 10 to 19 students. "All of my professors have been highly engaged with the students and always available to discuss class material," notes a student. W&M's Schools of Business and Education, and its major in history, are particularly strong; 58 majors are offered overall, in addition to the Charles Center's Structured Interdisciplinary Programs, which include linguistics, Africana studies, environmental science and policy, or self-designed majors.

"Academically talented" students can apply to the Charles Center's Departmental Honors program, under which students conduct a year-long research project with a faculty supervisor, write an Honors thesis, and defend it orally.

But Honors is not the most prestigious special program on offer at W&M: applicants who are exceptionally accomplished can be admitted to or invited to apply for, respectively, the James Monroe Scholars or Murray Scholars Programs. The Monroe Scholars Program provides ample funding for research projects: money is available for projects after the freshmen year and once more after sophomore or junior year. Students also have access to specialized advising and housing. The Murray Scholars Program provides hefty financial support as well as the opportunity for students to design their own interdisciplinary seminars and courses of study under faculty guidance and to undertake a capstone research project. Murray Scholars can also opt to spend a semester of study abroad at Oxford.

Many W&M students are involved with community service-based programs. In fact, more alumni from W&M go into the Peace Corps than graduates from any other research university. The Sharpe Community Scholars Program offers first-year students a service-oriented academic curriculum complemented by ongoing team-based service projects. Break Out also offers service trips to places within the confines of the United States, such as Washington DC, as well as excursions to foreign countries like Africa, South America and China.

Research is intense at William and Mary, characteristically unusual for a college with such a liberal-arts-based education; indeed, students are "expected to contribute significantly to the university's research efforts." W&M is affiliated with more than 20 research centers in all fields and offers unparalleled initiatives to support undergraduate research, particularly through its partnership with the Howard Hughes Medical Institute. All students can get involved in research by collaborating with faculty as early as their freshman year under the well-funded Faculty-Student Research Initiative.

W&M also offers exchange agreements for semester- or year-long study in 10 countries and language-intensive summer study-abroad programs in 11 countries. W&M has the highest study-abroad participation rate of any public university.

The school also boasts impressive statistics when it comes to students' post-graduation plans. The *Wall Street Journal* ranks W&M as one of the top 10 "feeder" schools for elite graduate (law, medical, and business) schools. W&M students also have the highest rate of Fulbright Scholarships acceptance among all top research schools.

Student Life

William and Mary's 400 student organizations range from performance groups, like the Seventh Grade Comedy Club or the Swing Club, to service groups that include AIDS Tanzania and Big Brothers Big Sisters. College-sanctioned events are quite popular, including the pre-Winter Break Yule Log ceremony, featuring hot cider, cookies, and the college president dressed as Santa reading *How the Grinch Stole Christmas*. One student comments, "we get to be kids again." The Triathlon consists of scaling the wall of the Governor's Palace and making it to the middle of the hedge maze, swimming in Crim Dell, and streaking across the Sunken Garden.

Parties thrown by any of W&M's 17 fraternities and 13 sororities are popular, given that more than a quarter of the student body belongs to the Greek system. Off-campus house parties are popular, or students will go out to a deli (bars are prohibited, so delis serve alcohol and function as bars in Williamsburg). Some secret societies exist at W&M (the *Flat Hat* student newspaper scoffs that they are "not a secret worth keeping") but these, which include the Bishop James Madison Society and Society of Sevens, are mostly philanthropic societies.

COLLEGE OF WILLIAM AND MARY

Highlights

Students
Total enrollment: 8,258
Undergrads: 6,171
Part-time students: 1%
From out-of-state: 34%
From public schools: 79%
Male/Female: 45%/55%
Live on-campus: 72%
In fraternities: 25%
In sororities: 30%
Off-campus employment rating: Excellent
Caucasian: 59%
African American: 7%
Hispanic: 9%
Asian / Pacific Islander: 6%
Native American: 0%
Mixed (2+ ethnicities): 4%
International: 4%

Academics
Calendar: Semester
Student/faculty ratio: 12:1
Class size 9 or fewer: 15%
Class size 10-29: 49%
Class size 30-49: 28%
Class size 50-99: 5%
Class size 100 or more: 2%
Returning freshmen: 96%
Six-year graduation rate: 91%

Most Popular Majors
Business administration
Government
Psychology

Admissions
Applicants: 13,660
Accepted: 4,394
Acceptance rate: 32.2%
Placed on wait list: 3,518
Enrolled from wait list: 106
Average GPA: 4.0
ACT range: 28-32
SAT Math range: 620-720
SAT Reading range: 630-740
SAT Writing range: 37-46
Top 10% of class: 79%
Top 25% of class: 97%
Top 50% of class: 100%

189

COLLEGE OF WILLIAM AND MARY

Highlights

Admissions Criteria
Academic criteria:
Grades: ☆ ☆ ☆
Difficulty of class schedule: ☆ ☆ ☆
Class rank: ☆ ☆ ☆
Standardized test scores: ☆ ☆ ☆
Teacher recommendations: ☆ ☆ ☆
Personal statement: ☆ ☆ ☆
Non-academic criteria considered:
Interview
Extracurricular activities
Special talents, interests, abilities
Character/personal qualities
Volunteer work
Work experience
Geographical location
Minority affiliation
Alumni relationship

Deadlines
Early Action: No
Early Decision: November 1
Regular Action: January 1 (final)
Notification of admission by: April 1
Common Application: Accepted

Financial Aid
In-state tuition: $10,428
Out-of-state tuition: $32,816
Room: $5,870
Board: $3,946
Books: Varies
Freshmen receiving need-based aid: 31%
Undergrads rec. need-based aid: 33%
Avg. % of need met by financial aid: 75%
Avg. aid package (freshmen): $14,812
Avg. aid package (undergrads): $16,407
Avg. debt upon graduation: $22,344

School Spirit
Mascot: Griffin
Colors: Green, gold, and silver

Students at W&M are enthusiastic about athletics, whether it's jogging on DoG Street, intramural mini golf, or following one of the Tribe's 21 Division I sports teams. The Tribe holds a conference-record of 101 conference titles, which have in recent years been won by men's cross-country, soccer, and football teams. Intramurals are available, as are the slightly more competitive Sports Clubs.

Students can ride free on the Williamsburg Area Transit trolleys to visit Williamsburg or DoG Street's many attractions; the street was named one of the "Top 10 Great Streets" in America by the American Planning Association. History buffs will enjoy visiting historic Williamsburg, Jamestown, and Yorktown, while more modern diversions include outlet shopping, an Anheuser-Busch brewery, and an amusement park. "You get so accustomed to it that you don't even take a second look when you see people dressed in period costumes," says a student. Jamestown Beach is only about eight minutes from campus.

The majority of students live on campus. Freshmen have the option of mostly dorm-style residences and some suites; upperclassmen can also elect to live in on-campus apartments. Special-interest housing is available, ranging from Africana to Eco to Language houses.

Student Body

W&M has a highly ethnically diverse student body, and is fairly geographically diverse as well. Students describe themselves as "independent thinkers" and "highly motivated," not surprising, given that nearly 80 percent of students graduated in the top 10 percent of their high school class.

You May Not Know

- A portion of the initial funds for the college were supposedly obtained from three English pirates who had been arrested in 1692; an English court ordered them to fork over 300 pounds of loot, which apparently translates to over $900,000 today.

- According to campus legend, if a couple kisses on the bridge over Crim Dell, they will get married. In order to reverse this effect, you must throw your significant other off the bridge.

- The Sir Christopher Wren Building is not only the oldest college building in the country, but also possibly the most flammable, having been destroyed by fire three times.

Distinguished Alumni

David Brown, Columbia Space Shuttle astronaut; Glenn Close, actress; Jon Stewart, host of Comedy Central's *The Daily Show*.

Admissions and Financial Aid

Under the Gateway William and Mary program, families whose income is $40,000 or less are eligible to receive financial aid in an amount that will completely cover expenses. In addition to the financial assistance offered by the Monroe and Murray Scholars Programs, the William and Mary Scholar Awards of in-state tuition and fees are made to students who have overcome adversity. As W&M is a state school, out-of-state admissions tend to be highly competitive.

COLLEGE OF WOOSTER

Overview

A small private liberal arts college in Wooster, Ohio—just 75 minutes away from Cleveland—the College of Wooster is home to a vibrant, tight-knit community of 2,000 undergrads. The castle-like academic building Kauke Hall sits as an iconic representation of the center of campus near Oak Grove, where each senior class plants a tree the day before graduation. This unique tree endowment makes for quite the verdant campus. In 2012, the College opened the Scot Center, a 123,000-square-foot recreation facility, part of its overall plan to build a campus center.

This suburban campus has a vibrant social life—perhaps because virtually all students live on campus, and there isn't much to do in agricultural Wooster. The traditional Amish farmers who come into town by horse and buggy for commerce are a far cry from the taxis and subways of major cities, so students looking for a metropolitan experience are better off looking elsewhere. The college also lacks the ethnic diversity often found at universities.

While the attractions of Wooster may not put this college on the map, its much-lauded Independent Study program certainly does. This program ensures that every graduate from the College completes a senior thesis or project in collaboration with a faculty mentor. If getting a good liberal arts education in a small community where you'll have close-knit relationships with faculty and students sounds like your cup of tea, you'll want to consider applying for the College of Wooster.

Academics

Wooster offers 47 areas of study, and students can also design their own majors. All students complete the First-Year Seminar in Critical Inquiry during their first semester. Other requirements include courses in Writing, Global and Cultural Perspectives, Religious Perspectives, and Quantitative Reasoning. Six courses in the "Learning Across Disciplines" requirement ensure breadth across academic areas, while seven to nine courses in one's department or program provide depth. Three independent-study courses, typically taken in junior and senior year, focus on developing research skills and completing the senior thesis.

Students enjoy close relationships with professors, as 87 percent of classes have fewer than 30 students. "Without exception, my professors have all been extremely helpful and responsive," says a student. Strong programs include chemistry, economics, religious studies, and sociology. First-Year Seminars provide small, writing-intensive classes of no more than 15 students that are led by professors who also serve as academic advisors to the students. Topics have included "The Drugs We Drink: Biological and Societal Perspectives" and "Heating Up the Planet: Response to a Catastrophe." Students from four sections of First-Year Seminar can participate in the First-Year Living and Learning Project, which coordinates their academic and residential experiences. "This is the easiest way to make friends during freshman year," notes a participant.

The College of Wooster is most famous for its Independent Study (I.S.) Program. Seniors write a thesis or complete a project then participate in an oral defense, which students describe as "the ultimate preparation for graduate school." Students can get a head start on building relationships with faculty through The Sophomore Research Program—where they not only gain knowledge, but also a salary, as research assistants to faculty members.

Each year, around 170 students choose to study off-campus in over 60 countries, typically in their sophomore or junior years. There is plenty of international education on campus too, with an international student body of about six percent, a residence hall with six language suites, and another residence hall for cross-cultural programming.

COLLEGE OF WOOSTER

Four-year private
Founded: 1866
Wooster, OH
Large town
Pop. 26,139

Address:
1189 Beall Avenue
Wooster, OH
44691

Admissions:
800-877-9905

Financial Aid:
800-877-3688

admissions@wooster.edu

www.wooster.edu

COLLEGE OF WOOSTER

The Scots Career Network is one of the many services offered by the Career Services Office. "I've used the service to find alums in my career field and arrange informational interviews," one student explains.

Student Life

With 120 student organizations and most students living on campus, student life at Wooster is vibrant in spite of the school's small size. Nearly a third of all students make music as a singer or instrumentalist through one of the many choirs, ensembles, bands, and a cappella groups on campus. Through the Jenny Investment Club students invest $1.3 million in the college's funds in the stock market as an educational experience, while the student-run coffee shop Common Grounds is open late to offer an alternative to the party scene.

The Common Grounds coffee shop doesn't serve alcohol, but College Underground does. You'll often find students hanging out at the campus's very own pub enjoying happy hour and entertainment from bands and comedians. "We get some locally famous performers," notes a student.

The Wooster Activities Crew (W.A.C.), the campus programming board, throws popular annual events such as Party on the Green—the biggest party of the year, showcasing a wide array of musical talent—and Springfest.

Wooster's most unique traditions relate to Independent Study. Upon completion, students receive a button that says "I Did It!" along with a single Tootsie Roll—more than a few alumni have had theirs bronzed for posterity. I.S. Monday, the day projects are due, features a jubilant parade of seniors being led to a celebratory dinner with their advisors, making for "an academic Mardi Gras," as it were. One student comments, "It seems silly to be so happy over a Tootsie Roll, but after months—or even years—of work, we celebrate that Tootsie Roll to the extreme."

Wooster has 10 Greek groups—six sororities and four fraternities—which are independent of national Greek organizations. "Many of the parties the Greek groups throw are open to the whole campus, so I don't see much benefit in joining," says a student.

Nearly one third of students compete on one or more of the 23 Division III varsity sports teams. The baseball and basketball teams have been strong in recent years. More than 80 percent participate in club and intramural sports, from Ultimate Frisbee to cricket. For those who enjoy less strenuous recreation, Scot Lanes offers billiards, bowling, and more.

Off-campus activities in the immediate vicinity won't satisfy big-city connoisseurs, but agriculture lovers may appreciate Local Roots, the collective year-round farmers' market for locally produced goods. Cleveland offers arts, culture, dining, and sports attractions.

Virtually all students (99 percent) live on campus. There are more than 20 different program houses for six to 16 students who share a common interest. All houses have a service aspect, such as volunteering for a local agency.

Student Body

Wooster's student body is a tight-knit bunch—everyone either knows everyone else or is a friend of a friend. Politically, students "range from moderate to slightly liberal," reports a student.

There is moderate ethnic diversity—15 percent of students are minorities—and moderate geographic diversity. Sixty-two percent of students hail from outside of Ohio, representing approximately 42 states and 55 countries.

You May Not Know

- The University of Wooster was founded as a co-ed institution in 1866 and didn't become the College of Wooster until 1915 so that it could deliberately emphasize its liberal arts identity.
- The college's Scot Marching Band adorns kilts.
- On graduation day, the senior class presents the president with a gift. Recent ones have included a puzzle piece, penny, and packet of hot sauce.

Distinguished Alumni

Donald Kohn, Vice Chair, Federal Reserve; Timothy Smucker, CEO of JM Smucker Co; Susan Stranahan, Pulitzer Prize winner.

Admissions and Financial Aid

The admissions office is looking for "good students who do good things." Successful applicants will want to demonstrate how they can contribute to a campus where campus life is vibrant and show that they are capable of undertaking a collaborative student-designed project with a faculty mentor. The Teacher Evaluation is waived for those using the Wooster Web Application.

Students are admitted without regard for financial need. Over $42 million in merit scholarships and need-based grants are awarded each year; there are an additional $6 million in loans and $1 million in campus employment.

All applicants are automatically considered for the Dean's Scholarship of $14,000 to $20,500 per year, while additional Competition-Based Scholarships and Special Interest Awards require an online application. The College Scholar award covers half to two thirds of tuition each year, as does the Clarence Beecher Allen Scholarship for African-American students. There are special awards for first-generation college students, performing artists, and members of the Presbyterian Church.

COLLEGE OF WOOSTER

Highlights

Admissions Criteria

Academic criteria:
Grades: ☆ ☆ ☆
Difficulty of class schedule: ☆ ☆ ☆
Class rank: ☆ ☆
Standardized test scores: ☆ ☆
Teacher recommendations: ☆ ☆
Personal statement: ☆ ☆
Non-academic criteria considered:
Interview
Extracurricular activities
Special talents, interests, abilities
Character/personal qualities
Volunteer work
Work experience
Geographical location
Minority affiliation
Alumni relationship

Deadlines

Early Action: November 15
Early Decision: November 15
Regular Action: February 15 (final)
Notification of admission by: March 15
Common Application: Accepted

Financial Aid

In-state tuition: $41,680
Out-of-state tuition: $41,680
Room: $4,750
Board: $5,170
Books: $1,000
Freshmen receiving need-based aid: 66%
Undergrads rec. need-based aid: 59%
Avg. % of need met by financial aid: 93%
Avg. aid package (freshmen): $36,045
Avg. aid package (undergrads): $35,763
Avg. debt upon graduation: $26,750

School Spirit

Mascot: Scottie
Colors: Black and old gold

Four-year private
Founded: 1874
Colorado Springs, CO
Major city
Pop. 426,388

Address:
14 East Cache La Pou-
dre Street
Colorado Springs, CO
80903

Admissions:
800-542-7214

Financial Aid:
800-260-6458

admission@colorado-
college.edu

www.coloradocollege.
edu

COLORADO COLLEGE

Overview

At the base of Pike's Peak and the Rocky Mountains, the buildings of the Colorado College campus peek out between expanses of leafy green trees. The campus and surrounding area of mountains, forests, and rivers—along with the 300 days of sunshine a year—provide ample incentive for students to enjoy the outdoor landscape. The 2,000 undergraduates at the private, liberal arts college are known for being driven yet laid-back, actively engaged in environmental activism, and enthusiastic about outdoor recreation.

Colorado College was first established in 1874, two years before Colorado was even a state. Cutler Hall was the college's first building and has been standing since 1880, first accompanied only by the mountains. Because much of the early growth of the college was pre-1900s, many of its buildings are on the National Register of Historic Places. Campus however has a fresh and modern feel, due to the numerous new residences which have been built since the mid-1950s. The start of the 21st century has seen new apartment-style living, a Science Center, and the revitalization of east campus.

At the heart of Colorado College's academic system is the Block Plan, which allows students to take one class at a time, over an intensive 3.5-week course. This reflects a determination to delve deep into experiential academic material, and, as the official college motto states, truly "acquire knowledge and live it."

Academics

Colorado College offers 52 majors, including a series of interdisciplinary programs. Strong areas include biology, English, and history; and popular options among students include geology, anthropology, botany, and sociology, which allow students to experience unique field studies. Students may self-design majors, or double major if they wish.

Along with the major requirements, students have a general core requirement to fulfill. All freshmen participate in a First-Year Program, which consists of a set of courses taken in the first two blocks as well as initiatives for learning opportunities outside the classroom.

CC's Block Plan was first adopted in 1970, in order to encourage focused, intensive classroom learning. Students take a total of eight courses over each year (two semesters of four blocks each). All classes are capped at 25 students, a ratio that creates a strong relationship between professors and the students they teach. Another advantage is that students immerse themselves wholly in their subject and have the opportunity to learn during field trips and in on-site classes. Archaeology classes can be held on the site of a dig or in a lab doing analysis. Classes are flexible, and meeting times are often determined by the subject and professor. A possible disadvantage is that "if you aren't into a class, you're stuck with it until the next block, and there's no way to slack," says a student.

The college boasts that the classroom experience is—and has always been—based on close relationships between students and professors. Faculty and staff members are encouraged to take part in the Breaking Bread program, which funds informal meals for students at a faculty member's home. "We've had some deep discussions with professors over a meal," explains one student. This, coupled with the small class sizes, encourages a strong sense of community on campus. There is a Phi Beta Kappa honor society on campus, and collaborative grants and Venture Grants are awarded in each division for student and faculty to engage in investigative research together.

According to CC, the college is one of the top five in the country for student opportunities to study abroad. The Block Plan is flexible for students who wish to go abroad, as they may take off any number of blocks to fit their program. Opportunities exist in Australia, Brazil, China, France, Japan, Mali, South Africa, and numerous other countries.

Colorado College is very helpful in working with students to find internships and job opportunities, both during and after college. Campus advisors help students prepare for post-graduate scholarships, fellowships, and internships. Colorado College reports that post-graduate success is common, with alumni filling positions as "successful artists, businesspeople, doctors, educators, lawyers, and professors."

Student Life

There are 135 official student organizations on campus. TWIG is a popular improvisational comedy show, and Dance Workshop puts on one show each semester. The Outdoor Recreation Committee offers student-led trips which include hiking, camping, backpacking, kayaking, and white-water rafting, as well as cycling. Students love to be outdoors and frequently hang out on campus at Armstrong Quad. "When the weather is nice or even half-way nice, everyone heads outdoors," remarks a student.

Outdoor concerts are popular on campus, especially the annual Llamapalooza, a day-long music festival in the spring, which features over 10 hours of music, inflatable obstacle course, slip 'n slide, and an art series. Traditional parties include the ABC Party (Anything But Clothes—be creative in covering yourself) and the Harley Party (get out your leather and tattoos). "Dressing up and costumes are a big part of what we do," comments a student. The Summer Festival of the Arts fills the campus with music, dance, and film, from June to August.

Athletics play a major role on campus, with 25 percent of students involved on varsity teams and 75 percent participating in club and intramural sports. "Intramurals are more about having fun than competition," explains one participant. All varsity teams are NCAA Division III, except for men's ice hockey and women's soccer, which are Division I. Men's hockey is arguably the most popular spectator sport, and the team has made it to the NCAA tournament 12 times since 1995.

Greek life is not especially prevalent on campus, with only three fraternities and three sororities. Residential housing includes theme houses, especially language-themed for international students and others with special interests.

After each semester, there is a four-day weekend, accompanied by a great deal of celebration, partying, and outdoor activities. More than three-quarters of students live on campus (students are required to live on campus their first three years and are guaranteed housing their fourth year if they choose to remain on campus), so there are plenty of social activities each weekend. Though Colorado Springs is a city of 400,000 people, the nightlife in the city does not draw a large crowd—most students socialize on campus.

Student Body

A majority of students are actively interested in environmental issues and outdoor recreation. This lends the student body a "granola" and "sustainable-friendly" vibe, say students. Though students say their classes are academically rigorous, the competition doesn't seep into students' relationships—they enjoy a cooperative and

COLORADO COLLEGE

Highlights

Students
Total enrollment: 2,026
Undergrads: 2,008
Freshmen: 540
Part-time students: 1%
From out-of-state: 82%
From public schools: 54%
Male/Female: 46%/54%
Live on-campus: 78%
In fraternities: 7%
In sororities: 11%
Off-campus employment rating: Fair
Caucasian: 73%
African American: 2%
Hispanic: 7%
Asian / Pacific Islander: 4%
Native American: 0%
Mixed (2+ ethnicities): 7%
International: 6%

Academics
Calendar: Other
Student/faculty ratio: 10:1
Class size 9 or fewer: 22%
Class size 10-29: 76%
Class size 30-49: 2%
Class size 50-99: -
Class size 100 or more: -
Returning freshmen: 95%
Six-year graduation rate: 90%

Most Popular Majors
Biology
Economics
Sociology

Admissions
Applicants: 5,606
Accepted: 1,289
Acceptance rate: 23.0%
Placed on wait list: 1,064
Enrolled from wait list: 6
Average GPA: Not reported
ACT range: 28-32
SAT Math range: 610-710
SAT Reading range: 630-720
SAT Writing range: 33-54
Top 10% of class: 62%
Top 25% of class: 90%
Top 50% of class: 98%

195

COLORADO COLLEGE

Admissions Criteria

Academic criteria:
Grades: ☆ ☆ ☆
Difficulty of class schedule: ☆ ☆ ☆
Class rank: ☆ ☆
Standardized test scores: ☆ ☆
Teacher recommendations: ☆ ☆
Personal statement: ☆ ☆
Non-academic criteria considered:
Interview
Extracurricular activities
Special talents, interests, abilities
Character/personal qualities
Volunteer work
Work experience
State of residency
Religious affiliation/commitment
Minority affiliation
Alumni relationship

Deadlines

Early Action: November 15
Early Decision: November 15
Regular Action: January 15 (final)
Notification of admission by: April 1
Common Application: Accepted

Financial Aid

In-state tuition: $43,812
Out-of-state tuition: $43,812
Room: $5,826
Board: $4,486
Books: $1,244
Freshmen receiving need-based aid: 40%
Undergrads rec. need-based aid: 35%
Avg. % of need met by financial aid: 98%
Avg. aid package (freshmen): $38,292
Avg. aid package (undergrads): $37,319
Avg. debt upon graduation: $19,970

School Spirit

Mascot: Tigers
Colors: Black and gold

encouraging atmosphere, supported by a fair "hippie population" on campus. "We're a pretty liberal campus, but we aren't extremists," says a student.

There is both a high level of ethnic diversity with 20 percent minority students and high geographic diversity—82 percent of students come from out of state, predominantly from the West coast and the Northeast.

Spiritual life at Colorado College is represented by a varied population and several student organizations. These range from Hillel and Chaverim to a Christian Science Organization, and from the Catholic Community to a Tibetan Buddhist Organization.

You May Not Know

- In 1994 students created a referendum to change the athletic teams' names to the Colorado College Cutthroats. The students' effort just barely lost.
- In 2009, the college had a 14-week campaign to reduce electricity, heat, and water usage by 14 percent across campus. The school estimates that they saved close to $100,000 and reduced greenhouse gas emissions by 378 metric tons of $CO2$.
- In 2009, Colorado Springs was ranked #2 "Fittest City in America" (*Men's Fitness Magazine*), #10 "Best Place to Be a Woman" (*Women's Health Magazine*), and #1 "Best Place to Live" (*Outside Magazine*).

Distinguished Alumni

Lynne Cheney, wife of former U.S. Vice President Dick Cheney; Peggy Fleming, Olympic figure skater, gold medalist; Glenna Goodacre, artist, designer of millennium Sacagawea Golden Dollar; James Heckman, Nobel Prize winner in Economic Sciences; Ken Salazar, U.S. Secretary of the Interior.

Admissions and Financial Aid

According to the college, it is in the student's best interest to provide as much information as possible about accomplishments, activities, and awards. Students who consider Colorado College as their first choice, or one of their top choices, should apply under Early Action or during one of their two Early Decision rounds.

In the fall of 2010, Colorado College adopted a Flexible Testing Policy regarding standardized test requirements. Applicants may now submit either SAT score, ACT score, or three approved exams of their choice such as AP exams, IB exams, or SAT and ACT subject tests.

Colorado College offers some merit-based scholarships, including the Barnes Scholarships, the El Pomar Fellowship, the Trustee Scholarships, Leadership Scholarships, and the Boettcher Scholarships. The El Pomar Fellowship covers full tuition, room, and board for students from Colorado with demonstrated financial need, who intend to pursue careers in public policy or nonprofit work. The Barnes Scholarships are full-tuition awards offered to students pursuing degrees in chemistry, mathematics, or the natural sciences.

COLORADO SCHOOL OF MINES

COLORADO SCHOOL OF MINES

Four-year public
Founded: 1874
Golden, CO
Major city
Pop. 19,035

Address:
1600 Maple Street
Golden, CO
80401

Admissions:
303-273-3220

Financial Aid:
303-273-3220

admit@mines.edu

www.mines.edu

Overview

The Colorado School of Mines combines strong programs in engineering, applied science, and (of course) mining with the natural beauty of Colorado. It's located in Golden, Colorado, about 15 miles west of Denver, and is near the Rocky Mountains. Rather than ivory towers, the school features architecture from the late 1800s and early 1900s along with some contemporary, glass-and-metal buildings.

Recent additions to the campus include a new, 291-bed residence hall opened in 2011 and a 78,000 square-foot addition to the Division of Engineering and Department of Mining Engineering's Brown Hall.

The school prides itself on combining a quality education in resource management with a more intimate environment than is found in most engineering schools and has several unique programs focusing on the intersection of leadership and engineering.

Academics

Students are expected to fulfill the requirements of the core courses. The curriculum is not for the faint of heart—its long list of courses includes Calculus I, II, and III; Differential Equations; and Physics I and II. The curriculum requires classes in mathematics, the basic sciences, humanities, the social sciences, physical education, and a Freshman Success Seminar. The rigorous curriculum, paired with demanding professors, means that Colorado School of Mines is challenging; however, the small size of the school means students won't be lost in the crowd if they're struggling.

The school has strong mining engineering, geology, and chemical engineering programs. The mining engineering department was started more than 100 years ago to "train gold rush miners" but has since incorporated "advance technologies and capitaliz(ed) on new scientific discoveries." The department of geology and geological engineering conducts research in areas including Alaska, Chile, California, Europe, Africa, and Asia. Students say it is "one of the best programs in the country." The department of chemical engineering has been in the top 10 for the number of students to receive their bachelor's degrees in the field.

Students in the prestigious McBride Honors Program complete 24 semester hours of coursework and off-campus learning in order to explore the connection between engineering and the social sciences, as well as the ethical ramifications of and requirements for leadership in their field of study. "This program is founded on the ideal that pure technical problems do not exist—only those embedded in political, cultural, ethical, and moral problems," says Dr. Robert E.D. Woolsey, emeritus professor.

The Hennebach Program in the Humanities sponsors visiting professors and a series of lectures on the intersection of humanities and engineering so as to enrich the student experience. Students interested in research can go to the school's departmental centers and institutional centers, through which professors work with teams of students on either small-scale or large-scale group research projects. These centers provide a way for students to take their learning into the field and look at practical applications of their skills.

Study-abroad programs are available in a variety of countries, including Belgium, China, Sweden, and Thailand. Students are encouraged to go abroad during semesters or in the summer. Students are also able to co-op, using the school to place them at an engineering company at which they may work for several semesters.

About 85 percent of students enter the work force after graduation, and 99 percent of them are in a career related to their major within a year of graduation—frequently at mining, petroleum, or government institutions; the school is noted for the high salaries of its graduates over the course of their careers.

COLORADO SCHOOL OF MINES

Students

Total enrollment: 5,632
Undergrads: 4,169
Freshmen: 949
From out-of-state: 38%
From public schools: 82%
Male/Female: 74%/26%
Live on-campus: 43%
In fraternities: 12%
In sororities: 16%
Off-campus employment rating: Good
Caucasian: 74%
African American: 1%
Hispanic: 7%
Asian / Pacific Islander: 5%
Native American: 0%
Mixed (2+ ethnicities): 3%
International: 6%

Academics

Calendar: Semester
Student/faculty ratio: 16:1
Class size 9 or fewer: 10%
Class size 10-29: 47%
Class size 30-49: 26%
Class size 50-99: 12%
Class size 100 or more: 5%
Returning freshmen: 89%
Graduates who immediately go to graduate school: 20%
Graduates who immediately enter career related to major: 85%

Most Popular Majors

Engineering
Petroleum engineering
Chemical engineering

Admissions

Applicants: 11,682
Accepted: 4,373
Acceptance rate: 37.4%
Placed on wait list: 1,533
Enrolled from wait list: 2
Average GPA: 3.8
ACT range: 27-31
SAT Math range: 630-720
SAT Reading range: 570-670
SAT Writing range: 8-42
Top 10% of class: 60%
Top 25% of class: 91%
Top 50% of class: 100%

Student Life

Most students live off campus. However, the school has 168 student organizations, and Greek life, minority engineering organizations, and religious organizations (particularly Christian) to keep them engaged with on-campus activities.

Campus traditions take advantage of the nearby terrain's natural beauty. In the fall, all the freshmen carry 10-pound rocks from campus up Mt. Zion outside of Golden, where they paint them white and build an "M" that can be seen from campus; seniors retrieve their rocks when they graduate. At Engineer's Days, in the spring, the campus puts aside work for a spectacular fireworks show, a cardboard canoe race, and a proclamation from the governor. Tradition dictates that graduating seniors receive engraved silver diplomas.

There are 10 Greek organizations (seven fraternities and three sororities), but the Greek presence on campus isn't overwhelming. "You don't feel left out if you aren't a member," says a student.

The school has 14 Division II teams, with cross country, football, and women's basketball deemed the most competitive. There are a variety of intramural teams, including breakdancing, lacrosse, cheerleading, kayaking, and the shooting club.

Off campus, students enjoy taking advantage of the nearby Rockies by skiing, hiking, and biking. "If you don't like the outdoors you may as well not go here," says a student. However, city life is not far. Denver is nearby and offers big-city entertainment and shopping for students.

Freshmen tend to live in dorms, though they are not required to, and upperclassmen typically move to Greek housing or off campus. The campus provides traditional double room housing, suite-style dorms, and apartments with shared bedrooms—all open to freshmen.

Student Body

The student body at Mines, like many engineering schools, is heavily skewed by gender—it's three-quarters male. "There are a lot of options if you're a female student, but they aren't necessarily good options," says a student. Because of the rigorous nature of their schoolwork and the competitive nature of admissions, students are very academically focused. "We have fun, but schoolwork is the highest priority for a lot of us," adds another student. The college is moderately ethnically diverse, with 16 percent minority students and six percent international. Students are primarily from Colorado, but 38 percent venture in from out of state.

You May Not Know

- The school's first silver diplomas awarded in 1934 took two men 500 hours to etch. Graduates still receive diplomas made from the precious metal.
- The first graduating class, in 1883, had two students. The first female graduate followed in 1898.
- The school operates its own mine, Edgar Mine, in Idaho Springs, CO.

Distinguished Alumni

Arden L. Bement, Jr., director, National Science Foundation; Mari Angeles Major-Sosias, vice president, International Network, AREVA, Inc.; Antonio Ermírio de Moraes, chairman, Grupo Votorantim, Brazil.

Admissions and Financial Aid

The school recommends that students take calculus in high school if it is offered to them and is specific about what kind of students it's looking for: it asks that students rank in the upper third of their graduating class and have strong ACT or SAT scores.

All admitted students are considered for merit scholarships, and they are awarded at the school's discretion. Admitted students find out if they've been offered a scholarship by March 1. There is one scholarship that requires separate application—the E-Days scholarship, which is only offered to Colorado residents. It is for full tuition for eight semesters. Selection is based on a competitive process involving an essay and consideration of academic performance.

COLORADO SCHOOL OF MINES

Highlights

Admissions Criteria
Academic criteria:
Grades: ☆ ☆ ☆
Difficulty of class schedule: ☆ ☆ ☆
Class rank: ☆ ☆ ☆
Standardized test scores: ☆ ☆ ☆
Teacher recommendations: ☆
Personal statement: ☆
Non-academic criteria considered:
Interview
Extracurricular activities
Special talents, interests, abilities
Character/personal qualities
Geographical location
Alumni relationship

Deadlines
Early Action: No
Early Decision: No
Regular Action: Rolling admissions
Common Application: Not accepted

Financial Aid
In-state tuition: $13,590
Out-of-state tuition: $28,620
Room: Varies
Board: Varies
Books: $1,500
Freshmen receiving need-based aid: 56%
Undergrads rec. need-based aid: 54%
Avg. % of need met by financial aid: 61%
Avg. aid package (freshmen): $12,239
Avg. aid package (undergrads): $12,214
Avg. debt upon graduation: $23,385

School Spirit
Mascot: Orediggers, Blaster, Marvin the Miner
Colors: Blue and silver
Song: *The Mines Fight Song*

COLORADO
STATE
UNIVERSITY

Four-year public
Founded: 1870
Fort Collins, CO
Medium city
Pop. 146,762

Address:
1062 Campus Delivery
Fort Collins, CO
80523

Admissions:
970-491-6909

Financial Aid:
970-491-6321

admissions@colostate.
edu

www.colostate.edu

COLORADO STATE UNIVERSITY

Overview

Since it's a university with a strong agricultural heritage, it's fitting that the campus of Colorado State University (CSU) is covered in green trees, and many of its 23,000 undergraduates are often decked out in green tees. The Oval at the center of campus is lined with elm trees, and you'll find students congregating at the Lory Student Center, where foot traffic nears 100,000 in a single week, and Morgan Library, which has over two million volumes to offer its readers.

The "Green University," as CSU calls itself, is a fitting nickname for a campus where students are passionate about the environment—whether academically or recreationally. With 300 days of sunshine each year and a location at the base of the Rocky Mountain foothills, there's no shortage of outdoor activities to choose from. Fort Collins, where the main campus is located, was ranked as number one in *Money* magazine's list of "America's Best Places to Live" based on criteria such as affordability, art and leisure, and park space.

CSU is a large enough public university to have top-rated facilities and a plethora of courses while still enabling students to get individualized attention, especially as they enter upper level classes. Still, a large university requires a lot of personal initiative: students can choose to seek out attention from professors or stay low-key. Applicants who consider CSU shouldn't be daunted by the prospect of carving out their own trails at the big university among big mountains.

Academics

CSU has more than 200 academic programs. The downside of this huge selection is that "you may not get the classes that you want," says a student. Lower level classes can be a couple hundred students but upper level classes get much smaller, and the most common course size is 10 to 19 students. More than 1,000 students participate in the honors program, which typically has the benefit of more personalized attention from faculty.

Undergraduate programs of study include majors, minors, concentrations within majors, and the interdisciplinary studies program, each with a minimum number of required credits. The strongest programs at CSU are career-focused: various engineering-related programs, graphic design, programs in the department of occupational therapy, psychology, social work, and zoology. The Department of Veterinary Medicine and Biomedical Sciences is ranked in the top three nationwide by *U.S. News & World Report*.

Undergrads must complete the All-University Core Curriculum, which consists of classes in intermediate and advanced writing, math, oral communications, biological/physical sciences, arts/humanities, social/behavioral sciences, historical perspectives, and global and cultural awareness. "The requirements are not overwhelming and pretty easy to meet," remarks one student.

Students interested in science research can take advantage of the Honors Undergraduate Research Scholars (HURS) Program. Undergrad HURS Scholars work closely with grad students, postdocs, and science faculty. The more business-minded can apply for one of the 15 highly-competitive spots in the Summit Student Investment Fund in the College of Business. The group meets twice a week to review and make decisions on the stock in their current portfolio.

About 900 students a year study abroad. There are a large number of programs to choose from, including CSU-sponsored, CSU-affiliated, and non-affiliated programs. "You can pretty much study anywhere in the world," notes a student.

CSU's Career Center, in the Lory Student Center, provides services for students and alumni. CareerRAM offers access to thousands of internships and job listings, including 200+ employers who interview students directly on campus, as well as networking opportunities among alumni.

Student Life

Though only about a quarter of students live on campus, there is still a vibrant social scene, as exemplified by the 500 student organizations. Greek organizations enjoy a strong presence, with about seven percent of the student body participating in 40 fraternities and sororities. KCSU, the college's radio station, reaches 250,000 listeners. The *Rocky Mountain Collegian* is the daily student newspaper and has been honored as one of the best student newspapers in the country.

CSU can boast as many performances, exhibitions, and arts events as sunny days each year. A student group traces CSU's "exuberant programming on campus" to the "golden age" of the 1960s, when bands such as The Rolling Stones and the Red Hot Chili Peppers performed on campus. Today, the famous people who come aren't just bands: for example, The Monfort Lecture Series has brought Jane Goodall, Archbishop Desmond Tutu, and Madeleine Albright to speak.

The President's Fall Address and University Picnic welcomes students back to campus in September. Not long afterwards, the university becomes a sea of green during Homecoming Weekend, a tradition that includes a 5K run, parade, and festival before the tailgate and homecoming football game. Ag Day celebrates Colorado's agricultural history and raises money for CSU agricultural science student scholarships. In the spring, Business Day and the Spring Career Fair have activities for the career-oriented.

Though technically a dry campus, alcohol can still be found at parties—especially off campus parties, frat parties, and, obviously, the bars in Fort Collins. "The party scene is a pretty big one," says a student. The Lory Student Center, purported as one of the best student centers in the country, underwent a $18 million renovation after a flash flood in 1997. Its three levels include over a dozen eateries, the CSU bookstore, and student groups and services.

Football is a popular spectator sport at CSU, even if the team doesn't have a spectacularly successful history. The Rams' biggest rival is the University of Colorado at Boulder, which explains why the annual Rocky Mountain Showdown between the two schools' football teams draws enormous crowds.

Fourteen percent of students participate in intramural sports. The 27 sports clubs, from alpine ski team to men and women's wrestling, also have high participation rates.

Many students have cars to help them take advantage of the plethora of outdoor activities in the Rocky Mountains and Horsetooth Reservoir: skiing, snowboarding, hiking, mountain biking, camping, white water rafting, and boating. "I head outdoors almost every day after class, and I'm definitely not alone," remarks a student.

Freshmen are required to live on campus and housing is assigned on first-come, first-served basis. The 13 residence halls on campus house more than 5,000 students and various halls house the Residential Learning Communities (RLCs). The Live Green community requires a freshman seminar and spring break service trips to the National Parks of Colorado. Key Academic Community for freshmen brings 190 academically-focused students together in

COLORADO STATE UNIVERSITY

Highlights

Students
Total enrollment: 30,647
Undergrads: 23,479
Freshmen: 5,835
From out-of-state: 26%
From public schools: 90%
Male/Female: 49%/51%
Live on-campus: 25%
In fraternities: 6%
In sororities: 9%
Off-campus employment rating: Excellent
Caucasian: 75%
African American: 2%
Hispanic: 9%
Asian / Pacific Islander: 2%
Native American: 0%
Mixed (2+ ethnicities): 3%
International: 2%

Academics
Calendar: Semester
Student/faculty ratio: 19:1
Class size 9 or fewer: 10%
Class size 10-29: 49%
Class size 30-49: 22%
Class size 50-99: 11%
Class size 100 or more: 7%
Returning freshmen: 84%
Six-year graduation rate: 64%
Graduates who immediately go to graduate school: 22%

Most Popular Majors
Business administration
Human development/family studies
Health/exercise science

Admissions
Applicants: 17,929
Accepted: 13,394
Acceptance rate: 74.7%
Average GPA: 3.6
ACT range: 21-27
SAT Math range: 520-640
SAT Reading range: 500-620
SAT Writing range: Not reported
Top 10% of class: 22%
Top 25% of class: 51%
Top 50% of class: 88%

201

COLORADO STATE UNIVERSITY

Admissions Criteria
Academic criteria:
Grades: ☆ ☆ ☆
Difficulty of class schedule: ☆ ☆ ☆
Class rank: ☆ ☆
Standardized test scores: ☆ ☆ ☆
Teacher recommendations: ☆ ☆
Personal statement: ☆ ☆
Non-academic criteria considered:
Extracurricular activities
Special talents, interests, abilities
Character/personal qualities
Volunteer work
Work experience
State of residency
Geographical location
Alumni relationship

Deadlines
Early Action: December 1
Early Decision: No
Regular Action: Rolling admissions
Common Application: Accepted

Financial Aid
In-state tuition: $7,494
Out-of-state tuition: $23,347
Room: $4,956
Board: $5,820
Books: $1,126
Freshmen receiving need-based aid: 54%
Undergrads rec. need-based aid: 53%
Avg. % of need met by financial aid: 69%
Avg. aid package (freshmen): $16,131
Avg. aid package (undergrads): $15,195
Avg. debt upon graduation: $22,039

School Spirit
Mascot: Rams
Colors: Green and gold

groups of 19, while about 50 percent of first-year honors students opt to live in the new Honors Academic Village.

Student Body

Only 26 percent of students are from out of state, although students hail from all 50 states and 79 countries. While the university has increased its ethnic diversity by more than one third in the past decade, the number of minority students still remains a moderate 16 percent of the total student body.

The large number of students enrolled at the university guarantees that all types of students are represented, as the enormous number of student groups can attest. "There are two things that unify us—a love of outdoors and an interest in the environment," explains one student.

You May Not Know

- CSU was founded in 1870 as the Colorado Agricultural College. Colorado became a state in 1876.
- The university's colors (green and gold) were selected as a symbolic link to the institution's history as an agricultural college.
- Thirty percent of *all* of Colorado's science, math, engineering, and technology majors study at CSU.

Distinguished Alumni

Mary Cleave, engineer and former NASA astronaut; Yusef Komunyakaa, Pulitzer Prize winning poet; Bill Ritter, Jr., Colorado Governor.

Admissions and Financial Aid

The admissions office states that "each application is given a careful, individual, holistic review" that focuses on academic achievement, community service and leadership, one's "ability to contribute to a diverse campus community," and uniquely compelling personal circumstances. Priority consideration is given to students with a minimum GPA of 3.25 who have completed 18 recommended high school units across a number of subjects. Students applying for certain majors—including art, biomedical sciences, business, computer science, engineering, and technical journalism—have more rigorous requirements.

Colorado residents who apply by February 1 are automatically considered for five merit-based scholarships ranging from $8,000 to $10,000 over four years. Three other awards for Colorado State residents require a separate application: there is an award for first generation students and the arts and the Monfort Scholarship, which covers all tuition and fees for four years. Applicants who are not Colorado residents also have a number of scholarships for which they are either automatically considered or can apply separately for. The largest of these is the Presidential Scholarship, which offers $36,000 over four years.

COLUMBIA UNIVERSITY

Overview

Undergrads at Columbia University have no shortage of statistics to boast about regarding the world-renowned liberal arts research university they attend: 79 Columbians have won a Nobel Prize—not to mention receipts of Pulitzer Prizes, MacArthur Genius Awards, and Academy and Oscar Awards. There are almost 500 student groups to choose from. There's even a small number to be proud of: zero student loans in financial aid packages, and no tuition for low-income students who qualify.

The Columbia campus in the Morningside Heights neighborhood of New York city acts as a park-like urban village with striking buildings such as the Butler Library—modeled after the Parthenon in Greece—and the glass and steel atrium of Alfred Lerner Hall. The location in NYC allows students access to world-class museums and culture, restaurants, shopping, and internships on Wall Street or in the media.

The bigness of the city and the largeness of Columbia University—with undergraduate schools that include Columbia College, The Fu Foundation School of Engineering and Applied Science, and The School of General Studies (for returning and nontraditional students)—can be overwhelming for some, and students from Barnard also attend Columbia classes. Guaranteed four years on-campus housing helps create closer-knit communities, though Columbia is by no means an insular university. High-achieving students with big ambitions may find a good fit in Columbia's vibrant academic and social scene and Manhattan's fast-paced culture.

Academics

Undergraduates choose from more than 90 majors and 40 concentrations. All undergrads take the Core Curriculum, designed to stimulate critical thinking in small and intensive discussion-based seminars. At the center of the Core is Contemporary Civilization in the West, a two-semester course required for all sophomores. All first-year students complete Literature Humanities, another two-semester course. "The Core classes allow us to have discussion that anyone in our class can participate in," says a student. Other Core courses cover arts, music, science, foreign language, writing, and more. Global Core courses engage students with a specific culture or civilization, or classes may involve comparative studies between cultures. There is also a physical education requirement that includes passing a swimming test or taking beginning swimming for one term.

Strong programs include chemistry, economics, English, physics, and political science. Research opportunities abound with Columbia's more than 200 research institutes and centers, and 22 libraries making up one of the top 10 library systems in the country. The Undergraduate Research Involvement Program (URIP) through The Fu Foundation School of Engineering and Applied Science gives students a chance to collaborate with faculty on research projects for a stipend or course credit on topics such as nanotechnology to tissue engineering. "I've done real, hands-on research on cancer," explains a science major. "I never thought that as an undergrad I'd have this kind of opportunity." Some students who are admitted are guaranteed that they will have four years of research experience.

One of the university's centers is the Columbia Center for Archaeology. Students and faculty are involved in field programs in areas including Argentina, the UK, Turkey, Israel, and Egypt. Columbia Neuroscience is a collection of more than 200 faculty members in different departments of the medical school, public health school, and Faculty of Arts and Sciences. The Jerome L. Green Science Center is planned to be established for neuroscience study by a $200 million donation on behalf of an alumnus.

Accelerated and Joint programs at Columbia include a five-year plan that enables students to attend Columbia College and The Fu Foundation School of Engineering and Applied Science to receive both BA and BS degrees. Talented juniors can also ap-

COLUMBIA UNIVERSITY

Four-year private
Founded: 1754
New York, NY
Major city
Pop. 8,244,910

Address:
2960 Broadway
New York, NY
10027

Admissions:
212-854-2522

Financial Aid:
212-854-3711

ugrad-ask@columbia.edu

www.columbia.edu

COLUMBIA UNIVERSITY

Students

Total enrollment: 26,471
Undergrads: 6,068
Freshmen: 1,415
From out-of-state: 76%
Male/Female: 53%/47%
Live on-campus: 94%
In fraternities: 15%
In sororities: 10%
Off-campus employment rating: Excellent
Caucasian: 40%
African American: 8%
Hispanic: 14%
Asian / Pacific Islander: 16%
Native American: 1%
Mixed (2+ ethnicities): 4%
International: 13%

Academics

Calendar: Semester
Student/faculty ratio: 6:1
Class size 9 or fewer: 14%
Class size 10-29: 73%
Class size 30-49: 6%
Class size 50-99: 5%
Class size 100 or more: 2%
Returning freshmen: 99%
Six-year graduation rate: 97%

Admissions

Applicants: 31,851
Accepted: 2,362
Acceptance rate: 7.4%
Average GPA: Not reported
ACT range: 32-35
SAT Math range: 710-790
SAT Reading range: 700-780
SAT Writing range: 77-21

ply for accelerated or joint degree options at Columbia Law School, The School of International and Public Affairs, and Juilliard School.

Columbia offers nearly 200 study-abroad opportunities, including university-sponsored study centers in Beijing, Berlin, and Kyoto; special programs at Oxford and Cambridge; and shorter term-focused research or summer internship opportunities. Columbia even has a research center in Antarctica.

The Center for Career Education Programs hosts career fairs as well as specialized ones for engineering, media, and non-profits. "The career fairs are filled with employers, which makes it extremely easy to network," comments one student. The office also directs several internship programs specifically for Columbia students, such as the Columbia Arts Experience, Columbia Experience Overseas, and Science Technology Engineering Program.

There are more than 270,000 Columbia alumni worldwide in every state in the U.S. and over 180 countries. Columbia's "Alumni and Outcomes" website highlights the achievements of Columbia alumni who became leaders in academia, business, literature, politics, and more.

Student Life

Each fall, Columbia's nearly 500 student clubs, organizations, and initiatives vie for new members on College Walk during Activities Day. Many of these opportunities claim long-standing traditions: the LGBTQ group is the oldest on an American college campus; the *Columbia Daily Spectator* is the second-oldest daily newspaper in the country; the entirely student-run *Varsity Show* has been staged for more than 120 years. Nearly 100 religious and cultural groups celebrate the diversity of the student body.

Many students manage not to have classes on Fridays, so weekends can start early. One student comments, "Thursdays, Fridays, and Saturdays are nights to party and go out." Students often pass the time on the steps of Low Memorial Library, a National Historic Landmark whose distinctive freestanding granite dome cap is the largest in the United States.

The aforementioned *Varsity Show* is one of Columbia's oldest traditions, with sold-out performances playing to the undergraduate community every April. An even noisier tradition features the Columbia University Marching Band. Members conduct jokes and music all over campus on the day before the Organic Chemistry final exam, beginning with inside Butler Library. Appropriately dubbed Orgo Night, the Band's antics are designed to add levity to an otherwise grueling study time.

Winter brings more peaceful events with the Tree-Lighting and Yule Log Ceremonies, which include free hot chocolate, a cappella performances and speeches, and caroling. Warmer weather brings Bacchanal, Columbia's annual weeklong spring festival, which features the much-anticipated free Spring Concert. "After a winter of cold and snow, we're ready to celebrate once spring rolls around," comments a student.

Greek life has a presence on campus with 14 fraternities, 11 sororities, and a number of multicultural Greek organizations. However, only about 15 percent of males and 10 percent of females pledge. "You'd hardly even know that there are fraternities and sororities on campus. There's so much else to do," says a student.

Though there are no athletic scholarships at Columbia, the university still boasts 15 Ivy League Athletic Championships since 2007. "We're the most successful Ivy League when it comes to athletics," notes a fan. As with other opportunities on campus, there are plenty of athletic opportunities to choose from: 31 NCAA Division I teams, 45+ club sports, and 40+ intramural sports.

And of course, there's always New York City itself, with its seemingly infinite number of activities including restaurants, bars, shopping, culture, museums, professional sports, etc. For big city lovers, the Big Apple sells itself.

The vast majority of students live on campus, and campus housing is guaranteed for all four years, a definite plus since rent in New York City is outrageous for most student budgets. There are more singles available at Columbia than at most colleges, and all rooms in the two-dozen residence halls are singles or doubles. Because so many students live on campus, there is an active on-campus life as well as off campus. Freshmen all live in five halls located directly on the University's main quadrangle.

Student Body

There is high ethnic diversity at Columbia with its 43 percent minority population, as well as high geographic diversity with three-quarters of undergrads hailing from out of state. This diverse student body is united, however, by a love of learning and focus on academics—not surprising given that 94 percent of students graduated in the top 10 percent of their class. "There is no typical Columbia student because every interest and talent is represented, which is a great thing," comments a student.

Columbia's students are known to be very liberal, with a history of promoting free speech. The university has hosted controversial speakers including Iranian President Mahmoud Ahmadinejad in 2007 and Minuteman founder Jim Gilchrist in 2006. The college describes the student body as "politically, environmentally, and socially conscious" and notes "a robust and avante garde performing arts community."

You May Not Know

- The movies *Hitch* and *Ghostbusters* were filmed on the Columbia campus.
- Columbia grew from a one-room classroom with a single professor and eight students to more than 4,000 faculty members and 6,000 undergraduate students today.
- Pupin Hall is where a uranium atom was first split and the laser and FM radio were invented.

Distinguished Alumni

Ruth Bader Ginsburg, Associate Justice of the U.S. Supreme Court; Stephen Jay Gould, historian of science; Maggie Gyllenhaal, actress; Langston Hughes, poet and writer.

Admissions and Financial Aid

The admissions office encourages prospective students to explore admissions procedures by individual schools or by a listing of academic departments and programs. Admissions is extremely

COLUMBIA UNIVERSITY

Highlights

Admissions Criteria
Academic criteria:
Grades: ☆ ☆ ☆
Difficulty of class schedule: ☆ ☆ ☆
Class rank: ☆ ☆ ☆
Standardized test scores: ☆ ☆ ☆
Teacher recommendations: ☆ ☆ ☆
Personal statement: ☆ ☆ ☆
Non-academic criteria considered:
Interview
Extracurricular activities
Special talents, interests, abilities
Character/personal qualities
Volunteer work
Work experience
State of residency
Geographical location
Minority affiliation
Alumni relationship

Deadlines
Early Action: No
Early Decision: November 1
Regular Action: January 1 (final)
Notification of admission by: April 1
Common Application: Accepted

Financial Aid
In-state tuition: $46,846
Out-of-state tuition: $46,846
Room: Varies
Board: Varies
Books: $1,040
Freshmen receiving need-based aid: 51%
Undergrads rec. need-based aid: 52%
Avg. % of need met by financial aid: 100%
Avg. aid package (freshmen): $43,087
Avg. aid package (undergrads): $42,716

School Spirit
Mascot: Lions
Colors: Columbia blue and white
Song: *Roar Lion Roar*

competitive, with over 31,000 applicants for just 2,300 students accepted; however, the university emphasizes its holistic admissions process that looks for "extraordinary academic work over the last four years" regardless of GPA, class rank, or test scores. The admissions committee also evaluates extracurricular participation, summer experiences, academic/personal responsibilities and interests, personal essay and short answer responses, and letters of evaluation. The university seeks "those that we believe will take the greatest advantage of the unique Columbia experience and will offer something meaningful in return to the community."

Admission to Columbia is need-blind and financial aid is need-based. There are no academic, athletic, or talent-based institutional scholarships. Columbia will meet 100 percent of demonstrated financial need for all admitted freshmen, including foreign students, and continues to meet demonstrated need for all four years of study. Since the 2008-2009 school year, loans were eliminated for all students receiving financial aid and replaced with university grants; furthermore, parents with calculated income below $60,000 are not required to contribute any income to tuition, room, board, and mandatory fees.

CONNECTICUT COLLEGE

Overview

New London serves as host to Connecticut College, a woodsy campus that overlooks the tidal marshes of the Long Island Sound. The college grounds are laced with hiking trails and double as an arboretum to which tree huggers beeline. But birches aren't the only thrill for those who give peace a chance. Connecticut College's relatively lax test-taking policy has also snagged a well-rounded crowd. Lackadaisical the college is not; its prestige and academic rigor have earned its "Little Ivy" status.

Founded to answer nearby Wesleyan's decision to cease admitting female students, Connecticut College continues to cater to a more heavily female student body. Festivals like the catchall Festivus further exemplify the school's inclusive spirit. Occasionally this love-in feel can seem sappy. Graduates are presented with an actual pine sapling upon receiving their diplomas.

The school boasts attractive bearings in the Northeast, as students have only a two-hour drive to Boston or New York City. Connecticut College also offers a tight-knit student body in a slower-paced but friendly environment.

Academics

Connecticut College profs often go by their first names. They also teach all classes on campus. This move for closer faculty-student relationships translates into most classes having no more than 20 students. "I don't have any class with more than 25 students," says a student, "and one of my classes has only five students."

Connecticut College has 49 majors, and it excels in such departments as botany, English, and psychology. The school mandates completion of a General Education core, which includes a freshman fall seminar that matches one class in each of seven areas (from creative arts and mathematics to philosophical and religious studies). Those interested in prelaw or premed programs should not gloss over the college. Nearly four-fifths of those who graduate Connecticut College and then apply to law school or graduate programs in the health professions are accepted.

The college's Honor Code allows students to schedule and take their own tests individually and at their convenience. "At first it seems like a lot of responsibility to administer your own exam, but after a while it is just so much more convenient," states a student. Five interdisciplinary academic centers offer programs in international studies, the environment, arts and technology, public policy and community action, and the study of race and ethnicity. Students may earn certificates through the centers.

Students may also participate in honors study and complete an honors thesis, working one-on-one with a faculty member. "It's a lot of extra work to do a thesis, but it's rewarding to work with a professor on a year-long project and produce a thesis as a result," says a student.

More than half of the student body studies abroad. The award-winning program shuttles students anywhere from Morocco to Mongolia, and the college's formidable language study curriculum ensures that they master the local lingo. A semester through Study Away/Teach Away brings up to 20 juniors to mingle close and personal with a professor and his or her line of study. Economics in Rome and Spanish in Oaxaca are also offered.

Connecticut College successfully supports its seniors with "life-changing," bountiful internships, often financially backed by the office of Career Enhancing Life Skills (CELS). In addition to assisting students with career planning, the office also guides them in applying for fellowships. Connecticut College has been a top producer of Fulbright Fellowships for the past three years.

CONNECTICUT COLLEGE

Four-year private
Founded: 1911
New London, CT
Large town
Pop. 27,569

Address:
270 Mohegan Avenue
New London, CT
06320-4196

Admissions:
860-439-2200

Financial Aid:
860-439-2058

admission@conncoll.edu

www.conncoll.edu

CONNECTICUT COLLEGE

Students
Total enrollment: 1,933
Undergrads: 1,926
Part-time students: 2%
From out-of-state: 83%
Male/Female: 40%/60%
Live on-campus: 99%
Off-campus employment rating: Good
Caucasian: 73%
African American: 4%
Hispanic: 7%
Asian / Pacific Islander: 3%
Native American: 0%
Mixed (2+ ethnicities): 2%
International: 4%

Academics
Calendar: Semester
Student/faculty ratio: 9:1
Class size 9 or fewer: 19%
Class size 10-29: 62%
Class size 30-49: 18%
Class size 50-99: 1%
Class size 100 or more: 1%
Returning freshmen: 92%
Six-year graduation rate: 85%
Graduates who immediately go to graduate school: 25%

Most Popular Majors
Economics
English
Government

Admissions
Applicants: 4,837
Accepted: 1,734
Acceptance rate: 35.8%
Placed on wait list: 1,152
Enrolled from wait list: 31
Average GPA: Not reported
ACT range: 28-31
SAT Math range: 615-700
SAT Reading range: 620-710
SAT Writing range: 44-49
Top 10% of class: 56%
Top 25% of class: 95%
Top 50% of class: 100%

Student Life

A night in New London certifies the claim that crickets haunt the campus! It's a fact: their sad music chirps throughout the sleepy town. Most students enjoy Fridays free of classes but that just means three potentially blasé days off. Luckily the Big Apple isn't too far away and organized trips to New York City are scheduled once a month. On the other weekends, students must rely on the restaurants and bars that are available in town. The campus does offer a series of Friday Night Live concerts, which features bands from both on and off the campus. Wintertime free-for-all Festivus celebrates, well, everything, and concert-packed Floralia enlivens the spring.

There are 55 student organizations on campus but no fraternities or sororities. "We are small enough that we are practically our own fraternity or sorority," laughs one student. "Purely recreational" intramural sports teams keep 1,000 participants busy. "More than half the school does intramural sports," remarks a student. "It's more about having fun than who wins." A 10,000-square-foot fitness center offers both "leading-edge exercise equipment" and a view of the Thames River. The college has 28 Division III varsity teams, with the women's volleyball team an especially strong standout.

Students generally choose between either of a pair of housing options. The North, home to the souped-up "Plex" residence, has a reserved feeling upon entering the complex. Ke$ha clones and clubbers boogie on the more outgoing South Campus. No matter your locale, you'll luck out with a single in your junior and senior years. Male and female students elbow each other as they floss and coif in the co-ed bathrooms.

Student Body

Students at Connecticut College number a cozy 1,900. The petite figure means that everyone finds a posse, no sweat. Minorities make the campus moderately diverse and account for 16 percent of the population. More abundant are differences in statehood, since 83 percent hail from outside of Connecticut. A bias toward the region of New England qualifies this variety in background. And most students are financially well-to-do, which might vouch for the healthy showing of international students. "It seems like everyone wears designer clothes and has a summer home," says a student.

There are more women at Connecticut College, and they roar. The female majority reflects itself in the gender-aware social scene and classroom interactions. "Women aren't afraid to speak up here," notes a student.

You May Not Know

- Nearby U.S. Coast Guard Academy students attend courses on the mainland campus, and vice versa.
- Playwright Eugene O'Neill wrote his first eight plays in the college's own New London.
- The Thames River, nearby to the campus, annually acts as host to the Boat Race, in which racers from Harvard and Yale compete.

Distinguished Alumni

Tim Armstrong, CEO of America Online; Joshua Green, editor of *The Atlantic* publication; John Krasinski, actor from *The Office*; members of the band Clap Your Hands Say Yeah; Estelle Parsons, Academy- and Tony Award-winning actress.

Admissions and Financial Aid

Apply to the campus via the Common Application and the school's own supplement, which requests two short answers to questions asking you to "share something about yourself." Interviews are not required but "highly recommended." Standardized tests are optional, and the college recommends that you do not submit your scores if they "do not reflect your full potential." The college does what it can to support students' aim for entry, even sharing successful essays for you to peruse.

Ah, to have been born in New London. Residents of the city can potentially qualify for a Jane Bredson Scholarship, which pays for half of one's tuition. "Local underrepresented students" who can demonstrate financial need compete for the Lois Taylor scholarship. A student committed to studies of race and diversity can earn the Cornel West Scholarship and enjoy four-year financial support. The college itself offers many need-based grants. The school also flaunts that their average grant award is "$29,000" covering about half of the cost of attendance.

CONNECTICUT COLLEGE

Highlights

Admissions Criteria
Academic criteria:
Grades: ☆ ☆ ☆
Difficulty of class schedule: ☆ ☆ ☆
Class rank: ☆ ☆ ☆
Standardized test scores: ☆
Teacher recommendations: ☆ ☆
Personal statement: ☆ ☆
Non-academic criteria considered:
Interview
Extracurricular activities
Special talents, interests, abilities
Character/personal qualities
Volunteer work
Work experience
Geographical location
Religious affiliation/commitment
Minority affiliation
Alumni relationship

Deadlines
Early Action: No
Early Decision: November 15
Regular Action: January 1 (final)
Notification of admission by: March 31
Common Application: Accepted

Financial Aid
In-state tuition: $46,085
Out-of-state tuition: $46,085
Room: Varies
Board: Varies
Books: $1,000
Freshmen receiving need-based aid: 49%
Undergrads rec. need-based aid: 50%
Avg. % of need met by financial aid:
    100%
Avg. aid package (freshmen): $34,688
Avg. aid package (undergrads): $35,200
Avg. debt upon graduation: $23,558

School Spirit
Mascot: Camels
Colors: Blue and white
Song: *CC by the Sea*

Four-year private
Founded: 1859
New York, NY
Major city
Pop. 8,244,910

Address:
30 Cooper Square
New York, NY
10003

Admissions:
212-353-4120

Financial Aid:
212-353-4113

admissions@cooper.
edu

www.cooper.edu

COOPER UNION

Overview

Cooper Union is a very small, highly competitive college with an impressive history. CU consists of three schools: the Irwin S. Chanin School of Architecture, the School of Art, and the Albert Nerken School of Engineering. Peter Cooper, founder of The Cooper Union, had a unique vision for his school. From the moment he established the school in 1859, he made education available to all—including women and people of color. Until 2014, Cooper Union offered a full tuition scholarship to every admitted student, making its degree not only prestigious but also free. Starting with freshmen entering in Fall 2014, that famous policy has changed—amidst vocal student protests. Students, aside from those receiving need-based financial aid, will have to pay half of the cost of tuition (to the tune of around $20,000).

Price tag aside, the academic rigor of Cooper Union is nearly unmatched. There are plenty of opportunities for interactions with professors given the eight-to-one student-to-faculty ratio. The school's East Village location allows students to go out and work, learn, and play in New York City.

Those who are looking for a very conventional, "collegiate" feel in their university may find Cooper Union a disappointment. Its urban location, lack of campus institutions like frat houses and dining halls, and labor-intensive curriculum are a stark contrast to what you might expect from the movies. You have to be ready to work hard if you come to Cooper Union, but if you are, you will find all the resources and opportunities you could wish for.

Academics

Cooper Union is a nerd's ideal playground. Academic standards and student work ethics are unbelievably high, with a consistent thread of interdisciplinary learning woven through the curriculum of all three of the college's schools.

The one component that all three programs share is the humanities core curriculum, a four-semester series. The core courses are: "The Freshman Seminar" ("a literature course concentrating on poetry and drama"), "Texts and Contexts: Old Worlds and New," "The Making of Modern Society," and "The Modern Context: Figures and Topics."

The School of Art affirms that it "is firmly committed to a generalist curriculum that encompasses all the fundamental disciplines and resources of the visual arts." As such, the curriculum precludes students from becoming too narrowly focused on their specialties. Students must complete core coursework in art history and a freshman Foundation Studio.

The Bachelor of Architecture program takes five years to complete. Students must take courses from "Freehand Drawing" to "Modern Physics" to "Introduction to Urban History" to "Theories of Construction Management." The final year includes a required thesis project and Professional Practice course.

Engineering is a four-year program with the opportunity for students to specialize in chemical, civil, electrical, or mechanical engineering. In year one, students take an innovative course called "Engineering Design and Problem Solving," in which they tackle urban engineering challenges. In their third and fourth year, students devote their time to advanced, specialized courses and individual and group design projects.

Cooper's study abroad options are more limited than those at most schools and are only open to third-year students. The college only partners with an extremely select group of art schools around the world, in places like Prague, Kyoto, and London.

There are many special academic opportunities at Cooper Union, including several fellowships to fund projects in one's senior year. Each of the three schools has its own awards, and there are a few general grants open to all CU students. For instance, the Benjamin Menschel Fellowship Program to Support Creative Inquiry provides funding for seniors to "further their intellectual investigations." Throughout their time at Cooper Union, students can apply to become Student Research Associates and to assist with professor-led research funded by the C.V. Starr Research Foundation, CU's research arm.

Cooper Union provides many resources to link students with career opportunities. Through the Professional Internship Program, art and architecture students in their final year at CU can receive up to $1,000 of funding for otherwise unpaid internships. The CU @ Lunch programs brings in successful young alumni to discuss job hunting post-graduation. CONNECT (Cooper's Own No-Nonsense Engineering Communication Training) is a series of workshops on interpersonal communication and public speaking to prepare engineers for the workplace.

Student Life

The traditional outlets for college students—corny bonding activities, frat parties, frisbee on the quad—aren't really a big thing at Cooper Union. There's not even a dining hall, although there is one small cafe. Students tend to be hard driving and to spend a lot of nights and weekends in the studio or working on engineering assignments. Although there's a comparative dearth of social activities on campus, students have easy access to all the varied nightlife, dining, and cultural opportunities of New York. Of course, the challenge is finding time to make the most of these opportunities. "If you're awake, you're pretty much studying," says one student.

CU students can take a uniquely active role in running the college. Founder Peter Cooper originally wanted to empower students to create "such rules and regulations as they, on mature reflection, shall believe to be necessary and proper;" those rules have evolved into the current student Code of Conduct.

There are 80 student-run organizations at CU. They tend to lean towards the nerdy, from the reading group Bookspotting to the Finance and Investment Club to the Whovian Club, dedicated to educating students about "the importance of Time And Relative Dimension In Space and Doctor Who." CU has one fraternity, Zeta Psi. Let's be honest: no one goes to CU for the sports. Nonetheless, some limited options are available such as varsity soccer, varsity basketball, varsity tennis, varsity volleyball, and cross country.

As every New Yorker will tell you, the major downside of living in the city that never sleeps is trying to find an affordable place to sleep. Like most New York schools, CU has limited housing options. Only 20 percent of all students live on campus. Eighty percent of freshmen do. About 180 freshmen can choose to live in the Student Residence. You can't beat it for convenience, as it's just across the street from the Foundation Building, home to art and architecture classes. CU explicitly tells students that its East Village neighborhood is really darn expensive, and recommends beginning an apartment search in early summer if you want to live nearby. If you don't want to spend an arm and a leg, you'll have to live in a different borough. "You can live close by, but you'll have a lot of roommates in a too-small space or you can commute to school," notes a student.

Student Body

The important thing to keep in mind about Cooper Union's student body is that it is very small. A freshman class will include 20-35

THE COOPER UNION

Highlights

Students
Total enrollment: 939
Undergrads: 862
Freshmen: 202
From out-of-state: 50%
From public schools: 65%
Male/Female: 63%/37%
Live on-campus: 20%
In fraternities: 1%
Off-campus employment rating: Excellent
Caucasian: 37%
African American: 6%
Hispanic: 8%
Asian / Pacific Islander: 19%
Native American: 1%
Mixed (2+ ethnicities): 4%
International: 11%

Academics
Calendar: Semester
Student/faculty ratio: 8:1
Class size 9 or fewer: 25%
Class size 10-29: 69%
Class size 30-49: 5%
Class size 50-99: -
Class size 100 or more: 1%
Returning freshmen: 90%
Six-year graduation rate: 82%
Graduates who immediately go to graduate school: 50%

Most Popular Majors
Fine art
Architecture
Electrical engineering

Admissions
Applicants: 3,573
Accepted: 251
Acceptance rate: 7.0%
Placed on wait list: 75
Enrolled from wait list: 15
Average GPA: 3.6
ACT range: 29-33
SAT Math range: 610-770
SAT Reading range: 620-710
SAT Writing range: 40-35
Top 10% of class: 93%
Top 25% of class: 98%
Top 50% of class: 99%

College Profiles

THE COOPER UNION

Admissions Criteria

Academic criteria:
Grades: ☆ ☆ ☆
Difficulty of class schedule: ☆ ☆ ☆
Class rank: N/A
Standardized test scores: ☆ ☆ ☆
Teacher recommendations: ☆
Personal statement: ☆ ☆
Non-academic criteria considered:
Interview
Extracurricular activities
Special talents, interests, abilities
Character/personal qualities
Volunteer work
Work experience
State of residency
Minority affiliation

Deadlines

Early Action: No
Early Decision: December 1
Regular Action: January 1 (final)
Notification of admission by: April 1
Common Application: Not accepted

Financial Aid

In-state tuition: $39,600
Out-of-state tuition: $39,600
Room: $11,000
Board: $4,000
Books: $1,400
Freshmen receiving need-based aid: 61%
Undergrads rec. need-based aid: 46%
Freshmen receiving merit-based aid:
   100%
Undergrads rec. merit-based aid: 100%
Avg. % of need met by financial aid: 91%
Avg. aid package (freshmen): $37,500
Avg. aid package (undergrads): $37,500
Avg. debt upon graduation: $15,684

School Spirit

Colors: Maroon and gold

architecture students, 65 art students, and 115 engineering students.

Data on diversity and the student population can thus change quite a lot from year-to-year based on small changes in actual student numbers. Thanks to the now-defunct tuition waiver, CU students have come from a wide variety of economic backgrounds. In the near future, that may change with the changing tuition policy. The student body is six percent African American, 19 percent Asian, eight percent Latino, and 11 percent international. Even though it is not a state school, 50 percent of the college's students come from New York state. Perhaps because of the presence of the engineering school, the overall student population skews male—63 percent of students are men. Students must have a good work ethic to survive here, where grade inflation is nearly unheard of and the admissions process is hyper-selective. "There's no room for slacking," one student mentions. Another notes, "We're pretty much open to anything so you can let your freak flag fly." As you would expect, students are pretty darn hip, so be prepared to see some avant-garde fashion choices on campus. Pack your hipster glasses.

You May Not Know

- Cooper Union's Great Hall has hosted speeches by an illustrious list of historic figures. Perhaps the Great Hall's greatest moment was Abraham Lincoln's 1860 delivery of the renowned "Right Makes Might" speech.
- The school offers continuing education courses, in which any (paying) member of the public can enroll, on topics like Book Arts and New York History.
- Researchers at Cooper Union created the prototype for the microchip.

Distinguished Alumni

Thomas Edison, world-famous inventor; Max Fleischer, cartoonist and creator of Betty Boop; Milton Glaser, co-founder of *New York Magazine*; Bob Kane, comic book artist and creator of Batman; Eleanore Pettersen, pioneering female architect; Augustus Saint-Gaudens, 19th-century American sculptor.

Admissions and Financial Aid

Cooper Union is so competitive that every applicant, no matter how talented, should consider it a "reach" school. Only seven percent of applicants are accepted. Admissions processes differ by college. Art and architecture applicants must complete a "home test," which the school mysteriously describes as "a number of visual projects" that must be returned to the school within three to four weeks. "If you don't use every minute of the time you have for the home test, you're either brilliant or you aren't trying hard enough," describes a student. Art students must also submit their portfolios, which the school recommends include 10 to 20 pieces. In addition to the SAT or ACT, prospective engineers must submit SAT Subject Test scores in mathematics and either physics or chemistry and complete a series of short answer questions. Recommendation letters are required for artists and recommended for engineers, but not for architects.

CORNELL COLLEGE

Overview

"We're not in Ithaca," Cornell College's website reminds its visitors. Cornell College in Mount Vernon, Iowa, and Cornell University in Ithaca, New York, do seem to share some surface similarities: students at both schools have to brave cold, snowy winters and steep inclines—hence Cornell College's nickname "The Hilltop" (not to be confused with the university's nickname, "The Hill").

However, there are many factors that unmistakably distinguish the liberal arts college from any other schools. Cornell's wooded 129-acre campus in Mount Vernon, Iowa is not only beautiful but historic: indeed, it was the first college to have its entire campus listed on the National Register of Historic Places. Unfortunately, being situated in Mount Vernon does limit the off-campus social scene; the nearest major city, Chicago, is 200 miles away. Cornell College may not have the brand-name recognition that the Ivy League university of the same name enjoys, but it ranks high in academics: *Forbes* magazine ranked Cornell the top college in Iowa, and the college was recently ranked on *U.S. News & World Report's* "Up-and-Coming Schools" list.

Perhaps the most distinguishing factor of Cornell College is its "One Course at a Time" (OCAAT) system, where academic terms involve studying—you guessed it—just one subject. This system, as well as the small size of the college, makes for a tight-knit student body. Students who are happy to live in Iowa, and want to attend a strong school where they can get their college education in focused "blocks," will thrive at Cornell.

Academics

Cornell College offers 35 majors, 25 minors, and 11 pre-professional programs. The strongest programs are biology, economics and business, elementary education, English, psychology, and pre-professional programs in law and medicine.

All students are required to complete a capstone project, but by far the most unusual requirement for Cornell students is participation in the college's unique One Course at a Time (OCAAT) system. What is normally covered in a semester at a typical university fits into less than 18 Cornell class days, allowing students to focus deeply in the three and a half weeks of each of these "blocks." There is a four-and-a-half day "block break" after each course ends. "I love the block plan because I can live and breathe a subject for an entire month," says a student. The "block plan" makes for strong relationships among students and between students and their professors. However, some participants feel it is less ideal for foreign language classes.

A class cap of 25 and low faculty-student ratio ensure that students get individualized attention. The Bachelor of Special Studies also allows students to carve an individualized path with the guidance of faculty: students design their own liberal arts program as outlined in their prospectus. The BSS offers flexibility since there are no general education requirements or constraints. Other special academic opportunities include the competitive Cornell Fellows Program, a chance for high-level internships and professional mentoring for a select group of about 30 students.

According to the college, students typically study in more than 20 countries each year. One-block Cornell courses provide a window to study abroad for those who don't want to go for an entire semester (semesters are broken down in blocks one to four and five to nine).

About 65 percent of Cornell students pursue graduate studies, and the college ranks 68th among U.S. private four-year colleges in the number of graduates who go on to earn PhDs. The Career Office offers a number of services for students and alumni, such as individual counseling, help with preparing for internships, and finding jobs. Half of students enter a career related to their major within one year of graduating.

CORNELL COLLEGE

Four-year private
Founded: 1853
Mount Vernon, IA
Small town
Pop. 4,549

Address:
600 First Street SW
Mount Vernon, IA
52314-1098

Admissions:
800-747-1112

Financial Aid:
877-579-4049

admissions@cornell-college.edu

www.cornellcollege.edu

CORNELL COLLEGE

Students

Total enrollment: 1,180
Undergrads: 1,180
Freshmen: 341
Part-time students: 1%
From out-of-state: 85%
Male/Female: 45%/55%
Live on-campus: 90%
In fraternities: 22%
In sororities: 26%
Off-campus employment rating: Fair
Caucasian: 65%
African American: 5%
Hispanic: 11%
Asian / Pacific Islander: 4%
Native American: 1%
Mixed (2+ ethnicities): 2%
International: 6%

Academics

Calendar: Other
Student/faculty ratio: 12:1
Class size 9 or fewer: 21%
Class size 10-29: 79%
Class size 30-49: -
Class size 50-99: -
Class size 100 or more: -
Returning freshmen: 85%
Six-year graduation rate: 70%
Graduates who immediately go to graduate school: 23%
Graduates who immediately enter career related to major: 50%

Most Popular Majors

Psychology
Economics/business
Biology

Admissions

Applicants: 2,716
Accepted: 1,436
Acceptance rate: 52.9%
Placed on wait list: 142
Enrolled from wait list: 43
Average GPA: 3.5
ACT range: 24-30
SAT Math range: 540-690
SAT Reading range: 535-685
SAT Writing range: 10-40
Top 10% of class: 38%
Top 25% of class: 66%
Top 50% of class: 91%

Student Life

With 90 percent of students living on campus, Cornell has a vibrant social life as exemplified by its impressive 100+ clubs, organizations, and special interest groups—about 1 club for every 10 students! A diversity of interests are represented: Mountaineering Club brings students together to socialize and enjoy rock climbing, camping, and other outdoor activities, while the creatively named Knot Just for Grannies brings together students who love to knit and crochet. One group that's impossible to miss is Pandemonium, Cornell's 20-member steel drum ensemble.

Cornell students' love of music extends beyond this unique percussion group. Music Mondays brings different performers to campus four times a year: past performers include the Chicago Brass Quintet and international acts like the Mozart Piano Quarter from Berlin.

About one fifth of Cornell students join one of the 15 non-national Greek groups on campus, making these groups a major part of the social scene. These local sororities and organizations, often called "social groups," focus on leadership development, community service, and relationship building. "You can choose a social group that's more focused on partying or one that's more low-key," says a student.

In a nod to Cornell's OCAAT system, the annual "Knock Your Block Off" celebration signals the end of the year with tie-dying, music, and other festivities. "By Knock Your Block Off time, we have a lot of steam to blow off so everyone's relaxed," comments a student. A more serious tradition is the Student Symposium in April where students display their scholarly and creative work. Freshmen learn about all these traditions during their weeklong New Student Orientation, which also clues them in to the "Ramspeak," common colloquialisms used at the college.

There are 19 intercollegiate sports at Cornell at the NCAA Division III level. The college's wrestling team has been particularly successful, producing a number of individual national title wins and even seven Olympic wrestlers. Cornell's football rivalry with Coe College is the oldest intercollegiate rivalry west of the Mississippi dating from 1891. Those looking for friendly sports competition can choose from nearly 40 intramural sports.

Mount Vernon is quiet city of about 4,500 residents with few attractions for college students besides the local bars. "There's not as much to do off campus, so we do a lot on campus," notes one student. Some prefer the 30-minute drive to the larger cities of Cedar Rapids (where Coe College is located) and Iowa City (where the University of Iowa is located). Palisades-Kepler State Park is only five miles away and offers hiking, camping, picnicking, fishing, and hunting on its 840 acres. Students use their "block breaks" to visit regional cities such as Chicago, Minneapolis, and St. Louis.

Cornell has nine residence halls, most of which house fewer than 100 students. Freshmen can choose to live on any of three first-year theme floors—known as "Connect Floors,"—where they can bond with other students who share a common interest. The Living and Learning Communities bring 4 to 12 students together in a residential program to explore an issue in society, such as children with disabilities and cultural diversity. The communities vary each year.

Student Body

Cornell College is geographically diverse, with 85 percent hailing from outside of Iowa. Twenty-three percent of the student body is comprised of minority students, making it highly ethnically diverse. Despite its Midwest location, Cornell students don't fit the stereotype of Midwest conservatism; more students are liberal than not. "Personally I know more liberal students, but no one is an extremist," remarks a student.

Thanks to the OCAAT system, students get a chance to form friendships with those they might not normally get to know. "Everyone is really friendly and open to meeting new people," says one student. Another commonality is that students get involved in on-campus activities. About 75 percent of students participate in student organizations, leadership programs, and/or volunteer service.

You May Not Know

- Cornell College calls itself the "original Cornell" since it was founded in 1853, 12 years before the Ivy League University in Ithaca, NY was founded with the same name.
- Cornell College in Iowa does have a link to Cornell University in New York: iron tycoon William Wesley Cornell (Cornell College's namesake) was a distant cousin of Ezra Cornell, who founded Cornell University.
- According to the college, it is the "first college west of the Mississippi to grant women the same rights and privileges as men." The first woman graduated from Cornell in 1858.

Distinguished Alumni

Christoper Carney, U.S. Congress representative; Dr. Lawrence Dorr, Director of Dorr Arthritis Institute at Centinela Hospital, CA; Dr. Campbell McConnell, economist, educator, and author.

Admissions and Financial Aid

All students must complete the Cornell College Preliminary Application to start the admissions process. This simple online form requires information including what term you plan to enroll. For students who submit their application online, the application fee is waived. The Common Application and Common Application Supplement can replace the Cornell application. Teacher recommendations are optional but recommended. Cornell encourages students to visit the campus, either by attending one of the Preview Days or arranging an overnight stay at a residence hall, an option open to high school seniors.

Scholarships include academic awards that range from $6,000 to full tuition, and Performing Arts Scholarships and Awards ranging from $1,000 to $15,000. There are no athletic scholarships. The college also offers 6,500 work-study jobs each year.

CORNELL COLLEGE

Highlights

Admissions Criteria
Academic criteria:
Grades: ☆ ☆ ☆
Difficulty of class schedule: ☆ ☆ ☆
Class rank: ☆
Standardized test scores: ☆
Teacher recommendations: ☆ ☆
Personal statement: ☆ ☆
Non-academic criteria considered:
Interview
Extracurricular activities
Special talents, interests, abilities
Character/personal qualities
Volunteer work
Work experience
Geographical location
Minority affiliation
Alumni relationship

Deadlines
Early Action: December 1
Early Decision: November 1
Regular Action: Rolling admissions
Common Application: Accepted

Financial Aid
In-state tuition: $36,205
Out-of-state tuition: $36,205
Room: $3,800
Board: $4,700
Books: $800
Freshmen receiving need-based aid: 78%
Undergrads rec. need-based aid: 75%
Avg. % of need met by financial aid: 84%
Avg. aid package (freshmen): $32,040
Avg. aid package (undergrads): $30,087
Avg. debt upon graduation: $27,227

School Spirit
Mascot: Rams
Colors: Purple and white

CORNELL UNIVERSITY

Four-year private
Founded: 1865
Ithaca, NY
Large town
Pop. 30,054

Address:
349 Pine Tree Road
Ithaca, NY
14850

Admissions:
607-255-5241

Financial Aid:
607-255-5145

admissions@cornell.edu

www.cornell.edu

Overview

Cornell University's campus is big enough to have its own zip code, not surprising given the seven Colleges and Schools that comprise this Ivy League University. You might catch a glimpse of an "Ithaca is Gorges" T-shirt hinting at the beauty of the hilly 745-acre campus with its gardens, gorges, and waterfalls. The spectacular views, Ithaca and Cayuga lakes, and a plethora of outdoor activities do have a few drawbacks though: getting to class can feel like a real trek, and Ithaca is a small and remote town.

Cornell's main campus is teeming with activity: over 260 university buildings, nearly 800 student groups, and a whopping 4,000 courses are just some of the offerings. Cornell is big enough to be divided into North Campus, West Campus, Central Campus, and East Hill as well as Collegetown (on south side) and Plantations, Vet Quad, and Orchards (on the east side).

Cornell is said to be the easiest Ivy to get into—though admission is still very competitive. Cornell's unique structure distinguishes it from the others: four of its colleges/schools are private and three are public, creating in-state tuition options.

As a top-notch research institution, Cornell offers students an enormous amount of resources, though some complain that their professors are more focused on personal advancement than teaching. The university also consistently ranks near the top of the list of *U.S. News & World Report*. Students who attend will have to be able to contend with rigorous classes and the pressure to succeed in a highly competitive environment.

Academics

Due to Cornell's decentralized structure, each of its seven undergraduate colleges and schools is fairly autonomous, managing its own admissions and academic programs. Required classes vary by college. The College of Arts and Sciences requires first-year writing seminars; foreign language courses; distribution courses in cultural analysis, historical analysis, knowledge, cognition, and moral reasoning, literature and the arts, social and behavioral analysis, and physical and biological sciences; two physical education courses; and passing the swim test. The College of Arts and Sciences has the most students, followed by the Agriculture and Life Sciences and Engineering Colleges—together these account for about three-quarters of the student population.

There are nearly 80 undergraduate majors, and while most professors are highly praised and many are well known in their fields, some are criticized for not being the best teachers, being more focused on their own advancement than imparting their knowledge to students. Some "aren't afraid to cancel class when they have a conference to attend" while others "give out their cell phone numbers just so students can reach them," say students. There are some large lecture courses such as Psych 101, which has more than 1,000 students, but this is atypical, especially as students enter upper level classes. The most common course size is 10 to 19 students.

With 98 percent of students in the top 25 percent of their high school class, the competitive atmosphere among students isn't surprising. The competition "isn't overt and doesn't stop us from cooperating on projects, but it is an underlying sense," comments a student. Cornell has a reputation for an intense workload. However, Cornell's label as a "suicide college" is statistically unwarranted: suicide rates aren't actually higher there than at any other colleges.

Strong programs include agricultural sciences, biological sciences, economics, engineering degrees (including computer science, environmental engineering, and mechanical engineering), English, and hotel administration. Cornell has the nation's first colleges for hotel administration, industrial and labor relations, and veterinary medicine, all of which are highly regarded programs, especially hotel administration. According to the university, its interdisciplinary research centers in nanotech, biotech, supercomputing, and genomics "sets Cornell apart from its Ivy League peers."

The First-Year Writing Seminars give a sense of the rigor of Cornell's classes as well as its breadth: each semester, over 100 courses are taught in more than 30 departments in the program, and requirements include six to nine formal essays. Students who dread writing might opt for some less typical classes like sailing, scuba diving, and wine tasting (Cornell is in a wine producing region). "My parents weren't too happy to hear that Cornell has a wine tasting course, but I think it'll come in handy in the future," remarks a student.

Cornell students can study anywhere in the world as long as their faculty advisors approve of the program. Cornell in Rome allows students to learn about architecture, urban studies, and art. Closer to home, Cornell in Washington enables students to study abroad in DC while the Urban Semester Program in the College of Human Ecology offers internships in New York City. Students may intern in the New York state legislature through the Capital Semester program.

With more than 255,000 living alumni, there are plenty of networking opportunities for Cornell grads. About one fifth of students find a job through the on-campus recruiting program. In addition to the main Cornell Career Services, there are career offices specifically for the Johnson School of Management, Law School, and College of Veterinary Medicine.

Student Life

Due to Cornell's remote location, a lot of socializing happens on campus. Greek parties are especially popular, not surprising given that 28 percent of men and 24 percent of women participate in the 64 Greek chapters and more than 50 fraternity and sorority houses. "It's the desire of every freshman to go to as many fraternity parties as possible," comments a student.

The college notes, "life at Cornell is relatively quiet, but never boring." There is certainly no shortage of activities—for instance, there are a mind-boggling 850+ official student organizations to choose from. On sunny days you might find students playing human chess on the Arts Quad. The distinctly gothic Willard Straight hall, one of the first student unions in the U.S., is the hub of student activity on campus with its music room, computer lab, movie theater, and more. The movie theater is home to Cornell Cinema, "Ithaca's year-round film festival" offering nearly 400 films a year.

A major, unique annual tradition is Cornell's Dragon Day parade in March. Each year, first-year architecture students parade an enormous model dragon of their own creation past the College of Engineering into the Arts Quad. Another major annual event is Slope Day, an end-of-the-school-year concert that dates back to 1901. A recent Slope Day brought 14,000 attendees. For freshman entering in the fall, the first point of commonality is the New Student Reading Project, where all incoming students read a book designed to create a point of connection. "It's nice that you have something to talk about with every person you meet," says a student.

Though Cornell does not offer athletic scholarships, its Division I sports are strong and definitely play an important role in the social scene. Hockey is an especially popular spectator sport. Recently the men's basketball team has done well, making it to the NCAA's Sweet 16, an accomplishment no other Ivy League team has achieved in

CORNELL UNIVERSITY

Highlights

Students
Total enrollment: 21,424
Undergrads: 14,261
From out-of-state: 68%
Male/Female: 49%/51%
Live on-campus: 57%
In fraternities: 28%
In sororities: 24%
Off-campus employment rating: Good
Caucasian: 44%
African American: 6%
Hispanic: 10%
Asian / Pacific Islander: 16%
Native American: 0%
Mixed (2+ ethnicities): 4%
International: 10%

Academics
Calendar: Semester
Student/faculty ratio: 9:1
Class size 9 or fewer: 17%
Class size 10-29: 51%
Class size 30-49: 13%
Class size 50-99: 12%
Class size 100 or more: 6%
Returning freshmen: 96%
Six-year graduation rate: 93%

Admissions
Applicants: 37,808
Accepted: 6,259
Acceptance rate: 16.6%
Placed on wait list: 3,098
Enrolled from wait list: 139
Average GPA: Not reported
ACT range: 30-33
SAT Math range: 670-780
SAT Reading range: 640-740
SAT Writing range: Not reported
Top 10% of class: 91%
Top 25% of class: 98%
Top 50% of class: 100%

CORNELL UNIVERSITY

Admissions Criteria
Academic criteria:
Grades: ☆ ☆ ☆
Difficulty of class schedule: ☆ ☆ ☆
Class rank: ☆ ☆
Standardized test scores: ☆ ☆ ☆
Teacher recommendations: ☆ ☆ ☆
Personal statement: ☆ ☆ ☆
Non-academic criteria considered:
Interview
Extracurricular activities
Special talents, interests, abilities
Character/personal qualities
Volunteer work
Work experience
Geographical location
Minority affiliation
Alumni relationship

Deadlines
Early Action: No
Early Decision: November 1
Regular Action: January 2 (final)
Notification of admission by: early April
Common Application: Accepted

Financial Aid
In-state tuition: $45,130
Out-of-state tuition: $45,130
Room: $8,112
Board: $5,566
Books: $850
Freshmen receiving need-based aid: 47%
Undergrads rec. need-based aid: 50%
Avg. % of need met by financial aid: 100%
Avg. aid package (freshmen): $42,248
Avg. aid package (undergrads): $40,942
Avg. debt upon graduation: $20,490

School Spirit
Mascot: Touchdown the Bear
Colors: Carnelian and white

more than 30 years. Cornell also offers more than 30 leagues and tournaments each year in intramural sports.

Off-campus opportunities offer more recreational sporting: skiing, kayaking, and the like. Even staying on campus can feel like a hike since you walk through the hills and pass streams, gorges, and waterfalls. "You can work up a sweat just walking to class," remarks a student.

Freshmen live in the North Campus dorms that are close to community centers, dining rooms, athletic facilities, and the Carl Tatkon Center for first year studies—there's also the added perk of being within a short walk of the academic buildings on central campus. Other options include co-op housing, Greek houses, and themed living and learning communities.

Cornell Dining is known for its exceptional food—thanks to Cornell's excellent school of agriculture and hotel administration, which supply some of the food and service. Plus, nearly half of the executive chefs are graduates of the Culinary Institute of America. "It's too easy to gain the freshman 15 here," laughs a student.

Student Body

Cornell has a sizeable population of in-state students (32 percent) due in part to the fact that the university offers in-state tuition. However, there is still significant geographic diversity, with every state in the U.S. and over 120 countries represented.

The private and public components of Cornell also make for socioeconomic diversity, and there is a sizeable minority population of 36 percent. Former U.S. Attorney General Janet Reno highlighted her alma mater's diversity when she noted, "I don't think I have ever been anywhere in the United States that had so many people with so many different interests."

As for the political climate on campus, one student explains that the majority is "either in the middle or more liberal politically." The caliber of student is exemplary. If students were big fish at the small pond of their high schools, Cornell is a huge ocean filled with other big fish: nearly all undergrads were in the top 25 percent of their high school.

You May Not Know

- Cornell has two medical school campuses in New York City and Doha, Qatar. The latter is the first American medical school outside of the U.S.

- Cornell's motto, "I would found an institution where any person can find instruction in any study," is a quotation from Ezra Cornell, who helped start the university by offering his farm and $500,000 for the initial endowment in 1865.

- Cornell was the first co-ed school among what we now call the Ivy Leagues: the university began admitting women n 1868.

Distinguished Alumni

Ruth Bader Ginsburg, U.S. Supreme Court Justice; Toni Morrison, winner of the Nobel Prize for Literature; Bill Nye the "Science

Guy"; Steven Squyres, Cornell professor and NASA Mars Rover science project leader.

Admissions and Financial Aid

Admission to Cornell is highly selective, with over 37,000 students vying for just 6,200 admission spots in each year's incoming freshman class. According to the admissions office, "there's no magical formula of grade-point average and standardized test scores." Rather, the university is looking for "intellectual potential, strength of character, and love of learning." Some colleges require an interview. Exceptional students have the option of applying to two of Cornell's colleges through the Primary/Alternate Admission system.

Cornell practices need-blind admission and meets all of a family's demonstrated need. Families earning $75,000 or less receive grants instead of loans, families earning between $75,000 and $120,000 have a cap on need-based loans of $3,000. All gift aid at Cornell is need-based; there are no merit or athletic scholarships. Those eligible for grant aid may also receive endowed scholarships, which does not change the total amount of financial aid awarded but often entails a direct relationship between the student and donor who established the scholarship.

Four-year private
Founded: 1878
Omaha, NE
Major city
Pop. 415,068

Address:
2500 California Plaza
Omaha, NE
68178

Admissions:
800-282-5835

Financial Aid:
402-280-2731

admissions@creigh-
ton.edu

www.creighton.edu

CREIGHTON UNIVERSITY

Overview

A medium-sized Jesuit university in Omaha, Nebraska that offers both liberal arts education as well as pre-professional training, Creighton University is unusual for a school of its size. Despite having only slightly over 4,000 undergraduates, Creighton has a business, law, and medical graduate school. Ranked first by *U.S. News & World Report* among the best Midwest universities, students here "learn about the life of the mind and the spirit while exploring different disciplines in the context of Jesuit, Catholic heritage."

Though most students stay on campus and steer clear of the Midwestern city of Omaha, the Council Bluffs area was recently ranked sixth in the country's most livable cities list published by *Forbes*. The biggest complaint on campus seems to be the quality of the school's food. But, overall, the university provides a well-rounded academic, social, and spiritual experience in addition to an impressively spirited athletic community.

Academics

With 95 percent of classes consisting of 50 students or fewer, Creighton students certainly get lots of face time and personal attention from professors. Core curriculum requirements are sometimes considered cumbersome by its students, as they include the completion of courses in five categories: 18 credits in Theology, Philosophy, and Ethics Requirements; 18 credits in Cultures, Ideas, and Civilizations; 7 credits in Natural Sciences; 6 Social and Behavioral Sciences; and 12-15 credits in skills (such as language, speech, or writing). "I wish we had more flexibility in choosing our classes," says a student. Strong programs at Creighton include biology, communication studies, and pre-med studies.

Creighton's honors program, rooted in Jesuit tradition and faith, aims to "foster a community committed to the ongoing education of students and faculty members as fellow seekers for truth." The program looks for well-prepared and academically adventurous students who want to immerse themselves in a rigorous program guided by a faculty mentor, who shares a love of learning. "The Study" is another special program at Creighton, as well as its own space. Providing opportunities for students to become successful, independent learners through academic support programs, the Study assists all students by offering one-on-one tutoring, helping with time management, and defining strategies that will help to raise their GPAs.

Upon earning their undergraduate degree, Creighton students also receive what is called the "Creighton Preference," which is priority placement for acceptance to any of their professional schools including medical, dental, law, pharmacy, and physical therapy. "This is a huge advantage and takes a lot of stress out of applying to graduate school," says a pre-med student.

Each year 250 students participate in the university's study-abroad program. The university's Office of International Programs hosts a study-abroad fair and Study Abroad 101 sessions. Unique to the university is its semester-long Encuentro Dominicano, a program in the Dominican Republic. "Encuentro Dominicano is a true immersion into life in the Dominican Republic," explains one student. "It's an experience you'll never forget."

Creighton University prides itself on its career, academic planning, and advising system. Each admitted student is assigned to a Faculty Preceptor who serves as an advisor throughout the first year, helping to guide the student in scheduling classes, finding jobs, or discussing academic paths. The Career Center, designed to augment the guidance of the faculty advising system, allows students to work with career advisors. Here, students can discuss practical life skills, including how to write a resume and cover letter, in addition to exploring their interests and abilities and developing job-marketing skills. The Writing Center is another resource for students looking to brainstorm ideas before beginning an essay or looking for tips on how to revise one.

After college, Creighton students have a fairly high success rate: more than 96 percent of students from the classes of 2011 and 2012 were employed, involved in volunteer work or furthering their education within 8 months after graduation (compared to the national average of 75 percent). In addition, Creighton has the highest admissions rate of graduating students into medical, dental, pharmacy, physical, and occupational therapy programs and 54 percent of students who graduate from the College of Arts and Sciences go directly to graduate or professional schools.

Student Life

Among the 182 official student organizations on campus, community service focused groups, such as Best Buddies of America, are the most popular. "People do public service not just because it looks good on a resume but because we really care," says a student.

Traditions at Creighton include the annual fall events known as Getting Blue BBQs, a series of on-campus barbeques where students and staff gather to support their sports teams and the Creighton Blue Crew (the school's yell leaders) who get fans pumped for games. Another popular event among students is the Greek Lip Sync contest when, during Welcome Week, Greek organizations compete for their claim to fame by embarrassing themselves with goofy lip sync spoofs. Before graduating, most students will participate in a retreat of some sort, such as the Come Away Retreat, a 24-hour retreat off campus which combines activities like canoeing and hiking with prayer and reflection.

Although there are five social fraternities and seven social sororities on campus, only one frat and one sorority are housed organizations. About 34 percent of the student body choose to join Greek life, making the Greek scene an influential, but relatively laid back part of the Creighton experience. "Greek life has its presence, but if you don't pledge you don't feel left out," explains a student.

The Creighton Bluejays are a Division I school competing in men and women's basketball, men and women's golf, softball, men and women's soccer, men and women's cross country, baseball, men and women's tennis, volleyball, and women's crew. Most students participate in intramural sports as well; the most popular teams are volleyball and flag football. Of the varsity sports, men's soccer and basketball draw in the biggest crowds, with tailgating and school spirit to compensate for the lack of having a football team at a southern school. The men's basketball has ranked at the top of the Missouri Valley Conference for the past seven years and had one of the top 15 attendances in the past four years.

Due to its rural location, Creighton students often participate in lots of outdoor activities such as hiking. However, the students tend to give off-campus activities mixed reviews. While some claim that there's lots to do around campus, like attending indie concerts, going to the zoo, or visiting the museum, others say that its rather isolated location creates "limited" offerings of things to do.

Students are required to live on campus their freshman and sophomore year. Freshmen can live in one of three dorms, which are either coed or all female.

CREIGHTON UNIVERSITY

221

CREIGHTON UNIVERSITY

Highlights

Admissions Criteria
Academic criteria:
Grades: ☆ ☆ ☆
Difficulty of class schedule: ☆ ☆ ☆
Class rank: ☆
Standardized test scores: ☆ ☆
Teacher recommendations: ☆
Personal statement: ☆ ☆
Non-academic criteria considered:
Extracurricular activities
Special talents, interests, abilities
Character/personal qualities
Volunteer work
Work experience
State of residency
Minority affiliation

Deadlines
Early Action: No
Early Decision: No
Regular Action: Rolling admissions
Common Application: Accepted

Financial Aid
In-state tuition: $32,812
Out-of-state tuition: $32,812
Room: $5,528
Board: $4,200
Books: $1,200
Freshmen receiving need-based aid: 63%
Undergrads rec. need-based aid: 59%
Avg. % of need met by financial aid: 83%
Avg. aid package (freshmen): $29,251
Avg. aid package (undergrads): $27,505
Avg. debt upon graduation: $36,333

School Spirit
Mascot: Bluejays
Colors: Blue and white
Song: *The Blue and the White*

Student Body

Students at Creighton are generally there to study and focus on religion and service. One student reports this helps to create a "friendly Midwestern vibe." More than three-quarters of the most recent entering class was involved in church or service organizations. Students are also athletically talented—almost three-quarters participate in varsity sports.

Though walking around campus you will notice the predominately Caucasian and uniform look of the students, Creighton tries hard to attract minority students despite its location in Nebraska, drawing in a high ethnic diversity of 23 percent. With 77 percent of student hailing from out of state, the school is highly geographically diverse as well.

You May Not Know

- Smoking was banned on campus in 2008.
- For three years, from 1998 to 2001, Creighton was one of three schools to send all of their basketball, soccer, and baseball teams to the NCAA.
- Some of the famous speakers Creighton has hosted include Warren Buffet and Jon Heder.

Distinguished Alumni

Bob Gibson, Major League Baseball Hall of Fame pitcher; Donald Keough, former president and chief operating officer of Coca Cola; J. Joseph Rickets, owner of the Chicago Cubs.

Admissions and Financial Aid

Creighton University looks for well-rounded students with strengths in and outside the classroom. The admission process weighs high school GPA, ACT and SAT scores, extracurricular activities, and a recommendation from a high school counselor. The school also believes that the personal statement is "an excellent way of demonstrating creative abilities and attributes not reflected through transcripts."

Creighton has a large variety of scholarship funds available to students coming from different high schools and parts of the country. Among the most notable are these: Creighton Academic Scholarships, competitive academic scholarships awarded to students with solid high school academic performance as well as national test scores; the Clare Boothe Luce Scholarship, funded to promote women in science, awarded to junior and senior women science majors, providing up to full tuition; and the Lynch-Heaston Scholarship for students with a GPA of 2.5 or higher who are planning a career in social work.

DARTMOUTH COLLEGE

DARTMOUTH COLLEGE

Four-year private
Founded: 1769
Hanover, NH
Small town
Pop. 10,850

Address:
6016 McNutt Hall
Hanover, NH
03755

Admissions:
800-443-3605

Financial Aid:
603-646-2451

admissions.office@
dartmouth.edu

www.dartmouth.edu

Overview

Located on the border with Vermont and along the Connecticut River, Dartmouth College in Hanover, New Hampshire, is the smallest of the Ivy Leagues and has the patina fitting of a venerable institution. The campus architecture is colonial style, Georgian American brick, organized around a central Green. The campus feels intimate at 269 acres, and the town of Hanover surrounding the college is quaint with a population of almost 11,000.

Dartmouth provides the arts and culture for its student body since the closest major cities aren't that close: Burlington, Vermont is 1.5 hours away and Boston is 2.5 hours. Nature is everywhere though, and the campus offers loads of opportunities for hiking, biking, skiing on Dartmouth's 100 acres of skiway, and sledding. The New England small downtown offers restaurants, shops, and friendly residents. The winters are long and rough, but the combination of great weather for winter and summer sports, a beautiful setting, the eclecticism of an Ivy League college, and the pleasures of small town life recently earned Hanover a second place ranking in *Money* magazine's "Best Places to Live."

The legacies of Dartmouth include stellar academics, sports, and a strong Greek presence (*Animal House* is based on a Dartmouth fraternity). It should be noted that the college certainly hasn't remained frozen in time and boasts new facilities including the McLaughlin Cluster and Tuck Mall residence halls, which feature communal lounges and kitchens, the MacLean Engineering Sciences Center, and a new visual arts center in the works.

Academics

The Dartmouth academic experience provides a foundation in the liberal arts. Only professors (that means no teaching assistants) teach undergrads, and over 60 percent of the classes contain fewer than 19 students, creating a dynamic and "intimate" class setting. Fifty majors are offered. Strong programs include biology, computer science, economics, and pre-health advising.

There are basic degree requirements for every student no matter the major. Broadly, the requirements are residence during the fall, winter, and spring quarters of the first year and final year, plus the summer quarter after the second year (also known as "sophomore summer"); 35 courses with passing grades, including writing, foreign languages, and general education; the physical education requirement; and, lastly, the specific course requirements (usually around 8-10 courses) for the chosen major. The requirements are "nothing to get worked up over," says a student.

Since students are required to stay on campus after their second year for sophomore summer (which students describe as the "ultimate bonding experience") and take courses, the overall four-year academic schedule is flexible. This is part of the Dartmouth plan (aka the "D-Plan") that allows time for studying abroad or pursuing an internship during the sophomore or junior years. Consequently about two-thirds of students do take advantage of studying abroad in more than 20 countries, and some even do it more than once.

For over-achievers, the James O. Freedman presidential scholars program chooses a select group of outstanding juniors to complete research with faculty members and readies students to carry out senior honor theses.

Female students pursuing studies in the sciences, engineering, and mathematics can participate in WISP, the Women in Science Project, which provides opportunities for mentoring, research, and forming community with fellow women scientists. The program encourages women to "enter fields that we are underrepresented in," says a student.

DARTMOUTH COLLEGE

Students

Total enrollment: 6,277
Undergrads: 4,193
Freshmen: 1,098
Part-time students: 1%
From out-of-state: 98%
From public schools: 55%
Male/Female: 50%/50%
Live on-campus: 86%
In fraternities: 66%
In sororities: 64%
Off-campus employment rating: Good
Caucasian: 47%
African American: 7%
Hispanic: 8%
Asian / Pacific Islander: 14%
Native American: 2%
Mixed (2+ ethnicities): 4%
International: 8%

Academics

Calendar: Quarter
Student/faculty ratio: 8:1
Class size 9 or fewer: 21%
Class size 10-29: 56%
Class size 30-49: 13%
Class size 50-99: 8%
Class size 100 or more: 1%
Returning freshmen: 97%
Six-year graduation rate: 96%
Graduates who immediately go to graduate school: 20%

Most Popular Majors

Economics
Government
Psychological/brain sciences

Admissions

Applicants: 23,109
Accepted: 2,260
Acceptance rate: 9.8%
Placed on wait list: 1,736
Enrolled from wait list: 82
Average GPA: Not reported
ACT range: 30-34
SAT Math range: 680-780
SAT Reading range: 670-780
SAT Writing range: 69-25
Top 10% of class: 90%
Top 50% of class: 100%

Dartmouth alumni keep in touch and actively offer advice and guidance to new alumni through the Dartmouth Career Network. Additionally, the Dartboard lists employment opportunities specifically geared toward Dartmouth college graduates. About one fifth of students attend graduate school within one year of graduating.

Student Life

Somehow between devotion to studying and frat parties, students find time to participate in student groups, sports, and annual celebrations with zeal. Remember, Dartmouth is located in the middle of nowhere, so the center of the social scene is campus, and participation in extracurricular activities on campus is high. One student comments, "We have to be creative about how to have fun."

Out of 300+ student groups—including intriguing offerings like the Thursday night salsa club, the medieval enthusiasts, and the creative writing club—the most popular is the Dartmouth outing club (DOC). It's the oldest and largest outing club in the United States. Over 1,500 students are involved and there are just as many alumni members. Besides organizing outdoor trips year-round, the DOC looks after more than 70 miles of the Appalachian Trail and teaches wilderness safety skills, environmental education, and stewardship activities. "The Outing Club isn't just a club," a student explains. "It's literally more than one third of our college." The DOC sparks freshman bonding with first-year wilderness trips. Small groups of students and group leaders spend five days together in activities like hiking, camping, organic farming, yoga, horse riding, nature writing, and more. The trip is considered the "perfect introduction" to Dartmouth culture.

The active student life also includes helping others through the Tucker Foundation on campus. Public service comes in many forms, including Habitat for Humanity and spring break trips to places such as Kentucky to work on issues of healthcare and poverty. Students may also live, learn, and work with the community at Cheyenne River Sioux Tribe Youth Center in South Dakota or volunteer in response to natural disasters. Other opportunities include crosscultural travel to volunteer in places like Nicaragua, Belarus, and Bangladesh.

Dartmouth is an old college with lots of history, and traditional events dot the campus calendar. Homecoming in the fall acts largely as a freshman initiation weekend. Alumni and upperclassmen cheer freshman on as they make 100 laps—plus extra laps for the last two numbers of their class year—around a great scaffold bonfire.

Winter Carnival, captured in a 1939 movie that F. Scott Fitzgerald was involved with (until his bender at the Dartmouth fraternities got him ousted from the picture), is the winter quarter celebration. Various winter "sports" occur during these days, such as the polar bear plunge into Occom pond. "You have to be crazy to take the plunge, and there are some people crazy enough to do it," remarks a student.

There's no denying that Greek life is huge at Dartmouth; 26 Greek organizations include 15 fraternities, 8 sororities and 3 co-eds. A whopping 66 percent of men and 64 percent of women pledge, and everyone goes to the parties. "Greek life is rampant. Fortunately the fraternities are open to non-members attending," relates a student. *National Lampoon's Animal House* is based on an alum's experience in Alpha Delta Phi.

But there's more going on than beer drinking on the weekends. There are sports activities galore. Three-quarters of students are on a team of some sort—there's Division I varsity, intramural, and club sports—golf, soccer, ice hockey, lacrosse, and more are played on men's and women teams. Sailing and skiing are coed. Beyond organized sports, hiking is popular and the Appalachian Trail runs through campus. Dartmouth also has its own skiway and Nordic center.

Eighty-six percent of students live on campus. Off-campus options do exist, but the surrounding town of Hanover doesn't present many options. Most students agree it's easier to live on campus since there's no true public transportation to speak of in town. Dorms in general vary greatly from small to large rooms, singles to quadruples, and single-sex to "gender neutral" rooms. A dorm favorite is Wheelock.

Student Body

A cozy total undergrad student body of 4,200 on a fairly small campus means everyone gets to know each other well, and at Dartmouth this means getting to know a diverse group of people. Thirty-five percent of the students identify as ethnic minorities and students come from all 50 states as well as 84 countries. Fifty-five percent of students come from a public high school background, but the boarding school world is well represented among those coming from private schools.

Perhaps it's the boarding school style that influences the "preppy" college style on campus, or maybe it's the two centuries as a bastion for elite WASPy male students that's hard to shake. Many students are "into fashion" and dress nicely in J.Crew and Banana Republic, but there are also jocks, and a popular half-hippie-half-rugged-woodsiness look as well. In the fall, winter, and spring, warmth is an issue, so students are also practical and outfit themselves in fleece and down, and everyone owns at least one North Face fleece jacket.

The New Hampshire state motto, "Live Free or Die" is reflected in the Dartmouth enclave too with students freely expressing their opinions. There are democrats, libertarians, independents, and republicans on campus, all making sure that their views are heard.

You May Not Know

- Dartmouth was established in 1769, and remained a men's college for over two centuries until 1972.
- There's no official Dartmouth mascot, but unofficial mascots have existed over time, the latest being "Keggy," a beer keg with legs and arms.
- In 2007, the Democratic Presidential candidates debated at Dartmouth College and students were in the audience to ask questions. New Hampshire is a Presidential primary battleground as the state with the earliest primary election in the country.

DARTMOUTH COLLEGE

Highlights

Admissions Criteria
Academic criteria:
Grades: ☆ ☆ ☆
Difficulty of class schedule: ☆ ☆ ☆
Class rank: ☆ ☆ ☆
Standardized test scores: ☆ ☆ ☆
Teacher recommendations: ☆ ☆ ☆
Personal statement: ☆ ☆ ☆
Non-academic criteria considered:
Interview
Extracurricular activities
Special talents, interests, abilities
Character/personal qualities
Volunteer work
State of residency
Geographical location
Minority affiliation
Alumni relationship

Deadlines
Early Action: No
Early Decision: November 1
Regular Action: January 1 (final)
Notification of admission by: April 10
Common Application: Accepted

Financial Aid
In-state tuition: $45,444
Out-of-state tuition: $45,444
Room: $7,755
Board: $4,710
Books: $1,980
Freshmen receiving need-based aid: 44%
Undergrads rec. need-based aid: 51%
Avg. % of need met by financial aid: 100%
Avg. aid package (freshmen): $42,419
Avg. aid package (undergrads): $41,200
Avg. debt upon graduation: $17,825

School Spirit
Colors: Green and white
Song: *Alma Mater*

Distinguished Alumni

Louise Erdrich, Guggenheim Fellow and National Book Critics Circle Award winning poet and writer; Theodor Seuss Geisel (aka Dr. Seuss), children's author; C. Everett Koop, United States Surgeon General from 1982–89; Nelson Rockefeller, United States Vice President from 1974–77.

Admissions and Financial Aid

Dartmouth doesn't let "just anybody" in; the acceptance rate is highly selective at 10 percent. So, what's the secret to getting admitted? Unfortunately, there's no secret code or handshake, but the senior assistant director of admissions gives the following advice:

"Here's what you don't need to be armed with to stand out in the college admissions process...A defined career path or course of study. Your life calling. Clear passions. A cure for cancer. Here's what you should consider articulating in your essays, interviews, conversations...You. A clear, honest picture of who you are and what matters to you (all subject to growth and change, I hope). What you find interesting and intriguing. What you enjoy reading about and discussing. What choices you've made. What (and how) you've learned."

Dartmouth's approach to financial aid backs up the idea that the admissions committee is interested in the passion and potential of the student and not his or her pocketbook. Admissions is need-blind, and accepted students who have an annual family income of $75,000 or less receive free tuition—that's right, no loans. For families whose income exceeds $75,000, loans are capped at $5,500. All in all, Dartmouth doles out over $80 million in financial aid to students, and the average package is $38,000. If a student has secured acceptance to Dartmouth, then they've proved they're special enough for the college to help them attend. As with all the Ivy Leagues, Dartmouth doesn't offer athletic or merit-based scholarships.

DAVIDSON COLLEGE

Overview

Based in the college town of Davidson, North Carolina, Davidson College provides a unique blend of idyllic setting, accessible resources, and well-rounded education. The college offers a dedicated faculty, a unique student body that leans conservative, strong Division I athletics, and a vibrant alumni network. In fact, *U.S. News & World Report* recently ranked Davidson among the top ten liberal arts colleges in the nation.

With an enrollment of almost 1,800 students, this private institution offers a 450-acre campus and recreational lake that is located in the city of Davidson, 20 miles north of Charlotte. The college is affiliated with the Presbyterian Church. According to the college, Davidson aims to "embrace diversity in all forms, and students are encouraged to express and explore their beliefs and values through any of a number of student faith organizations."

To determine whether Davidson is indeed a fit for you, it is important to keep a few things in mind. You probably won't find bustling social scenes more commonly associated with larger state schools or a particularly diverse student body. Given that the town is roughly 11,000 people-strong, the surrounding town's community life might not be the most active, and shopping and restaurants available to you will be limited. However, students mention that the school still caters very well to its student body.

What you *can* look forward to is a tightly knit body of students who respect each other. You'll rub shoulders with celebrated athletes on a daily basis, recognize faces all over campus, and expect great parties, though it is unlikely that they will define your collegiate experience. Additionally, you would engage with top-notch academics in superb facilities. Given all of these perks, what more could you ask for? Oh right, free laundry service, which the college has provided for the past 80 years and continues to offer to all students!

Academics

The majority of students say that the Davidson experience is demanding but incredibly rewarding. There are 850 courses offered per year, including those in the college's 23 majors. Some of the strongest programs are chemistry, English, prelaw, and premed. There are also numerous minors, self-designed majors, and interdisciplinary possibilities to those who would like the additional challenge. Given that there are no graduate programs, students enjoy ready access to their professors and tend to interact heavily with them. Students also mention that the science classes are "especially rigorous," remarking that there is "no grade inflation."

The school has a general core requirement, which includes classes in writing, foreign language, cultural diversity, physical education, literature, fine arts, history, religion and philosophy, natural science and mathematics, and social sciences. There are a number of challenging pre-professional programs in premed, law, business, ministry, and management. Davidson also offers a number of special academic programs that appeal to a range of students, including self-designed majors such as computational biophysics, religion and literature, and genomics. Students can further customize their academic tracks through independent study, double majors, and a strong honors program. Depending on the academic field, the honors program has a set GPA that must be maintained and requires independent research, the writing of an honors thesis, and oral defense. "It's a lot of extra work so you need to brace yourself for it," says a student.

For students who might wish to venture beyond the walls of campus, the Dean Rusk International Studies Program features 12 Davidson-directed study-abroad programs, including Cyprus, France, Ghana, India, Kenya, Peru, Spain, the United Kingdom, and Zambia. Over 70 percent of students study abroad. Study abroad is "quintessential to a Davidson education," remarks a student. Both overseas and abroad,

DAVIDSON COLLEGE

Students

Total enrollment: 1,790
Undergrads: 1,790
Freshmen: 490
From out-of-state: 71%
From public schools: 51%
Male/Female: 50%/50%
Live on-campus: 92%
In fraternities: 36%
In sororities: 45%
Off-campus employment rating: Excellent
Caucasian: 71%
African American: 7%
Hispanic: 6%
Asian / Pacific Islander: 5%
Native American: 1%
Mixed (2+ ethnicities): 3%
International: 5%

Academics

Calendar: Semester
Student/faculty ratio: 10:1
Class size 9 or fewer: 31%
Class size 10-29: 59%
Class size 30-49: 10%
Class size 50-99: -
Class size 100 or more: -
Returning freshmen: 97%
Six-year graduation rate: 93%
Graduates who immediately go to graduate school: 28%
Graduates who immediately enter career related to major: 55%

Most Popular Majors

Political science
Biology
Psychology

Admissions

Applicants: 4,770
Accepted: 1,184
Acceptance rate: 24.8%
Average GPA: 4.1
ACT range: 29-32
SAT Math range: 635-720
SAT Reading range: 625-720
SAT Writing range: 41-43
Top 10% of class: 79%
Top 25% of class: 97%
Top 50% of class: 100%

228

students adhere to Davidson's strong Honor Code tradition of what the college describes as "self-scheduled and unproctored exams" as well as a unique spirit rooted in commitment to community service.

Upon graduation, Davidson offers a number of resources to help students with job placement or further studies. The committed Career Services Center provides guidance in the job search and for graduate school selection, as well as access to a career services library. One-quarter of students attend graduate school within one year of graduating.

Student Life

With 92 percent of students living on campus, the school provides plenty of social activities throughout the academic year. Students can often be found in the Knobloch Campus Center, which houses the Alvarez College Union and the Duke Family Performance Hall. "If you hang out for a half hour, you'll see at least a dozen people you know," comments a student. When in need of a change of scenery, students can also enjoy Lake Campus, which, as described by the college, encompasses "109.6 acres of water front property on beautiful Lake Norman." Seven miles from campus, the recreational campus provides a setting for water activities and serves as the base for the sailing clubs and crew teams.

Popular campus events include Homecoming in November, which is the time for class receptions and reunions among current students, alumni, and former and current faculty members. Additional events to look forward to are the Campus Christmas Party and Spring Frolics, a time for "many, many parties," says a student.

Students partake in more than 150 official student organizations. Popular groups include InterVarsity Christian Fellowship, Davidson Outdoors, and the Greek system, which includes eight fraternities and six sororities, as well as female "eating houses" which are "more or less sororities," comments a student. Overall, 36 percent of men join a fraternity, and 45 percent of women join a sorority or eating house.

Davidson College has 21 Division I athletic teams that have an overall graduation rate of more than 90 percent. Intramural sports include, but are not limited to, basketball, beach volleyball, flickerball, and soccer. General recreation facilities provide areas for basketball, racquetball, tennis courts, a swimming pool, and weight training and fitness centers.

Davidson offers 11 residence halls and six apartment complexes located throughout campus. Options include coed dorms, single-student apartments, and cooperative housing. One example is the popular Martin Court, which houses 300 students in six apartment buildings; four or five students live in an apartment with a kitchen. Students say that most of the dorms have been "modernized" or "fixed up" in the last few years.

Student Body

In terms of ethnic diversity, the campus is roughly 22 percent ethnic minority with more than 70 percent hailing from out of state. Forty-nine states and DC and 36 countries are represented. Students often mention that their peers are "heavily focused on their studies," not surprising given that four-fifths graduated in the top

10 percent of their high school class. They also say that more tend to "lean conservative but not super-conservative."

According to the editor of the student newspaper, the *Davidsonian*, students are "honest" and "value integrity", with the Honor Code providing "the most distinct characteristic of Davidson. Students leave their iPhones on library desks, doors are always left unlocked, and exams are self-scheduled. I have known a student to leave 25 cents on a copy machine for several days and come back to find it there untouched."

You May Not Know

- The college has had 23 Rhodes Scholars.
- According to the college, in 2007 it became the first national liberal arts college to eliminate student loans from financial aid packages.
- The college has held an annual Freshman Cake Race since 1934. It was originally a mandatory race designed to find track talent among the entering class but is now optional. As the name suggests, participants are rewarded with cake.

Distinguished Alumni

Patricia Cornwell, contemporary American crime writer; Tony Snow, American journalist and political commentator; Woodrow Wilson, 28th President of the United States.

Admissions and Financial Aid

Davidson spells out exactly what it is looking for in its future students. These are the factors that are considered by admissions personnel, in order of importance: rigor, as demonstrated by the difficulty level of high school classes; success, measured by grades; "writing ability and personal impact," demonstrated by essays and recommendations; extracurricular activities; and test scores. There are no evaluative interviews, but students may meet with members of the admissions office to gather information and ask questions.

Davidson meets 100 percent of financial need, and more than 40 percent of its students receive financial aid. Merit-based aid includes scholarships ranging from $30,000 to full tuition, but also smaller general scholarships based on availability. The most competitive scholarships include the Bryan Scholarship, Belk Scholarship, and Charles Scholarship. Some merit-based aid requires separate application forms and special nominations.

International students should apply for financial assistance early, as the university is not able to offer financial aid to all students who are not U.S. citizens or U.S. permanent residents.

DAVIDSON COLLEGE

Highlights

Admissions Criteria
Academic criteria:
Grades: ☆ ☆ ☆
Difficulty of class schedule: ☆ ☆ ☆
Class rank: ☆
Standardized test scores: ☆ ☆
Teacher recommendations: ☆ ☆ ☆
Personal statement: ☆ ☆
Non-academic criteria considered:
Interview
Extracurricular activities
Special talents, interests, abilities
Character/personal qualities
Volunteer work
State of residency
Alumni relationship

Deadlines
Early Action: No
Early Decision: November 15
Regular Action: January 2 (final)
Notification of admission by: April 1
Common Application: Accepted

Financial Aid
In-state tuition: $42,425
Out-of-state tuition: $42,425
Room: $6,249
Board: $5,585
Books: $1,000
Freshmen receiving need-based aid: 47%
Undergrads rec. need-based aid: 47%
Avg. % of need met by financial aid: 100%
Avg. aid package (freshmen): $32,022
Avg. aid package (undergrads): $34,121
Avg. debt upon graduation: $23,904

School Spirit
Mascot: Wildcats
Colors: Red and black

Two-year private
men's college
Founded: 1917
Dyer, NV
Rural
Pop. 1,350

Address:
HC 72, Box 45001
Dyer, NV
89010

Admissions:
760-872-2000

apcom@deepsprings.
edu

www.deepsprings.edu

DEEP SPRINGS COLLEGE

Overview

Deep Springs is a very, very small, all-male, private college on a cattle ranch and alfalfa farm in Eastern California (even though its mailing address is in Nevada). The school charges no tuition and provides free room and board; students only pay for travel, books and incidentals. Deep Springs is affiliated with Telluride Association, a non-profit, educational organization that also facilitates self-governing scholarship houses at the University of Michigan and Cornell University. The student body consists of just 26 men, who attend for two years, and then transfer to other institutions to complete a degree. It is common for "Springers" to go on to attend Ivy League universities and other prestigious schools.

The campus is extremely isolated. It is located in Deep Springs Valley—called "the Valley" by students—a hiker's paradise in the desert. According to the student-imposed Ground Rules, students are not allowed to leave the Valley during terms; but there's really not much temptation to venture away since there is absolutely zero to do nearby.

Deep Springs is nothing if not idiosyncratic. On the plus side, it offers a unique, formative experience that combines practical labor with intellectual pursuits—and the price is right. For those up to the challenge, Deep Springs can be an ideal place to seek self-awareness. On the minus side, it epitomizes the concept of the "college bubble" and lacks the range of activities and social outlets common to other schools.

Academics

Deep Springs does not offer majors. Rather, students choose a mixture of classes that interest them. In addition to introductory courses, students take on studies more advanced than the standard freshman and sophomore fare. The strongest programs are in the humanities and social sciences. There are always three long-term professors in residence: one in the humanities, one in the social sciences, and one in the natural sciences and mathematics. These professors stay for two to six years and work side by side with three visiting professors or artists that complement the faculty each semester. "You need to either like or learn to like your professors because there isn't much selection," says a student.

The only mandatory courses at Deep Springs are Composition and Public Speaking. Students take a four-credit composition course in their first fall term. As part of the public speaking curriculum, students give a total of 15 speeches over the course of their stay at Deep Springs—three graded speeches each semester in Terms 2-5 and one ungraded speech in Term 1 and Term 6. With so much practice listening to themselves talk, it's little wonder Deep Springers can spend 10 hours debating at Student Body Meetings. "We talk and talk some more," one student notes.

Students are also required to take a Summer Seminar during their first term at Deep Springs. What better way to get to know your new classmates than engaging in a team-taught, interdisciplinary exploration of political theory? The class content encourages students to directly address how they want to implement self-government at Deep Springs.

The level of academic commitment among students at Deep Springs is the college's true strength. "It's not uncommon to pull all-nighters in preparation for debates," says a student. Strong relationships with professors are part of the norm, and faculty members often hang out informally with students in their free time. If you can picture yourself excitedly noting your professor's lit porch light, the customary Deep Springs welcome signal, and wandering over to his or her house for an in-depth talk, then Deep Springs may be for you

Each year at Deep Springs is divided into six terms. Students must stay for 11 of the 12 terms of their two years. They can choose to stay for either Term 6 of their

The Ultimate
Guide to America's
Best Colleges

first year or Term 1 of their second year. During Term 1, they get to meet new students and take a Summer Seminar. Term 6 courses are shorter than other courses and tend to be focused on specific topics not included in the normal curriculum. During any term, interested students (and, really, no Springers suffer a lack of academic interest) can take student-designed Independent Study courses or professor-designed Directed Study courses. Study abroad does not exist at Deep Springs for the simple reason that, save for one term, students aren't allowed to leave.

Springers flex their muscles as well as their gray matter. Deep Springs isn't just a school—it's also a working ranch, with a cattle herd and an alfalfa farm, staffed by the Hegel-reading, beard-stroking students themselves who work 20 hours a week. Each term, the men are assigned a labor position based on their preferences. Every student serves two terms as "BH"—a member of the Boardinghouse Crew—owning the responsibility of keeping the dining area tidy. Other jobs include birthing, raising, and killing cows; tamer, plant-related agricultural tasks; and indoor jobs like staffing the library and cooking. The lucky might win the job title of "Cowboy."

In addition to their labor, students serve on committees to do the nitty-gritty work that comes with self-government. The students themselves review applications, make curriculum decisions, and take on certain responsibilities associated with academic life at Deep Springs.

Over two-thirds of Deep Springs alumni eventually earn graduate degrees. Many pass from Deep Springs to the equally insular world of academic careers without ever dirtying their cowboy boots on the mean streets of the "real world."

Student Life

There are no organized activities at Deep Springs. Students have to take the initiative to start up the activities that they want. The college claims that since students have to "build the fun from scratch ... the fun feels more a part of [them]." Students spend the scarce free time they have hanging out and talking, watching movies, tramping around the lovely desert environs, working on crafts, and playing Dungeons and Dragons. "You have to be inventive," one student notes. Because of concerns about fire safety, no smoking is allowed. Alcohol and drugs are also prohibited. There are no Greek organizations at Deep Springs.

Deep Springs has several traditional events to stave off cabin fever. The Turkey Bowl pits students from East of the Mississippi against those from the West in a Black Friday football game. "Boogies" (pronounced *boo-jies*) are spontaneous, crazy dances; in fact, "Boogie" is Springish for "super dorky dance party." The men break it down to notoriously bad music and often shed their clothing in the process. On a slightly more refined note, "DSPACs" (Deep Springs Music and Performing Arts Committee events) are music and spoken-word performances. Every other year, students enjoy "Sludgefest," which consists of dredging mud and slime out of the Upper Reservoir. It's no joke; the effort even entails the use of a dump truck. The "Death March," another appealingly-named tradition, is a yearly, week-long hike around the entire valley.

There are no formal sports teams at Deep Springs. Nonetheless, in addition to hiking, there are plenty of pick-up soccer and Fris-

DEEP SPRINGS COLLEGE

Highlights

Students
Total enrollment: 26
Undergrads: 26
Part-time students: Not reported
From out-of-state: 80%
From public schools: 50%
Male/Female: 100%/0%
Live on-campus: 100%
Off-campus employment rating: Poor
Caucasian: Not reported
African American: Not reported
Hispanic: Not reported
Asian / Pacific Islander: Not reported
Native American: Not reported
Mixed (2+ ethnicities): Not reported
International: Not reported

Academics
Calendar: Semester
Student/faculty ratio: 4:1
Class size 9 or fewer: Not reported
Class size 10-29: Not reported
Class size 30-49: -
Class size 50-99: -
Class size 100 or more: -
Returning freshmen: Not reported
Six-year graduation rate: Not reported

Most Popular Majors
Liberal arts and sciences
Humanities

Admissions
Applicants: 170
Accepted: 7
Acceptance rate: 4%
Average GPA: Not reported
ACT range: Not reported
SAT Math range: 700-800
SAT Reading range: 750-800
SAT Writing range: Not reported
Top 10% of class: 86%
Top 25% of class: 93%
Top 50% of class: 100%

College Profiles

DEEP SPRINGS COLLEGE

Admissions Criteria
Academic criteria:
Grades: ☆ ☆ ☆
Difficulty of class schedule: ☆ ☆ ☆
Class rank: ☆
Standardized test scores: ☆
Teacher recommendations: ☆ ☆ ☆
Personal statement: ☆ ☆ ☆
Non-academic criteria considered:
Interview
Extracurricular activities
Special talents, interests, abilities
Character/personal qualities
Volunteer work
Work experience
Geographical location
Religious affiliation/commitment
Minority affiliation
Alumni relationship

Deadlines
Early Action: No
Early Decision: No
Regular Action: November 15 (Part I),
    January 15 (Part II)
Notification of admission by: April 15
Common Application: Not accepted

Financial Aid
In-state tuition: $0
Out-of-state tuition: $0
Room: $0
Board: $0
Books: $600
Freshmen receiving need-based aid:
    100%
Undergrads rec. need-based aid: 100%
Avg. % of need met by financial aid:
    100%
Avg. debt upon graduation: $0

bee games as well as the opportunity for frigid swims in the Upper Reservoir. Off-campus activities all take place in the great outdoors. Hiking, skiing, and climbing in the High Sierras are popular pursuits. In keeping with Springers' apparent abhorrence of clothing, naked sledding on sand dunes is also a hit. "What happens in the Valley, stays in the Valley," one student laughs.

The dorm situation at Deep Springs is unconventional but comfortable. The dorm has just 11 rooms and one guest room. Each room has a loft ceiling and houses two to five students. Pets are allowed. Students enjoy the fireplace in the Rumpus Room and the movie collection in the Alpine Lodge.

Student Body

Springers are hard workers. They take their academics seriously; 86 percent graduated in the top 10 percent of their high school classes. Their vision of intellectual life isn't limited to classes, and they tend to be deep thinkers. "There isn't much else to do except think," one student notes. Geographic diversity is high.

You May Not Know

- Deep Springs has an ever-growing collection of clothes— affectionately known as the "Bonepile"—left by former students. Hypothetically, students could get by without bringing any clothes of their own to school.
- The metaphorical ancestors of modern-day Springers were hired by Telluride Power Company tycoon L.L. Nunn as round-the-clock, live-in staff. In exchange for monitoring electricity transmission to mines, they received an education and a small salary.
- Students can check the collected hiking lore of generations of Springers in the "Horse Book," which includes maps and suggested routes.

Distinguished Alumni

William vanden Heuvel, former Deputy U.S. Ambassador to the United Nations; William T. Vollmann, National Book Award-winning author; Silas Warner, programmer and video game creator.

Admissions and Financial Aid

Deep Springs is highly competitive since there are so few spots available. You had best sharpen your SAT scores to above the 700 level for a strong shot. The two-part application process is intensive. Students are chosen for Round 2 based on SAT scores, high school transcripts, and three essays. In the second round, hopefuls write even more essays and visit for three to four days in February.

DENISON UNIVERSITY

Overview

The Great Lakes nestle the crown jewel of Granville, Ohio—Denison University. Founded in 1831, this private liberal arts institution chose to uniquely focus on undergraduate education in the 1920s. Generations of science-minded freshmen and sophomores who can study in the pastoral campus' massive biological reserve have forever demonstrated gratitude. Denison has experienced societal upgrades similar to its academic refocusing: it became fully coeducational in 1900, and oil magnate John D. Rockefeller spearheaded the move to open campus to all Ohio residents, regardless of religion. Such moves have contributed to the close-knit feeling among students that permeates the campus.

Granville's hushed city life has also encouraged Denison's animated social scene. A newly instated "Campus Common" provides an elliptically shaped, verdant lawn to encourage campus residents to socialize; this complements the spacious efforts of Denison's original architects, Frederick Law Olmsted and Sons (of New York City's Central Park fame). That Denison stands nearly 30 miles east of major city Columbus also means that attendees can concentrate on shoring up their resumes as both partiers and pupils. Nearly 50 Fulbright Scholarships and a dozen National Science Foundation fellowships attest to the success of Denison students' focus. The university's test-optional admissions policy may mean less sweat on your part to savor the goods of the campus.

Academics

There are 39 majors at Denison. Economics, communication, biology, political science, and history rank as the school's flagship programs. Current stars of both the big and small screens vouch for the helpfulness of Denison's theater program; it places majors in New York City-based training programs or internships for at least one semester. Queer Studies also help to distinguish Denison's offerings.

The General Education Program requires that students take two seminars during the first year. "The seminars acquaint us with college academics," notes a student. In addition, students must take two courses each in fine arts, sciences, social sciences, and humanities as well as one course in interdisciplinary and world issues and two to three semesters of a foreign language.

Choosing Denison also means that you value thorough student-to-professor interaction, a quality of pride for the campus. Grade inflation "just doesn't happen," say students, and classes prove rigorous. Yet professors offset their stringent standards with assistance for students; in fact, the staff works deeply to support their students.

First-Year program requires freshmen to undergo summer orientation, seminars, and academic advising. Nearly 200 full-time faculty members demonstrate enough of an investment in their students to earn a student-to-faculty ratio of 10:1, and most classes will hold no more than 18 fellow students. "The instructors are always available to help," remarks a student.

World trekkers who hanker for international study will satisfy cultural thirst here; study abroad is available in locales as varied as Mali and the Caicos Islands. During their junior year, 35 percent of students study off campus. "There are so many opportunities, it's hard to pass over studying abroad," explains a student.

The school flaunts an internship program that informs residents of positions available both on campus and around the country, stipends included. Denison's Summer Scholar Program funds students for 10 weeks' worth of professorial-partnered research. Government-minded students take up places in the Lugar Program and season themselves in political acumen. Of those who work after graduating, 40 percent work in a career related to their major within one year of graduating. Students that graduate from Denison's bachelor programs often find that graduate school beckons;

DENISON UNIVERSITY

Four-year private
Founded: 1831
Granville, OH
Large town
Pop. 5,662

Address:
1 Main Street
Granville, OH
43023

Admissions:
740-587-6276

Financial Aid:
740-587-6279

admissions@denison.edu

www.denison.edu

DENISON UNIVERSITY

Students
Total enrollment: 2,336
Undergrads: 2,336
Freshmen: 642
From out-of-state: 73%
From public schools: 69%
Male/Female: 42%/58%
Live on-campus: 99%
In fraternities: 35%
In sororities: 41%
Off-campus employment rating: Good
Caucasian: 71%
African American: 6%
Hispanic: 7%
Asian / Pacific Islander: 3%
Native American: 0%
Mixed (2+ ethnicities): 4%
International: 7%

Academics
Calendar: Semester
Student/faculty ratio: 10:1
Class size 9 or fewer: 34%
Class size 10-29: 63%
Class size 30-49: 3%
Class size 50-99: -
Class size 100 or more: -
Returning freshmen: 92%
Six-year graduation rate: 86%
Graduates who immediately go to graduate school: 26%

Most Popular Majors
Economics
Communication
Biology

Admissions
Applicants: 4,757
Accepted: 2,355
Acceptance rate: 49.5%
Placed on wait list: 207
Average GPA: 3.5
ACT range: 27-31
SAT Math range: 600-680
SAT Reading range: 600-720
SAT Writing range: Not reported
Top 10% of class: 49%
Top 25% of class: 88%
Top 50% of class: 100%

26 percent of alums continue their education either immediately or within a year of receiving the undergrad diploma.

Student Life

Granville, Ohio sports a five-o'clock shadow. Namely, everything closes and goes dark at a time when Happy Hours launch elsewhere. Besides the most riveting option—slinking away to Columbus—the university notes how most students "hang out at the Bandersnatch Coffee House and Slayter (student) Union." "The Snatch" is one of campus' most popular coffeehouses, of which there are plenty: The Roost, Brews, Del Mar, Whit's Custard, and Village Coffee all seem to whisper, "the better to keep you awake." Caffeinated spirits have translated into 180 student organizations and a bustling Greek scene, in which hefty numbers of both men (35 percent) and women (41 percent) participate. Ten fraternities and eight sororities mean that most every house is an Animal House. "There isn't much to do in Granville, which intensifies the role of the Greek scene," says a student.

Ever-energized Denison students continue to work off steam in their support of campus athletics. The Division III swim team has found the most ink and press, but the squash, tennis, lacrosse, soccer, baseball, and softball teams are also strong. Intramurals are offered in nine sports including men's and women's flag football, four types of basketball, and dodgeball. "You don't have to be the greatest athlete to participate," comments a student.

Just as the coffee never finishes, the party never ends; the crowd continues to live it up at the Vail Concert Series, where the Laura Reed Trio has recently jammed. Previous performers in the high-profile concert series include Yo-Ya Ma, Dizzy Gillespie, and Wynton Marsalis. Volcanoes ooze unctuous chocolate to smite strawberries at the annual Homecoming Gala, and dozens of students all seem to celebrate a birthday in the buff during Naked Week. "It's exhilarating that it's so chilly and there's still snow on the ground during Naked Week," laughs a student.

Campus housing is broad enough to encompass all residents and fill almost every need. Freshmen live together in first-year-only housing; seniors count down to commencement in their own exclusive dwellings. Notable among Denison residences is the sustainable Homestead. Here the diet is strictly vegan or vegetarian, and chores such as feeding animals and chopping wood please the lumberjacks among us. "You have to be a hard-core environmentalist to live at the Homestead," explains a student.

Student Body

Ethnic diversity is moderate at Denison; 20 percent of the community identifies as minority. Three-quarters of Denison denizens call somewhere outside of Ohio home. The prevalent political mindsets seem to be "mostly conservative or moderate," say students. Tuition of almost $43,000 translates into a relatively high socioeconomic status for the campus. "You see people with designer clothes all the time," remarks a student. Bountiful need-based scholarships are on offer, however, and one out of every eight students is the first in his or her family to seek a college education.

You May Not Know

- A good deal of Denison's nearby buildings may have served as shelters to slaves along the passage of the Underground Railroad.
- The historic Alligator Effigy Mound is located in home city Granville.
- Nearby Columbus was recently named the country's second manliest city.

Distinguished Alumni

Joe Banner, President and CEO of the Philadelphia Eagles; William Bowen, President Emeritus of the Andrew W. Mellon Foundation and President of Princeton University; Steve Carrell, actor in *The Office*; Jennifer Garner, award-winning actress; Richard Lugar, United States Senator and Chairman of the Senate Committee on Foreign Relations; Bobby Rahal, Indianapolis 500 champion; Jack Thompson, anti-video game activist.

Admissions and Financial Aid

An interview is "suggested," which means that if you are able to visit the campus, you should make every effort to set up an interview. Test scores are optional when applying but must be supplied when matriculating. The university accepts the Common Application with a supplement.

Each year the university awards more than 1,000 merit-based scholarships. All awards are renewable for four years. Highlights include Wells Scholarship in the Sciences and Dunbar Scholarship in the Humanities, each with a price tag of $35,000 to subtract from the cost of attendance. To be considered for the merit-based awards, students must apply by January 15.

DENISON UNIVERSITY

Highlights

Admissions Criteria
Academic criteria:
Grades: ☆ ☆ ☆
Difficulty of class schedule: ☆ ☆ ☆
Class rank: ☆
Standardized test scores: ☆
Teacher recommendations: ☆ ☆ ☆
Personal statement: ☆ ☆ ☆
Non-academic criteria considered:
Interview
Extracurricular activities
Special talents, interests, abilities
Character/personal qualities
Volunteer work
Work experience
Geographical location
Religious affiliation/commitment
Minority affiliation
Alumni relationship

Deadlines
Early Action: No
Early Decision: November 15
Regular Action: December 1 (priority)
January 15 (final)
Notification of admission by: April 1
Common Application: Accepted

Financial Aid
In-state tuition: $42,990
Out-of-state tuition: $42,990
Room: $4,060
Board: $4,300
Books: $650
Freshmen receiving need-based aid: 56%
Undergrads rec. need-based aid: 52%
Avg. % of need met by financial aid: 96%
Avg. aid package (freshmen): $37,445
Avg. aid package (undergrads): $36,688
Avg. debt upon graduation: $20,162

School Spirit
Mascot: Big Red
Colors: Red and white
Song: *Denison Marching Song*

DEPAUL
UNIVERSITY

Four-year private
Founded: 1898
Chicago, IL
Major city
Pop. 2,707,120

Address:
1 East Jackson Bou-
levard
Chicago, IL
60604-2287

Admissions:
800-433-7285

Financial Aid:
312-362-8091

admission@depaul.
edu

www.depaul.edu

DEPAUL UNIVERSITY

Overview

With the motto, "I will show you the way of wisdom," DePaul University provides a powerful combination of location, diversity, broad academic offerings, and access to resources. Over a century since its founding, DePaul has become the largest Catholic university and the eighth largest private university in the United States. Based in Chicago, and in close proximity to the most dynamic aspects of this renowned city, DePaul is more diverse than you might expect.

There are six DePaul campuses in the Chicago area—two main campuses, one of which is based in the Lincoln Park area of Chicago and the other in the downtown Loop, and four suburban campuses. Located on 36 acres, the Lincoln Park Campus is DePaul's "largest and most active" campus. This campus is more of a traditional college setting and houses the College of Liberal Arts and Sciences, the School of Education, the Theater School, and the School of Music. The downtown campus at the Loop is home to the College of Commerce, College of Law, School of Computer Science, Telecommunications and Information Systems, School for New Learning, and School of Accountancy and Management Information Systems. The suburban campuses cater mostly to part-time adult students. New facilities include the $40 million McGowan Science Building opened in 2009 and the new four-story Arts and Letters Hall opened in 2012.

Academics

DePaul has nine colleges and schools, and the university offers over 275 undergraduate and graduate programs of study. Strong programs exist within the colleges of commerce, communication, law, computing and digital media, and music. At DePaul, professors teach 98 percent of classes as opposed to teaching assistants taking on instruction. Given that the university operates on a quarterly system, students have noted that classes can often feel rushed. "It's time for exams before you know it," comments a student.

The Liberal Studies Program is the core curriculum, which the university states is aimed at developing "students' writing abilities, computational and technological proficiencies, and critical and creative thinking skills." The requirements vary by college but typically include courses in writing; quantitative reasoning; multiculturalism; experiential learning; arts and literature; philosophical inquiry; scientific inquiry; self, society, and the modern world; religious dimensions; and understanding the past.

The university maintains a unique First-Year Program, and in the autumn quarter, all freshmen take a course that introduces them to the intellectual resources of the city and emphasizes DePaul's role as a part of the city. In the winter or spring quarter, freshmen take a Focal Point Seminar. One student explains that during this seminar, students "discuss and debate readings."

DePaul University's Honors Program offers small, seminar-style classes. Benefits include "academic advising, an Honors Lounge, a student government, peer mentoring," and service activities. The Honors Program is "deeply intellectually challenging," says a student.

The School of Music is nationally recognized with faculty members who perform with the Chicago Symphony Orchestra and the Lyric Opera of Chicago. The school offers degrees in traditional areas such as jazz studies, performance, and composition but also programs in sound recording technology and performing arts management. Many students gain experience by performing in professional groups or interning with professional recording studios.

According to the university, the Theatre School is the Midwest's oldest theatre training conservatory. Reflecting a university focus on experiential education, theatre students play a major role in more than 40 productions a year.

Students have the opportunity to study abroad in more than 30 countries. Over 700 graduates and undergraduates study abroad each year in more than 40 locations. In conjunction with the Irwin W. Steans Center for Community-based Service Learning, the study-abroad program also "supports programs in economically marginalized regions" according to the college.

The university's Career Center provides on-campus interviewing, recruiting days, job and internship fairs, and an online database of jobs and internships. There is also an Internship and Co-op Program, including funds of up to $1,300 for first-generation students to work in unpaid internships. "Graduates stick close to Chicago," says a student.

Student Life

On-campus activities feature over 300 student organizations. For instance, the Intercollegiate Broadcasting System recently named Radio DePaul the best college radio station in the nation.

Major events include DePaul's annual concert, Fest, which takes place during each spring and recruits a number of popular bands. DePaul also hosts the Concerto Festival, an annual festival for young musicians to perform with an orchestra. Given the university's proximity to Chicago, there has also been a strong connection with the city's music, theatre, and film scene.

DePaul has nine fraternities and 15 sororities. "With so much to do off campus, there aren't too many people who are really into the Greek scene," comments one student.

DePaul's 24 intercollegiate athletic teams compete in NCAA Division I. Easily identified by the Blue Demons mascot, the school's renowned basketball program last gained prominence in the late 1970s but still has many fans. "Without a football team, everyone pours their energy into cheering on the basketball team," says a student. DIBS, or Devil in a Blue Suit, is often present at sporting events. School rivals include Notre Dame and Loyola. There are over 30 intramural activities, including soccer, scrabble, chess, and badminton.

Although students socialize on campus—especially at the Student Center—many tend to return home during weekends and students say that the campus can be a "ghost town." But there are plenty of diversions in nearby Chicago. Along with a diverse population in the city, there are countless museums, restaurants, bars, cultural performances, professional athletic events, and shopping venues.

The Lincoln Park campus offers traditional residence halls and apartments for freshmen and sophomores and townhouse buildings for upperclassmen. Loop housing options are through the 18-story University Center of Chicago, which houses students from DePaul, Roosevelt University, and Columbia College. However, more than 80 percent of students live off campus—especially juniors and seniors—and this makes a definite impact on student life. "You make friends during freshman and sophomore year when more people live on campus," notes a student, "but then as people move off campus, it's hard to keep in touch."

DEPAUL UNIVERSITY

Highlights

Students
Total enrollment: 24,966
Undergrads: 16,498
Freshmen: 3,029
Part-time students: 17%
From out-of-state: 36%
From public schools: 77%
Male/Female: 46%/54%
Live on-campus: 17%
In fraternities: 3%
In sororities: 9%
Off-campus employment rating: Good
Caucasian: 56%
African American: 8%
Hispanic: 17%
Asian / Pacific Islander: 8%
Native American: 0%
Mixed (2+ ethnicities): 3%
International: 2%

Academics
Calendar: Quarter
Student/faculty ratio: 16:1
Class size 9 or fewer: 14%
Class size 10-29: 57%
Class size 30-49: 28%
Class size 50-99: 1%
Class size 100 or more: -
Returning freshmen: 85%
Six-year graduation rate: 68%
Graduates who immediately enter career
    related to major: 45%

Most Popular Majors
Accounting
Psychology
Finance

Admissions
Applicants: 18,160
Accepted: 11,318
Acceptance rate: 62.3%
Average GPA: 3.6
ACT range: 23-28
SAT Math range: 510-630
SAT Reading range: 530-640
SAT Writing range: Not reported
Top 10% of class: 23%
Top 25% of class: 52%
Top 50% of class: 85%

237

College Profiles

DEPAUL UNIVERSITY

Admissions Criteria
Academic criteria:
Grades: ☆ ☆ ☆
Difficulty of class schedule: ☆ ☆ ☆
Class rank: ☆ ☆
Standardized test scores: ☆ ☆ ☆
Teacher recommendations: ☆ ☆
Personal statement: ☆ ☆ ☆
Non-academic criteria considered:
Interview
Extracurricular activities
Special talents, interests, abilities
Character/personal qualities
Volunteer work
Work experience
Geographical location
Religious affiliation/commitment
Minority affiliation
Alumni relationship

Deadlines
Early Action: November 15
Early Decision: No
Regular Action: November 15 (priority)
February 1 (final)
Notification of admission by: March 15
Common Application: Accepted

Financial Aid
In-state tuition: $33,390
Out-of-state tuition: $33,390
Room: $6,756
Board: $1,407
Books: $1,134
Freshmen receiving need-based aid: 72%
Undergrads rec. need-based aid: 70%
Avg. % of need met by financial aid: 60%
Avg. aid package (freshmen): $21,917
Avg. aid package (undergrads): $20,150
Avg. debt upon graduation: $28,284

School Spirit
Mascot: Blue Demons
Colors: Royal blue and scarlet
Song: *DePaul Fight Song*

Student Body

The university takes significant pride in recruiting a wide range of students, noted by the fact that 36 percent of the student body is of minority background. Geographically, however, it's a different story; roughly two-thirds of students hail from Illinois. Collectively students come from all 50 states and almost 100 countries.

DePaul also targets first-generation and economically disadvantaged students. According to the college, about 35 percent of full-time freshmen have parents who do not hold a college degree.

The general impression is that DePaul is more politically and religiously diverse than you would expect from a Catholic college. "There is actually a pretty strong liberal presence," says a student.

You May Not Know

- DePaul journalism students helped staff the press office at the 2010 Winter Olympics.
- The School of Music was named as one of the "Schools That Rock" by *Rolling Stone* magazine.
- On Vincentian Service Day, 1,400 students and faculty members volunteer at more than 80 local organizations.

Distinguished Alumni

Jack Greenberg, former President and CEO, McDonald's USA.; Gillian Anderson, actress; Karl Malden, actor; Hon. Anne Burke, Justice, Illinois Supreme Court; George Mikan, former NBA Player; George Perle, Pulitzer Prize-winning composer; Samuel Magad, Chicago Symphony Orchestra concertmaster.

Admissions and Financial Aid

According to the admissions office, "a lot of factors go into an admission decision." While the university typically seeks applicants who "rank in the top half of their graduating class and present strong SAT or ACT scores," other factors are taken into account such as essays, recommendations, interviews, and achievements.

DePaul offers more than $9 million in merit-based scholarships. There are five major academic scholarships, three service and leadership scholarships, and five talent scholarships available, in addition to scholarships for transfer students. The Free Application for Federal Student Aid (FAFSA) is required for a number of scholarships.

DEPAUW UNIVERSITY

Overview

Forty miles west of Indianapolis in Greencastle, Indiana, DePauw University provides private, liberal arts education to approximately 2,300 undergraduate students. The new Janet Prindle Institute of Ethics and Sue Bartlett Reflection Center are the latest additions to the classically beautiful 175-acre campus, but the oldest parts of DePauw are the most notable. The university boasts all of these elements: a historic East Campus, a place on the National Register of Historical Monuments, the oldest music school in the country, a Theater and Center for Performing Arts, and a nature park that was once a limestone quarry. Affiliated with the United Methodist Church, the university has been co-ed since 1837.

Traditional quality education meets progressive innovation with a low faculty ratio and a winter term for students to study and intern off campus. Education is as rigorous as the Greek system is lively, with more than 60 percent of the students pledging Greek organizations. If the Greek system isn't your idea of fun, this may not be the school for you; but if you are as excited about public service and quality liberal arts education as you are about togas and tradition, read on.

Academics

As a liberal arts university, the core curriculum emphasizes breadth of study, critical and creative thinking, and communication skills. These are highlighted in a First Year Seminar and Senior Capstone. To graduate, students must be proficient in expository writing, quantitative reasoning, and oral communication, as well as complete distribution requirements in arts and humanities, science and mathematics, social science, and language.

DePauw offers 47 majors, as well as individually designed majors, which are an option for the more independent student. Music is a very strong program, and talented students often perform for the university and surrounding communities. The shows are "unbelievable," according to one student. Computer and information sciences and other technological majors are popular as well; in fact, all students are required to purchase a laptop at the beginning of freshman year.

For those who are looking for even more rigorous study, DePauw provides five honors programs. The Science Research Fellows conduct hands-on scientific research, working with a faculty member during the summer. The Media Fellows gain experience through off-campus internships and a speaker series through the Eugene S. Pullam Center for Contemporary Media. You can also participate in the Management Fellows Program, the Information Technology Associates Program, and the more classic Honor Scholars Program.

Even if you don't take advantage of the personalization of an honors track, virtually all classes have 50 or fewer students and the student faculty ratio is an intimate 10:1. It is not unusual for students to call professors by their first name or go to their houses for dinner. "I was impressed when our professor invited the entire class to his home for tea," says a student.

DePauw's Winter Term occurs during the month between fall and spring semesters and allows students to take unique classes, do internships, or travel abroad. Faculty members offer courses that take students to study education in Ghana or creativity and art in New Mexico. Many winter terms are devoted to service, such as a trip to Ecuador where students work at a biological reserve. Some students forge out their own in independent studies or take courses at other universities. All experiences are graded satisfactory/not satisfactory. "I love Winter Term because we travel to places and study courses we normally wouldn't and without the stress of grades," comments a student.

DEPAUW UNIVERSITY

Four-year private
Founded: 1837
Greencastle, IN
Small town
Pop. 10,316

Address:
313 South Locust Street
Greencastle, IN 46135

Admissions:
765-658-4006

Financial Aid:
765-658-4030

admission@depauw.edu

www.depauw.edu

DEPAUW UNIVERSITY

Highlights

Students
Total enrollment: 2,336
Undergrads: 2,336
Freshmen: 609
Part-time students: 1%
From out-of-state: 58%
Male/Female: 45%/55%
Live on-campus: 95%
In fraternities: 76%
In sororities: 65%
Off-campus employment rating: Good
Caucasian: 69%
African American: 6%
Hispanic: 4%
Asian / Pacific Islander: 3%
Native American: 0%
Mixed (2+ ethnicities): 4%
International: 11%

Academics
Calendar: 4-1-4 system
Student/faculty ratio: 10:1
Class size 9 or fewer: 14%
Class size 10-29: 81%
Class size 30-49: 5%
Class size 50-99: -
Class size 100 or more: -
Returning freshmen: 89%
Six-year graduation rate: 78%
Graduates who immediately go to graduate school: 23%

Most Popular Majors
Communication
Economics
Biology

Admissions
Applicants: 4,913
Accepted: 3,023
Acceptance rate: 61.5%
Average GPA: 3.5
ACT range: 24-30
SAT Math range: 550-680
SAT Reading range: 530-650
SAT Writing range: 9-40
Top 10% of class: 44%
Top 25% of class: 77%
Top 50% of class: 98%

Over 80 percent of students study off campus at some point during their four years. Apart from the Winter Term, students can also complete a semester or more at one of DePauw's abroad campuses in over 60 countries on six continents.

About one fourth of DePauw graduates pursue advanced degrees, while 90 percent of students entering the workforce are employed within six months. The Civic, Global, and Professional Opportunities Center coordinates career advising, alumni speaker series, internships, and resume and interview help.

Student Life

Over 111 organizations keep DePauw students busy. After long hours in the school's impressive library, students who can choose from groups such as X-Cell, a stepping and dance team, or the Rock Climbing Club. For those who want to continue exercising their minds, they might want to try out the Philosophy Club, Society of Physics Students, Model United Nations, and more. Over 70 percent of students also participate in some sort of public service, through a student group such as DePauw Community Services, an alternative spring break, or a winter term in-service project. Dance Marathon, one of the largest events on campus, is a 24-hour fundraiser for children with AIDS and "something every student must do at least once," says a participant.

Events on campus range from college-classic to downright quirky. The intellectual drive at DePauw is nurtured during the Ubben Lecture series, which brings world leaders, activists, entertainers, and entrepreneurs to DePauw for lectures that are free to students. The creative face of DePauw is revealed during ArtsFEST, which celebrates the lively arts scene with performances and exhibits tuned to a different theme every year. Finally, the active side of the school is exemplified in late April, during the 500 bike race. In 1956, the race started as a fundraiser for the American Cancer Fund. Today, a musical revue called Cyc-Sing, mud volleyball, and tomato dodge ball complete the festivities for those who are not cyclers.

In general, sports don't play that large of a role at DePauw; that is, except for the Monon Bell Classic or "The Game," the football game between DePauw and Wabash College. The bell is an antique 300-pound train bell. Started in 1890, this is the oldest football rivalry west of the Alleghenies. "Even people who don't care about sports go to The Game," says a student. The women's basketball team also won the Division III national championship, the college's first national title.

Greek life—more than sports—defines social life at DePauw. Consistently ranked as the number one college to be a part of a fraternity or sorority, 76 percent of men are members of a fraternity and 65 percent of women are members of a sorority. It's fairly easy to join the Greek system and those who don't usually have friends who are involved, which makes it easy for everyone to attend the parties. "Unless you're socially inept, you're pretty much joining a fraternity or sorority," comments a student. For those not living in fraternities or sororities, coed dorms and single-student apartments house 95 percent of students.

The surrounding small town of Greencastle has limited offerings, but students of age do frequent the bars and the traditional favorite, Marvin's, where the garlic cheeseburger brings out the students to satisfy all-nighter munchies. For more excitement, students can drive into Indianapolis, 40 miles east, to frequent the concerts, bars, and clubs.

Student Body

Depauw University boasts respectable racial and geographic diversity, especially for a small Midwestern university, with 17 percent minority and 58 percent from out of state. Many of these out-of-state students do, however, hail from the surrounding states of Michigan, Illinois, and Ohio. Students describe themselves as "friendly because everyone pretty much knows everyone else." Depauw has only slightly more women than men, (55 percent to 45 percent). Campus politics generally lean from moderate to right according to one student.

You May Not Know

- The first sorority in the United States, Kappa Alpha Theta, started at DePauw in 1870.
- DePauw is home to impressive print and radio communications; WGRE-FM went on air in 1949 as the first 10-watt college radio station in the country, and award-winning student run newspaper *The DePauw* was the first college newspaper in Indiana.
- A scenic escape for students and community members, the DePauw Nature Park, features 10.5 miles of trails in the abandoned limestone quarry.

Distinguished Alumni

Karen Koning AbuZayd, Commissioner-General of the U.N. Relief and Works Agency; Bret Baier, anchor for FOX News; Joseph Flummerfelt, internationally acclaimed conductor; Lee Hamilton, former Congressman and Vice Chair of the 9/11 Commission; Barbara Kingsolver, author; Ferid Murad, 1998 Nobel Prize Winner in medicine; Steve Sanger, CEO of General Mills; Dan Quayle, 44th U.S. Vice President.

Admissions and Financial Aid

The acceptance rate at DePauw is a substantial but not impossible 61.5 percent. According to DePauw admissions, secondary school record is very important, including GPA and teacher recommendations. More than 40 percent of DePauw students are in the top 10 percent of their high school classes. Of course, for a school that values community service and energy, extracurricular involvement is also key.

Once accepted, about 41 percent of students receive merit aid and 55 percent receive need-based aid, though only 88 percent of demonstrated need is met. With the goal of increasing diversity, DePauw participates in the Posse Family scholarship, which offers mentoring and financial assistance to minority students. And in keeping with the school's religious roots, United Methodist scholarships are awarded to nine students who are members of the church. Many other general merit awards are given upon admission.

DEPAUW UNIVERSITY

Highlights

Admissions Criteria
Academic criteria:
Grades: ☆ ☆ ☆
Difficulty of class schedule: ☆ ☆ ☆
Class rank: ☆ ☆
Standardized test scores: ☆ ☆ ☆
Teacher recommendations: ☆ ☆
Personal statement: ☆ ☆
Non-academic criteria considered:
Interview
Extracurricular activities
Special talents, interests, abilities
Character/personal qualities
Volunteer work
Work experience
Geographical location
Alumni relationship

Deadlines
Early Action: December 1
Early Decision: November 1
Regular Action: Rolling admissions
Common Application: Accepted

Financial Aid
In-state tuition: $40,150
Out-of-state tuition: $40,150
Room: Varies
Board: Varies
Books: $350
Freshmen receiving need-based aid: 64%
Undergrads rec. need-based aid: 55%
Avg. % of need met by financial aid: 88%
Avg. aid package (freshmen): $31,834
Avg. aid package (undergrads): $31,812
Avg. debt upon graduation: $26,570

School Spirit
Mascot: Tiger
Colors: Old gold and black
Song: *Here's to DePauw*

Four-year private
Founded: 1783
Carlisle, PA
Large town
Pop. 19,072

Address:
P.O. Box 1773
Carlisle, PA
17013-2896

Admissions:
800-644-1773

Financial Aid:
717-245-1308

admit@dickinson.edu

www.dickinson.edu

DICKINSON COLLEGE

Overview

Set in the historic town of Carlisle, Pennsylvania, Dickinson College was chartered just days after the signing of the Treaty of Paris. The oldest campus building, Old West, was completed in 1804 and is a registered National Historic Landmark. Despite being steeped in history, Dickinson has a progressive vision focused on global education. Classes are designed to have a global focus, and the college offers extensive opportunities for students to study and research abroad.

Dickinson is also actively committed to sustainability and its two newest buildings were awarded Gold LEED (Leadership in Energy and Environmental Design) certification. Dickinson has also pledged to be carbon neutral by 2020. The Center for Sustainable Living, a residential house better known as the Treehouse, is evidence of Dickinson's commitment to sustainable practices.

The small size of the college means that students can get individual attention and can feel that they belong to an intimate community. However, without a nearby city to escape to, the small college and quiet town of Carlisle may be stifling for some.

Academics

Dickinson students have a choice of 42 majors, including 22 disciplinary majors and 19 interdisciplinary majors. In addition, Dickinson also offers specialized advising and recommends courses for pre-business management, pre-engineering, pre-health, and prelaw students. Other strong programs include business, English, and foreign language studies.

Freshmen are required to take a First-Year Seminar, small-group sessions intended to introduce freshmen to the "community of inquiry" and liberal learning. Uniquely, the professor of the First-Year Seminar acts as the students' initial academic advisor. In the second year, students are required to take a Writing Intensive Course designed to focus on the writing process and to introduce students to academic writing. Complementing the writing requirement is a mandatory Quantitative Reasoning Course that focuses on analysis of quantitative data and analytical reasoning. A variety of courses can satisfy either requirement. Finally, students are required to fulfill distribution requirements in three categories: arts and humanities, social sciences, and laboratory sciences. "It seems like a lot of required classes, and it is, but it's do-able," says a student.

Overall, students report that classes are "a lot of work but not overwhelming." Since virtually all classes have 50 or fewer students, professors are able to provide a high level of individual attention. "They genuinely care about teaching and put a lot of effort into classes," comments a student.

A recently established Center for Sustainability Education helps to make "the study of the environment a defining characteristic of a Dickinson education," according to the college. Courses offered include Sustainable Business, Eco-feminism, and Buddhism and the Environment. Because the college also set a goal to become completely carbon-neutral by 2020, it was named on *Forbes Magazine's* list of America's Greenest Colleges and Universities.

The Community Studies Center assists students in doing hands-on research in the social sciences and humanities that works to achieve "greater equality, peace, and social justice." A recent project allows students to study climate change through four classes at Dickinson and two weeks abroad in Durban, South Africa, and also includes attending the United Nations Framework on Climate Change Convention.

Dickinson has an exceptionally strong study-abroad program, which reflects their goal to "turn the campus from a single site into the hub of a truly global network." Dickinson boasts more than 40 programs in 24 countries, including academic year programs, semester programs, summer programs, and other specialized opportunities.

Dickinson's study-abroad programs include such diverse locations as Yaoundé, Cameroon; Querétaro, Mexico; and Beijing, China.

Upon graduation, alumni have access to an online alumni directory and career network. Through this source, they may get help applying to graduate school. The Career Center also sponsors a Networking Day in which alumni speak with current students about careers.

Student Life

Dickinson students have an eclectic gamut of clubs and activities to choose from, ranging from traditional language-interest groups to more unique organizations such as the archeology-focused Chimaera Club and the Japanese Animation Club. There is a strong emphasis on community service, with 21 clubs working on both local and international projects. Particularly interesting is the number of groups that assist ESL (English as a Second Language) students and adults in the area.

Popular events on and around campus include the yearly OcTUBAfest, an open-air concert hosted by the Keystone Tuba Ensemble, and the local Amani Festival, an annual street fair that celebrates global cultures and ethnicities. Members of the faculty seem eager to participate in campus life, as evidenced by the performance of the Faculty Jazz Quartet during last year's Homecoming weekend. "The faculty are game for almost anything," laughs a student. Off-campus events are limited for the typical broke college student, but students enjoy skiing and hiking on the nearby Appalachian Trail.

When it comes to room and board, Dickinson students have a range of choices. Besides traditional residential halls, Dickinson also has special interest houses for sophomores, juniors, and seniors, such as language houses or the Music Society.

Greek life also has a strong presence on campus, with four fraternities and five sororities. About one in five students participates in Greek life. "If you want the most social interaction, you should probably join a fraternity or sorority, but you can still have options if you're not a member," comments a student. Frat activities are often open to non-members, creating an active party atmosphere on campus. For those who prefer not to drink, The Quarry is a popular pizza-and-milkshake place to hang out, and it stays open until 2 a.m. on Fridays and Saturdays. "You'll pretty much run into someone you know every weekend night at the Quarry," says a student.

Dickinson has 12 women's and 11 men's Division III varsity sports, besides intramural sports and physical education classes. The Red Devils' longstanding football rivals are Franklin and Marshall for the Conestoga Wagon Trophy, and Gettysburg College for the Little Brown Bucket. For those who want to try a non-traditional sport, Dickinson has a Chidokwan Karate Club as well as an Equestrian Club.

Student Body

Dickinson's small student population—2,400 students—means that it is not hard to know everyone on campus. Dickinson has a relatively high number of international students (eight percent) hailing from 41 countries, while 13 percent identify as ethnic minorities. However, a large number of students come from the New England

DICKINSON COLLEGE

Highlights

Students
Total enrollment: 2,386
Undergrads: 2,386
Freshmen: 602
Part-time students: 2%
From out-of-state: 79%
From public schools: 61%
Male/Female: 45%/55%
Live on-campus: 95%
In fraternities: 11%
In sororities: 29%
Off-campus employment rating: Fair
Caucasian: 77%
African American: 3%
Hispanic: 6%
Asian / Pacific Islander: 2%
Native American: 0%
Mixed (2+ ethnicities): 2%
International: 8%

Academics
Calendar: Semester
Student/faculty ratio: 10:1
Class size 9 or fewer: 25%
Class size 10-29: 66%
Class size 30-49: 9%
Class size 50-99: -
Class size 100 or more: -
Returning freshmen: 91%
Six-year graduation rate: 85%

Most Popular Majors
International business/management
Political science
Economics

Admissions
Applicants: 5,844
Accepted: 2,340
Acceptance rate: 40.0%
Placed on wait list: 1,157
Enrolled from wait list: 17
Average GPA: Not reported
ACT range: 27-30
SAT Math range: 600-690
SAT Reading range: 590-690
SAT Writing range: 21-53
Top 10% of class: 48%
Top 25% of class: 78%
Top 50% of class: 96%

College Profiles

DICKINSON COLLEGE

Admissions Criteria
Academic criteria:
Grades: ☆ ☆ ☆
Difficulty of class schedule: ☆ ☆ ☆
Class rank: ☆ ☆
Standardized test scores: ☆ ☆
Teacher recommendations: ☆ ☆ ☆
Personal statement: ☆ ☆ ☆
Non-academic criteria considered:
Interview
Extracurricular activities
Special talents, interests, abilities
Character/personal qualities
Volunteer work
Work experience
Geographical location
Minority affiliation
Alumni relationship

Deadlines
Early Action: December 1
Early Decision: November 15
Regular Action: February 1 (final)
Notification of admission by: March 20
Common Application: Accepted

Financial Aid
In-state tuition: $45,644
Out-of-state tuition: $45,644
Room: $5,966
Board: $5,602
Books: $1,021
Freshmen receiving need-based aid: 56%
Undergrads rec. need-based aid: 56%
Avg. % of need met by financial aid: 96%
Avg. aid package (freshmen): $34,269
Avg. aid package (undergrads): $36,221
Avg. debt upon graduation: $25,574

School Spirit
Mascot: Red Devils
Colors: Red and white

area, leading to a large "preppy" population. "You'll fit right in if you dress in designer brands and drive a brand-name car," remarks a student. "But if you don't, that's fine too."

You May Not Know

- The college was founded by Dr. Benjamin Rush, a signer of the Declaration of Independence.
- John Dickinson, the college's namesake, signed the United States Constitution.
- Dickinson was chartered five days after the Treaty of Paris, making it the first college chartered in the "newly-recognized United States."

Distinguished Alumni

Chief Bender, Hall of Fame baseball pitcher; James Buchanan, 15th President of the United States; Jennifer Haigh, author and PEN/Hemingway Award winner; Roger B. Taney, Chief Justice of the United States; Robert J. Wise, founder of Wise Foods Inc.

Admissions and Financial Aid

Applicants to Dickinson have an unusually large number of options, as Dickinson has four different application processes: Early Decision I, Early Action, Early Decision II, and Regular Decision. Each has different deadlines; the first on November 15 and the last on February 1. Dickinson recommends applying Early Decision for a more personal review process due to a smaller pool.

The school also stresses the importance of getting in touch with a regional admissions counselor, who may advocate for students during the admissions process.

Besides financial aid, Dickinson also has three merit-based scholarships ranging from $10,000 to $20,000 per year. An unusual Community College Partnership Program provides an opportunity for a student to attend one of the region's five community colleges for two years, then transfer to Dickinson for his final two years, with a $15,000 per year scholarship. Finally, Dickinson also participates in the Posse Foundation Program, which recruits minority students from urban public high schools.

DREW UNIVERSITY

Overview

Madison, New Jersey—home to the Liberal Arts College, graduate school, and theological school of Drew University—may not ring a bell for many people, but rest assured that it is hardly the middle of nowhere. More than fifty Fortune 500 companies are located in Morris County, one of the 10 wealthiest counties in the nation. And one of Drew's major perks is its enviable location 30 miles west of midtown Manhattan, where opportunities for internships at the UN, Wall Street, and top art museums abound, not to mention a plethora of social activity.

While it's close to the city life of Manhattan, Drew also offers almost 200 acres of nature-filled campus, giving it the nickname "University in the Forest." Most of the 1,600 "Drewid" undergrads live on campus, where theater and arts are celebrated. However, students who want Greek organizations, strong athletic programs, or a large number of student groups are better off looking elsewhere.

Some may find the extensive General Education Requirements somewhat constricting, though these same requirements also ensure that all students study off campus. While the university's advertisement of its high achieving alumni working at Morgan Stanley and the U.S. Department of State may seem at odds with the stereotypes of a liberal arts education, Drew does indeed have a strong focus on "womyn's (sic) issues" as well as Pan-African culture—putting the "liberal" back in liberal arts—and yes, even a strong theater *arts* program.

Academics

Drew offers over 30 undergraduate majors—programs which all provide minors except neuroscience, behavioral science, and the joint mathematics and computer science major. There are an additional 21 interdisciplinary minors, as well as dual degree programs in medicine (BA/MD) and engineering and applied science (BA/BS or BA/BEng). Other strong programs include chemistry, English, environmental studies and sustainability, history, political science, prelaw, premed, and theatre arts.

There are a large number of General Education Requirements. First-year students must enroll in the College Seminar and College Writing Course and are housed in residence halls close to the other members of their seminar to encourage interaction. The entire freshman class gets the chance to bond through The Common Hour, a weekly hour-long shared experience where students can meet regularly in small groups with undergrad peer mentors. Students in The Common Hour receive training through Campus Life Seminars, academic planning and advising seminars, and other activities. All students are required to complete a Capstone project. Students receive plenty of attention from professors, with the most common course size being 10 to 19 students. Professors know students on a "first-name basis" and "even call or text when we don't show up for class," says a student.

Students are required to have an off-campus experience and choose from a wide array of options, from internships to a full semester abroad. Wall Street Semester takes advantage of Drew's proximity to the nation's central financial district by structuring a program around twice-a-week field trips to Wall Street. During these excursions, Wall Street hopefuls may look at the economics, history, and ethics of the financial sector. Semester in New York on Contemporary Art is a similar program with a focus on modern art that includes visiting museums and even meeting prominent artists. Semester on the United Nations also takes students to NYC twice a week and includes a research project and optional internship component. "We're right next door to the largest metropolitan classroom in the world, New York City," explains a student.

Drew International Seminars (DIS) are an excellent opportunity for first-year students to get a taste of studying abroad without interfering with other first-year requirements. These seminars combine coursework on campus with a month-long

DREW UNIVERSITY

Four-year private
Founded: 1867
Madison, NJ
Small town
Pop. 15,924

Address:
36 Madison Avenue
Madison, NJ
07940-1493

Admissions:
973-408-3739

Financial Aid:
973-408-3112

cadm@drew.edu

www.drew.edu

DREW UNIVERSITY

Highlights

Students
Total enrollment: 2,447
Undergrads: 1,636
Freshmen: 363
Part-time students: 4%
From out-of-state: 37%
Male/Female: 40%/60%
Live on-campus: 78%
Off-campus employment rating: Fair
Caucasian: 56%
African American: 10%
Hispanic: 14%
Asian / Pacific Islander: 5%
Native American: 0%
Mixed (2+ ethnicities): 2%
International: 2%

Academics
Calendar: Semester
Student/faculty ratio: 10:1
Class size 9 or fewer: 17%
Class size 10-29: 71%
Class size 30-49: 11%
Class size 50-99: 1%
Class size 100 or more: -
Returning freshmen: 75%
Six-year graduation rate: 69%
Graduates who immediately go to gradu-
    ate school: 28%

Most Popular Majors
Political science
Psychology
Economics

Admissions
Applicants: 3,872
Accepted: 3,294
Acceptance rate: 85.1%
Average GPA: 3.3
ACT range: 21-28
SAT Math range: 480-600
SAT Reading range: 490-620
SAT Writing range: 5-26
Top 10% of class: 31%
Top 25% of class: 58%
Top 50% of class: 85%

period of off-campus study, allowing for intensive on-site study of another culture. Internship opportunities in New York City on Wall Street, at the UN, at museums, for major publishers, and the like may explain why 90 percent of Drew's newest alumni are employed or in top graduate, law, and medical schools within six months of graduation. Recent graduates have found jobs at Morgan Stanley, CNN, the U.S. Department of State, *Vogue*, and the Museum of Modern Art.

Student Life

With so many students living on campus, the social scene at Drew is active to say the least, and there's even a Pub on campus that has been serving students since 1974. Another hangout is The Other End Coffeehouse and Cabaret, featuring nachos and quesadillas and events such as a cappella performances. The Shakespeare Theater of New Jersey—one of 22 professional theaters in the state—is housed on campus and, along with Drew's strong theater arts department, contributes to the popularity of theater productions on campus. The Drew Forum lecture series brings major speakers to campus such as Thomas Freidman and Elie Wiesel.

There are about 85 student groups at Drew University. Notable organizations include the University Program Board (UPB), a student-run volunteer group; Women's Concern Club, which promotes feminism and awareness of women's issues; and Kuumba, the Pan-African organization that offers films, excursions, and discussions. There are no Greek organizations at Drew, though there are a number of honor societies. "There is no yearning for Greek organizations," comments a student.

September brings the annual Community Day at Drew, a free afternoon of crafts, food, and entertainment open to local residents and Drew students alike. The biggest annual events are clustered around the spring. Ninety-nine Nights, as one Drew student blogger wrote, is "mostly a night to...party with class solidarity" in a place called the Space, a late-night dining area popular among students. The event is not just about inebriated abandon though—there's a hint of the bitter sweet, as the event marks 99 nights until graduation day. The First Annual Picnic (FAP) is a long-standing tradition where current students and alumni come together and celebrate the beginning of spring. A recent FAP theme, Jersey Shore, featured funnel cake and other boardwalk food, inflatable slides, and laser tag. "Everyone comes out for the picnic," recalls one participant.

The Drew Rangers compete at the NCAA Division III level in 11 sports. Intramurals include flag football, indoor/outdoor soccer, basketball, and billiards, with awards and occasional travel to regional and national tournaments.

The college explains students' options for off-campus excursions like this: "Small-town Madison is a two-block walk, hipster-historic Morristown is a four-mile jaunt, and the ultimate big-city adventure—Manhattan—is a mere 45-minute train ride." One student remarks, "We have the best party in the world by being so close to the city."

The dorms at Drew are acceptable, though nothing to brag about. About 78 percent of students live on campus, and housing is guaranteed for all four years. Six theme houses embrace various

cultures—Asian, Latino, Pan-African—and others promote ecology/
sustainability, spirituality/interfaith dialogue, and "womyn's issues."

Student Body

The 1,600 undergraduates at Drew comprise a diverse student
body, with 31 percent minority students and 37 percent from out
of the state. The university is 60 percent female, which affects the
dating scene on campus. "There is a dearth of eligible men here,"
one female student explains, "but fortunately, Farleigh Dickinson
University is as close as the city." Drew is affiliated with the United
Methodist Church and many of the Theological School's students
and faculty are United Methodist; however, no religious demands
are made on students.

You May Not Know

- Many of the buildings on Drew University's campus date
  from the 19th and early 20th centuries.
- In 1984, two psychology professors made Drew Uni-
  versity the first liberal arts college to provide a personal
  computer and software to all incoming freshman.
- Several motion pictures and TV shows have used Drew
  University as a filming location, including episodes of *The
  Sopranos* and *The Daily Show*.

Distinguished Alumni

Amy Introcaso-Davis, Senior Vice President for Original Program-
ming and Development at Oxygen Media; Leo H. Grohowski,
Chief Investment Officer of The Bank of New York Mellon; Tim
Rothwell, Chairman of Sanofi-Aventis.

Admissions and Financial Aid

According to the admissions office, Drew aims to create "a diverse,
energetic, and talented first-year class." Besides the binding Early
Decision program, Drew also offers a non-binding Priority Admission program with benefits that include early notification, waiving
the application fee, and first consideration for scholarships. Special
admission programs include the Dual-Degree (BA/MD) Medical
Program. Drew has taken the unusual step of not requiring either
the SAT or ACT but allowing students to submit a graded paper
from one of their high school classes instead.

Drew offers a number of merit-based scholarships, though
there are no athletic scholarships. All applicants are automatically
considered for three scholarships: 1) renewable Baldwin Honors
Scholarships for academic achievement, which provide financial
support along with acceptance into the Baldwin Honors Program.
2) Drew Merit-Based Scholarships; these range from $3,000 to
$22,000 and are also renewable. 3) RISE Scholarship for Excel-
lence in Science, renewable as long as the student is a major in the
natural or physical sciences, mathematics, or computer science.
Other scholarships rewarding civic engagement and talent in the
arts require separate applications.

DREW UNIVERSITY

Highlights

Admissions Criteria
Academic criteria:
Grades: ☆ ☆ ☆
Difficulty of class schedule: ☆ ☆ ☆
Class rank: ☆
Standardized test scores: ☆
Teacher recommendations: ☆ ☆
Personal statement: ☆ ☆
Non-academic criteria considered:
Interview
Extracurricular activities
Special talents, interests, abilities
Character/personal qualities
Volunteer work
Work experience
State of residency

Deadlines
Early Action: January 15
Early Decision: November 1
Regular Action: Rolling admissions
Common Application: Accepted

Financial Aid
In-state tuition: $42,936
Out-of-state tuition: $42,936
Room: $7,684
Board: $4,260
Books: $1,128
Undergrads rec. need-based aid: 68%
Avg. % of need met by financial aid: 72%
Avg. aid package (freshmen): Not re-
  ported
Avg. aid package (undergrads): $30,732
Avg. debt upon graduation: $24,470

School Spirit
Mascot: Rangers
Colors: Green and blue

247

DREXEL
UNIVERSITY

Four-year private
Founded: 1891
Philadelphia, PA
Major city
Pop. 1,536,471

Address:
3141 Chestnut Street
Philadelphia, PA
19104-2875

Admissions:
800-237-3935

Financial Aid:
215-895-2537

enroll@drexel.edu

www.drexel.edu

DREXEL UNIVERSITY

Overview

Drexel's approach to higher learning is focused on career preparation and driven by its cooperative education program. The Drexel Plan/Drexel Co-op is one of the oldest cooperative programs in the country, and many students find jobs at the companies where they intern.

Drexel's almost 16,000 undergraduate students include a large contingency of part-time, adult, and online students. Pair the non-traditional student body with the fact that most students live off campus and the result is a subdued student life.

Drexel University was founded in 1891 and its main campus is on 74 acres located in the University City district of Philadelphia, Pennsylvania. The downtown district is just a 10-minute walk from campus. While students say they feel safe on campus, the main campus's proximity to some lower income areas of Philadelphia means that students take common sense safety measures. The university provides walking escorts and staff at residence hall main entrances 24 hours a day.

Academics

Drexel not only requires students to enroll within a major at the beginning of their undergraduate career, but even has a prescribed curriculum for those who are undecided. Drexel's Still-Deciding Students programs provide some freedom to explore classes while fulfilling some of the requirements for a specific field of study. "I like that I'm not wasting time even though I haven't decided exactly what I'd like to major in," says a student.

Drexel is a college that is perhaps geared toward a different kind of student: the B-student, the returning student, or the commuting student. It offers a useful degree for students who are working toward a specific career path. Fifty-six percent of students enter a field related to their major upon graduation, which means that majors at Drexel can be rather specific. Some examples include business administration, nursing, army reserve officers' training corps, culinary arts, and information systems.

Many Drexel students have already done the proverbial, "finding themselves" and are focused on a chosen career upon enrolling. Drexel calls itself a pioneer in co-operative education, and in fact, it is this program that distinguishes it from a traditional undergraduate experience. During their freshmen year, students attend classes full-time; after, they alternate between attending classes and working full-time. Students may repeat this pattern up to three times and work as many as 18 months by graduation. The internships are paid, and the average salary for six months of employment is just under $15,000. "This is the best possible job training program you can ask for," says a student. "I'm learning the same skills as college graduates." The down side to this Drexel Plan is that the average student should expect at least a five-year undergraduate experience.

Drexel has a significant adult, part-time, and online undergraduate population. To accommodate this non-traditional student population, Drexel does not impose a core curriculum but instead offers various routes by which to obtain a bachelors degree. "The reason that I chose Drexel is so I can fit my education around the other things in my life such as my job and family," comments a student. Drexel offers 73 majors, 85 minors, and certificate programs for undergraduate students. Many majors may be completed as a part-time program.

Drexel also allows for some bachelors degrees to be completed online. Programs include criminal justice, education, property management, and health and nursing. In essence, Drexel takes a vocational training approach to undergraduate education. Important to note: although Drexel allows a great deal of flexibility in how a degree may be attained, the university is on a quarter system, which means that students are expected to master material in a short 10 weeks. "The pace of the classes can be a little overwhelming," notes a student. All lectures are posted online, regardless of the program.

Drexel's study-abroad programs are designed to fulfill a degree or university requirement, thus enabling students to participate in internships or cooperative education programs abroad while still staying on track to graduate in the time allotted to their degree program. Nineteen programs are open to the general student body, and 36 additional programs are available to certain majors. The Commuter, Graduate, and Transfer Student Programs and Services Center offers advice and guidance to students during their Drexel experience.

Student Life

Clubs on campus are diverse and include both pre-professional and social groups. There are over 180 student organizations, which include Tango Club, Ultimate Frisbee, Society of Women Engineers, and the Drexel Players (theater club). However, students say that the campus community is "not all that lively," perhaps due in part to off-campus coeducational activities. Since intramural sports are among the most popular activities on campus, there are commuter teams that are scheduled to play at earlier times so that students who take the train don't miss their ride.

"If you want the quintessential college experience, you may need to look elsewhere," says a student. Still, Drexel offers several traditions and activities that are more in line with what one would expect on most college campuses. For example, there is Greek Week for students who are interested in pledging, and a recent schedule of events included a powder-puff football tournament and a Jeopardy-style quiz game. Additionally, there is an annual semi-formal Crystal Ball. There are 17 fraternities and 12 sororities represented on campus with nine percent of men and eight percent of women pledging. Community service projects that have a strong Greek presence are Habitat for Humanity, St. Agatha/St. James Soup Kitchen, and the AIDS Walk.

Intramural sports are popular with students and include flag football, basketball, and soccer. Drexel has eight men's and eight women's NCAA Division I teams, and varsity basketball is the most popular spectator sport. Football lovers beware—there's no team. "We root for basketball since we don't have football as an option," says a student. The John A. Daskalakis Athletic Center, known to students as "the Dac," includes a fully-equipped gym, swimming pool, and basketball and squash courts.

Given that so many students live off campus after their first year, and that campus is located smack in the middle of Philadelphia, a lot of socializing happens off campus. Philadelphia is home to the 76ers and the Phillies. Philadelphia is a historical playground full of monuments, museums, and markers: Independence Hall and the Liberty Bell, the Philadelphia Museum of Art, the Philadelphia Zoo, the Rodin Museum. All of these tell great stories and all are easily accessible by way of public transportation. New York City is a 90-minute Amtrak trip away as well.

Sixty-five percent of students live off campus, and on-campus housing is only guaranteed for freshman year. Ten residence halls are available with either double-occupancy or suite-style options.

DREXEL UNIVERSITY

Highlights

Students
Total enrollment: 25,500
Undergrads: 15,876
Freshmen: 3,116
Part-time students: 18%
From out-of-state: 50%
From public schools: 70%
Male/Female: 54%/46%
Live on-campus: 35%
In fraternities: 9%
In sororities: 8%
Off-campus employment rating: Excellent
Caucasian: 58%
African American: 7%
Hispanic: 6%
Asian / Pacific Islander: 12%
Native American: 0%
Mixed (2+ ethnicities): 2%
International: 11%

Academics
Calendar: Quarter
Student/faculty ratio: 11:1
Class size 9 or fewer: 26%
Class size 10-29: 59%
Class size 30-49: 10%
Class size 50-99: 3%
Class size 100 or more: 2%
Returning freshmen: 85%
Six-year graduation rate: 65%
Graduates who immediately enter career related to major: 56%

Most Popular Majors
Engineering
Business administration
Health professions

Admissions
Applicants: 40,586
Accepted: 30,382
Acceptance rate: 74.9%
Average GPA: 3.6
ACT range: 24-29
SAT Math range: 580-680
SAT Reading range: 540-640
SAT Writing range: 8-36
Top 10% of class: 34%
Top 25% of class: 65%
Top 50% of class: 92%

249

College Profiles

DREXEL UNIVERSITY

Admissions Criteria
Academic criteria:
Grades: ☆ ☆ ☆
Difficulty of class schedule: ☆ ☆ ☆
Class rank: ☆ ☆ ☆
Standardized test scores: ☆ ☆ ☆
Teacher recommendations: ☆ ☆
Personal statement: ☆ ☆
Non-academic criteria considered:
Interview
Extracurricular activities
Special talents, interests, abilities
Character/personal qualities
Volunteer work
Work experience
State of residency
Alumni relationship

Deadlines
Early Action: No
Early Decision: November 15
Regular Action: Rolling admissions
Common Application: Accepted

Financial Aid
In-state tuition: $35,135
Out-of-state tuition: $35,135
Room: $8,730
Board: $5,685
Books: $2,000
Avg. aid package (freshmen): $16,890 for grants or scholarship aid, $10,896 for student loans
Avg. aid package (undergrads): $15,422 for grants or scholarship aid, $7,546 for federal student loans

School Spirit
Mascot: Dragons
Colors: Blue and gold

Students can choose to live in a learning community based on their academic interests.

Student Body

The university has high diversity with about one-quarter of students identifying as minority and high geographic diversity with half of students from out of state. Students freely describe themselves as "geeky," which in this case, translates into being more focused on getting in and out than spending a lot of time socializing on campus.

According to the college, about 90 percent of graduating students are either employed, in graduate school, or in a service organization. The co-op program has a lot to do with that number since most students find that they are able to become employed with the companies for which they intern.

You May Not Know

- In 1983, Drexel became the first university in the United States to require every student to own a computer; in 2000, Drexel was the first major university to have a completely wireless campus.
- Operating out of the College of Media Arts and Design, Mad Dragon Records is a student-run record label that promotes local and student talents.
- Drexel's co-op program works with more than 1,500 companies in 27 states and 12 countries. The law school at Drexel is only one of two in the country to operate a co-op model.

Distinguished Alumni

Earle I. Mack, former U.S. Ambassador to Finland; Joan McConnon, co-founder and CFO of Project H.O.M.E. in Philadelphia; John Rittenhouse, retired Senior Vice President and General Manager of General Electric Aerospace; Sandra Schultz Newman, Pennsylvania Supreme Court Justice.

Admissions and Financial Aid

Drexel prefers that prospective students apply online and use the online application available at the college's website. Both the Common Application and Universal College Application are accepted, but the application fee is waived for students who apply online. Drexel requires a one- to two-page essay from every applicant, and topics vary by major. The admissions committee looks for quality of writing, depth of analysis, and the skill with which a student justifies his or her conclusions.

Over 30 percent of incoming freshmen are awarded some form of academic scholarship. All first-time freshman applicants who complete their applications by the January admissions deadline will be automatically reviewed for the academic achievement A.J. Drexel Scholarship. This award is available in amounts up to $26,000. Other scholarships include the Presidential Scholarship (full tuition), the Dean's Scholarship (partial tuition), and the Drexel Legacy Scholarship (available to children and grandchildren of Drexel Alumni). Athletic scholarships, performing arts scholarships, and ROTC scholarships are also available.

DUKE UNIVERSITY

Overview

Situated on nearly 9,000 acres in the City of Medicine—Durham, North Carolina—Duke University is home to 6,700 undergrads and about 8,700 graduate students. The university is large enough to have three contiguous campuses: East, West, and Central. Frequent shuttles bus students between classes, passing by the Collegiate Gothic structures of West Campus, as exemplified by the Duke Chapel with its 210-foot tower, and the stately Georgian architecture of East Campus, which is home to all first-year students. Students appreciate the shuttles, as walking from one end of East campus to the other end of West campus can easily be a two-mile trek.

Surrounding forests can belie the closeness of downtown Durham, making the many undergrads that live on campus feel they are part of a self-contained center for academic, research, and social opportunities. A private liberal arts college with highly regarded academics, Duke was recently rated in the top 10 national universities by *U.S. News & World Report*. The university is also known for its outstanding basketball program and its die-hard school spirit—what other school features students camping out in tents for months before a game? Students who are happy to live in North Carolina and are looking for rigorous classes, a large Greek scene, and lots of sports lovers will want to apply for the chance to join the classrooms—and the tents—of Duke University.

Academics

Duke offers 40 majors and 16 certificate programs. Students can pursue up to three majors/minors/certificates. Programs are offered through the Trinity College of Arts and Sciences, where 80 percent of undergrads enroll, the Pratt School of Engineering, and the Graduate School. Ninety-four percent of classes have 50 or fewer students. In general, students say that courses "range from tough to downright panic attack-inducing," not surprising given that Duke students are academically focused and 92 percent graduated in the top 10 percent of their high school classes.

General education requirements for Trinity College include courses in two of five Areas of Knowledge, plus two courses in each of six Modes of Inquiry: cross-cultural, ethical, science technology and society, foreign language, writing, and research. All first-year students take a writing course and seminar, and all students must complete two Small Group Learning Experiences—seminars, tutorials, thesis courses, and independent study courses—after their first year. Strong programs include the various degrees in the divinity school and nursing school, the various engineering majors, and the majors of economics, environmental sciences, and public policy studies. Prelaw and premed are also strong. The biomedical engineering department is the "best in the country," says a student, aligning with similar rankings from the *Chronicle of Higher Education*.

Duke's resources for research abound, beginning with its extensive library resources—one of the nation's 10 largest private research library systems. Students interested in the environment will appreciate the Duke University Marine Laboratory in coastal Beaufort, North Carolina and the Duke Forest, a 7,200 acre outdoor laboratory. Lemur lovers will discover the world's only university-based facility devoted to the study of prosimian primates. The French Family Sciences Center, a $115 million, 280,000-square-foot center that opened in 2007, offers research and teaching labs for genomics, biochemistry, nanoscience, biology, and other sciences. There's a "ton of support and opportunities" for undergraduate research, notes a student.

The Baldwin Scholars Program is a four-year program for female undergraduates that supports the classroom, leadership, and professional endeavors of women. Eight students are selected each year to participate in two academic seminars, a sophomore residential experience, and an internship. The Focus Program for first- and second-

DUKE UNIVERSITY

Four-year private
Founded: 1838
Durham, NC
Medium city
Pop. 233,252

Address:
2138 Campus Drive,
Box 90586
Durham, NC
27708

Admissions:
919-684-3214

Financial Aid:
919-684-6225

undergrad-admissions@duke.edu

www.duke.edu

DUKE UNIVERSITY

Students
Total enrollment: 15,386
Undergrads: 6,655
Freshmen: 1,724
From out-of-state: 90%
From public schools: 67%
Male/Female: 50%/50%
Live on-campus: 81%
In fraternities: 29%
In sororities: 42%
Off-campus employment rating: Excellent
Caucasian: 47%
African American: 10%
Hispanic: 6%
Asian / Pacific Islander: 20%
Native American: 1%
Mixed (2+ ethnicities): 2%
International: 8%

Academics
Calendar: Semester
Student/faculty ratio: 7:1
Class size 9 or fewer: 24%
Class size 10-29: 60%
Class size 30-49: 10%
Class size 50-99: 4%
Class size 100 or more: 2%
Returning freshmen: 97%
Six-year graduation rate: 94%
Graduates who immediately go to graduate school: 36%

Most Popular Majors
Economics
Psychology
Public policy

Admissions
Applicants: 30,374
Accepted: 4,077
Acceptance rate: 13.4%
Average GPA: Not reported
ACT range: 30-34
SAT Math range: 690-790
SAT Reading range: 670-760
SAT Writing range: 69-25
Top 10% of class: 92%
Top 25% of class: 98%
Top 50% of class: 99%

year students offers an Interdisciplinary Seminar of no more than 18 students and a freshman residential experience.

Almost half of undergraduates study abroad before graduation. The DukeEngage program, launched in 2007, provides funding for undergrads to pursue an intensive civic engagement experience abroad. There are more than 30 semester and summer-abroad programs, plus other programs not administered by Duke but accessible to their students.

More than 135,000 Duke alumni make up a strong network. Internship opportunities abound since Duke is right in the heart of the Research Triangle Park. The Health Careers Exploration Program allows pre-health students to intern at the Duke University Medical Center or another health facility. According to the university, the experience allows students an opportunity to "work in direct patient clinical care, shadow a health professional, work on a service project, or participate in laboratory research."

Student Life

There are more than 400 student organizations that are showcased at the much-anticipated Student Activities Fair on East Campus at the beginning of each academic year. "Everyone is pretty much involved in at least one activity," explains a student. Popular groups include the Outing Club, Circle K, College Republicans, and Duke Democrats. More than 75 percent of students are involved in community service while at Duke, contributing more than 100,000 hours each year. Three bars on campus serve as popular locations to hang out. A 40,000 square-foot plaza completed in 2006 serves as an outdoor performance and gathering space. The plaza links Bryan Center, a hub of student activity, with the main residential quad on West campus.

The Annual Events Committee on campus is committed to creating large-scale campus-wide events such as cocktail parties and scavenger hunts. Some events are traditional, such as the popular Springternational, which is an international cultural festival with food, music, and performances. Joe College Day is another one-day festival that brings food, arts and crafts, tie-dying, and music to campus.

Greek life is a major part of Duke's social scene, with 29 percent of men and 42 percent of women participating in one of 25 fraternities and sororities on campus. Fraternity parties are often open to non-members. "Frat parties are most commonly frequented by underclassmen," one student comments. Every fall, fraternity and sorority members celebrate Greek Weekend with events like a freshman BBQ, trivia competition, and Gala at the Gardens.

The Blue Devils have won 12 national titles, including four by the men's basketball team. "Basketball is nothing short of a religion here," explains a student. Fans are often referred to as Cameron Crazies, an apt moniker considering how they queue up hours or even overnight before games, and, most famously "tenting" for the University of North Carolina Chapel Hill game up to three months ahead of time. Tenting means students camp outside of Cameron Indoor Stadium in Kryzewskiville. Those who aren't competing in Division I sports (even if they're probably cheering them on) can choose from 35 club sports and nearly as many intramural options.

Durham has restaurants and bars, but Raleigh and Chapel Hill, each about 30 minutes away, provide more options for off-campus outings. "For the most part, everything we need is on campus," says a student.

Freshmen, sophomores, and juniors are required to live on campus. First-year students live in the dorms on East Campus, while upperclassmen live on West and Central campus. There are 11 Select Living Groups for students wanting self-selecting living arrangements that are similar to Greek houses but generally co-ed.

Student Body

Students say that they "have the perfect balance," that they are focused on their academic and career goals but know how to let loose too. They describe themselves as "more laid-back" than students at the Ivies and other top-rated schools—it helps that there is such a strong school spirit, a lot of it surrounding basketball.

There is very high ethnic diversity at Duke, with 39 percent minority students. Geographic diversity is also high, with 90 percent of students hailing from out of state. "You will meet every kind of person from every kind of background here," notes a student.

You May Not Know

- Duke started as Brown's School in 1838. The current name honors Washington Duke, the father of James Buchanan Duke, a tobacco company founder, who donated $40 million to establish the endowment for the university in 1924.

- The Blue Devils are named after an elite World War I French military unit that received global attention during WWI and its aftermath. The French fighters wore blue caps and blue berets as part of their uniforms.

- The Duke Lemur Center houses more than 200 lemurs and according to the university is the "world's largest sanctuary for rare and endangered prosimian primates."

Distinguished Alumni

Elizabeth Dole, United States Senator; Melinda French Gates, co-founder of the Bill and Melinda Gates Foundation; Sean McManus, President of CBS News and Sports; William Styron, Pulitzer-prize winning author.

Admissions and Financial Aid

Duke's admissions office says the school looks for "multi-faceted, multi-talented" students and chooses each year's student body as a whole by looking at both academic and personal factors. The six main factors that Duke considers are the academic program rigor, academic performance, letter of recommendation, extracurricular activities/personal qualities, the personal statement, and test scores. Artistic materials and interviews are optional.

Admission to Duke is need-blind, so students are admitted regardless of their families' ability to pay, and 100 percent of demonstrated financial need is met for four years. About 45 percent of undergrads receive need-based aid. Families with incomes less than $60,000 are not required to have parental contributions and those

DUKE UNIVERSITY

Highlights

Admissions Criteria
Academic criteria:
Grades: ☆ ☆ ☆
Difficulty of class schedule: ☆ ☆ ☆
Class rank: ☆ ☆ ☆
Standardized test scores: ☆ ☆ ☆
Teacher recommendations: ☆ ☆ ☆
Personal statement: ☆ ☆ ☆
Non-academic criteria considered:
Interview
Extracurricular activities
Special talents, interests, abilities
Character/personal qualities
Volunteer work
Work experience
Geographical location
Religious affiliation/commitment
Minority affiliation
Alumni relationship

Deadlines
Early Action: No
Early Decision: November 1
Regular Action: January 2 (final)
Common Application: Accepted

Financial Aid
In-state tuition: $44,020
Out-of-state tuition: $44,020
Room: $7,240
Board: $5,662
Books: $1,300
Freshmen receiving need-based aid: 48%
Undergrads rec. need-based aid: 45%
Avg. % of need met by financial aid: 100%
Avg. aid package (freshmen): $40,561
Avg. aid package (undergrads): $40,821
Avg. debt upon graduation: $21,713

School Spirit
Mascot: Blue Devils
Colors: Blue and white
Song: *Fight Blue Devils*

253

with income less than $40,000 will not have loans. There are also a limited number of merit scholarships endowed by individuals, foundations, and corporations for which any and every applicant is considered. The most prestigious is the A.B. Duke Scholarship, which uses a rigorous selection process that includes inviting 45 finalists from around the world for a three-day visit, including an interview. There are also awards for arts, athletics, and ROTC.

EARLHAM COLLEGE

Overview

Tucked away in the small city of Richmond, Indiana, about 75 miles east of Indianapolis, is the verdant 800-acre campus of Earlham College. The main quad is called the "Heart" and is in the center of a number of brick buildings. Most of campus is forested, including a "back campus" used for research and as the site for the Hash, an all-seasons weekly running group prominent on campus.

This private liberal arts college of 1,200 undergraduates is often compared to other top small schools of the Midwest. The school's Quaker heritage has a strong influence on campus culture, where people address each other on a first-name basis (no "doctor" or "professor" needed) in support of equality. The athletic mascot and a minor in Quaker Studies also hint at the religious affiliations of those who founded Earlham in 1847. Earlham has a dry campus policy (though some students call the reality "pleasantly moist") and no Greek system. However, students interested in a strong liberal arts education in Indiana will have access to personalized attention from professors, plus research opportunities at Earlham and, through the study-abroad and May Term programs, around the world.

Academics

Earlham offers more than 40 programs and courses and even a minor in Quaker Studies. While primarily an undergraduate college, there are also two graduate programs: an MA in teaching and MA of education for students who plan to become licensed educators. Students can also take courses at the Earlham School of Religion and Bethany Theological Seminary. Strong programs include psychology, English, and biology.

Earlham's General Education Requirements begin with three first-year courses, including an interactive seminar class. Other courses must cover analytical reasoning, scientific inquiry, perspectives on diversity, arts, and wellness.

Students say that academics at Earlham are challenging. But professors are very accessible, thanks in part to the small student body. "All of my professors have been very helpful, incredibly knowledgeable, and easy to find outside of class. I've had coffee with three of my professors already," says a student.

Students and faculty can conduct research with the help of Ford/Knight grants that promote collaboration in research and scholarship. Past Ford/Knight projects have included biology research on tropical spider diversity and research on Toni Morrison in the humanities. Those who are eager to add a strong self-directed learning component to their education can teach Student-Designed and Initiated Courses, which are capped at 12 people. Another academic elective is May Term, a period following spring semester when some Earlham faculty offer intensive courses designed to be experimental. Several May Term courses are held off campus or include an off-campus component; past destinations included Mexico, Senegal, and the Galapagos. There are four $2,500 Julian Neil Hawkins May Term Scholarships awarded to support travel during this special term.

Almost two-thirds of students participate in a study-abroad program for a semester, which takes them to countries such as Tanzania, Japan, and New Zealand. There are also year-long programs in China, Japan, and Senegal. "Study abroad is really popular. With so few students, it's a nice way to expand our horizons," says a student.

Earlham ranks eighth in the nation for graduates receive Ph.D.'s in biological sciences, and 26th in the nation for Ph.D.'s in all fields. The Bonner Center for Service and Vocation helps students with vocational planning, service opportunities, internship and job searches, and one-on-one consultations.

EARLHAM COLLEGE

Four-year private
Founded: 1847
Richmond, IN
Large town
Pop. 36,670

Address:
801 National Road
West
Richmond, IN
47374

Admissions:
765-983-1600

Financial Aid:
765-983-1217

admission@earlham.
edu

www.earlham.edu

EARLHAM COLLEGE

Students
Total enrollment: 1,211
Undergrads: 1,087
Freshmen: 300
Part-time students: 2%
From out-of-state: 67%
From public schools: 66%
Male/Female: 44%/56%
Live on-campus: 96%
Off-campus employment rating: Good
Caucasian: 45%
African American: 9%
Hispanic: 6%
Asian / Pacific Islander: 2%
Native American: 1%
Mixed (2+ ethnicities): 2%
International: 18%

Academics
Calendar: Semester
Student/faculty ratio: 10:1
Class size 9 or fewer: 37%
Class size 10-29: 52%
Class size 30-49: 8%
Class size 50-99: 3%
Class size 100 or more: -
Returning freshmen: 94%
Six-year graduation rate: 72%
Graduates who immediately go to graduate school: 25%

Most Popular Majors
Psychology
Biology
Interdisciplinary

Admissions
Applicants: 1,408
Accepted: 1,055
Acceptance rate: 74.9%
Placed on wait list: 37
Enrolled from wait list: 13
Average GPA: 3.4
ACT range: 23-30
SAT Math range: 530-660
SAT Reading range: 550-700
SAT Writing range: 7-39
Top 10% of class: 30%
Top 25% of class: 61%
Top 50% of class: 93%

Student Life

There are more than 70 student-run organizations on campus, including the student-managed public radio station WECI. You'll find classes on New Testament Greek at Earlham, but no Greek organizations. The Runyan Center is Earlham's student center and offers a space to hang out, rent movies, and watch cable television.

While Earlham's campus is technically "dry," i.e., alcohol free, the campus group Point Oh Eight advocates responsible alcohol use and acknowledges the reality that some students drink on campus. "There is alcohol on campus," admits one student, "but it's not crazy like at other schools. And there's no pressure to drink."

Earlham's student-led Hash House Harriers running group was founded in 1989 and is loosely connected with the noncompeting running and drinking clubs by the same name. The Earlham student group, known as "The Hash," maintains weekly runs that take place on the "back campus" during all seasons. Other popular events include Sunsplash, which brings free food, games, and live music at Beane Stadium to campus. Springfest turns Earlham into a festival ground complete with slip and slide, bouncy castles, popcorn stands, music, arts and crafts sales, and more.

The college's 16 varsity teams (eight men's, eight women's) compete in Division III, with the soccer teams being the most competitive. Earlham students may participate in any of six club sports, including rugby and horse riding. The Athletics and Wellness Center has an indoor running track and climbing wall, a pool, tennis courts, and gymnasium that seats 1,800.

Richmond, a city of about 37,000, offers low-key dining and recreation for students. On Saturday nights, the Richmond shuttle takes students to different locations around town: movies, restaurants, groceries, and the coffeehouse. For bigger city entertainment, students may road trip to Indianapolis or Cincinnati. The Student Activities office also plans weekend day trips to Indianapolis Mall, Pacers Games, King's Island amusement park, and more. "It's a necessity to get out of Richmond every once and a while," confides a student. "Fortunately, it's easy to do so."

Freshmen are guaranteed housing, while upperclassmen obtain housing through a lottery system. Most students live on campus in eight residence halls and 28 theme and friendship houses with topics ranging from interfaith to vegetarian to literary arts.

Student Body

Earlham's Quaker heritage influences much of the campus culture. Students are generally laid back and run on "Earlham Time," which is indicative of the relaxed atmosphere. Being laid back doesn't translate into slacking off though; students tend to be academically focused.

There is high ethnic diversity, with minority students making up 20 percent of the student body. Geographic diversity is in the moderate range, with 67 percent of students hailing from outside Indiana. A large international student population makes up 18 percent of the student body.

You May Not Know

- One of Earlham's fight songs goes like this: "Fight, fight, inner light! Kill, Quakers, kill! Beat 'em, kick 'em, knock 'em senseless! Do we really have consensus?"
- Students at Earlham can study aardvarks in the Kakamega Forest.
- The Joseph Moore Museum is a student- and faculty-managed natural history museum; the museum showcases Indiana's natural history.

Distinguished Alumni

Gertrude Bonin, writer and Native American activist; Liza Donelly, cartoonist whose work has been featured in *The New Yorker*; Michael C. Hall, star of the Showtime series *Dexter*; Frances Moore Lappe, author of *Diet for a Small Planet*.

Admissions and Financial Aid

Earlham notes that there is no "strict formula to compute a student's acceptance." Two admissions counselors read each application. Important aspects include high school coursework and achievements, opinions of teachers/guidance counselors, and other factors such as jobs, awards, and activities. Interviews are encouraged and are requested of students who visit campus.

Merit scholarships include the Presidential Honors Scholarship, the Bonner Scholarship giving distinction to volunteer service, the achievement based Cunningham Cultural Scholarship, and Carleton B. Edwards Chemistry Scholarship. There are also two scholarships specifically for Quaker students: the Quaker Fellows Scholarship and the Wilkinson Award. Quaker Fellows commit to weekly programming and receive $5,000 per year. Earlham awards more than $20 million in aid each year, a figure that includes grants, scholarships, campus employment, and loans.

EARLHAM COLLEGE

Highlights

Admissions Criteria
Academic criteria:
Grades: ☆ ☆ ☆
Difficulty of class schedule: ☆ ☆ ☆
Class rank: ☆ ☆ ☆
Standardized test scores: N/A
Teacher recommendations: ☆ ☆
Personal statement: ☆ ☆
Non-academic criteria considered:
Interview
Extracurricular activities
Special talents, interests, abilities
Character/personal qualities
Volunteer work
Work experience
Alumni relationship

Deadlines
Early Action: December 1
Early Decision: December 1
Regular Action: January 1 (priority)
February 1 (final)
Notification of admission by: March 1
Common Application: Accepted

Financial Aid
In-state tuition: $40,600
Out-of-state tuition: $40,600
Room: $4,190
Board: $4,070
Books: $1,000
Freshmen receiving need-based aid: 62%
Undergrads rec. need-based aid: 61%
Avg. % of need met by financial aid: 96%
Avg. aid package (freshmen): $39,734
Avg. aid package (undergrads): $33,818
Avg. debt upon graduation: $24,018

School Spirit
Mascot: Quakers
Colors: Maroon and white

ECKERD COLLEGE

ECKERD COLLEGE

Four-year private
Founded: 1958
St. Petersburg, FL
Medium city
Pop. 244,997

Address:
4200 54th Avenue
South
St. Petersburg, FL
33711

Admissions:
727-864-8331

Financial Aid:
727-864-8334

admissions@eckerd.
edu

www.eckerd.edu

Overview

A huge part of the appeal of private liberal arts college Eckerd College can be summed up in one word: location. The 188-acre campus on Frenchman's Creek and Boca Ciega Bay in St. Petersburg, Florida is close to Gulf of Mexico beaches, and it boasts an average temperature of 74 degrees, a plethora of water sports, hammocks to lounge in, and—not surprisingly—a laid-back atmosphere. Even the college's mascot, the Triton, celebrates the aquatic environment, as do the glass and external views available from many buildings on campus. Wildlife may be viewed including dolphins, pelicans, and alligators.

Life at Eckerd isn't all beach resort bumming around: academics can be rigorous, especially in the strongest programs of marine sciences and international studies. Though it is a fairly young college founded in 1958, Eckerd has distinguished itself by pioneering the 4-1-4 calendar and offering strong study-abroad programs for its one-month intensive term and throughout the school year. Indeed, as gorgeous as campus may be, about half of the school's students have traveled overseas by the time they graduate.

The almost 1,900 students at Eckerd hail from all over the U.S. and 35 countries, though ethnic diversity remains low. Students with a love of the environment and sustainability will fit in well on a campus where it's typical to see students getting to class or the campus pub on free, communal yellow bikes, part of the nationally recognized Yellow Bike program. Students with a love of sea, sun, and surf will want to apply as early as possible.

Academics

There are 38 majors at Eckerd that lead to BA or BS degrees, and students can design their own interdisciplinary concentrations. The "four-year, interdisciplinary, values oriented" general education curriculum is required for all students. General Education includes Western Heritage in a Global Context, a two-course sequence that all freshmen take; College Program Series events required for freshmen and sophomores; Environmental and Global Perspective courses; and the senior-level Quest for Meaning course.

Strong academic programs include environmental science, international business, international relations and global affairs, marine science, writing workshop (the creative writing program), and the interdisciplinary concentration of organizational studies. Eckerd students praise their professors' teaching—faculty members, not grad students or TAs, teach courses. This facilitates close relationships between students and professors since each student has a faculty mentor, and students can even share a soda or pitcher of beer with their professors while discussing classes—or other topics—through the distinctive Pitchers with Professors program. "It's just more personal when you can have an informal drink with your professor," says a student.

As the first college to have the 4-1-4 schedule, with a one-month term for special projects and studying abroad, Eckerd has distinguished itself as a forerunner in special programs. Sea Semester gives students a chance to study oceanography, nautical science, and maritime studies in Woods Hole, Massachusetts for six weeks—the shore component—followed by six weeks of practical laboratory experience at sea. Eckerd College Search and Rescue is the only program of its kind in the U.S. and responds to more than 500 calls a year. "Our location enables us to have some very unique learning opportunities," comments a student. The Academy of Senior Professionals (ASPEC) is a group that interacts regularly with Eckerd College students and faculty as mentors, colleagues, and friends; ASPEC's ranks include Nobel Prize winner Elie Wiesel.

Almost half of all Eckerd graduates have studied abroad by the time of graduation. In 2003, the *Chronicle of Higher Education* named Eckerd the top baccalaureate institute in the United States for highest percentage of undergrads that study abroad. One student notes, "I wanted to attend a college where studying abroad is almost required." There are semester, year-long, and winter term opportunities, as well as the newest "spring-into-summer" model, where students take a class spring semester that prepares them for travel that begins at the end of the semester. Eckerd's London Study Center has hosted over 1,500 students since 1970. Other opportunities include internships through International Practicum and studying international organizations in New York and Geneva.

According to Eckerd, more than 40 percent of each graduating class goes on to pursue advanced degrees and the college is "among the nation's leaders in the percentage of its graduates who earn doctoral degrees." The Office of Career Resources found that 33 percent of recent graduates found a job within one month of graduation and 69 percent are employed full time.

Student Life

Eckerd has about 40 student arts and entertainment, pre-professional, media, religious, multicultural, service, and political groups. There are also nearly two dozen athletic clubs, from bowling to things you won't find in more land-locked colleges, such as surfing, kiteboarding, and wakeboarding, as well as water-ski clubs. Keep in mind that students don't have to join clubs to take advantage of free boats and kayaks, sailing and windsurfing lessons, and private waterfront. It's all right there. "There's nothing like heading out to sail every day after class," says a student.

The alcohol policy doesn't allow kegs on campus or alcohol at college events, but there is a bar on campus, the Triton Pub, with a grill and deli. There are no Greek organizations. Still, this doesn't prevent students from partying. "The nickname Camp Eckerd was given to us because of the amount of partying we do," one student notes.

With about 80 percent of students living on campus, there are plenty of social activities. One of the longest running traditions on campus is the annual Kappa Karnival, a waterfront celebration of the end of each year. It features games, food, music, and giveaways. Another annual event has a more serious theme: the Festival of Hope, which is the closing celebration of the senior class' Quest for Meaning Project. Upon completing service learning projects through the Tampa Bay Community during fall semester, seniors present their projects and reflections to the community. According to Eckerd, students have contributed 70,000 hours of service through this program. To showcase Eckerd's strong international programs, the annual Festival of Cultures celebrates the food, music, dress, and history of countries around the world.

There is no football team at Eckerd, though the volleyball teams have had recent successes, along with the men's lacrosse team. There are 11 Division II teams. An outdoor swimming pool next to the new 7,500-square foot gymnasium (built in 2008) is open to all students. "Our equipment is on par with some of the best gyms," comments a student.

ECKERD COLLEGE

Highlights

Students
Total enrollment: 1,893
Undergrads: 1,893
Freshmen: 589
Part-time students: 2%
From out-of-state: 81%
From public schools: 75%
Male/Female: 41%/59%
Live on-campus: 81%
Off-campus employment rating: Good
Caucasian: 79%
African American: 3%
Hispanic: 8%
Asian / Pacific Islander: 2%
Native American: 0%
Mixed (2+ ethnicities): 3%
International: 5%

Academics
Calendar: 4-1-4 system
Student/faculty ratio: 13:1
Class size 9 or fewer: 10%
Class size 10-29: 81%
Class size 30-49: 8%
Class size 50-99: 1%
Class size 100 or more: -
Returning freshmen: 81%
Six-year graduation rate: 60%

Most Popular Majors
Marine science
Environmental studies
International business

Admissions
Applicants: 3,910
Accepted: 2,776
Acceptance rate: 71.0%
Placed on wait list: 111
Enrolled from wait list: 34
Average GPA: 3.3
ACT range: 23-28
SAT Math range: 500-610
SAT Reading range: 510-620
SAT Writing range: Not reported

ECKERD COLLEGE

Admissions Criteria

Academic criteria:
Grades: ☆ ☆ ☆
Difficulty of class schedule: ☆ ☆ ☆
Class rank: ☆
Standardized test scores: ☆ ☆
Teacher recommendations: ☆ ☆
Personal statement: ☆ ☆
Non-academic criteria considered:
Interview
Extracurricular activities
Special talents, interests, abilities
Character/personal qualities
Volunteer work
Work experience
State of residency
Alumni relationship

Deadlines

Early Action: November 15
Early Decision: No
Regular Action: Rolling admissions
Common Application: Accepted

Financial Aid

In-state tuition: $37,046
Out-of-state tuition: $37,046
Room: $5,106
Board: $5,038
Books: $1,200
Freshmen receiving need-based aid: 66%
Undergrads rec. need-based aid: 59%
Avg. % of need met by financial aid: 86%
Avg. aid package (freshmen): $29,923
Avg. aid package (undergrads): $26,201
Avg. debt upon graduation: $33,957

School Spirit

Mascot: Triton
Colors: Teal, black, navy, and white

Off campus, the Saturday Morning Market in downtown St. Petersburg, the largest market in Florida, is a delicious way to spend a weekday morning. Nearby BayWalk has 150,000 square feet of shopping, restaurants, and a movie theatre. Students also frequent the bars and clubs of Ybor City. To top it all off, Disney World is less than two hours away. "You have to visit Disney World at least once while you're here," says a student.

Residences at Eckerd house over 1,800 students and range from air-conditioned dorms to apartment suites with stunning views of the Boca Ciega Bay. All residence halls are smoke-free. The newest residences are four interconnected houses in the Iota Complex, which includes a Health and Wellness House and an all-female house. Dorms have air conditioning and views of the water. As a pet-friendly campus, Eckerd students live with over 300 pets: the pet photo gallery shows puppies, kittens, turtles, ducklings, bunnies, and more.

Student Body

Eckerd's students are known to be "politically more liberal," and many are "passionate about environmental and sustainability issues." There is strong geographic diversity with 81 percent of students from out of state, though ethnic diversity is moderate: 16 percent are minority students. "It's very homogenous here and it would be nice to have more diversity," comments one student.

You May Not Know

- According to the college it was founded to "accommodate returning GIs eager to earn a college education." The first classes were held in 1960 with 155 first-year students.
- The namesake of the college is Jack M. Eckerd, who founded the Eckerd drugstore chain.
- There are 15 hammocks on campus for studying or just enjoying the sunshine.

Distinguished Alumni

Dorothy Allison, writer; Dennis Lehane, award-winning novelist; Brian Sabean, General Manager of the San Francisco Giants.

Admissions and Financial Aid

Eckerd has rolling admissions, so students should apply as early as possible. Applications are reviewed in October and a decision is made within four weeks. While most students begin in the fall, it is also possible to start in January for the intensive one-month mini-term. Application requirements for first-year applicants are straight-forward and include a letter of recommendation, personal essay, application (either Eckerd's or the Common Application), and SAT/ACT scores.

Merit-based academic achievement scholarships are available to all students who qualify and are based on high school GPA and test scores. All admitted students are considered for these awards. In addition, Artistic Achievement Awards are offered, which require a separate application. Athletic aid is also available.

ELON UNIVERSITY

ELON UNIVERSITY

Four-year private
Founded: 1889
Elon, NC
Large town
Pop. 9,516

Address:
2700 Campus Box
Elon, NC
27244

Admissions:
336-278-3566

Financial Aid:
336-278-7640

admissions@elon.edu

www.elon.edu

Overview

A private, mid-sized liberal arts school in North Carolina, Elon University sits in a small town that is geographically situated between mountains and beaches. Many students can call Elon home because they barely have to leave their front lawns to reach campus: in other words, about 18 percent of the student body is from North Carolina. Just over two decades ago, the great majority of Elon students were residents of the state, but the university has been striving to diversify in recent years.

The Elon campus itself contains nearly 600 acres of oak trees, lakes, fountains, and brick paving. Despite Elon's less diverse population and rather rural location, these students are not "hicks out in the sticks." Boasting a low ratio of committed student to committed faculty, as well as a national reputation for spirited public service, Elon students are active and involved.

Furthermore, with a less than 30-minute drive, students can escape the sleepy college town to the more nocturnal Greensboro. And larger universities like Duke and Chapel Hill are less than an hour away. Considering Elon's overwhelmingly female gender ratio and colonial-style red brick architecture, Elon students could be appropriately described as the "chicks from the bricks."

Academics

What Elon loses in small school isolation, it wins back in the administration's commitment to "a close relationship between student and faculty." More than half of all classes contain fewer than 20 students. Professors are very "hands-on" and "focused on teaching," say students. Over 250 students conduct undergraduate research under the mentorship of faculty.

First-year Elon students must complete The Core, which includes four courses, as well as the Experiential Learning Requirement, which can consist of study abroad, internships, or community service. The general education requirements include courses in expression (literature, philosophy, or fine arts), civilization (history, foreign languages, or religion), society (economics, geography, political science, psychology, or sociology/anthropology), and science (mathematics, science, and computer science). Students must also either pass an exam or take courses in foreign language. The requirements are "better than at other colleges because of the choices involved," remarks a student. There are 71 majors offered, and ambitious students may even design their own independent majors. Some of Elon's strongest programs are biology, business administration, communications, and education. The communications department is nationally recognized and is recognized as one of 18 private colleges and universities that has an accredited program. Students are blessed with "professional-level video editing suites, a recording studio, a film screening room, and top-of-the-line equipment," says a student.

Through the Honors Program, students have access to a $10,000 Honors Scholarship, peer mentors, Honors housing, and grants for thesis research and study abroad. "There are huge benefits to joining the Honors Program," says a participant. In addition to the general Honors Program for students of any major, there are also Elon College Fellows for students in the arts and humanities, as well as social sciences; natural and mathematical sciences; Business Fellows; Communications Fellows; Teaching Fellows; Isabella Cannon Leadership Fellows; and International Fellows. Students must complete an application for these programs.

Opportunities for research are available through the Undergraduate Research Program. Students may present their results through the Spring University Research Forum (SURF) or work with faculty mentors during the Summer Undergraduate Research Experience (SURE). Research and travel grants are awarded.

ELON UNIVERSITY

Students

Total enrollment: 6,029
Undergrads: 5,357
Freshmen: 1,495
Part-time students: 3%
From out-of-state: 82%
From public schools: 68%
Male/Female: 41%/59%
Live on-campus: 60%
In fraternities: 22%
In sororities: 38%
Off-campus employment rating: Fair
Caucasian: 82%
African American: 6%
Hispanic: 4%
Asian / Pacific Islander: 2%
Native American: 0%
Mixed (2+ ethnicities): 1%
International: 2%

Academics

Calendar: 4-1-4 system
Student/faculty ratio: 13:1
Class size 9 or fewer: 7%
Class size 10-29: 76%
Class size 30-49: 16%
Class size 50-99: -
Class size 100 or more: -
Returning freshmen: 90%
Six-year graduation rate: 83%
Graduates who immediately go to graduate school: 15%
Graduates who immediately enter career related to major: 77%

Most Popular Majors

Strategic communications
Marketing
Finance

Admissions

Applicants: 10,241
Accepted: 5,293
Acceptance rate: 51.7%
Placed on wait list: 3,297
Enrolled from wait list: 41
Average GPA: 4.0
ACT range: 25-29
SAT Math range: 560-660
SAT Reading range: 570-660
SAT Writing range: 14-50
Top 10% of class: 26%
Top 25% of class: 65%
Top 50% of class: 91%

Elon's academic calendar encompasses two four-month semesters with an intermediary one-month term in January. During the winter term, many students study abroad. Recent options have included studying jungle service in Costa Rica, ecotourism in Australia, or "paths for China's modernization" in the Flying Dragon course. As such, it's not surprising that according to the college, "Elon is #1 in the country among master's-level institutions for the number of students who study abroad." "It's almost a given that you'll study abroad," notes a student, "and it's the best use of the winter term." Students can take a semester or two with programs located in nearly 50 different countries.

Apparently, the accessibility and engagement of faculty members pays off as evidenced by Elon's alumni: 15 percent pursue a graduate degree within one year of completing their bachelors degrees. Among those who seek employment post-graduation, approximately 77 percent of alumni secure a job in a related field within one year, perhaps due in part to the fact that 80 percent of students complete internships during their time in school.

Student Life

Elon proudly maintains 150 student groups ranging in type from 26 honors societies to ethnic clubs, and from political groups to philanthropy organizations. Impressively, Elon is ranked among the top three universities nationwide for its community service. One third of students take on leadership roles in one or more student organizations or programs. "We are heavily involved," says a student.

The Student Union Board hosts Midnight Meals on Thursday nights, complete with movie screenings, karaoke, and game show nights. There are also comedy shows and concerts ranging from Gavin DeGraw to Girl Talk. The administration organizes College Coffee on Tuesday mornings, a time for students and faculty to share in "refreshments and fellowship." Other notable campus hang-outs include Lighthouse Tavern, which offers pool tables and live performances, as well as The Zone, which is buzzworthy for its tasty Irazú coffee. Students are encouraged to outsource their school pride through Discover NC, a school-sponsored opportunity to visit North Carolina hotspots—such as the State Fair and Asheboro Zoo—and attend a Panther's Football Game.

Greek society welcomes 22 percent of male and 38 percent of female students and "dominates" the party, if not the entire social scene, on campus. Consisting of 12 social fraternities and 12 social sororities, Elon Greeks permeate the school's greater population with their school spirit. In fact, prospective Greek students arrive one week early for spring semester in order to attend the rush events of Greek Week.

For students seeking a more athletic role on campus, Elon has 16 Division I sports. In terms of athletic performance, Elon ranks with fellow private, mid-sized liberal arts institutions. In terms of athletic enthusiasm, the university *is* in the South, so we can understand if its bark is bigger than its bite. The college claims that tailgating in the Rhodes Stadium parking lot is "rapidly becoming a school tradition." What this really means is that Elon students are "super-fanatical" about supporting athletics. For those students who are not satisfied with the sidelines, Elon also hosts nearly 40 intramural and club sports. As for the weekends, if students should choose to pass on the parties in favor of more low-key relaxation, they can take a road trip to the beach or spend an afternoon at the mall.

Housing options at Elon span from single apartments and flats to typical double rooms in dormitories. Students can also choose to live in one of six learning communities, which include four modern languages as well as Business and Sustainability. Of course, we must not forget Elon's 16 Greek houses. All freshmen live on campus.

Student Body

Despite its ongoing campaign for demographic diversity, Elon remains a rather homogeneous student body with only 13 percent minority students and less than one-fifth North Carolinians; another one fifth of students hail from either New Jersey or Massachusetts. The university has managed to attract and enroll students from 49 nations and 47 states.

Students say that most tend to be "upper middle class." One student comments, "We have a reputation of having a lot of rich white girls, and it's not entirely unfounded." Students say the campus is fashion-focused, and it's typical for women to "wear full makeup, even at the gym."

Elon's religious affiliation spans back to its founding in 1889 by the United Church of Christ. Despite this continued presence, the university professes an open and affirming policy toward other religious communities. For example, the Hillel center on campus reaches out to the Jewish community, which consists of a couple hundred students each year.

You May Not Know

- Just what is the origin of the "Phoenix" mascot? In 1923, much of the campus was destroyed by a fire; rebuilding began immediately.
- Until 1999, Elon's mascot was the "Fightin' Christians."
- Elon has been designated as a botanical garden.

Distinguished Alumni

Kerrii Anderson, former Chief Executive Officer and President of Wendy's International Inc.; Rich Blomquist, writer on *The Daily Show*; Ward Burton, NASCAR auto racer; Isabella Cannon, first female mayor of Raleigh, NC; Terrell Hudges, Dallas Cowboys wide receiver; Deborah Yow, Athletics Director, University of Maryland.

Admissions and Financial Aid

Considered a "best buy" college by the *Kiplinger's* guide, students pay a yearly tuition that is about half that of the average big-name private liberal arts school. However, Elon wants to break away from its reputation as a "bargain school attended by students in designer fashions." The student body is pooled from the top half of their respective secondary schools.

Eighteen percent of freshmen receive merit-based grants, a testament to the university's efforts to bring in the top scholars. The university offers six Fellows programs developed to entice the overachievers with such privileges as special courses, tutoring, study-abroad grants, and scholarships.

ELON UNIVERSITY

Highlights

Admissions Criteria
Academic criteria:
Grades: ☆ ☆ ☆
Difficulty of class schedule: ☆ ☆ ☆
Class rank: ☆
Standardized test scores: ☆ ☆ ☆
Teacher recommendations: ☆ ☆
Personal statement: ☆ ☆
Non-academic criteria considered:
Extracurricular activities
Special talents, interests, abilities
Character/personal qualities
Volunteer work
Work experience
Geographical location
Minority affiliation
Alumni relationship

Deadlines
Early Action: November 10
Early Decision: November 1
Regular Action: November 10 (priority)
January 10 (final)
Notification of admission by: March 15
Common Application: Not accepted

Financial Aid
In-state tuition: $29,750
Out-of-state tuition: $29,750
Room: $4,953
Board: $4,944
Books: $900
Freshmen receiving need-based aid: 35%
Undergrads rec. need-based aid: 35%
Avg. % of need met by financial aid: 63%
Avg. aid package (freshmen): $16,094
Avg. aid package (undergrads): $17,378
Avg. debt upon graduation: $28,183

School Spirit
Mascot: Phoenix
Colors: Maroon and gold

263

EMERSON COLLEGE

Overview

Emerson College sits in the center of Boston, bordering the Boston Common, theatre district, and Chinatown. Founded in 1880, the college is a unique private liberal arts school focusing on communication and the arts. The setting is undeniably urban, and campus looks the part, with modern glass and sleek metal structures. Those who are confident that an arts or communication discipline is their true pursuit will fit right in.

The college is within walking distance of many Boston landmarks, including the Massachusetts State House, Freedom Trail, restaurants, and museums. However, the Emerson campus isn't confined to Boston proper; there are also centers in Washington, DC and Los Angeles. While Boston is an exceptional and exciting location to go to school, the price of urban living isn't cheap. Also keep in mind that the winters are wickedly bitter and the summers are muggy.

Academics

There are 65 majors at Emerson and approximately 700 courses offered each semester. Unlike other colleges with a similar arts focus, Emerson is not a conservatory, but provides both pre-professional training in communication and the arts and a liberal arts education. All students are required to complete the general education curriculum, and the courses are grouped into three requirement areas. Foundations coursework includes written communication, oral communication, and quantitative reasoning; Perspectives coursework covers aesthetics, ethics and values, historical, interdisciplinary, literary, scientific and social and psychological; and, Global and U.S. Diversity coursework encompasses global diversity, U.S. Diversity, and world languages.

In particular, the standout programs are communication sciences and disorders, communication studies, journalism, marketing communication, performing arts, visual and media arts, and writing, literature, and publishing. The facilities, labs, and studios at Emerson are professional and technologically advanced; audio post-production, costume shops, hearing and speech therapy centers, editing suites, professional television studios, sound stage, film screening rooms, digital newsroom, theatre design, four theatres including the Majestic and Paramount theatres, and much more are the reasons that Emerson is a special place for professional artistic development. "Our facilities are ultra-modern and at the professional level," says a student.

In addition to having the right equipment, students also have the right teachers. Scholarly-type professors and real-world arts professionals at the top of their discipline teach at Emerson. "The professors don't just teach, they do things in their field," comments a student. Virtually all classes have 50 or fewer students.

On the main Emerson campus in Boston, a unique, hands-on minor program called the Emerson experience in entrepreneurship (E3) turns students into savvy entrepreneurs with a business plan. The annual E3 exposition is a chance for students to present their business ideas and marketing platforms. About 35 percent of ventures presented at E3 have become a reality since the program's inception in 2005.

Study abroad is easy since the campus maintains a castle in the Netherlands where students take classes, eat, and live and then take excursions to other European cities. Other study-abroad options are in Prague for film studies and Taiwan for language, marketing, and other liberal arts. Domestically, Emerson maintains a campus in Los Angeles where students hold internships in the entertainment industry and take courses, a "perfect entrée into a hard-to-break-into field," says a student. A program is also available in DC where students spend a fall semester taking courses and interning at nonprofits and social advocacy groups.

With 28,000 alumni worldwide and many Emerson graduates making headlines and receiving awards at the top of their artistic fields, there's a great network of contacts for graduates. The career services center helps with employment resources, mock interview preparation, and speed-networking events.

Student Life

In many respects, student life at Emerson is not the typical college experience. The fraternity and sorority scene is "small" to virtually "nonexistent" (seven organizations) in the eyes of most students. Sure, there are varsity sports, but almost no one plays them; and, there are no lush lawns where students sprawl in the sun or play frisbee between classes. Instead, students have the city as a part of their campus experience: public sidewalks, urban streets, and Boston Common. Living in the middle of a metropolis, much of the social life takes place in coffeeshops, local bars, clubs, and off-campus student apartments. The Cutler Majestic Theatre on campus shows student and professional dance, music, theater, and opera that draws students as well as crowds from Boston.

Student clubs and annual events are what make the campus coherent, and they do, of course, evolve around communications and the performing arts. Sixty student organizations exist on campus, including the likes of comedy and stand-up, children's theatre, dance, and choreography. Community service, sexual health and wellness outreach, and peace and justice clubs, have an advocacy presence as well. Professional organizations also give students a chance to make contacts and participate in the community of their discipline. WERS-FM, the oldest national noncommercial radio station located at Emerson, is student-run. "Everyone is involved in something. We're a motivated group," notes a student.

Campus events include the annual Emerson Recognition and Achievement (ERA) celebration, which applauds those on campus who have made outstanding contributions to the community. The EVVYs is an award show that recognizes excellent student work, and creative and arts professionals are the judges. This is no small affair—the dress is gowns and suits—and acceptance speeches are made. The EVVYs are the largest student award show in the country. "It's our version of the Oscars," remarks one student.

Last, and perhaps least, Emerson teams are known as the "lions," but they don't really have a loud roar. It's not uncommon to attend Emerson and not know there are Division III varsity and intramural sports teams; but for those who are interested the basics like basketball, soccer, baseball, and volleyball do exist. "We're so involved in everything else we don't have much time to support athletics," says a student.

Freshmen are guaranteed housing but aren't required to live on campus, and half of all upperclass students live off campus. Off-campus housing is plentiful in Boston, even if pricey. For those who decide that the dorm experience is a good way to transition into college and the city, there are four residence halls with rooms that range from singles to six-person suites. Residence learning communities are available where those with common interests live together. Those students in learning communities are housed on specific floors or room groupings in the residence halls, and include Digital Culture, Living Green, Performing Cultures, Wellness, and Writers' Block.

EMERSON COLLEGE

Highlights

Students
Total enrollment: 4,513
Undergrads: 3,675
Freshmen: 866
From out-of-state: 81%
From public schools: 70%
Male/Female: 38%/62%
Live on-campus: 57%
In fraternities: 3%
In sororities: 3%
Off-campus employment rating: Excellent
Caucasian: 60%
African American: 3%
Hispanic: 10%
Asian / Pacific Islander: 4%
Native American: 0%
Mixed (2+ ethnicities): 4%
International: 4%

Academics
Calendar: Semester
Student/faculty ratio: 13:1
Class size 9 or fewer: 6%
Class size 10-29: 78%
Class size 30-49: 15%
Class size 50-99: 1%
Class size 100 or more: -
Six-year graduation rate: 82%
Graduates who immediately go to graduate school: 9%

Most Popular Majors
Film production
Writing/literature/publishing
Marketing

Admissions
Applicants: 7,465
Accepted: 3,615
Acceptance rate: 48.4%
Placed on wait list: 1,229
Enrolled from wait list: 191
Average GPA: 3.6
ACT range: 26-29
SAT Math range: 560-650
SAT Reading range: 590-680
SAT Writing range: 17-54
Top 10% of class: 38%
Top 25% of class: 77%
Top 50% of class: 93%

265

EMERSON COLLEGE

Admissions Criteria
Academic criteria:
Grades: ☆ ☆
Difficulty of class schedule: ☆ ☆
Class rank: ☆ ☆
Standardized test scores: ☆ ☆ ☆
Teacher recommendations: ☆ ☆
Personal statement: ☆ ☆
Non-academic criteria considered:
Extracurricular activities
Special talents, interests, abilities
Volunteer work
Work experience
State of residency
Geographical location
Minority affiliation
Alumni relationship

Deadlines
Early Action: November 1
Early Decision: No
Regular Action: January 5 (final)
Notification of admission by: April 1
Common Application: Accepted

Financial Aid
In-state tuition: $35,072
Out-of-state tuition: $35,072
Room: Varies
Board: Varies
Books: $1,000
Freshmen receiving need-based aid: 65%
Undergrads rec. need-based aid: 57%
Avg. % of need met by financial aid: 72%
Avg. aid package (freshmen): $19,193
Avg. aid package (undergrads): $18,643
Avg. debt upon graduation: $22,844

School Spirit
Mascot: Lion
Colors: Purple and gold

Student Body

It's pretty obvious that Emerson students are "highly creative," and their artistic expression bleeds into their wardrobes. The "look" includes lots of piercings, dyed hair, mohawks, skinny black jeans, and black t-shirts, as well as creative and individual street fashion. Students aren't slobs but look like urban artists, which is exactly what they are.

Geographically speaking, students come from all over: 81 percent are from out of state. The ethnic diversity is high with 21 percent minority. Students are very accepting of those from different racial, ethnic, socio-economic, and ideological backgrounds. Students "lean very far liberal," says a student.

It's apparent that there are slightly more female students on campus than males. The student body is 62 percent female.

You May Not Know

- Students have the opportunity to live in a 14th century castle in Kasteel Well, The Netherlands, while studying abroad. The castle is replete with two moats and a tower.
- In 1937, Emerson began its undergraduate broadcasting program, one of the first in the country.
- Athletics aren't a high priority at Emerson, the school was without even a gym until 2006.

Distinguished Alumni

Bobbi Brown, makeup artist; Jay Leno, talk show host; Max Mutchnick, *Will & Grace* television producer; Princess Noor Hamzah of Jordan, Jordanian Embassy attaché.

Admissions and Financial Aid

Getting into Emerson is competitive. As a communications and arts school, the college is interested in accessing a student's art during the admissions process. All applicants in the performing arts must complete additional requirements. For example, those applying in the performing arts for an acting BFA must submit a resume and have an acting audition; a BFA in theatre design and technology requires a portfolio, resume, and interview; film major applicants provide a script or a short film; and, anyone applying for the Honors program submits an honors application, short essay, and graded writing sample.

Merit scholarships are awarded and don't require an additional application: the Deans Scholarship, $14,000 per year, for academic excellence and leadership skills; the Emersonian scholarship, $10,000 per year, for academic and leadership achievement and community involvement; a half tuition scholarship called the Trustees scholarship for Honors program students, as well as other merit scholarships are available.

EMORY UNIVERSITY

Overview

Not only is Emory University a nationally recognized private college ranked among the top 20 universities by *U.S. News & World Report*, it strikes an ideal balance between academics and location in Atlanta, Georgia. Interactions with the impressive faculty at Emory University—which include the Dalai Lama as a Presidential Professor and annual Carter Town Halls held by former U.S. President, Jimmy Carter—provide unique academic opportunities for students.

Emory University is located in the idyllic and pedestrian-friendly Druid Hills, one of Atlanta's first suburbs. The cosmopolitan city of Atlanta, rich in both history and diversity, is easily accessible by Emory students. The equal abundance of both verdant greenery and pink and gray marble-clad buildings on campus presents a pleasant compromise between the influence of nature and the influence of man. With architecture heavily influenced by the style of the Italian Renaissance, Emory is a church-affiliated university with an extensive library and museums readily available for enjoyment. Predominately Greek, there is a healthy party scene at Emory and opportunities for recreation exist both on and off campus.

Academics

Because Emory University offers 149 majors, students are presented with many options when choosing a discipline for study. Some of the strongest academic programs include biomedical engineering, English/creative writing, history, music, nursing, political science, psychology, public health, and sociology. Pre-business administration, prelaw, and premed are among the most popular pre-professional programs.

The General Education Requirements include first-year seminar classes; first-year and continuing writing requirements; math; science, nature, technology; history, society, cultures; humanities, arts, performance; and physical education and dance. Students describe the requirements as "pretty easy to fulfill."

Emory also offers students a unique academic experience, given that there are four possible tracks students can decide between. Incoming students may choose to either enroll at Emory College or Oxford College; Oxford College, located 38 miles east of Atlanta on Emory's original campus, provides students with a small-college feel while retaining the same level of academic rigor/opportunity provided at Emory College. Upon reaching their junior year, all students return to Emory's main campus and have the ability to earn a degree at Emory College, Goizueta Business School (bachelor of business administration), or the Nell Hodgson Woodruff School of Nursing. "It's nice to have the option of having two years in a more close-knit setting and still graduate with an Emory degree," notes a student.

Given the many options available to students considering different majors, Emory University has an extensive mentoring program. Pre-Major Advising Connections at Emory (PACE) emphasizes individualized attention for students and is "really helpful especially during freshman year," says a student. Additionally, Emory encourages a global perspective by offering study-abroad programs in more than 40 countries, some of which include Switzerland, Israel, Tanzania, and Vietnam.

Not only do students experience academic and personal success on campus, but many students are successful in finding employment after college as well. Indeed, notable corporations like Bain & Company, the Central Intelligence Agency, Teach for America, General Electric and Deloitte and Touche, and others are reported to frequently hire Emory graduates. There are also many internship opportunities with companies including Coca-Cola, CNN, Delta Air, and Turner Broadcasting. Atlanta itself is ranked fourth in hosting the most Fortune 500 companies in the country.

EMORY UNIVERSITY

Four-year private
Founded: 1836
Atlanta, GA
Large town
Pop. 432,427

Address:
Boisfeuillet Jones
Center
Atlanta, GA
30322

Admissions:
800-727-6036

Financial Aid:
404-727-6039

admiss@emory.edu

www.emory.edu

EMORY UNIVERSITY

Students
Total enrollment: 14,677
Undergrads: 7,656
Freshmen: 1,363
From out-of-state: 78%
From public schools: 60%
Male/Female: 44%/56%
Live on-campus: 66%
In fraternities: 29%
In sororities: 27%
Off-campus employment rating: Excellent
Caucasian: 40%
African American: 10%
Hispanic: 5%
Asian / Pacific Islander: 23%
Native American: 0%
Mixed (2+ ethnicities): 2%
International: 14%

Academics
Calendar: Semester
Student/faculty ratio: 7:1
Class size 9 or fewer: 14%
Class size 10-29: 64%
Class size 30-49: 14%
Class size 50-99: 6%
Class size 100 or more: 3%
Returning freshmen: 95%
Six-year graduation rate: 90%
Graduates who immediately go to graduate school: 43%
Graduates who immediately enter career related to major: 30%

Most Popular Majors
Business administration
Economics
Biology

Admissions
Applicants: 17,475
Accepted: 4,602
Acceptance rate: 26.3%
Placed on wait list: 3,457
Enrolled from wait list: 37
Average GPA: 3.8
ACT range: 29-32
SAT Math range: 650-750
SAT Reading range: 620-710
SAT Writing range: 48-45
Top 10% of class: 80%
Top 25% of class: 98%
Top 50% of class: 100%

Student Life

Emory University offers more than 250 student organizations, which means multiple opportunities to pursue interests and passions. Examples of organizations at Emory include Colleges against Cancer, RACES (Racial and Cultural Education Sources), SEED (Student Educators on Eating Disorders), Swing Club, and Amnesty International.

Emory University also hosts academic, informational, cultural, and entertaining events. During the Carter Town Hall Meetings, students have the opportunity to write questions to President Carter which are pulled at random and addressed in a public forum by the influential world leader himself. "It's amazing to be able to sit in the same room with a former President," remarks a student.

Intellectual activity characterizes the prestigious university, but Dooley, the historic biology skeleton, safeguards the spirit of Emory and serves as the unofficial mascot. Students are secretly selected to embody Dooley (literally) during a week dedicated to him. The week concludes with Dooley's Ball in the center of campus. Not only does Emory have an active history, but it also embraces the technology of the future; for instance, the iMovie Fest allows budding cinematographers to create films which are judged during the film festival. Given guidelines, a theme, and a five-minute time limit, students can showcase their creativity and talent during this campus-wide event. Emory also strives to expose its students to different cultural perspectives and fosters a community in which students can feel comfortable learning about and from each other. The International Cultural Festival provides a platform upon which a mutual appreciation of different cultures can occur. Dances, songs, and short skits by students provide a glimpse of the cultural diversity at Emory.

With 29 percent of men and 27 percent of women in fraternities and sororities, there is a "very loud, and very lively" Greek community on campus, according to students. Many of the 17 social fraternities and the 12 social sororities on campus are housed. Fraternity parties are popular and inclusive of non-members.

Although Emory doesn't have a football team, there are many other athletic programs which Emory students can rally around. Emory has almost 20 intramural teams, which include badminton, flag football, court hockey, table tennis, and others. There are eight men's and eight women's Division III teams. Recent strong teams have been in swimming and diving, tennis, and volleyball.

There are many opportunities to explore life off campus. Indeed, clubs, restaurants, and shopping venues like the Lenox Mall are prevalent in Atlanta. Professional teams, like the Atlanta Braves and the Atlanta Hawks, can serve as a source of entertainment for the sports aficionado. "Atlanta is the perfect college city with enough nightlife, shopping, and entertainment to last well beyond four years," notes a student.

Many upperclassmen move off campus, but both freshman and sophomores are required to live on campus. Housing options include traditional residence hall doubles, suites, and apartments. "The best dorms for freshmen are Evans, Few, and Turman," says a student.

Student Body

Considering that 80 percent of Emory students graduated in the top 10 percent of their high school class, it is not surprising that students are "very dedicated" to their studies. The abundance of students enrolled in strong pre-profession programs reveals that Emory students are "truly focused on future careers," says a student. Additionally, students at Emory have the opportunity to mingle with many different perspectives given that 40 percent of students are from minority backgrounds. Emory's commitment to diversity, in every definition of the word, is upheld, as evidenced by the fact that more than 78 percent of students are from out of state.

You May Not Know

- Emory received sponsorship from the founder of The Coca-Cola Company, Asa Candler, who offered seed money and donated land in 1915.
- With 18 NCAA Division III varsity sports teams, Emory University ranked among the top 20 schools in the nation with the best-all around athletics program, as determined by the Directors Cup of the National Association of Collegiate Directors of Athletics.
- Desmond Tutu, a former cleric and South African activist who heavily influenced the movement against apartheid, was a visiting Robert W. Woodruff professor.

Distinguished Alumni

Thomas J. Donohue, U.S. Chamber of Commerce President and CEO; Marjorie J. Hill, Gay Men's Health Crisis CEO; Alice Hoffman, *New-York Times* best-selling author; Jonathan Larson, author of Pulitzer Prize-winning Broadway musical *RENT*.

Admissions and Financial Aid

Although the transcript, course rigor, and student performance are determining admission factors, extracurricular activities, essays, recommendations, and standardized test scores are also taken into consideration. Of all these factors, the college notes that the "transcript, including course rigor and student performance, weighs most heavily in the decision-making process." Interviews with Emory alumni are available in certain cities, like Chicago, Houston, and San Francisco, but an on-campus interview is not included in the admissions process.

Recently ranked in the top 15 for best values among private universities by *Kiplinger's Personal Finance*, Emory has a very strong financial aid program of which merit-based scholarships play a prominent role. Incoming students who are nominated by appropriate high school officials and complete the applications are offered generous merit-based scholarships. Packages range from partial to full coverage of tuition, fees, and room and board. The Emory Advantage Program, a financial aid initiative to make college affordable for students from homes with incomes of $100,000 or less, is a notable financial aid program. This program is composed of two parts: the Loan Replacement Grant addresses the needs of families who make $50,000 or less and replaces the loans which students would have been forced to withdraw, and the Loan Cap Program restricts the cumulative need-based debt to $15,000 for students from families who make between $50,000 and $100,000.

EMORY UNIVERSITY

Highlights

Admissions Criteria
Academic criteria:
Grades: ☆ ☆ ☆
Difficulty of class schedule: ☆ ☆ ☆
Class rank: ☆
Standardized test scores: ☆ ☆ ☆
Teacher recommendations: ☆ ☆ ☆
Personal statement: ☆ ☆ ☆
Non-academic criteria considered:
Interview
Extracurricular activities
Special talents, interests, abilities
Character/personal qualities
Volunteer work
Work experience
Geographical location
Minority affiliation
Alumni relationship

Deadlines
Early Action: No
Early Decision: November 1
Regular Action: January 15 (final)
Notification of admission by: April 1
Common Application: Accepted

Financial Aid
In-state tuition: $43,400
Out-of-state tuition: $43,400
Room: $7,360
Board: $5,000
Books: $1,200
Freshmen receiving need-based aid: 44%
Undergrads rec. need-based aid: 48%
Avg. % of need met by financial aid: 95%
Avg. aid package (freshmen): $35,945
Avg. aid package (undergrads): $37,552
Avg. debt upon graduation: $27,737

School Spirit
Mascot: Eagles
Colors: Blue and gold

EUGENE LANG COLLEGE THE NEW SCHOOL FOR LIBERAL ARTS

EUGENE LANG COLLEGE THE NEW SCHOOL FOR LIBERAL ARTS

Four-year private
Founded: 1985
New York, NY
Major city
Pop. 8,391,881

Address:
66 West 12th Street
New York, NY
10011

Admissions:
877-528-3321

Financial Aid:
212-229-8930

lang@newschool.edu

www.newschool.edu/
lang

Overview

Less than 30 years old, the Eugene Lang College The New School for Liberal Arts was founded with the goal of "pursuing social justice, political responsibility, and cultural awareness in order to effect positive change in the world." Lang is a small school with only 1,500 students, all seminar classes, and a reputation for rigorous, unconventional education. Lang students are free-spirited and fiercely creative, filling their time with theater productions and fundraising fashion shows.

Students can choose from 20 majors or design their own plan of study, while taking advantage of special programs such as the BA/BFA track, the Tishman Environmental Merit Scholars Program, and courses at NYC cultural institutions. Speaking of NYC, the campus itself is practically indistinguishable from the rest of Greenwich Village, and about three-quarters of students live off campus. With plays, concerts, clubs, movies, museums, and poetry slams a walk or subway ride away, there is no better college town than the Big Apple.

Academics

Many students at Lang opt for a self-designed "liberal arts" major, but 17 established majors are offered. The Literary Studies and the Arts offer Dance, Theater, Visual Arts, Music, and Arts in Context. Cluster offerings such as Jewish Studies and Civic Engagement can be also incorporated into majors. Each focus area has its own minimal requirements, but all first-year students are required to take a course in writing and research skills, just as seniors must complete a senior seminar or independent project.

Lang is intellectually and artistically challenging, but the atmosphere is "cooperative rather than competitive." Professors go by their first names and are readily accessible to students. "Every professor I have has been willing to answer questions after class," says a student. Being a very small school with a 14:1 faculty ratio, classes are often under 15 students and always seminar style. In fact, the Princeton Review ranked Lang No. 1 for in-class discussions. And for a fully rounded education, Lang Outdoors provides Wellness Courses such as Lang Urban Park Rangers, Public ArtSquad, and Buddhist Meditation.

Perhaps because Lang focuses on student-directed education, there are an impressive variety of special academic opportunities. One of the most recently added is the Tishman Environmental Merit Scholars Program. Students interested in environmental studies and activism can apply to spend one summer working with the Alaska Conservation Foundation, coupled with a series of five related courses.

The artistically inclined take courses arranged every semester around shows and exhibits at important NYC cultural institutions such as the New York Historical Society, the Museum of Modern Art (MOMA), and the Public Theater. "There's no better place to be exposed to real-world art than New York," says a student. For those serious about pursuing a career in art, the BA/BFA Program offers a five-year tract where students can study the Eugene Lang liberal arts curriculum while simultaneously attending one of the graduate schools at the New School, for example, Parsons Design or the New School for Jazz and Contemporary Music.

During breaks, faculty led trips out of the city are popular for courses such as "Tibet: Living Buddhist Culture," and "South Africa: Democracy and Diversity Institute." Lang also supports semester long study-abroad programs in many European countries; and through other programs, anywhere in the world.

In preparation for life after Lang, the ELC Internship Program coordinates career building by helping students find the perfect internship in New York City or elsewhere. Students have recently worked at HBO, Beth Israel Hospital, the *Village Voice*, Gay Men's Health Crisis, and the ACLU. Community activism is encouraged alongside internships through the Institute for Urban Education, Alternative Spring breaks, and service-learning projects.

Student Life

Lang isn't your typical American college. There are many Greek plays, but no Greek organizations. There are also no varsity or intramural sports. In fact, the school has been called America's worst sports college. That said, active students can train with the marathon team, take yoga and Pilates, or join the bicycle team that works with an organization promoting sustainable transport by reclaiming and rebuilding bicycles.

Since students are privy to just about anything in NYC, it would require a reprint of the culture section from *The New York Times* just to list the off-campus activities within throwing distance of Lang. The young vibrancy of the Village and Chelsea mean there are always clubs open until dawn, poetry readings at the famed Nuyorican Poets Café, live jazz, cinema, theater at the SoHo Play-house, contemporary art galleries, dance companies, and world-class museums. Lang in the City provides discount tickets to some of NYC's best shows and events. As one student explains, "24/7, 365 days a year, there's always something to do."

In addition to a plethora of off-campus activities, there are 34 on-campus student groups. Some of the most popular are the bi-weekly newspaper *The New School Free Press*, the Change Forum, and the Theater Collective. Groups such as the Low Income Student Alliance and the Sustainable Design Review are testaments to social activism on campus. One student explains, "It seems like someone is protesting something or raising funds every other day."

Student groups and the school itself put on a number of events throughout the year. International Education Week invites students to share their culture, food, and ideas with the campus community and also includes a cultural festival, trip to the United Nations, photo contest, and film festival. Sisters on the Runway fashion show harnesses the art skills of Lang to raise money for Shelter our Sisters, an agency providing support for victims of domestic abuse. Other popular events include the Lang Theater Produc-tions, where students perform for public audiences in November and March. Previous shows have included *Measure for Measure* and the *Laramie Project*.

Freshmen are guaranteed housing, while most students move off campus by their sophomore year. Cost of living in the area around campus can be expensive, so many students move to Brooklyn or other affordable areas. While at any other school, such a migration off campus can mean a lack of student social life, but luckily, in New York City, there is no such thing.

Student Body

Chock full of artists, hipsters, budding social scientists, and envi-ronmental activists, "normal" is not in Eugene Lang's vocabulary. Students are politically liberal, and many are so academically focused that the average GPA is 3.3. Ethnic diversity is high, with only 56 percent of students reporting as Caucasian. Geographic diversity is less impressive, with a moderate 20 percent from out of state. Male students make up only one third of the student body.

EUGENE LANG COLLEGE THE NEW SCHOOL FOR LIBERAL ARTS

Highlights

Students
Total enrollment: 1,511
Undergrads: 1,511
Freshmen: 531
Part-time students: 6%
From out-of-state: 80%
Male/Female: 33%/67%
Live on-campus: 27%
Off-campus employment rating: Good

Academics
Calendar: Semester
Student/faculty ratio: 14:1
Class size 9 or fewer: 11%
Class size 10-29: 83%
Class size 30-49: 4%
Class size 50-99: 1%
Class size 100 or more: -
Returning freshmen: 75%
Six-year graduation rate: 56%

Most Popular Majors
Liberal arts
Culture/media
Psychology

Admissions
Applicants: 1,661
Accepted: 1,211
Acceptance rate: 72.9%
Placed on wait list: 107
Enrolled from wait list: 18
Average GPA: 3.4
ACT range: 22-27
SAT Math range: 470-610
SAT Reading range: 530-660
SAT Writing range: 10-37
Top 10% of class: 16%
Top 25% of class: 47%
Top 50% of class: 87%

271

College Profiles

EUGENE LANG COLLEGE THE NEW SCHOOL FOR LIBERAL ARTS

Admissions Criteria
Academic criteria:
Grades: ☆ ☆
Difficulty of class schedule: ☆ ☆
Class rank: ☆ ☆
Standardized test scores: ☆
Teacher recommendations: ☆ ☆
Personal statement: ☆ ☆ ☆
Non-academic criteria considered:
Interview
Extracurricular activities
Special talents, interests, abilities
Character/personal qualities
Volunteer work
State of residency
Alumni relationship

Deadlines
Early Action: No
Early Decision: November 15
Regular Action: Rolling admissions
Common Application: Accepted

Financial Aid
In-state tuition: $37,710
Out-of-state tuition: $37,710
Room: $12,600
Board: Varies
Books: $2,050
Freshmen receiving need-based aid: 68%
Undergrads rec. need-based aid: 57%
Avg. % of need met by financial aid: 80%
Avg. aid package (freshmen): $33,675
Avg. aid package (undergrads): $34,210
Avg. debt upon graduation: $30,830

School Spirit
Colors: Yellow, orange, and red

Tolerance is a natural part of the Lang community, not surprising with so many students studying cultural, gender, and racial issues on a campus in NYC with a diverse student body. Ethnic and spiritual groups facilitate meetings, film screenings, and forums.

You May Not Know

- The Institute for Urban Education (IUE) at The New School partners with K-12 schools in New York to promote equal, innovative, and effective inner-city education. Many Lang students take part in research and projects with IUE.
- Parsons the New School for Design, where Eugene Lang students can pursue a BA/BFA, is the location for the hit Bravo TV Series *Project Runway*.
- In 1933, the New School created the "University in Exile" to serve as a safe haven for European Intellectuals escaping the Hitler and Mussolini regimes.

Distinguished Alumni

Ani DiFranco, musician; Elisa Donovan, actress; Emily Gould, former Co-Editor of Gawker; Jacqueline Lewis, writer, Managing Editor of *Chief Magazine*; Matisyahu, musician; Sufjan Stevens, musician.

Admissions and Financial Aid

The admissions board evaluates applicants based on their academic preparation first, and their "individuality, creativity, and intellectual promise" second. Year-round interviews can be scheduled, though they are more informative than evaluative. While Lang does accept the Common Application, submitting standardized test scores is optional (but still recommended). If you choose not to submit your SAT/ACT scores, you must instead submit a graded paper with teacher comments.

A host of scholarships and grants are available, both need- and merit-based. The Global Scholarship awards exemplary international students with interdisciplinary interests and leadership abilities. The Brian Watkins Memorial Scholarship provides financial assistance to a student who "demonstrates outstanding academic ability, community involvement, and a commitment to helping others."

EVERGREEN STATE COLLEGE

Overview

Located in a 1,000-acre forest on the shores of the Puget Sound, Evergreen State College is a leading school in environmental studies and sustainability. The campus has its own organic farm, community gardens, forest trails for running and hiking, a Native American long home, and a salt water beach for research, swimming, and kayaking. Within driving distance of the campus are many famous outdoor recreation areas, including Olympic National Park and Mount Rainer National Park. While the campus itself may seem like a national park, a quick drive brings students to downtown Olympia, the moderate-sized capital city of Washington (and for those wishing to explore a larger city, Seattle is just one hour away).

The student body and administration at Evergreen are dedicated to sustainable living. One hundred percent of the energy used by the school comes from renewable sources. Much of the produce in the cafeteria comes directly from Evergreen's organic farm. There are also community gardens and Teaching Gardens, which showcase sustainable landscaping and native plants.

Founded in 1969, Evergreen State College is Washington's first public liberal arts school (making it a great tuition bargain, especially for in-state residents). The curriculum is highly unique in that students do not receive grades but rather written evaluations from their teachers. Moreover, students enroll in single programs, such as "Food, Health, and Sustainability," each quarter rather than taking a number of different courses. While this may not suit students wanting to explore multiple interests at the same time, it's ideal for students who want to delve into a particular area of study. The programs—each with about 23 students per professor—involve seminars, discussions, field trips, and hands-on laboratories. Evergreen State has a national reputation as being a school where students interact closely with professors and learn about topics through a practical, multifaceted approach.

Academics

While Evergreen is most renowned for environmental studies, biology, and other sciences, it offers more than 64 areas of focus ranging from art to prelaw. Evergreen students do not declare majors; rather, they choose an area of study. Students can even design their own area of study with the help of an academic advisor. All freshmen participate in two freshmen-specific programs. Sophomore, junior, and senior year, Evergreen students choose advanced-level programs.

Evergreen has no general education requirements; students enroll in a total of 12 programs throughout their studies at Evergreen, which is on the quarter system. Even without the grade system and multiple courses in different subjects, students say that their programs are "challenging" and "require a lot of time for studying," but still that they "don't mind the heavy workload because it's on subjects we care about."

Evergreen's programs offer a personalized and multifaceted approach to learning; students design their own projects, and participate in field trips and hands-on laboratories. Past field trips have included rafting through the Grand Canyon while surveying its geology, visiting local sawmills for classes in forest health, and community discussion forums in local cities. "The field trips help us see what we're learning firsthand," explains a student. "You can internalize the information so much better when you experience it." Students are encouraged to collaborate with peers on projects and in discussion seminars. With the small size of the programs, students also get to know their professors extremely well and recommend researching the professors to see who matches your interests before applying to programs each quarter.

Evergreen offers study-abroad opportunities on a quarterly basis, with programs taught in places like New Zealand, Argentina, Egypt, and Turkey. The programs are not language-intensive, and most do not involve living with a host family. Rather,

EVERGREEN
STATE
COLLEGE

Four-year public
Founded: 1967
Olympia, WA
Large town
Pop. 47,266

Address:
2700 Evergreen Park-
way, NW
Olympia, WA
98505

Admissions:
360-867-6170

Financial Aid:
360-867-6205

admissions@ever-
green.edu

www.evergreen.edu

EVERGREEN STATE COLLEGE

Students
Total enrollment: 4,509
Undergrads: 4,193
Freshmen: 595
Part-time students: 8%
From out-of-state: 47%
Male/Female: 47%/53%
Live on-campus: 18%
Off-campus employment rating: Fair
Caucasian: 67%
African American: 5%
Hispanic: 7%
Asian / Pacific Islander: 3%
Native American: 2%
Mixed (2+ ethnicities): 6%
International: 1%

Academics
Calendar: Quarter
Student/faculty ratio: 21:1
Class size 9 or fewer: 14%
Class size 10-29: 52%
Class size 30-49: 27%
Class size 50-99: 7%
Class size 100 or more: -
Returning freshmen: 71%
Six-year graduation rate: 54%

Admissions
Applicants: 1,650
Accepted: 1,624
Acceptance rate: 98.4%
Average GPA: 3.0
ACT range: 21-27
SAT Math range: 460-590
SAT Reading range: 510-640
SAT Writing range: 3-24
Top 10% of class: 13%
Top 25% of class: 30%
Top 50% of class: 58%

students live and travel with their peers as a part of their program, taught by Evergreen faculty. Program examples include learning about Mediterranean conflict history in Turkey and biodiversity in Argentina.

More than half of Evergreen graduates go on to graduate or professional school within five years of earning a bachelor degree. Of those, 80 percent to 90 percent are accepted into their first or second choice of schools. Evergreen graduates are employed in a variety of fields, from governmental and non-profit agencies to media and entertainment. An education at Evergreen is designed to equip students with skills in collaboration, self-directed learning, and a multi-disciplinary approach to problem-solving.

Student Life

There are over 75 student organizations at Evergreen, including Sustainable Entrepreneurs, Amnesty International, and a number of religious, cultural, and performing arts groups. The school also has a student-run newspaper and radio station.

There are no sororities or fraternities at Evergreen. "Greek life would be mocked if we had it here," laughs a student. However, even without Greek life, Evergreen students throw parties and enjoy the local bar scene. While it's not considered a party school, students say there is a "happening" campus social scene. Campus traditions include Super Saturday, a June community event near graduation that showcases entertainment, food, arts and crafts vendors, and community service groups. Other popular events include the Longhouse Native Arts Fair, the autumn Harvest Festival, and the Synergy Sustainability Conference.

Evergreen has NAIA intercollegiate basketball, cross country, soccer, track and field, and volleyball teams. However, there is no football team. There are club sports such as crew and baseball, and intramural sports that include Ultimate Frisbee, softball, tennis, badminton, basketball, soccer and volleyball. To stay fit, students enjoy the gymnasium, Olympic-sized swimming pool, climbing wall, dance rooms, and tennis and racquetball courts. Although it rains a lot at Evergreen, especially during the winter, outdoor recreation remains a favorite activity. The on-campus Outdoor Program is one of the most popular student organizations, since the area boasts incredible scenery and many opportunities to run, hike, kayak, canoe, sail, ski downhill and cross-county, rock climb, road and mountain bike, surf, and much more. "This is an outdoor paradise," claims one student. Students are very fit and healthy in general, valuing time outdoors and healthy (preferably organic and local) food.

When students want to enjoy nature scenery away from their own forest and beach, they can visit Olympic National Park, Mount Rainer National Park, and a number of ski slopes. For city life, Olympia has an active bar scene with music, especially on the 4th Avenue Strip. There's also a popular Farmer's Market in Olympia with fresh local produce that's "very popular," as described by one student. Seattle is also just one hour away and offers plenty of shopping, multicultural restaurants, arts and music and nightlife.

Evergreen freshmen typically live in on-campus dorms, which is where many students say they make their closest friendships. After freshmen year, students can live in on-campus apartments, with vegetarian/vegan, quiet space, community action and sustainable living options. Most upperclassmen live off campus or even commute from home.

Student Body

The student body at Evergreen is generally liberal, politically active, outdoorsy, and environmentally conscious. One junior said, "There's a definite 'green' and activist feel on campus, and there's a lot less concern about who's wearing what or who belongs to what group than you'd see at some schools."

Evergreen is diverse both ethnically and geographically—23 percent are non-white and 47 percent are from out of state. A sizeable minority of students are adults. Evergreen has a "tight-knit" feel where "everyone knows everyone else."

You May Not Know

- The Sierra Club named Evergreen State as one of the "Top 20 Cool Colleges."
- Evergreen received the Environmental Protection Agency (EPA) Award for "Top Green Power Purchaser among Colleges and Universities" because Evergreen purchases 100 percent of its electricity from green sources.
- Evergreen has its own private recreational beach on campus that can be reached via picturesque forest trails.

Distinguished Alumni

Lynda Barry, graphic novelist and cartoonist; Matthew Groening, cartoonist and creator of *The Simpsons*; Rosalund Jenkins, Executive Director, Washington State Commission on African American Affairs.

Admissions and Financial Aid

Evergreen has a rolling admissions policy, with applications accepted for fall quarter admission from September through March. The college advises students to submit their applications as early as possible to ensure a full admission review and timely financial aid consideration.

Official transcripts and SAT/ACT scores are required with the application. Evergreen recommends that students who have experienced a personal challenge or overcome an obstacle submit a personal statement to explain their academic performance. Evergreen also welcomes letters of recommendation from teachers, counselors, or employers who are familiar with applicants' academic preparation and ability to succeed in college. Interviews are not required for admission; however, many applicants meet with Evergreen admissions counselors to help them decide if the school is a good fit for them., and Evergreen admissions counselors travel to cities across America.

In addition to need-based aid (both federal and from the state), Evergreen offers a number of merit-based scholarships from specific donor funds to incoming freshmen and returning students. Qualifications for these scholarships vary, and include factors such as ethnic background, field of study, academic achievement, community service, and others.

EVERGREEN STATE COLLEGE

Highlights

Admissions Criteria
Academic criteria:
Grades: ☆ ☆ ☆
Difficulty of class schedule: ☆ ☆ ☆
Class rank: N/A
Standardized test scores: ☆ ☆
Teacher recommendations: ☆
Personal statement: ☆ ☆ ☆
Non-academic criteria considered:
Interview
Extracurricular activities
Volunteer work
Work experience
State of residency

Deadlines
Early Action: No
Early Decision: No
Regular Action: Rolling admissions
Common Application: Not accepted

Financial Aid
In-state tuition: $7,812
Out-of-state tuition: $18,978
Room: $6,150
Board: $3,090
Books: $999
Freshmen receiving need-based aid: 59%
Undergrads rec. need-based aid: 63%
Avg. % of need met by financial aid: 67%
Avg. aid package (freshmen): $8,012
Avg. aid package (undergrads): $8,790
Avg. debt upon graduation: $15,706

School Spirit
Mascot: Geoducks
Colors: Forest and white
Song: *The Geoduck Fight Song*

Four-year private
Founded: 1942
Fairfield, CT
Large town
Pop. 57,340

Address:
1073 North Benson
Road
Fairfield, CT
06824-5195

Admissions:
203-254-4100

Financial Aid:
203-254-4125

admis@fairfield.edu

www.fairfield.edu

FAIRFIELD UNIVERSITY

Overview

Founded in 1942 by The Society of Jesus, this Jesuit Catholic University is located in Fairfield, Connecticut, two miles from the Long Island Sound and 60 miles from New York City. The school features a beautiful 200-acre campus with sprawling green lawns and elegant manor houses. Fairfield is known as the Dogwood capital of the world. When the trees are in bloom the first of spring, it is indeed a sight to behold. This private four-year coeducational institution attracts students from 36 states and 46 international countries. *Business Week* ranks Fairfield University as 63rd in the U.S., and 2nd in Connecticut for best value on the return investment it provides its students.

The town of Fairfield has been routinely named one of the safest cities in the U.S. and has been praised as one of the best places to live in the Northeast with an extremely low crime rate and a great downtown scene. While the town may be breathtaking, the location is definitely suburbia, without the excitement and constant hive of activities that an urban location may offer. But Fairfield University is in a great location in terms of offering a cohesive campus feel and having strong educational programs. According to the college, "students are committed to broad intellectual inquiry, based on lifelong learning with Jesuit values integrated into their graduate and professional studies."

Academics

Undergraduate students may choose from 34 majors and 16 minors. Virtually all classes have 50 or fewer students. Strong programs range from finance and communications/journalism to nursing. There is a general core curriculum which provides a basis for a liberal education in a range of classes in mathematics and the natural sciences, history and the social sciences, philosophy and religious studies, and English, along with the visual/performing arts.

Students who are intellectual self starters—described by the college as "inquisitive and passionate about ideas in a range of disciplines"—are encouraged to ask about the Honors Program, which is by invitation only. Students are invited to apply before entering college, and those who have excelled academically after their first semester at Fairfield are also invited. According to the college, the Honors Program "highlights the skills of critical thinking, graceful writing, and cogent argumentation, skills that are crucial to success in any field." Participation is also noted on students' transcripts.

Fairfield University offers academic support through several different programs. The Office of Service Learning assists students in connecting with community organizations for service-learning courses and for internships. Through the Writing Center, students gain access to writing tutors and a comfortable space for writing. In addition, the university offers top-notch facilities such as the center for the arts, the language lab, art galleries, a television studio, and a business experimental simulation and trading floor classroom. "Through formal and informal channels, we can get the help we need," says a student.

Around 40 percent of the students at Fairfield University study abroad. There are 35 different countries—and even more cities than that—for students to choose from. An interesting program some students opt to pursue is a study abroad during their one week January intersession. Participants travel to Italy and study Early Renaissance Art in Florence. Students also have the opportunity to earn three credits while immersed in a different culture during their winter break. "There is no better place in the world to study art than Florence," says a student.

All these experiences through service, community, and the diverse curriculum contribute to creating a well-rounded student. The average freshman GPA is 3.2 and 87 percent of freshman students return for sophomore year. Approximately 23 percent of students pursue a graduate degree immediately after graduation, and among students who enter the work force, 70 percent enter a field related to their major within six months of graduation.

Student Life

The majority of students live on campus, and that helps shape student life. There is never a dull moment for a student looking for something to do on campus since Fairfield University boasts 20 Division I athletic teams and 114 student organizations. Many students are also involved in public service. Popular gathering spots include Jazzman's Café, downtown Fairfield, Barone Campus Center, and the RecPlex.

There are no Greek organizations at Fairfield. But with the number of other organizations and events available, students hardly miss it. When it comes to athletics, basketball, lacrosse, and soccer are where Fairfield Stags really shine. Intramurals are popular as well, with the Equestrian Club, men's hockey, men's rugby, and men's volleyball polled as favorites.

Campus events include glee club concerts, Multicultural Mondays, dance ensemble recitals, the Presidential Ball, and the Dogwood Dance. Noche Caliente is an annual formal dance hosted by SALSA, featuring salsa and meringue. For those who are looking for service-based activity, Hunger Club consists of 500 students and faculty volunteering for a one day serve-a-thon at more than 40 local agency sites in the Connecticut area. Senior Week is another popular tradition. This program facilitates seven different events that are catered to the graduating class as they reflect on their years at Fairfield. Activities include the Jesuit Social, Pub Night, the Commencement Ball, and a Senior Picnic. "Everyone lets loose during Senior Week," remarks a student. Other well received groups on campus include the student government, Theatre Fairfield, and Campus Ministry.

On a typical weekend night, parties in lowerclassmen dorms or the upperclassmen townhouses are not uncommon. A very popular off-campus activity is to go to "The Beach," property along the Long Island Sound where many seniors live and throw parties. "The Beach is the hot spot for seniors and those who aspire to live like the seniors," laughs a student. If going to the beach doesn't fulfill a student's craving for adventure, NYC is just an hour away by train.

Many students do take advantage of New York City's close proximity to enhance their college experience without having to be immediately entrenched in an urban, fast paced atmosphere all the time. The country's largest city and the home of the most Fortune 500 companies in the U.S., NYC offers students numerous internships and varied educational opportunities. Ample cultural fair is available for students to explore, such as museums, restaurants, and some of the most diverse neighborhoods you can find.

For students who dorm, there are many housing options. Besides the non-school affiliated houses on the Beach, there are school-affiliated townhouses that are most-sought-after by students. All freshmen and a portion of the sophomore class live together in traditional-style halls. Some sophomores are able to take advantage of suite-style accommodations. Seniors live in townhouses, apartments, or in other off campus housing, with juniors following suit depending on space availability.

FAIRFIELD UNIVERSITY

Highlights

Students
Total enrollment: 4,999
Undergrads: 3,879
Freshmen: 990
Part-time students: 11%
From out-of-state: 77%
From public schools: 57%
Male/Female: 41%/59%
Live on-campus: 83%
Off-campus employment rating: Good
Caucasian: 67%
African American: 3%
Hispanic: 8%
Asian / Pacific Islander: 2%
Native American: 0%
Mixed (2+ ethnicities): 1%
International: 2%

Academics
Calendar: Semester
Student/faculty ratio: 11:1
Class size 9 or fewer: 11%
Class size 10-29: 71%
Class size 30-49: 17%
Class size 50-99: 1%
Class size 100 or more: -
Returning freshmen: 87%
Six-year graduation rate: 81%
Graduates who immediately go to graduate school: 23%

Most Popular Majors
Nursing
Marketing
Communication

Admissions
Applicants: 9,254
Accepted: 6,585
Acceptance rate: 71.2%
Placed on wait list: 1,668
Enrolled from wait list: 43
Average GPA: 3.4
ACT range: 24-27
SAT Math range: 550-630
SAT Reading range: 530-620
SAT Writing range: 5-39
Top 10% of class: 34%
Top 25% of class: 64%
Top 50% of class: 91%

277

College Profiles

FAIRFIELD UNIVERSITY

Admissions Criteria
Academic criteria:
Grades: ☆ ☆ ☆
Difficulty of class schedule: ☆ ☆ ☆
Class rank: ☆
Standardized test scores: ☆
Teacher recommendations: ☆ ☆ ☆
Personal statement: ☆ ☆ ☆
Non-academic criteria considered:
Interview
Extracurricular activities
Special talents, interests, abilities
Character/personal qualities
Volunteer work
Work experience
State of residency
Geographical location
Minority affiliation
Alumni relationship

Deadlines
Early Action: November 1
Early Decision: January 1
Regular Action: January 15 (final)
Notification of admission by: April 1
Common Application: Accepted

Financial Aid
In-state tuition: $42,320
Out-of-state tuition: $42,320
Room: $7,920
Board: $5,010
Books: $1,150
Freshmen receiving need-based aid: 54%
Undergrads rec. need-based aid: 53%
Avg. % of need met by financial aid: 88%
Avg. aid package (freshmen): $27,725
Avg. aid package (undergrads): $29,491
Avg. debt upon graduation: $28,507

School Spirit
Mascot: Stags
Colors: Cardinal red

Student Body

Not surprisingly, many students are Catholic. There is moderate ethnic diversity with 14 percent of students identifying themselves as minorities, although the race or ethnic background is unknown for 17 percent of students. The university has high geographic diversity with 77 percent of students from out of state. The part-time student population is significant, with 11 percent of undergraduates carrying less than a full load. The university is making efforts to increase diversity. Several innovative programs, such as the Ally Network, The Cura Personalis Mentoring Program, and the Pathway to Success, promote understanding and smooth transitions from a student's former environment into college.

You May Not Know

- Most of the buildings on campus are named after Jesuit priests who have committed their lives to exemplary service.
- Fairfield University has produced 55 Fulbright Scholars since 1993, and 94 percent of the faculty hold the highest degrees in their fields.
- The oldest club on campus is the Fairfield University Glee Club.

Distinguished Alumni

E. Gerald Corrigan, Managing Director of Goldman, Sachs & Co; Christopher McCormick, CEO of L.L.Bean; Eileen Clarkin Rominger, Chief Investment Officer at Goldman, Sachs & Co.

Admissions and Financial Aid

Fairfield made the submission of SAT/ACT results optional in fall 2010. However, if students opt not to submit test scores, they will need to answer an additional question on the application regarding how a student might see themselves as a member of the Fairfield community.

Fairfield University offers merit-based and athletic scholarships, with seven percent of freshmen and six percent of undergraduates receiving merit-based aid. The Magis Scholarship is awarded to students who have "made the most of the opportunities presented to them through high school, their community, or their church." This scholarship provides a $20,000 annual grant that is renewable for four years, providing that the student maintains a 3.0 GPA. All first-year candidates are considered for the scholarship automatically; there is no separate application.

FLORIDA INSTITUTE OF TECHNOLOGY

FLORIDA INSTITUTE OF TECHNOLOGY

Four-year private
Founded: 1958
Melbourne, FL
Medium city
Pop. 76,095

Address:
150 West University
Boulevard
Melbourne, FL
32901-6975

Admissions:
800-888-4348

Financial Aid:
800-666-4348

admission@fit.edu

www.fit.edu

Overview

Founded in the midst of the Space Race to provide continuing education for engineers working at Cape Canaveral (what is now Kennedy Space Center), Florida Institute of Technology occupies a prime spot on the subtropical east coast of Florida. The 130-acre suburban campus in Melbourne, Florida, includes a botanical garden and one of the largest collections of palm trees in the United States and is minutes from beaches and the Atlantic Ocean. Florida Tech's location is not just a perk for surfers and beach bums, though. Students on Florida's "Space Coast" have easy access to NASA, Kennedy Space Center, a number of high-tech companies, as well as the bio-diverse Indian River Lagoon.

Florida Tech's facilities, location, and relatively small size lend themselves to plenty of opportunities for undergraduate research, internships, and job preparation. Minimal core requirements allow students to get right down to business in their chosen fields—which is probably good, since the wealth of distractions and the year-round good weather could make it hard to focus on school, and probably play a role in the school's relatively low freshmen retention rates. But for students who can balance hefty work with playtime, Florida Tech offers high-level and diverse educational opportunities and endless ways to relax, both on campus—including the recently-constructed state-of-the-art Clemente Center for Sports and Recreation—and off.

Academics

Florida Tech offers 187 majors. Studies in aerospace and mechanical engineering, marine biological sciences, aviation management, and psychology are heavyweight. This should come as no surprise, given that NASA is a next-door neighbor, and that Florida's lakes, rivers, and particularly the Indian River Lagoon offer students in the field of the marine biological sciences hands-on experience in manatee preservation, beach erosion, and sea turtle research.

Florida Tech academics are competitive and demanding. Fortunately Florida Tech's small size means that students get plenty of support from professors; half of the classes have fewer than 20 students. Florida Tech also prides itself in that its students begin work in their majors starting their very first year—but this does come in the form of a comprehensive general education. Florida Tech explains that "a common purpose of all undergraduate programs at Florida Tech is to impart an understanding of our current technology-centered civilization and its historical background," translating into much more than a cursory and technology-centric overview of humanities and social sciences.

Florida Tech's Undergraduate Core Requirements include one to three courses each in communication, humanities, mathematics, physical and or life sciences, and social sciences, as well as a computer literacy requirement and a one-credit University Experience course. "You're expected to know what you want to do when you start rather than spend a year or two exploring yourself and picking a major," says one student.

A large part of Florida Tech's education emphasizes preparation for jobs: students in the College of Engineering can get a jump start in the workforce through the ProTrack Cooperative Education Program, which allows students to gain three paid semesters of work experience related to their majors during sophomore and junior years while also earning their bachelor's degree. While cooperative education programs at other schools usually take five years, Florida Tech's takes four, as it requires summer term participation; limited core requirements probably also factor in. Students generally earn about $30,000 over the course of the ProTrack program and can explore as many as three different jobs. Students interested in ProTrack can apply as part of their application to Florida Tech. A similar practicum is offered to

FLORIDA INSTITUTE OF TECHNOLOGY

Students

Total enrollment: 5,384
Undergrads: 2,978
Freshmen: 1,049
Part-time students: 6%
From out-of-state: 43%
From public schools: 36%
Male/Female: 72%/28%
Live on-campus: 49%
In fraternities: 14%
In sororities: 11%
Off-campus employment rating: Good
Caucasian: 45%
African American: 5%
Hispanic: 6%
Asian / Pacific Islander: 2%
Native American: 0%
Mixed (2+ ethnicities): 2%
International: 29%

Academics

Calendar: Semester
Student/faculty ratio: 9:1
Class size 9 or fewer: 15%
Class size 10-29: 67%
Class size 30-49: 14%
Class size 50-99: 4%
Class size 100 or more: -
Returning freshmen: 79%
Six-year graduation rate: 55%
Graduates who immediately go to gradu-
    ate school: 42%
Graduates who immediately enter career
    related to major: 49%

Most Popular Majors

Mechanical engineering
Aerospace engineering
Electrical engineering

Admissions

Applicants: 7,428
Accepted: 4,386
Acceptance rate: 59.0%
Average GPA: 3.6
ACT range: 22-28
SAT Math range: 540-640
SAT Reading range: 500-610
SAT Writing range: Not reported
Top 10% of class: 31%
Top 25% of class: 58%
Top 50% of class: 85%

students in business, while co-ops are available to students in other majors on an individual basis. Many majors also require a final project: psychology students must complete a faculty-guided three course internship sequence as part of the Scholarly Inquiry Project. Engineering students must participate as part of an interdisciplinary team that will design and construct a senior project. Students appreciate these programs, as one student points out, "The co-op program is a huge advantage because I will graduate with work experience, and I also have contacts at the companies where I worked."

Students in biological sciences can participate in Summer Field Programs, two to six-week travel courses that explore diverse temperate or tropical ecosystems in locations such as the Appalachian Mountains, the Rocky Mountains, the African Savannah, Costa Rica, Peru, the Caribbean Coral Reef, and Australia. Students in other majors can go abroad via Florida Tech's International Academic Programs, which offer study abroad in Norway, Hungary, Belgium, Argentina, France, and England, some of which are specialized for students in management or aviation.

Florida Tech students who enter the work force generally enjoy a good record of success: within six months of graduation, about half find work in their fields, while three quarters find work in a field related to their major within a year.

Student Life

Almost 150 student organizations function on campus, including the College Players, who present biannual plays; the university Jazz Band; and WFIT, the college radio station. On-campus sports events introduce a healthy element of competition to students' social lives as well as academics: Florida Tech's eight fraternities and three sororities square off against one another during Greek Week with games and competitions ranging from very traditional soccer and basketball to bocce ball, "can-struction," and the multi-component event called "Doug Englar." Fourteen percent of men and eleven percent of women join Greek organizations. Engineering Week operates on a similar premise: teams of engineering students compete against teams from other companies in projects such as building a climbing device out of rope and a mouse trap. In spring, international students put on a cultural showcase of music and dance as part of the International Festival.

Athletics and outdoor activities are a major attraction in sunny Florida. Places to go surfing, swimming, biking, hiking, and canoeing are all within reasonable distance, if not on campus, which offers multiple outdoor pools and lighted tennis and sand volleyball courts. *Surfline* has named Florida Tech one of the top surfing schools in the U.S., while *Boat US Magazine* lists it as one of the "Boatiest" schools in America. "Sometimes it's hard to focus on studying when there's so much to do outdoors," admits one student. Intramurals include some nontraditional sports, such as cricket, while several of Florida Tech's 21 Division II varsity sports teams have enjoyed competitive success—most recently the women's soccer team appeared in the NCAA semifinals. Off-campus escapes can include beach towns like Miami, Key West, and Tampa, or Orlando for Disney World and Sea World as well as shopping and restaurants.

All freshmen must live on campus in traditional dorm-style residence halls. Upperclassmen may live in on-campus traditional, suite, or apartment-style residences, but many opt to move off campus.

Student Body

As at most technical institutes, students at Florida Tech tend to be concentrated in tech-related fields and are academically-oriented; traditionally, the population is pretty heavily male. "There are a few not socially awkward guys, but social awkwardness comes with the territory," says a female student. Diversity, both ethnically and geographically, is moderate, with 43 percent of students coming from outside Florida.

You May Not Know

- A small brick kiosk on campus known as the "atomic toilet" is the last trace of an experiment conducted at Florida Tech in the 1960s using radiation to purify sewage water as a potential source of drinking water.
- In 1974, 500 Florida Tech students organized the largest mass streak in history, which included streakers on stilts. The local police station posted pictures of the streakers at the local police station and asked parents to come identify their children: no one showed.
- Florida Tech's seven residence halls are named for and dedicated to the memory of each of the seven astronauts aboard the Shuttle Columbia.

Distinguished Alumni

Ann E. Dunwoody, first female four star general in the United States military; Joan Higginbotham, NASA astronaut; Sunita Williams, NASA astronaut.

Admissions and Financial Aid

Florida Tech looks for applicants who have participated in certain teams or extracurriculars or have taken classes that encourage teamwork on projects, research, and problem solving. The transcript, however, is "most important." Interviews on campus are not required by highly recommended.

Merit scholarships of up to $18,500 annually are available to all applicants based on high school academic performance. Graduates from National Consortium of Specialized Secondary Schools of Mathematics, Science, and Technology are eligible for at least $15,000 annually, while applicants who participated in FIRST Robotics teams, or Eagle or Girl Scout Gold Award recipients, are eligible for a minimum of $10,000 with verification of participation and submission of application by February 1. Florida residents with qualifying GPAs and test scores are eligible for Florida Bright Futures Scholarships: students must apply to Florida Tech by February 1, submit a FAFSA, and fill out a specific scholarship application.

FLORIDA INSTITUTE OF TECHNOLOGY

Highlights

Admissions Criteria
Academic criteria:
Grades: ☆ ☆ ☆
Difficulty of class schedule: ☆ ☆ ☆
Class rank: ☆
Standardized test scores: ☆ ☆ ☆
Teacher recommendations: ☆
Personal statement: ☆
Non-academic criteria considered:
Interview
Extracurricular activities
Character/personal qualities
Work experience
State of residency
Alumni relationship

Deadlines
Early Action: No
Early Decision: No
Regular Action: Rolling admissions
Common Application: Not accepted

Financial Aid
In-state tuition: $35,460
Out-of-state tuition: $35,460
Room: $6,940
Board: $4,880
Books: $1,200
Freshmen receiving need-based aid: 63%
Undergrads rec. need-based aid: 58%
Avg. % of need met by financial aid: 83%
Avg. aid package (freshmen): $32,855
Avg. aid package (undergrads): $32,459
Avg. debt upon graduation: $38,953

School Spirit
Mascot: Panther
Colors: Crimson and gray
Song: *Florida Tech All Hail*

Four-year private
Founded: 1883
Lakeland, FL
Medium city
Pop. 98,589

Address:
111 Lake Hollings-
worth Drive
Lakeland, FL
33801-5698

Admissions:
800-274-4131

Financial Aid:
800-205-1600

fscadm@flsouthern.
edu

www.flsouthern.edu

FLORIDA SOUTHERN COLLEGE

Overview

Aspiring Moccasins visiting campus will likely begin their wanderings at the "Child of the Sun" Visitor Center. If the soaring building appears classic Frank Lloyd Wright, it's because it is—and if many buildings you pass also have hallmarks of the renowned American architect, it's because they do. With 18 structures designed by Wright, Florida Southern College is a Nationally Registered Historic Place, home to the largest collection of Wright architecture in a single location.

Sun shines on Florida Southern 330 days out of the year, making suburban Lakeland, Florida, a small oasis for its 2,000 undergraduates. The location—45 miles from bustling Orlando and Tampa—and campus design make time spent on campus nearly idyllic. The stunning architecture is complemented by surrounding manicured lawns, an enviable lakefront setting, and state-of-the-art athletic facilities. Nestled in such a sublime environment, the small student population reaps the benefits of an established academic program and thriving student life. Class sizes allow for close student-professor relationships and the school's ongoing commitment to its founding Judeo-Christian principles (Florida Southern is a Methodist-affiliated school) contributes to the tight-knit student body.

This comfort does not come without its sacrifices, however. Perhaps what contributes in part to the strong sense of community can also be a detriment: the undergraduate population is fairly demographically homogenous, with 64 percent hailing from within Florida. For those seeking a vibrant community of students from very different backgrounds, Florida Southern might feel too provincial.

Academics

Florida Southern College's academic rigor consistently garners national and state recognition. It has been named one of the top baccalaureate colleges in Florida by *U.S. News & World Report*. In the spirit of a well-rounded liberal arts education, students must complete a prescribed set of courses called the "Cornerstone Curriculum," which requires students to take classes across a variety of disciplines—including writing, computer competency, Western Civilization, math, biology, and the fine arts. In all classes, students and their professors forge close relationships in a classroom environment in which class sizes are typically between 10 and 19 students. "Professors greet me by name while I'm walking around campus," says a student.

Florida Southern College offers a range of academic opportunities, with 47 majors and pre-professional programs. Standout programs include biology, business and economics, and education as well as premed studies. The academic approach espoused by the college is "engaged learning," which prioritizes taking knowledge out of the classroom and into labs, workplaces, and service-learning opportunities. All freshmen entering Florida Southern are guaranteed an internship placing during their undergraduate career. One student explains, "the hands-on experience is invaluable because it takes learning from theoretical to practical."

For those intellectuals who wish to take their academic studies to the next level, Florida Southern offers a structured Honors Program, which requires a minimum of six semesters of Honors courses that culminate in either an Honors Thesis or "Honors within the Major." Offered only by certain departments, the "Honors within the Major" track includes project-based endeavors. In Honors Thesis coursework, students work in a group with their classmates and professor of the course on research projects focused on a central theme.

Forty percent of Florida Southern students take advantage of the school's "amazing" study-abroad program, which currently offers semester-, summer-, and year-abroad programs in England, Spain, Italy, France, and China, with a program in Germany in the works. Each destination has an academic focus specifically tailored to the uniqueness of the location; for example, students who want to study in Italy can concentrate their studies on either art or religion.

Separate from the abroad program is Junior Journey. All freshmen are guaranteed an abroad experience—at no additional costs—during summer term or other breaks. "I chose FSC specifically because of the guaranteed study abroad," says a student. All Junior Journeys have course credit, are themed, and culminate in a final project.

After graduation, 96 percent of recent graduates who report back to their alma mater say that they have either bagged a job or that they are enrolling in graduate studies. Of the premedical students who have taken the MCAT and applied for medical school, 100 percent have been accepted. Florida Southern's Career Center has programming, resources, and networking opportunities to support their students as they prepare to enter the workforce.

Student Life

The student-run Association of Campus Entertainment (ACE) brings concerts, comedians, dances, movies, and other revelry to campus. Each April, they throw the Fair-well Festival, a carnival-like extravaganza with rides, carnival food, and other attractions to mark the nearing of summer. "The festival is a last celebratory hurrah," laughs a student. The Festival of Fine Arts is another initiative that puts world-renowned performers on the stage and in conversation with students.

The student body gathers every month for the mandatory Faith and Life Convocation Series that is designed to "expose students to a broad range of issues—religious, aesthetic, moral, as well as intellectual"—as part of the liberal arts education experience. Alumni throng back to campus each year at Homecoming in March, where they are treated to live music, food, and other gaiety. During Founder's Week, students engage with the university's history through a special convocation, the traditional Founder's Ball, and other programming.

Greek life thrives at FSC, involving 31 percent of men and 27 percent of women. There are seven fraternities and six sororities, all situated within the "Greek Village"—campus-provided housing. Because the fraternities and sororities do not have their own houses, the party scene is not so much focused on the house party as it is in many other schools with strong Greek life. Florida Southern is technically dry, but room parties and off-campus options keep the party scene alive. "There's definitely somewhere to party every weekend," notes a student. Lakeland lacks a hot bar and club scene, so students typically venture to Orlando or Ybor City in Tampa.

The Florida Southern College Moccasins have a strong NCAA Division II record, with 26 National Championship titles and more than 420 All-American athletes. The Mocs field particularly strong golf teams: between the men's and women's sides, Moccasin Golf boasts 15 national championships. In the absence of a football team, popular spectator sports include baseball and softball. Intramural sports are also popular at FSC, with 50 percent of the student body involved in the 12 offered sports.

Florida Southern has a booming outdoor recreational program which aids in getting students off campus. Activities include horse-

FLORIDA SOUTHERN COLLEGE

Students
Total enrollment: 2,238
Undergrads: 2,040
Freshmen: 600
From out-of-state: 36%
From public schools: 81%
Male/Female: 42%/58%
Live on-campus: 70%
In fraternities: 31%
In sororities: 27%
Off-campus employment rating: Good
Caucasian: 73%
African American: 6%
Hispanic: 9%
Asian / Pacific Islander: 2%
Native American: 0%
Mixed (2+ ethnicities): 4%
International: 5%

Academics
Calendar: Semester
Student/faculty ratio: 13:1
Class size 9 or fewer: 24%
Class size 10-29: 61%
Class size 30-49: 16%
Class size 50-99: -
Class size 100 or more: -
Returning freshmen: 76%
Six-year graduation rate: 55%
Graduates who immediately enter career related to major: 70%

Most Popular Majors
Business administration
Biology
Nursing

Admissions
Applicants: 4,448
Accepted: 2,477
Acceptance rate: 55.7%
Average GPA: 3.6
ACT range: Not reported
SAT Math range: 500-600
SAT Reading range: 500-590
SAT Writing range: 2-14
Top 10% of class: 21%
Top 25% of class: 42%
Top 50% of class: 75%

283

FLORIDA SOUTHERN COLLEGE

back riding, kayaking, paint ball, rock climbing, and camping. The program also organizes day, overnight, and break trips throughout the state. "Recreation is a high priority," notes a student. The programs are well received by the student body, perhaps because most activities are free!

Seventy percent of Florida Southern students live on campus in one of 18 residence halls. First-year students live in single-sex halls, supported by a strong residence staff that leads programming events designed to foster connections and ease the transition into college life. Florida Southern recently launched the Second-Year Experience Living Learning Community initiative to continue creating community for its second-year students.

Student Body

Motivated by philanthropic drive and the school's commitment to engaged learning experiences, Mocs are very involved in their community, dedicating more than 10,000 hours a year to service endeavors. As an affiliate of the United Methodist Church, the school has a large number of students who identify as being religious, but "no one feels pressured to be religious," remarks a student.

Socially and politically, Florida Southern tends to lean more conservatively than many other colleges.

You May Not Know

- The college holds a Cardboard Regatta on Lake Hollingsworth. They provide the materials, while teams of up to four students compete to build the trophy-winning vessel.
- Frank Lloyd Wright could be often seen striding about campus, wielding a walking stick and wearing a cape and either a beret or pork pie hat.
- Whenever the shallow section of Florida Southern's 328,000-gallon pool is open, students can use the school's equipment to play water basketball or water volleyball.

Distinguished Alumni

John Antoon, United States District Judge; Lee Janzen, two-time U.S. Open-winning professional golfer; R. Fred Lewis, Florida Supreme Court Justice; Lance Niekro, professional baseball player.

Admissions and Financial Aid

Florida Southern is moderately selective, and students can apply Early Decision or Regular Action, which accepts students on a rolling basis.

Florida Southern offers over $15 million per year in aid through merit scholarships, need-based assistance, loans, and a work-study program. Merit scholarships are automatically determined during the admissions process. Presidential Scholarships are based upon GPA and SAT scores, while talent-based scholarships recognize talented performing and visual artists. Men and women can both earn athletic scholarships offered for nine sports. Various special interest awards carry more specific eligibility requirements.

FLORIDA STATE UNIVERSITY

Overview

As one of Florida's two flagship universities, Florida State University has a lot going for it. A very large school, it can offer unparalleled diversity of options. It has also been designated as a Carnegie Research University, indicating very high levels of research activity. The university's premier programs boast state-of-the-art facilities. FSU athletics regularly appear in national competitions. The 500-acre campus provides ample green space, like Landis Green, where students can hang out, play Frisbee, and enjoy the fact that even in the winter the average temperature hovers in the 50s. Residence halls are attractive historic red-brick buildings. And just a short walk away, Tallahassee, Florida's state capital, is a "just right" college town.

FSU isn't without its drawbacks, and they are fairly common to universities of its size. Classes are large, and it's an uphill struggle to get attention from professors; the social scene can be intimidating, especially if Greek isn't your thing. For academically-focused students, however, FSU has extensive special offerings and can be a nurturing environment. If you're less into academics, no one will make you work too hard. What FSU is really about is offering endless opportunities that students can take advantage of (or not)—ranging from academic opportunities to new social scenes—and tailgating and cheering on the FSU football team with almost 70,000 of your closest friends.

Academics

FSU offers about 200 degrees and is best known for its College of Motion Picture Arts, but its College of Education, majors in religion, meteorology, and creative writing program (under the English major) stand out as well. In addition to major studies requirements, students must complete the Common Requirements: Liberal Studies, the mysteriously named "X/Y," and Oral and Computer Competency. Liberal Studies breaks down into two or three courses each in mathematics, English, history/social science, humanities/fine arts, and natural science. Students satisfy the "X/Y" requirement by taking two multicultural courses (designated as "X") and diversity in Western culture ("Y"). Each major offers courses that satisfy the oral communication and computer competency components as well.

Unsurprisingly, most classes at FSU have a large number of students; in fact, more than half of classes have more than 20 students. This affects professor/student relationships, as one student explains, "some professors are very responsive, but others require a little chasing down to get an answer."

Any freshman can participate in the Freshmen Interest Group (FIG) program. A FIG is a predetermined menu of classes. Freshman liberal studies courses are grouped according to certain academic or pre-professional interests so that when students in the same FIG (about 20-25 people) take the same courses, they will know at least some classmates even in large lectures.

Like FIGs, freshman Living-Learning Communities are organized around certain academic interests and generally feature a weekly colloquium with distinguished FSU faculty; unlike FIGs, though, they are also residential programs. "LLCs are the best way to meet friends who have similar interests and to have a built-in study group," notes a student.

High-achieving freshmen can apply to the Honors Program. If selected, students take small Honors-only sections or elective Honors seminars taught by distinguished tenured faculty members. Honors students can also apply for special study-abroad grants and housing in the Honors-only hall and they get to register for classes as early as possible. Prelaw or premed students can get a "head start" on law or med school, respectively, in the Honors Legal Scholars Program or the Honors Medical Scholars Program. The students in these programs can observe classes and shadow current

FLORIDA STATE UNIVERSITY

Four-year public
Founded: 1851
Tallahassee, FL
Medium city
Pop. 182,965

Address:
A2500 University
Center
282 Champions Way
Tallahassee, FL
32306

Admissions:
850-644-6200

Financial Aid:
850-644-5871

admissions@admin.
fsu.edu

www.fsu.edu

285

College Profiles

FLORIDA STATE UNIVERSITY

Highlights

Students
Total enrollment: 40,695
Undergrads: 32,171
Freshmen: 5,738
Part-time students: 11%
From out-of-state: 11%
From public schools: 89%
Male/Female: 45%/55%
Live on-campus: 20%
In fraternities: 16%
In sororities: 19%
Off-campus employment rating: Good
Caucasian: 67%
African American: 9%
Hispanic: 16%
Asian / Pacific Islander: 3%
Native American: 0%
Mixed (2+ ethnicities): 2%
International: 1%

Academics
Calendar: Semester
Student/faculty ratio: 26:1
Class size 9 or fewer: 13%
Class size 10-29: 52%
Class size 30-49: 21%
Class size 50-99: 8%
Class size 100 or more: 6%
Returning freshmen: 91%
Six-year graduation rate: 75%
Graduates who immediately go to graduate school: 35%
Graduates who immediately enter career related to major: 70%

Most Popular Majors
Finance
English
Psychology

Admissions
Applicants: 30,040
Accepted: 16,124
Acceptance rate: 53.7%
Average GPA: 3.9
ACT range: 25-29
SAT Math range: 560-640
SAT Reading range: 560-640
SAT Writing range: 7-43
Top 10% of class: 41%
Top 25% of class: 80%
Top 50% of class: 98%

286

law or med students. They are eligible for automatic admission to the FSU Colleges of Law and Medicine, respectively, and can earn a bachelors and MD or JD in seven years.

FSU's College of Motion Picture Arts is among the best in the nation. Its students have won Emmys and Oscars and featured screenings at the Cannes Film Festival. Students have 24-hour access to state-of-the-art cameras, sound stages, digital editing and production rooms, and back-lots. FSU is also the only film school in the U.S. that foots the bill for the production of all student films. "There are so many opportunities to get hands-on experience," explains a student, "and the support from alumni after graduation is unsurpassed." An extensive film-school alumni network serves as mentors to every student, helping nearly 100 percent of graduates find work within a year of graduation. Success rates are also heavily boosted by the Torchlight Program, a non-degree program in business practices in the film industry.

About 20 percent of FSU students study abroad with FSU's International Programs, which rank among the top 15 in the nation. Programs are available in countries including Argentina, China, Croatia, France, Israel, Russia, and South Africa; students may also opt to spend their first semester or year in Florence, London, Valencia, or Panama City.

FSU's strength when it comes to career preparation is in internships—the Film School offers access to internships with major companies, and students interested in the political process can get in on the action at the Florida State Legislature located just a short walk from campus. One student comments, "our location is one of the best for finding internships, and the career office helps out a lot." Thirty-five percent of students attend graduate school within one year of graduating.

Student Life

Students can learn about FSU's 550 student organizations at Market Wednesdays, when groups set up their tables and congregate in the Oglesby Union courtyard. If you're limber, you can join the FSU Flying High Circus, one of only two college circuses in the nation. FSU's 31 fraternities and 27 fraternities are pretty prominent, accounting for 16 percent of men and 19 percent of women. While a very large portion of students live off campus, on-campus events are still a big draw due to the prominence of football and athletic events. Campus has its own bowling alley and billiards room, Crenshaw Lanes. And Club Downunder offers free shows that students actually want to see: past acts have included the White Stripes, Modest Mouse, Soundgarden, and the Yeah Yeah Yeahs.

Homecoming is a major event on campus, both because of the football team and the myriad events that accompany it. Fun activities include a "Warchant" concert (which most recently featured Ludacris), a Chili Cook-Off, Pow Wow, campus-wide tailgate, and a parade with the Budweiser Clydesdales. Seven Days of Opening Nights offers more cultural diversions, featuring artists and speakers such as B. B. King, Joanna Newsom, Bill Cosby, and David Sedaris.

Athletics are a big deal at FSU. The Seminoles have eight men's and nine women's Division I teams. Whereas football has probably already seen its heyday as the "winningest" team in the country in the 1990s, the baseball team is experiencing a high now as the "winningest" team since 2000. Win or lose, athletic events are still holidays for FSU. One student remarks, "football games are an all-weekend affair between the tailgating before and after the games." Students also say that intramurals at FSU are "ultra-competitive," but less combative Seminoles can get their workouts in at the three-story Leach Recreation Center.

Tallahassee itself offers a wide variety of distractions, including the Strip's shops, restaurants, and clubs. An hour's drive will take you to the beach.

Freshmen can live in traditional dorm-style or suite-style residences; upperclassmen can live in apartments on campus. "There's a mix of old and new dorms," says a student. "The old are habitable, but the new are much more desirable."

Student Body

FSU was known as the "Berkeley of the South" in the 1960s and 70s and was the scene of a number of major student protests. Since then, the student body has made a significant move to the right. "Most people I know are politically in the middle," one student comments.

As large as the school is, plenty of diversity is represented, particularly ethnic diversity: FSU is the leader in graduation of African American undergraduates and doctoral students. The vast majority of students come from Florida.

You May Not Know

- FSU was turned into a military school during the Civil War: in 1865, at the Battle of Natural Bridge, FSU defeated the Union army.
- Streaking is said to have originated at FSU during the 1970s on Landis Green.
- FSU uses the name "Seminole" with the official permission of the Seminole Tribe of Florida, Inc., and the Seminole Nation of Oklahoma.

Distinguished Alumni

Stephanie Abrams, Weather Channel meteorologist; Alan Ball, screenwriter and director; Matt Chapman, creator of Homestarrunner.com; Charlie Crist, Florida Governor; Richard Simmons, fitness personality; Leonard Skinner, high school gym teacher and namesake for the band Lynrd Skynrd.

Admissions and Financial Aid

Grades and test scores make up a large part of the admissions decision process; however, admissions officers also look at the rigor of the student's course of study, trends in grades, and educational goals. Students with high achievements in the visual and performing arts and athletics will be given additional consideration, as will students who apply to the CARE Summer Bridge Program, a college-prep program for disadvantaged and first-generation college students.

Merit scholarships of between $8,000 and $24,000 over four years are available. Students do not need a separate application, but must submit their applications to FSU by January 1.

FLORIDA STATE UNIVERSITY

Highlights

Admissions Criteria
Academic criteria:
Grades: ☆ ☆ ☆
Difficulty of class schedule: ☆ ☆ ☆
Class rank: ☆
Standardized test scores: ☆ ☆
Teacher recommendations: ☆
Personal statement: ☆
Non-academic criteria considered:
Extracurricular activities
Special talents, interests, abilities
Character/personal qualities
Volunteer work
Work experience
Geographical location
Alumni relationship

Deadlines
Early Action: No
Early Decision: No
Regular Action: January 14 (final)
Common Application: Accepted

Financial Aid
In-state tuition: $6,467
Out-of-state tuition: $21,633
Room: $5,980
Board: $3,932
Books: $1,000
Freshmen receiving need-based aid: 46%
Undergrads rec. need-based aid: 48%
Avg. % of need met by financial aid: 67%
Avg. aid package (freshmen): $9,470
Avg. aid package (undergrads): $9,850
Avg. debt upon graduation: $22,405

School Spirit
Mascot: Seminoles
Colors: Garnet and gold
Song: *Alma Mater - High Over Towering Pines*

FORDHAM UNIVERSITY

Overview

As a Jesuit institution with separate campuses around New York City, Fordham doesn't offer the quintessential college experience that many students envision. However, that doesn't keep it from being the perfect fit for many. Incredibly close to New York City, Fordham University students rave about its great location and ample access to major cultural and learning centers, in addition to the not-too-small, not-too-large size of its student body.

Fordham's Jesuit foundation may be frustrating for some students. Aside from the fact that the campus is largely populated by "well-to-do white Catholic school graduates," students also have to grapple with a strict administration that, for example, will not let male and female students share a room past a certain point in the evening. For others, though, the Jesuit institution is a positive aspect which infuses both campus and classroom environment. Affirming the complementary roles of faith and reason in learning, Fordham's mission is to encourage the growth of moral and intellectual development. And, with two separate campuses in New York, ranging from urban to gothic and green sceneries, Fordham provides many wide-ranging opportunities.

Rose Hill is the original campus sprawling 85-acres in the Bronx between the Bronx Zoo and Botanical Gardens, and Lincoln Center is a six-acre campus in the center of Manhattan. Students attending Fordham have the ability to reside on or commute to either campus. Both campuses offer liberal arts majors but the Fordham College at Rose Hill is home to the College of Business Administrations; by contrast the Lincoln Center, a smaller, urban campus in the heart of Manhattan, is home to the Graduate Schools of Business, Social Service, Education, and the School of Law.

Academics

Fordham strives to provide its students with an education in both heart and mind, expecting them to complete a series of core classes which blend traditional and new-age thinking, thereby imparting to students a truly liberal arts background. Beginning in the fall of 2009, Fordham updated its core requirements, obliging students to take 18 courses in a range of subjects, including classes in rhetoric, literature, philosophy, theology, history, mathematical reasoning, natural science, social science, fine arts, and modern or classical language. Additionally, students must complete courses in American pluralism and global studies as well as four Eloquentia Perfecta seminars (classes focused on written and spoken expression), which include a capstone senior seminar on values. "The core requirements are good because I take classes I normally wouldn't, but they make it harder to take the classes I want to take," remarks a student.

Class sizes at Fordham tend to be small, with virtually all classes having fewer than 50 people. Students say that classes tend to be rigorous and "most people don't get A's." Fordham offers 206 majors, though students can also choose to design their own majors. The strongest programs at the Rose Hill Campus are psychology, philosophy, business economics, and the pre-health professions program. While Fordham has no particular prelaw program, it does have a prelaw advising program that assists students interested in applying to law school. At the Lincoln Center campus, students are attracted to the school's strong theatre and dance programs.

An exciting opportunity for prospective Fordham students is the school's Manresa Program where students are taught by an internationally recognized teacher-scholar who also serves as their advisor. According to the university, Manresa scholars have the opportunity to "explore questions about the value and meaning of liberal arts education in the Jesuit tradition and integrate their in-class learning with extracurricular activities."

Fordham has numerous study-abroad opportunities for students interested in exploring other cultures for a semester, summer, or a full year (known as full-term).

One student explains, "I not only learned the language but also about the way of life in France."

In addition to its study-abroad programs, Fordham's G.L.O.B.E. Program (Global Learning Opportunities and Business Experiences) is designed to prepare students for careers on multinational levels. Courses are taught from an international perspective and hone students' international understanding of topics such as business economics, entrepreneurship, and human resource management.

With more than 150,000 alumni and great access to Wall Street, the media, art museums, and more, Fordham is able to offer ample internships and career/networking opportunities. The Office of Career Services is also available to provide students with a variety of resources which assist in their professional development, lending a hand in everything from picking a major to conducting a job search.

Student Life

Of the more than 8,000 undergraduates at Fordham, 56 percent live in university-managed housing. This makes Fordham somewhat of a "commuter college." The university has 143 official student organizations. Among the most popular activities are band, theatre, film study, public speaking, global outreach, community service, and other cultural/social clubs. The official school newspaper, *Observer*, is published weekly.

Amongst the school's most important events of the year is the annual alumni Jubilee, which draws thousands of successful alumni to cocktail parties and other activities. Two more important events are Fordham Week, which showcases many clubs and programs on campus, and Spring Week, which celebrates the final weekend of programming before students begin final exams. The events associated with Spring Week include big screen movie nights, dance parties, comedy shows, and a Saturday concert.

For those interested in sports, there are a multitude of intramural teams such as baseball, basketball, flag football, and volleyball. In addition, the university sponsors 23 Division I men's and women's varsity sports teams. School spirit reaches an all-time high at the biggest football game of the year when Fordham plays Colombia. "Even if we don't win any other game, it's a winning season if we beat Columbia," says a fan.

Fordham does not have Greek Life on campus. If students really wish to join a sorority or fraternity, they will sometimes pledge at another New York university such as NYU or Columbia, although this is not very common. "There are so many alternative activities that we don't need fraternities or sororities," notes a student. Popular off-campus activities include taking advantage of the cultural performances, restaurants, shopping, and museums in the vicinity of the Lincoln Center campus, or taking the train to Arthur Avenue (the Bronx's Little Italy) from the Rose Hill Campus.

Student Body

With 31 percent minority students, and 60 percent from out of state, Fordham is both ethnically and geographically diverse. The Rose Hill and Lincoln Center campuses, though united, are known for their dissimilarities. Students describe Rose Hill campus as "serious and more conservative" and those at Lincoln Center as "hip, urban artists." One student sums it up by saying, "despite

FORDHAM UNIVERSITY

Highlights

Students
Total enrollment: 15,170
Undergrads: 8,325
Part-time students: 7%
From out-of-state: 60%
Male/Female: 47%/53%
Live on-campus: 56%
Off-campus employment rating: Excellent
Caucasian: 62%
African American: 5%
Hispanic: 14%
Asian / Pacific Islander: 9%
Native American: 0%
Mixed (2+ ethnicities): 3%
International: 5%

Academics
Calendar: Semester
Student/faculty ratio: 13:1
Class size 9 or fewer: 9%
Class size 10-29: 61%
Class size 30-49: 29%
Class size 50-99: 1%
Class size 100 or more: -
Returning freshmen: 88%
Six-year graduation rate: 81%

Most Popular Majors
Business administration
Communications
Psychology

Admissions
Applicants: 34,069
Accepted: 14,621
Acceptance rate: 42.9%
Placed on wait list: 5,749
Enrolled from wait list: 748
Average GPA: 3.6
ACT range: 26-30
SAT Math range: 580-680
SAT Reading range: 570-670
SAT Writing range: 20-50
Top 10% of class: 50%
Top 25% of class: 87%
Top 50% of class: 99%

FORDHAM UNIVERSITY

Admissions Criteria

Academic criteria:
Grades: ☆ ☆ ☆
Difficulty of class schedule: ☆ ☆ ☆
Class rank: ☆ ☆ ☆
Standardized test scores: ☆ ☆ ☆
Teacher recommendations: ☆ ☆
Personal statement: ☆ ☆
Non-academic criteria considered:
Extracurricular activities
Special talents, interests, abilities
Character/personal qualities
Volunteer work
Work experience
State of residency
Geographical location
Minority affiliation
Alumni relationship

Deadlines

Early Action: November 1
Early Decision: No
Regular Action: November 1 (priority)
January 15 (final)
Notification of admission by: April 1
Common Application: Accepted

Financial Aid

In-state tuition: $42,845
Out-of-state tuition: $42,845
Room: $7,910
Board: $4,850
Books: Varies
Freshmen receiving need-based aid: 67%
Undergrads rec. need-based aid: 66%
Avg. % of need met by financial aid: 73%
Avg. aid package (freshmen): $27,170
Avg. aid package (undergrads): $26,539

School Spirit

Mascot: Ram
Colors: Maroon and white
Song: *Fordham Ram*

the differences between the campuses, we still have a lot of overall shared school spirit."

You May Not Know

- Due to the great number of tunnels which connect old buildings to one another on campus, there are tales of haunted buildings, including some of the dorms.
- Among other historical figures who have pursued Jesuit educations, like the one offered at Fordham, are Descartes, Alfred Hitchcock, Sting, and James Joyce.
- In 2009, Fordham launched a campaign to raise $500 million in time for their 175th anniversary in 2016.

Distinguished Alumni

Thomas Cahill, best-selling author; Vince Lombardi, football coach; Anne Mulcah, Chairman and CEO, Xerox; John E. Potter, U.S. Postmaster General and CEO of the U.S. Postal Service; Amanda Seyfried, actress, *Mean Girls*; Donald Trump, business executive; Denzel Washington, Academy Award-winning actor.

Admissions and Financial Aid

Fordham University, which does *not* accept the Common Application, reflects carefully on student essays. The admissions office evaluates essays on the basis of their creativity and clarity, looking for an essay that most accurately reflects a student's individuality. Fordham does not offer interviews; however, if students feel they have not had an adequate opportunity to express themselves, they are welcome to submit a short personal statement in addition to their application essay. They are also able to meet and ask questions to members of the admissions office if they are visiting campus.

Fordham offers a variety of merit-based and athletic scholarships which can cover full or part tuition. All freshmen applying to the university are reviewed for the Dean's scholarship which covers $10,000 (or more if needed) of tuition. The university's Metro Grant, a non-need-based scholarship, is a $6,000 grant given to incoming freshmen and transfers who commute to Fordham from their permanent residences in NYC. It may be renewed up to eight academic year semesters, as long as the student continues to commute and uphold certain academic standards.

FRANKLIN & MARSHALL COLLEGE

Overview

Occupying a green 170 acres in Pennsylvania's Amish country, Franklin and Marshall is a small, private college. F&M has strengths to offer, particularly in its science programs, small size, and its research opportunities and funding. And while the science-heavy emphasis of the school and the strength of its programs may make it an uncomfortable environment for non-science majors, the community—both inside and outside of the classroom—is a friendly and close-knit one. F&M guarantees a ready-made network of friends and neighbors through its College House system; and since everyone lives on campus, this sense of community persists throughout all four years.

F&M's location contributes to this sense of community and ensures that campus is the hub of student social life. The campus is pleasant, featuring a mix of historic and modern red-brick buildings and lots of open green spaces (that turn into snowball battlefields come the first snow). The surrounding area, including neighboring Lancaster, is scenic and quaint but sleepy. Because of this, most college socializing takes place on campus and is dominated by Greek parties. Fortunately, not-so-sleepy Philadelphia and New York City are within reach for big outings.

For students who want strong science backgrounds and boundless research opportunities without the meat-market feel of a large research institution, F&M is a first-rate option. Additionally, the environment on campus offers limited but lively distractions and promotes long-lasting relationships with peers, advisors, and professors.

Academics

F&M offers 37 majors, of which its science majors are the strongest: these include biology, chemistry, geosciences, environmental studies, environmental science, mathematics, physics, astrophysics, astronomy, and psychology. Several joint majors are offered as well, ranging from bioinformatics to animal behavior to public health. Business, organizations, and society is also a strong major.

F&M's General Education requirements offer some flexibility in choosing classes to satisfy each of its requirements: two "Foundations" courses, which explore major questions of human inquiry; distribution requirements in the arts, humanities, social sciences, natural sciences, and non-western culture; a writing requirement; and three semesters of a foreign language. Students can also fulfill the Writing Requirement by enrolling in a First-Year Seminar. Groups in the same seminar (usually 16 or fewer) are housed together in a College House, combining residential life with in-class learning. "Being able to walk down the hall to discuss homework is very helpful," notes a student.

Most classes at F&M have no more than 29 students, and many have fewer than that. According to students, this makes working closely with professors a "given." The academic environment tends to privilege the sciences and science majors, and divisions are perceptible between science and non-science majors, with the former tending to claim that the latter have much easier classes and majors. This can be an inhospitable environment for non-science majors, but not an impossible one. "We joke that the non-science majors are just along for the ride," one student comments. If students can't find a class they need or want at F&M, they can also cross-register at nearby Dickinson and Gettysburg colleges.

F&M boasts an abundance of funding for research in all fields, but with special emphasis on the science. The Committee on Grants doles out a hefty sum to support student-initiated, faculty-supervised research or collaborations with faculty. These include Leser and Nissley Grants of up to $1,000 for natural science and humanities, social sciences, and arts students, respectively; small Student Research Grants to augment departmental research funding; college-wide Summer Travel Awards; and Conference Travel Funds. Students may also receive funding from their own

FRANKLIN & MARSHALL COLLEGE

Four-year private
Founded: 1787
Lancaster, PA
Large town
Pop. 60,058

Address:
P.O. Box 3003
Lancaster, PA
17604-3003

Admissions:
877-678-9111

Financial Aid:
717-291-3991

admission@fandm.edu

www.fandm.edu

FRANKLIN & MARSHALL COLLEGE

Highlights

Students
Total enrollment: 2,365
Undergrads: 2,365
Freshmen: 599
Part-time students: 2%
From out-of-state: 71%
From public schools: 63%
Male/Female: 48%/52%
Live on-campus: 99%
In fraternities: 28%
In sororities: 34%
Off-campus employment rating: Excellent
Caucasian: 65%
African American: 4%
Hispanic: 6%
Asian / Pacific Islander: 3%
Native American: 0%
Mixed (2+ ethnicities): 2%
International: 10%

Academics
Calendar: Semester
Student/faculty ratio: 9:1
Class size 9 or fewer: 18%
Class size 10-29: 77%
Class size 30-49: 4%
Class size 50-99: -
Class size 100 or more: -
Returning freshmen: 92%
Six-year graduation rate: 83%
Graduates who immediately go to graduate school: 25%

Most Popular Majors
Business/organizations/society
Government
Psychology

Admissions
Applicants: 5,174
Accepted: 2,034
Acceptance rate: 39.3%
Placed on wait list: 1,330
Enrolled from wait list: 31
Average GPA: Not reported
ACT range: 28-31
SAT Math range: 613-710
SAT Reading range: 600-690
SAT Writing range: Not reported

departments, the study-abroad office, or the Ware Institute for Civic Engagement, depending on the project. The Hackman Summer Scholars Program offers students funding for 10 weeks of faculty-supervised summer research in any field (again, with special funding for science and econ research). "For a school as small as ours, we have a significant number of research opportunities," says a student.

With nearly three quarters of the student body involved in some kind of community service, Community Based Learning (CBL) through the Ware Institute is also a major part of most F&M students' study plans. CBL course leaders partner with local and international organizations, making these courses a forum for students to integrate their volunteer experiences with in-class readings and lectures. The Ware Institute also coordinates independent projects, such as Putting It Together (PIT) in the Community, summer mentoring, and the Project LAUNCH summer camp for local high school students. International CBLs and Alternative Service Breaks can include travel to South Africa, Ecuador, Honduras, and Guatemala.

Study abroad, independent of the CBL projects, is also available. Approximately one third of the student body elects to study abroad in faculty-led, exchange, or pre-approved third-party programs. Faculty-led trips usually are part of specific courses or are facilitated by certain departments. These can offer visits to Greece, Italy, and Japan in the summer; a semester program in France is another choice. Exchanges are available in Turkey, Hong Kong, Japan, Germany, France, Austria, Belgium, Denmark, Italy, Spain, Sweden, Switzerland, and the UK.

Career Services offers a Career Day, workshops, networking opportunities with alumni and parents, and individual career-coaching sessions. The Satell Scholar Program "for life after college success" helps juniors map out their post-graduation goals and plans through venues such as special speakers and dinners, workshops, coaching, and networking.

Student Life

Of F&M's 115 student clubs and organizations, Greek, ethnic (for example, the International Club), and service groups (such as, Habitat for Humanity) tend to be the most popular. Ben's Underground offers plenty of on-campus entertainment like movies, concerts, and comedy performances with a side of student-friendly fried food and milkshakes. Homecoming, with its tailgates and concerts, is an exciting time, now conjoined with Family Weekend. F&M shows its flair for alliteration in its other popular events: Flapjack Fest, the midnight pancake feed before finals, and "Fum Follies," the faculty variety show featuring musical performances and skits. "We have some pretty talented professors who aren't afraid to let loose," notes a student. But given that more than a quarter of students are involved in F&M's eight fraternities and four sororities, Greek parties are the "biggest social events" on campus.

F&M's 28 varsity sports teams compete in Division III (except for wrestling, which is Division I). Women's lacrosse and men's basketball and swimming are the Diplomats' strongest contenders. The few intramurals offered at F&M aren't terribly imaginative, but House Teams—in addition to regular open league—introduce an extra element of competition. "You don't have to be super athletic to play," one student says.

Lancaster itself is within walking distance of campus, offering historical buildings, art galleries, and Central Market, the oldest farmers market in the country. The first Friday of each month features gallery openings and extended shop and restaurant hours for an enjoyable evening of browsing the town. For those seeking bigger diversions, Philadelphia is only about an hour and a half away, and New York City is three hours.

Students are required to live on campus for all four years. Entering freshmen are assigned to College Houses, small clusters of residence halls organized around the same common green, and they continue to belong to these communities for the remainder of their time at F&M. Houses have their own funds to put on events, like pizza parties, dances, and field trips, and are supervised by a faculty don. Upperclassmen may continue to live in the residence halls or can branch out into houses organized around themes like French language, sustainability, or the arts, or move to on-campus apartments.

Student Body

F&M students have a reputation for being upper-class white students—a reputation that is in part substantiated. "Most students are white and wear designer labels," comments a student. "That's not to say that if you don't fit the type, you won't fit in. It's a welcoming environment for everyone." F&M has moderate levels of ethnic diversity. Seventy-one percent of students are from out of state.

You May Not Know

- F&M was established in 1787 with a donation of 200 pounds from Benjamin Franklin.
- Franklin College (the precursor of F&M) was the first bilingual college in the country, offering classes in both English and German.
- F&M was temporarily closed in 1979 due to the nuclear meltdown at Three Mile Island.

Distinguished Alumni

Kenneth Duberstein, White House Chief of Staff for President Ronald Reagan; Danielle Ganek, author; Jennifer Gareis, actress; James Lapine, playwright; Mary Schapiro, Chairwoman of the Securities and Exchange Commission (SEC); Franklin Shaffner, film director; Treat Williams, actor.

Admissions and Financial Aid

Applicants to F&M who believe their standardized test scores do not accurately represent their academic aptitude may submit two graded essays instead of their test scores.

All applications are considered for merit scholarships; no separate application is needed. Thirty-four percent of first-year students receive some kind of merit-based aid, ranging from $5,000 to the full cost of tuition. National Merit Finalists receive a $2,000 scholarship. The Courtney Adams Music Award is a $5,000 scholarship.

FRANKLIN & MARSHALL COLLEGE

Highlights

Admissions Criteria
Academic criteria:
Grades: ☆ ☆ ☆
Difficulty of class schedule: ☆ ☆ ☆
Class rank: ☆ ☆ ☆
Standardized test scores: ☆ ☆
Teacher recommendations: ☆ ☆
Personal statement: ☆ ☆
Non-academic criteria considered:
Interview
Extracurricular activities
Special talents, interests, abilities
Character/personal qualities
Volunteer work
Work experience
State of residency
Geographical location
Minority affiliation
Alumni relationship

Deadlines
Early Action: No
Early Decision: November 15
Regular Action: January 15 (final)
Notification of admission by: April 1
Common Application: Accepted

Financial Aid
In-state tuition: $46,185
Out-of-state tuition: $46,185
Room: $7,330
Board: $4,680
Books: $700
Freshmen receiving need-based aid: 53%
Undergrads rec. need-based aid: 47%
Avg. % of need met by financial aid: 100%
Avg. aid package (freshmen): $40,679
Avg. aid package (undergrads): $38,286
Avg. debt upon graduation: $37,432

School Spirit
Mascot: Diplomats
Colors: Blue and white

FURMAN UNIVERSITY

Four-year private
Founded: 1826
Greenville, SC
Medium city
Pop. 60,379

Address:
3300 Poinsett Highway
Greenville, SC
29613

Admissions:
864-294-2034

Financial Aid:
864-294-2204

admissions@furman.
edu

www.furman.edu

Overview

Furman University is a private, liberal arts university five miles north of downtown Greenville, South Carolina. A scenic lake is the highlight of the 750-acre, beautifully landscaped campus, nicknamed the "Country Club of the South." However, if you can't stomach the words "quaint" and "proper" being associated with your undergraduate experience, Furman is probably not for you. Attire, manners, religion, and politics swing towards the conservative end of the spectrum. The student body is not remarkable for its ethnic diversity; and, as you might expect, Greek life is a large part of the social scene.

Off campus, picturesque Greenville does not provide the hustle and bustle of a large city, but it does offer the requisite restaurants, bars, and shops for students seeking a night out.

Academically, Furman is no slouch. Two major selling points are small classes and abundant summer opportunities. Most classes have just 10 to 19 students; so while your professor may not be a "big name," he or she will definitely know *your* name. During the summer, the Furman Advantage program provides a large number of students with stipends for enrichment experiences on campus and off. Furman recently debuted its May Experience, a three-week mini-semester for students to sample out-of-the-ordinary courses on campus and abroad. Furman enjoys a strong academic reputation in the South and is ranked in the top 60 liberal arts colleges by *U.S. News & World Report*.

If you're looking for classes that will challenge you, a landscape that will inspire you, and classmates who will call you ma'am, then Furman just might be for you. Don't forget to pack your pearls and bowties, ladies and gents.

Academics

Furman offers 42 majors and eight interdisciplinary concentrations. The computer science, music, and political science programs are especially strong. In addition to completing a major, students may complete an interdisciplinary concentration. Options include Black cultures in the Americas, Latin American studies, poverty studies, and women's and gender studies.

All students must complete general education requirements that include both run-of-the-mill categories like freshman seminars (one in writing) as well as categories like "Ultimate Questions" (hip liberal arts speak for "Religious Studies") and "Body and Mind." One unique academic requirement is the Cultural Life Program. To graduate, students must attend 32 approved concerts, lectures, performances, or film screenings over the course of four years. "I actually liked the cultural requirement because it forced me to go to performances I normally wouldn't have," admits one student.

Ninety-five percent of courses have fewer than 30 students. It's not uncommon for students to be on a first-name basis with their professors or even to score an invite to dine at a professor's house. But some students say they did not expect the challenging workload they encountered. "I'm definitely studying more than I anticipated I would," a student notes.

A relatively new special academic opportunity at Furman is the May Experience (May X), an extra mini-semester included in regular tuition. After the spring semester ends, students may choose to sign up for a three-week course either on campus or abroad. Courses tend to be spicier than the normal offerings. Recent May X trips abroad have included living "off the grid" in Fiji, studying volcanoes in Iceland, and geology in the Appalachians. Seventeen school-sponsored study-abroad programs are available, including "faculty-led travel study" with Furman professors. The programs include Australia, the United Kingdom, Africa, and Japan.

Furman stands out for its abundance of summer research opportunities that are available for underclassmen. Through the Research Fellows program, students receive $3,000 stipends and do research full time during the summer with a Furman faculty member. The Furman Advantage program provides stipends for academic summer internships relevant to students' career goals, whether they are on campus or around the world. According to the university, 70 percent of students eventually go on to graduate school.

Student Life

Furman has over 140 student organizations dedicated to a respectable range of interests. (It's not every university that boasts a bridge club.) Religious organizations make a strong showing. Also, the highly popular Heller Service Corps links students to over 40 volunteer opportunities in Greenville.

Heller Service Corps brings the whole campus, and the individuals they have served throughout the year, together for a "May Day Play Day" celebration at the end of the year. Homecoming, complete with music and spirited floats, also draws crowds. The Inter-Fraternity Council takes the lead in organizing "Beach Weekend," when students flock to Myrtle Beach for a weekend of partying. To keep students entertained between these big events, the Student Activities Board regularly schedules smaller activities, from concerts and dance workshops to trips to amusement parks.

With seven social fraternities and seven social sororities present, Greek life is prominent on campus. Thirty-eight percent of men and 51 percent of women pledge. "While the Greek parties are the best, joining a fraternity or sorority is about more than the social aspects. Volunteering is key," says a student.

Small but mighty, Furman is a Division I school. The university has won 12 Southern Conference football titles and one national title for the NCAA Football Championship Subdivision. Women's golf, men's soccer, men's tennis, and rugby are also standout teams. For the less intense athletes out there, Furman offers a smattering of intramural sports.

Students can hop a university-run shuttle to downtown Greenville on weekends to get a breather from the secluded campus and to check out the restaurant and bar scene. "Downtown Greenville has a ton of restaurants and bars. There's plenty to do," says a student. You can stroll the main thoroughfare, which has been named one of America's Great Main Streets. Granted, it's not New York City, but Greenville does have some large events venues that draw nationally-known acts, especially bands with a country flavor. The shopping isn't bad, since malls abound in the area. And for the adventurous, a two-hour trip to Atlanta or Charlotte will be well worth the travel time to enjoy the added entertainment options and nightlife.

Since almost all students live on campus, dorms are social hubs. Hallmates bond through planned social activities like movie nights and trips. Students can also choose to live in "Engaged Living" dorms where faculty members plan dorm activities and discussions in conjunction with a class. Many upperclassmen live in apartment-style university housing.

FURMAN UNIVERSITY

Highlights

Students
Total enrollment: 2,915
Undergrads: 2,753
Freshmen: 697
From out-of-state: 71%
From public schools: 52%
Male/Female: 43%/57%
Live on-campus: 96%
In fraternities: 38%
In sororities: 51%
Off-campus employment rating: Excellent
Caucasian: 81%
African American: 5%
Hispanic: 3%
Asian / Pacific Islander: 2%
Native American: 0%
Mixed (2+ ethnicities): 2%
International: 3%

Academics
Calendar: Semester
Student/faculty ratio: 11:1
Class size 9 or fewer: 14%
Class size 10-29: 80%
Class size 30-49: 5%
Class size 50-99: -
Class size 100 or more: -
Six-year graduation rate: 83%
Graduates who immediately go to graduate school: 44%

Most Popular Majors
Political science
Health sciences
Business administration

Admissions
Applicants: 6,035
Accepted: 4,676
Acceptance rate: 77.5%
Placed on wait list: 76
Enrolled from wait list: 3
Average GPA: Not reported
ACT range: 25-29
SAT Math range: 560-660
SAT Reading range: 550-650
SAT Writing range: 12-42
Top 10% of class: 40%
Top 25% of class: 72%
Top 50% of class: 92%

295

FURMAN UNIVERSITY

Admissions Criteria

Academic criteria:
Grades: ☆ ☆ ☆
Difficulty of class schedule: ☆ ☆ ☆
Class rank: ☆ ☆
Standardized test scores: ☆
Teacher recommendations: ☆
Personal statement: ☆ ☆
Non-academic criteria considered:
Interview
Extracurricular activities
Special talents, interests, abilities
Character/personal qualities
Volunteer work
Work experience
State of residency
Minority affiliation
Alumni relationship

Deadlines

Early Action: November 15
Early Decision: November 1
Regular Action: January 15 (final)
Notification of admission by: April 2
Common Application: Accepted

Financial Aid

In-state tuition: $42,784
Out-of-state tuition: $42,784
Room: $6,262
Board: $5,022
Books: $1,200
Freshmen receiving need-based aid: 41%
Undergrads rec. need-based aid: 39%
Avg. % of need met by financial aid: 73%
Avg. aid package (freshmen): $26,910
Avg. aid package (undergrads): $30,492
Avg. debt upon graduation: $26,661

School Spirit

Mascot: Paladins
Colors: Purple and white

Student Body

Furman is full of proper Southerners prone to saying, "yes, ma'am." One student explains, "if you aren't from the South, you may feel a little like a fish out of water; but you'll find everyone to be friendly to help you acclimate." Preppy is definitely the order of the day. When it comes to politics, students tend to be "more conservative than not." On Sunday mornings, a large portion of the student body will be warming pews rather than their beds.

Ethnic diversity is not Furman's strong suit. Twelve percent of students identify as minorities. Geographic diversity, on the other hand, is high, with 71 percent of students hailing from out of state.

You May Not Know

- The best birthday attire at Furman may be a bathing suit; it's a tradition to throw friends into the campus lake on their birthdays.
- Furman was named one of the 362 most beautiful places in the country by the American Society of Landscape Architects.
- The university was founded in 1826 and was originally affiliated with the South Carolina Baptist Convention. Its motto is *Christo et Doctrinae* ("For Christ and learning").

Distinguished Alumni

Keith Lockhart, Director of Boston Pops Orchestra; Richard Riley, former Secretary of Education; Charles Townes, Nobel Prize winner in physics.

Admissions and Financial Aid

The university looks for students who have taken the most challenging courses available (in most cases, AP courses) in five major subject areas: English, math, social science, science, and foreign language. Furman uses the Common Application exclusively and waives the application fee if you apply online.

In addition to many relatively small and targeted scholarships for specific academic interests, Furman offers several general and more generous scholarship programs. Four entering freshmen displaying "exceptional academic achievement and distinctive personal accomplishment" win the Herman W. Lay Scholarship each year. The comprehensive, renewable award covers tuition, fees, weighted average room cost and board; and it is valued at over $180,000 for four years. Ten academically gifted freshmen will receive free tuition through James B. Duke Scholarships.

Hollingsworth Scholars from South Carolina and Townes Scholars from out of state receive $25,000 a year towards tuition, $1,000 for study abroad, support for summer experiences or research, and the chance to attend seminars that connect them to "government and civic leaders." Applicants to the Hollingsworth and Townes leadership programs need a recommendation from a "Community Leader."

Athletic scholarships, including full rides, are available in 17 sports; but Furman keeps information on these scholarships close to the chest. Contact the relevant coach or athletic director for the scoop.

GEORGE MASON UNIVERSITY

Overview

It may not have a lot of history to back it up yet, but all eyes are on George Mason University as an up-and-coming school. The university invested more than $1 billion between 2007 and 2013. Several new buildings were constructed, including an on-campus conference center and hotel, and one of the largest academic residential communities in the state. Not impressive enough? Mason ranks first, nationally, in research grants for public policy, public administration, public affairs, and political science.

The university is still in its infancy, having been founded in 1972 as a public post-secondary school; but in the short time that Mason has been around, it has carved for itself the reputation of an innovative institution. *U.S. News & World Report* "Up-and-Coming Schools" named Mason the number two school to watch. Professors are respected leaders in their fields, students enjoy internship opportunities in and around the nation's capital, and the university enjoys one of the most extensive study-abroad programs in the country.

In a show of their commitment to forward thinking, Mason recently opened a 40,000 square-foot state-of-the-art sustainable dining facility called Southside. It is designed to not only meet, but *exceed*, green standards.

Like any "up-and-coming" school that hasn't yet established a solid rep, George Mason has a few downsides that should be carefully considered. For one, it's still mostly a commuter college. While this may be a negative for students looking for the on-campus experience, George Mason scores well in the ultimate test of real estate: location, location, location! George Mason is located on 677 acres in Fairfax, Virginia, 18 miles from Washington, DC.

Academics

One of George Mason's strongest assets is the professor pool. Many of the instructors at George Mason are still very involved in their fields, and among these ranks are two Nobel Prize winners. Even those professors just starting out have received recognition; Merav Opher, an assistant professor in the Department of Physics and Astronomy, recently won the Presidential Early Career Award, the highest honor given by the U.S. government for outstanding research. "All of my professors have been amazing," says a student.

The average class size is 20-30 students, and students say they "need to make an effort to develop a close relationship with their professors." Mason offers 71 undergraduate majors. Strong programs include dance, economics, journalism, management, prelaw, and public policy.

Mason does have an honors program, as well as the self-designed major option and independent study opportunities. The university's general education requirements include courses in written and oral communication, quantitative reasoning, ethics, literature, arts, natural science, Western civilization/world history, global understanding, and social and behavioral sciences as well as a synthesis course that draws on "knowledge attained through the ...core elements of the General Education program."

One particularly unique opportunity Mason students have at their fingertips is the Smithsonian Semester. A partnership between the university and the Smithsonian Institute, the program allows students to live at the Conservation and Research Center of the Smithsonian's National Zoo. Students who participate in the program study sustainability issues and civic concerns.

The Institution of International Education has ranked George Mason University second among U.S. doctoral institutions for the number of students who study abroad. The university has programs in more than 30 countries, including reciprocal rela-

GEORGE MASON UNIVERSITY

Four-year public
Founded: 1972
Fairfax, VA
Medium city
Pop. 22,549

Address:
4400 University Drive
Fairfax, VA
22030

Admissions:
703-993-2400

Financial Aid:
703-993-2353

admissions@gmu.edu

www.gmu.edu

GEORGE MASON UNIVERSITY

Highlights

Students
Total enrollment: 32,961
Undergrads: 20,653
Freshmen: 2,694
Part-time students: 21%
From out-of-state: 20%
From public schools: 90%
Male/Female: 48%/52%
Live on-campus: 28%
In fraternities: 3%
In sororities: 3%
Off-campus employment rating: Excellent
Caucasian: 46%
African American: 9%
Hispanic: 11%
Asian / Pacific Islander: 18%
Native American: 0%
Mixed (2+ ethnicities): 5%
International: 4%

Academics
Calendar: Semester
Student/faculty ratio: 16:1
Class size 9 or fewer: 10%
Class size 10-29: 51%
Class size 30-49: 26%
Class size 50-99: 10%
Class size 100 or more: 3%
Returning freshmen: 86%
Six-year graduation rate: 66%
Graduates who immediately go to graduate school: 14%

Most Popular Majors
Psychology
Communication
Biology

Admissions
Applicants: 14,703
Accepted: 9,667
Acceptance rate: 65.7%
Placed on wait list: 1,737
Enrolled from wait list: 158
Average GPA: 3.7
ACT range: 23-28
SAT Math range: 530-630
SAT Reading range: 520-620
SAT Writing range: Not reported
Top 10% of class: 21%
Top 25% of class: 57%
Top 50% of class: 94%

tionships with universities in Russia, Korea, China, and Germany. Mason was also the first university in Virginia to establish a Confucius Institute with the Beijing Language and Culture University.

Students will find they have the opportunity to intern for several nationally recognized organizations, from Fortune 500 companies to the Kennedy Center. Some examples of well known companies that hire graduates from George Mason include the following: AOL/Time Warner, the World Bank, Fannie Mae, AFLAC, National Public Radio, and the Federal Government. This should go almost without saying, but due to Mason's close proximity to Washington, DC, internship opportunities involving politics are "plentiful," according to students.

Student Life

Almost three-fourths of the student body live off campus. This is not entirely a bad thing, as most freshmen still get the dorm experience, though a whopping 27 percent of freshmen do live off campus. The majority of freshmen live in Presidents Park, which one student describes as "cramped but a central place for meeting other freshmen."

On campus, students hang out at the George W. Johnson Center (JC), which has a food court, movie theater, ballroom, and bookstore. The Greek scene is also active, with 21 fraternities and 15 sororities represented on campus. There are more than 250 student clubs and organizations. Students who get a thrill out of public speaking can try out for Mason's debate and forensics team. For those who prefer powerful phrases in print, *Phoebe* is the University's literary magazine, and *So To Speak* is a feminist journal. *The Broadside* is the university's newspaper, which has won national awards for journalism.

Every Freakin' Friday (EFF) is a bi-weekly program of "very fun nights that appeal to pretty much everyone," says a student. Past EFF weekends have included Rock the Runway, Slam Poet, Murder Mystery Dinner, Swing Dance Lessons, and live bands. For those first-year students still learning the ropes, Mason on Location takes groups of students to explore significant locations in the Virginia and DC areas.

The Patriots have 20 Division I teams. Basketball games are the most popular, especially after the team's Final Four appearance in 2006 and appearance in the NCAA tournament in 2008. Mason's Recreation Sports Complex features six basketball courts, seven tennis courts, seven volleyball courts, a batting cage, fencing lanes, and saunas. Swimmers will find the Freedom Aquatic and Fitness Center a little slice of heaven with a competition and leisure pool as well as a waterslide.

Off campus, Washington, DC has a plethora of bars, restaurants, concerts, and museums. Free shuttle service to the metro makes getting off campus convenient. Exploring the local music scene will eventually lead students to such clubs as Busboys and Poets, Black Cat Club, and Jammin Java. And to satisfy more refined interests, well, it's Washington, DC! The Kennedy Center, the Smithsonian, Georgetown, Old Town Alexandria, and the Basilica of the National Shrine of the Immaculate Conception are all national landmarks just a few minutes away by car. Wolf Trap National Park for the Performing Arts is popular for hosting a wide range of concerts.

The historic Chesapeake and Ohio Canal is a national park with great biking trails. Great Falls Park is another favorite spot for picnicking and hiking.

Student Body

George Mason is a large public university, and as with most large, public universities, most every type of student imaginable is represented. Because of its proximity to the nation's capital, a common interest among many students is an avid interest in politics. As a whole, the student body is "slightly more conservative than liberal" one student explains.

Though only about one fifth of the student body hails from out of state, the university still has geographic representation from all 50 states and 125 countries. Mason has a high level of ethnic diversity with 43 percent of its undergraduate population self-identifying as being part of a minority group. Some say that there are no outward problems with discrimination, but as one student comments, "many divide themselves by racial or ethnic group." Students vary in their academic career trajectories, with 21 percent of undergraduates attending school on a part-time basis.

You May Not Know

- The George Mason Bronze on Mason's campus is the first three-dimensional portrait in the U.S. of George Mason, one of the Nation's founding fathers.
- The State Council of Higher Education for Virginia recently approved five new degrees, offered for the first time in 2010: bioengineering, environmental science, geoinformatics, nursing, and sport and recreation studies.
- The Patriot Center is a 10,000 seat arena on Mason's campus that has seen such concerts as Bruce Springsteen, Bob Dylan, Keith Urban, and Enrique Iglesias.

Distinguished Alumni

Anousheh Ansari, Vice President and General Manager, Intelligent IP Division of Sonus Networks; Carolyn Kreiter-Foronda, Virginia Poet Laureate; Zainab Salbi, founder and President of Women for Women International.

Admissions and Financial Aid

Mason takes into consideration a student's cumulative high school GPA, SAT and/or ACT scores, high school course load, a secondary school report, a counselor recommendation, and a personal statement. Letters of recommendation are encouraged, but not required.

Mason recommends that students take both the ACT and the SAT but does offer Score Optional Consideration. This means that students who feel that their standardized test scores do not adequately reflect their academic prowess are able to submit their application without submitting their ACT or SAT test scores.

Students who wish to be considered for a merit scholarship must submit their admissions application by December 1; no additional application is required. Merit scholarships are renewable for up to four years for students who maintain a minimum 3.0 GPA at Mason.

GEORGE MASON UNIVERSITY

Highlights

Admissions Criteria
Academic criteria:
Grades: ☆ ☆ ☆
Difficulty of class schedule: ☆ ☆ ☆
Class rank: ☆ ☆
Standardized test scores: ☆
Teacher recommendations: ☆
Personal statement: ☆
Non-academic criteria considered:
Extracurricular activities
Special talents, interests, abilities
Character/personal qualities
Volunteer work
Work experience
State of residency
Alumni relationship

Deadlines
Early Action: November 9
Early Decision: No
Regular Action: November 1 (priority)
January 15 (final)
Notification of admission by: April 1
Common Application: Not accepted

Financial Aid
In-state tuition: $9,908
Out-of-state tuition: $28,592
Room: $5,690
Board: $3,010
Books: Varies
Freshmen receiving need-based aid: 52%
Undergrads rec. need-based aid: 50%
Avg. % of need met by financial aid: 61%
Avg. aid package (freshmen): $11,987
Avg. aid package (undergrads): $11,790
Avg. debt upon graduation: $25,822

School Spirit
Mascot: The Patriot
Colors: Green and gold
Song: *GMU Alma Mater*

Four-year private
Founded: 1821
Washington, DC
Major city
Pop. 617,996

Address:
2121 Eye Street, NW
Washington, DC
20052

Admissions:
800-447-3765

Financial Aid:
202-994-6620

gwadm@gwu.edu

www.gwu.edu

GEORGE WASHINGTON UNIVERSITY

Overview

Chartered by the U.S. Congress, George Washington University (GW) is a large private college in a prime DC location, just walking distance from the White House. First Lady Michelle Obama was the speaker at the 2010 commencement held in the National Mall, a true indication of the university's ties to politics.

Budding politicians, poets, and scientists alike enjoy two sides of DC life: the main campus, Foggy Bottom, is integrated with the city, while the Mount Vernon campus is a smaller, woodsy escape in an upscale residential neighborhood. A shuttle, the Vern Express, helps students move from class to home to class between these two campuses. Cultural activities and internship opportunities abound on and around the GW campus, while world-class professors teach small classes and the Colonial's basketball team brings out crowds.

Academics

GW's educational goal is to prepare students as citizens, equipping them with skills that will aid them in thinking critically and quantitatively to solve the problems of our country as they relate to the world. GW offers 213 majors, with the most popular being international affairs and political science. "We have the best location in the world to study political science," one student notes. Other strong programs are biology, finance, and political communications. As a more traditional liberal arts school, GW requires students to complete classes in writing, quantitative and logical reasoning, natural sciences, social and behavioral sciences, arts, literature, humanities, and foreign language.

As with most high profile universities, there are professors who some students say are more focused on "promoting themselves" than teaching. On the other hand, who better to learn mechanical and aerospace engineering from than the former director of the Fluid Dynamics and Hydraulics Program at the National Science Foundation? The good news is that most classes are between 10-19 students and are reported to be very "discussion-oriented."

To get involved in George Washington University life, freshmen can take part in the living and learning Elizabeth Somer's women's leadership program, become Scholars in Quantitative and Natural Sciences, or opt to excel as Dean's Scholars in Shakespeare. "Living with students who share your interests expands learning well beyond the hours that we're in class," explains a student. The Honors Program also engages exceptional students in a series of small, interdisciplinary seminars and rigorous courses, complemented by the professors-on-the-town program that encourages cooperation between students and faculty on service projects. The program opens doors to fellowships, internships, and jobs internationally.

Honors or not, GW students have rich extracurricular resources. The Luther Rice Collaborative Fellowship Program, Gamow Research Awards, and Major-Specific Awards all provide funding for student-initiated or faculty-led research during all years of undergraduate study. Off campus options include four GW-only programs in Latin America, England, Madrid, and Paris, complimented by 240 affiliated study-abroad schools, including 20 in Africa and four in Israel.

You don't have to go far, however, to find fantastic internship opportunities. Many students find internships at term-time because they aren't competing against students from other colleges who flock to DC during the summer. In fact, more than 90 percent of students take on an internship, research project, or other career-building experience before graduation. GWork, an exclusive online database of jobs and internships, facilitates this process, and students have worked at the *Washington Post*, Miramax Films, IBM, and the United States Congress. "You'd be missing out if you didn't do an internship," remarks a student. "When else will you have the opportunity to be in the heart of the most powerful city in the world?"

For those students who want to pursue studies past a bachelor's degree, accelerated degree programs are also offered. Freshmen can begin BA/MA programs, or a combined seven-year BA-MD progam, while juniors can participate in joint and dual degree programs as well.

Student Life

According to the college, Marvin Student Center is the "hub of campus life," with televisions, bowling, billiards, and a host of—according to students—mediocre and overpriced fast food joints. Tonic, a restaurant on GW's grounds, is a popular spot for happy hour and brunch.

But there is much more to do than eat and drink on campus; popular events include classic festivals such as Fall Fest, cultural shows like the Bhangra Blowout and Taste of Africa, and spirit events such as the Colonial Invasion at the end of Spirit week, where the cheer and dance teams give their first performance of the season to live music. The charity event "Buzzing 4 Change" is becoming popular as well. Dubbed "lazy man's walkathon," students voluntarily shave their heads to raise funds for children battling cancer. "You'll never see as many nearly-bald people in your life," one student comments.

Greek organizations and international student groups influence student life in a big way. There are 22 fraternities and 18 sororities with almost one quarter of students pledging. "Joining is about more than the parties," notes a member. "We do a ton of service and form lifelong friendships." Other official student organizations keep everyone else busy, with 70 cultural clubs, 75 academic organizations including the student newspaper, 45 political groups, and 27 religious communities—all organized by the Student Activities Center. Fourteen student guides of the GW TRAiLs program guide rafting, backpacking, kayaking, and climbing trips to places as varied as Shenandoah National Park to the Florida Keys. Creative students find outlets in any of the dance, theater, improv, and musical ensembles.

George Washington is a Division I member of the Atlantic 10 Conference and the Collegiate Water Polo Association. Basketball games are "crazy and filled with school spirit," and the team has made three appearances in the NCAA tournaments since 2005. A host of intramural activities keep students active, from shotokan karate to roller hockey.

Off campus, students hang out in Adams Morgan, DuPont Circle, and Georgetown areas, which offer lots of bars and clubs that cater to students. "There's something going on every day of the year," says a student. Plus the monuments, professional athletic teams, and cultural offerings of DC are virtually limitless, with the national mall just down the street.

GW students must live on campus during their first and second years; but most don't mind, since GW has been ranked in the top 10 by Princeton Review for "Dorms Like Palaces." Off-campus housing can be very pricey. According to the college, the unique living and learning cohorts "are student-led interest groups within

GEORGE WASHINGTON UNIVERSITY

Highlights

Students
Total enrollment: 25,653
Undergrads: 10,464
Part-time students: 7%
From out-of-state: 99%
Male/Female: 45%/55%
Live on-campus: 67%
In fraternities: 23%
In sororities: 23%
Off-campus employment rating: Excellent
Caucasian: 59%
African American: 7%
Hispanic: 7%
Asian / Pacific Islander: 10%
Native American: 0%
Mixed (2+ ethnicities): 2%
International: 8%

Academics
Calendar: Semester
Student/faculty ratio: 13:1
Class size 9 or fewer: 11%
Class size 10-29: 60%
Class size 30-49: 19%
Class size 50-99: 6%
Class size 100 or more: 3%
Returning freshmen: 93%
Six-year graduation rate: 80%
Graduates who immediately go to graduate school: 19%

Most Popular Majors
International affairs
Political science

Admissions
Applicants: 21,753
Accepted: 7,197
Acceptance rate: 33.1%
Placed on wait list: 2,865
Enrolled from wait list: 26
Average GPA: Not reported
ACT range: 27-31
SAT Math range: 600-700
SAT Reading range: 600-690
SAT Writing range: 28-53
Top 10% of class: 58%
Top 25% of class: 86%
Top 50% of class: 99%

301

College Profiles

GEORGE WASHINGTON UNIVERSITY

Highlights

Admissions Criteria
Academic criteria:
Grades: ☆ ☆ ☆
Difficulty of class schedule: ☆ ☆ ☆
Class rank: ☆ ☆
Standardized test scores: ☆ ☆
Teacher recommendations: ☆ ☆
Personal statement: ☆ ☆
Non-academic criteria considered:
Interview
Extracurricular activities
Special talents, interests, abilities
Character/personal qualities
Volunteer work
Work experience
State of residency
Geographical location
Minority affiliation
Alumni relationship

Deadlines
Early Action: No
Early Decision: November 10
Regular Action: December 1 (priority)
January 10 (final)
Notification of admission by: April 1
Common Application: Accepted

Financial Aid
In-state tuition: $47,290
Out-of-state tuition: $47,290
Room: Varies
Board: $3,400
Books: $1,275
Freshmen receiving need-based aid: 48%
Undergrads rec. need-based aid: 50%
Avg. % of need met by financial aid: 88%
Avg. aid package (freshmen): $38,163
Avg. aid package (undergrads): $39,207
Avg. debt upon graduation: $33,398

School Spirit
Mascot: Colonials
Colors: Buff and blue

a particular House, which focus on a year-long investigation of an experiential co-curricular activity."

Student Body

GW is a highly political school, and with the diversity of students, intense debating at the coffee shop is not uncommon. "Stereotypical" students are rich and planning a future in government; but while this is clearly an exaggeration, it is indicative of the general tenor of GW. "There are some students I can see running for political office in the future, but most of us are more normal," states a student.

GW boasts high ethnic diversity, with 26 percent of the student body a minority. The geographic diversity is no less impressive, with 99 percent of students from out of state and eight percent of students hailing from other countries entirely.

You May Not Know

- George Washington is only four blocks from the White House.
- The university has $172 million in research funding.
- The Hippo is GW's unofficial mascot. A statue in one of the quadrangles is reminiscent of the "river horses" that are rumored to have lived in the Potomac, and were believed to bring good luck to Martha and George Washington's plantation.

Distinguished Alumni

Alec Baldwin, actor; Eric Cantor, House Majority Leader; John Foster Dulles, former Secretary of State; Frank Freyer, former Governor of Guam; J. William Fulbright, former U.S. Senator and creator of the Fulbright scholarships; Ina Garten, chef, author and Food Network host; Vincent Gray, Mayor of the District of Columbia; Jacqueline Kennedy Onassis, former First Lady; Colin Powell, former Secretary of State; Harry N. Reid, Senate Majority Leader; Mark Warner, former Governor of Virginia.

Admissions and Financial Aid

Students apply directly to one of the six different schools, and a big part of the application is making it personal. For example, the George Washington admissions staff suggests, for your essay, that you "choose a topic which conveys an important aspect of you, your character, or your personality that is not apparent anywhere else in your application." And according to the admissions office, interviews are not required but are encouraged because of their "evaluative" contribution.

As one of the priciest colleges in the country, scholarships certainly help, and the school meets approximately 88 percent of demonstrated need. More than 10 percent of students also receive merit-based aid, such as the Seven-Year Integrated BA/MD scholarship ($105,000 total merit discount) and Arts Scholarships. Students may only be awarded one scholarship even if they qualify for multiple, and all awards are determined upon initial application.

GW follows a fixed tuition scheme, where the amount due for a student's first semester will remain the same for the full undergraduate program (in contrast to other colleges' tuition rates that can rise on average 6.3 percent per year).

GEORGETOWN UNIVERSITY

Overview

Georgetown is the country's oldest Catholic University, and over two centuries after its founding still holds deep roots in the Catholic faith and Jesuit tradition. Overlooking the beautiful Potomac River and with the United States capital in the background, the 110-acre campus provides a scenic backdrop. Students gather and study in majestic, historic buildings; for example, Healy Hall, a trademark of the university's architecture, was built in the Flemish Romanesque style and towers in a gorgeous and stately fashion over one of campus' main quadrangles.

Georgetown is ranked by the *U.S. News & World Report* as one of the top 20 universities across the nation—you'll definitely get that "wow" response when you can claim Georgetown as your alma mater. With a steady focus outside the nation's borders, Georgetown has an internationally acclaimed School of Foreign Service and a renowned Faculty of Languages and Linguistics. For the would-be senator or foreign dignitary, DC is the place to be, and Georgetown is the place to get your degree.

Receiving buzz for their successful basketball team and the accompanying rabid Hoya student section, Georgetown offers more than just a deep immersion in the American political scene—you'll find plenty of fun school traditions and pride, the vibrant social and cultural setting that is the DC area, and opportunities to really get to know and work with the professors who will be teaching you. At just over 7,500 undergraduate students, Georgetown has both that big school rallying excitement and just enough smallness and familiarity to ensure that you'll recognize a face or two walking across campus.

Though the university's Catholic ties prevent the progress and freedom that many students would hope for on a college campus, hot topic issues such as sexual health resources, abortion, and diversity provide ample opportunities for the student who wants to try his or her hand at lobbying.

Academics

Georgetown offers 191 majors, and with so many options, many students choose to double major or add a minor. All undergraduate academic programs are offered through Georgetown College, the School of Foreign Service, the School of Business, or the School of Nursing and Health Studies. As a prospective, you select one school to apply to, and take most of your coursework there. Freshmen find their friends within the main community of that school.

Undergraduates say that classes are "very challenging," and filled with students who graduated at the top of their class in high school. Despite rigorous courses, students say Georgetown is not ultra-competitive. A very attractive trait of the academic scene is that classes are taught by professors, not by TAs, and professors are "easy to get in touch with and open to talking with students."

All students across each of the four schools must complete the Georgetown core curriculum, dedicated to providing undergraduates with a broad understanding of the liberal arts as well as an expanded and inclusive world view. The core requirements include two courses in each of the following areas: theology, philosophy, humanities and writing, history, math and science, and social sciences. Students must also achieve intermediate proficiency in a foreign language.

The strongest majors and departments at Georgetown are economics, government, and the international programs offered through the Walsh School of Foreign Service, one of the foremost institutions worldwide for the study of international affairs. Georgetown also has a unique Faculty of Languages and Linguistics (FLL), dedicated to the serious study of languages and cultures. Over 25 percent of students major or minor in a foreign language or linguistics, often coupling that with another major.

GEORGETOWN UNIVERSITY

Students

Total enrollment: 17,357
Undergrads: 7,552
Freshmen: 1,665
Part-time students: 4%
From out-of-state: 99%
From public schools: 48%
Male/Female: 44%/56%
Live on-campus: 67%
Off-campus employment rating: Good
Caucasian: 60%
African American: 6%
Hispanic: 8%
Asian / Pacific Islander: 9%
Native American: 0%
Mixed (2+ ethnicities): 3%
International: 11%

Academics

Calendar: Semester
Student/faculty ratio: 11:1
Class size 9 or fewer: 19%
Class size 10-29: 59%
Class size 30-49: 16%
Class size 50-99: 5%
Class size 100 or more: 2%
Returning freshmen: 96%
Six-year graduation rate: 93%

Most Popular Majors

Government
Finance
International politics

Admissions

Applicants: 20,115
Accepted: 3,413
Acceptance rate: 17.0%
Placed on wait list: 2,217
Enrolled from wait list: 84
Average GPA: Not reported
ACT range: 29-33
SAT Math range: 660-750
SAT Reading range: 650-750
SAT Writing range: Not reported
Top 10% of class: 92%
Top 25% of class: 99%
Top 50% of class: 100%

Study abroad is very popular for Georgetown students, with about 60 percent of the student body participating in a study-abroad program during their undergraduate years. Georgetown has many programs and connections with universities in over 40 countries—you're likely to find your ideal study-abroad experience here.

The Alumni Career Services organization at Georgetown works to provide a network for Hoya students and alumni, creating career development resources and regional networking events. "Hoya alumni are very supportive of recent graduates and willing to make connections and provide informational interviews," says a student. Within six months of graduation, about 68 percent have entered the work force in a field related to their major. Approximately 29 percent pursue graduate school after college, and many obtain prestigious fellowships such as the Rhodes, Marshall, and Truman scholarships.

Student Life

Georgetown boasts 144 official student organizations, including 14 honors societies and a myriad of political, theater, music, community service, academic, athletic, and religious groups. Popular organizations include the Student Association (student government), class committees, and the two student newspapers. Georgetown does not officially recognize any Greek organizations on campus. But if you're craving that brother- or sisterhood, there are a handful of fraternities dedicated to community and foreign service, business, and socializing. These are complemented by just one sorority and are organized around foreign service. "There is no wild fraternity party scene here," remarks a student.

Georgetown has 23 varsity athletic teams, and in 2007, *U.S. News & World Report* listed the Georgetown athletic program as one of the top 20 Division I schools in the nation. The most popular sports are men's and women's basketball. The men's team sees success on a regular basis, both in conference and NCAA tournament play. "Whether it's a good season or a bad one—and there are more good than bad—we come out to support the basketball team," notes a student. For those who want to stay active as well as watch others do so, there are plenty of intramural sports teams, from flag football to floor hockey, and soccer to golf. You can even have a whack at walleyball if you feel so inclined.

Sixty-seven percent of undergraduates live on campus, which provides plenty of social opportunities for students. Housing options include coed dorms, single-student apartments, and special housing for disabled students. Because of the university's location, it's fairly normal to hear prominent politicians such as Bill Clinton, Hillary Clinton, and Barack Obama speak on campus. Popular special events include the Hoya Halloween celebration, accompanied by public viewings of *The Exorcist* (see "You May Not Know" fact #2!) and costumed students dancing through the streets. Georgetown Day, a full-day carnival each April, recognizes the best professor of the year as voted on by the students. Midnight Madness is a spirit event held each year to introduce the men's and women's basketball teams after midnight of the first day they are allowed to practice. And of course there is the Diplomatic Ball, an annual spring event where students can rub elbows with statesmen, foreign dignitaries, and other bigwigs.

As far as parties go, the university cracks down seriously on underage drinking, so most parties take place in local area bars and off-campus apartments rather than in dorms. According to the *Georgetown Voice*, the weekly student newsmagazine, "students tend to spread out on the weekends" to a series of favorite nearby haunts, such as the Tombs, Hoya's, and Booeymongers.

Another issue brought up by university policy is the how Georgetown's religious affiliation affects on-campus sexual health resources. To purchase condoms or birth control, students must venture into DC, because they are banned from being sold on campus. The pro-choice student group, H*ya's for Choice, is not officially recognized by the university, and therefore cannot hold the Hoya name. "If you're a staunch liberal, this is not the place for you," comments a student.

DC provides endless areas to explore, including museums and monuments, restaurants, and shopping districts. And you might want to also take in some cultural performances. These aren't exactly easy to reach, however, because the Metro doesn't stop at Georgetown. If you are determined, you can scout out the best of the vibrant city; but if not, you'll most likely find yourself on campus or in the surrounding few blocks. "DC has so much to offer, if only we could get to it all," says a student.

Student Body

There is a high level of ethnic diversity at Georgetown, with a 26 percent minority population and an 11 percent international population representing 120 countries. U.S. students come primarily from the Middle Atlantic region, though there is a fairly even geographic spread across the rest of the country. Because of Georgetown's need-blind admissions and financial aid policy, students come from a variety of socioeconomic backgrounds.

Georgetown students, though statistically diverse, definitely fit a "type." A common trait among students is an "intense interest in politics," one student explains. Georgetown's strength as a politically and internationally focused university, combined with the resources of the nation's capital, make the school ideal for students aiming for a career in government or international affairs. Both Democrats and Republicans find support among students on campus. The religious affiliation of the university does also seem to affect the makeup of the student body. Of the students who indicate a religious preference, approximately half report they are Catholic.

One serious issue within the Georgetown community is that of diversity and acceptance—though it exists statistically, a 2009 report shows that nearly 80 percent of students report witnessing discrimination by fellow students—and nearly 50 percent choose to ignore it. The Hoya report found that 76 percent of students see racial "self-segregation" on campus. "We'd like to portray ourselves as one big happy family, but there are many cases where we aren't," notes a student.

You May Not Know

- The official Georgetown colors are blue and grey, first adopted in 1866, after the end of the Civil War. The university colors symbolize the reunion of the North and South.

GEORGETOWN UNIVERSITY

Highlights

Admissions Criteria
Academic criteria:
Grades: ☆ ☆ ☆
Difficulty of class schedule: ☆ ☆ ☆
Class rank: ☆ ☆ ☆
Standardized test scores: ☆ ☆ ☆
Teacher recommendations: ☆ ☆ ☆
Personal statement: ☆ ☆ ☆
Non-academic criteria considered:
Interview
Extracurricular activities
Special talents, interests, abilities
Character/personal qualities
Volunteer work
Work experience
Geographical location
Minority affiliation
Alumni relationship

Deadlines
Early Action: November 1
Early Decision: No
Regular Action: January 10 (final)
Notification of admission by: April 1
Common Application: Not accepted

Financial Aid
In-state tuition: $44,280
Out-of-state tuition: $44,280
Room: $9,330
Board: $4,290
Books: $1,200
Freshmen receiving need-based aid: 43%
Undergrads rec. need-based aid: 41%
Avg. % of need met by financial aid: 100%
Avg. aid package (freshmen): $34,238
Avg. aid package (undergrads): $33,566
Avg. debt upon graduation: $28,035

School Spirit
Mascot: Hoyas
Colors: Blue and gray
Song: *Georgetown Fight Song*

305

- Scenes from *The Exorcist*, written by Georgetown alum William Peter Blatty, were filmed on the Georgetown campus in 1972.
- *Hoya Saxa!* This Greek- and Latin-derived phrase translates roughly to *What Rocks*, and was the inspiration for the Georgetown mascot: the Hoya. In the 1960s however, students rallied for a more "tenacious" mascot, and received a puppy bulldog, which stubbornly refused to answer to the name "Hoya." So, Jack the Bulldog it is!

Distinguished Alumni

Bill Clinton, former United States President; Laura Chinchilla, current and first female President of Costa Rica; Bradley Cooper, actor; Margaret Edson, Pulitzer Prize-winning author of *Wit*; George J. Mitchell, former Chairman, Walt Disney Company; Antonin Scalia, Supreme Court Justice; Maria Shriver, author; George Tenet, former Director, Central Intelligence Agency.

Admissions and Financial Aid

Georgetown admits 17 percent of applicants, making it the dream school of many. The admissions committee says they are "most interested in the quality of a student's work, general promise, and seriousness of purpose." Georgetown admits are generally students who have been at the top of their class, tested well on a variety of exams, and have an active and involved résumé of leadership and involvement.

Georgetown does not offer any merit-based scholarships, other than those for athletics. There are a substantial amount of scholarships provided for student athletes—a number are based on a pairing of athletic ability and financial need.

Georgetown admits and enrolls students on an entirely need-blind basis—a family's financial status is not a factor in admission. Georgetown pledges to meet 100 percent of demonstrated financial aid for eligible students, ranging from $1,000 to $45,000 annually, on an average of $23,000 per recipient. Much of this money is provided by the Georgetown Scholarship Program—a community of university affiliates dedicated to supporting Georgetown students through scholarship funds.

GEORGIA INSTITUTE OF TECHNOLOGY

Overview

Georgia Tech is ranked seventh among *U.S. News & World Report's* top public universities, and its engineering programs are among the premiere in the nation. Georgia Tech is best described as a research powerhouse: the university sinks a significant chunk of change into science and technology research ($525 million annually), making it one of the nation's biggest research spenders without a med school.

Add to the description that Georgia Tech is settled on a large campus with plenty of green space, and you are beginning to see just what this university can offer.

Central Campus—with newly constructed classroom and administrative buildings—divides East Campus—with historic Collegiate Gothic architecture, freshman residences, and Greek houses—from West Campus—with more recently-built undergraduate dorms and apartments. A Campus Recreation Center, completed in 2004, includes not only the swimming pool built for the 1996 Atlanta Olympic Games, but also a leisure pool with a waterslide. Now put all of this in the busy urban setting of Midtown Atlanta, with cafes, bookstores, and bars right next to campus. Factor in some serious Division I sports and devoted fans, and you have Georgia Tech.

Georgia Tech is a heavyweight research institution that works hard to earn and maintain its reputation. With such emphasis on research, undergraduates may not always feel that they are their instructors' first priority. Professors "can be consumed with their own research at the expense of the class," notes an undergrad. You must be serious about studying, students say, even choosing academics over the social and cultural scene at times. But if you are passionate about technology, science, and engineering and have the discipline to stay on top of your studies, Georgia Tech can be an extremely rewarding college environment.

Academics

Education at Georgia Tech is divided into five schools, which offer a total of 126 majors. It goes without saying that the bulk of students at Georgia Tech major in science and technology. But Georgia Tech puts some effort into giving its students a liberal arts foundation. Core Curriculum requirements mandate basic courses in English, foreign languages, and social studies, most of which are located in the Cherry Street academic area. Students generally knock out these requirements in their freshmen year and rarely visit the Cherry Street area as upperclassmen unless they are majoring in liberal arts subjects, sticking instead to the Life Sciences Complex or research facilities on Central Campus. This division can create some friction: technical majors claim that their classes are harder and more competitive than liberal arts classes, which can make Georgia Tech an environment where humanities and social sciences students "feel a little like second-class citizens," as reported by one student.

Undergraduates may have to compete with grad students for research positions. Introductory classes, particularly in the hard sciences and engineering, can be extremely large—22 percent of classes have over 50 students. But the strength of Georgia Tech's undergraduate programs and research opportunities is undeniable. *U.S. News* recently rated Georgia Tech's industrial engineering program as the top program in the nation, while GT's architecture, engineering, engineering mechanics, information technology/information systems, and materials science and engineering programs are similarly respected. Undergraduates can gain research experience as part of the Undergraduate Research Opportunities Program (UROP), which aims to help students find labs or projects with open positions, funding, and workshops. Students can also apply for President's Undergraduate Research Awards (PURA), which funds student research with faculty members.

It can be hard to find the time to study abroad, but almost 40 percent of Georgia Tech students do. Georgia Tech offers 20 faculty-led summer-abroad programs in

GEORGIA
INSTITUTE OF
TECHNOLOGY

Four-year public
Founded: 1885
Atlanta, GA
Major city
Pop. 432,427

Address:
225 North Avenue, NW
Atlanta, GA
30332-0530

Admissions:
404-894-4154

Financial Aid:
404-894-4160

admission@gatech.
edu

www.gatech.edu

307

GEORGIA INSTITUTE OF TECHNOLOGY

Students

Total enrollment: 21,557
Undergrads: 14,527
Freshmen: 3,048
Part-time students: 9%
From out-of-state: 41%
Male/Female: 67%/33%
Live on-campus: 56%
In fraternities: 23%
In sororities: 29%
Off-campus employment rating: Excellent
Caucasian: 57%
African American: 6%
Hispanic: 6%
Asian / Pacific Islander: 18%
Native American: 0%
Mixed (2+ ethnicities): 3%
International: 9%

Academics

Calendar: Semester
Student/faculty ratio: 18:1
Class size 9 or fewer: 19%
Class size 10-29: 42%
Class size 30-49: 16%
Class size 50-99: 15%
Class size 100 or more: 7%
Returning freshmen: 95%
Six-year graduation rate: 79%
Graduates who immediately go to gradu-
    ate school: 24%
Graduates who immediately enter career
    related to major: 74%

Most Popular Majors

Mechanical engineering
Management
Industrial engineering

Admissions

Applicants: 14,645
Accepted: 8,045
Acceptance rate: 54.9%
Placed on wait list: 978
Enrolled from wait list: 43
Average GPA: 3.9
ACT range: 28-32
SAT Math range: 660-760
SAT Reading range: 600-700
SAT Writing range: 27-55
Top 10% of class: 74%
Top 25% of class: 94%
Top 50% of class: 99%

various countries in South America, Western Europe, and Asia, as well as Ghana and Russia. Faculty members also lead semester- or year-long programs, including Architecture Senior Year in Paris. Students may also attend approved exchange programs at more than 80 universities worldwide.

Georgia Tech offers an Undergraduate Cooperative Education Program, a five-year plan in which students alternate semesters of school with semesters of work (including overseas placements). Undergrads are matched with employers in fields directly related to their majors. In addition to gaining work experience, co-op students can make up to $50,000 during the program and many are hired by their co-op employers upon graduation.

In general, students seeking work post-graduation are well provided for. In addition to a Career Services Center, Georgia Tech's Alumni Association also offers career advice and the opportunity to network with "clubs" of alumni throughout the world. These groups focus on similar interests or fields. "The alumni network is quite strong," says a student. About 24 percent of students continue to post-graduate education immediately after graduation.

Student Life

More than 500 student organizations are active on campus, including the Musician's Network, student rock musicians; DramaTech, a theatre group; and WREK, the student-run radio station. These groups put on events throughout the year. Additionally, Under the Couch, the Musician's Network's performance venue, hosts student and non-student music and comedy acts.

Since the Greek system is a central part of life at Georgia Tech (more than a quarter of students are in fraternities or sororities), Greek Week draws a crowd of Greeks and non-Greeks alike to watch fraternities and sororities compete in games like tug of war and musical contests. The Greek system's major philanthropic events, Relay for Life and Tech Beautification Day, also take place during Greek Week.

Homecoming features the Ramblin' Wreck Parade of student-created vehicle "contraptions." One of the biggest events of the year is unappealingly named RATS (Recently Acquired Tech Students) Week—an orientation program for incoming freshmen and transfer students that takes place just before term begins. It puts on a smorgasbord of social activities and information sessions designed to help students get acquainted with their new environment and each other. "It's a lot of fun and paves the way for bonding within the freshman class," says a student.

Football at Georgia Tech is popular and successful: the team has won four national championships. Basketball runs a close second, with that team making it to the Final Four. Intramural options include the less-traditional billiards and innertube water polo. Students also turn out for the Mini 500, an annual tricycle race. But if your tricycling isn't what it used to be, it's okay: "drivers" must make "pit stops," so you can apply your Georgia Tech engineering education and be a part of the pit crew. "There's nothing funnier than seeing a bunch of college kids try to ride tricycles," notes a student.

Students can also take advantage of Georgia Tech's urban setting to venture out into Atlanta. Midtown houses cultural performances, museums, bars, cafes, and restaurants, while nearby Buckhead is a major shopping destination. Campus is well connected to the rest of Atlanta via MARTA (Metro Atlanta Rapid Transit Authority), which stops at Tech Square. "We don't go out every weekend, but it's nice to have the option," says a student.

With so much happening on campus, a fair number of students choose to live in dormatories. Freshmen are guaranteed housing and describe the dorms as "pretty standard" and "not the nicest or newest but passable."

Student Body

Georgia Tech's demographic breakdown reflects its status as a major technical research institute. The school has a staggering male-female ratio of about 67-33. "You would think the ratio would help the dating pool, but the pool is still very small," says a female student. Another student notes, "we aren't afraid to let our geekiness show." Ethnic diversity and out-of-state and international student representation are similarly high.

You May Not Know

- Georgia Tech was the first school in the Deep South to voluntarily admit African-American students.
- Buzz, Georgia Tech's Yellow Jacket mascot, was voted best mascot in the nation.
- The ubiquitous term "Ramblin' Wreck" originally referred to the buggies that Tech students created in the 1920s to improve transportation systems in South America.

Distinguished Alumni

Michael Arad, architect, designer of World Trade Center Memorial; G. Wayne Clough, secretary, Smithsonian Institution; Jeff Foxworthy, comedian; John Salley, co-host, Fox Sports, *Best Damn Sports Show Period*.

Admissions and Financial Aid

Georgia Tech's admission rate is high, but don't assume that means it's easy to get in. Most students need to be pretty committed to the idea of spending four years working hard on science or technology in a heavily male-dominated environment in order to apply.

Georgia Tech offers merit-based scholarships, including the President's Scholarship Program, which covers the full cost of attendance and offers priority housing registration, specialized advising, and study-abroad stipends. The Gobold Family Foundation Scholarship meets 100 percent of need for qualified students from certain counties in South Carolina, Florida, North Carolina, and Tennessee. Through the G. Wayne Clough Georgia Tech Promise Program, families that earn $33,300 or less per year earn scholarships to cover the gap between their financial aid package and the rest of the costs of tuition, fees, books, housing and meals. Georgia also offers HOPE Scholarships to state residents, which cover tuition, various fees, and books.

GEORGIA INSTITUTE OF TECHNOLOGY

Highlights

Admissions Criteria
Academic criteria:
Grades: ☆ ☆ ☆
Difficulty of class schedule: ☆ ☆ ☆
Class rank: N/A
Standardized test scores: ☆ ☆
Teacher recommendations: N/A
Personal statement: ☆ ☆
Non-academic criteria considered:
Extracurricular activities
Special talents, interests, abilities
Character/personal qualities
Volunteer work
Work experience
Geographical location
Minority affiliation
Alumni relationship

Deadlines
Early Action: October 15
Early Decision: No
Regular Action: October 15 and November 1 (priority)
January 10 (final)
Notification of admission by: mid-March
Common Application: Accepted

Financial Aid
In-state tuition: $8,258
Out-of-state tuition: $27,562
Room: $5,822
Board: $3,992
Books: $1,200
Freshmen receiving need-based aid: 44%
Undergrads rec. need-based aid: 45%
Avg. % of need met by financial aid: 62%
Avg. aid package (freshmen): $19,073
Avg. aid package (undergrads): $18,030
Avg. debt upon graduation: $26,412

School Spirit
Mascot: Buzz, Rambling Wreck
Colors: Old gold and white
Song: *Ramblin' Wreck*

GETTYSBURG
COLLEGE

Four-year private
Founded: 1832
Gettysburg, PA
Large town
Pop. 7,622

Address:
300 North Washington
Street
Gettysburg, PA
17325

Admissions:
800-431-0803

Financial Aid:
717-337-6611

admiss@gettysburg.
edu

www.gettysburg.edu

GETTYSBURG COLLEGE

Overview

Civil War reenactors and future scholars alike unite in their huzzahs for Gettysburg College in Pennsylvania. The historic campus sits adjacent to Gettysburg National Military Park, founded on the site of the famed 1863 battle. Theologian Samuel Simon Schmucker founded Pennsylvania College in 1832, but the school didn't settle on its current name until nearly seven years after its inception. The campus oozes presidential grace, thanks to Abraham Lincoln offering the Gettysburg Address at the nearby National Cemetery. The muck of the Gettysburg warfare lives on in the soggy climate and poor drainage, meaning that Gettysburg College's campus did occasionally flood over in the past and led to the name "Stine Lake" for a section of the campus. Technology has dried things over, but the catchy name still holds.

Gettysburg students revel over their award-winning *Gettysburg Review* publication when not enjoying the musical stylings of the Sunderman Conservatory of Music. The private liberal arts college especially caters, naturally, to those looking to study and intern in Civil War studies. Sports buffs will beam over the brand new Center for Athletics and Recreation. The college advertises an apparent proximity to several major American cities. Yet 90 minutes to DC and two hours to Philadelphia won't allow you to march for your rights or show brotherly love as often as it might seem.

Academics

Gettysburg College fields 35 majors and 36 minors to students, some of the strongest of them being business, history, and political science. First-year seminars for freshmen help them bond with fellow classmates and expose them to topics as varied as "Samurais and Geishas" and "Green Eggs and Government Cheese." Four pillars uphold Gettysburg's unique curriculum: the challenge to students to vary their approaches to learning by the use of Multiple Inquiries; Integrative Thinking's bid to generate novel thinking; Communication Skills; and language study via Informed Citizenship. Professors exclusively lead the college's classes, 89 percent of which have fewer than 30 students.

Warheads won't be gun-shy over the chance to immerse themselves in an authentic Civil War experience through the celebrated Gettysburg Semester. Gettysburg's true claim to fame has organically emerged from its Civil War Era Studies program, in which pupils bone up on "The American Civil War on Film" and "African American Activism in the Nineteenth Century." The prestigious Civil War Institute can augment the course of study with prime lectures and conferences. "This is the premier location in the country to learn about the Civil War because you are literally in the center of where it occurred," says a student. Public policy students get cozy in the Eisenhower Institute to delve head-first into a Mecca for leadership and policy making, while gleaning lessons from such speakers as Bob Herbert and Chris Matthews.

Gettysburg College also privileges its students with the Washington Semester, the opportunity to focus on governmental themes in the nation's capital. Domestically, students may also participate in programs at the United Nations in New York City, marine research labs, or the Smithsonian Museum of International and Contemporary Art. More than half of Gettysburg students take advantage of the more than 200 options for study abroad. One student notes, "study abroad is really integrated here so you don't feel like you're missing out when you leave campus for a semester."

The Career Development Center offers a week of workshops during Career Week as well as weekly drop-in hours for advice on resumes, internships, and federal jobs. You might earn an internship and join about half of Gettysburg graduates who do the same before leaving campus. "The career center really helps out with finding internships," one student comments.

Student Life

Eight hundred events annually and 120 student organizations do not lie: there's quite a bit to do at Gettysburg. Take advantage of the campus' close range to the Majestic Theater, and catch a film or celebrity sighting there. During the school's annual all-you can-eat Crab Fest, you can consume one of 1,500 crabs. "You'll never see more seafood in one place in your life," says a student. Freeze in fashion during the Snowball winter formal; thaw out over the three-day long Springfest's concerts and novelty items.

Greek life is prominent on campus, as 36 percent of women and 32 percent of men participate in nine frats and seven sororities—but Greek parties welcome the entire campus. (The sororities do not house their members.) "Even though so many people join," explains one student, "you can still get in on the best parties if you're not a member but have friends who are."

The Center for Athletics, Recreation, and Fitness drummed up $25 million to offer new fitness equipment to students and staff. The Gettysburg Recreation and Adventure Board (GRAB) organizes recreational outings such as hiking, kayaking, and rock climbing locally as well as in Alaska, Yosemite, and Baja. "Whether you're an outdoor recreational expert or novice, there's an activity for you," notes a student. The college has 24 NCAA Division III sports. Football and lacrosse court many campus fans for Bullet games. Intramural leagues are popular at Gettysburg yet do not raise the heat of the campus nearly as high as Gettysburg's rivalry with nearby Dickinson, marked by the decades-long jockeying for ownership of the Little Brown Bucket.

Off campus, there are a smattering of bars and restaurants that students frequent, but Gettysburg is a "pretty sleepy little town." During the spring and summer it is filled with tourists seeking out the historical sites.

Most Gettysburg students live on campus and enjoy acclaimed high-speed internet and cable TV in their rooms. There are six residence halls that include apartments, suites, singles, and theme houses. Freshmen are assigned to halls based on their First-Year Seminar or College Writing course. Sophomores, juniors, and seniors enter a lottery system based on seniority and GPA.

Student Body

Gettysburg's 11-percent minority diversity is low, and some of the student body deplore the campus' overwhelming "whiteness." Seventy-one percent of the students hail from out-of-state, mostly from the Northeast, and "many come from upper-class backgrounds," comments one student. Though the college is not very diverse ethnically or geographically, there is diversity of interests. "Some are focused 100 percent on studying, some on having a good time, and a lot in between," says a student, adding, "most students here are highly involved, love the outdoors, and love our college."

You May Not Know

- Some of the food students eat is from the student garden, and waste from the dining halls is used as compost.
- Pennsylvania Hall was used as a field hospital and signal station as the Battle of Gettysburg took place.

GETTYSBURG COLLEGE

Highlights

Students
Total enrollment: 2,597
Undergrads: 2,597
Freshmen: 770
Part-time students: 1%
From out-of-state: 71%
From public schools: 70%
Male/Female: 47%/53%
Live on-campus: 92%
In fraternities: 36%
In sororities: 32%
Off-campus employment rating: Excellent
Caucasian: 81%
African American: 3%
Hispanic: 4%
Asian / Pacific Islander: 2%
Native American: 0%
Mixed (2+ ethnicities): 2%
International: 2%

Academics
Calendar: Semester
Student/faculty ratio: 10:1
Class size 9 or fewer: 19%
Class size 10-29: 70%
Class size 30-49: 11%
Class size 50-99: -
Class size 100 or more: -
Returning freshmen: 91%
Six-year graduation rate: 84%
Graduates who immediately go to graduate school: 30%

Most Popular Majors
Management
English
Political science

Admissions
Applicants: 5,620
Accepted: 2,264
Acceptance rate: 40.3%
Average GPA: 3.4
ACT range: Not reported
SAT Math range: 610-670
SAT Reading range: 600-690
SAT Writing range: Not reported
Top 10% of class: 72%
Top 25% of class: 92%
Top 50% of class: 99%

311

College Profiles

GETTYSBURG COLLEGE

Admissions Criteria

Academic criteria:
Grades: ☆ ☆ ☆
Difficulty of class schedule: ☆ ☆ ☆
Class rank: ☆ ☆ ☆
Standardized test scores: ☆ ☆
Teacher recommendations: ☆ ☆ ☆
Personal statement: ☆ ☆
Non-academic criteria considered:
Interview
Extracurricular activities
Special talents, interests, abilities
Character/personal qualities
Volunteer work
Work experience
State of residency
Geographical location
Minority affiliation
Alumni relationship

Deadlines

Early Action: No
Early Decision: November 15
Regular Action: February 1 (final)
Notification of admission by: April 1
Common Application: Accepted

Financial Aid

In-state tuition: $45,870
Out-of-state tuition: $45,870
Room: $5,870
Board: $5,080
Books: $1,000
Freshmen receiving need-based aid: 53%
Undergrads rec. need-based aid: 53%
Avg. % of need met by financial aid: 100%
Avg. aid package (freshmen): $33,259
Avg. aid package (undergrads): $33,315
Avg. debt upon graduation: $29,067

School Spirit

Mascot: Bullets
Colors: Orange and blue
Song: *Loyalty to Gettysburg*

- A medical school founded by the College closed in 1861 due in part to students from Southern states, then seceding, who returned home.

Distinguished Alumni

J. Michael Bishop, Nobel Laureate; Ron Paul, Presidential candidate; Stephanie Sellars, author; Karen Sosnoski, author; John Yovicsin, NFL football player.

Admissions and Financial Aid

According to the admissions office, students' grades, difficulty of courses, and class rank are "highly significant." The college also seeks students "of character who will make positive contributions," judging this by essays and recommendations. The interview is strongly recommended, which means that if Gettysburg is one of your top-choice colleges, you should make every effort to visit the campus and arrange for an interview.

Merely applying to Gettysburg may avail you to its many merit scholarships, of which the $25,000 Abraham Lincoln Scholarship shows the most glamour. Music prodigies can earn Sunderman or Wagnild Scholarships with an audition. Need-based financial aid is also available upon completion of the FAFSA documents. The Post-9/11 Veterans Educational Act has instated the Yellow Ribbon GI Education Enhancement Program on the campus, providing funding for students who qualify. Should your parents or family members work for a participating institution, you may benefit from the Tuition Exchange recognized by Gettysburg.

An exception exists for students "who believe that standardized test scores do not accurately reflect the strength of their academic achievements"— check Box 3 on Gettysburg's College Application Supplement and declare yourself test-optional. Do not do so if you are aiming for consideration for a merit scholarship, as they require SAT or ACT test scores.

GOUCHER COLLEGE

Overview

Goucher College may not be a household name, nor have most people heard of the suburb the 287-acre campus is located in—Towson, Maryland—but this tight-knit liberal arts college is one to be noticed. It's proximity to Baltimore provides plenty of internship opportunities as well as easy access to nearby colleges; students can even enroll in some classes at Johns Hopkins. The college's strong artistic programs in dance and creative writing attract plenty of creative students to the undergraduate student body of almost 1,500.

Goucher's mascot, the Gophers, is fitting for a college set off from the surrounding suburb by extensive woods where wildlife such as deer thrive. The school's slightly hilly grounds offer hiking and riding trails. Buildings are tan-hued in a stone called Butler Stone, and campus visitors are sure to marvel at the Athenaeum, a 100,000-square-foot building constructed in 2009 that houses a library, art gallery, café, and more—"the center piece of Goucher's campus and community," as the college describes it.

The first college in the nation to require study abroad for all undergrads, Goucher is a good fit for students who want to gain an international perspective at some point before they graduate. The college's origins as an all-women's college are still evident on campus; though Goucher became co-ed in 1987, two-thirds of students are female.

Academics

Goucher offers 31 majors and six interdisciplinary programs. In 2006, Goucher launched a new liberal arts curriculum that includes proficiency in English composition and foreign language, and a breadth of other course requirements. Freshmen are introduced to campus through special introductory courses.

Academics at Goucher vary in difficulty depending on the major. Most students call their professors by first name, evidence of just how accessible professors are at this college. "One of my professors invites everyone over to his house for coffee as his office hours," says a student. The most common course size is 10 to 19 students. Strong programs include dance, English, the Kratz Center for Creative Writing, political science and international relations, prelaw, and premed studies. Students can cross-register for some classes at Johns Hopkins.

The Kraz Center for Creative Writing brings prominent authors to the campus for lectures and residencies. Students may receive funding of up to $3,000 for travel, internships, or conferences related to writing through the center's Summer Writing Fellowships. *Verge* is the "peer-reviewed journal for undergraduate research and writing," according to the publication. Recent articles have included "Facebook: Surveillance and Changing Notions of Privacy in the Social Networking Era" and "How to Perform the Laundry Ritual—and Keep Your Blacks Blacker than Black."

All undergrads are required to have an off-campus experience through an internship or study-abroad, and all students must study abroad at least once to graduate. A popular choice for fulfilling this requirement is a three-week Intensive Course Abroad in which students take a course on campus and then study abroad for three weeks. There are also semester- and year-long study-abroad programs offered by Goucher and by other schools as well. The college gives each student a $1,200 stipend to assist with travel costs. "I love that study abroad is built into the curriculum," notes a student.

According to the college, Goucher ranks among the top 10 percent of colleges whose graduates go on to earn doctoral degrees in the sciences.

Student Life

There are more than 60 student organizations on campus, and students are encouraged to start their own through the Student Government Organization if they can't find what they're looking for. The student newspaper, *The Quindecim*—a.k.a. *The Q*—has

GOUCHER COLLEGE

Four-year private
Founded: 1885
Baltimore, MD
Large town
Pop. 55,197

Address:
1021 Dulaney Valley
Road
Baltimore, MD
21204

Admissions:
410-337-6100

Financial Aid:
410-337-6141

admissions@goucher.edu

www.goucher.edu

GOUCHER COLLEGE

Students
Total enrollment: 2,254
Undergrads: 1,484
Freshmen: 498
Part-time students: 3%
From out-of-state: 74%
From public schools: 64%
Male/Female: 34%/66%
Live on-campus: 86%
Off-campus employment rating: Good
Caucasian: 65%
African American: 9%
Hispanic: 7%
Asian / Pacific Islander: 3%
Native American: 0%
Mixed (2+ ethnicities): 5%
International: 3%

Academics
Calendar: Semester
Student/faculty ratio: 9:1
Class size 9 or fewer: 17%
Class size 10-29: 79%
Class size 30-49: 3%
Class size 50-99: 1%
Class size 100 or more: -
Returning freshmen: 84%
Six-year graduation rate: 66%
Graduates who immediately go to gradu-
ate school: 23%

Most Popular Majors
English
Communication
Psychology

Admissions
Applicants: 3,615
Accepted: 2,593
Acceptance rate: 71.7%
Placed on wait list: 201
Enrolled from wait list: 20
Average GPA: 3.2
ACT range: 22-28
SAT Math range: 480-620
SAT Reading range: 510-640
SAT Writing range: 6-32
Top 10% of class: 26%
Top 25% of class: 57%
Top 50% of class: 87%

314

been in publication for over 90 years, while the aptly named Pizzazz puts on music theater for the student body. The Goucher Privateer Alliance is one of the most distinctive social clubs: as the club notes, it is "for anyone interested in the historical actions of pirates, people who enjoy pirate music and sea shanties, or people who like to hang out and say 'yarrr' a lot." The Privateer Alliance takes a trip to the Maryland Renaissance festival each fall and Pyratefest at the end of the school year.

With no Greek scene, parties at Goucher tend to be small ones hosted in dorm rooms. The Gopher Hole, an on-campus coffee house, is a popular student hangout known for its live music on weekends. Other student pastimes are a bit less conventional; for example, Goucher students are credited with founding Humans vs. Zombies (HvZ), a game of moderated tag where human players use Nerf guns to fight against the "zombies." "The game can easily become all-consuming," laughs a student. This quirky game has gained national press coverage and an international fan base.

Another famous Goucher tradition is GIG, Get into Goucher Day. This springtime annual festival has a different theme each year and features a huge BBQ, a concert by a major band/performer, games, and more. Goucher's annual spring formal, Gala, is another eagerly anticipated event, usually held at a venue in Baltimore, though in 2004 the event took place on a yacht in the harbor.

It should be noted that one Goucher tradition has been discontinued. In 2003, the student newspaper wrote "Goucherdales, House Council's annual male stripping competition, had been postponed until further notice due to a lack of participation."

Goucher offers 18 intercollegiate sports as part of the NCAA Division III Landmark Conference. Especially strong teams in which the college has won conference titles are field hockey, women's lacrosse, and men's basketball. Equestrian fans will appreciate Goucher's on-campus horse stables as well.

Although Towson—where Goucher is located—has restaurants and bars, there are many more to choose from in Baltimore and Washington, DC, both about an hour's drive away. Baltimore's Inner Harbor is an especially popular hangout with its shops, National Aquarium, Hard Rock Café, and more. Closer to campus, there is plenty of hiking on nearby trails. Getting to nearby colleges is especially easy with the free Baltimore Collegetown Shuttle network; local buses also help make local transportation a breeze.

Freshmen are required to live on campus, a good way to develop strong friendships their first year. There are six residence halls, each with its own distinct history and a student Community Assistant, along with four special interest houses that students can apply for: Live Music House, Healthy Living House, Gaming House, and Green House.

Student Body

Goucher has high ethnic diversity with 24 percent minority students. Seventy-four percent of students are from out of state, though this geographic diversity is diminished by the fact that many students are from nearby states.

Two-thirds of the student body is female, which affects the environment and social atmosphere, but, as one female explains, "there are plenty of available men at nearby colleges like Towson

University." Thanks to its strong dance and arts programs, Goucher attracts many "super creative and artsy" types.

You May Not Know

- Goucher was founded as The Woman's College of Baltimore in 1885 by Methodist ministers Dr. John Goucher and John B. Van Meter; the school was renamed in 1910.
- Deer thrive at Goucher in a fenced area that protects the animals from natural predators; however, the school decided to hire bowmen to thin the population for ecological reasons in 2007 despite the objection of some students and community members.
- The college houses a collection of books about dogs in honor of Jacques Pierre, a black toy poodle owned by a Goucher dance professor.

Distinguished Alumni

Emily Newell Blair, feminist and a founder of the League of Women Voters; Jonah Golberg, journalist and conservative commentator; Sherry Cooper, economist; Phyllis A. Kravitch, Senior Circuit Judge on the U.S. Court of Appeals for the Eleventh Circuit.

Admissions and Financial Aid

Admission to Goucher is quite competitive and students are chosen based on their academic credentials and the ability to contribute to a "diverse community of scholars." According to the college, "Chosen from over (3,700) applicants, the 400 new students attending Goucher represent 36 states and territories and six foreign countries." SAT and ACT scores are no longer required for admission, a policy Goucher adopted in 2006.

Goucher makes its admissions without regard to financial circumstances. About 82 percent of undergraduates receive need-based or merit-based financial assistance, including approximately $19 million in institutional grants. Merit scholarships, such as the prestigious Deans' Scholarships, range up to the full cost of tuition.

All students who complete applications are automatically considered for first-year student scholarships. Almost 20 percent of freshmen were awarded academic merit scholarships. The renewable Global Citizen Scholarships award academic credentials and special talents and range from $10,000 to $15,000. Arts Scholarships are need-blind and are as high as $7,000.

GOUCHER COLLEGE

Highlights

Admissions Criteria
Academic criteria:
Grades: ☆ ☆ ☆
Difficulty of class schedule: ☆ ☆ ☆
Class rank: ☆
Standardized test scores: ☆
Teacher recommendations: ☆ ☆
Personal statement: ☆ ☆
Non-academic criteria considered:
Interview
Extracurricular activities
Special talents, interests, abilities
Character/personal qualities
Volunteer work
Work experience
Geographical location
Minority affiliation
Alumni relationship

Deadlines
Early Action: December 1
Early Decision: November 15
Regular Action: February 1 (final)
Notification of admission by: April 1
Common Application: Accepted

Financial Aid
In-state tuition: $38,462
Out-of-state tuition: $38,462
Room: $6,664
Board: $3,566
Books: $800
Freshmen receiving need-based aid: 71%
Undergrads rec. need-based aid: 63%
Avg. % of need met by financial aid: 76%
Avg. aid package (freshmen): $30,410
Avg. aid package (undergrads): $28,225
Avg. debt upon graduation: $29,135

School Spirit
Mascot: Gophers
Colors: Blue and gold

Four-year private
Founded: 1846
Grinnell, IA
Small town
Pop. 9,169

Address:
1103 Park Street
Grinnell, IA
50112

Admissions:
800-247-0113

Financial Aid:
800-247-0113

askgrin@grinnell.edu

www.grinnell.edu

GRINNELL COLLEGE

Overview

Recently ranked 17th nationally in *U.S. News & World Report's* list of liberal arts colleges, Grinnell is not what you'd expect from a school surrounded by cornfields. Located 55 miles east of Des Moines, in one of the "best small towns in America," Grinnell is an internationally respected private institution home to almost 1,700 stellar undergraduate students.

On the 120-acre campus you will find the architecturally renowned Noyce Science Center and the Bucksbaum Center for the Arts designed by Cesar Pelli. Getting off campus presents students with an array of outdoor activities in the rural prairie landscape, including a bicycle path to nearby Black Rock State Park and the college-owned 365-acre Conard Environmental Research Area (CERA). But it is the intellectual life at Grinnell that makes it stand out, not the remote location.

As socially progressive as it is intellectually challenging, students are (mostly) happy to brave the four months of Midwest winter for the small classes, diverse community, and academic freedom.

Academics

In the spirit of academic freedom, Grinnell only has one core requirement, the first-semester tutorial. This intensive, inquiry-based course delves into a specific topic, such as Cancer Survivorship; The Origins of Capitalism; or Folktales, Fairy Tales, and Fantasy. Within classes of only 13 participants, the tutorial trains students in written and oral communication, as well as introducing them to the rigorous academics of the college. "The debates and discussions in our tutorial were some of the most engaging I've ever had," says a student. After the tutorial, students form close relationships with their chosen advisor who helps them navigate the over 500 courses, 150 professors, and 27 majors in their futures. While some of the strongest majors are biology, English, history, and political science, students can also study interdisciplinary topics from gender, women's, and sexuality studies to neuroscience. Not satisfied with the listed courses? You can design an independent study or complete a "plus-2," which adds 2 credits to an existing course with outside, in-depth work in the subject area.

Another option for the self-motivated student is the Mentored Advanced Project. This provides an opportunity to work closely with a faculty member to undertake research or a creative project and, as a capstone, present the results through publication or exhibition.

That said, students don't have to engage in any extra study to be involved with professors. Almost all classes have fewer than 30 students, creating many chances for students to get to know their professors—and for professors to get to know their students. This means instructors don't just know students' names; they may even call when they're absent from class! "I wouldn't go as far to say my professors are my friends," a student explains, "but they're pretty close."

Students are encouraged to not just take advantage of the academic opportunities on campus, but to venture off campus and out of the country as well. Over half of students study abroad at some point. "You're missing out if you don't take advantage of study abroad," one student comments. Over 70 international programs are available, and students typically are guided to a location that meshes with their broader academic life. Are you an aspiring environmental scientist? Study Ecology in Tanzania. Or perhaps a mathematician? Head to Budapest, Hungary.

Grinnell's Career Development Office encourages and coordinates a vast array of internships for the academic year and summertime. The diverse alumni base provides a starting point for many students to get credit and funding for their forays into the working world. As a result, a recent graduating class saw half of their students employed within three months, in fields ranging from business to health care. Almost a third immediately enrolled in graduate school, and the remainder engaged in community service or travel.

Student Life

While 1,700 students on a 164-acre campus may seem socially small, the community offers plenty of diverse activities, events, and clubs. There are over 200 student groups and organizations. Students may follow interests in the Dahogir Swordfighting Club; Film Writing, Acting, and Directing; or the Student Peace and Action Network, as well as a bevy of other selections. Students interested in journalism can join the Student Publications and Radio Committee, an elected student group overseeing 10 campus newspapers, journals, humor magazines, and one radio station.

The college also supports a changing array of concerts, lectures, art exhibitions, and creative readings through programs such as Grinnell Concerts, the Rosenfeld Program for Public Affairs Symposium, and Writers@Grinnell. The Joe Rosenfield '25 Campus Center houses the many multicultural community offices, which can always be counted on for organizing exciting events. The Titular Head Student Film Festival—which debuts student films every spring—is only one event in the bustling arts scene one would expect from a liberal arts school, which also includes the One-Act Play Festival, Jazz nights in Bob's Underground Café, the formal Winter and Spring waltzes, and the volunteer Prison Writers Workshop. Since 1980, the wacky Alice and Wonderland Festival has been a time for tie-dying, human chess matches, drum circles, and general merriment. "It's really an excuse for a big party, with a crazy theme," laughs a student.

For the athletically inclined, Grinnell offers 18 varsity sports in the Division III Midwest Conference and many more intramural sports, the most popular being Ultimate Frisbee, kickball, and volleyball. For those who are athletic but don't necessarily enjoy competitive sports, the Grinnell Outdoor Recreation Program devotes school resources to the training, equipping, and organizing of kayak, climbing, backpacking, biking, sailing, and cave exploration events. You can join in on an established trip or just rent equipment and forge out with a group of friends.

While Grinnell is truly a small town, a three-screen movie theater, the popular Lonnski's Pub and Deli, numerous coffee shops, and a plentiful bi-weekly farmers market take students off campus to relax, study, stock up on fresh produce, and listen to free music on Thursday evenings. "It's not the best college town," notes one student, "but there's enough to keep us busy."

There are no fraternities or sororities on campus, but the college hosts free parties almost every week at the Harris Center, DJ and all. Students live in on-campus dorms, and housing is guaranteed for four years. Supervised by live-in Residence Life Coordinators, student-staffed dorms operate through self-governance, which means students hold each other accountable, and as a result, enjoy a great deal of freedom. North, South, and East Campus all have their distinct personalities, with East being "more subdued" and South being the "rowdiest."

GRINNELL COLLEGE

Highlights

Students
Total enrollment: 1,674
Undergrads: 1,674
Freshmen: 444
Part-time students: 4%
From out-of-state: 84%
From public schools: 68%
Male/Female: 46%/54%
Live on-campus: 88%
Off-campus employment rating: Good
Caucasian: 57%
African American: 5%
Hispanic: 7%
Asian / Pacific Islander: 7%
Mixed (2+ ethnicities): 4%
International: 12%

Academics
Calendar: Semester
Student/faculty ratio: 9:1
Class size 9 or fewer: 19%
Class size 10-29: 78%
Class size 30-49: 2%
Class size 50-99: -
Class size 100 or more: -
Returning freshmen: 95%
Six-year graduation rate: 90%
Graduates who immediately go to graduate school: 29%

Most Popular Majors
Psychology/general
English
Biology

Admissions
Applicants: 4,021
Accepted: 1,458
Acceptance rate: 36.3%
Placed on wait list: 1,191
Enrolled from wait list: 111
Average GPA: Not reported
ACT range: 29-33
SAT Math range: 650-750
SAT Reading range: 630-750
SAT Writing range: Not reported
Top 10% of class: 62%
Top 25% of class: 88%
Top 50% of class: 99%

317

GRINNELL COLLEGE

Admissions Criteria
Academic criteria:
Grades: ☆ ☆ ☆
Difficulty of class schedule: ☆ ☆ ☆
Class rank: ☆ ☆ ☆
Standardized test scores: ☆ ☆ ☆
Teacher recommendations: ☆ ☆ ☆
Personal statement: ☆ ☆
Non-academic criteria considered:
Interview
Extracurricular activities
Special talents, interests, abilities
Character/personal qualities
Volunteer work
Work experience
Geographical location
Minority affiliation
Alumni relationship

Deadlines
Early Action: No
Early Decision: November 15
Regular Action: January 15 (final)
Notification of admission by: April 1
Common Application: Accepted

Financial Aid
In-state tuition: $43,656
Out-of-state tuition: $43,656
Room: Varies
Board: Varies
Books: $900
Freshmen receiving need-based aid: 75%
Undergrads rec. need-based aid: 72%
Avg. % of need met by financial aid:
    100%
Avg. aid package (freshmen): $38,718
Avg. aid package (undergrads): $38,306
Avg. debt upon graduation: $16,226

School Spirit
Mascot: Pioneers
Colors: Scarlet and black

Student Body

Particularly commendable for a school in a prairie setting, Grinnell harbors a diverse and international community with 84 percent of the students from out of state and 12 percent from out of the country. Moderately ethnically diverse as well, 23 percent of Grinnell students are minorities. Not so surprising for a diverse liberal arts school, many of the students are politically liberal.

On the institutional level, Grinnell actively supports diversity. But despite the spectrum of country, state, and race, Grinnell students don't consider themselves unusual—just universally "active and intelligent."

You May Not Know

- Warren Buffett is a trustee of Grinnell, which is one reason that the college is one of only about 50 colleges in the country with an endowment of more than $1 billion.
- The most common course size is an intimate 10 to 19 students.
- At the beginning of a long social justice legacy, Grinnell was the first college west of the Mississippi to admit African Americans and women.

Distinguished Alumni

Benjamin Barber, political theorist and author of *Jihad vs. McWorld*; Thomas R. Cech, PhD, Noble Laureate in chemistry; Herbie Hancock, Academy Award and Grammy Award-winning jazz pianist and composer; Harry Hopkins, WPA administrator and architect of the New Deal; Robert Noyce, co-founder of Intel, co-inventor of integrated circuit, recipient of National Medal of Science.

Admissions and Financial Aid

Grinnell is very clear about what they are looking for in their incoming students. Standardized test scores count for 25 percent, while high school records—including GPA and academic rigor—count for 50 percent. The remainder of their decision, the admissions department says, depends on extracurriculars, recommendations, and the essay. An interview is not required but recommended, which means that if at all possible, students should do it.

Grinnell attempts (and often succeeds) to lure top tier students to their out-of-the-way campus by offering an abundance of merit scholarships. Automatically upon application, Grinnell puts together a merit package for qualified students, including the Grinnell Trustee Honor. But the best news is that Grinnell is need-blind, meaning they admit all qualified students regardless of their ability to pay, and then promise to meet 100 percent of demonstrated need for domestic students (this includes capping any institutional loans to $2,000). Currently only 85 percent of international student-demonstrated need is met, but Grinnell is working to make this full aid as well.

GUILFORD COLLEGE

GUILFORD COLLEGE

Four-year private
Founded: 1837
Greensboro, NC
Large town
Pop. 273,425

Address:
5800 West Friendly
Avenue
Greensboro, NC
27410

Admissions:
800-992-7759

Financial Aid:
336-316-2165

admission@guilford.
edu

www.guilford.edu

Overview

Providing an education instilled with liberal arts and Quaker philosophies, Guilford College stands strong as an institution of integrity that respects the individual. Drawing on the Quaker values of compassion, honesty, and courage, Guilford takes a unique approach to the liberal arts education, preparing its students with the tools they need to be leaders on the global scene.

Guilford is a small, private, church-affiliated college located in the naturally beautiful and peaceful city of Greensboro, North Carolina. The red brick architecture of the institution reflects a Georgian Colonial influence and is set amidst bountiful areas of greenery. Campus facilities include a well-stocked library, art gallery, language lab, science center, and observatory, among other useful and aesthetically pleasing resources. Furthermore, there are seven other colleges and universities within a 25-mile radius at which Guilford students may also take courses.

The values-rich educational experience one gleans at Guilford takes into account more than academics—the college has a strong devotion to community service and a commitment to the promotion of diversity. Abundant community events, student employment opportunities, and internships provide trips into the community to improve living conditions for all, in missions filled with passion and purpose.

As part of its commitment to diversity and openness to new ideas, Guilford welcomes students of all faiths, regions, and backgrounds into its community of purposeful living and higher education.

Academics

General education requirements at Guilford include a core curriculum with classes separated into five tiers. The first tier, Foundations, includes classes in writing, oral communication, research, information technology, and quantitative reasoning. The second tier, Explorations, includes classes in arts, business studies, humanities, mathematics, and social sciences, as well as intercultural and diversity studies and social justice. The third and fourth tiers require students to choose a major as well as a minor. The final requirement is Capstone, an interdisciplinary studies course taken by seniors.

Academics at Guilford are rigorous and competitive, with a heavy emphasis on writing involved with the coursework. "If you don't know how to write well before you start here, you will by the time you graduate," says a student. There are 39 majors offered, and strong programs include psychology, political science, and English.

In keeping with the Quaker value of equality, the Honors Program at Guilford does not separate its students from the general student body; rather, Honors students typically take one Honors course per semester. These students are selected not only for having a high GPA, but also based on outstanding achievement in spite of adverse circumstances.

Other special academic programs at Guilford include the Principled Problem Solving Scholars Program, which combines classroom, experiential, and integrative learning and includes a summer internship; the Bonner Scholars Program, a program of extensive community service awarded to dedicated and financially-lacking students; and the Quaker Leadership Scholars Program, a program that expands involvement in the Religious Society of Friends.

Cultural appreciation is a central tenet to the Guilford education; thus, study-abroad programs are highly encouraged and are offered in over 13 countries across the globe. Whether it's working in a Mexican community or studying German politics in Munich, each Guilford-led program has its own unique characteristics that make it, as students consistently report, an invaluable educational experience.

GUILFORD COLLEGE

Students

Total enrollment: 2,462
Undergrads: 2,462
Freshmen: 322
Part-time students: 16%
From out-of-state: 48%
From public schools: 72%
Male/Female: 42%/58%
Live on-campus: 77%
Off-campus employment rating: Fair
Caucasian: 62%
African American: 25%
Hispanic: 5%
Asian / Pacific Islander: 3%
Native American: 0%
Mixed (2+ ethnicities): 3%
International: 1%

Academics

Calendar: Semester
Student/faculty ratio: 15:1
Class size 9 or fewer: 6%
Class size 10-29: 88%
Class size 30-49: 5%
Class size 50-99: -
Class size 100 or more: -
Returning freshmen: 71%
Six-year graduation rate: 57%
Graduates who immediately go to graduate school: 20%
Graduates who immediately enter career related to major: 65%

Most Popular Majors

Business/marketing
Social sciences
Psychology

Admissions

Applicants: 2,549
Accepted: 2,040
Acceptance rate: 80.0%
Placed on wait list: 101
Enrolled from wait list: 2
Average GPA: 3.2
ACT range: 21-26
SAT Math range: 490-660
SAT Reading range: 480-620
SAT Writing range: 4-23
Top 10% of class: 11%
Top 25% of class: 38%
Top 50% of class: 76%

320

Career preparation and networking are made easy through Guilford's Career Development Center, where students can connect with faculty and alumni for internships and career options during and after their undergraduate experience.

Student Life

With over 30 active student organizations on campus, Guilford offers a wide variety of extracurricular activities to its students. From Cooking Club, to Chinese Culture Club, to Fancy Feet, an organization that introduces different types of American dances to the Guilford community, students with all types of interests have opportunities to find their niche at Guilford. "We don't have as many organizations as they do at large public universities, but there is something for everyone," comments a student.

Events held on campus throughout the year keep Guilford students happily entertained. One such event, Serendipity, is a spring festival that features performances by hip-hop and rock artists, as well as a service project. The Bryan Series at Guilford is a lecture series featuring such prominent figures as Bill Clinton and Jean-Michel Cousteau. In addition, the Eastern Music Festival is a five-week festival that presents over 100 music-related events, including performances by the world class Eastern Festival Orchestra as well as two student orchestras and guest artists from around the globe.

There is no Greek life at Guilford, but there is an active athletics scene. Sixteen teams play in a Division III conference, with men's golf, women's basketball, and women's rugby being the most competitive teams. Intramurals such as baseball, bowling, and cheerleading are popular among students on campus as well.

As far as off-campus diversions, students enjoy heading to Greensboro for shopping, dining, and low-key entertainment. "Greensboro is not a big city, but it has what we need," says a student. Many also embark on longer road trips to the beach or mountains for outdoor activities.

Housing at Guilford offers a variety of options, from classic dormitories to co-ops. The majority of students live on campus; if they choose to live off campus, students must first gain permission from the housing department. Most students prefer campus housing, as one student explains, "it's more convenient and pretty economical to live on campus."

Student Body

The student body as a whole leans towards the Quaker roots of the school, and politically leans left. The typical Guilford student describes himself as quirky or different in some aspect, with a strong desire to become a functional societal contributor.

Ethnic diversity at Guilford is high, with 36 percent of the student population being of minority status. Geographic diversity is moderate with 48 percent of students hailing from out of state.

You May Not Know

- The Guilford campus was a station for the Underground Railroad as well as a center for resistance against Confederate conscription.
- Guilford is the fourth-oldest college in the state.

- Guilford has 200 solar panels, the largest solar thermal system on a college campus in the country.

Distinguished Alumni

M. L. Carr, former ABA/NBA player, head coach and executive; Howard Coble, member of U.S. House of Representatives (6th District, N.C.); David M. Dobson, creator of *Snood*; Rick Elmore, judge, North Carolina Court of Appeals; John Hamlin Folger, U.S. Representative; William Queen, author of *New York Times* bestseller *Under and Alone*; Tony Womack, Major League Baseball player.

Admissions and Financial Aid

A unique aspect of the Guilford admissions process is that SAT/ACT test scores are optional—students may instead submit an academic portfolio of written work. In addition to academic success, the admissions committee considers creativity, leadership, and school and community involvement. Interviews are encouraged but not required.

Merit-based scholarships at Guilford include a number of $20,000 Presidential Scholarships, based on a 3.6 GPA and SAT scores over 1250, as well as a number of $12,000 Thompson Scholarships, based on a 3.2 GPA and SAT scores over 1100.

GUILFORD COLLEGE

Highlights

Admissions Criteria
Academic criteria:
Grades: ☆ ☆ ☆
Difficulty of class schedule: ☆ ☆ ☆
Class rank: ☆
Standardized test scores: ☆ ☆
Teacher recommendations: ☆
Personal statement: ☆ ☆
Non-academic criteria considered:
Interview
Extracurricular activities
Special talents, interests, abilities
Character/personal qualities
Volunteer work
Work experience
Geographical location
Religious affiliation/commitment
Minority affiliation
Alumni relationship

Deadlines
Early Action: Rolling
Early Decision: No
Regular Action: Rolling admissions
Common Application: Accepted

Financial Aid
In-state tuition: $32,090
Out-of-state tuition: $32,090
Room: Varies
Board: Varies
Books: $1,600
Freshmen receiving need-based aid: 82%
Undergrads rec. need-based aid: 78%
Avg. % of need met by financial aid: 80%
Avg. aid package (freshmen): $22,998
Avg. aid package (undergrads): $17,587
Avg. debt upon graduation: $25,025

School Spirit
Mascot: Quakers
Colors: Dark red and grey

GUSTAVUS ADOLPHUS COLLEGE

GUSTAVUS ADOLPHUS COLLEGE

Four-year private
Founded: 1862
St. Peter, MN
Small town
Pop. 11,223

Address:
800 West College
Avenue
St. Peter, MN
56082

Admissions:
800-487-8288

Financial Aid:
800-487-8288

admission@gustavus.
edu

www.gustavus.edu

Overview

You'll find Gustavus Adolphus—a private liberal arts college affiliated with the Lutheran Church—60 miles southwest of Minneapolis-St. Paul, in the quiet town of St. Peter. The College's Christ Chapel, which seats 1,500 people, is at the heart of campus, while sculptures by Paul Granlund are scattered throughout the grounds. The college owes its name to a Swedish king, and you don't have to look far to see the school's Swedish roots—whether it's the Scandinavian architecture on campus, Swedish House residence, the plant-filled Linnaeus Arboretum, or the annual Nobel Conference featuring Nobel-prize winning speakers and other scholars.

Several of Gustavus' buildings were rebuilt after a devastating F3 tornado hit in 1998. While tornados are far from an annual occurrence, subzero temperatures every winter may scare off those not used to the weather. Other students may be put off by Gustavus' lack of ethnic and geographic diversity—more than four-fifths of students are from Minnesota. However, students appreciate small classes, abundant opportunities for study abroad during the month-long January term and other times, and a lively campus where most students live.

Academics

There are two general education choices for Gusties: Curriculum I and Curriculum II. The first (CI) involves fulfilling area requirements, while Curriculum II (CII) is an integrated sequence of courses that emphasizes interdisciplinary learning and is limited to no more than 60 students. Though not an honors program, CII's limited size makes for a strong sense of community within the group that is further enhanced by retreats and trips to cultural events in the Twin Cities. "It's like our own little exclusive club," describes a student. Students not in CII enroll in a required First-Term Seminar course, which offers an introduction to a liberal arts education in a small-group setting with a professor/advisor.

Students choose from Bachelors of Arts in 71 majors—including 15 honors majors—in 24 departments and three interdisciplinary programs, including elementary and secondary education, music, and nursing, which are the strongest. According to the college, Gustavus Writing across the Curriculum has received national recognition for curriculum innovation by combining required writing intensive courses (three courses from two departments are required) with a thriving College Writing Center.

Students appreciate the small class sizes and availability of professors. The most common class size is 10 to 19 students, and higher-level classes can be very small. "I have a class where I'm the only student," explains a student. "That's a lot of pressure and attention at the same time," she laughs. Almost all classes are taught by professors rather than teaching assistants.

During "J-term," the one-month January term, students have four weeks to immerse themselves in one topic through courses or independent study. They may also choose to do an institutional exchange at an American college or even study abroad during this time. Gustavus' defining academic special opportunity is the Nobel Conference, an annual tradition that began in 1963 when 26 Nobel Laureates gathered on campus to dedicate the Alfred Nobel Hall of Science. Thus far, the annual science conference has brought 62 Nobel Laureates as speakers.

Carl Linnaeus is another famous Swede (besides Alfred Nobel) that has a building named after him on campus. The Linnaeus Arboretum, established in 1973, offers hands-on interaction in botany and other classes, serving as a living museum for research as well as formal and informal education.

According to Gustavus, the college is "routinely ranked in the top 10 baccalaureate institutions for the number of Gustavus students who study abroad"—50 percent of graduating seniors have studied abroad. A number of options are available, including the Gustavus faculty-led, interdisciplinary programs of Semester in India and Semester in Sweden.

There are more than 25,000 living alumni, and the online Gustie Network portal helps students find a job or internship. "Alums are pretty open to helping out current undergrads, and when we graduate I'm sure we'll do the same," says a student.

Student Life

The majority of students live on campus, making for a lively campus scene—in the winter you'll even find students sledding down hills on dining trays. There are more than 100 official recognized campus organizations across a dozen categories, from academic to religious to special interest. The forensics team is nationally ranked and a number of music ensembles and theatre groups perform throughout the year.

With about 12 percent of students in the 10 fraternities and sororities, Greek life exerts a strong influence on the social scene. "You don't have to be a member to go to the parties, but it opens up options," says a member.

The Dive, a non-alcoholic dance club, is a favorite hang-out on campus. Additionally, the college promotes and provides a free movie every weekend, which is billed as one of many alternatives to social events with alcohol. "The parties are decent, and you don't have to drink to have a good time, although most people do," one student comments.

At the beginning of December, the Christmas in the Chapel program brings together alumni, students, staff, and faculty for five services to celebrate the holidays together. The theme changes each year and about 1,200 people attend each service to enjoy music, dance, spoken word, and prayer. Later in the school year, the student-initiated, student-led "Building Bridges" conference on diversity addresses global and social issues by offering workshops and performances. The annual MAYDAY! Peace Conference focuses on human rights and social justice and features plenty of participatory activities for the audience.

Gustavus' Intercollegiate Division III athletics are popular to watch, especially games against rival St. Olaf. The college has had three players drafted in the NFL, most recently in 2003. There are 25 varsity teams and more than 40 intramural and club sports.

St. Peter doesn't have a lot of offerings so students trek to nearby Mankato, which has more restaurants, shopping, and bars due to the presence of Minnesota State-Mankato. The Twin Cities of St. Paul and Minneapolis are about an hour away by car. "Every once in a while we head into the Twin Cities for a concert or just if we want a taste of city life," says a student.

Freshmen and sophomores are required to live on campus, and most students live in dorms, college-owned houses, and themed residences. Gustavus' South Side dorms have a reputation for being quiet while the North Side dorms have a more lively reputation. On the North Side, Norelius Hall—nicknamed Coed because it was the first residence at Gustavus to open to both male and female students in 1967—includes various sections that are reserved for substance-free living. The Carlson International Center houses three programs for globally engaged students.

GUSTAVUS ADOLPHUS COLLEGE

Highlights

Students
Total enrollment: 2,524
Undergrads: 2,524
Freshmen: 694
From out-of-state: 19%
From public schools: 93%
Male/Female: 44%/56%
Live on-campus: 86%
In fraternities: 11%
In sororities: 12%
Off-campus employment rating: Excellent
Caucasian: 84%
African American: 3%
Hispanic: 3%
Asian / Pacific Islander: 4%
Native American: 1%
Mixed (2+ ethnicities): 2%
International: 2%

Academics
Calendar: 4-1-4 system
Student/faculty ratio: 12:1
Class size 9 or fewer: 14%
Class size 10-29: 66%
Class size 30-49: 19%
Class size 50-99: 2%
Class size 100 or more: -
Six-year graduation rate: 83%
Graduates who immediately go to graduate school: 26%

Most Popular Majors
Business administration
Biology
Education

Admissions
Applicants: 4,881
Accepted: 3,096
Acceptance rate: 63.4%
Placed on wait list: 11
Average GPA: 3.7
ACT range: 25-30
SAT Math range: Not reported
SAT Reading range: Not reported
SAT Writing range: 15-44
Top 10% of class: 37%
Top 25% of class: 74%
Top 50% of class: 96%

323

GUSTAVUS ADOLPHUS COLLEGE

Admissions Criteria
Academic criteria:
Grades: ☆ ☆ ☆
Difficulty of class schedule: ☆ ☆ ☆
Class rank: ☆ ☆
Standardized test scores: ☆
Teacher recommendations: ☆ ☆
Personal statement: ☆ ☆
Non-academic criteria considered:
Interview
Extracurricular activities
Special talents, interests, abilities
Character/personal qualities
Volunteer work
Work experience
State of residency
Geographical location
Minority affiliation
Alumni relationship

Deadlines
Early Action: November 1
Early Decision: No
Regular Action: Rolling admissions
Common Application: Accepted

Financial Aid
In-state tuition: $38,660
Out-of-state tuition: $38,660
Room: $5,820
Board: $3,230
Books: $900
Freshmen receiving need-based aid: 77%
Undergrads rec. need-based aid: 73%
Avg. % of need met by financial aid: 86%
Avg. aid package (freshmen): $31,279
Avg. aid package (undergrads): $29,160
Avg. debt upon graduation: $28,124

School Spirit
Mascot: Gus the Lion
Colors: Black and gold
Song: *Gustie Rouser*

Student Body

Of the 2,500 undergrads at Gustavus, less than one fifth are from out of state and about 13 percent are minority students, making for low geographic and moderate ethnic diversity. As might be expected for a college affiliated with the Evangelical Lutheran Church in America, religious groups are popular. However, students say that "even if you aren't religious, you will feel welcome."

You May Not Know

- The college's namesake is Swedish King Gustavus Adolphus, a.k.a. "The Lion of the North;" hence, their mascot, Gus the Lion.
- Gustavus Adolphus was not originally located in St. Peter, but the town enticed the college to move in 1876 with an offer of $10,000 and a large campus.
- The college's motto is *E Caelo Nobis Vires*, Latin for "Our Strength Comes From Heaven."

Distinguished Alumni

George Lindbeck, Yale University Professor of Theology; James M. McPherson, Pulitzer Prize winner in history; Semanti Mustaphi, Deputy Press Secretary for Michelle Obama; Patsy O'Connell Sherman, chemist and co-inventor of 3M Scotchgard.

Admissions and Financial Aid

Gustavus' admissions office emphasizes the college's "holistic approach to admission," which means they "evaluate all the information—not simply 'the numbers.'" In line with this policy, Gustavus is the first private college in Minnesota to adopt a test-optional admissions policy. The college also seeks those who can add geographic diversity since so many students are from within the state.

There is no application fee, whether applying on paper or online. Applications are reviewed on a rolling basis beginning November 1, and though there is no formal application deadline, most applications are received by early winter and the class is filled by early spring. The deposit deadline for enrolling at Gustavus is May 1, but students who send in their deposits earlier have priority for class registration and housing selection.

Gustavus offers merit-based scholarships and need-based grants. All students automatically are considered for five scholarships, including a diversity scholarship, with a maximum amount of $24,500 annually (or $98,000 over four years) for students who are awarded both the Dean's Scholarship and the National Merit College-Sponsored Scholarships. Eight other scholarships require an application. No athletic scholarships are offered.

HAMILTON COLLEGE

Overview

Nestled on a hill in upstate New York, Hamilton College offers a well-respected liberal arts education for its students, with a key emphasis on writing. The college is ranked 14th among liberal arts colleges in the country by *U.S. News & World Report*. Advisors assigned to each individual student encourage both achievement in the rigorous liberal arts curriculum and exploration for personal interests and goals. It is a requirement for all students to complete a senior project prior to graduation. However, unlike most liberal arts colleges, Hamilton does not have a core set of classes, allowing students eight semesters to take classes of their choice.

This private university—founded in 1812 and located just north of the village of Utica, New York and a short drive from Syracuse—offers an environment that can be thought of as both very secluded in a small town in the rural country and also as a college with city access by way of a mere 45-minute drive. The architecture on campus is for the most part colonial style, white with green roofing, reminiscent of the era in which the college was founded and the surrounding region. Campus itself is divided into two parts by a hillside, Hamilton on the north and Kirkland on the south. Because of its geographic location, students can expect harsh winters with temperatures ranging in the twenties from late November until March.

Academics

Hamilton College offers 53 areas of study, with academic strengths in English, history, prelaw, and premed. Unlike the majority of colleges in the United States, Hamilton offers almost complete independence and freedom to students when picking their courses and their majors. "You'll do best if you're the kind of person who can shape your own academic course rather than need a course given to you," says a student. Such loose requirements and small class settings create a place where students are all truly interested in the subject matter. Many students appreciate this approach to education and feel it far surpasses traditional methods where the majority of students drift off to sleep in required courses with two-hour-long lectures on subjects like Galileo's philosophy.

There are, however, two programs that Hamilton requires for their students. The first meets the college's main goal of creating competent writers during their four undergraduate years. To fulfill this, students must complete "three writing intensive courses offered throughout the curriculum." These courses are not universal in subject matter; rather, they are tailored to fit specific areas of studies. If you're not entirely confident with your writing background, don't fret. Hamilton offers to all students a writing center supported by almost 30 writing tutors. Students even admit to the success of the writing program, stating that they felt as though their writing "greatly improved" during the four years.

The second program, which usually incorporates the ideology of competent writing, is known as the Senior Program. During this, students normally compile a senior honors thesis in their area of study. This offers a unique way for all students to bring together their own specific interests while utilizing Hamilton's reputable writing program. "It's a big project but a rewarding one," notes a student.

Through the Arthur Levitt Public Affairs Center, students may conduct research with faculty as well as attend lectures that "connect Hamilton students with the non-Hamilton community," according to the center. The center focuses on programs on inequality and equity, security, and sustainability. Students also take courses, attend workshops, and receive one-on-one tutoring through the Oral Communication Center. According to this center, its goal is to "help students develop thinking and communication skills."

HAMILTON COLLEGE

Four-year private
Founded: 1812
Clinton, NY
Rural
Pop. 1,939

Address:
198 College Hill Road
Clinton, NY
13323

Admissions:
800-843-2655

Financial Aid:
800-859-4413

admission@hamilton.edu

www.hamilton.edu

HAMILTON COLLEGE

Highlights

Students
Total enrollment: 1,884
Undergrads: 1,884
Freshmen: 475
Part-time students: 1%
From out-of-state: 68%
From public schools: 59%
Male/Female: 49%/51%
Live on-campus: 98%
In fraternities: 26%
In sororities: 17%
Off-campus employment rating: Poor
Caucasian: 63%
African American: 4%
Hispanic: 7%
Asian / Pacific Islander: 8%
Native American: 0%
Mixed (2+ ethnicities): 2%
International: 5%

Academics
Calendar: Semester
Student/faculty ratio: 9:1
Class size 9 or fewer: 31%
Class size 10-29: 58%
Class size 30-49: 10%
Class size 50-99: 1%
Class size 100 or more: -
Returning freshmen: 96%
Six-year graduation rate: 91%

Most Popular Majors
Economics
Mathematics
Political science/government

Admissions
Applicants: 5,107
Accepted: 1,389
Acceptance rate: 27.2%
Placed on wait list: 1,016
Enrolled from wait list: 3
Average GPA: Not reported
ACT range: 29-33
SAT Math range: 650-740
SAT Reading range: 650-740
SAT Writing range: 52-36
Top 10% of class: 79%
Top 25% of class: 97%
Top 50% of class: 100%

For those who want to study abroad, Hamilton offers programs specifically affiliated with the college in France, China, Spain, Australia, Sweden, and India, but it is willing to work with nearly 180 programs around the world so that students have the ability to transfer credits from their schools of choice. Most students study abroad during their junior year.

The college emphasizes a Career Related Experience (CRE) before graduation. Each student is recommended to complete at least one CRE, either an "Initial" or "Advanced." The Initial is for students who have completed their first or second years. They work in their hometowns during the summer so they can network and acquire experience. The Advanced is usually an internship that can be paid. During a CRE or internship that is unpaid, Hamilton grants students funds to cover their costs of living. College credit may be given in some instances.

Hamilton's Career Center is extremely helpful in outlining what students need for grants, applications, recommendations, and other opportunities. "There's a lot of support to help us get hands-on experience," one student comments.

Student Life

Life on Hamilton's campus is filled with activities and more than 150 organizations ranging from musical a cappella choirs to cultural and academic groups. Hamilton also offers annual traditions for all students. Class and Charter day is Hamilton's most well known tradition and biggest party. The college shuts down all classes and students celebrate the end of their spring semester with a picnic and an event known as "G-road" at the end of the night. Febfest, Hamilton's week-long winter carnival, offers everyone a chance to get out and enjoy the cold fluffy white stuff (snow), along with live music, food, and drinks. Another tradition, albeit a new one recently created by student organizations, is known as Mayday when bands and singers perform outdoors. Some previous performers have been The New Pornographers, Citizen Cope, and Catch-22. "There's pretty much always something going on," says a student.

More than a quarter of the men and 17 percent of the women pledge the very popular non-housed fraternities and sororities, of which there are seven sororities and nine fraternities with national charters. The Emerson Literary Society is co-ed and is not affiliated with any national Greek organization. "You meet a ton of people by pledging," one student notes.

There are 25 NCAA Division III sports teams, the most esteemed being women's lacrosse and men's and women's crew. Also, students with any athletic ability can participate in one of 30 intramural sports. Students cheer on the Continentals at the annual Citrus Bowl, traditionally the first ice hockey game of the season where everyone dons orange to remember a time when they could chuck oranges at the opposing team. "It's rousing to see everyone in a sea of orange," remarks a student.

Since you won't find much nightlife in the small town of Utica, most nightlife is on campus. There aren't many restaurants or shopping facilities for college aged students, but many utilize Syracuse for a big-city atmosphere fix with concerts, shopping, and sporting events. For those interested in hiking, skiing, or snowboarding, upstate New York also offers a beautiful landscape that can fulfill any outdoorsman's needs.

If you're wondering why Hamilton's sororities and fraternities are all without houses, it is because the university requires that all students live on campus for the duration of their undergrad career. "That everyone lives on campus builds school spirit," says a student. Housing can be either in dormitory style living or in university-owned houses that are all within campus. The north side of campus is known for being more "loud" than the southern "quieter" Kirkland side.

Student Body

Sixty-eight percent of the student body is from out of state, giving Hamilton great geographic diversity. Ethnically, the school states that they have roughly 21 percent of students who identify themselves as multicultural or minority. The student body, according to the students themselves, is "more conservative than liberal, although there are lots of liberals too," as one student notes.

You May Not Know

- Hamilton is the third oldest university in New York named after the first secretary of U.S. Treasury, Alexander Hamilton, who was also the first member of the Board of Trustees.
- Al-Ham—short for Alexander Hamilton—is the school mascot, who can be seen wearing his traditional clothing and cheering at sporting events.
- To commemorate the 40th anniversary of the Stonewall Riots of 1969, a Hamilton alum led the organization of Pride March in 2010.

Distinguished Alumni

Paul Greengard, neuroscientist and 2000 Nobel Prize Winner for Physiology or Medicine; Ezra Pound, modern poet; James S. Sherman, Vice President to Howard Taft.

Admissions and Financial Aid

Taking on the newer trend in financial aid for students, Hamilton offers only need-based scholarships rather than merit or athletic based. The college meets 100 percent of students' demonstrated financial need.

Like their curriculum and requirements, Hamilton lets students have an element of choice in presentation for admissions. When applying to Hamilton, you may submit either your SAT/ACT scores or three standardized exams of your choice which must include a "quantitative" exam and a "verbal or written" exam.

HAMILTON COLLEGE

Highlights

Admissions Criteria
Academic criteria:
Grades: ☆ ☆ ☆
Difficulty of class schedule: ☆ ☆ ☆
Class rank: ☆ ☆ ☆
Standardized test scores: ☆ ☆
Teacher recommendations: ☆ ☆
Personal statement: ☆ ☆
Non-academic criteria considered:
Interview
Extracurricular activities
Special talents, interests, abilities
Character/personal qualities
Volunteer work
Work experience
State of residency
Geographical location
Minority affiliation
Alumni relationship

Deadlines
Early Action: No
Early Decision: November 15
Regular Action: January 1 (final)
Notification of admission by: April 1
Common Application: Accepted

Financial Aid
In-state tuition: $45,620
Out-of-state tuition: $45,620
Room: $6,400
Board: $5,310
Books: $1,300
Freshmen receiving need-based aid: 54%
Undergrads rec. need-based aid: 46%
Avg. % of need met by financial aid: 100%
Avg. aid package (freshmen): $40,594
Avg. aid package (undergrads): $39,386
Avg. debt upon graduation: $18,568

School Spirit
Mascot: Continentals
Colors: Buff and blue

HAMPDEN-
SYDNEY
COLLEGE

Four-year private
men's college
Founded: 1775
Hampden-Sydney, VA
Rural
Pop. 1,450

Address:
P.O. Box 667
Hampden-Sydney, VA
23943

Admissions:
800-755-0733

Financial Aid:
434-223-6119
hsapp@hsc.edu

www.hsc.edu

HAMPDEN-SYDNEY COLLEGE

Overview

The 1,100 men who attend Hampden-Sydney Colley (H-SC) enjoy a spacious, 1,340-acre wooded campus about 90 minutes from Richmond, Virginia. Federal-style buildings are spread throughout the rural campus on rolling hills which are also home to cattle. Renovations since 2004 have resulted in a new fitness center, parking lot, lacrosse field, the 1850-seat Lewis C. Everett Stadium, and most notably the 85,000-square-foot Walter M. Bortz III Library.

According to H-SC, the small private liberal arts college "expects its students to be gentlemen of good moral character and to be active and informed participants in the life of their communities." The emphasis on morality is not just lip service: H-SC's Honor System is highly regarded. While frats form a big part of social life at Hampden-Sydney, freshmen's introduction to H-SC is more sober than the average induction party: in a formal ceremony, incoming students pledge not to lie, cheat, steal, or tolerate those who do so.

The Honor Code, plus tough core academic requirements and a rigorous Rhetoric Program, contribute to the formation of a tight-knit "brotherhood" that continues after graduation. The campus lacks ethnic and geographic diversity; and being surrounded largely by genteel, Southern men isn't for everyone. Nearby colleges help ensure that the social scene can be co-ed, though the remote campus can still feel isolated. Still, the college is certainly unique for its eclectic offerings: as a *New York Times* article put it, "Hampden-Sydney's approach is part Southern gentleman, part good-ol'-boy club, with an emphasis on liberal arts, rhetoric and public speaking as well as a gun locker where students store the shotguns and rifles they take on hunting trips."

Academics

There are 29 majors offered and a number of minors and pre-professional and other academic programs. The Core Requirements at H-SC are rigorous and include requirements in writing, math, Western Culture, science, and foreign language. The writing requirement is particularly rigorous, including two freshman-year classes and a written proficiency exam during sophomore year. "It's pretty much a guarantee that you'll know how to write after all of the writing requirements," states a student. Four math and science classes, plus a three-semester sequence in the history and culture of Western Civilization, is a higher requirement than most colleges.

In keeping with the spirit of rigorous core requirements, classes are no breeze either. Students say that there isn't grade inflation and C's are "more common that you'd like them to be." The most common class size is 10 to 19 students. While difficult, the Rhetoric Program—one requirement of which is to write 10 papers per semester—is appreciated by alums who remark on the post-graduation usefulness of the faculty resolution that "all Hampden-Sydney graduates will write competently."

Strong majors include biology, classical studies, economics, and the prelaw program is also well-regarded. The Honors program at Hampden-Sydney is "simultaneously a scholarship program, an academic enrichment program, and a cultural enrichment program," according to the college. A uniquely Hampden-Sydney academic opportunity is the Caveman Chemistry class with Professor Kevin Dunn, a course that explores chemical technologies "from the campfires of the stone age to the plastic soft drink-bottle," which means students don't just learn about technologies but recreate and experience them, for example, making bronze from metal ores, soap from fat, and alcohol from honey.

Hampden-Sydney's offers study-abroad opportunities in over 30 countries abroad. There are language immersion programs in France, China, and other countries, plus topic-specific programs such as art and architecture in Cairo and marine sciences in

Australia. There are also month-long May Term Abroad programs designed by H-SC faculty in special topics in their disciplines.

Students say the alumni network is "stronger than at other colleges" because of the "brotherhood" that alums want to maintain even after graduating. This strong alumni network is, of course, helpful for job searching.

Student Life

With 95 percent of students living on campus or in campus-owned housing, it's not surprising that much of social life revolves around the school. With about 32 percent of students involved in Greek life, the eight social fraternities have a strong presence on campus and are a major driver of the social scene. Fraternity Circle is the central focus of party life on campus. To make sure that social life isn't all about men, women from nearby colleges such as the all-female Hollins University and Sweet Briar College, come to campus and Hampden-Sydney students also visit their campuses. "We have plenty of opportunities to meet women," says a student. For daytime and midnight munchies, the Tiger Inn, known to students as T.I., is a favorite hangout with its famous wrap sandwiches and entertainment in the form of TVs, pool tables, video games, and more.

Besides the two dozen social and honorary fraternities, student life at H-SC features service and religious clubs, three publications, an FM radio station, debating, drama, and musical groups, and 30 other student organizations. Notable service opportunities include the nonprofit Hampden-Sydney Volunteer Fire Department. "Beyond the Hill" community service trips include Alternative Spring Break programs that take students to countries such as Belize and Honduras.

H-SC freshmen begin their induction to the college through the ceremonial Signing of the Honor Code. Students meet in small-group sessions with members of the Student Court to discuss the Honor Code; and then they participate in a signing ceremony that lasts 45 minutes and is conducted in complete silence, with each student individually congratulated and welcomed by the President upon signing. "It's a tradition that ties us all together," says a student.

Less sobering major campus events include ODAC (Old Dominion Athletic Conference) Basketball. Hampden-Sydney's team has captured 10 championships—four in the new millennium alone. There's even more fanfare during April, when the fraternities show off their campus presence by throwing Greek Week, the annual festival that draws thousands of students from around the region. "Ours is the only Greek Week where people will literally take road trips to attend," notes a student.

Hampden-Sydney has eight varsity teams at the NCAA Division II level. Football is a popular sport where you'll find student spectators wearing jackets and ties, part of a long-standing tradition. "The other schools think it's strange we dress up for games," explains a student, "but it's just one of those things we do." There are also club teams; but intramurals are unrivaled in popularity, with 65 percent of students participating in the dozen or so options.

Off-campus, outdoor activities abound: hunting, fishing, camping, and hiking. Freshmen can get a taste of this through Outdoor Options, the College's pre-orientation wilderness program that brings together 6-10 freshmen, upperclassmen, and a faculty, staff,

HAMPDEN-SYDNEY COLLEGE

Highlights

Students
Total enrollment: 1,080
Undergrads: 1,080
Freshmen: 342
From out-of-state: 72%
From public schools: 66%
Male/Female: 100%/ 0%
Live on-campus: 95%
In fraternities: 32%
Off-campus employment rating: Fair
Caucasian: 80%
African American: 9%
Hispanic: 2%
Asian / Pacific Islander: 1%
Native American: 1%
Mixed (2+ ethnicities): 4%
International: 1%

Academics
Calendar: Semester
Student/faculty ratio: 11:1
Class size 9 or fewer: 24%
Class size 10-29: 73%
Class size 30-49: 3%
Class size 50-99: -
Class size 100 or more: -
Returning freshmen: 78%
Six-year graduation rate: 68%
Graduates who immediately go to graduate school: 25%

Most Popular Majors
Economics
History
Economics/business

Admissions
Applicants: 2,630
Accepted: 1,463
Acceptance rate: 55.6%
Average GPA: 3.4
ACT range: 21-26
SAT Math range: 510-615
SAT Reading range: 490-620
SAT Writing range: Not reported
Top 10% of class: 8%
Top 25% of class: 40%
Top 50% of class: 63%

329

HAMPDEN-SYDNEY COLLEGE

Admissions Criteria
Academic criteria:
Grades: ☆ ☆ ☆
Difficulty of class schedule: ☆ ☆ ☆
Class rank: ☆ ☆
Standardized test scores: ☆ ☆ ☆
Teacher recommendations: ☆ ☆ ☆
Personal statement: ☆
Non-academic criteria considered:
Interview
Extracurricular activities
Special talents, interests, abilities
Character/personal qualities
Volunteer work
Work experience
State of residency
Minority affiliation
Alumni relationship

Deadlines
Early Action: January 15
Early Decision: November 15
Regular Action: March 1 (final)
Notification of admission by: April 15
Common Application: Accepted

Financial Aid
In-state tuition: $36,224
Out-of-state tuition: $36,224
Room: Varies
Board: Varies
Books: $1,450
Freshmen receiving need-based aid: 66%
Undergrads rec. need-based aid: 83%
Avg. % of need met by financial aid: 81%
Avg. aid package (freshmen): $29,766
Avg. aid package (undergrads): $28,572
Avg. debt upon graduation: $30,048

School Spirit
Mascot: Tiger
Colors: Garnet and gray

or alumni member for an outdoor adventure. Farmville has very little "city life" to offer students, but other, larger campuses, such as The University of Richmond, University of Virginia, and Longwood University, are just a drive away.

Freshmen are required to live on campus in one of three freshmen dorms—Cushing is one of the most popular—while upperclassmen may live in off-campus college-owned dorms. The Housing Lottery is determined by seniority followed by GPA.

Student Body

H-SC's student body of about 1,100 is moderate on diversity, with 15 percent minority students and 28 percent from out of state. Only about half the states in the U.S. are represented each year. Students lean politically conservative, and, in fact, describe themselves as "mostly conservatively dressed and conservatively-minded Southerners."

You May Not Know

- Opening its doors in 1775, Hampden-Sydney was the last college founded before the American Revolution and is the 10th oldest college in the nation.
- Hampden-Sydney is one of the country's three four-year all-men liberal arts colleges: the other two are Morehouse College and Wabash College.
- The first fraternity house in North America can be found on Hampden-Sydney's campus: Beta Theta Pi used Atkinson Hall beginning in 1850.

Distinguished Alumni

Dr. Randall Chitwood, Chairman of Surgery at East Carolina University; Stephen Colbert, comedian and host of *The Colbert Report*; Dr. Eugene Hickcock, U.S. Deputy Secretary of Education.

Admissions and Financial Aid

Freshman admission requirements are fairly straightforward, with one required personal reference and the option to send in other references and even a photograph. The admissions office notes that it "seeks candidates who have demonstrated aptitude in the classroom through a series of rigorous classes" as well as those who excel in their extracurricular activities. Prospective students are encouraged to interview with an admissions counselor.

Every student is evaluated for academic merit-based scholarships, with the top-level scholarships covering nearly all of tuition. Students receive aid that totals $31 million. There are no athletic scholarships. However, there are need-based and non-need-based programs, the latter including a number of Honors Scholarships and Achievement Awards. The highest of these, the Allan Scholarships, offer a $30,000 grant plus 100 percent of remaining financial need.

HAMPSHIRE COLLEGE

HAMPSHIRE COLLEGE

Four-year private
Founded: 1965
Amherst, MA
Large town
Pop. 34,874

Address:
893 West Street
Amherst, MA
01002

Admissions:
877-937-4867

Financial Aid:
413-559-5484

admissions@hamp-
shire.edu

www.hampshire.edu

Overview

The forested and rural landscape of Pioneer Valley in Western Massachusetts is the home of Hampshire College. Small towns dot the valley and provide cultural comforts like independent bookstores, a variety of restaurants, indie music performances, art galleries, and good old-fashioned political protests.

Huffington Post named Hampshire one of the top 10 hipster schools. What began as a higher education experiment has thrived. Hampshire is known for its true focus on independence as there are no majors at the college. Instead, students design their own courses of study. Additionally, there are no grades but written narrative evaluations, and there is no freshman, sophomore, junior, or senior year but a Divisional System instead.

Walking around campus, it's easy to survey the student body and one notices that the school attracts alternative students and a good number of hippies. Don't be thrown off by the plain, and sometimes aesthetically questionable, architecture; the school got its start only 50 years ago, and the buildings reflect a utilitarian late 60's-early 70's cement and brick style. While Hampshire is a small campus, there are four other colleges in the immediate vicinity, and together they make up a five-college consortium. Students at Hampshire have access to courses and events at Amherst, Mt. Holyoke, Smith, and the University of Massachusetts at Amherst. Boston and its city life is a 90-mile trek away, so the outdoors takes the place of urban life; bicycling, walking paths, hiking, camping, winter sports, and gardening are major activities.

Academics

Initiative and independence will help a student get the most out of the Hampshire academic experience. The system that replaces traditional majors is referred to as "divisions," with the three divisions of study non-dependent on class year. In fact, the idea of freshman year, sophomore year, etc. just doesn't apply to the Hampshire model; according to the college, "… after exploring widely and deeply, students become the architects and builders of their own academic programs." Division I courses include two semesters of Basic Studies, while Division II is called The Concentration and occupies four semesters of a student's time at the college. Division III is an Advanced Study that encompasses two semesters. In order to graduate with a degree from Division III, major projects are completed. These can be artwork, a performance, research, or writing, depending on the student's concentration. "We love the amount of freedom that we're given and that we can choose the classes we want to take versus what the college prescribes," says a student. Communications/media studies (one class is Alien/Freak/Monster: Race, Sex, and otherness in Sci-Fi and Horror), creative writing (small workshops in poetry, fiction, playwriting, and literary journalism), and film/video/photography are considered strong programs at Hampshire.

Class sizes are small. Almost all classes have fewer than 30 students, and students and professors alike expect to get to know one another. However, students must take advantage of courses in which they are interested, as they aren't necessarily offered on a steady rotation and can't be expected to reappear in the course catalog the following year. While limited offerings may seem like a downside to Hampshire's small size, the opportunity to take classes at any of the other colleges in the five-college consortium more than compensates for it, opening up unlimited potential for study. Free shuttles run between the campuses. "This is a huge advantage," explains a student. "I've already taken courses at two of the other colleges."

Off-campus learning experiences away from the academic lair of the five-college consortium are also a popular student option. Short-term field courses are offered during January between the semesters, and in May at the end of the spring semester.

HAMPSHIRE COLLEGE

Students
Total enrollment: 1,461
Undergrads: 1,461
Freshmen: 361
From out-of-state: 82%
Male/Female: 42%/58%
Live on-campus: 80%
Off-campus employment rating: Fair
Caucasian: 64%
African American: 3%
Hispanic: 10%
Asian / Pacific Islander: 2%
Native American: 0%
Mixed (2+ ethnicities): 5%
International: 6%

Academics
Calendar: 4-1-4 system
Student/faculty ratio: 12:1
Class size 9 or fewer: 11%
Class size 10-29: 85%
Class size 30-49: 4%
Class size 50-99: -
Class size 100 or more: -
Returning freshmen: 78%
Six-year graduation rate: 63%
Graduates who immediately go to graduate school: 10%
Graduates who immediately enter career related to major: 15%

Most Popular Majors
Creative writing
Film/photo/video
Fine arts

Admissions
Applicants: 2,856
Accepted: 1,819
Acceptance rate: 63.7%
Placed on wait list: 388
Enrolled from wait list: 47
Average GPA: 3.5
ACT range: 25-29
SAT Math range: 540-650
SAT Reading range: 600-700
SAT Writing range: 19-49

Topic-oriented field courses include Ireland (West Ireland's Land and Landscape), the Netherlands (the Hague), China (a summer intensive language program), and France (filmmaking in Paris). Longer-term semester or year-long study-abroad programs via exchange are offered in 30 countries, and around 150 students take advantage of them per year.

After graduation, students can receive career support from Hampshire via networking and career counseling. Alumni have the opportunity to takes classes at Hampshire and even teach a January term course.

Student Life

Make no mistake, Hampshire doesn't want to be like every other college; there are no fraternities and sororities here, and there are no varsity sports. When the school mascot is a frog, it's pretty clear that the agenda is different than elsewhere. "We aren't afraid to steer away from the traditional college scene," says a student.

Intramural sports do exist at Hampshire; Ultimate Frisbee and intramural basketball have popular—if not seriously competitive—teams. The over 100 student groups provide one of the major organized social outlets on campus and reflect the myriad unique interests. The GNU+Linux Users Group, HaFTA (Hampshire Fair Trade Alliance), Friends of Fermentation, Buddhist Resource Group, Burlesque for All, and more clubs are all active on campus.

School spirit manifests in the mass participation in annual events. Hampshire Halloween in the fall is an extravaganza with art shows, Halloween fireworks, and dancing; creative costumes are a must. The spring drag ball is another well-attended event hosted by LGBT campus groups, the Women's center, and other student groups. The ball is a chance for students to express themselves as another gender and dance away the night. Another spring event is the infamous keg hunt at Easter, where instead of hunting for eggs, students hunt for kegs with a cup in hand. "We have a twist on the typical college traditions, usually with either alcohol or cross-dressing involved," laughs a student.

The officially unsponsored social life does include partying. Hampshire students have a reputation for drinking, which may be reflect the campus's independent atmosphere. "Whatever you want, you can pretty much find, but the great majority of us know our limits," notes a student. Many student parties happen in the mods (modular housing), and since approximately 80 percent of students live on campus, it's easy to access the party circuit.

In town, the Eric Carle Museum of Picture Book Art exhibits the art for which it is named, and there's a studio where visitors can create their own picture books. Amherst has unique shops and restaurants, and students do participate in activities at the other colleges in the consortium. The occasional road trip to Boston or New York is another getaway option.

As far as dorm life goes, first-year students are mainly housed in Dakin House and Merrill House, which offer traditional dorm-style singles and some doubles. Upper division students live in the modular housing residences Prescott House, Greenwich House, and Enfield House, featuring apartments with a common living/dining room combo, kitchen, and bathroom. Prescott House's loft-style rooms and cathedral ceiling rooms make it a desirable choice.

Student Body

Hampshire attracts students who are "extremely independent," liberal, and left-leaning, and often into alternative culture, whether that be activist, hippy, or hipster. There's high ethnic diversity on campus with a 20 percent minority population. Students come to Hampshire from all over the country and internationally, with 82 percent of students from out of state.

Experimentation, self-expression, and values seem to dictate the style of students. From dreadlocks and hemp skirts to hiking boots and worker pants to trucker hats and flannel, there are obvious subculture trends in wardrobe choices. But, these looks aren't just about style—they are ways in which students exercise independent thinking. Hampshire students are notorious for being "very active politically" and "passionate about social and environmental issues."

You May Not Know

- There are no grades at Hampshire College; instead, students receive narrative evaluations for their work.
- The idea for the college was created in 1965 to add to the options for a liberal arts education, and the first students were admitted in 1970.
- The National Yiddish Book Center, a 37,000-square-foot museum and rescue mission for one million Yiddish books, began as the project of a 23-year old graduate student attending Hampshire.

Distinguished Alumni

Gary Hirshberg, CEO of organic yogurt producer, Stonyfield Farm; Elliott Smith, musician; Jessamyn West, librarian, activist and blogger.

Admissions and Financial Aid

One notable difference in Hampshire's application process is their test-optional policy for most students. That said, approximately 87 percent of students do submit test scores and AP exam scores as part of their application, and the college does encourage this if substantive high school narrative evaluations or grades are unavailable. Local interviews are available through a network of alumni and counselors and are also strongly recommended as part of the admission process. All in all, the college aims to find students who are good fits, using the college essay as a way to demonstrate this.

Merit-based scholarship recipients are selected from among all applicants to receive annually renewable awards of $1,000 to $12,500. Merit awards include the Andrew Salkey Memorial scholarship for a student of "exceptional writing promise" and the Scholarship in the Sciences for students who show promise to carry out innovative and passionate research or activism in the sciences.

HAMPSHIRE COLLEGE

Highlights

Admissions Criteria
Academic criteria:
Grades: ☆ ☆
Difficulty of class schedule: ☆ ☆
Class rank: ☆
Standardized test scores: ☆
Teacher recommendations: ☆ ☆
Personal statement: ☆ ☆ ☆
Non-academic criteria considered:
Interview
Extracurricular activities
Special talents, interests, abilities
Character/personal qualities
Volunteer work
Work experience
State of residency
Minority affiliation
Alumni relationship

Deadlines
Early Action: December 1
Early Decision: November 15
Regular Action: November 15 (priority)
January 1 (final)
Notification of admission by: April 1
Common Application: Accepted

Financial Aid
In-state tuition: $45,100
Out-of-state tuition: $45,100
Room: $7,680
Board: $4,350
Books: $700
Freshmen receiving need-based aid: 59%
Undergrads rec. need-based aid: 60%
Avg. % of need met by financial aid: 97%
Avg. aid package (freshmen): $34,430
Avg. aid package (undergrads): $36,741
Avg. debt upon graduation: $20,430

School Spirit
Colors: Blue and green

HARVARD
UNIVERSITY

Four-year private
Founded: 1636
Cambridge, MA
Medium city
Pop. 106,038

Address:
86 Brattle Street
Cambridge, MA
02138

Admissions:
617-495-1551

Financial Aid:
617-495-1581

college@fas.harvard.
edu

www.harvard.edu

HARVARD UNIVERSITY

Overview

Founded in 1636, Harvard University is the country's first institution of higher learn-ing and is generally regarded as the top school in the nation. It is situated in picturesque Cambridge, just minutes from the historical city of Boston. Harvard shares many values with its host city of Cambridge, such as protecting the environment, maintaining the town's quaint aesthetic nature, and accommodating the constant stream of tourism. In fact, tourists are such a consistent presence on the Harvard campus that students don't think twice about detouring off paths blocked by tour groups or having their pictures snapped on the way to dinner.

Harvard Yard in the fall is the ultimate picture of the Ivy League campus, with tall elms and red brick residential halls casting shadows on the yard where students read or toss Frisbees. Since the campus has developed over time, its architecture cannot be neatly categorized. The architectural backbeat of the Harvard campus is solemn, 17th century red brick, interrupted by structures like the bulky, concrete Science Center or the edgy Carpenter Art Center designed by Le Corbusier.

Academics

Harvard academics are undeniably rigorous, but nearly everyone adjusts to the school's academic wavelength within a semester. Most students are competent enough upon arrival to handle the heavy workload without any significant problems. An aspect of the Harvard curriculum is Freshman Seminars, which are focused, pass/fail courses offered exclusively to the incoming freshman class. The idea behind Freshman Seminars is to allow new students to work closely with faculty in a more inventive environment than the typical classroom setting. The courses are composed of 15 students or fewer and deal with specific themes in the professor's field of expertise. Students describe the Freshman Seminars as a "good way to ease into Harvard academics" and as "mixed" in their academic rigor.

Harvard offers its students over 40 concentrations—or majors—and while the vast majority of the school's departments are regarded as excellent, some of the the strongest programs are economics, biology, government, and English. Harvard re-placed its Core Curriculum with a General Education requirement, which is more flexible and aims to familiarize students with key domains of knowledge, rather than forcing them to sample a single course in every discipline. Expository Writing is a required course for freshmen, designed to hone their topical writing skills and better equip them to succeed in the rest of their Harvard courses. Every student must also demonstrate proficiency in a foreign language by the end of the junior year, either by passing a language test or by taking two semester-long courses of a foreign language.

Study-abroad experiences are highly encouraged at Harvard, and students can choose from 300 approved host programs and over 60 destination countries. But even with the wealth of options, many students think twice about missing a semester of Harvard classes. Instead, a huge number of students opt for summertime study-abroad programs or overseas internships, which the administration will usually fund in part.

The Fellows Program is a mutually beneficial program in which political practi-tioners, journalists, and academics spend a semester at Harvard to pursue personal projects and participate in the intellectual life of the school. Through study groups and conversations with Fellows, students learn first-hand about application of ideas and concepts in the public sector. Students also have access to several research op-portunities, including the Faculty Aide Program, where they can work as paid research assistants to faculty members, and the Harvard College Research Program, where they may receive funding for independent research projects.

After graduation, Harvard's incredibly large alumni base often helps to facilitate effective career and internship searches. The Office of Career Services provides

Crimson Careers, an online database of job and internship postings; an on-campus interview program; graduate school advising; and premedical and health careers advising. "Interviewing on campus is the most competitive time at Harvard, unless you're a premed major, in which case every day is a little competitive," says a student.

Student Life

At any given moment, Harvard's campus is teeming with activities and events hosted by one of its 400 student organizations. These events range from concerts and drama productions, to colorful shows such as Cultural Rhythms, a hugely anticipated celebration of ethnic diversity that includes student performances emceed by celebrities like Queen Latifah, Jackie Chan, and Halle Berry. The administration organizes several events like pep rallies, exam-week study breaks, and the Freshman Formal for first-year students. One of the school's biggest annual events is YardFest, an outdoor autumn festival that typically features barbecues, carnival rides, and concerts by well known artists.

On the weekends, finals clubs and house parties dominate the campus social life, and most students choose to remain on campus rather than traveling into Boston for entertainment. While Greek life exists at Harvard, it is not a key element of campus activity since 99 percent of undergraduates live in school-provided student housing. Finals clubs, which are similar to fraternities in concept, are private social clubs that own real estate in Cambridge and host social events on a regular basis. Students describe the Finals clubs as "exclusive" and "remnants of the old boys' network."

Housing at Harvard is excellent, and much of the campus social scene revolves around residential life. Freshmen live in dormitories in or near the Yard, which gives the freshman class a sense of cohesiveness as they adjust to university life together. Near the end of the year, students are divided into one of twelve upper-class houses located throughout Cambridge, where they will live, eat, and socialize for the remainder of their time at Harvard. Each House has a distinct reputation on campus, and students tend to become loyal to their houses very quickly. Each House has defining characteristics, including mascots (such as the Dunster moose) and annual, hallmark intra-house parties (such as the Kirkland Incest Fest). While dining hall quality and room size may vary from house to house, most students consider their house to be the best.

Harvard may not have a reputation for being a "jock school," but its athletic program is one of the best in the nation and fields 41 Division I intercollegiate varsity sports teams. The school's most competitive sports are ice hockey, rowing, fencing, and sailing. The basketball team enjoyed its first NCAA tournament victory in 2013. Harvard also has more than 30 student-run club teams and recreational sports teams, and an estimated 75 percent of the student body participates in athletic activity on some level. Harvard's most intense athletic rivalry is with Yale, which culminates in the annual Harvard-Yale football game. "There's usually more school spirit for hockey games than football games, except for when it's The Game," remarks a student.

The Boston-Cambridge area is ideal for the college lifestyle. Students who wish to escape the infamous "Harvard bubble" can get to the city within a few minutes on the T, Boston's subway

HARVARD UNIVERSITY

Highlights

Students
Total enrollment: 10,559
Undergrads: 6,658
Freshmen: 1,675
From out-of-state: 84%
Male/Female: 51%/49%
Live on-campus: 99%
Off-campus employment rating: Excellent
Caucasian: 48%
African American: 6%
Hispanic: 9%
Asian / Pacific Islander: 15%
Native American: 0%
Mixed (2+ ethnicities): 5%
International: 11%

Academics
Calendar: Semester
Student/faculty ratio: 7:1
Class size 9 or fewer: 43%
Class size 10-29: 44%
Class size 30-49: 6%
Class size 50-99: 4%
Class size 100 or more: 3%
Returning freshmen: 97%
Six-year graduation rate: 97%

Most Popular Majors
Economics
Political science/government
Sociology

Admissions
Applicants: 34,303
Accepted: 2,076
Acceptance rate: 6.1%
Average GPA: 4.0
ACT range: 32-35
SAT Math range: 710-790
SAT Reading range: 700-800
SAT Writing range: 81-16
Top 10% of class: 95%
Top 25% of class: 98%
Top 50% of class: 99%

335

College Profiles

HARVARD UNIVERSITY

Admissions Criteria
Academic criteria:
Grades: ☆
Difficulty of class schedule: ☆
Class rank: N/A
Standardized test scores: ☆
Teacher recommendations: ☆
Personal statement: ☆
Non-academic criteria considered:
Interview
Extracurricular activities
Special talents, interests, abilities
Character/personal qualities
Volunteer work
Work experience
State of residency
Geographical location
Minority affiliation
Alumni relationship

Deadlines
Early Action: November 1
Early Decision: No
Regular Action: January 1 (final)
Notification of admission by: April 1
Common Application: Accepted

Financial Aid
In-state tuition: $38,891
Out-of-state tuition: $38,891
Room: $8,667
Board: $5,448
Books: $1,000
Freshmen receiving need-based aid: 58%
Undergrads rec. need-based aid: 60%
Avg. % of need met by financial aid: 100%
Avg. aid package (freshmen): $46,519
Avg. aid package (undergrads): $45,307
Avg. debt upon graduation: $12,560

School Spirit
Mascot: Crimson
Colors: Crimson and white
Song: *10,000 Men of Harvard*

system—either to see shows and performances, or to support the Red Sox, Celtics, Patriots, and Bruins during their respective sports seasons. When it comes to eating out, students need to look no farther than Cambridge's huge host of restaurants, where they can find everything from exotic Algerian cuisine to the ever-present Dunkin Donuts. Running and biking paths along the Charles River also make Cambridge the perfect place for exercising outdoors. Students describe Cambridge as the "perfect college town" and the "ideal location in the best college town in the country."

Student Body

For years, the stereotypical Harvard student has been infamously portrayed as a white New England prep-school student in a blazer and boat shoes. While a sliver of the student body still fits this profile, the undergraduate population at Harvard today is incredibly diverse, with students from over 100 international countries and all 50 states. Sixteen percent of undergraduates are Massachusetts residents. Harvard's ethnic diversity is also extremely high—the student body is only 48 percent Caucasian, and nearly every ethnic group is represented by one or more student clubs on campus. In reality, the stereotype of the white, preppy Harvard kid is not the rule; instead, the campus is an unmatched melting pot of cultures and backgrounds. Because Harvard only accepts about 2,000 out of 34,000 talented applicants, the administration can handcraft the demographics of the student body to ensure that a huge range of cultures is represented on campus.

The atmosphere at Harvard is certainly politically liberal, but every political group has several active student groups and publications on campus. "Conservatives are few and far between," says a student. Many religions are represented at Harvard, and while the college attempts to provide spaces to practice faith, many religious students opt to join a local, off-campus religious community. Harvard's Hillel is the campus center of Jewish life, and includes a kosher cafeteria, religious discussion times, and relaxed study spaces.

Because of their heavy workloads, Harvard students are necessarily focused when it comes to academics. Most do not stop at school, however, but cram their schedules with student clubs, sports, volunteer work, internships, politics, and speaking events. Heavily overloaded schedules are the norm at Harvard, and students with free time often feel self-conscious about the gaps in their schedules. While Harvard kids may be under pressure, most still find the time on weekends to cultivate their social lives—contrary to popular opinion, the typical Harvardian is not bent over a laptop during every waking hour. "There are some students who only study, but they are definitely the minority," a student remarks. Rather, the hallmark of a Harvard kid is a plurality of interests and the desire to take advantage of every available opportunity. Many students try to pile the whole buffet on their plates at first, but upperclassmen usually learn to whittle down their interests into a slightly more healthy set of obligations before they graduate.

You May Not Know

- Harvard's official mascot is John Harvard, the founder. Since "John Harvard" is awkward to scream at football

games or to print on T-shirts, Harvard students just yell,
"Go Crimson!"

- Depending on the season, 35 to 70 percent of Harvard's
dining hall food is grown locally.
- Harvard's Library contains over 16 million volumes, making it the largest private library system in the world.

Distinguished Alumni

John Adams, president of the U.S.; John Quincy Adams, U.S. President; Samuel Adams, Governor of Massachusetts; John Ashbery, poet; Elaine Chao, U.S. Secretary of Labor; e.e. cummings, poet; W.E.B. Du Bois, civil rights leader; T.S. Elliot, Nobel Prize in literature; Ralph Waldo Emerson, writer; Al Gore, Vice President of the U.S. and Nobel Peace Prize winner; John Hancock, first Governor of Massachusetts; Oliver Wendell Holmes Jr., Justice of the U.S. Supreme Court; Tommy Lee Jones, actor; Ashley Judd, actress; John F. Kennedy, U.S. President; Henry Kissinger, U.S. Secretary of State and Nobel Peace Prize winner; Yo-Yo Ma, cellist; Conan O'Brien, comedian; Soledad O'Brien, television host; Frank O'Hara, poet; Bill O'Reilly, journalist and political commentator; Natalie Portman, actress; David Rockefeller, banker and philanthropist; Franklin D. Roosevelt, U.S. President; Theodore Roosevelt, U.S. President; Gertrude Stein, poet and novelist; Henry David Thoreau, writer and philosopher; John Updike, writer.

Admissions and Financial Aid

Because Harvard receives a daunting number of applications per year, their application process is efficient, with only one large essay and an optional supplementary essay. The applicant's proficiency with expository prose is an important criterion in the evaluation process, since ideas are only useful insofar as they can be clearly conveyed. While the Harvard admissions team considers a student's academic promise first and foremost, they also seek individuals with distinctive traits and talents, i.e. students who excel in one or more non-classroom domains and who will raise the bar on campus in their relevant berth of expertise and influence. Students who stand out to the admissions team are the ones who took the most challenging courses available to them and developed their non-classroom talents with passion and persistence—students who did not let opportunities for personal growth pass them by.

Harvard financial aid is excellent and its recent policy goal is for every student to graduate without debt; thus, the college promises to meet 100 percent of each student's demonstrated need. Student loans are not required by the college. Through the Harvard Financial Aid Initiative, there is no parent contribution for students whose families make less than $60,000 in income. Those with family incomes between $60,000 and $180,000 have reduced expected parent contributions, on a scale from 0 to 10 percent. Harvard does not offer merit scholarships.

HARVEY MUDD COLLEGE

Four-year private
Founded: 1955
Claremont, CA
Large town
Pop. 35,143

Address:
301 Platt Boulevard
Claremont, CA
91711

Admissions:
909-621-8011

Financial Aid:
909-621-8055

admission@hmc.edu

www.hmc.edu

Overview

Located in the suburb of Claremont, California, about 35 miles east of downtown LA, Harvey Mudd College (HMC) is small in size—more than 700 undergraduates live and study on this 38-acre campus—and big in reputation for its excellent science, mathematics, and engineering courses.

The campus features symmetrical buildings designed with '50s architecture, much of it covered with thousands of square concrete features that students refer to as "warts" and which sometimes double as storage space for skateboards. Indeed, the unofficial mascot of the college is a concrete block, affectionately dubbed "Wally the Wart."

Though known for its strength as a technical school, Harvey Mudd offers students a strong backbone in the liberal arts, thanks to its membership in the Claremont Colleges. Students share resources from libraries to dining halls to student groups with Pitzer, Scripps, Claremont McKenna, and Pomona College, which provides a sense of a larger university community. To join their ranks, you'll want to have a real passion for math, science, and/or engineering, and be willing to work very hard. If a small community of fellow techies and accessible professors in sunny Southern California is your ideal college experience, Harvey Mudd is a great choice.

Academics

Harvey Mudd offers six department majors and three interdisciplinary majors, all centered around science/math/engineering. Students can also opt for an Independent Program of Study (IPS), which a handful of students do each year. Finally, students can choose an off-campus major at another Claremont College as long as they minor in a technical field at Harvey Mudd. Strong programs include engineering, mathematics, and computer science.

HMC's curriculum is divided into four parts: The Common Core is meant to provide a strong foundation for upper-division courses and includes 12 semester-long classes across various technical fields. Humanities and social sciences classes make up the second part and give breadth to students' experiences. The third component encompasses courses in each student's major. Finally, there is the Integrative Experience, which addresses the interface between society and science and technology and includes a required research project as a part of this component.

Academics at Harvey Mudd are intense—not surprising for a school that requires 128 credit hours of courses. Students work hard to earn their BS degrees. One student describes classes as "much more challenging than you'd think." Fortunately, due to small class sizes, professors and faculty members are often involved with students' academic progress and are very willing to help. And the college makes sure students don't sit in classrooms or labs all day by requiring three physical education classes. "I guess the physical education classes are good for us, but most of us would prefer to skip them," says a student.

Community and college interaction are encouraged at Harvey Mudd. The Clinic Program for juniors and seniors is a hallmark of the college. Students are given the chance to develop solutions to real-world technical problems for industrial clients. Since the Clinic Program's inception in 1963, almost 1,300 year-long projects have been completed by teams of students. This arrangement provides companies with an inexpensive student workforce, while students gain hands-on experience and are often recruited by the sponsoring company after graduation or named on patents that come out of projects. Additionally, Harvey Mudd students who want to share their love of science can participate in the Science Bus Program, which helps teach science to underprivileged children.

Students looking to earn accelerated master's degrees can do a 3-2 program in economics and engineering. Claremont Graduate University also offers the 4+1 BS

+ MBA program through the management school, and a 4+1 BS + MSIS through the graduate school of Information Science.

Most Harvey Mudd students who study abroad do so in their junior year through approved programs vetted by HMC as well as non-approved programs. Cultural Immersion Programs, created in partnership with Pitzer College, allow Mudders to take core engineering courses while still getting a field-based study-abroad experience. Students who aren't able to study abroad can consider the Domestic Exchange Program with Swarthmore College and Rensselaer Polytechnic Institute, where they can study for a semester at the same cost as attending HMC.

Harvey Mudd is the leading undergraduate producer of science and engineering Ph.D.s and the second highest among all universities and colleges based on a 2008 National Science Foundation report. Graduates are also among the highest-earning in the nation, with an average starting salary of $75,000 to $80,000.

Student Life

Harvey Mudd's student organizations range from academic (mainly science and engineering clubs) to cultural to community service to arts to recreational. There is no Greek system at the college; however, there is a plethora of opportunities for group interaction. HMC has some of its own groups—for instance, *The Muddraker*, HMC's student newspaper, and The etc. Players, a campus theater group—and students can also join clubs at the other Claremont Colleges. A community service fair is held each fall, and the Strauss Internship for Social Understanding gives students a chance to intern for a nonprofit social service agency for 10 weeks during the summer.

The student-led group, Increasing Harvey Mudd's Traditional Practices, aims to support old college traditions and start new ones. Annual events it hosts include Wednesday Nighters (think happy hour), Frosh/Soph Games, and more. One quirky tradition dates back to the 1970s, when the Gonzo Unicycle Madness club was formed. They still organize a 9.6 mile ride named the Foster's Run, where its completion is rewarded with strawberry donuts. Some students are even known to play unicycle hockey. You don't have to balance on a single wheel to enjoy being a Mudder though: there's also the popular annual Suds Party, aka Foam Party, and Long Tall Glasses, a formal affair that's as elegant as it sounds, complete with chocolate-covered strawberries.

Harvey Mudd fields 19 varsity teams (eight men's, nine women's, and two co-ed) jointly with Claremont McKenna and Scripps College, which compete in Division III. The women's teams are called the Athenas while the male athletic teams are the Stags. Cross country, track and field, water polo, tennis, and women's basketball are the most competitive. Intramural sports are also popular, facilitating keen rivalry among residence halls.

Off campus, Claremont offers low-key days and nights out on the town. For more glamorous entertainment, students can take road trips to Los Angeles, San Diego, Las Vegas, or Mexico.

Virtually everyone lives on campus at Harvey Mudd. Dorm areas are divided into North, South, East, and West, and each maintains a distinct personality. Dorm-based party traditions have included Halloween's Trick or Drink and the tequila-center TQ Nite, both thrown by the West.

HARVEY MUDD COLLEGE

Highlights

Students
Total enrollment: 783
Undergrads: 783
From out-of-state: 59%
From public schools: 80%
Male/Female: 56%/44%
Live on-campus: 98%
Off-campus employment rating: Good
Caucasian: 54%
African American: 1%
Hispanic: 7%
Asian / Pacific Islander: 22%
Native American: 0%
Mixed (2+ ethnicities): 2%
International: 8%

Academics
Calendar: Semester
Student/faculty ratio: 8:1
Class size 9 or fewer: 33%
Class size 10-29: 49%
Class size 30-49: 13%
Class size 50-99: 4%
Class size 100 or more: 1%
Returning freshmen: 98%
Six-year graduation rate: 88%
Graduates who immediately go to graduate school: 36%
Graduates who immediately enter career related to major: 55%

Most Popular Majors
Engineering
Mathematics
Physics

Admissions
Applicants: 336
Accepted: 642
Acceptance rate: 191.1%
Placed on wait list: 501
Enrolled from wait list: 27
Average GPA: Not reported
ACT range: 33-35
SAT Math range: 740-800
SAT Reading range: 680-770
SAT Writing range: 68-30
Top 10% of class: 96%
Top 25% of class: 100%
Top 50% of class: 100%

339

College Profiles

HARVEY MUDD COLLEGE

Admissions Criteria

Academic criteria:
Grades: ☆ ☆ ☆
Difficulty of class schedule: ☆ ☆ ☆
Class rank: ☆ ☆
Standardized test scores: ☆ ☆
Teacher recommendations: ☆ ☆ ☆
Personal statement: ☆ ☆ ☆
Non-academic criteria considered:
Interview
Extracurricular activities
Special talents, interests, abilities
Character/personal qualities
Volunteer work
Work experience
Geographical location
Minority affiliation
Alumni relationship

Deadlines

Early Action: No
Early Decision: November 15
Regular Action: January 1 (final)
Notification of admission by: April 1
Common Application: Accepted

Financial Aid

In-state tuition: $44,159
Out-of-state tuition: $44,159
Room: $7,763
Board: $6,708
Books: $800
Freshmen receiving need-based aid: 53%
Undergrads rec. need-based aid: 51%
Avg. % of need met by financial aid: 100%
Avg. aid package (freshmen): $41,827
Avg. aid package (undergrads): $37,184
Avg. debt upon graduation: $20,374

School Spirit

Mascot: Stags (men)/Athenas (women)
Colors: Maroon and gold

Student Body

Mudders are techies—no surprise there. They're also very academically focused, again not surprising, given that a third of the student body are National Merit Scholars and 96 percent graduated in the top 10 percent of their class. As with many technical schools, there is a heavy male skew in the student population. "The dating situation is what you'd expect—a handful of attractive, not socially awkward guys among the masses," says a female student.

There is moderate geographic diversity, with about 59 percent of students from out of state and nearly all 50 states, plus 25 foreign countries, represented. Ethnic diversity is very high with more than 32 percent minority students.

You May Not Know

- The college's namesake is an early investor in the Cyprus Mines Corporation.
- As of 2010, only seven students at the college have ever earned a 4.0 GPA.
- Harvey Mudd was the first undergraduate-only college to win first prize in the ACM International Collegiate Programming Contest.

Distinguished Alumni

Karl Mahlburg, mathematician; George "Pinky" Nelson, astronaut and first American to walk in space without a tether to a spacecraft; Amanda Simpson, senior technical adviser to the Department of Commerce.

Admissions and Financial Aid

Harvey Mudd doesn't mince words: when it comes to what kind of student the college is looking for, they state simply, "the best." They look for "students who take, and excel in, challenging courses." There are eligibility requirements for minimum amounts of coursework, with a strong emphasis on math, science, and also English. Three letters of recommendation are required: from the school counselor, a math/science teacher, and a humanities teacher. Interviews for prospective students are recommended.

Harvey Mudd's admissions process is need-blind for U.S. citizens and permanent residents. The most frequently granted merit award is the $10,000-per-year Harvey S. Mudd award, which requires no separate application. The President's Scholars Program provides a four-year full tuition scholarship for students traditionally underrepresented in math, science, and engineering.

HAVERFORD COLLEGE

Overview

Haverford College is sometimes confused in name with its Ivy League neighbor to the north, but the attitude at this Pennsylvania private liberal arts college differs vastly from that of 'Hahvahd.' Haverford, located on 204 acres of beautiful gardens and woodlands just 10 miles outside of Philadelphia, combines close location to a bustling metropolis with a calm and natural setting ideal for pursuing academics. The college boasts the oldest planned college campus in the country—designed after an English landscape by gardener William Carvill—and features award-winning stately brick and stone architecture. Haverford is also a nationally-recognized arboretum, containing over 400 species of trees and shrubs. Students can enjoy a contemplative stroll along the 2.25-mile Nature Walk or relax by the centrally-located duck pond.

Haverford is small—only about 1,200 undergraduates—but the college takes advantage of its size to provide strong faculty attention to students, as well as a close-knit community that continues discussions of academia and social justice outside of the classroom. Haverford was founded in 1833 to educate Quaker boys, and Quaker values still make up the college principles: during their four years, students acquire a strong work ethic, individuality, and tolerance for others. The Haverford Honor Code, almost completely student-run, is held in high respect, and makes up the cornerstone of both academic and college life. Students know they can leave backpacks and laptops safely alone in the library and hold the responsibility of scheduling and taking their exams without proctors. This freedom and respect for self-accountability fosters an environment of genuine interaction and trust.

Haverford is ranked ninth in *U.S. News & World Report's* rankings of liberal arts college, and its close proximity to Bryn Mawr and Swarthmore Colleges—along with Haverford, they form the Tri-College Consortium , through which students can take classes on any of the three schools—provides even more academic and social variety. Haverford truly combines the best of both worlds, maintaining a small and intimate school in the middle of a plethora of intellectual and metropolitan opportunities.

Academics

Haverford offers 34 majors and boasts strong programs in biology, economics, history, physics, and premed studies. Curriculum requirements are designed to expand and broaden thinking. Students must take classes in the social sciences, humanities and natural sciences, and all freshmen take a writing seminar. Students are required to take 32 classes to graduate, 19 of which must be outside of the major. Upon declaring a major by the end of sophomore year, students begin work on a comprehensive senior thesis, which allows deep pursuit of a specific topic. "With a thesis that can take up to three years to do, we produce a more cumulative work," explains a student.

Since almost all classes contain fewer than 50 members, absences are definitely noticed, and students must come prepared to actively participate in discussions. "There's no hiding out," notes a student. Many of Haverford's 115 full-time and 17 part-time faculty members live on campus, allowing students to connect with their professors.

If students have a particular passion they wish to pursue, they can take a class through Experimental College, a student-run organization that provides non-credit education in topics ranging from Beginning Ceramics to The History of Punk Rock and the Role of Punk Rock in Contemporary Western Society.

Students also have numerous opportunities to expand their cultural knowledge and language skills by pursuing a semester or year abroad through Haverford's International Academic Programs office. Those interested can apply to a university-approved program in one of over 40 countries around the world, and many students choose to do so. In fact, typically more than 40 percent of the junior class studies abroad.

HAVERFORD COLLEGE

Four-year private
Founded: 1833
Haverford, PA
Large town
Pop. 48,491

Address:
370 Lancaster Avenue
Haverford, PA
19041-1392

Admissions:
610-896-1350

Financial Aid:
610-896-1350

admission@haverford.edu

www.haverford.edu

HAVERFORD COLLEGE

Highlights

Students
Total enrollment: 1,205
Undergrads: 1,205
Freshmen: 323
From out-of-state: 88%
From public schools: 55%
Male/Female: 47%/53%
Live on-campus: 99%
Off-campus employment rating: Excellent
Caucasian: 67%
African American: 6%
Hispanic: 9%
Asian / Pacific Islander: 7%
Native American: 0%
Mixed (2+ ethnicities): 6%
International: 4%

Academics
Calendar: Semester
Student/faculty ratio: 8:1
Class size 9 or fewer: 36%
Class size 10-29: 56%
Class size 30-49: 8%
Class size 50-99: -
Class size 100 or more: -
Returning freshmen: 96%
Six-year graduation rate: 94%
Graduates who immediately go to graduate school: 13%
Graduates who immediately enter career related to major: 60%

Most Popular Majors
Psychology
Biology
Political science

Admissions
Applicants: 3,626
Accepted: 830
Acceptance rate: 22.9%
Placed on wait list: 869
Enrolled from wait list: 3
Average GPA: Not reported
ACT range: Not reported
SAT Math range: 660-760
SAT Reading range: 650-760
SAT Writing range: 60-34
Top 10% of class: 92%
Top 25% of class: 100%
Top 50% of class: 100%

Haverford offers numerous internships and summer research opportunities. Students can choose, for example, to pursue a Senior Bridge Internship through the Center for Peace and Global Citizenship, where they will study issues of peace and social justice. Would-be writers or reporters can apply for the Andrew Silk Summer Journalism Internship, a program in which they will work in a print or broadcast field. Students can also apply for a research internship in one of the seven integrated natural sciences departments (biology, chemistry, physics, mathematics, computer science, astronomy, and psychology).

Student Life

Haverford's proximity to Bryn Mawr and Swarthmore Colleges, as well as to Philadelphia, provides ample social activities, while campus itself always bustles with events. There are nearly 150 student organizations. Public transportation makes traveling to the nearby colleges, shopping malls, professional sporting events, bars, and restaurants an easy option that doesn't require a car. "Public transportation or a friend with a car are key," notes a student.

Haverford hosts joint parties with Bryn Mawr, and although the college does not have Greek organizations, it has numerous events, activities, and annual traditions. These range from dances, including the Snowball and Sun Dances, to Haverfest, a weekend to let loose and have fun at the end of the school year. Other events include the Collection speaker series and a cappella concerts.

Because students value the Honor Code so highly, one of the most important traditions on campus is Plenary, held every autumn and spring. The Student Association meets to discuss and propose changes to the constitution and the Honor Code. True to the school's roots, Plenary allows all student voices and ideas to be heard; Experimental College was actually started by an idea that emerged during a Plenary session. "As students, we make so many critical decisions about how we want our community to be," says a student. In addition, because the Honor Code is student-run and modified, Haverford's alcohol policy allows students to self-monitor underage drinking and to trust each other to provide a safe community.

Haverford has 21 varsity athletic teams that compete in Division III athletics. The men's cross country team is particularly strong, ranking in the top 10 in its division. Over 40 percent of Haverford students participate in varsity sports, and another 15 percent compete at the club level. Haverford also boasts the country's only varsity cricket team—the oldest sport at the college. Although singular in its varsity status, the team competes with club cricket teams around the country.

Ninety-nine percent of Haverford students, and all freshmen, live on campus, which creates a close-knit social and academic community. Freshmen live in one of three living spaces: Barclay Hall, Gummere Hall, or Haverford College Apartments (HCA). Barclay and Gummere offer single and double rooms, while HCA houses groups of four students in single-sex two-room apartments, complete with a kitchen and bathroom. Students are guaranteed housing all four years and can choose a variety of living options. One of the most aptly-named houses on campus, Drinker House, was built by William Comfort, who became president in 1917; the house, featuring seven double and four single rooms, is often the chosen living space for those who enjoy imbibing.

Student Body

Haverford's ideals of tolerance and acceptance of diversity draw a fittingly varied crowd, with 88 percent of students hailing from outside of the state and 28 percent identifying as minorities. Students share a common strength in, and love for, academics. "We actually love going to classes, not just to earn grades, but because we get involved in the material," says a student.

Haverford has numerous clubs promoting awareness of other cultures, religions, and backgrounds. Groups range from Men Against Sexual Assault and Rape (MASAR) to the AIDS Service Network and Students for Justice in Palestine.

You May Not Know

- Haverford's Magill Library houses The Quaker Collection, which includes over 42,000 works dating back to the 17th century.
- The college also has a cricket library, which, according to the college, is the largest collection in the Western hemisphere.
- Haverford owns a copy of the first printing of Shakespeare's complete plays.

Distinguished Alumni

Dave Barry, humor columnist; Gerald M. Levin, CEO Time Warner Inc.; Christopher Morley, poet and Rhodes Scholar; Philip J. Noel-Baker, winner of the Nobel Prize for Peace; Maxfield Parrish, artist; Norman Pearlstine, Editor-in-chief of Time Inc.; Joseph H. Taylor Jr., Nobel Laureate in physics; John C. Whitehead, former Deputy Secretary of State under President Ronald Reagan.

Admissions and Financial Aid

Admission to Haverford is rigorous, as the school looks for students who will be strong matches with its ideals of high academic excellence, drive for social justice, and desire to make a difference in the world. Haverford uses the Common Application plus a brief supplement. The secondary school transcript is the most important part of the application to Haverford, as it determines how rigorous a course load students took on in high school. Haverford also recommends an interview—especially for students living within 150 miles of the college—as a way to distinguish the strongest applicants and best fits to the school. Haverford does not offer merit-based scholarships but does have a need-blind admissions policy.

HAVERFORD COLLEGE

Highlights

Admissions Criteria
Academic criteria:
Grades: ☆ ☆ ☆
Difficulty of class schedule: ☆ ☆ ☆
Class rank: ☆ ☆
Standardized test scores: ☆ ☆
Teacher recommendations: ☆ ☆ ☆
Personal statement: ☆ ☆ ☆
Non-academic criteria considered:
Interview
Extracurricular activities
Special talents, interests, abilities
Character/personal qualities
Volunteer work
Work experience
State of residency
Geographical location
Minority affiliation
Alumni relationship

Deadlines
Early Action: No
Early Decision: November 15
Regular Action: January 15 (final)
Notification of admission by: April 15
Common Application: Accepted

Financial Aid
In-state tuition: $45,018
Out-of-state tuition: $48,018
Room: $7,870
Board: $5,940
Books: Varies
Freshmen receiving need-based aid: 51%
Undergrads rec. need-based aid: 50%
Avg. % of need met by financial aid: 100%
Avg. aid package (freshmen): $41,352
Avg. aid package (undergrads): $40,321
Avg. debt upon graduation: $14,171

School Spirit
Mascot: Fords
Colors: Black and scarlet
Song: *How'er Our Fathers*

HENDRIX COLLEGE

Four-year private
Founded: 1876
Conway, AR
Medium city
Pop. 60,470

Address:
1600 Washington
Avenue
Conway, AR
72032

Admissions:
800-277-9017

Financial Aid:
800-277-9017

adm@hendrix.edu

www.hendrix.edu

Overview

Hendrix College cannot claim Jimi Hendrix as a namesake, even though the school name is spelled just like the musician's. The Methodist Church-affiliated private college is tucked away in the suburb of Conway, Arkansas, 25 miles north of Little Rock and more than 2,000 miles from the acclaimed electric guitarist's birthplace of Seattle. Hendrix College's 160 acres include academic, residential, and recreational spaces, as well as an arboretum. A major campus expansion project has resulted in a $24 million Wellness and Athletics Center, new student apartments, upgraded science facilities, and the $26 million Student Life and Technology Center, the largest capital project in the college's 130+ year history.

While impressive, these new campus improvements may not convince some prospective students from outside the South to live in suburban Arkansas—and in a dry county, no less. In a different location, admissions might be more competitive, as the college has strong statistics and a unique Odyssey Program that emphasizes experiential learning.

Hendrix does defy stereotypes of the South and the expectations some might have for a church-affiliated college: there is a moderate minority student population, a fair number of liberals on campus, and the academic program is secular. Add to that a fun-loving bunch of students who introduce activities such as one where freshmen don underwear (for the men) and boxer shorts (for the women) and participate in a campus-wide dance contest, and you've got a well-rounded environment.

Academics

Hendrix offers 32 undergraduate majors and 33 minors, along with a master's degree in accounting. The academic program at Hendrix includes three required one-semester classes through the Collegiate Center; seven classes across six Learning Domains; and a Capacities component with course requirements for writing, foreign language, quantitative skills, and physical activity. Explorations—a required one-semester course for freshmen—assists incoming students in their transition to college. Virtually all classes at Hendrix have fewer than 50 students, which facilitates strong relationships between students and faculty. "The classes are intimate, and we get to know not only the other students, but our professors," says a student. Strong programs include biology, English, politics, and sociology/anthropology.

The distinctive Odyssey Program, launched in 2006, requires Hendrix students to complete at least three experiential learning projects. The program offers credit and competitive grants for extracurricular projects and activities across three categories such as artistic creativity, global awareness, and undergraduate research. "The experiences not only add to our resumes, but they also add to our sense of personal fulfillment," notes a student. Hendrix students and faculty have shared more than $1 million in grant funding for opportunities as simple as growing a vegetable garden on campus to grander interventions such as teaching English in rural China.

Maymester is Hendrix's three-week mini-semester during which students can earn credit for one course. Participants meet two and a half hours a day, five days a week, during the May to June period, including Memorial Day. "It's a nice break to have classes only during the morning and have the rest of the day free to study some but also socialize," one student comments.

Hendrix's study-abroad program offers students a plethora of international travel opportunities as it invites students to "study abroad through more than 150 universities or programs covering the six inhabited continents." Thanks to many independent and external programs that supplement Hendrix's own study-abroad programs, students may participate in trips to locations such as Ghana, South Africa, Bulgaria, Poland, Peru, and Thailand.

According to Hendrix, the college is ranked 28th in the nation for percentage of graduates who earn PhDs within six years of graduation, and more than half of Hendrix's students enroll in graduate or professional school within two years of graduation. Hendrix graduates' acceptance rate to law school is 90 percent and the acceptance rate at medical schools is 85 percent.

Student Life

Hendrix's 80 student organizations include multicultural, religious, academic/professional, and special interest groups. KHDX, Hendrix's student-run radio station, sponsors a concert each year for Welcome Week—past performers include Ted Leo and The Pharmacists, The Pharcyde & Rahzel, and OK GO. There are honor societies at Hendrix, including Phi Beta Kappa, but no fraternities or sororities. Dorm parties are popular, as are parties in the Brick Pit, an outdoor area in the center of campus. In general, campus is a hub for the school's social activity since so many students live on campus and the surrounding city of Conway "doesn't have a lot going on," as explained by a student. The Office of Student Activities plans weekend events (called Weekenderz) and Wednesday evening entertainment in a relaxed coffeehouse setting (called Hump Nights).

The first major event for incoming freshmen begins before classes with the weeklong New Student Orientation. Highlights include Playfair, a fast-paced icebreaker that the entire first-year class participates in; Pizza Wars, which features a band and free pizza from local vendors, and a three-day Orientation Trip with 15-25 students and titles like "Dude Ranch – Round 'Em Up," "Service in Fayetteville," and "Waterskiing at Brady Mountain." Students return from these trips to kick off Welcome Week, which culminates in the long-standing traditional Shirttails dance competition. All first-year students in residence halls walk from dorm to dorm performing their routines, the guys in white shirts, ties, and underwear, the girls in white shirts and boxer shorts. "You really get to know your classmates—and what they look like in their skivvies—before school even starts," one student laughs.

Students with a flair for performing will also appreciate Coffeehouse, a campus talent showcase. Many social traditions at Hendrix seem to revolve around costumes, and the annual toga party is a favorite. An event based on New York's Studio 54, students dress in 70s attire and feature cage dancers. Ghost Roast, the annual Halloween Party, serves as a forum for students to dress outrageously.

Hendrix is a member of the Southern Collegiate Athletic Conference (Division III) and recently added women's field hockey and men's lacrosse to its roster of intercollegiate sports. There are over 15 intramural sports, as well as a handful of club sports. The Hendrix College Wellness and Athletic Center, a $23 million construction, provides a 100,000-square-foot facility for athletics on campus.

When students need a little more excitement than what is provided on campus, they can take to the road. Some go to Little Rock, which is approximately 30 miles from campus, for restaurants, bars, and shopping. Faulkner County, where campus is located, is a dry county, so students wanting to purchase alcohol also venture out.

Residences include co-ed and single sex options, residence halls, theme houses, and apartment buildings. Students must live

HENDRIX COLLEGE

Highlights

Students
Total enrollment: 1,388
Undergrads: 1,373
Freshmen: 394
Part-time students: 1%
From out-of-state: 55%
From public schools: 82%
Male/Female: 43%/57%
Live on-campus: 91%
Off-campus employment rating: Excellent
Caucasian: 72%
African American: 3%
Hispanic: 5%
Asian / Pacific Islander: 3%
Native American: 1%
Mixed (2+ ethnicities): 3%
International: 5%

Academics
Calendar: Semester
Student/faculty ratio: 11:1
Class size 9 or fewer: 19%
Class size 10-29: 68%
Class size 30-49: 12%
Class size 50-99: 1%
Class size 100 or more: -
Returning freshmen: 86%
Six-year graduation rate: 72%
Graduates who immediately go to graduate school: 22%

Most Popular Majors
Social science
Biology
Psychology

Admissions
Applicants: 1,656
Accepted: 1,374
Acceptance rate: 83.0%
Placed on wait list: 11
Enrolled from wait list: 3
Average GPA: 3.9
ACT range: 26-32
SAT Math range: 540-670
SAT Reading range: 550-690
SAT Writing range: Not reported
Top 10% of class: 51%
Top 25% of class: 77%
Top 50% of class: 96%

345

HENDRIX COLLEGE

Admissions Criteria

Academic criteria:
Grades: ☆ ☆ ☆
Difficulty of class schedule: ☆ ☆ ☆
Class rank: ☆ ☆
Standardized test scores: ☆ ☆ ☆
Teacher recommendations: ☆ ☆
Personal statement: ☆ ☆ ☆
Non-academic criteria considered:
Interview
Extracurricular activities
Special talents, interests, abilities
Volunteer work
State of residency
Minority affiliation

Deadlines

Early Action: November 15 and February 1
Early Decision: No
Regular Action: February 1 (priority)
June 1 (final)
Notification of admission by: December 15 and March 1
Common Application: Accepted

Financial Aid

In-state tuition: $37,516
Out-of-state tuition: $37,516
Room: $5,480
Board: $5,140
Books: $1,100
Freshmen receiving need-based aid: 66%
Undergrads rec. need-based aid: 60%
Avg. % of need met by financial aid: 83%
Avg. aid package (freshmen): $29,273
Avg. aid package (undergrads): $28,189
Avg. debt upon graduation: $24,492

School Spirit

Mascot: Warriors
Colors: Orange and black
Song: *Go Hendrix*

on campus during their first year, and most continue to do so—91 percent of students live in college-owned housing.

Student Body

Hendrix's undergraduate student body of approximately 1,400 has moderate ethnic diversity with minority students making up 15 percent. There is moderate geographic diversity with about 55 percent of students from out of state, though most are from the South.

As Hendrix is tied to the Methodist Church, the presence of a large number of religious students is not surprising. What is surprising, however—given the college's location in the conservative South—is that there are what students deem "more than a handful of liberals."

You May Not Know

- Three of Hendrix College's buildings are listed on the National Register of Historic Places: Ellis Hall (Office of Admissions and Financial Aid), Galloway Hall (a female residence hall), and Martin Hall (a male residence hall).
- Hendrix College's name has no relationship to the famous American guitarist/singer. Hendrix College was named in 1889 in honor of Bishop Eugene Hendrix of Kansas City.
- In 1981, a 7'5", 160 lb. mounted alligator gar (a primitive ray-finned fish) was given to the biology department; it is still on display today.

Distinguished Alumni

Douglas Blackmon, writer and Pulitzer Prize winner; Sarah Caldwell, National Medal of Arts winner; Margaret Pittman, first female head of a National Institute of Health laboratory.

Admissions and Financial Aid

Hendrix has a high acceptance rate perhaps because its location is not a prime destination for many high school students outside of the South. Hendrix's admissions office emphasizes the importance of "academic competence and preparation, dedication to learning, and motivation to participate fully in the Hendrix community."

The college is nonsectarian and looks for diversity in applicants. Recommendations are encouraged but not required. The application fee is waived for students applying through the online Common Application. Admission is rolling, beginning in late October until the class is full.

Hendrix offers need-based grants and achievement-based aid scholarships and grants, though no awards for athletic achievement. According to Hendrix, "100 percent of students receive some form of achievement-based and/or need-based state, federal, or institutional assistance" and the average award is more than $24,000. All applicants are automatically considered for academic scholarships, which range from $4,000 to full tuition. The Hays Memorial Scholarship, given to four first-year students, supplies four years of full tuition, room, and board as well as opportunities for grants for summer research and travel.

HIRAM COLLEGE

Overview

Hiram College is a small liberal arts college affiliated with the Disciples of Christ church and located in Hiram, Ohio, a town numbering 1,400. The college offers a strong sense of community and a focus on undergraduate education. It is also renowned for its distinctive academic schedule and for its study-abroad programs. Hiram's academic calendar follows "The Hiram Plan," which divides two 15-week semesters into a 12-week period (three courses) and a three-week period (one course).

Located 40 miles southeast of Cleveland, the campus is covered in verdant green and features nineteenth century, distinguished Western Reserve architecture. Newer college buildings are designed to complement the natural beauty of the campus and include a recreation center and a career services office.

Academics

Hiram focuses almost exclusively on undergraduate education, though the college does have a small number of graduate students. Students also have the opportunity to pursue a dual degree in engineering with Washington University in St. Louis or Case Western Reserve University.

The core curriculum at Hiram comprises one third of the coursework. First-year students encounter General Education requirements right away, including a first year seminar, first year colloquium, two interdisciplinary courses, and eight core curriculum requirements. Many of the classes are seminar sized, which allows for personal attention. Strong programs include biology, management, biomedical humanities, accounting, and education.

There are 32 majors to choose from, as well as an additional nine minors. With almost all classes having fewer than 30 students, there is a lot of opportunity for students to engage in lectures. Majors typically require an independent project. In this sense much of the onus is placed on the student to be self motivated and really take ownership of his or her work, much like a graduate student. "We take it above and beyond," explains a Hiram student. "Usually only graduate students do a defense of their dissertations."

There are a number of special programs available to students. Hiram has created seven Centers of Distinction in which teaching and learning are collaborative. The aim of these centers is to "apply interdisciplinary approaches to complex questions that are not straightforward to solve." They bring to campus notable scholars and authors and create research opportunities for undergraduates.

The Garfield Scholars program is a program through which students participate in seminars, engage public leaders on and off campus, and demonstrate scholarship. The program is not designed for slackers: it requires students to take initiative and demonstrate leadership.

Another special program available to business-minded students is the Entrepreneurship Residential Learning Community. The ERLC is located in the suites in East Hall where students are provided with an environment that encourages entrepreneurship. It's a lifestyle choice on campus; students who live in the ERLC will be surrounded by aspiring businesspeople, assist in event planning, interact with visiting entrepreneurs, and actively network. It's a program offering students a great many opportunities but comes with a cost of added responsibility. Students who are involved in the program feel it provides them an advantage that will become apparent after graduation. One participant explains, "ERLC is perfect for networking because you know that everyone you live with will be working in a similar field in the future."

Hiram places a strong emphasis on becoming a world citizen, and its study-abroad programs reflect this. More than half of students study abroad. Hiram College has formal exchange agreements in Istanbul, Turkey; Osaka, Japan; and Rome, Italy. There

HIRAM COLLEGE

Four-year private
Founded: 1850
Hiram, OH
Rural
Pop. 1,407

Address:
P.O. Box 67
Hiram, OH
44234

Admissions:
800-362-5280

Financial Aid:
330-569-5107

admission@hiram.edu

www.hiram.edu

HIRAM COLLEGE

Students
Total enrollment: 1,324
Undergrads: 1,293
From out-of-state: 24%
Male/Female: 44%/56%
Live on-campus: 82%
In fraternities: 10%
In sororities: 10%
Off-campus employment rating: Good
Caucasian: 74%
African American: 12%
Hispanic: 3%
Asian / Pacific Islander: 1%
Native American: 0%
Mixed (2+ ethnicities): 1%
International: 6%

Academics
Calendar: Other
Student/faculty ratio: 12:1
Class size 9 or fewer: Not reported
Class size 10-29: Not reported
Class size 30-49: Not reported
Class size 50-99: Not reported
Class size 100 or more: Not reported
Graduates who immediately go to graduate school: 23%
Graduates who immediately enter career related to major: 23%

Most Popular Majors
Biology
Management
Biomedical humanities

Admissions
Applicants: 2,378
Accepted: 1,474
Acceptance rate: 62%
Average GPA: Not reported
ACT range: 20-25
SAT Math range: 440-570
SAT Reading range: 440-560
SAT Writing range: 410-550
Top 10% of class: 20%
Top 25% of class: 46%
Top 50% of class: 74%

are also special programs available in countries such as Guatemala, China, France, the UK, Bhutan, and South Africa.

The career center has both an online and offline presence. Through the website a student can locate internships, graduate programs, and prepare for employment. Add to that on-campus counseling and two courses (career exploration, job search skills) that help students prepare for their futures.

Approximately 23 percent of undergraduates pursue a graduate degree within one year of graduating. Among students who enter the work force, around 23 percent enter a related field within six months.

Student Life
Student life at Hiram College is quieter than at larger universities but boasts a slew of activities and groups to keep undergrads busy. Moreover, Hiram's convenient location close to Akron and Cleveland means students can get out into an urban setting at their whim. Cleveland is known for great dining, shopping, and nightlife and is also home to the Cavaliers and Browns for sports entertainment. There are also golf courses and ski slopes nearby for students to take advantage of.

The college has around 90 student organizations. A few notable ones include the investment club, where students are given a real cash portfolio to manage; the Kennedy Center Programming Board, which organizes student events; and WHRM, a campus radio station that's incredibly popular with students.

Hiram abounds with special events. Campus Day is an annual tradition where classes are cancelled and students engage in community service. Destressfests are also popular before exams and offer relaxation to stressed-out studiers. Another popular event is Bowler First Friday. These end-of-the-week activities help celebrate the cultural diversity on campus and are fun as well as informative. On the first Friday of the month, there's a presentation about a foreign country, followed by ethnic food associated with that culture.

Hiram has abolished national fraternities or sororities. Greek social clubs, however, do exist. These are similar but have no affiliations with national fraternities. These organizations operate as venues for students to connect and meet new people. Some would say this offers all the benefits of a fraternity without the pressures that come with it. The Greek social clubs "focus on friendships and service. Sure, there's some drinking but it's not *Animal House* style," says a student.

Varsity athletics are offered with teams participating in the NCAA's Division III. Volleyball remains the most competitive sport for the college, but football and soccer are the most popular. The community feeling of the college extends to sports, as one student reports. "Sports are not our strength, but it's still fun to go to a game or two since we always know someone on the field."

Most students live on campus. In fact, residential houses offer a mix of underclassmen and upperclassmen. There's also an international house, and all residence halls are smoke-free. Dorms can range from very lively to very quiet, but they are designated as "dry." Upperclassmen have the option of keeping their rooms from year to year if they choose to.

Student Body

There's a close sense of community at Hiram. "You not only know everyone, but you pretty much know their life stories," confides a student. Remaining anonymous is not an option, and students get to know their classmates. Students are academically focused, and many truly wish to take on leadership roles and make a difference.

Ethnically, the majority of students are Caucasian (74 percent) and gender skews slightly female (56 percent). There are a moderate number of minorities, but no minority group tends to dominate. Twenty-four percent of the student body hails from out of state.

You May Not Know

- The college's basketball team competed as the national team in the 1904 Olympics and won the gold medal.
- Hiram's volleyball team was named the 2005 NCAC Champions.
- Nearby museums include the Rock & Roll Hall of Fame, Pro-Football Hall of Fame, and Inventor's Hall of Fame.

Distinguished Alumni

Joseph Fernandez, biotechnology entrepreneur, cofounder of Invitrogen; James A. Garfield , President of the United States; Jan Hopkins, CNN journalist and businesswoman; Dean Scarborough, CEO, Avery Dennison Corp.; Claude Steele, Provost of Columbia University; Bill White, former MLB first baseman; Allyn Abbott Young, American economist.

Admissions and Financial Aid

Hiram College uses a "rolling" admission plan. This means that prospective students may continuously apply for admission and Hiram will admit qualified students on a space-available basis. Students may apply using a Common Application or Hiram's own application. Admissions is generally selective, but Hiram pays attention to intangibles when evaluating applicants, so keep in mind that recommendations—and the optional interview—will weigh heavily.

Merit scholarships are offered for exceptional students and include a Dean's Scholarship of $16,000, and other scholarships ranging from $10,000 - $14,000 depending on high school GPA and achievement. Hiram also has a Tuition Guarantee, which guarantees that tuition will be the same for students all four years of college.

HIRAM COLLEGE

Highlights

Admissions Criteria
Academic criteria:
Grades: ☆ ☆ ☆
Difficulty of class schedule: ☆ ☆ ☆
Class rank: ☆
Standardized test scores: ☆ ☆
Teacher recommendations: ☆ ☆
Personal statement: ☆ ☆
Non-academic criteria considered:
Interview
Extracurricular activities
Special talents, interests, abilities
Character/personal qualities
Volunteer work
State of residency
Alumni relationship

Deadlines
Early Action: No
Early Decision: No
Regular Action: Rolling admissions
Common Application: Accepted

Financial Aid
In-state tuition: $29,065
Out-of-state tuition: $29,065
Room: $4,820
Board: $5,040
Books: Varies
Avg. aid package (freshmen): $19,429 for grants or scholarship aid, $8,582 for student loans
Avg. aid package (undergrads): $17,054 for grants or scholarship aid, $8,560 for federal student loans

School Spirit
Mascot: Terriers

Four-year private
Founded: 1822
Geneva, NY
Large town
Pop. 13,268

Address:
337 Pulteney Street
Geneva, NY
14456

Admissions:
315-781-3622

Financial Aid:
315-781-3315

admissions@hws.edu

www.hws.edu

HOBART AND WILLIAM SMITH COLLEGES

Overview

Mention Hobart and William Smith Colleges and most people will say they've never heard of them. With only 2,300 undergraduate students, Hobart College for men and William Smith College for women are private, liberal arts colleges in New York's Upstate Finger Lakes region. Though separated by genders, Hobart and William Smith Colleges share their campus, classes, and facilities. A 200-acre combined campus situated in Geneva, the colleges boast a serene campus filled with greenery and beautiful views of the lakes.

Although Hobart College was founded in 1822 as a private liberal arts college for men, the two colleges became co-ed in 1908. Through the Fisher Center for the Study of Women and Men, the university provides its students with a multitude of activities and events. Rooted in their unique history as distinct, gender-specific colleges, Hobart and Williams Colleges celebrate their individualism with ceremonial and social traditions.

Saturated with wealthy students—many of whom come from New England— HWS colleges offer an environment with little ethnic diversity but plenty of other advantages. Given its small size, students generally appreciate the opportunities they have to develop personal relationships with professors. Athletics are popular and school spirit is generally high. There is also an omnipresent sense of safety on campus.

Academics

According to the university, Hobart and William Smith strongly believe in educating their students "broadly and deeply through a curriculum that requires students to complete courses that are both disciplinary and interdisciplinary." Although the colleges do not have a core curriculum, they do require that students complete a major and a minor or second major. They also require that each student address each of the institution's eight educational goals, pass a first-year seminar, complete any faculty-mandated writing requirements, and pass 32 courses. "It's nice to have more flexibility to choose what we want to learn," says a student.

The university offers 47 majors. Amongst the most popular are English and economics. Other strong programs at HWS are American studies, history, the prelaw program, and the environmental studies program (where students can participate in environmental research and internships through Finger Lake's Institute).

The First-Year Seminar is a unique part of the HWS experience. The colleges state that the program was created "without regard for future major or minor choices, seminars were constructed around different faculty interests—from peace movements to ancient warfare, Mozart, and rock-and-roll." Carefully crafted to hone students' writing, speaking, and critical thinking skills, each seminar hosts 13-15 students and allows plenty of opportunities for discussion and debate, as well as field trips and other special events throughout the year.

The colleges also offer several joint degree programs for promising, motivated students who are interested in pursuing pre-professional certifications. The program usually entails a set amount of time and classes at specific departments in universities in the vicinity. For example, the joint degree program in engineering requires students to spend three years at HWS and then two years at Columbia University or Dartmouth. At the end of five years, the student receives a BA or BS from HWS as well as a BS from the cooperating university. Students may also choose to pursue joint degrees in business, architecture, or nursing.

For those students looking to get involved in summer research and wanting to build a strong relationship with a faculty mentor, the Student Summer Research Program is the perfect opportunity. Students work side by side with a faculty research mentor who helps them develop research skills and gain laboratory experience. The program is also known to produce a good amount of publications and as one student notes, "provides incredible hands-on experience" in the sciences and social sciences.

While class size varies by major, the most common is between 10 and 19 students. Many students relish the opportunity to meet professors for coffee or office hours. Students find classes to be "a medium amount of work."

HWS colleges offer study-abroad opportunities all over the world and boast that the program is one of the "most ambitious off-campus programs in the country." The Center for Global Education prepares students to make the most of their time in another culture, and many students even end up publishing photographs or writings in school publications or exhibits on campus that document their experiences.

HWS' Pathways programs assist students in their individualized career development and success. A four-year program, Pathways pairs its students with mentors who play a key role in empowering them to explore their various interests and talents, while also developing career goals and gaining experience in their career path.

Student Life

Despite their small size, Hobart and William Smith colleges provide ample opportunities for students to get involved. There are over 80 official student organizations and a wide range of interests represented. Among the most popular are the Debate Team, 12 Windows Film Series, and the Jazz Ensemble.

With 18 percent of the male student body involved in a fraternity, Greek life has a rather visible presence. There are six social fraternities and six fraternity houses on campus; however, there are no sororities. "Greek life is pretty prominent but it doesn't dominate," says a student. Partying is common on campus during the weekend or weekdays since Geneva does not hold many nightlife attractions.

Members of the student body say they feel they are generally "overall social," though many students complain about the "scarce dating scene" on campus. Important annual events include Charter Day, which commemorates the school's founding; Moving Up Day, a ceremony which marks the "move up" up each class; and Volunteer Day, a day that brings various members of the college's community and residents from Geneva together to focus on community service

Hobart sponsors 10 Division III and one Division I (lacrosse) programs while William Smith sponsors 11 Division III sports. There are intramural men and women's teams in basketball, cross country, golf, racquetball, soccer, softball, table tennis, and volleyball.

Off-campus activities are limited. While Geneva does have shopping, a few restaurants and bars that are student-friendly, it does not have a reputation for being a great college town. In fact, according to students, Hobart and William Smith seem to be "pretty isolated." However, this may foster camaraderie among students, as all HWS students live on campus. Many students state that this, along with the small dorm size, really enhances the "massive amount of school spirit" at Hobart and William Smith. Dorms are safe and

HOBART AND WILLIAM SMITH COLLEGES

Students
Total enrollment: 2,300
Undergrads: 2,292
Part-time students: 1%
From out-of-state: 57%
Male/Female: 45%/55%
Live on-campus: 90%
In fraternities: 18%
Off-campus employment rating: Good
Caucasian: 66%
African American: 4%
Hispanic: 4%
Asian / Pacific Islander: 2%
Native American: 1%
Mixed (2+ ethnicities): 0%
International: 5%

Academics
Calendar: Semester
Student/faculty ratio: 11:1
Class size 9 or fewer: 24%
Class size 10-29: 66%
Class size 30-49: 10%
Class size 50-99: -
Class size 100 or more: -
Returning freshmen: 88%
Six-year graduation rate: 76%
Graduates who immediately go to graduate school: 12%

Most Popular Majors
English
Economics
History

Admissions
Applicants: 4,465
Accepted: 2,370
Acceptance rate: 53.1%
Placed on wait list: 517
Enrolled from wait list: 25
Average GPA: 3.3
ACT range: 26-29
SAT Math range: 565-660
SAT Reading range: 570-650
SAT Writing range: 9-42
Top 10% of class: 34%
Top 25% of class: 63%
Top 50% of class: 90%

351

College Profiles

HOBART AND WILLIAM SMITH COLLEGES

Admissions Criteria
Academic criteria:
Grades: ☆ ☆ ☆
Difficulty of class schedule: ☆ ☆ ☆
Class rank: ☆ ☆
Standardized test scores: ☆ ☆
Teacher recommendations: ☆ ☆
Personal statement: ☆ ☆
Non-academic criteria considered:
Interview
Extracurricular activities
Special talents, interests, abilities
Character/personal qualities
Volunteer work
Work experience
State of residency
Geographical location
Minority affiliation
Alumni relationship

Deadlines
Early Action: No
Early Decision: November 15
Regular Action: February 1 (final)
Notification of admission by: April 1
Common Application: Accepted

Financial Aid
In-state tuition: $45,180
Out-of-state tuition: $45,180
Room: Varies
Board: Varies
Books: Varies
Freshmen receiving need-based aid: 72%
Undergrads rec. need-based aid: 72%
Avg. % of need met by financial aid: 79%
Avg. aid package (freshmen): $27,793
Avg. aid package (undergrads): $30,891
Avg. debt upon graduation: $34,463

School Spirit
Mascot: Statesmen/Herons
Colors: Orange and purple/green and white

friendly environments where students often leave their doors open throughout the day.

Student Body

With only 11 percent ethnic minorities, Hobart and William Smith colleges are certainly not diverse college campuses. Students also report a mild amount of cliques amongst the athletic teams and ethnic groups.

Most students on campus can be seen wearing sweatpants and sweatshirts to class when it is cold; when it's warmer, women wear skirts or sun dresses and men wear khaki shorts and t-shirts. Some students complain that "those from less privileged backgrounds may not fit in as well." Students report that many are heavily focused on drinking, and someone who chooses not to drink "might have limited options."

Generally, students are proclaimed to be politically aware and lean towards the left, while there certainly is a fair amount of conservative students to maintain a good balance of political affiliations.

You May Not Know

- HWS is the first New York college to use wind power.
- In the 1960s, when many single-sex institutions became co-ed, Hobart and William Smith chose to retain their gender separate identities.
- Hobart's sports team became known as the "Statesmen" after a football game against Amherst College in 1936 when the *New York Times* referred to them as the "statesmen from Geneva."

Distinguished Alumni

Rodney Frelinghuysen, New Jersey Congressman, U.S. House of Representatives; Dr. Reynold Levy, President, Lincoln Center for the Performing Arts.

Admissions and Financial Aid

The colleges look for students who have challenged themselves with rigorous high school courses. Most unique to their application process, however, is the fact that students are not required to submit standardized test scores. HWS believes that reliance on these tests scores is not an accurate reflection of a student's ability or character. As a result, students' transcripts, essays, and extracurricular activities are more heavily weighted.

Merit-based scholarships that are offered include the full-tuition Hersh and Wood Scholarship as well as scholarships for students in the arts and those who are planning to enter careers in medicine. The largest merit-based program is the Trustee Scholarship, a $20,000 award given to 50-60 students. Some of the scholarship programs require a separate application.

HOFSTRA UNIVERSITY

Overview

Hofstra is a private university with 6,900 undergraduates located in Hempstead, New York, an area in suburban Long Island about 25 miles from New York City. The school currently hangs in the balance—even as its academic programs grow in sophistication and rigor, its admission rate has not yet tightened in response.

Students attending Hofstra enjoy modern buildings and architecture without losing the distinct East Coast feel or the rustic allure of the surrounding city. The campus is nothing if not green—it holds both an arboretum and bird sanctuary and bursts into bloom each spring with tens of thousands of tulips.

Students can choose from hundreds of activities and societies. Social life on campus is stimulated by many sources—from Honors College to Greek life—and the big city is only a short train ride away.

Academics

Hofstra's fairly indiscriminate admissions policy belies the breadth of its academic excellence. It is fully accredited in 19 disciplines, an achievement matched by fewer than 100 other American schools. In total, Hofstra offers 150 academic programs in liberal arts, the sciences, engineering, business, communication, and education. Its strongest programs are marketing and internal business; speech communication, rhetoric and performance studies; and English.

The business programs in particular are up and coming. The school established a state-of-the-art trading room equipped with 34 Bloomberg terminals. At each of these, students and faculty can access professional-quality market data, analysis, and news. "The hands-on experience in business is a segue to internships and work after college," says a student. The Hofstra chapter of the American Marketing Association is very active and has won international recognition. Hofstra added a medical school in 2011.

One student reports that Hofstra professors are "very open to meeting with students" but encourages students to schedule appointments due to the busy schedules of many faculty members. Students say the difficulty of classes and exams depends on the program. One student notes that science and engineering courses are known to be "the most challenging."

An ideal opportunity for intellectual challenge and one-on-one time with a professor comes in the form of First Year Connections seminars. Topics offered include "The Psychology of Everyday Life" and "Fairy Tale in Literature and Film." One student comments, "I highly recommend that you take a first-year seminar because college academics are so different from high school academics, and this will give you a first taste." The common size for most classes is 10 to 19 students.

Hofstra requires six general education courses in addition to courses required for the completion of majors and minors. Students must take courses in the humanities, natural science, social sciences, cross-cultural studies, English, and foreign language. Its residency requirements are fairly relaxed, allowing students plenty of time to study abroad at one or more of Hofstra's 60 programs in 30 countries.

The school also offers several honors programs and societies, which include academic opportunities and requirements as well as social events. Honors College—at which the acceptance rate is much lower than the rest of the school—consists of a shared first-year experience, after which students can design their programs and thesis essays to suit their own interests.

When it comes time to look beyond Hofstra, students don't have to go it alone. Counseling and critiques are available through the Career Center, which sponsors career fairs in addition to offering a variety of online resources such as tips about resume writing and the job hunt. Some services are also available to alumni.

HOFSTRA UNIVERSITY

Four-year private
Founded: 1935
Hempstead, NY
Medium city
Pop. 759,757

Address:
100 Hofstra University
Hempstead, NY
11549

Admissions:
800-HOFSTRA

Financial Aid:
516-463-8000

admission@hofstra.edu

www.hofstra.edu

HOFSTRA UNIVERSITY

Highlights

Students

Total enrollment: 11,023
Undergrads: 6,893
Freshmen: 1,488
Part-time students: 8%
From out-of-state: 46%
Male/Female: 47%/53%
Live on-campus: 46%
In fraternities: 11%
In sororities: 9%
Off-campus employment rating: Excellent
Caucasian: 61%
African American: 9%
Hispanic: 11%
Asian / Pacific Islander: 8%
Native American: 0%
Mixed (2+ ethnicities): 3%
International: 2%

Academics

Calendar: Semester
Student/faculty ratio: 14:1
Class size 9 or fewer: 13%
Class size 10-29: 63%
Class size 30-49: 21%
Class size 50-99: 4%
Class size 100 or more: -
Returning freshmen: 78%
Six-year graduation rate: 61%
Graduates who immediately go to graduate school: 23%

Most Popular Majors

Psychology
Marketing
Public relations

Admissions

Applicants: 22,733
Accepted: 13,346
Acceptance rate: 58.7%
Placed on wait list: 407
Enrolled from wait list: 31
Average GPA: 3.5
ACT range: 23-28
SAT Math range: 540-630
SAT Reading range: 530-630
SAT Writing range: Not reported
Top 10% of class: 28%
Top 25% of class: 61%
Top 50% of class: 87%

354

Student Life

Over a hundred activities, clubs, and organizations are at students' fingertips, including groups that focus on academics, performance, politics, the media, diversity and cultural identity, religion, social life, and pre-professional development. Hofstra is known for its radio station, Long Island's oldest public station, and for its ROTC battalion that has caused some controversy on campus for almost 60 years.

One of Hofstra's most popular events is its annual Shakespeare festival, held in the campus replica of the Globe Theater. Other activities include the Hofstra Idol singing extravaganza and Midnight Breakfast, a finals week study break. "The Midnight Breakfast is the perfect last push we need before taking exams," says a student.

Hofstra has 14 active fraternities and 10 active sororities. Greek life is not the center of the student experience, though, as only about 10 percent of students are affiliated with a Greek organization. "Whether you choose to join a fraternity or sorority or not, you'll have plenty of opportunities to go to parties and meet people," notes a student. Greek organizations are known primarily for philanthropy, school spirit, and social life on campus.

Hofstra's 17 NCAA Division I varsity athletic teams play in the Colonial Athletic Association. "The Pride" wears blue, gold, and white. There are 18 intramural sports teams at Hofstra, as well as a fitness center with a cycle, yoga, and aerobics studio and an indoor track. Students looking for a big state school football game culture won't find it, though—Hofstra terminated its football program in 2009. "That has put a damper on school spirit," one student says.

Off-campus social activities range from going to nearby beaches and hitting the bars in Hempstead to traveling by train or car to New York City, some 45 minutes away.

Forty-six percent of undergraduates live on campus, a percentage figure that becomes smaller as students become older. Housing options on campus include traditional dorms, high rises, suites, and two-story houses. The Netherlands houses first-year students in doubles as well as living/learning communities for students with interests such as arts, health sciences, American politics, environmental sustainability, and leadership. "If you are passionate about one of the areas, I'd highly recommend you choose a living/learning community so you can meet people who share your interests," says a student.

Student Body

Many Hofstra students belong to one of over 20 multicultural societies, and 31 percent of students come from minority backgrounds. Geographically, 54 percent of students come from the state of New York.

Students say that the school has "no overt" religious or political leanings.

For students who are extremely focused on academics and their future careers, many opportunities for networking with those of similar mind are made possible through the Career Center and other student-run organizations. However, students sometimes complain that many of their peers seem to be in college just to party—classes are merely an interruption. "I like to have fun too," explains a student, "but I wish there were more students who were focused primarily on their academics and careers."

You May Not Know

- Though the school has strong Dutch roots, its motto is in French. "Je maintiendrai" means "I stand steadfast" or "I shall maintain."
- Hofstra has hosted a series of prominent Presidential conferences, at which leading political figures and intellectuals debate the administrations of former U.S. Presidents. It also hosted the third and final 2008 Presidential debate.
- The school's sports teams' unofficial nickname used to be "The Flying Dutchmen," but when in 2004 it was uncovered that this name had ties to a former slave ship, Hofstra named its mascot "The Pride" after a pair of lions that have served as mascots since the 1980s.

Distinguished Alumni

Francis Ford Coppola, producer and director; Nelson DeMille, author; Kathryn V. Marinello, Chairman/CEO, Stream Global Services.

Admissions and Financial Aid

With an acceptance rate of almost 59 percent and only 28 percent of students graduating in the top 10 percent of their high school classes, Hofstra's admission policies can be described as fairly lenient. The current time is ideal for students wishing to apply to Hofstra—the strength of its academic programs seems to have outpaced its admissions rate.

The admission process at Hofstra includes an interview. Factors given great weight are secondary school record, class rank, teacher recommendations, standardized test scores, and the student's personal statement. Alumni relationship, geographical location, and minority affiliation are also considered. Students can apply using the Hofstra application or the Common Application.

Hofstra offers few school-specific merit-based scholarships. For example, even students making the Dean's or Provost's Lists are instructed to contact their major departments to inquire about additional available funding. Program-specific scholarship offerings include Communication and LGBT studies grants. Representatives are also available on campus to help students prepare for—and apply to—a variety of prestigious scholarships for post-graduate study in the U.S. and abroad.

HOFSTRA UNIVERSITY

Highlights

Admissions Criteria
Academic criteria:
Grades: ☆ ☆ ☆
Difficulty of class schedule: ☆ ☆ ☆
Class rank: ☆ ☆ ☆
Standardized test scores: ☆ ☆ ☆
Teacher recommendations: ☆ ☆ ☆
Personal statement: ☆ ☆ ☆
Non-academic criteria considered:
Interview
Extracurricular activities
Special talents, interests, abilities
Character/personal qualities
Volunteer work
Work experience
State of residency
Geographical location
Minority affiliation
Alumni relationship

Deadlines
Early Action: November 15
Early Decision: No
Regular Action: Rolling admissions
Common Application: Accepted

Financial Aid
In-state tuition: $36,350
Out-of-state tuition: $36,350
Room: $8,750
Board: $4,050
Books: $1,000
Freshmen receiving need-based aid: 73%
Undergrads rec. need-based aid: 67%
Avg. % of need met by financial aid: 59%
Avg. aid package (freshmen): $24,000
Avg. aid package (undergrads): $23,000

School Spirit
Mascot: Kate and Willie Hofstra (Lioness and Lion)
Colors: Blue, gold, and white
Song: *March On, Hofstra*

Four-year private wom-
en's college
Founded: 1842
Roanoke, VA
Medium city
Pop. 96,714

Address:
P.O. Box 9707
Roanoke, VA
24020

Admissions:
800-456-9595

Financial Aid:
540-362-6332
huadm@hollins.edu

www.hollins.edu

HOLLINS UNIVERSITY

Overview

Nestled in a valley surrounded by the Blue Ridge Mountains, the setting of Hollins University in Roanoke, Virginia, could not be more picturesque. The private four-year women's college satisfies any craving for statuesque Southern architecture, with Corinthian columns, red brick, and white-framed windows. It's not difficult to imagine Hollins' many internationally-celebrated novelists letting their imaginations cultivate in such a landscape.

The 600 undergraduates traversing the lush lawns and lazing under the abundant trees on campus call Hollins home—77 percent of students live on campus—and with such a small student body, traditions are key aspects of student life. *Forbes Magazine* ranked Hollins one of the top 100 best American colleges: the school is committed to all aspects of education that turn out well-rounded and well-read citizens. And Hollins grads keep their alma mater close at heart, providing invaluable network-ing opportunities for current students and supporting an endowment that helps the university provide need-based financial aid to 76 percent of Hollins undergrads.

With such a commitment to closeness, Hollins might not be the best fit for everyone—the tight-knit community could quickly become claustrophobic for the free spirits out there. And while a close drive to other area colleges and to the city of Roanoke allow for more mingling with new people, adding variety to social life at Hollins requires a concerted effort. Still, those who choose to attend Hollins find that the inconveniences are often offset by some real advantages: lunches at profes-sors' homes, very close ties with peers, and a quirky school personality that celebrates every student's individuality.

Academics

At Hollins, it is not uncommon to go grab dinner with your professor at her home. More than 85 percent of classes have fewer than 20 students each, facilitating close student-teacher relationships. The university offers 34 majors, granting Bachelor of Arts, Bachelor of Arts and Fine Arts, and Bachelor of Science degrees. The Hollins Creative Writing program is particularly distinguished, turning out an impressive list of Pulitzer Prize winners. Other notably strong programs include concentrations within the English major, prelaw, and psychology.

To graduate, students divide their required credits between coursework within their major, electives, and general education courses. The general education courses, known as ESP—Education through Skills and Perspectives—ensure Hollins students receive a well-rounded liberal arts education. Each course in the series offers either one of eight unique "perspectives" (e.g. scientific inquiry or aesthetic analysis) or fulfills a skill requirement (such as writing or information technology).

Additionally, Hollins women must complete two physical education classes and participate in a freshman seminar. In the first year, all students must take one of 15 seminars targeting essential skill groups. Each seminar is kept small—no more than 15 students command any one teacher's attention at a time. And attention from men-tors is a key feature of First-year Seminars: the instructor also serves as the student's first-year advisor, and an upper-class Student Success Leader provides support from the student perspective. "I'm still friends with the student I was paired with," says a student.

The Batten Leadership Institute offers a Certificate of Leadership Studies to undergraduates who complete a series of classes, skill-building groups, and seminars. Pre-professional programs like premed, prelaw, and prevet prepare students for gradu-ate schools, while the Arts Management Certificate program allows fine arts students to explore another potential career path. During January Short Term, students can test out an internship, take a course that involves travel, or explore a new intellectual curiosity through a seminar.

If the Hollins campus starts feeling a bit too cozy, students can choose to spend a term or a full year at any one of six other participating area colleges through the Seven College Exchange Program. And if the city of Roanoke starts feeling claustrophobic, Hollins has a plethora of off-campus study opportunities. Stateside, Hollins students can be found spending a semester at the American University in Washington, DC. Hollins was one of the first American universities to offer abroad opportunities and runs two overseas programs itself—in London and Paris. Through affiliates, Hollins sends students to Argentina, Cuba, Germany, Ghana, Greece, Italy, Ireland, Japan, Mexico, South Africa, and Spain.

After such an opportunity-filled undergraduate career, Hollins alumnae are more than equipped to find career openings after graduation. Attending their five-year high school reunions, Hollins women find that seven out of 10 classmates have already landed jobs and more than a quarter are en route to graduate or professional schools. Part of this success is attributable to the close networking that happens during the undergraduate years—the "intimate" community during college translates to an equally supportive alumni network.

Student Life

Hollins University is dedicated to providing a well-rounded education that extends beyond academics and into the community. Students are required to live on campus all four years, based on the premise that a residential campus yields students who "perform stronger academically, learn greater leadership skills, gain a larger network of friends and contacts, and enhance physical and spiritual development." Housing options include apartments, dormitories, and dorms with themes such as community service, French language and culture interest, and even one on anime.

Traditions like Tinker Day bring the whole school together: the president declares classes cancelled one day each fall, and the students and faculty climb Tinker Mountain for a picnic. While Hollins does have its own parties on campus, it is not a party school and as one student notes, "there's no pressure to imbibe if you don't want to." Luckily, its proximity to other area colleges and the city of Roanoke facilitates meeting new people—including guys!—just a drive away.

Hollins students can fill their time on campus by participating in 30 organizations, including the Wilderness Adventure Club, the Fencing Club, and Students for Environmental Action. While there are no sororities, there are some secret societies, including Freya, an invitation-only, anonymous society dedicated to responding to unaddressed needs within the college.

Hollins is steeped in community and tradition. The ADA group exists to oversee general "zaniness" and the tradition of wearing purple on Tuesdays; only members of this secret society know what the acronym stands for. On Ring Night, each senior secretly has a junior ring sister, who must complete various fun tasks in order to earn her ring and discover the identity of her senior. "It sounds hokey, but it's a really fun tradition," one student laughs.

HOLLINS UNIVERSITY

Highlights

Students
Total enrollment: 794
Undergrads: 613
Freshmen: 134
Part-time students: 3%
From out-of-state: 50%
From public schools: 80%
Male/Female: 0%/100%
Live on-campus: 77%
Off-campus employment rating: Good
Caucasian: 72%
African American: 10%
Hispanic: 5%
Asian / Pacific Islander: 2%
Native American: 0%
Mixed (2+ ethnicities): 3%
International: 5%

Academics
Calendar: 4-1-4 system
Student/faculty ratio: 9:1
Class size 9 or fewer: 46%
Class size 10-29: 52%
Class size 30-49: 2%
Class size 50-99: -
Class size 100 or more: -
Returning freshmen: 70%
Six-year graduation rate: 56%

Most Popular Majors
English
Psychology
Studio art

Admissions
Applicants: 814
Accepted: 537
Acceptance rate: 66.0%
Placed on wait list: 7
Enrolled from wait list: 7
Average GPA: 3.6
ACT range: 21-27
SAT Math range: 460-590
SAT Reading range: 500-650
SAT Writing range: 10-25
Top 10% of class: 18%
Top 25% of class: 61%
Top 50% of class: 89%

357

College Profiles

HOLLINS UNIVERSITY

Highlights

Admissions Criteria
Academic criteria:
Grades: ☆
Difficulty of class schedule: ☆
Class rank: ☆
Standardized test scores: ☆ ☆ ☆
Teacher recommendations: ☆ ☆
Personal statement: ☆ ☆
Non-academic criteria considered:
Interview
Extracurricular activities
Special talents, interests, abilities
Character/personal qualities
Volunteer work
Work experience
State of residency
Alumni relationship

Deadlines
Early Action: December 1
Early Decision: November 1
Regular Action: Rolling admissions
Common Application: Accepted

Financial Aid
In-state tuition: $32,710
Out-of-state tuition: $32,710
Room: Varies
Board: Varies
Books: $1,000
Freshmen receiving need-based aid: 75%
Undergrads rec. need-based aid: 76%
Avg. % of need met by financial aid: 78%
Avg. aid package (freshmen): $29,987
Avg. aid package (undergrads): $27,277
Avg. debt upon graduation: $31,104

School Spirit
Colors: Green and gold
Song: *The Green and the Gold*

The most celebrated Division III athletic team on Hollins campus is the equestrian team, which consistently advances full hunt seat equitation teams to the Intercollegiate Horse Show Association National Championship Horse Show. Its state-of-the-art riding facilities, top coaching staff, and stable full of quality horses draws equestriennes from across the nation. Those interested in cross-country running, fencing, martial arts, or softball can participate through student club sports. And if organized team sports aren't your thing, the Hollins Outdoor Program takes advantage of Hollins' ideal location to bring students rock climbing, camping, and caving.

Student Body

While the Hollins student body is moderately ethnically diverse—with 20 percent of students representing minority racial backgrounds—the school enjoys the diversity of having students from out of state and from other countries. About 50 percent of the student body is from Virginia. In general, "there are more liberals than conservatives, although all are welcome," notes a student.

Students report that the school is "too small" for cliques, but that everybody pretty much knows or knows of everybody else. An abundance of opportunities to get involved brings the school together—25 percent of students are involved with community service organizations.

You May Not Know

- It's a good thing that "Hollins" is just two syllables long, because the school has neither a mascot nor an official nickname to yell out during sports matches.
- The Rock is a large, centrally-located boulder that serves as an outlet for creative, political, and celebratory expression.
- On Viking Day, students dress in Viking garb and "pillage" campus, soliciting charitable donations.

Distinguished Alumnae

Mary Ashworth, Pulitzer Prize winning historian; Annie Dillard, Pulitzer Prize winning author; Ellen Malcolm, founder of EMILY's List; Sally Mann, named America's Best Photographer by *Time Magazine*; Carol Semple Thompson, World Golf Hall of Famer.

Admissions and Financial Aid

Students may apply to Hollins via its own application or the Common Application. The university offers a three-year accelerated program for first-time, first-year students.

Students may apply for one of three Academic Excellence Scholarships or for one of the Outstanding Achievement awards granted each year. The Batten Scholar Award, recognizing academic achievement and leadership potential, grants awards to students at different amounts all the way up to full tuition. Also available are grants for Virginia students and endowed, need-based scholarships.

HOPE COLLEGE

Overview

Hope College is a private, four-year college located in Holland, Michigan that is affiliated with the Reformed Church. It is a place of faith. Religious convictions permeate approaches to academics, extracurricular activities, and student life. It is a place that doesn't differentiate between everyday life and spiritual life—at Hope College, the two are one and the same.

The city of Holland, not surprisingly, has Dutch origins. Much of the early Dutch influence can be found today in its customs and religious fervor. Like the country of Holland, this U.S. college town is known for its tulips, even celebrating a Tulip Time Festival each spring. Holland has a beautiful view of Lake Michigan. The city enjoys lovely weather in the summer and is a sought-after resort area; the winter, however, can get very cold with temperatures hovering around 25 degrees.

Hope is known for its emphasis on research, especially in the stem field and for its strong arts programs, especially music, dance, and theatre. Hope is also a notable athletic school. Its campus is striking, combining both 19th century and modern architectural styles.

Academics

Hope is a school with small classes and plenty of individual attention and mentorship. The average class size is 10 to 19 students, and the student-to-faculty ratio is 12:1. The academic rigor of Hope varies depending on the major the student chooses, as some plans of study can be more intensive than others. "There are impossible classes in every discipline, but the sciences have the reputation for being the hardest," says a student. English, psychology, chemistry and biochemistry, and biology are all strong academic programs.

Freshmen must complete a First Year Seminar, which serves as a transition for students into interdisciplinary college work. Expository Writing is another academic requirement, as is Health Dynamics, which teaches students stress-management, diet, and exercise skills, and facilitates the creation of an individual life-style program for each student. Knowledge of a foreign language is also required; students must pass a placement exam or take classes at the college. The liberal arts Core Curriculum includes 10 credits of mathematics and the natural sciences, six credits of religious studies, six credits of the social sciences, six credits of arts, eight credits of cultural heritage, and four credits of cultural diversity classes.

Completion of the Senior Seminar is a graduation requirement; students contemplate philosophical and religious questions of meaning and value. They examine how faith can inform and transform their lives, and write a culminating life view paper that articulates this. "I've never reflected on the meaning of life in general and my life in particular more than I have in my Senior Seminar," comments one student.

Opportunities for academic growth at Hope College include The Phelps Scholars Program, which provides an avenue for students to build new relationships and experience various cultures. Any student may apply for the Phelps Scholars Program; there is no academic requirement. Phelps Scholars participate in the First Year Seminar as a group and then engage in different activities and trips together, such as the Underground Railroad Re-enactment at Connor Prairie near Indianapolis. The Hughes Research Scholars is another popular and rewarding academic program, admission to which is based on college academic record. Students who are interested in the sciences may conduct a 10-week research project with faculty during the summer, while receiving a stipend from the college.

Hope offers a number of off-campus programs within the United States. The Border Studies Program explores cultures in the regions of Texas, New Mexico, and Chihuahua, while the Chicago Semester is a program affiliated with eight other

HOPE COLLEGE

Four-year private
Founded: 1866
Holland, MI
Medium city
Pop. 33,270

Address:
P.O. Box 9000
Holland, MI
49422-9000

Admissions:
800-968-7850

Financial Aid:
888-439-8907

admissions@hope.edu

www.hope.edu

HOPE COLLEGE

Highlights

Students

Total enrollment: 3,343
Undergrads: 3,343
Freshmen: 903
Part-time students: 4%
From out-of-state: 35%
Male/Female: 40%/60%
Live on-campus: 81%
In fraternities: 10%
In sororities: 12%
Off-campus employment rating: Fair
Caucasian: 86%
African American: 2%
Hispanic: 6%
Asian / Pacific Islander: 2%
Native American: 0%
Mixed (2+ ethnicities): 2%
International: 2%

Academics

Calendar: Semester
Student/faculty ratio: 12:1
Class size 9 or fewer: 20%
Class size 10-29: 66%
Class size 30-49: 12%
Class size 50-99: 2%
Class size 100 or more: -
Returning freshmen: 90%
Six-year graduation rate: 77%
Graduates who immediately go to graduate school: 26%
Graduates who immediately enter career related to major: 76%

Most Popular Majors

Management
Psychology
Communication

Admissions

Applicants: 3,493
Accepted: 2,970
Acceptance rate: 85.0%
Average GPA: 3.8
ACT range: 23-29
SAT Math range: 520-670
SAT Reading range: 510-660
SAT Writing range: Not reported
Top 10% of class: 37%
Top 25% of class: 66%
Top 50% of class: 92%

Midwestern Christian colleges. Students in this seminar have the opportunity to take classes and participate in a four-day-a week internship in their academic area of choice while learning about the Chicago urban environment. The Newberry Seminar in the Humanities also takes place in Chicago, taking advantage of the many resources of the Newberry Library.

The New York Arts Program provides students with the opportunity to act as apprentices to an artist or arts organization while taking academic classes. A similar program is the New York Center for Arts and Media Studies. In this program, internships can be found in galleries and media institutions as well as with working artists.

Study programs in the sciences are also a part of Hope College offerings. The Oak Ridge Science Semester allows students to work at the Oak Ridge National Laboratory in Tennessee, while the Oregon Extension Program combines academic work with questions of Christian faith and peace and provides a tranquil environment for reflection and study. The Washington Honors Semester Program allows students to learn more about government and politics by interning for two-week periods in Congress, while taking academic seminars. Additionally, Hope offers study-abroad programs in 60 countries.

After graduation, about 26 percent of students at Hope College enter graduate school and continue their education. Others find jobs in the U.S., while still others pursue careers in other countries. For those graduates who are interested in living abroad, the Paul G. Fried International Center is a resource for international alumni to connect with Hope students and help them find jobs.

Student Life

Social life thrives at Hope College, which supports almost 70 different official student organizations. The most popular include Fellowship for Christian Athletes and Gospel Choir. Greek life is also very prominent on campus; there are seven fraternities and seven sororities.

"The Pull" and the Nykerk Cup are popular events that involve competition between the freshman and sophomore classes. "The Pull" is a giant tug of war across Black River. The male students tug, and the female students offer support. Conversely, freshmen and sophomore female students compete in music, drama, and public-speaking for the Nykerk Cup, while the male students act as supporters. A weekly popular social event is called "The Gathering," a Sunday night worship service meeting. "There are a lot of fun things to do even if you don't drink, and there's no pressure to drink," remarks a student.

Hope College is a Division III school, competing in the MIAA conference. It hosts 18 varsity female and male teams. There are 27 intramural sports teams, which are also very popular. In 2010, the women's basketball team won the national title; and the men's basketball team has won six titles since 2000. "It's fun to go to basketball games and scream your head off," laughs a student. In addition to basketball, soccer is another well-liked sport on campus.

Holland, MI is a good location for both rural and urban off-campus fun. Some students like to participate in water activities at Lake Michigan. Others opt for the shopping and culture of Holland, while an adventurous few enjoy taking road trips to Chicago.

Over 80 percent of students live on campus, and upperclassmen housing is determined by a lottery. A student at Hope could live anywhere from a traditional dorm to an apartment to a house; all are viable campus-living options.

Student Body

Students at Hope College tend to be academically motivated and devoted to exploring their faith. "Faith is very important here," explains a student. "It's not unusual to spend Friday nights worshipping." With a higher population of female students (60 percent) than males, students say that the dating scene is a little "warped" but that the female students aren't afraid to participate in college life on all levels and even "speak up in class."

The ethnic diversity of the school is low, as only 12 percent of students come from minority backgrounds. The geographic diversity is moderate; 35 percent of students attend Hope College from out of state.

You May Not Know

- Hope College has two mascots: the Flying Dutchmen for their men's athletic teams, and the Flying Dutch for their women's athletic teams.
- The symbol of Hope College is an anchor, the top of which resembles a cross to emphasize the importance of faith in one's life foundation.
- Hope College's colors are blue and orange, indicating its Dutch heritage.

Distinguished Alumni

Pete Hoekstra, U.S. Representative from Michigan; Craig Morford, former U.S. Deputy Attorney General; Robert H. Schuller, televangelist; Sufjan Stevens, musician; Guy Adrian Vander Jagt, U.S. Representative from Michigan.

Admissions and Financial Aid

Class rank is an important factor for admissions officers to consider when making a decision about a student's application. The college has an Early Notification program in which students applying before November 1 receive word of acceptance or non-acceptance by Thanksgiving.

Hope College offers a number of merit scholarships. The Trustee Scholarship of $17,000 per year is based on academic record, test scores, and signs of leadership. The National Merit Scholarship, also $17,000 per year, is awarded to National Merit Scholarship Finalists who indicate that Hope is their first-choice college. The Presidential Scholarship, $6,000 to $15,000 per year, is determined by academic record, class rank, and test scores.

HOPE COLLEGE

Highlights

Admissions Criteria
Academic criteria:
Grades: ☆ ☆ ☆
Difficulty of class schedule: ☆ ☆ ☆
Class rank: ☆ ☆
Standardized test scores: ☆ ☆ ☆
Teacher recommendations: ☆
Personal statement: ☆ ☆
Non-academic criteria considered:
Interview
Extracurricular activities
Special talents, interests, abilities
Character/personal qualities
Volunteer work
Work experience
Geographical location
Religious affiliation/commitment
Minority affiliation
Alumni relationship

Deadlines
Early Action: No
Early Decision: No
Regular Action: Rolling admissions
Common Application: Accepted

Financial Aid
In-state tuition: $28,550
Out-of-state tuition: $28,550
Room: $4,040
Board: $4,770
Books: $870
Freshmen receiving need-based aid: 68%
Undergrads rec. need-based aid: 63%
Avg. % of need met by financial aid: 78%
Avg. aid package (freshmen): $23,044
Avg. aid package (undergrads): $22,197
Avg. debt upon graduation: $37,010

School Spirit
Mascot: Flying Dutchmen/Flying Dutch
Colors: Orange and blue
Song: *Fight on You Big Dutchmen*

Four-year private
Founded: 1867
Washington, DC
Major city
Pop. 632,323

Address:
2400 Sixth Street, NW
Washington, DC
20059

Admissions:
800-822-6363

Financial Aid:
800-433-3243

admission@howard.
edu

www.howard.edu

HOWARD UNIVERSITY

Overview

Howard University is frequently described as America's leading historically black college and university (HBCU). The university describes itself as an environment that "engenders and nurtures an environment that celebrates African-American culture in all its diversity." Small classes provide the opportunity to work closely with well known professors, and Howard is practically peerless for students interested in Afro-American studies. To top things off, the university boasts an illustrious history and can claim such famous names as author Zora Neale Hurston, former Supreme Court Justice Thurgood Marshall, and actress Phylicia Rashad as alumni.

Howard's campus, home to many historic buildings, sits in one of the nation's best university locations. Washington, DC offers access to a vibrant social life and incomparable internships. Students never lack for something interesting to do, be it on-campus or off. On the other hand, Howard's surroundings present a safety challenge. Still, Howard's strong academics, supportive and empowering environment, great location, proud history, and bounteous merit scholarships make it an excellent choice.

Academics

Howard offers 187 majors. Some of its strongest programs are Afro-American studies, business degrees, engineering, and political science. Howard also has a strong reputation in preparing students for law and medical school, although there is no specific prelaw or premed major. To fulfill Howard's core requirements, all students complete two composition courses and choose one Afro-American studies course. In addition, most students must take courses in mathematics, freshman orientation, humanities, social sciences, natural sciences, and physical education. Students should expect to benefit from lots of personalized attention from professors, since the most common course size is two to nine students. "All of my professors know my name," comments a student, "and I've spoken with all of them outside of class."

The required Freshman Seminar at Howard is "hard work but a good introduction to college-level courses," notes a participant. Students gain insight into the history of Howard as an institution and, more broadly, according to the college, "become engaged participants in the intellectual and cultural life of African peoples throughout the Diaspora by exploring this rich history and legacy and this legacy's vibrant contemporary work and institutional life." The course includes a group research project, the creation of an e-portfolio of written work, guest lectures, and a day trip to the African Burial Ground in New York City.

The Writing Across the Curriculum program encourages students to develop strong writing skills for use in their disciplines. Writing-intensive courses in each department are capped at 20 students to maximize the possibility of feedback from professors. "My writing class was the best that I've taken. I feel like I've improved immensely as a writer," says a student.

The Honors Program at Howard emphasizes composition, literature, natural and social sciences in the first years, seminar courses in the following two years, and directed research to produce an honors thesis in the final year. Honors students have plenty of independent study opportunities. Students say the program "attracts the most academically motivated students."

For students in a hurry to begin their medical or dental career (or in a hurry to save a bundle on tuition), Howard offers accelerated BS/MD and BS/DDS degrees through "Combined Programs." Both last six years. The accelerated medical curriculum consists of four semesters and one summer in the College of Arts and Sciences and four years in the College of Medicine. The accelerated dental curriculum, on the other hand, consists of two or three years in the College of Arts and Sciences followed by the remaining three to four years in the College of Dentistry.

Howard offers study-abroad options in 13 countries. The study-abroad application is surprisingly simple and streamlined. Students of Howard and Hampton are eligible for the Luard Scholarship which provides an opportunity to study at a university in the UK during the junior year.

Students note that the alumni network at Howard is "one of the strongest in the country." It's common for undergrads to network with alumni to find jobs. Each spring, the career services office sponsors a "Career Exploration Week," which includes a large career fair and other career development activities, such as résumé critiques by corporate recruiters.

Student Life

Howard has over 225 official student organizations. The Howard University Student Association (HUSA) is one of the largest groups. In addition, the student newspaper *The Hilltop* has won many accolades, including recently being honored by *The New York Times* as a "premier college news source." Despite the fact that only a small minority of students join Greek organizations, there is still an active Greek scene at Howard—not just for parties but also for community service. Informally, hanging out and people-watching at the Punchout Café and the Yard are popular on-campus pass-times.

Homecoming at Howard is serious business. More than 100,000 alumni return to campus for the event Ludacris described as "you just can't miss." Each year, the homecoming has a classy one-word title. A recent title is "Legendary: The Essence of Icons." One of the biggest homecoming activities is a competitive step show that brings representatives from African-American Greek letter organizations across the country together to battle for top honors. In addition, students and alums enjoy a fashion show, comedy show, multiple concerts, a "Coronation Ball" to welcome the Homecoming King and Queen, and the requisite homecoming football game.

In a younger Howard tradition, born in 2002, students compete in ResFest, a more well-rounded version of the Olympics. Students representing each residence hall compete in games, debates, athletic events, dance competitions, and even beauty pageants in an attempt to win glory for their dorm. "While it's all for fun, there's a lot of pride at stake," notes a student.

Finally, each year the formal Bison Ball honors outstanding Howard students and faculty with awards like "Underclassmen of the Year," the "Faculty Cup," and "Sorority of the Year." It's also a last hurrah for seniors, as it marks their final formal at Howard.

Howard fields 19 Division I teams (eight men's, 11 women's). In general, athletic events are not terribly popular, although basketball has a following. The football team has a rather poor record. "We're not known for our athletics," states a student. The usual selection of intramural sports are offered for those "non-varsity" athletic types.

Off campus, students must always keep a sharp eye on their surroundings, since the university is located in the Shaw district, which has experienced high levels of crime. For restaurants, bars, and night life, students frequent Georgetown, U Street, and Adams Morgan. Of course, the high-quality free museums, professional athletics, and cultural offerings of DC are close at hand. "We're in the most exciting college town in the country," says a student. Thanks to its extensive Metro system, DC is a car-less student's dream.

HOWARD UNIVERSITY

Highlights

Students
Total enrollment: 10,002
Undergrads: 6,688
From out-of-state: 96%
Male/Female: 33%/67%
Live-on campus: 55%
In fraternities: 2%
In sororities: 1%
Off-campus employment rating: Good
Caucasian: 1%
African American: 93%
Hispanic: 0%
Asian / Pacific Islander: 1%
Native American: 2%
Mixed (2+ ethnicities): 0%
International: 2%

Academics
Calendar: Semester
Student/faculty ratio: 10:1
Class size 9 or fewer: 37%
Class size 10-29: 44%
Class size 30-49: 15%
Class size 50-99: 3%
Class size 100 or more: 1%
Graduates who immediately go to graduate school: 40%
Graduates who immediately enter career related to major: 65%

Most Popular Majors
Biology
Psychology
Journalism

Admissions
Applicants: 9,015
Accepted: 4,868
Acceptance rate: 54%
Average GPA: Not reported
ACT range: 21-26
SAT Math range: 480-580
SAT Reading range: 490-580
SAT Writing range: 470-570

HOWARD UNIVERSITY

Howard's residence hall options include co-ed and gender-segregated buildings as well as freshmen-only halls. Undergraduate honor students can live in the upscale apartments of Howard Plaza Towers East, a privilege otherwise reserved for grad students. Most upperclassmen choose to move off campus. When it comes to food on campus, the most popular days at the Howard Cafeteria are the self-explanatory Soul Food Thursdays and Barbecue Tuesdays. "The fried chicken is very tasty," remarks a student.

Student Body

While the college is predominantly African-American, there is a lot of diversity on campus in terms of geographic origin, with 96 percent of students hailing from outside Washington, DC and two percent from outside of the country. The student body is two-thirds female, a demographic that is "a big downside of the university," as noted by one female student.

Howard students describe themselves as "politically active" and "liberal" as well as "focused on the future career-wise." Most undergrads have a good sense of what they want to do after graduating. On the lighter side, fashion is an important part of life at Howard, so be prepared to dress up just to go to class. "The entire campus is like a fashion catwalk," laughs a student.

You May Not Know

- Howard is named after General Oliver O. Howard, who served with distinction in the Civil War, and afterward founded the university. He was Commissioner of the Freedman's Bureau.
- Howard did not have its first black president until 1926—Dr. Mordecai Wyatt Johnson.
- The popular Punch-Out dining hall is modeled after a mall food court and includes franchises of real restaurant chains.

Distinguished Alumni

Zora Neale Hurston, author; Thurgood Marshall, Supreme Court Justice; Toni Morrison, Nobel and Pulitzer Prize-winning author; Phylicia Rashad, Emmy Award-winning actress.

Admissions and Financial Aid

Howard has merit scholarships galore. For entering freshmen, there are five separate merit scholarship programs for academic excellence that cover full tuition. The most prestigious award, the Presidential Scholarship, includes tuition, fees, a $950 book voucher, room and board, and a laptop. Separate applications are not required for freshman scholarships.

After freshman year or after transferring to Howard, students become eligible for yet more scholarships based on their performance. In addition to academic scholarships, athletic grants are also available.

ILLINOIS INSTITUTE OF TECHNOLOGY

Overview

The 120-acre main campus of the Illinois Institute of Technology (Illinois Tech or IIT) is located at 33rd and State Streets in Chicago. In keeping with the historic flavor of the Bronzeville neighborhood in which it's located, the campus features 20th century architecture, much of it designated on the National Register of Historic Places.

You won't find students immersed in studies of history here, though. This small private technical school's strengths lie in engineering, business, and architecture. Even the names of the school's music groups have a technological ring to them: the TechTonics, the Crown Joules, and the X-Chromotones, for example. Though the general education requirements include seven courses in the humanities and social sciences, the bulk of the tough academics are centered on the technical courses. Opportunities for research and real-world projects cater to the career-minded objectives of most students.

Women are outnumbered by the men, who make up almost 70 percent of the student population, and geeks will be quite at home on campus. While IIT does not offer a very "traditional" college experience, career-minded techies who want to take advantage of living in a big city may want to count themselves among the 2,800 undergrads at Illinois Tech.

Academics

There are 16 undergraduate majors available through six of IIT's eight academic divisions: the Armour College of Engineering, College of Architecture, College of Letters and Sciences, Institute of Psychology, School of Applied Technology, and Stuart School of Business. General Education Requirements include one math course and one computer science course, plus seven courses in the humanities and social studies. In addition, even students not studying the sciences or engineering are required to complete courses in the fields. Within each program, there is an introductory course for first-year students that is designed to acclimate them to their profession.

IIT's hallmark Interprofessional Projects (IPROs) unite 10-15 students from cross disciplines to work on a "real-world project." Under the guidance of faculty and the leadership of students, IPROs have produced patents and products and consequently connected students with potential employers. "I learned more from our IPRO project than I could have learned in any traditional classroom," says a student.

Courses are challenging with lots of technical work in science and math. "It's not unusual to pull all-nighters before projects are due," remarks a student. Fortunately, professors are helpful and accessible, not surprising, given the 12:1 faculty-student ratio. Strong programs include the five degrees in the engineering college, architecture, and business administration.

Dual Admission Programs enable ambitious IIT students to accelerate the process of earning professional degrees in medicine, pharmacy, law, and business. Freshmen interested in research can participate in the Undergraduate Research Scholar's Program, which offers a stipend for conducting research the summer between their freshman and sophomore years. This competitive program is open to students who scored in the top 10 percent of their high school class and show a clear interest in the medical field.

For the career-minded student, IIT's Co-operative Education program integrates learning in the classroom and on-the-job application. Students usually work with practicing engineers to get more first-hand knowledge of their career field, and co-op students put in a minimum of three full-time work terms with the same employer. Students do not pay tuition or receive a credit for a co-op experience, but they may still live on campus and take advantage of campus life perks.

Study-abroad opportunities include a Semester in Paris for electrical and computer engineering courses taught in English. "Can you think of a better place in the

ILLINOIS INSTITUTE OF TECHNOLOGY

Four-year private
Founded: 1890
Chicago, IL
Major city
Pop. 2,707,120

Address:
3300 South Federal Street
Chicago, IL
60616

Admissions:
800-448-2329

Financial Aid:
312-567-7219

admission@iit.edu

www.iit.edu

ILLINOIS INSTITUTE OF TECHNOLOGY

world to learn electrical engineering?" asks a student. The school's study-abroad office provides general resources for going overseas, though students must often take a proactive role in designing their programs.

There are more than 62,000 living alumni of IIT. Historically, 85 percent of students have been admitted to graduate or professional school and/or have decided on their first full-time job position at the time of graduation. Alumni have launched careers at Boeing, Compaq, Dow Chemical, NASA, Xerox, and other well known companies.

Student Life

There are more than 100 student groups at IIT. Many have a techie bent. The IIT Model Railroad Club runs a model railway that covers much of the sixth floor of the Main Building. Other campus groups include the Programming Team, American Society of Civil Engineers Steel Bridge Team, and the Formula Hybrid Team, which have all done well in their respective competitions in recent years. The campus newspaper, *TechNews*, has been publishing since 1930.

The distinctive McCormick Tribune Campus Center, notable architect Rem Koolhaas' first building in the U.S., centralizes the campus bookstore and post office into one location. The futuristic building is underneath a stainless steel tube that shields the southbound Green Line train and earned the building the former, unflattering nickname of BUTT (Building Under The Tracks), though now MTCC is more common. The BOG, an on-campus pub and bowling alley, is another favorite student hangout.

Greek life has been established for over 100 years at IIT, and about 14 percent of the student body joins one of the seven fraternities and three sororities on campus. Traditional activities at IIT kick off as early as the first week of fall classes with Taste of the Quad, an event hosted by the fraternities and sororities. One of the largest social events on campus, Taste of the Quad brings food, music, and carnival games to entertain and feed Greek and non-Greek students alike.

Other key social events include the International Fest and Spring Formal. International Fest brings the flavors of IIT's diverse student population to campus every semester. Students may taste food from around the world and watch their friends perform songs, dances, and skits associated with different cultures. Spring Formal gets students out for a night in Chicago. "It's very elegant with everyone all dressed up," comments a student.

IIT's eight athletic teams (four men's, four women's) compete in NAIA Division I. Men's swimming and diving are among the most competitive sports. Baseball, men's cross-country, men's basketball, and women's volleyball are the most popular. Intramurals/recreational events range from soccer league to tango. And if a disc flies past you while walking on Main Campus, don't be alarmed: IIT hosts a nine-hole disc golf course constructed in 2007.

Off campus, Chicago provides endless possibilities for big city nightlife, entertainment, dining, and shopping. Students go to Lake Michigan for activities by or on the water. Nearby Chinatown offers a taste and glimpse of another culture in the nation's second-largest Chinatown after New York.

While 59 percent of freshmen live on campus, many students also commute. However, freshmen not living with their families are required to live on campus. All but one of the seven dorms on campus are co-ed. Those who live in on-campus housing praise their accommodations. Hall leaders organize social events such as concert outings, film screenings, and intramural sports. "We don't have much to complain about with the dorms," agrees a student.

Student Body

IIT students are very academically focused, and—as can be expected—tend to be technically inclined. Geeks will find themselves in good company. "We're proud to call ourselves geeks," says a student. Women are outnumbered by men by more than 2:1. There is low geographic diversity, with 21 percent of students from out of state but a sizable international student population of 23 percent. There is high ethnic diversity, with 31 percent of undergrads identifying as minority students.

You May Not Know

- IIT formed in 1940 when the Armour Institute of Technology and Lewis Institute merged.
- The Paul V. Galvin Library on campus was home to many famous African-Americans during the mid-20th century, including civil rights activist Ida B. Wells, bandleader Louis Armstrong, author Gwendolyn Brooks, and pilot Bessie Coleman.
- The neighborhood in which the main campus is located is known as the Black Metropolis District.

Distinguished Alumni

Harry Callihan, photographer; Marvin Camras, pioneer in magnetic recording; Susan Solomon, discoverer of the cause of the hole in the ozone layer; Jack Steinberger, Noble Prize in Physics winner.

Admissions and Financial Aid

IIT's admissions officers look for hard-working students who have performed well academically and have strong community ties. Online recommendations are strongly preferred over paper recommendations. Besides looking at academic achievement and extracurricular activities, IIT also looks at future career goals, "whether there's a specific answer or not." The admissions office notes that good candidates tend to be in college prep classes or attending a school with curriculum that includes four years of mathematics, including pre-calculus, three years of science (with two years of lab work). Technology and computer courses are recommended but not required.

There are a variety of merit-based scholarships available, including four- and five-year full-tuition grants. Freshmen are automatically considered for the Heald and University Scholarships of up to $10,000 annually. Full-tuition scholarships include IIT's highest undergraduate academic award, the Camras Scholars Program, which challenges the top one percent of the applicant pool to apply and interview with a faculty member for the honor. The need-based Collens Scholars Program also covers full tuition.

ILLINOIS INSTITUTE OF TECHNOLOGY

Highlights

Admissions Criteria
Academic criteria:
Grades: ☆ ☆ ☆
Difficulty of class schedule: ☆ ☆ ☆
Class rank: ☆ ☆
Standardized test scores: ☆ ☆ ☆
Teacher recommendations: ☆ ☆
Personal statement: ☆
Non-academic criteria considered:
Interview
Extracurricular activities
Special talents, interests, abilities
Character/personal qualities
Volunteer work
Work experience
State of residency
Alumni relationship

Deadlines
Early Action: December 1
Early Decision: No
Regular Action: Rolling admissions
Common Application: Accepted

Financial Aid
In-state tuition: $38,512
Out-of-state tuition: $38,512
Room: Varies
Board: Varies
Books: $1,200
Freshmen receiving need-based aid: 68%
Undergrads rec. need-based aid: 62%
Avg. % of need met by financial aid: 76%
Avg. aid package (freshmen): $33,988
Avg. aid package (undergrads): $29,712
Avg. debt upon graduation: $29,581

School Spirit
Mascot: Scarlet Hawks
Colors: Scarlet and gray

ILLINOIS WESLEYAN UNIVERSITY

ILLINOIS WESLEYAN UNIVERSITY

Four-year private
Founded: 1850
Bloomington, IL
Large town
Pop. 77,071

Address:
Box 2900
Bloomington, IL
61702-2900

Admissions:
800-332-2498

Financial Aid:
309-556-3096

iwuadmit@iwu.edu

www.iwu.edu

Overview

Right in the heart of the Prairie State—about two hours south of Chicago—the 80-acre Midwestern campus of Illinois Wesleyan University stands proudly. A small, liberal arts college filled with a couple thousand young, eager minds, IWU is a pretty classic college scene: brick buildings, grass quads, and seasonal gardens. But the school also offers an interesting mix of old and new, with buildings like the Buck Memorial library, the former central library, and the Center for Natural Sciences with its glass-ceiling atrium. Additionally, IWU presents some unique academic opportunities, like the month-long May term, and its own abroad/exchange program with Keio University in Japan. Clearly, the school manages to keep a lot of options available to students despite its size.

Small still means small, though: the school has just over 2,000 undergraduate students, with a social scene pretty dependent on Greek life and athletics. With the help of Illinois State University, college bars in both Bloomington (the college's home) and nearby Normal provide for a fun alternative when the campus scene gets old.

Academics

Including liberal arts, interdisciplinary, and pre-professional programs, Illinois Wesleyan has 50 majors and programs. Some of the strongest of these are nursing, English, and biology. Nursing majors are admitted to the School of Nursing and graduate with Bachelor of Science in Nursing. The English department has two sequences: one on literature, and the other on writing. These include both journalism and creative writing.

The average class size is 17 students, and the professors are renowned for their outside-of-class accessibility. "Professors will call me if I don't show up for class," notes a student. "That's really personal treatment."

The general education requirements are extensive, crossing over 12 different categories, including a physical fitness and a language requirement (though students can place out of this, based on their proficiency). Some of the categories can be fulfilled through overlapping classes with major requirements, and students can place out of requirements with 4s and 5s on AP Exams.

All freshmen take the Gateway Colloquium seminar, a discussion-based class that develops writing skills and public speaking. The classes are small, and each syllabus focuses on a different overall subjects. "An Introduction to the Nature of the Creative Process" and "Who Killed Classical Music?" are examples of topics on a relatively expansive list. Appreciation for the seminar classes depends on who you talk to. "The seminars are hit and miss, depending on your professor and the other students in the class," remarks one student.

To promote independent undergraduate student research (for credit), the school founded the John Wesley Powell Research Conference held every April. It provides a forum for students to publicly present their work through either a 15-minute oral presentation or a poster session, and all students—regardless of field of study or graduation year—can participate.

Though the school has only three study-abroad programs of its own, it's one of the few schools to offer an exchange program: students may opt to study at Keio University in Japan. IWU also recognizes hundreds of affiliate programs around the world through organizations like IES and CIEE.

May term is a three-week intensive study that counts as a full-credit course and allows students to do community service, have internships, take unconventional classes, travel both domestically and abroad, or do independent research projects in collaboration with, or under the guidance of, faculty. "I look forward to the May term each year because it lets me get hands-on experience," says a student.

Beyond academic advisors who guide students in learning time management and study habits, the school provides help through the IWU Writing Center, available to students at all stages of the writing process; the Language Resource Center; and tutoring centers in the residence halls—all free to students. The Career Center has an online database accessible to both students and alumni with internship and job opportunities. It also has career specialists, resume help, and a mock interview program.

Student Life

There are 165 student organizations on campus, ranging from the Birdie Bashers (a badminton club) to Only Punks Pull Triggers (a group against violence among youth) to Lyrical Graffiti (a slam poetry group).

The school also boasts the over-20-year-running Gospel Festival, an annual tribute to Martin Luther King Jr. that IWU hosts as a memorial to the two visits King made to its campus during his lifetime. IWU introduces new students and new activities at its annual activity fair, the Far left Carnival, where clubs and groups set up stands to attract members or to give out information. Other popular events include Earthapalooza, jazz band and civic orchestra concerts, International Carnivale, and the International Film Series.

Greek life is huge on campus, with almost one in three students involved in one of the 11 fraternities and sororities. On a campus as small as Illinois Wesleyan's, that's where most of the parties are going to be, which makes "it a challenge for those who don't join and who want an active social life," says a student.

Athletics are another way to socialize. There's usually a great turnout at the school's basketballs games. IWU is an NCAA Division III school, with 18 varsity sports teams (nine men's, nine women's), including NCAA championship winning baseball, men's basketball, and women's track (both indoor and outdoor) teams. "School spirit is pretty high during games," notes a student. Club sports include dance team, cheerleading, and Ultimate Frisbee.

If sports aren't your thing, the surrounding Bloomington-Normal area—home to over 110,000 people—has museums, concert venues, and a decent nightlife in the downtown area thanks to college bars and great restaurants.

Though about 29 percent of students live off campus in Bloomington, all freshmen and sophomores are required to reside on campus. There are 12 residence halls, housing between 23 and 204 students each, all air-conditioned. Every room has cable, "Titan TV" (the student senate-run movie and school programming channel), as well as access to the campus network. "The dorms are the best places to meet people because there's always someone in the common areas," comments a student.

All students can bring their cars, regardless of class year, and there's no charge, just registration. Having a means to get away on the weekend can make a huge difference in a small college, especially after freshman year.

Student Body

The student body at IWU is not all that diverse; though there is some ethnic diversity, white students make up 73 percent of the population, and 88 percent of the student body is from Illinois,

ILLINOIS WESLEYAN UNIVERSITY

Highlights

Students
Total enrollment: 2,013
Undergrads: 2,013
From out-of-state: 12%
Male/Female: 42%/58%
Live on-campus: 71%
In fraternities: 31%
In sororities: 33%
Off-campus employment rating: Good
Caucasian: 73%
African American: 5%
Hispanic: 5%
Asian / Pacific Islander: 6%
Native American: 0%
Mixed (2+ ethnicities): 0%
International: 4%

Academics
Calendar: 4-4-1 system
Student/faculty ratio: 11:1
Class size 9 or fewer: 23%
Class size 10-29: 71%
Class size 30-49: 6%
Class size 50-99: 1%
Class size 100 or more: -
Returning freshmen: 90%
Six-year graduation rate: 89%
Graduates who immediately enter career
   related to major: 60%

Most Popular Majors
Business administration
Psychology
English

Admissions
Applicants: 3,297
Accepted: 1,963
Acceptance rate: 59.5%
Placed on wait list: 200
Enrolled from wait list: 5
Average GPA: 3.5
ACT range: 25-30
SAT Math range: 570-700
SAT Reading range: 540-650
SAT Writing range: Not reported
Top 10% of class: 45%
Top 25% of class: 82%
Top 50% of class: 98%

369

ILLINOIS WESLEYAN UNIVERSITY

Highlights

Admissions Criteria
Academic criteria:
Grades: ☆ ☆ ☆
Difficulty of class schedule: ☆ ☆ ☆
Class rank: ☆ ☆
Standardized test scores: ☆ ☆
Teacher recommendations: ☆
Personal statement: ☆ ☆
Non-academic criteria considered:
Interview
Extracurricular activities
Special talents, interests, abilities
Character/personal qualities
Volunteer work
Work experience
Geographical location
Minority affiliation
Alumni relationship

Deadlines
Early Action: November 15
Early Decision: No
Regular Action: Rolling admissions
Common Application: Accepted

Financial Aid
In-state tuition: $39,136
Out-of-state tuition: $39,136
Room: $5,752
Board: $3,384
Books: $780
Freshmen receiving need-based aid: 71%
Undergrads rec. need-based aid: 65%
Avg. % of need met by financial aid: 87%
Avg. aid package (freshmen): $27,634
Avg. aid package (undergrads): $26,643
Avg. debt upon graduation: $32,964

School Spirit
Mascot: Titans
Colors: Green and white
Song: *Titan Cheer Song*

specifically the Chicago area. The male to female ratio is about 42:58. "There's some justified grumbling about the lack of eligible guys," a female student comments.

Politically, as one might expect from a swing-state, the students are pretty balanced in terms of views. It's a politically active campus, with 17 politically involved groups as well as the Action Resource Center, which connects students with community leaders in Central Illinois.

There is a growing focus on environment sustainability: the GREENetwork is open to all members of the IWU community, including professors, students, administration, and staff, and the school even has a student-run clothing store, PreShrunk.

You May Not Know

- IWU played its first organized football game in 1887, when its colors were navy blue and gray (as opposed to green and white, first reported as the school colors in 1898).
- Local businesspeople and alumni raised $600,000 in 1920 to keep IWU from moving from Bloomington to Springfield.
- In 1855, IWU suspended operations for two years due to low enrollment, but President Oliver Munsell was able to turn the school prospects around and increase enrollment.

Distinguished Alumni

Bill Damaschke, head of animation and creative production for Dreamworks; Richard Jenkins, American character actor; Carl Marvel, "The Father of Polymer Chemistry;" Wayne Messmer, "The Voice of the Chicago Cubs;" Christine Moore, actress; Brian Udovich, producer of *A Necessary Death* and co-producer of *The Wackness*.

Admissions and Financial Aid

IWU has early action and regular decision. School of Theatre applicants are not eligible for early action because decisions are made after all of the auditions have finished, which is after the EA deadline. The school has its own application but also accepts the Common Application (with supplement) and the Universal College Application (with supplement). There is no application fee for any of these.

There are two merit-based scholarships and one merit award. The Alumni Scholarship awards between $2,000 and $15,000 per year, and the Alumni Fine Arts Scholarship awards between $2,000 and $12,000. The merit award is for international students, covering anywhere between $1,000 per year and full tuition.

INDIANA UNIVERSITY - BLOOMINGTON

Overview

With over 32,000 undergraduate students, Indiana University Bloomington is a very large public college located in the quintessential college town of Bloomington, Indiana. Despite its overwhelming size, the university carries a mid-western community feel and is oozing with school spirit specifically surrounding the men's basketball team, the Hoosiers. A research university, IU is stronger in its humanities programs than in the hard sciences.

Fifty miles southwest of Indianapolis, Bloomington is often described as an excellent "college town." The campus features architecture ranging from brick to Gothic and even has a creek that runs through it. The school boasts one of the top five university museums in the country, designed by I.M. Pei.

Academics

With strengths in its business, music, communication, and culture programs, IU offers 436 majors, providing students a wide range of academic possibilities. There is no single set of requirements that apply to all IU students; rather, degree requirements vary by major, but most include some sort of math/science, humanities, social sciences, writing, and foreign language prerequisite.

Most students report the academic environment as surprisingly laid back. Despite the large student body, professors are quite accessible to students and most students seem to revel in the collaborative, rather than competitive, nature of classes. "I've never seen any overt competition. I have seen students who've finished their homework staying up all night to help another student," says a student. In order to graduate, students must complete between 120-128 credit hours (averaging 15-16 hours per term and maintaining a minimum of 12 hours). Students must also maintain a minimum 2.0 GPA.

Special academic opportunities at IU include the chance to become a Cox Research scholar. Forty exemplary high school students are selected for this program each year to work on research and scholarly activities, often related to their major, under a faculty mentor. The scholarship, which provides full-tuition over four years, is valued at more than $60,000 and includes a research stipend.

IU's Honors College, which offers a range of small, challenging courses, attracts highly motivated students who are seeking an enriched academic and social experience. The program offers opportunities to work closely with IU's top faculty in addition to a variety of extracurricular and service programs. Another special opportunity for freshmen is the school's Intensive Freshman Seminar, a three-week program that occurs before the start of the fall semester.

IU also offers study-abroad opportunities through more than 100 IU-administered and co-sponsored programs and more than 250 IU-approved programs. In some cases, IU financial aid may be applied toward studying abroad. The Office of Overseas Study also administers more than $100,000 in need- and merit-based scholarships for study abroad.

Indiana University has a strong advising program and the school states that academic advisors are "the single most useful planning guides that you have available to you at IU to help you plan and make the best decisions for you and your unique circumstances and educational goals." The college provides support for students' post-college plans through the Career Development Center, which offers career advising, job and internship listings, and job fairs. "The career office has been extremely helpful," comments a student. "I found two summer internships by working with them."

INDIANA UNIVERSITY BLOOMINGTON

Four-year public
Founded: 1820
Bloomington, IN
Medium city
Pop. 81,381

Address:
107 South Indiana Avenue
Bloomington, IN
47405-7000

Admissions:
812-855-0661

Financial Aid:
812-855-0321

iuadmit@indiana.edu

www.iub.edu

INDIANA UNIVERSITY BLOOMINGTON

Students
Total enrollment: 42,133
Undergrads: 32,371
Freshmen: 7,962
Part-time students: 4%
From out-of-state: 32%
Male/Female: 49%/51%
Live on-campus: 38%
Off-campus employment rating: Good
Caucasian: 74%
African American: 4%
Hispanic: 4%
Asian / Pacific Islander: 4%
Native American: 0%
Mixed (2+ ethnicities): 3%
International: 11%

Academics
Calendar: Semester
Student/faculty ratio: 18:1
Class size 9 or fewer: 11%
Class size 10-29: 53%
Class size 30-49: 18%
Class size 50-99: 11%
Class size 100 or more: 7%
Returning freshmen: 88%
Six-year graduation rate: 75%

Most Popular Majors
Finance
Management
Accounting

Admissions
Applicants: 35,247
Accepted: 26,228
Acceptance rate: 74.4%
Average GPA: 3.6
ACT range: 24-29
SAT Math range: 540-660
SAT Reading range: 510-620
SAT Writing range: 6-27
Top 10% of class: 34%
Top 25% of class: 70%
Top 50% of class: 95%

Student Life

There are a plethora of student organizations to stimulate campus involvement. Some of the most popular of campus activities are the Apparel Merchandising Organization, Cinephile Film Arts Organizations, Student Philanthropy Organization, and IU's Cigarette Clean Up Organization.

The university also hosts a number of important traditional activities each year, the biggest of which is the Little 500 Weekend, a men's bike race. This event is considered one of the biggest intramural events in the country with over 20,000 attendees. It also includes a women's bike race, a regatta, and shows by musical artists. Proceeds are used to give aid to working students.

IU shows their philanthropic spirit with Dance Marathon and IU Sing. Dance Marathon, a 36-hour dance competition, occurs every November to raise money for Riley Hospital for Children in Indianapolis; while IU Sing, a scholarship fundraiser, features students from all across campus who write, produce, and choreograph song-and-dance skits.

Unlike a lot of other schools of its size, IU has a strong but not overly dominant Greek life. Less than 20 percent of students join the 39 fraternities and 33 sororities. "For those who are in fraternities and sororities, they are the most important thing in their lives. For those who aren't, you don't really notice them," says a student.

Athletics are an integral part of the IU experience with 22 teams (10 men's, 12 women's) that compete in Division I. While the soccer teams and women's golf and tennis teams are competitive, men's basketball is practically a religion on campus and students take their tailgating and sportswear very seriously. "Even if the team isn't that strong, everyone goes to the Hoosier basketball games," explains a student. Intramural sports for every skill level are also very popular and run the gamut of activities from indoor soccer to sports trivia.

Bloomington is consistently ranked as one of the best college towns in the nation. Its layout makes it favorable for students who must walk to their destinations. The area surrounding campus offers plenty of dining, shopping, and outdoor activities. Road trips to Indianapolis, St. Louis, and Chicago are also quite popular.

While all freshmen are guaranteed housing, most students choose to move off campus after their first year. Dorms feature an "academic floor" for students who must maintain a minimum GPA and show that they are focused on their studies.

Student Body

Because IU is such a large school, pretty much all "types" of students can find their niche. Overall, there seems to be a well-struck balance between students who come for the social aspects of the college, and those who come to work hard. "If you want to be a partier, you can," remarks a student. "But if you want to focus on your future, you can do that too."

With 17 percent ethnic minorities and 32 percent of students hailing from out of state, IU is a moderately diverse ethnic and geographic campus.

The university works hard to maintain a tolerant viewpoint toward all types of diversity, despite the conservative viewpoints that come with the campus's location near the Bible Belt.

You May Not Know

- IU was one of the first universities to admit women in 1867: its first female student, Sarah Parke Morrison, became the first female professor five years later.
- The Kinsey Institute, a Research Center for Sex, Gender, and Reproduction on campus, contains the largest pornography collection in the world.
- Even though it is a disputed fact by the college, the Herman Wells library is rumored to sink over an inch every year due to the weight of all the books that the architect did not take into account in its construction.

Distinguished Alumni

Evan Bayh, former U.S. Senator and Governor of Indiana; Larry Bird, legendary NBA player; Kevin Kline, actor; Jimmy Wales, co-founder of Wikipedia; James D. Watson, Nobel Prize in Medicine award winner for his groundbreaking work on the DNA structure.

Admissions and Financial Aid

Although there are no required essays or letters of recommendation needed as a part of IU's application process, the university's admissions board will consider them if they are submitted. Preference for acceptance into the school is given to Indiana residents who rank in the top 40 percent of their class or to non-Indiana residents who rank in the top 30 percent.

IU awards millions of dollars to hard-working students in academic, international, and transfer scholarships. Students who submit their applications by November 1 are automatically considered for the university's Automated Academic scholarships. These include the IU Excellence award, which provides $9,000 for four years, and is given to Indiana residents with a 3.8 or above and a minimum SAT score of 1340; and the IU Distinction Scholarship, which provides the same financial compensation for students who meet the same requirements but live out of state. The university's most prestigious scholarship, the Wells Scholarship, covers full tuition, fees, and a living stipend for four years. To be eligible for the Wells Scholarships, students must be nominated by a high school teacher or counselor.

INDIANA UNIVERSITY BLOOMINGTON

Highlights

Admissions Criteria
Academic criteria:
Grades: ☆ ☆ ☆
Difficulty of class schedule: ☆ ☆ ☆
Class rank: ☆ ☆ ☆
Standardized test scores: ☆ ☆
Teacher recommendations: ☆
Personal statement: ☆
Non-academic criteria considered:
Interview
Extracurricular activities
Special talents, interests, abilities
Character/personal qualities
Volunteer work
Work experience
Geographical location
Minority affiliation
Alumni relationship

Deadlines
Early Action: No
Early Decision: No
Regular Action: Rolling admissions
Common Application: Not accepted

Financial Aid
In-state tuition: $10,209
Out-of-state tuition: $32,350
Room: Varies
Board: Varies
Books: $1,500
Freshmen receiving need-based aid: 45%
Undergrads rec. need-based aid: 44%
Avg. % of need met by financial aid: 87%
Avg. aid package (freshmen): $12,218
Avg. aid package (undergrads): $11,747
Avg. debt upon graduation: $28,769

School Spirit
Mascot: Hoosiers
Colors: Cream and crimson
Song: *Indiana, Our Indiana*

IOWA STATE UNIVERSITY

IOWA STATE UNIVERSITY

Four-year public
Founded: 1858
Ames, IA
Large town
Pop. 59,042

Address:
100 Enrollment Ser-
vices Center
Ames, IA
50011

Admissions:
800-262-3810

Financial Aid:
800-478-2998

admissions@iastate.
edu

www.iastate.edu

Overview

Taking a walk through Iowa State University's 1,795-acre campus, you'll find much to support its status as one of the 25 most beautiful college campuses in the nation—the leafy green park-like Central Lawn; the Reiman Gardens, one of the best public rose gardens in the United States; or perhaps the largest collection of public art on any campus in the country.

It could be easy to underestimate Iowa State. A very large public university found in a small town, located in one of the most homogenous states in the country—you might think the school is too big, the town is too small, and there's just not much flavor to be found. However you would be overlooking much that the university has to offer: the renowned academic programs, the rich history of scientific research, the Big 12 athletic powerhouse, and the friendliness that a Midwestern locale provides. Home of the first electronic computer, George Washington Carver's innovations, and one of the leaders of the women's suffrage movement, ISU is not trapped in the past but rather looking forward to the future.

Though the college town of Ames, Iowa has a population of just 59,000, residents say it is full of small-town charm, yet alive with the heartbeat of a big city. And located 30 miles north of Des Moines, students aren't too far from a big city. Iowa State isn't cosmopolitan by any stretch of the imagination, but if you're fond of smaller communities, rich with cultural and historical gems, it could be just the place for you.

Academics

Iowa State has 100 majors, offered through seven distinct colleges. Its academic quality ranks the university in the top 50 public colleges by *U.S. News & World Report*. The strongest programs and departments include aerospace engineering, agriculture, counseling, engineering, architecture, chemistry, higher education administration, industrial and manufacturing systems engineering, marketing, statistics, and veterinary medicine. Iowa State is recognized internationally for its comprehensive research programs.

Iowa State students complete general education requirements, which include a series of courses in the arts and humanities, natural sciences, mathematics, and social sciences. The academic rigor is as to be expected for a public university, as are large classes, especially when fulfilling the GenEds—nine percent of classes have over 100 students. However, according to the students, professors are "easier to connect with than you might expect."

Many individual colleges within the university have led forays into new academic fields. The College of Agriculture and Life Sciences—described by students as "nationally recognized"—is currently enjoying the highest enrollment of the past 30 years and is leading the nation with the development of a new, one-of-a-kind major, Global Resource Systems.

Other colleges are of equal notoriety. The College of Veterinary Medicine was the first public veterinary college in the nation and sponsors a Summer Scholars Program that allows students to pursue unique mentor-supervised research projects. The College of Engineering is home to the nation's first agricultural engineering major, which served as the model for all subsequent universities; it also boasts the Ames Laboratory, the only U.S. Department of Energy research laboratory located on a university campus. The Ames Laboratory has received 17 R&D 100 awards (nicknamed the "Oscar of Science") and according to the laboratory, "produces the purest rare-earth materials used in academic and industrial research today."

About four percent of Iowa State students decide to study abroad—though the number isn't great, it ranks high for a research university. Students choose from 54 countries and are eligible for ISU financial aid.

ISU Career Services provides a network for students and alumni to explore careers. According to *U.S. News & World Report*, Iowa State is one of 10 public universities nationwide commended for providing outstanding internships and co-op work opportunities. "There are career fairs especially focused on areas like business, engineering, and agriculture so you can find a job or internship that's related to your field," notes a student.

Student Life

Iowa State is home to 800 student organizations. The possibilities are virtually endless, with arts, religious, academic, service, and multicultural groups and more. All these are complemented by the Greek community, which is very active—there are 32 fraternities and 20 sororities. With 15 percent of men and 16 percent of women going Greek, it's no surprise that for the past four years, the ISU Greek community was named best large Greek community in the Midwest by the Association for Fraternal Leadership and Values. A student quoted in the *ISU Daily* says, "students can socialize without having to do drugs or alcohol."

Students often hang out at Memorial Union, complete with food options, a bowling alley, and an arcade. And ISU AfterDark is a student group that plans free late night activities on Friday nights. Other special events on campus include VISHEA, a week-long festival held each spring, and Homecoming, which features traditions such as the "Yell Like Hell!" cheering competition, firework displays, and innumerable tailgate parties.

One of the biggest draws of Iowa State University is its athletic prominence (and dominance). ISU is home to 18 Division I teams. Students should expect to be swayed by the Cyclone success—the football team has earned 10 trips to bowl games since 1971; the women's basketball team has won three conference titles; the men's wrestling team has been conference champions 199 times; and the university boasts the Most Dominant College Mascot on Earth according to CBS Sportsline.com. Students who are itching to get in the arena—besides cheering for the varsity athletes—will find over 80 intramural and club sport teams. *Muscle and Fitness* magazine ranked Iowa State as having the third most-fit student body in the nation. "If you're not playing on a team, then you're rooting for one," remarks a student.

If you want to venture around campus or into Ames, you can hop on a CyRide or Moonlight Express (weekend) bus. Though not a major city, Ames draws performers such as Kenny Chesney, Dave Matthews, and Widespread Panic, hosts many cultural festivals, and provides acres of parks and bike paths. No, you won't find Bright Lights and Big City in Ames, but just remember that the city was named the second most-livable small city in the nation. "Ames is pretty quiet, but the people are friendly, and there's enough to keep us busy," one student comments.

About 86 percent of freshmen live on campus—fewer upperclassmen—so as a first-year student, you'll have a supportive newbie community and can choose to live in residence halls or apartment complexes.

IOWA STATE UNIVERSITY

Highlights

Students
Total enrollment: 30,748
Undergrads: 25,555
Freshmen: 6,375
Part-time students: 5%
From out-of-state: 36%
From public schools: 91%
Male/Female: 56%/44%
Live on-campus: 37%
In fraternities: 15%
In sororities: 16%
Off-campus employment rating: Good
Caucasian: 78%
African American: 3%
Hispanic: 4%
Asian / Pacific Islander: 3%
Native American: 0%
Mixed (2+ ethnicities): 2%
International: 8%

Academics
Calendar: Semester
Student/faculty ratio: 18:1
Class size 9 or fewer: 10%
Class size 10-29: 48%
Class size 30-49: 20%
Class size 50-99: 13%
Class size 100 or more: 9%
Returning freshmen: 86%
Six-year graduation rate: 71%
Graduates who immediately enter career related to major: 74%

Most Popular Majors
Mechanical engineering
Finance
Marketing

Admissions
Applicants: 16,539
Accepted: 13,648
Acceptance rate: 82.5%
Average GPA: 3.6
ACT range: 22-28
SAT Math range: 530-680
SAT Reading range: 460-620
SAT Writing range: Not reported
Top 10% of class: 26%
Top 25% of class: 56%
Top 50% of class: 90%

375

IOWA STATE UNIVERSITY

Admissions Criteria

Academic criteria:
Grades: ☆ ☆ ☆
Difficulty of class schedule: ☆ ☆ ☆
Class rank: ☆ ☆ ☆
Standardized test scores: ☆ ☆ ☆
Teacher recommendations: ☆
Personal statement: ☆
Non-academic criteria considered:
Interview
Extracurricular activities
Special talents, interests, abilities
Character/personal qualities
Volunteer work
Work experience
Geographical location

Deadlines

Early Action: No
Early Decision: No
Regular Action: Rolling admissions
Common Application: Accepted

Financial Aid

In-state tuition: $7,726
Out-of-state tuition: $20,278
Room: Varies
Board: Varies
Books: $1,046
Freshmen receiving need-based aid: 57%
Undergrads rec. need-based aid: 54%
Avg. % of need met by financial aid: 82%
Avg. aid package (freshmen): $12,000
Avg. aid package (undergrads): $11,821
Avg. debt upon graduation: $30,374

School Spirit

Mascot: Cy
Colors: Cardinal and gold
Song: *ISU Fights*

Student Body

All 50 states and 110 countries are represented by members of the ISU student body. However, the levels of ethnic and geographic diversity are low, with only a 12 percent ethnic minority population, and two-thirds of the student body hailing from Iowa. It's fabulous to be a single female at ISU, with women representing 44 percent of the undergraduate student population.

Students say that while every type of student is represented, a commonality among everyone is a "Midwestern friendliness" and an "open" spirit. It's common to see people wave hello or strike up a conversation on the way to class.

You May Not Know

- The Campanile bell tower is a major symbol of ISU. Folklore states that you aren't a true Iowa State student until you have been kissed underneath the Campanile at the stroke of midnight.
- The Cyclone has been the ISU mascot since 1895, when underdog Iowa State defeated Northwestern in a football game. The *Chicago Tribune* reported that "Northwestern might as well have tried to play football with an Iowa cyclone as with the Iowa team it met yesterday"—and the nickname stuck.
- According to the university's Ames Laboratory, the world's first computer was invented on campus by professor John Atanasoff and graduate student Clifford Berry in the late 1930s.

Distinguished Alumni

George Washington Carver, botanist and inventor; Carrie Chapman Catt, leader of the women's suffrage movement; Ted Kooser, Pulitzer Prize winner; Nawal El Moutawakel, first African and Muslim woman to win an Olympic Gold Medal; Henry A. Wallace, U.S. Vice President; Tom Whitney, inventor of the pocket calculator.

Admissions and Financial Aid

Admission decisions are based on the Regent Admission Index (RAI), which takes into account four factors: ACT composite score, high school GPA, high school percentile rank, and the number of high school courses in core subject areas. The RAI equation adds 2 X ACT score + 1 X high school rank + 20 X high school GPA + 5 X number of core courses completed. Students who have completed the minimum high school course requirements and achieve an RAI score of at least 245 are automatically offered admission to Iowa State.

Iowa State provides a number of automatic four-year awards for incoming freshmen, based on academic records. These awards do not require a separate application. As they are based solely on a calculation of your academic record, you can find out how much aid you are currently eligible to receive by going to the ISU admissions website. Other merit awards require extra submissions.

ITHACA COLLEGE

Overview

During the fall before this private, mid-sized upstate New York campus is blanketed by foot upon foot of snow, Ithaca students can admire the foliage along 11 miles of walkways and 700 acres of hillside campus overlooking the breathtaking Cayuga Lake.

To many Ithaca College students, the grass may *not* be greener on the other side of Ithaca, namely, at Cornell University. Despite its status as a mid-range undergraduate school, Ithaca College has nationally preeminent music, communications, and health science programs that are reflected back in Ithaca's thriving artistic, athletic, and interconnected campus community.

The surrounding area is nature at her best. Off-campus highlights include the grandeur of waterfalls, lakes, and gorges that present almost endless opportunities for recreation. But with winter temperatures in the teens, Ithaca College must be thought of as a paradise for the cold-blooded—but warm at heart—student.

Academics

Ithaca offers a menu of more than 100 majors and 60 minors. The general education requirements include courses in self and society, science, math, language, and visual and performing arts. If students don't score high enough on the AP exam or the college's assessment test, they must also take a writing course.

Founded as a conservatory of music in 1892, Ithaca continues to mark itself among the strongest music programs nationwide. Faculty members and live-in residents meet with students on a weekly basis for both private lessons and repertoire class meetings. Among the 24 musical ensembles are chamber groups, a chamber orchestra, a symphony orchestra, six vocal ensembles, and three jazz ensembles. Between these groups, Ithaca puts on over 300 concerts each year. "Whether you are a music major or not, your Ithaca experience will be filled with music," says a student.

Ithaca was the first college to have its own TV channel. According to one student, the School of Communications "is nationally recognized and attracts top employers." Communications students work locally on innumerable ventures involving community service, consulting, and internships, and they are often presented with opportunities to travel internationally.

Students can run talk-shows or disc-jockey either of the two campus radio stations, WICB and VIC. WICB is highly acclaimed, having won the MTVU Woodie Award for the Best College Radio Station. *The Ithacan*—a paper whose staff gets extensive hands-on knowledge of filming and reporting—has won collegiate journalism awards, including a five-time acceptance run of the Associated Collegiate Press' National Pacemaker Award.

While taking a semester at the James B. Pendleton Center in Los Angeles, students can penetrate the entertainment business through internships with such big-names as Universal Pictures, Atlantic Records, and the *Los Angeles Times*. Other students might opt to study in a national capital city, either London or Washington, DC, with guaranteed internships.

The School of Health Science and Human Performance is most appreciated for its "very strong" occupational sciences/occupational therapy and clinical health studies/physical therapy programs, but it produces a number of future therapists, researchers, educators, and athletic professionals. Students enter the field to work or complete internships across the country, securing placements in over 1,700 organizations.

Ithaca students can take a Washington Semester that is individually tailored to provide internships and other experiences relevant to their majors. Ithaca invites students to participate in study-abroad programs established in over 50 countries around the world. Students also have the opportunity to take classes in nearby Wells College and Cornell University.

ITHACA COLLEGE

Four-year private
Founded: 1892
Ithaca, NY
Large town
Pop. 30,054

Address:
953 Danby Road
Ithaca, NY
14850

Admissions:
800-429-4274

Financial Aid:
800-429-4275

admission@ithaca.edu

www.ithaca.edu

ITHACA COLLEGE

Students
Total enrollment: 6,759
Undergrads: 6,281
Freshmen: 1,853
Part-time students: 2%
From out-of-state: 56%
From public schools: 82%
Male/Female: 44%/56%
Live on-campus: 70%
Off-campus employment rating: Fair
Caucasian: 70%
African American: 4%
Hispanic: 6%
Asian / Pacific Islander: 3%
Native American: 0%
Mixed (2+ ethnicities): 3%
International: 2%

Academics
Calendar: Semester
Student/faculty ratio: 11:1
Class size 9 or fewer: 15%
Class size 10-29: 67%
Class size 30-49: 13%
Class size 50-99: 3%
Class size 100 or more: 1%
Returning freshmen: 84%
Six-year graduation rate: 77%

Most Popular Majors
Business administration
Television/radio
Physical therapy

Admissions
Applicants: 13,813
Accepted: 8,963
Acceptance rate: 64.9%
Placed on wait list: 1,887
Average GPA: Not reported
ACT range: Not reported
SAT Math range: 530-640
SAT Reading range: 520-630
SAT Writing range: 7-33
Top 10% of class: 33%
Top 25% of class: 69%
Top 50% of class: 92%

Many Ithaca alumni continue on to successful careers with celebrated symphonies and opera companies; others can be spotted on Broadway. "When you're looking for a job, you'll find that alums are in most every top area of music," comments a student.

Student Life

There are over 180 student groups, ranging from the Bureau of Concerts to IC Feminists to IC Habitat for Humanity. As for volunteerism, nothing says it better than Ithaca's tagline "You can't spell service without 'IC.'" In many instances at Ithaca, co-curricular activities complement students' areas of study. Communications students can work on the college newspaper, TV station, or radio stations. Business students can join American Marketing Association or the Core Trading Consultants. And according to one student, "the pre-professional clubs are great for networking."

The Student Activities Board is committed to bringing arts and culture to campus. Since many students are aspiring artists, the Board doesn't have to look far for talent. Notable are the film screenings. Ithaca hosts such events as the Finger Lakes Environmental Film Festival and the Out of the Closet and Onto the Screen film series. Artists at Ithaca—students and faculty—have ample opportunities to contribute to student life by showcasing their art at Handwerker Gallery or producing theater performances.

To give incoming freshmen the opportunity to make friends before the year begins, Ithaca provides four Jumpstart programs. These include Community Plunge (public service), Experience Connections (camping on Finger Lakes Trail), Lead-In (leadership through a challenge course), and Sustainable Community Challenge (studying the neighboring bioregion including a Native American farm).

Although the origin of the nickname Ithaca "Bombers" has historically been a point of contention, there is little argument that the 26 athletics teams to which it refers are among the strongest competitors in NCAA Division III. The Bombers boast an impressive 15 NCAA championships, including three National Football Championships. You would be unlikely to find an Ithaca student who would dare skip the Cortaca Jug, a matchup with rival SUNY Cortland. Other strong teams are women's crew and women's soccer.

Ithaca constructed a $65.5 million athletics center which includes outdoor tennis courts, an indoor pool, and an indoor track. There are about 30 fitness classes available each semester, about 35 registered sports clubs, and a whopping 60 club sports. Furthermore, the Outdoor Recreation Equipment Center hooks up Ithaca students with climbing wall memberships as well as camping, skiing, and other rental equipment. "We take full advantage of the outdoors here," one student notes, "even in the dead of winter."

Students looking for a party head to an off-campus house or apartment on Prospect Street. And those looking for an even bigger college scene attend nearby Cornell fraternity parties, since Ithaca itself has no Greek institutions of its own. Students are careful about drinking and smoking in dormitories and around campus, since campus security is "pretty strict about underage drinking," as one student explains.

Off campus, students can take a cab or the T-Cat bus downtown to the Ithaca Center or the Commons. Both the Center and the

Commons have an array of restaurants and bars. For those students who want breakfast early, there is a delivery service that students say is "well used." It runs to both dormitories and off-campus homes until 3 a.m. The downtown Commons also hosts various annual festivals, including Chili Fest, Beer Fest and Apple Fest.

Seventy percent of students live on campus in any of the 27 residence halls and two apartment complexes. Undergraduates are guaranteed housing throughout their four years, but seniors have the option of living off campus. Ithaca contains four major residential areas. Many of these can be subdivided among Ithaca's noteworthy Specialty Housing programs, which include Sustainably Conscious living, Honors housing, Outdoor Adventure Learning housing, and freshman-only housing.

Student Body

Ethnic diversity at Ithaca is not particularly impressive, but—according to students—you will find an "unusual balance between the jocks and artsy types" due to the prominent athletic and music programs. There is a moderate level of minority students, 16 percent. Fifty-six percent of the student body is composed of New York outsiders representing almost every state, as well as 78 nations.

As for religion, there is considerable diversity, including active Catholic and Jewish communities. As an extension of such religious involvements, there is a "Kosher Kitchen."

You May Not Know

- Ithaca was founded when a local violin teacher rented four rooms and began instructing eight students.
- The alternative *Buzzsaw Magazine* has won numerous national awards among college publications, including an award for "Best Political Commentary" in 2005.
- Ithaca's School of Business is a pioneer of sustainability, becoming the first business school in the world to achieve LEED Platinum Certification.

Distinguished Alumni

Michelle Federer, theater and film actress, Broadway's *Wicked*; Barbara Gaines, Emmy Award-winning *Late Show* with David Letterman Executive Producer; Robert Iger, The Walt Disney Company President and CEO; Chris Regan, *Daily Show* Emmy Award-winning writer; Jessica Savitch, first female network news anchor.

Admissions and Financial Aid

Almost 65 percent of applicants are accepted to Ithaca, but the pool of applicants continues to rise and selectivity varies by specific school of admittance. Applicants use the Common Application, but some programs have special requirements such as an interview, audition, or portfolio, including but not limited to music, theater, art, business, and physical therapy. According to the college, it is looking for, "involvement, creativity, and personal achievement."

Ithaca offers merit-based scholarships that generally range from $7,500 to $10,000. Many of these are renewable, and some require a separate application from the admissions application.

ITHACA COLLEGE

Highlights

Admissions Criteria
Academic criteria:
Grades: ☆ ☆ ☆
Difficulty of class schedule: ☆ ☆ ☆
Class rank: ☆ ☆
Standardized test scores: ☆
Teacher recommendations: ☆ ☆
Personal statement: ☆ ☆
Non-academic criteria considered:
Interview
Extracurricular activities
Special talents, interests, abilities
Character/personal qualities
Volunteer work
Work experience
State of residency
Minority affiliation
Alumni relationship

Deadlines
Early Action: December 1
Early Decision: November 1
Regular Action: February 1 (final)
Notification of admission by: April 15
Common Application: Accepted

Financial Aid
In-state tuition: $38,400
Out-of-state tuition: $38,400
Room: $7,480
Board: $6,420
Books: $1,458
Freshmen receiving need-based aid: 72%
Undergrads rec. need-based aid: 69%
Avg. % of need met by financial aid: 86%
Avg. aid package (freshmen): $31,780
Avg. aid package (undergrads): $30,772

School Spirit
Mascot: Bomber
Colors: Blue and gold
Song: *Ithaca Forever*

JAMES MADISON UNIVERSITY

Overview

James Madison University, named after the fourth American President, is a large public university located in Harrisonburg, Virginia, known for its excellent business and education programs. Students—who call themselves the "Dukes"—are offered a wide range of educational opportunities as is evidenced by JMU's foundation in liberal arts, inclusion of professional and pre-professional programs, and its emphasis on learning experiences outside the classroom. Located on a 696-acre campus, clean and classic architectural lines with red roofs and gray stone characterize the buildings.

Harrisonburg is considered to be the shopping hub of Shenandoah Valley. In addition to national retailers, there are thrift stores, antique shops, and storefront boutiques in the historic downtown area. Although the city is currently undergoing a revitalization effort, the mix of the historic and new architecture is both quaint and quirky.

For those who enjoy the great outdoors, there are plenty of trails, slopes, rivers, and forests. For those who prefer city life, in addition to an active night scene, there are a variety of food options, ranging from traditional Southern food to ethnic cuisine. Artsy types will appreciate the many small coffee shops, galleries, and museums which serve as incubators for creativity.

JMU has thousands of students and although there are many opportunities for students to find their own niche, one can sometimes feel like just another face in the crowd. Because many JMU students live off campus, the on-campus vibe is definitely affected. However, if you are one who sees "big" as a world of options to explore and challenges to conquer, then James Madison University may be the perfect school for you.

Academics

With 86 majors offered, the JMU student truly enjoys a variety of choices. All students are required to complete the General Education Core, which is divided into five clusters. Cluster titles include "Skills for the 21st Century," which places an emphasis on reasoning, writing, and speaking skills, and "Individuals in the Human Community," which challenges students to learn more about their own identity and to see themselves as members of other communities.

As is typical for public universities, there are large lecture classes, especially in lower-level classes. However, students say that "for the most part, professors are accessible, some more than others." Students have many opportunities to further their education by doing research, enrolling in a practicum, finding an internship, or obtaining a student teaching position. Around 80 percent of JMU students take advantage of at least one of these academic options.

Although the programs at JMU offer students a strong background in their specific field, a few programs—specifically business, education, and music—deserve increased attention. The business program is ranked third among public schools and fourth among undergraduate business schools in the U.S. by *Business Week* for return investment. This major is divided into various specialties, which range from hospitality and tourism management to quantitative finances. Juniors in the College of Business have the unique opportunity to enroll in an integrated course that is team-taught by professors from all of the business disciplines. One participant explains that through this course, students "see all aspects of business through the lens of different disciplines."

The College of Education claims to produce "more teachers each year than any other Virginia college or university." In addition to traditional student-teaching assignments, a field-based approach to teacher preparation enables students to gain exposure to teachers and school children under the guidance and instruction of JMU professors.

Music attracts many JMU students as well. There are traditional music-education concentrations like instrumental and vocal in addition to a music industry program in which students enroll in a variety of music and business courses.

The Honors Program presents a unique opportunity for students to explore their intellectual passions at an accelerated pace. There are three honors tracks. Track I is for incoming freshman who are enrolled in an honors study for their bachelor's degree program. All classes are honors courses, and they are required to complete a senior honors project. Students graduate as Honors Scholars. Track II is available for students who are recruited into the program. Track III entails the completion of a senior honors project, open to all students in their junior year with a cumulative GPA of 3.5 or higher. Students graduate with distinction in their field.

JMU students also enjoy a variety of learning opportunities in other countries such as Belgium, China, Spain, and the United Kingdom. According to the *Chronicle of Higher Education*, JMU was ranked second in the country among master's level schools for the number of students who study abroad.

Life after JMU is filled with opportunities. Of the students who enter the work force within six months of graduation, 81 percent are successfully employed in a field related to their major. Roughly 32 percent of students choose to pursue a graduate degree.

Student Life

The college's 300 student organizations include Amnesty International, the Anthropology Club, and Breakdance Club. Unique to JMU is Taylor Down Under, or TDU, which is a creative space for students to hang out. It is full of comfy couches, pool tables, and places to relax. TDU also has its own coffee bar. Some scheduled programs at TDU include Late Night, during which students can enjoy performances and activities, and Open Poetry.

Annual school events include James Madison Week, which is focused around the achievements of the college's namesake. During Masterpiece Season, acclaimed performers are invited to sing, act, dance, and play instruments. Exhibits featuring the work of artists from around the world are also on display at the Sawhill Gallery. During International Week, a thematic focus is chosen and the music, food, dances, and cultural activities coherent with that theme are provided at various locations on campus. "You can literally eat food from around the world," one student comments.

JMU is the home of a thriving Greek community with 24 sororities and fraternities on campus. The *Greek Vine* is an online publication that serves as the center of information for all Greek events. "If you're in a fraternity or sorority, it's a big deal. If not, then it's not," notes a student. Only sororities are housed on campus.

With 18 intercollegiate athletic programs competing in the Division I level of the NCAA, die-hard JMU fans decked in purple and gold are serious competitors. Indeed, the football team recently won the Division IAA title while the Women's Field Hockey Team won the Division I national title. Intramural teams range from fly fishing, sand volleyball, and Ultimate Frisbee to other traditional sports.

Off campus, students take advantage of the outdoor activities in the surrounding area and head to downtown Harrisonburg for shopping and eating. "It's a small college town," explains a student,

JAMES MADISON UNIVERSITY

Highlights

Students
Total enrollment: 19,927
Undergrads: 18,107
Freshmen: 4,028
From out-of-state: 32%
Male/Female: 41%/59%
Live on-campus: 35%
In fraternities: 10%
In sororities: 12%
Off-campus employment rating: Good
Caucasian: 79%
African American: 4%
Hispanic: 4%
Asian / Pacific Islander: 5%
Native American: 0%
Mixed (2+ ethnicities): 3%
International: 2%

Academics
Calendar: Semester
Student/faculty ratio: 16:1
Class size 9 or fewer: 10%
Class size 10-29: 55%
Class size 30-49: 22%
Class size 50-99: 9%
Class size 100 or more: 4%
Six-year graduation rate: 80%
Graduates who immediately go to graduate school: 32%

Most Popular Majors
Health sciences
Kinesiology
Communication studies

Admissions
Applicants: 22,648
Accepted: 14,392
Acceptance rate: 63.5%
Placed on wait list: 3,335
Enrolled from wait list: 7
Average GPA: Not reported
ACT range: Not reported
SAT Math range: 530-630
SAT Reading range: 520-620
SAT Writing range: 4-31
Top 10% of class: 28%
Top 25% of class: 44%
Top 50% of class: 98%

381

College Profiles

JAMES MADISON UNIVERSITY

"but the people are friendly and with some creativity, you can keep yourself occupied."

No alcohol is allowed in freshman dorms and JMU enforces a three-strike policy for underage drinking on campus. Most parties occur in upperclassman apartments, many of which are off campus. Only freshmen are guaranteed housing so most of the university population lives near campus in the housing intended for students. Students can opt for special housing such as the Living and Learning Center for Honors Program students and Substance Free Housing.

Student Body

Although it began as a woman's industrial college, JMU has been co-educational since 1966. Virginia itself has both a liberal and conservative region and "we range the gamut from liberal to conservative," says a student. Although relatively diverse in opinions and ideas, JMU is not very diverse in terms of ethnicity. All ethnic groups combined account for 16 percent of the population. Geographic diversity could be considered moderate, with 32 percent of the student body hailing from out of state. However, only two percent of students are international.

You May Not Know

- JMU students are referred to as "Dukes" in honor of the university's second president, Samuel Page Duke.
- JMU is ranked 21st in the nation among large colleges and universities with volunteers in a U.S. service program.
- Based on results from student surveys, JMU was ranked by the Princeton Review as third in the nation for the best campus food.

Distinguished Alumni

Marcia Angel, former Executive Editor, *The New England Journal of Medicine*; Barbara Hall, movie/TV writer and producer; Charles Haley, all pro-NFL linebacker.

Admissions and Financial Aid

Students have the option of applying to JMU through early action or regular decision. To be admitted early, students must have "superior" academic achievement, although 35 to 42 percent of students deferred were later admitted in the past two years. There is no competitive advantage to applying either early or regular.

According to the admissions office, the order of importance for criteria begins with high school academics. Admissions personnel also consider academic achievement, test scores, secondary school report forms, extracurricular activities, and the optional personal statement.

Financial aid is awarded based on the number of credit hours a student enrolls in, and there are many work opportunities available. Merit-based scholarships are awarded and include six Thomas and Karyn Dingledine Scholarships for full in-state tuition and 350 Madison Achievement Scholarships of $2,000-$3,500 per year.

JOHNS HOPKINS UNIVERSITY

JOHNS HOPKINS UNIVERSITY

Four-year private
Founded: 1876
Baltimore, MD
Major city
Pop. 619,493

Address:
3400 North Charles
Street
Baltimore, MD
21218

Admissions:
410-516-8171

Financial Aid:
410-516-8028

gotojhu@jhu.edu

www.jhu.edu

Overview

Johns Hopkins University is a serious school for serious students. This medium-sized private college has an impressive academic reputation, ranking in the top 15 national universities according to *U.S. News & World Report*. Thirty-three Nobel Laureates grace the ranks of JHU faculty members and graduates. JHU is a great fit for students who cannot wait to jump into significant research, as research opportunities are abundant. As might be expected of a school connected with a renowned hospital, premed programs are top-notch. There is more to JHU than premed, though. The international relations department is very well-regarded, as is the Writing Seminars program.

Coursework is highly challenging, and you can rest assured that your professors are leaders in their fields. In freshman year, course grades are reported only as "Satisfactory" or "Unsatisfactory," presumably to protect the egos of high-achievers adjusting to the difficulty level at JHU. (By the way, if you want to earn the privilege of stressing out at JHU, you had better polish up your high-achiever credentials to meet very tough admissions standards.) Students say that JHU's reputation for cut-throat competition is misleading though.

The Johns Hopkins University campus feels like a park full of Georgian-style brick buildings, with a location that is convenient to the Charles Village neighborhood of north Baltimore and the Inner Harbor, a picturesque tourist destination. Baltimore has a wealth of cultural life and entertainment options, although safety can be a concern.

Contrary to popular opinion, it is possible to have a social life on campus. You can enjoy getting to know the highly diverse student body by joining one of JHU's 360-plus student organizations. Those craving some quality toga time will find a lot of company. But if you envision spending time cheering on your school, you'll have to develop an interest in lacrosse.

If you're looking for carefree collegiate bliss, keep looking. But if you're an over-achieving premed type, ready to throw on your safety goggles and hit the lab, Johns Hopkins is calling your name.

Academics

There are 124 majors at Johns Hopkins, and students can create their own interdisciplinary major. The university requires all students to complete distribution requirements by taking courses in five general subject areas: humanities, natural sciences, social and behavioral sciences, quantitative and mathematical sciences, and engineering. Arts and Sciences students must also earn 12 credits in writing-intensive classes.

Courses at Johns Hopkins are "10 times harder than your hardest high school class," says a student. Your first semester freshman grades will appear on your transcript only as "Satisfactory" (for C- and up) or "Unsatisfactory," but they can still satisfy distribution and major requirements. This represents the last time the university will go easy on you.

Many classes are graded on a curve. Hitting the books has to be top priority if you want to keep up. "I study for several hours every night," a student explains, "and I still don't get everything done." The workload may be intense, but the opportunities to learn are incredible. The star-studded faculty includes three Nobel Prize winners, 45 American Academy of Arts and Sciences Fellows, and seven MacArthur Fellows. There are especially strong offerings in biology, chemistry, engineering, English (and writing seminars), international relations, and premed.

Aspiring writers can major or minor in the Writing Seminars program, which boasts a top-10 ranking from the *Atlantic Monthly* and was one of the first of its kind. "Graduates have published best-selling books and won Emmys. Here, you hone your writing skills to perfection," notes a student.

JOHNS HOPKINS UNIVERSITY

Highlights

Students
Total enrollment: 7,221
Undergrads: 5,192
Freshmen: 1,331
Part-time students: 1%
From out-of-state: 90%
From public schools: 58%
Male/Female: 52%/48%
Live on-campus: 54%
In fraternities: 20%
In sororities: 23%
Off-campus employment rating: Good
Caucasian: 50%
African American: 6%
Hispanic: 9%
Asian / Pacific Islander: 18%
Native American: 0%
Mixed (2+ ethnicities): 4%
International: 10%

Academics
Calendar: 4-1-4 system
Student/faculty ratio: 13:1
Class size 9 or fewer: 25%
Class size 10-29: 54%
Class size 30-49: 9%
Class size 50-99: 7%
Class size 100 or more: 5%
Returning freshmen: 97%
Six-year graduation rate: 94%
Graduates who immediately go to graduate school: 37%

Most Popular Majors
Public health studies
International studies
Biomedical engineering

Admissions
Applicants: 20,502
Accepted: 3,626
Acceptance rate: 17.7%
Placed on wait list: 2,730
Enrolled from wait list: 1
Average GPA: 3.7
ACT range: 30-34
SAT Math range: 670-770
SAT Reading range: 640-740
SAT Writing range: Not reported
Top 10% of class: 84%
Top 25% of class: 99%
Top 50% of class: 99%

384

Johns Hopkins is a premed paradise. "Look to the person to your left and to your right, and one of them will be premed," says a student. The Johns Hopkins School of Medicine and Bloomberg School of Public Health are very highly regarded, winning accolades from the National Institute of Health and receiving impressive amounts of federal research funding.

During Intersession, which occurs over winter break, students can take up to three credits of "Academic Exploration" courses. For those who want to venture off campus, Johns Hopkins offers "Experiential Learning" courses with leaders in different career fields as well as several exciting (and pricey) courses abroad, like "Renaissance Art in Florence."

Research is an integral and well-supported part of the Johns Hopkins experience. No other school receives more federal research and development funding. About two thirds of undergrads undertake some research while at JHU, and the school has a lengthy list of affiliated research centers and opportunities sorted by areas of interest. The university lays claim to a litany of important discoveries—when you do research at Johns Hopkins, you can be sure it's significant and cutting-edge. We have Johns Hopkins to thank for clearing up how SSRI antidepressants work, mapping dark matter, linking a modified Atkins diet to a reduction in epileptic seizures, finding a 3,400-year-old statue in Luxor, Egypt, and much more.

While the university sponsors only five study-abroad programs, students can study through a large number of other university-vetted programs or get approval to enroll directly in a foreign university.

According to the university, six months after graduation, 90 percent of JHU graduates are settled at a job or a graduate school. While at Johns Hopkins, students have ample opportunities to further their career path. The Robins Internship Program grants $5,000 for summer business internships in Asia, and the Second Decade Society Internship grants $5,000 for summer internships that are unpaid or sponsored by non-profits. The Edge Program does not offer funding, but it does give JHU students the first crack at applying to a database of internships.

Student Life

There are many on-campus events to break up those long hours of studying. The Milton S. Eisenhower Symposium brings world-famous speakers like Malcolm Gladwell to campus to expound on of-the-moment themes. The free lecture series is entirely run by undergrads.

On a lighter note, Fall Fest promises a lot of free food and big name musical performances. Also in the fall, Culturefest embodies a week of events showcasing JHU's diversity. The highlights include student performances at the Culture Show and ethnic cuisine at the International Night Market. Spring Fair is a bonanza featuring arts and crafts vendors, stands run by local non-profits, a beer garden, and a concert.

Students can choose from over 300 extracurricular groups. These range from pre-professional groups like the Hopkins Organization for Pre-Health Education and the Pre-Law Society to more laidback options like the Arcade Gaming Club and Outdoor Pursuits. Organizations for the visual and performance arts abound.

JHU has 13 social fraternities and 12 sororities. Greek life is a significant part of campus culture, as about one in five students pledge. "We know how to have fun too," says a member.

The JHU Blue Jays are a Division I Lacrosse team. All other sports at JHU are Division III. The men's lacrosse team has an impressive record, winning 44 national championships. "I never thought I'd be interested in lacrosse until I came here and saw how exciting the sport can be," notes a fan. The men's water polo team has earned nine NCAA Division III national titles. Intramural sports include the usual offerings, plus quirkier options like inner tube water polo.

Off campus, students have easy access to downtown Baltimore and the Inner Harbor, and Washington, DC is an hour away by train. In Baltimore's Inner Harbor, you can enjoy waterfront views and check out the National Aquarium. It's also a great place for nightlife and dining. The Fells Point area, convenient to JHU's main Homewood campus, is a favorite student hangout.

Baltimore has a high crime rate. For students concerned about safety, the university runs a night-time shuttle service from 5 p.m. to 3 a.m. "I don't really go anywhere at night by myself," remarks a student. "You just have to use common sense."

Freshmen and sophomores must live on campus. There are four buildings solely for freshman: two Alumni Memorial Residences (AMRs) and Buildings A and B. The AMRs have a traditional dorm layout with hallways of singles and doubles, while Buildings A and B are organized into suites. Meal plans are mandatory in all-freshman housing. Charles Commons, built in 2006, houses mainly upperclassmen. Its two buildings feature two- and four-person suites with their own kitchens. Best of all, everyone gets a single room. Those living off campus gravitate towards row homes in the walkable Charles Village neighborhood.

Student Body

By their own descriptions, students at JHU are "intense" and "focused on their careers." Eighty-four percent of students are culled from the top 10 percent of their high school graduating class. Despite this, students are quick to point out that the rumors about JHU as a hotbed of cut-throat premeds is misleading. "Even though we all want to do well, we still cooperate and would never undermine another student," one student comments.

The university is highly ethnically diverse, with 37 percent minority students. Almost one fifth of the student body is of Asian/Pacific Islander descent. Geographic diversity is very high as well (90 percent from out-of-state), and international students make up 10 percent of the student body.

You May Not Know

- Why is there an odd, extra "S" at the end of Johns? Johns Hopkins, the school's founder, was named after his great-grandmother, Margaret Johns.
- When the Wolman Hall dorm was an apartment building, F. Scott Fitzgerald lived there.
- The JHU Archaeological Collection boasts an Egyptian mummy affectionately known as "Boris."

JOHNS HOPKINS UNIVERSITY

Highlights

Admissions Criteria
Academic criteria:
Grades: ☆ ☆ ☆
Difficulty of class schedule: ☆ ☆ ☆
Class rank: ☆ ☆
Standardized test scores: ☆ ☆
Teacher recommendations: ☆ ☆ ☆
Personal statement: ☆ ☆
Non-academic criteria considered:
Interview
Extracurricular activities
Special talents, interests, abilities
Character/personal qualities
Volunteer work
Work experience
Geographical location
Minority affiliation
Alumni relationship

Deadlines
Early Action: No
Early Decision: November 1
Regular Action: January 1 (final)
Notification of admission by: April 1
Common Application: Accepted

Financial Aid
In-state tuition: $45,470
Out-of-state tuition: $45,470
Room: $7,920
Board: $5,912
Books: $1,200
Freshmen receiving need-based aid: 50%
Undergrads rec. need-based aid: 44%
Avg. % of need met by financial aid: 100%
Avg. aid package (freshmen): $37,917
Avg. aid package (undergrads): $36,312
Avg. debt upon graduation: $23,092

School Spirit
Mascot: Blue Jay
Colors: Columbia blue and black

Distinguished Alumni

Rachel Carson, biologist and author of *Silent Spring*; Wes Craven, film director; Woodrow Wilson, 28th President of the United States and Nobel Peace Prize winner.

Admissions and Financial Aid

JHU accepts the Common Application plus a supplement. A recent supplemental essay question asked students to write about their current interests and how they will "build upon them" at JHU. The admissions website helpfully includes four "essays that worked" with comments from admissions readers to help guide students. Applicants are encouraged to take up to three SAT subject tests, and engineering applicants must submit the Math Level 2 subject test and at least one science subject test. For a fighting chance, your math, reading, and writing SAT scores *each* had better be well-nigh 700—at least.

The Hodson Trust Scholarship grants $26,500 per year to incoming freshman with remarkable "academic and personal achievement, leadership, and contribution." The Hodson-Gilliam Success Scholarship is awarded to outstanding students who belong to under-represented minority groups and demonstrate financial need. Two engineering students receive the Charles R. Westgate Scholarship in Engineering, which provides full tuition and a living stipend for four years.

The only athletic scholarships are for men's and women's lacrosse. There are 25 four-year, endowed lacrosse scholarships.

JUNIATA COLLEGE

Overview

Located in the small college town of Huntingdon in central Pennsylvania, Juniata offers students a personal and distinctive educational experience. The 110-acre campus features traditional architecture, brick buildings, and sprawling green lawns.

More than anything, Juniata College prides itself on its individual attention to students. Small classes, great advising, and the ability to design and control your own major and POE (Program of Emphasis) are certainly benefits of attending the university. However, students looking for clubbing, frat parties, or a city close by that is brimming with plenty of activities would be better off at another school—those things are nonexistent here. Still, if you are interested in a school that puts a premium on personal guidance and support, Juniata is worth checking out.

Academics

Juniata College offers 41 majors, and 90 percent of classes have fewer than 30 students. "We get to know our professors and our classmates too," one student comments.

In order to graduate students must complete requirements in six different areas: a college writing seminar; a cultural analysis requirement; four courses in communication skills; a quantitative skills class; distribution requirements (six credits in each of five categories including fine arts, international studies, social sciences, humanities, and natural sciences); and finally a Program of Emphasis (POE). Students may also complete the optional service learning requirements, which entail two hours of community service per week, earning students one credit per semester.

A large part of what distinguishes the Juniata experience from other colleges is the Programs of Emphasis (POE), an opportunity for students to design any program of study that fits their interests. Juniata students may pick from a large list of POEs ranging in topics from accounting, business, and economics, to peace and conflict studies. Thirty percent of students choose to design their own major or POE.

Among the most noted programs at Juniata are business and the natural sciences. The latter is centered at the von Liebig Center, which offers 25,000 square feet of laboratory space, featuring capabilities such as cell and tissue culture, atomic and magnetic resonance spectroscopy, and biological separations. The business program is acclaimed for its entrepreneurial spirit; for example, the Sill Business Incubator allows students and faculty to lease business space and the Seed Capital program funds students $5,000 to start as entrepreneurs.

Special academic opportunities at Juniata include Inbound Retreats, a program that gives 10 students a chance to experience Juniata before classes begin. The participants experience outdoor exploration, artistic expression, spiritual retreats, or service learning. "You can make friends even before the school year starts," one student notes.

The unique Peace and Conflicts (PAC) major at Juniata explores how and why humans use violence to resolve conflicts and aims to "practice peace, prevent violence, and provide post-conflict resolution." Students have the opportunity to pursue an internship at a related firm or participate in any of 39 locations in 19 countries to study resolutions for these issues. "I chose to study at Juniata because of PAC and the knowledge of world affairs I'd gain," says a student.

The Liberal Arts Symposium celebrates the most impressive accomplishments of Juniata students. The symposium occurs one day during the spring when classes are cancelled. Recognition is given to research, project development, and student performance.

Thanks to the college's On-Time Graduation Guarantee, 92-96 percent of Juniata students complete their degrees in four years or less. The university is committed to

JUNIATA COLLEGE

Four-year private
Founded: 1876
Huntingdon, PA
Small town
Pop. 7,066

Address:
1700 Moore Street
Huntingdon, PA
16652

Admissions:
814-641-3420

Financial Aid:
814-641-3142

admissions@juniata.
edu

www.juniata.edu

JUNIATA COLLEGE

Students

Total enrollment: 1,565
Undergrads: 1,558
Freshmen: 426
Part-time students: 4%
From out-of-state: 39%
From public schools: 83%
Male/Female: 45%/55%
Live on-campus: 81%
Off-campus employment rating: Good
Caucasian: 78%
African American: 3%
Hispanic: 4%
Asian / Pacific Islander: 2%
Native American: 0%
Mixed (2+ ethnicities): 2%
International: 9%

Academics

Calendar: Semester
Student/faculty ratio: 13:1
Class size 9 or fewer: 21%
Class size 10-29: 69%
Class size 30-49: 8%
Class size 50-99: 2%
Class size 100 or more: 1%
Returning freshmen: 90%
Six-year graduation rate: 75%
Graduates who immediately go to graduate school: 34%
Graduates who immediately enter career related to major: 60%

Most Popular Majors

Biology
Business
Education

Admissions

Applicants: 2,418
Accepted: 1,605
Acceptance rate: 66.4%
Placed on wait list: 91
Average GPA: 3.7
ACT range: Not reported
SAT Math range: 530-645
SAT Reading range: 520-640
SAT Writing range: Not reported
Top 10% of class: 42%
Top 25% of class: 74%
Top 50% of class: 99%

ensuring that students are well-informed about College Degree and Program of Emphasis requirements as well as advised on planned semester activities.

More than 40 percent of students study abroad. Juniata has international exchange/study abroad agreements with colleges and universities in 19 countries and every POE offers at least one study-abroad program.

The majority of Juniata students speak highly of the university's career advising and alumni network. In fact, 85 percent of students complete an internship before graduating. Students also have an extremely high rate of acceptance into graduate programs with 97 percent of Juniata graduates being accepted into medical, podiatry, dental, occupational therapy, physical therapy, and chiropractic schools.

Student Life

Juniata students can choose to participate in one of over 100 student organizations. Some of the most notable are Big Brothers, Big Sisters, All Ways of Loving, Dodgeball, and Laughing Bush (Outdoor Recreation).

Juniata features several annual events revered across campus. To kick off the year, the school welcomes students back to campus with Lobsterfest, a picnic that features whole Maine lobsters as well as live music and entertainment. The Madrigal dinner and dance is another well-loved tradition on campus. Organized into sections, students sit at tables named after a verse of "The 12 Days of Christmas" and sing the carol as a group. But the most popular—and the oldest— tradition at Juniata is Mountain Day, when classes are cancelled on a previously unannounced day. Students enjoy a day of picnics and games. "You can feel the excitement we all have on Mountain Day," one student comments.

If you're looking for a college experience centered on Greek life, Juniata is not for you. There are no fraternities or sororities on campus. However, students generally report that this is not an issue. Many of the natural social groups that form on campus center on athletic teams and activities. "Our college is small enough that we are like our own fraternity," one student says.

Juniata has 19 Division III varsity athletic teams. Sports do not constitute a big part of Juniata's campus life, and as one student says, "I wish we had more school spirit." However, the men's and women's volleyball teams have a large group of loyal fans—both teams have earned recent championship titles. Club sports are quite popular as well, with many students choosing to participate in the soccer, indoor field hockey, Ultimate Frisbee, and rugby teams.

Off campus, there is not a great deal to do in the extremely small town of Huntingdon. While students do tend to appreciate the small-town feel of Huntingdon, full of family-owned stores and specialty shops, they are easily frustrated by its limited offerings. Many say that the best shopping is the Walmart Supercenter, although Route 22 has some fast food and clothing stores. For the most part, students say, "We create our own fun."

Freshmen are required to live on campus at Juniata. All dorms are only a short walk to the major places on campus.

Student Body

The majority of Juniata's student body is composed of "white, middle- to upper-class" students. Not very ethnically diverse, 11 percent of the student body is comprised of minority students. The college is moderately geographically diverse, with 39 percent of students hailing from out of state. Despite the limited diversity due to its location in a small town in Pennsylvania, the college draws from a variety of different political and religious views. It also is endowed with an impressive percentage of international students.

Juniata students tend to be "open to new ideas" and "more liberal than conservative" especially when it comes to socially charged issues.

You May Not Know

- Held as a charity benefit, the Mr. Juniata Beauty Pageant creates an intense competition among the university's male students.
- The Goal Post Trophy, a section of an actual goal post, is awarded to the winner of the Susquehanna University football game.
- To accommodate all students' dietary needs, some of Juniata's dining halls feature vegan options.

Distinguished Alumni

Chuck Knox, former NFL coach; John Kuriyan, winner of the Lounsbery Award for extraordinary scientific achievement; Wayne Meyers, President, International Leprosy Association; William Phillips, atomic physicist awarded the Nobel Prize in Physics.

Admissions and Financial Aid

When applying, students may submit two graded papers instead of their SAT or ACT scores. Interviews—opportunities to get a real sense of the college and assess a student's "fit" with the institution—are also highly recommended.

Juniata's competitive scholarships are awarded to students who do well academically as well as involve themselves in their schools and local communities. Among some of the scholarships available are the Distinguished Scholars Award, full tuition plus room and board for students who have achieved National Merit or National Achievement Finalist status; the James Quinter Scholarship, $18,000 annually awarded to students with a 3.75 GPA and a 1320 (math and verbal) SAT score; Elizabeth Baker Scholarships, $10,000 each year awarded to students balancing academic and extracurricular activities with a 3.25 minimum GPA; and Heritage Awards, up to $8,000 awarded to students who are committed to academic excellence and community service among diverse groups.

JUNIATA COLLEGE

Highlights

Admissions Criteria
Academic criteria:
Grades: ☆ ☆ ☆
Difficulty of class schedule: ☆ ☆ ☆
Class rank: N/A
Standardized test scores: ☆ ☆ ☆
Teacher recommendations: ☆ ☆ ☆
Personal statement: ☆ ☆ ☆
Non-academic criteria considered:
Interview
Extracurricular activities
Special talents, interests, abilities
Character/personal qualities
Volunteer work
Geographical location
Minority affiliation
Alumni relationship

Deadlines
Early Decision I: November 15
Early Decision II: February 15
Regular Action: Rolling admissions
Common Application: Accepted

Financial Aid
In-state tuition: $36,410
Out-of-state tuition: $36,410
Room: $5,380
Board: $4,820
Books: $600
Freshmen receiving need-based aid: 72%
Undergrads rec. need-based aid: 70%
Avg. % of need met by financial aid: 81%
Avg. aid package (freshmen): $29,241
Avg. aid package (undergrads): $28,211
Avg. debt upon graduation: $31,213

School Spirit
Mascot: Eagles
Colors: Blue and gold

KALAMAZOO COLLEGE

Four-year private
Founded: 1833
Kalamazoo, MI
Medium city
Pop. 74,743

Address:
1200 Academy Street
Kalamazoo, MI
49006

Admissions:
800-253-3602

Financial Aid:
800-632-5760

admission@kzoo.edu

www.kzoo.edu

KALAMAZOO COLLEGE

Overview

Quaintly nicknamed "K-Zoo," Kalamazoo College lives up to its quirky name by providing a unique liberal arts experience to its students. The college is nestled in the quiet residential area of Kalamazoo, immersed in the rustic, rolling hills of southwest Michigan. The city sits a mere 35 miles from Lake Michigan and 140 miles from both Detroit and Chicago, proving a desirable location for lakeside and metropolitan activities alike. For those without the luxury of a vehicle, the college is within walking distance of the city of Kalamazoo's charming downtown area, consisting of abundant shopping, movies, and restaurants. These nearby amenities are especially valuable during the harsh Michigan winters, with temperatures averaging in the 30s for three months of the year.

This private, liberal arts college sits on a 60-acre campus. Such a small size allows the college to commit to a true liberal arts philosophy, emphasizing students' complete ownership of their education. The college offers a wide breadth of vigorous majors, focusing strongly on study abroad and service-learning programs, culminating for each student in a custom Senior Individualized Project.

While Kalamazoo caters to each student's individual pursuits academically, the college also provides bountiful opportunities for recreational pursuits, such as the famed Monte Carlo Night. At this annual event, students "gamble" with their "Monte Carlo bucks" and can splurge with their winnings at the Millionaire Shop on prizes donated by the community.

Emphasizing its efforts to provide a tight-knit atmosphere, K-Zoo recently renovated the Hicks Student Center, a 24-hour gathering place for students, professors, and community members that serves as the heart and hub of campus activity. With coffee shops, the campus bookstore, and numerous meeting spaces for the many student organizations, the Student Center helps to cultivate the integrated liberal arts education students experience at Kalamazoo College.

Academics

Kalamazoo College provides a highly individualized academic program with unique requirements. Referred to as the "K-Plan," this educational model requires students to explore four areas of study: liberal arts and sciences, learning through experience, international engagement, and the Senior Individualized Project. The Plan begins with three Shared Passages Seminars and one First-Year Seminar, which are general graduation requirements focusing on development of written, oral, and critical thinking skills. After freshman year, students begin to delve into cultural education with a Sophomore Seminar, specializing in one of the 31 majors offered at the college and preparing for study abroad. Senior year focuses on integrating the "K-Plan education" into a focused topic through a Disciplinary or Interdisciplinary Senior Seminar. Strong academic programs include biology, English, and prelaw.

Other graduation requirements include learning a second language, participating in physical education, and completing a Senior Individualized Project. The Project requires year-long research, often integrated with an internship or creative enterprise and culminating in a final written report, performance, or exhibit. "The senior project is a big deal and the opportunity to do graduate-level work," explains a student.

The college works on the trimester system, meaning classes are only 10 weeks long and, as a result, fast-paced. "It feels like you're just getting into a class when it's winding down," notes a student. However, this also affords students the opportunity to take fewer classes per trimester, producing a stronger focus on each class. Class size is often very small, averaging 10-19 students per class.

Although not required, the college strongly encourages students to expand their cultural horizons through study abroad. Extremely popular among the students (85 percent of the student body participates in a study-abroad program), Kalamazoo offers 34 sites in 25 different countries. The programs consist largely of home-stays and often include an Integrative Cultural Research project. "You live authentically in a foreign country rather than as a tourist," one student says.

Kalamazoo also heartily emphasizes career preparation during the undergraduate years with its prevalent internship and externship opportunities. Strong alumni networking and unique programs such as the Discovery Externship Program and the Field Experience Program prove effective, with 80 percent of students partaking in such an internship or externship program. The college ranks 18th in the nation for graduates going on to earn doctorate degrees.

Student Life

Even before arriving at K-Zoo, students have the opportunity to jumpstart their social lives by participating in the LandSea Wilderness Experience, an optional two-week long trip to the Killarney Provincial Park in Sudbury, Ontario. Backpacking, canoeing, and climbing are just some of the activities in which students participate. "It's nice to have a tight group of friends before classes even start," says a participant.

Upon arriving on campus, Kalamazoo students are presented with over 40 student organizations that cover a wide range of interests, from the Environmental Organization, to the Frelon Dance Company, to the campus radio station, WJMD. Considering that 75 percent of Kalamazoo students choose to live on campus, it is no wonder that the majority of students place themselves in a position to take advantage of these numerous group options.

Plentiful social opportunities are also available by joining the Student Activities Committee (SAC), a group that organizes major campus events. The Extravaganza takes place the weekend before final exams and provides students a time to relax with music, delicious treats, and entertainment such as comedians or trivia game shows. Spring Fling supplies a day of moonwalks, dunk tanks, and a picnic on the quad. And finally, the Air Band/Talent Show provides the opportunity for students to show off their stage skills in a day-long contest of lip-syncing and yo-yoing. "We have some crazy lip-syncing talent," brags a student. Although there is no Greek life on campus, the SAC excels in satisfying the social needs of Kalamazoo students.

K-Zoo students are also encouraged to pursue recreation through athletics. An NCAA Division III school with 16 varsity teams, the college boasts a men's tennis team that has won over 70 consecutive Michigan Intercollegiate Athletic Association championships. Other notable teams include men's swimming and diving and women's cross country. Though the football team is not stellar, it incites rigorous competition with rival Hope College, with whom the Kalamazoo Hornets battle for the desired "wooden shoes." For those seeking a less competitive athletic atmosphere, there is also an extensive intramural program.

Off-campus activities provide another way for students to unwind. A nearby movie theater in Kalamazoo offers affordable tickets to students, a chamber music society welcomes listeners, and a shopping mall beckons a short drive away. "It's not the big city, but there are enough diversions," notes a student. When they

KALAMAZOO COLLEGE

391

KALAMAZOO COLLEGE

Admissions Criteria
Academic criteria:
Grades: ☆ ☆ ☆
Difficulty of class schedule: ☆ ☆ ☆
Class rank: N/A
Standardized test scores: ☆ ☆
Teacher recommendations: ☆ ☆
Personal statement: ☆ ☆
Non-academic criteria considered:
Interview
Extracurricular activities
Special talents, interests, abilities
Character/personal qualities
Volunteer work
Work experience
State of residency
Geographical location
Minority affiliation
Alumni relationship

Deadlines
Early Action: November 20
Early Decision: November 10
Regular Action: November 20 (priority)
February 1 (final)
Notification of admission by: April 1
Common Application: Accepted

Financial Aid
In-state tuition: $39,027
Out-of-state tuition: $39,027
Room: Varies
Board: Varies
Books: $900
Freshmen receiving need-based aid: 65%
Undergrads rec. need-based aid: 59%
Avg. % of need met by financial aid: 86%
Avg. aid package (freshmen): $32,931
Avg. aid package (undergrads): $31,025
Avg. debt upon graduation: $27,845

School Spirit
Mascot: Hornets
Colors: Orange and black

tire of the metropolitan area, students often head to the nearby Western Michigan University for larger-scale social engagements.

On-campus housing offers several options. Coed residence halls include single, double, and triple rooms, as well as suites. The college also offers the unique option of living/learning housing units that combine living with a particular educational focus.

Student Body

The student body at Kalamazoo is 64 percent white, with high minority presence of 21 percent. Geographic diversity is moderate, with 33 percent of last year's freshman class hailing from out of state. The undergraduate population skews slightly more female with 58 percent women and 42 percent men.

The lack of Greek life, combined with the majority presence of students living on campus, provides a unified campus community with everyone, for the most part, knowing everyone else. "You can't walk 10 steps without seeing someone you know," laughs a student.

You May Not Know

- In 2009, every Kalamazoo Fulbright finalist was awarded a grant.
- On one day every spring, the school calls for a "Day of Gracious Living," and all classes are cancelled in the spirit of a stress-free lifestyle.
- Kalamazoo produces the greatest number of Peace Corps volunteers per capita.

Distinguished Alumni

Selma Blair, actress; Lisa Kron, Tony Award-nominated actress and playwright; Mike McFall, Biggby Coffee Company President; Paige Simpson, film producer.

Admissions and Financial Aid

Kalamazoo College does accept the Common Application. Admission considerations include the personal statement, ACT or SAT scores, and teacher recommendations. The admissions board does not look at class rank; however, it does consider extracurricular activities, special talents, volunteer work, minority status, and alumni affiliation. The average GPA of admitted students is a 3.7, with an average ACT score of 28 and average SAT Reasoning score of 1300.

In addition to need-based aid, all students entering Kalamazoo are considered for merit-based scholarships, ranging between $5,000 and $14,000 annually. The scholarships are considered upon processing the general application and are based 60 percent on the student's academic record and 40 percent on his or her co-curricular record.

The college also offers various Enlightened Awards, or merit-based scholarships, in different community-based areas such as social activism/civil engagement and sustainability/environmental activism. All students are eligible for these scholarships, and five scholarships are given in each of the areas.

KANSAS STATE UNIVERSITY

Overview

Known for its strengths in agriculture, Kansas State University is a large public university in the Midwest. The school, divided into nine colleges, provides a fair amount of academic variety and a lively campus scene that turns purple on football game days.

Located in Manhattan, Kansas, about 55 miles west of Topeka, the campus features architecture ranging from limestone to red brick. K-State students are generally spirited about their school, swearing by the friendly Midwestern vibe of the people and proud of the great college town so abundant with popular bars and coffee shops.

Academics

KSU offers 203 majors with each college having its own University General Education. Though course requirements vary by specific college, most have requirements in English/writing, math, and foreign language; all requirements are in place to ensure adequate breadth of learning at K-State through "the diversity of knowledge and the ability to make connections between disciplines." Despite the large student body, students say that professors are easy to get in touch with and responsive to their needs. Additionally, each student receives a faculty member as an academic advisor. Among the strongest programs available at K-State are agriculture, architecture planning and design, and veterinary medicine.

Kansas State University's Honors Programs offer motivated students the chance to tackle several disciplines at once and conduct original research. Honors program students take special classes and work with the university's top professors while combining their interests and experience to write an honors project or thesis in any field of study. To be eligible for admission, students must have a minimum 3.75 GPA, an ACT store of 28 or above, and complete a short entrance application.

The School of Leadership Studies is another special learning opportunity at K-State: a chance to pursue an interdisciplinary minor in Leadership Studies as well as to explore and apply leadership theories across academic disciplines.

PILOTS, a year-long freshman retention program that provides academic structure, assists new students in making a strong connection to the campus community during a sometimes overwhelming transition. With small class sizes, access to faculty, free tutoring, peer assistants, and leadership training, students who are seeking guidance for early academic success can find the support they need.

Kansas State offers study-abroad opportunities in nine different countries: Australia, Canada, France, Germany, Ireland, Italy, Japan, Spain, and the UK. In addition to traditional study abroad, the university also offers faculty-led and exchange programs. Because of the two-way flow of students, the exchange program is a cost effective program that makes different universities around the world available to interested students.

The career center on campus is another available resource for students looking for professional guidance. However, most students report that the large alumni database is the most useful tool when searching for a job. "I know a couple of grads who got their first jobs basically because they were K-State alums," affirms a student.

Student Life

With over 450 student organizations, there are plenty of opportunities to get involved with activities at Kansas State. Some of the most popular groups include debate team, baton twirling, and madrigal ensemble.

The Little Apple Jazz Festival—with jazz music on the KSU lawn, potluck dinner, and coolers filled with students' favorite drinks—is a popular annual event. The night often features artists who have appeared in nationally recognized arenas.

KANSAS STATE UNIVERSITY

Four-year public
Founded: 1863
Manhattan, KS
Large town
Pop. 53,678

Address:
119 Anderson Hall
Manhattan, KS
66506

Admissions:
800-432-8270

Financial Aid:
877-817-2287

k-state@k-state.edu

www.k-state.edu

KANSAS STATE UNIVERSITY

Students
Total enrollment: 24,378
Undergrads: 19,853
Freshmen: 5,130
Part-time students: 10%
From out-of-state: 18%
Male/Female: 52%/48%
Live on-campus: 25%
In fraternities: 17%
In sororities: 25%
Off-campus employment rating: Good
Caucasian: 77%
African American: 4%
Hispanic: 6%
Asian / Pacific Islander: 1%
Native American: 0%
Mixed (2+ ethnicities): 3%
International: 7%

Academics
Calendar: Semester
Student/faculty ratio: 20:1
Class size 9 or fewer: 13%
Class size 10-29: 53%
Class size 30-49: 21%
Class size 50-99: 7%
Class size 100 or more: 5%
Returning freshmen: 80%
Six-year graduation rate: 59%
Graduates who immediately enter career
  related to major: 70%

Most Popular Majors
Business administration
Animal science
Mechanical engineering

Admissions
Applicants: 9,273
Accepted: 9,180
Acceptance rate: 99.0%
Average GPA: 3.4
ACT range: 21-27
SAT Math range: Not reported
SAT Reading range: Not reported
SAT Writing range: Not reported
Top 10% of class: 20%
Top 25% of class: 45%
Top 50% of class: 74%

394

Service opportunities are also available at K-State with plenty of chances to volunteer in the local community of Manhattan. Students can choose "to go Greek" to become involved with community service as the various Greek chapters have individual projects to raise funds for charity, or they may choose to participate in Up 'Til Dawn, which assists St. Jude Children's Research Hospital.

Greek life composes a large part of the KSU experience. While only 20 percent of students chooses to join a fraternity or sorority, the Greek social scene has a large presence on campus. "If you're in a sorority or fraternity, it pretty much consumes all your time outside of classes and homework," explains one student.

Home football games are another big event at K-State, complete with massive tailgate parties, fight songs, and tons of school spirit. In fact, while the K-State athletes were originally known as the "Aggies," their name was changed to the "Wildcats" in 1915 by the football coach because of their fighting spirit. On game days, Willie the Wildcat becomes a local hero and the town "bleeds purple," students and fans alike. "You know it's a game day from the buzz among students and the sea of purple everywhere," says a student. The Wabash, a musical piece, is played at all games and known by almost every student in the crowd. Complemented by spring tailing and alumni barbeques, the spring football scrimmage is another football-centered tradition that measures how successful the team will be in the upcoming fall.

K-State competes in Division I athletics with four men's, six women's, and two mixed varsity teams. For men, football and basketball are the most popular sports and they are big competitors on the national level. For women's sports, basketball and volleyball, along with the equestrian team, are the most notable. Intramural sports are popular in many shapes and forms, including the parachuting and inner tube water polo teams.

Typically, students looking for low-key recreational activity, dining, and shopping are pleased with what is available in the Manhattan area; those looking for a large array of things to do can take a road trip to Kansas City two hours away.

Although they are not required to do so, most freshmen live on campus and move off campus after their first year. "Don't expect much from the dorms, especially freshman year," comments a student, "but living in the dorm is the best way to make friends."

Student Body

Kansas State University is a "not so diverse" student body. With moderate ethnic diversity, ethnic minorities compose 14 percent of students. Geographic diversity is quite low with 18 percent of students hailing from out of state. Some students complain that minorities tend to segregate themselves but there is a general Midwestern, welcoming feel pervasive throughout the campus. The student body tends to lean politically right but there is also a notable liberal presence.

You May Not Know

• Kansas State is one of only 25 universities in the world to have a nuclear reactor on campus.

- The "Wabash Cannonball," commonly played at sporting events, was the only piece of music to survive a campus fire in 1968.
- Purple Pride blueberry ice cream was developed in the late 1960s by professor Harold Roberts to spark interest in football and to promote school pride.

Distinguished Alumni

Erin Brockovich, environmental activist; Herbert Dimond, inventor of the snooze alarm; Mitch Richmond, NBA all-star; Pat Roberts, U.S. Senator; Eric Stonestreet, star of NBC show *Modern Family*; Earl Woods, father of golfer Tiger Woods.

Admissions and Financial Aid

K-State has specific admissions requirements (GPA, test scores, or class rank) that, if met, make students eligible for admission. More specifically, students must have a 21 or higher on the ACT or 980 or higher on the SAT Critical Reading and Math, should be ranked in the top third of their high school class, and/or must have completed the Kansas precollege curriculum with a minimum 2.0 GPA (minimum 2.5 GPA for out-of-state students). Those students who do not meet these criteria may still apply to the school by contacting the Office of Admissions (about 10 percent of students are admitted in this fashion).

The Putnam Scholarship is a merit award offered by Kansas State, given to students on the basis of merit (semifinalists and finalists from the National Merit, National Achievement, or National Hispanic Scholarship programs). It totals $7,500 in value and is renewable for three years. The Foundation Scholarship is awarded to students on the basis of merit and totals $1,250 per year with an additional $1,000-$2,500 available dependent on ACT or SAT score. The Heritage Scholarship is given to the out-of-state children of alumni. Recipients pay 150 percent of in-state tuition, accounting for $7,000 in annual savings.

KANSAS STATE UNIVERSITY

Highlights

Admissions Criteria
Academic criteria:
Grades: ☆ ☆ ☆
Difficulty of class schedule: ☆ ☆ ☆
Class rank: ☆ ☆ ☆
Standardized test scores: ☆ ☆ ☆
Teacher recommendations: ☆
Personal statement: N/A
Non-academic criteria considered:
State of residency

Deadlines
Early Action: No
Early Decision: No
Regular Action: November 1 (priority)
February 1 (programs with application deadlines)
Common Application: Not accepted

Financial Aid
In-state tuition: $7,830
Out-of-state tuition: $20,775
Room: Varies
Board: Varies
Books: $1,100
Freshmen receiving need-based aid: 53%
Undergrads rec. need-based aid: 52%
Avg. % of need met by financial aid: 81%
Avg. aid package (freshmen): $11,289
Avg. aid package (undergrads): $11,182
Avg. debt upon graduation: $25,147

School Spirit
Mascot: Willie the Wildcat
Colors: Purple and white
Song: *Wildcat Victory*

KENYON
COLLEGE

Four-year private
Founded: 1824
Gambier, OH
Rural
Pop. 2,396

Address:
Ransom Hall, 106 College Park Drive
Gambier, OH
43022-9623

Admissions:
800-848-2468

Financial Aid:
740-427-5430

admissions@kenyon.edu

www.kenyon.edu

KENYON COLLEGE

Overview

Rural Gambier, Ohio (population 2,396) might not be where you would expect to find Ohio's oldest private college. But there it is—Kenyon College—a small liberal arts college, located about an hour northeast of Columbus, set atop a hill on a thousand acres. With Collegiate Gothic architecture and a 380-acre nature preserve, Kenyon is on the National Register of Historical Places, and the campus is known for its aesthetics.

A sense of history underpins a tight-knit community where students live on campus all four years and form close relationships with professors in their small classes. Some traditions go back more than a century: for example, all incoming students take a Matriculation Oath and sign the Matriculation Book. First-years also join together in the First-Year Sing to learn Kenyon songs; they'll enjoy these same lyrics and melodies at Senior Sing, the tradition having carried them back full circle.

Not everything is old history though. The fresh new faces that have arrived in recent years have been able to enjoy brand new facilities, including a $32 million science center, $70 million athletic center, and a second building for Kenyon's well-regarded English Department. These new buildings hint the importance of student research and athletics (nearly a third of students participate in intercollegiate sports) at the college. For some, a small college in such a remote location may feel stifling. Those who are instead excited to spend four years learning and playing in a closely-woven community will want to show off their smart, well-rounded selves in their Kenyon applications.

Academics

Kenyon has 18 departments along with 13 interdisciplinary programs. Students can choose a minor or concentration to supplement their major. Everyone is required to complete a Senior Exercise in their major, and each major has an Honors Program option. Degree requirements include distribution, second language, and quantitative reasoning courses. Students are able to select courses that satisfy these categories; they aren't required to take any single course.

Classes are taught by professors with no teaching assistants. That, plus the student-faculty ratio of 10 to 1, makes for tight relationships with professors. Strong fine arts programs include dance, drama, and a film program that claims Paul Newman as a graduate. The department publishes the highly regarded *Kenyon Review*, and as one student brags, it "is a huge opportunity to get hands-on literary publishing experience."

The Senior Exercise is an original research project or creative piece that each student completes during his or her major. This capstone experience is unique to each student and tailored to the student's department. It may take the form of a paper, presentation, art exhibit, multimedia project, or another creative format.

The Summer Science Scholars Program offers competitive awards for students who want to work with faculty mentors in the lab sciences. Students and faculty work as a team to create a research plan, complete the project, and present results. Recent scholars studied topics as varied as binding proteins, caterpillar behavior, and Kenyon students' food preferences.

The Brown Family Environmental Center is a resource for students and the broader community, with several thousand people attending a large number of free programs each year. The Center has a 400 acre preserve with diverse habitats. Major annual events include an Earth Day Health Expo and the Harvest Festival in autumn.

Kenyon's Center for Global Engagement offers more than 150 programs in more than 50 countries. The school also has its own programs in England (at the University of Exeter), Honduras (an archeology and anthropology program), and Italy (the study of Italian art and culture). Most students who major in Modern Languages and Literatures study abroad in their target language area during junior year.

Kenyon's Career Development Office, located in the lower level of Gund Commons, has drop-in hours and regular events for students. The Extern Program gives students a chance to shadow a professional for three to five days, while the Kenyon Career Network has 7,000 volunteers who students can contact for advice on jobs and graduate school. "There's a lot of support for after college," one student comments.

Student Life

Luckily for those living on campus—which is almost everyone—Kenyon offers more than 140 organizations to keep students entertained. As the college notes, "from the linguistics club, to the Snowden Fried Chicken Cook-off, to six a cappella singing groups, to a 4:00 a.m. romp in the snow, there's endless activity here." WKCO, the student-run radio, streams worldwide, while the literary journal *The Kenyon Review* publishes emerging writers from diverse communities. The Renegade Theater is a group exclusively for first-year students.

The amusingly titled Philanderer's Phebruary Phling isn't just a made-up moniker: the annual semi-formal dance is named after the founder of Kenyon College, Philander Chase. The evening includes dance, casino games, and a special theme. "It's one of the biggest events of the year," one student comments. Then when warmer weather comes around, Summer Sendoff brings students together for a full-day outdoor festival with music, free meals, balloon art, and other fun activities. Harry Potter fans will delight in Harry Potter Day when the whole campus goes all out with a scavenger hunt, Quidditch match, and costumed, themed meal in the Great Hall.

There are 11 Greek organizations on campus with a history that goes back more than 150 years. The 10 days of Rush Week honor traditions that started in 1852. Peeps O' Kenyon is a co-ed society, and the Archon society is a co-ed community service organization. "There are some people who only socialize with other Greeks, but most aren't so exclusive," one student describes.

Kenyon's 22 Division III teams are known as the Lords and Ladies. Nearly one third of students participate in varsity sports, with many more enjoying intramurals. The men's swimming team has won 31 consecutive national titles since 1980 and the women's swim team has won 23 national titles. The $70-million, 263,000-square-foot Kenyon Athletic Center is a light-filled wonderland for fitness, with indoor tennis squash courts, a 22-lane pool, spaces for yoga, and more. Even those who aren't so athletic can go to use wifi, sit at the café, or meet in a conference room.

If you hear students saying "Meet me at the Middle Ground," they're referring to the popular café in downtown Gambier. Gambier does have a few restaurants and bars, but students tend to head to Mount Vernon for more options.

Students are required to live on campus all four years, and all first-years live in five residence halls, all of which are near Gund Commons. Upperclassmen may choose from apartment-style living.

KENYON COLLEGE

Highlights

Students
Total enrollment: 1,667
Undergrads: 1,667
Freshmen: 447
From out-of-state: 85%
From public schools: 53%
Male/Female: 47%/53%
Live on-campus: 99%
In fraternities: 14%
In sororities: 16%
Off-campus employment rating: Poor
Caucasian: 76%
African American: 3%
Hispanic: 5%
Asian / Pacific Islander: 7%
Native American: 1%
Mixed (2+ ethnicities): 1%
International: 4%

Academics
Calendar: Semester
Student/faculty ratio: 10:1
Class size 9 or fewer: 20%
Class size 10-29: 71%
Class size 30-49: 7%
Class size 50-99: 1%
Class size 100 or more: -
Six-year graduation rate: 90%
Graduates who immediately go to graduate school: 16%

Most Popular Majors
English
Psychology
Economics

Admissions
Applicants: 3,947
Accepted: 1,421
Acceptance rate: 36.0%
Placed on wait list: 931
Enrolled from wait list: 15
Average GPA: 3.9
ACT range: 28-32
SAT Math range: 610-680
SAT Reading range: 630-730
SAT Writing range: 41-44
Top 10% of class: 52%
Top 25% of class: 86%
Top 50% of class: 98%

397

College Profiles

KENYON COLLEGE

Admissions Criteria
Academic criteria:
Grades: ☆ ☆ ☆
Difficulty of class schedule: ☆ ☆ ☆
Class rank: ☆ ☆
Standardized test scores: ☆ ☆
Teacher recommendations: ☆ ☆ ☆
Personal statement: ☆ ☆ ☆
Non-academic criteria considered:
Interview
Extracurricular activities
Special talents, interests, abilities
Character/personal qualities
Volunteer work
Work experience
Geographical location
Minority affiliation
Alumni relationship

Deadlines
Early Action: No
Early Decision: November 15
Regular Action: January 15 (priority)
January 15 (final)
Notification of admission by: April 1
Common Application: Accepted

Financial Aid
In-state tuition: $43,900
Out-of-state tuition: $43,900
Room: $4,870
Board: $6,300
Books: $1,900
Freshmen receiving need-based aid: 42%
Undergrads rec. need-based aid: 39%
Avg. % of need met by financial aid: 94%
Avg. aid package (freshmen): $37,805
Avg. aid package (undergrads): $37,283
Avg. debt upon graduation: $20,992

School Spirit
Mascot: Lords and Ladies
Colors: Purple and white

Student Body

Kenyon students describe themselves as "close" and "very friendly." The college has moderate diversity, with about 17 percent of students identifying as students of color. The Snowden Multicultural Center puts on events for Latino, Native American, Asian American, and Black History months, as well as programs with the delectable titles of "Global Café" and "Dessert and Discussion."

There is high geographic diversity, with 85 percent of students from out of state and all 50 states represented. International students from more than 40 countries make up about four percent of the student body. Most students are from the Midwest, mid-Atlantic, and New England areas.

You May Not Know

- Kenyon is the oldest private college in the state of Ohio.
- Kenyon, Minnesota derives its name from Kenyon College.
- During the 2004 presidential elections, some Kenyon students waited as long as 13 hours in line to place their votes.

Distinguished Alumni

Carl Djerassi, developer of the birth control pill; Rutherford B. Hayes, U.S. President; Allison Janney, Emmy Award–winning actress; Olof Palme, Swedish Prime Minister.

Admissions and Financial Aid

Applicants to Kenyon should complete 18 academic units of a college preparatory program—a program that ideally includes AP, IB, and/or honors courses. Interviews are recommended, though not required. These can be done on campus or with an alumni outside of Ohio. The online application to Kenyon is free. The admissions office paints a picture of the bright, well-rounded student that the college seeks with the following statement: "Kenyon students are achievers but are also creative and know the value of community."

About 39 percent of students are offered need-based financial assistance and about 12 percent are offered merit-based aid from Kenyon, and the average aid package is more than $37,000. There are Kenyon College Need-based Grants as well as a number of merit-based Academic Scholarships. The latter include the coveted Kenyon Honor, Science, and Trustee Opportunity Scholarships, with award amounts ranging up to $20,000. Distinguished Academic Scholarships of up to $12,000 are given to students with leadership potential and high academic achievement. There are also special awards for the arts.

KNOX COLLEGE

Overview

As the site of one of the seven Lincoln-Douglas debates in 1858, and the first at which Abraham Lincoln denounced slavery, Knox College has a long history of belief in equality. Knox, located in the classic red-brick prairie town of Galesburg, Illinois, embodies its Midwestern roots by providing an atmosphere of free thought and friendly informality. The 82-acre campus, founded in 1837, was established at the same time as Galesburg, creating a community of open interaction between the college and the town. Knox and Galesburg provide the perfect mix of a small-town welcoming and casual attitude with the cultural excitement of a big city, including several museums and theatres, the Galesburg Civic Art Center, and numerous coffee shops and restaurants.

Students at Knox fully embrace their college's values of equality, and their course loads reflect Knox's ideals of interacting with other cultures and learning outside the classroom. The college appropriates a great deal of money toward undergraduate research—which almost all students take advantage of—and for one of the graduation requirements, the "Experiential Learning" course.

Academics

Knox academics are based on its principles of giving students the freedom to discover for themselves what they are interested in learning. Every student has a faculty advisor with whom they work to map out their course of study. Knox offers 37 majors and 51 minors but also helps students design their own majors. Especially strong areas of study include creative writing and premedical studies.

The school year at Knox is divided into three 10-week terms, during which students take three courses. "It's nice to be able to focus on fewer classes, but you're forced to learn the material very quickly," notes a student. Freshmen must take a First-Year Preceptorial—an intensive seminar that provides an introduction to liberal arts with an emphasis on writing skills—during their first term. The Preceptorial, fittingly called "Conversations in a World of Strangers," engages students in examining questions and conflicts surrounding human self-identification and interactions with others. Students must also complete at least one course in arts, humanities, mathematics and natural sciences, and history and social science. No class has more than 50 students, which lends an atmosphere of informality.

Knox offers several unique programs that allow students to take independent learning a step further. Through its College Honors Program, seniors pursue advanced independent study in a specific subject, culminating in a research or creative project. Knox also offers access to over $200,000 in research grants, including the Ford Foundation Research Fellowship Program, which funds students interested in teaching careers, and the Ronald McNair Program, which supports students from under-represented groups in the pursuit of academic careers. "There's a lot of support for finding research opportunities and getting the funds to do the work," says a student.

In keeping with its belief that students learn many of their most valuable lessons outside the traditional classroom setting, Knox has a requirement that all students must engage in "Experiential Learning," a setting in which they apply their skills to real-life situations. The activity to fulfill this requirement can be anything from study abroad to summer research to leadership in an on-campus group, but students must write up a plan for learning about potential careers as well as personal growth. "Studying off campus is not just about having fun—you're compelled to learn something about your future and yourself," one student comments. Knox offers numerous off-campus programs, both in the United States and in other countries. From a semester at Knox's very own Green Oaks Biological Field Station just off campus or a summer working in the arts in Chicago, to a year studying classics in Greece or

KNOX COLLEGE

Four-year private
Founded: 1837
Galesburg, IL
Large town
Pop. 32,193

Address:
2 East South Street
Galesburg, IL
61401

Admissions:
309-341-7100

Financial Aid:
309-341-7149

admission@knox.edu

www.knox.edu

KNOX COLLEGE

trekking across the Serengeti, students at Knox can explore a gamut of opportunities all over the world.

The college provides financial support for internships through the Hirsch-Zucker Endowed Fund for Non-Profit Internships and the Conservation/Rural Development Internship Fund. The career center also administers the Fall Institute, when classes are cancelled and events "provide practical, hands-on time to shape and define individual goals."

Student Life

Although a small school in a small town, Knox always has numerous activities and varied forms of entertainment. Knox's "101 Fun Things to Do"—a list compiled by Knox students—ranges from the physicality of "playing pick-up soccer in the rain for the sole purpose of getting dirty," to wandering among the trees of Standish Park Arboretum next to campus. Students can also choose activities from about 100 organizations, including such groups as the Chemistry and Rocketry Clubs to the Knox College Choir and Knox Jazz Ensemble.

Knox College has a host of other traditions. The annual Pumphandle Day sums up Knox in a handshake (literally). The first day of each school year begins with every student and faculty member lining up to shake everyone else's hand. Students appreciate the chance to "greet old friends and make new ones," explains a student. Students also enjoy Flunk Day—a surprise day at the beginning of spring when the secretly-chosen leaders of Flunk run through campus and announce the cancellation of classes in favor of games and mud wrestling. Knox has several other seasonal traditions: in the winter, students sled or ride trays at the football stadium, and in the spring, the community gathers to ritualize the importance of prairie fires at the Green Oaks Biological Station.

Fraternities and sororities are a popular choice at Knox, with approximately one out of six students joining Greek organizations. Students can choose from six fraternities and four sororities, including the Gentlemen of Quality and the Women of Influence, which promote understanding among different cultures. The fraternity houses are popular party destinations, but Greek members also put a lot of effort into community service, with some houses serving more than 800 hours a year. True to the college's founding belief in learning outside the classroom, Knox students "prioritize community service," as one student points out. The Knox Peace Corps Preparatory Program, which grooms students to serve in the Peace Corps after graduation, is the first of its kind at any college.

Knox also offers numerous club and intramural sports, including the aptly-named Xonk Ultimate Frisbee team and the LARC, or Live-Action Role-playing Club. Knox's 21 Division III sports create ample opportunities for school spirit to abound. Nearby Monmouth College is Knox's top football rival, and the two teams battle every fall for the Bronze Turkey Trophy.

Eighty-five percent of the college—and almost all freshmen—choose to live on campus. Several of the fraternities are also housed, and students may opt for theme houses. The International House is open to both international and domestic students, while Peterson House provides places for 14 seniors who wish to live with their close friends. Professors live right next to campus, and students often visit their homes to explore ideas presented in class.

Student Body

Knox students embrace the school's values associated with freedom of thought. They come from 45 states and 48 countries, as well as numerous ethnicities and religions. One student explains that despite their differences, students share a common "focus on academics and careers."

Knox began admitting women and students of different races in 1850, making it one of the earliest co-educational schools; its founders were social reformers who strongly opposed slavery. Students carry that legacy, and are generally "more liberal and accepting of those who are different," says a student.

Although the student body is 64 percent Caucasian, a 23 percent minority community promotes a desire among students to give all members of the community an equal voice. Less than half of the student body comes from out of state.

You May Not Know

- Three U.S. Presidents have received honorary degrees from Knox.
- Knox has not given a proctored exam in 58 years.
- Knox was originally called Knox Manual Labor College, and students worked on the college's farm in order to pay their way through school.

Distinguished Alumni

Barry Bearak, Pulitzer Prize winning journalist; Ismat Kittani, former President, UN General Assembly; Thomas E. Kurtz, co-creator, BASIC programming language.

Admissions and Financial Aid

Knox is most interested in applicants who embody the college's values. High school course loads, grades, personal statements, and teacher recommendations are important, but Knox goes beyond this to verify that its incoming student body will embrace Knox's ideals and will contribute to the community. The submission of standardized test scores is optional for most applicants, except those who are home-schooled or from high schools which do not give grades.

Knox was founded on the belief that any applicant worthy of a Knox education should be admitted to the school, regardless of economic standing. Academic-based scholarships range from $5,000 to $16,000 per year and are awarded for academic excellence in high school. Knox also offers scholarships in several academic disciplines, including visual and performing arts, mathematics, and writing, and well as National Merit and National Achievement Scholarships.

KNOX COLLEGE

Highlights

Admissions Criteria
Academic criteria:
Grades: ☆ ☆ ☆
Difficulty of class schedule: ☆ ☆ ☆
Class rank: ☆ ☆
Standardized test scores: ☆
Teacher recommendations: ☆ ☆
Personal statement: ☆ ☆ ☆
Non-academic criteria considered:
Interview
Extracurricular activities
Special talents, interests, abilities
Character/personal qualities
Volunteer work
State of residency
Geographical location
Minority affiliation
Alumni relationship

Deadlines
Early Action: November 1 (Early Action I), December 1 (Early Action II)
Early Decision: No
Regular Action: February 1 (final)
Notification of admission by: March 31
Common Application: Accepted

Financial Aid
In-state tuition: $38,286
Out-of-state tuition: $38,286
Room: $4,206
Board: $4,194
Books: $900
Freshmen receiving need-based aid: 80%
Undergrads rec. need-based aid: 77%
Avg. % of need met by financial aid: 87%
Avg. aid package (freshmen): $30,376
Avg. aid package (undergrads): $28,374
Avg. debt upon graduation: $27,542

School Spirit
Mascot: Prairie Fire
Colors: Purple and gold
Song: *Hail Knox*

LAFAYETTE COLLEGE

Overview

Ninety miles from the Philadelphia city center, 2,500 students make Lafayette College their home. This private Presbyterian college strongly supports the sciences and engineering while encouraging students to take advantage of excellent study abroad, research, and internship programs. Consistently listed among the top 40 liberal arts schools, Lafayette's students play as hard as they work, with a strong Greek life and Division I sports.

The campus itself is park-like and classically "college," with stone buildings, a recently expanded library, an impressive athletic complex, and state-of-the-art classrooms. Venturing down college hill leads students into the small city of Easton, which hosts a charming farmers market, live jazz, and affordable living for artists and entrepreneurs who enjoy the proximity to New York and Philadelphia just as much as the students do.

Academics

Lafayette offers 37 majors, along with the opportunity for independent study and interdisciplinary work, and especially prides itself in its programs in biology, engineering studies, English, and psychology.

While the school does not have a general core requirement, all sophomores must participate in the Values and Sciences/Technology (VAST) program. Exemplifying the focus of Lafayette, courses use an interdisciplinary approach to solve modern problems in science and technology. "I took the Dog Course in which we studied dogs in literature, biology, and history and even did a dog show," recalls a student.

Whether in engineering or English, almost all classes have 50 students or fewer, so it is easy for students to get a lot of "one-on-one attention" from their professors. Students say that the professors know their names and "will readily meet for a cup of coffee or lunch." The small class experience begins for most with the First-Year Seminar program. Classes of fewer than 16 students learn basic strategies of writing, discussion, and research. Nearly 40 different courses are offered each year, and professors work closely with students in all of them, often organizing field-trips, guest lectures, or other forms of active learning. "I loved my seminar because we had great discussions and all became friends," notes a student.

Lafayette is full of other above-and-beyond academic opportunities in addition to First-Year Seminars. For example, the school hosts a Technology Clinic, in which "students from different majors team up to attack real-world problems posed by business firms, non-profit organizations, and government agencies." Students rate participation in the Tech clinic as one of "the best programs at Lafayette," and, consequently, admission into this program is very competitive.

Moving beyond the classroom, the Excel Scholars program is Lafayette's generous way of fostering undergraduate research. When nominated by a professor, students can engage in independent research. Working on original—rather than routine or clerical—projects, students become research assistants for faculty members. They are paid $8-10 per hour, and during interim and summer, are offered free housing. The program currently has about 160 students and a budget of over $500,000. Past projects have included researching the decision-making of Supreme Court Justices, measuring the effect of steroid hormones, and co-directing a dramatic performance.

Many students continue research during Lafayette's two three-week-long Interim sessions every January and May. During this time, other students choose to participate in off-campus internships coordinated by faculty members or the Career Services office. Past internships have included testing motor oil dispersants for Mobil Chemical Corp., assisting with licensing at Jim Henson Enterprises, and helping with client management at Mutual of New York.

The college also offers optional programs led by Lafayette faculty during Interim sessions. These take students to one of a dozen or so different countries and address a range of different subjects. "It's a huge opportunity to be able to study off campus without missing out on the regular school year," says a student. A recently instated program takes geology students through all major National Parks of the American West—a rare program by any measure!

For a longer international experience with semester study abroad, Lafayette offers over 80 affiliated programs worldwide, many of which provide internships. Students can also choose to take part in the Semester in Environmental Science at the Marine Biological Laboratory's Ecosystems Center, Woods Hole, Massachusetts, or in the Washington Semester program, based at American University.

After graduation, approximately 26 percent of students pursue a graduate degree immediately. Among students who enter the work force, approximately 58 percent enter a field related to their major within six months of graduation.

Student Life

With 250 student organizations ranging from 20 academic honor societies to the "Holla Back" voting mobilization club, there is something for everyone. All sorts of ethnic, religious, and international community organizations keep the campus vibrant, while artistic programs, such as the Marquis Players theater group, engage the creative. Model UN, Neuroscience Club, and Chess Club keep the intellectual student challenged outside the classroom. The Landis Community Outreach Center coordinates over 30 service groups.

The Lafayette Activity Forum (LAF) organizes open mikes at Gilbert's coffee-house, all-night parties in the campus's own dance club "The Spot," and performances in the Limburg Theater at the Farinon College Center. Larger events include the popular All-college day, a day-long festival culminating in a Midnight Breakfest, the Block pARTy showcasing campus arts, and the Lafayette Leadership Institute, which invites 200 students for workshops.

As if there isn't enough to distract people from school work, Greek organizations are very prominent with 19 percent of men and 39 percent of women joining the four fraternities and six sororities. "Greek parties are the best," says one student.

Other than All-college day, the biggest on-campus event is the Lafayette-Lehigh football game. This match-up has been played 145 times and is always well-attended by "rowdy, hyped up" fans. Despite being a small college, the school offers Patriot Division I sports. The football team has played in the NCAA Football Championship Subdivision tournament for three consecutive years, and the men's basketball team also tends to make a strong showing. A remarkably quirky list of 40 intramural sports includes Scrabble, Mini Golf, Ping Pong, Uno, and arm wrestling as well as traditional sports. The non-varsity athlete can participate in 40 club sports, including the requisite soccer, fencing, and of course, Ultimate Frisbee.

Students can also drive into Philadelphia or even New York City for big city entertainment. More often, though, they can be found in the classic town of Easton at the College Hill Tavern,

LAFAYETTE COLLEGE

403

College Profiles

LAFAYETTE COLLEGE

hanging out on campus at the Farinon College Center or partying at a fraternity house.

Incoming freshmen complete a survey to be assigned to housing while upperclass students participate in a housing lottery. Ninety-two percent of students live on campus, with many in the 12 Greek houses. Twenty exceptional students are nominated each year to join the competitive McKelvy House Scholars program.

Student Body

As a church-affiliated school, Lafayette students lean a little "more conservatively," remarks a student. That said, the university itself encourages ethnic, religious, and social diversity, with a moderately diverse student population that describes itself as 16 percent minority. The geographic diversity is high: five percent of students come from abroad, and 78 percent from out of state. Students describe themselves as "very active and involved" and "pretty friendly because you more or less know everyone else or at least recognize their faces."

You May Not Know

- In 1844, Lafayette graduated David K. McDonogh, arguably the first "legalized" slave to receive a college degree.
- The school's namesake, the Marquis de Lafayette, asked the King of France to finance his journey to America to assist in the revolution. When the King refused, 19-year-old Lafayette bought his own ship and added the phrase "cur non" to his family crest. This saying, meaning "Why not?" is now the motto of Lafayette College.
- Lafayette's endowment per student is in the top two percent of all U.S. institutions.

Distinguished Alumni

Charles Bergstresser, co-founder of Dow Jones and Company; Haldan K. Hartline, winner of 1967 Nobel Prize in Physiology or Medicine; Roger Newton, Pfizer Global Research and Development, co-discoverer of Lipitor; Joel Silver, producer of *Die Hard*, *Lethal Weapon*, and *The Matrix*.

Admissions and Financial Aid

Secondary school records, strong teacher recommendations, and personal statements are very important in admissions decisions. The admissions board also makes clear that they are not just looking for good students, but good citizens, in particular ones that display "motivation, social awareness, ambition, individualism, and potential for leadership as exhibited through involvement in community and extracurricular activities."

Once accepted, Lafayette happily meets 100 percent of student's demonstrated need, with just over half of students receiving need-based aid and six percent receiving merit-based aid. Top students are offered the Marquis Scholarship, which provides $20,000 per year and an extra $4,000 for a faculty-led study-abroad program. Athletic scholarships are also offered for men's and women's basketball, men's soccer, and women's field hockey.

LAKE FOREST COLLEGE

Overview

American writer F. Scott Fitzgerald wrote to his daughter in 1940, "once I thought that Lake Forest was the most glamorous place in the world. Maybe it was." Lake Forest College is indeed a beautiful and lush campus, with 107 acres of wooded land right next to Lake Michigan. Residents of Lake Forest see all the seasons, with snowy winters and green springs.

Besides its charming environment, Lake Forest benefits from its proximity to Chicago—it is just 30 miles north of downtown Chicago. The college organizes programs and events in the city, and internship opportunities abound.

While the school is small, students are offered multiple opportunities to research and work independently, and are encouraged to make full use of all the opportunities available on and off campus. This is a school where you can craft your own experience.

Academics

Lake Forest College is known for its strong liberal arts education, which provides a strong foundation in the humanities, social and natural sciences, and offers a wide range of additional programs for students who want more challenges. Students may pick from over 40 majors, which include more specialized interdisciplinary majors such as Islamic World Studies and Environmental Studies, besides the more traditional areas of study. Motivated students are also allowed to participate in the Independent Scholar Program, which allows students to design their own majors. Particularly strong majors are English and pre-health.

The school asks students to complete a General Education Curriculum, but the requirements are relatively few compared to many colleges. The three main requirements are First Year Studies, which includes a writing requirement; "Academic Divisions," which means two credits each of humanities, social sciences, and natural sciences; and two "Cultural Diversity" courses. "I love that we have the freedom to choose the classes we want to take," says one student.

Lake Forest encourages its students to push themselves, providing opportunities for students to work and research independently. Honors Fellows are selected every year to produce independent research and senior theses, which are presented at the Student Symposium, an annual event that celebrates the student scholarship.

Students in law, communications, nursing, engineering, and international relations also have the option of a fast-track accelerated program, in which they may opt to complete their degree in three years instead of the usual four, or complete their bachelor's degree while simultaneously beginning a graduate degree with a partner university.

Somewhat less impressive is the study-abroad selection which, while diverse, is unfortunately quite small. Students have five choices—Beijing, Granada, Greece, Paris, or the border between Mexico and America. However, students may also participate in Associated Colleges of the Midwest study-abroad programs.

During the summer, students are given the chance to work one-on-one with a faculty member as part of the Richter Scholars program. The Scholars live and work together, participating in a weekly colloquium.

Students and alumni may use an online career center to search for jobs and internships, and the school provides assistance to those applying to graduate school. More unique is a Mentor Program where students and alumni are paired based on their interests for a one-year relationship.

Student Life

With over 50 extracurricular groups and organizations to pick from, Lake Forest students are spoiled for choice. Unique groups include I-SEE, a business and en-

LAKE FOREST COLLEGE

Four-year private
Founded: 1857
Lake Forest, IL
Small town
Pop. 19,375

Address:
555 North Sheridan
Road
Lake Forest, IL
60045

Admissions:
800-828-4751

Financial Aid:
847-735-5103

admissions@lakeforest.edu

www.lakeforest.edu

LAKE FOREST COLLEGE

Highlights

Students
Total enrollment: 1,570
Undergrads: 1,552
Freshmen: 416
Part-time students: 1%
From out-of-state: 40%
From public schools: 70%
Male/Female: 42%/58%
Live on-campus: 72%
In fraternities: 7%
In sororities: 11%
Off-campus employment rating: Fair
Caucasian: 60%
African American: 6%
Hispanic: 13%
Asian / Pacific Islander: 5%
Native American: 0%
Mixed (2+ ethnicities): 3%
International: 11%

Academics
Calendar: Semester
Student/faculty ratio: 12:1
Class size 9 or fewer: 9%
Class size 10-29: 81%
Class size 30-49: 9%
Class size 50-99: 1%
Class size 100 or more: -
Returning freshmen: 83%
Six-year graduation rate: 70%
Graduates who immediately go to gradu-
    ate school: 21%

Most Popular Majors
Communication
Education
Biology

Admissions
Applicants: 3,479
Accepted: 1,981
Acceptance rate: 56.9%
Placed on wait list: 45
Enrolled from wait list: 15
Average GPA: 3.6
ACT range: 23-28
SAT Math range: 530-670
SAT Reading range: 560-640
SAT Writing range: Not reported
Top 10% of class: 35%
Top 25% of class: 63%
Top 50% of class: 88%

406

trepreneurial student group; LEAP, an environmental awareness group; and Synapse, a group focused on neuroscience. Notably, Lake Forest students produce four serious publications—*Tusitala*, a literary magazine dating back to 1935; *Stentor*, the weekly paper; *Collage*, a foreign language magazine; and *Eukaryon*, a science research journal. There are also seven Greek organizations on campus, both fraternities and sororities. Tri Beta is uniquely focused on biology. Though there are many Greek organizations, their presence is not overwhelming.

Besides student activities, there are also events open to the entire student population. Traditional on-campus events are less about school spirit and more about serving the community. Mr. CASAnova, an annual male beauty pageant put on by Kappa Alpha Theta, may sound like a facetious and superficial event, but the money raised goes to CASA, an organization that helps children in foster care. Another community service-oriented event is the Gates Day of Service, an annual event where students, staff, and faculty all pitch in to paint schools and churches, or play Bingo with residents at nearby community centers. Ra Fest is a two-day music festival with different bands.

On a regular school day, the Mohr Student Center is the self-named "living room" of the college, a place where students eat, relax, and play pool or table tennis. For students who want to get off campus, a nearby train makes a quick getaway to Chicago for shopping, museums, movies, or just hanging out. The school's Center for Chicago Programs also organizes trips and events in the cities.

In terms of athletics, Lake Forest has 17 Varsity (Division III) sports teams. Besides the more traditional sports, they also have a strong handball team, which has won 30 national championships and claimed the men's, women's, and combined titles at the latest Collegiate National Championships. There are also multiple student-organized club sports, ranging from cheerleading to sailing to golf. Intramural sports include flag football and Ultimate Frisbee. Athletes enjoy a new recreation, sport, and fitness center that includes multiple courts, a training room, and a dance studio.

Students at Lake Forest are guaranteed housing. Most incoming students live in quads, some which consist of two doubles connected by a private bathroom, and others that are just single large rooms. "The dorms are so-so for freshman year, but it gets better," says one student. Upperclass students go through a lottery for housing.

Student Body

Lake Forest is a small school, with a total enrollment of around 1,500. This makes it easy to meet everyone on campus. While the stereotype of Lake Forest students is that they are wealthy, three quarters of the student population receives financial aid. In terms of diversity, around 11 percent are international students, and 27 percent identify as ethnic minorities.

You May Not Know

- There are nearly 250 species of naturalized plants on campus.
- Lake Forest students maintain a campus garden where they grow pesticide-free fruits, vegetables and herbs.

- The founders of Lake Forest College also founded the town of Lake Forest.

Distinguished Alumni

Herbert Block, Pulitzer Prize-winning political cartoonist; Allan Carr, Tony Award winner; Diana Nyad, world-record holding swimmer and sports commentator.

Admissions and Financial Aid

There are three ways to apply to Lake Forest: by Early Decision (deadline Dec. 1), Early Action (also Dec. 1), or Regular Decision (Feb. 15). While Lake Forest uses the Common Application, it also requires a graded writing sample. Students have the option to omit their test scores, but students who choose this option must sit for an interview. Students who submit their test scores are still encouraged to do an interview.

There are seven merit-based scholarships offered at Lake Forest but no athletic scholarships. Two geographically based scholarships, the In-State Scholarship for Illinois residents, and the Presidential Scholarship for students outside of Illinois, both offer $12,000 per year. Chicago Public School Full-Tuition Scholarships are offered to 25 graduates of Chicago Public Schools. There are also two scholarships for international students, and one for transfer students. In total, the school awards up to $20,000 per year.

LAKE FOREST COLLEGE

Highlights

Admissions Criteria
Academic criteria:
Grades: ☆ ☆ ☆
Difficulty of class schedule: ☆ ☆ ☆
Class rank: ☆
Standardized test scores: ☆
Teacher recommendations: ☆ ☆ ☆
Personal statement: ☆ ☆
Non-academic criteria considered:
Interview
Extracurricular activities
Special talents, interests, abilities
Character/personal qualities
Volunteer work
Work experience
State of residency
Geographical location
Alumni relationship

Deadlines
Early Action: December 1
Early Decision: December 1
Regular Action: February 15 (priority)
Notification of admission by: March 20
Common Application: Accepted

Financial Aid
In-state tuition: $39,168
Out-of-state tuition: $39,168
Room: $4,480
Board: $4,812
Books: Varies
Freshmen receiving need-based aid: 75%
Undergrads rec. need-based aid: 79%
Avg. % of need met by financial aid: 84%
Avg. aid package (freshmen): $32,000
Avg. aid package (undergrads): $31,000
Avg. debt upon graduation: $30,801

School Spirit
Mascot: Black Bear
Colors: Red and black

LAWRENCE UNIVERSITY

LAWRENCE UNIVERSITY

Four-year private
Founded: 1847
Appleton, WI
Medium city
Pop. 73,243

Address:
711 East Boldt Way
Appleton, WI
54911

Admissions:
800-227-0982

Financial Aid:
920-832-6583

admissions@lawrence.
edu

www.lawrence.edu

Overview

"Liberal Arts College + Conservatory = Lawrence University," notes this small private liberal arts university. About a quarter of students at this exclusively undergraduate institution are part of the conservatory, and their private lessons explain the statistic that two thirds of Lawrence's classes have just one student. Even non-music majors will benefit from Lawrence's focus on "individualized learning" since 75 percent of classes have fewer than 20 students.

The picturesque 84-acre main campus is nestled on a bluff overlooking the historic Fox River, next to downtown Appleton, a growing metropolis of 73,000 in the northeast of Wisconsin. Northern Campus has a definite tongue-twister for a name—Björklunden vid Sjön—and represents the 425-acre estate on Lake Michigan that hosts weekend student retreats and seminars. While spring and fall make for beautiful scenery, winter is—well, the university says, "we like to think of it as 'character-building' weather." By "it," they mean four feet of snow per winter and an average January high/low of 24°F/7°F.

A recent campus construction phase resulted in the renovation of every existing academic building and the construction of new facilities, including a residence hall and the impressive 107,000-square-foot Warch Campus Center. For musicians or liberal arts students who don't mind being located in the Midwest rather than a larger city, who enjoy individualized attention, and who own heavy winter coats, Lawrence may be a good fit.

Academics

The Lawrence Conservatory of Music, usually referred to as "the Con," was founded in 1894. Most students at Lawrence earn a bachelor's of arts or bachelor's of music, with about three percent of students completing both degrees through a five-year program. There are also a number of co-op programs in fields including engineering, health sciences, and environmental studies. Lawrence offers over 40 courses in study/areas of interest.

BA students' requirements are spread equally in three areas: Freshman Studies and General Education, a declared major, and elective study. General Education mandates include courses in the humanities, fine arts, social sciences, laboratory natural sciences, global and comparative studies, diversity, writing or speaking, math, and foreign language or passing an approved exam. Bachelor of Music students spend about two thirds of their curriculum on music courses, with the remaining third devoted to Freshman Studies and General Education requirements. All students must complete a Senior Experience course or activity.

Lawrence's three ten-week trimesters make for intensive classes, since information is presented within the constraints of a short period of time; but some students find this desirable. "Being able to focus on just three classes makes organizing my time easier," says a student. Strong programs include chemistry, English, history, and, most notably, music.

The Freshman Studies Program, Lawrence's "introduction to liberal learning," has been part of the curriculum for over 60 years. Freshmen take the course during their first two trimesters on campus, and each section of the course has about 15 students. "We discuss Plato, Shakespeare, and *A Pocket Style Manual*," explains a student. "Discussions can get heated."

It's unusual to have a conservatory within a liberal arts university, and Lawrence's is a vibrant institution, with more than 350 music majors. "For a school of our size, we have more musical talent per capita than any other liberal arts school in the country," brags a student. A big plus is that the conservatory's many resources are available exclusively for undergraduates.

There are nearly 30 countries to choose from for off-campus study, with the most popular being the Lawrence University London Centre, founded in 1970. Juniors and seniors have an option to intern in London. Other study-abroad options also come with an internship component, and there are scholarships that support overseas study. Lawrence administers a Marine Biology term at the Francophone Seminar in Dakar, Senegal.

Lawrence's career center offers an online internship database, an alumni contact program to put students in touch with alums in their field of interest, and access to Workforce, an annual career and internship fair for the state's 20 private colleges and universities.

Student Life

The more than 100 student organizations at Lawrence attest to the diversity of the student body. The organizations are categorized as political/activism organizations, academic groups, spiritual organizations, publications and campus involvement, sports and games (including LU Tree Climbers), Greek organizations, and music/drama (from Artistic Masturbation Theater Troupe to WLFM, the campus radio station). Other miscellaneous groups are equally intriguing, from Anime Club to the Society for Creative Anachronism.

The Warch Campus Center is an impressive 107,000-square-foot eco-friendly building with open spaces, high ceilings, natural stone, and beautiful views of the surrounding Fox River. It instantly became a popular gathering spot for students.

One of Lawrence's most famous events is the Great Midwest Trivia Contest, broadcast over the college radio in January for 50 consecutive hours. It is known as the "World's Longest Running Trivia Contest" because of the tradition of asking the last question from one year as the first question of the next. "The contest is the essence of Lawrence," comments a student. "Everyone gets excited even though it's so old school."

Other events include the annual Lawrence Jazz Celebration Weekend, an educational festival where professional jazz artists visit campus, and Shack-a-thon, an annual event to raise funds for Habitat for Humanity and raise awareness about homelessness. "We build temporary shacks out of scrap metal and compete for Best Shack," says a student.

Of the eight Greek organizations, the most unique is definitely Phi Mu Alpha Sinfonia, a fraternity composed of musicians. Founded at Lawrence in 1938, the group spearheads many events, from philanthropic activities such as clinics with high school and middle school bands to helping with Lawrence University Jazz Weekend.

Lawrence's boasts 22 varsity teams, with Division III basketball the best known. In fact, the team has played in the NCAA national tournament five times since 2004. "Fans really come out for basketball," one student remarks. Club sports include teams for Ultimate Frisbee and crew, as well as individual competitions including rock climbing, swing dancing, and martial arts. A wide variety of intramurals are also offered.

Off campus, Appleton's College Avenue provides restaurants, coffee shops, and stores within walking distance. A half-mile away, the $45 million Fox Cities Performing Arts Center seats 2,100 for performances. Those who prefer the outdoors can run, hike, cycle, row, and simply enjoy themselves at nearby High Cliff State Park, Fox River, and dozens of local parks.

LAWRENCE UNIVERSITY

Highlights

Students
Total enrollment: 1,525
Undergrads: 1,525
Freshmen: 412
From out-of-state: 72%
From public schools: 70%
Male/Female: 46%/54%
Live on-campus: 98%
In fraternities: 18%
In sororities: 9%
Off-campus employment rating: Good
Caucasian: 76%
African American: 3%
Hispanic: 4%
Asian / Pacific Islander: 3%
Native American: 1%
Mixed (2+ ethnicities): 3%
International: 9%

Academics
Calendar: Trimester
Student/faculty ratio: 9:1
Class size 9 or fewer: 32%
Class size 10-29: 58%
Class size 30-49: 7%
Class size 50-99: 2%
Class size 100 or more: -
Six-year graduation rate: 73%
Graduates who immediately go to graduate school: 18%

Most Popular Majors
Visual/performing arts
Biology
Social sciences

Admissions
Applicants: 2,599
Accepted: 1,980
Acceptance rate: 76.2%
Placed on wait list: 61
Enrolled from wait list: 12
Average GPA: 3.6
ACT range: 25-31
SAT Math range: 580-710
SAT Reading range: 580-720
SAT Writing range: 23-47
Top 10% of class: 46%
Top 25% of class: 71%
Top 50% of class: 92%

409

College Profiles

LAWRENCE UNIVERSITY

Admissions Criteria

Academic criteria:
Grades: ☆ ☆ ☆
Difficulty of class schedule: ☆ ☆ ☆
Class rank: ☆ ☆ ☆
Standardized test scores: ☆
Teacher recommendations: ☆ ☆
Personal statement: ☆ ☆
Non-academic criteria considered:
Interview
Extracurricular activities
Special talents, interests, abilities
Character/personal qualities
Volunteer work
Work experience
State of residency
Geographical location
Minority affiliation
Alumni relationship

Deadlines

Early Action: December 1
Early Decision: November 1
Regular Action: January 15 (final)
Notification of admission by: April 1
Common Application: Accepted

Financial Aid

In-state tuition: $40,926
Out-of-state tuition: $40,926
Room: $3,975
Board: $4,521
Books: $900
Freshmen receiving need-based aid: 69%
Undergrads rec. need-based aid: 63%
Avg. % of need met by financial aid: 88%
Avg. aid package (freshmen): $31,608
Avg. aid package (undergrads): $31,400
Avg. debt upon graduation: $30,724

School Spirit

Mascot: Vikings
Colors: Blue and white
Song: *O'er the Fox*

Students are generally required to live on campus all four years. In addition to seven residence halls, Lawrence offers small houses (ranging from 8-27 beds) where upperclassmen live. Group-style living arrangements are also available for student organizations united around a common cause or programmatic theme. Hiett Hall, Lawrence's newest residence, overlooks the Fox River; Hiett's suites are reserved for upperclass students.

Student Body

Lawrence's small student body of about 1,500 undergraduates is geographically diverse, hailing from almost all 50 states. International students from more than 50 other countries make up nine percent of the student body. The international population gives the college a unique perspective—and students from equatorial countries must be commended for surviving Appleton's brutal winters.

There is moderate ethnic diversity with 14 percent minority students. Students say that with so many music majors, they "have an interesting mix between the creative music types and the rest of the students, but it seems to work."

You May Not Know

- Chartered in 1847, Lawrence was the second college in the U.S. to be founded as a co-ed institution.
- On August 20, 1882, Appleton became the first city to generate electricity commercially (New York City was a close runner-up two weeks later).
- "*Light! More Light!*" are believed to be the last words uttered by Goethe and can be found on Lawrence University's seal.

Distinguished Alumni

Jennifer Baumgardner, feminist writer and activist; Michael Hammond, Chairman of the National Endowment for the Arts; Barbara Lawton, Lieutenant Governor of Wisconsin; Fred Sturm, jazz composer.

Admissions and Financial Aid

According to the college, admissions officers consider "each applicant's course of study, grades, standardized test scores (if submitted), recommendations, and extracurricular activities, roughly in that order." Test scores are optional, though about three-quarters of students submit their scores. Conservatory applicants must complete additional information on the Lawrence supplement to the Common Application and submit a music resume.

Admission to Lawrence is need-blind for domestic students. Besides need-based aid, there are also a variety of merit-based awards: academic ($7,000 to $15,000 a year), music (also $7,000 to $15,000 a year), "more light!" ($1,000 to $7,000 awards that honor leadership and community engagement), and others.

LEHIGH UNIVERSITY

LEHIGH UNIVERSITY

Four-year private
Founded: 1865
Bethlehem, PA
Medium city
Pop. 75,266

Address:
27 Memorial Drive
West
Bethlehem, PA
18015

Admissions:
610-758-3100

Financial Aid:
610-758-3181

admissions@lehigh.
edu

www.lehigh.edu

Overview

"Oh little town of Bethlehem, how still we see thee lie"…unless, of course, we're talking about Bethlehem, Pennsylvania, home of Lehigh University. With just over a third of all undergraduates active in frats or sororities, campus is anything but "still" on a Friday night. However, don't let the preeminence of the Greek system fool you; given that the students here attend the research university ranked 41st in the nation by *U.S. News & World Report*, they clearly know how to hit the books.

About a third of undergraduates major in engineering and applied sciences, and another third major in business, two of the strongest majors. However, Lehigh isn't interested in producing one-dimensional grads; they encourage students to take classes from across disciplines and to tailor their own majors to their academic interests.

Students at Lehigh can forget about the gym—their campus is built into the side of a valley, so they get a workout just walking to and from class (though if you really love exercising indoors, they do have a gym, too). The buildings on campus are largely gothic, (think medieval cathedrals and castles), though that doesn't mean facilities are all old-fashioned. A brand new multidisciplinary science building, which uses green technology, was built in 2009.

If students get bored with life on campus, they can always venture into Bethlehem itself. With a population of approximately 75,000, Bethlehem makes for a relatively calm college town—not huge—but active. And if you really feel like a big fish in a little pond, New York and Philadelphia are both within easy driving distance.

Academics

Lehigh has three undergraduate colleges: the College of Arts and Science, the College of Business and Economics, and the College of Engineering and Applied Physical Sciences. There are more than 150 majors, and students from one college may choose a minor from one of the other colleges. Students may also craft their own major with an advisor's approval.

In the vein of encouraging students to experience different facets of academia, Lehigh requires all students to fulfill distribution requirements in the humanities, social science, natural science, and math, as well as three courses in writing (two of which are taken freshman year, and the third of which is taken junior year). There is, however, a way to get out of the distribution requirements: the Eckhardt Scholars program, composed of a select group of high achieving students, allows students to replace university requirements with their own carefully crafted program of courses. Eckhardt Scholars must consult with an advisor and ultimately produce a thesis. "We get extra attention from professors and get to interact with them outside of the classroom," says a participant.

Lehigh has a variety of specially tailored degree programs. For those set on becoming a doctor, Lehigh has a seven-year combined BA/MD program. More interested in nurturing minds than fixing bodies? Lehigh offers a five-year BA plus MA in education and Teacher Certification Program.

For the business-minded student, Lehigh has a wide variety of resources and programs. These include the Integrated Degree Engineering, Arts, and Sciences Honors Program (IDEAS), which is a BS program combining two focus areas, one from business and one from arts/sciences. "In this program, I've already had to write multiple papers and give a number of presentations," notes a student. "I'm really learning how to communicate effectively."

High-achievers may set their sights on the Martindale Student Associates Program, in which a small group of juniors are given the opportunity to travel overseas on the university's dime. The purpose is to interact with some of today's most influential business leaders and decision makers.

LEHIGH UNIVERSITY

Students
Total enrollment: 7,080
Undergrads: 4,883
Freshmen: 1,217
Part-time students: 1%
From out-of-state: 74%
Male/Female: 57%/43%
Live on-campus: 70%
In fraternities: 38%
In sororities: 44%
Off-campus employment rating: Good
Caucasian: 69%
African American: 4%
Hispanic: 8%
Asian / Pacific Islander: 6%
Native American: 0%
Mixed (2+ ethnicities): 3%
International: 6%

Academics
Calendar: Semester
Student/faculty ratio: 10:1
Class size 9 or fewer: 15%
Class size 10-29: 51%
Class size 30-49: 21%
Class size 50-99: 9%
Class size 100 or more: 3%
Returning freshmen: 94%
Six-year graduation rate: 88%
Graduates who immediately go to graduate school: 30%
Graduates who immediately enter career related to major: 63%

Most Popular Majors
Finance
Mechanical engineering
Accounting

Admissions
Applicants: 11,529
Accepted: 3,756
Acceptance rate: 32.6%
Placed on wait list: 3,595
Enrolled from wait list: Not reported
Average GPA: Not reported
ACT range: 28-31
SAT Math range: 630-730
SAT Reading range: 570-670
SAT Writing range: Not reported
Top 10% of class: 64%
Top 25% of class: 92%
Top 50% of class: 100%

412

There are other opportunities to travel abroad. In fact, Lehigh approves over 150 study-abroad programs all over the world, and it also offers programs during winter and summer break. Anyone up for Art and Architecture in Vicenza? How about Sustainable Development in Costa Rica? If you can think of a location and a project, Lehigh will work with you to try and make it a reality.

To help students with planning for their futures, the Career Services office provides an annual career fair, career networking with 26,000 alumni through the Lehigh University Career Advisory Network, and on-campus interviewing with 200 employers each year. "Every time I've sought help, I've gotten more help than I've expected," one student comments.

Student Life

Ever hung on to the side of a bed and had your friends push you in a race? Come to Lehigh and you can do just that during the week of parties and rallying that precede The Rivalry—the annual football game between Lehigh and Lafayette. This is the longest uninterrupted football rivalry in college history. "Even if you're not into sports, you'll get excited about the game against Lafayette," says a student. The frats and sororities come out for the event, and they make quite the force; with 21 fraternities and 11 sororities on campus, about 40 percent of the undergraduate population decides to go Greek.

If football isn't really your sport, you should still be able to find a team more to your liking amongst the 25 NCAA Division I varsity sports at Lehigh. If you're not quite up to varsity caliber yet, you can always go for one of the 40 intramural and club teams. Wrestling is a stand-out among the varsity programs, while Frisbee is a favorite with the club teams.

Lehigh is not just for jocks. The Zoellner Arts Center on campus offers plays, concerts, and speaker series. There are more than 150 student organizations, focusing on everything from volunteering to anime (and if somehow no one has thought to start a club for your favorite activity, you can always recruit some friends, an advisor, and start one yourself). About a third of the students at Lehigh participate in religious activities, and Lehigh has a rabbi and a chaplain on staff.

Off campus, students enjoy Musikfest, a 10-day music festival held in Bethlehem that recently featured 300 performances including those by Norah Jones, Martina McBride, and Lynyrd Skynyrd and the Celtic Classic Festival. "It's amazing to have such top-notch performers come to our small town of Bethlehem," one student comments.

Housing at Lehigh changes as students move up the ranks as undergrads. Freshmen and sophomores are required to live on campus, though they change housing between their first and second year. Freshmen submit a housing preference when they pay a deposit for their first year of tuition. When deciding where to live, some things to keep in mind: McClintic-Marshall is closer to the Hill and therefore affords greater proximity to parties. However, Lower Cents has some of the only AC units and requires less hiking. "You'll appreciate the AC because it can get pretty humid," says a student. CHOICE housing is always, well, a choice. This is a specially designated section of housing for students who have a common commitment to living in an alcohol- and tobacco-free environment. And of course you can always pledge. Upperclassmen have a variety of options on and off campus, including dorms, theme houses, and apartments.

Student Body

Lehigh is not known for being terribly diverse. The student body comes largely from the Northeast, with 27 percent from New Jersey, 24 percent from Pennsylvania, and 15 percent from New York. "Those from outside of the Northeast are few and far between," notes a student. International students make up a small percentage of the student body. The school is 69 percent white, and the predominant atmosphere is on the "preppy" side. Still, students claim that while they may be somewhat underrepresented, minorities are "obviously welcome."

You May Not Know

- Lehigh has made *Playboy's* List of Top 25 Party Schools.
- Lehigh used to be affiliated with the Episcopal Church.
- The Lehigh mascot was originally the Engineers (though it switched to the slightly more fearsome Mountain Hawks in 1995).

Admissions and Financial Aid

Lehigh accepts the Common Application, but requires students to fill out a supplemental form specific to the university. The questions on the supplement reflect Lehigh's emphasis on entrepreneurship and unique majors, asking questions such as this one: "If you founded your own college or university, what topic of study would you make mandatory for all students to study?" If you've ever wanted to justify World of Warcraft 101, now's your chance.

Lehigh only requires one teacher recommendation, and while interviews are considered, they aren't mandatory. Over-achievers should note that Lehigh offers a limited number of Academic Merit-Based scholarships, valued at either full or half tuition. Dean's Scholars are students who excel once they're at Lehigh and are offered $10,000 per year in recognition of their hard work. Lehigh offers a few smaller scholarships for the arts, as well as small awards for National Merit Finalists.

LEHIGH UNIVERSITY

Highlights

Admissions Criteria
Academic criteria:
Grades: ☆ ☆ ☆
Difficulty of class schedule: ☆ ☆ ☆
Class rank: ☆
Standardized test scores: ☆ ☆
Teacher recommendations: ☆ ☆ ☆
Personal statement: ☆ ☆
Non-academic criteria considered:
Interview
Extracurricular activities
Special talents, interests, abilities
Character/personal qualities
Volunteer work
Work experience
State of residency
Geographical location
Minority affiliation
Alumni relationship

Deadlines
Early Action: No
Early Decision: November 15
Regular Action: January 1 (final)
Notification of admission by: April 1
Common Application: Accepted

Financial Aid
In-state tuition: $43,220
Out-of-state tuition: $43,220
Room: $6,640
Board: $4,920
Books: $1,000
Freshmen receiving need-based aid: 44%
Undergrads rec. need-based aid: 44%
Avg. % of need met by financial aid: 95%
Avg. aid package (freshmen): $36,189
Avg. aid package (undergrads): $36,771
Avg. debt upon graduation: $31,122

School Spirit
Mascot: Clutch the Mountain Hawk
Colors: Brown and white
Song: *The Lehigh Alma Mater.*

LEWIS AND
CLARK
COLLEGE

Four-year private
Founded: 1867
Portland, OR
Major city
Pop. 593,820

Address:
0615 SW Palatine Hill
Road
Portland, OR
97219-7899

Admissions:
800-444-4111

Financial Aid:
503-768-7090

admissions@lclark.edu

www.lclark.edu

LEWIS & CLARK COLLEGE

Overview

In what might just be the most perfect synchronicity ever, funky, unconventional, environmentalist Lewis & Clark College is located in quirky, alternative, outdoorsy Portland, Oregon—a match made in heaven. This small private college is known for its highly environmentally and socially conscious students, who benefit from L&C's 137-acre campus location in the wooded hills of an unremarkable Southwest Portland suburb that is also well connected to downtown. Reflecting its students' concern for sustainability, campus features a very high number of LEED-certified buildings, including an $11.5 million LEED platinum-rated residence hall completed in 2012.

L&C students are probably better known for their environmental and social consciousness and commitment to service than they are for their academics; but although L&C's academic offerings are limited, a few programs offer stand-out, holistic preparation for grad school or careers augmented by small class size and plenty of personal attention from faculty. L&C's size may limit the availability of certain resources—like library books or even academic opportunities—but what L&C does have, they do well. Liberal, passionate students looking to break out of the cookie-cutter college experience should consider Lewis & Clark.

Academics

Lewis & Clark offers 32 majors and 25 minors, of which some of the strongest are its biology and international affairs majors, and its interdisciplinary major and minor in environmental studies and ethnic studies, respectively. While its size certainly limits the number of courses available, it also means that classes tend to have fewer than 20 students. Professors are accessible and enthusiastic about teaching and interacting with undergrads and graduate students alike, most notably those who attend Lewis & Clark's Law School or Graduate School of Education and Counseling. "I've had lunch with almost every one of my professors," one student comments.

All students at L&C must begin their studies with the two-semester Exploration and Discovery course. Additional mandates include one semester of writing- and discussion-laden liberal arts, with a semester-long seminar taught on a subject of the instructor's interest. L&C further requires two courses in international studies, three in scientific and quantitative reasoning, one in creative arts, as well as foreign language proficiency and two semesters of physical education.

L&C puts an emphasis on "holistic" education—which may sound hippie-dippy, especially at a place like Lewis & Clark—but in the context of L&C's educational programs, it translates into highly interdisciplinary programs that transcend the traditional teaching of the same subjects at other schools. "It's invaluable to not just learn a subject but to learn how subjects are interrelated," says a student.

International affairs, one of L&C's premier programs, is its own department rather than subordinate to political science, offering students a broader foundation in foreign policy and international law, international economics, national security, and national development. The department also administers a Model UN team, and students organize a yearly International Affairs Symposium. Internships locally as well as globally are available, and the department encourages students to go beyond proficiency in a foreign language and to study abroad—which nearly everyone at L&C does.

A holistic and international mindset also governs the environmental studies program, which combines teachings and faculty from departments as disparate as biology and geology with philosophy and history. The major encourages independent thinking and research, as all students must design their own concentration in addition to the major core. Hefty funding from the Andrew W. Mellon Foundation allows students to participate in the department's research in ecologically diverse Oregon as well as throughout the world. Internships, local or abroad, are also encouraged.

Opportunities are also available in other science disciplines such as the John S. Rogers Science Research Program, which funds collaborative student-faculty summer projects. Through the Howard Hughes Medical Institute-Collaborative Research Team (HHMI-CRT) summer program, L&C students can be paired with a faculty mentor from L&C or Oregon Health Sciences University with whom they conduct research. These students also collaborate with high school or community college students, acting as mentors.

With their focus on international affairs and social awareness, L&C students tend to go abroad in very high numbers—about 60 percent of the student body. "We want to see firsthand what's happening around the world," one student notes. Since 1962, over 10,000 students have studied abroad, which is impressive when you consider that L&C is so small. They run their own programs, offering a large and diverse selection. Semester-long General Culture or Language Intensive programs are available in Australia, Brazil, Chile, China, Cuba, the Dominican Republic, Ecuador, Italy, Japan, Kenya, Morocco, Senegal, New Zealand, Tanzania, France, Greece, Spain, India, Japan, Russia, and the UK.

L&C's Center for Career and Community Engagement provides comprehensive career counseling, ranging from resume critique and practice interview to advice on choosing a major. Approximately 900 alums are active in the L&C Net, the alumni career networking database. L&C ranks in the top 25 of small schools sending grads to the Peace Corps.

Student Life

There's a good chance that L&C is smaller than your high school; and, except for the environmental, liberal, slightly hippie atmosphere, socializing on campus might feel a lot like high school too. Such a small, close-knit community can make for cabin fever, but student organizations help take up the slack. About 90 groups are active on campus. Service and social justice groups, like Students Engaged for Eco-Defense, account for a large portion of that, but you'll find a wide range of choices, from the Ski and Snowboard Club to the Beekeeping Society and Apocalips spoken word.

The entirely student-run coffee shop and multi-use arts space, the Co-Op, is a very popular student hangout, offering regular student musical performances and celebrating the end of the school year with Critical Blast, an event that sponsors live music and a barbeque. The Co-Op's mission is to "promote political, social, artistic, and environmental awareness" and you'll find granola, trail mix, brown rice, and not much else on the menu. Casino Night—where faculty, students, and staff come together to gamble with fake money for prizes—might remind you of high school but it's lots of fun nonetheless. L&C students also get a big kick out of streaking, with an annual Naked Mile that passes through the library. As you might also expect, there is no Greek system. "Fraternities and sororities are too conventional to be accepted," one student explains.

The Pioneers men's rowing team is the standout among its nine men's and 10 women's NCAA Division III teams. Non-varsity aspiring athletes can get their kicks by participating in organized intramurals, which include dodgeball and kickball, or kayaking,

LEWIS AND CLARK COLLEGE

Highlights

Students
Total enrollment: 3,703
Undergrads: 2,150
Freshmen: 555
Part-time students: 1%
From out-of-state: 88%
From public schools: 72%
Male/Female: 40%/60%
Live on-campus: 70%
Off-campus employment rating: Fair
Caucasian: 59%
African American: 2%
Hispanic: 7%
Asian / Pacific Islander: 4%
Native American: 1%
Mixed (2+ ethnicities): 4%
International: 9%

Academics
Calendar: Semester
Student/faculty ratio: 12:1
Class size 9 or fewer: 21%
Class size 10-29: 67%
Class size 30-49: 10%
Class size 50-99: 1%
Class size 100 or more: -
Returning freshmen: 89%
Six-year graduation rate: 73%

Most Popular Majors
Psychology
Sociology/anthropology
Biology

Admissions
Applicants: 6,524
Accepted: 4,187
Acceptance rate: 64.2%
Average GPA: 3.8
ACT range: 26-31
SAT Math range: 590-670
SAT Reading range: 600-700
SAT Writing range: 23-50
Top 10% of class: 37%
Top 25% of class: 76%
Top 50% of class: 98%

415

LEWIS AND CLARK COLLEGE

Admissions Criteria

Academic criteria:
Grades: ☆ ☆ ☆
Difficulty of class schedule: ☆ ☆ ☆
Class rank: ☆ ☆
Standardized test scores: ☆ ☆
Teacher recommendations: ☆ ☆
Personal statement: ☆ ☆
Non-academic criteria considered:
Interview
Extracurricular activities
Special talents, interests, abilities
Character/personal qualities
Volunteer work
Work experience
Geographical location
Minority affiliation
Alumni relationship

Deadlines

Early Action: November 1
Early Decision: No
Regular Action: January 15 (final)
Notification of admission by: April 1
Common Application: Accepted

Financial Aid

In-state tuition: $41,568
Out-of-state tuition: $41,568
Room: $5,722
Board: $4,914
Books: $1,050
Freshmen receiving need-based aid: 63%
Undergrads rec. need-based aid: 62%
Avg. % of need met by financial aid: 86%
Avg. aid package (freshmen): $32,748
Avg. aid package (undergrads): $33,842
Avg. debt upon graduation: $25,134

School Spirit

Mascot: Pio the Newfoundland Dog
Colors: Orange and black

hiking, or skiing through College Outdoors, which organizes trips and provides equipment. Very popular are L&C's two homegrown sports, Ninja and Wolvetch.

A free shuttle known as the Raz transports students to downtown Portland, where the haunt of choice is the Hawthorne District, famed for its hippies and hipsters as well as shops and restaurants. "It's actually an approachable but lively college town," says a student. Portland's proximity to mountains and the Oregon Coast means that there's plenty of opportunity for outdoor recreation, which L&C students eat up with a relish.

Students are required to live on campus for freshman and sophomore years. Residence halls are either traditional dorm-style layouts or smaller community-based living blocks. Themed housing, including Multicultural and Outdoor Pursuits, is also available. Apartment-style residences are offered to upperclassmen, but more often they choose to live off campus.

Student Body

Although most students at L&C are not from Oregon, they tend to come from the Pacific Northwest. They are liberal, outdoorsy, and focused on environmental sustainability. Students describe themselves as "independent" and "free-thinking"—there is more than a "touch" of hippie.

A moderate level of ethnic diversity is represented with 18 percent of students identifying as minority.

You May Not Know

- L&C's self-fashioned sports include Ninja (sometimes called Boffing), a "goal-oriented combat system" where players capture the flag with padded foam stick weapons; and Wolvetch, soccer played on all fours, without knees touching the ground. Biting is not allowed.
- Several hauntings and ghosts have been reported on campus.
- Watzek Library houses an extensive collection of high-quality printed materials on the Lewis and Clark expedition.

Distinguished Alumni

Earl Blumenauer, U.S. Congressman; Ahmed Al Badi, CEO, Belbadi Enterprises in UAE; Monica Lewinsky, former White House intern; Lewis Sharp, Director, Denver Art Museum.

Admissions and Financial Aid

Students who do not feel that their standardized test scores accurately represent their ability may apply via the Portfolio Path, by submitting two graded pieces of work, one piece of analytical writing, and one quantitative or scientific assignment.

Applicants do not need to apply separately for merit scholarships. Awards include the Barbara Hirschi Neely Scholarship worth up to $146,500 over four years, Trustee Scholarships worth up to $73,000, and Dean's Scholarships worth 25 percent of tuition and fees.

LOUISIANA STATE UNIVERSITY

Overview

Louisiana State University (LSU) is known for its football team, prominent Greek scene, and larger-than-life Mardi Gras celebrations. In short, LSU is the party school Hollywood uses as a model for movies. Those who still want to sport Tiger colors while being challenged in the classroom can apply to LSU's Honors College.

LSU was founded in 1860, and is the flagship institution of Louisiana. With more than 24,000 undergraduate students, it is a very large public university and one of 25 universities in the country that is both a land-grant and sea-grant institution. The campus is set on 2,000 acres in Baton Rouge where the humidity is thick enough to slice and the oak trees are majestic. Baton Rouge is Louisiana's capital, and the state's second-largest city. Those who somehow don't find enough to do on campus will have plenty to do in Baton Rouge. The city is well known for its singles scene, and area clubs and bars cater to young adults and the college crowd.

LSU is a community in every sense of the word, with an active alumni presence, close-knit Greek institutions and residential colleges, service-learning programs, and study-abroad opportunities. But whether students go the route of jock, nerd, or Greek, LSU students have this in common: they all bleed purple and gold!

Academics

LSU offers bachelor's degrees in 77 fields, with stand-out programs in biochemistry and mass communications and the premed program. As is the case with such a large university, access to professors outside of class is "not a strong suit." However, other students say, "if you make the effort, you can get one-on-one time with your professors." Almost one fifth of undergraduate classes have 50 or more students, and introductory-level classes can have several hundred students. Class sizes do get smaller as students move toward upper-level courses, but in general, students say "there's often more interaction with TAs than professors."

LSU has a general core requirement. Students must complete 39 hours of course work in six areas: English composition, analytical reading, arts, humanities, natural sciences, and social sciences. Many LSU students choose to complete premed requirements by earning a degree in the College of Science. The Manship School of Mass Communication is also popular with undergraduate students.

The university offers students the opportunity to design their own majors, participate in independent study, double major, earn a dual degree, and graduate with honors. LSU students may apply to the Honors College at any point in their undergraduate career. These are only a few of the more standard academic opportunities available to LSU students. Over 40 countries are listed as part of LSU's Study Abroad program.

The University College Center for Freshman Year is a unique program available to freshmen and transfer students. The program is designed to prepare new students for success at LSU and to aid in defining academic and career goals. "At a large school like LSU, this is especially helpful," comments a student.

Most students enter the workforce after graduation, but about 29 percent of students decide to continue on to graduate school. Employers that most frequently hire LSU graduates include JP Morgan Chase Bank, United States military, BP, Deloitte & Touche, Dow Chemical, and Teach for America. Alumni-current student mentoring programs assist LSU students in connecting with opportunities beyond graduation.

Student Life

The Greek scene at LSU is huge. Fifteen percent of male students join one of 23 fraternities, and one quarter of female students join one of the 15 sororities. "If you're not part of the Greek scene, you're really missing out," says a member. Greek organizations annually welcome over 1,000 new pledges to their ranks and host a variety

LOUISIANA STATE UNIVERSITY

Four-year public
Founded: 1860
Baton Rouge, LA
Medium city
Pop. 230,139

Address:
110 Thomas Boyd Hall
Baton Rouge, LA
70803

Admissions:
225-578-1175

Financial Aid:
225-578-3103

admissions@lsu.edu

www.lsu.edu

LOUISIANA STATE UNIVERSITY

Highlights

Students

Total enrollment: 30,225
Undergrads: 24,626
Freshmen: 7,200
Part-time students: 8%
From out-of-state: 21%
From public schools: 59%
Male/Female: 49%/51%
Live on-campus: 27%
In fraternities: 15%
In sororities: 24%
Off-campus employment rating: Excellent
Caucasian: 76%
African American: 11%
Hispanic: 5%
Asian / Pacific Islander: 3%
Native American: 0%
Mixed (2+ ethnicities): 2%
International: 2%

Academics

Calendar: Semester
Student/faculty ratio: 23:1
Class size 9 or fewer: 8%
Class size 10-29: 54%
Class size 30-49: 19%
Class size 50-99: 10%
Class size 100 or more: 9%
Returning freshmen: 83%
Six-year graduation rate: 67%
Graduates who immediately go to graduate school: 29%
Graduates who immediately enter career related to major: 59%

Most Popular Majors

Biological sciences
Kinesiology
Mass communication

Admissions

Applicants: 16,169
Accepted: 12,326
Acceptance rate: 76.2%
Average GPA: 3.4
ACT range: 23-28
SAT Math range: 520-630
SAT Reading range: 500-620
SAT Writing range: Not reported
Top 10% of class: 24%
Top 25% of class: 50%
Top 50% of class: 80%

418

of activities throughout the year, including Songfest, which features song and dance routines.

LSU has over 300 official student organizations, including 31 honor societies. The African American Cultural Center implements an academic, cultural, and social context for students of color at LSU. The center also provides programming designed to create bridges and to build a better understanding of the African American experience. Service groups such as Sisters Keeping it Real Through Service (SKIRTS) and Uganda Education Project provide unique ways for Tigers to give back to the local and global communities. The official school newspaper is *The Daily Reveille*.

The Greek scene is huge at LSU, but the football scene is even bigger. The university is a member of the Southeastern Conference, Division I, and has the sixth largest college football stadium in the country. In other words, LSU can pack 92,400 fans screaming at 122 decibels into its stadium. "Game days are out of control," laughs a student. "We have more school spirit than any other school." Major rivals include the University of Florida and the University of Alabama. LSU fans come from far and wide to "Death Valley" to cheer on the Tigers. When filled to capacity, Tiger Stadium lists as the sixth largest city in the state of Louisiana.

For students who are not quite on the varsity level but still want to play on a team, LSU has a wide range of intramural sports. Flag football, basketball, softball, sand volleyball, and Ultimate Frisbee are popular intramural choices. Working out and staying healthy is easy at LSU. Great recreational facilities include outdoor fields, indoor basketball courts, a swimming pool, weight rooms, a challenge course, and a climbing gymnasium.

LSU has 17 residence halls. Some feature traditional rooms with free-standing furniture that students may arrange as they like. Others have more modern rooms that are compact but feature built-in furniture that maximizes space. The majority of students (almost three quarters) live off campus, and freshman are not required to live on campus. "There's a lot of inexpensive housing off campus," notes a student.

Student Body

With a university the size of LSU, every background and interest is represented, though most students come from in state (79 percent). "It's more a question of what part of Louisiana you're from," notes a student. Overall, students "aren't bookworms" like at more selective colleges; and while the college's reputation for partying has decreased—a little—there is still a "large crowd" who is more interested in having a good time than studying.

LSU has a large minority student population, and its official cultural center is the African American Cultural Center (AACC). The student body is represented by 21 percent minorities, with African Americans composing the largest population at 11 percent.

You May Not Know

- The LSU Press is a nonprofit book publisher, according to the university, one of the "oldest and largest" university presses in the South, and is "the only university press to have won a Pulitzer Prize in both fiction and poetry."

- While LSU is known for its football program, its only Heisman winner was Billy Cannon in 1959.
- LSU's choice of mascot can be traced back to the Civil War. A volunteer company organized in New Orleans tagged itself the "Tiger Rifles," and in time, all Louisiana troops were called, simply, *Tigers*.

Distinguished Alumni

Kenneth Brown, host of HGTV show *ReDesign*; Cassandra Chandler, one of FBI's highest-ranking African-American women; Bill Conti, Academy Award-winning composer; Carlos Roberto Flores, former President of Honduras; Hubert Humphrey, 38th Vice President of the United States; Shaquille O'Neal , four-time NBA Champion.

Admissions and Financial Aid

Students looking into LSU need to keep in mind three important criteria. First, all incoming freshmen must have earned a minimum high school GPA of 3.0 calculated from academic courses. Second, prospective students are also expected to have completed at least 18 units of college-prep courses. Finally, to be initially considered, incoming students must have a minimum composite ACT score of 22, or a combined critical reading and math SAT score of 1030.

For those who are just way too excited about becoming Tigers, but don't quite meet the above requirements, all is not lost. LSU still encourages those students to apply for admission. Other factors that can positively impact a student's chances of being accepted are class rank, rigor of high school course load, participation in extracurricular activities, letters of recommendation, and choice of degree program.

An advantage that Louisiana high school students enjoy is the Taylor Opportunity Program for Students (TOPS). TOPS provides Louisiana high school graduates with scholarships, should they choose to attend a Louisiana public college or university. This scholarship pays an amount equal to LSU tuition along with some of the student fees. The Louisiana Office of Student Financial Assistance (LOSFA) annually evaluates all high school student records in the state to determine eligibility for TOPS and notify high school graduates regarding their eligibility during the summer following graduation. The TOPS program has three award levels based on each student's academic eligibility, and students will be notified of their TOPS level in their initial eligibility letter. Additional scholarship opportunities exist for Louisiana residents and out-of-state applicants.

LOUISIANA STATE UNIVERSITY

Highlights

Admissions Criteria
Academic criteria:
Grades: ☆ ☆ ☆
Difficulty of class schedule: ☆ ☆ ☆
Class rank: ☆
Standardized test scores: ☆ ☆ ☆
Teacher recommendations: ☆
Personal statement: ☆
Non-academic criteria considered:
Extracurricular activities
Special talents, interests, abilities
State of residency
Alumni relationship

Deadlines
Early Action: No
Early Decision: No
Regular Action: Rolling admissions
Common Application: Not accepted

Financial Aid
In-state tuition: $5,891
Out-of-state tuition: $23,808
Room: $6,900
Board: $3,904
Books: $1,500
Freshmen receiving need-based aid: 44%
Undergrads rec. need-based aid: 40%
Avg. % of need met by financial aid: 70%
Avg. aid package (freshmen): $12,600
Avg. aid package (undergrads): $13,772
Avg. debt upon graduation: $20,125

School Spirit
Mascot: Mike VI (live Bengal tiger)
Colors: Purple and gold

Four-year private
Founded: 1911
Los Angeles, CA
Major city
Pop. 3,819,702

Address:
One LMU Drive
Los Angeles, CA
90045-2659

Admissions:
310-338-2750

Financial Aid:
310-338-2753

admissions@lmu.edu

www.lmu.edu

LOYOLA MARYMOUNT UNIVERSITY

Overview

Perennially sunny skies paint the backdrop to the palm trees and Spanish and modern architecture of picturesque Loyola Marymount University (LMU). Campus sits atop a bluff in the Westchester area of Los Angeles (about 20 minutes southwest of downtown), offering views of the LA Basin and Pacific Ocean. The grassy lawns of Alumni Mall and Sunken Garden are verdant and fetching, and also represent Loyola's focus on sustainability. In fact, LMU was home to the first campus-wide college recycling program in California, was one of the first campuses in the state to recycle *all* its green waste, and uses solar rooftop systems to generate a portion of the university's electricity.

This medium, private Roman Catholic university has a strong sense of community, much of it due to the school's religious affiliation. A tight-knit community, Loyola boasts a great location and strong programs in a diverse set of fields, including engineering, film, and business. The student body is heavily diversified, with a large Hispanic student population. LMU is a good fit for students who are looking to be close to dynamic LA and yet comfortable in a small school with a strong sense of Catholic identity and religious heritage.

Academics

LMU offers 53 majors and 57 minors for undergraduates. There are seven colleges and schools including the law School, each with its own degree requirements. Every school slightly tailors LMU's Core Curriculum, which includes coursework or demonstrated proficiency in American cultures, college writing, communication, theological studies, and more. All undergraduates take at least one ethics course. Foreign language study is recommended though not required.

The rigor of academics varies from school to school and course to course. "The more difficult classes tend to be in the sciences, although you can get a hard class in any department," says a student. The smaller size of the student body allows greater access to professors.

Strong programs include those in the College of Business Administration, the School of Film and Television, and the College of Science and Engineering. The School of Film and Television offers programs such as Acting for Filmmakers, Screenwriters Showcase, the Distinguished Artists and Mentors Program, and an annual film festival. "You can't beat our location if you want to go into the entertainment industry," boasts a student.

The University Honors Program offers students a "qualitatively different intellectual experience" rather than using a "harder and more" approach to honors classes, according to the college. Honors students enjoy smaller class sizes, faculty mentors and directors who help with research, and priority registration. Incoming freshmen live in the Honors Living Learning Community, and about 30-40 students are accepted each year. Honors Research Fellowships ($5,000) fund summer research and study abroad.

Students majoring in biology, natural sciences, engineering, and psychology also have their own Living Learning Communities. "It's really helpful for studying and socializing to live with students who share a common interest," one student remarks.

The Institute for Leadership Studies aims to prepare students for leadership positions through a variety of activities, including an annual conference, internships in DC, and special fellowships and scholarships. Domestic and International Alternative Breaks give students a chance to combine service and travel. Past destinations have included Tanzania, Cambodia, Mexico, and India.

Over 500 LMU students study abroad each year through semester and summer programs. There are exchange programs with universities around the world, opportunities through the Association of Jesuit Colleges and Universities, and in special situations, students may apply for non-LMU programs.

Nearly 44,000 alumni, the bulk of which live in California and about half of whom stay in the LA area, make for a strong local network.

Student Life

Loyola Marymount University has over 130 clubs and organizations on campus. Service organizations are popular: students volunteer more than 170,000 service hours with 350 community organizations. *The Los Angeles Loyolan*, the campus award-winning newspaper, has been publishing for over 80 years, and the campus radio, KXLM, has been broadcasting for over 50 years.

As a way to assist new students in learning about the on-campus organizations, Club Fest is held at the beginning of the school year. Representatives of the various groups man tables on the picturesque lawn of the Sunken Gardens. Students may visit the tables to speak with club members and pick up any literature that is available.

LMU hosts World Fest, also known as International Education Week, every fall, with events as varied as "beer tasting from around the world" to documentary film screenings. College Fest is an annual outdoor concert that has recently featured Third Eye Blind. Charity Ball in the spring is a fundraiser for a community organization while giving students the chance to get creative with the annual theme—a recent one was The Great Gatsby. The dance is the biggest of the year. "Everyone dresses to the theme and goes all out for the Charity Ball," explains a student.

There are 16 fraternities and sororities on campus. Sixteen percent of men and 33 percent of women join the six fraternities and 10 sororities. "It can be a little socially isolating if you don't pledge," comments one young woman, "especially if you're female."

LMU's 19 teams (nine men's, 10 women's) compete in Division I. Men's basketball and women's water polo are the most competitive and the most popular. Loyola's softball is also very successful, with the most titles in its conference. Club sports are divided into highly competitive (men's ice hockey, lacrosse, and rugby) and semi-competitive (skiing, snowboard, and surf team); and students also compete in other intramurals as well.

Off campus, students can explore stretches of beach within easy access while Los Angeles offers big city entertainment, dining, shopping, and outdoor activities. Popular destinations for road trips include San Diego and Las Vegas.

There are 12 residence halls and six apartment buildings, with options ranging from traditional dorms to "Living Learning Communities" to theme housing. First-year theme houses include the Los Angeles Experience (LAX) and Recreation Outdoor Adventure in Rosecrans (ROAR), while upper class communities include houses oriented towards service and interaction. Six Living Learning Communities include COMPASS, a community for freshmen who are still exploring their majors.

Student Body

Many of LMU's students appear to fit the LA "stereotype." "You'll see a lot of too-skinny, too-tan, too-beautiful, and too-rich people,"

LOYOLA MARYMOUNT UNIVERSITY

Highlights

Students
Total enrollment: 9,492
Undergrads: 6,085
Freshmen: 1,525
From out-of-state: 25%
From public schools: 49%
Male/Female: 43%/57%
Live on-campus: 52%
In fraternities: 16%
In sororities: 33%
Off-campus employment rating: Excellent
Caucasian: 50%
African American: 6%
Hispanic: 22%
Asian / Pacific Islander: 10%
Native American: 0%
Mixed (2+ ethnicities): 7%
International: 4%

Academics
Calendar: Semester
Student/faculty ratio: 11:1
Class size 9 or fewer: 12%
Class size 10-29: 74%
Class size 30-49: 12%
Class size 50-99: 2%
Class size 100 or more: -
Returning freshmen: 89%
Six-year graduation rate: 75%

Most Popular Majors
Business administration
Communication studies
English

Admissions
Applicants: 11,913
Accepted: 5,975
Acceptance rate: 50.2%
Placed on wait list: 1,477
Enrolled from wait list: 9
Average GPA: 3.8
ACT range: 24-29
SAT Math range: 560-660
SAT Reading range: 550-640
SAT Writing range: 12-47
Top 10% of class: 26%
Top 25% of class: 70%
Top 50% of class: 96%

421

College Profiles

LOYOLA MARYMOUNT UNIVERSITY

Admissions Criteria
Academic criteria:
Grades: ☆ ☆ ☆
Difficulty of class schedule: ☆ ☆ ☆
Class rank: ☆
Standardized test scores: ☆ ☆
Teacher recommendations: ☆
Personal statement: ☆ ☆
Non-academic criteria considered:
Extracurricular activities
Special talents, interests, abilities
Character/personal qualities
State of residency
Alumni relationship

Deadlines
Early Action: November 1
Early Decision: No
Regular Action: Rolling admissions
Common Application: Accepted

Financial Aid
In-state tuition: $39,344
Out-of-state tuition: $39,344
Room: $9,150
Board: $4,400
Books: $1,710
Freshmen receiving need-based aid: 58%
Undergrads rec. need-based aid: 58%
Avg. % of need met by financial aid: 64%
Avg. aid package (freshmen): $23,356
Avg. aid package (undergrads): $26,246
Avg. debt upon graduation: $34,629

School Spirit
Mascot: Iggy the Lion
Colors: Crimson and navy
Song: *LMU Fight Song*

laughs one student. But many students also defy that stereotype in their appearance, strong focus on academics, and the range of socioeconomic backgrounds represented. Spirituality is also a major presence, since the school is religiously affiliated. There is moderate geographic diversity, with a quarter of students from out of state, though the large number of Californians certainly contributes to the sunny campus culture.

Ethnic diversity is very high, with 45 percent minority students. Hispanics (22 percent) and Asian Americans (10 percent) make up the largest minority groups.

You May Not Know

- LMU is the largest Catholic university on the West Coast.
- LMU draws 12 percent of its electric power from renewable resources, such as a large solar electric rooftop array.
- Iggy the Lion has been a mascot at LMU for more than 70 years, though its origin is debated. Some credit an enthusiastic fan for suggesting the mascot in 1919; others say it was inspired by the abundance of mountain lions that roamed the land before LMU existed.

Distinguished Alumni

John Anderson, businessman and one of 400 richest Americans according to *Forbes Magazine*; Anthony Coelho, former U.S. congressman from California; Mila Kunis, actress; Beverly Mitchell, actress and country music singer.

Admissions and Financial Aid

According to the college, an applicant's academic record is the primary consideration in deciding whether to accept a student to Loyola. Also significant are extracurricular accomplishments, recommendations, test scores, and "relationship to the university." There are no minimum GPAs or test scores, though there is a recommended high school course of study. There are additional coursework requirements for students applying to specific fields, including business, engineering, and the arts.

Applicants will want to give extra care to writing their application essay, which is a factor in evaluating academic scholarship recipients. The only LMU merit scholarship that requires a separate application is the Jesuit Community Scholarship ($30,000 over four years for graduates of Jesuit or Catholic secondary schools). The Arrupe Scholarship is awarded to up to 10 percent of applicants and begins at $12,500 annually, renewable over four years. The Trustee and Presidential Scholarships are the most prestigious awards; students interview during the Presidential Preview Weekend to compete for these awards, which cover up to full tuition, room, and board for four years.

LOYOLA UNIVERSITY CHICAGO

Overview

Established in 1870, Loyola University Chicago is now the largest Jesuit Catholic University in the United States—with a total enrollment of almost 16,000 students—and the only Jesuit institution in Chicago. As a Jesuit Catholic University, Loyola not only prides itself on a strong academic heritage, but also seeks to prepare its students to "lead extraordinary lives."

Each of Loyola's campuses fills a distinct academic role. The Lake Shore Campus (LSC), which borders Lake Michigan, is Loyola's primary residential and undergraduate campus. It serves as the home to almost 4,000 students as well as the College of Arts and Sciences (the largest of Loyola's 10 schools), the Graduate School, and the Marcella Niehoff School of Nursing. The LSC houses more than 40 buildings, including the main campus library, a state-of-the-art Life Sciences Education and Research Center, and a multi-purpose fine arts and theatre programming facility.

The Water Tower Campus (WTC) boasts a downtown location close to Michigan Avenue, otherwise known as Chicago's "Magnificent Mile." The WTC provides space for many of Loyola's graduate-level classes, though some undergraduate courses are also offered there. The downtown setting of the WTC helps students connect with Chicago-based businesses for internships.

Loyola has two additional campuses: the Medical Center Campus in the Maywood suburb of Chicago, and the John Felice Rome Center in Italy, just four miles outside downtown Rome in Monte Mario.

Academics

One of the hallmarks of Loyola's academic program is its undergraduate Core curriculum. The Core curriculum focuses on three main areas—knowledge, skills, and values—and is made up of 15 required courses covering 10 different knowledge areas. Although the number of courses and knowledge areas required to complete the Core are set by the university, students have the freedom to choose from among a variety of approved courses to complete the requirements. "Some of the classes have been stronger than others, but overall I've enjoyed the core classes," says a student.

Some students may find that courses taken to meet requirements of the Core curriculum can also be applied toward the requirements of their major or minor. The university offers more than 70 undergraduate majors. Of the six undergraduate schools at Loyola, The Marcella Niehoff School of Nursing and the School of Business Administration are particularly strong.

Those seeking to pursue an even more rigorous course of study may apply to the Interdisciplinary Honors Program, which offers undergraduates the same broad education provided by the Core curriculum, but with a greater focus on interdisciplinary education and service learning. Course requirements for the Honors Program are often team taught and are taken in a sequence. Freshman Honors students who live on campus are placed together in Regis Hall. By living and taking courses together, honors students form an intellectual community that includes an Honors Student Association that plans social and service events, an Honors Lounge, and an Honors Council of elected officers and representatives. There's a "strong Honors community," notes a student.

In addition to the Interdisciplinary Honors Program, high-achieving students are invited to apply to the Loyola Undergraduate Research Opportunities Program (LUROP), which facilitates collaboration between students and professors. Another scholarship offered to promote student-faculty relationships is the Mulcahy Scholars Program. It offers students in the College of Arts and Sciences up to $2,000 of financial support to pursue research projects.

LOYOLA UNIVERSITY CHICAGO

Four-year private
Founded: 1870
Chicago, IL
Major city
Pop. 2,707,120

Address:
1032 West Sheridan Road
Chicago, IL
60660

Admissions:
800-262-2373

Financial Aid:
773-508-7704

admission@luc.edu

www.luc.edu

LOYOLA UNIVERSITY CHICAGO

Students
Total enrollment: 15,720
Undergrads: 9,723
Freshmen: 2,425
Part-time students: 8%
From out-of-state: 40%
From public schools: 68%
Male/Female: 37%/63%
Live on-campus: 41%
In fraternities: 6%
In sororities: 12%
Off-campus employment rating: Fair
Caucasian: 63%
African American: 4%
Hispanic: 12%
Asian / Pacific Islander: 10%
Native American: 0%
Mixed (2+ ethnicities): 5%
International: 3%

Academics
Calendar: Semester
Student/faculty ratio: 14:1
Class size 9 or fewer: 8%
Class size 10-29: 54%
Class size 30-49: 31%
Class size 50-99: 5%
Class size 100 or more: 2%
Returning freshmen: 87%
Six-year graduation rate: 70%

Most Popular Majors
Biology
Psychology
Nursing

Admissions
Applicants: 19,657
Accepted: 11,395
Acceptance rate: 58.0%
Average GPA: 3.8
ACT range: 25-29
SAT Math range: 540-650
SAT Reading range: 550-650
SAT Writing range: 7-37
Top 10% of class: 35%
Top 25% of class: 69%
Top 50% of class: 94%

Among the LUROP's myriad opportunities is the Ricci Scholars Program, which gives select students scholarships to travel and study abroad at Loyola's John Felice Rome Center or the Beijing Center for Chinese Studies. If Italy and China do not align with a student's academic or travel goals, he or she is free to select from more than 70 other programs spanning 32 different countries.

The university's Career Development Center provides "extensive help" through job fairs, resume workshops, and RamblerLink, a job search database. Students can also earn academic credit for internships through the Center for Experiential Learning. These internships may be paid or unpaid and require roughly 10 hours of work per week.

Student Life

The Office of Student Activities and Greek Affairs (SAGA) supports more than 175 student groups. Notable ones include the 45 Kings, self-proclaimed "Loyola's Premier Improv Comedy Team;" the Growers' Guild, a gardening club; and the Silhouettes, an all-female a cappella group.

Popular SAGA traditions are equally as noteworthy. They include Finals Breakfast, a late-night breakfast served by faculty and staff—a "much needed break," a student explains. The New Year's Festival kicks off the beginning of each new academic year with fireworks, live performances, and of course, free prizes!

Greek life is "pretty small" on campus, as noted by one student. While there are seven social fraternities and 10 social sororities, the Greek community is tightly knit while maintaining an innocuous presence on campus for those students who do not wish to participate. The Office of Student Activities and Greek Affairs puts on special events like the President's Ball, a free formal gala that is open to all students.

For those students who want to cheer on LUC athletics, there are a total of 11 varsity teams, all competing in NCAA Division I. Although Loyola hasn't had a varsity football team since 1930, athletics remain popular on campus through organizations like the Rambler Rowdies, the student section that cheers on the men's basketball team alongside LU Wolf, the school mascot. There are also plenty of intramural and club sports, including a Quidditch league!

As part of encouraging a robust residence life, Loyola requires that all students live on campus for their first two years. Loyola also allows first-year students the unique opportunity to select a roommate over the summer, provided the students are assigned to the same residence hall. "I much preferred choosing my own roommate to living with a stranger," one student comments. Freshmen live in traditional dorms, while upperclassmen have the option of living in apartment-style housing, including Baumhart Hall, located in the downtown Water Tower Campus.

Even for those who do not live at the Water Tower Campus, LUC's proximity to downtown Chicago allows students to access all the city has to offer. All students receive a CTA U-Pass, which provides them with unlimited bus and train rides, and there is a CTA train station located next to the Lake Shore Campus. Downtown Chicago's museums, concerts, shows, professional sports, and bars and restaurants are only a short train ride away. "There's always something to do," remarks a student.

Student Body

The ethnic diversity of Loyola's student body is high, with 31 percent of students identifying themselves as minorities. The university's geographic diversity is also high, with 40 percent of students coming from outside Illinois and hailing from all 50 states and 82 countries.

As a Jesuit University, there are many Catholic students at Loyola, but the university also encourages inter-faith dialogue. Through the university's Ministry, Hillel provides services to Jewish students, and there are Hindu and Muslim Student Organizations, as well as a Protestant Ministry. "You'll be in the minority if you're not Catholic, but of course you'll be accepted," says a student.

Loyola's student body is politically diverse, with College Democrats, Republicans, and Libertarians all maintaining a presence on campus. Although Catholic, the university is not known for being politically conservative and hosted Ralph Nader and Howard Dean during their runs for the White House in 2004.

You May Not Know

- The school's athletes are referred to as Ramblers, the name originally given the football team in 1926 because of their extensive travels around the United States.
- The university encompasses the Saint Joseph College Seminary and the Jesuit First Studies Program, one of three such programs in the country that provide aspiring Jesuit priests the first three years of their eleven-year training.
- The largest of Loyola's campuses is actually the Loyola University Medical Center.

Distinguished Alumni

Leslie David Baker, actor, *The Office*; Brenda Barnes, CEO, Sara Lee Corp.; Ian Brennan, creator and writer of *Glee*; James Iha, The Smashing Pumpkins and A Perfect Circle guitarist; Stephen McGowan, former CFO Sun Microsystems.

Admissions and Financial Aid

Admission to Loyola is based on demonstrated academic ability. Prospective students must apply using Loyola's online application. In addition to reviewing the application, admissions officers look closely at the writing sample, counselor recommendation, student activities, grades, and standardized test scores.

Although applications are accepted on a rolling basis, students must have completed the application process and have been admitted by the first of February if they are interested in being considered for merit-based scholarships. Students who apply to the Interdisciplinary Honors Program are automatically considered by the University for one of three full-tuition Ignatian Scholarships. Loyola also awards several four-year, merit-based scholarships totaling as much as $14,000 per year, to academically qualified students. Other merit-based scholarships requiring additional applications are available as well.

LOYOLA UNIVERSITY CHICAGO

Highlights

Admissions Criteria
Academic criteria:
Grades: ☆ ☆ ☆
Difficulty of class schedule: ☆ ☆ ☆
Class rank: ☆
Standardized test scores: ☆ ☆ ☆
Teacher recommendations: ☆ ☆
Personal statement: ☆
Non-academic criteria considered:
Interview
Extracurricular activities
Special talents, interests, abilities
Character/personal qualities
Volunteer work
Work experience
Geographical location
Alumni relationship

Deadlines
Early Action: No
Early Decision: No
Regular Action: Rolling admissions
Common Application: Not accepted

Financial Aid
In-state tuition: $35,500
Out-of-state tuition: $35,500
Room: $8,110
Board: $4,790
Books: $1,200
Freshmen receiving need-based aid: 74%
Undergrads rec. need-based aid: 73%
Avg. % of need met by financial aid: 79%
Avg. aid package (freshmen): $30,940
Avg. aid package (undergrads): $29,572
Avg. debt upon graduation: $36,328

School Spirit
Mascot: Wolf
Colors: Maroon and gold
Song: *LU Fight Song*

425

LOYOLA UNIVERSITY NEW ORLEANS

Overview

Traditional values, modern times, and culture intersect at Loyola University New Orleans, a small, private Roman Catholic school tucked away on a compact campus in the slightly-more-upscale residential Uptown New Orleans across from Audubon Park and Zoo. Buildings on both the uptown campus on St. Charles Avenue as well as its Broadway Street adjunct campus a few blocks away vary from Tudor and Gothic styles to more modern architecture.

Backed by nearly 500 years of Jesuit teaching and scholarship, Loyola offers strengths in the more traditional disciplines that are a part of the humanities, as well as majors in business, journalism, and mass communication. Loyola University New Orleans consistently ranks among the top 10 Southern regional universities, according to *U.S. News & World Report*. The Jesuit emphasis on community service forms a major hub of education at Loyola and couldn't be better placed in such a critical-need location as New Orleans.

But that doesn't mean that tradition and the demands of the present day always mesh seamlessly: just 20 minutes downtown, students will find the French Quarter and downtown Nola, with its modern-day delights ranging from tamer shopping, dining, and entertainment options to the full-blown wild party scene that accompanies Mardi Gras in the Big Easy. Loyola's library website reminds students that "if you celebrate Mardi Gras, then you should practice Lenten sacrifice as well." But Loyola sees outside-of-the-classroom teachable moments everywhere, and so when Loyola's omnipresent spirituality and Catholic mission come into conflict with its modern and secular surroundings, the university seeks to translate that into a learning opportunity.

To students seeking a Catholic education as well as a firm foundation in liberal arts, Loyola offers its students an environment where spirituality, intellectual inquiry, service, and aid to others are virtually synonymous.

Academics

Loyola offers 76 majors in five colleges (the Colleges of Business, Humanities and Natural Sciences, Law, Music and Fine Arts, and Social Sciences), as well as a small selection of interdisciplinary minors that include Catholic Studies, Environmental Studies, Middle East Peace Studies, and the unique New Orleans Studies. All students must complete the Common Curriculum, which begins with a First-Year Seminar that is small and faculty-taught. These interdisciplinary seminars are said to address "questions of enduring value." The Common Curriculum also includes a selection of introductory and advanced courses in liberal arts and religious studies. Students must either already demonstrate or achieve proficiency in a foreign language and complete electives, which vary according to major.

Students with qualifying high school GPAs and test scores may apply to the Honors Program, which offers an Honors curriculum in place of much of the Common Curriculum, as well as further upper division Honors small-group seminars that emphasize working with primary sources, writing, and conducting independent research. Honors students must also complete a senior project—either a research project, thesis, or creative work—with a faculty advisor. "It was nerve-wracking to present my project," says a student, "but all of the positive feedback made it a worthwhile experience."

Loyola's small size means that the majority of its classes are on the intimate side, which allows students, in Honors courses or not, an "abundance" of personal attention from faculty. Loyola fosters an environment in which intellectual inquiry is pervasive—first-year students especially are immersed in an atmosphere of discussion and thought, as they are housed in Learning Communities according to which First-Year Seminar they are taking. "It's nice to live next door to someone you can discuss class with," notes a student.

Service learning is a major component of education and life at Loyola; classes across the five colleges require or offer a service learning component in which students are placed with local charities, non-profits, or volunteer organizations for 10-20 hours over the course of the class. Loyola makes it easy for students to access these organizations through a partnership with nearby Tulane University, which allows Loyola students to ride the University Shuttle for free; students performing community service can also rent a bike for free via Cycloserve.

The College of Business boasts one of Loyola's most exciting professional development plans, the Executive Mentor Program. This program matches up a small group of business students with a local business executive who serves as a mentor to the group. During the students' freshman year, mentors will meet with and advise their groups and may even bring students along to informal meetings and networking opportunities, giving students a healthy and early leg-up on the job market. "My mentor has been extremely helpful and even helped me find an internship," comments a participant in the program.

Loyola's own study-abroad opportunities are summer travel courses and are specific to each college: students can travel to the Bahamas, Belgium, Costa Rica, India, the UK, France, and Spain. The college offers other options through its exchange agreements. Students spend a semester studying at universities in Japan, the Netherlands, Mexico, Germany, Italy, and New Zealand.

The Career Development Center helps students with job and internship listings, career fairs, employer campus visits, and interview preparation. Of Loyola graduates who enter the workforce, more than 60 percent find work in a field related to their major within six months of graduation.

Student Life

More than 80 student groups are active on campus: music groups, such as Genesis Gospel Choir, and volunteer organizations, including Big Brothers/Big Sisters of Loyola, are particularly popular. The Society of Professional Journalists named the student newspaper *Maroon* one of the top in the country. Loyola holds a nation-wide community service event, called Wolves on the Prowl, in which students and alumni volunteer with charities and nonprofits across the country.

Other activities on Loyola's campus help students unwind, particularly the hilariously-named "Sneaux" event, which creates a "Winter Wonderland" and features a giant pre-finals snowball fight. "It's the perfect stress reliever," relates a student. Loyolapalooza is a concert in spring semester that showcases both local and student bands as well as major artists, and it also features one of the first crawfish boils of the year.

Students can also venture off campus, either as part of a Loyola-organized scavenger hunt in the French Quarter or on their own, to enjoy New Orleans' entertainment, shopping, and gastronomic delights. Mardi Gras is of course a huge draw for students—it is a school holiday for religious reasons—many participate in or at least attend the parades. Despite the rate of crime of some areas of New Orleans, Loyola has been recognized as one of the safest colleges in the country.

LOYOLA UNIVERSITY NEW ORLEANS

Highlights

Students
Total enrollment: 4,933
Undergrads: 3,200
Freshmen: 899
From out-of-state: 62%
From public schools: 47%
Male/Female: 42%/58%
Live on-campus: 65%
In fraternities: 9%
In sororities: 6%
Off-campus employment rating: Good
Caucasian: 52%
African American: 15%
Hispanic: 15%
Asian / Pacific Islander: 4%
Native American: 1%
Mixed (2+ ethnicities): 2%
International: 4%

Academics
Calendar: Semester
Student/faculty ratio: 10:1
Class size 9 or fewer: 21%
Class size 10-29: 58%
Class size 30-49: 20%
Class size 50-99: 2%
Class size 100 or more: -
Returning freshmen: 74%
Six-year graduation rate: 58%
Graduates who immediately go to graduate school: 68%

Most Popular Majors
Music business
Communications
Psychology

Admissions
Applicants: 6,486
Accepted: 4,257
Acceptance rate: 65.6%
Average GPA: 3.7
ACT range: 22-27
SAT Math range: 510-620
SAT Reading range: 530-650
SAT Writing range: 7-42
Top 10% of class: 27%
Top 25% of class: 47%
Top 50% of class: 77%

427

College Profiles

LOYOLA UNIVERSITY NEW ORLEANS

Admissions Criteria
Academic criteria:
Grades: ☆ ☆ ☆
Difficulty of class schedule: ☆ ☆ ☆
Class rank: ☆
Standardized test scores: ☆ ☆ ☆
Teacher recommendations: ☆ ☆
Personal statement: ☆ ☆
Non-academic criteria considered:
Interview
Extracurricular activities
Special talents, interests, abilities
Character/personal qualities
Volunteer work
Work experience
Geographical location
Alumni relationship

Deadlines
Early Action: No
Early Decision: No
Regular Action: Rolling admissions
Common Application: Accepted

Financial Aid
In-state tuition: $35,504
Out-of-state tuition: $35,504
Room: $7,250
Board: $4,935
Books: $1,200
Freshmen receiving need-based aid: 76%
Undergrads rec. need-based aid: 69%
Avg. % of need met by financial aid: 72%
Avg. aid package (freshmen): $30,148
Avg. aid package (undergrads): $26,626
Avg. debt upon graduation: $23,178

School Spirit
Mascot: Wolfpack
Colors: Maroon and gold
Song: *Loyola Fight Song*

Greek life plays a small role on campus: four fraternities and four sororities are present, with sororities slightly more of a draw than fraternities. "Most people don't participate because there are larger parties to be had in New Orleans," explains a student.

Sports and recreation take place in the formidable six-story University Sports Complex, which features sport courts and a natatorium with a sauna and steam room in addition to a jogging track and a gym. A small smattering of intramural sports are on offer, while the university's eight varsity athletic teams compete in Division I. Basketball is the most popular and competitive; the women's team won its conference championship in 2009.

Freshmen are housed in the Learning Communities in traditional dorm-style or suite-style residences. Upperclassmen who choose to live on campus are assigned to suites or apartment-style housing.

Student Body

Academic and spiritual values are emphasized on campus. As one student explains, "almost everyone is motivated, overly friendly, and open to meeting new people." For most Loyola students, the school's Catholic spiritual mission is a major draw and they take it to heart.

More than 60 percent of the student body comes from out of state; ethnic diversity is quite high with African Americans (15 percent) and Hispanics (15 percent) well represented.

You May Not Know

- Twenty tons of snow are shipped in for Sneaux's giant snowball fight.
- Loyola's Monroe Library, built in 1999, has been ranked as one of the most beautiful college libraries in the country.
- The land on which Loyola's St. Charles Avenue campus is located was originally a plantation owned by the son-in-law of Etienne de Bore, who invented the process of granulating sugar.

Distinguished Alumni

Joseph Cao, U.S. Representative, first Vietnamese-American member of Congress; Philip Carroll, former CEO of Shell Oil; Harry Connick, Jr., singer and pianist; Donald Wetzel, inventor of the automatic teller machine; Robert L. Wilkie, Assistant Secretary of Defense for Legislative Affairs.

Admissions and Financial Aid

All students with qualifying GPAs and test scores who submit applications by January 15 are considered automatically for academic merit scholarships, which can range from $2,000 to $20,000 annually; however, an interview before December 1 is required for the 10 Ignatian Scholarships for Academic Excellence awarded annually and recommended for the Dean's Scholarship and Loyola Scholarship. Significant community involvement is also a criterion for all of these awards.

MACALESTER COLLEGE

Overview

Ranked the 24ᵗʰ best liberal arts school in the country by *U.S. News & World Report*, Macalester College is a small private college that focuses on international studies. Located only 10 minutes from both downtown St. Paul and Minneapolis, Mac offers the job opportunities and internships of a big city with Midwestern friendliness and a rustic charm. The campus is filled with red brick buildings that give it a historic feel, yet, the large grassy quads lend themselves to less formal laid-back enjoyment of the changing of the seasons. Beware of the frigid winters though, where temperatures average in the single digits and the teens. Nicknamed "Tangletown" for the windy streets adorned with trees, Mac's campus is known for its pleasing aesthetics.

Macalester College boasts a new and completely "green" building, Markim Hall, which houses the Institute for Global Citizenship. International education is vital at Mac. This building meets the Platinum certification of the U.S. Green Building Council and was the first of its kind in the metropolis. Both the building and the program within it are innovative and progressive. If you're interested in global citizenship and leadership, then Mac might be perfect for you.

Academics

Similar to liberal arts schools around the country, Macalester requires that students complete a core set of classes for graduation. The Macalester basic course menu includes entrees in the social sciences, mathematics, natural sciences, humanities, and fine arts. However, in addition to its core curriculum, Macalester focuses its students on an international studies curriculum where all students are required to take classes that meet internationalism and multiculturalism mandates. All seniors are required to fulfill a capstone requirement as well.

There are 36 majors and over 800 courses to choose from. Students say, however, that sometimes they feel the "the academic offerings are somewhat limited." Many participate in First-Year Courses, which are intimate classes of 10 to 15 students and a professor. The topics covered are extremely diverse, ranging from "3D Design" to "Rivers, Lakes, and Streams." One student notes, "I enjoyed my freshman class because not only did I get to know my classmates, but many of them lived nearby so that we had a built-in study group."

Research is a big part of the Macalester experience. Over 90 percent of students receive research grants to work with professors during the summer or throughout the year. Students with at least a 3.3 GPA, depending on the department, can apply the honors program where they formulate and publish their own research and findings in an honors thesis. Some topics range from avant-garde to Islam, market competition, and how Facebook and Internet networking keeps friends together.

If you're looking to study abroad, you should know that Mac students choose from over 45 locations throughout six continents. Destinations include Istanbul, Mali, Santiago, Vietnam, and Amsterdam, just to name a few. Most students study abroad during their junior years. The universities that students attend abroad are not Mac campuses, but they transfer credit upon approval.

Internships are also very common for students who take advantage of their metropolis. Two thirds of students complete an internship during their undergrad career. The Twin Cities offers many internship opportunities, and Mac also offers programs in New York and DC.

After receiving a diploma from Macalester, 16 percent of students pursue an advanced degree within one year. Also, 90 percent of students with a GPA of 3.6 or higher are admitted to medical school. Others that do not pursue an advanced degree often join the workforce in scientific and technical jobs or media and communications. The Mac alumni network is extremely strong and provides networking that is

MACALESTER COLLEGE

Four-year private
Founded: 1874
St. Paul, MN
Major city
Pop. 288,448

Address:
1600 Grand Avenue
St. Paul, MN
55105

Admissions:
800-231-7974

Financial Aid:
800-231-7974

admissions@macalester.edu

www.macalester.edu

MACALESTER COLLEGE

Students

Total enrollment: 2,070
Undergrads: 2,070
Freshmen: 534
Part-time students: 2%
From out-of-state: 83%
From public schools: 69%
Male/Female: 40%/60%
Live on-campus: 62%
Off-campus employment rating: Excellent
Caucasian: 66%
African American: 3%
Hispanic: 6%
Asian / Pacific Islander: 7%
Native American: 0%
Mixed (2+ ethnicities): 5%
International: 13%

Academics

Calendar: Semester
Student/faculty ratio: 10:1
Class size 9 or fewer: 14%
Class size 10-29: 77%
Class size 30-49: 7%
Class size 50-99: 1%
Class size 100 or more: -
Returning freshmen: 94%
Six-year graduation rate: 90%
Graduates who immediately go to graduate school: 16%
Graduates who immediately enter career related to major: 60%

Most Popular Majors

Biology
Economics
English

Admissions

Applicants: 6,030
Accepted: 2,214
Acceptance rate: 36.7%
Placed on wait list: 469
Enrolled from wait list: 55
Average GPA: Not reported
ACT range: 28-32
SAT Math range: 640-730
SAT Reading range: 630-740
SAT Writing range: 35-50
Top 10% of class: 65%
Top 25% of class: 93%
Top 50% of class: 99%

essential to students. The school's reputation for internationalism, multiculturalism, and community service is often favored in the application process for competitive schools.

Student Life

Whether you're looking for a cultural club, religious organization, club sport, or an organization inspired by a political movement, Mac has it. With over 100 clubs and organizations, students are able to find something that piques their interests. There are dance groups and art organizations like MacSalsa, which has weekly Latin dance instruction; the *Mac Weekly*, the school's weekly newspaper which is completely student run; and in keeping with the school's international focus, organizations with a global initiative like Europa or Afrika. Many organizations have a campus presence so that students are able to easily fulfill service requirements for graduation. One example is FaceAIDS, and HIV/AIDS awareness group.

More than 90 percent of Mac students participate in community service. As a part of their motto, the school encourages "civic engagement" for all students throughout their careers. There are 50 classes offered that include service-based learning. Mac also offers specific programs—like the Bonner Community Scholars and The Lives of Commitment program for freshman and first-generation college students—to engage participants in service and leadership roles. Some students participate in service trips over their spring break and summer domestically and abroad. "Service is pretty much a given for everyone," says a student.

During the year there are many activities on campus to help students get a taste of each other's cultures. One such event is Diversity Weekend, where students can learn through the means of dance and art. The MacPlayers, the college's theatre program, puts together a Player's Ball in December where they showcase at least two performances in one weekend. Students also organize educational events like the International Roundtable where speakers and guest lecturers speak on student-chosen topics concerning global initiatives. In the fall, the music department hosts its annual Extravaganza where all different genres are showcased over a weekend. "In the classroom and out, we learn a lot about multiculturalism," comments a student.

There is no Greek life at Mac. Students usually socialize around sporting events and shows in the area. The Twin Cities offers a lot of choices off campus for student nightlife like concerts, clubs and bars, restaurants, ice skating, and theatre shows.

Macalester sports, known as the Scots in blue and orange, are all NCAA Division III. There are 19 varsity sports offered to both men and women. The women's soccer team recently won the NCAA championship, and students say that the soccer games are the "most popular to attend and root the team on." During the football season, Mac faces off with Carleton Knights rivals in the Brain Bowl. If you're not interested in trying out for a varsity team, don't sweat it!—there are many club sports run by students like climbing, rugby, and Ultimate Frisbee.

Students are required to live on campus for their first two years. Options include typical college dorms or more unique cultural or themed housing like the Veggie Co-op, the EcoHouse, or the Spanish house.

Student Body

The school is Presbyterian affiliated and many students do identify with the denomination, but students say, "you won't feel out of place if you're not religious." Despite the conservative background of the college, students describe themselves as "mostly liberal or even very liberal" politically.

Students at Mac come from over 46 states and 93 countries, with an international student base of 13 percent. There is a moderate minority population of 16 percent. Geographically, the college is extremely diverse with 83 percent of students from out of state. States with the most representation are California, Minnesota, Illinois, New York, Massachusetts, and Washington.

You May Not Know

- The founder of the college, Reverend Edward Neill, served in three U.S. presidential administrations.
- DeWitt and Lila Wallace, the founders of *Reader's Digest*, were significant donors to the college.
- Esther Suzuki was freed from a Japanese American internment camp when she was admitted to the college in 1942.

Distinguished Alumni

Kofi Annan, Nobel Peace Prize recipient and United Nations Secretary General; Catharine Lealtad, the college's first African-American graduate; Walter Mondale, Vice President of the U.S.

Admission

Macalester strongly considers high school GPA, as evidenced by the fact that over 34 percent of the freshman class was a valedictorian or salutatorian. The college also recommends an in-person interview, which is usually done on campus or at select locations off campus. Mac only offers regular and early decision.

Because of the focus on geographic diversity and multicultural education, Macalester notes students' personal stories in admissions decisions. Personal qualities, which are best gauged through interviews and essays, are extremely important. Also considered are high school activities, recommendations, standardized scores, and course selections.

Merit scholarships are granted to minority students and students with great academic ranking. Mac offers National Merit Scholars' finalists $5,000, and semifinalists $3,000 annually. Also, the Catherine Lealtad Scholarship is offered to minority students in the amount of $3,000. Beyond this, Macalester will meet full need for all admitted students through need-based scholarships.

MACALESTER COLLEGE

Highlights

Admissions Criteria
Academic criteria:
Grades: ☆ ☆ ☆
Difficulty of class schedule: ☆ ☆ ☆
Class rank: ☆
Standardized test scores: ☆ ☆
Teacher recommendations: ☆ ☆
Personal statement: ☆ ☆
Non-academic criteria considered:
Interview
Extracurricular activities
Special talents, interests, abilities
Character/personal qualities
Volunteer work
Work experience
State of residency
Minority affiliation
Alumni relationship

Deadlines
Early Action: No
Early Decision: November 15
Regular Action: January 15 (final)
Notification of admission by: March 30
Common Application: Accepted

Financial Aid
In-state tuition: $45,167
Out-of-state tuition: $45,167
Room: $5,412
Board: $4,656
Books: $1,050
Freshmen receiving need-based aid: 74%
Undergrads rec. need-based aid: 72%
Avg. % of need met by financial aid: 100%
Avg. aid package (freshmen): $37,945
Avg. aid package (undergrads): $37,519
Avg. debt upon graduation: $23,285

School Spirit
Mascot: The Scots
Colors: Blue and orange
Song: *Dear Old Macalester*

431

MANHATTAN-VILLE COLLEGE

Four-year private
Founded: 1841
Purchase, NY
Large town
Pop. 8,000

Address:
2900 Purchase Street
Purchase, NY
10577

Admissions:
800-32-VILLE

Financial Aid:
914-323-5357

admissions@mville.
edu

www.mville.edu

MANHATTANVILLE COLLEGE

Overview

Why live in the city when you can visit whenever you want? Manhattanville College combines all the charm of a 100-acre rural campus with the excitement of New York City just 30 minutes away. On campus, you will see the turrets of the college's castle-like, yet environmentally-friendly buildings; and if you long for the city's skyscrapers, they're within reach too. For a student who desires the stimulation of both rural and urban settings, Mville just might be the perfect place.

Students incorporate themselves into the surrounding area through 30,000 hours of community service each year. Just as Manhattanville allows integration of country and city life, the Portfolio System allows students to integrate their studies and extra-curriculars with long-term goals, creating plans of study and reflecting on the skills they will need in their real-life career. Mville is like a small village hidden away from the big city; a tight-knit community that values ethical and charitable behavior, which could be stifling for someone who relishes more freedom and variety, or comforting to the student who wants a little of both.

Academics

Manhattanville College offers 32 different majors for bachelor degrees, as well as certain majors in fine arts, special programs in management and teaching, and self-designed majors. Students need a minimum of 90 credits with an overall average of a C to graduate with a Bachelor of Arts degree and must pursue both a major and a minor. The general education curriculum requires students to take classes in quantitative reasoning, critical analysis and reasoning, scientific reasoning, oral communication, written communication, a foreign language, technological competency, and information literacy. Students must also write a Global Awareness Essay, in which they discuss how at least two of their classes have developed their understanding of other cultures, and complete credit requirements within the humanities, the social sciences, mathematics, science, and the fine arts.

First-years are required to take a seminar and a writing class to help them begin to analyze information at the college level and to build relationships with faculty early on. After the First-Year Program, additional credits in writing competency must also be taken. The Portfolio System applies structure to students' choices, pushing them to plan out their studies well in advance and asking them to reflect on their choices afterwards, analyzing and trying to improve their education while still at school. Though all of these requirements might seem overwhelming, they also provide students with the opportunity to balance their education and to make sure that they leave college with an understanding of their goals and their skills. "Some people complain about the Portfolio System, but for me it's been very helpful to map out a plan," says a student. That being said, students should consider that Manhattanville doesn't offer the option of a looser educational plan.

Manhattanville offers small classes and individual attention, particularly excelling in art, education, and music, and featuring special programs that combine a major with a master's. The average class size is 17, guaranteeing a lot of interaction with professors, whether desired or not. There is also a wide variety of study-abroad programs in Spain, Italy, South Africa, Japan, Puerto Rico, Germany, and Mexico. And if you're tired of just visiting New York City on the weekends, you can spend a semester living in Manhattanville's dorms in Brooklyn Heights, while you take classes in NYC. You can also spend a semester in Washington, DC or Oakland, California. Likewise, opportunities abound in Purchase, where Morgan Stanley, PepsiCo, and MasterCard all have corporate offices that often hire Manhattanville undergrads as interns. Select students intern with the United Nations. With all these opportunities, many students graduate with skills that lead to successful careers in business or PR, as well as teaching, arts, and advocacy.

Student Life

There are more than 50 clubs on campus, from Irish Step Dance to the Ascend Business Society to the radio station. The Office of Student Activities plans events on campus, such as movies on the quad, as well as New York City trips to shows and museums, often at discounted prices. There are plenty of opportunities to get involved in the community, with the Duschene Center for Religious and Social Justice cultivating alliances with over 40 different service organizations in the country. The college strongly emphasizes the importance of social action, and almost all students do some form of community service.

There are no Greek organizations on campus, but Manhattanville students party in other ways. Events like the winter and spring formals in the Castle entice participants, as well as the International Bazaar, where students give performances and enjoy international cuisine. The Quad Jam music festival is also a popular event.

Students may also want to watch their friends play one of the 19 NCAA Division III sports in which the Valiants participate. Most colleges' sports life centers on the football team; but Manhattanville doesn't have a football team, and the biggest sport on campus is ice hockey. The women have been in the national championship game three times, and the men frequently appear in NCAA tournaments. There are also numerous intramural and club sports, such as the Equestrian Club.

Seventy-nine percent of students live in one of four residence halls on campus. First-year students generally live in Spellman Hall in double rooms. Founder's Hall offers singles to four-person quads, and Dammann and Tenney Halls have suites built to accommodate six people who share a living room and bathroom and sleep in bedrooms that are either double or single.

Students often go to White Plains, and, of course, New York City. In fact most student life used to occur off campus, but recently the on-campus social scene has been reviving. "Of course there are limitless things to do in the city," shares one student, "but it's nice that there are options on campus too."

Student Body

The student body is highly diverse geographically, hailing from 48 states and 76 countries, and highly diverse ethnically with 24 percent of students reporting as minorities.

There are almost twice as many women as men on campus, which some male students describe as a "paradise." One woman comments, "it takes some getting used to, being in an environment with so many women, but there are plenty of ways to meet guys off campus."

Manhattanville is a college for people who value serving the community, and many students are either business- or arts-oriented.

You May Not Know

- Students celebrate with the 200 Nights Halloween party, 100 Nights party, and 50 Nights toga party, marking the number of days until graduation.

MANHATTANVILLE COLLEGE

Highlights

Students
Total enrollment: 2,796
Undergrads: 1,736
Freshmen: 584
Part-time students: 5%
From out-of-state: 42%
Male/Female: 36%/64%
Live on-campus: 79%
Off-campus employment rating: Excellent
Caucasian: 40%
African American: 8%
Hispanic: 14%
Asian / Pacific Islander: 2%
Native American: 0%
Mixed (2+ ethnicities): 0%
International: 7%

Academics
Calendar: Semester
Student/faculty ratio: 11:1
Class size 9 or fewer: 31%
Class size 10-29: 64%
Class size 30-49: 6%
Class size 50-99: -
Class size 100 or more: -
Returning freshmen: 69%
Six-year graduation rate: 56%
Graduates who immediately go to graduate school: 22%
Graduates who immediately enter career related to major: 35%

Most Popular Majors
Finance/management
Visual/performing arts
Psychology

Admissions
Applicants: 4,772
Accepted: 2,863
Acceptance rate: 60.0%
Average GPA: 3.0
ACT range: 22-26
SAT Math range: 500-610
SAT Reading range: 500-620
SAT Writing range: Not reported
Top 10% of class: 21%
Top 25% of class: 47%
Top 50% of class: 80%

433

College Profiles

MANHATTANVILLE COLLEGE

Admissions Criteria

Academic criteria:
Grades: ☆ ☆ ☆
Difficulty of class schedule: ☆ ☆ ☆
Class rank: N/A
Standardized test scores: ☆ ☆ ☆
Teacher recommendations: ☆ ☆
Personal statement: ☆ ☆
Non-academic criteria considered:
Interview
Extracurricular activities
Special talents, interests, abilities
Character/personal qualities
Volunteer work
Work experience
State of residency
Geographical location
Alumni relationship

Deadlines

Early Action: No
Early Decision: December 1
Regular Action: Rolling admissions
Notification of admission by: December 1
Common Application: Accepted

Financial Aid

In-state tuition: $34,020
Out-of-state tuition: $34,020
Room: $8,680
Board: $5,840
Books: $800
Freshmen receiving need-based aid: 76%
Undergrads rec. need-based aid: 72%
Avg. % of need met by financial aid: 84%
Avg. aid package (freshmen): $29,397
Avg. aid package (undergrads): $28,484
Avg. debt upon graduation: $23,833

School Spirit

Mascot: Valiants
Colors: Red and white

- The Midnight Brunch is a Manhattanville tradition, which occurs each semester before finals. The faculty serve the students a meal to energize them for the exams ahead and to provide a break from studying.
- *The Thomas Crown Affair* (1999) included a character from Manhattanville and filmed inside Reid Hall.

Distinguished Alumni

Sila Calderon, Governor of Puerto Rico; Rose Kennedy, mother of John F. Kennedy; Maria Elena Lagomasino, Chairman and CEO JP Morgan; Rosemary Murphy, Broadway and film actress; Olga Nolla, poet, journalist and professor.

Admissions and Financial Aid

Manhattanville is not a particularly selective school, as it accepts more than half its applicants. If students want to attend Manhattanville but don't have the highest SATs or GPA, they should include interviews and graded writing samples, as recommended by the admissions office.

Manhattanville is well known for its excellence in the arts. Students wishing to be accepted into the fine arts program should include a portfolio, and music students must audition.

Although the college does not meet 100 percent of students' demonstrated financial need with aid, it does have merit-based academic, fine arts, and Sacred Heart scholarships. The Chairman Award ($18,000 freshman year), the Elizabeth J. McCormack Scholarship (100 percent of financial need), and transfer scholarships of up to $15,000 a year are examples.

MARLBORO COLLEGE

Overview

Marlboro College is not for those tied to the status quo: this tiny, private liberal arts college in Marlboro, Vermont has an alternative approach to nearly every aspect of the college experience. This is perhaps most easily seen in the college's use of academic "Plans" (focused programs of study designed by the students themselves) rather than majors, intended to promote student responsibility and investment in their own learning. The admissions office promises that "if you are an independent thinker and have a passion for learning, you will find here a community of scholars unlike that at any other college."

The town of Marlboro is remote, isolated by the Green Mountains. The closest "big" town is Brattleboro, which has a population of 12,000 people and contains limited cultural offerings in the form of art galleries, book shops, restaurants, and coffee shops. Marlboro's location may be attractive to lovers of the outdoors: the school is 30 minutes from the Appalachian Trail, 20 minutes from the Mount Snow ski resort, and surrounded by farmland and cross-country skiing trails.

Academics

Marlboro offers 34 degree fields from which students can create a Plan. First-year students are expected to take classes in at least three academic areas as part of the school's liberal arts commitment to a wide range of study. The only required class is a writing seminar which must be taken within the first three semesters, and students must submit a 20-page writing portfolio to fulfill the school's Clear Writing requirement. Because of the school's size, classes are small: virtually all classes have fewer than 30 students, and the average class size is 10. Students say that classes are rigorous because of the workload and "you can't really hide out from your professor when the classes are so small"—a sentiment echoed by many students at small liberal arts colleges.

With the assistance of faculty advisors, Marlboro students create their own Plans of study for their junior and senior years. By junior year, students are well into the course work outlined in their Plans and learning to strike a balance between that and tutorials. By senior year, students are expected to focus mostly on tutorials and independent work, and students abandon a traditional A-F grading system for a satisfactory/unsatisfactory system. At the end of the program, students are evaluated by a board made up of at least two Marlboro faculty members and one person outside the college, similar to the way a PhD candidate might be interviewed. "The Plan experience is really like a graduate school experience and forces us to think beyond college," explains a student.

Interested students can participate in the World Studies Program, which is a four-year program that integrates liberal arts learning with a six-to-eight month internship abroad. Students earn a bachelor's of arts or science in international studies and an area of concentration.

Those students interested in more traditional study-abroad programs can design their own with the help of a faculty member. There are long-term options through external programs and shorter-term options with faculty-led trips. Also offered is a two-week Outdoor Program to locations such as Canada, Costa Rica, Galapagos, and Belize during spring break and winter break. The Outdoor Program pairs recreational activities with either service or academic research. Some recent internship opportunities have included teaching in Brazil and Ghana, research on malnutrition in Kenya, and disaster relief in Guatemala. "This experience literally changes your life because you are working day to day to truly make a difference and you can see the effect that you have," notes a student.

MARLBORO COLLEGE

Four-year private
Founded: 1946
Marlboro, VT
Rural
Pop. 978

Address:
P.O. Box A, 2582
South Road
Marlboro, VT
05344-0300

Admissions:
800-343-0049

Financial Aid:
802-258-9237

admissions@marlboro.edu

www.marlboro.edu

MARLBORO COLLEGE

Like students at many liberal arts schools, most of Marlboro's graduates—69 percent—go to grad school, typically in education, law, or library science. Eighty-three percent of graduates say that their Marlboro education helped them in their careers. Because the school is so small and relatively young (it was founded in 1946), the alumni network is limited; however, students can get in touch with past graduates through Nook, the school's social network for alumni.

Student Life

The liberal-leaning campus has 22 student organizations, including Pride (the LGBT group), a political action group, and Dead Tree Radio (an online radio station). The school is governed by consensus in town meetings, in which everyone—students, faculty, and staff—gets an equal vote; individual sub-committees of students meet as they see fit. "There's no other college in the country that's run this way," one student comments.

The campus enjoys quirky traditions like Apple Day, which celebrates the famous fruit by bobbing for apples, listening to music, and making apple doughnuts. Word Day is another unique experience in which students, faculty, and staff set aside one day a semester for the entire campus to work on assigned maintenance, from weeding the daffodil beds to chopping wood. "Other schools show school spirit by cheering at football games. We show it by picking up trash," explains a student.

Marlboro has no Greek life and no varsity sports teams, though students will play pick-up games of Frisbee or four-square. The school does have two organized sports teams: soccer (the team competes with nearby schools) and fencing. And the school has one unofficial sport it's serious about: the slightly ridiculous broomball. Students compete for the top prize in the annual tournament, which involves a frozen lake, brooms, and a healthy dose of school pride.

Athletic students can take part in the Marlboro Outdoor Program, which helps students take advantage of the school's location in the Green Mountains by sea kayaking, caving, hiking, and skiing near the local resorts. "No matter what the season, there's something to do outdoors," says a student.

Students can live on campus in one of nine residence halls, three houses, six cottages, two cabins, or four apartments; on-campus housing is overseen by RAs. "What's more important than the actual dorms is who's living in them," remarks a student. "You could be in the craziest or quietest dorm depending on who's there." Students are guaranteed housing for the first year.

Student Body

Marlboro pulls students from 36 states and eight countries, though that can change drastically each year due to the small size of the entering class. The students are "very, very liberal," primarily white (56 percent), and politically engaged. Because the school is so small, everybody knows everyone else as well as their background—some say there are no Greek organizations because the school itself is one big fraternity or sorority. "You're not going to find the cheerleader- or frat boy-type here," says a student.

Students respect each other, as evidenced by their honor-system-controlled library. Though students might be afraid of small-town cliquishness, 25 percent of each year's new students are transfer students. This infuses the social scene with new people.

You May Not Know

- The school's fencing program was introduced 10 years ago by a student whose Plan focused on medieval weaponry.
- A Marlboro professor recently spoke about the influence of the game Monopoly on Americans' economic attitudes.
- Chris North, aka "Mr. Big" on *Sex and the City*, went to Marlboro—though he dropped out.

Distinguished Alumni

Sophie Cabot Black, American poet; Robert MacArthur, ecologist famous for his studies of ecological niches; Jock Sturges, portrait photographer known for his controversial nudes of children.

Admissions and Financial Aid

According to the admissions office, the college is looking for students with "intellectual promise, a high degree of self-motivation, self-discipline, personal stability, social concern, and the ability and desire to contribute to the college community." Marlboro requires interviews for transfer applicants and encourages them for freshmen, either in person or by phone.

Reflecting the college's non-traditional bent, students are invited to submit poetry, creative writing, and CDs or DVDs of their artwork as part of the application process—the college wants to get a feel for who, exactly, their applicants are. Test scores are not required but are accepted. Though the school has a high acceptance rate, students are in part self-selecting by seeking out and applying to Marlboro; the school attracts a certain kind of applicant and, in turn, a certain kind of student.

Any applicant with a GPA of 3.0 or higher is eligible for merit scholarships ranging from $7,500 to $12,500 at Marlboro. If a student doesn't come from a school setting that assessed his or her work by means other than a GPA (if they were home schooled, for example), the admissions board makes a decision based on the student's individual application.

MARLBORO COLLEGE

Highlights

Admissions Criteria
Academic criteria:
Grades: ☆ ☆ ☆
Difficulty of class schedule: ☆ ☆ ☆
Class rank: ☆
Standardized test scores: ☆
Teacher recommendations: ☆ ☆
Personal statement: ☆ ☆ ☆
Non-academic criteria considered:
Interview
Extracurricular activities
Special talents, interests, abilities
Character/personal qualities
Volunteer work
Work experience
Geographical location
Minority affiliation
Alumni relationship

Deadlines
Early Action: January 15
Early Decision: November 15
Regular Action: Rolling admissions
Common Application: Accepted

Financial Aid
In-state tuition: $37,200
Out-of-state tuition: $37,200
Room: $5,660
Board: $4,620
Books: $1,200
Freshmen receiving need-based aid: 82%
Undergrads rec. need-based aid: 75%
Avg. % of need met by financial aid: 75%
Avg. aid package (freshmen): $29,719
Avg. aid package (undergrads): $29,090
Avg. debt upon graduation: $20,051

School Spirit
Mascot: The Fighting Dead Trees

College Profiles

MARQUETTE UNIVERSITY

MARQUETTE UNIVERSITY

Four-year private
Founded: 1881
Milwaukee, WI
Major city
Pop. 594,833

Address:
P.O. Box 1881
Milwaukee, WI
53201

Admissions:
800-222-6544

Financial Aid:
414-288-0200

admissions@mar-
quette.edu

www.marquette.edu

Overview

Wisconsin wins acclaim for its cheeses. Marquette, its largest university, earns top cheddar as one of the state's flagship institutions. Sitcom *Laverne and Shirley* may have put capital Milwaukee on the map; but Marquette continues to draw top-tier support from its hometown for its strong educational opportunities. *U.S. News & World Report* ranked Marquette 75th among other schools, which ensures that Marquette is your best educational bet—especially if you stick to Wisconsin.

The university, founded in 1881, prides itself in its deep Catholic and Jesuit traditions, though following the faith is not a requirement for entrance. The 8,000 undergraduates revel in the school's proximity to Lake Michigan and enjoy a campus architecture that embraces Art Deco. The Beatles themselves got in on Marquette's groove during their brief 1964 stay in Mashuda Hall.

The stately and urban downtown setting that serves as home to the campus encourages Marquette students to pursue an active social life—at least until single-digit temperatures prohibit play in the winter. *Playboy* recently proclaimed Marquette the top party school among Catholic places of higher learning. Numerous student organizations, a rabid basketball fan base, and traditions that include caroling and lighting the campus Christmas tree provide options for the less party-focused.

Academics

Marquette offers 65 majors, with stand-outs in engineering and the prelaw program. According to the university, the "intellectual heart" of study at Marquette is the Core of Common Studies, a Jesuit-themed collection of required classes that students must complete before graduation. The requirements include rhetoric, mathematical reasoning, theology, human nature and ethics, science and nature, individual and social behavior, literature and performing arts, diverse cultures, and histories of cultures and societies. All students must take Introduction to Theology, and then another class on a topic such as the Hebrew scriptures, New Testament, or Christianity. Students don't seem to mind, as one student explains, "even if you aren't religious, you can probably appreciate having an understanding of religion."

Enrollment in some introductory courses may number in the hundreds, but overall, most Marquette classes (88 percent) sport no more than 50 students. "I've had no trouble getting attention from my professors," notes a student.

The university provides several distinctive academic opportunities. The Les Aspin Center for Government offers such popular prospects as special courses and internships atop Capitol Hill. Since the program began in 1984, students have had internships at political locales including the State Department, United States Secret Service, The White House, and the Department of Defense. "During my internship I wasn't just making photocopies," recalls a participant. "I worked on communicating with constituencies in a Congressional district."

Marquette's Honors Program offers students exclusive seminars and introductory courses, post-college guidance, and Honors housing. "The best professors teach the Honors courses," one student says. Honors students may conduct research during their junior year, and a senior capstone experience is required of all students.

The school's Educational Opportunity Program assists first-generation and low-income college students and those from under-represented groups. Through the program students receive academic support while in college. Assistance in graduate school preparation is offered through the Ronald E. McNair Scholars Program. Those who are both disadvantaged and envision a medically focused career will find a trove of directed assistance through the Health Careers Opportunity Program.

Marquette offers its own sponsored study-abroad options, student exchanges with partner universities, faculty-led trips, and affiliated programs. To assist students with their selections, the Office of International Education conducts a study-abroad fair each year as well as informational sessions.

Those graduating with a Marquette diploma find themselves well-situated amongst nearly 20 Fortune 500 companies in the Milwaukee area. "A lot of graduates stay in the area because there are so many opportunities right here," says a student. The Career Services Center offers assistance to students in securing jobs in their fields through activities such as the fall career fair, WorkForce fair, Big East Career Consortium, and spring career fair. Students must register with the center in order to access the online listings of full-time jobs and internships.

Student Life

If the Jesuit tradition promotes selflessness, Marquette students have gravitated to at least one teaching of the religion. "Community service is what everyone does," says a student. Nearly 85 percent of students volunteer annually. A Community Service Center helps field the demand, and class credit is awarded for special service learning opportunities. More than 1,500 students make for Marquette's service crème de la crème: Hunger Clean-Up Day unites the campus as they seek to do their part in fighting both hunger and homelessness.

Students get information about the university's 250 organizations during the annual Organization Fest—or O-Fest, as it is sometimes called—where student groups table up to recruit new members. The Miracle of Central Hall is another annual event. Students gather to watch the lighting of the campus Christmas tree as carolers provide aural ambience and individual candles are lit from person to person. Heavenly peace aside, the Midnight Madness Basketball Kickoff is anything but calm. The Golden Eagles' renowned B-ball team whoops it up for their season premiere each October.

Greek life lives on in the campus' 14 sororities and 15 frats. Only 11 percent of men and 14 percent of women pledge. Students say this means that "while Greek life exists, it doesn't affect most people on a day to day basis."

Besides basketball, Marquette's golf squad proves solid for the school. It has made nearly 30 NCAA Tournament appearances. In all, the university has 14 Division I teams. For those not playing at the varsity level, there are 30 club sports, including the usual suspects, as well as some that are more original and make use of the school's plethora of outdoor locations. These are skiing, snowboarding, waterskiing, and wakeboarding. The more than 20 intramural sports include sand volleyball, bag toss, futsal, inner tube water polo, floor hockey, and a free-throw contest.

When not screaming their heads off in the week of March Madness, students journey into Milwaukee to take advantage of the city's nightlife, pro teams, and famed breweries. "The Miller Brewery Tour is a must," says a student. "Besides seeing how the beer is brewed, you get samples!"

There are nine residence halls and seven university apartment buildings. Special housing options include living/learning communities, Inclusive Leadership CommUNITY, and the Dorothy Day Social Justice Community.

MARQUETTE UNIVERSITY

Highlights

Students
Total enrollment: 11,749
Undergrads: 8,293
Freshmen: 2,197
From out-of-state: 70%
From public schools: 53%
Male/Female: 48%/52%
Live on-campus: 54%
In fraternities: 11%
In sororities: 14%
Off-campus employment rating: Excellent
Caucasian: 75%
African American: 5%
Hispanic: 9%
Asian / Pacific Islander: 5%
Native American: 0%
Mixed (2+ ethnicities): 2%
International: 3%

Academics
Calendar: Semester
Student/faculty ratio: 14:1
Class size 9 or fewer: 14%
Class size 10-29: 48%
Class size 30-49: 26%
Class size 50-99: 8%
Class size 100 or more: 4%
Six-year graduation rate: 80%
Graduates who immediately go to graduate school: 23%

Most Popular Majors
Marketing
Biomedical sciences
Finance

Admissions
Applicants: 22,900
Accepted: 12,644
Acceptance rate: 55.2%
Placed on wait list: 3,789
Enrolled from wait list: 505
Average GPA: Not reported
ACT range: 24-29
SAT Math range: 550-650
SAT Reading range: 520-630
SAT Writing range: 7-34
Top 10% of class: 38%
Top 25% of class: 67%
Top 50% of class: 94%

439

College Profiles

MARQUETTE UNIVERSITY

Admissions Criteria

Academic criteria:
Grades: ☆ ☆ ☆
Difficulty of class schedule: ☆ ☆ ☆
Class rank: ☆ ☆
Standardized test scores: ☆ ☆
Teacher recommendations: ☆ ☆
Personal statement: ☆ ☆
Non-academic criteria considered:
Extracurricular activities
Special talents, interests, abilities
Character/personal qualities
Volunteer work
Geographical location
Minority affiliation
Alumni relationship

Deadlines

Early Action: No
Early Decision: No
Regular Action: December 1 (priority)
December 1 (final)
Notification of admission by: January 31
Common Application: Accepted

Financial Aid

In-state tuition: $34,200
Out-of-state tuition: $34,200
Room: Varies
Board: Varies
Books: $960
Freshmen receiving need-based aid: 62%
Undergrads rec. need-based aid: 60%
Avg. % of need met by financial aid: 74%
Avg. aid package (freshmen): $22,661
Avg. aid package (undergrads): $22,236
Avg. debt upon graduation: $34,602

School Spirit

Mascot: Golden Eagles
Colors: Blue and gold
Song: *Ring Out Ahoya*

Student Body

The stereotypical Marquette student is "white and conservative," says a student, adding, "many students fit the stereotype, but there is more to us than that." There's a high 21 percent minority population with 70 percent of students from out of state. Many out-of-staters are from neighboring Illinois, especially the Chicago area.

As for the conservative label, one student says, "you will find more conservatives than liberals, but most conservative students are still socially moderate or liberal." Students say that a commonality is an "interest in serving the community."

You May Not Know

- In 1809, Marquette welcomed its first women and made history as the first co-educational Catholic institution in the world.
- Nearby locale Harambee translates into the Swahili for "all pull together."
- Marquette alum Joyce Delhi joined the Pulitzer Prize Board in 2008.

Distinguished Alumni

Gail Collins, author and *New York Times* columnist; Chris Farley, comedian, *Saturday Night Live*; Patrick Eugene Hagerty, co-founder, Texas Instruments; Glenn "Doc" Rivers, head coach of the Boston Celtics; Dwyane Wade, NBA player.

Admissions and Financial Aid

At least two admissions officers review each application. If you've taken both the ACT and SAT exams, Marquette will only use your highest score on either of them as they evaluate your academic future. "Most important" in consideration of prospective freshmen is high-school ranking. Equivalent in an evaluation are not only grades, but the classes in which those grades were earned. The admissions office understands that "a B in an AP course is not the same as an A in a regular course."

The admissions office offers this advice: "Relax [as you] write" your Marquette essay. Then match your cool, calm attitude with an exceptional revision as you "proofread your essay and read it backward."

Merit-based scholarships are on offer to students, including the Diederich Scholarship for disadvantaged students who see a communications-related career in their sights. This full-scale offering covers it all: tuition, housing, and school fees, with a stipend to boot. Those students who do not hail from the Midwest, but who can still imagine themselves at Marquette, may find themselves selected for a Pere Marquette Explorer Scholarship, worth $5,000.

MASSACHUSETTS INSTITUTE OF TECHNOLOGY

Overview

Founded in 1891, MIT is a private university with a history rooted in laboratory instruction and an emphasis on applied technology. The MIT campus sits on the banks of the Charles River in the medium-sized city of Cambridge, just a hop, skip, and a jump away from vibrant Boston proper. The 154-acre campus showcases a historic display of statuesque domes and columns, accompanied by new and inventive architectural buildings (all of which are referred to, unsurprisingly perhaps, by numbers and codes). Perhaps in anticipation of bitter Northeastern winters, nearly all the buildings on campus are interconnected.

Famous, or perhaps infamous, for the level of course difficulty, students are sure to be in for the hardest four years of their lives at MIT. But with the passion with which students and faculty members approach problems and problem-solving, they are also bound to be some of the "most incredible" years of your life, according to students.

At MIT, a student's brain will be put to use for both work and play. MIT "hacks," or clever and impressive pranks, have gained nationwide recognition. Hacks include a police car on top of the Great Dome, a rocket with an "MIT" banner shooting up from beneath the field in a Harvard-Yale football game, or the sudden appearance of the Caltech Cannon on the MIT campus. The MIT hacks represent much of the philosophy of the Institute, which "prides itself on first and foremost teaching its students how to think."

Academics

You would have to live under a rock to not know the level of academic rigor at MIT. Because 98 percent of students graduated in the top 10 percent of their high school class, courses are bound to be rigorous. However, students say that the atmosphere is one of cooperation, not competition, and that cutthroat competition is "rare." Freshmen don't receive official letter grades their first semester, receiving instead pass or fail grades; this allows new students a grace period, so they may adjust to college-level courses. "I chose MIT because I knew I'd need time to adjust academically," says a student.

All students must complete General Institute Requirements, which not surprisingly seem weighted toward the sciences. These include courses in science, communication, writing, humanities, arts, and social sciences. Other required classes are Restricted Electives in Science and Technology (REST), laboratory, and physical education, which does have a swimming component.

MIT boasts many excellent programs, with several standouts. The School of Engineering has been ranked top in the country by *U.S. News* for the past 10 years, and the business department was recently ranked second in the nation. There are a myriad of opportunities for academic exploration at MIT. Freshman Learning Communities offer full-year programs of study for groups of 25-100 freshmen. The Experimental Study Group offers small classes, tutorials, and self-paced study, while Concourse emphasizes creative connections between fields of study. Terrascope uses the Earth System as context for core disciplines, and Media Arts and Sciences Program explores the intersection of technology and communication. These courses allow freshmen to orient their studies to an individualized interest.

The Undergraduate Research Opportunities Program is extensive, allowing students the chance to work on cutting-edge research with established faculty members. Students can receive academic credit, project funding, or work on a voluntary basis. Projects run the gamut of academia, from using programming to benefit farming cooperatives in Latin America to creating "animated maps of street life in Ho Chi Minh City." According to students, research opportunities are "abundant."

MASSACHUSETTS INSTITUTE OF TECHNOLOGY

Four-year private
Founded: 1861
Cambridge, MA
Medium city
Pop. 106,038

Address:
77 Massachusetts Avenue
Cambridge, MA 02139

Admissions:
617-253-3400

Financial Aid:
617-253-4971

admissions@mit.edu

web.mit.edu

MASSACHUSETTS INSTITUTE OF TECHNOLOGY

Highlights

Students
Total enrollment: 11,189
Undergrads: 4,503
Freshmen: 1,141
From out-of-state: 91%
From public schools: 65%
Male/Female: 55%/45%
Live on-campus: 90%
In fraternities: 42%
In sororities: 31%
Off-campus employment rating: Excellent
Caucasian: 37%
African American: 6%
Hispanic: 15%
Asian / Pacific Islander: 24%
Native American: 0%
Mixed (2+ ethnicities): 4%
International: 10%

Academics
Calendar: 4-1-4 system
Student/faculty ratio: 8:1
Class size 9 or fewer: 39%
Class size 10-29: 38%
Class size 30-49: 10%
Class size 50-99: 9%
Class size 100 or more: 4%
Returning freshmen: 97%
Six-year graduation rate: 93%
Graduates who immediately go to graduate school: 39%

Most Popular Majors
Computer science/engineering
Electrical engineering/computer science
Mechanical engineering

Admissions
Applicants: 18,109
Accepted: 1,620
Acceptance rate: 8.9%
Placed on wait list: 849
Enrolled from wait list: Not reported
Average GPA: Not reported
ACT range: 32-35
SAT Math range: 740-800
SAT Reading range: 670-770
SAT Writing range: 70-26
Top 10% of class: 98%
Top 25% of class: 100%

442

Students can also study abroad all over the world with a fair amount of ease due to opportunities such as the Cambridge-MIT Exchange Program, the MIT-Madrid Program, and the Delft University and Hong Kong University Exchanges.

MIT graduates find phenomenal success after college, with almost 60 percent going straight into the workforce, and 39 percent immediately enrolling in graduate or professional school. Each year, over 400 companies visit MIT to actively recruit its students, and MIT hosts a series of career fairs. The school offers career counseling, resume workshops, and practice interviews. "Going to MIT is pretty much a golden ticket to getting a job," says a student.

Student Life

With over 450 student-run clubs and activities, you can get involved in basically any extracurricular you could dream up at MIT—and they're not all math or chess clubs either. There is an incredibly wide spectrum of focus—from comedy improv to ethnic and cultural awareness to Model UN. Some of the more unique activities include an Origami Club, the Underwater Hockey Group, and the Laboratory for Chocolate Science, which as you might expect, is quite tempting to many.

If you're hoping you'll also be able to get some of that "Animal House" feel at MIT, you're both in and out of luck. With 26 social fraternities and six social sororities, Greek life is huge at MIT, with 42 percent of the male population and more than a quarter of the female population belonging to a Greek organization. However, it's probably not Greek life as you've imagined it—the focus is not as much on partying as it is on supporting academics and community service. As one student explains, "There are massive Greek parties, but everyone knows deep down why we're here—to study."

Despite the scholarly bent of students, athletics is alive and well on campus. Most of the varsity sports at MIT compete as Division III NCAA teams (crew being the exception, at Division I). The university has the most number of Academic All-Americas in Division III in the country with more than 200 recipients. MIT has won recent national titles in pistol and swim. There are over 800 participants in the 35 club sports teams, with one third of these weighing in as martial arts groups. More than 4,000 students and faculty members participate in 18 intramural sports.

As an MIT student, you have guaranteed housing all four years. Freshmen are required to live on campus, in one of the 11 residence halls. After freshman year, a small number decide to live off campus, but overall, 90 percent of all students live on campus.

On-campus activities are flavored by the MIT atmosphere. Students can head to a fraternity party on the weekend but many also treasure nerdy delights such as the Orange Tour. Held every fall under the darkness of night, this tour introduces students to secret spots on campus. Companion activities of the same nature include the MIT Mystery Hunt, a campus-wide puzzle competition held during the January Independent Activity period, and Spring Weekend, a festival and concert held annually which has featured artists such as N.E.R.D., Busta Rhymes, The Roots, Blues Traveler, and 10,000 Maniacs. Students that have participated in these events comment that they are "legendary and a must-do."

Off campus, Cambridge is easily accessible; you can try a variety of cuisines at Kendall Square, and experience the local music scene at Central Square. Boston—the largest college town in the country with one in four residents being a college student—is just a quick trip across the bridge. Students can opt to see a Bruins, Celtics, or Red Sox game, take advantage of free admission to the Museum of Science, see a performance at the Boston Symphony Orchestra, or go clubbing at Middle East and TT The Bear's Place.

Student Body

There is a high level of ethnic diversity among students at MIT, with almost half of students identifying as minorities. It's not an overwhelming East Coast population either, with a fairly even geographic distribution across the States: 20 percent from the West, 17 percent from the Southeast and Puerto Rico, 16 percent from the Mid-Atlantic, and 13 percent each from the Midwest, Plains states, and New England. Because of the need-blind admission policy, students represent many levels of socioeconomic status—65 percent of students attended a public high school.

The population at MIT has historically been dominated by men, but the gender ratio is steadily becoming more balanced—the female population is currently up to 45 percent. "As a woman, I've never felt out of place," says a female student.

The predominant stereotype for MIT students is "geek and social misfit." While this may be true for some students, it does not define the student body as a whole. A commonality among MIT students is a passion for learning, not simply a focus on earning good grades. "Grades are secondary. What really counts is understanding the material," says a student.

You May Not Know

- MIT has never awarded an honorary degree—the university has however awarded two honorary professorships to Winston Churchill and Salman Rushdie.
- Students and alumni wear the "Standard Technology Ring," which is fondly referred to as the "Brass Rat." Though the three faces of each year's ring vary slightly, they always feature the same images—a beaver on the front face, flanked by the MIT seal and class year on either side.
- In 2005, MIT held a Time Traveler Convention to make contact with time travelers from the future. Though no confirmed time travelers attended, the organizers state that "many time travelers could have attended incognito to avoid endless questions about the future."

Distinguished Alumni

Buzz Aldrin, Apollo 11 Pilot, second man to land on the moon; Kofi Annan, Former UN Secretary-General; Capt. Catherine Coleman, astronaut; H. Robert Horvitz, Nobel Laureate in Physiology/Medicine; Linda Muri, three-time world champion rower; I.M. Pei, architect; Alex Rigopulos, developer of Guitar Hero and Rock Band.

MASSACHUSETTS INSTITUTE OF TECHNOLOGY

Highlights

Admissions Criteria
Academic criteria:
Grades: ☆ ☆
Difficulty of class schedule: ☆ ☆
Class rank: ☆
Standardized test scores: ☆ ☆
Teacher recommendations: ☆ ☆
Personal statement: ☆ ☆
Non-academic criteria considered:
Interview
Extracurricular activities
Special talents, interests, abilities
Character/personal qualities
Volunteer work
Work experience
State of residency
Geographical location
Minority affiliation

Deadlines
Early Action: November 1
Early Decision: No
Regular Action: January 1 (final)
Notification of admission by: March 20
Common Application: Not accepted

Financial Aid
In-state tuition: $43,210
Out-of-state tuition: $43,210
Room: $7,970
Board: $4,774
Books: $1,000
Freshmen receiving need-based aid: 56%
Undergrads rec. need-based aid: 58%
Avg. % of need met by financial aid: 100%
Avg. aid package (freshmen): $41,756
Avg. aid package (undergrads): $41,703
Avg. debt upon graduation: $20,794

School Spirit
Mascot: Beaver
Colors: Cardinal red and silver gray

Admissions and Financial Aid

At an acceptance rate of less than 10 percent of those who apply, it is no wonder that MIT is considered one of the most elite schools in the nation. In fact, it is so difficult to be admitted, that the MIT admissions office provides resources for parents on how they can help their child (and themselves) deal with the disappointment of not being accepted to the school.

MIT students are generally those who were at the top of their graduating class, elicited excellent teacher recommendations, and have performed very well on standardized test scores. Despite the outstanding caliber of applicants' success, the college is not looking for "a batch of identically perfect" students, but rather for "a richly varied team of capable people who will support, surprise, and inspire each other."

An interview is highly recommended, and there are more than 3,000 alumni interviewers around the world.

MIT does not offer any athletic or merit-based scholarships. However, the financial aid program is very generous—MIT reports that 90 percent of all undergraduate students receive some form of need-or merit-based financial aid. Families earning less than $75,000 a year do not need to pay any tuition and will not have any student loans.

MCGILL UNIVERSITY

Overview

McGill University's main campus lies in the heart of Montreal, Canada at the foot of Mount Royal. The park-like campus' main buildings are constructed using local gray limestone, and students enjoy access to two nearby metro stations. A very large public university, McGill boasts diversity in its students, who hail from more than 150 countries, as well as its wide range of academic offerings.

While Montreal is French-speaking, the university is English-speaking, so knowledge of French is helpful but not absolutely necessary. A growing number of American students—who make up nearly 10 percent of the undergrad population—attend the university, perhaps drawn by the dynamic city of Montreal and the relatively low cost of tuition. The Faculty of Science is particularly strong at McGill, with extensive resources for undergraduate research, including a $100 million, 340,000-square-foot Life Sciences Complex, a collection of a dozen buildings that will house 600 researchers. About 30 kilometers west of the downtown campus is the waterfront Macdonald Campus, where students study the natural sciences, environment, agriculture, and food.

Evidence of McGill's support of sustainability includes a student-run bicycle collective and weekly Farmer's Market during the fall. While there's plenty to do both on and off campus, students do have to withstand frigid winters (think *minus* 15 Celsius). American students will also need to acclimate in other ways: to a country and school where Greek life doesn't play a major role, to the British system of spelling, and—not everyone will complain about this—to a lower legal drinking age of 18.

Academics

McGill offers degrees and diplomas in over 300 fields of study across 21 faculties and professional schools. English is the language of instruction, though students can submit graded work in English or French. About 22 percent of students are enrolled in the Faculty of the Arts, the largest school at the university; other larger faculties include Science, Medicine, Engineering, and Management.

Students pursuing a BA or BS degree are required to complete a Freshman Program of 30 credits, including foundational courses in math, science, and arts (which includes humanities, languages, and social sciences). Students looking to combine different fields of study may complete a Department Program such as Multi-track, Honors, Joint Honors, and Interfaculty.

Students say that courses "for the most part are pretty challenging." The faculty-student ratio is fairly low, despite the large size of the university. "It doesn't take a lot of effort to develop a professional relationship with professors," says a student. Strong programs include engineering, linguistics, management, and the sciences (especially for premed students).

Discover McGill is a one-day orientation that kicks off the first week for incoming freshmen. Students are divided into groups based on their faculty and spend time with upper-year students in various information sessions. "It's a day where everyone is super-friendly and open to making friends," notes a student.

The Faculty of Science is one of the most competitive and offers 16-month internships, field study abroad, tropical research in Barbados, and even a stay at an Arctic Research Station. Undergraduate research in science has an impressive array of resources and as one student describes, "plentiful opportunities"—as the fact that there are 396 undergraduate research project courses attests.

The Office of Sustainability at McGill supports the university's commitment to social, economic, and environmental sustainability. There is a Sustainability Projects Fund that has spawned projects with titles like "Meatless Mondays McGill" and "Water is Life! Sustaining McGill's eau de vie."

MCGILL UNIVERSITY

Four-year public
Founded: 1821
Montreal, CN
Major city
Pop. 3,635,571

Address:
845 Sherbrooke Street
West
Montreal, CN
H3A 2T5

Admissions:
514-398-3910

Financial Aid:
514-398-6013

admissions@mcgill.ca

www.mcgill.ca

MCGILL UNIVERSITY

Students
Total enrollment: 38,779
Undergrads: 26,349
Part-time students: 16%
Male/Female: 41%/59%
Live on-campus: 12%
Off-campus employment rating: Good
International: 21%

Academics
Calendar: Semester
Student/faculty ratio: 16:1
Class size 9 or fewer: 12%
Class size 10-29: 40%
Class size 30-49: 16%
Class size 50-99: 20%
Class size 100 or more: 11%

Most Popular Majors
Political science
General management
International development studies

Admissions
Acceptance rate: 53.6%
Average GPA: 3.5
ACT range: 29-32
SAT Math range: 650-720
SAT Reading range: 640-740
SAT Writing range: 650-730

McGill offers student exchanges and study-abroad opportunities in more than 30 countries. There are also field-studies opportunities for studying social conditions in Africa, environmental issues in Panama, and more.

McGill has around 200,000 living alumni worldwide, making for an extensive network. The university boasts the most Rhodes Scholars of any Canadian University. The McGill Career Planning Service (CaPS) offers workshops, advising, and assistance with finding jobs and internships.

Student Life

The Students' Society of McGill University (SSMU), i.e. the student union, supports over 200 student clubs and throws the self-proclaimed "best parties in Montreal." Students often hang out in the William Shatner University Centre, with diverse offerings including the campus bar Gerts (with live bands on Thursdays), a lounge, and various eateries. There's even an organic food co-op and a bicycle co-op! For those who love the arts, the Players' Theatre hosts shows throughout the year, including the popular McGill Drama Festival.

For incoming students who may feel overwhelmed by the many activities available at McGill, there's a First Year Office to help them get acclimated. "It's nice to have somewhere to turn when you have questions," says a student. McGill's Orientation Week, aka Frosh Week, takes place the week before classes start, and the Orientation Centre showcases student clubs in a centralized location.

Another source of celebration is the Open Air Pub, which takes place at the beginning of the year and brings the entire McGill community together to hang out under the late summer sun. Students enjoy inexpensive food and cool beverages, plus live music, late into the evening.

The annual 4 Floors Party is extremely popular and sells out its 1,500-student capacity quickly. The SSMU transforms the Orientation Centre's four floors into a giant party with different themes on each floor, like Halloween bash and Sheesha lounge. "It's a whole school party that you don't want to miss," notes a student.

Greek life is not dominant at McGill—about two percent of the student body joins, which seems low compared to American universities but is average for a Canadian school. Canada's sole national fraternity, Phi Kappa Pi, was founded at McGill and the University of Toronto about 100 years ago and continues to operate.

McGill Athletics and Recreation has 29 different intercollegiate teams, numerous competitive clubs, 700 intramural teams, and an extensive fitness and recreation program. Facilities include a pool, tennis courts, and the 25,000-seat Molson Stadium, home to the Montreal Alouettes, the university's football team. Indeed, the first game of American football was played between McGill and Harvard in the late 19th century. This rivalry continues in the form of the biannual rugby games between the two schools. Attesting to the strength of sports at McGill, a McGill alumnus or alumna has competed at every Olympic Games since the early 1900s.

Off campus, Montreal offers shopping, museums, restaurants, bars on Ste. Denis and St. Laurent, cultural venues, and professional athletics. It's legal to drink at age 18, so you'll even see freshmen out at the bars. "Montreal is the perfect college town," one student comments.

Housing is only guaranteed for first-year students in the "rez" or residence halls. The New Residence Hall (New Rez), a converted four-star hotel, is not surprisingly the most coveted. The vast majority of students live off campus, many in the "McGill Ghetto," the neighborhood directly to the east of downtown campus.

Student Body

McGill has a diverse student population with the largest international student population (21 percent) of any Canadian university—the plurality of whom are American students. There is moderate geographic diversity, with 57 percent of students from Quebec and 24 percent from the rest of Canada. Though the university is located in a French-speaking province, only about 17 percent of students claim French as their first language (English is the first language for more than half of the student body).

You May Not Know

- McGill is named after James McGill, a successful businessman in furs and ammunition.
- Built in 1839, the Arts Building is the oldest building on campus still standing.
- Radon was discovered at McGill by physicist Ernest Rutherford. McGill was also where the first artificial cell and first Internet search engine were developed.

Distinguished Alumni

Samantha Bee, correspondent on the *Daily Show*; Steven Pinker, cognitive scientist; Vivienne Poy, first Canadian Senator of Asian ancestry; William Shatner, *Star Trek* actor.

Admissions and Financial Aid

Students apply to a specific faculty or department at McGill rather than the university itself. The admissions team evaluates academic performance in courses related to one's intended program—e.g., math and science courses for science-based programs; auditions for music; portfolios for architecture. Unlike many American colleges, "extracurricular activities are not significant in the admission decision, although they are an important factor in the awarding of certain entrance scholarships."

All eligible applicants are automatically considered for Basic Scholarships (one-year awards of $3,000). Separate applications are needed for Major Scholarships, which range from $3,000 to $10,000 and are renewable. Awardees of these scholarships enjoy the extra perk of being guaranteed their first choice of residence. There are also athletic awards for a number of sports.

Need-based aid includes loans and bursaries, which do not need to be repaid. McGill recently offered $3.6 million in entrance bursaries to 868 entering undergrads; Quebec/Canadian offers averaged $3,400 each while United States and/or overseas students received offers averaging $8,300.

MCGILL UNIVERSITY

Highlights

Admissions Criteria
Academic criteria:
Grades: ☆ ☆ ☆
Difficulty of class schedule: ☆ ☆ ☆
Class rank: ☆ ☆
Standardized test scores: ☆ ☆ ☆
Teacher recommendations: ☆
Personal statement: N/A
Non-academic criteria considered:
State of residency

Deadlines
Early Action: No
Early Decision: No
Regular Action: Rolling admissions
Common Application: Not accepted

Financial Aid
In-state tuition: $2,421
Out-of-state tuition: $14,891
Room: $6,347
Board: $4,900
Books: $1,000
Avg. aid package (freshmen): Not reported
Avg. aid package (undergrads): Not reported

School Spirit
Colors: Red and white

Four-year public
Founded: 1809
Oxford, OH
Small town
Pop. 21,444

Address:
501 East High Street
Oxford, OH
45056

Admissions:
513-529-2531

Financial Aid:
513-529-8734

admission@miamioh.
edu

www.miamioh.edu

MIAMI UNIVERSITY

Overview

There are certain things you learn to expect from the Midwest: it's a little white bread, a little conservative, very hospitable, and man, does it like football! At Miami University in Ohio, there aren't a whole lot of things that break the mid-western mold. There's a strong sense of community—students get involved on campus, be it through Greek life, athletics, one of the many clubs, or research—but if you're looking for diversity, Miami University might not be the place you find it. However, whatever MU might lack in diversity, it makes up for in beauty. The 2,000-acre campus is breathtaking: lots of green, lots of brick, and even a so-called "Natural Area," complete with hiking trails and bird-watching opportunities.

At a school as big as Miami, it can be easy to get lost among the thousands, but MU seems to make a pretty big effort to make sure there's always some way to feel like you belong.

Academics

Miami University was ranked 3rd in commitment to undergraduate teaching by *U.S. News & World Report*, a reflection of the school's determination to make the students' classroom experiences worthwhile. Almost 90 percent of the school's classes have less than 50 students. "You can tell that the professors really care about teaching," says a student. "I had a professor actually call me when I was absent."

The school has a strong Interior Design program in its School of Fine Arts, particularly interesting because it shares an administration with the architecture program, allowing for a lot of interdisciplinary work. The School of Engineering and Applied Science has a noted program as well, and Accountancy and Interdisciplinary Business Management have strong national reputations.

Students at Miami have to fulfill the school's Foundation requirements, which fall into five categories: two courses in English Composition; four courses and at least three hours in each of fine arts, humanities, and social science; two courses in cultures; three courses in natural science with at least one in biology and one in physical science; and one course in mathematics, formal reasoning, or technology. Among these, at least one course has to count for Historical Perspective. AP courses can fulfill the requirements. The Honors Program at Miami allows for its students to shape their own curriculum through normal classes, faculty-led research projects, internships, teaching courses, and community service.

Academic advising at Miami is extensive and accessible. For first-year, on-campus students, an advisor lives and works in their dorms. Commuting students have their own advising center. After their first year, Miami students are assigned departmental advisors. ROTC students, athletes, study-abroad participants, and honors students are among the groups that have specialized additional advisors available to them.

Some students complain that it's harder for non-honors undergraduates to get into the classes they want because of priority given to the graduate and Honors Program students. "I guess it's to be expected at a public school that you can't always get the classes that you want," says a student.

Miami requires its seniors to take part in a Capstone project to encourage critical analysis and the communication of ideas and information among students. The projects can take pretty much any form: individual studio work, research seminars, group projects, etc., and they don't have to relate to the students' majors, though certain majors require it as part of the track. There are also a number of specialized research programs open to undergraduate students, including the Interdisciplinary Technology Development Research Challenge, an annual competition that has teams of students looking at the whole process of technology development from the construction to the politics and business sides of innovation.

The Career Center at Miami offers workshops throughout the year in interviewing techniques, preparing resumes, and strategies to help with the job search. The center also provides access to several online databases and tools, mini career development courses, and peer advising.

Miami University offers some interesting study-abroad choices. The school has its own center in Luxembourg, the Dolibois Center, as well as exchange and direct enrollment in foreign universities around the world. Additionally, Miami recognizes many programs from other schools or organization. All said, the study-abroad program offers opportunities to go to almost 100 different countries through hundreds of different programs.

Student Life

Miami has more than 400 student organizations, from the Anime Club to the Investment Club and the Paintball team to whichever political orientation with which you happen to agree. MU even has a Parkour Club, the form of "freerunning" made famous by David Belle in the 90s that calls for its members to overcome any obstacle in their paths by jumping, ducking, rolling, and generally contorting.

The most popular student groups are the fraternities and sororities. With 24 percent of students participating in 50 fraternities and sororities, Greek life runs the social scene. If you're not a part of it, it's probably still a part of your life. Even between parties and pre-games, the Greeks have a strong presence on campus. "If you want to have a social life, you really should join a fraternity or sorority," says a student.

Athletics are a big part of life at MU. It's a Division I school, so competition is fierce among the eight men's and 10 women's varsity teams. The football games are well attended, and the basketball team has been a part of the NCAA tournament 16 times. The school even has a winning synchronized skating team, one of the most decorated programs in the country. Miami takes great pride in its sports and the students who perform them.

Besides its sporting events, Miami hosts Make a Difference Day, an annual volunteer coordination that gets students involved in projects around the Oxford community. The University's Natural Areas has an annual Hike-a-thon and Bird Watch that maps out one-, three-, and five-mile hikes. And if watching people fall over themselves in valiant efforts to dignify broomball gets you cheering, then After Dark Broomball and skating—hosted by the Groggin Ice Center—is probably right up your alley.

The Oxford area has some good choices for restaurants and bars. Off-campus housing is popular; in fact, half the student body lives off campus. This makes the off-campus social scene dominant, especially for upperclassmen. "I don't know any upperclass students who still live on campus," says one student.

Miami on-campus housing has great dorm and apartment-style living options, but most students only take part freshman and sophomore year.

Student Body

Diversity isn't huge at Miami, but let's face it, it's an Ohio state school. Ohio isn't exactly known for its diversity. The school does make an effort to keep things a little bit mixed up and has managed a

MIAMI UNIVERSITY – OXFORD

Highlights

Students
Total enrollment: 17,683
Undergrads: 15,081
Freshmen: 4,177
From out-of-state: 36%
From public schools: 74%
Male/Female: 48%/52%
Live on-campus: 48%
In fraternities: 24%
In sororities: 25%
Off-campus employment rating: Good
Caucasian: 82%
African American: 4%
Hispanic: 3%
Asian / Pacific Islander: 2%
Native American: 0%
Mixed (2+ ethnicities): 2%
International: 6%

Academics
Calendar: Semester
Student/faculty ratio: 17:1
Class size 9 or fewer: 5%
Class size 10-29: 58%
Class size 30-49: 25%
Class size 50-99: 9%
Class size 100 or more: 4%
Returning freshmen: 89%
Six-year graduation rate: 80%

Most Popular Majors
Finance
Accountancy
Marketing

Admissions
Applicants: 20,314
Accepted: 14,788
Acceptance rate: 72.8%
Placed on wait list: 1,715
Enrolled from wait list: 6
Average GPA: 3.6
ACT range: 24-29
SAT Math range: 550-660
SAT Reading range: 530-630
SAT Writing range: Not reported
Top 10% of class: 36%
Top 25% of class: 68%
Top 50% of class: 96%

449

College Profiles

MIAMI UNIVERSITY – OXFORD

Admissions Criteria
Academic criteria:
Grades: ☆ ☆ ☆
Difficulty of class schedule: ☆ ☆ ☆
Class rank: ☆ ☆ ☆
Standardized test scores: ☆ ☆ ☆
Teacher recommendations: ☆ ☆ ☆
Personal statement: ☆ ☆ ☆
Non-academic criteria considered:
Extracurricular activities
Special talents, interests, abilities
Character/personal qualities
Volunteer work
Work experience
Geographical location
Alumni relationship

Deadlines
Early Action: December 1
Early Decision: November 15
Regular Action: February 1 (final)
Notification of admission by: March 15
Common Application: Accepted

Financial Aid
In-state tuition: $13,266
Out-of-state tuition: $29,056
Room: $5,328
Board: $5,572
Books: $1,250
Freshmen receiving need-based aid: 47%
Undergrads rec. need-based aid: 43%
Avg. % of need met by financial aid: 56%
Avg. aid package (freshmen): $10,647
Avg. aid package (undergrads): $11,437
Avg. debt upon graduation: $27,817

School Spirit
Mascot: RedHawks
Colors: Red and white
Song: *Love and Honor to Miami*

moderate 11 percent ethnic minority, and a 36 percent out-of-state population. Given that most of the students are white and from Ohio, it doesn't come as too much of a surprise that it's pretty much a preppy school. It's even earned itself the nickname "J Crew U."

And while Ohio is a swing state, the students at Miami tend toward more conservative political views. "There are some liberal students," says a student, "but I'd say the majority here are more conservative."

You May Not Know

- Miami University was called the "Yale of the West" soon after it opened its doors in 1809.
- Craig Williamson, a Miami Ecosystem Ecology scholar, was invited to join the United Nations Environmental Panel (UNEP).
- When Miami University students marry each other, it's known as a Miami Merger.

Distinguished Alumni

Art Clokey, creator of Gumby and Pokey toys; Rita Dove, former U.S. Poet Laureate; Benjamin Harrison, the 23rd President of the United States; Richard Smucker, President of Smucker's brand foods; Matt Yuricich, Academy-Award winning special effects artist.

Admissions and Financial Aid

Miami uses the Common Application with its own supplement. Applicants to the Farmer School of Business have to complete a computer skills exam that tests knowledge of Microsoft Excel and Access.

The School of Fine Arts students have special application procedures, as well, though that's pretty standard for art programs.

Merit-based scholarships are awarded formulaically based on GPA and ACT/SAT scores, with higher amounts corresponding with higher test score and more money for out-of-state students (because their tuition is more expensive). Qualified in-state students receive from $2,000 to $6,500, out-of-state from $4,500 to $10,000.

The Harrison Scholarship is available to Honors students. This award grants the equivalent of in-state tuition for all four years. Scholarships are available through certain departments, as well, so make sure to look through the website of the department in which you're interested.

MICHIGAN STATE UNIVERSITY

Overview

Michigan State University, founded in 1855 as the first land-grant university in the nation, truly embodies a pioneering spirit of discovery. First known as the Agricultural College of the State of Michigan, MSU still embraces its roots, and boasts a campus of 5,200 acres and over 15,000 acres total throughout Michigan for research in agriculture and forestry. The campus includes nearly 600 buildings, ranging from historic ivy-covered halls to modern facilities, as well as over 100 miles of walkways and roads. The Red Cedar River cuts through the center of campus, and the many leafy trees create a park-like atmosphere.

MSU is a strong research university, recently ranked the 29th best public university in the country by the *U.S. News & World Report*. It is also one of only 60 universities in the nation to be a member of the Association of American Universities. MSU is big, with more than 37,000 undergraduates, but the school provides ample opportunities for any area of study or interest. Students choose to study through one of MSU's 17 colleges and the Honors College or to live in one of three Residential Colleges.

Although the student body center can spread out and move away from campus dorms, MSU still bonds together, especially for sports games against the University of Michigan. Over 500 clubs allow students to pursue any interest they can imagine, and campus events range from Safe Halloween to *Spartan Idol*. MSU provides challenging courses, and the winters can be long and cold—average January lows can drop into the teens—but students thrive on the endless opportunities to learn, engage, and grow.

Academics

Michigan State University grants 150 majors through 17 colleges. Strong programs include agriculture and natural resources, business, communications, engineering, political science and public policy, premedical studies, and pre-veterinary studies. In order to graduate, all students must fulfill requirements in mathematics, writing, and integrative studies. The math and writing requirements are not very demanding in terms of number: only two classes each. The Integrative Studies Program is a bit more extensive: designed to provide the benefits of a core curriculum in a liberal arts education, courses encourage students to think critically and to understand and appreciate different cultures.

To help create a smaller community within the larger university campus, the school offers an Honors College for students who were in the top five percent of their high school classes and achieved a score of at least 30 on the ACT or 1360 out of 1600 on the SAT. The Honors College provides students the freedom to pursue their own interests and programs, rather than taking a prescribed set of courses, and allows them the opportunity to study in small classes and work closely with their professors. They may also pursue studies in any number of research and international programs, and engage in social and cultural activities. "You have to work a lot harder to get the same amount of attention from faculty members if you aren't in the Honors College," says a student.

MSU also offers close-knit community through its system of Residential Colleges, in which students interested in studying similar topics live and learn together. Students apply to join a college, and are carefully selected—each college has a maximum class size of 25 students. There are three residential colleges: Arts and Humanities, for students interested in history, literature, languages, and visual and performing arts; Lyman Briggs College, which focuses on the sciences, although it strives to reconcile science and humanities; and James Madison College, a college focused on social sciences and public policy. "Even though MSU is 'humongous,' the residential colleges make it seem not as large," notes a student.

MICHIGAN STATE UNIVERSITY

Four-year public
Founded: 1855
East Lansing, MI
Medium city
Pop. 48,666

Address:
Administration Building
East Lansing, MI
48824

Admissions:
517-355-8332

Financial Aid:
517-353-5940

admis@msu.edu

www.msu.edu

451

MICHIGAN STATE UNIVERSITY

Students

Total enrollment: 48,906
Undergrads: 37,454
Part-time students: 8%
From out-of-state: 13%
Male/Female: 50%/50%
Live on-campus: 42%
In fraternities: 8%
In sororities: 7%
Off-campus employment rating: Excellent
Caucasian: 71%
African American: 7%
Hispanic: 4%
Asian / Pacific Islander: 4%
Native American: 0%
Mixed (2+ ethnicities): 2%
International: 11%

Academics

Calendar: Semester
Student/faculty ratio: 16:1
Class size 9 or fewer: 6%
Class size 10-29: 52%
Class size 30-49: 21%
Class size 50-99: 9%
Class size 100 or more: 12%
Returning freshmen: 91%
Six-year graduation rate: 79%
Graduates who immediately enter career related to major: 95%

Most Popular Majors

Psychology
Accounting
Finance

Admissions

Applicants: 30,224
Accepted: 21,327
Acceptance rate: 70.6%
Average GPA: 3.6
ACT range: 23-28
SAT Math range: 540-680
SAT Reading range: 430-590
SAT Writing range: 4-17
Top 10% of class: 27%
Top 25% of class: 64%
Top 50% of class: 94%

As the five-year leader of study-abroad participation among public universities, MSU provides ample opportunities for its students to explore other cultures. MSU's 260 programs in over 60 countries provide a great deal of flexibility as well as variety—students can choose to study for as little as one or two weeks or as long as a semester or year. MSU also offers seminars abroad, in which students can spend several weeks after their freshman year studying a specific question in one of a couple of countries. Students can also complete international internships during a semester or the summer.

The Career Services Network provides more than 20 career fairs a year, including specialized ones for accounting, nursing, supply chain management, packaging, criminal justice, and engineering. One-on-one counseling, workshops, and speed networking events are also offered.

Student Life

With such a large student body and campus, MSU is bound to have something for everyone with over 500 student organizations. Notable annual events include the Homecoming Parade in October, which had a theme of environmental sustainability last year, and the popular Spartan Idol, MSU's version of *American Idol*, in which students audition for best school singer by singing *a cappella* songs and by telling jokes onstage.

Greek life is "very visible" on campus, and although only about eight percent of the student body rushes, they can choose from 31 social fraternities and 19 social sororities, as well as several business and co-ed Greek organizations. One notable event held jointly by MSU fraternities and sororities is Safe Halloween, in which Greek members host a carnival of fun Halloween activities for families of East Lansing in order to provide safe Halloween activities for local children.

Sports at Michigan State University are a *huge* deal, especially against rival University of Michigan. MSU has especially strong men's and women's basketball teams and holds a record for being the only school to have won multiple national championships in football, basketball, and hockey. The university boasts 25 Division I varsity teams in the Big Ten Conference, and students and alumni always turn out in green and white to cheer their team on. School spirit abounds: Spartan Stadium, which can hold 76,000 fans, is often full during football season, and "Sparty," the school mascot, has been voted the nation's best mascot several times. "Tailgating for football games is like a sport in and of itself," laughs a student. Numerous club sports teams, as well as intramural sports, also keep students active. Choices include lacrosse, soccer, volleyball, men's handball, and women's fast pitch softball. In addition to numerous activities on campus, students embrace the surrounding area, including the community of East Lansing, the nearby capital of Lansing, and the beautiful beaches of Lake Michigan. "You can tell we're in a college town because of all of the restaurants, bars, shopping, and movie theatres," says a student.

Although MSU offers on-campus housing to 22,000 students and has several unique residential learning programs, more than half of students choose to live off campus. Freshmen are required to live on campus, which helps create a community during the first year.

Student Body

MSU is a state school, and nearly 90 percent of its students are from Michigan. MSU has moderate ethnic diversity, with 17 percent of students identifying as minority. The school does strive to incorporate cultural diversity into college life through numerous organizations, including the Office for Inclusion and Intercultural Initiatives and the Office of Cultural and Academic Transitions.

"You will find students from all walks of life here," notes a student. "The one thing that probably binds us all together is rooting for the football team."

You May Not Know

- MSU is the only university in the country with three on-campus medical schools, for allopathic and osteopathic physicians, and veterinarians.
- The cross-fertilization of corn was discovered at MSU in the 1870s, and the anticancer drug cisplatin was discovered in the 1960s.
- MSU is the sixth largest producer of Peace Corps volunteers.

Distinguished Alumni

Richard Ford, author and Pulitzer Prize winner; Kay Koplovitz, founder of the USA Network.

Admissions and Financial Aid

Admission to MSU is selective and competitive. In fact, most MSU students had a high school GPA between 3.4 and 3.85 and engaged in activities outside of the classroom. With a rolling admissions policy, students will learn their results within three months. Interested students should apply as early as possible, preferably between August and November 1 of their senior year of high school, in order to be considered for scholarships. In addition to visiting campus and taking tours, applicants to MSU have the option of chatting online with current students.

MSU offers numerous scholarships, and all students who apply are automatically considered, although some scholarships require a supplemental application. Scholarships come in a variety of forms, including academic merit scholarships, special criteria awards, and scholarships for both Michigan residents and students from other states. Academic scholarships are plentiful and varied, and range from awards of $1,500 per year to complete coverage of tuition, fees, and room and board, plus $1,000 annually. Special criteria scholarships are awarded for a variety of reasons, ranging from talent or interest in performing arts or humanities, to 4-H students and students in several counties in Michigan whose families have been affected by cancer.

MICHIGAN STATE UNIVERSITY

Highlights

Admissions Criteria
Academic criteria:
Grades: ☆ ☆
Difficulty of class schedule: ☆ ☆
Class rank: ☆
Standardized test scores: ☆ ☆ ☆
Teacher recommendations: ☆
Personal statement: ☆ ☆
Non-academic criteria considered:
Interview
Extracurricular activities
Special talents, interests, abilities
Character/personal qualities
Volunteer work
Work experience
State of residency
Geographical location

Deadlines
Early Action: October 16
Early Decision: No
Regular Action: Rolling admissions
Common Application: Accepted

Financial Aid
In-state tuition: $12,863
Out-of-state tuition: $33,750
Room: $3,636
Board: $5,170
Books: $1,044
Freshmen receiving need-based aid: 47%
Undergrads rec. need-based aid: 49%
Avg. % of need met by financial aid: 61%
Avg. aid package (freshmen): $11,718
Avg. aid package (undergrads): $11,509
Avg. debt upon graduation: $24,987

School Spirit
Mascot: Spartans
Colors: Green and white
Song: *MSU Fight Song*

MIDDLEBURY
COLLEGE

Four-year private
Founded: 1800
Middlebury, VT
Rural
Pop. 8,183

Address:
131 South Main Street
Middlebury, VT
05753

Admissions:
802-443-3000

Financial Aid:
802-443-5158

admissions@middle-
bury.edu

www.middlebury.edu

MIDDLEBURY COLLEGE

Overview

Middlebury College is one of the oldest liberal arts colleges in the U.S. and one of the most top-rated. Recently ranked fourth among liberal arts colleges by the *U.S. News & World Report*, this school of 2,500 undergraduates stands out for its excellence in languages and outdoor recreation.

Located in the Champlain Valley near the historic village of Middlebury in central Vermont, the college's main campus boasts its own golf course, plus a host of new buildings erected in the past two decades. These include the 100,000-square-foot Center for the Arts and the 220,000-square-foot McCardell Bicentennial Hall. Bread Loaf Mountain Campus, 12 miles east of Middlebury, is nestled in the middle of 30,000 acres of forested land and serves as a ski center in the winters.

Students with a passion for environmental and sustainability issues will feel at home at Middlebury, and those who appreciate a plethora of snow-centered activities in winter will find it easier to brave the cold temperatures. While the student body is diverse, you're likely to fit in best if you are academically stellar, engaged in volunteerism, and appreciative of international perspectives.

Academics

There are more than 45 departments and programs at Middlebury that offer majors and minors. Strong programs include environmental studies, international studies, and literature. The academic calendar follows a 4-1-4 format, with 13-week fall and spring semesters and a four-week winter term in January where students can take a single intensive course, complete an internship, or work on independent projects. Middlebury's Honor Code allows students to schedule their own exams and take them without the professors being there. "The Honor Code isn't just lip service; it guides us academically, socially, and personally," says a student.

All incoming freshmen take a First-Year Student Seminar, which is comprised of writing intensive courses taught by faculty in groups that are capped at 15 students. Topics cover over 40 academic areas, with courses such as "Beyond Cowboys: The Literary West" and "Sustainable Lands, Wild Lands: Toward a Conservation Paradigm."

Middlebury's distribution requirements are specific and extensive. Besides a First Year Seminar, students must also complete at least one other writing-intensive class within their first two years. Additionally, students are required to take at least one course in seven of eight academic categories and meet the Cultures and Civilizations requirement, which mandates one course in each of four categories representing different world cultures and civilizations.

As is typical for a private liberal arts college, classes at Middlebury are smaller in size than large public schools. Virtually all classes have fewer than 50 students, and the academic caliber is high. Students say, "you want to be the best in the class, but you're not going to jeopardize your integrity by being overly competitive either."

Middlebury's Language Schools transform main campus each summer into the site of study for 10 languages and cultures. Participants make the Language Pledge, a promise to communicate solely in their language of study for the duration of the program. "Besides going to the country itself, there is no better way to learn a language," notes a student. For those who want to do language study beyond a summer, Middlebury's C.V. Starr Schools Abroad offer international study in 13 countries and more than 30 cities. These immersion programs require students to complete their entire curriculum in the language of their host country.

Career resources include MiddNet, an online database of 8,000 Middlebury alumni who have volunteered to offer career advice to pre-graduates. These alumni are available to students on a drop-in basis for professional counseling and are often involved in The Senior Program (a job recruiting source).

Student Life

According to the college, "Middlebury students lead rich, engaged, complicated, active lives…" and that is no wonder since opportunities to get involved on campus abound. Students can choose from more than 120 student organizations that range from the African American Alliance to Xenia, a substance free social house, and plenty in between. "I guarantee you'll find a club of interest," promises a student. Volunteering is a big part of the campus identity, with over 1,300 students and a large percentage of faculty contributing over 65,000 hours of local service each year.

Students also take time to sleep in the sun (weather permitting) and hang out at 51 Main, Middlebury's lounge and social space, whose hours are posted as "11 a.m. – Late." A brainchild of Middlebury students who wanted "a sophisticated, international social space where people … could come together for conversation, good music, and art," it is something students are proud of and feel that they have ownership in.

Annual campus events at Middlebury kick off with Orientation Week, a memorable week featuring activities for students and parents, from the informative (academic forums) to the delicious (ice cream social) to the social (square dance, slam poetry, stargazing). Homecoming Weekend highlights the beauty of fall in Vermont, while the February Celebration honors students who began Middlebury as February first-years. Seniors snowboard, walk, and snowshoe in their caps and gowns. February is also the month of the three-day, student-run Winter Carnival, started in 1923. There is no shortage of festivities: bonfire, fireworks, snowball fights, the carnival ball, and skiing competitions add to the fun.

There are no Greek organizations, though Middlebury offers the opportunity for upperclass students to be part of co-ed, self-governed social houses. "The social houses are like fraternities and sororities but not quite as wild and definitely not as exclusionary," says a student.

Middlebury's 31 varsity teams compete in Division III. The Panthers have won 30 national championships in the past 16 years, including recent victories in men's soccer, rugby, and women's cross-country. There are plenty of scholar-athletes at Middlebury, with 28 percent of students participating in varsity sports, not to mention dozens of club sports (including Quidditch, which Middlebury students founded in 2005 and which has since spread nationwide) and intramurals.

Off-campus recreational activities are popular, and those who tire of the small town of Middlebury can make the 30-minute drive to slightly larger Burlington. "Besides outdoor activities and a few bars and restaurants, there isn't a ton to do in Middlebury," explains a student.

The Commons Residential System, a plan by which residence halls are grouped into "living-learning communities" known as Commons, is a cornerstone of the Middlebury student life experience. There are over 400 students in each of the five Commons, and each Common is led by a team that advises and supports student residents. The Commons model makes for integrated social, academic, and residential experiences. There is a single fee that includes tuition, room, and board, so it is no surprise that the vast majority of students live on campus.

MIDDLEBURY COLLEGE

Highlights

Students
Total enrollment: 2,516
Undergrads: 2,516
Freshmen: 598
Part-time students: 1%
From out-of-state: 95%
Male/Female: 49%/51%
Live on-campus: 97%
Off-campus employment rating: Fair
Caucasian: 67%
African American: 2%
Hispanic: 7%
Asian / Pacific Islander: 6%
Native American: 0%
Mixed (2+ ethnicities): 4%
International: 10%

Academics
Calendar: 4-1-4 system
Student/faculty ratio: 9:1
Class size 9 or fewer: 18%
Class size 10-29: 66%
Class size 30-49: 14%
Class size 50-99: 2%
Class size 100 or more: -
Returning freshmen: 97%
Six-year graduation rate: 94%
Graduates who immediately go to graduate school: 11%

Most Popular Majors
Economics
Political science
Environmental studies

Admissions
Applicants: 8,847
Accepted: 1,518
Acceptance rate: 17.2%
Placed on wait list: 1,679
Enrolled from wait list: 78
Average GPA: Not reported
ACT range: 31-33
SAT Math range: 640-740
SAT Reading range: 630-740
SAT Writing range: 57-32

MIDDLEBURY COLLEGE

Admissions Criteria
Academic criteria:
Grades: ☆ ☆ ☆
Difficulty of class schedule: ☆ ☆ ☆
Class rank: ☆ ☆ ☆
Standardized test scores: ☆ ☆
Teacher recommendations: ☆ ☆
Personal statement: ☆ ☆
Non-academic criteria considered:
Interview
Extracurricular activities
Special talents, interests, abilities
Character/personal qualities
Volunteer work
Work experience
Geographical location
Minority affiliation
Alumni relationship

Deadlines
Early Action: No
Early Decision: November 10
Regular Action: January 1 (final)
Notification of admission by: March 30
Common Application: Accepted

Financial Aid
In-state tuition: $44,919
Out-of-state tuition: $44,919
Room: Varies
Board: Varies
Books: $1,000
Freshmen receiving need-based aid: 44%
Undergrads rec. need-based aid: 41%
Avg. % of need met by financial aid: 100%
Avg. aid package (freshmen): $38,670
Avg. aid package (undergrads): $39,079
Avg. debt upon graduation: $17,246

School Spirit
Mascot: Panthers
Colors: Blue and white

Student Body

According to Middlebury, students are marked by a diversity of perspectives, a respect for the environment and sustainability, and an international focus. The high geographic diversity—95 percent of students are from out of state and all 50 states plus over 70 countries are represented—and high ethnic diversity provide a rich variety of perspectives. The large international student population (10 percent) contributes to Middlebury's worldwide focus. "You will literally meet people from around the world," says a student.

Among this diversity, students do share traits in common. Students describe themselves as "liberal or at least socially liberal" and "passionate about the outdoors and environmentalism." Many are involved in outdoor activities—granted, it's hard *not* to be, given that the college has so many fabulous facilities, including its very own ski center. Grants fairs for campus sustainability projects exemplify student's passion for environmental issues right in their home (or college) town; and the fact that Middlebury was selected as one of 20 teams for the Solar Decathlon, a competition to build a solar-powered house for the United States Department of Energy, attests to students' successes in their sustainability projects.

You May Not Know

- Middlebury awarded the first bachelor's degree to an African American in the U.S. when the college graduated Alexander Twilight in 1823.
- Middlebury offered the first undergraduate program in environmental studies in 1965.
- The college hosts the oldest writer's conference in the country, the Bread Loaf Writers' Conference.

Distinguished Alumni

Ron Brown, first African American U.S. Secretary of Commerce; Eve Ensler, creator of *The Vagina Monologues*; Ari Fleischer, White House Press Secretary; Ted King, professional cyclist.

Admissions and Financial Aid

Middlebury's application offers flexibility with standardized tests: students may take the ACT, the SAT, or three SAT Subject Tests in different subject areas. Admitted students start either in the fall or in February. According to the college, Middlebury "does not have a set formula that applies to each application." However, a rigorous academic curriculum and academic success in high school, along with "contributions outside the classroom" demonstrating that applicants will fit in with Middlebury's "community of very active and engaged citizens," are major factors in admissions decisions.

Merit or athletic scholarships do not exist at Middlebury. Admission is need-blind for domestic students and "need-aware" for international students. Loans are offered at graduated rates depending on family income.

MILLS COLLEGE

Overview

This all-women's liberal arts college in northern California was founded in 1852 to accommodate the daughters of gold miners, farmers, and merchants who were forging new communities in the West. The pioneering spirit that was integral to the founding of Mills College is still evident today in the independent spirits of its students. Indeed, Mills is characterized by innovation and path-forging—it was the first business school in the West for women, and the first woman's college in the nation to offer a computer science major. Today, Mills students are proactive about political causes, passionate about their own education, and on occasion, they even contribute to the college's administrative decisions. In 1990, for example, the student body went on strike to protest making Mills a co-ed college until the Board of Trustees revoked their decision.

U.S. News & World Report recently ranked Mills College fifth among colleges in the West, and for good reason—not only does Mills have an academically inquisitive and politically charged environment, but the college is also a leader in the arts. Since 1940, Mills has offered its students a modern dance degree that is well respected, and the school has earned the reputation for being "the national center of modern dance outside New York City."

Located just twenty minutes south of San Francisco on a large, wooded campus, Mills provides its students with the opportunity to have a foot in both worlds—the edgy cosmopolitanism of the city by the bay as well as the wonders of nature. Students grow to appreciate the beauty of their campus, Mediterranean-style architecture amongst 135 acres of groves and meadows.

Academics

Mills offers over 54 majors, though its five strongest programs are English, psychology, ethnic studies, studio art, and their multidisciplinary version of an economics program entitled PLEA. Another option open to Mills students is the dual degree; this five-year's master program is offered in computer science, education, engineering, infant mental health, math, and public policy. Classes at Mills are, without fail, composed of 15 students or less—so if you are hoping to blend into the back row of a classroom, Mills is not for you. On the flip side, most students form relationships with several of their professors by the time they graduate. "The professors know when you miss class and even when you're behind on an assignment," says a student.

The General Education program is a 10-course, nine-credit requirement for undergrads. It can be fulfilled through a huge number of courses, including those that count toward the student's major and even AP courses taken previously. The General Education program aims to equip students with basic proficiency in a few key domains of knowledge, rather than forcing students to take a rigid set of courses.

For their first year at Mills, students are divided into Living Learning Communities—a system of residential halls designed to group students according to their academic and extracurricular interests. First-year students can designate their LLC preferences before arriving at school, and most Mills students find themselves placed in a challenging community with classmates whose interests overlap their own. For many students, Living Learning Communities are also an effective way to establish connections with key faculty and upperclassmen in their fields of study.

Studying abroad is strongly encouraged at Mills, both in international and domestic destinations. The college offers opportunities for study abroad in a huge number of international locations, and has pre-formed exchange agreements with 11 acclaimed East Coast colleges, including American University in DC and Mount Holyoke in Massachusetts. In keeping with the school's ethos of exploration and

MILLS
COLLEGE

Four-year private women's college
Founded: 1852
Oakland, CA
Major city
Pop. 395,817

Address:
5000 MacArthur Boulevard
Oakland, CA
94613

Admissions:
800-87-MILLS

Financial Aid:
510-430-2000

admission@mills.edu

www.mills.edu

MILLS COLLEGE

improvisation, students may tailor their study-abroad experience to best complement their area of focus, working with several approved host programs.

The Mills graduate programs are open to both men and women. In some circumstances, students may cross-register for courses at UC Berkeley, Cal State University, and several other Bay Area colleges. Mills also provides several great segues into the professional world through internships; for example, students have held local internship positions in numerous professional fields, including journalism, medicine, government, and nonprofit.

Student Life

Due to the closed campus, the small student body, and the larger-than-normal percentage of students with families, the party scene at Mills is nearly nonexistent. The majority of single students head to Berkeley, Oakland, or into San Francisco for weekend activities. Transportation to and from the city is convenient and close, since all the major bus lines run by the college campus. "While there isn't much of a night life on campus, there's almost too much to do off campus," says a student.

On campus, Mills students are highly involved in the more than 50 clubs and extracurricular activities, and student events are usually well attended. Some of these include the Earth Day Fair, an event designed to raise environmental awareness; the *Vagina Monologues*, a theatrical production to promote healthy female sexuality; and the Spring Fling, a dance event with a focus on "keeping it green."

More than half of Mills students live on campus in school-owned housing. The other half usually live in nearby apartments in Berkeley or Oakland, and their commute takes about 20 minutes or less. There is no Greek life at Mills. During the day, students will generally enjoy lunch together in the central, cafeteria-style dining area called Founders Commons, a light and open area to eat and socialize. There are also two on-campus restaurants, the Tea Stop and Café Suzie.

Mills competes in seven intercollegiate sports, though historically, its athletics department has never been prominent, save for its dance programs. In an effort to provide students with a rounded college experience, Mills College recently started a successful intramural sports program that includes Ultimate Frisbee, indoor soccer, and basketball.

Student Body

At Mills, you can expect to find a higher-than-normal percentage of typical nor-Cal hipsters—think band T-shirts, skinny jeans, knitted beanies and Moleskins. Although 74 percent of undergraduates are California residents, there is still an impressive range of ethnicities and backgrounds represented within the student body. Mills has students from 49 states, and 50 percent of the student body classify themselves as women of color. The majority of students are politically liberal and many are vocal activists for various causes. Environmental sustainability has taken the spotlight on campus in the last decade, and has even leaked into classroom—Mills recently began offering a course called "The Greening of Mills."

As a rule, students at Mills are extremely focused academically. Because many students have taken time off from school and have already started a career or a family, their primary motivation in attending Mills is to earn an academic degree—not to indulge in the typical "debaucheries" of the undergraduate life. Intellectual rigor is the default lifestyle at Mills and is generally practiced across the board, even in the younger and more experimental demographic of the student body. Mills' younger students report that having older students in class often enriches classroom discussions, especially when they incorporate their real-life and professional experiences into the learning process. At times, however, these veteran students tend to dominate academic discussions. "It's a weird mix, but you get used to it," says a student.

You May Not Know

- The Upward Bound program was first launched at Mills in 1966.
- Mills was the first college in the nation to offer a graduate degree in book art and creative writing.
- Past speakers at Mills College include Ansel Adams, Martin Luther King, Jr., Nancy Pelosi, and Chelsea Clinton.

Distinguished Alumni

Katherine Eltrich, Budget Management for the Clinton Administration; Bonnie Guiton Hill, first African American woman to direct the United States Office of Consumer Affairs; Liz Holman, Emmy-award-winning producer of the *Animaniacs*; Meredith May, journalist for the *San Francisco Chronicle*; Toraya Ahmed Obaid, Under-Secretary General for the United Nations; Jennifer Basye Sander, bestselling author and columnist for *USA Today*.

Admissions and Financial Aid

Applicants must submit a graded writing sample to illustrate their analytical skills. While not required, the interview is an important part of the Mills application process, and can be conducted remotely as well as locally.

Several merit-based scholarships are available to students and are outlined in detail on the college website. Dean's Scholarships can be as high as $14,000 per year, while field-specific scholarships are available for science and music majors and range from $5,000 to $10,000 per year. Athletic scholarships are not available.

MILLS COLLEGE

Highlights

Admissions Criteria
Academic criteria:
Grades: ☆ ☆ ☆
Difficulty of class schedule: ☆ ☆ ☆
Class rank: ☆ ☆
Standardized test scores: ☆ ☆
Teacher recommendations: ☆ ☆
Personal statement: ☆ ☆
Non-academic criteria considered:
Interview
Extracurricular activities
Special talents, interests, abilities
Character/personal qualities
Volunteer work
Work experience
Geographical location
Alumni relationship

Deadlines
Early Action: November 15
Early Decision: No
Regular Action: January 15 (final)
Notification of admission by: April 1
Common Application: Accepted

Financial Aid
In-state tuition: $40,210
Out-of-state tuition: $40,210
Room: $5,720
Board: $5,370
Books: $1,430
Freshmen receiving need-based aid: 85%
Undergrads rec. need-based aid: 84%
Avg. % of need met by financial aid: 79%
Avg. aid package (freshmen): $38,795
Avg. aid package (undergrads): $36,185
Avg. debt upon graduation: $27,021

School Spirit
Mascot: Cyclones
Colors: Yellow, white, and blue
Song: *Fires of Wisdom*

Four-year private
Founded: 1890
Jackson, MS
Medium city
Pop. 175,561

Address:
1701 North State
Street
Jackson, MS
39210-0001

Admissions:
800-352-1050

Financial Aid:
800-352-1050

admissions@millsaps.
edu

www.millsaps.edu

MILLSAPS COLLEGE

Overview

Located in the heart of Mississippi, in the state's capital of Jackson, Millsaps is a small college of 800 undergraduates. Though Jackson isn't a city without crime, most students claim that common sense is enough to ensure a safe experience, and with the abundance of culture and entertainment in Jackson, the city has been named among the "The Best of the New South." The 100-acre campus holds three new suite-style dorms. The oldest building on campus is the James Observatory, built in 1901 and renovated to currently allow for star-gazing.

Particularly strong in its business program, Millsaps attracts many students because of its proximity to the state government and access to political internships. A fervently—yet respectfully—conservative campus, Millsaps College prides itself on its southern history and small student-to-faculty ratio. Though its small size and lack of diversity is unappealing to some, the college does offer many characteristics not usually expected of a small school, such as a football team and a bustling Greek life. Such unpredictable qualities have led the college to claim that "the closer you look, the more you'll like Millsaps."

Academics

Millsaps College offers 35 majors to its students. Among its strongest programs are the English, business administration, prelaw, and pre-health programs. A large part of its educational experience is focused on the school's "core curriculum," which Millsaps refers to as the "heart of liberal education." By the end of the sophomore year, Millsaps students must complete a series of nine courses, ranging in subjects from fine arts and history to business and computer science. In their senior year, students must complete a final and tenth core class that requires them to reflect on their liberal and interdisciplinary education.

With 98 percent of classes having fewer than 30 students, Millsaps provides students ample opportunities for close interactions with professors and classmates. Additionally, students say that with no graduate teaching assistants or student teachers, they "get the full attention of the professors." Students also comment that classes tend to focus more on discussions rather than lectures, creating a much more active learning experience. With such an intimate learning environment, academics at Millsaps are fairly rigorous and the school prides itself on being one of the few liberal arts colleges in the United States to have a Phi Beta Kappa chapter and accreditation at both the graduate and undergraduate level.

There are also a number of special academic opportunities at Millsaps. The Heritage Program, for example, is the equivalent of two yearlong courses focusing on the problems, religions, cultures, and ideas that have shaped the world as we know it today. The Faith and Work initiative studies character and career development; the college states that the aim of this program is to "help students become persons of passion and compassion who will lead lives shaped by a deep understanding of calling and purpose, a true understanding of self, and a broad understanding of the needs of the world." For those with more ecological interests, the Living in Yucatan program offers students the chance to live and study in the heart of the Yucatan peninsula on a bio-cultural reserve. And finally, Millsaps offers business undergraduates the chance to get their MBA in a five-year program.

Millsaps believes that studying abroad gives students the tools for understanding a complex world. In addition to participating in exchange programs with Japan and Ireland, there are study-abroad locations in countries including Belgium, China, Costa Rica, France, Ghana, Greece, Israel, Italy, Japan, Mexico, and Tanzania.

Millsaps' location in the state capital also opens other doors. Students at Millsaps have plenty of access to networking opportunities through internships in the state government.

Student Life

Millsaps College has 70 official student organizations. Some of the most popular groups on campus include Student Government, MCA Diversity Group, Habitat for Humanity, and One Campus One Community service organization.

Unlike many other small liberal arts colleges of a similar size, Millsaps has an active Greek community. In fact, 56 percent of the male student body joins one of the six social fraternities, and 55 percent of the female students join one of the four sorority houses on campus, prompting some students to claim that Greek parties dominate the social scene on campus.

In a state where football reigns supreme, Millsaps follows suit and has its own football team despite its size. The Millsaps Majors don the colors of purple and white and are members of the NCAA Division III. Intramural sports are also popular and range from basketball to table tennis to walleyball.

Exciting annual events at Millsaps include the Southern Circuit Film Series, where innovative independent filmmakers screen and discuss their films (admission is free for students and directors stay after the films to answer questions). Major Madness, a spring music festival that features a crawfish boil, is also a popular event among students, and Purple Pride is a day dedicated to school spirit and getting students fired up about Millsaps' athletics.

Off campus, the city of Jackson provides plenty of entertainment. Students can visit one of four museums, ten historic sites, and three parks. Fondren, a funky art district, is also less than five minutes from campus and boasts plenty of art galleries, boutiques, a bakery, coffee shops, and some of the best restaurants in town.

With 84 percent of Millsaps students choosing to live on campus, residence halls bustle with activity. "There's always something going on in the dorms," notes one student, "and they're close to classes." All residence halls are designed for traditional double, apartment, or suite style living. Freshmen live on the North Side of campus and are assigned housing. After freshman year there is a lottery for dorm assignments based on class and GPA.

Student Body

Ethnic diversity is moderate, at best, with 75 percent of students being white, many from the upper-middle class. The political leaning of the student body is overwhelmingly conservative. Nonetheless, minority groups are well-acknowledged on campus through the school's newspaper and multi-cultural festival, and students are generally respectful of political opinions.

Geographic diversity is moderate with 66 percent of students hailing from out of state. However, the school is almost purely southern and the majority of those not from Mississippi are from the surrounding southern states.

MILLSAPS COLLEGE

Highlights

Students
Total enrollment: 909
Undergrads: 843
Freshmen: 228
Part-time students: 2%
From out-of-state: 66%
From public schools: 63%
Male/Female: 51%/49%
Live on-campus: 84%
In fraternities: 56%
In sororities: 55%
Off-campus employment rating: Good
Caucasian: 75%
African American: 11%
Hispanic: 2%
Asian / Pacific Islander: 5%
Native American: 1%
Mixed (2+ ethnicities): 0%
International: 2%

Academics
Calendar: Semester
Student/faculty ratio: 8:1
Class size 9 or fewer: 48%
Class size 10-29: 50%
Class size 30-49: 2%
Class size 50-99: -
Class size 100 or more: -
Returning freshmen: 77%
Six-year graduation rate: 72%
Graduates who immediately go to graduate school: 40%

Most Popular Majors
Business administration
Psychology
Biology

Admissions
Applicants: 2,255
Accepted: 1,235
Acceptance rate: 54.8%
Average GPA: 3.6
ACT range: 23-29
SAT Math range: 420-610
SAT Reading range: 490-610
SAT Writing range: 3-13
Top 10% of class: 35%
Top 25% of class: 60%
Top 50% of class: 85%

461

College Profiles

MILLSAPS COLLEGE

Admissions Criteria
Academic criteria:
Grades: ☆ ☆ ☆
Difficulty of class schedule: ☆ ☆ ☆
Class rank: ☆ ☆
Standardized test scores: ☆ ☆ ☆
Teacher recommendations: ☆ ☆
Personal statement: ☆ ☆
Non-academic criteria considered:
Interview
Extracurricular activities
Special talents, interests, abilities
Character/personal qualities
Volunteer work
Work experience
State of residency

Deadlines
Early Action: December 1
Early Decision: No
Regular Action: Rolling admissions
Common Application: Accepted

Financial Aid
In-state tuition: $30,500
Out-of-state tuition: $30,500
Room: $6,416
Board: $4,952
Books: $1,100
Freshmen receiving need-based aid: 67%
Undergrads rec. need-based aid: 60%
Avg. % of need met by financial aid: 81%
Avg. aid package (freshmen): $27,094
Avg. aid package (undergrads): $27,049
Avg. debt upon graduation: $28,965

School Spirit
Mascot: Majors
Colors: Purple and white

You May Not Know

- Major Reuben Webster Millsaps founded the college in 1890 with $100,000, half of which he personally contributed.
- Dean Martin and Jerry Lewis were the celebrity judges for the college's beauty contest in 1953.
- According to the college, it was the "first all-white college in Mississippi to integrate voluntarily" in 1965.

Distinguished Alumni

Johnny Carson, TV host; Chris Jackson, professional football player; Robert McElvaine, noted historian/political commentator; Tate Reeves, Mississippi State Treasurer.

Admissions and Financial Aid

Millsaps recommends that all prospective students visit the campus before applying. Visits—which can even feature a regional favorite catfish feast—are personalized with specialized options for student athletes, science/premed students, and fine arts students.

For many minority students, Millsaps is attractive due to the school's plentiful financial aid packages, which generously fund underrepresented students in a hope of bridging economic gaps. In fact, 60 percent of students received need-based aid and 34 percent of students receive merit-based aid.

Scholarships are awarded for musical, extracurricular, or academic prowess; however, no athletic scholarships are offered. Scholarships range from $500 to the full tuition given to the recipient of the President Scholarship, awarded to incoming freshmen with outstanding academic records. Academic scholarships are competitive and are awarded independent of financial need. However, scholarships are awarded on a rolling basis, encouraging students to prioritize applying to Millsaps.

MONTANA TECH OF THE UNIVERSITY OF MONTANA

Overview

As the name suggests, Montana Tech of the University Montana—Montana Tech, for short—is the technical-institute cousin of the University of Montana family. Perched on top of Tech Hill, the so-called "shoulder of Big Butte," Montana Tech overlooks the small, historic town of Butte, Montana. A few buildings, particularly Main Building, are built in red-brick Renaissance Revival style, while the rest of the campus consists mostly of nondescript modern brick construction. Montana Tech is a regional leader in engineering and hard sciences and offers the benefit of its small size and plenty of personalized attention and tutoring to its students.

For the outdoor-recreation junkie, Montana Tech might just be paradise: in the midst of the Rocky Mountains, Montana Tech is in between Yellowstone and Glacier National Parks and provides year-round opportunities for skiing, snowboarding, camping, hiking, and biking. Otherwise, quaint but small Butte has probably already seen its best days during the mining boom in the early 19th century: its endless supply of Gold-Rush-era Americana sites and tours aren't likely to keep college students engaged for long, and the next nearest outpost of urban civilization is 120 miles away. However skiing and snowboarding opportunities abound, and for the outdoorsy types, or the tech types—or better yet, the outdoorsy tech types—Montana Tech provides solid academics in an unparalleled outdoor setting.

Academics

Montana Tech offers 47 majors, most of which are engineering and science. As part of its general education requirements, students must complete two courses each in communications, humanities, mathematics, physical and/or life sciences (including a lab course), and the social sciences; otherwise, students are free to get down to business in their chosen majors. Predictably, Montana Tech's strengths lie in its engineering programs in the School of Mines and Engineering and its science majors; the major in business and information technology stands out as well.

As with most technical institutes, Montana Tech's academics can be demanding, but Montana Tech's small size benefits students, allowing for access to professors and more personalized attention inside and outside of class. Montana Tech also touts its tutoring services, which are provided free of charge to students at the Tech Learning Center. "These are some of the toughest classes I've ever taken, so it's helpful to have free tutoring available," says a student.

Motivated students with qualifying high school GPAs and standardized test scores may make an application to the Honors Program, which consists of a Freshman Honors Seminar and Freshman Honors Writing as a substitute for one of the communications courses stipulated by the general education requirements. Students must then participate in Honors Seminars for four of their remaining six semesters, as well as conduct or participate in original research, and complete an Honors thesis. The program particularly encourages applications from "students with varied life experiences, non-traditional students, students with diverse backgrounds and from varied racial and ethnic backgrounds."

All students can apply to the Undergraduate Research Program, which provides funding for student research. Participating students develop a research question or a creative project under the supervision of a faculty mentor, and are eligible for funding of research-related or conference travel. Students additionally receive a small stipend.

Science and engineering majors can also participate in research as part of MIT's Summer Research Program and the AmGen UROP (Undergraduate Research Opportunities Program). Students spend the summer at MIT working on research in

MONTANA TECH OF THE UNIVERSITY OF MONTANA

Four-year public
Founded: 1893
Butte, MT
Large town
Pop. 33,704

Address:
1300 West Park Street
Butte, MT
59701

Admissions:
800-445-TECH

Financial Aid:
800-445-TECH

enrollment@mtech.edu

www.mtech.edu

MONTANA TECH OF THE UNIVERSITY OF MONTANA

Students
Total enrollment: 2,816
Undergrads: 2,646
Freshmen: 1,190
Part-time students: 17%
From out-of-state: 12%
From public schools: 91%
Male/Female: 59%/41%
Live on-campus: 11%
Off-campus employment rating: Good
Caucasian: 82%
African American: 0%
Hispanic: 2%
Asian / Pacific Islander: 1%
Native American: 2%
Mixed (2+ ethnicities): 0%
International: 6%

Academics
Calendar: Semester
Student/faculty ratio: 15:1
Class size 9 or fewer: 29%
Class size 10-29: 48%
Class size 30-49: 13%
Class size 50-99: 9%
Class size 100 or more: 1%
Returning freshmen: 66%
Six-year graduation rate: 48%
Graduates who immediately enter career
    related to major: 47%

Most Popular Majors
Petroleum engineering
General engineering
Nursing

Admissions
Applicants: 822
Accepted: 737
Acceptance rate: 89.7%
Average GPA: 3.4
ACT range: 21-27
SAT Math range: 550-610
SAT Reading range: 500-620
SAT Writing range: 1-14
Top 10% of class: 22%
Top 25% of class: 47%
Top 50% of class: 79%

areas ranging from mechanical engineering to brain and cognitive sciences; housing, food, and transportation to and from Boston are included, as is a stipend.

Aside from these research and travel opportunities (or the occasional road trip to Missoula or Yellowstone), Montana Tech students are probably going to stay close to campus: Montana Tech does not seem to offer its own study-abroad programs or exchange agreements.

Of those entering the workforce, about 47 percent find work in a field related to their majors within six months of graduating; average starting salary sits a little under $49,000. About 11 percent of Montana Tech graduates go on to graduate school immediately upon graduating.

Student Life

Depending on your perspective, there is either nothing or everything to do at Montana Tech. About 50 student organizations operate on campus. The vast majority of these are pre-professional organizations; others include the Copper Guard, the school spirit group, and outdoor recreation groups like Fly-Fishing Club. The student newspaper, the *Technocrat*, is published every two weeks.

Campus events are largely geared toward those living in dorms, and as such, are playing to a very limited crowd of 11 percent of the student body. "Even though so many students live off campus," explains a student, "life on campus is still lively. Most students live nearby and participate in activities." Orientation events kick off on-campus programs, featuring Digger Hunt, a campus-wide scavenger hunt in which freshmen race to find Charlie Oredigger, the school mascot, and prizes scattered around campus.

Although Montana Tech isn't big on the party scene (there are no fraternities or sororities, unless you count Sigma Rho, the mining "fraternity"), the school works hard to provide social events on campus. Mulletfest is a traditional event where sports, mullet haircuts, and partying combine to attract students to an outdoor softball game held in the spring, sometimes while snow is still on the ground.

On M-Day, students make the hike up the giant iconic "M" on Big Butte (which stands for "miners") and make a day of fixing up the M—which has fallen into disrepair in recent years—by giving it a fresh coat of sodium sulfide, changing light bulbs, and repairing fencing.

Athletics, particularly outdoor recreation, are a major part of life, whether it is camping in nearby national parks or fishing or mountain biking; the school even offers intramural hiking and fishing. Montana Tech has six varsity athletic teams, which compete in the National Association of Intercollegiate Athletics; football and volleyball tend to draw the most attention. "Whether you're playing on a team or hiking on your own, you're going to be active if you come here," says a student.

If skiing, camping, and hiking aren't your thing, then Butte may offer some quaint distractions, but once you've been on one historic tour of the town's mining sites, you may have seen it all. For those truly enterprising and determined to make it out of Butte, Billings is 230 miles east; Missoula is 120 miles to the north; and if you can make it that far, you might as well drive 130 more miles to the Canadian border, although you'll have to put in even more drive time to get to an actual city.

Montana Tech offers standard dorm- or suite-style residences to those living on campus, which is mandatory for freshmen; otherwise, living in Butte is eminently affordable and preferable to many students.

Student Body

Predictably, the population at this technical institute skews male and focused on engineering and science. Also not surprising, outdoorsy types prevail. Ethnic diversity is on the low side—unusual for a technical school—and the majority of students come from within the state.

One student says. "It's worth noting that Montana is a socially conservative and religiously fundamentalist area."

You May Not Know

- The "M" on Big Butte was constructed out of 441 tons of rhyolite; originally it measured 75 feet wide and 91 feet long, but with the addition of serifs, it now measures 90 feet wide.
- The incongruous gargoyle wearing a vintage football uniform outside the entrance to the Science and Engineering building is a holdover from the building's original function as a gymnasium.
- Montana Tech's campus is tobacco-free.

Distinguished Alumni

Mel Brekhus, director, president, and chief executive officer, Texas Industries, Inc.; Tom Dyk, founding partner and COO, Orion Energy Partners; Gary Kolstad, chief executive officer, president and director, CARBO Ceramics Inc.; Gordon Parker, CEO, Newmont Mining.

Admissions and Financial Aid

Applicants to Montana Tech must meet certain criteria in terms of class rank, GPA, AP and SAT or ACT test scores to qualify for admission; curiously, they must also be immunized against measles, mumps, and rubella to even be considered.

Montana Tech offers a range of merit scholarships, including two tuition-reduction scholarships for out-of-state students. The Western Undergraduate Exchange Scholarship is available to academically qualified students from the Western U.S.; recipients' tuition will be reduced to 150 percent of in-state tuition for all four years. The Advantage Scholarship offers the same to out-of-state students interested in select engineering and science programs.

Incoming freshmen with qualifying GPAs, test scores, and class rank are eligible for the annually-renewable President's Scholarship, which waives fees, reduces tuition, and offers a stipend of $2,000 - $3,000 a year. Students can apply for all scholarships with a separate application due by January 1.

MONTANA TECH OF THE UNIVERSITY OF MONTANA

Highlights

Admissions Criteria
Academic criteria:
Grades: ☆ ☆ ☆
Difficulty of class schedule: ☆ ☆ ☆
Class rank: ☆ ☆ ☆
Standardized test scores: ☆ ☆ ☆
Teacher recommendations: N/A
Personal statement: N/A
Non-academic criteria considered:
State of residency

Deadlines
Early Action: No
Early Decision: No
Regular Action: Rolling admissions
Common Application: Not accepted

Financial Aid
In-state tuition: $5,177
Out-of-state tuition: $17,955
Room: $3,524
Board: $4,404
Books: $1,000
Freshmen receiving need-based aid: 64%
Undergrads rec. need-based aid: 59%
Avg. % of need met by financial aid: 84%
Avg. aid package (freshmen): $9,592
Avg. aid package (undergrads): $10,505
Avg. debt upon graduation: $25,360

School Spirit
Mascot: Orediggers
Colors: Green and copper
Song: *Forward Tech*

Four-year private
men's college
Founded: 1867
Atlanta, GA
Major city
Pop. 432,427

Address:
830 Westview Drive,
SW
Atlanta, GA
30314

Admissions:
800-851-1254

Financial Aid:
800-873-9041

admissions@more-
house.edu

www.morehouse.edu

MOREHOUSE COLLEGE

Overview

Morehouse College is a small, private historically black men's liberal arts college that takes pride in molding the African-American leaders of tomorrow. Morehouse describes its students as "Renaissance Men with a social conscience and global perspective who are Well-Read, Well-Spoken, Well-Traveled, Well-Dressed, and Well-Behaved." Among its impressive list of alumni are Dr. Martin Luther King Jr., Spike Lee, and Samuel L. Jackson.

The red-brick college is relatively small, but as the campus is located just minutes from downtown Atlanta, students have a wide range of options for activities both on and off campus. Not only is the school academically focused, but the students are also encouraged to volunteer and give back to the community. The college emphasizes leadership, with a Leadership Center on campus to host events and workshops.

Academics

Morehouse is known to be academically "grueling," offering a limited selection of 26 majors within three academic divisions—humanities and social sciences, science and mathematics, and business administration and economics. Particularly strong programs are business administration, African-American studies, and political sciences. The college also offers a dual-degree "three-two" program in engineering with Georgia Tech, in which students pursue a general science curriculum at Morehouse for three years then study a field of engineering at Georgia Tech for two years.

Morehouse students are required to complete a core curriculum, which includes coursework in the humanities, mathematics, and natural and social sciences. These requirements include classes in English composition, a modern foreign language, and health and physical education. Freshmen also participate in a year-long pass/fail freshman orientation course that familiarizes students with the academic and social life at Morehouse. The course is intended to help ease the transition into college, though some first-years aren't so sure. "It's pretty painless," one student remarks, "but I can think of better uses of my time."

Students who wish to pursue a more rigorous course of study may participate in a number of special academic opportunities. The Honors Program is a four-year program that emphasizes leadership and social outreach. Honors students also enjoy smaller classes and special resources. "The biggest advantage is being able to enroll in smaller classes, which has helped me to get more out of them," one student notes. Students are admitted based on their test scores, GPA, and a profile form at the time of their admittance. Second-semester freshmen and first-semester sophomores may also apply to the program.

The Leadership Center provides opportunities for the study of ethical leadership described "as a historical and analytical discipline." Students can minor in leadership studies. The center also organizes research projects and workshops for students to participate in.

Morehouse requires that its students attend a minimum of six Crown Forum events per semester. According to the college, the Crown Forum aims to "expose students to issues affecting our common humanity." The forums include major events of the college, such as Opening Convocation and Founder's Day. "This requirement helps build school spirit," says a student.

The Andrew Young Center for International Affairs (AYC) assists students with study abroad and administers 250 programs that almost 100 students participate in each year.

After graduating, the "Morehouse Men" tend to find that they have a very good network of support through the National Alumni Association. There are career-planning services specifically designated for business majors, non-business majors, research careers, and dual degree majors in the engineering and health fields.

Student Life

There are over 50 student organizations on campus, many of which emphasize social and political awareness or service. All eight fraternities on campus have outreach programs that include service events so that their members can give back to the community. Other notable organizations that address social and political concerns include Students for Enlightened Environmental Decisions and Actively Changing Tomorrow Through Service. There are also a large number of religious organizations on campus.

The Glee Club, founded in 1911, has an impressive record. Its performances include Martin Luther King Jr.'s funeral, President Jimmy Carter's inauguration, Super Bowl XXVIII, and the 1996 Atlanta Summer Olympics.

Not surprising, Rev. Dr. Martin L. King, Jr. Week is one of the biggest annual events at Morehouse. Activities include speakers and movie screenings related to the historical leader. Homecoming, which takes place in October, is shared with Morehouse's sister school, Spelman College. The week includes such eclectic events as a Fashion Show, Hip Hop Concert, Coronation Ball, and Pan Hellenic Greek Step Show. In April, the Campus Alliance for Student Activities throws a Spring Fest, which includes a Drive In Movie, a Beauty Pageant, and various performances.

About one fifth of the student body joins one of the eight Greek organizations. "We're about more than parties," explains a student. "We're also about service and the step show."

Seven teams compete in Division II athletics: football, basketball, baseball, tennis, cross country, golf, and track and field. The marching band—known as the "House of Funk"—combines dance and music ranging from rap to pop music during their half-time performances. The band has performed on the *Today Show*, in the Krewe of Zulu Parade of Mardi Gras, and for the Atlanta Falcons. Students who are athletic, but not on the varsity level, can participate in intramurals. Popular ones include flag football, tennis, and fishing. The college also provides classes in aerobics, yoga, and bodybuilding.

Students can easily go to downtown Atlanta for entertainment and dining and often visit their sister school Spelman College to interact with the women. "There are a lot of bar and restaurant options," notes a student.

Only 65 percent of the student body lives on campus, due to inadequate housing. Freshmen are required to live in the dorms, but most upperclassmen opt to move off campus. There are special housing options such as Business Opportunities for the Sophisticated Scholar (BOSS), Signifying (creative arts), iSTEM (medical sciences), W.E.B. DuBois International House, Soul House (development of the "mind, body, and soul" with a zone to "curtail the use of expletives and inappropriate attire"), REBEL (career and academic support), and White Hall Center for Social Change and Empowerment.

MOREHOUSE COLLEGE

Highlights

Students
Total enrollment: 2,377
Undergrads: 2,377
Freshmen: 660
From out-of-state: 71%
From public schools: 76%
Male/Female: 100%/ 0%
Live on-campus: 65%
In fraternities: 19%
Off-campus employment rating: Good
Caucasian: 0%
African American: 96%
Hispanic: 0%
Asian / Pacific Islander: 0%
Native American: 0%
Mixed (2+ ethnicities): 0%
International: 3%

Academics
Calendar: Semester
Student/faculty ratio: 12:1
Class size 9 or fewer: 21%
Class size 10-29: 66%
Class size 30-49: 13%
Class size 50-99: 1%
Class size 100 or more: -
Returning freshmen: 80%
Six-year graduation rate: 55%
Graduates who immediately go to graduate school: 25%
Graduates who immediately enter career related to major: 68%

Most Popular Majors
Business administration
Biology
Political science

Admissions
Applicants: 2,576
Accepted: 1,711
Acceptance rate: 66.4%
Average GPA: 3.2
ACT range: 19-24
SAT Math range: 460-570
SAT Reading range: 450-570
SAT Writing range: 1-11
Top 10% of class: 20%
Top 25% of class: 45%
Top 50% of class: 71%

467

MOREHOUSE COLLEGE

Admissions Criteria

Academic criteria:
Grades: ☆ ☆
Difficulty of class schedule: ☆ ☆
Class rank: ☆ ☆
Standardized test scores: ☆ ☆ ☆
Teacher recommendations: ☆ ☆
Personal statement: ☆ ☆
Non-academic criteria considered:
Interview
Extracurricular activities
Special talents, interests, abilities
Character/personal qualities
Volunteer work
State of residency
Geographical location
Minority affiliation
Alumni relationship

Deadlines

Early Action: December 15
Early Decision: November 1
Regular Action: November 1 (priority)
February 15 (final)
Notification of admission by: April 1
Common Application: Accepted

Financial Aid

In-state tuition: $23,380
Out-of-state tuition: $23,380
Room: $7,510
Board: $5,670
Books: Varies
Freshmen receiving need-based aid: 96%
Undergrads rec. need-based aid: 96%
Avg. % of need met by financial aid: 61%
Avg. aid package (freshmen): $21,252
Avg. aid package (undergrads): $20,350
Avg. debt upon graduation: $40,081

School Spirit

Mascot: Maroon Tigers
Colors: Maroon and white
Song: *Dear Old Morehouse*

Student Body

Morehouse students are "very academically-focused" and, perhaps feeling the pressure to follow in the footsteps of so many famous alumni, can be quite competitive when vying for internships and job placements. According to students, the small population is "very tight knit" and "active in athletics, extracurriculars, and socializing."

Morehouse students hail from all over the country, with 71 percent from out of state. However, there are only a handful of international students.

You May Not Know

- Morehouse houses 7,000 original documents written by Martin Luther King, Jr., valued around $30 million.
- As part of its Appropriate Attire Policy started in 2009, students may not wear attire such as dresses, makeup, sagging pants, or do-rags.
- Morehouse College is the first Historically Black College to produce a Rhodes Scholar.

Distinguished Alumni

Sandford D. Bishop, U.S. Congressman, Georgia; Samuel L. Jackson, actor; Martin Luther King, Jr., Nobel Peace Prize winner and Civil Rights leader; Spike Lee, filmmaker; Edwin Moses, Olympic gold medalist.

Admissions and Financial Aid

In line with their vision of Morehouse Men as future leaders, the admissions office at Morehouse stresses that students are not merely assessed on their academic achievements. According to the school, they seek students who are "highly motivated and possess a social conscience." Keeping in mind their focus on service and volunteering, the admissions board looks for an applicant who has engaged in extracurricular activities that have "added value to his high school community."

Students can seek early admission, though the college stresses that early admission applicants be in the top 25 percentile of their classes, usually with at least a 3.5 GPA.

Morehouse provides a number of merit-based scholarships, ranging from Academic Scholarships to Athletic Grants and Talent Grants for music. There are also departmental awards.

MOUNT HOLYOKE COLLEGE

Overview

Mount Holyoke College is a small, private women's college in western Massachusetts with 2,300 undergraduate students. It started life as the first of the Seven Sisters, a group of all-women alternative schools dating from when the Ivy League was still all-male. It continues a tradition of academic excellence for women, and is now part of the Five College Consortium with Amherst, Hampshire, Smith, and UMass Amherst; students shouldn't worry about Holyoke's small size because the consortium gives them access to the 5,300 courses available at the five sister institutions for no additional cost.

The college is nationally recognized and recently ranked 38th among liberal arts colleges by *U.S. News & World Report*. It is also deemed one of the most beautiful in the country, full of New England foliage in the fall and classic-looking college buildings. Nearby Skinner Park and Mount Holyoke Range State Park offer unparalleled scenery and breathtaking views of the Connecticut River from Mount Holyoke, the college's namesake.

Academics

Mount Holyoke offers 53 majors and an option to design your own. Students are required to earn 32 credits in their major, with 12 of these at the 300 level. They must also take on a minor or a second major. There are distribution requirements in the humanities, science and math, foreign language, multicultural perspectives, and physical education. Classes are small and intensive; 95 percent of classes having fewer than 50 students.

Strong majors include chemistry, biochemistry, politics, and pre-health. For women in the sciences, this is the place to be. In the 1990s, 25 percent of all female chemists in the United States received their degrees from Mount Holyoke, and the National Science Foundation ranked the college first among selective liberal arts colleges for the number of women who received their doctorates in the life and physical science fields. Mount Holyoke built a new Science Center, complete with scanning and transmission electron microscopes and DNA sequencing equipment available to the school's all-undergraduate student body.

Mount Holyoke offers first-year seminars to "introduce students to the idea of the liberal arts." These courses encourage students to engage in interdisciplinary thinking on the college level. Available in a variety of subjects, first-year seminars touch on many issues, such as Visions of Hell and Paradise, forensic science, the geology of diamonds, and Biblical women. Once first-year students have finished their first semester, they can take advantage of "J-Term" during January. Between normal academic semesters, the college encourages students to take these short classes outside their majors to learn new skills, relax, and recharge.

Holyoke's Weissman Center for Leadership and the Liberal Arts brings speakers to campus and hosts an annual student conference that continues the school's goal of producing women who are "effective agents of change" in their communities. Additionally, students can widen their "community" to global scale through study-abroad opportunities in more than 50 countries. Of particular interest is a Shanghai program, which focuses on "economic transformation and business challenges" in China. Students are guaranteed financial aid through Laurel Fellowships, and more than 95 percent of Laurel Fellowship grants are approved.

The college does well in getting students into graduate school or the workforce—86 percent of the class was either working or in a graduate program six months after graduation. Indeed, 75 percent of alumnae eventually go to graduate school. The college has a vibrant and active alumnae network maintained independently of the college for those interested in networking opportunities.

MOUNT HOLYOKE COLLEGE

Four-year private women's college
Founded: 1837
South Hadley, MA
Small town
Pop. 17,196

Address:
50 College Street
South Hadley, MA
01075

Admissions:
413-538-2023

Financial Aid:
413-538-2291

admission@mtholyoke.edu

www.mtholyoke.edu

MOUNT HOLYOKE COLLEGE

Highlights

Students
Total enrollment: 2,344
Undergrads: 2,322
Freshmen: 506
Part-time students: 2%
From out-of-state: 80%
From public schools: 58%
Male/Female: 0%/100%
Live on-campus: 95%
Off-campus employment rating: Fair
Caucasian: 48%
African American: 6%
Hispanic: 8%
Asian / Pacific Islander: 7%
Native American: 0%
Mixed (2+ ethnicities): 4%
International: 23%

Academics
Calendar: Semester
Student/faculty ratio: 10:1
Class size 9 or fewer: 17%
Class size 10-29: 63%
Class size 30-49: 15%
Class size 50-99: 4%
Class size 100 or more: 1%
Returning freshmen: 92%
Six-year graduation rate: 81%
Graduates who immediately go to graduate school: 23%

Most Popular Majors
English
Biology
Politics

Admissions
Applicants: 3,876
Accepted: 1,631
Acceptance rate: 42.1%
Placed on wait list: 974
Enrolled from wait list: 30
Average GPA: 3.7
ACT range: 28-31
SAT Math range: 610-700
SAT Reading range: 610-720
SAT Writing range: 38-48
Top 10% of class: 56%
Top 25% of class: 82%
Top 50% of class: 97%

There are paid internships exclusively for Mount Holyoke students through the Miller Worley Center for the Environment. Participating employers include The Nature Conservancy, Harvard Forest, and Worldwatch Institute. Students may also apply for funding to do an internship or conduct research abroad through the McCulloch Center for Global Initiatives. Such funding was recently awarded to 60 Mount Holyoke students.

Student Life

Mount Holyoke has more than 100 student-run organizations. These include the Roosevelt Institute, which pushes for nonpartisan progressive ideals; Nice Shoes, a feminist music group; and Love Across the Coast, which connects Holyoke students with orphans in China for mentorships and fundraising. There's even a handbell club!

The college has its own set of traditions—for instance, students are served milk and cookies several times a week. There's also Mountain Day, announced by a surprise ringing of the bell tower each fall; students take advantage of the free day and hike on Mount Holyoke. There's also a Five Colleges Drag Ball, where students hop on stage to strut their stuff to the delight of their peers.

There is no Greek system on campus, as students feel like the school is one big sisterhood. There are, however, 14 varsity sports and a variety of club sports that compete against nearby schools. Intramural sports are available, including Ultimate Frisbee and wiffleball. Because the women's athletics aren't competing with men's for funding or resources, the school is a haven for women scholar-athletes. "Women's sports aren't second-rate like at other co-ed colleges," says one student. There's an 18-hole golf course and the Fitness Center, which offers cardio equipment and fitness classes to students. The jewel in the athletic department's crown is its equestrian team: they've won the national championship twice since 2000.

For those students who are interested in venturing off campus, there are free buses to the other Five College schools, and Holyoke students frequently take advantage of Northampton and Amherst for more varied shopping and dining opportunities, as well as co-ed student bodies. The school's New England location provides skiing at Berkshire East, biking at Norwottuck Rail Trail, and whitewater rafting on the Deerfield River, all just minutes from campus.

Students are guaranteed on-campus housing for four years, but the dorms vary a great deal, as there are older (and smaller) Victorian-era dorms side by side with modern, uniform halls. Housing is determined by lottery, and members of each college class live in each dorm as part of the school's commitment to on-campus community. On the whole, students are pleased with the housing options. "I don't have any complaints about the dorms," says a student.

Student Body

Students at Mount Holyoke are steadfastly liberal—they're women who've specifically chosen to learn in a community that encourages them to be leaders in and out of the classroom. The school has no official religious affiliation, but there are a variety of on-campus religious organizations for interested students.

Ethnic and geographic diversity is high—25 percent of students are minorities, and 80 percent of students are from out of state. Geographically, most students hail from New England (26 percent); the international population weighs in at 23 percent as well, followed by the Mid-Atlantic region (16 percent) and the West (13 percent).

You May Not Know

- The school was founded by pioneering female chemist Mary Lyon in 1837—nearly 100 years before female suffrage.
- Mount Holyoke has five green, LEED-certified buildings on campus.
- Just before graduation, students go to the Canoe Sing where lantern-decked boats are paddled by seniors singing school songs. When they reach the shore, they are received by their classmates.

Distinguished Alumnae

Nita Lowey, New York Congresswoman; Suzan-Lori Parks, Pulitzer-prize winning playwright; Mona Sutphen, White House Deputy Chief of Staff.

Admissions and Financial Aid

Standardized test scores are optional for applicants, and if submitted, they only account for about 10 percent of the admissions process. The school says the optional scores came about "because the SAT does not measure the range of intellectual and motivational qualities that [their] educational environment requires." Consequently, the college decided "to de-emphasize its (SAT) role in admission decisions."

Admissions officers review applicants' transcripts, essays, a graded paper, and the short answer. The focus on writing is to make sure that applicants are prepared for the writing-intensive curriculum at Mount Holyoke. After these are considered, the committee looks at activities, involvement, and recommendations—especially useful if they're on the fence about a candidate.

Interviews are not required but are strongly recommended so that the admissions officers can get a feel for a candidate; the interviews are conducted by alumnae throughout the U.S. and internationally. On-campus interviews are conducted by current students. The admissions process attempts to be holistic; Holyoke tries to admit women who will thrive in Holyoke's environment rather than just those with the best grades and scores.

Mount Holyoke offers merit aid through programs such as the 21st Century Scholars Program. Scholars receive $20,000 a year renewable for four years, funding for an internship, and admission to a first-year honors tutorial with a faculty member.

MOUNT HOLYOKE COLLEGE

Highlights

Admissions Criteria
Academic criteria:
Grades: ☆ ☆ ☆
Difficulty of class schedule: ☆ ☆ ☆
Class rank: ☆ ☆ ☆
Standardized test scores: ☆
Teacher recommendations: ☆ ☆ ☆
Personal statement: ☆ ☆ ☆
Non-academic criteria considered:
Interview
Extracurricular activities
Special talents, interests, abilities
Character/personal qualities
Volunteer work
Work experience
State of residency
Geographical location
Minority affiliation
Alumni relationship

Deadlines
Early Action: No
Early Decision: November 15
Regular Action: January 15 (final)
Notification of admission by: April 1
Common Application: Accepted

Financial Aid
In-state tuition: $41,270
Out-of-state tuition: $41,270
Room: $5,940
Board: $6,200
Books: $950
Freshmen receiving need-based aid: 60%
Undergrads rec. need-based aid: 70%
Avg. % of need met by financial aid: 100%
Avg. aid package (freshmen): $31,846
Avg. aid package (undergrads): $35,643
Avg. debt upon graduation: $22,691

School Spirit
Mascot: Lyons
Colors: Blue and white
Song: *Alma Mater*

471

MUHLENBERG
COLLEGE

Four-year private
Founded: 1848
Allentown, PA
Large town
Pop. 119,141

Address:
2400 West Chew
Street
Allentown, PA
18104

Admissions:
484-664-3200

Financial Aid:
484-664-3174

admissions@muhlen-
berg.edu

www.muhlenberg.edu

MUHLENBERG COLLEGE

Overview

Located in Allentown, Pennsylvania—an average-sized city 90 miles west of the Big Apple and 55 miles north of Philadelphia—Muhlenberg College offers students a quiet learning environment with a liberal arts focus. Surrounded by the lush Lehigh Valley, students enjoy the shops and restaurants of a typical town (both urban and suburban), the opportunities and connections of New England's big cities, and the serene comfort of nature. Founded in 1848 as a haven for the Evangelical Lutheran Church in America, the four-year college continues to honor its religious roots by teaching in the Judeo-Christian tradition.

'Berg emphasizes small classes, extremely accessible faculty, a strong premedical program, and DIII opportunities for both recruited and walk-on athletes. Muhlenberg is often referred to as "The Caring College" and strives to cultivate compassionate graduates dedicated to "leadership and service"—students with an appreciation for "traditions of diverse civilizations and cultures." Unfortunately, 'Berg's lack of diversity may at times impede this goal.

Academics

While 'Berg offers many academically challenging options for the over-achiever, including honors programs, double majors, dual degrees, and independent study, the college also provides an exceptional learning environment for the B-student. Muhlenberg prides itself on small classes, accessible faculty, and an impressive student-to-faculty ratio of 12:1, all of which provide students with the personal attention and support key to academic success.

The college offers 43 different majors; some of the strongest are business administration, English, and theatre. All students must complete at least one class in writing, oral expression, reasoning, language, literature and the arts, meaning and value, human behavior and social institutions, historical studies, physical and life sciences, diversity and difference, physical education, and a first-year seminar, which is a key component to a Muhlenberg education. In this writing-intensive, semester-long course, students learn how to research, formulate a thesis, and eloquently present an argument. Students also get to work closely with faculty who specialize in their respective course topics, some of which include "Musical Revolutions," "Dancing with the Nuclear Genie," and "Cuisine as Culture." Academics at Muhlenberg commonly return to the college's religious background.

Other academic opportunities include the three honors programs: the Muhlenberg Scholars Program, the Dana Associates Program, and the R.J. Fellows Program. All three provide students an "enriched academic experience," as well as a $4,000 annual stipend. Both the Muhlenberg Scholars Program and the R.J. Fellows Program are offered to 15 students each year. They emphasize "small seminar-style classes, research and independent study opportunities with a faculty mentor, and an active learning style." The Dana Associates Program is somewhat different from its counterparts in that it focuses on internship experience and coordination of a liberal arts education with "real-world" situations. Each honors program also provides students with a preferential financial aid package that tends towards grants and away from loans. Whether part of an honors program or not, students can take advantage of the Lehigh Valley Association of Independent Colleges (LVAIC). This program allows 'Berg students to take classes and use the libraries at DeSales University, Lafayette College, Lehigh University, Moravian College, and Cedar Crest College.

Upon entering, freshmen begin the advising process in early June, planning classes, getting involved on campus, and outlining future plans. They can also consider participating in the study-abroad program, which offers destinations in 60 countries, including Cameroon, Cyprus, and Turkey.

The Career Center helps students plan for post-graduate success by providing programs such as the Shadow Program during which students job shadow an alumnus during the semester break and the Muhlenberg Career Network, a database of 900 alumni who have volunteered to help students with career planning.

Student Life

Muhlenberg offers around 125 official student groups and organizations, including the Muhlenberg Theatre Association and the 'Berg Organization of Music (BOOM). In addition, the school is home to 14 honors societies and a variety of interest clubs.

The Muhlenberg Activities Council coordinates all organizations and campus-related events. Students repeatedly rank the Henry Awards, the Scotty Wood Tournament, and Candlelight Carols as three of the best annual campus events. The "Henry's" are a Muhlenberg specialty patterned after the Academy Awards— a night of grandeur where students and faculty are showcased for their outstanding achievements. Started in 1982, the Scotty Wood Tournament has gained great support for the 'Berg basketball teams and has garnered enthusiasm for their weekend-long, spirit-filled season opener. In contrast, the Candlelight Carols event brings a peaceful conclusion to the first semester, as students and faculty gather in Egner Memorial Chapel the weekend before finals and enjoy performances by the Muhlenberg College Choir.

Another component of 'Berg's social scene are the four fraternities and five sororities. Unlike other universities, however, Greek life at Muhlenberg only represents for 16 percent of men and 17 percent of women. "The fraternities and sororities are there," explains a student, "but you certainly don't have to be a part of them to have a good time."

The women's basketball team currently leads Muhlenberg's 22 DIII varsity sports teams in number of national titles, followed by football and rugby. Although the Mules may not be the most competitive in the Centennial Conference, 'Berg athletics offer an opportunity for teamwork and leadership to both recruited and non-recruited athletes. Students who wish to be active can also participate in intramurals, which range from Frisbee golf to volleyball.

Due to the high level of activity on campus, students primarily work, play, and live within the campus grounds. The four-year housing guarantee makes staying on campus even more desirable, although some students opt for MILE housing, situated just off campus and still maintained by the school. Housing is determined on a lottery basis.

Student Body

'Berg's student body is commonly criticized for its lack of ethnic diversity, with 11 percent of students identifying as a minority. Muhlenberg does, however, do an excellent job of bringing in students from out of state, with only 19 percent of students hailing from Pennsylvania. Although diversity levels are low, students at "The Caring College" strive to treat one another kindly, with understanding and respect. "It sounds corny, but it's true. Students here really are nicer than at other colleges," says one student.

Religious ties are prominent at 'Berg as most students identify as conservative Christians. Muhlenberg students are academically

MUHLENBERG COLLEGE

Highlights

Students
Total enrollment: 2,422
Undergrads: 2,422
Freshmen: 581
From out-of-state: 81%
From public schools: 74%
Male/Female: 41%/59%
Live on-campus: 92%
In fraternities: 16%
In sororities: 17%
Off-campus employment rating: Good
Caucasian: 77%
African American: 3%
Hispanic: 3%
Asian / Pacific Islander: 2%
Native American: 0%
Mixed (2+ ethnicities): 3%
International: 11%

Academics
Calendar: Semester
Student/faculty ratio: 12:1
Class size 9 or fewer: 26%
Class size 10-29: 70%
Class size 30-49: 3%
Class size 50-99: -
Class size 100 or more: -
Six-year graduation rate: 87%
Graduates who immediately go to graduate school: 25%

Most Popular Majors
Business administration
Biology
Psychology

Admissions
Applicants: 5,023
Accepted: 2,316
Acceptance rate: 46.1%
Placed on wait list: 1,691
Enrolled from wait list: 22
Average GPA: 3.3
ACT range: 25-31
SAT Math range: 560-680
SAT Reading range: 560-680
SAT Writing range: 16-48
Top 10% of class: 45%
Top 25% of class: 77%
Top 50% of class: 96%

473

MUHLENBERG COLLEGE

Admissions Criteria

Academic criteria:

Grades: ☆ ☆ ☆
Difficulty of class schedule: ☆ ☆ ☆
Class rank: ☆ ☆
Standardized test scores: ☆ ☆
Teacher recommendations: ☆ ☆
Personal statement: ☆ ☆

Non-academic criteria considered:

Interview
Extracurricular activities
Special talents, interests, abilities
Character/personal qualities
Volunteer work
Work experience
State of residency
Minority affiliation
Alumni relationship

Deadlines

Early Action: No
Early Decision: February 1
Regular Action: Rolling admissions
Notification of admission by: March 15
Common Application: Accepted

Financial Aid

In-state tuition: $42,470
Out-of-state tuition: $42,470
Room: Varies
Board: $3,965
Books: $1,295
Freshmen receiving need-based aid: 51%
Undergrads rec. need-based aid: 50%
Avg. % of need met by financial aid: 93%
Avg. aid package (freshmen): $26,110
Avg. aid package (undergrads): $26,328
Avg. debt upon graduation: $30,351

School Spirit

Mascot: Mule
Colors: Cardinal red and gray

driven but also focus on extracurricular activities like theatre, dancing, and vocal performance.

You May Not Know

- Muhlenberg maintains a 40-acre arboretum as well as a separate 40-acre wildlife sanctuary.
- Miller Tower was inspired by the Tom Tower at Oxford University. It is named for David A. Miller, who founded the Allentown newspaper.
- Berg's party scene is said to rival that of Penn State.

Distinguished Alumni

Frank N. D. Buchman, founder of the Oxford Group (now Initiates of Change) and two-time Nobel Peace Prize nominee; Barbara Crossette, United Nations Bureau Chief from 1994 to 2001; David Fricke, senior editor at *Rolling Stone* magazine; John McKeon, United States Representative from New York; Theodore Weiss, American poet.

Admissions and Financial Aid

Fortunately for many prospective students, Muhlenberg College accepts the Common Application. If, however, applicants seek admission to one of Muhlenberg's dual programs with Drexel University College of Medicine or Columbia University Engineering Program, they must also submit application supplements, which can be found on Muhlenberg's website. Students must also submit two teacher recommendations, a mid-year evaluation from a counselor, and ACT or SAT test scores. Notably, however, Muhlenberg has made test scores optional. If applicants wish to withhold test scores, they must submit an SAT Optional Form (found online), as well as participate in a personal interview.

Apart from the honors programs, Muhlenberg also offers several merit-based scholarships, ranging from $1,000 to $16,000 annually. While the financial aid awards are based on need, these merit-based scholarships are awarded to students who excel in academics, music and performance arts, visual art, and campus ministry.

NEW COLLEGE OF FLORIDA

Overview

Located in Sarasota Bay, Florida, New College of Florida is an innovative institution without grades and with a reputable liberal education. *U.S. News & World Report* ranked New College fifth among public liberal arts colleges in the country. The school's affordable tuition and solid reputation for turning out students who do well in the graduate school and job market arenas is a huge lure for many students. The workload is rigorous, with all students being required to complete a senior research-based thesis or oral baccalaureate exam before receiving their degree, but the effort seems to pay off in the end.

New College of Florida was founded less than 60 years ago on the western side of Florida with the specific goal of providing students a learning environment in which they can concentrate on their own independent research and writing skills. The architecture of the buildings is reminiscent of regal 1920s southern mansions fitted with arches, balconies and wrap-around porches, and surrounded by gorgeous palm trees representative of a climate that has average yearly temperatures ranging from 60 to 95 degrees throughout the year.

In a setting that overlooks the water, NCF provides beautiful views of the Sarasota Bay and offers a short drive to Gulf of Mexico beaches. The campus is situated in a fairly suburban area, only 50 miles south of Tampa, a location that can be perfect for people of all ages. This translates to retirement facilities not too far from campus for seniors who hope to spend their winters in the warmth. You shouldn't worry too much though; social life is still busy and fun!

Academics

Classes are based on a pass/fail system. In order to graduate, students must receive a satisfactory in a liberal arts core, mathematics core, three ISPs (Introductory Study Projects that represent a student's own individual research), a senior thesis and an oral defense of a senior project and research. Not exactly a simple task, but not without reason: the administration and founders believe that students should be "free spirited" in their studies and should be motivated by a desire to learn rather than a want for a specific grade. Rather than a level of achievement, all students receive a written evaluation from their professors of each course so that they are aware of their progress. "You need to be able to take criticism that goes beyond a letter grade and take charge of your own education," stresses a student.

Just in case you do want guidelines, you should know that NCF requires all students to draft a semester personal contract for study in which they write out their goals for the upcoming term. Professors hold students to their contracts and grant "satisfactory" accordingly. This system requires personal involvement of professors at a high level and is unique—but do-able, with only 800 students—and it appears to be successful. Of the 41 majors offered, some of the strongest are biology, physics, and political science.

Class settings are "small and discussion-based" and the relationships with professors are "very individual," with classes hardly ever exceeding 50 students. The academic calendar is divided into two semesters, like most schools, but the college divides each semester into halves, seven weeks each. A professor can choose to offer a course for seven or 14 weeks with either one or two evaluation periods for students. This gives students a great deal of time to explore different areas of study or to specifically concentrate in one area. "The choices that we have are unprecedented," notes a student.

Between the two 14-week semesters is a month long period where students can be on campus and focus solely on their research. It is during this time that many fulfill their ISP requirements. Sometimes research is individual or with a group but always facilitated by a professor from the college.

NEW COLLEGE OF FLORIDA

Four-year public
Founded: 1960
Sarasota, FL
Large town
Pop. 52,341

Address:
5800 Bay Shore Road
Sarasota, FL
34243

Admissions:
941-487-5000

Financial Aid:
941-487-5000

admissions@ncf.edu

www.ncf.edu

NEW COLLEGE OF FLORIDA

Students looking to study abroad can use this interim time as well. New College does not have its own individual campuses or study programs abroad, but students can choose from international programs offered by the Florida State School Program or any accredited university or college, pending credit approval. Some students even get off campus by domestic exchange with other public colleges.

After graduation—and sometimes before—a competitive number of students are offered Fulbright Scholarships to finish their research in graduate studies. Since the college graduates less than 200 students a year, the alumni count is small, making networking difficult. However, "graduates are in high demand for jobs," notes a student, adding, "we have a reputation for being go-getters and being able to work independently, qualities that employers want."

Student Life

Since most students live on campus in the gorgeous and what some even describe as "luxurious" apartments and dormitories, campus is often teeming with people and activities. Most students participate in at least one of the 45 clubs on campus. Some stand-outs include Multicultural Society, Ben & Jerry's Devotional Society, and Anarchy Death Sticks Club, which knits for charitable purposes. "We have clubs you wouldn't find on any other campus," says a student.

Politically, many students are liberal, and the clubs reflect this. There are numerous green-living, organic-eating, and multicultural organizations. If you're a Republican though, there is also a conservative society. Pride week is a big event on campus, organized by PRIDE and the Queer Culture groups. There are often performances on campus as well, like the annual *Vagina Monologues* and Arts Festival.

There is no Greek life on campus and not many clubs in Sarasota. To have fun, students organize "Walls," an all-night outdoor party in the center of campus where speakers hang from the walls. People can be found dancing throughout any Friday and Saturday night. "We really let loose," notes a student. More themed parties are hosted throughout the year in the Palm Court; for example, Halloween and Valentine's Day celebrations.

If you're a student from the south who isn't really involved in athletics, this may be just the school for you. Unlike the stereotypical Southern university, there are no varsity sports teams at NCF and most students do not participate in intramural sports. "A rah-rah school we are not," states a student. But that doesn't mean that students aren't active. The fitness center boasts equipment, weights, a swimming pool, racquetball courts, a basketball court, and tennis courts as well as offers free sailing and kayaking lessons. The one athletic affiliation that NCF has is the Intercollegiate Sailing League.

Getting off campus usually means going to the Bay and sailing or relaxing on the beach. The smaller city of Sarasota offers restaurants and shopping, but "is light on" bar or night life. Many students enjoy seeing exhibits at the local Ringling Museum of Art, literally less than a mile from the center of campus.

Students who opt to live on campus will most likely be in the newly built and renovated student living spaces. Five new residence halls were designed by architect I.M. Pei. About 75 percent of students live on campus, and nearly the entire freshman class will dorm for the year. The living arrangements, for the cost, are "much better than you'd expect," comments a student.

Student Body

The learning environment, academic policies, and atypical nature of this Southern school lead to a "very, very liberal" student body. The community within NCF is extremely accepting of different types of students and embraces this in its identity. As the editor of the school newspaper says, "we're the most interesting social misfits around because everyone fits in here."

On a whole the student body is predominantly Caucasian but still has high ethnic diversity with 22 percent of students reporting as minorities. Geographically, about 16 percent of students come from out of state, but mostly from the nearby southern states.

This college is seen as a "liberal haven" in the South, although it is surrounded by a "largely upperclass and conservative" community.

You May Not Know

- NCF was originally a private institution but was made public in order to be more affordable for students.
- In only 13 years, students have been granted 31 Fulbright Fellowships.
- NCF teamed up with Lovelace Respiratory Research Community, giving students more research opportunities in bioinformatics and biology.

Distinguished Alumni

William Dudley, President and CEO, Federal Reserve Bank of New York; Lincoln Diaz-Balart, Representative, United States House of Representatives; Carol Flint, Emmy Award-winning television and film writer/producer.

Admissions and Financial Aid

Requirements are typical: Common Application and supplement, transcript, standardized test scores, and letter of recommendation. If denied, students may appeal with a written petition.

Florida high school graduates with high academic achievement may be eligible for Bright Futures Scholarships, i.e. the Florida Academic Scholars (FAS) and Florida Medallion Scholars (FMS) awarded by the state. In addition, the college provides merit awards which include the Four Winds Awards of up to $3,500 per year based on test scores and GPA. The New College National Scholarship Program is based on performance in the National Merit Scholarship Program, National Achievement Scholarship Program, or National Hispanic Recognition Program and provides a renewable scholarship of up to $4,000 per year.

NEW COLLEGE OF FLORIDA

Highlights

Admissions Criteria
Academic criteria:
Grades: ☆ ☆ ☆
Difficulty of class schedule: ☆ ☆ ☆
Class rank: ☆
Standardized test scores: ☆ ☆
Teacher recommendations: ☆ ☆
Personal statement: ☆ ☆ ☆
Non-academic criteria considered:
Interview
Extracurricular activities
Special talents, interests, abilities
Character/personal qualities
Volunteer work
Work experience
Geographical location
Alumni relationship

Deadlines
Early Action: No
Early Decision: No
Regular Action: November 1 (priority)
April 15 (final)
Common Application: Accepted

Financial Aid
In-state tuition: $6,783
Out-of-state tuition: $29,812
Room: Varies
Board: Varies
Books: $1,200
Freshmen receiving need-based aid: 58%
Undergrads rec. need-based aid: 58%
Avg. % of need met by financial aid: 80%
Avg. aid package (freshmen): $12,104
Avg. aid package (undergrads): $12,186
Avg. debt upon graduation: $18,276

Four-year public
Founded: 1881
Newark, NJ
Major city
Pop. 277,540

Address:
University Heights
Newark, NJ
07102-1982

Admissions:
973-596-3300

Financial Aid:
973-596-3479

admissions@njit.edu

www.njit.edu

NEW JERSEY INSTITUTE OF TECHNOLOGY

Overview

A medium-sized public technical research university, The New Jersey Institute of Technology (NJIT) has six specialized colleges, including the Newark College of Engineering (NCE), an earlier name that some still use when they refer to the university. The small campus is composed of 45 acres and 26 buildings ranging from Gothic to modern style. NJIT has doubled in size in the past decade. The Campus Center with its eateries, rooftop gardens, and bowling alley was recently added, and the Alumni Center and athletic facilities were also renovated. Fans of *The Sopranos* can catch glimpses of campus on episodes filmed after an $83.5 million campus makeover in 2005.

As befits its name, New Jersey Institute of Technology boasts strengths in engineering, math, and science. The vast majority of students hail from New Jersey, so you won't find wide geographic representation in the student body; however, NJIT can certainly boast about its success in achieving ethnic diversity. The school ranks #1 in the state for awarding engineering degrees to African-American and Hispanic students, and minority students make up more than half of the student population.

While you'll definitely find tech nerds, the school's location doesn't lend itself to holing up in labs all day. Located in downtown Newark, in the vibrant University Heights neighborhood, NiJits (to use a moniker coined in the 1970s) enjoy the college-town feel of New Jersey's largest city with an added bonus of proximity to New York's largest city. If you're excited by the prospect of attending a diverse tech- and innovation-oriented university located twenty minutes by train to NYC, NJIT may be the perfect choice for you.

Academics

NJIT offers 44 degree programs disbursed among 27 undergraduate majors. There are six colleges and schools: Newark College of Engineering, College of Architecture and Design, College of Science and Liberal Arts, Albert Dorman Honors College, School of Management, and College of Computing Sciences. The university also provides graduate programs. In keeping with the school's tech and innovation emphasis, studies span a wide range of fields—there are even courses in Video Game development. All students must complete General University Requirements (GUR). These include courses in computer science, English/communication and cultural history, humanities and social sciences, management, math, natural sciences, physical education, and social sciences.

The rigor of student's workloads varies from major to major, and some academic programs are more laid back than others. Engineering tends to be more demanding. Many of NJIT's professors are heavily involved in research. Students feel this can be good or bad, depending on how the professor balances his or her responsibilities. One student comments, "Most of my professors have been top-notch but a few seem to be more concerned with advancing their own personal research projects." Strong programs include electrical engineering, biomedical engineering, computer science, and information systems.

There are more than 650 students across all majors in the Honors College at NJIT. The program is by admission for students with outstanding records. Those selected take 11 Honors courses over four or five years, and are guaranteed on-campus housing, participation in Honors Colloquia each semester, and exclusive access to the Honors lounge and study areas. Honors courses are small and in-depth, making the program a good way to build a network of "academically-minded high-achievers," according to the university.

The McNair Achievement Program supports low-income, first-generation, and underrepresented students who plan to earn PhDs in science, engineering, and mathematics. McNair scholars do research with faculty mentors and can participate in summer research during junior year.

Cooperative Education and Internships offer off-campus work experience for students who want to try hands-on application of their studies during their undergraduate years. Students earn wages as well as academic credit. In the last 10 years, nearly 2,600 different companies—including Johnson & Johnson to Citigroup to Lockheed Martin—have hired NJIT students for co-op assignments. "There's no better way to get hands-on work experience than while you are still a student," one participant notes.

NJIT offers exchange programs with a number of partner universities in France, Germany, Italy, and Sweden. There are also a number of summer-abroad programs, primarily in Europe. Architecture and Honors College students can spend a summer at the University of Siena, and Copenhagen is the newest addition to study-abroad options.

With more than 44,000 NJIT alumni, the Career Resource Center can tap into a substantial network to offer job search tools and graduate school application tips. Career Development Services also manages cooperative education and internship opportunities.

Student Life

The Campus Center serves as a gathering place for members of the NJIT community to eat, meet, watch films, play games, and socialize. It houses various entities, including the Center for First Year Students and the Diversity and Wellness Program. There are more than 70 student organizations, from Amateur Radio Club to Habit for Humanity.

NJIT Day is the university's annual fall festival for students and their families, faculty and staff, and alumni. With music, games, food, men's soccer and women's volleyball, this weekend in October is an eagerly anticipated one. The weekend also features the Tour de Tech, where teams of students, faculty, and staff take bike laps around the campus in a race for cash prizes. "Fifty laps around campus is pretty intense," says a student.

The campus celebrates its diversity during One World Week in April. Themes from past years include a Global Dinner, "Dancing with the Staff" Latin dance competition, and a campus memorial for Holocaust Remembrance Day.

There are 23 on-campus fraternities and sororities at NJIT. Greek Week in April emphasizes Greek life for seven days, enticing students to participate by tempting them with competitions (everything from Sudoku to boat building and racing), service events (campus clean-up, Relay for Life), food, and entertainment. "There aren't strong lines dividing members from non-members," comments a student.

NJIT's nine men's and seven women's sports teams compete in Division I. Men's soccer, basketball, and baseball, as well as women's volleyball, are the most competitive. Students not on varsity teams stay active through club sports and intramurals. The athletic center offers students a facility for fitness activities.

NEW JERSEY INSTITUTE OF TECHNOLOGY

Highlights

Students
Total enrollment: 8,667
Undergrads: 6,154
Freshmen: 1,626
From out-of-state: 8%
From public schools: 80%
Male/Female: 79%/21%
Live on-campus: 26%
In fraternities: 8%
In sororities: 5%
Off-campus employment rating: Excellent
Caucasian: 35%
African American: 9%
Hispanic: 14%
Asian / Pacific Islander: 21%
Native American: 0%
Mixed (2+ ethnicities): 8%
International: 4%

Academics
Calendar: Semester
Student/faculty ratio: 16:1
Class size 9 or fewer: 4%
Class size 10-29: 60%
Class size 30-49: 30%
Class size 50-99: 5%
Class size 100 or more: 1%
Returning freshmen: 82%
Six-year graduation rate: 55%
Graduates who immediately go to graduate school: 18%

Most Popular Majors
Architecture
Civil and mechanical engineering
Digital, industrial and interior design

Admissions
Applicants: 4,216
Accepted: 2,684
Acceptance rate: 63.7%
Average GPA: Not reported
ACT range: Not reported
SAT Math range: 550-660
SAT Reading range: 470-600
SAT Writing range: 4-18
Top 10% of class: 20%
Top 25% of class: 52%
Top 50% of class: 85%

479

College Profiles

NEW JERSEY INSTITUTE OF TECHNOLOGY

Admissions Criteria
Academic criteria:
Grades: ☆ ☆ ☆
Difficulty of class schedule: ☆ ☆ ☆
Class rank: ☆ ☆ ☆
Standardized test scores: ☆ ☆ ☆
Teacher recommendations: ☆
Personal statement: ☆
Non-academic criteria considered:
Interview
Extracurricular activities
Special talents, interests, abilities
Character/personal qualities
Volunteer work
Work experience
Geographical location
Religious affiliation/commitment
Minority affiliation
Alumni relationship

Deadlines
Early Action: No
Early Decision: No
Regular Action: Rolling admissions
Notification of admission by: November 15
Common Application: Accepted

Financial Aid
In-state tuition: $12,800
Out-of-state tuition: $25,856
Room: $8,400
Board: $3,166
Books: $3,075
Freshmen receiving need-based aid: 68%
Undergrads rec. need-based aid: 68%
Avg. % of need met by financial aid: 50%
Avg. aid package (freshmen): $12,163
Avg. aid package (undergrads): $12,201
Avg. debt upon graduation: $34,867

School Spirit
Mascot: Highlander
Colors: Scarlet and black

Students head to Newark for low-key dining or entertainment, and New York City for everything else. Newark is New Jersey's largest urban center and a college town in its own right, with more than 30,000 students from the four public institutes of higher learning in University Heights. "There are tons of restaurants and bars that cater to students," one student notes.

Freshmen and students who live far away from campus get priority for housing and receive two years guaranteed housing if placed. There are four dormitories, none older than the late 1970s, that are furnished and fully wired. Most upperclassmen move off campus. Forty-three percent of freshman and 26 percent of the entire student body live on campus.

Student Body

According to students, there seems to be a wide range between the "social" and the "nerdy" on campus. "We have a mix—the partiers, the people who spend 24/7 in the library, and the rest of us who are in between," one student explains. There's also a heavy male skew in the gender ratio (4:1).

The vast majority of NJIT students are from New Jersey, making for low geographic diversity; however, about 33 states and more than 100 countries are represented in the student body. There is very high ethnic diversity: the university ranks eighth in the nation for diversity and, according to the university, "is consistently listed as one of the leading schools for graduating minority students."

You May Not Know

- The university is often referred to as Newark College of Engineering, which was its name from 1919 to 1975.
- NJIT was the first university to obtain (and retain) Yahoo's "Most Wired University Award."
- The term "Virtual Classroom" is trademarked by NJIT.

Distinguished Alumni

Gerard Foschini, telecommunications engineer; Beatrice Hicks, founder of the Society of Women Engineers; TJ O'Malley, NASA aerospace engineer; Ellen Pawlikowski, Commander of Air Force Research Laboratory.

Admissions and Financial Aid

NJIT's admissions office lists three important criteria for applicants: high school academic record, standardized test scores, and class rank. The university looks for students in the top 30 percent of their class—a "B" average for schools without ranking systems. There are rolling admissions, so students are notified within two to three weeks about the admissions decision.

Merit scholarships include those open to New Jersey residents, out-of-state residents, and all students. There are also academic and athletics department scholarships. The Science, Mathematics and Research for Transformation (SMART) Scholarship for Service Program, established by the Department of Defense, gives recipients full scholarships and employment upon completion of the degree. Honors students are eligible for awards up to the cost of attendance.

NEW MEXICO INSTITUTE OF MINING AND TECHNOLOGY

Overview

New Mexico Institute of Mining and Technology—or New Mexico Tech, as it is often called—is a public technical institute with intense academics in a small town setting. The school is located in Socorro, NM, about 75 miles south of Albuquerque. The campus itself features adobe buildings and trees aplenty, but the overall availability of social/night life is nearly nonexistent.

New Mexico Tech is so academically challenging that students will have little time to notice how little else there is to do. There is ample opportunity to participate in meaningful research on campus, and the school maintains good ties to industry and government, both for undergraduate research and for career opportunities after graduation. Beyond academics, there are relatively few student organizations and no varsity sports. Men drastically outnumber women at the university. The school lacks the name recognition of other grueling technical institutes but the curriculum and research opportunities are solid.

Academics

There are 49 majors available at New Mexico Tech, with especially strong programs in engineering, earth science, and technical communication. General education requirements include courses in communications, mathematics, laboratory sciences, social sciences, and humanities. No one—not even psychology majors—can escape the six required basic science courses: Calc I and II, Physics 121 and 122, and Chemistry 121 and 122. All students complete a capstone project in their senior year. Engineers complete a Senior Design Clinic. According to the school, senior projects "are team-based, real-world projects that often pair students with private companies, government agencies, or branches of the military." In general, the academic atmosphere at New Mexico Tech is highly intense. Many students do not manage to fulfill the demanding requirements within the space of four years. "If running one marathon is painful, this is like running three of them with a nail in your foot," says a student.

To help freshmen survive its rigors, the university offers a Freshman First-Year Experience course. Students take a freshman seminar led by an upperclass peer educator in their major. The course emphasizes developing the academic skills needed to avoid crashing and burning at such a tough school. There are also special social events for freshmen to help them get to know one another. Even after freshman year, Community Education courses provide an outlet for students to unwind a bit. Free, fun courses like Zumba and Stained Glass are a break from academic work.

Outside the classroom, many students are involved in part-time research with faculty members, and it is not uncommon for undergrads to co-author published papers. In addition to research with faculty members, undergrads can land jobs within the university's many research divisions, which cooperate with industry leaders, the government, and other universities.

New Mexico Tech doesn't offer any of its own study-abroad programs; however, New Mexico Tech does participate in a consortium with seven other New Mexico schools so that Tech students can study abroad through affiliated programs.

New Mexico Tech's career services office coordinates on-campus interviews with major corporations. Despite the remote location, employers are willing to travel to New Mexico Tech to seek its highly-qualified students as employees. "I'm not worried at all about finding a job after graduation," comments a student. "Graduates from New Mexico Tech usually have their pick of jobs." The school also sponsors two career fairs each year to help students explore their career options.

NEW MEXICO INSTITUTE OF MINING AND TECHNOLOGY

Four-year public
Founded: 1889
Socorro, NM
Small town
Pop. 9,055

Address:
801 Leroy Place
Socorro, NM
87801

Admissions:
800-428-TECH

Financial Aid:
800-428-TECH

admission@admin.nmt.edu

www.nmt.edu

NEW MEXICO INSTITUTE OF MINING AND TECHNOLOGY

Students
Total enrollment: 2,105
Undergrads: 1,565
Freshmen: 426
Part-time students: 13%
From out-of-state: 17%
Male/Female: 70%/30%
Live on-campus: 59%
Off-campus employment rating: Fair
Caucasian: 60%
African American: 2%
Hispanic: 26%
Asian / Pacific Islander: 3%
Native American: 3%
Mixed (2+ ethnicities): 3%
International: 2%

Academics
Calendar: Semester
Student/faculty ratio: 12:1
Class size 9 or fewer: 29%
Class size 10-29: 47%
Class size 30-49: 17%
Class size 50-99: 6%
Class size 100 or more: 1%
Returning freshmen: 74%
Six-year graduation rate: 49%
Graduates who immediately enter career
    related to major: 79%

Most Popular Majors
Mechanical engineering
Computer science
Petroleum engineering

Admissions
Applicants: 1,188
Accepted: 369
Acceptance rate: 31.1%
Average GPA: 3.7
ACT range: 23-29
SAT Math range: 590-700
SAT Reading range: 550-670
SAT Writing range: Not reported
Top 10% of class: 35%
Top 25% of class: 63%
Top 50% of class: 91%

Student Life

There are just 65 official student organizations on campus, as might be expected for a small and academically-intensive university. The most popular student groups, like the Association for Computing Machinery and American Society of Mechanical Engineers, are associated with academic interests.

There are no varsity sports at the university, but there are 14 club sports groups, including soccer and rugby. The caving, climbing, martial arts, and paintball clubs are also popular options for physical activity. Outside of organized events, students congregate at the Joseph A. Fidel Student Services Center, home to several study and event spaces as well as the Fire and Ice Coffee Shop. Greek life is not a large part of the social experience. "We're not the typical rah-rah type of school, but we're so busy we don't really miss it," says a student.

There are moments of light-hearted fun interspersed throughout the grueling academic year. Early in the fall, students let their hair down for four days of fun at the Annual '49ers Celebration. Recent attractions included a headlining comedian, human foosball, swing dancing, a heavy metal fest with live music and food, and a zombie-themed parade. At Halloween, students go all-out to take top honors at the costume contest.

The '49ers Celebration also features the traditional Bordello Night, during which audience members try to outbid one another to win the right to remove the on-stage dancers' garters. Proceeds benefit charities fighting to prevent violence against women. Spring Fling is a slightly tamer event, with a barbecue, live music, mud wrestling, glow in the dark golf, and prom dress rugby scrimmage.

Off campus, the Socorro Springs Brew Pub is popular with some students. Beyond that, students enjoy watching tumbleweeds cross the Socorro horizon. "Life in Socorro can be boring, but we just have to be creative with entertaining ourselves," laughs a student. Those with time and wheels head to Albuquerque or El Paso for entertainment. Outdoorsy types will appreciate the hiking, mountain biking, and other outdoor activities available nearby.

Many students live off campus, since off-campus housing is cheap. On campus, there are two all-female and two all-male residence halls, and the rest are co-ed. The only way to get a single room is to live in one of the three apartment-style buildings.

Student Body

Students are academically focused and more likely to be found in the lab than at a bar. "We don't care if we have a reputation for being nerds," explains a student. "We can't deny who we are and it's just nice to be in an environment with like-minded people." The student body is skewed heavily male. "Don't come here if you're looking for an active dating scene," says a student. Ethnic diversity is high, with a large percentage of Hispanic students, but geographic diversity is low.

You May Not Know

- Socorro has over 300 days a year of sunshine.
- When the university broke ground on its Magdalena Ridge Observatory in 2002, Prince William was there to watch.

- New Mexico Tech's golf course has been called one of the 500 best courses in America by *Golf Digest*.

Distinguished Alumni

Dr. John F. Alderete, professor of microbiology at the University of Texas Health Science Center; John Kruppenbach, seismologist and entrepreneur; Dr. Van Romero, physicist, *MythBusters* guest.

Admissions and Financial Aid

New Mexico Tech has specific admission requirements regarding GPA and standardized test scores: a minimum of 2.5 high school GPA and an ACT composite score of 21 or SAT combined score (critical reading and math) of 970. Students who go above and beyond these minimum requirements are automatically considered for merit scholarships based upon their GPA and National Merit status. The awards range from the Gold Award ($6,000 per year) to the Bronze Award ($1,000 per year). New Mexico residents who completed high school in the state can win the New Mexico Legislative Lottery Scholarship for full tuition if they earn a 2.5 GPA during their first semester at New Mexico Tech.

NEW MEXICO INSTITUTE OF MINING AND TECHNOLOGY

Highlights

Admissions Criteria
Academic criteria:
Grades: ☆ ☆ ☆
Difficulty of class schedule: ☆ ☆ ☆
Class rank: ☆
Standardized test scores: ☆ ☆ ☆
Teacher recommendations: N/A
Personal statement: N/A
Non-academic criteria considered:
Extracurricular activities
Special talents, interests, abilities
State of residency

Deadlines
Early Action: No
Early Decision: No
Regular Action: Rolling admissions
Common Application: Not accepted

Financial Aid
In-state tuition: $5,714
Out-of-state tuition: $17,074
Room: Varies
Board: Varies
Books: $1,038
Freshmen receiving need-based aid: 52%
Undergrads rec. need-based aid: 51%
Avg. % of need met by financial aid: 81%
Avg. aid package (freshmen): $11,261
Avg. aid package (undergrads): $12,026
Avg. debt upon graduation: $18,834

NEW YORK UNIVERSITY

Four-year private
Founded: 1831
New York, NY
Major city
Pop. 8,244,910

Address:
70 Washington Square
South
New York, NY
10012

Admissions:
212-998-4500

Financial Aid:
212-998-4444

admissions@nyu.edu

www.nyu.edu

NEW YORK UNIVERSITY

Overview

New York University (NYU) is one of the largest private universities in the country, and one of only 60 members of the prestigious Association of American Universities. For students interested in an urban campus, the Greenwich Village location is unbeatable. The intellectual environment is rigorous, and the faculty is star-studded. Arts and business programs stand out among the wide range of majors.

The campus is integrated into Greenwich Village, so it lacks a traditional, insular campus feel. Public Washington Square Park takes the place of a private college quad. The university maintains 330 uniformed public safety officers and a safe ride program for students concerned about safety, but the neighborhood isn't especially dangerous for those who keep their wits about them. The university guarantees housing for four years, a major plus for those worried about exorbitant New York rent.

There is so much to do off campus that only the truly unmotivated can feel bored. And NYU is no place for unmotivated students—the student body here is a focused and sophisticated group that balances serious bar-hopping with serious academics. If life in the Big Apple ever becomes overwhelming, NYU has remote campuses in locations around the world, from Abu Dhabi to Florence to Shanghai.

NYU is not a good option for those who want to enjoy a cozy, green campus oasis steeped in tradition, frats, and football, away from the cares of the world. However, if you want to immerse yourself in the "real world" and experience the thrills of one of the world's greatest cities, NYU is ideal.

Academics

The university as a whole offers a whopping 522 majors, so a student's interests would have to be pretty obscure not to be represented. Students in the College of Arts and Sciences take a core curriculum called the Morse Academic Plan (MAP). MAP consists of four components: expository writing program, study of a foreign language, Foundations of Contemporary Culture (FCC), and Foundations of Scientific Inquiry (FSI). Most students complete their required courses by the end of sophomore year. "As far as core curriculums go, MAP isn't bad," says a student.

NYU is a rigorous intellectual environment. Faculty members have impressive trophy shelves—68 have been elected to the American Academy of Arts and Sciences, 147 have received Guggenheim Fellowship recipients, and four are Pulitzer Prize winners. Students interested in business, dance, and drama will find especially strong programs. The Tisch School of the Arts is a nationally-renowned powerhouse with such famous alumni as Woody Allen, Joel Coen, Angelina Jolie, Martin Scorsese, and Oliver Stone. "You're really surrounded by the most talented people you'll ever meet here," says a student.

Research options include the Dean's Undergraduate Research Fund, which provides grants of $250 to $2,000 for students' research expenses. The Undergraduate Research Conference, where students can apply to give individual or team presentations, demonstrates how seriously the university feels about its program.

NYU is a great option if you can't wait to study abroad. The school describes itself as a "Global Network University." In addition to the usual study-abroad offerings at other universities, NYU has an Abu Dhabi campus as well as research/study outposts in Accra, Ghana; Berlin, Germany; Buenos Aires, Argentina; Florence, Italy; London, England; Madrid, Spain; Paris, France; Prague, the Czech Republic; Shanghai, China; Tel Aviv, Israel; and elsewhere.

NYU has almost 350,000 alums, and there are ample internship opportunities at places like Time Warner, NBC Universal, Conde Nast Publications, EMI, BBDO, Major League Baseball, the National Football League, and DKNY. You won't be alone if you want or need to work as an undergrad, since 85 percent of students are holding down an internship or job in addition to their studies. The Wasserman Center for Career Development provides job and internship fairs, career counseling, and even funding for internships with non-profit organizations.

Student Life

The focus of student life at NYU is off campus, which is really not surprising for a campus that is smack-dab in the middle of "the city that never sleeps." If you're looking for a cozy, coherent campus feel, NYU isn't the place. Washington Square Park is the closest you'll come to a traditional quad. But if you long for the chance to sample all that NYC cultural life has to offer, you'll find that city lights more than compensate for the lack of a well-manicured, private green where you can act like you're posing for photos in a college brochure.

New York City should keep you occupied and entertained, but—just in case you want more—the college also offers a smattering of cheesy, traditional collegiate events. The annual StrawberryFest is the most delicious of these. You can enjoy a carnival atmosphere and take a bite of New York City's longest strawberry shortcake. The black-tie optional Violet Ball has a classier feel than most college parties with hors d'oeuvres and dancing replacing shortcake and dunk tanks. There's no beating the Halloween experience at NYU. Over two million spectators and participants flock to take in the over-the-top entertainment value of the Greenwich Village Halloween Parade. It's the biggest public Halloween event in the United States.

Greek life is practically nonexistent at NYU. Only about six percent of students go Greek, perhaps because the appeal of frat parties pales in comparison to real New York City nightlife.

Sports aren't a large part of life at NYU either. There isn't even a football team. All sports are Division III except for Division I volleyball and the very popular Division I fencing. "That fencing is one of our most prominent sports says a lot about us," one student notes. Intramural sports offerings are few and conventional (basketball, soccer, etc.), but there are more options for club sports.

On campus, students meet up at the Loeb Student Center. There are a ton of student activities to explore, including the Flaneur Club, which takes walking—and eating—tours of the city. But the heart of social life is off campus in East Village. Bar-hopping is a major weekend (and weeknight) activity; bars like Bar None and Josie Woods owe their existence to crowds of NYU students. During the day, devoted shoppers will find their paradise in nearby SoHo. Of course, those with a taste for the art and music scene will never be disappointed with all that New York City has to offer.

NYU guarantees housing for four years, which can be a blessing since off campus, students face astronomical rent. Traditional dorms and apartment-style housing are available. While dorms are generally well-integrated into neighborhoods, you might find yourself living blocks and blocks from the center of campus. "Unless you're incredibly wealthy—and some of the students here are—you'll want to live in campus housing," says a student.

NEW YORK UNIVERSITY

Highlights

Students
Total enrollment: 44,516
Undergrads: 22,498
Freshmen: 5,140
Part-time students: 6%
From out-of-state: 72%
Male/Female: 40%/60%
Live on-campus: 50%
In fraternities: 8%
In sororities: 5%
Off-campus employment rating: Excellent
Caucasian: 40%
African American: 5%
Hispanic: 10%
Asian / Pacific Islander: 19%
Native American: 0%
Mixed (2+ ethnicities): 3%
International: 12%

Academics
Calendar: Semester
Student/faculty ratio: 10:1
Class size 9 or fewer: 15%
Class size 10-29: 66%
Class size 30-49: 10%
Class size 50-99: 7%
Class size 100 or more: 3%
Returning freshmen: 92%
Six-year graduation rate: 85%
Graduates who immediately go to graduate school: 14%
Graduates who immediately enter career related to major: 76%

Most Popular Majors
Business/marketing
Social sciences
Visual/performing arts

Admissions
Applicants: 42,807
Accepted: 14,998
Acceptance rate: 35.0%
Average GPA: 3.6
ACT range: 28-32
SAT Math range: 630-740
SAT Reading range: 620-710
SAT Writing range: 43-47

485

NEW YORK UNIVERSITY

Admissions Criteria
Academic criteria:
Grades: ☆ ☆ ☆
Difficulty of class schedule: ☆ ☆ ☆
Class rank: ☆ ☆ ☆
Standardized test scores: ☆ ☆ ☆
Teacher recommendations: ☆ ☆
Personal statement: ☆ ☆
Non-academic criteria considered:
Extracurricular activities
Special talents, interests, abilities
Character/personal qualities
Volunteer work
Work experience
State of residency
Geographical location
Minority affiliation
Alumni relationship

Deadlines
Early Action: No
Early Decision: November 1
Regular Action: January 1 (final)
Notification of admission by: April 1
Common Application: Accepted

Financial Aid
In-state tuition: $42,469
Out-of-state tuition: $42,469
Room: $12,008
Board: $4,614
Books: $1,070
Freshmen receiving need-based aid: 55%
Undergrads rec. need-based aid: 54%
Avg. % of need met by financial aid: 55%
Avg. aid package (freshmen): $28,920
Avg. aid package (undergrads): $29,367
Avg. debt upon graduation: $35,104

School Spirit
Mascot: Bobcat
Colors: Purple and white
Song: *The Palisades*

Student Body

Students are generally liberal-leaning. The student body is highly ethnically and geographically diverse with 37 percent minority students and 72 percent from out of state, and students tend to mix across ethnic and geographic lines. However, many are from well-off backgrounds and there are cliques of especially wealthy students. "You hear about a few students who travel in private jets or who have their own chauffeur," one student notes.

You May Not Know

- Samuel Morse, professor of sculpture and painting (and namesake of the Morse Academic Program), first demonstrated his working model of the telegraph in Washington Square Park.
- NYU acquired La Pietra, a villa in Florence, Italy, as a bequest in 1994 and now runs academic programs, including the study of Tuscan gardening, from that location.
- NYU is home to "Max," the fastest computer in the United States.

Distinguished Alumni

Jake Burton Carpenter, founder of Burton Snowboards; Candace Bushnell, author of *Sex and the City*; Spike Lee, film director.

Admissions and Financial Aid

NYU describes its application process as more holistic than formulaic, so the whole application should be polished and well-rounded. The university is "interested in how well you have made use of the opportunities available to you, however great or limited they may have been." The admissions office points to students' academic records as the most important factor in the application. Students may apply Early Decision in either November or January.

NYU does not promise to meet all of every student's need with financial aid. AnBryce scholarships for first-generation college students who demonstrate financial need can cover as much as all of your tuition for four years. Perks include mentoring and special educational activities. The university also awards ARCH scholarships to students "committed to having a positive impact." ARCH scholarships meet full need and include access to specialized internships and career-planning resources. There are a few other merit scholarship programs available.

NORTH CAROLINA STATE UNIVERSITY

Overview

When students think of "going off to college," they might picture historic red brick buildings, bell towers, and a buzzing college town. This archetypal image may well have been inspired by North Carolina State University in Raleigh. Classic brick buildings and red sidewalks abound on campus, complementing a central plaza known as "The Brickyard." Memorial Bell Tower offers another distinctive architectural feature for NC State, though ironically it does not actually house the university bells.

NCSU is a very large land-grant university, and its proximity to the other universities of the Research Triangle translates to incredible research opportunities. NCSU has traditionally had strong agriculture, engineering, and design programs; and given their over 100 bachelor programs available, every student should be able to find something of interest.

For those looking for a great college town, Raleigh is tough to beat. *Money* magazine ranked it the fourth best large U.S. city in which to live, and *The Daily Beast* calls it America's Smartest City. For once, the economists and the intellectuals agree.

Academics

Going to a school with over 34,000 students means that some of the classes may be a little big. Introductory classes at NCSU can easily have enrollments of a couple hundred students, and 22 percent of the classes on campus have 50 students or more. At least students never have to worry about finding a study buddy. On the plus side, the opportunities available are as vast as the student body. The university is comprised of 10 separate colleges: Agriculture and Life Sciences, Design, Education, Engineering, Humanities and Social Sciences, Management, Natural Resources, Physical and Mathematical Sciences, Textiles, and Veterinary Medicine. Not sure which of those is the right fit? Not to worry; NCSU has developed the First Year College specifically for incoming students who need a little guidance freshman year before they settle on a college.

NCSU offers 110 different degrees, including very strong programs in business, design, engineering (especially agricultural, chemical, environmental, and industrial/manufacturing), physics, and textiles. However, no one will get away with just taking science classes, since all undergrads are required to fulfill core requirements not only in math and natural science, but also in writing and the humanities. The research opportunities offered on the Centennial campus are a dream come true for anyone interested in biomanufacturing and the biopharmaceutical industry, thanks to the extensive Biomanufacturing Training and Education Center (where the synthetic aorta and the artificial retina were developed, among other things). "Whatever kind of research you want to do, you can do it here," says one student.

Those students wanting to gain "real-world experience" while at school will find that NCSU's Cooperative Education Program offers students the chance to work in different professions and provides over 1,000 work rotations each year. For another type of real world experience, students can consider going abroad on one of the more than 20 NCSU programs, or one of the many outside programs that NCSU approves. Last but not least, internships are always an option; the University Career Center and Human Resources can help students find internships in their chosen field, making them that much more employable upon graduation.

Student Life

One might expect campus living to be especially crowded with such a large student population. However, while most freshmen live on campus, it's not required, and most upperclassmen live off campus (about 68 percent of all undergraduates decide to live in non-university housing). Nevertheless, there's still plenty of action at NCSU.

NORTH CAROLINA STATE UNIVERSITY – RALEIGH

Four-year public
Founded: 1887
Raleigh, NC
Major city
Pop. 416,468

Address:
Box 7001
Raleigh, NC
27695

Admissions:
919-515-2434

Financial Aid:
919-515-2421

undergrad_admissions@ncsu.edu

www.ncsu.edu

NORTH CAROLINA STATE UNIVERSITY – RALEIGH

Students
Total enrollment: 34,340
Undergrads: 24,833
Freshmen: 5,076
Part-time students: 12%
From out-of-state: 13%
From public schools: 80%
Male/Female: 56%/44%
Live on-campus: 32%
In fraternities: 11%
In sororities: 14%
Off-campus employment rating: Good
Caucasian: 75%
African American: 8%
Hispanic: 4%
Asian / Pacific Islander: 5%
Native American: 0%
Mixed (2+ ethnicities): 2%
International: 2%

Academics
Calendar: Semester
Student/faculty ratio: 18:1
Class size 9 or fewer: 5%
Class size 10-29: 48%
Class size 30-49: 24%
Class size 50-99: 14%
Class size 100 or more: 8%
Returning freshmen: 92%
Six-year graduation rate: 72%
Graduates who immediately enter career
    related to major: 62%

Most Popular Majors
Engineering
Business
Communication

Admissions
Applicants: 20,435
Accepted: 10,137
Acceptance rate: 49.6%
Average GPA: 4.4
ACT range: 23-28
SAT Math range: 580-670
SAT Reading range: 550-630
SAT Writing range: 5-30
Top 10% of class: 49%
Top 25% of class: 87%
Top 50% of class: 99%

About 11 percent of men and 14 percent of women decide to go Greek, graciously providing an open party scene with invitations to all. There are over 500 student organizations to partake in as well, so students not into the frat scene still have lots to occupy their time. NCSU offers everything from a cappella groups and academic honor societies to the Wolfpack Drag Strip Club.

NCSU features 24 varsity athletic programs, 45 club sports, and 18 intramural leagues. Football and basketball are the most popular spectator sports, especially when the NCSU Wolfpack are playing their rivals, the UNC Tar Heels. The basketball team has more than 20 NCAA tournament appearances, so students should be ready to cheer for a team that is used to winning! "Basketball is pretty much a religion here," says a student. Students who really aren't into organized sports can still get their exercise fix with the Outdoor Adventures program, which offers a climbing wall, Frisbee golf, hiking, and camping trips.

Among events on campus, NCSU's Homecoming week is one of the biggest and best attended; run entirely by students, it features a parade, pep rallies, and a concert starring major artists. Other notable events include the Center Stage Performing Arts Series, which brings big names in jazz, dance, music, and drama to the auditorium on campus throughout the year. On the other end of the spectrum, students may enjoy the traditional Krispy Kreme Challenge: competitors race 2 miles from the Belltower to the local donut shop, wolf down a dozen glazed donuts, and run back to the starting point, all within an hour. *Sports Illustrated* listed the run as one of the "102 Things You Gotta Do Before you Graduate."

Student Body

The student body at NCSU is, as one would expect, largely from North Carolina. State law requires that 82 percent of the students be from in state. NCSU has a moderate percentage of minority students (19 percent), with African Americans having the largest representation at eight percent of the undergraduate population. With its focus on engineering and the sciences, some might not be surprised to hear that there are slightly more men than women on campus. "There aren't as many women in the sciences, so if you are one, please come here. Please," says a male student.

Politics on campus tend to lean to the right, though all perspectives are represented.

You May Not Know

- NCSU's sports teams got their nickname the Wolfpack from a disgruntled alum who likened the student body's behavior at a sporting event to that of a "pack of wolves." Formerly NCSU teams were known as the Aggies or the Techs.
- NCSU is the only university to have Mr. and Ms. Mascots—Mr. and Ms. Wuf.
- Story has it that the original bricks for Halladay Hall were donated by the state prison and were made by the inmates.

Distinguished Alumni

Bill Cowher, Super Bowl winning NFL coach; John Edwards, former U.S. Senator and Vice Presidential candidate; Robert Gibbs, White House Press Secretary; James B. Hunt Junior, four-term Governor of North Carolina; Rajendra Kumar Pachauri, 2007 Nobel Peace Prize recipient; Henry Shelton, former Chairman of the United States Armed Forces Joint Chiefs of Staff.

Admissions and Financial Aid

Good news for the ladies: the slight gender imbalance at NCSU means women have a small advantage when applying. Classes taken and grades earned are the most important factors determining admission, though extracurriculars receive secondary attention. Teacher recommendations are not part of the application.

In order to be admitted, students must first satisfy general university standards, and then also be approved by the college of their choice. In other words, the student applying to the college of Natural Resources might have a better shot than the one applying to the College of Engineering simply because he picked a less competitive college. The most selective programs are agriculture and life sciences, design, education, engineering, management, physical and mathematical sciences, and the First Year College.

For students who want the most for their buck, *Kiplinger* magazine has ranked NCSU as the 10th best value among university educations. NCSU also offers some notable scholarships. The Park Scholarship Program is merit-based and pays full tuition for 35 in-state students and 15 out-of-state students. The College of Textiles offers the Centennial Scholarship for students who have shown strong academic and leadership skills. Centennial Scholars have close to 80 percent of all their NCSU expenses paid, and they receive a $7,500 stipend with which to pursue "enrichment opportunities." NCSU is also committed to offering generous aid to low-income students through a combination of scholarships and work-study programs.

NORTH CAROLINA STATE UNIVERSITY – RALEIGH

Highlights

Admissions Criteria
Academic criteria:
Grades: ☆ ☆ ☆
Difficulty of class schedule: ☆ ☆ ☆
Class rank: ☆ ☆ ☆
Standardized test scores: ☆ ☆ ☆
Teacher recommendations: ☆
Personal statement: ☆
Non-academic criteria considered:
Extracurricular activities
Special talents, interests, abilities
Character/personal qualities
Volunteer work
Work experience
Geographical location
Minority affiliation
Alumni relationship

Deadlines
Early Action: October 15
Early Decision: No
Regular Action: November 1 (priority)
February 1 (final)
Common Application: Not accepted

Financial Aid
In-state tuition: $8,206
Out-of-state tuition: $21,661
Room: $6,034
Board: $3,400
Books: $1,000
Freshmen receiving need-based aid: 48%
Undergrads rec. need-based aid: 49%
Avg. % of need met by financial aid: 84%
Avg. aid package (freshmen): $12,846
Avg. aid package (undergrads): $12,652
Avg. debt upon graduation: $22,626

School Spirit
Mascot: Wolf
Colors: Red and white
Song: *Red & White*

Four-year private
Founded: 1898
Boston, MA
Major city
Pop. 625,087

Address:
360 Huntington Avenue
Boston, MA
02115

Admissions:
617-373-2200

Financial Aid:
617-373-3190

admissions@neu.edu

www.northeastern.edu

NORTHEASTERN UNIVERSITY

Overview

Set in the heart of Boston, Northeastern is a large private university with over 16,000 undergraduates. Northeastern students are exposed to a dazzling array of opportunities—being in the city means the students are not limited to campus life and can enrich their lives with cultural activities in and around Boston.

The Northeastern graduate programs also create a trickle-down effect, encouraging undergraduate students to get involved with research early. The school's famous co-op program allows students to alternate semesters of study with semesters working full-time jobs, allowing them a taste of the real world before completing their bachelor's. While the opportunities at a big school are endless, Northeastern may not be the place for students seeking an intimate experience and a sense of tight community. But if you are looking for a chance to be involved in high energy, top level research along with the rush of a big city, then fill out your paperwork!

Academics

Northeastern offers 80 majors and concentrations within the following nine schools: Arts Media and Design, Business Administration, Computer and Information Sciences, Health Studies, Profession Studies, Science, Social Science and Humanities, and Law. Business and computer and information science are some of the strongest majors. Students can also craft their own major.

Core course requirements are split into "knowledge domains" (arts/humanities, social science, science/technology, and one upper-level course outside the student's major); writing; mathematical/analytical thinking; comparative cultures; integrated experiential learning; a capstone course; and "first-year learning communities," which are designed so that freshmen bond and get to know faculty. The core requirements at Northeastern make up a relatively large portion of a student's classes compared to other colleges, and some students find them constraining. "I'd like it better if we could choose the classes we wanted to take," says one student.

Northeastern is famous for its co-op program—started more than 100 years ago—which allows students to alternate periods of academic study with two or three six-month programs of full-time paid internships related to their majors, which start in their sophomore year. Many students in the co-op program take five years to graduate instead of the typical four, but the program gives them hands-on work experience and the chance to make business connections before graduation. "I found that I learned more during my co-op time than I did in any classroom," notes a student.

Students who wish to work internationally can apply for grants through the Presidential Global Scholars Program, which supports up to 200 students annually. "It's the best way to study abroad," one student comments. The Scholarship grants up to $6,000 for one co-op, and a select few candidates are granted a Presidential Global Fellowship, a full-tuition scholarship for the remainder of their undergraduate degree. The most popular overseas locations are the UK, France, Spain, Germany, Costa Rica, Argentina, Peru, China, Singapore, Turkey, and South Africa.

Besides the co-op program, Northeastern has International Study Programs for students who want to study abroad. There are two options—a "traditional" study-abroad program, where students can study at any of the 60 Northeastern-approved institutions around the world for a semester, or the "Dialogue of Civilizations" program, a summer program where students hold discussions with other local students, government, and community leaders.

For students less inclined to go abroad, there is an Honors Program for incoming freshmen who want a more intellectually rigorous undergraduate experience. The Honors Program invites a select group of high school seniors to join the program each fall, based on their application materials. These Honors Program students are residents in one of four "Living and Learning communities:" Science, Technology and Human Values; Social Development; Conflict and Peace Building; or Inquiry, Advocacy, and the Social World. Students participate in small-sized Honors courses and are encouraged to complete a junior/senior project, though it is not required.

Northeastern encourages undergraduates to participate in research. This focus is so strong that the university holds an annual Research and Scholarship Expo to feature the findings of their undergraduates involved in research. The Honors program and the Provost's office provide funding for projects.

Northeastern's 200,000 alumni stay connected mostly through the web. The website encourages alumni to join the Alumni Facebook page, or receive up-to-date information about news and events through Twitter. There is also a quarterly alumni magazine published by the university.

Student Life

There are over 300 student organizations at Northeastern, so students are spoiled for choice. A particularly large number of ethnic and cultural organizations span from Filipino to Cape Verdean to Haitian to Saudi Arabian students. Other more diverse groups include the Deaf Club, the Emergency Medical Services Interest Group, Students for a Sensible Drug Policy, and Vegetarians United.

Each season also brings with it large school-wide events. November's homecoming is an annual tradition where alumni can participate in discussions, listen to faculty lectures, and cheer on the Huskies in various games. February and March bring the International Carnevale, a two-month festival celebrating cultural diversity through music, art, dance, poetry, song, food, and fashion. "You can see Filipino dance and Cambodian theater but also celebrate Persian New Year," summarizes a student. In the spring, the university hosts Springfest, a week of fun events with comedians, graffiti artists, magicians, concerts, scavenger hunts, and karaoke nights.

There are 28 Greek chapters at the university that are split into four groups: the Interfraternity Council, the Multicultural Greek Council, the National Pan-Hellenic Council, and the Pan-Hellenic Sororities. Some chapters were founded at Northeastern as long ago as 1969, while others were founded as recently as 2009. However, Greek life is not dominant on campus. "None of my close friends have joined," remarks one student, "and so I never considered it."

Northeastern has 18 varsity sports at the NCAA Division I level, 40 club teams that serve around 1,000 athletes, and another 14 intramural sports with nearly 1,200 teams involving over 8,000 students. Intramural sports include sand volleyball, broomball, and flag football. While there is no football team, hockey is particularly popular on campus. The Beanpot—the annual hockey competition between Boston College, Boston University, Harvard, and Northeastern—is held at the university's Matthew's Arena. The crew team is also particularly strong.

Off campus, it is easy for students to enjoy the social and cultural offerings of the city. The campus is located between the Museum of Fine Arts and the Symphony Hall, and students are also encouraged to give back to the city by participating in community service.

NORTHEASTERN UNIVERSITY

Highlights

Students
Total enrollment: 24,540
Undergrads: 16,685
Freshmen: 2,664
From out-of-state: 77%
Male/Female: 50%/50%
Live on-campus: 53%
In fraternities: 3%
In sororities: 5%
Off-campus employment rating: Excellent
Caucasian: 49%
African American: 5%
Hispanic: 6%
Asian / Pacific Islander: 8%
Native American: 0%
Mixed (2+ ethnicities): 11%
International: 18%

Academics
Calendar: Semester
Student/faculty ratio: 13:1
Class size 9 or fewer: 15%
Class size 10-29: 58%
Class size 30-49: 21%
Class size 50-99: 5%
Class size 100 or more: 2%
Returning freshmen: 96%
Six-year graduation rate: 79%

Most Popular Majors
Business administration
Criminal justice
Psychology

Admissions
Applicants: 44,208
Accepted: 14,084
Acceptance rate: 31.9%
Average GPA: Not reported
ACT range: 29-32
SAT Math range: 650-740
SAT Reading range: 630-720
SAT Writing range: 31-51
Top 10% of class: 63%
Top 25% of class: 88%
Top 50% of class: 99%

491

College Profiles

NORTHEASTERN UNIVERSITY

Admissions Criteria
Academic criteria:
Grades: ☆ ☆ ☆
Difficulty of class schedule: ☆ ☆ ☆
Class rank: ☆
Standardized test scores: ☆ ☆ ☆
Teacher recommendations: ☆ ☆ ☆
Personal statement: ☆ ☆ ☆
Non-academic criteria considered:
Interview
Extracurricular activities
Special talents, interests, abilities
Character/personal qualities
Volunteer work
Work experience
State of residency
Geographical location
Minority affiliation
Alumni relationship

Deadlines
Early Action: November 1
Early Decision: No
Regular Action: January 15 (final)
Notification of admission by: April 1
Common Application: Accepted

Financial Aid
In-state tuition: $40,780
Out-of-state tuition: $40,780
Room: $7,530
Board: $6,570
Books: $1,000
Freshmen receiving need-based aid: 49%
Undergrads rec. need-based aid: 44%
Avg. % of need met by financial aid: 69%
Avg. aid package (freshmen): $29,409
Avg. aid package (undergrads): $22,787

School Spirit
Mascot: Paws
Colors: Red and black
Song: *All Hail!*

Freshmen at Northeastern are housed together in 11 co-ed residential halls, with between 100 and 700 students per hall. There are a very limited number of single rooms, and most students live in doubles. Upperclassmen are mainly housed in apartment-style accommodations, from single studios to six-person apartments with kitchenettes. There are over 10 apartment complexes for upperclassmen to pick from, some which are strategically located close to Fenway Park, home of the Red Sox, or the Symphony Hall, home to the Boston Pops. "The location is unbeatable," brags a student.

Student Body

Northeastern has a high level of ethnic diversity, with 30 percent minority students and 18 percent international students, hailing from 125 countries. The highest proportion of international students comes from Asia, followed by Europe, then Central and South America.

Students say "there is no typical Northeastern student," adding, "You'll find people from all walks of life who are into anything you can think of."

You May Not Know

- Famed science fiction writer Isaac Asimov set his 1957 story Galley Slave at Northeastern University in 2033.
- Northeastern chemical engineering students recently placed first in the National Chem-E-Car Competition by building a "chemically powered vehicle."
- There is a network of underground tunnels, which are especially utilized during snowstorms.

Distinguished Alumni

Kevin Antunes, musical director for Justin Timberlake; Shawn Fanning, founder of Napster; Mark P. Fitzgerald, Vice Admiral for the United States Navy; Wendy Williams, talk show host; Sy Sternberg, Chairman and CEO, New York Life Insurance.

Admissions and Financial Aid

While Northeastern does not have a minimum score or GPA requirement for applicants, the university emphasizes its desire to enroll students who have gone "beyond the minimum graduation requirements" and have taken advantage of their high school's courses. The university suggests recommendation letters from guidance counselors and teachers.

Northeastern has several merit-based scholarships. The Trustee Scholarship, which covers full tuition, room and board, is given to students in the top one percent of the admitted freshman applicant pool. Another full scholarship is the Torch Scholars Program, which includes a Summer Immersion Program prior to freshman year. Students attending a Boston Public High School, who are in the top 10 percent of their high school class, are eligible for full scholarships. Applicants must be nominated by their high school. There are also merit scholarships ranging from $5,000-$17,000 for freshmen applicants, which are given to the top 25 percent of freshmen applicants. After the first year, amounts are awarded on a per semester basis and range from $2,500-$8,500.

NORTHWESTERN UNIVERSITY

Overview

With the waves of Lake Michigan lapping at one edge of the campus, Northwestern University is one of those great schools whose rigorous academics are matched by a rousing school spirit. Ranked 12th in the country by *U.S. News & World Report*, the school houses the nationally respected Medill School of Journalism, the McCormick School of Engineering, and the Kellogg School of Management, along with impressive arts and sciences programs. Interdisciplinary work and world class research are also a given.

That said, Northwestern's appeal is not just in the classroom, but on the field, where as a Big Ten school, the Wildcats draw rowdy student excitement. This is not to mention, of course, that Northwestern's enviable location in Evanston is only 12 miles north of the heart of Chicago, putting nightlife, museums, culture, and internships easily within reach.

Academics

In order to obtain a degree from the College of Arts and Sciences, students must fulfill a distribution requirement by taking courses in six different academic areas, participate in freshman seminars, become proficient in a foreign language and in English writing, and must specialize in one of 70 majors. Students also have the opportunity for interdisciplinary and independent work, with the additional option of self-designing a non-traditional major.

Northwestern is renowned for its Specialized Schools in communications, education, and music, as well as for its social sciences, prelaw, premed, and theatre programs. And uniquely, Kellogg Business School offers a one-of-a-kind business certificate for undergraduates.

With an international reputation, the Medill School of Journalism itself is worth describing in more detail. It is no wonder that the student-run newspaper has received national accolades, given that juniors take an 11-week Journalism Residency in which they get hands-on experience in a professional newsroom. As a result of such experience, the starting salary of Medill graduates is approximately $5,000 more than the average of graduates from other journalism schools. Medill alumni include Pulitzer Prize winners, the former president of the National Organization for Women, and the former president of NBC. "This is the premier destination if you want to have a career in journalism," says a student.

Through the separate School of Communication, undergraduates are able to take classes in anything ranging from audiology and hearing sciences to language pathology to screen writing. The school overlaps artists, engineers, technicians, and scholars to create a holistic, interdisciplinary approach to communications. Providing ample opportunities for hands-on work, Northwestern operates research laboratories, as well as theatre spaces, and organizes performances, readings, and radio broadcasts.

All these programs operate on the quarter system, which means students can take more classes (four each quarter, up to five for engineering students). On the flip side, however, this means that classes move at a very rapid pace and sometimes do not go into as much depth as a semester system would allow. Luckily for students, professors, rather than teaching assistants, teach 97 percent of classes. With so many classes to choose from, the Course and Teacher Evaluation Council is an invaluable resource where students can access evaluations of classes written by previous students.

But it's not all inside the classroom for Northwestern academics. As a university that received $557 million in sponsored research grants last year, it is no surprise that students have abundant opportunities to participate in (and get paid for) cutting edge work outside their courses. Research grants for academic and creative undergraduate work are awarded both during the school year ($1,000) and during the summer

NORTH-WESTERN UNIVERSITY

Four-year private
Founded: 1851
Evanston, IL
Medium city
Pop. 74,785

Address:
1801 Hinman Avenue
Evanston, IL
60208

Admissions:
847-491-7271

Financial Aid:
847-491-7400

ug-admission@northwestern.edu

www.northwestern.edu

493

NORTHWESTERN UNIVERSITY

Highlights

Students
Total enrollment: 21,215
Undergrads: 9,376
Freshmen: 2,138
Part-time students: 9%
From out-of-state: 67%
Male/Female: 49%/51%
Live on-campus: 65%
In fraternities: 32%
In sororities: 38%
Off-campus employment rating: Excellent
Caucasian: 55%
African American: 5%
Hispanic: 8%
Asian / Pacific Islander: 17%
Native American: 0%
Mixed (2+ ethnicities): 4%
International: 6%

Academics
Calendar: Quarter
Student/faculty ratio: 7:1
Class size 9 or fewer: 15%
Class size 10-29: 58%
Class size 30-49: 21%
Class size 50-99: 5%
Class size 100 or more: 2%
Six-year graduation rate: 94%

Most Popular Majors
Engineering
Economics
Journalism

Admissions
Applicants: 31,991
Average GPA: Not reported
ACT range: 31-34
SAT Math range: 680-780
SAT Reading range: 680-760
SAT Writing range: 67-27
Top 10% of class: 90%
Top 25% of class: 91%
Top 50% of class: 100%

($3,000). The final products of these projects are exhibited in the Undergraduate Research Symposium.

If you are itching to get off-campus experience, you can choose to participate in 120 Northwestern-affiliated study-abroad programs in any of 45 different countries. Often students choose to spend their entire junior year away from the university.

The school prides itself on setting up internships all over the world, both during the school year and summer. The Office of University Career Services holds informational classes such as InternQuest 101, job fairs, and alumni panels. Northwestern's impressive list of alumni, over 190,000 strong, is a testament to the career opportunities students have upon graduating.

Student Life

Northwestern's spirit manifests in student-run events throughout the year, perhaps most notably with Dillo Day—which marks the end of month-long Mayfest (a series of musical celebrations including Battle-of-the-bands and Sing-a-long-Mulan)—a day honoring the Armadillo. Dillo Day includes events such as a concert festival, lakeside games, vendors, and performers. Socially conscious students organize countless awareness events such as Take Back the Night, a march against sexual abuse, or fundraising events such as Dance Marathon, where students boogie for 24 hours.

Some of the biggest events, of course, are those that center on sports. Division I in the Big Ten conference, Northwestern is one of the rare schools that couples top-notch academics with a healthy dose of school spirit. "Athletics is just one of the ways that we're better than the Ivies," says a student. The women's lacrosse team recently won five consecutive NCAA national titles. Unfortunately, their football team has not fared as well and holds the record for losses in Division I-A, but that doesn't stop face-painted, flag-waving students from supporting the Wildcats at games. Competitive club teams and intramural sports teams such as basketball, football, Ultimate Frisbee, ice hockey and even ju-jitsu are always popular as well.

If athletics isn't your cup of tea, you can try some of the other clubs—more than 400 of them—honor societies, newspapers, theater, music, academic, service, and special-interest groups. Can't find a niche? It is easy to create new groups, though we'd wonder why you'd need to, given there is already every club imaginable, including a Happiness Club and Northwestern Model Arab League.

Greek life is also a large force on campus, with 32 percent of men and 38 percent of women involved. House parties in the surrounding neighborhoods are held by brothers, sisters, and non-Greeks alike.

Speaking of housing, all freshmen are required to live on campus in both co-ed and single sex dorms, but many upperclassmen move off campus to apartments. North side of campus, which houses the Greeks and a lot of the engineering and science majors, is known for being louder and having more parties than the south side, which houses many theatre and communications majors.

With Chicago so close, there is truly no shortage of things to do off campus; restaurants, bars, clubs and museums, shopping, and professional sports are all within a short train ride. Chicago is like an "amusement park for college students," says one student.

Journeying to the city takes some doing, though, so students spend a lot of time in Evanston itself. The city has enough bars and eateries to keep you busy, certainly enough to generate controversial articles in the student paper about "the best nachos in Evanston." Feeling more cultured? The campus itself is the home to the Block Museum of Arts and the Block Theater.

Student Body

As expected for a school so near Chicago, Northwestern has high diversity, with 5 percent African American, 17 percent Asian American, and 8 percent Hispanic. The school also boasts relatively high geographic diversity, with 41 percent of students from the Midwest, 17 percent from the Middle Atlantic States, and 15 percent from the West. In fact, students represent all 50 states and more than 50 countries. Such diversity nurtures a tolerant and liberal community, with minority organizations such as the Black Board, the student magazine for the black community.

Most importantly, with 90 percent of students having graduated in the top 10 percent of their high school class, students share a passion for learning. "Northwestern students are simply brilliant," says a student.

You May Not Know

- Northwestern actually has three campuses: the main campus in Evanston, 25 acres in central Chicago, and an international base in Doha, Qatar.
- Northwestern was ranked in 2013 as the second best school in the Midwest by *Forbes*.
- In 1916, Northwestern ran a field hospital in France to serve over 60,000 World War I and World War II soldiers.

Distinguished Alumni

Zach Braff, actor, writer, and director; Stephen Colbert, actor and comedian; Rahm Emanuel, Chief of Staff for President Barack Obama; John Paul Stevens, U.S. Supreme Court Justice; Mary Zimmerman, Tony Award-winning director.

Admissions and Financial Aid

In order to call yourself a Northwestern student, you have to prove your academic worth with a strong secondary school record and respectable SAT scores. The admissions board says, "the qualities we look for in each candidate are independent thinking, a sense of humor, self-confidence, energy, enthusiasm, and an interest in activities, people, and ideas," qualities best shown through essays, extracurriculars, and teacher recommendations. There are no evaluative interviews, but there are optional informational opportunities to meet with an alum in selected cities.

Northwestern offers no academic merit scholarships, but there are athletic scholarships, and the college guarantees to meet 100 percent of the demonstrated need of its students. Plus, through the No-Loan Program, families with the greatest financial need (generally those who make less than $55,000 a year) receive grants so that they don't need to take out any student loans. All other students who take out subsidized Stafford or Perkins loans have their loans capped at a total of $20,000 for all four years.

NORTHWESTERN UNIVERSITY

Highlights

Admissions Criteria
Academic criteria:
Grades: ☆ ☆ ☆
Difficulty of class schedule: ☆ ☆ ☆
Class rank: ☆ ☆ ☆
Standardized test scores: ☆ ☆ ☆
Teacher recommendations: ☆ ☆
Personal statement: ☆ ☆ ☆
Non-academic criteria considered:
Interview
Extracurricular activities
Special talents, interests, abilities
Character/personal qualities
Volunteer work
Work experience
State of residency
Minority affiliation
Alumni relationship

Deadlines
Early Action: No
Early Decision: November 1
Regular Action: January 1 (final)
Notification of admission by: April 15
Common Application: Accepted

Financial Aid
In-state tuition: $45,120
Out-of-state tuition: $45,120
Room: Varies
Board: Varies
Books: $1,878
Freshmen receiving need-based aid: 47%
Undergrads rec. need-based aid: 48%
Avg. % of need met by financial aid: 100%
Avg. aid package (freshmen): $37,835
Avg. aid package (undergrads): $36,827
Avg. debt upon graduation: $21,754

School Spirit
Mascot: Wildcats
Colors: Purple and white
Song: *Go U Northwestern*

OBERLIN COLLEGE

Overview

A place of music, arts, culture, and an intense dedication to learning, Oberlin College stands as a highly reputable institution for liberal arts. The college was recently ranked 25th in the nation for liberal arts colleges by *U.S. News & World Report* and boasts more alumni going on to attain PhDs than any other liberal arts college. Dynamic in academics, athletics, and community, Oberlin provides an overall stellar experience for those who attend.

Nestled in the stately city of Oberlin, Ohio, Oberlin College displays charming 19th-century sandstone buildings. The city was an active part of the abolitionist movement with the college as a station for the Underground Railroad. The rich history of Oberlin's progressive nature inspires in its students a compassion for all.

Home to the country's oldest continuously operated conservatory, Oberlin is praised for cultivating one of the richest musical environments of any American school. The Oberlin Conservatory Symphony Orchestra boasts an impressive reputation, with a performance at Carnegie Hall's Isaac Stern Auditorium as well as hundreds of other concerts local and country-wide. The Artist Recital Series at Oberlin attracts some of the finest classical musicians in the country, providing a uniquely enriching experience for Oberlin students.

With the same vigor as in the musical arena, Oberlin is dedicated to rigorous academics. Professors at Oberlin hold teaching as their primary priority, and this dedication shows in the quality of education students receive. Classes are also small, allowing students more academic flexibility; students often undertake double majors or get involved in research positions with faculty.

Oberlin is an institution infused with passion, inspiring its students through both a leading College of Arts and Sciences and a world-class Conservatory of Music.

Academics

True to its commitment to academic excellence, Oberlin requires classes in three arenas: arts and humanities, social sciences, and natural sciences and math. The college also has a cultural diversity class requirement, as well as several writing and quantitative proficiency mandates. Small class sizes (90 percent of classes have 30 or fewer students), combined with the dedication of passionate professors, allow students to delve thoroughly into their studies. "Almost everyone has a real passion for learning for the sake of learning," says a student.

As an institution of creativity and progressive attitudes, Oberlin offers 60 majors with strong academic programs including creative writing, environmental studies, and music. The Music Conservatory attracts the brightest young musicians from around the globe, with 615 undergraduate students from 45 U.S. states and 22 countries. "It's not just marketing hype when we say that we have a nationally recognized music conservatory," one student notes. Majors offered at the Conservatory include music education, performance, composition, and a double major in piano performance and vocal accompaniment.

Oberlin abounds with special academic opportunities, such as Experimental College. This unique program allows any student to teach his or her own class, providing exposure to untraditional material such as Brazilian Jujitsu or the History of Piracy. "My parents probably wouldn't approve," a student laughs, "but I took a class in Dungeons and Dragons, and my friend took one in Pokémon."

Another unique aspect of academics at Oberlin is the Winter Term, when students have an entire month free of regular classes and instead pursue an individual project. Students may choose to work intensely with a faculty member on a research topic relative to their major, to begin intense study of a foreign language, or perhaps to volunteer with a community group or improve a particular hobby or skill. The purpose of the term is to expand students' experiences, breaking the boundaries of traditional, structured education.

The college encourages its students to study abroad, and, in addition to 80 programs affiliated with the college, offers four of its own programs to different destinations in Europe. Students may opt to study literature in London; literature, history, music, and other topics in Cordoba, Spain; Italian culture in Arezzo, Italy; or economics in Austria and the Netherlands. During study-abroad programs, Oberlin maintains its high academic standards in tandem with the goal of complete cultural immersion.

As far as life after Oberlin, the Office of Career Services provides guidance for networking, internships, careers, and graduate school. Students may make appointments with advisors or use the drop-in hours. There are workshops and information sessions almost every day of the week with recent offerings including "Careers in Writing," "Start Smart Workshop Get Paid Fairly," and "Law Scholars Information Session."

Student Life

Students at Oberlin have a variety of available extracurricular options. With over 122 student groups established on campus—from Bike Co-op, to Student Senate, to Swing Dance—students are never restricted in attending to their recreational interests. The conservatory provides plenty of student-run performance groups, and the college also has an Art Rental Program in which students may rent original works of art from such prominent artists as Picasso and Monet. "For $5, I had art by Warhol in my dorm room for a semester," notes a student.

The social calendars of Oberlin students are bustling with intriguing events to keep even the most outgoing student satisfied. One rather unconventional event is the Drag Ball, a party where everyone who attends must come dressed in drag. In fact, several nationally-known drag queens and kings attend each year. The college also devotes a week to Earth Day, scheduling a slew of speakers, volunteer opportunities, and activities intended to educate attendees about the environmental issues. Also popular on campus is the Friday Night Organ Pump Concert, an organ concert held at midnight one Friday of every month. Attendance at school events in general is usually more than satisfactory, perhaps partly due to the lack of Greek life on campus.

Athletics, as well as sororities and fraternities, have an underwhelming role on Oberlin's campus. The college has 20 Division III varsity sports teams, 10 for men and 10 for women, with the football team ranking as the worst in all of the division. "We have so many other strengths, we're not ashamed that sports is not one of them," says a student. However, the men's Ultimate Frisbee team boasts a national ranking, and the women's cross-country team consistently is rated among the top 30 in the country.

For those that are craving off-campus excitement, downtown Oberlin, though small, offers several student-friendly bars and restaurants. "We could have more to do, but it just forces us to be creative," remarks a student. And, for big-city entertainment, Cleveland is only a 40-minute drive away.

Most students, however, are satisfied with the spread of activities offered on campus. Almost 90 percent of students live on campus,

OBERLIN COLLEGE

Highlights

Students
Total enrollment: 2,944
Undergrads: 2,930
Freshmen: 764
Part-time students: 1%
From out-of-state: 92%
From public schools: 66%
Male/Female: 45%/55%
Live on-campus: 88%
Off-campus employment rating: Fair
Caucasian: 71%
African American: 5%
Hispanic: 7%
Asian / Pacific Islander: 4%
Native American: 0%
Mixed (2+ ethnicities): 5%
International: 6%

Academics
Calendar: 4-1-4 system
Student/faculty ratio: 10:1
Class size 9 or fewer: 34%
Class size 10-29: 56%
Class size 30-49: 8%
Class size 50-99: 1%
Class size 100 or more: 1%
Returning freshmen: 93%
Six-year graduation rate: 85%
Graduates who immediately go to graduate school: 16%

Most Popular Majors
Biology
English
Music

Admissions
Applicants: 7,172
Accepted: 2,248
Acceptance rate: 31.3%
Placed on wait list: 1,106
Enrolled from wait list: 50
Average GPA: 3.6
ACT range: 28-32
SAT Math range: 620-720
SAT Reading range: 640-740
SAT Writing range: 41-47
Top 10% of class: 64%
Top 25% of class: 86%
Top 50% of class: 98%

497

College Profiles

OBERLIN COLLEGE

Admissions Criteria

Academic criteria:
Grades: ☆ ☆ ☆
Difficulty of class schedule: ☆ ☆ ☆
Class rank: ☆ ☆ ☆
Standardized test scores: ☆ ☆ ☆
Teacher recommendations: ☆ ☆
Personal statement: ☆ ☆
Non-academic criteria considered:
Interview
Extracurricular activities
Special talents, interests, abilities
Character/personal qualities
Volunteer work
Work experience
State of residency
Minority affiliation
Alumni relationship

Deadlines

Early Action: No
Early Decision: November 15
Regular Action: January 15 (final)
Notification of admission by: April 1
Common Application: Accepted

Financial Aid

In-state tuition: $46,250
Out-of-state tuition: $46,250
Room: $6,550
Board: $6,054
Books: $830
Freshmen receiving need-based aid: 55%
Undergrads rec. need-based aid: 54%
Avg. % of need met by financial aid: 100%
Avg. aid package (freshmen): $31,983
Avg. aid package (undergrads): $33,632
Avg. debt upon graduation: $16,812

School Spirit

Mascot: Yeomen/Yeowomen
Colors: Crimson and gold

498

with freshmen, sophomores, and juniors required to do so. Students tend to be content with housing, though, with the student-run housing organization having the largest participation rate of any campus in America.

Student Body

The average student at Oberlin College is "politically involved," socially aware, and "politically liberal." Most important at Oberlin is the focus on individuality. Oberlin has proved this stance throughout its history as the first institution to admit students of color (1835) and the first to educate men and women together in a baccalaureate program (1837). "Individuality is emphasized and honed here," emphasizes a student.

Students at Oberlin also prove their intense love for learning, as they attend graduate school at a higher rate than undergraduates from any other four-year institution. Ethnic diversity is high with 19 percent minority students, as is geographic diversity, with 92 percent of students hailing from out of state.

You May Not Know

- Oberlin owns 207 Steinway pianos, filling the concert halls, teaching studios, and practice rooms.
- The college's Allen Memorial Art Museum is among the top five campus museums in the country and has a collection of over 14,000 works of art.
- Ninety-five percent of Oberlin's science faculty in the last five years received grants for research, equipment, or curriculum development from sources such as NASA and the National Science Foundation.

Distinguished Alumni

Mark Boal, screenwriter for *The Hurt Locker*; Stanley Cohen, Nobel Physiology and Medicine Laureate; Marc Cohn, Grammy Award winning singer-songwriter; Erwin Griswold, former Solicitor General of the United States and Dean of Harvard Law School; Liz Phair, singer/songwriter.

Admissions and Financial Aid

Oberlin takes a holistic approach to the admissions process, looking at the high school transcript in addition to what the applicant is like as a person. The goal at Oberlin is to have an incoming class with a wide spread of talents, viewpoints, and backgrounds, and the admissions board looks at the application with this goal in mind. If applying to the Conservatory, a Unified Application for Music is required in addition to an audition and music teacher recommendations.

The college sponsors several merit-based scholarships including National Merit and National Achievement Scholarships for up to $2,000, Conservatory Dean's Awards; and John F. Oberlin Scholarships for those in the College of Arts and Sciences.

OCCIDENTAL COLLEGE

Overview

Occidental College, affectionately nicknamed "Oxy," is a small, private, liberal arts college with strong academic offerings across many fields, making it a viable alternative to the Claremont Colleges. The school can now claim a particularly prominent alumnus: Barack Obama.

Oxy's campus is located minutes from downtown Los Angeles and features Mediterranean architecture. Students have no excuse to be bored at such a dynamic location, with access to all the nightlife, dining, and entertainment readily available in LA.

While the atmosphere on campus is relaxed, academic standards are high. Special academic opportunities include an impressive range of Community Based Learning courses as well as cooperative programs with schools in the area and with prestigious law and bioscience graduate programs. The diverse student body promotes an active political environment on campus—mostly swinging toward the left side of the political spectrum.

Occidental is a progressive school that puts its money where its mouth is when it comes to promoting diversity, social justice, and environmental awareness. The laidback California atmosphere, the pleasant weather, the happening location, and the non-competitive academic culture at Oxy make for an enjoyable college experience with all the academic rigor of other liberal arts schools.

Academics

Occidental coursework tends to be challenging, but manageable. The small average class size—10 to 19 students—allows undergrads to form relationships with professors in a relaxed environment. "My professors have always been available," reflects a student. "Several of them call or email me to follow up on classes or assignments." There are 33 majors available, with especially strong programs in chemistry, English and comparative literary studies, and diplomacy and world affairs.

The Core Program includes first-year courses in writing, foreign language, fine arts, sciences, and mathematics. In addition, a global literacy requirement consists of three courses touching on at least three different geographic regions (Africa and the Middle East; Asia and the Pacific; Europe; Latin America; the United States; and Intercultural). Students must pass a senior comprehensive exam, which may be given in the form of a seminar, creative project, fieldwork, an oral exam, a thesis, or a field research project.

Occidental's special academic opportunities reflect its emphasis on fostering diversity and social justice. When you apply to Occidental, you are automatically considered to attend a free Multicultural Summer Institute for a month the summer before you matriculate. Fifty students participate in this program that is created "for students of color, first generation students, and students who have expressed interest in diversity and multiculturalism." For the month, you'll spend *all* of your time on MSI activities, including an intensive academic seminar team-taught by Occidental professors, field trips, community service projects, and diversity training. The program comes with plenty of perks. Not only will you earn four college credits at no cost, but you'll also have a chance to get acquainted with some of your classmates, the campus, and LA before you start in the fall. Students describe the Multicultural Summer Institute as "amazing" and the "best possible introduction to Oxy and other students."

Community Based Learning courses connect the classroom to the rest of LA, engaging students by the introduction of theoretical issues and then putting them to work. Occidental stands out from other institutions for the range of Community Based Learning courses it offers across different departments. The service components of such courses range from clerking at a public interest law firm to tutoring high school students in math to getting involved with an architectural venture, as well as many

OCCIDENTAL
COLLEGE

Four-year private
Founded: 1887
Los Angeles, CA
Major city
Pop. 3,819,702

Address:
1600 Campus Road
Los Angeles, CA
90041-3314

Admissions:
800-825-5262

Financial Aid:
323-259-2548

admission@oxy.edu

www.oxy.edu

OCCIDENTAL COLLEGE

Highlights

Students
Total enrollment: 2,178
Undergrads: 2,176
Part-time students: 1%
From out-of-state: 53%
Male/Female: 44%/56%
Live on-campus: 80%
In fraternities: 10%
In sororities: 16%
Off-campus employment rating: Fair
Caucasian: 54%
African American: 4%
Hispanic: 15%
Asian / Pacific Islander: 13%
Native American: 0%
Mixed (2+ ethnicities): 8%
International: 3%

Academics
Calendar: Semester
Student/faculty ratio: 10:1
Class size 9 or fewer: 18%
Class size 10-29: 69%
Class size 30-49: 12%
Class size 50-99: -
Class size 100 or more: -
Returning freshmen: 94%
Six-year graduation rate: 84%
Graduates who immediately go to gradu-
    ate school: 25%

Most Popular Majors
Diplomacy/world affairs
English
Economics

Admissions
Applicants: 6,135
Accepted: 2,412
Acceptance rate: 39.3%
Placed on wait list: 970
Enrolled from wait list: 41
Average GPA: 3.6
ACT range: 28-32
SAT Math range: 600-700
SAT Reading range: 600-700
SAT Writing range: 28-53

other projects. "I've learned as much outside the classroom as I have in it," says a student about the courses.

Occidental participates in several exchange and cooperative programs to supplement the college's own offerings. Students can take courses for credit at the California Institute of Technology or at the Art Center College of Design in Pasadena. Pre-law students with high GPAs and LSAT scores may be accepted into Columbia Law School's Accelerated Interdisciplinary Program in Legal Education and earn their Occidental bachelor's together with a Columbia law degree in just six years. Similarly, biochemistry majors with a minimum 3.2 GPA can get guaranteed admission to Keck Graduate Institute's bioscience graduate program.

Occidental has study-abroad programs in 34 countries. In addition to programs during the academic year, students can apply for full funding to do research abroad for eight to 12 weeks in the summer. Occidental also sends students to New York City to take courses and intern with the United Nations.

The Career Development Center offers a yearly dinner for students to practice professional business etiquette, skills which will be useful in meetings and lunch interviews. In addition, the unique "Interview with a Tiger" program brings alumni and employers to campus to facilitate mock interviews for students.

Student Life

There is plenty to do on campus at Occidental. Students hang out at the Student Quad or Samuelson Pavilion (which includes a lovely outdoor deck for enjoying the SoCal weather) or grab a bite at the Taco Truck. The Oxy Dance Team, Oxy Poker Club, Bad Movie Club, and Environmental Action Coalition are among the most popular of 112 official student organizations. Finance-minded students might want to get involved with the Blyth Fund, a six-figure investment portfolio within the college's endowment that is entirely managed by students.

Oxy boasts several yearly events that bring students together for a night of entertainment. Apollo Night features student performances in which performers can win cash prizes based on how loudly the audience makes their approval known. The event honors the legacy of the famous Apollo Theater in Harlem, the place where many famous African American performers began their ascent to stardom.

The annual Dance Production offers students, faculty, and alums the opportunity to showcase their talents and is one of the most popular events on campus. Those who prefer fun and games to performances will enjoy "Da Getaway," an on-campus casino night that traditionally caps a week of "Mafia wars" in which student teams try to eliminate each other by squirting opponents with water guns. Students describe the "Mafia wars" as "out of control" and an event that some students "take much more seriously than homework."

Greek life isn't very prominent at Occidental, with just four social fraternities and four social sororities. There are only two sorority houses and one frat house on campus. Ten percent of men and 16 percent of women participate. "There's so much to do around campus that Greek life just isn't very important," says a student.

Oxy fields 21 teams—10 men's, 11 women's—that compete in Division III. Football is the most popular sport, while women's basketball and soccer are the most competitive. Intramural sports offerings are limited, with just three sports a semester.

The eventful and varied downtown Los Angeles is a major asset for Oxy students. Beyond that, students also head to Old Pasadena for entertainment, nightlife, and dining. Outdoorsy types may strike out to the San Gabriel Mountains to snowboard, or to Malibu to surf. Popular road trip destinations include Las Vegas, San Diego, or Tijuana. "If you can bear the traffic, there's so much to do," says a student.

Freshmen, sophomores, and juniors are required to live on campus. Dorms are student-governed and co-ed, and they house students from all four classes. A high percentage of students stay in dorms throughout their entire tenure at Oxy.

Student Body

The highly diverse student body is politically active and leans to the left. Geographic diversity is moderate. "Even though we're a small school, we have a lot of different types of people which makes everyone welcome," comments a student.

Students cite the openness at Oxy. "It's so easy to make friends because you can go up and talk to pretty much anybody," notes a student.

You May Not Know

- Oxy's campus has been featured in over 75 movies and TV shows.
- The first two graduates, who received diplomas in 1893, were women.
- Demonstrating its environmental awareness, the college buys only Energy Star appliances, Green Seal cleaning products, and organic pesticides.

Distinguished Alumni

Terry Gilliam, movie producer, director, writer; Robinson Jeffers, poet; Barack Obama, President of the United States.

Admissions and Financial Aid

In keeping with the school's spirit of diversity and open-minded approach, Occidental College considers not just standardized test scores but also applicants' "motivation, character, and creativity." Oxy offers a variety of merit scholarships, ranging from $500 to $47,000 a year. One of the largest academic merit scholarships is the Margaret Bundy Program, which provides $20,000 a year to select students who maintain a 3.0 GPA.

OCCIDENTAL COLLEGE

Highlights

Admissions Criteria
Academic criteria:
Grades: ☆ ☆ ☆
Difficulty of class schedule: ☆ ☆ ☆
Class rank: ☆ ☆
Standardized test scores: ☆ ☆
Teacher recommendations: ☆ ☆
Personal statement: ☆ ☆
Non-academic criteria considered:
Interview
Extracurricular activities
Special talents, interests, abilities
Character/personal qualities
Volunteer work
Work experience
State of residency
Geographical location
Minority affiliation
Alumni relationship

Deadlines
Early Action: No
Early Decision: November 15
Regular Action: January 2 (priority)
January 10 (final)
Notification of admission by: April 1
Common Application: Accepted

Financial Aid
In-state tuition: $45,190
Out-of-state tuition: $45,190
Room: Varies
Board: Varies
Books: $1,244
Freshmen receiving need-based aid: 56%
Undergrads rec. need-based aid: 56%
Avg. % of need met by financial aid: 100%
Avg. aid package (freshmen): $38,084
Avg. aid package (undergrads): $39,160
Avg. debt upon graduation: $23,703

School Spirit
Mascot: Tigers
Colors: Orange and black
Song: *Occidental Fair*

Four-year private
Founded: 1835
Atlanta, GA
Major city
Pop. 432,427

Address:
4484 Peachtree Road,
NE
Atlanta, GA
30319-2797

Admissions:
800-428-4484

Financial Aid:
404-364-8356

admission@ogletho-
rpe.edu

www.oglethorpe.edu

OGLETHORPE UNIVERSITY

Overview

Named for Georgia state founder James Oglethorpe, Oglethorpe University's 100-acre campus, with its attractive Collegiate Gothic buildings, sits in the suburbs of Atlanta, Georgia. This liberal arts school is small—with an enrollment of about 1,100 undergraduates—and selective. Central to the school's educational approach is the "Oglethorpe Idea," which strives to educate students to "make a life and make a living." Career development and leadership programs form a major part of Oglethorpe's offerings as well.

As with most small schools, its size can be both an advantage and a drawback, allowing for plenty of personal attention from faculty while at the same time limiting class and extracurricular options. But the resources this college has are quality, including the recently renovated and expanded Philip Weltner Library, whose third floor is occupied by the Oglethorpe University Museum's exhibitions.

Oglethorpe's on-campus social scene is a small one, with tradition and some peculiar Anglophile aspirations forming the core of events; cliques tend to form, particularly around the Greek system.

Since most students like to take breaks from the on-campus scene, it is fortunate that the campus is well-connected to downtown Atlanta, which offers diverse cultural, sports, entertainment, and dining options. Overall, Oglethorpe offers a strong, if limited, liberal arts foundation along with career-oriented development programs; the intimate setting allows student-faculty interaction and lively intellectual discussion, and its location allows for plenty of escape to vibrant downtown Atlanta.

Academics

Oglethorpe offers 27 undergraduate majors, of which business administration, English, politics, and psychology are particularly strong. Students whose academic interests don't coincide with pre-existing majors have the option to design their own. The Individually Planned Major (IPM) program allows students to work with an academic advisor to define and plan their courses of study. Oglethorpe does not offer such flexibility when it comes to its core requirements, however. The four-year core requires students to take year-long, two-class sequences for their first three years; these course sequences are interdisciplinary across the liberal arts and thematically organized around concepts of "Narratives of Self," "Social Order," and "Historical Perspectives on Social Order," respectively. Seniors must take either the biological or physical science core class and must also satisfy fine arts, mathematics, and foreign language requirements. "While it's confining to be forced to take the core classes, it's nice in some ways that everyone is going through the same experience," says a student.

In such a small setting as Oglethorpe, the variety of classes may be disappointing to students looking for diversity in their academic programs; fortunately, the classes that Oglethorpe does offer will invariably be small, allowing students to engage both with faculty and classmates—making for an engaging intellectual experience. "There's never been a time that I haven't been able to get help from my professors," says a student. Academics are fairly demanding at Oglethorpe, and students are focused.

Students can augment core classes with Oglethorpe's Honors Program, which emphasizes working with primary sources and collaborative learning, while not overburdening students' schedules. Interested students take an introductory seminar in their first semester before applying to the program; they then take two Honors seminars taught by a team of faculty members. Students must also complete an Honors thesis or project supervised by a faculty reading committee. "Being in the honors program helps because we get priority registration," says a student.

Oglethorpe's unique Urban Leadership Program offers a variety of leadership skill-development experiences. The program's academic curriculum requires four courses, three core classes and one elective, and supplements those classes with off-campus workshops, internships, and student-organized conferences and symposia. Students with qualifying GPAs can apply and interview for the program after the first semester of their freshman year.

Oglethorpe does display diversity in terms of its study-abroad options. Oglethorpe runs its own short-term, faculty-led travel program with courses that last one to three weeks. Students may visit Costa Rica, Spain, Peru, Russia, Japan, Greece, Italy, France, and the UK. An Alternative Spring Break service trip to Guatemala is also available. "Special" partnerships are in place with Oxford and institutions in Italy, where "student associates" may take advantage of Oglethorpe's exchange agreements. Countries involved include Argentina, Austria, Belgium, Brazil, Ecuador, France, Germany, Iceland, Japan, Mexico, Monaco, the Netherlands, Spain, Turkey, and the UK. Students may also participate in third-party-abroad programs.

Oglethorpe puts a strong emphasis on career preparation. Students are encouraged to enroll in its Sophomore Choices seminar, which helps students explore their career and internship options and develop crucial decision-making, resume-writing, and interview skills. "I found the seminar very useful," comments a student. "I improved my interviewing skills dramatically." About a quarter of students attend graduate school within a year of graduating.

Student Life

Student organizations at Oglethorpe number over 40, including the student newspaper, *The Stormy Petrel*. The OU Playmakers take advantage of the new state-of-the-art Conant Performing Arts Building, which is also the home for the professional company, Georgia Shakespeare. Academic honor societies are very common as well.

Traditional events make up the bulk of on-campus happenings, including the not-very-informatively-named "Oglethorpe Day." Oglethorpe, seeking to make the most of its namesake James Oglethorpe's English origins and Oxford education, is "steeped in English tradition"—or rather, has steeped itself in Anglophile traditions. Oglethorpe Day strives to raise awareness of those traditions, summoning students with a bagpipe to witness footraces around campus.

The background story behind the holiday party called Boar's Head is equally Anglophilic. It involves a 14th century Oxford student killing a boar by ramming a book of Aristotle down its throat. Oglethorpe also has an annual muddy tug-of-war that pits student teams against faculty. One Oglethorpe event has a particularly creative name—the "Battle of Bloody Marsh"—an event that is named after James Oglethorpe's victory over Spanish troops in Georgia in 1742. "The Battle of Bloody Marsh is especially fun to watch," says a student.

Although Oglethorpe only has three fraternities and three sororities, about 16 percent of the student body belongs to the Greek system. "The fraternities and sororities are a pretty big deal," explains a student.

For students interested in athletics, limited intramural options are available each semester, including less-traditional ping-pong and pool. Seven men's and seven women's varsity teams compete

OGLETHORPE UNIVERSITY

Students
Total enrollment: 1,079
Undergrads: 1,053
Part-time students: 8%
From out-of-state: 25%
From public schools: 70%
Male/Female: 41%/59%
Live on-campus: 57%
In fraternities: 20%
In sororities: 12%
Off-campus employment rating: Excellent
Caucasian: 35%
African American: 21%
Hispanic: 8%
Asian / Pacific Islander: 3%
Native American: 0%
Mixed (2+ ethnicities): 2%
International: 6%

Academics
Calendar: Semester
Student/faculty ratio: 13:1
Class size 9 or fewer: 35%
Class size 10-29: 65%
Class size 30-49: -
Class size 50-99: -
Class size 100 or more: -
Returning freshmen: 80%
Six-year graduation rate: 56%
Graduates who immediately go to graduate school: 25%

Most Popular Majors
Business administration
Accounting
Psychology

Admissions
Applicants: 2,463
Accepted: 2,036
Acceptance rate: 82.7%
Average GPA: 3.4
ACT range: 22-26
SAT Math range: 510-610
SAT Reading range: 530-620
SAT Writing range: 4-22
Top 10% of class: 25%
Top 25% of class: 54%
Top 50% of class: 81%

503

College Profiles

OGLETHORPE UNIVERSITY

Highlights

Admissions Criteria
Academic criteria:
Grades: ☆ ☆ ☆
Difficulty of class schedule: ☆ ☆ ☆
Class rank: ☆ ☆
Standardized test scores: ☆ ☆ ☆
Teacher recommendations: ☆ ☆
Personal statement: ☆ ☆
Non-academic criteria considered:
Interview
Extracurricular activities
Special talents, interests, abilities
Character/personal qualities
Volunteer work
Work experience
State of residency
Alumni relationship

Deadlines
Early Action: November 15
Early Decision: No
Regular Action: Rolling admissions
Common Application: Accepted

Financial Aid
In-state tuition: $31,000
Out-of-state tuition: $31,000
Room: Varies
Board: Varies
Books: $1,100
Freshmen receiving need-based aid: 72%
Undergrads rec. need-based aid: 79%
Avg. % of need met by financial aid: 72%
Avg. aid package (freshmen): $28,042
Avg. aid package (undergrads): $27,081
Avg. debt upon graduation: $22,692

School Spirit
Mascot: Stormy Petrels
Colors: Black and gold

in Division III of the NCAA; while men's golf is the standout team among them. Men's basketball tends to draw the most spectators.

The Metropolitan Atlanta Rapid Transit Authority (MARTA) connects campus to downtown and the greater Atlanta area. Atlanta offers something to suit everyone's tastes, ranging from art museums, galleries, professional sports teams to a zoo, Six Flags, and Coca-Cola World Headquarters. Outdoor recreation is also available in nearby national parks.

Freshmen and sophomores must live on campus in suite-style residences, and juniors must live on campus in apartment-style residences.

Student Body

With most of the student body hailing from within the state, Oglethorpe students tend to fall on the conservative side of the political spectrum. "There are some liberals," explains a student, "but it's a pretty conservative campus." However, ethnic diversity is high. Students share that cliques tend to form around certain social circles. "Everyone knows everyone else so even though there are cliques, you pretty much know someone in each group," says a student.

You Might Not Know

- Franklin D. Roosevelt gave his first "New Deal" speech as the commencement speaker for Oglethorpe's 1932 graduating class.
- Lil Wayne's music video "Fireman" was filmed on the Oglethorpe campus.
- Oglethorpe is home to the "Crypt of Civilization," listed by the *Guinness Book of World Records* as the first time capsule. It is scheduled to be opened in 8113 AD.

Distinguished Alumni

Sidney Lanier, post-Civil War era poet, critic, and musician; Vincent Sherman, film director and actor; Tim Tassopoulos, Senior Vice President of Operations, Chick-fil-A.

Admissions and Financial Aid

Merit scholarships at Oglethorpe can range from $3,500 to the full cost of tuition. HOPE Scholarships of $3,500 or Out-of-State HOPE Equivalents are available to Georgia residents or non-residents, respectively, with qualifying GPAs. Based on their applications (it is worth noting that the application essays are part of the evaluation), qualified students may also receive invitations to Oglethorpe's Scholarship Weekend competition. Runners-up at the competition are awarded Oglethorpe Scholars Awards ranging from $5,000 to $17,000. Up to five winners with excellent academic achievements and potential for community contributions will be awarded James Edward Oglethorpe Scholarships, which include the full cost of tuition, plus a host of perks, monetary and otherwise.

OHIO STATE UNIVERSITY - COLUMBUS

Overview

With more than 43,000 undergraduates, 1,400+ student groups and organizations, 175+ majors, and 100+ study-abroad opportunities, Ohio State University (OSU) can be summed up in one word—*large*. Indeed, Ohio State was the nation's largest university in 2008. This quantity doesn't come at the expense of quality, though; *U.S. News & World Report* ranked OSU 16th in the country among public universities.

Ohio State's urban campus is just 2.5 miles north of downtown Columbus, with the Olentangy River weaving its way through campus' traditional and modern buildings. The 11-acre Oval in front of the main library is in the center of campus. The largest city in Ohio, Columbus offers professional sports, culture, entertainment, and access to government internships.

Thanks to its enormity, OSU offers virtually every opportunity imaginable. All this choice can be a mixed blessing—so many options can be overwhelming for some. But students who aren't afraid to carve out their own niche in a huge sea of options, and who don't mind donning scarlet and gray and cheering at football games, might find a comfortable home for their undergraduate years at OSU.

Academics

There is no shortage of majors at OSU with over 175 to choose from, not to mention the hundreds of specializations within those majors, double majors, pre-professional programs, and self-designed majors through the Personalized Study Program. Students in the Arts and Sciences are required to take the General Education Curriculum, which includes distribution mandates for taking courses that fall into five categories: Skills (including writing, quantitative, and foreign language), Breadth, Historical Study, Diversity, and Issues of the Contemporary World. The strongest majors include those in the colleges/schools of business, education and human ecology, and engineering, along with the prelaw program and psychology major.

Not surprising for a school of this size, there are large classes of several hundred students. Indeed, nine percent of classes have more than 100 students. Despite these large class sizes, students say that professors are accessible if you make the effort. "If you don't take the time to get to know your professors, they won't go out of their way to get to know you," explains a student.

To help incoming freshmen navigate this enormous university, OSU's First Year Experience program runs from the summer before students arrive on campus through their entire first year. Students learn about the university's traditions and resources at the President's Convocation, which kicks off Welcome Week, Buckeye Welcome, a networking event in winter and spring, and other events. The first-year class also functions as a book club of sorts. Students read a book over the summer and come to campus to hear the author and attend book discussions. Alternative Spring Break and the Leadership Collaborative offer opportunities for community service and leadership.

Freshman seminars give students a chance to connect with faculty in small-group, discussion-based settings. Past seminars include "A Look in the Mirror: Body Image and Wellness," "Innovation and Entrepreneurship; Rocket Fuel for Creative Minds," and "Why Do Fools Fall in Love?"

The Honors and Scholars programs offer two distinct paths for motivated students. The Honors Program provides a rigorous curriculum and undergraduate research opportunities, while The Scholars Program takes learning beyond the classroom by connecting students with similar interests and career goals through living and learning communities. "The Honors Program is a good way to get into smaller classes," says a student.

OHIO STATE UNIVERSITY – COLUMBUS

Four-year public
Founded: 1870
Columbus, OH
Major city
Pop. 797,434

Address:
Student Academic Building, 281 West Lane Avenue
Columbus, OH 43210

Admissions:
614-292-3980

Financial Aid:
800-678-6440

askabuckeye@osu.edu

www.osu.edu

OHIO STATE UNIVERSITY – COLUMBUS

Students

Total enrollment: 56,387
Undergrads: 43,058
Part-time students: 10%
From out-of-state: 18%
From public schools: 85%
Male/Female: 53%/47%
Live on-campus: 25%
Off-campus employment rating: Good
Caucasian: 74%
African American: 6%
Hispanic: 3%
Asian / Pacific Islander: 5%
Native American: 0%
Mixed (2+ ethnicities): 2%
International: 8%

Academics

Calendar: Semester
Student/faculty ratio: 19:1
Class size 9 or fewer: 10%
Class size 10-29: 46%
Class size 30-49: 22%
Class size 50-99: 14%
Class size 100 or more: 9%
Returning freshmen: 92%
Six-year graduation rate: 82%

Most Popular Majors

Biology
Finance
Psychology

Admissions

Applicants: 25,816
Accepted: 16,521
Acceptance rate: 64.0%
Placed on wait list: 1,191
Average GPA: Not reported
ACT range: 26-30
SAT Math range: 610-710
SAT Reading range: 540-650
SAT Writing range: 9-41
Top 10% of class: 54%
Top 25% of class: 89%
Top 50% of class: 99%

The Denman Undergraduate Research Forum, created in 1996, showcases outstanding student research in a dozen categories. Another stand-out is the Student Investment Management Program, in which students manage a $20 million investment fund.

OSU has more than 100 study-abroad programs in over 40 different countries. Nearly 20 percent of undergrads study abroad before they graduate.

Ohio State's Career Services operates many resources for OSU community. With over 425,000 living alumni, there are plenty of opportunities for networking with fellow Buckeye alums.

Student Life

As befits a university with such a large student population, there are a huge number of student organizations. While the Poultry Science Club probably won't draw a large following, the Marching Band is a long-standing OSU tradition and is famous for performances at football games. Started in 1875, the Ohio State Men's Glee Club is the oldest organization on campus.

First-year students have a chance to kick off their college experience at Camp Buckeye, a three-day off-campus retreat that weaves outdoor team adventure activities into the framework of learning about OSU traditions and, of course, camping. Homecoming Weekend and the biggest football game of the year (against the University of Michigan Wolverines) draw huge crowds clad in scarlet and gray and buckeye necklaces, while later in the spring, the weeklong African-American Heritage Festival brings poetry, music and dance to campus. Another celebratory spring tradition is the Medieval and Renaissance Faire, which transforms South Oval into an English village replete with dancing and swordplay, merchants and minstrels, and even acrobats and storytellers. "It's an excuse to dress in costume," laughs a participant.

Although the percentage of students who participate in Greek life isn't high—six percent of men and seven percent of women—because of the size of the school, this represents an enormous Greek scene, with 47 fraternities and 22 sororities. The fraternities provide some of the biggest parties in some of the frat houses located on Indianola Avenue. "You'll see a stream of mostly underclassmen every weekend night on Indianola," says a student.

The Buckeyes' 39 varsity teams all compete at the Division I level. The university is one of only three to have won a national title in baseball, basketball, and football. Of these three sports, football is the most popular, and the team has won seven national titles. Football games involve all-day tailgating, with more than 102,000 spectators packed into Ohio Stadium, the fourth largest stadium in the NCAA. One student warns, "sellouts are a given."

OSU students have plenty of opportunities to be more than spectators in sports. The Recreation and Physical Activity Center (RPAC) in the heart of campus has 27,500 square feet of fitness space. Outdoor enthusiasts will appreciate the nearby rivers, hiking trails, and ski slopes, not to mention the 70 acres of outdoor facility space right on campus.

For off-campus activities, students say that High Street's bars and restaurants in downtown Columbus are popular. Plus, Columbus is home to "museums and an orchestra for culture" and "attracts some big-name performers" like Lil Wayne, Taylor Swift, and Keith Urban.

Freshmen are required to live on campus unless they commute from home. Ohio State operates 31 on-campus residences in three geographic clusters: South Campus, North Campus, and "The Towers." South Campus has a reputation for being louder and having more parties. There are four honors residence halls and 40 smaller living and learning environments within the residence hall system.

Student Body

With a university of this size, every interest is represented. Perhaps one commonality that unites such a splendid panoply of students is school spirit over athletics. Not every student is a rah-rah fan, but on game day, it sure feels like it. "We live, eat, and breathe football on game day," says a student.

There is low geographic diversity, with 82 percent of students hailing from Ohio, and moderate ethnic diversity with a 16 percent minority student population. While these percentages could be higher, in sheer numbers, OSU boasts plenty of diversity. In 2007, more than 22 percent of freshmen were first-generation college students (compared to the nation's average of 16 percent).

You May Not Know

- OSU was founded as a land-grant university in 1870 under the name of Ohio Agricultural and Mechanical College.
- The "Buckeye Bullet," an electric car designed by a team of engineering students, has traveled at more than 300 miles per hour, a record for an electric vehicle.
- Ohio State's marching band is the "largest all-brass and percussion band in the world."

Distinguished Alumni

Dorothy Canfield Fischer, education reformer, social activist, and author; Yang Huiyan, Chinese real estate developer; Roy Lichtenstein, American Pop artist; Jesse Owens, four-time Olympic gold medalist in track and field.

Admissions and Financial Aid

According to Ohio State University, admissions officers emphasize a rigorous high school curriculum, high school academic performance, and standardized test scores. The admissions office also values writing skills as shown through exam scores. The first batch of admissions decisions are sent out in mid-December, after which decisions are given on a rolling basis 10-12 weeks after OSU receives a completed application.

OSU offers a number of merit scholarships, most of which are competitive, available for 12 academic quarters. Two scholarships are the Morrill Scholars Program, which covers full expenses, and the Cooperative Scholarship Housing, given on the basis of academic merit and demonstrated financial need. The Land Grant Opportunity Scholarship for Ohio Residents covers the full in-state cost of education as a part of a program to support one student from a low-income background in each of Ohio's 88 counties.

OHIO STATE UNIVERSITY – COLUMBUS

Highlights

Admissions Criteria
Academic criteria:
Grades: ☆ ☆ ☆
Difficulty of class schedule: ☆ ☆ ☆
Class rank: ☆ ☆ ☆
Standardized test scores: ☆ ☆ ☆
Teacher recommendations: ☆
Personal statement: ☆ ☆
Non-academic criteria considered:
Interview
Extracurricular activities
Special talents, interests, abilities
Character/personal qualities
Volunteer work
Work experience
Geographical location
Minority affiliation

Deadlines
Early Action: No
Early Decision: No
Regular Action: Rolling admissions
Common Application: Accepted

Financial Aid
In-state tuition: $10,010
Out-of-state tuition: $25,726
Room: Varies
Board: Varies
Books: $1,248
Freshmen receiving need-based aid: 53%
Undergrads rec. need-based aid: 52%
Avg. % of need met by financial aid: 64%
Avg. aid package (freshmen): $12,201
Avg. aid package (undergrads): $11,671
Avg. debt upon graduation: $26,409

School Spirit
Mascot: Brutus Buckeye
Colors: Scarlet and gray
Song: *Fight the Team*

OHIO UNIVERSITY

Overview

Ohio University (OU) is a big university—22,000 undergrads who know how to party. In fact, the school ranks as the #3 party school in the nation according to the Princeton Review. The location leaves something to be desired, unless you're an aficionado of the relatively rural, Appalachian scene. Athens, Ohio is a small town and off-campus activities for the most part have a rural flavor. Still, those looking for music and theater won't suffer total cultural starvation. And if you're interested in the fields of journalism or engineering, you'll find the school a plethora of opportunities.

Academically, the school has its strengths and weaknesses. The roughly 220 students in the Honors Tutorial College get a unique chance to work one-on-one or in small groups. Other students have relatively small classes for such a large university, but the level of challenge varies greatly by course. The E.W. Scripps School of Journalism is well-respected.

OU could be a good deal if you're a native Ohioan with a penchant for parties. But if you don't fit at least part of that bill, you may not be satisfied.

Academics

OU has a 32-credit general education requirement in which students take courses in applied science and mathematics, cross-cultural perspectives, humanities and literature, natural sciences, and social sciences. Unlike many other schools, Ohio also requires students to take courses in fine arts. If you haven't flexed your artistic skills since your coloring book days, there's no need to worry—you can always get by with art history. Seniors must also complete a capstone class or project. General education requirements amount to about one full year of coursework altogether.

There are 157 majors at Ohio U. Programs in engineering and communications are strong. *Writer's Digest* ranked the E.W. Scripps School of Journalism one of the top five journalism programs in the country. The McClure School of Information and Telecommunications is the second of its kind in the country. If you're interested in experiential learning, you might find yourself among the 250 McClure students who work in real radio and TV stations.

The level of academic rigor is a mixed bag, depending on the courses you take. "If you're in the sciences or engineering, you're going to have a rougher time," says one student. Eighty-six percent of classes have fewer than 50 students. Numbers get smaller as students climb the academic ladder since most of the bigger classes are introductory courses for freshmen.

The Honors Tutorial College, modeled after Oxford and Cambridge, allows about 220 students to learn one-on-one from faculty or in small groups. It's a great chance to craft an individualized, challenging education. The catch? Admission is highly competitive, involving essays beyond the normal application, high SAT scores, and often supplemental material like a creative portfolio, writing sample, or recommendation letters. You can't apply if you are undecided about your major.

Students in learning communities take courses in common and sometimes live together. Peer-led tutoring labs are a major perk of living communities for biological sciences, math, and chemistry majors.

Those ready to take on the world can get a two-year certificate (not a degree) from the Global Leadership Center. In GLC classes, active projects on global issues replace traditional coursework. Past stand-outs have included collaborating with students at the University of Liberia to study successes and failures of microfinance programs in Africa and working on postwar reconstruction in Iraq.

There are 52 study-abroad programs, about half of them in Europe. The university also sends interns to the National Assembly of Wales.

Ohio University has the typical career services offerings, with a unique teacher recruitment job fair in addition to general career fairs offered in the fall, winter, and summer.

Student Life

OU ranked #3 in Princeton Review's list of Top Party Schools. Many of you can stop reading here. You might also like to know that OU has an unofficial block party each spring called "Palmerfest" where the partying gets so raucous that the event often ends in arson and arrests. "Palmerfest gets shut down by the riot police every year," comments one student.

If you're still reading, you'll be pleased to hear about some fun, wholesome traditions at Ohio U. Millfest and Halloween are both blowout parties similar to Palmerfest. For those seeking tamer entertainment, the International Street Fair is a popular event. After a week of international programming—from movie screenings to international cuisine tastings to service projects—the street fair showcases student and community organizations. Students can sample food and check out crafts while taking in music and dance performances.

Greek life is a fairly big part of the OU scene, with eight percent of men and 12 percent of women pledging. There are 18 social frats and 10 social sororities on campus. Additionally, there are 420 student organizations to choose from, the most popular options being Comedy for the Masses, Hip-hop Congress, Jitterbug Club, and Stand up Comedian Club.

Ohio U's athletic environment is a bit out of the ordinary, with basketball drawing more attention than football. The men's basketball team has been in 13 NCAA tournaments. Baseball, volleyball, and women's swimming and diving are also strong. Intramural sports make a good showing, including quirky options like walleyball, sandball, and broomball.

Athens, Ohio is a small town that takes pride in its Appalachian traditions. While a lot of the events off campus have a distinctly rural flavor—barbeque festivals, farmer's markets, etc.—the music and theater scene is better than you might expect. Courtside Pizza and Sports Bar is a popular destination for all, as are more upscale restaurants uptown. Outdoorsy types can hit "Old Man's Cave" at Hocking Hills State Park.

Freshmen and sophomores are required to live on campus, but many move off campus as upperclassmen. There are—count 'em!—42 residence halls and one apartment complex on three separate greens at Ohio U. Several dorms are for freshmen only. Single dorm rooms are few and far between.

Student Body

Naturally there are exceptions, but in general, OU students aren't as highly driven regarding academics as at other more selective colleges. Only 16 percent of students graduated in the top 10 percent of their high school class. Still, students feel there is quality education at OU. "If you are really focused on studying," a student explains, "you will find your niche. You just won't be in the majority."

The level of ethnic diversity at OU is low with 10 percent of students identifying as minority. Geographic diversity is very low

OHIO UNIVERSITY

Highlights

Students
Total enrollment: 27,402
Undergrads: 22,685
Freshmen: 3,888
Part-time students: 26%
From out-of-state: 12%
From public schools: 83%
Male/Female: 40%/60%
Live on-campus: 40%
In fraternities: 8%
In sororities: 12%
Off-campus employment rating: Good
Caucasian: 84%
African American: 5%
Hispanic: 2%
Asian / Pacific Islander: 1%
Native American: 0%
Mixed (2+ ethnicities): 2%
International: 4%

Academics
Calendar: Semester
Student/faculty ratio: 19:1
Class size 9 or fewer: 9%
Class size 10-29: 52%
Class size 30-49: 23%
Class size 50-99: 10%
Class size 100 or more: 5%
Returning freshmen: 79%
Six-year graduation rate: 64%

Most Popular Majors
Nursing
Health administration
Communication studies

Admissions
Applicants: 17,466
Accepted: 13,571
Acceptance rate: 77.7%
Placed on wait list: 440
Enrolled from wait list: 113
Average GPA: 3.4
ACT range: 21-26
SAT Math range: 490-610
SAT Reading range: 480-590
SAT Writing range: 3-17
Top 10% of class: 16%
Top 25% of class: 42%
Top 50% of class: 81%

509

College Profiles

OHIO UNIVERSITY

Admissions Criteria

Academic criteria:
Grades: ☆ ☆ ☆
Difficulty of class schedule: ☆ ☆ ☆
Class rank: ☆ ☆
Standardized test scores: ☆ ☆ ☆
Teacher recommendations: ☆
Personal statement: ☆ ☆
Non-academic criteria considered:
Extracurricular activities
Special talents, interests, abilities
Character/personal qualities
Volunteer work
Work experience
Geographical location
Minority affiliation
Alumni relationship

Deadlines

Early Action: No
Early Decision: No
Regular Action: February 1 (priority)
Notification of admission by: September 15
Common Application: Not accepted

Financial Aid

In-state tuition: $10,380
Out-of-state tuition: $19,344
Room: $5,846
Board: $5,428
Books: $886
Freshmen receiving need-based aid: 60%
Undergrads rec. need-based aid: 55%
Avg. % of need met by financial aid: 53%
Avg. aid package (freshmen): $8,562
Avg. aid package (undergrads): $8,458
Avg. debt upon graduation: $27,060

School Spirit

Mascot: Bobcats
Colors: Hunter green and white
Song: *Stand Up and Cheer*

also with only 12 percent of students from out of state. Those who aren't native Ohioans might feel out of place.

Distinguished Alumni

Matt Lauer, *Today Show* host; Clarence Page, syndicated columnist; George Voinovich, Ohio Senator.

You May Not Know

- OU is one of the most haunted universities in the United States, notably the Alpha Omicron Phi sorority building and Brown House.
- OU students consume 305,910 lbs of French fries at campus dining halls.
- The university has a nine-hole golf course, which makes a fun outing for students.

Admissions and Financial Aid

Academic factors weigh the most heavily at OU with attention paid not just to grades but also to the difficulty level of courses you've taken. The college pays strong attention to academic performance in the junior year. Selective programs at the university and their class rank and ACT/SAT score guidelines are as follows: business (top 20 percent, 24/1100), engineering and technology (top 30 percent, 21/990), journalism (top 15 percent, 25/1140), media arts (top 40 percent, 23/1060), visual communication (top 30 percent, 21/990), and the Honors Tutorial College (top 10 percent, 30/1300).

The Gateway Award Program has merit-based and need-based awards, and the Gateway Excellence Scholarship for academic merit covers four years of in-state tuition. The Gateway Scholarship provides amounts from $500 up to full in-state tuition depending on GPA and SAT/ACT scores. The Gateway Grant is on a sliding scale according to merit and need, and the Gateway Trustee Award provides $6,000 a year to be applied to the out-of-state surcharge.

OHIO WESLEYAN UNIVERSITY

Overview

Located 30 miles north of Columbus, Ohio, Wesleyan University (OWU, affectionately known as "oh-woo") occupies more than 200 acres in the small town of Delaware, Ohio. The campus features architecture ranging from historic Colonial to modern, all spread neatly along landscaped paths. The first building on campus, Elliot Hall, is the state's oldest collegiate Greek Revival building, while the castle-like University Hall on the academic quad is an elegant example of Neoromanesque architecture.

This small private liberal arts school historically has had a reputation as a party school, but it is working to become known more for academic offerings. The school is recognized for its preparation of students for graduate or professional school; one third of graduates go on to further studies. Founded in 1842 by Methodist leaders, religion is still prominent on campus—there are three chapels for students to use—though in an interfaith, nonsectarian context. The Methodist tie-in also explains Ohio Wesleyan's unusual athletic mascot: the Battling Bishops.

Not everyone will feel inspired at a small school in a small community, though luckily, a number of study-abroad (or study-in-bigger-U.S.-cities) programs provide a portal into the broader world. The large international student population also lends diversity to the campus. Students study hard, but know how to have fun and like to stay politically engaged (the proximity to Ohio's state capital, Columbus, may influence this) to boot.

Academics

Ohio Wesleyan offers Bachelor of Arts, Bachelor of Fine Arts, and Bachelor of Music degrees through 22 academic departments and nine interdisciplinary programs. There are also combined degree programs over five years in engineering, physical therapy, and optometry.

Distribution Requirements fall into four categories known as "Groups": Social Sciences; Natural Sciences, Mathematics, and Computer Science; Humanities/Literature; and Arts. There is also a foreign language requirement. "The requirements are pretty manageable," one student notes. Courses are challenging, but students say they are "cooperative rather than competitive." At such a small school, it is not uncommon for students to get to know their professors. Strong programs include economics, microbiology, and psychology.

The Leland F. and Helen Schubert Honors Program can span four years of a student's undergraduate career. There is a GPA requirement, and University Honors students must pass a comprehensive exam in their major. Honors tutorials, independent study, and honors courses make for a more rigorous academic program. The Schubert Honors Scholarship, valued at $17,000, is renewable over four years.

The annual Sagan National Colloquium addresses an issue of international importance. Past colloquia speakers have included Gloria Steinem, who headlined "Women, Activism, and Change on a Global Level," as well as President Gerald Ford and author Kurt Vonnegut.

The Woltemade Center provides a wide array of opportunities for economics majors. Corns Business and Entrepreneurship Scholars complete at least two internships, either during the school year or summer, along with a Senior Research Project. Corns Scholars in their junior and senior years can apply for a $5,000 scholarship. There are also grants for summer internships and research with faculty.

Students in the Summer Science Research Program have 10 weeks to conduct research with faculty. Past topics have included the distribution of native bird and soil bacteria, the behavior of stickleback fish, and the memory capacity of younger and older adults.

OHIO WESLEYAN UNIVERSITY

Students
Total enrollment: 1,821
Undergrads: 1,821
Freshmen: 560
Part-time students: 1%
From out-of-state: 47%
Male/Female: 45%/55%
Live on-campus: 90%
In fraternities: 40%
In sororities: 32%
Off-campus employment rating: Excellent
Caucasian: 76%
African American: 5%
Hispanic: 3%
Asian / Pacific Islander: 2%
Native American: 0%
Mixed (2+ ethnicities): 3%
International: 8%

Academics
Calendar: Semester
Student/faculty ratio: 11:1
Class size 9 or fewer: 26%
Class size 10-29: 64%
Class size 30-49: 9%
Class size 50-99: -
Class size 100 or more: -
Returning freshmen: 83%
Six-year graduation rate: 68%
Graduates who immediately go to graduate school: 32%
Graduates who immediately enter career related to major: 80%

Most Popular Majors
Psychology
Economics management
Politics/government

Admissions
Applicants: 3,835
Accepted: 2,823
Acceptance rate: 73.6%
Placed on wait list: 182
Enrolled from wait list: 77
Average GPA: 3.5
ACT range: 23-28
SAT Math range: 520-640
SAT Reading range: 510-620
SAT Writing range: 6-29
Top 10% of class: 32%
Top 25% of class: 63%
Top 50% of class: 89%

OWU offers study-abroad programs in more than 20 countries. The New York Arts Program offers fine arts, theater, and English majors a semester of study in NYC while apprenticing with professional artists or organizations. The Wesleyan in Washington Program includes a full-time internship in DC—some students may land internships at CNN or the White House. "Interning in DC was a once-in-a-lifetime opportunity," one student reminisces.

The Office of Career Services helps student find internships and jobs, prepare for grad school, and even plan a gap year. The office also tracks student outcomes. In 2011, 99 percent of students reported being either employed full-time or enrolled in a full-time graduate program.

Student Life

OWU has almost 100 clubs and organizations that cover a range of categories. Arts and media organizations include the improv comedy troupe, Babbling Bishops, and two a cappella groups. The weekly student-run newspaper, *The Transcript*, holds the honor of being the oldest continuously published college newspaper in the country. Special interest clubs range from anime lovers to water polo players. There are three chapels, a number of religious groups, and four religious chaplains, which makes for a vibrant religious life on campus.

Among the traditions at OWU is the Mock Convention, which was first held in 1884 and has occurred in every presidential election year since 1920. The convention informs the university and local community about key issues in the coming election. It's not all serious, as Oprah garnered 24 percent of the vote for vice president in a recent mock election. "It's an event that gets everyone excited," remarks a student.

Other campus events include football and music. Homecoming draws crowds of students with a bonfire, 5K run, and of course a football game against one of OWU's traditional rivals. In December, the President's Gala offers a stylish evening of music, dance, and fine food. Two events, Unity through Music and Springfest, bring together musical acts in a carnival style atmosphere.

Greek life dates back to OWU's first fraternity in 1853. The Greek population has fluctuated throughout the years: fraternities were banned in 1870 and reinstated in the 1920s; in the 1960s and 1990s, more than half the student population belonged to a fraternity or sorority. Today, more than 30 percent of the student body belongs to one of the 17 fraternities and sororities. "The Greek organizations play a big role in campus life," one student notes.

The Battling Bishops have 21 teams (10 men's, 11 women's) that compete at the Division III level. Men's soccer, lacrosse, and golf are the most competitive. A dozen intramural sports are offered each year, such as flag football in the fall and sand volleyball in the spring.

Off campus, Delaware offers low-key recreation, while Columbus is a 30-minute drive away for bigger city opportunities. In the area surrounding campus, there are lakes and farms for those who enjoy rustic scenery.

All freshmen live in the dorms, and all dorms except one are co-ed. Students have an opportunity to live in Small Living Units, or SLUs, which are themed houses of about 10 to 15 students reserved for upperclassmen. Current houses include the Tree House (focused on environmentalism), Women's House, Creative Arts House, and Inter-Faith House.

Student Body

The student body "leans right" politically. Students take their academics seriously but they also like to have fun. "We are balanced," one student says. There is moderate ethnic diversity, and 13 percent of the student body is multicultural; the Office of Multicultural Student Affairs offers programs, events, and support for diversity. OWU has moderate geographic diversity, with about half of students hailing from out of state. Students come from 47 U.S. states and 50 foreign countries, and international students make up nine percent of the student body.

You May Not Know

- The "Battling Bishops" nickname goes back to 1925. Before that, OWU's teams were known as "The Red and Black" and "The Methodists."
- Ohio Wesleyan is affiliated with the United Methodist Church, and many bishops from the Church have come from the ranks of OWU.
- Mildred Sisk, an alumna of OWU, was the first American woman convicted of treason. She completed her bachelor's degree after serving a 12-year sentence.

Distinguished Alumni

Charles Fairbanks, 26th Vice President of the United States; Mary King, activist who worked with Dr. Martin Luther King, Jr.; Wendie Malick, Emmy-nominated actress; Branch Rickey, baseball manager who signed former professional baseball player Jackie Robinson.

Admissions and Financial Aid

According to the university, "a college-preparatory background is essential to enter OWU." A teacher recommendation is suggested but not required. There is no application fee for applications submitted online. It is possible to defer admission for one year, and students also have the option to begin their bachelor's degree program midyear.

All students who apply for admissions are automatically considered for merit-based scholarships. Exceptional first-year students can receive the Leland F. and Helen Schubert Scholarship for four years. Two full-tuition awards honor outstanding women leaders. There are also limited departmental awards, along with awards for students with a sibling at OWU or a connection to an OWU alumnus.

OHIO WESLEYAN UNIVERSITY

Highlights

Admissions Criteria
Academic criteria:
Grades: ☆ ☆ ☆
Difficulty of class schedule: ☆ ☆ ☆
Class rank: ☆ ☆
Standardized test scores: ☆ ☆
Teacher recommendations: ☆ ☆ ☆
Personal statement: ☆ ☆ ☆
Non-academic criteria considered:
Interview
Extracurricular activities
Special talents, interests, abilities
Character/personal qualities
Volunteer work
Work experience
State of residency
Geographical location
Minority affiliation
Alumni relationship

Deadlines
Early Action: January 15
Early Decision: November 15
Regular Action: Rolling admissions
Common Application: Accepted

Financial Aid
In-state tuition: $40,250
Out-of-state tuition: $40,250
Room: $5,690
Board: $4,980
Books: $1,100
Freshmen receiving need-based aid: 71%
Undergrads rec. need-based aid: 65%
Avg. % of need met by financial aid: 80%
Avg. aid package (freshmen): $28,940
Avg. aid package (undergrads): $27,376
Avg. debt upon graduation: $30,900

School Spirit
Mascot: Battling Bishops
Colors: Red and black

OREGON STATE
UNIVERSITY

Four-year public
Founded: 1868
Corvallis, OR
Large town
Pop. 54,674

Address:
104 Kerr Administra-
tion Building
Corvallis, OR
97331

Admissions:
800-291-4192

Financial Aid:
541-737-2241

osuadmit@oregon-
state.edu

www.oregonstate.edu

OREGON STATE UNIVERSITY

Overview

Known for its accessibility to students and breadth of solid academics, Oregon State University is a very large public school in the Pacific Northwest. Despite its relatively overwhelming size, community feel and a healthy level of school spirit permeate campus.

OSU is situated in Corvallis, a college town located in Willamette Valley, the heart of Oregon's agriculture country, just 80 miles south of Portland and 50 miles east of the Pacific Ocean. The campus features a range of architecture from ivy-covered buildings to contemporary structures.

Academics

OSU offers 249 majors to students. Some of the strongest programs are engineering, agricultural sciences, biology, and forestry. The forestry program is particularly notable, managing 14,000 acres of forests and located near the facilities of the U.S. Forest Service, EPA, and U.S. Geological Survey. "If you want to go into forestry, this is the place to be," remarks a student.

According to the university, OSU's Baccalaureate Core "represents what the OSU faculty believes is the foundation for students' further understanding of the modern world." Students are required to take courses in the following categories: skills, perspective, difference, power and discrimination, synthesis, and writing. The goal of the core requirements is to inspire students to synthesize ideas, think creatively, and understand the interrelationships of major societal issues.

A significant portion of students' classes their first two years are filled with large lecture courses that fulfill the Baccalaureate Core requirements. While students have noted that some of these classes are not overly challenging, options are limited and classes are large. Some students have commented that they feel lost in the sheer mass of other students around them. However—despite the large size of the student body—students still find professors to be accessible and willing to help when needed. "You have to make the effort," says a student.

The University Honors College provides motivated students with special opportunities. UHC students travel the world researching, studying, and earning a second degree in international studies. Other special academic opportunities include the chance to take courses at the Hatfield Marine Science Center, a large collaboration of partners, with a combined budget exceeding $37 million. Students can work alongside HMSC staff and become involved in research and management of the marine environment. HMSC's mission is to "improve scientific understanding of marine systems, coastal processes, and resources, and apply this knowledge to social, economic, and environmental issues."

The University's Exploratory Studies Program provides students with academic advising and career assistance. Students can declare the UESP as their "academic home" while they explore their interests and the work environment that would be most suited to them.

Oregon State University offers international experience through more than 200 study-abroad programs, internships, and bachelor's degrees in international studies. More than 400 students study abroad each year, some of whom receive scholarships to do so.

Student Life

Some of the most popular of the 300 official student organizations on campus include the Flying Club, Salsa Club, and Cycling Club. The Flying Club owns four aircraft and is "one of the oldest continuously active flying clubs in the U.S."

School spirit soars each year when OSU competes against its long-lived rival, the University of Oregon. Known as Civil War Football Weekend, the event is one of the most contested rivalries in the nation. "There's nothing else but football on our minds during the Game," says a student. Fall Festival is another popular event each year on campus, featuring a race, artist booths, food and wine vendors, and live music. University Sing, a competition between Greeks, is also very popular in engaging students each year.

Greek life at Oregon State is visible, but not overwhelmingly dominant. There are 25 social fraternities and 14 fraternity houses on campus and 14 social sororities and 12 sorority houses. Overall, approximately 10 percent of the student body joins Greek life. "If you want it to be big, Greek life can be," states a student.

With 17 teams (seven men's and 10 women's) competing in Division I, athletics is a notable part of the OSU experience. In fact, the university is home to the oldest marching band in the PAC-10. Football is the school's most popular sport and competes on a national level. More recently, baseball has been strong, while wrestling is a perennial contender. For those who'd like to participate in intramurals sports, there are over 35 leagues and tournaments offered throughout the academic year.

Off campus, students enjoy the fun town of Corvallis—filled with good dining and entertaining. Mountains and beaches are nearby, which provide Oregon State with ample opportunities for outdoor activities. "It's an outdoor heaven," says a student.

Though not strictly enforced, all freshmen are "expected" to live on campus. In addition to traditional dorms and Greek houses, there are also other housing options, including co-op houses and off-campus apartments. "The dorms are not the best but they're not the worst either," comments one student.

Student Body

Politically, students at OSU tend to lean towards the conservative side. They enjoy many extracurriculars and many tend to be the outdoorsy type. With a vibrant level of school spirit and such a large student body, there is a niche for practically everyone.

With 21 percent minorities, the university is high in ethnic diversity; but with just 24 percent of students from out of state, it is low in geographic diversity.

You May Not Know

- Maraschino cherries were accidentally invented by students at OSU during a science experiment.
- OSU was the third public university in the U.S. to admit women.
- OSU is the only college in the country with a nuclear power facility, a fact that attracts students from all over the world.

Distinguished Alumni

Chad Javon Johnson, NFL player; Michael Lowry, actor; Linus Pauling, recipient of two Nobel Peace Prizes; Leonard Shoen, founder of U-Haul.

OREGON STATE UNIVERSITY

Highlights

Students
Total enrollment: 26,393
Undergrads: 21,812
Freshmen: 4,640
Part-time students: 18%
From out-of-state: 24%
Male/Female: 53%/47%
Live on-campus: 20%
In fraternities: 12%
In sororities: 9%
Off-campus employment rating: Excellent
Caucasian: 69%
African American: 1%
Hispanic: 7%
Asian / Pacific Islander: 7%
Native American: 1%
Mixed (2+ ethnicities): 5%
International: 6%

Academics
Calendar: Quarter
Student/faculty ratio: 22:1
Class size 9 or fewer: 8%
Class size 10-29: 50%
Class size 30-49: 18%
Class size 50-99: 14%
Class size 100 or more: 9%
Returning freshmen: 81%
Six-year graduation rate: 60%

Most Popular Majors
Human development/family sciences
Liberal studies
Business administration

Admissions
Applicants: 12,330
Accepted: 9,720
Acceptance rate: 78.8%
Average GPA: 3.6
ACT range: 21-27
SAT Math range: 490-630
SAT Reading range: 480-600
SAT Writing range: 3-17
Top 10% of class: 26%
Top 25% of class: 55%
Top 50% of class: 90%

515

College Profiles

OREGON STATE UNIVERSITY

Admissions Criteria

Academic criteria:
Grades: ☆ ☆ ☆
Difficulty of class schedule: ☆ ☆ ☆
Class rank: ☆ ☆
Standardized test scores: ☆
Teacher recommendations: ☆
Personal statement: ☆ ☆ ☆
Non-academic criteria considered:
Interview
Extracurricular activities
Special talents, interests, abilities
Character/personal qualities
Volunteer work
Work experience
State of residency

Deadlines

Early Action: February 1
Early Decision: No
Regular Action: Rolling admissions
Common Application: Not accepted

Financial Aid

In-state tuition: $6,876
Out-of-state tuition: $22,068
Room: Varies
Board: Varies
Books: $1,965
Freshmen receiving need-based aid: 59%
Undergrads rec. need-based aid: 58%
Avg. % of need met by financial aid: 53%
Avg. aid package (freshmen): $10,651
Avg. aid package (undergrads): $10,515

School Spirit

Mascot: Benny the Beaver
Colors: Orange and black
Song: *OSU Fight Song*

Admissions and Financial Aid

In order for students to be considered for acceptance into Oregon State, they must have a minimum cumulative GPA of 3.0 and have completed 14 subject area courses. In addition to grades and SAT scores, the admissions office considers a variety of other factors such as a student's creativity, initiative, intellectual curiosity, unusual talent, and substantial experience with other cultures.

OSU offers the Presidential Scholarship, $6,000 renewable for four years, which is given to incoming freshmen who are residents of Oregon with a 3.87 GPA or over 1900 on their SAT. The Provost Scholarship, varying in amount from $4,000-$7,000 for four renewable years, is available for non-resident or transfer students with a GPA of 3.75 and SAT of 1800 or above. Students with a documented disability, a member of an ethnic minority community or low-income status can apply for the Diversity Achievement Award to receive up to $1,800 for each year of enrollment.

PENNSYLVANIA STATE UNIVERSITY – UNIVERSITY PARK

PENNSYLVANIA STATE UNIVERSITY – UNIVERSITY PARK

Four-year public
Founded: 1855
University Park, PA
Large town
Pop. 42,034

Address:
University Park Campus
University Park, PA 16802

Admissions:
814-865-5471

Financial Aid:
814-865-6301

admissions@psu.edu

www.psu.edu

Overview

From its founding in 1855, Pennsylvania State University has been rapidly expanding as a place that values both scholarship and community involvement. The school was founded as an agricultural institute and has evolved into a research university with twenty undergraduate campuses.

University Park is the largest of Penn State's campuses with a total enrollment of more than 45,000 students. Its location near the center of the state—seventy miles northwest of Harrisburg—makes it the most attractive campus for applicants, contributing to the lowest acceptance rate of any Penn State campus.

The campus itself sprawls over 15,984 acres in the State College Borough of Pennsylvania, known for its beautiful foliage and ranked as one of the least stressful places to live in the United States. It's also known as being a great "singles" city, with 65 percent of the population between 18-24 years of age and many enrolled at Penn State. The university provides on-campus housing in 6,975 units that can accommodate 13,656 students, with options that include co-ed and single-sex dorms, sorority houses, apartments, disabled, and international housing. Penn State has been rated as a top party school; that said, there's not much in the way of urban surroundings, so university life becomes the students' universe.

Academics

Penn State offers a multitude of majors and fields of study within an environment conducive to more than just partying. The university has 2,392 full-time and 353 part-time faculty members and a 17:1 student-to-faculty ratio. With a school this size there will inevitably be large classes, but the most common is between 20 and 29 students, and class sizes tend to become smaller with progression to upper division courses. "Especially after your freshman year, you don't get lost in your classes," says a student.

The university has a General Education core curriculum which composes about one third of the undergraduate coursework. The curriculum is made up of skills courses to sharpen quantitative and communication abilities, a writing course, and required humanities, foreign cultures, and sciences courses. There are 160 majors to choose from, but double majors are allowed, as is independent study. Penn State is known for a few stand-out programs, including business, chemistry, computer science, engineering, environmental science, psychology, and sociology.

First-year seminars are given to help accustom new students to the university. These are generally survey courses and are meant to give students perspective on what's available to them. Introduction to Business is a popular seminar course that feeds into the equally popular business major. Some other interesting and perhaps less conventional seminars include things like intrapersonal communication, and introduction to digital music. Additionally, all undergraduates are given the opportunity to do research in their field of study and work with faculty members on projects. Summer research is a popular option and offers a stipend for work done during the summer break.

For students of exceptional ability, the Schreyer Honors College offers an honors program with specialized classes taught by select faculty. The program also provides advising and grants for study abroad, service learning, and internships. Students must submit a supplemental application to be selected, and the program is open to only 300 undergraduates each year.

Penn State students have the opportunity to spend time on two campuses during their undergraduate experience. The 2+2 program allows students to transfer to a different campus after the first two years. This option has been historically popular, with 60 percent of the student body opting to move.

PENNSYLVANIA STATE UNIVERSITY – UNIVERSITY PARK

Students
Total enrollment: 45,783
Undergrads: 39,192
Part-time students: 3%
From out-of-state: 40%
Male/Female: 54%/46%
Live on-campus: 36%
In fraternities: 14%
In sororities: 14%
Off-campus employment rating: Excellent
Caucasian: 73%
African American: 4%
Hispanic: 5%
Asian / Pacific Islander: 5%
Native American: 0%
Mixed (2+ ethnicities): 2%
International: 8%

Academics
Calendar: Semester
Student/faculty ratio: 17:1
Class size 9 or fewer: 16%
Class size 10-29: 50%
Class size 30-49: 19%
Class size 50-99: 8%
Class size 100 or more: 7%
Returning freshmen: 92%
Six-year graduation rate: 87%
Graduates who immediately enter career
   related to major: 64%

Most Popular Majors
Business
Engineering
Communications

Admissions
Applicants: 47,552
Accepted: 25,772
Acceptance rate: 54.2%
Average GPA: 3.6
ACT range: 25-29
SAT Math range: 560-670
SAT Reading range: 530-630
SAT Writing range: 8-38
Top 10% of class: 41%
Top 25% of class: 84%
Top 50% of class: 98%

Studying abroad is something that many students end up looking back on as a major turning point in how they view the world. Penn State recognizes this and offers study-abroad programs in 51 different countries. Advisors help at each step of the process and many students take advantage of the program. The university is ranked eighth nationally for students that participate in the study-abroad program.

Penn State offers a plethora of resources in its Career Services department for life after graduation; for example, students can receive interview coaching and resume advice. Employers are invited to interview students at Penn State for both internship and full-time positions. Some major corporations such as Bank of America, DuPont, IBM, and others regularly interview on campus. The university maintains an alumni network that students also have access to for networking.

Student Life

Most students at Penn State live off campus, which makes the social scene a bit less centralized than at other colleges. There isn't necessarily going to be the "floor life" where those who live together in a dorm bond, but that doesn't mean students don't have fun. "At all hours of the day, there's something going on," says a student.

There are many popular events at Penn State. Several thousand students dance and stand for 48 hours as a part of the charity-benefit Dance Marathon (THON). The student section at home football games is one of the largest in the nation, and football games are immensely popular. And the annual Pennsylvania Center Stage offers performances by the professional arm of the Penn State School of Theatre.

There are 800 student organizations, and it goes without saying that Greek life is a large part of Penn State's social scene. There are 56 social fraternities and 31 social sororities on campus; a lot of these have their own houses and play host to parties and events. The other student organizations include special interest groups, theatre, music, and journalism, among others.

Penn State is also a member of the NCAA (Division I) for sports and a member of the Big Ten. The football team has won two national titles. Despite the 2012 conviction of former assistant coach Jerry Sandusky for sexual abuse and the subsequent $60 million fine and four-year postseason ban, football games are very popular and home games are played in Beaver Stadium, the second-largest stadium in the country, seating more than 107,000. Besides football, the university is also strong in women's volleyball, men's and women's fencing, women's rugby, and men's gymnastics. For those who may not make the school's official teams, there are intramural teams available for most sports.

Housing on campus is mandatory as a freshman. Suites are an on-campus option after the first year, but many students decide to move off campus. There are a good number of things to do off campus that ensure your social life doesn't suffer: the downtown area of State College borough is very close to campus and hosts activities like the Central Pennsylvania Festival of the Arts, Blue and White Weekend, and the Homecoming Parade. The area is also peppered with restaurants and bars sure to entertain off-campus dwellers.

Student Body

It is true that Penn State University is sometimes flagged as a "party school," but with various study-abroad options, research opportunities, and the honors program, suffice to say all students don't fit the party mold. "We aren't all hard partiers," remarks a student.

There are students from myriad ethnic and socioeconomic backgrounds. The minority population is moderate (16 percent), and the university represents 50 states and 131 countries.

You May Not Know

- Penn State won its first of two Football National Championships in 1982 in the Sugar Bowl.
- One in 122 Americans with a college degree is an alumnus of Penn State.
- More than a thousand corporations and government agencies interview annually at the University Park campus.

Distinguished Alumni

William Schreyer, Chairman and CEO of Merrill Lynch; Fred M. Waring, musician, co-inventor of the Waring Blender.

Admissions and Financial Aid

Admissions to Penn State – University Park is considerably more selective than other Penn State campuses. Because of its central location, it's the campus most applicants want. Furthermore, it was ranked as one of *Kiplinger's* 100 best values in public colleges. While roughly two-thirds of the decision process is based on grades alone, admission is based on various factors, including GPA, standardized test scores, and intangibles like the personal statement and activities. These last two items are not required for admission, but are recommended to increase the admission committee's understanding of you as an applicant.

Applicants may complete applications online. Admissions decisions are also communicated through the web. For applicants to the Honors College, recommendations are an additional requirement.

Penn State offers five school-sponsored scholarships (ranging from $1,000-$2,000) each year to National Merit finalists naming Penn State as their first choice school. The $3,500 Academic Excellence Scholarship is also awarded annually to Honors College entrants.

PENNSYLVANIA STATE UNIVERSITY – UNIVERSITY PARK

Highlights

Admissions Criteria
Academic criteria:
Grades: ☆ ☆ ☆
Difficulty of class schedule: ☆ ☆ ☆
Class rank: ☆
Standardized test scores: ☆ ☆ ☆
Teacher recommendations: ☆
Personal statement: ☆
Non-academic criteria considered:
Extracurricular activities
Special talents, interests, abilities
Character/personal qualities
Volunteer work
Work experience
State of residency
Alumni relationship

Deadlines
Early Action: No
Early Decision: No
Regular Action: Rolling admissions
Common Application: Not accepted

Financial Aid
In-state tuition: $16,090
Out-of-state tuition: $28,664
Room: $3,660
Board: $3,790
Books: $1,536
Freshmen receiving need-based aid: 47%
Undergrads rec. need-based aid: 51%
Avg. % of need met by financial aid: 61%
Avg. aid package (freshmen): $9,481
Avg. aid package (undergrads): $10,552
Avg. debt upon graduation: $35,100

School Spirit
Mascot: The Nittany Lion
Colors: Blue and white
Song: *Hail to the Lion*

PEPPERDINE UNIVERSITY

Overview

Overlooking the Pacific Ocean in picturesque Malibu, California, Pepperdine University offers a breathtaking educational experience to those who attend. A medium-sized private university with almost 3,500 undergraduate students, Pepperdine draws students from all over the U.S. and from more than 90 countries worldwide, boasting catered and specialized commitment to each and every one of its students in both academia and development of general life skills.

Academics at Pepperdine are split up into five colleges, with Seaver College taking on the responsibility for the education of undergraduates. The heart of academic pursuits at Seaver College is total development of the student as a person; therefore, courses are offered in letters, arts, and sciences. The college is renowned for its high academic standards and unique international opportunities, with undergraduate programs in Florence, Heidelberg, London, Lausanne, Shanghai, and Buenos Aires.

Pepperdine is a Christian institution, emphasizing moral and ethical values in all of its teachings. As a whole, the university shares a commitment to integrating Christian values and learning; all faculty members are devoted to Christianity, with official ceremonies and events opened in prayer. The spirit of the college is based on the idea that acquiring knowledge calls for lives of service, and the Pepperdine atmosphere prepares students for lives of purpose and leadership.

Although affiliated with the Church of Christ, Pepperdine accepts students of all religious backgrounds. Set in one of the most beautiful campuses in the country, Pepperdine continues to draw great numbers of students of all backgrounds to indulge in its awe-inspiring atmosphere and wholesome spirit.

Academics

In order to create well-balanced lives for its students, Seaver College requires a General Education Curriculum with courses in Western heritage, religion, literature, and the American experience. All students must take three courses in Christianity and culture; first-year students are also required to take a First Year Seminar and juniors must create a Junior Writing Portfolio. "Even if you aren't very religious," explains a student, "it's enlightening to learn about the Old Testament, New Testament, and the role of religion in our society."

In addition to general requirements, students may pursue majors in 39 different fields and minors in 37 fields. Virtually all classes have fewer than 50 students, with an average student-to-faculty ratio of 13:1, allowing for a great deal of individual attention from professors. "If you want a college where you can hide in class, this is not the place for you," notes a student.

Strong academic programs at Seaver include business administration and communications. Within the business administration division, the Service Leadership class provides a special academic opportunity. Required for business administration majors, this course blends academics with community service by forming student consulting teams to assist nonprofit organizations with business concepts and skills. In this course, students have served programs such as the Boys and Girls Club and United Cerebral Palsy.

The communications department offers programs such as the AD club, a National Honor Society for Advertising Students sponsored by the American Advertising Federation, and a chapter of the Public Relations Student Society of America, which hosted a national conference on different aspects of public relations last year and had in attendance corporations such as Jaguar, Quiksilver, Make-A-Wish Foundation, and Disney.

The Summer Undergraduate Research Program at Seaver is also growing in popularity, offering students hands-on experience—with the aid of faculty members—on individualized projects across disciplines. Recently, students have researched biotechnology and its role for pharmaceutical companies, the works of Leo Tolstoy, and contemporary political philosophy.

Studying abroad is highly encouraged at Seaver, with six different programs offered during the academic year, two Summer Language Intensive programs in France and Spain, and Summer Special Interest programs in seven different countries. "I studied Spanish through a home-stay program in Madrid," one student shares. "The family I lived with was incredibly generous." The college also offers summer internship programs abroad in five different countries.

Internship opportunities are also available on campus, with a Career Office prepared to connect students with faculty and alumni, and abundant student mentorships offered between students and alumni.

Student Life

Seaver College at Pepperdine hosts hundreds of student organizations, from student government and student programming, to clubs, sport club councils, and Greek life. Many of the on-campus activities center on the university's commitment to Christianity, with popular organizations being the Christianity and Public Policy Organization, a group dedicated to the practical applications of the Christian faith; and the Churchill Society, dedicated to the study of leadership and prudence in community public policy.

Among many notable events on campus are SongFest, Midnight Madness, and CultureFest. SongFest is a musical variety show put on each year with a cast of hundreds of students and six performances. Groups of students congregate to put together short, 12-minute shows featuring creative costuming, acting, singing, and dancing, with completely original scripts and choreography. Always boasting sold-out audiences, this variety show is a strongly embraced tradition at the college. "I was shocked that the quiet guy from my history class is a real performer," says a student. Midnight Madness promotes the start of a new basketball season, featuring dunk contests, silly player introduction videos, and other means of raising basketball excitement. Finally, CultureFest celebrates the university's cultural diversity with three hours of multicultural attractions such as live music, food, and performances.

Greek life on campus also has its influence on the social scene, with seven sororities and five fraternities dedicated to making a positive impact and holding positions of leadership on campus. "The fraternity parties can get pretty large, and you'll meet a lot more people if you join a fraternity or sorority," says a pledge.

As far as athletics, Pepperdine has 14 Division I teams in the West Coast Conference, with strong contenders for men's volleyball and tennis. For those interested in intramurals, Pepperdine offers basketball, dodgeball, flag football, and Ultimate Frisbee, among many others.

When students tire of the campus scene, they venture to nearby Westwood and bustling Los Angeles to enjoy endless restaurants, shopping, and nightlife. Students tend, however, to enjoy their time on campus, what with their praise-worthy dorm facilities and copious views of the ocean. "We have some of the most breathtaking scenery of any college," comments a student.

PEPPERDINE UNIVERSITY

Highlights

Students
Total enrollment: 7,319
Undergrads: 3,488
Part-time students: 12%
From out-of-state: 48%
Male/Female: 43%/57%
Live on-campus: 56%
In fraternities: 18%
In sororities: 31%
Off-campus employment rating: Good
Caucasian: 45%
African American: 7%
Hispanic: 15%
Asian / Pacific Islander: 13%
Native American: 1%
Mixed (2+ ethnicities): 5%
International: 8%

Academics
Calendar: Semester
Student/faculty ratio: 13:1
Class size 9 or fewer: 29%
Class size 10-29: 60%
Class size 30-49: 8%
Class size 50-99: 2%
Class size 100 or more: 1%
Returning freshmen: 91%
Six-year graduation rate: 80%
Graduates who immediately go to graduate school: 20%
Graduates who immediately enter career related to major: 44%

Most Popular Majors
Business administration
Psychology
Telecommunications

Admissions
Applicants: 8,567
Accepted: 2,505
Acceptance rate: 29.2%
Average GPA: 3.6
ACT range: 25-30
SAT Math range: 570-680
SAT Reading range: 550-650
SAT Writing range: 18-44
Top 10% of class: 39%
Top 25% of class: 77%
Top 50% of class: 95%

521

College Profiles

PEPPERDINE UNIVERSITY

Admissions Criteria

Academic criteria:
Grades: ☆ ☆ ☆
Difficulty of class schedule: ☆ ☆ ☆
Class rank: N/A
Standardized test scores: ☆ ☆
Teacher recommendations: ☆ ☆
Personal statement: ☆ ☆ ☆
Non-academic criteria considered:
Extracurricular activities
Special talents, interests, abilities
Character/personal qualities
Volunteer work
Work experience
State of residency
Religious affiliation/commitment
Minority affiliation
Alumni relationship

Deadlines

Early Action: No
Early Decision: No
Regular Action: January 5 (final)
Notification of admission by: April 1
Common Application: Accepted

Financial Aid

In-state tuition: $44,650
Out-of-state tuition: $44,650
Room: $9,890
Board: $3,000
Books: $1,500
Freshmen receiving need-based aid: 64%
Undergrads rec. need-based aid: 57%
Avg. % of need met by financial aid: 82%
Avg. aid package (freshmen): $40,045
Avg. aid package (undergrads): $39,439
Avg. debt upon graduation: $30,101

School Spirit

Mascot: Willie The Wave
Colors: Blue, orange, and white
Song: *We're Gonna' Fight for Pepperdine*

Almost 60 percent of students live on campus and indulge in the notably spacious and aesthetically-pleasing dormitory housing. "I have to admit that our dorms rock," one student remarks.

Student Body

The typical student at Pepperdine tends to be devoutly Christian, "politically conservative," and academically motivated. "Not everyone fits this mold," notes a student, "but you'll acclimate better if you at least partially fit it." The university's conservative tendencies even led to a ban on dancing until the late 1980s.

Ethnic diversity within the student body is high, with 41 percent minority students. Geographic diversity is high as well, with almost half of students hailing from out of state. Of those, 12 percent are from the rest of the West and eight percent from the Southwest.

You May Not Know

- The university was founded in 1937 by George Pepperdine, a businessman who founded the Western Auto Supply Company.
- In 1937, tuition plus room and board were $420, and tuition was $135 for commuter students. A hamburger and soda cost 20 cents.
- Pepperdine's school colors of blue and orange came from a vote in 1937: blue symbolizing the ocean, orange symbolizing the state of California.

Distinguished Alumni

Rod Blagojevich, former Governor of Illinois; Kim Fields Freeman, President, Victory Entertainment; Tia and Tamera Mowry, television actresses best known for their roles on ABC's *Sister, Sister*; Michael Shermer, founder of The Skeptics Society; Laura Skandera Trombley, President, Pitzer College; Neil Clark Warren, Chairman and co-founder, eHarmony.com.

Admissions and Financial Aid

All students are encouraged to apply to Pepperdine regardless of where they stand on the spectrum of test scores. The admissions committee takes a holistic approach to the process, considering all attributes of the student to see what he or she will bring to the university.

Campus tours are held daily and are very helpful in providing information to the prospective student. Admissions counselors are always ready to answer questions, and interested students may even request to sit in on classes.

Many departments award scholarships to students who show outstanding talent in certain areas, such as natural sciences, business, theatre, communication/journalism, social science, fine arts, as well as athletics. Awards vary depending on the area and the particular scholarship. Pepperdine also awards restricted scholarships, which are privately funded by donors who wish to assist worthy students. Details vary on an individual basis.

PITZER COLLEGE

Overview

Pitzer College in Claremont, California is situated 30 miles east of downtown Los Angeles. The student body of this small, private liberal arts college is encouraged to take academic risks and to explore what interests them. In fact, academic freedom is key to the school's learning environment.

Pitzer's campus combines 1960s architecture with more modern structures. There are no "ivory towers;" but for adventurous, open-minded students looking to study in an intimate environment on the West Coast, Pitzer definitely has something to offer.

Academics

Students are required to complete a core curriculum focused on service and the liberal arts. These studies include three courses in Interdisciplinary and Intercultural Exploration, a Social Responsibility course (or out-of-class experience), two humanities courses, two social/behavioral science courses, a natural science course, a math or reasoning course, and a writing class.

The school offers 46 majors (and the option to choose a major from another one of the Claremont Colleges if it's not offered at Pitzer); and though the courses are challenging, they are not unmanageable. Students rely on each other for help rather than competing; and because of small classes, students quickly form close bonds with professors. However, small classes also mean accountability. "You can't slack," a student says. "The professor will notice if you cut class." The school has particularly strong psychology, sociology, and media studies programs. "The media studies program is boosted by access to all of the media outlets in LA," says a student.

Pitzer students can participate in a host of special programs. Because the college is a member of the Claremont College consortium—comprising a group of five nearby colleges—students can study in areas which take advantage of all of the colleges' resources. There are 16 available Intercollegiate Programs, including Intercollegiate Media Studies, Cross Cultural Health and Healing, and Chicana/o-Latina/o Studies.

Interested students may choose to be part of the college's Community Engagement Center. Here, students can become involved with the local programs. They may tutor GED hopefuls, volunteer at a GLBT youth center, or help with the Borrowed Voices hip-hop program which nurtures students' literary abilities by producing a literary magazine. The school also offers several special degree programs, including a seven-year medical degree from Western University of Health Sciences and BA/MA programs in a variety of areas including cultural studies, information systems, and women's studies.

Students can participate in a variety of study-abroad options, including exchange-style programs where students live as they would if they were students in the host program. Pitzer offers its own programs where students go in small groups and live with local families, traveling as far abroad as Botswana, Nepal, or Thailand. In fact, a remarkably high number of students study abroad—more than 70 percent.

After graduation, 15 percent of Pitzer students immediately enter graduate school, somewhat less of a "grad mill" than most comparable colleges. Because the school is small (with an enrollment of about 1,100 students), its alumni network is correspondingly small. "There aren't a lot of alums, but it's a tight-knit network," says a student.

Student Life

There are 68 official school clubs at Pitzer, including a club dedicated to home brewing (charmingly named "The Rotten Orange"), Ohlone Sandwich (which brings together Native and non-Native students), and Feel Good (a club that raises funds to end world hunger by selling grilled cheese sandwiches). The school also hosts the

PITZER COLLEGE

Four-year private
Founded: 1963
Claremont, CA
Large town
Pop. 35,143

Address:
1050 North Mills Avenue
Claremont, CA 91711-6101

Admissions:
800-PITZER1

Financial Aid:
909-621-8208

admission@pitzer.edu

www.pitzer.edu

PITZER COLLEGE

Students

Total enrollment: 1,084
Undergrads: 1,084
Freshmen: 261
Part-time students: 4%
From out-of-state: 53%
From public schools: 52%
Male/Female: 39%/61%
Live on-campus: 65%
Off-campus employment rating: Fair
Caucasian: 48%
African American: 5%
Hispanic: 15%
Asian / Pacific Islander: 8%
Native American: 1%
Mixed (2+ ethnicities): 4%
International: 4%

Academics

Calendar: Semester
Student/faculty ratio: 10:1
Class size 9 or fewer: 19%
Class size 10-29: 75%
Class size 30-49: 5%
Class size 50-99: -
Class size 100 or more: -
Returning freshmen: 90%
Six-year graduation rate: 87%
Graduates who immediately go to graduate school: 15%
Graduates who immediately enter career related to major: 50%

Most Popular Majors

Psychology
Sociology
Media studies

Admissions

Applicants: 4,228
Accepted: 663
Acceptance rate: 15.7%
Average GPA: 3.8
ACT range: 24-30
SAT Math range: 590-680
SAT Reading range: 580-710
SAT Writing range: Not reported
Top 10% of class: 59%

Green Bike Program, a student-run bike collective. Students are able to join any number of clubs hosted at the other consortium colleges as well.

On-campus events incorporate the new and the old, relying on tradition in some instances. Since 1974, the school has hosted the Kohoutek Music and Arts Festival, a multi-day event with music, vendors, and art. Since 2003, the school has hosted BobFest, named for Bob Marley, which features reggae music and food for the community. During November, school community members are encouraged to bring hammocks to the Pitzer Mound, a grassy lawn at the school, and nap in them. The school officially sanctions the activity—or non-activity, as it were—and even donates some of the hammocks.

As might be predicted in such a small school, there's no Greek life at Pitzer. The school does have 21 Division III sports teams (10 men's, 11 women's), with particularly competitive football, basketball, and women's water polo teams.

Students confess that there's not much to do in Claremont itself, so those with cars take trips to Pasadena, LA, San Diego, or Las Vegas; students without transportation often opt to get involved with the numerous school clubs.

Pitzer's dorms have been recognized for being eco-friendly— three of them are LEED gold certified—and many of the students live on-campus for all four years. Students in on-campus housing can live in co-ed dorms in traditional double rooms or single-student apartments.

Student Body

Pitzer students are known for marching to the beat of their own drummer; they both are different and tolerate that difference in others. The student body leans to the left and students have a reputation as hippies. "The hippie reputation isn't true for everyone, but it's definitely not unfounded," says a student. The success of the Green Bike Program indicates a strong do-it-yourself spirit running through the school and the community; students have a feeling that they can change the world.

The school is highly ethnically diverse, with 33 percent of its students identifying as non-white (and 15 percent choosing not to disclose). There's moderate geographic diversity, with 53 percent of Pitzer students coming from out of state and four percent coming from abroad.

You May Not Know

- Pitzer actually started as a women's college in 1963 and went co-ed in 1970.
- Science majors at the school are required to complete a comprehensive research project before graduation.
- The school runs the Firestone Center for Restoration Ecology in Costa Rica, a 145-acre nature preserve where students can study rainforest ecology.

Distinguished Alumni

Jenniphr Goodman, filmmaker; John Landgraf, president and general manager, FX Networks; Susan Patron, author of *The Higher*

Power of Lucky; Debra Yang, first Asian American Assistant U.S. Attorney.

Admissions and Financial Aid

Students who do particularly well in high school—in the top 10 percent of their class or with an unweighted 3.5 GPA—don't have to submit standardized test scores. Alternatively, students may submit AP scores instead of SAT or ACT scores. Students are encouraged to schedule their interviews (which take place from May of the junior year through mid-December) in the summer or fall.

Students who show a commitment to academics and service, or who demonstrate great talent, are eligible for the Trustee Community Scholarship, which is worth $5,000 and can be renewed for up to four years. There are also a variety of merit scholarships offered by organizations other than the college, including the Udall Scholarship, which targets Native American students, and various scholarships to help defray the costs of studying abroad.

PITZER COLLEGE

Highlights

Admissions Criteria
Academic criteria:
Grades: ☆ ☆ ☆
Difficulty of class schedule: ☆ ☆ ☆
Class rank: ☆ ☆ ☆
Standardized test scores: ☆
Teacher recommendations: ☆ ☆ ☆
Personal statement: ☆ ☆ ☆
Non-academic criteria considered:
Interview
Extracurricular activities
Special talents, interests, abilities
Character/personal qualities
Volunteer work
Work experience
State of residency
Geographical location
Minority affiliation
Alumni relationship

Deadlines
Early Action: No
Early Decision: November 15
Regular Action: January 1 (final)
Notification of admission by: April 1
Common Application: Accepted

Financial Aid
In-state tuition: $44,752
Out-of-state tuition: $44,752
Room: $8,330
Board: $6,068
Books: Varies
Freshmen receiving need-based aid: 34%
Undergrads rec. need-based aid: 39%
Avg. % of need met by financial aid: 100%
Avg. aid package (freshmen): $41,456
Avg. aid package (undergrads): $39,231
Avg. debt upon graduation: $20,900

School Spirit
Mascot: Sagehen
Colors: Orange and white

POMONA COLLEGE

Overview

At the foot of the San Gabriel Mountains—within striking distance of beaches, ski resorts, and the desert—sits Pomona College, a component not only of the circle of mountains, but also within the circle of the five Claremont Colleges and the wider Los Angeles metropolitan area. With its small population, a blend of Colonial and Spanish architecture, and quaint little Claremont "Village" nearby, Pomona may seem idyllic and isolated. But the resources and recreation of the four other Claremont colleges, as well as the city of Los Angeles, are also open to Pomona students.

Considered one of the best American liberal arts institutions, Pomona is competitive with the top East Coast colleges and consistently ranks among *U.S. News & World Report's* top 10 liberal arts colleges. Walk across its beautiful campus, complete with Organic Farm, and you may just get the chance to hear the Smith Tower bell ringing again after 10 years of silence, that is, if it happens to be the 47th minute of the hour, a number with mystical significance for the Sagehens.

Academics

Pomona College offers 45 majors, and all the academic resources of the other Claremont colleges. This means that Pomona classes are small and intimate, and professors are easily accessible. Conversely, other classes, professors, students, and intercollegiate majors are available within one square mile because of the Consortium. The artistic and library resources are also much greater than those of the individual college, while the events and guest speakers are more varied and interesting. "I've taken full advantage of taking classes at the other colleges," remarks a student. "It's the best balance to have a small college atmosphere but to also be able to access the full resources of the other Claremont Colleges."

Students must complete at least 16 classes at Pomona College. They must take a physical education and foreign language requirement as well the first-year critical inquiry seminar, which helps students learn to form persuasive arguments. The breadth of study requirements compel students to take courses in creative expression; social institutions and human behavior; history, values, ethics, and cultural studies; physical and biological sciences; and mathematical reasoning.

Dynamics of difference and power (DDP) is a component of the general education program that is not required but is strongly encouraged. According to the college, a DDP course "uses class, ethnicity, gender, race, religion, and/or sexuality as categories of analysis and that examines power at the interpersonal, local, national and/or international levels." Course offerings include Archeology, Race and the U.S. Economy, and the Economics of Gender and the Family.

Pomona academics are generally "very challenging," and the economics, sciences, and political science departments are especially strong. The Hart Institute for American History brings prominent researchers to lecture and awards grants for student summer research in American history.

Special academic opportunities include the Summer Undergraduate Research Program, which allows students to work on a personal research project under the guidance and supervision of a faculty member. A public announcement of their findings at the end of the summer is made to the Pomona community and often leads to a larger presentation at a national conference or to a year-round research project. "Presenting academic material is preparation for graduate school," notes a student.

Students with wanderlust can participate in one of nearly 50 Pomona programs for study abroad, which have an on-site director, serving as the student's liaison with the foreign college and coordinating things like extracurricular activities and living arrangements. "There's so much support to ease you into being in an unfamiliar environment," one student remarks.

The Pomona College Internship Program gives students paid opportunities to work in the greater LA area with over 50 organizations in all kinds of industries. Students have recently interned at numerous venues including Foothill AIDS Project, marketing companies, and non-profit organizations. Along with this unusual term-time opportunity, students also have a lot of assistance when looking for jobs after graduation, including on-campus recruiting, career fairs, personalized marketing assistance, and customized recruiting plans. Nearly a quarter of students receive a graduate degree directly after graduation.

Student Life

With nearly everyone living on campus, Pomona has a strong residential and extracurricular community. There are 227 student clubs and organizations, including the other Claremont school clubs. The Pep band, music, and dance organizations on campus are extremely popular, but the Cheese Club, Pomona Lawn Sports Club, and Druids, though quirky, are just as active.

Students also enjoy events like Ski-Beach Day, when they take to the mountains and the beach in a single day. "There aren't many places where you can snowboard and then sunbathe at the beach all in the same day," laughs a student. Death by Chocolate is another popular tradition, which occurs on the last day of classes each fall, bringing students and faculty alike flooding into the Smith Campus Center, where chocolate fountains flow, and other chocolate treats fill the room. Once a year, a truck dumps a pile of snow on the front lawn, where snow-starved California students can frolic. The more intellectual students can ponder the "Mystery of 47," a tradition that started with a professor's math proof and has turned into a student quest to see if the number 47 appears more often in nature than other numbers.

There are three fraternities, although few students participate in them, and none have fraternity houses. "We don't have the typical Greek scene with parties, parties, parties," explains a student, "although there are a few parties."

Pomona competes in the Southern California Intercollegiate Athletic Conference (Division III) in 21 varsity sports. Along with Pfizer, with whom it is paired in an athletic rivalry against the three other colleges, Pomona is most competitive in basketball, football, and women's water polo. Students who want to compete at the intramural level can participate in foosball, billiards, and chess.

While Claremont may be a quiet place, students often drive into Los Angeles for greater cultural or entertainment opportunities and might even drive to San Diego or Las Vegas. The mountains, desert, and ocean provide all kinds of opportunities for the more outdoorsy types. "We're not in the heart of the city so you'll need a car for decent nightlife," notes a student.

Students are guaranteed housing all four years, and nearly everyone takes advantage of it, even if they opt for a less traditional language hall. In its 12 co-ed residence halls, nearly two thirds of the rooms are singles. The courtyards are student gathering places, while the basements provide space for bands to practice. The residence halls even have their own outings. There are also many dining halls on campus, but beware if you drop a plastic cup in Frary

POMONA COLLEGE

Highlights

Students
Total enrollment: 1,607
Undergrads: 1,607
Part-time students: 1%
From out-of-state: 67%
From public schools: 67%
Male/Female: 48%/52%
Live on-campus: 98%
In fraternities: 5%
Off-campus employment rating: Good
Caucasian: 45%
African American: 6%
Hispanic: 14%
Asian / Pacific Islander: 11%
Native American: 0%
Mixed (2+ ethnicities): 6%
International: 7%

Academics
Calendar: Semester
Student/faculty ratio: 8:1
Class size 9 or fewer: 23%
Class size 10-29: 67%
Class size 30-49: 8%
Class size 50-99: 1%
Class size 100 or more: -
Returning freshmen: 97%
Six-year graduation rate: 96%
Graduates who immediately go to graduate school: 23%

Most Popular Majors
Economics
Mathematics
English

Admissions
Applicants: 7,456
Accepted: 966
Acceptance rate: 13.0%
Placed on wait list: 634
Enrolled from wait list: 11
Average GPA: Not reported
ACT range: 29-34
SAT Math range: 680-760
SAT Reading range: 680-770
SAT Writing range: 70-25
Top 10% of class: 91%
Top 25% of class: 97%
Top 50% of class: 100%

527

College Profiles

POMONA COLLEGE

Admissions Criteria

Academic criteria:
Grades: ☆ ☆ ☆
Difficulty of class schedule: ☆ ☆ ☆
Class rank: ☆ ☆ ☆
Standardized test scores: ☆ ☆ ☆
Teacher recommendations: ☆ ☆ ☆
Personal statement: ☆ ☆ ☆
Non-academic criteria considered:
Interview
Extracurricular activities
Special talents, interests, abilities
Character/personal qualities
Volunteer work
Work experience
State of residency
Minority affiliation
Alumni relationship

Deadlines

Early Action: No
Early Decision: November 1
Regular Action: January 1 (final)
Notification of admission by: April 1
Common Application: Accepted

Financial Aid

In-state tuition: $43,255
Out-of-state tuition: $43,255
Room: Varies
Board: Varies
Books: $900
Freshmen receiving need-based aid: 55%
Undergrads rec. need-based aid: 52%
Avg. % of need met by financial aid: 100%
Avg. aid package (freshmen): $40,093
Avg. aid package (undergrads): $39,273
Avg. debt upon graduation: $7,540

School Spirit

Mascot: Sagehens
Colors: Blue and orange

Dining Hall, all the other students will proceed to simultaneously do the same!

Student Body

Sagehens are diverse, "academically motivated," and "politically liberal." One student says, "It's not unusual to be discussing philosophy or the country's economy at 2 a.m." Another describes students as "appearing to be California laid-back but studying like crazy behind closed doors." The fact that more than 90 percent of students graduated in the top 10 percent of their high school classes is a testament to their studiousness. The student body is highly ethnically diverse and moderately geographically diverse.

You May Not Know

- Pomona has a secret society of punksters called Mufti, who glue pieces of paper all over campus with double-entendre social commentary.
- The campus has a ghost named Gwendolyn Rose, who haunts Sumner Hall wearing a long, white dress, and occasionally moaning or crying.
- Pomona has set the scene for dozens of films and television shows over the years, including *Pearl Harbor*, *The Gilmore Girls*, and *The West Wing*.

Distinguished Alumni

Myrlie Evers, Civil Rights activist and NAACP Chairman; Bill Keller, *New York Times* Executive Editor; Kris Kristofferson, actor and musician; Robert Shaw, Grammy-winning conductor.

Admissions and Financial Aid

Pomona is a highly selective college, taking only the highest performing high school students. Applicants must have good test scores and high class ranks, which Pomona admissions officers use instead of a minimum GPA requirement. Interviews are encouraged, though not required, and they are "expected" for Southern California students.

Admission is need-blind, and more than half the students attending Pomona receive some form of financial aid. Pomona meets all of a student's demonstrated financial need but does not award any merit-based scholarships.

PRINCETON UNIVERSITY

Overview

As one of the oldest, most selective, and highly regarded institutions in the country, Princeton University—ranked first in the country by *U.S. News & World Report*—doesn't need much of an introduction. Princeton's prestige is built on nationally top-ranked programs like the Woodrow Wilson School of Public and International Affairs, the School of Engineering and Applied Science, and the economics program. Additional draws are the emphasis on original, independent research, internship experience, and its medium size. Princeton has the smallest student body of its Ivy League peer institutions, Harvard and Yale, and as such can offer a distinct advantage when it comes to class size and student-faculty ratio.

Princeton also offers a unique and particular social scene; dominated by the eating clubs, life at Princeton is heavily preppy and even elitist at times, which means that the bulk of on-campus fun isn't accessible to everyone. Those who aren't interested in or can't afford to join an eating club may find their options wanting in such a limited setting as small-town Princeton. Fortunately, about an hour away from Princeton's 500-acre, Collegiate Gothic campus are New York City and Philadelphia, offering endless distractions from some of the nation's most demanding academics and the eating-club-centric life on campus.

Academics

Princeton offers 122 majors, with particularly strong programs in economics, engineering, and public and international affairs. Its General Education Requirements are minimally invasive and include the completion of a writing course, up to two years of foreign language, one course each that satisfy the categories of Epistemology and Cognition, Ethical Thought and Moral Values, Historical Analysis, and Quantitative Reasoning, two courses each in Literature and the Arts, Science and Technology (with lab components), and Social Analysis. All students must complete independent, original research, beginning in the junior year with the Junior Paper or Papers and culminating in a senior thesis. "The research for the thesis is on par with graduate school work," says a student. Requirements for students in School of Engineering and Applied Science differ but are also challenging.

Princeton's academics are some of the most challenging in the country, particularly in light of recent efforts at grade deflation. Fortunately, with a third of its classes enrolling under 10 students, there's plenty of access to faculty support. "The professors are the reason that I chose Princeton," one student explains. "There are the famous professors like Cornell West and Paul Krugman, but even the professors who aren't famous are at the top of their fields."

Princeton makes provisions for students with talent—academic or creative—that can't be accommodated in the regular curriculum, or interests that don't fall under a single major. The University Scholar Program allows a select few students to be exempted from general requirements and to take a reduced major course load. Undergrads apply after their first year and must have faculty support and excellent academics. Students whose academic interests are outside a single major may design an Independent Concentration under the guidance of at least two faculty advisors.

Princeton offers a unique twist on classroom interaction by offering students the opportunity to propose their own course to teach. Once approved, students develop reading lists and course material, and enroll other students in Student-Initiated Seminars. These count as full, regular courses (although they can't fulfill distribution requirements). Past Student-Initiated Seminars have included "Contemporary American Indians," "Computer Animation," and "Toward an Ethical CO_2 Emissions Trajectory for Princeton." One participant explains, "everyone is so amazing that it's not surprising that we teach our own classes."

PRINCETON UNIVERSITY

Four-year private
Founded: 1746
Princeton, NJ
Small town
Pop. 16,265

Address:
110 West College
P.O. Box 430
Princeton, NJ
08544

Admissions:
609-258-3060

Financial Aid:
609-258-3330

uaoffice@princeton.edu

www.princeton.edu

PRINCETON UNIVERSITY

Highlights

Students

Total enrollment: 8,010
Undergrads: 5,336
Freshmen: 1,364
Part-time students: 1%
From out-of-state: 80%
From public schools: 59%
Male/Female: 51%/49%
Live on-campus: 98%
Off-campus employment rating: Good
Caucasian: 48%
African American: 7%
Hispanic: 7%
Asian / Pacific Islander: 19%
Native American: 0%
Mixed (2+ ethnicities): 4%
International: 10%

Academics

Calendar: Semester
Student/faculty ratio: 6:1
Class size 9 or fewer: 33%
Class size 10-29: 50%
Class size 30-49: 7%
Class size 50-99: 6%
Class size 100 or more: 4%
Returning freshmen: 98%
Six-year graduation rate: 96%

Most Popular Majors

Economics
Politics
Public administration

Admissions

Applicants: 26,664
Accepted: 2,094
Acceptance rate: 7.9%
Placed on wait list: 1,472
Enrolled from wait list: Not reported
Average GPA: 3.9
ACT range: 31-35
SAT Math range: 710-800
SAT Reading range: 700-790
SAT Writing range: 81-17
Top 10% of class: 96%
Top 25% of class: 99%
Top 50% of class: 100%

Princeton offers a Community-Based Learning Initiative. Reflecting the university's emphasis on research, this program supports "Community-Based Research" (CBR), in which students research an issue affecting the community and share their findings with relevant organizations. Rather than emphasizing hands-on volunteer work, CBLI offers courses with a Community-Based Research component and can help with internship placement.

Studying abroad can be a challenge at Princeton—only about 10 percent of students go abroad—largely because juniors and seniors are occupied with independent research. If upperclassmen choose to go abroad, they must complete their independent research just the same, and do it while abroad. "The opportunities are pretty limited," says a student. The best option to study abroad is through Princeton's own summer programs in France, Italy, Germany, Russia, Spain, Bermuda, China, Japan, and Tanzania. Princeton does not run its own semester or year-long programs but offers affiliated programs or exchanges in Hungary, Germany, China, Spain, France, Italy, Sweden, Japan, the UK, South Africa, Cuba, and Australia. Students can also attend pre-approved summer, semester, or year-long third-party programs. The International Internship Program places students around the world.

The Office of Career Services critiques resumes, cover letters, or personal statements, and conducts practice interviews. They also facilitate career and internship fairs and help students network. The TigerTracks program and Alumni Careers Network can draw on more than 4,000 alumni who are available to speak with students. Alumni also offer externships for students, one to three days of job shadowing. "There's a lot of support for finding a job and for using the Princeton network," says a student.

Student Life

More than 250 student groups exist at Princeton. A cappella groups are especially popular; many have been in existence since the 40s and 50s, including the Katzenjammers, the Ivy League's oldest a cappella group. Ethnic interest groups are also well supported.

Princeton's massive four-day-long Homecoming is the best-attended college reunion in the world, featuring a massive "P-Rade" where participants emerge in elaborate themed costumes. Other events include concerts, performances, fireworks, and "oceans of beer" (it is the second-largest single order of beer in the country, after the Indy 500). "If you're in the U.S. and you're an alum, you pretty much come back for Homecoming," one student states.

Princeton branches out into its community for Communiversity, which attracts students and locals with music performances, art, food, and games. Princeton's six residential colleges also arrange their own events, which include high-profile speakers like Edward Norton, and field trips to performances and sporting events in New York City.

But the focal point of life outside the classroom is the tradition of eating clubs, mansions that line Prospect Avenue (known as "the Street"). These organizations are part (co-ed) fraternity, part dining hall: upperclass members take their meals there, but eating clubs' main function is social. Eating clubs put on weekend parties open to all campus. They also plan Lawn Party concerts that have featured major artists, like Lupe Fiasco, MGMT, Rihanna, and Girl Talk, and weekend-long, members-only formal and semi-formal House Parties. Some eating clubs accept members by a selection process called "bickering," in which bickerees must complete tasks—which can range from interviews to all-out competitions—to be accepted; others accept members via lottery. Nearly three-quarters of Princeton students are members of an eating club, and they are generally seen as a bastion of old-school, East Coast elitism, as their fees are prohibitively expensive (Princeton alum Woodrow Wilson despised the eating clubs' elitism). "As a student who can barely afford to be here, I'm not a big fan of the eating clubs," comments one student. "It feels exclusionary." A handful of fraternities and sororities exist at Princeton, but these are not recognized by the university and members usually also join eating clubs.

The Ivies aren't known for their athletics, but Princeton is the exception to that rule. Princeton's athletic program—which encompasses 36 Division I varsity teams (19 men's and 17 women's)—has been ranked first in *Time's* "Strongest College Sports Teams" and as a top 10 school for athletics by *Sports Illustrated*. Princeton excels in the preppy mainstay sports: squash, lacrosse, crew, and field hockey. "Besides being the best Ivy," a student explains, "Princeton has the best athletic teams too." Princeton's intramural program—in which residential colleges and eating clubs compete—is extensive, featuring sports, athletic tournaments, and special events. Sports can range from the standard to broomball and "Xtreme" dodgeball to bingo, cardboard canoe races, and even snowman-building.

Princeton is a tree-lined town full of specialty shops and restaurants, but other than the Tony Award-winning McCarter Theatre Centre, there's very little to do. Fortunately, a shuttle train called the "Dinky" connects campus to the Princeton Junction Train Station, which offers service to New York City and Philadelphia.

Students start out living in one of six residential colleges, most of which are outdated dorm buildings; upperclassmen can elect to continue living in the residential colleges or can move to upperclass residences.

Student Body

Princeton has a reputation as being more conservative than most Ivies, as well as overwhelmingly East Coast, wealthy, and preppy. "The wealth is visible in students' clothes, where they vacation, and their zip codes," notes a student. While a large part of the student body hails from ethnic minorities and out of state, *U.S. News & World Report* still ranks the school as having "little economic diversity."

Princeton students are also known for their active social lives, although you'll need to have plenty of spare cash to keep up or even participate in the fun. "I am friends with a concert pianist, a nationally ranked debater, and a guy who earned $300,000 in a startup he founded," one student states.

You May Not Know

- Newman's Day is an event on April 24, in which students attempt to drink 24 beers in 24 hours. The day is named for Paul Newman, who supposedly said, "24 beers in a case; 24 hours in a day. Coincidence? I think not." Newman condemned the tradition.

PRINCETON UNIVERSITY

Highlights

Admissions Criteria
Academic criteria:
Grades: ☆ ☆ ☆
Difficulty of class schedule: ☆ ☆ ☆
Class rank: ☆ ☆ ☆
Standardized test scores: ☆ ☆ ☆
Teacher recommendations: ☆ ☆ ☆
Personal statement: ☆ ☆ ☆
Non-academic criteria considered:
Interview
Extracurricular activities
Special talents, interests, abilities
Character/personal qualities
Volunteer work
Work experience
State of residency
Geographical location
Minority affiliation
Alumni relationship

Deadlines
Early Action: November 1
Early Decision: No
Regular Action: January 1 (final)
Notification of admission by: March 31
Common Application: Accepted

Financial Aid
In-state tuition: $40,170
Out-of-state tuition: $40,170
Room: $7,220
Board: $5,860
Books: $1,200
Freshmen receiving need-based aid: 59%
Undergrads rec. need-based aid: 59%
Avg. % of need met by financial aid: 100%
Avg. aid package (freshmen): $36,912
Avg. aid package (undergrads): $36,411
Avg. debt upon graduation: $5,096

School Spirit
Mascot: Tigers
Colors: Orange and black

531

- The first football game (which was played under soccer-style rules) was played in 1869 between Rutgers and the College of New Jersey, as Princeton was then known.
- Up until 1993, campus legend held that a ghostly figure haunted the mathematics department, writing complex equations on blackboards. It turned out that the "Phantom" was actually John Forbes Nash, inventor of the Nash Equilibrium and subject of the film *A Beautiful Mind*.

Distinguished Alumni

Ben Bernanke, Chairman of the Federal Reserve; Jeff Bezos, founder of Amazon.com; Ethan Coen, Academy Award-winning filmmaker; David Duchovny, actor; Jonathan Safran Foer, author; James Madison, fourth President of the United States; Ralph Nader, political activist and four-time erstwhile Presidential candidate; Queen Noor of Jordan; Michelle Obama, First Lady of the United States; Donald Rumsfeld, former Secretary of Defense, Eric E. Schmidt, CEO of Google; Brooke Shields, actress.

Admissions and Financial Aid

Princeton looks for a wide variety of talents, interests, backgrounds, and experiences in its applicants, as well as academic promise and potential contribution to the Princeton community. The admissions office underscores the importance of essays, which should complement the rest of the application; interviews are encouraged but not required. The university states, "there are some qualities we hope all Princeton students share: integrity, a deep interest in learning, and a devotion to both academic and nonacademic pursuits."

Princeton does not offer merit scholarships. Instead, it offers one of the most extensive financial aid policies in the country, covering 100 percent of demonstrated need without using loans.

PURDUE UNIVERSITY

Overview

Located in industrial West Lafayette, Indiana, Purdue University's main campus lies 65 miles northwest of Indianapolis near the Wabash River. This lovely campus, with its redbrick architecture, is divided into northern and southern portions and is large enough that students can take free bus rides on eight different campus loop routes. A very large public university, not just in physical size but also in total student body numbers (almost 40,000), Purdue is known for its strengths in engineering and science as well as solid liberal arts and healthcare programs. The university also boasts the second largest number of international students and third largest Greek community in the nation.

While academics are rigorous, students take study breaks to greet each other on the sidewalks of Memorial Hall, appropriately named Hello Walk, and to show off their school spirit with renditions of "Hail Purdue!" whether they're at a football game or not. Some students may feel lost at such a huge university, and others won't appreciate the fact that there are many more men than women—though today's ratio is much better than in 1930, when 85 percent of the student body was male. Students who are ready to study hard, and feel they can fit in among a more conservative student body, will no doubt enjoy Purdue's plentitude of academic and social offerings.

Academics

Purdue has more than 200 undergraduate majors across 10 schools, each of which has its own requirements. Most of the schools include required courses in English composition, mathematics, laboratory science, and foreign language. Academics in general are rigorous at Purdue. Though Purdue is large, university officials and faculty work to provide students with personal attention. Freshman class sizes tend to be smaller. One Purdue student sums it up this way: "I always knew I could get help from my advisor or professors."

Strong programs include the various options in the College of Engineering and the College of Science, as well as business in the Krannert School of Management. Students eager to earn an MBA can take advantage of the 3+2 BS/MBA Combined Degree Program. "The engineering and business students are pretty much the elites," says a student.

Students with excellent high school academic records and SAT/ACT scores are invited to University Honors Programs (UHP) from all the academic colleges. Honors students have access to special small classes taught by engaging faculty who propose new courses every year. There are also honors programs within some of the colleges; these programs often provide an excellent opportunity to conduct research with a faculty mentor.

A great way for freshman to navigate the large university is to enter into a learning community, which is either a group of 20-30 students who take two or three of the same courses together, or a group of students who live in the same residence hall and share a common academic interest. Some students do both.

Purdue has more than 200 study-abroad options ranging from a week to a year. Many programs last for a semester or six to eight weeks during the summer. There are several scholarships available for students studying abroad.

The Center for Career Opportunities offers a host of services to students, from walk-in appointments to career counseling to internships. Recently, 1,200 to 1,400 employers per year visited the campus.

Student Life

There are more than 900 student organizations on campus. The *Purdue Exponent*, the university's student newspaper, has 150 student staff members. "Students who

PURDUE UNIVERSITY

Students

Total enrollment: 39,256
Undergrads: 30,147
Freshmen: 6,291
Part-time students: 5%
From out-of-state: 35%
Male/Female: 57%/43%
Live on-campus: 35%
In fraternities: 10%
In sororities: 8%
Off-campus employment rating: Good
Caucasian: 68%
African American: 3%
Hispanic: 4%
Asian / Pacific Islander: 5%
Native American: 0%
Mixed (2+ ethnicities): 2%
International: 16%

Academics

Calendar: Semester
Student/faculty ratio: 14:1
Class size 9 or fewer: 15%
Class size 10-29: 45%
Class size 30-49: 23%
Class size 50-99: 10%
Class size 100 or more: 7%
Returning freshmen: 91%
Six-year graduation rate: 68%
Graduates who immediately enter career
   related to major: 66%

Most Popular Majors

Mechanical engineering
Computer science
Management

Admissions

Applicants: 30,903
Accepted: 18,951
Acceptance rate: 61.3%
Placed on wait list: 1,393
Enrolled from wait list: 165
Average GPA: 3.7
ACT range: 24-30
SAT Math range: 550-680
SAT Reading range: 510-620
SAT Writing range: 5-28
Top 10% of class: 41%
Top 25% of class: 76%
Top 50% of class: 97%

work on the newspaper go on to work at the largest papers in the country," comments a student. The Boiler Volunteer Network connects students with service opportunities in the Great Lafayette area and organizes six community action days and three annual special events each year.

Greek life is a major part of Purdue's campus culture, with 81 fraternities and sororities, 18 of which have a multicultural emphasis. Indeed, Purdue has the nation's third largest Greek community with almost 3,000 students participating. "If you're not in a fraternity or sorority you won't get the full Purdue experience," says one fraternity member.

One of the best-known annual traditions at Purdue is the Grand Prix, a 50-mile go-kart race that is part of Gala Week. The karts are made by hand. Another popular event is Spring Fest, a two-day attraction that draws tens of thousands of participants of all ages to learn about animals, arts, astronomy, and other topics, making for a fun, hands-on learning experience. During winter, students find their fun at the Slayter Center for Performing Arts amphitheater, which morphs into a popular sled run.

Purdue's 18 varsity teams (nine men's, nine women's) compete in Division I. Football and men's basketball are nationally competitive and are the most popular. Women's golf has also been very competitive in recent years. There are 30 club sports, including a Rifle and Pistol club and Trap and Skeet club, as well as sports such as rugby and Ultimate Frisbee which are likely to be found on many large campuses. Golf fans will appreciate the on-campus Birck Boilermaker Golf Complex with its two 18-hole championship golf courses.

The surrounding town of West Lafayette is a classic college town, and everything is reachable by foot. Harry's Chocolate Shop is a favorite gathering place for students and alumni—the family business has operated for more than 80 years and serves not just fountain drinks but also beer and liquor. On weekends, students often take road trips to Chicago and Indianapolis.

Most freshmen live on campus, though they are not required to do so. Of the 15 residence halls, two are single sex. The rest are "co-ed" dorms—though the living areas are separated by gender. There are 12 cooperative houses, where students prepare meals and perform chores.

Student Body

Purdue's student body of almost 40,000, about three-quarters of whom are undergraduates, is known to be a very academically focused bunch. The student body leans right politically. "If you're conservative, you'll feel at home," says a student. There is a heavy male skew in gender distribution—57 percent male, which translates into a big numerical difference—over 4,000 more men on campus.

There is moderate geographic diversity, with over half of students from Indiana and about 35 percent from the other 49 states and DC. Purdue has an especially large international student population of 16 percent representing 128 countries. There is moderate ethnic diversity, with 14 percent minority students.

You May Not Know

- Purdue has the second most students in Indiana and the second most international students among public universities in the country.
- Purdue and the University of Alabama have produced the most quarterbacks to have won the Super Bowl.
- Purdue's nickname is Cradle of Astronauts—not surprising, given that 22 graduates have gone on to become astronauts.

Distinguished Alumni

Neil Armstrong, astronaut; Dorothy Colwell, National Science Foundation director; Chesley Sullenberger, heroic US Airways pilot; Robert Griese, Pro Football Hall of Fame quarterback.

Admissions and Financial Aid

Purdue evaluates individual applications once all required materials are received, including the transcript, SAT or ACT score, and application fee. The college states that "first and foremost, applicants must be prepared academically" for the rigors of college as well as for the specific Purdue college, school, or program to which they are applying. Successful applicants typically go beyond the minimum coursework requirements listed on the admissions website, and students interested in technical programs such as engineering and science should take advanced coursework in math and science.

The essay is a key part in evaluating students for merit scholarships. All first-time college students who finish their application by November 15 and are admitted are put in the running for University-wide scholarships. The Trustees Scholarship offers $12,000-$16,000 a year to nonresidents and $10,000 to residents for up to 100 students each year. The Presidential Scholarship awards somewhat less, and both scholarships award academic achievement and demonstrated leadership. There are also scholarships specific to Indiana residents. These awards are tied to the majors that students choose, so students who switch majors relinquish their awards.

PURDUE UNIVERSITY

Highlights

Admissions Criteria
Academic criteria:
Grades: ☆ ☆ ☆
Difficulty of class schedule: ☆ ☆ ☆
Class rank: ☆
Standardized test scores: ☆ ☆ ☆
Teacher recommendations: ☆
Personal statement: ☆ ☆
Non-academic criteria considered:
Extracurricular activities
Special talents, interests, abilities
Character/personal qualities
Volunteer work
Work experience
Geographical location
Minority affiliation
Alumni relationship

Deadlines
Early Action: No
Early Decision: No
Regular Action: March 1 (priority)
Notification of admission by: December
Common Application: Accepted

Financial Aid
In-state tuition: $9,900
Out-of-state tuition: $28,702
Room: Varies
Board: Varies
Books: $1,370
Freshmen receiving need-based aid: 52%
Undergrads rec. need-based aid: 49%
Avg. % of need met by financial aid: 85%
Avg. aid package (freshmen): $12,668
Avg. aid package (undergrads): $12,300
Avg. debt upon graduation: $27,798

School Spirit
Mascot: Boilermaker Special
Colors: Old gold and black
Song: *Hail Purdue*

QUINNIPIAC UNIVERSITY

Four-year private
Founded: 1929
Hamden, CT
Large town
Pop. 56,913

Address:
275 Mount Carmel
Avenue
Hamden, CT
06518

Admissions:
800-462-1944

Financial Aid:
800-462-1944

admissions@quinnipiac.edu

www.quinnipiac.edu

QUINNIPIAC UNIVERSITY

Overview

Quinnipiac is a warm and fuzzy, student-centered university in a small, suburban Connecticut town. Undergraduates receive a lot of TLC, given the average class size of 25 students. There's an emphasis on building a supportive community among the almost 6,500 undergraduates, as well as on developing students' leadership skills and encouraging them to give back to the community. Students interested in communications and medical careers will find especially ample opportunities here.

QU is located in Hamden, Connecticut, a town about 15 minutes from more bustling New Haven. Hamden's main claim to fame is the Sleeping Giant Mountain, giving new meaning to the phrase "sleepy town." The Mt. Carmel campus, the main hub of activity among the university's three campuses, has many new brick buildings that mimic an older, classic collegiate style.

Given the university's almost 69 percent acceptance rate, getting in won't be a nail-biter. However, from extensive university programming on weekends to popular Division I hockey games to student jobs at Quinnipiac's famous polling center, undergraduates will find a campus that keeps them happy and occupied.

Academics

Quinnipiac "is in the midst of an institutional transformation" as it shifts to become centered around a "learning paradigm." That is, QU is attempting to make sure that its academics, extracurricular programs, and student life contribute to interdisciplinary learning that better prepares students for the 21st-century world. This may all sound like educationese mumbo jumbo, but the university promises to prioritize students' learning (rather than, say, faculty research achievement) and to make sure students graduate with a skill-set that goes beyond major-specific knowledge.

The core curriculum at Quinnipiac includes an unusual number of required freshman seminars. In addition to two freshman composition courses, first-years must also take three interdisciplinary seminars. The quantitative literacy requirement mandates a three-credit math course, and the breadth component of the core requires students to take 28 hours of coursework. For breadth, all students must complete seven credits in the sciences, including a four-credit course with a lab. This may be a groan-inducing fact for humanities-minded students, since few universities with science requirements mandate that students set foot in a lab. "I thought I was done with lab work in high school," bemoans a humanities major. They must also earn six credits in the social sciences, six in the humanities, three in the fine arts, and six credits of electives. When it comes to the strongest programs at QU, the School of Communications is very well regarded, and offers some of Quinnipiac's most popular majors.

A few twists differentiate Quinnipiac's honors program from those at other colleges. Freshmen admitted to the program are not cordoned off in honors housing, but rather housed in quads composed of two honors students and two non-honors students. Another unique aspect of the honors program is the senior-year Honors Symposium. Honors students take a research-based course in their major in their senior year and get together with other honors students from various majors to discuss their work, giving them the opportunity for meaningful exchange outside their own field. "We get different perspectives on our work," notes a senior.

Students interested in studying abroad may do so through Quinnipiac-affiliated programs in 12 countries or through other university-approved programs. The university's showcase study abroad program is QU at University College Cork in Ireland. In addition to semester-long study abroad programs, students can participate in short-term trips with a humanitarian bent organized by the school's Albert Schweitzer Institute.

Quinnipiac's research centers offer a few surprises. You may have heard of Quinnipiac polls without necessarily connecting them with the university. The QU

Polling Institute is a highly regarded source of information on public opinion. The university is also home to a research center and museum on Ireland's Great Hunger (the politically correct name for the potato famine).

Each college of the university has its own career development office that offers the full range of career advising resources. Career development is particularly strong in the School of Communications, which requires students in most majors to complete a 120-hour internship for three credits. "I gained so much valuable on-the-job experience in my internship," says a student. The Quinnipiac in LA program gives communications students the chance to spend a year interning in LA while taking courses with QU professors. The College of Arts and Sciences also allows students to complete internships for credit. All QU students can benefit from the school's 30,000-strong alumni network.

Student Life

If you're talking sports at Quinnipiac, chances are you're talking hockey. Basketball has its moments of glory as well, but the action on the ice tends to get the most consistent attention from fans. While the school plays in Division I, it lacks both a football team and the hyped-up fan culture that you might find at larger schools. "We still have enough rah-rah spirit and don't miss having a football team," notes a student. There are nine fall intramural sports on offer, including beach volleyball, and eight in the spring.

QU hosts five fraternities and six sororities and the Order of Omega, an academic honor society for Greeks. The frats and sororities work together to host Greek Week each year, with goofy sports competitions and awards for academic, community service, and leadership accomplishments.

There are many opportunities for students to gain practical experience in communications-related fields through extracurriculars, from the student-staffed Quinnipiac Bobcat Sports Network, exclusive broadcaster of most QU sports, to the *The Chronicle* newspaper, to QuinniPR, a student-run PR agency.

Students interested in leadership and community service may find the many extracurricular offerings enticing. The Leadership Development Program offers conferences and forums. Community service receives a lot of emphasis, too. Students and faculty alike participate in "The Big Event," a national day of service, each year.

"We are a tight-knit community because so many of us live on campus," states a student. Housing is guaranteed for the first three years, and it's usually not difficult to find university housing for senior year. Quinnipiac's focus on building a strong sense of community affects residential life, beginning with the First-Year Residential Experience (FYRE). Freshmen are clustered into seven dorms and must complete roommate contracts after a discussion of common sources of roommate friction, such as study and sleep schedules, cleaning duties, and guests. (Talk about university hand-holding.) Freshmen and sophomore housing is located on the Mt. Carmel campus, while junior and senior housing is located predominantly on York Hill campus, about a half-mile away.

Students can find a lot to do on campus at QU, but will be limited by its small-town location. A lot of the cultural life is campus-based, since Hamden is a quiet, small town. The university provides regular programming on weekend nights, but don't expect frequent

QUINNIPIAC UNIVERSITY

Highlights

Students
Total enrollment: 8,614
Undergrads: 6,430
Freshmen: 1,785
From out-of-state: 78%
From public schools: 65%
Male/Female: 38%/62%
Live on-campus: 80%
In fraternities: 12%
In sororities: 11%
Off-campus employment rating: Excellent
Caucasian: 79%
African American: 4%
Hispanic: 8%
Asian / Pacific Islander: 2%
Native American: 0%
Mixed (2+ ethnicities): 1%
International: 1%

Academics
Calendar: 4-1-4 system
Student/faculty ratio: 12:1
Class size 9 or fewer: 10%
Class size 10-29: 70%
Class size 30-49: 18%
Class size 50-99: 2%
Class size 100 or more: -
Six-year graduation rate: 77%
Graduates who immediately go to graduate school: 34%

Most Popular Majors
Management
Nursing
Communications

Admissions
Applicants: 18,813
Accepted: 12,919
Acceptance rate: 68.7%
Placed on wait list: 1,640
Enrolled from wait list: 180
Average GPA: 3.4
ACT range: 22-26
SAT Math range: 500-600
SAT Reading range: 490-580
SAT Writing range: 2-19
Top 10% of class: 24%
Top 25% of class: 69%
Top 50% of class: 91%

537

College Profiles

QUINNIPIAC UNIVERSITY

Highlights

Admissions Criteria

Academic criteria:
Grades: ☆ ☆ ☆
Difficulty of class schedule: ☆ ☆ ☆
Class rank: ☆ ☆
Standardized test scores: ☆ ☆
Teacher recommendations: ☆ ☆
Personal statement: ☆ ☆
Non-academic criteria considered:
Interview
Extracurricular activities
Character/personal qualities
Volunteer work
Work experience
State of residency
Minority affiliation
Alumni relationship

Deadlines

Early Action: No
Early Decision: November 1
Regular Action: Rolling admissions
Common Application: Accepted

Financial Aid

In-state tuition: $37,830
Out-of-state tuition: $37,830
Room: $11,850
Board: $2,400
Books: $800
Freshmen receiving need-based aid: 66%
Undergrads rec. need-based aid: 64%
Avg. % of need met by financial aid: 64%
Avg. aid package (freshmen): $23,867
Avg. aid package (undergrads): $22,679
Avg. debt upon graduation: $42,730

School Spirit

Mascot: Bobcats
Colors: Navy and gold

big-name concerts or a thumping nightlife. Entertainment options include free weekend movies, the Hamden Symphony Orchestra, which QU students are welcome to join, and student theater productions. "Do we sometimes wish for more entertainment options? Yes, but we always manage to have fun," notes a student. Hamden also offers hiking opportunities at Sleeping Giant State Park (named for a mountain that looks like a drowsy giant). If you're into museums, galleries, theaters, movies, and restaurants, you'll likely find yourself heading over to New Haven to glom onto some of the offerings clustered around that other university—you know, Yale. QU sponsors shuttles that take students to New Haven and nearby shopping areas for free.

Student Body

Quinnipiac's student body has a significantly larger female population (62 percent). It has moderate ethnic diversity at 15 percent minority students. QU is very geographically diverse, as 78 percent of its students are from out-of-state. Among all undergraduates, 12 percent of men and 11 percent of women belong to Greek organizations. Campus style tends toward the dully conventional, with women decked out in a standard Uggs, leggings, and North Face uniform come winter.

You May Not Know

- The university's name comes from an American Indian word meaning either "people from the long-water land" or "to make change in the direction of travel," depending on whom you ask.
- In the 2012-2013 season, QU men's hockey advanced all the way to the Frozen Four—unfortunately, only to be defeated by arch-nemesis Yale.
- University President John Lahey earned $1.2 million in 2011, according to *The Chronicle of Higher Education*, making him the 26th highest-paid in the U.S.

Distinguished Alumni

Susan Filan, MSNBC legal analyst; Eric Hartzell, Pittsburgh Penguins goalie; Murray Lender, former CEO of Lender's Bagels; William Weldon, CEO of Johnson & Johnson.

Admissions and Financial Aid

QU offers both a rolling admissions process and an early decision option. Students applying for programs in nursing, physician assistant, and physical therapy are advised to apply by Nov. 15. Students can apply online either with the Common Application or the specific Quinnipiac Application. There are no separate scholarship applications, as students are automatically considered for scholarships.

Quinnipiac emphasizes the individualized nature of its admissions process, but tends to accept students whose high school average is at least a B+ and who have a combined critical reading and math score of 1050 on the SAT. Applicants can apply to a specific school even if undecided about their major within that school.

The university notes that 53 percent of freshmen come from families with incomes over $150,000 or families who did not apply for financial aid, although among all Quinnipiac students, 64 percent received need-based aid and 16 percent received merit-based aid.

RANDOLPH COLLEGE

Overview

Randolph is a tiny college tucked away in idyllic Lynchburg, Virginia, at the foot of the Blue Ridge Mountains and on the James River. Although only 500 students attend the college, Lynchburg has three other schools, making it a haven for athletic, outdoor-oriented college students. For anyone who loves hiking, biking, and camping, Randolph's proximity to the Blue Ridge and Blackwater Creek are a huge draw. Even the campus itself has plenty of attractions with classic redbrick buildings, 100 acres of rolling lawns and towering trees, two nature preserves, an observatory, and an outstanding equestrian center.

Although Randolph was formerly a private women's college, the decision was made in 2007 to admit men—a change that was highly contested by many students and alumni—making 2011's graduation ceremony the first to include male students. The school is in a slightly awkward transition stage, gradually moving from all-women to co-ed. Still, the college has an excellent reputation for liberal and fine arts education and should continue to attract good students of both genders. Student body population is currently skewed with more women than men.

Academics

There are 30 different majors at Randolph, including the option to design your own major. Some of the strongest programs are biology, psychology, and English. Randolph also offers a master's in education. To graduate, students must take writing, math, and foreign language classes, an interdisciplinary forum, as well as distribution requirements in literature or rhetoric. Additional classes are creative writing or fine arts, history, philosophy or religion, social or behavioral sciences, natural sciences, constructions and implications of gender. Courses in United States or European countries, Asia, Africa, Middle East, or Latin America and Global Issues complete the list of required studies. Each student must also graduate with one physical education credit.

Every Randolph graduate should leave with a firm understanding of the liberal arts. "The requirements are challenging, but every class has blown my mind away," says a student. It is a rigorous school, but the small size of the classes—some have as few as three students—facilitates individual attention and one-on-one time with professors.

Randolph emphasizes global education with International Study Seminars, short faculty-led trips to places such as Japan or Ecuador, and study abroad. Nearly half the students study abroad at some point, through partnerships with universities in England, Denmark, France, Greece, Ireland, Mexico, Italy, Japan, and Spain.

The American Culture Program invites students to utilize a new approach in their study of America: they treat America as a foreign country and study American history, politics, literature, music, and art from that perspective. The program involves lectures, guest speakers, and trips, and may be completed during a semester or over the summer. Another benefit is that students from all over the country and other parts of the world enroll in Randolph's American Culture Program.

The Summer Research Program offers interested students the option of conducting laboratory and field studies with a professor over the summer and presenting the results of the research at a mini-retreat at the end of the course.

Other special opportunities at Randolph include the Davenport Global Leadership Program for Women, which trains female students in community service and ethical leadership throughout all four years of college.

Randolph promotes hands-on learning and incorporating experiences outside of the classroom into an education. All of this leads to excellent prospects after graduation, with graduates getting into medical school at a rate 29 percent higher than the national average. Randolph is also in the top 10 percent nationally for the percentage

RANDOLPH COLLEGE

Four-year private
Founded: 1891
Lynchburg, VA
Medium city
Pop. 76,504

Address:
2500 Rivermont Avenue
Lynchburg, VA
24503-1555

Admissions:
800-745-7692

Financial Aid:
434-947-8128

admissions@randolph-college.edu

www.randolphcollege.edu

RANDOLPH COLLEGE

of students who get doctoral degrees. The Experiential Learning Center encourages students to pursue educational opportunities off campus such as internships and job-shadowing.

Student Life

Randolph has more than 40 student organizations and clubs, from *Hail, Muse!*, a magazine that publishes student artwork and writing, to Humans vs. Zombies, a tag survival game that takes place on campus over several days, to Jemila Raks, the belly-dancing club. Randolph has very little Greek life.

There are also 14 varsity sports teams that compete in NCAA Division III, in the Old Dominion Athletic Conference. Wildcats are especially competitive in riding and women's swimming. A lot of Wildcats enjoy other recreational sports, such as hiking in the nearby Blue Ridge Mountains or along the Appalachian Trail or skiing at the nearby Wintergreen Resort. Many students also volunteer at local homeless shelters or Habitat for Humanity sites. On campus, students gather at the Skeller or Student Center, and off, students may get together at the Cavalier and Rivermont Pizza. Those who are willing to go a little farther afield plan road trips to Washington, DC.

There is plenty to get involved in at Randolph, with its rich inheritance of campus activities. The oldest tradition is the Even and Odd rivalry that pits freshmen and juniors against sophomores and seniors based upon whether their graduation year is even or odd. The year-long competition ends every spring with Bury the Hatchet. Skeller Sings brings all the classes together to serenade and out-sing each other.

MacDoodle day is one of the most anticipated days of the year, even though the exact date is a secret. Classes are canceled and other activities are planned for this surprise vacation. Now entering its second century, the Greek Play is another highly anticipated event, with students performing a Greek drama in the outdoor amphitheatre. "Everyone goes to the Greek Play. It's something that only Randolph has," boasts a student.

On-campus student life is lively, as the vast majority of students live on campus. Freshmen fill out preference forms and are placed in one of the six residential halls, which combine upper and lower classmen. The campus cafes and bistros also bring students together, where they catch a quick bite with their meal plan or dining dollars.

Student Body

Randolph is a school where people care about community. Its students are spirited and active in both indoor and outdoor events, as demonstrated by the number of students who participate in school traditions. They are dedicated to their schoolwork, but become involved in other things also of great value to them. Students say that they "study hard" but also "make the time to form lasting friendships."

The college has moderate ethnic diversity (19 percent) and international students from more than 30 countries, with a moderate amount of geographic diversity (61 percent from out-of-state). It is clearly a school dominated by women at the present time. Some did not welcome the switch to a co-educational college. There is even a Feminist Majority Leadership Alliance that works to pursue feminist goals.

You May Not Know

- In 1916, Randolph College was the first Southern women's college to have a Phi Beta Kappa charter.
- During Ring Week, the first-years make scavenger hunts that lead their sisters in the junior class to their class rings.
- Randolph's Maier Museum of Art has one of the best collections of American art in the country with works by Arthur B. Davies and Ben Shahn.

Distinguished Alumni

Pearl S. Buck, author of *The Good Earth*; Candy Crowley, CNN senior political correspondent; Blanche Lincoln, Senior Democratic U.S. Senator from Arkansas; Emily Squires, director of *Sesame Street*.

Admissions and Financial Aid

Randolph College is relatively easy to get into (83 percent of students are accepted), not because it's not academically challenging once you get there, but because it receives very few applicants. The admissions office explains that admissions officers consider "much more than grades and test scores when [they] evaluate each admission application."

Most students receive a combination of merit and need-based financial support. The Presidential Scholars Program awards as much as full tuition. There are also academic scholarships from $2,000 to $18,000 a year, originally based on GPA and test scores and then renewed annually based upon academic performance.

RANDOLPH COLLEGE

Highlights

Admissions Criteria
Academic criteria:
Grades: ☆ ☆
Difficulty of class schedule: ☆ ☆
Class rank: ☆ ☆
Standardized test scores: ☆ ☆ ☆
Teacher recommendations: ☆ ☆
Personal statement: ☆ ☆
Non-academic criteria considered:
Interview
Extracurricular activities
Special talents, interests, abilities
Character/personal qualities
Volunteer work
Work experience
State of residency
Alumni relationship

Deadlines
Early Action: December 1
Early Decision: No
Regular Action: Rolling admissions
Common Application: Accepted

Financial Aid
In-state tuition: $32,750
Out-of-state tuition: $32,750
Room: Varies
Board: Varies
Books: $2,600
Freshmen receiving need-based aid: 69%
Undergrads rec. need-based aid: 69%
Avg. % of need met by financial aid: 78%
Avg. aid package (freshmen): $27,128
Avg. aid package (undergrads): $26,644
Avg. debt upon graduation: $33,737

School Spirit
Mascot: WildCats
Colors: Black and yellow

REED COLLEGE

Overview

Located just five miles from downtown Portland, Oregon, Reed College's campus is covered in green and protected wetlands, with buildings that feature architecture ranging from brick to limestone to Gothic. Reed College Canyon, a forested canyon wilderness preserve, sits at the center of campus, dividing academic buildings from residential ones. Reed is a small private liberal arts college known for its intellectualism and nonconformist student body; its students are required to research, write, and defend a senior-year thesis—which may be what prepares so many of them to go on to earn PhDs.

Though small, Reed is certainly distinctive: the campus houses the only nuclear reactor run by undergraduates; the annual 10-day Paideia is a festival that's a teaching-and-learning free-for-all (Giant Concrete Gnome Construction class, anyone?); and many students graduate without even knowing their GPAs, as professors focus on lengthy commentaries rather than grades. Not everyone will find a small and liberal school with no Greek system or competitive varsity sports appealing; but students who want a liberal arts education surrounded by liberal, oftentimes-quirky peers and the beautiful Portland outdoors will want to consider Reed for their undergraduate studies.

Academics

Reed offers 26 department majors, 12 interdisciplinary majors, six dual-degree programs with other colleges and universities, as well as premed and pre-veterinarian programs. Distribution Requirements include Humanities 110, five "Group" requirements in different subject areas, three semesters of physical education, and competency in a foreign language. Students must take a qualifying examination in their major field at the end of their junior year, and seniors complete a one-year research project that culminates in a thesis that they must defend.

Academics at Reed are intense with a highly intellectual, rather than competitive, feel. Professors de-emphasize letter grades and instead evaluate students through lengthy commentaries. "The evaluations are immensely more helpful than letter grades because you get feedback on what you're doing well on and where you need to improve," says a student. Strong programs include English, physics, biology, and psychology.

The Reed Research Reactor, established in 1968, is the only nuclear reactor operated primarily by undergraduates. Each year there is a seminar for students interested in learning more about the reactor, and about 40 undergraduates are licensed to operate it. For students who prefer peace studies to nuclear physics, the Davis Projects for Peace offers $10,000 to undergraduate students to design grassroots projects: past projects have included building a language Resource Center in South Africa and teaching conflict resolution to traumatized orphans in Rwanda. Other student fellowships and grants include Summer Creative Scholarships, internship awards for students in public or nonprofit sectors, science research fellowships, and more.

Reed offers domestic exchange programs at Howard University, Sarah Lawrence College, and through The Sea Education Association, which offers field programs in marine and environmental studies. There are 18 countries to choose from when students consider studying abroad.

Reed is among the top 10 of undergraduate institutions ranked by percentage of graduates who go on to earn a PhD. "We're here because we love to learn," notes a student. "A lot of us don't want to stop learning after college and we continue to graduate school." The top employers of Reed graduates are institutions of higher education. Among liberal arts colleges, Reed has produced the second-highest number of Rhodes scholars among liberal arts college.

Student Life

There are around 150 student organizations at Reed, with descriptions that range from quirky ("We oppose the idea that the bagel is a boring breakfast food") to fun ("We shall play laZZZer Tag in THE FUN DOME") to delicious ("We bake delicious pies for the community free of charge"). One student explains it this way, "No matter how strange your interest, you will most likely find at least a handful of other people willing to join an organization in support of it." KRRC, the campus radio, has been broadcasting since 1954, the campus newspaper the *Quest* has been published since 1913, and *The New York Times On Campus Program* puts papers in the hands of students every weekday.

Many of the student organizations attest to Reedies' love of the environment and outdoors. Reed Outdoor Programs and Education offers a large array of activities for skiers, rock climbers, kayakers, and backpackers. The Gray Fund, an endowed fund established in 1992, funds recreational trips—snow-shoeing, a wildflower hike, cross-country skiing—as part of its broader efforts to enhance the lives of students, faculty, and staff outside the classroom.

Freshmen at Reed get acquainted with the college through a five-day orientation. The optional and highly popular Orientation Odysseys give students a chance to backpack, river raft, or rock climb or address social issues through service trips. "It's helpful to know people the first day of class," says a student.

Just before the start of second semester, Reed holds Paideia, a festival of learning that lasts 10 days and is chock full of classes taught by professors, faculty, or even students. A long-standing tradition is a popular underwater basket weaving class; other classes can be more structured, though not necessary less obscure.

At the end of spring semester, Reed holds Renn Fayre, a three-day celebration that began as a Renaissance fair in the 1960s but now has a new theme every year. Renn Fayre begins with the Thesis Parade, where seniors deliver their theses en masse to the registrar and burn the year's notes in a fiery pit. In keeping with a general sense of mayhem, events have included a naked Slip 'n' Slide, full-contact human cheese, fire-dancing performance, bug-eating contests, and other such events.

Reed has no fraternities or sororities. And Reed does not have competitive athletic teams, though there are five varsity club sports: rugby, soccer, Ultimate Frisbee, basketball, and squash. The men's and women's rugby teams have competed in regional championships. Interestingly enough, six quarters of physical education classes are required for graduation.

Portland offers music, shopping, eating—and, for the less city-oriented—wilderness. Students also roadtrip to Oregon's other gorgeous natural offerings: beaches, mountains, and high desert. "If you don't hike or camp before you come here, you surely will after," notes a student.

Freshmen are guaranteed campus residency and upperclassmen usually get singles by participating in a housing lottery. There are 26 dorms on campus, including many "theme dorms" that usually house 30 students or less. Examples are the Chinese, French, German, Russian, and Spanish language houses.

REED COLLEGE

Highlights

Students
Total enrollment: 1,455
Undergrads: 1,432
Freshmen: 320
Part-time students: 3%
From out-of-state: 91%
From public schools: 58%
Male/Female: 46%/54%
Live on-campus: 63%
Off-campus employment rating: Good
Caucasian: 60%
African American: 3%
Hispanic: 9%
Asian / Pacific Islander: 8%
Native American: 1%
Mixed (2+ ethnicities): 1%
International: 6%

Academics
Calendar: Semester
Student/faculty ratio: 10:1
Class size 9 or fewer: 30%
Class size 10-29: 62%
Class size 30-49: 4%
Class size 50-99: 2%
Class size 100 or more: 1%
Returning freshmen: 91%
Six-year graduation rate: 73%
Graduates who immediately go to graduate school: 17%

Most Popular Majors
Biology
English literature
Psychology

Admissions
Applicants: 3,131
Accepted: 1,125
Acceptance rate: 35.9%
Placed on wait list: 748
Enrolled from wait list: 56
Average GPA: 3.9
ACT range: 28-32
SAT Math range: 630-720
SAT Reading range: 670-770
SAT Writing range: 49-44
Top 10% of class: 63%
Top 25% of class: 85%
Top 50% of class: 98%

College Profiles

REED COLLEGE

Student Body

Reed's 1,400 students are known to be "moderately to radically liberal" and very academically focused. The unofficial motto of Reed, found on T-shirts and sweaters in the College Bookstore, hints at the nonconformist reputation of the school: "Communism, Atheism, Free Love." A wide range of socioeconomic backgrounds are represented on campus, something that students are "thankful" for.

There is high racial diversity, with 22 percent minority students, the biggest populations being Hispanic and Asian. About six percent of students are international. There is high geographic diversity, with most students from out of state, though about 40 percent are from the west coast, and most students hail from California.

You May Not Know

- Japhy Ryder from Jack Kerouac's *The Dharma Bums* is one of several fiction Reed alumni; Lambert Somers from Judy Blume's *Summer Sisters* is another.
- Reed's namesakes are entrepreneurial pioneer Simeon Gannett Reed and his wife Amanda Reed, who established the school following her husband's request in his will.
- Reed does not participate in college rankings including those of *U.S. News & World Report* or *Money* magazine.

Distinguished Alumni

Kate Christensen, PEN/Faulkner award-winning novelist; Larry Sanger, co-founder of Wikipedia; John Sperling, businessman and founder of the University of Phoenix; Howard Wolpe, former Congressman.

Admissions and Financial Aid

According to Reed College's admissions office, admission to Reed depends on a variety of factors, with academic accomplishment given the most consideration. Honors and advanced courses in high school improve an applicant's chance of getting in. There are standardized requirements or cutoff points for grades and exam scores. Students are allowed to defer enrollment for up to a year if accepted.

Reed does not offer merit-based scholarships, but the school does attempt to meet needs through grants and loans. The college gives $21 million in grant funds, with individual awards ranging from $1,000 to $54,300. Work-study, typically about 5-10 hours a week, is another option, and more than half of all Reed students work at least part of the school year.

RENSSELAER POLYTECHNIC INSTITUTE

RENSSELAER POLYTECHNIC INSTITUTE

Four-year private
Founded: 1824
Troy, NY
Medium city
Pop. 50,120

Address:
110 Eighth Street
Troy, NY
12180-3590

Admissions:
518-276-6216

Financial Aid:
518-276-6813

admissions@rpi.edu

www.rpi.edu

Overview

Located in upstate New York, Rensselaer Polytechnic Institute (RPI) boasts a 275-acre campus that sits on a bluff overlooking the historic city of Troy and the Hudson River. The campus features ivy-covered brick buildings alongside modern architecture. In the spirit of research, innovation, and entrepreneurship, RPI operates an on-campus business incubator and a Technology Park designed to take technology from the laboratory to the marketplace. A medium private technical school oriented toward engineering and the sciences, RPI is generally ranked among the top 50 colleges in America and the top 50 technological schools worldwide.

The Rensselaer Plan, initiated in 1999, has increased funding for research, including the construction of the Center for Biotechnology and Interdisciplinary Studies and a $100 million supercomputing center. While there are plenty of hardworking students who fit the nerdy engineer stereotype, there's also a strong Greek scene, and athletics are huge on campus—though granted, the sports teams are called the RPI Engineers and have been known to feature math in their cheers.

As is typical at a technologically-focused school, women are outnumbered at the university, though the 187-year-old school has made great strides since going co-ed in 1942. Students who are up for the intense academic challenge of living and breathing all-things-technology in a collaborative environment of athletic geeks (or geeky athletes?) will feel right at home at RPI.

Academics

RPI offers 123 degree programs in 60 fields that culminate in degrees at the bachelor, masters, and doctoral levels. The university consists of five schools: architecture; engineering; humanities, arts, and social sciences; science; and management and technology. Each major has its own requirements, but every RPI student must take classes in the humanities and social sciences, in addition to two communication-intensive courses.

Academics at RPI are intense. Students work hard—think 30+ hours a week outside of class doing homework/labwork/problem sets—but are not cutthroat. "We try to work together rather than being competitive," says a student. Strong programs include engineering, computer science, and management.

In keeping with RPI's emphasis on research and innovation, the Rensselaer Incubation Program has been "giving life to new ideas" since 1980. Results of the Incubator have been impressive: a more than 85 percent survival rate for participating companies, creation of 2,500 jobs, hundreds of employed RPI students, and two thirds of participating companies started by RPI alumni or from research projects at the university.

Rensselaer Technology Park allots 1,250 acres to technology ventures seeking a unique environment. The park joins industry and education, with research ranging from electronics to physics research, from biotechnology to software. "To have access to these kinds of research opportunities as an undergrad is amazing," notes a student.

Accelerated programs at RPI include a BS/MD in only seven years through RPI's Biology Department and nearby Albany Medical College and two BS/JD programs. There is also a newly added co-terminal program that enables students to earn a bachelor's and master's degree in five years.

Rensselaer offers study-abroad and exchange opportunities in more than 15 countries on five continents. Rensselaer Education Across Cultural Horizons (REACH), launched in spring 2009 as an exchange program for engineering students, encourages and expects all undergraduates to study abroad at some point, whether through semester or short term programs, internships, or service learning. "Studying abroad helps broaden our perspective as future engineers," explains a student.

RENSSELAER POLYTECHNIC INSTITUTE

Students

Total enrollment: 6,999
Undergrads: 5,391
Freshmen: 1,326
From out-of-state: 70%
From public schools: 77%
Male/Female: 71%/29%
Live on-campus: 57%
In fraternities: 30%
In sororities: 16%
Off-campus employment rating: Good
Caucasian: 67%
African American: 2%
Hispanic: 6%
Asian / Pacific Islander: 9%
Native American: 0%
Mixed (2+ ethnicities): 5%
International: 7%

Academics

Calendar: Semester
Student/faculty ratio: 15:1
Class size 9 or fewer: 25%
Class size 10-29: 43%
Class size 30-49: 19%
Class size 50-99: 11%
Class size 100 or more: 2%
Returning freshmen: 94%
Six-year graduation rate: 84%
Graduates who immediately enter career
    related to major: 49%

Most Popular Majors

Engineering
Computer science
Biological/life sciences

Admissions

Applicants: 15,222
Accepted: 6,634
Acceptance rate: 43.6%
Placed on wait list: 2,690
Enrolled from wait list: 63
Average GPA: 3.7
ACT range: 26-31
SAT Math range: 660-760
SAT Reading range: 610-700
SAT Writing range: Not reported
Top 10% of class: 66%
Top 25% of class: 95%
Top 50% of class: 99%

There are almost 95,000 RPI alumni. RPI was recently named to *Forbes'* list of schools with the highest-earning graduates, and alumni generosity helped RPI reach a $1.4 billion fundraising goal recently.

Student Life

RPI's Student Union is entirely student-run and funds about 170 student organizations. Another 30 organizations, mostly political and religious ones, are self-supporting. RPI's Senior Honor Society, Phalanx, has honored the students most active in leadership, service, and devotion to their alma mater. The student newspaper *The Poly* prints about 7,000 copies each week, and the college radio WRPI serves the greater Albany Area. Theater and music groups are popular, such as the improv comedy group Sheer Idiocy, and the on-campus theater group The Players, who have staged over 260 productions since its inception in 1929.

The Greek system is popular, with almost one third of the men and one sixth of women belonging to the university's 29 fraternities and five sororities.

With RPI's proximity to the Berkshires, Green Mountains, and Adirondacks, it's not surprising that Ski Club and Outing Club are very well attended—Ski Club offers weekly trips in the winter. "One of the main reasons I chose RPI is for the skiing," admits a student.

RPI has 23 teams (12 men's, 11 women's) that compete in Division III, except for men's and women's ice hockey, which compete in Division I. Hockey is by far the most popular sport, though there are plenty of football fans too. "Everyone pretty much goes to the hockey games because they're exciting even when we lose," notes a supporter. There are 50 intramural and club sports and 70 percent of undergrads are actively engaged in athletics, making it a major cornerstone of campus life.

Memorable events are plentiful. Freshmen enter RPI through the award-winning weeklong "Navigating Rensselaer and Beyond" first-year experience program. Homecoming weekend brings 2,000 to 3,000 alumni, family, and friends back to campus for days of festivities, from the President's Address to the FanFest carnival. And hockey fans come out in droves to the Big Red Freakout!, RPI's last home game of the season, which fills Houston Field House with thousands of fans dressed in red and white.

For students who care for politics over sports, Grand Marshall Week celebrates the election of new student government representatives, including the highest elected student office of Grand Marshal. A recent week featured a kickoff Casino Night and DJ-Off, mid-week BBQ, and closing cocktail hour, along with the expected debates and elections. Many student groups plan special activities and events during this activity-filled week.

Albany, a half-hour's drive away, gives students an outlet for shopping and entertainment. Road trips to nearby mountains or lakes—or to Boston and Montreal for city lovers—add to the menu of off-campus attractions.

Freshmen and sophomores are required to live on campus as part of the "Clustered Learning Advocacy and Support for Students" (CLASS) initiative. "Living on campus builds school spirit and helps you meet a lot of people," one student comments. Upperclassmen get rooms on campus or move off campus to college-owned apartments. There are freshmen residence halls, upperclass residence halls, and four-year halls, as well as special interest housing options.

Student Body

RPI's 5,400 undergrads are typically "nerdy" and "very focused" on studying, although students say, "not everyone fits that stereotype." There is a heavy male skew in the gender ratio. "The uneven number of males to females is not an issue because there's not much interest in dating anyway," one student notes. High ethnic diversity can be attributed to 22 percent minority students. RPI has moderate geographic diversity, with 70 percent of students hailing from out of state.

You May Not Know

- Founded in 1824 by Stephen Van Rensselaer, RPI is, according to the college, the "nation's oldest technological university."
- Alumnus George Ferris was the inventor of the first Ferris wheel.
- During the 1970s and 80s, one RPI cheer was: "*E to the x, dy/dx, E to the x, dx; Cosine, secant, tangent, sine; 3.14159; Square root, cube root, log of pi; Disintegrate them, RPI!*"

Distinguished Alumni

Myles Brand, President of the National Collegiate Athletic Association; Claire Fraser-Liggett, President and Director of The Institute for Genomic Research; Ivar Giaever, physics Nobel Prize Laureate; Ed Zander, Chairman of Motorola, Inc.

Admissions and Financial Aid

In keeping with a technologically-oriented college, RPI encourages freshmen to apply online. Applicants should have completed four years of English, four years of math through pre-calculus, three years of science, and three years of social studies or history. According to the admissions office, the committee also "pays particular attention to candidates who demonstrate qualities and talents that will contribute to the richness of the Rensselaer community." Architecture and electronic arts applicants must submit a creative portfolio.

Sixty-five percent of students receive need-based aid, 29 percent receive merit-based aid, and all applicants are automatically considered for merit scholarships. Rensselaer Medalists are guaranteed $60,000 over four years, and undergraduates can receive an additional year of aid to pursue a master's degree while completing their bachelor's degree through the co-terminal program.

RENSSELAER POLYTECHNIC INSTITUTE

Highlights

Admissions Criteria
Academic criteria:
Grades: ☆ ☆ ☆
Difficulty of class schedule: ☆ ☆ ☆
Class rank: ☆ ☆ ☆
Standardized test scores: ☆ ☆ ☆
Teacher recommendations: ☆ ☆
Personal statement: ☆ ☆
Non-academic criteria considered:
Extracurricular activities
Special talents, interests, abilities
Character/personal qualities
Volunteer work
Work experience
State of residency
Geographical location
Minority affiliation
Alumni relationship

Deadlines
Early Action: No
Early Decision: November 15
Regular Action: January 15 (final)
Notification of admission by: March 20
Common Application: Accepted

Financial Aid
In-state tuition: $45,100
Out-of-state tuition: $45,100
Room: $7,390
Board: $5,570
Books: $2,591
Freshmen receiving need-based aid: 69%
Undergrads rec. need-based aid: 65%
Avg. % of need met by financial aid: 79%
Avg. aid package (freshmen): $34,436
Avg. aid package (undergrads): $30,208
Avg. debt upon graduation: $31,000

School Spirit
Mascot: Engineers, Redhawks
Colors: Cherry and white

RHODE ISLAND SCHOOL OF DESIGN

Four-year private
Founded: 1877
Providence, RI
Medium city
Pop. 178,053

Address:
2 College Street
Providence, RI
02903

Admissions:
401-454-6300

Financial Aid:
401-454-6661

admissions@risd.edu

www.risd.edu

Overview

Rhode Island's small capital city Providence might look like a sleepy New England town, but Providence is home to a vibrant arts and cultural scene. At the heart of that arts scene is Rhode Island School of Design, or RISD, one of the nation's premier art and design colleges. Intense artsy types work long hours in design and drawing studios at RISD, and have access to RISD's attractive, award-winning Fleet Library, world class museums and galleries on campus, and study-abroad programs as well as the facilities at their Ivy-League neighbor, Brown University, just up the hill.

RISD's 13 acres of renovated historic Victorian and Colonial buildings occupy a residential neighborhood perched on the lower slope of College Hill just above the scenic Providence River. Lively shopping, cafes, and restaurants can be found on College Hill, if students can take time from their demanding in-studio workload and their extensive liberal arts education requirements to enjoy them. If art, creativity, and experimentation are your M.O.—both in your academic work and your social life—there can be no more perfect place for you than RISD.

Academics

As one of the nation's top art and design schools, RISD offers 16 intense majors, of which architecture, graphic design, and illustration are the most popular and particularly strong. As part of RISD's emphasis on studio-based education, RISD also requires that its students are well-versed in skills essential to any artistic discipline. The required first-year Foundation Studies program mandates that students take studio courses in drawing and two- and three-dimensional design before going on to pursue a major starting in their sophomore year. Classes are generally small—fewer than 20 students—and studio sections are taught by a team of faculty.

But RISD also requires that its students gain a foundation in humanities, literature, and social science. As such, Foundation Studies puts students through extensive courses in the Division of Liberal Arts, including core and elective courses in English literature and composition, history, philosophy, social sciences, and the history of art and architecture. In addition to their professional majors, students may also complete a concentration—similar to a minor—in the Division of Liberal Arts. "The liberal arts classes we take differentiate us from a trade school and give us a foundation to pursue a wide range of careers," says a student.

RISD also offers a full complement of special academic programs. For six weeks between fall and spring semester, students participate in the shortened Wintersession semester, which offers more experimental classes. Wintersession's abroad course offerings include classic art destinations, such as "Photography" in Paris or "Renaissance Painting Techniques" in Florence, Italy as well as more exotic courses, including "Creature-Creation" in Bali, "Signs and Symbols" in Ghana, and "Spirituality in Pueblo Art" in New Mexico. Students staying in Providence can take the opportunity to explore outside their majors, or can sample more adventurous offerings, including the class enigmatically named "Toaster." "Wintersession lets us explore and take a class we wouldn't normally take," one student explains.

Opportunities to go abroad abound with three summer study-abroad programs in Copenhagen, Denmark; Switzerland; and Rome. Well-qualified juniors and seniors can participate in the European Honors Program, 21-week fall/summer or winter/spring sessions during which students live and study in Rome. RISD offers additional exchange agreements with 47 universities in 22 countries.

Back at home in Providence, students have access to cutting-edge studio and gallery facilities, including the RISD Museum of Art and 14 galleries for displaying student work. All RISD students have access to Brown's libraries, including its singularly ugly Rockefeller Library. For students who are as academically driven and ambitious as

The Ultimate
Guide to America's
Best Colleges

they are artistic, RISD and Brown have partnered to offer a Dual Degree Program. This allows students to earn an AB from Brown and a BFA from RISD in just five years. Students must apply individually to both institutions and then make further application to the Dual Degree Program.

While an education at RISD sets its alumni up for a good deal of success post-graduation, the job market for artists can be inhospitable: RISD itself makes the sobering statement that they recognize "not all students will ultimately be practicing in their professions: they may in fact choose other professional endeavors." But their liberal arts backgrounds provide solid foundations for related endeavors, and RISD alumni have also gone on to pursue careers with such companies as Apple, Disney, Houghton-Mifflin, Martha Stewart Living, NASA, Nike, and Pixar.

Student Life

Outside the studio, RISD students participate in a small but lively campus social scene: 31 student groups operate on campus, including the popular Anime Culture Club and skiing and snowboarding group Snow Club.

Students' creativity reigns supreme in their social lives: dressing up and creating costumes is a major part of nearly every party, whether it is university sponsored, held in a classmate's apartment, or a theme night at a local bar. "We never pass up an opportunity to make or wear a costume," one student laughs. The annual fall Artists' Ball and the bi-annual Electro-flo feature crazy dancing and performances from artists that have included GrandMaster Flash and DJ Scratch. Most important of all, creative and funky costumes that students design and create add to the fun. RISD by Design is a weekend-long alumnus and parent event in October that includes an outdoor art sale, class dinners, and studio demonstrations.

RISD has no Greek system, so much of the on-campus student party scene centers on university events, house parties, and local bars. "Fraternities and sororities are too mainstream to exist here," one student comments. For those who really need their frat-house fix, Brown Greek parties are usually open to RISD students.

Recreational sports and fitness are popular at RISD, and students frequently make rock-climbing and skiing or snowboarding expeditions. Organized sports teams, on the other hand, are literally a joke (RISD's two varsity sports teams, hockey and basketball, don't participate in any NCAA division and are called the Nads and the Balls, respectively). "We would lose every game if we had actual varsity teams. We're artists not athletes," one student laments.

Providence offers varied opportunities for distraction: with the wealth of restaurants and cafes on Thayer Street on College Hill, no artist at RISD is starving. Thayer Street and downtown Providence also feature shopping, nightclubs, and bars. RISD students can also take advantage of Tillinghast Estate, RISD's recreational facility, 20 minutes from Providence. Known as "the farm," it features large wide open spaces and volleyball and basketball courts as well as a beach on Narragansett Bay. RISD also arranges regular charter buses to New York City for students and free local shopping shuttles; Boston is less than an hour away by train.

First-year students live on campus in traditional dorm- or suite-style residence halls. Two themed houses are also available to fresh-

RHODE ISLAND SCHOOL OF DESIGN

Highlights

Students
Total enrollment: 2,386
Undergrads: 1,971
Freshmen: 460
From out-of-state: 93%
Male/Female: 33%/67%
Live on-campus: 62%
Off-campus employment rating: Excellent
Caucasian: 34%
African American: 2%
Hispanic: 7%
Asian / Pacific Islander: 18%
Native American: 0%
Mixed (2+ ethnicities): 3%
International: 21%

Academics
Calendar: 4-1-4 system
Student/faculty ratio: 9:1
Class size 9 or fewer: 12%
Class size 10-29: 86%
Class size 30-49: 1%
Class size 50-99: 1%
Class size 100 or more: -
Returning freshmen: 95%
Six-year graduation rate: 86%
Graduates who immediately go to graduate school: 1%
Graduates who immediately enter career related to major: 45%

Most Popular Majors
Illustration
Architecture
Industrial design

Admissions
Applicants: 3,113
Accepted: 790
Acceptance rate: 25.4%
Average GPA: 3.5
ACT range: Not reported
SAT Math range: 570-690
SAT Reading range: 550-670
SAT Writing range: 20-43

RHODE ISLAND SCHOOL OF DESIGN

Admissions Criteria
Academic criteria:
Grades: ☆ ☆ ☆
Difficulty of class schedule: ☆ ☆ ☆
Class rank: ☆
Standardized test scores: ☆ ☆
Teacher recommendations: ☆ ☆
Personal statement: ☆ ☆
Non-academic criteria considered:
Extracurricular activities
Special talents, interests, abilities
Character/personal qualities
Volunteer work
Work experience
State of residency
Minority affiliation
Alumni relationship

Deadlines
Early Action: No
Early Decision: November 1
Regular Action: February 1 (final)
Notification of admission by: March 15
Common Application: Accepted

Financial Aid
In-state tuition: $42,622
Out-of-state tuition: $42,622
Room: $6,958
Board: $5,314
Books: $2,781
Freshmen receiving need-based aid: 48%
Undergrads rec. need-based aid: 42%
Avg. % of need met by financial aid: 50%
Avg. aid package (freshmen): $23,033
Avg. aid package (undergrads): $19,942
Avg. debt upon graduation: $32,207

men: a Music house and a substance-free Healthy Living Healthy Choices house. Most students move off campus after their first year.

Student Body

RISD students are usually a highly ethnically diverse set of intensely-focused, alternative, creative types, nearly all of whom come from outside of Rhode Island. "If you're afraid to be yourself, you probably won't fit in here," says a student. Another student comments, "That weird kid with the purple hair and tattoos from high school, you'll find her times 100 here."

As is more or less expected from an art school, the male-female ratio is hopelessly skewed in favor of women.

You May Not Know

- RISD was founded in 1877, when a women's group decided to put their leftover money toward creating a school of design rather than a commemorative drinking fountain.
- RISD's unofficial mascot, Scrotie, is exactly what you think he is. Cheerleaders for the Nads hockey team are known as the Jockstraps.
- The first of any applicant's three required drawing samples must be a bicycle.

Distinguished Alumni

Dale Chihuly, glass artist; Deborah Coolidge, film director; Seth MacFarlane, animator and creator of *Family Guy*; Gus Van Sant, film director; Tina Weymouth, bassist, *Talking Heads*.

Admissions and Financial Aid

In addition to the standard application materials (letters of recommendation, writing samples, test scores), students must submit three drawing samples and a portfolio of their work. The entire RISD application process encourages and rewards experimentation. Creativity, process, and potential are more important than polished finish products. The school recommends taking risks with drawing samples, and one of its personal statement prompts asks for a short story or poem rather than the traditional personal essay.

For students who demonstrate artistic and academic achievement as well as financial need, merit scholarships ranging from $500 to $27,500 annually are available. Students with "outstanding" artistic and academic records who do not demonstrate need can participate in the Arts Recognition and Talent Search (ARTS) or Scholastics competitions, which each make two awards of at least $10,000. Five additional Trustee Scholarships of at least $10,000 annually are awarded; no participation in competition or application is needed for these.

RHODES COLLEGE

Overview

Known for its tight-knit community, Rhodes College is a small, private liberal arts college in the mid-south. With a Presbyterian history and a homogeneous student body, Rhodes provides students the opportunity for an intimate and challenging learning experience in an environment that is less focused on athletics than many colleges.

Situated in Memphis, Tennessee, near a park that houses an art museum, golf course, and the Memphis Zoo, the Rhodes campus features Gothic architecture. Rhodes students have opportunities for involvement in extracurriculars and the Greek social scene, as well as volunteer projects and student-interest organizations to join. They also may enjoy the variety of activities and entertainment in Memphis, soaking up southern culture.

Academics

Rhodes College offers 34 majors. In addition to the courses necessary for their majors, students must complete mandates in four basic areas. Either of the courses "The Searches for Values in the Light of Western History and Religion" or "Life: Then and Now" fulfills the Search and Life Program credential, while a writing seminar is the second of the four obligatory requirements. Add a foreign language (for one semester or a placement equivalent) and physical education (three half-semester courses which can also be fulfilled through varsity athletics and club sports) to complete the requirements. "I wasn't enthused about the physical education requirement," says a student, "but it actually turned out to be great stress reliever."

With challenging courses, Rhodes is well known for its tough academic expectations. But, with a small student body, students can anticipate that most of their classes will have 25 or fewer students, and that they will no doubt find professors very accessible. "Professors keep close tabs on us," says a student. Some of the school's strongest programs are biology, chemistry, business, and administration.

Special academic opportunities at Rhodes include the school's Honors Research program in which a student works with a faculty committee to craft a 50-to-60-page research paper. Those students participating in the Honors Research are also encouraged to apply to the Directed Inquiry Program, an independent study coordinated by a faculty member. Research opportunities are extended through the Rhodes Institute for Regional Studies, which encourages students' pursuit of history projects in local and regional archives. Students interested in pursuing a master's in education or nursing may also benefit from the school's joint-partnership program with Vanderbilt University.

Students may also pursue a multitude of service and learning opportunities through Rhode's Buckman Center for International Education. Rhodes offers study-abroad programs in Switzerland, Italy, Morocco, France, Australia, Spain, Ireland, Costa Rica, South Africa, Senegal, Denmark, Argentina, Chile, and China.

Rhodes students report the Career Services Center to be extremely useful. The center provides assistance for students creating a four-year plan, choosing a major, finding an internship, evaluating graduating schools, writing an effective resume, or conducting a successful job interview.

Student Life

With 120 student organizations, extracurricular involvement runs deep in the hearts of these passionate Rhodes College students. Among the most popular groups are the Art Club, Dance Company, Lipstick Your Collar, and the Rhodes Activities Board.

The biggest annual events and traditions at Rhodes are "The Rites." The Rites of Spring—a three-day music festival in April—attracts several nationally-known bands such as Dr. Dre and Better Than Ezra, while Rites to Play, organized and executed

---

RHODES COLLEGE

Four-year private
Founded: 1848
Memphis, TN
Major city
Pop. 652,050

Address:
2000 North Parkway
Memphis, TN
38112

Admissions:
901-843-3700

Financial Aid:
901-843-3810

adminfo@rhodes.edu

www.rhodes.edu

RHODES COLLEGE

Students
Total enrollment: 1,927
Undergrads: 1,915
Freshmen: 554
Part-time students: 1%
From out-of-state: 73%
From public schools: 53%
Male/Female: 41%/59%
Live on-campus: 71%
In fraternities: 37%
In sororities: 54%
Off-campus employment rating: Good
Caucasian: 73%
African American: 6%
Hispanic: 3%
Asian / Pacific Islander: 6%
Native American: 1%
Mixed (2+ ethnicities): 2%
International: 4%

Academics
Calendar: Semester
Student/faculty ratio: 10:1
Class size 9 or fewer: 25%
Class size 10-29: 69%
Class size 30-49: 5%
Class size 50-99: 1%
Class size 100 or more: -
Returning freshmen: 90%
Six-year graduation rate: 81%

Most Popular Majors
Biology
Political science
Business administration

Admissions
Applicants: 4,138
Accepted: 2,258
Acceptance rate: 54.6%
Placed on wait list: 435
Enrolled from wait list: Not reported
Average GPA: 3.8
ACT range: 26-31
SAT Math range: 580-680
SAT Reading range: 570-690
SAT Writing range: Not reported
Top 10% of class: 49%
Top 25% of class: 78%
Top 50% of class: 96%

552

by Rhodes students, brings elementary-school children to campus for carnival rides and other fun activities.

Another fun event centers on exams and food, a likely pairing at a college so devoted to rigorous study. Pancake breaks are a tradition popular at exam times when faculty and staff cook blueberry and chocolate chip pancakes for anyone who needs a break from studying.

With 37 percent of the male student body and 54 percent of the female student body choosing to join a sorority or fraternity, the Greek scene is a very dominant part of the social life at Rhodes and, despite the large amount of Greek pride, most students report no major rivalry or separation among students. Most events, philanthropic activities, and parties hosted by Greek organizations are open to all students. "There's not much division between Greeks and independents," explains one student. "I've always felt welcome at Greek events."

Although Rhodes is a Division III school with nine men's and 10 women's sports teams, students in general are not as enthusiastic toward sports as the population at many other colleges. The strongest and most competitive of the teams are cross country and women's golf. A large number of students do choose to participate in intramural and club sports. The most popular clubs are Ultimate Frisbee, crew, basketball, and volleyball. "Intramurals are more about having a good time than being competitive," says a student.

Students looking for off-campus activities can benefit from the plethora of offerings in Memphis, from eating and nightlife to shopping and country music. Generally, Rhodes students come away with very positive feelings towards Memphis, where you can almost always be sure to find a country concert of some sort or find other forms of entertainment like Memphis Grizzlies (NBA) games, gallery openings, or Broadway musical productions.

All Rhodes students are randomly assigned a roommate their freshman year and are required to live on campus for the first two years of their undergrad experience. Most freshmen are assigned to live in Glassell or Williford, while upperclassmen usually select the East Village apartments. All dorms are air-conditioned, most halls are single-sex, and the rooms have a reputation for being more spacious when compared with those of other college dorms.

Student Body

Although Rhodes is a moderately ethnically and geographically diverse campus—18 percent of the Rhodes student body is a minority and 73 percent hail from out of state—the student body as a whole is rather homogenous. The majority of students seen walking around campus are Southern, Caucasian, and Christian. The diversity of student opinions and interests, however, is reflected in the large array of student and service organizations in which most people are heavily invested.

You May Not Know

- Rhodes students are nicknamed "Rhodents."
- As an unofficial rite of passage, many students at Rhodes will take a trip to Graceland, the former estate of Elvis Presley, before they graduate.

- One of the most common complaints among Rhodes students is campus dining and its limited options—the only two places on campus with a meal plan are called "The Rat" and "The Lair."

Distinguished Alumni

Bill Alexander, U.S. Congressman from Arkansas; John H. Bryan, former CEO of Sara Lee and board member of Goldman Sachs; Abe Fortas, U.S. Supreme Court Justice; Charlaine Harris, best-selling mystery writer.

Admissions and Financial Aid

Rhodes admissions officials look for students who will add diversity to its campus population. Students should show an invested interest in a variety of extracurricular activities, while simultaneously applying themselves to challenging academic courses. To increase their chances of admission to Rhodes, the university suggests students visit campus, talk to Rhodes students about what they love about the school, or speak with professors about potential majors. Students are invited to visit classes and experience everything the school has to offer.

Rhodes College prides itself on the fact that students are never prevented from attending the university because of financial reasons. With half of students receiving need-based aid and 41 percent of students receiving merit-based aid, the school gives an average of $3.3 million away in scholarships and fellowships each year. Fellowships provide students with financial support in addition to research and service. A multitude of scholarships are also available for incoming students ranging from the Belingrath Scholarship, which provides full tuition and room and board, to the Rhodes scholarship, which totals approximately $11,000 a year. Most scholarships are renewable for all four years.

RHODES COLLEGE

Highlights

Admissions Criteria
Academic criteria:
Grades: ☆ ☆ ☆
Difficulty of class schedule: ☆ ☆ ☆
Class rank: ☆ ☆ ☆
Standardized test scores: ☆ ☆
Teacher recommendations: ☆ ☆
Personal statement: ☆ ☆
Non-academic criteria considered:
Interview
Extracurricular activities
Special talents, interests, abilities
Character/personal qualities
Volunteer work
Work experience
Geographical location
Minority affiliation
Alumni relationship

Deadlines
Early Action: November 15
Early Decision: November 1
Regular Action: January 15 (final)
Notification of admission by: April 1
Common Application: Accepted

Financial Aid
In-state tuition: $39,484
Out-of-state tuition: $39,484
Room: Varies
Board: Varies
Books: $1,170
Freshmen receiving need-based aid: 56%
Undergrads rec. need-based aid: 50%
Avg. % of need met by financial aid: 90%
Avg. aid package (freshmen): $34,271
Avg. aid package (undergrads): $34,042
Avg. debt upon graduation: $26,372

School Spirit
Mascot: Lynx
Colors: Red and black

Four-year private
Founded: 1912
Houston, TX
Major city
Pop. 2,145,146

Address:
P.O. Box 1892
Houston, TX
77251-1892

Admissions:
713-348-7423

Financial Aid:
713-348-4958

admi@rice.edu

www.rice.edu

RICE UNIVERSITY

Overview

The campus of Rice University is, in a word, *gorgeous*. In fact, visitors to the campus are often enamored by the beautiful architecture and struck by the coziness of the residential college system. The main entranceway in Lovett Hall, with its grand sallyport arches, is reminiscent of a castle. According to the college, the design was "inspired by the medieval architecture of Southern Europe, and uniquely adapted [to] the conventions of the collegiate, Gothic Revival style." Architects also kept in mind "the hot and humid coastal plain of Texas" when drawing plans.

Rice is a relatively small research university with 3,800 undergraduate students located on 300 acres. Recently ranked 18th in the nation by *U.S. News & World Report*, Rice highlights the opportunities students have for a strong education in a closed campus in a big city, while fostering close relationships with professors and peers. Three miles from downtown Houston, Rice possesses a prime location in the ever-growing metroplex. The price tag for Rice has generally been lower than other peer universities, offering a great value for the quality of its education. With an endowment of $3.99 billion and a small student population, the endowment per student is among the highest in the nation.

Academics

The strong academic focus at Rice is the main reason many students choose to attend. There are 119 majors offered, with biochemistry and cell biology popular majors since many students go on to medical school. Three general education requirements are mandated for graduation: 12 credits each in the arts or humanities, social sciences, and science or engineering.

Students come from all over the world to study architecture, engineering, and music at Rice. Undergrads work for a year in architecture firms to get hands-on experience. "The architecture program is nationally recognized," notes a student. Rice's engineering programs are among the strongest in the nation, and 65 percent of undergraduates in those majors participate in research, partnerships with the oil and gas industry, NASA, and MD Anderson Cancer Center. The school is academically rigorous, but "there's a lot of attention from professors," says a student. For ambitious students who know they want to attend medical school after graduating Rice, the Rice/Baylor Medical Scholars Program is a great opportunity to get a head start. It is an extremely competitive program, with only 14 incoming freshmen admitted each year.

Students who are interested in graduate school or pursuing careers in certain academic fields should check out the Rice Undergraduate Scholars Program. According to the university, juniors and seniors "act" as graduate students "for an academic year, with a faculty member selected by the student who serves as a mentor." The Humanities Research Center Undergraduate Fellowship is another competitive program that supports undergraduates with interdisciplinary research projects.

Studying abroad is a popular option among students since Rice has over 500 programs and approximately 70 countries to choose from, as well as sister schools in different countries that facilitate a direct exchange of students. Study abroad through several other approved third-party programs is also possible. Study Abroad Peer Advisors are available to guide interested students through the process.

According to students, Rice does an "incredible" job preparing students for life after graduation. Many enter the workforce, but approximately 36 percent of students pursue a graduate degree immediately after graduation. Among students who enter the work force, approximately 32 percent enter a field related to their major within six months of graduation. Being located in the fourth largest city in the nation has its advantages. Houston has the third most Fortune 500 company headquarters, allowing plentiful opportunities for internships. In addition, there is a strong network of alumni located all over the world. Students can find resources through the Center for Student Professional Development.

Student Life

There are many events hosted by different residential colleges. Among these are the "public parties" that all Rice students are invited to attend. Popular public parties include NOD (Night of Decadence), a Halloween lingerie party; Bacchanalia, a toga party; School Girls; and 80's.

There are 215 official clubs at Rice, but the more popular ones include the Rice Student Volunteer Program, the Rice Philharmonics, and the *Rice Thresher*, the official school newspaper. The picturesque campus offers many places to hang out, from lounging on the grassy lawns to having coffee outside Brochstein Pavilion. Rice also has an on-campus undergraduate Pub run by students in the Rice Memorial Center.

Inarguably, the most popular event on campus is Beer Bike. Nearly everyone on campus participates. It all starts with a campus-wide water balloon fight between the colleges; then students chug water and compete in a bike race. "Even alumni return to campus for Beer Bike," says a student. Other big events include Screw Yer Roommate (sic), a campus-wide blind date night, where people dress up in paired costumes to find their dates. Homecoming is a weekend full of activities, including its formal dance, Esperanza. Baker 13 is a tradition where students streak with only shaving cream on at 10 p.m. on every 13th and 31st (or 26th) of the month. "We know how to let loose," laughs a student.

Rice has 14 Division athletic teams. The only national title for team sports is in baseball—the Rice Owls have won four consecutive conference championships. The football team at one time held the second longest streak for not appearing in a bowl game but has recently improved, even winning its first bowl game in 45 years. The women's volleyball, basketball, and track and field teams are strong. Popular intramural sports include badminton, soccer, flag football, Ultimate Frisbee, and volleyball.

Off campus, students can visit the Galleria and Katy Malls, choose from a plentiful assortment of restaurants, or head to Galveston Beach, which is just a 45-minute drive from Rice. Downtown Houston is also easily reached by the light rail. The Museum District, which includes the Houston Museum of Fine Arts and the Museum of Natural Science, is directly adjacent to campus. "Everything is accessible," says a student.

There are 11 residential colleges, each with its own dining hall and public spaces. Whichever college a student is placed in largely influences his or her experience at Rice. Each college has its own set of traditions, norms, governing student body, and culture. There are no fraternities or sororities at Rice, but the college system essentially replaces a need for that. The people in a student's college become like family, and students live with them all four years. Each college has a college master (a faculty member who has tenure) and his/her family, RAs, and a college coordinator. "You identify yourself not as a Rice student or an architecture major but by which college you're in," explains a student.

RICE UNIVERSITY

Highlights

Students
Total enrollment: 6,484
Undergrads: 3,848
Freshmen: 935
Part-time students: 1%
From out-of-state: 49%
From public schools: 76%
Male/Female: 51%/49%
Live on-campus: 72%
Off-campus employment rating: Excellent
Caucasian: 41%
African American: 7%
Hispanic: 14%
Asian / Pacific Islander: 21%
Native American: 0%
Mixed (2+ ethnicities): 5%
International: 11%

Academics
Calendar: Semester
Student/faculty ratio: 6:1
Class size 9 or fewer: 30%
Class size 10-29: 51%
Class size 30-49: 10%
Class size 50-99: 6%
Class size 100 or more: 2%
Returning freshmen: 96%
Six-year graduation rate: 92%
Graduates who immediately go to graduate school: 36%

Most Popular Majors
Psychology
Economics
Biochemistry/cell biology

Admissions
Applicants: 15,133
Accepted: 2,528
Acceptance rate: 16.7%
Placed on wait list: 2,304
Enrolled from wait list: 38
Average GPA: Not reported
ACT range: 30-34
SAT Math range: 700-780
SAT Reading range: 660-750
SAT Writing range: 61-29
Top 10% of class: 90%
Top 25% of class: 97%
Top 50% of class: 100%

555

RICE UNIVERSITY

Admissions Criteria

Academic criteria:
Grades: ☆ ☆ ☆
Difficulty of class schedule: ☆ ☆ ☆
Class rank: ☆ ☆ ☆
Standardized test scores: ☆ ☆ ☆
Teacher recommendations: ☆ ☆ ☆
Personal statement: ☆ ☆ ☆
Non-academic criteria considered:
Interview
Extracurricular activities
Special talents, interests, abilities
Character/personal qualities
Volunteer work
Work experience
Geographical location
Minority affiliation
Alumni relationship

Deadlines

Early Action: No
Early Decision: November 1
Regular Action: January 1 (final)
Notification of admission by: April 1
Common Application: Accepted

Financial Aid

In-state tuition: $38,260
Out-of-state tuition: $38,260
Room: $8,800
Board: $4,200
Books: $800
Freshmen receiving need-based aid: 44%
Undergrads rec. need-based aid: 42%
Avg. % of need met by financial aid: 100%
Avg. aid package (freshmen): $35,549
Avg. aid package (undergrads): $33,004
Avg. debt upon graduation: $18,133

School Spirit

Mascot: Owl
Colors: Blue and gray
Song: *Rice's Honor*

Student Body

With 90 percent of students having graduated in the top 10 percent of their high school class, there are many students who are "very focused on academics." Still, "not everyone spends 24/7 in the library," says a student. There is a high percentage of minorities at 47 percent and almost half of students are from out of state.

Many may mistakenly believe Rice to be a conservative school because of its location in the South, but students describe the political atmosphere as "almost non-participatory" and "very" liberal leaning.

The 61st mayor of Houston, elected in 2009, is the second woman to be elected mayor in Houston, and an alumna of Rice.

You May Not Know

- Yankee Stadium was owned by Rice from 1962-1971, as a gift from '27 graduate John William Cox. Rice later sold it to the City of New York for $2.5 million.
- The Super Bowl was held at Rice in 1974, and the Economic Summit of Industrialized Nations was held on campus in 1990. Rice is the only university ever to have hosted both events.
- The football stadium is so large that all the university's alumni, dead or alive, would not fill it up completely.

Distinguished Alumni

Robert Curl, winner of the Nobel Prize in Chemistry; Larry McMurtry, Pulitzer Prize-winning author (*Lonesome Dove*) and two-time Oscar winner (*The Last Picture Show* and *Brokeback Mountain*); Hector Ruiz, Chairman and CEO of Advanced Micro Devices Inc.

Admissions and Financial Aid

When applying to the university, students must choose one of six academic divisions, but the selection is not binding until the second semester of sophomore year. The interview is not required but recommended.

Rice has a need-blind admissions process and meets 100 percent of students' demonstrated financial need. It has recently been ranked fourth by *Kiplinger's Personal Finance* magazine's 100 best values in private colleges.

The university has a policy that allows families with incomes less than $80,000 to avoid taking out loans. In fact, the cap for loans to need-eligible incoming students has been lowered to $10,000 for the duration of a student's time at Rice. Merit-based scholarships are offered, and 16 percent of undergrads receive this type of financial aid. The Century Scholars Program provides a faculty mentor, two-year merit scholarship, and a research stipend.

RIPON COLLEGE

Overview

Ripon College is a small, private, liberal arts and sciences college in the north-central United States that has a warm sense of community. Ripon takes particular pride in its success rate and history of sending students on to graduate school—especially medical school—and in its high-powered forensics team. High percentages of the student body participate in athletics, from intramural to varsity. Academically, the school's special opportunities promote a holistic vision of the truly well-educated individual.

Ripon's campus is equidistant from Milwaukee and Madison (80 miles either way) and features a range of 19th and 20th century buildings amidst plenty of trees and natural areas. Ripon owns 130 acres of land on which it is recreating a prairie environment—an environment that is wholesome and family-oriented. There's little reason not to enjoy the friendly atmosphere and range of strong academic programs at Ripon.

Academics

Thirty-two majors are available at Ripon, with strong programs in biology (especially for pre-meds), education, and business management. Students enjoy a moderate level of academic competition. "Because our school is small and you know pretty much everyone, there is some competition," says a student. Professors push students to try hard, but also work to ensure their success.

The college describes its academic program with the phrase "Explore-Select-Connect." First-year students are expected to "explore," completing three credits in each of the following divisions: behavioral and social science, fine arts, humanities, and natural sciences. First-years must also complete a First-Year Studies course in any department, take a First-Year Writing course, and sweat their way through an Exercise Science class. After the first year, students "select" a major and then "connect" all the dots in their senior year with a capstone project. All must also fulfill a Global and Cultural Studies requirement through study abroad, foreign language study, or approved courses.

The Communicating Plus program is woven into the liberal arts curriculum at Ripon. This initiative, tailored to each individual major, aims to sharpen students' skills in oral and written communication, critical thinking, and problem solving. One student describes the program as "especially helpful since we just didn't practice those skills in high school." The college further demonstrates its emphasis on producing well-rounded citizens with the Ethical Leadership Program, which teaches students how to make ethical decisions even when times are tough. In addition to Ethical Leadership courses, students get the chance to hear professionals describe how they handled real-life ethical dilemmas in their careers.

Forensics is serious business at Ripon. Unlike most schools, the college covers all costs for travel, competition entry fees, and materials for members of its nationally respected team. Forensics whizzes can even win up to $5,000 per year in scholarships.

Two more special academic opportunities show the diverse interests Ripon nurtures—from consulting to conserving. Working at the Creative Enterprise Center allows students to get real-world experience offering consultancy services to local businesses, all under the wings of professors and professional mentors. Students interested more in the backwoods than the boardroom will enjoy exploring the Ceresco Prairie Conservancy. Ripon sponsors efforts to restore acres of prairie, savanna, and wetland, providing fertile ground for student research.

Ripon is affiliated with 25 study-abroad programs in 18 countries. Ambitious students with a specific plan of study in mind can independently design a semester off-campus pursuing their own project for up to 16 credits. Students taking this option will still have to pay tuition to Ripon.

RIPON COLLEGE

Four-year private
Founded: 1851
Ripon, WI
Rural
Pop. 7,733

Address:
300 Seward Street
Ripon, WI
54971-0248

Admissions:
800-94-RIPON

Financial Aid:
920-748-8101

adminfo@ripon.edu

www.ripon.edu

RIPON COLLEGE

Students

Total enrollment: 968
Undergrads: 968
From out-of-state: 28%
From public schools: 60%
Male/Female: 49%/51%
Live on-campus: 91%
Off-campus employment rating: Good
Caucasian: 85%
African American: 2%
Hispanic: 5%
Asian / Pacific Islander: 1%
Native American: 1%
Mixed (2+ ethnicities): 1%
International: 3%

Academics

Calendar: Semester
Student/faculty ratio: 13:1
Class size 9 or fewer: 20%
Class size 10-29: 66%
Class size 30-49: 12%
Class size 50-99: 2%
Class size 100 or more: -
Returning freshmen: 81%
Six-year graduation rate: 70%
Graduates who immediately go to graduate school: 21%
Graduates who immediately enter career related to major: 63%

Most Popular Majors

History
English

Admissions

Applicants: 1,115
Accepted: 837
Acceptance rate: 75.1%
Average GPA: 3.4
ACT range: 21-27
SAT Math range: 460-610
SAT Reading range: 430-550
SAT Writing range: Not reported
Top 10% of class: 30%
Top 25% of class: 61%
Top 50% of class: 84%

The Career Development office at Ripon offers standard services, including an alumni network to aid in the job search. The office also maintains a library of print and video resources. Nearly half of Ripon grads continue on to graduate school within a year after graduation. "There's an advantage to being at a small school," explains a student. "I've gotten one-on-one help with writing my resume and also practice interviewing."

Student Life

For a small college, Ripon has great cultural events like lectures and concerts on campus on a regular basis. In addition, there are over 70 official student organizations. One of the most popular groups is the Student Media and Activities Committee, the group responsible for the college's thriving cultural and entertainment programming. Pep band, dance groups, and pre-professional societies also make a strong showing. Greek organizations are very prominent on campus, with three sororities and five fraternities, one of which has a frat house on campus. "The party scene is pretty strong considering how small we are," remarks one student.

Each year students enjoy a good old-fashioned murder at Murder Mystery night. It's all in good fun; small teams of students compete to find the solution to a murder mystery show put on by student actors. In less macabre fashion, Springfest celebrates the end of classes with low-key outdoor games and a headlining musical performance. Before classes wind down, the Couch Potato Playoffs are a great breather from intellectual exertions. Students compete to answer pop-culture trivia questions to prove their couch potato cred. In a similar vein, Extrava-Game-Za brings popular TV game shows to life with Ripon students as enthused participants and amused spectators.

The college boasts 21 varsity teams (10 men's, 11 women's) that compete in Division III. Football and men's basketball are among the most popular, while baseball and softball are also competitive. There are a good number of intramurals available as well, including inner tube water polo. A healthy 65 percent of the student population try their luck at intramurals. "Intramurals are not competitive so everyone gets involved," explains a student.

Ripon itself is a small town with some shopping and dining opportunities. Students take road trips to larger, nearby towns like Oshkosh or to big cities like Milwaukee, Madison, or even Chicago. "For the best concerts and bar scenes, you need to get out of the area," confides a student. During the winter, skiing and other cold weather activities are available close by as well.

Ripon wants to keep its students close—students must make a special petition to live off campus. "It's nice that pretty much everyone lives on campus. It builds school spirit," says a student. There are only nine residence halls, and freshmen live together.

Student Body

The town of Ripon itself is conservative, as one might expect from a small Wisconsin hamlet. On campus, jocks should feel comfortable, since a large percentage (~35 percent) of the student body participates in varsity sports. Still, even non-athletes will find a warm welcome on Ripon's remarkably friendly campus. "You pretty much say hi or smile to everyone even if you don't know them," says a student. Among the student body, ethnic diversity is low, and geographic diversity is moderate.

You May Not Know

- The NFL was founded at Ripon in 1931. No, not *that* NFL—the National Forensics League.
- The school paper, *College Days*, is the oldest student paper continuously published in Wisconsin.
- *Newsweek* ranked Ripon number eight on its list of "25 Top Schools for Do-Gooders."

Distinguished Alumni

Harrison Ford, actor; Al Jarreau, Grammy-winning musician; Spencer Tracy, actor.

Admissions and Financial Aid

Ripon suggests a minimum of 17 units of college preparatory work. These credits should include four years of English, three years each of social studies and natural science, and Algebra, Geometry, and Algebra II.

Ripon offers a variety of merit-based scholarships, ranging from under $2,000 to full tuition. Most scholarships are in the $5,000 range. The most prestigious scholarship is the Pickard Scholarship for $13,000 to full tuition. It is awarded to students with a minimum 3.8 GPA, a top-5 percent rank in their high school class, and high SAT or ACT scores.

RIPON COLLEGE

Highlights

Admissions Criteria
Academic criteria:
Grades: ☆ ☆ ☆
Difficulty of class schedule: ☆ ☆ ☆
Class rank: ☆
Standardized test scores: ☆ ☆
Teacher recommendations: ☆ ☆
Personal statement: ☆ ☆ ☆
Non-academic criteria considered:
Interview
Extracurricular activities
Special talents, interests, abilities
Character/personal qualities
Volunteer work
Work experience
State of residency
Minority affiliation
Alumni relationship

Deadlines
Early Action: December 1
Early Decision: No
Regular Action: Rolling admissions
Common Application: Accepted

Financial Aid
In-state tuition: $31,327
Out-of-state tuition: $31,327
Room: $4,665
Board: $4,150
Books: $800
Avg. aid package (freshmen): $18,763 for grants or scholarship aid, $8,052 for student loans
Avg. aid package (undergrads): $18,678 for grants or scholarship aid, $6,994 for federal student loans

School Spirit
Mascot: Red Hawks
Colors: Crimson and white

ROCHESTER INSTITUTE OF TECHNOLOGY

Overview

Set in upstate New York, the Rochester Institute of Technology is a bastion of engineering and computer research. As a master's university with research centers in everything from Imaging Science to Cyber Infrastructure, the undergraduate academic life is enriched with opportunities for research and specialized study. However, RIT also has a strong program in arts and design; and as the home of the National Technical Institute for the Deaf, has a varied and diverse population of students as well as course offerings.

The campus is set in a lush woodland and swamp area, and is affectionately referred to as "Brick City" because almost all the buildings on campus are composed of red brick. Student life on campus is vibrant, with many unique student organizations that support the diverse interests of the RIT students.

The school is professionally focused, as students apply into an academic program. This is great for students who know what they want to do, as they can take advantage of the RIT Co-op program right from the beginning.

Academics

RIT has nine colleges, from the more traditional Colleges of Engineering and Business to the Colisano Institute for Sustainability and the College of Applied Science and Technology. The colleges offer undergraduates 212 majors to choose from, as well as minors and concentration options. RIT is noted for its engineering programs, particularly the microelectronic engineering program, and the College of Imaging Arts and Sciences was the first of its kind in the nation. RIT has also been ranked highly in its fine arts programs, with attention given to glass art, industrial design, and graphic design. In addition, RIT is home to the National Technical Institute for the Deaf and offers a bachelor's degree in ASL-English interpretation as well as a master's degree in deaf education.

Undergraduates complete a Liberal Arts General Education Curriculum. This involves an introductory core—writing, two humanities courses, and two social science courses, an Arts of Expression course, and some advanced course work. Students pursuing a Bachelor of Science degree are required to complete courses in science and mathematics. Finally, students are also required to complete the Wellness Education Requirement, courses "designed to help students develop and maintain a well-balanced, healthy lifestyle that encourages the use of free time in an enjoyable and constructive manner." These courses are essentially sports and activity courses; intercollegiate athletes are exempt, and students participating in club sports are also given credit. The Wellness Education Requirement is "easy and actually fun" to fulfill, says a student. Freshmen can schedule a heavy course-load early on so that they can space out their requirements over a longer period of time.

Students who wish to get real-world experience during their undergraduate years can participate in RIT's co-op program, which is the fourth-oldest in the world and one of the biggest in the nation. The program allows students to alternate quarters of study with three to five quarters of employment. The RIT co-op program partners with close to 2,000 employers worldwide. "Almost everyone does a co-op because there's no better way to get hands-on work experience," explains one student.

RIT also has an Honors program, structured around the three ideals of leadership, scholarship, and citizenship. Students participate in a special curriculum with seminar-style classes, live together in the honors residence hall, and are required to participate in leadership or service activities. Honors students are granted a yearly scholarship of $1,000.

The University Studies Program was launched in 2009 to help undecided undergraduate students choose their majors. Students in the program focus on core general education courses during their first year to expose them to a variety of fields. They also must enroll in a Career Exploration Seminar and spend time in personalized academic advising.

Another option for students who wish to make the most out of their years at RIT is an Accelerated Dual Degree, in which students earn a bachelor's and master's degree in five years. A common option is a BS combined with a business MBA.

Rochester students are encouraged to study abroad, either during the year or over the summer. The school has its own study-abroad programs, supplemented by affiliated programs at other schools, giving students choices from a wide range of countries and cities. The gamut extends from China to Hungary to Nicaragua.

After graduation, most students enter the work force, and 13 percent attend graduate school within one year of graduating. Companies that often hire graduates from RIT include Microsoft, Lockheed Martin, Toyota, and Intel. Alumni are supported by the Office of Cooperative Education and Career Services, which provides networking opportunities. There is also an Alumni Online Community with a directory of over 100,000 alumni records.

Student Life

RIT has over 200 student organizations, many which reflect the unique interests of RIT students, such as the Jewelry and Metals Association, and a wide variety of Deaf Clubs to support the large population of deaf students. Another unique organization on campus is RIT's Tech Crew, comprised entirely of student employees, which supports on-campus activities, providing lighting, sound, staging, and power for everything from dance parties to rock concerts to commencement. There are also 29 Greek organizations on campus, which have a small but significant presence with five percent of students participating. Some of the organizations have their own special housing on campus.

Major events on campus also reflect the character of the school. Besides the annual Homecoming activities, more unique events include the annual Brick Bash, where student-designed brick-bashing machines are used to crush bricks. The event arose from a machine design class, where the machines were the final student project. The students are evaluated on their design and the amount of brick pieces left after the machine has done its work. "Only at RIT would we get so excited about smashing bricks," laughs a student.

A bigger event is the annual Imagine RIT Festival, which showcases innovative and creative activity specific to RIT. Open to the public, some 30,000 visitors can view new ideas for products and services and attend theatrical and musical performances. For those who wish to get off campus, the city of Rochester offers shopping, restaurants, and cultural opportunities. Students describe Rochester as "having more than you'd expect" although they also take road trips to Buffalo, Syracuse, and Canada.

RIT has 23 varsity sports teams (11 men's and 12 women's) which compete in Division III, with the notable exception of men's hockey, which competes in Division I. There is also a wide variety

ROCHESTER INSTITUTE OF TECHNOLOGY

Highlights

Students
Total enrollment: 16,362
Undergrads: 13,711
Freshmen: 2,757
From out-of-state: 49%
From public schools: 83%
Male/Female: 68%/32%
Live on-campus: 68%
In fraternities: 5%
In sororities: 5%
Off-campus employment rating: Excellent
Caucasian: 61%
African American: 5%
Hispanic: 6%
Asian / Pacific Islander: 5%
Native American: 0%
Mixed (2+ ethnicities): 2%
International: 5%

Academics
Calendar: Semester
Student/faculty ratio: 13:1
Class size 9 or fewer: 16%
Class size 10-29: 57%
Class size 30-49: 23%
Class size 50-99: 4%
Class size 100 or more: 1%
Six-year graduation rate: 62%
Graduates who immediately go to graduate school: 13%

Most Popular Majors
Computer science
Mechanical engineering
Electrical engineering

Admissions
Applicants: 16,353
Accepted: 9,562
Acceptance rate: 58.5%
Placed on wait list: 376
Average GPA: 3.6
ACT range: 25-30
SAT Math range: 570-680
SAT Reading range: 540-650
SAT Writing range: 7-32
Top 10% of class: 35%
Top 25% of class: 66%
Top 50% of class: 93%

561

College Profiles

ROCHESTER INSTITUTE OF TECHNOLOGY

Admissions Criteria
Academic criteria:
Grades: ☆ ☆ ☆
Difficulty of class schedule: ☆ ☆ ☆
Class rank: ☆ ☆
Standardized test scores: ☆ ☆
Teacher recommendations: ☆
Personal statement: ☆
Non-academic criteria considered:
Interview
Extracurricular activities
Special talents, interests, abilities
Character/personal qualities
Volunteer work
Work experience
State of residency
Geographical location
Minority affiliation
Alumni relationship

Deadlines
Early Action: No
Early Decision: December 1
Regular Action: February 1 (priority)
Common Application: Accepted

Financial Aid
In-state tuition: $33,932
Out-of-state tuition: $33,932
Room: $6,530
Board: $4,648
Books: $1,025
Freshmen receiving need-based aid: 79%
Undergrads rec. need-based aid: 69%
Avg. % of need met by financial aid: 88%
Avg. aid package (freshmen): $22,800
Avg. aid package (undergrads): $22,600
Avg. debt upon graduation: $24,200

School Spirit
Mascot: Tiger
Colors: Burnt umber, orange, and white

of club and intramural teams, which include flag football, Ultimate Frisbee, and racquetball. There is also a Deaf Basketball Association.

Freshmen are required to live on campus at RIT, and most are assigned to a residence hall. There are many options for finding a good match, such as Lifestyle Floors, which include substance free and smoke free floors or intensified study floors. There are also seven Special Interest Houses, where members share a particular passion. These include the Art, Computer Science, Engineering, General Science, Photo, International, and Unity House. Many upperclassmen opt to live in off-campus apartments.

Student Body

RIT's student population is moderately diverse, with about half of each class hailing from out of state. There are also 1,200 deaf or hard-of-hearing students on campus, and a number of the professors are also deaf. Many hearing students participate in the RIT Sign program to learn sign language.

You May Not Know

- The RIT campus is largely covered with fresh-water swamp and woodland, making it home to rare plant species.
- RIT boasts the largest sculpture on any American university campus—a 70 ft. high, 110 ton steel structure called *The Sentinel*.
- To support the deaf and hard-of-hearing students on campus, RIT has the largest number of interpreters among universities in the country.

Distinguished Alumni

Bernie Boston, photojournalist; Tom Curley, president and CEO of the Associated Press; Bob Duffy, New York Governor; N. Katherine Hayles, critical theorist; Bruce James, 24th Public Printer of the United States.

Admissions and Financial Aid

RIT does not have any specific grade requirements for applicants but states that "the most successful RIT students have a positive attitude toward learning, the desire to get involved in campus life, and a significant interest in developing professional potential."

Students do not apply to RIT as a whole; instead, they apply to a specific academic program. However, applicants are encouraged to select second-choice programs when applying for admission, as they might qualify for a second or third choice if they are not accepted into their first-choice program.

RIT also offers a number of merit-based scholarships, especially for freshmen, many of which are based on SAT scores and high school academic records. These include scholarships that are subject specific, such as the Computing Medal scholarships, and scholarships for business, arts, or robotics. Most scholarships range from $6,000 to $9,000 per year.

ROLLINS COLLEGE

Overview

Rollins College is a small private liberal arts school near Orlando, Florida that—according to students—has a reputation for attracting "wealthy students who like to party." Naturally, not all students fit this mold, and students say that "everyone finds their own group."

Founded in 1885, the Rollins campus features beautiful lakeside Spanish Mediterranean architecture set on 70 acres. The college highlights its students' accomplishments in "writing, collaboration, discussion, and community-based learning" as well as its "unique" programs in sustainable development, Australian studies, and international business.

Academics

Rollins students tend to excel while learning in cooperative settings. In fact, it is not uncommon for students to work closely with faculty to publish collaborative research. The college prides itself on providing a practical liberal arts education. With 193 full-time and 44 part-time faculty members, Rollins has a 10:1 student-to-faculty ratio with only one percent of classes exceeding 30 students. "If you want one-on-one interaction with professors, this is the place to be," states a student.

Rollins offers 35 majors, with particularly strong programs in economics, international business, and psychology. Minors and practical concentrations are also available. "Many of us are serious about our studies," a student comments. To be eligible to graduate with a BA, students must complete one course from each of 10 general education areas: Expressive Arts, Non-Western Cultures, Western Society and Culture, Foreign Language, Literature, Organic and Physical Sciences, Quantitative Reasoning, Contemporary American Society, Values, and Writing.

Students who want a more rigorous approach to their academics may be eligible for the Honors Degree Program. Freshmen who are in the top 10 percent of their entering class are eligible to be invited to participate in the Honors Degree Program. A small number of sophomores are invited to participate each year.

Rollins has a 3/2 Accelerated Management Program that allows students to complete their undergraduate and graduate work in five years, receiving both a BA and an MBA from the Crummer Graduate School of Business at Rollins College. Students who want to apply to the program can do so during the regular admission process by indicating that they are interested in being considered. Admission is very selective, but students who are not selected as entering freshmen can reapply after the first semester of their first year.

The college has a fairly comprehensive study-abroad program, with classes in Australia, China, Costa Rica, France, Germany, Greece, Hong Kong, Italy, Peru, Spain, Turkey, the United Kingdom, the Dominican Republic, and the Czech Republic.

And what happens after Rollins? The Office of Career Services has an active job posting board on their website for current students and alumni. About 22 percent of Rollins graduates pursue a higher degree immediately after undergrad, while 31 percent enter graduate school within a year after graduation.

Student Life

Rollins is a small college and doesn't provide the kind of breadth and variety in extracurricular activities that a larger campus would. Still, there is plenty to do, and students can find outlets through 100 official student organizations. The most popular include College Democrats, College Republicans, the *Sandspur* (Rollins' official school newspaper), and the Interfraternity Council.

Other social activities include Snowed In, the signature event at Rollins that serves as the official welcome-back of the spring. Since snow in Florida—also known

ROLLINS COLLEGE

Four-year private
Founded: 1885
Winter Park, FL
Large town
Pop. 28,398

Address:
1000 Holt Avenue
Winter Park, FL
32789-4499

Admissions:
407-646-2161

Financial Aid:
407-646-2395

admission@rollins.edu

www.rollins.edu

ROLLINS COLLEGE

Students

Total enrollment: 2,459
Undergrads: 1,884
Freshmen: 518
From out-of-state: 54%
From public schools: 58%
Male/Female: 41%/59%
Live on-campus: 68%
In fraternities: 29%
In sororities: 35%
Off-campus employment rating: Good
Caucasian: 64%
African American: 7%
Hispanic: 16%
Asian / Pacific Islander: 3%
Native American: 0%
Mixed (2+ ethnicities): 2%
International: 5%

Academics

Calendar: Semester
Student/faculty ratio: 10:1
Class size 9 or fewer: 28%
Class size 10-29: 71%
Class size 30-49: 1%
Class size 50-99: -
Class size 100 or more: -
Returning freshmen: 84%
Six-year graduation rate: 72%

Most Popular Majors

Economics
Psychology
International business

Admissions

Applicants: 4,542
Accepted: 2,533
Acceptance rate: 55.8%
Placed on wait list: 188
Enrolled from wait list: 13
Average GPA: 3.3
ACT range: 24-29
SAT Math range: 540-640
SAT Reading range: 550-640
SAT Writing range: 10-35
Top 10% of class: 38%
Top 25% of class: 69%
Top 50% of class: 95%

564

as the Sunshine State—is practically nonexistent, Rollins students take matters into their own hands, and with a little help from a snow machine, the Cornell Campus Center is transformed into a true winter wonderland. "It's the first time to see snow for some students," recalls a student, "even if it's manmade."

Lip Sync—a friendly competition between student organizations faculty, fraternities, and sororities—is a battle for the trophy that represents one of the college's biggest traditions. Fox Day is another time-honored event. Once a year, the college president places a statue of a fox outside on Mills Lawn, signifying that classes for that day have been cancelled.

The Greek scene is enormously popular. Almost one third of all students join the seven sororities and five fraternities on campus. "To get the most social mileage," a student advised, "you should probably pledge."

Rollins boasts 21 NCAA Division II national championships and 52 Sunshine State Conference championships. Fans need a closet of blue and gold to cheer their varsity teams, which include golf and waterskiing. Several options are available for intramural sports, including basketball, bowling, flag football, kayaking, soccer, rock climbing, tennis, and volleyball. Most students participate in at least one intramural sport during their time at Rollins, and many students participate in more than one.

More than 65 percent of students live on campus in either one of the six residential halls or one of the 11 small houses reserved for fraternities, sororities, and residential organizations. While plenty of students choose to live off campus after their first year, living in the dorms offers a more active social life.

Student Body

Rollins has a strong affluent and conservative vibe. "It's not unusual to overhear students talk about their family's vacation homes," says a student.

The largest minority group at Rollins is represented by Hispanics at 16 percent of the student population. African-American, Asian or Pacific Islander, and mixed ethnicity students make up an additional 12 percent of the students.

You May Not Know

- Rollins' Mayflower Hall has a 15-inch piece from the original Mayflower on display.
- The first Fox Day happened in the Spring of 1956, when college president, Hugh McKean, put a statue of a fox on the lawn, cancelled all classes, and invited students and faculty to spend time doing things together at the college.
- Fred Rogers, creator of "Mister Rogers Neighborhood," is a Rollins graduate. His signature sweater and sneakers are on display in Olin Library.

Distinguished Alumni

F. Duane Ackerman, Chairman and CEO, BellSouth Corporation; Donald J. Cram, Nobel Prize winner in chemistry; Karen Moyer Garrison, President and CEO of Pitney Bowes Services; Dana R.

Ivey, stage and screen actress; Hunt Lowry, film producer of *Last of the Mohicans*, *A Time to Kill*, and *Donnie Darko*.

Admissions and Financial Aid

Rollins considers a student's academic record, talents, interests, and potential to contribute to the Rollins community. Applicants are required to submit a representation of their strengths or talents. They can be creative in this venture, so much so that the presentation mode is often as unique as the student. Past submissions have included YouTube videos, DVDs or slideshows of a musical or artistic talent, scrapbooks, and CDs. Rollins also requires one letter of recommendation from a teacher. The recommender must have taught the student in a core academic class during junior or senior year.

Students have the option of applying without their standardized test scores using the "Test Score Waived Option." There are two rounds of early decision deadlines and the regular decision deadline. Applicants who want to be considered for Cornell Scholarships, Deans' Scholarships, and Donald Cram Scholarships should submit all application materials by the January deadline. Students who want to be considered for the Centennial and Presidential Scholarships should submit all application materials by the February deadline. Cornell Scholarships are for full tuition, and Deans' Scholarships are for up to $20,000 per year.

ROLLINS COLLEGE

Highlights

Admissions Criteria
Academic criteria:
Grades: ☆ ☆ ☆
Difficulty of class schedule: ☆ ☆ ☆
Class rank: ☆
Standardized test scores: ☆ ☆
Teacher recommendations: ☆ ☆
Personal statement: ☆ ☆
Non-academic criteria considered:
Extracurricular activities
Special talents, interests, abilities
Character/personal qualities
Volunteer work
Work experience
State of residency
Alumni relationship

Deadlines
Early Action: No
Early Decision: November 15
Regular Action: January 15 (priority)
February 15 (final)
Notification of admission by: April 1
Common Application: Accepted

Financial Aid
In-state tuition: $41,460
Out-of-state tuition: $41,460
Room: $5,080
Board: $5,340
Books: $818
Freshmen receiving need-based aid: 53%
Undergrads rec. need-based aid: 57%
Avg. % of need met by financial aid: 80%
Avg. aid package (freshmen): $33,676
Avg. aid package (undergrads): $34,058
Avg. debt upon graduation: $24,096

School Spirit
Mascot: Tars
Colors: Blue and gold

Four-year private
Founded: 1874
Terre Haute, IN
Large town
Pop. 60,961

Address:
5500 Wabash Avenue
Terre Haute, IN
47803

Admissions:
812-877-8213

Financial Aid:
812-877-8259

admissions@rose-
hulman.edu

www.rose-hulman.edu

ROSE-HULMAN INSTITUTE OF TECHNOLOGY

Overview

Rose Hulman is a small, private technical school that balances academic rigor and personal attention with a somewhat relaxed environment. While it may not have the name recognition as other technical schools, Rose-Hulman has a reputation for highly rigorous coursework. Expect a nose-to-the-grindstone study experience here with less time for college frivolity than might be expected in other schools. Upon graduation, though, you will have a well-respected degree and you will be ready for a technical career. In addition to its small class sizes, one of Rose-Hulman's major benefits is the school's strong connections to leaders in industry. Programs like Rose Hulman Ventures and the Consulting Engineering Program give students an excellent, practical preparation for technical careers.

The tree-lined campus—home to two lakes—is located among the rolling hills of Terre Haute, IN. The architecture ranges from traditional to modern. Terre Haute itself is not a hotbed of activity, so social life centers on dorms and Greek houses. The heavily male skew of the student population, preponderance of white Midwesterners, and obvious technical bent of the majority of the student body create a social environment that's rather "geekish. " Still, if nerdy activities like Nerf gun fights and elaborate pranks appeal to you, Rose-Hulman is a good option.

Academics

Twenty-six majors are available at Rose-Hulman. The school's strong suits are electrical engineering, mechanical engineering, and computer science. The core requirements must be fulfilled during the freshman year, which is quite possible since they are short and sweet: a one-credit course in "College and Life Skills," one rhetoric and composition course, a humanities and social science elective, and calculus I, II, and III (for those students who don't place out through testing). Beyond that, each program of study is clearly mapped out, with little choice of courses and few electives. The academic calendar runs on a trimester system. Coursework tends to be challenging but not cutthroat. Students say the first two years are the hardest, and if you can make it through the intensive sophomore year you should be fine from then on. The sophomore year is part of the "weeding out process," confides a student, adding, "only the fittest survive."

Selected freshmen who score a minimum of 700 on the math section of the SAT may qualify to take Fast Track Calculus courses that cover integral and multivariable calculus over the summer before freshman year. There are several other special programs to round out your academic experience at Rose-Hulman as well. The Consulting Engineering Program supplements students' engineering preparation with business and communications courses that prepare them for lucrative careers in the world of consulting. Interested students should be prepared to take on even more credits than are required to earn the already-demanding BS degree. Similarly, the Management Studies Program teaches students managerial strategy, ethical management, and economics in addition to their technical degree. Like the Consulting Engineering Program, it often entails an intensive course load for engineering majors, but it is more manageable for other majors.

Study abroad is offered in 14 different countries. For high-achieving juniors with what Rose-Hulman deems "academic and personal maturity," the Foreign Studies program is an opportunity to study engineering and science at prestigious universities abroad.

Rose-Hulman's Career Services administers an alumni mentoring program to put students in contact with successful alumni with whom they may network to their hearts' content. In addition to teaming up with alumni, the Partnership Program forges links to major corporations. This year, 12 companies, including Proctor & Gamble and Texas Instruments, will be recruiting on campus, holding speakers' series, and funding students to attend conferences. "Companies know we're a goldmine of future employees," says a student.

Rose-Hulman Ventures connects students with big ideas to companies with big wallets. Through this program, students get to do hands-on work with large technological companies in a facility that is just a five-minute walk from campus. The focus is on innovation and development, providing an excellent way for students to get practical experience while they prepare for their careers.

Student Life

A somewhat small percentage of Rose-Hulman students live on campus. Most socializing happens off campus at student or frat houses. Fraternities and sororities play a large role in the social life of Rose-Hulman with about one quarter of students participating. There are eight frats, each with a house on campus, and three sororities, two of which have houses on campus. Students describe the social scene as "small" and "not our strongest asset." If you're looking for a bigger party scene, nearby Indiana State University's reputation as a big party school attracts hopeful Rose-Hulman students for weekend shenanigans.

Freshmen rally together to build a huge bonfire at Homecoming each year, an activity that has been a tradition since 1923. Over the course of a week, students build a 25-foot tall structure—topped by an outhouse—to be burned down. As they see it, what better symbol of camaraderie and school spirit is there than a flaming outhouse? Rose-Hulman is also known for impressive senior pranks. Continuing the nerdy theme of campus-wide events, many students get involved in playing "Zombies" several times a year. Basically, engineers attack "zombies" (their fellow engineers) with Nerf guns around campus.

In terms of organized activities, there are 98 official student organizations, ranging from the nerdy (such as the role-playing club) to the run-of-the-mill (for example, the film club). As you might expect, many of the groups have a scientific bent. Rose-Hulman also fields 19 sports teams, 10 men's and nine women's, that compete in Division III. Basketball is the most popular, while baseball, softball, and soccer are the most competitive. Intramural sports include the usual options but also a "Strongest Engineer" competition, which is unique to the school. Additionally, chess is a competitive activity.

Though students feel off-campus recreation and entertainment is limited in Terre Haute, they are pleased to receive free tickets for Terre Haute Symphony concerts, and there are a few places in town to grab a bite to eat. There's also shopping at the Honey Creek Mall. Still, considering the low-key nature of the town and the heavy workload, it's not surprising that hanging out at dorms, apartments, or frats is the main social outlet at Rose Hulman. "Terre Haute is not a very active college town," explains one student, "but it has the basics of what we need." The adventurous might be able to swing a road trip to Indianapolis, Chicago, Cincinnati, or St. Louis.

Freshmen and sophomores are guaranteed housing, and freshmen must live on campus. On the up side, there's a weekly maid service. On the down side, students complain about unappetizing

ROSE-HULMAN INSTITUTE OF TECHNOLOGY

Highlights

Students
Total enrollment: 2,214
Undergrads: 2,121
Freshmen: 621
From out-of-state: 66%
Male/Female: 79%/21%
Live on-campus: 62%
In fraternities: 26%
In sororities: 23%
Off-campus employment rating: Good
Caucasian: 79%
African American: 2%
Hispanic: 3%
Asian / Pacific Islander: 4%
Native American: 0%
Mixed (2+ ethnicities): 3%
International: 8%

Academics
Calendar: Quarter
Student/faculty ratio: 13:1
Class size 9 or fewer: 14%
Class size 10-29: 74%
Class size 30-49: 11%
Class size 50-99: -
Class size 100 or more: -
Six-year graduation rate: 82%

Most Popular Majors
Mechanical engineering
Chemical engineering
Biomedical engineering

Admissions
Applicants: 4,469
Accepted: 2,926
Acceptance rate: 65.5%
Placed on wait list: 95
Enrolled from wait list: 3
Average GPA: 3.9
ACT range: 27-32
SAT Math range: 630-730
SAT Reading range: 560-670
SAT Writing range: 9-37
Top 10% of class: 60%
Top 25% of class: 90%
Top 50% of class: 100%

567

College Profiles

ROSE-HULMAN INSTITUTE OF TECHNOLOGY

Admissions Criteria

Academic criteria:
Grades: ☆ ☆ ☆
Difficulty of class schedule: ☆ ☆ ☆
Class rank: ☆ ☆ ☆
Standardized test scores: ☆ ☆
Teacher recommendations: ☆ ☆
Personal statement: ☆
Non-academic criteria considered:
Interview
Extracurricular activities
Special talents, interests, abilities
Character/personal qualities
Volunteer work
Work experience
State of residency
Alumni relationship

Deadlines

Early Action: No
Early Decision: No
Regular Action: Rolling admissions
Common Application: Not accepted

Financial Aid

In-state tuition: $39,462
Out-of-state tuition: $39,462
Room: $7,041
Board: $4,443
Books: $1,500
Freshmen receiving need-based aid: 71%
Undergrads rec. need-based aid: 69%
Avg. % of need met by financial aid: 72%
Avg. aid package (freshmen): $28,031
Avg. aid package (undergrads): $26,703
Avg. debt upon graduation: $44,965

School Spirit

Mascot: Dear Old Rose
Colors: Red and black
Song: *Fightin' Engineers*

food at the dining halls. Students say the food is "edible but barely" and "a good motivator to eat out." Upperclassmen tend to move into Greek houses or off campus. Those who do live on campus might be lucky enough to stay in Apartment Hall, built in 2004. As the name suggests, rooms are apartment-style with full kitchens to give students their own cooking options.

Student Body

Most Rose-Hulman students are academically motivated, Midwestern males. Almost 80 percent of the student body is male. That means very good dating odds for straight women, but also a college experience lacking in female companionship. "Of course we miss having more women, but at the same time, there's not much time for dating outside of schoolwork," says a student. Ethnic diversity is moderate (12 percent minority students) and geographic diversity is moderate (66 percent from out-of-state). While the student body overall leans a bit conservative, the campus environment is apolitical—probably a result of a demanding workload that leaves little time for activism.

You May Not Know

- If your class schedule doesn't include a lunch break, Rose-Hulman has a special lunch-packing service.
- The "Hulman" in the school's name comes from a Terre Haute family that donated its farmland to the growing school in 1917.
- There are live-in tutors in sophomore dorms who are available round the clock to get you through the toughest year at Rose-Hulman.

Distinguished Alumni

Ernest Davidson, recipient of the National Medal of Science for quantum chemistry research; Robert Wilkins, president, National African American Museum and Cultural Complex; Jason Zielke, President and COO, Precise Path Robotics.

Admissions and Financial Aid

Quantitative types who shudder at the thought of writing a college essay will love Rose-Hulman's application. No essay is required, but students are allowed to provide additional information to support their application, which could include an essay, SAT Subject Test results, or anything else. If you apply before December 1, the application fee is waived.

The Rose-Hulman Merit Scholarship is awarded based on academic achievement and/or extracurricular involvement, leadership, and community service. There are a limited number of named scholarships. Full scholarships are available to underrepresented populations in science and math. No separate scholarship applications are required.

RUTGERS – THE STATE UNIVERSITY OF NEW JERSEY

RUTGERS,
THE STATE
UNIVERSITY OF
NEW JERSEY

Four-year public
Founded: 1766
Piscataway, NJ
Large town
Pop. 55,444

Address:
65 Davidson Road
Piscataway, NJ
08854-8097

Admissions:
732-932-4636

Financial Aid:
848-932-7057

admissions@ugadm.
rutgers.edu

nb.rutgers.edu

Overview

The largest university within New Jersey's state university system—with a total enrollment of almost 40,000, including more than 31,000 undergrads—Rutgers offers a wide range of academic opportunities and boasts one of the most diverse student bodies in the nation. While the school itself is spread across three campuses, the New Brunswick campus has the largest concentration of students. Located along the Raritan River, the main campus features ivy-covered traditional brick buildings, some of which go back to Colonial times, and verdant open spaces. A 24-hour-a-day bus service shuttles students from each campus. Nearby New Brunswick offers an urban vibe, and Philadelphia and New York City are both within road-trip distance.

Everything about Rutgers screams big: the university can feel like a small city, with 6,400 acres, 863 buildings, and 18 libraries. While this means there's certainly something for everyone, it also means extra effort in seeking out the right academic opportunities and social niche. Those who aren't afraid of getting lost in the crowd, who jump at the opportunity to be part of a sea of red at the Scarlet Knights' home football games, and are proactive in seeking out their learning options, might find Rutgers to be the perfect place for their undergraduate years.

Academics

Rutgers offers more than 100 bachelors programs (plus 100 masters and 70 doctoral degree programs) in 175 academic departments. The main New Brunswick campus includes 10 undergraduate schools, including the School of Arts and Sciences, School of Engineering, College of Nursing, and more. Strong programs include the social sciences and majors in pharmacy and engineering.

Each school has its own requirements, but all students must fulfill writing skills, humanities and arts, and social science and life science mandates. Students also must pass an "Expository Writing" requirement. Students say the workload is fairly steady. Academic opportunities abound but require a proactive attitude to seek out. "Professors are accessible if you make the effort," says a student.

The School of Arts and Sciences Honors Program offers an enriched curriculum with interdisciplinary honors seminars taught by leading faculty members, discipline-specific honors courses, and a Capstone Project senior year. There is also funding for research, a Peer Mentor and Faculty Mentor program, and a Summer Reading program.

Students looking to interweave their academic and residential lives will appreciate the learning communities where they can take shared courses with their housemates. Another great way to meet students as a freshman is to participate in the First-year Interest Group Seminars (FIGS), one-credit seminars taught by upper-class students. The impetus of FIGS is to help first-year students transition to college while exploring an academic interest area. Those looking for faculty connection can participate in The Byrne Family First-Year Seminar Program, which links first-year students to prominent professors in small (20 students or less) seminars that have no letter grades and no formal exams.

Study-abroad options include the Rutgers International Service Learning Program in five countries, incorporating a course on interventionist work with grassroots women in Ghana and another focused on child welfare in Translyania. There are study-abroad scholarships and peer advisors plus regional coordinators to help students navigate all the options.

The career services office hosts more than a dozen career days a year for students to meet future potential employers as well as CareerKnight, an online database of job and internship listings and on-campus interviews. According to the Rutgers Alumni

RUTGERS, THE STATE UNIVERSITY OF NEW JERSEY

Students

Total enrollment: 40,434
Undergrads: 31,268
Freshmen: 6,170
Part-time students: 5%
From out-of-state: 8%
Male/Female: 51%/49%
Live on-campus: 53%
Off-campus employment rating: Fair
Caucasian: 47%
African American: 8%
Hispanic: 12%
Asian / Pacific Islander: 26%
Native American: 0%
Mixed (2+ ethnicities): 3%
International: 3%

Academics

Calendar: Semester
Student/faculty ratio: 14:1
Class size 9 or fewer: 13%
Class size 10-29: 49%
Class size 30-49: 18%
Class size 50-99: 11%
Class size 100 or more: 9%
Returning freshmen: 92%
Six-year graduation rate: 77%
Graduates who immediately enter career
    related to major: 20%

Most Popular Majors

Business administration
Psychology
Pharmacy

Admissions

Applicants: 28,635
Accepted: 17,436
Acceptance rate: 60.9%
Average GPA: Not reported
ACT range: Not reported
SAT Math range: 540-670
SAT Reading range: 500-620
SAT Writing range: 13-36
Top 10% of class: 41%
Top 25% of class: 77%
Top 50% of class: 98%

Association, it is "one of the oldest continuously operating alumni associations" in the United States, founded in 1831. There are more than 310,000 Rutgers alumni, with about 60 percent of whom live in New Jersey.

Student Life

Rutgers is home to over 400 student organizations. These include the second-oldest college newspaper, *The Daily Targum* (after *The Dartmouth*). The Rutgers University Glee Club was started in 1872 and exists today. Every fall, thousands of students flock to the Fall Involvement Fair on the Voorhees Mall to learn more about clubs and activities.

The New Brunswick campus has over 40 fraternities and sororities, including African American, Hispanic, multicultural, and Asian Greek organizations. The first fraternity was founded in 1845 on campus and Greek life continues to be a major part of campus interaction. "Greeks are a minority, but a loud minority," says a student.

At such a large university, annual events always bring much fanfare. Football games turn campus into a sea of scarlet-clad fans. Spring is particularly festive: Rutgersfest brings together 30,000 people for the annual end-of-the-year carnival and free concert, with nationally recognized performers, boardwalk style carnival games, and plenty of food and snacks. Also in spring is Rutgers Agricultural Field Day, a farm-oriented event with hands-on demonstrations, exhibits, lectures, plant sales, animal fairs, and department-specific events like the entomology department's cockroach races. Commencement brings a touch of tradition to campus as undergraduates smash clay pipes over the Class of 1877 Cannon monument, symbolizing the breaking of their ties with the college.

The Rutgers Scarlet Knights compete in 22 sports (nine men's, 13 women's) at the Division I level. Football is the most popular sport and is nationally competitive. Baseball, basketball, tennis, and soccer are also standouts. Recently, men's basketball coach Mike Rice was fired from the university after being caught on tape hitting, kicking, and name-calling players. "What an embarrassment," says one student. Nearly 1,000 men and women actively participate in the sports programs. There are also over 50 intramural sports and a hefty list of club sports, from aikido to wrestling.

Students head to the city of New Brunswick for dining and entertainment. Those looking for a big city vibe take road trips to NYC and Philadelphia.

Dorms at Rutgers are large, and there are also special interest housing options, from living-learning communities to co-op living and recovery housing. Students split evenly between living on campus and living off campus, though upperclassmen tend to move off campus. Douglass Residential College is an all-female housing option.

Student Body

With such a large student body, the composition of people at Rutgers is diverse. Students seem to find a balance between academics and social life. There is high ethnic diversity, with minority students making up 49 percent of the student body. Geographic diversity, however, is low, with 92 percent of students coming from New Jersey and the vast majority coming from the Northeast.

You May Not Know

- The graduating class of 1774 consisted of just one student, Matthew Leydt.
- Rutgers is the eighth-oldest university in the nation and one of only two colleges to predate the founding of the country to become public universities (College of William and Mary is the other).
- In 2008, Rutgers University members broke the Guinness World Record for "Largest Gathering of People Dressed as Ninja Turtles" (786). In 2009, they captured the Guinness World Record for "Largest Gathering of People Dressed as Waldo" as a fundraiser (1,052) for New Brunswick public schools.

Distinguished Alumni

Kristen Davis, actress; Milton Friedman, economics Nobel Laureate; Paul Robeson, African-American concert singer, recording artist, athlete, and actor; Barry Schuler, former CEO of AOL.

Admissions and Financial Aid

The admissions office notes that preference is given to students who submit all application materials by the priority deadline. Factors considered for acceptance include high school performance as measured by class rank, GPA, grade trends, and advanced classes. Additionally, standardized test scores, and completion of entrance requirements—including those in English, foreign language, math, science, and other areas—are carefully weighed. For the Mason Gross School of Arts, a formal talent assessment is a large part of the admissions decision.

The essay that students must complete with the application is used to consider eligibility for academic scholarships. Rutgers' merit scholarships are competitive awards. No set of "numbers" can guarantee receipt of these awards. The most prestigious is the Presidential Scholarship of $23,000 per year, plus guaranteed on-campus housing for four years and admission to the Honors Program. The James Dickson Carr Scholarship honors the first African-American Rutgers graduate and reflects a commitment to diversity.

RUTGERS, THE STATE UNIVERSITY OF NEW JERSEY

Highlights

Admissions Criteria
Academic criteria:
Grades: ☆ ☆ ☆
Difficulty of class schedule: ☆ ☆ ☆
Class rank: ☆ ☆ ☆
Standardized test scores: ☆ ☆ ☆
Teacher recommendations: ☆
Personal statement: ☆
Non-academic criteria considered:
Extracurricular activities
Special talents, interests, abilities
Volunteer work
Work experience
Geographical location
Minority affiliation

Deadlines
Early Action: No
Early Decision: No
Regular Action: December 1 (priority)
Notification of admission by: April 16
Common Application: Not accepted

Financial Aid
In-state tuition: $10,718
Out-of-state tuition: $24,742
Room: $7,092
Board: $4,486
Books: $1,550
Freshmen receiving need-based aid: 61%
Undergrads rec. need-based aid: 58%
Avg. % of need met by financial aid: 52%
Avg. aid package (freshmen): $12,992
Avg. aid package (undergrads): $12,393
Avg. debt upon graduation: $23,212

School Spirit
Mascot: Scarlet Knight
Colors: Scarlet
Song: *On the Banks of the Old Raritan*

SANTA CLARA UNIVERSITY

SANTA CLARA UNIVERSITY

Four-year private
Founded: 1851
Santa Clara, CA
Medium city
Pop. 118,263

Address:
500 El Camino Real
Santa Clara, CA
95053

Admissions:
408-554-4700

Financial Aid:
408-554-4505

www.scu.edu

Overview

A medium-sized private Jesuit university in the Bay Area of California, Santa Clara University (SCU) features a beautiful mission campus with Spanish architecture and an abundance of trees and gardens. Recent expansion projects include a new baseball field, the campus' first green building, and a new facility for the School of Business.

With an average 300 days of sunshine a year, you'll find students focused on coursework and their tans at the same time. Located just minutes west of San Jose and about 45 miles south of San Francisco, students—at least those with cars—can enjoy a plethora of off-campus activities. On campus, students develop a liberal arts and sciences foundation over four years while also taking programs in business and engineering.

Students won't find a Greek system at Santa Clara, and not all will feel comfortable in the fairly political conservative environment. However, "conservative" doesn't mean stodgy—after all, this is a school that has a commencement tradition of students taking their dads out for 6:00 a.m. drinks at the local bar on the day of graduation. Religion and spirituality are a major influence on campus—Jesuits make up about around seven percent of the permanent faculty, and there's even a Residential Learning Community devoted to faith and social justice. All told, students who appreciate great weather and a solid liberal arts education at a diverse school that values service, religion, and—as befits Silicon Valley—innovative and interdisciplinary research, may find SCU to be a good fit for their undergraduate studies.

Academics

Santa Clara's undergraduate schools include the College of Arts and Sciences, Leavey School of Business, and the School of Engineering. The School of Education Counseling and Psychology and Jesuit School of Theology offer graduate level courses. There are more than 45 undergraduate majors.

SCU's Core Curriculum is broken down into requirements in Foundations (introductory courses), Explorations (linking one's major to other areas of learning), and Integrations (experiential learning, advanced writing, and a cluster of related courses). The curriculum includes classes in critical thinking, writing, mathematics, a second language in the first year; courses on ethics, arts, civic engagement, and sciences in the second year; and science, technology, and society courses in the third year. Students are required to take courses in religion, theology, and culture for three years.

The academic climate at SCU is rigorous. "Almost everyone studies pretty hard, and it's not easy to find classes you can cruise through," says a student. Strong programs include the various majors in the Leavey School of Business and the School of Engineering and communication in the College of Arts and Sciences.

Students wanting an extra challenge can participate in the Honors Program in any major. Honors students take small, seminar-style classes with no more than 17 students. These replace many core courses. Students in the Honors Program enjoy priority registration. "The most motivated students are in the program," explains a student.

The Roeland Fellows Grant Program provides funding for research in Science and Technology for Social Benefit for students and faculty, with innovative past projects such as developing a mobile application for monitoring labor rights issues and using solar energy to provide clean water. Students interested in research in other fields are encouraged to connect with faculty and apply for undergraduate research funding—summer research awards range upwards to $7,000.

SCU offers over 100 study-abroad programs in 50 countries. Students with high language proficiency can enroll in a number of Catholic or Jesuit universities overseas. "The best way to become truly immersed is to learn alongside foreign students," remarks one student. The university runs a number of programs, including one in Australia with an internship component.

There are more than 71,000 SCU alumni. The Career Center on campus offers a number of services. The Center found that in 2012, 81 percent of recent graduates were employed full time, attending graduate school, or participating in a service program within six months of graduation.

Student Life

There are more than 100 student organizations at SCU, including KSCU FM, the student-operated radio station; *The Santa Clara* weekly newspaper; and the Santa Clara Community Action Program, a volunteer service organization where students can tutor, help with the Special Olympics, and more. SCU's Activities Programming Board brings comedians and other entertainment to campus. Past events facilitated by this board have included concerts by Maroon 5, The Roots, and Mos Def. Community service is popular on campus: every quarter, 500 students enroll in courses that integrate academics and direct experience with underserved populations through the Eastside Project. "We believe in giving back," shares a student. "To be able to learn while doing so is the best of both worlds."

Many of the annual events on campus are organized by the Residential Learning Communities. These include an East Campus vs. West Campus "capture-the-flag" game; Dormal Formal, a free campus-wide formal dance attended by hundreds; and the even more popular Mr. RLC competition—think Miss America with Mr. representatives from each RLC. Students crowd Market Square every year to cheer on their favorites in categories such as talent, formal attire, and a choreographed group dance.

Midnight Breakfast is an ever-popular effort every quarter to stave off the hunger of stressed-out students before finals. Likewise, certain student initiatives are associated with graduation festivities. Dads and Grads is a commencement tradition where graduates take their dads to the Hut, a local Santa Clara dive bar, in the early hours of the morning. After graduation, recent grads return to the Hut to pin their business cards and first dollar made from their first job out of college on the ceiling. "The whole place is covered in dollar bills and business cards," says a student.

SCU's 19 teams (nine men's, 10 women's) compete in Division I. Men's and women's soccer are nationally competitive. Men's basketball is also competitive, and basketball games against the rival teams of St. Mary's and Gonzaga are always highly attended.

Off-campus, students head to San Jose for dining or shopping. San Francisco offers bigger city entertainment, while Santa Cruz and Monterey have beach and ocean-front activities for those willing to make longer road trips. "A car is a must," comments a student.

Housing is guaranteed for at least the first two years; many students move off campus starting junior year. Students live in Residential Learning Communities, which focus on programming to foster a strong sense of community among undergrads—some are even multi-year. There are eight communities in all, including Loyola for students interested in faith and justice, da Vinci for those

SANTA CLARA UNIVERSITY

Highlights

Students
Total enrollment: 8,519
Undergrads: 5,250
Freshmen: 1,278
Part-time students: 2%
From out-of-state: 41%
From public schools: 45%
Male/Female: 50%/50%
Live on-campus: 53%
Off-campus employment rating: Excellent
Caucasian: 46%
African American: 3%
Hispanic: 18%
Asian / Pacific Islander: 14%
Native American: 0%
Mixed (2+ ethnicities): 6%
International: 3%

Academics
Calendar: Quarter
Student/faculty ratio: 12:1
Class size 9 or fewer: 8%
Class size 10-29: 65%
Class size 30-49: 25%
Class size 50-99: 1%
Class size 100 or more: -
Returning freshmen: 95%
Six-year graduation rate: 86%
Graduates who immediately go to graduate school: 15%

Most Popular Majors
Communications
Psychology
Finance

Admissions
Applicants: 14,339
Accepted: 7,344
Acceptance rate: 51.2%
Placed on wait list: 2,057
Enrolled from wait list: 71
Average GPA: 3.6
ACT range: 27-31
SAT Math range: 610-700
SAT Reading range: 590-680
SAT Writing range: Not reported
Top 10% of class: 44%
Top 25% of class: 81%
Top 50% of class: 96%

573

College Profiles

SANTA CLARA UNIVERSITY

Admissions Criteria

Academic criteria:
Grades: ☆ ☆ ☆
Difficulty of class schedule: ☆ ☆ ☆
Class rank: ☆ ☆
Standardized test scores: ☆ ☆
Teacher recommendations: ☆ ☆
Personal statement: ☆ ☆ ☆
Non-academic criteria considered:
Extracurricular activities
Special talents, interests, abilities
Character/personal qualities
Volunteer work
Work experience
Geographical location
Religious affiliation/commitment
Minority affiliation
Alumni relationship

Deadlines

Early Action: November 1
Early Decision: November 1
Regular Action: November 1 (priority)
January 7 (final)
Notification of admission by: Late March
Common Application: Accepted

Financial Aid

In-state tuition: $42,156
Out-of-state tuition: $42,156
Room: Varies
Board: Varies
Books: $1,710
Freshmen receiving need-based aid: 49%
Undergrads rec. need-based aid: 44%
Avg. % of need met by financial aid: 68%
Avg. aid package (freshmen): $26,310
Avg. aid package (undergrads): $27,067
Avg. debt upon graduation: $28,672

School Spirit

Mascot: Broncos
Colors: Red and white
Song: *Fight for Santa Clara*

passionate about Italian culture, and Cyphi for sustainability and the arts aficionados.

Student Body

SCU's undergraduates lean conservative politically, in contrast to the reputation of the broader Bay Area as a politically liberal area. Students tend to come from upper-middle class backgrounds and students describe themselves as "focused but not overly focused."

There is very high ethnic diversity. Forty-one percent identified as an ethnic group other than Caucasian. There are large groups of Hispanic, Asian, and multi-ethnic students. There is moderate geographic diversity, with 41 percent of students from out of state.

You May Not Know

- According to the university it is "California's oldest operating higher-education institution."
- The university was founded at the site of one of the original California missions.
- Hubert Flynn, S.J., a philosophy professor at the university, created the athletic teams' nickname in 1923 when he wrote, "the Bronco is a native westerner, a chunk of living dynamite... He can kick and oh boy how he can buck."

Distinguished Alumni

Dee Dee Myers, author, political commentator, and former Press Secretary; Janet Napolitano, Secretary of Homeland Security; Steve Nash, professional basketball player; Peter Oppenheimer, Senior Vice President and CFO of Apple.

Admissions and Financial Aid

In considering applications for admission, SCU looks at the rigor of high school coursework, cumulative GPA, standardized test scores, a letter of recommendation, and involvement in school and community activities. SCU recommends that students take both the SAT and ACT and submit the stronger test score. Students are encouraged to use the personal essay to let their personalities shine through and to include something not apparent from the rest of the application. SCU does not conduct interviews.

Scholarships include the Presidential at Entry Scholarship for freshman admitted with distinction, a merit-based award that covers four years of tuition. The Provost Scholarship honors student leaders and covers half tuition for four years. There are a number of other awards, including those for students in theater, dance, and music.

SARAH LAWRENCE COLLEGE

Overview

Sarah Lawrence College, a small liberal arts college in the New York City suburb of Bronxville, has been honored by the *Huffington Post* as the 5th-ranked "Top Hipster School" in the nation. What they mean by that, they say, is that Scary Larry or Sadie Lou, as SLC students colloquially call it, is one of the places "witty-independent-artist-intellectuals most often float to—places where the pants are tight, the hearts are bleeding, the conversation is postmodern, and gender is nothing more than a social construct." Sarah Lawrence's particular brand of hipster likes its winter coats distressed and/or vintage, prefers to get naked in the spring, worships *Rocky Horror*, and gender-bends at will. At Sarah Lawrence, if the pants aren't tight, they're not on at all, and, as students gleefully demonstrate at the annual Sleaze Ball, gender is more of a playground than a construct.

But "witty-independent-artist-intellectual" isn't just a descriptor for the social environment at SLC: for SLC's academically-focused students, independence and the arts—both liberal and fine—are the name of the game inside the Tudor- or red-brick-style classroom buildings as well. SLC's unique curriculum has no real majors and requires students to design their own paths of study and concentrations in close consultation with faculty advisors, or "dons." SLC additionally puts a heavy emphasis on the creative and fine arts, and requires it as part of its loosely-defined curriculum. If you are seriously passionate about the humanities and fine arts, are creative and self-disciplined enough to design and monitor your own course of studies, and don't have qualms with events that feature optional clothing, then Sarah Lawrence is a match made in hipster heaven for you.

Academics

SLC nominally has no majors or required curriculums. Instead, students' main areas of interest are called "concentrations;" students can concentrate in one of 32 writing-intensive disciplines. A set of loose stipulations gently nudges students' courses of study in an interdisciplinary direction: no more than 50 of the 120 credits required for the BA can be earned in a single discipline. Courses are divided into four main areas (creative and performing arts, history and the social sciences, humanities, and natural sciences and mathematics), and the number of credits students can take in each area is capped, meaning that students must explore multiple areas. SLC also has a requirement of four quarters of physical education, half of which must be completed during freshman year. Grades are awarded only for the purposes of transcripts; what really matters is the written evaluations professors give.

If this sea of wide-open possibilities overwhelms or confuses you, don't worry: every student at SLC is assigned a faculty advisor, called a "don," who advises the student and helps to develop an individual course of study tailored to the student's needs and interests. Students' dons teach their First-Year Studies Seminar, and students continue to meet with their dons on a weekly basis. "I love my don! She has guided me through my whole time here," says a student.

As part of their required three courses per semester, students at SLC take a variety of types of courses, beginning with the First-Year Studies Seminar. These seminars are offered in several different disciplines and, in addition to in-depth study of an academic topic, introduce methods of critical thinking and exploration and emphasize written and oral communication. All classes at SLC are taught by full professors, not graduate students, and nearly all classes at SLC are seminar-style—lecture classes are almost non-existent—and have fewer than 20 students. Nearly every class requires independent research and writing supervised by the professor.

The most common type of course for upperclassmen is the Seminar/Conference system, in which a small, interactive seminar is accompanied by biweekly one-on-one conferences with the professor. During these conferences, professors and students

SARAH LAWRENCE COLLEGE

Four-year private
Founded: 1926
Bronxville, NY
Large town
Pop. 195,976

Address:
1 Mead Way
Bronxville, NY
10708-5999

Admissions:
800-888-2858

Financial Aid:
914-395-2570

slcadmit@sarahlawrence.edu

www.slc.edu

SARAH LAWRENCE COLLEGE

Highlights

Students
Total enrollment: 1,744
Undergrads: 1,413
Freshmen: 413
Part-time students: 3%
From out-of-state: 83%
Male/Female: 28%/72%
Live on-campus: 85%
Off-campus employment rating: Excellent
Caucasian: 66%
African American: 4%
Hispanic: 8%
Asian / Pacific Islander: 7%
Native American: 1%
International: 6%

Academics
Calendar: Semester
Student/faculty ratio: 9:1
Class size 9 or fewer: 30%
Class size 10-29: 66%
Class size 30-49: 3%
Class size 50-99: 1%
Class size 100 or more: -
Returning freshmen: 89%
Six-year graduation rate: 70%

Admissions
Applicants: 2,012
Accepted: 1,225
Acceptance rate: 60.9%
Average GPA: 3.6
ACT range: 27-30
SAT Math range: 550-650
SAT Reading range: 600-700
SAT Writing range: 590-680
Top 10% of class: 37%
Top 25% of class: 59%
Top 50% of class: 91%

plan independent research and writing projects related to the course. Students say that the conferences give "amazing access to professors" and "guarantee face time." SLC offers about 10 lecture courses per year, of which students may take two. Designed to give a broad overview of a single topic, these classes are capped at 45 students and usually complemented by group conferences.

Sarah Lawrence College's year-long abroad programs in Florence, Catania, Paris, Oxford, and Havana are distinct in their emphasis on small seminars and conference work. SLC also offers exchanges with five American and one British university as well as a semester in London that offers students professional experience with the British American Drama Academy.

A few special programs allow students to further tailor their course work to suit their interests. Upperclassmen have the option of signing up for either a "Language Third" or "Science/Math Third," both of which allow students to take two language courses or two science and/or math courses, respectively, as a third of their programs. Service Learning Seminars provides a hands-on outlet where students' conference work for the course consists of working with a local social service or social change organization. The Pre-Health Program is another avenue for augmenting coursework, adding MCAT and medical school preparation classes, original research and conference work, and a pre-health advisor to supervise and coach participants through the medical school admissions process. The Spring Writing Semester, open to SLC and non-SLC students alike, offers intensive writing workshops and lectures and field trips to readings and events in New York City.

About 10 percent of SLC graduating seniors immediately go on to grad school, with another 10 percent entering grad school within a year of graduation. Most enter the workforce.

Student Life

SLC's 61 student organizations range from identity groups, such as the Queer Voice Coalition, to performance groups, such as Porcelain Baby Burlesque and Midnight Cabaret. The college's clubs are as varied as the school's curriculum options, including, for example, the anime club Kamikazes Anonymous and arts-and-crafts club Stitch'n'Bitch.

Absence of a Greek system doesn't impede SLC's social life; on-campus events at SLC are far more provocative than most Greek activities at other campuses. Events run the gamut from the G-rated Mayfair carnival, with arts and crafts, obstacle courses, mini-golf, and carnival games; to Midnight Breakfast, where students stay up late cramming during end-of-semester Conference Week and then head to the dining hall in Bates to munch on pancakes; to the storied not-so-G-rated events.

SLC's most infamous event is Sleaze Week, a week dedicated to raising awareness about safe sex and open discussion of sexuality, promoting activism, and raising funds for HIV/AIDS charities. Put on by the student group TransAction, it features classes like "Tranny 101" and sexual etiquette. Midnight Cabaret has a special "Sleaze" theme; an aphrodisiac buffet is on offer; and the week culminates in the "Sleaze Ball," where you're likely to see most men wearing ball gowns and heels. Coming Out Month features a Coming Out Ball, which entails a lot of nudity. "You literally need to be comfortable in your own skin," says a student.

SLC's 12 varsity sports teams compete at Division III level; women's swimming and tennis are the most competitive. In addition to satisfying their physical education requirement, SLC students can play on intramural soccer, basketball, Ultimate Frisbee, and volleyball leagues.

Off campus, students may visit quaint Bronxville for its restaurants, including the popular Slave to the Grind, or the city of Yonkers for shopping and movie theatres. A half-hour train ride on the Metro North train will leave you at Grand Central Station, putting all of New York City's entertainment possibilities at your feet.

Most SLC students spend their first two years living on campus, which offers a range of options, including co-ed or single-sex traditional residence halls, apartments, converted houses, cooperative living areas, and themed-community dorms. Juniors and seniors generally move off campus to Yonkers.

Student Body

Reflective of its beginnings as an all-female college, SLC has a female-to-male ratio of almost 3:1. The student body is mostly from out of state and displays a high level of ethnic diversity. Students are generally the artsy-intellectual type. "We know we have a hipster stereotype," laughs a student. "And to be honest, it's pretty accurate," she adds.

You May Not Know

- Deb Ball, as Sleaze Ball was known when it began in 1983, was the first college-level AIDS fundraiser in the country.
- During the time that SLC was all-female, part of its early curriculum included "productive leisure," which included modeling, applying make-up, and gardening.
- The Black Squirrel, of which the campus has many, is SLC's unofficial mascot.

Distinguished Alumni

J.J. Abrams, film producer and creator of *Lost*; Rahm Emanuel, White House Chief of Staff; W. Ian Lipkin, molecular neurobiologist, discoverer of West Nile Virus; Julianna Margulies, actress; Yoko Ono, artist; Carly Simon, singer and songwriter; Alice Walker, writer; Barbara Walters, broadcast journalist; Vera Wang, fashion designer; Joanne Woodward, actress.

Admissions and Financial Aid

SLC does not look at standardized test scores for admissions, so high school transcripts and admissions essays are the most important components of the application for admittance. In addition to writing a traditional personal essay, applicants must also submit an analytical paper as a writing sample.

Sarah Lawrence awards more than 80 annually-renewable scholarships to applicants demonstrating academic promise and achievement in addition to need-based aid. Some of the scholarships also focus on students with financial need. No extra application is needed.

SARAH LAWRENCE COLLEGE

Highlights

Admissions Criteria
Academic criteria:
Grades: ☆ ☆ ☆
Difficulty of class schedule: ☆ ☆ ☆
Class rank: ☆
Standardized test scores: Test-optional
Teacher recommendations: ☆ ☆ ☆
Personal statement: ☆ ☆ ☆
Non-academic criteria considered:
Interview
Extracurricular activities
Special talents, interests, abilities
Character/personal qualities
Volunteer work
Work experience
State of residency
Geographical location
Minority affiliation
Alumni relationship

Deadlines
Early Action: No
Early Decision: November 1
Regular Action: January 1 (priority)
January 1 (final)
Notification of admission by: April 1
Common Application: Accepted

Financial Aid
In-state tuition: $47,640
Out-of-state tuition: $47,640
Room: $9,416
Board: $4,520
Books: $600
Freshmen receiving need-based aid: 66%
Undergrads rec. need-based aid: 60%
Avg. % of need met by financial aid: 89%
Avg. aid package (freshmen): $31,959
Avg. aid package (undergrads): $33,525
Avg. debt upon graduation: $18,360

School Spirit
Mascot: Gryphons
Colors: Hunter green and white

577

SCRIPPS COLLEGE

Four-year private women's college
Founded: 1926
Claremont, CA
Large town
Pop. 35,143

Address:
1030 Columbia Avenue
Claremont, CA
91711

Admissions:
909-621-8149

Financial Aid:
909-621-8275

admission@scrippscollege.edu

www.scrippscollege.edu

Overview

Visitors to Scripps College will find a verdant 30-acre campus with Spanish and Mediterranean architecture, a rose garden, and olive trees scattered throughout. The campus is listed on the National Historic Register of Places. Scripps Green—actually its own color—can be found throughout campus, from doors in the residence halls to the caps and gowns worn at Commencement.

Though very small in terms of size and enrollment (less than 1,000), the private women's college is recognized as one of the best liberal arts institutions in the nation. As a member of the five Claremont Colleges (5C), Scripps can offer students the advantage of resources no less than those found at a very large university.

Students looking for a bigger city than Claremont can drive to L.A., an hour away, though campus certainly provides a much calmer setting for the challenging academics. Women looking for an excellent liberal arts education with an intimate community of bright fellow peers will want to consider becoming a "Scrippsie"—as long as they don't mind the lack of Greek life and a demanding Core Curriculum.

Academics

There are 22 departments at Scripps, though over 60 total courses of study are available to students thanks to the 5C arrangement. Strong programs include art, biology, math, politics and international relations, and psychology.

Central to the Scripps educational experience is the Core. The three-part Core sequence goes through fall semester of sophomore year. Core I consists of a lecture/discussion course with a common syllabus; Core II choices are selected by students for more intensive study; and Core III offers a chance to develop independent research and projects. General requirements also include classes in fine arts, letters, natural sciences, social sciences, foreign language, women's/gender studies, and race/ethnic studies. First-year students must also take a writing course, and each student must complete a senior thesis or project.

Academics are challenging but not competitive. "There are many brilliant and talented women," says a student. At such a small school it is easy for students to get to know professors. "I've had lunch at the homes of two of my professors," notes a student. The school shares facilities with the other Claremont Colleges, including Honnold/Mudd Library and the Keck Science Center.

The Joint Science Program offered in conjunction with Claremont McKenna and Pitzer Colleges offers 10 majors, including biology and engineering. Students majoring in the sciences usually finish their four years with a research experience or thesis.

The Scripps Post-Baccalaureate Premedical Program is open to women and men who have received a BA in a field other than science from any four-year university. The small, selective program offers an educational foundation in the basic science prerequisites and boasts a nearly-universal acceptance rate into medical and professional schools for its graduates.

The Collaborative Gender and Women's Studies Research Grant Program, begun in 2003, has created opportunities for student/faculty research in the area of Gender and Women's Studies, part of the Intercollegiate Women's Studies of the Claremont Colleges. This means that students have access to "a greater offering of classes, speakers, and even scholarship opportunities," a student explains.

Off-Campus Study has more than 100 programs in 41 countries, and approximately 60 percent of students participate. Of Scripps students who go abroad, about 80 percent study a foreign language.

After graduation, about 60 percent of Scripps alumnae work, eight percent receive competitive fellowships and grants for full-time study and research, and 28 percent pursue graduate or professional degrees. Nearly two-thirds of Scripps students complete graduate degrees within five years of graduation. Life Connections, a database of 1,000 alumnae and friends, keeps Scrippsies connected post-graduation.

Student Life

Scripps College has more than 30 student clubs and organizations, plus those offered by the Smith Campus Center at Pomona College. Several clubs are service-oriented, including the Community Tutoring Program, Crepes for a Cause, and S.W.E.E.T (Scrippsies Who Endow Edible Treats) Bakery, a club that bakes birthday treats for children in an after-school care program.

A central part of campus is the Motley, a nonprofit coffee shop collectively run by students since 1974. Students go to the Motley to enjoy fair trade espresso, study, hang out, and listen to evening concerts. "I've spent many, many hours studying there," says a student.

There are a number of charming traditions at Scripps. At the beginning of each year the Dean of students holds the Dean's Desserts, a semi-formal party. For those who enjoy such activities, every Wednesday will be a treat since Afternoon Tea is a weekly tradition. The annual Medieval Dinner is a community event that promises dinner and a dance. It is held under tents on the lawn outside Denison Library. Four times a year, there are also Candlelight Dinners.

There are no sororities at Scripps, and indeed, no Greek life at all in any of the 5Cs. "With less than 1,000 students on a small, tight-knit campus, we're like one big sorority already," one student comments.

Scripps' 11 varsity teams compete in Division III. The athletic programs are held in conjunction with Claremont McKenna College and Harvey Mudd, and the women's teams compete as the Athenas (the men's teams are the Stags). Water polo, tennis, and swimming are the most competitive. Intramurals also fall under the umbrella of Claremont-Mudd-Scripps Athletics. The college houses the Sallie Tiernan Field House, a 24,000-square-foot recreation and fitness facility with a 25-meter pool and soccer/lacrosse fields.

Off campus, the city of Claremont offers a place for low-key days/nights out. Students can take road trips to Los Angeles, San Diego, Las Vegas, and even Mexico or make treks to participate in outdoor activities as part of the Scripps Outdoor Adventure Program (SOAP), Claremont Colleges Ski Club, and Harvey Mudd Sailing Club.

Most students live in one of nine residence halls or apartments. Dorms receive rave reviews for being spacious and aesthetically pleasing. "The dorms truly are beautiful and peaceful," notes a student. Indeed, all the residences halls have courtyards and fountains, and many rooms have balconies.

Student Body

Many students are "upper-middle class" women interested in feminist issues. "In class or outside of class, almost every day of the week, you'll hear discussions about women's issues. If that's not for you, this may not be the place for you," says a student.

There is high student diversity on campus, with 35 percent students of color. There is moderate geographic diversity, with 48 percent of students from out of state. There are also many students

SCRIPPS COLLEGE

Students
Total enrollment: 962
Undergrads: 945
Freshmen: 235
Part-time students: 1%
From out-of-state: 46%
Male/Female: 0%/100%
Live on-campus: 95%
Off-campus employment rating: Good
Caucasian: 52%
African American: 4%
Hispanic: 9%
Asian / Pacific Islander: 19%
Native American: 0%
Mixed (2+ ethnicities): 3%
International: 5%

Academics
Calendar: Semester
Student/faculty ratio: 10:1
Class size 9 or fewer: 16%
Class size 10-29: 82%
Class size 30-49: 2%
Class size 50-99: 1%
Class size 100 or more: -
Returning freshmen: 92%
Six-year graduation rate: 90%

Most Popular Majors
Psychology
Political science/government
Fine/studio arts

Admissions
Applicants: 2,373
Accepted: 769
Acceptance rate: 32.4%
Placed on wait list: 499
Average GPA: 4.1
ACT range: 28-32
SAT Math range: 620-700
SAT Reading range: 640-730
SAT Writing range: 50-45
Top 10% of class: 70%
Top 25% of class: 96%
Top 50% of class: 100%

SCRIPPS COLLEGE

Admissions Criteria

Academic criteria:
Grades: ☆ ☆ ☆
Difficulty of class schedule: ☆ ☆ ☆
Class rank: ☆ ☆ ☆
Standardized test scores: ☆ ☆ ☆
Teacher recommendations: ☆ ☆ ☆
Personal statement: ☆ ☆ ☆
Non-academic criteria considered:
Interview
Extracurricular activities
Special talents, interests, abilities
Character/personal qualities
Volunteer work
Work experience
State of residency
Geographical location
Minority affiliation
Alumni relationship

Deadlines

Early Action: No
Early Decision: November 15
Regular Action: January 2 (final)
Notification of admission by: April 1
Common Application: Accepted

Financial Aid

In-state tuition: $45,350
Out-of-state tuition: $45,350
Room: $7,280
Board: $6,188
Books: $800
Freshmen receiving need-based aid: 37%
Undergrads rec. need-based aid: 42%
Avg. % of need met by financial aid:
   100%
Avg. aid package (freshmen): $36,473
Avg. aid package (undergrads): $39,422
Avg. debt upon graduation: $17,487

School Spirit

Mascot: Stags (men)/Athenas (women)
Colors: Maroon and gold

from Washington and Oregon, though Massachusetts and New York make it into the top 10 list of 45 states represented.

You May Not Know

- Scripps mascot, La Semeuse, means "she who sows."
- The college was founded by newspaper publisher and philanthropist Ellen Browning Scripps in 1926.
- Scripps has its own font, named "Goudy Scripps" or "Scripps College Old Style" as well as its own color, "Scripps Green," which can be found throughout campus.

Distinguished Alumnae

Anne Hopkins Aitken, a "modern mother" of Zen Buddhism in the west; Gabrielle Giffords, U.S. Congresswoman; Rosemary Radford Ruether, theologian; Alison Saar, artist.

Admissions and Financial Aid

The admissions team at Scripps reviews applications holistically, with a focus on academic performance, SAT or ACT test scores, the personal essay, recommendations, and extracurricular activities. Interviews are encouraged, though not required.

Students who wish to be considered for scholarships must submit all application materials by November 1 and check the merit-based scholarship box on the front of the Common Application. These can range from half of tuition to the full cost of attendance. Scripps College pays for finalists to come to campus in early February for final interviews.

The James E. Scripps Award is given to between 20 and 35 scholars each year. The New Generation scholarship and Loenetti scholarship are competitive and highly prestigious awards that cover tuition, fees, room, board, three roundtrip airfares home annually, and $3,000 summer research stipend.

SEATTLE UNIVERSITY

Overview

True to its Jesuit-Catholic roots, Seattle University boasts a tradition of dedication to social justice, claiming the responsibility of empowering the leaders of the next generation. The university offers committed teachers, vigorous course work, and extracurricular activities aimed to equip students with the tools necessary to address the difficult issues in our world.

Founded in 1891, this private, church-affiliated institution lies in the heart of bustling Seattle, a city known for its eccentric culture and international community. In this exciting Pacific Northwestern setting, students socialize amidst green gardens and redbrick buildings, including the well known Chapel St. Ignatius.

Located a short distance from endless restaurants, shopping, and nightlife, Seattle University provides plenty of entertainment for its students. The university is also just minutes from the waterfront, allowing opportunities for plenty of maritime recreation.

New facilities on campus include the Lemieux Library and the McGoldrick Learning Commons.

Academics

Seattle University offers 61 bachelors degree programs. All students must follow the Core Curriculum, which includes three phases—Foundations of Wisdom, Person in Society, and Responsibility and Service. The first phase emphasizes critical thinking and includes subjects such as composition and argument, quantitative reasoning, historical origins, and fine arts. First-year students also take a Core Freshman Seminar. The second stage explores the nature of society, with a focus on the social sciences as well as theology and religious studies. The third stage educates students on how to make a positive impact on the world through ethics. This includes an interdisciplinary course on social problems and a senior synthesis.

The rigor of academics at Seattle University varies by major; however, students agree that the intimate nature of the student body and the accessibility of professors make the workload manageable and intellectually stimulating. Strong programs at the university include nursing, business, and public affairs. "The public affairs department is amazing," remarks a major. "We get hands-on experience through internships that prepare us for careers in public and non-profit organizations."

The University Honors Program is a special academic opportunity to which students are invited to apply. As a part of this program, exceptional students may take part in a select, two-year-long academic experience dedicated to providing in-depth study of philosophy, literature, and history. "I've not only learned so much because of the program, but I've also made some of my best friends through it," says a student.

The Academic Salons Local Immersion Program offers day-long excursions to local communities where students may explore the cultural, economic, health, and religious aspects of the community. The focus of these events is to better equip students for futures in public service. Students typically work in small groups with a faculty member.

Premajor Studies is a program designed to assist and direct students as they search academia for a field of study that is right for them. One of the largest programs at the university, Premajor Studies provides academic advising for the freshmen and sophomores who participate. "It's a relief to know that there's guidance when you're not really sure what you want to do," comments a student.

Studying abroad at Seattle University is popular, with 500 students studying in 45 different countries each year. Destinations include such exotic locations as Belize, Austria, and Ecuador. Although studying abroad is not a general graduation requirement, several majors either require or heartily encourage an international experience.

SEATTLE UNIVERSITY

Students
Total enrollment: 7,484
Undergrads: 4,589
Freshmen: 1,029
Part-time students: 5%
From out-of-state: 57%
From public schools: 65%
Male/Female: 41%/59%
Live on-campus: 41%
Off-campus employment rating: Excellent
Caucasian: 49%
African American: 4%
Hispanic: 9%
Asian / Pacific Islander: 17%
Native American: 1%
Mixed (2+ ethnicities): 5%
International: 10%

Academics
Calendar: Quarter
Student/faculty ratio: 12:1
Class size 9 or fewer: 12%
Class size 10-29: 70%
Class size 30-49: 18%
Class size 50-99: -
Class size 100 or more: -
Returning freshmen: 87%
Six-year graduation rate: 77%

Most Popular Majors
Nursing
Management
Liberal arts

Admissions
Applicants: 6,862
Accepted: 4,904
Acceptance rate: 71.5%
Placed on wait list: 924
Enrolled from wait list: 14
Average GPA: 3.6
ACT range: 24-29
SAT Math range: 540-640
SAT Reading range: 530-640
SAT Writing range: 7-38
Top 10% of class: 26%
Top 25% of class: 58%
Top 50% of class: 89%

582

Networking for careers after graduation is made easy at the University with the Redhawk Network, which students use to connect with alumni for employment and internship opportunities.

Student Life

With the Club Connections group working with students to create new organizations every day, Seattle University provides more than 300 clubs and groups on campus. Popular ones include the charity event organizers for Dance Marathon, the Student Events and Activities Council, and Dinner Club. Although there is no Greek system at the University, the busy student body never complains for lack of an active social scene. "Our school is small enough I'm glad we aren't divided up by a Greek scene," says a student.

Popular events on campus include Quadstock, an annual all-day music festival that takes full advantage of Seattle's eclectic music scene. Besides the music, there is sumo suit wrestling, inflatable obstacle courses, dunking booths, and a henna booth. "It's an all-day party," says a student. The Shaft Dance, for which roommates pick each other's dates, and the All School Picnic and BBQ, held the first week after students get back from summer break, are also standout events.

Athletics at the University are spread across Division I and Division II, with 17 teams (eight men's, nine women's) competing. The Redhawks are typically most competitive in men's basketball, with women's tennis, women's golf, and baseball trailing close behind. More than 1,200 students participate in the 30 intramural sports, and students participate in "trail, climbing, snow, water, cycling, and service project activities" through the Outdoor Adventure and Recreation (OAR) program.

When students itch to explore off campus, the grand city of Seattle lies at their fingertips. Students head to downtown Seattle for shopping, dining, and extensive nightlife, while those more interested in the outdoors have the mountains nearby for snow activities and hiking. "Seattle really has everything you'd want in a college town," notes a student, "and it's all very accessible."

All first- and second-year students must live on campus unless they are commuting students or are at least 21 years old. "The dorms are above average," says a student. A unique housing opportunity is Learning Communities, which integrate studies into the housing experience. Third- and fourth-year students, however, often choose to live off-campus in apartments.

Student Body

There is a heavy female skew in this Jesuit-Catholic student body, with almost 60 percent women. The typical student is also very "outdoor-oriented and passionate to the point of being almost crazy about the environment," reports a student. Additionally, the student body is high in ethnic diversity, with 36 percent of students of minority status. Geographic diversity among the student body is moderate, with 57138 percent of students hailing from out of state.

You May Not Know

• Seattle University is the largest private university in the Pacific Northwest.

- The university was ranked sixth in the west by the *U.S. News & World Report* as a master's-level institution.
- Sustainable operations at Seattle University have won 18 awards and eight environmental recognitions.

Distinguished Alumni

Elgin Baylor, former NBA player; Major General Patrick Henry Brady, Medal of Honor recipient; General Peter W. Chiarelli, Vice Chief of Staff of the U.S. Army; John E. Hopcroft, renowned theoretical computer scientist; Frank Murkowski, former Governor of Alaska and former U.S. Senator from Alaska; Jim Whittaker, first American to reach the summit of Mount Everest.

Admissions and Financial Aid

The admissions committee evaluates each applicant by considering the whole person, weighing the student's academic record against any life experiences and strengths the applicant might bring to positively affect the campus community. The university emphasizes sending all test scores, as the committee will look at the best sub-scores rather than just overall scores.

Merit scholarships at the university include the Trustee Scholarship, which awards $16,000 per academic year and requires a minimum GPA of 3.5; the Campion Scholarship, which awards $12,000 per academic year and requires a GPA of 3.4; the Bellarmine Scholarship, which awards $9,000 per academic year and requires a GPA of 3.25; and the Arrupe Scholarship, which awards $7,000 per year and requires a GPA of 3.0.

SEATTLE UNIVERSITY

Highlights

Admissions Criteria
Academic criteria:
Grades: ☆ ☆ ☆
Difficulty of class schedule: ☆ ☆ ☆
Class rank: ☆
Standardized test scores: ☆ ☆ ☆
Teacher recommendations: ☆ ☆
Personal statement: ☆ ☆
Non-academic criteria considered:
Interview
Extracurricular activities
Special talents, interests, abilities
Character/personal qualities
Volunteer work
Work experience
Geographical location
Religious affiliation/commitment
Minority affiliation
Alumni relationship

Deadlines
Early Action: November 15
Early Decision: No
Regular Action: Rolling admissions
Common Application: Accepted

Financial Aid
In-state tuition: $35,865
Out-of-state tuition: $35,865
Room: $6,555
Board: $3,990
Books: $1,485
Freshmen receiving need-based aid: 69%
Undergrads rec. need-based aid: 63%
Avg. % of need met by financial aid: 69%
Avg. aid package (freshmen): $27,375
Avg. aid package (undergrads): $29,210
Avg. debt upon graduation: $29,498

School Spirit
Mascot: Redhawks
Colors: Scarlet and white

SEWANEE: THE UNIVERSITY OF THE SOUTH

Four-year private
Founded: 1857
Sewanee, TN
Rural
Pop. 2,311

Address:
735 University Avenue
Sewanee, TN
37383

Admissions:
800-522-2234

Financial Aid:
931-598-1312

admiss@sewanee.edu

www.sewanee.edu

SEWANEE – THE UNIVERSITY OF THE SOUTH

Overview

A small, private university, Sewanee–The University of the South sits atop the Cumberland Plateau in southeastern Tennessee. The campus, affectionately known as "The Domain," consists of 13,000 acres of scenic mountain property featuring lakes, forests, and distinctive Gothic architecture. With sandstone buildings, garden pathways, and soaring bell towers, the campus circles around the All Saint's Chapel, modeled on great European cathedrals. Grounded in scholarship and faith, according to the university "Sewanee welcomes people of all faiths and offers a lively environment for active worship in the Episcopal tradition."

Steeped with tradition, Sewanee has many customs that all students abide by. One of the most distinctive is the fact the students dress up for class—females often wear dresses or skirts and males wear coats and ties, and most professors wear black academic gowns when they teach. A rather homogenous campus, the Greek scene and alcohol seem to drive the social life on campus.

Academics

Sewanee offers 33 majors. The university prides itself in the fact that "classes define the rhythm of each week." Filled with collaborative work, discussion, and frequent writing assignments, the liberal arts curriculum at Sewanee is broken down into thirds: general education requirements, major requirements, and electives (opportunities for students to explore a subject for the sheer joy of it).

General education requirements mandate students to take courses in the following categories: English, foreign language, mathematics/computer science, natural sciences, history, social sciences, philosophy, religion, and art/art history. Students must also pass two writing-intensive courses. In addition, students are required to take one physical education course by the end of their freshman year and one by the end of the sophomore year. Some of the strongest programs at Sewanee are English and theatre arts.

Most students seem to appreciate the personal attention they get due to the fact that all classes are taught by professors rather than teaching assistants (TAs). "Classes can be very difficult so it's nice to know that we always have someone to turn to when we have questions," says a student.

Home of the internationally-recognized *Sewanee Review*, the school is known as a crossroads where many of America's best writers gather. *The Review* annually provides the funding for one student to participate in a postgraduate internship. Additionally, as part of the Tennessee Williams writers-in-resident program, contemporary poets, novelists, and playwrights conduct various writing classes, readings, and workshops annually. "There is no better place to be for students interested in writing," notes a student. "We are exposed to some of the country's most prominent writers." The Sewanee Writer's Conference also features an annual roster of well known authors each summer who guide new and young writers.

The university's Writing Center provides peer support to students seeking assistance with their writing projects. Available to help with any stage of the writing process, tutors come from a wide range of educational backgrounds and strive to give students objective and constructive feedback.

Another special academic opportunity is the Sewanee Environmental Institute, which "facilitates interdisciplinary student-faculty research across disciplines and enhances academic programs." The Institute works to promote student-faculty research opportunities as well as undergraduate field courses and post-Baccalaureate student Fellowships.

Sewanee offers study-abroad options in over 25 locations and recommends a number of programs that "blend easily with your work at Sewanee," according to the Office of Study Abroad. Such programs include studies in Spain, South Asia, France, China, and Russia. Grades earned in these programs are counted in the overall college GPA.

The University Career and Leadership Development Center offers students many opportunities to meet and network with alumni each year through luncheons and talks hosted by alumni in various fields. The center also assists students in developing resumes and applying for internships and jobs. "A benefit of attending a school of our size is the personalized attention we get when it comes to job-hunting," explains a student. "We aren't just told to look through an online database of jobs."

Student Life

On campus, students love to hang out, eat, and drink at the Tiger Bay Pub, which is open until 2 a.m. and offers burgers, fries, onion rings, and late-night breakfast. Thursday night is band night, which features some of the best local bands. "It's a better alternative than the Waffle House. Better food and better music," notes a student.

Popular annual events include the Tennessee Williams Festival, a week-long, free event open to the public that features a one-man show, lectures, and plays. Jazz Festival features a week of hip and swanky local jazz musicians. The popular "Party Weekend" stands out among student favorites and occurs once per season, kicked off on Thursday night and carried through Friday. Students take drinks to class, listen to live music, and "everyone is happy and friendly," as described by one student.

Greek life is an "extremely" prominent part of student life at Sewanee. Overall, almost 70 percent of the students go Greek. Parties are very popular and most students claim that you will be "socially limited" by choosing not to participate. "Almost everyone who is socially involved joins, although you don't have to join to go to the parties," one student comments.

Sewanee has 24 Division III Athletics teams. Although the athletic prowess of their teams isn't students' main focus, they do enjoy another chance to dress up, wearing coats and ties to football games. "We dress up to go to class so it's not surprising that we also dress up for games," says a student. Intramural sports are common amongst students as well, whether it be through Greek life or other groups. Offerings include flag football, doubles badminton, floor hockey, basketball, and volleyball.

Popular off-campus activities include hikes in the nearby mountain areas and treks to Nashville or Chattanooga. Students don't have to venture far for outdoor activities. According to the college, the campus is an "outdoor classroom" that hosts its own hiking trails.

With 27 housing options to choose from, almost all students live on campus at Sewanee. Students can live in traditional dorm-style residences, sorority houses, or small theme houses such as the German House, which offers six students the chance to improve their language skills as they live and learn together. Other theme houses include the Richardson House for community engagement and Emery Hall for Asian studies.

SEWANEE: THE UNIVERSITY OF THE SOUTH

Highlights

Students
Total enrollment: 1,557
Undergrads: 1,478
Freshmen: 453
From out-of-state: 75%
From public schools: 42%
Male/Female: 48%/52%
Live on-campus: 98%
In fraternities: 67%
In sororities: 71%
Off-campus employment rating: Fair
Caucasian: 84%
African American: 4%
Hispanic: 3%
Asian / Pacific Islander: 2%
Mixed (2+ ethnicities): 4%
International: 3%

Academics
Calendar: Semester
Student/faculty ratio: 10:1
Class size 9 or fewer: 22%
Class size 10-29: 77%
Class size 30-49: 1%
Class size 50-99: -
Class size 100 or more: -
Six-year graduation rate: 78%

Most Popular Majors
English
Economics
History

Admissions
Applicants: 3,369
Accepted: 1,980
Acceptance rate: 58.8%
Placed on wait list: 507
Enrolled from wait list: 18
Average GPA: 3.6
ACT range: 26-30
SAT Math range: 580-660
SAT Reading range: 590-690
SAT Writing range: 16-46
Top 10% of class: 34%
Top 25% of class: 65%
Top 50% of class: 93%

585

SEWANEE: THE UNIVERSITY OF THE SOUTH

Highlights

Admissions Criteria

Academic criteria:
Grades: ☆ ☆ ☆
Difficulty of class schedule: ☆ ☆ ☆
Class rank: ☆
Standardized test scores: ☆ ☆
Teacher recommendations: ☆ ☆ ☆
Personal statement: ☆ ☆
Non-academic criteria considered:
Interview
Extracurricular activities
Special talents, interests, abilities
Character/personal qualities
Volunteer work
Work experience
State of residency
Geographical location
Minority affiliation
Alumni relationship

Deadlines

Early Action: December 1
Early Decision: November 15
Regular Action: February 1 (final)
Notification of admission by: March 17
Common Application: Accepted

Financial Aid

In-state tuition: $35,484
Out-of-state tuition: $35,484
Room: $5,302
Board: $4,912
Books: $800
Freshmen receiving need-based aid: 51%
Undergrads rec. need-based aid: 59%
Avg. % of need met by financial aid: 94%
Avg. aid package (freshmen): $33,849
Avg. aid package (undergrads): $29,202
Avg. debt upon graduation: $23,721

School Spirit

Mascot: Tigers
Colors: Purple and white

Student Body

Although students typically don't like the stereotype associated with the Sewanee student body, the university is a very white campus generally composed of "rich Southerners." Many students are also religious. "Southern hospitality" pervades the campus so "you hear a lot of 'ma'ams' and 'sirs.'" With 13 percent minority students, the student body is moderately ethnically diverse; but with 75 percent of students hailing from out of state, it is highly geographically diverse though a part of the Bible Belt.

You May Not Know

- The university has had 25 Rhodes Scholars, 36 Watson fellows, and dozens of Fulbright Scholars.
- Sewanee alumni, Rt. Reverend Gene Robinson, was the first openly gay Episcopal bishop.
- Many Sewanee students tap the roof of the car when entering or exiting campus in order to summon a "Sewanee angel" to protect them.

Distinguished Alumni

Ellis Arnall, Governor of Georgia; Mallory Ervin, Miss American contestant and *Amazing Race* finisher; Joe Hall, University of Kentucky head basketball coach; Jon Meacham, Pulitzer Prize winner and editor of *Newsweek*.

Admissions and Financial Aid

Although it offers no athletic awards, Sewanee provides need-based financial aid to almost 60 percent of students and merit-based aid to 26 percent of students. Academic scholarships average $11,871 each year thanks to generous support from the university's alumni and $315 million endowment. Many scholarships are awarded on the basis of need and applicants are automatically considered without special forms or addendums.

Additionally, a number of merit-based scholarships are available named in honor of university alumni. For example, the Wilkin's Scholarship funds approximately 25 students each year with strong leadership and academic records. These amount to $16,000 in scholarship money.

SKIDMORE COLLEGE

Overview

Skidmore College has an impressive neighbor—the Adirondacks. Campus is as idyllic as it is woodsy, as vibrant and peaceful as the town of Sarasota Springs, New York, where it's located. Students can go white water-rafting, hiking, or canoeing, or, for the less adventurous, simply put out a blanket and recline on the expansive green ground. And when they are done doing that, they may bask in the one-on-one attention given by faculty members, test their intellectual and creative limits with the many cross- and interdisciplinary options, or conduct research with an award-winning faculty member.

Founded originally as a women's college, but made coeducational in 1971, Skidmore has become increasingly diverse throughout the years. Today its student population is made up of almost 2,700 students from 40 states and 30 countries. Its undergraduate class is eclectic, much like its architecture, which combines both Victorian and more contemporary styles. Skidmore has a number of new facilities, including the Tang Teaching Museum and Art Gallery, which has earned national recognition since the unveiling in 2000. The Arthur Zankel Music Center, a building that seats 600, opened in 2009.

Known for its small student population and low professor-to-student ratio, Skidmore is a place where you'll have much individual time with faculty. Students in the know come to Skidmore for the excellent liberal and fine arts education, but students *really* in the know come for its spectacular science courses as well.

What is small for some, however, may be too small for others. What is outdoorsy and fun for some may be too rural and sweat-inducing for others. Here, all you'll have for those precious four years is your college, and, for some, that's all you'll need—a cozy haven you'll never want to leave.

Academics

Faculty members at Skidmore have earned a number of distinctions, including Pulitzer, Guggenheim, and Emmy awards, and Fulbright, MacArthur, and National Science Foundation funds. The student-to-faculty ratio is 9:1, allowing for an extensive advising system that gives each student guidance in choosing a major. There are 58 different majors offered, with standout programs in business and the arts including dance, music, studio art, and theater. "We aren't a conservatory, but our arts programs are so strong that we may as well be," says a student.

Skidmore's academic life is based much more on the seminar than the lecture. "It's mandatory to be able to discuss the material," notes a student. The most common class size at Skidmore is between 10 and 19 students, but classes can be even smaller. More than one fifth of the undergraduate courses offered have only two to nine students, and only six percent of classes at Skidmore are larger than 30 students. There is no hiding among the crowd in classes this small. "You need to come to class prepared," one student remarks.

For first years, academic life is very much tied up with social and residential life, as students choose a Scribner Seminar of study from over 50 options and then live with students who have chosen the same seminar. The Scribner Seminar was developed to foster an environment of rich intellectual thought and discussion that is interactive with both professors and peers. First years receive guidance from their Peer Mentors, upperclassmen who have chosen to act as counselors to newer students.

Academically, Skidmore is a place where students facilitate their own plans of study. Students have the option of developing their own major that is tailored to their specific curiosities. About half of the undergraduates at Skidmore choose to combine two areas of interest—not necessarily related—in order to make a double major. Examples can include dance and medicine or math and philosophy.

In order to graduate, students must fulfill foundational requirements in expository writing and mathematics, as well as a total of 90 hours of liberal arts classes. Students

SKIDMORE COLLEGE

Four-year private
Founded: 1903
Saratoga Springs, NY
Large town
Pop. 26,727

Address:
815 North Broadway
Saratoga Springs, NY
12866

Admissions:
800-867-6007

Financial Aid:
518-580-5750

admissions@skidmore.edu

cms.skidmore.edu/index.cfm

SKIDMORE COLLEGE

Highlights

Students
Total enrollment: 2,689
Undergrads: 2,660
Part-time students: 1%
From out-of-state: 68%
From public schools: 55%
Male/Female: 39%/61%
Live on-campus: 86%
Off-campus employment rating: Good
Caucasian: 65%
African American: 4%
Hispanic: 8%
Asian / Pacific Islander: 6%
Native American: 0%
Mixed (2+ ethnicities): 5%
International: 6%

Academics
Calendar: Semester
Student/faculty ratio: 9:1
Class size 9 or fewer: 21%
Class size 10-29: 73%
Class size 30-49: 5%
Class size 50-99: 1%
Class size 100 or more: -
Returning freshmen: 92%
Six-year graduation rate: 88%
Graduates who immediately go to graduate school: 11%

Most Popular Majors
Social sciences
Visual/performing arts
Business

Admissions
Applicants: 5,702
Accepted: 2,389
Acceptance rate: 41.9%
Placed on wait list: 1,396
Enrolled from wait list: 41
Average GPA: Not reported
ACT range: 26-30
SAT Math range: 560-670
SAT Reading range: 560-670
SAT Writing range: 17-45
Top 10% of class: 43%
Top 25% of class: 78%
Top 50% of class: 95%

must also complete twenty-four hours of maturity-level courses. In terms of which courses students are required to select more specifically, certain areas of study are required for graduation. These include the arts, humanities, natural and social sciences, foreign literature and language, non-western study, and cultural diversity study. Each major also requires certain specific courses of study.

Skidmore offers an Honors Forum, an enhanced intellectual community for students hoping to broaden their academic college experience. Students may gain entrance in the Honors Program after their admission to Skidmore if they have an especially promising academic and extracurricular record. Students may also become members if they make the Dean's List once enrolled, which requires a GPA of 3.5 or higher. Once inducted into the program, members must complete three honors courses, as well as a senior "Capstone" Project, a culminating work such as a thesis, artwork, or presentation. Those in the Honors Forum must participate in a Citizenship Project of community engagement and service.

Skidmore also encourages students to seek academic experiences separate from campus. The college offers 125 study-abroad programs and the opportunity for undergraduates to take semesters at other colleges, including traditionally black and Latino schools.

The Career Services Office is available to help Skidmore students and alumni connect with job and internship opportunities. Even after graduation, alumni are able to make appointments with the office in person or by phone to discuss overall career goals, graduate study concerns, networking, and strategies for job searching. Over 2,100 alumni and parents are connected through the Skidmore Career Network, a service that provides numerous job listings. For undergraduates seeking summer opportunities, Skidmore CareerLink offers connections to summer jobs and internships.

Student Life

There are over 80 student organizations, the most popular being a cappella groups, concert band, volunteer organizations, dance troupes, and environmental action groups. Undergraduates interested in journalism might want to get involved with Skidmore's newspaper, the *Skidmore News*. There are no fraternities or sororities.

Skidmore hosts a number of days a year devoted to social life. Junior Ring Weekend offers a student art show, tree lighting ceremony, and the Junior Ring Formal. During Oktoberfest, students celebrate the new season with fall-themed food and activities. The Morbid Halloween Ball is a huge, campus-wide costume party. "The costumes are very creative and an excuse to be wild," says a student.

Some students go off campus for their fun, making trips to New York or Montreal, or staying in the town of Sarasota Springs, which often hosts such culturally phenomenal guests as the New York City Ballet.

Skidmore has 19 teams (nine male, 10 female) that play in Division III athletics. Baseball, crew, and lacrosse are popular, but women's field hockey is the most competitive sport at the college. Intramurals include basketball, dodgeball, power volleyball, racquetball, and soccer.

First-year students live on campus, and their housing is largely determined by their Scribner Seminar. Upperclassmen occasionally elect to live off campus, although 86 percent of undergraduates remain in the dormitory housing. It is common for students choosing to stay on campus to have singles after their first year. While the residential options are not exceptional, they are by no means uninviting. "If you want more parties, pick South Quad," notes a student.

Student Body

Students say their classmates tend to be "artsy" and "artistically talented," many coming from affluent backgrounds. There are significantly more female than male students, and many of the males are "not into dating," according to one student.

With about 23 percent minority students, Skidmore is highly ethnically diverse. Its geographic diversity is likewise moderate, as 68 percent of students come from outside the state of New York.

You May Not Know

- Skidmore students have the option of cooking their own meals in the dining halls.
- In 1981, Skidmore's mascot changed from the Wombat to the Thoroughbred.
- Skidmore's campus moved in 1961 from downtown Sarasota Springs to its present location, requiring major new building projects.

Distinguished Alumni

Lake Bell, actress; Joseph L. Bruno, New York State Senate Majority Leader; Arwa Damon, CNN correspondent in the Middle East; David Miner, television producer; Ratatat, rock band.

Admissions and Financial Aid

The primary criteria Skidmore admissions officers use to evaluate candidates is academic performance, which includes grades, test scores, and teacher recommendations. Additionally, Skidmore looks at the essay and the interview to determine whether an applicant has desired qualities of intellectual curiosity, open-mindedness, and strong character.

Financial-aid officers at Skidmore determine a "package" comprised of grants, loans, and on-campus jobs for each incoming student. About 44 percent of the undergraduate class receives financial aid. In addition, Skidmore offers several merit scholarships including the Filene Music Scholarship, which is awarded based on a competitive performance process of interested applicants. The Porter Presidential Scholarship in Science and Mathematics is another merit-based program, recipients of which are chosen according to standards of academic performance and science or math teacher recommendations. Skidmore also provides the Scholars in Science and Mathematics scholarship, a combined need and merit award. NSF-scholarships may be provided for candidates exhibiting aptitude for math and the sciences.

The Skidmore Opportunities Program provides financial assistance for those in economic or social circumstances that would make the tuition fee a difficulty.

SKIDMORE COLLEGE

Highlights

Admissions Criteria
Academic criteria:
Grades: ☆ ☆ ☆
Difficulty of class schedule: ☆ ☆ ☆
Class rank: ☆ ☆
Standardized test scores: ☆
Teacher recommendations: ☆ ☆
Personal statement: ☆ ☆
Non-academic criteria considered:
Interview
Extracurricular activities
Special talents, interests, abilities
Character/personal qualities
Volunteer work
Work experience
State of residency
Geographical location
Minority affiliation
Alumni relationship

Deadlines
Early Action: No
Early Decision: November 15
Regular Action: January 15 (final)
Notification of admission by: April 1
Common Application: Accepted

Financial Aid
In-state tuition: $44,820
Out-of-state tuition: $44,820
Room: $7,214
Board: $4,988
Books: $1,300
Freshmen receiving need-based aid: 46%
Undergrads rec. need-based aid: 44%
Avg. % of need met by financial aid: 95%
Avg. aid package (freshmen): $37,067
Avg. aid package (undergrads): $37,824
Avg. debt upon graduation: $22,753

School Spirit
Mascot: Thoroughbreds

Four-year private wom-
en's college
Founded: 1871
Northampton, MA
Medium city
Pop. 28,549

Address:
Seven College Lane
Northampton, MA
01063

Admissions:
413-585-2500

Financial Aid:
413-585-2530

admission@smith.edu

www.smith.edu

SMITH COLLEGE

Overview

Smith College is a private, independent liberal arts college for women in the small town of Northampton, Massachusetts. It's one of the best women-only colleges in the nation and is the largest member of the Seven Sisters, a group of historically women's liberal arts colleges located on the East Coast. It's also a member of the Five Colleges consortium—a group of four liberal arts colleges and one research university, all in Massachusetts.

The Smith campus is located in a beautiful natural setting in the heart of New England. Northampton is a small town of almost 30,000 people, and the school itself has about 2,600 undergraduates. The campus today consists of 147 contiguous acres with more than 100 buildings. One of the more modern buildings is the Campus Center, which is located at the intersection of the town of Northampton and Smith College, and provides students, faculty, and staff with a multi-purpose setting for various activities. A popular campus attraction is the Botanical Gardens, which is spread throughout the campus.

Overall, the campus gives a rustic, natural feeling, and its location in a small town gives students a sense of peace and calm that creates a pleasant environment for scholarship and student interaction.

Academics

The academic program at Smith College offers a certain amount of freedom to students in choosing their courses, contrasting with many large research universities that have a core curriculum. Only two such requirements are placed on students: that they enroll in and pass a writing course during the first year of study, and that half of their cumulative courses are taken in classes outside a major concentration. There are 48 majors and 26 minors offered at Smith College, and students also have the option to create their own major with the help of faculty. Students at Smith describe the programs as "academically challenging" and "rigorous but not to the point of complete exhaustion." Particularly strong programs include psychology, political science, and economics.

There are a number of special academic opportunities. The Smith Scholars Program, for instance, is designed for students who want to spend two to four semesters working on projects independently. The STRIDE program offers a paid research position with a Smith professor—unusual in most academic environments in that it is not something that normally is available to undergraduates. This acts as an extension of academic learning for a group of lucky and successful applicants. Students say that research opportunities are "abundant" and "more widely available than at other colleges."

The Phoebe Reese Lewis Leadership Program is a highly regarded course of study designed to provide undergraduates with hands-on learning experiences and training in developing leadership skills. About 25 participants are chosen annually, based on academic performance and motivation. Successful applicants come from many different majors, so anyone who is interested and feels they want to develop useful leadership skills should apply.

The Five College Consortium allows roughly 5,000 students to cross-register for classes at one or more of the five campuses. This spirit of collaboration brings students from other universities to Smith, and allows Smith students to explore other course offerings at one of the other campuses. Other special programs include Semester-in-Washington, which is open to Smith juniors and seniors, and provides students with an opportunity to study the processes of public policy at a national level. There's also the Smith Program at the Smithsonian, which allows upperclassmen to work with prominent curators and scholars.

There are several study-abroad options at Smith. Leaders in international education, Smith's four Junior Year Abroad programs remain popular. These programs are offered in Switzerland, Germany, France, and Italy. Smith also has affiliations with other institutions allowing students to study abroad in India, Mexico, Spain, and Japan.

In terms of career opportunities after graduation, Smith has a career services office that provides "individualized advising and access to industry programs, career resources, jobs and internships, alumnae networking, grad school information, recruiting events, and career fairs." Many graduates of Smith choose to go on to graduate school.

Student Life

Smith is a vibrant community filled with energetic, intriguing individuals who come from diverse backgrounds. Smith always has something going on around campus, and students enjoy taking part in the many activities. Smith's Student Government Association (SGA) supports projects and programs for all the organizations on campus. There are roughly 100 different student groups, including notable ones such as Celebrations (a multicultural dance company), Student Events Committee, Investment Club, and cultural organizations for a variety of ethnic groups.

There are special events throughout the year. Convocation symbolizes the beginning of the school year. The night before classes start, students meet in John M. Greene Hall for an opening speech and a Glee Club performance. Another popular event is Mountain Day, which is a surprise holiday from classes for students chosen by the President. It usually happens on a beautiful fall day. One notorious Halloween tradition is the Immorality Party, held at Talbot House, one of the college residences. It's a classic evening of partying that students have enjoyed for many years. Rally Day is also popular, when students meet in Sweeney Concert Hall for alumnae to be given medals for their distinctions.

Smith does not have official Greek or sorority life, but there are more than 30 houses on campus, each with their own distinctive personalities and histories. Each house fosters a sense of community similar to that of a sorority, and many of the residents also reach out to the larger community and participate in service events, mirroring Greek organizations. "It's like being in a sorority without being in one," says a student.

When it comes to athletics, there are 14 varsity level sports offered at Smith in NCAA Division III. Among the most competitive sports at the college are crew, soccer, and volleyball. Smith also offers club and intramural sports, some of the popular ones being taekwondo, fencing, and Ultimate Frisbee.

Smith students take part in plenty of off-campus activities. Northampton features a number of galleries, shops, and restaurants. There are also several downtown night clubs for nocturnal fun, including the Calvin Theatre, which features acts ranging from Wynton Marsalis to comedian Margaret Cho. "We have more entertainment than typical for a city of this size because of all of the college students in the Five College Consortium," a student remarks.

SMITH COLLEGE

Highlights

Students
Total enrollment: 3,212
Undergrads: 2,664
Part-time students: 1%
From out-of-state: 78%
From public schools: 61%
Male/Female: 0%/100%
Live on-campus: 95%
Off-campus employment rating: Excellent
Caucasian: 47%
African American: 5%
Hispanic: 9%
Asian / Pacific Islander: 12%
Native American: 0%
Mixed (2+ ethnicities): 4%
International: 12%

Academics
Calendar: Semester
Student/faculty ratio: 9:1
Class size 9 or fewer: 17%
Class size 10-29: 69%
Class size 30-49: 9%
Class size 50-99: 5%
Class size 100 or more: -
Returning freshmen: 93%
Six-year graduation rate: 85%

Most Popular Majors
Government
Psychology
Economics

Admissions
Applicants: 4,341
Accepted: 1,842
Acceptance rate: 42.4%
Placed on wait list: 562
Enrolled from wait list: 118
Average GPA: 3.9
ACT range: 27-31
SAT Math range: 600-710
SAT Reading range: 610-720
SAT Writing range: 34-51
Top 10% of class: 66%
Top 25% of class: 90%
Top 50% of class: 99%

591

SMITH COLLEGE

Admissions Criteria

Academic criteria:
Grades: ☆ ☆ ☆
Difficulty of class schedule: ☆ ☆ ☆
Class rank: ☆ ☆
Standardized test scores: ☆
Teacher recommendations: ☆ ☆ ☆
Personal statement: ☆ ☆
Non-academic criteria considered:
Interview
Extracurricular activities
Special talents, interests, abilities
Character/personal qualities
Volunteer work
Work experience
State of residency
Minority affiliation
Alumni relationship

Deadlines
Early Action: No
Early Decision: November 15
Regular Action: January 15 (final)
Common Application: Accepted

Financial Aid
In-state tuition: $42,840
Out-of-state tuition: $42,840
Room: Varies
Board: Varies
Books: $800
Freshmen receiving need-based aid: 65%
Undergrads rec. need-based aid: 63%
Avg. % of need met by financial aid: 100%
Avg. aid package (freshmen): $39,440
Avg. aid package (undergrads): $39,120
Avg. debt upon graduation: $23,071

School Spirit
Mascot: Pioneers

Students at Smith live in one of the 30 houses on campus, which fosters a strong sense of community from the get-go. Most houses are mixed-class, so you can find both under- and upperclassmen with whom you can interact. While many students remain in the same house for the entirety of their four years at Smith, they are not obligated to do so, and may move around if they like.

Student Body

The student body at Smith is, in general, very liberal minded. Students are often involved in a plethora of activities outside of class and are cause-oriented individuals. The student body is fairly diverse, with a moderate number of Asian Americans, and a lower percentage of both African American and Hispanic students. There is also a small proportion of international students. Eleven percent of the student body doesn't identify their ethnic background. One student explains, "We don't want to be placed in a box." Geographically 78 percent hail from out of state.

You May Not Know

- Smith actually has some male graduates, hailing from its co-ed graduate program.
- The first women's basketball game was held at Smith College in 1892.
- The Calvin Theatre on King Street was named for President Calvin Coolidge, who practiced law in Northampton and later became its mayor.

Distinguished Alumnae

Barbara Bush, former First Lady; Julia Child, star of *The French Chef*; Madeleine L'Engle, author of *A Wrinkle in Time*; Betty Friedan, author of *The Feminist Mystique*; Sylvia Plath, author of *The Bell Jar*; Nancy Reagan, former First Lady; Gloria Steinem, founder of *Ms. Magazine*.

Admissions and Financial Aid

Smith is one of the few colleges that has made SAT and ACT test scores optional for admission. That said, admission to the college is still selective. Smith takes a broad-based approach when evaluating applicants. The admissions board states, "beyond meeting the normal requirements, we expect each candidate to pursue in greater depth academic interests of special importance to her."

Merit scholarships are offered to a limited number of students, with awards based on merit rather than need. Some notable ones include the Zollman Scholarship, which offers a $20,000 annual scholarship for exceptional incoming applicants, STRIDE scholarships of $15,000 annually, and Phi Theta Kappa scholarships offering $5,000 annually.

SOUTHERN METHODIST UNIVERSITY

Overview

Located minutes from downtown Dallas—Texas' third-largest city (and America's ninth-largest)—sits the beautiful campus that comprises Southern Methodist University (SMU), a medium-sized private school with a reputation for training the Dallas area/Texas business elite. Covered in well-manicured green, the main campus features Georgian architecture on 230 acres.

The university's focus on leadership brings national and world leaders to campus—a glance at the Tate Distinguished Lecture Series shows speakers Henry Kissinger and Jonas Salk from the program's beginnings in the 1980s and Colin Powell and Vicente Fox more recently. SMU's 10 libraries house the largest private collection of research materials in the Southwest.

While there are undoubtedly a wealth of resources, the university does have a reputation for being most comfortable for those who are wealthy, white, and conservative in their politics. Students with alternative lifestyles may not find SMU the best fit, and not all students will delight in sharing campus with a 227,000-square-foot complex that includes the George W. Bush Presidential Library and George W. Bush Policy Institute. However, students looking for strong connections in the business world and who are excited by a university in Texas where about half of 11,000 students are Methodist or Catholic, and where Greek life and sports play a major part of the school spirit and traditions, may want to apply to become an SMU Mustang.

Academics

SMU offers more than 100 majors and 75 minors. There are a total of seven degree-granting schools, including the Dedman College of Humanities and Sciences, the Meadows School of the Arts, the Lyle School of Engineering, and the Perkins School of Theology. Students can double and even triple major, and there are accelerated 4+1 master's degree programs as well.

The General Education Curriculum is made up of 41term hours of coursework that include classes in written English/rhetoric, mathematics, IT, science and technology, and wellness. There are also required "perspectives" courses that cover different approaches to reasoning; for example, religious and philosophical thought, cultural formations, and human diversity courses.

The academic environment is "rigorous" but "for the most part students cooperate rather than compete," a student explains. Strong programs include general business, English, political science, and religious studies.

The University Honors Program gives high-achievers opportunities to take small classes that foster student debate and interaction. Participants also live in the Honors residential community, meet speakers and attend special receptions, and apply for Richter Fellowships, which enable students to study abroad on a student-designed research project.

The Hilltop Scholars program is a living-learning environment for first-year students with high academic ability and strong leadership qualities. The program provides a cohesive academic and social environment and increased access to faculty.

Those wanting a break from the big city can go to SMU-in-Taos, the 295-acre campus in Northern New Mexico that offers hands-on educational experiences such as mountain skies for astronomy students, archeology field programs, and quiet, stunning natural surroundings open to students of all disciplines. "It's like going to school while on vacation," one student comments. Additionally, SMU's study-abroad program offers 24 offerings that cover 12 countries. Students can choose to do research, service, internships, and co-ops overseas.

The Hegi Family Career Development Center provides career development resources and counseling. There is active campus recruiting and a job referral program

SOUTHERN METHODIST UNIVERSITY

Four-year private
Founded: 1911
Dallas, TX
Medium city
Pop. 1,223,229

Address:
P.O. Box 750181
Dallas, TX
75275-0181

Admissions:
800-323-0672

Financial Aid:
800-323-0672

ugadmission@smu.edu

www.smu.edu

SOUTHERN METHODIST UNIVERSITY

Students
Total enrollment: 10,893
Undergrads: 6,249
Freshmen: 1,586
Part-time students: 4%
From out-of-state: 56%
Male/Female: 49%/51%
Live on-campus: 32%
In fraternities: 34%
In sororities: 47%
Off-campus employment rating: Fair
Caucasian: 66%
African American: 6%
Hispanic: 12%
Asian / Pacific Islander: 7%
Native American: 0%
Mixed (2+ ethnicities): 2%
International: 7%

Academics
Calendar: Semester
Student/faculty ratio: 11:1
Class size 9 or fewer: 26%
Class size 10-29: 49%
Class size 30-49: 18%
Class size 50-99: 6%
Class size 100 or more: 2%
Returning freshmen: 91%
Six-year graduation rate: 79%

Most Popular Majors
Finance
Economics
Psychology

Admissions
Applicants: 11,217
Accepted: 6,031
Acceptance rate: 53.8%
Placed on wait list: 1,057
Enrolled from wait list: 125
Average GPA: 3.6
ACT range: Not reported
SAT Math range: 600-690
SAT Reading range: 590-680
SAT Writing range: 19-48
Top 10% of class: 47%
Top 25% of class: 76%
Top 50% of class: 96%

that includes full-time positions, internships, part-time jobs, and summer jobs.

Student Life

More than 200 student organizations are a large part of SMU's social resources; these include a large number of academic and religious groups. The *Daily Campus* publishes Tuesday through Friday during fall and spring and has been an independent student newspaper since 1915. The Center for Academic-Community Engagement and Office of Leadership and Community Involvement offer plenty of opportunities to serve others. There's even Service House, a co-ed residence for 28 students that contributes well over 1,000 hours of community service annually.

Greek life began with the campus newspaper in 1915 when four fraternities were established. Nearly a century and tens of thousands of members later, there is a vibrant Greek scene, with 27 fraternities and sororities on campus.

Special events are numerous. Mustang Corral gathers up all first-year students in a three-day, off-campus retreat with highlights that include keynote speakers, team-building "Olympics," and a candle-light ceremony where seniors share about their experience. "It's an incredible bonding experience," says a student. There's also plenty of education focused on school spirit, which students need as soon as Homecoming rolls around with the Kick-off Party, tug-of-war games, music, loud fun, student-made floats, and tailgate gatherings. Before every football game, Bishop Boulevard, SMU's main street, is packed with tents and booths that offer free food and drinks, body painting, pom-poms, and other fan gear. On game days, students wear red and flashing two bent fingers—"Pony Ears"—as a gesture of school pride. Winter brings the Christmas-themed Celebration of Lights on the Main Quad, while the campus celebrates spring at the Mane Event, a student-run festival of live music, food, and fun.

SMU's 16 varsity teams (six men's, 10 women's) compete in Division I. Football is the most popular sport, while men's golf, and both men's and women's soccer and swimming teams are among the most competitive. Over 3,000 students participate in intramurals that encompass more than 30 different sports throughout the year. The extensive club sports list ranges from badminton to wakeboarding.

Students frequent Dallas and the immediate surrounding area for entertainment of all sorts: amusement parks, museums, pro sports teams, dining, and more. Road trips to New Orleans and Austin are also popular getaways from the enclave of University Park.

First-year students are required to live in the dorms, while upperclassmen tend to move into Greek houses or to off campus locations. Theme halls and apartments include the Honors Community, Multicultural House, and Fine Arts Community. "I really liked living on campus freshman year because I made so many friends in the dorms," recalls a student.

Student Body

The student body at SMU leans right politically. The university has a reputation for schooling the rich, as the nickname "Southern Millionaire University" attests. About 6,000 of the university's

11,000 students are undergraduates. Two-thirds of undergrads and 42 percent of graduate students report a religious affiliation; 23 percent are Methodist and 23 percent are Catholic.

For a school with a rich, white, and conservative reputation, SMU's ethnic diversity is fairly high, with 27 percent minority students. However, a 2009 article entitled "Diversity declining, SMU seeing white" in the SMU *Daily Campus* critiqued declining enrollment and lower retention rates for minority students.

There is moderate geographic diversity, with a little less than half of students hailing from Texas. "There's a strong Southern slant with the friendliest people you'll ever meet," notes a student. Students come from all 50 states and almost 100 different countries.

You May Not Know

- The official mascot of the SMU Mustangs is the Peruna, a live black Shetland pony that has been present at every SMU home football game for over 70 years. "Peruna" also refers to the costumed mascot and SMU's fight song.
- In 1915, Dallas Hall housed the entire university along with a bank and barbershop. The Hall, which was built on a hill, inspired SMU's nickname "The Hilltop."
- In 2001, nearly 100 SMU Mustang Band members and alumni, cheerleaders, and pom squad members performed in the George W. Bush Inauguration Parade.

Distinguished Alumni

Kathy Bates, Academy Award-winning actress; Laura Bush, First Lady and wife of former President George Bush; James Cronin, Nobel Prize-winning physicist; Cecil Williams, Pastor of Glide Memorial Church in San Francisco.

Admissions and Financial Aid

SMU looks at its applicant pool for high school students that have fulfilled certain course requirements that the best candidates generally exceed. The university emphasizes a holistic assessment so that coursework is just one factor among many. Interviews are not required but are strongly recommended; for those unable to visit campus, phone interviews are possible. Students interested in studying the performing arts must audition.

Candidates who apply for admission by January 15 are automatically considered for every merit-based scholarship they are eligible to receive. The most prestigious award is the President's Scholarship, given to 30-35 students each year. This scholarship covers full tuition and fees, including travel expenses and tuition for study abroad. The Hunt Leadership Scholarship rewards exceptional leadership, while the Meadows Scholars Program is specifically for students in the arts and communications fields. Forty percent of students receive need-based aid, and 31 percent of students receive merit-based aid.

SOUTHERN METHODIST UNIVERSITY

Highlights

Admissions Criteria
Academic criteria:
Grades: ☆ ☆ ☆
Difficulty of class schedule: ☆ ☆ ☆
Class rank: ☆ ☆ ☆
Standardized test scores: ☆ ☆ ☆
Teacher recommendations: ☆ ☆ ☆
Personal statement: ☆ ☆ ☆
Non-academic criteria considered:
Extracurricular activities
Special talents, interests, abilities
Character/personal qualities
Volunteer work
Work experience
State of residency

Deadlines
Early Action: November 1
Early Decision: No
Regular Action: Rolling admissions
Common Application: Accepted

Financial Aid
In-state tuition: $38,870
Out-of-state tuition: $38,870
Room: Varies
Board: Varies
Books: $800
Freshmen receiving need-based aid: 41%
Undergrads rec. need-based aid: 40%
Avg. % of need met by financial aid: 87%
Avg. aid package (freshmen): $35,683
Avg. aid package (undergrads): $35,182
Avg. debt upon graduation: $30,987

School Spirit
Mascot: Mustangs
Colors: Red and blue
Song: *Peruna*

595

SPELMAN COLLEGE

Overview

As an all-woman, historically black institution, Spelman College offers its students a strong and specialized liberal arts and sciences education. The compact campus features plenty of green spaces and attractive traditional red-brick, ivy-clad, columned buildings. Just five minutes to the west is downtown Atlanta, with its vibrant cultural, social, and entertainment scene, and across the street is Spelman's brother college, Morehouse.

Spelman offers a mix of forward-thinking education and highly traditional, fairly conservative environment. Its strengths lie in its science programs, including its recently-constructed Science Center, and its highly specific curriculum, tailored to suit the needs of African-American women in higher education. Emphasis is placed on the development of leadership skills and service.

Spelman relies heavily on its own long-standing campus traditions to form a cohesive school spirit and campus atmosphere, which some may find comforting, and others may find outdated and off-putting. But even if traditional dress and ceremonies don't appeal to you, downtown Atlanta is right next door and offers anything but traditional places for students to shop, eat, drink, and socialize.

Academics

Students at Spelman can choose from 30 majors and must fulfill two sets of general education requirements. The first range of courses include "African Diaspora and the World," (required by all incoming students), computer literacy, English composition, foreign language, physical education, mathematics, and international or women's studies; some of these classes may be replaced with AP or IB test scores. Under further divisional requirements, students must take a course each in the divisions of the social sciences, humanities, natural sciences, and fine arts. Spelman's flagship programs are its sciences, particularly biology, and its premed and prelaw tracks. Students intending to enter health sciences can take advantage of Spelman's Health Careers Program, which offers standardized test preparation, medical professional school application development, summer programs, job shadows, and interview practice through workshops, mentoring, tutoring, and peer support groups.

Spelman expects a great deal from its students, and academics can be challenging. The school's size allows students to receive plenty of individual attention from professors. "Coffee breaks with professors are not unusual," says a student.

The interdisciplinary Ethel Waddell Githii Honors Program offers Honors core curriculum courses plus electives for students with qualifying SAT/ACT scores and high school GPAs; all Honors students must write a thesis in their majors. "The Honors students are incredibly bright and motivated," notes a student. All Honors courses are small seminars, allowing discussion and interaction with peers and professors; students also have the opportunity to conduct independent research with faculty. Some perks come with Honors student status, including special advising, eligibility for scholarships and awards, priority housing in the Honors community dorm, a special Honors retreat, and funding for conference and workshop travel and research.

Spelman's Independent Scholars (SIS) also have the opportunity to conduct independent, original research as part of their participation in a two-semester oral history project: under the direction of an SIS faculty mentor, students from all majors conduct research and interview African-American women who are leaders from all backgrounds, augmenting their hands-on experience with weekly seminars and guest lectures on oral history, research, and archiving. SIS is administered under the leadership skill development program LEADS, which also offers training and mentoring opportunities in the Student Leadership Program, and the Women of Excellence Leadership Series, a seven-week leadership-skill development competition and seminar series for juniors and seniors. LEADS also runs a Women of Color Student Leadership Conference and Student Community Service Programs.

Spelman's five-year Dual Degree Engineering Program allows students to earn a liberal arts education and Bachelor of Science degree in three years from Spelman as well as a Bachelor of Engineering in two years at a number of partner schools, including Columbia, Dartmouth, Auburn, Rochester Institute of Technology, and University of Michigan.

Spelman offers exchanges with domestic and international universities in the West Indies, England, the Czech Republic, Japan, and Chile. The college does not have its own study-abroad programs; instead it taps into external study-abroad opportunities. Spelman does offer a three-week Summer Art Colony program in Panama that participants say is "amazing." The trip features visual arts instruction to arts students and project supervision to students conducting academic research, along with gallery and artists' studio visits, swimming, snorkeling, and hiking in the rainforest.

A large proportion—41 percent—of Spelman graduates pursue postgraduate studies. The rest entering the workforce enjoy a good record of success: about half find jobs related to their major within six months of graduation.

Student Life

Community service is a major focus of many of Spelman's 82 student organizations, which include the Up Til Dawn Community Service Group and Class Council, a civic engagement organization. The African Sisterhood and Spelman's Greek system, which comprises four sororities, are also major presences on campus. "We have the best parties and social life," one member remarks.

The P.U.L.S.E. Programming Board is responsible for planning a number of on-campus events, which include the traditional Homecoming activities as well as Welcome Back Jam, movie sneak previews, and poetry slams. A number of joint events with Spelman's brother college Morehouse also take place on campus.

Traditional events and ceremonies play a major role in campus life, including the semi-formal Senior Soiree and Class Day, which includes an "Ivy Oration" and planting by the valedictorian and the ceremonial procession through the Alumnae Arch—by unwritten tradition, students wear white dresses for most of these ceremonies, so definitely pack a few when you leave home. "While it's very quaint, it's also very beautiful to see everyone wearing a white dress," one student recalls. "There are some very specific rules about the dress' length though," she adds.

Spelman's athletics are a small but thriving part of life on campus: its seven varsity teams compete at Division III level, and the competitive basketball, volleyball, and tennis teams draw the most support. Students can compete in intramurals, but they don't seem to be a major draw.

The greater Atlanta downtown area offers nearly endless opportunities for entertainment—a number of major-league sports teams, malls, cafes, restaurants, bars, and museums, as well as Atlanta's historic cultural center, the Sweet Auburn district. Students at Spelman are frequent customers at the Shark Bar, Three Dollar Café, and Gladys Knight and Ron Winans' Chicken and Waffles.

SPELMAN COLLEGE

Highlights

Students
Total enrollment: 2,145
Undergrads: 2,145
Freshmen: 631
From out-of-state: 78%
From public schools: 84%
Male/Female: 0%/100%
Live on-campus: 65%
In sororities: 10%
Off-campus employment rating: Good
Caucasian: 0%
African American: 82%
Hispanic: 0%
Asian / Pacific Islander: 0%
Native American: 0%
Mixed (2+ ethnicities): 2%
International: 1%

Academics
Calendar: Semester
Student/faculty ratio: 11:1
Class size 9 or fewer: 23%
Class size 10-29: 63%
Class size 30-49: 11%
Class size 50-99: 4%
Class size 100 or more: -
Returning freshmen: 90%
Six-year graduation rate: 73%
Graduates who immediately go to graduate school: 33%

Most Popular Majors
Psychology
Biology
English

Admissions
Applicants: 6,081
Accepted: 2,312
Acceptance rate: 38.0%
Placed on wait list: 621
Enrolled from wait list: 250
Average GPA: 3.6
ACT range: 19-27
SAT Math range: 467-545
SAT Reading range: 446-608
SAT Writing range: Not reported
Top 10% of class: 40%
Top 25% of class: 73%
Top 50% of class: 95%

597

College Profiles

SPELMAN COLLEGE

Admissions Criteria
Academic criteria:
Grades: ☆ ☆ ☆
Difficulty of class schedule: ☆ ☆ ☆
Class rank: ☆
Standardized test scores: ☆ ☆ ☆
Teacher recommendations: ☆ ☆ ☆
Personal statement: ☆ ☆
Non-academic criteria considered:
Extracurricular activities
Special talents, interests, abilities
Character/personal qualities
Volunteer work
Work experience
State of residency
Geographical location
Alumni relationship

Deadlines
Early Action: November 15
Early Decision: December 31
Regular Action: February 1 (final)
Notification of admission by: April 1
Common Application: Accepted

Financial Aid
In-state tuition: $21,309
Out-of-state tuition: $21,309
Room: Varies
Board: Varies
Books: $2,000
Freshmen receiving need-based aid: 94%
Undergrads rec. need-based aid: 93%
Avg. % of need met by financial aid: 39%
Avg. aid package (freshmen): $13,904
Avg. aid package (undergrads): $14,391
Avg. debt upon graduation: $33,898

School Spirit
Mascot: Jaguar
Colors: Columbia blue
Song: *Spelman Hymn*

Underground Atlanta's shops, restaurants, and festivals are also popular student haunts.

Freshmen are required to live in campus housing, most of which is traditional dorm-style; upperclassmen who wish to live on campus can also live in apartment-style suites. Most, however, don't—students find campus housing's quality singularly underwhelming. "There are a lot of better options off campus," explains a student.

Student Body

Students say that Spelman's students tend to be "motivated academically," and fall on the "conservative" side in terms of socializing and drinking, in particular. "Even though we're all black and female, there is no single Spelman type," notes a student. A very large portion of the student body comes from outside Georgia.

You May Not Know

- Spelman's Women's Research and Resource Center was the first of its kind on a black women's college campus.
- When it was built in 1927, campus' Grover-Werden Memorial Fountain was the only place where cold water was available on campus.
- Spelman's was originally called the Atlanta Baptist Female Seminary when it was founded in 1881.

Distinguished Alumnae

Cassi Davis, actress; Marian Wright Edelman, founder and President of the Children's Defense Fund (CDF); Marcelite J. Harris, first African-American woman to earn the rank of General in the U.S. Air Force; Bernice King, President of the Southern Christian Leadership Foundation and daughter of Dr. Martin Luther King, Jr.; Audrey Forbes Manley, physician and public health professional.

Admissions and Financial Aid

Spelman's notes that it is "particularly interested" in applicants who have taken the most academically rigorous path possible in high school.

Merit scholarships are available to students who demonstrate both academic and extracurricular merit, leadership, and community involvement. Five Presidential Scholarships, which cover the full cost of attendance, are awarded; 65 Dean's Scholarships up to the full cost of attendance are awarded and are annually renewable. The Bonner Scholarship is awarded to a student who displays outstanding commitment to community service and good citizenship.

Applicants interested in engineering, physics, computer science, chemistry, or math are eligible for Women in Science and Engineering (WISE) Scholarships, which cover half the cost of attendance. HOPE Scholarships are also available to residents of Georgia who have qualifying GPAs. No extra application is necessary, but application materials must be submitted early to be considered for these scholarships.

ST. JOHN'S COLLEGE

Overview

St. John's College is a small private school with two very different locations—Annapolis, Maryland and Santa Fe, New Mexico. Historic Annapolis is a seaport town about 30 miles from the attractions of the bigger cities of Washington, DC and Baltimore. Santa Fe, the nation's oldest capital city, is a gateway into the cultural attractions of the Southwest.

The Annapolis campus is located in a historic area one block from the State Capitol. The school's front lawn is a popular place for the annual croquet match with rival United States Naval Academy. The campus' McDowell Hall, whose construction dates back to 1742, is a major landmark in town as well as a site for waltz and swing dance parties featuring champagne and strawberries. In contrast to the deep historical roots of the Annapolis campus, the Santa Fe campus was opened in 1964 to accommodate increased enrollment. This campus has an expansive view of Santa Fe and a secluded environment that lends itself to outdoor activities and even training in Search and Rescue.

Students admitted to one location can apply for transfer to the other. However, there's not much choice beyond that when it comes to an undergrads' four-year program of study, since St. John's students—known as Johnnie's—take an all-required liberal arts curriculum for four years. The fact that there are no majors, just one course of study spanning several disciplines, makes for a strong sense of academic cohesion that may be limiting to some but much needed structure to others. If studying Greek and Roman philosophers for two solid years doesn't excite you, St. John's would not be the best fit. However, if you feel you would benefit from a strong curriculum guide, then check out what St. John's has to offer.

It isn't just the curriculum that's unique, but St. John's entire educational philosophy. There are no professors—only "tutors"—and virtually no lectures—only discussions. There are no textbooks or exams; class participation and papers are the only criteria for grades, though they are released only at the request of the student so that the focus remains on learning rather than assessment. It's not surprising that St. John's recommends visiting either or both of the college campuses to get a better sense of whether this unique model of undergraduate education is a good fit for a prospective student.

Academics

St. John's College offers only one undergraduate degree: the Bachelor of Arts. The required course of study is the Great Books program, which the college has used since 1937. This distinctive, interdisciplinary curriculum is based on the great books of the Western tradition and includes four years each of Seminars on mathematics and language, three years of science, and one year of music.

There is an unusually low student-to-"tutor"(professor) ratio of eight to one, making for tight-knit classes. "We know all our tutors on an academic and personal level," one student states. Learning is emphasized above grades, and the college encourages prospective students to check out the interactive seminar courses.

The Seminar readings include selections in literature, philosophy, theology, political science, and more, and are roughly chronological: they cover Greeks (Homer, Plato, Aristotle) in freshman year, selections from the Hebrew Bible and classical Roman poetry in sophomore year, and readings from the 17th and 18th centuries in junior year. Seniors arrive at more contemporary readings of the 20th century.

The college describes its Seminar as "a small group of students and two faculty members [who] wrestle together with important and difficult texts, without agenda or lesson plan." Students set the course of discussion and tutors act as guides and fellow inquirers. This emphasis on professors as fellow learners is obvious from their

ST. JOHN'S COLLEGE

Four-year private
Founded: 1696
Annapolis, MD
Large town
Pop. 38,880

Address:
P.O. Box 2800
Annapolis, MD
21404

Admissions:
800-727-9238

Financial Aid:
410-626-2502

admissions@sjca.edu

www.stjohnscollege.edu

Founded: 1964
Santa Fe, NM
Large town
Pop. 68,642

Address:
1160 Camino Cruz Blanca
Santa Fe, NM
87505

Admissions:
800-331-5232

Financial Aid:
505-984-6058

admissions@sjcsf.edu

www.sjcsf.edu

ST. JOHN'S COLLEGE

Highlights

Students
Total enrollment: 509/430
Undergrads: 489/349
Freshmen: 120/Not reported
From out-of-state: 85%/77%
From public schools: 64%/75%
Male/Female: 56%/44% and 57%/43%
Live on-campus: 70%/82%
Off-campus employment rating: Good
Caucasian: 76%/64%
African American: 2%/1%
Hispanic: 7%/11%
Asian / Pacific Islander: 2%/3%
Native American: 0%/1%
Mixed (2+ ethnicities): 3%/6%
International: 9%/14%

Academics
Calendar: Semester
Student/faculty ratio: 8:1/7:1
Class size 9 or fewer: 4%/8%
Class size 10-29: 95%/92%
Class size 30-49: -
Class size 50-99: -
Class size 100 or more: 1%/ -
Returning freshmen: 81%/70%
Six-year graduation rate: 67%/58%
Graduates who immediately go to graduate school: 12%/15%
Graduates who immediately enter career related to major: 37%/Not reported

Most Popular Majors
Liberal arts

Admissions
Applicants: 378/251
Accepted: 311/211
Acceptance rate: 82.3%/84.1%
Average GPA: Not reported
ACT range: 28-30/25-29
SAT Math range: 570-680/550-680
SAT Reading range: 620-730/580-740
SAT Writing range: Not reported
Top 10% of class: 12%/16%
Top 25% of class: 32%/41%
Top 50% of class: 48%/70%

The Ultimate
Guide to America's
Best Colleges

titles as "tutors" (though most hold doctorates). "There have been times when I've felt like the students have deeper insights than the tutor," one student notes.

Seminars have 20 students. Daytime tutorials in language, mathematics, and music are smaller, ranging from 12 to 16 students. Preceptorials are the most intimate with between three and nine students. For seven to eight weeks in the middle of the year, seminars are suspended for juniors and seniors so that they may meet in smaller groups to explore more deeply a particular subject or reading—these are the closest things to electives at St. John's. Laboratories have 14 to 16 students and meet twice a week with experiment and discussion components. Freshmen cover biology and chemistry; juniors cover physics, while seniors cover biology, genetics, and more physics.

The required curriculum does not leave room for study abroad during the school year, though many students travel over the summers. The Career Services Offices keeps information on study-abroad opportunities, which is available to interested students. The office also emphasizes building personalized relationships with students to help them determine a fitting career path. Students can drop in or set up appointments with the director, associate director, and internship coordinator. "Before I came, people told me that I needed to major in something practical like business or computer science, but I've seen how employers appreciate our graduates' ability to think and analyze," one student comments.

Student Life

Both campuses offer extracurricular art classes and facilities to support creative endeavors, from soundproof music practice rooms to art galleries. While student organizations can be fairly informal and change based on students' interests, mainstays on both campuses include student government, newspaper, theater groups, and community service. The King William's Players have put on productions (Shakespeare and non-Bard) since the 1940s.

Both campuses have extracurricular events that seem to follow the seasons. On the Annapolis campus, students arrange rock dances, waltz parties, and community gatherings such as the Halloween Masked Ball, Christmas Party, and Mid-Winter Ball. In the spring, the Croquet Match, paired with the Croquet Cotillion (a formal dance), is a popular event. Seniors celebrate the completion of their senior essays by ringing the bell in McDowell Hall at midnight. On the Santa Fe campus, Reality Weekend is a spring festival than includes student skits, picnicking, and athletic competition.

While you'll find students studying Greek philosophers, you won't find them participating in Greek life, since there are no fraternities or sororities on campus. The college also lacks varsity sports but makes up for this with extensive intramurals. In Annapolis, flag football, basketball, soccer, team hand all, and softball are especially popular. There are also club sports including crew, fencing, and croquet.

Outdoor activities abound. In Santa Fe, students can easily head to the Sangre de Cristo Mountains to ski, snowboard, mountain bike, and hike. The Rio Grande and Chama rivers provide opportunities to enjoy whitewater canoeing, kayaking, and rafting. The Annapolis campus has easy access to boating, sailing, and crew.

More than 70 percent of students live on campus, and freshmen are guaranteed rooms on campus. Annapolis students can choose from eight dorms, six of which are historic buildings arranged around a central quad. The Santa Fe dorms are modern units clustered around central courtyards.

Student Body

At a school with such a unique educational approach, it isn't surprising that students have a passion for learning, not just for grades. "We often continue discussions outside of class, sometimes well into the night," one student notes.

There is moderate ethnic diversity; 14 percent (Maryland) and 22 percent (New Mexico) of undergrads are minority students. There is high geographic diversity on both campuses, with the vast majority of students hailing from out of state.

You May Not Know

- The college faced near-bankruptcy when the state withdrew its funding in 1805.
- Four of the college's founders were signers of the Declaration of Independence.
- Both campuses have outdoor Ptolemy Stones.

Distinguished Alumni

Ahmet Ertegun, founder of Altantic Records; Steven Holland, National Institutes of Health, Research Director and physician; Paul Mellon, philanthropist; Lisa Simeone, National Public Radio producer and host.

Admissions and Financial Aid

St. John's admissions committee consists of five tutors and the director of admissions from each campus. According to the committee, each application is seen as a question from the prospective student: "Do you think I am ready to profit from the program of studies at St. John's?" The committee evaluates essays, academic records, and letters of reference. SAT or ACT test scores are optional but "may prove helpful"—in practice, over 80 percent of applicants do submit them. Interviews and campus visits are recommended.

Both available spots and financial aid are given on a first-come, first-serve basis, which should be an incentive for students to apply early. St. John's does not offer any merit awards: as a small college with limited resources, they prefer scholarship aid to go to students with financial need (more than 70 percent receive some form of assistance), and they also prefer an egalitarian view of students.

ST. JOHN'S COLLEGE

Highlights

Admissions Criteria

Academic criteria:
Grades: ☆ ☆ ☆/☆ ☆
Difficulty of class schedule: ☆ ☆ ☆/☆ ☆
Class rank: ☆
Standardized test scores: ☆
Teacher recommendations: ☆ ☆ ☆/☆ ☆
Personal statement: ☆ ☆ ☆
Non-academic criteria considered:
Interview
Character/personal qualities
State of residency

Deadlines

Early Action: November 15 and January 15/November 15
Early Decision: No
Regular Action: Rolling admissions
Common Application: Accepted

Financial Aid

In-state tuition: $45,846/$44,554
Out-of-state tuition: $45,846/$44,554
Room: $5,358/Varies
Board: $5,596/Varies
Books: $620/$630
Freshmen receiving need-based aid: 82%/79%
Undergrads rec. need-based aid: 71%/85%
Avg. aid package (freshmen): $36,407/$36,445
Avg. aid package (undergrads): $33,665/$37,352
Avg. debt upon graduation: $29,265/$26,750

School Spirit

Mascot: The Great Book
Colors: Orange and black

ST. LAWRENCE
UNIVERSITY

Four-year private
Founded: 1856
Canton, NY
Small town
Pop. 6,305

Address:
23 Romoda Drive
Canton, NY
13617

Admissions:
800-285-1856

Financial Aid:
800-355-0863

admissions@stlawu.
edu

www.stlawu.edu

ST. LAWRENCE UNIVERSITY

Overview

Many people are surprised by the beauty of St. Lawrence's rustic 1,000-acre campus, which features research and recreational natural habitats, in addition to the university's own golf course. More commonly referred to by its nickname, "SLU," St. Lawrence University is located in Canton, New York, close to the border of Canada. The school's almost 2,400 undergraduates often take advantage of what this scenic region has to offer, traveling to the beautiful St. Lawrence Seaway—only 20 minutes away—and immersing themselves in the outdoors.

Despite its many undeniable advantages, some students often complain of New York's bitter winters. At times, some students feel stifled by the overwhelmingly small size of the school. The tiny village of Canton has a population of 6,000, making the university a big presence in the community.

Academics

SLU offers 32 majors. Students must complete a series of distribution and diversity requirements consisting of six total units from six different departments or programs at the university. Students must pass at least one unit in each of the following categories: arts/expression, humanities, social sciences, and mathematics or foreign language. In addition, they must complete at least two units in natural science/science studies. The Diversity Requirement requires students to pass two units in two different programs that expand their knowledge and grasp of issues such as nationality, ethnicity, gender, class, sexual orientation, and religious/cultural differences.

Classes at SLU are extremely small and there are no teaching assistants. While this is generally a very positive aspect of the school—because it means professors teach classes and are directly involved with students—it does have its challenges: students can have a hard time getting into classes that they want, and some complain that the discussion-based format can be a little intense. "With a small school, there are limitations," says a student.

Among the strongest programs offered at SLU are economics, English, and psychology. Other special academic opportunities include the First-Year Program, a living/learning program that helps students develop writing, speaking, and research skills. During their first semester, students live in one of 18 residential colleges with other students enrolled in their FYP seminar in addition to their academic advisor. In the spring, students enroll in First-Year Seminars which—given their small sizes—give them the chance to build close relationships with other students and faculty.

Many students also choose to participate in the Adirondack Semester, which immerses them in nature by taking classes in a yurt village among ancient treks and an Adirondack lake. The program consists of classes revolving around the field trips and daily life that reinforces the themes of academic study. Students rave about this four and a half unit program, with "amenities including a composting toilet and a wood-fired sauna," as well as the opportunity to create a camp favorite—calzones made from over open camp fires. "I felt so creative during the woodworking class that I took," recalls a participant.

The university's Fellows Program gives students new opportunities for intellectual growth by promoting student-faculty collaboration. Students awarded a fellowship receive a $3,500 stipend to replace earnings from summer employment. Recent examples of Fellowship topics range from "The Effect of Cell Membrane Composition on Protein Aggregation into Fiber," to "Shades of Grey: Fairy Tales for a Modern Audience."

SLU offers study-abroad programs in 17 countries and six continents including China, Costa Rica, England, and New Zealand. Students commonly take courses through the SLU study abroad that can be applied to their minor and can also choose to undertake research abroad that can form the basis for the capstone requirement.

St. Lawrence offers a full range of career services to students, including career planning advice and graduate school guidance. Based on a survey, more than 95 percent of the Class of 2010 found places in employment or graduate school.

Student Life

Students at SLU are active in 125 official organizations. Groups with an influence on campus social life include student government and the Association for Campus Entertainment (ACE), which provides a wide array of social and cultural activities from movies to plays to art openings. The Outing Club, which sponsors various backpacking, canoeing, snowshoeing, and ice climbing trips throughout the whole year, is very popular. The Outdoor Program leads students into the Adirondacks and is especially well received, as are other skiing and climbing trips.

Annual events on campus include Winterfest, a weekend filled with winter-based activities such as sledding, skating, and a snow sculpture competition, in addition to an abundance of cocktails. "Drinking is an *unofficial* competition," laughs a student. Peak Weekend, a three-decade tradition, takes around 140 students each year to reach the top of all of the Adirondack's highest peeks (those over 4,000 feet). "It makes us appreciate the outdoor recreation right around us," notes a student. Tree Holiday (now called "Moving-Up Day") was initiated in 1869 as a day in the spring when classes do not meet so that students and faculty may transplant trees to the campus. Today, the day serves as a day to recognize student achievement.

Greek life does not constitute a particularly huge part of life at SLU but it is certainly available for those who wish to join it: there are four social sororities, four sorority houses, and two social fraternities on campus. "There isn't an extensive Greek party scene—it's pretty low key," says a student. Nine percent of men and 17 percent of women participate.

St. Lawrence has 32 intercollegiate teams, including the NCAA Division I men's hockey team, which is extremely popular, especially during its game against its biggest rival—Clarkson. All other teams, including men's squash, Nordic skiing, baseball, basketball, crew, and equestrian teams, are Division III. For those interested in intramurals, top choices are basketball, broomball, flag football, ice hockey, and the quadatholon teams.

Off campus, there are a few chain restaurants and local restaurants in the tiny town of Canton. "There's not a ton going on in Canton," says a student. Students will often choose to take road trips to Ottawa, Montreal, or Syracuse—the closest major cities. Since the drinking age in Canada is 18, trips across the border are quite popular.

All students are required to live on campus but upperclassmen may choose to live in Greek or theme housing. Most seniors look forward to the chance of living in the recently built townhouses, which boast five single bedrooms, two bathrooms, a kitchen, and living room space. Students who wish to live in the senior townhouses must complete an application process.

ST. LAWRENCE UNIVERSITY

Highlights

Students
Total enrollment: 2,488
Undergrads: 2,398
Freshmen: 644
From out-of-state: 55%
From public schools: 69%
Male/Female: 45%/55%
Live on-campus: 99%
In fraternities: 9%
In sororities: 17%
Off-campus employment rating: Fair
Caucasian: 81%
African American: 3%
Hispanic: 4%
Asian / Pacific Islander: 2%
Native American: 0%
Mixed (2+ ethnicities): 2%
International: 7%

Academics
Calendar: Semester
Student/faculty ratio: 12:1
Class size 9 or fewer: 20%
Class size 10-29: 70%
Class size 30-49: 9%
Class size 50-99: 1%
Class size 100 or more: -
Six-year graduation rate: 80%

Most Popular Majors
Economics
Psychology
Biology

Admissions
Applicants: 4,067
Accepted: 1,962
Acceptance rate: 48.2%
Placed on wait list: 203
Enrolled from wait list: 20
Average GPA: 3.5
ACT range: 25-29
SAT Math range: 570-660
SAT Reading range: 560-650
SAT Writing range: 7-48
Top 10% of class: 44%
Top 25% of class: 76%
Top 50% of class: 94%

603

ST. LAWRENCE UNIVERSITY

Admissions Criteria
Academic criteria:
Grades: ☆ ☆ ☆
Difficulty of class schedule: ☆ ☆ ☆
Class rank: ☆ ☆
Standardized test scores: ☆
Teacher recommendations: ☆ ☆ ☆
Personal statement: ☆ ☆ ☆
Non-academic criteria considered:
Interview
Extracurricular activities
Special talents, interests, abilities
Character/personal qualities
Volunteer work
Work experience
State of residency
Geographical location
Minority affiliation
Alumni relationship

Deadlines
Early Action: No
Early Decision: November 1
Regular Action: February 1 (final)
Notification of admission by: Late March
Common Application: Accepted

Financial Aid
In-state tuition: $45,705
Out-of-state tuition: $45,705
Room: $6,385
Board: $5,475
Books: $650
Freshmen receiving need-based aid: 64%
Undergrads rec. need-based aid: 63%
Avg. % of need met by financial aid: 88%
Avg. aid package (freshmen): $39,811
Avg. aid package (undergrads): $38,941
Avg. debt upon graduation: $25,058

School Spirit
Mascot: Saints
Colors: Scarlet and brown
Song: *Alma Mater*

Student Body

At first glance, the students at SLU are often described as "Abercrombie and-Fitch-esque," but one student says, "despite our reputation, there's more to us than good-looking, well-dressed preppy types. We're passionate about the outdoors, the environment, and contributing to the community."

The student body is moderately ethnically diverse, with 11 percent of the student body consisting of minorities. With 55 percent of students from out of state, the campus is moderately geographically diverse as well.

You May Not Know

- The St. Lawrence art collection includes pieces by Andy Warhol and Pablo Picasso.
- There are 26 stained glass windows on campus, honoring a gamut of individuals from King Arthur to Mahatma Gandhi.
- J. Kimball Gannon, the composer of the university's alma mater, also wrote one of the most popular holiday songs ever published—*I'll Be Home for Christmas*.

Distinguished Alumni

Irvin Bacheller, newspaper syndicator and best-selling author in the early 1900s; Kirk Douglas, actor; Dave Jennings, punter for the New York Giants; Kim Whitehead Puckett, founder of Caribou Coffee; Holton D. Robinson, inventor of suspension bridge cable/architect of the Manhattan and San Francisco Bay Bridge.

Admissions and Financial Aid

The admissions process at SLU is test optional, meaning that students may choose whether or not they would like the results from the SAT or ACT to be used during the evaluation process. In general, students are strongly encouraged to visit campus (where interviews may be scheduled). In some areas, off-campus interviews are also available.

University grants, awarded based upon a student's financial need, are the most sought after type of financial assistance at SLU. Students will receive grants varying in amount based on their respective need. Students applying for grants do not need to complete a separate application—they simply need to fill out the Free Application for Federal Student Aid (FAFSA) prior to March 1 every year.

Several four-year merit-based scholarships, ranging in value from $3,000 to $16,000 per year, are also available to incoming freshmen. All students who apply for admission are automatically considered for four various scholarships. However, applications for the Presidential Scholarship and Martin Luther King Jr. Scholarship do require separate applications.

ST. OLAF COLLEGE

Overview

With five Rhodes scholars, 49 Fulbright recipients, and a number eight ranking among baccalaureate colleges in the number of graduates going on to earn doctoral degrees last year, St. Olaf College certainly proves itself a high-achieving academic institution worth the perusal of any serious student. This private, Lutheran-affiliated college is recognized as a leading contender in the liberal arts, known for its rigorous programs in mathematics, natural sciences, and music.

The 300-acre campus is located in Northfield, Minnesota, just 35 miles south of Minneapolis, and includes quaint 19th-century architecture amidst a naturalistic setting. On-campus events such as outside speakers and musical concerts attract large numbers from the local community, and a weekend bus running from campus to Minneapolis provides easy access to municipal diversions. In this tight-knit campus community, students often commune in "The Pause," the multi-faceted student facility, or the Goodbye Blue Monday Coffee House, to snack, socialize, and collaborate on academic ventures.

Adding to the elite academic accomplishments of the college is its intense focus on environmentalism. Recently installed on campus is a composter that can process up to one ton of food waste a day, as well as a wind turbine that can generate enough energy to replace one third of the college's energy use. In a world where environmental threats are a growing concern, St. Olaf stands at the forefront of the "green" movement.

Through its rigorous academics, dedication to the Lutheran faith, and commitment to the environment, St. Olaf provides students an invaluable experience that allows them to cultivate their characters and grow to become devoted members of society.

Academics

General education requirements at St. Olaf include Foundation Studies, which focus on oral and written communication skills as well as quantitative reasoning and physical education; Core Studies, which focus on multicultural studies; artistic studies; religion; natural sciences; and Integrative Studies, which focus on human behavior in society and ethical issues. "You don't have to be religious to do well in the Biblical and theology classes," explains a student, "but it can help so you don't have to learn from scratch."

Though the academic spread is demanding, students praise the amount of individual attention they receive, as 94 percent of classes contain less than 40 students. Strong programs, in addition to those listed above, are economics, mathematics, education, music, and nursing, as well as various special academic programs, such as The Great Conversation, a five-course spread tracing the development of Western intellectual and religious thought from the ancient Greeks and Hebrews to modern times. "The discussions sparked are very intellectual," notes a student. Another unique program is the music department at the college, the faculty of which plays with such prestigious orchestras as the Minnesota Orchestra and the St. Paul Chamber Orchestra.

All students partake in the unique class schedule of the college, which runs on two four-month semesters with a one-month "Interim" period in January. During this time, students can dedicate themselves intensively to one course, pursue an internship, or choose to study abroad. Recent Interim courses offered have been "Historical Geography and the Bible in the Holy Land" in the Middle East, "Theatre in London," and "Environmental Psychology" in the Rocky Mountains. Studying abroad at St. Olaf is incredibly popular, with over two thirds of students participating in study-abroad programs offered in Europe, Asia, the Middle East, Africa, North, South and Central America, and the Pacific. "There are so many opportunities to

ST. OLAF COLLEGE

Four-year private
Founded: 1874
Northfield, MN
Small town
Pop. 20,084

Address:
1520 St. Olaf Avenue
Northfield, MN
55057

Admissions:
800-800-3025

Financial Aid:
877-235-8386

admissions@stolaf.edu

www.stolaf.edu

ST. OLAF COLLEGE

study abroad, especially with Interim, that you have no excuse to not take part," one student comments.

As far as life after college, St. Olaf has an active Career Network designed to provide students connections with alumni as well as educate them about careers and internships in their fields of study.

Student Life

With over 200 student organizations present on campus—including such interesting choices as Herpetology Club, HipHip Skool, and Dream Box—students at St. Olaf never tire of extracurricular activities. Though technically a dry campus, the college does not fail to entertain its lively student body.

A unique business opportunity at St. Olaf is participating in the management of the Lion's Pause, a student-run night club/lounge/snack bar that offers daytime and late night nourishment and entertainment to students, including musical performances from students and community musicians. "I hang out there at least a couple times a week to meet up with friends," says a student.

Events on campus are often associated with tradition. The St. Olaf Christmas Festival boasts a title as one of the oldest Christmas musical celebrations in the country. Created by the founder of the renowned music department, the festival showcases over 500 student musicians from the St. Olaf Orchestra and choirs. "It really puts you in the spirit of Christmas to be surrounded by music," recalls a student. Another event, Fun for Finals, is a week-long string of activities, from Snow Creation Competition to barbeques and dunk tanks, providing students a delightful break from studying. Yet another event, Glam Ball, is a charity dance event with proceeds going toward the support of services for people with HIV/AIDS.

Although there is no Greek system at St. Olaf, the athletics scene offers a place for students to unite in school spirit, with 13 men's and 12 women's Division III sports teams. The swimming and diving teams are strong, with Nordic and alpine skiing also being very popular. Football draws in large numbers, especially when St. Olaf plays cross-town rival Carleton College in the Cereal Bowl, named to honor the Malt-O-Meal company in town. As far as non-varsity activities, the college has its own rock-climbing wall, the Tostrud Climbing Wall, as well as over 10 intramural sports.

Students at St. Olaf relish the outdoors and often participate in cross-country skiing or broomball in nearby outdoor facilities. Although Northfield is far from bustling in terms of nightlife, students often mingle with nearby Carleton College students and sometimes drive 45 minutes to Minneapolis or St. Paul for nighttime entertainment. "If you're willing to drive," says one student, "the Twin Cities have all the big-city entertainment."

Housing at St. Olaf is split into 11 residence halls and 18 honors houses, which are either academically-oriented or have a "special interest" theme, such as women's concerns or environmental issues. Ninety-one percent of students choose to live on campus all four years. "That so many people live on campus helps us develop strong friendships and school spirit that I just don't see at other schools," comments a student.

Student Body

Though often thought of as being composed of entirely blond, Scandinavian Lutherans, one student explains that they "don't all fit the stereotype, although some do." The student body at St. Olaf is not "overly religious." Though the influence of religion is "very strong" on campus, an even stronger uniting force within the student body is concern for the environment.

Ethnic diversity within the student body is moderate, with 14 percent being of minority status. Geographic diversity is moderate, with 52 percent of students hailing from out of state.

You May Not Know

- The fight song contains the lyrics, "Um! Yah! Yah!" repeated 14 times.
- An average of six St. Olaf students receive the Fulbright Scholarship each year.
- The St. Olaf Band was the first American college musical organization to perform a concert tour abroad when it traveled to Norway in 1906.

Distinguished Alumni

Russel A. Anderson, former Chief Justice of the Minnesota Supreme Court; Anton Armstrong, conductor of the St. Olaf Choir; Siri Hustvedt, novelist and poet; Barry Morrow, Academy Award-winning screenwriter; Elizabeth G. Nabel, President of Brigham and Women's/Faulkner Hospitals; Al Quie, former Governor of Minnesota; Ole Rolvaag, writer and professor.

Admissions and Financial Aid

The admissions committee considers GPA, test scores, and the difficulty of classes taken in high school. However, they also look at qualitative factors such as breadth of academic interests and leadership skills. They prefer students taking more difficult classes with lower grades than easier classes with impeccable GPAs.

St. Olaf awards merit-based scholarships to students who demonstrate academic excellence or leadership within their communities or churches. Some of the scholarships available include the St. Olaf Academic Scholarship Program, which awards $6,500-$16,000 a year, the National Merit Scholarship Program, which awards $7,500 a year, and the St. Olaf Service Leadership Scholarship, which awards $6,000 a year. Also available are music, theater, and dance scholarships of various monetary amounts.

ST. OLAF COLLEGE

Highlights

Admissions Criteria
Academic criteria:
Grades: ☆ ☆ ☆
Difficulty of class schedule: ☆ ☆ ☆
Class rank: ☆ ☆
Standardized test scores: ☆ ☆
Teacher recommendations: ☆ ☆
Personal statement: ☆ ☆ ☆
Non-academic criteria considered:
Interview
Extracurricular activities
Special talents, interests, abilities
Character/personal qualities
Volunteer work
Work experience
Geographical location
Religious affiliation/commitment
Minority affiliation
Alumni relationship

Deadlines
Early Action: No
Early Decision: November 15
Regular Action: January 15 (priority)
January 15 (final)
Notification of admission by: March 15
Common Application: Accepted

Financial Aid
In-state tuition: $40,700
Out-of-state tuition: $40,700
Room: $4,340
Board: $4,920
Books: $1,000
Freshmen receiving need-based aid: 68%
Undergrads rec. need-based aid: 68%
Avg. % of need met by financial aid: 100%
Avg. aid package (freshmen): $35,190
Avg. aid package (undergrads): $33,967
Avg. debt upon graduation: $27,637

School Spirit
Mascot: Ole the Lion
Colors: Black and gold
Song: *Um! Yah! Yah!*

STANFORD UNIVERSITY

Overview

On any given day at the largest contiguous university campus in the world, you'll find squirrels scurrying around palm trees under blue skies, students in cardinal red Stanford T-shirts biking past Spanish-influenced architecture and modern buildings, and tourists taking photos of the renowned beauty of Stanford University's campus. This stellar private school is consistently rated among the top universities in the nation.

With a strong reputation for academics, the school also provides an expansive slate of research opportunities and boasts one of the nation's top athletic programs. Located near Silicon Valley in the Bay Area of California, less than a one-hour drive to San Francisco, Stanford is famous for incubating entrepreneurs like the founders of Hewlett-Packard, Google, and Yahoo! Not surprisingly, Wi-Fi is available across campus and Apple's strong presence can be seen in the laptops and iPhones many students carry as they go from class to dorm to various extracurricular pursuits on the picturesque campus.

While the Stanford Bubble, as some students call campus, is famous for its beauty, it's also notoriously difficult to get admitted, and academics are very challenging—as can be expected among a pool of exceptionally talented and highly ambitious students. While games of Frisbee in the Oval in front of Stanford's photogenic Memorial Church certainly demonstrate that students have fun, it may also be a symptom of "duck syndrome" used to describe some students: calm on the surface, paddling furiously underneath. Nonetheless, for students who are eager to be around dynamic, well-rounded peers in an almost-always sunny campus overflowing with resources and opportunities, Stanford is hard to beat.

Academics

Stanford offers over 80 majors with plenty of subfields and concentrations within these. There are also departmental honors programs and options to double major, complete a "secondary major," minor, and even design one's own major. All students must fulfill a two-quarter writing requirement called the Program in Writing and Rhetoric (PWR, or "Power"), a language requirement, and general education mandates, which include the three-quarter sequence Introduction to the Humanities (IHUM), five courses in Disciplinary Breadth, and two courses within the areas of Education for Citizenship, Ethical Reasoning, the Global Community, American Cultures, and Gender Studies. "IHUM is the common experience that everyone pretty much dreads," says a student. Strong programs include biology, economics, engineering, English, international relations, and sociology.

Academics at Stanford are challenging. Students study hard and often participate in research or leadership opportunities. "We all pretty much put in hours devoted to the books, and there are a few people who essentially live in the library," notes a student. Given the community feel of the school, it is easy to get to know faculty outside the classroom; some professors who teach seminar courses even hold classes in their homes, as many professors live on or near campus.

Special academic opportunities include Introductory Seminars—popularly known as IntroSems—small-group courses for freshmen and sophomores that are taught by esteemed faculty and that are known for their competitive enrollment. Sophomore College also fosters close relationships between faculty and students by providing a three-week residential summer program for 12-14 sophomores before beginning fall quarter in various disciplines. Students who talk about "co-terming" are referring to Stanford's co-terminal degree program, which enables a student to begin a master's degree while completing the bachelor's; for many, this means completing a master's degree within an additional year rather than two.

The Bing Overseas Studies Program offers 13 quarter-long study-abroad opportunities, each with different prerequisites and topical focuses. For example, the Berlin study-abroad program comes with the option for a paid internship, while the Cape Town program enables students to engage in service learning and community-based research in South Africa.

The Career Development Center offers free one-on-one career counseling for students up to one year after they graduate. Students may also network with alumni. There are an estimated 211,706 living Stanford degree holders, including more than 75,000 undergraduate alumni, more than 95,000 graduate alumni, and 20,000 dual-degree holders. Stanford alumni can be found in 142 countries, 18 territories, and all 50 states and the District of Columbia. "I found an internship through the alumni email list," notes a student.

Student Life

The more than 650 student organizations on campus make for a plethora of options that can often feel overwhelming to incoming freshman during New Student Orientations (NSO's) Fall Activities Fair, when White Plaza is filled with student groups advertising their clubs and organizations. "You're guaranteed to find a group that meets your interests," says a student. The Associated Students of Stanford University (ASSU) allocates $1 million to the student organizations and represents the entire student body. A number of a cappella groups prove popular on campus, from the rich multicultural voices of Talisman to the hilarious antics of Fleet Street. *The Stanford Daily* has been in existence since Stanford's inception in 1892 and is always visible on campus, not surprising given its circulation size of 10,000 throughout campus and the city of Palo Alto.

The Haas Center for Public Service at Stanford provides a centralized resource for over 600 volunteer, internship, and research opportunities. Over 3,000 students engage in service each year, totaling more than 96,000 volunteer hours. The Alternative Spring Break (ASB) Program is popular and has won accolades.

Incoming freshmen arrive a week before classes begin in the fall for New Student Orientation, during which many engage in the tradition of fountain hopping, running around and leaping or swimming in the various fountains on campus—such as the distinctive Claw fountain in White Plaza, or the Red Fountain in front of Green Library. "It's the best time to meet people because everyone is open to making new friends," one student explains. Another famous (or perhaps infamous) tradition is Full Moon on the Quad, which began as seniors stealing kisses from freshmen but now involves an evening of music and, for many, indiscriminate kissing among students of all class ranks. One of the most anticipated events of the fall is Big Game, the football game against Stanford rival UC Berkeley. An entire week of festivities and activities lead up to the event, including the performance of Gaieties, an entirely student-run musical.

More than a quarter of undergraduates are part of Stanford's 13 sororities and 17 fraternities. Many of the parties on campus are thrown by Greek organizations, such as the well-attended Moonsplash and Sunsplash parties. "The Greek presence is there," one student comments, "but most people feel like you don't miss out on much by not joining."

STANFORD UNIVERSITY

Highlights

Students
Total enrollment: 18,217
Undergrads: 7,063
From out-of-state: 53%
From public schools: 58%
Male/Female: 52%/48%
Live on-campus: 91%
In fraternities: 24%
In sororities: 28%
Off-campus employment rating: Good
Caucasian: 37%
African American: 6%
Hispanic: 17%
Asian / Pacific Islander: 19%
Native American: 0%
Mixed (2+ ethnicities): 11%
International: 7%

Academics
Calendar: Quarter
Student/faculty ratio: 5:1
Class size 9 or fewer: 33%
Class size 10-29: 44%
Class size 30-49: 9%
Class size 50-99: 8%
Class size 100 or more: 5%
Returning freshmen: 98%
Six-year graduation rate: 95%
Graduates who immediately go to graduate school: 35%

Most Popular Majors
Computer science
Human biology
Engineering

Admissions
Applicants: 36,632
Accepted: 2,423
Acceptance rate: 6.6%
Placed on wait list: 789
Enrolled from wait list: Not reported
Average GPA: Not reported
ACT range: 31-34
SAT Math range: 700-790
SAT Reading range: 680-780
SAT Writing range: 76-21
Top 10% of class: 94%
Top 25% of class: 99%
Top 50% of class: 100%

609

STANFORD UNIVERSITY

Admissions Criteria
Academic criteria:
Grades: ☆ ☆ ☆
Difficulty of class schedule: ☆ ☆ ☆
Class rank: ☆ ☆ ☆
Standardized test scores: ☆ ☆ ☆
Teacher recommendations: ☆ ☆ ☆
Personal statement: ☆ ☆ ☆
Non-academic criteria considered:
Interview
Extracurricular activities
Special talents, interests, abilities
Character/personal qualities
Volunteer work
Work experience
State of residency
Geographical location
Minority affiliation
Alumni relationship

Deadlines
Early Action: November 1
Early Decision: No
Regular Action: January 1 (final)
Notification of admission by: April 1
Common Application: Accepted

Financial Aid
In-state tuition: $42,690
Out-of-state tuition: $42,690
Room: Varies
Board: Varies
Books: $1,500
Freshmen receiving need-based aid: 51%
Undergrads rec. need-based aid: 53%
Avg. % of need met by financial aid: 100%
Avg. aid package (freshmen): $41,894
Avg. aid package (undergrads): $42,354
Avg. debt upon graduation: $18,833

School Spirit
Mascot: Tree
Colors: Cardinal and white
Song: *All Right Now*

Stanford boasts one of the top athletics programs in the nation with 36 sports teams (17 men's, 19 women's) that compete in Division I. The university has won the NACDA Director's Cup—given to the nation's top ranked collegiate athletic program—for 16 years in a row. Football and basketball are the most popularly attended events. Baseball, tennis, swimming, water polo, gymnastics, soccer, volleyball, rowing, golf, and cross-country are among perennial national contenders.

About 800 students at Stanford participate in intercollegiate sports. There are also 20 club sports and intramurals that more than 9,000 students, faculty, and staff participate in each year, not to mention the thousands of students who enroll in PE courses throughout the year.

Nearby downtown Palo Alto has restaurants and shopping and the free Marguerite Shuttle goes to the Stanford Shopping Center, though neither of these places cater to student budgets—not surprising given that Palo Alto is among the most expensive cities in the U.S. "We could use some more cheap eats," notes a student. Students can travel to San Francisco, San Jose, or the East Bay (Oakland, Berkeley) for eating, shopping, nightlife, and outdoors excursions via public transport, though having a car is always helpful.

All first-year students are required to live on campus and housing is guaranteed for all four years. Housing options vary from small self-operated houses of 25 residents to large dorms of 200+ people. In fact, there are a total of 77 different houses, including 67 University-assigned houses, seven residential fraternities, and three residential sororities to choose from. Nearly all students are on a dining plan; luckily for them, there is a wide variety of excellent food: Stanford Dining operates a dozen dining halls and eateries on campus and has won awards both for culinary excellence and sustainability.

Student Body

The 7,000 undergraduates at Stanford are often separated, geographically and socially, from the 11,000 graduate students, though intermingling does happen in some classes and clubs. Undergraduates "lean left" and are "very passionate" about their studies and research. There is a strong sense of both service and entrepreneurship that pervades the student body, in keeping with Silicon Valley's history of innovation. "Everyone knows we're among the next founder of a Google," laughs a student.

Stanford's student body is highly diverse: more than half of undergraduates are students of color, and approximately 17 percent are the first in their families to attend college. Fifty-three percent are from out of state; it's not uncommon for out-of-state freshmen to find themselves paired with a Californian as a roommate. There is also a fairly large international student community, adding to the vibrant culture found on campus.

You May Not Know

- Leland Stanford founded the university in 1891 in honor of his son Leland Stanford, Jr., who died of typhoid at age 16—hence the official name, Leland Stanford Junior University.

- Stanford is often referred to as "The Farm," a reference to the fact that the university is on land that was formerly Leland Stanford's horse farm. Today, Stanford's Red Barn houses horses for the equestrian team and other interested riders.
- Stanford University is actually its own census-designated place within unincorporated Santa Clara County, which explains why it has its own post office on campus.

Distinguished Alumni

Sergey Brin and Lawrence Page, Google founders; Jennifer Connelly, actress; Sandra Day O'Connor, former U.S. Supreme Court Justice; Daniel Pearl, journalist.

Admissions and Financial Aid

Admission to Stanford is among the most competitive in the nation. However, there are no magic formulas for getting in. Stanford's admissions office encourages students to fill out the Common Application thoroughly and thoughtfully, ideally highlighting a deeper commitment in a few areas of achievement rather than a more shallow engagement with a broad range of activities. The admissions office also advocates using the Stanford Supplement to write "thoughtful and insightful short essays" that let the admissions officers get to know students personally. Stanford looks for a student body that consists of both well-rounded students and "angular" students who excel in one or two areas.

Stanford offers around 300 athletic scholarships but no other merit scholarships; however, Stanford does have an extensive financial aid program that is entirely need-based. For parents with total annual income below $60,000, Stanford does not expect any parental contribution for students; for parents with income below $100,000, tuition charges are covered with a combination of need-based scholarships and grants.

SUNY –
BINGHAMTON
UNIVERSITY

Four-year public
Founded: 1946
Binghamton, NY
Medium city
Pop. 46,996

Address:
P.O. Box 6000
Binghamton, NY
13902-6000

Admissions:
607-777-2171

Financial Aid:
607-777-2428

admit@binghamton.
edu

www.binghamton.edu

STATE UNIVERSITY OF NEW YORK – BINGHAMTON UNIVERSITY

Overview

Binghamton is a large public university that ranks 44th among public universities according to *U.S. News & World Report*. Although the tuition is a steal even for out-of-staters, the majority of the student body hails from New York State. For those ready to seek them out, there are myriad special academic opportunities and challenging courses, especially in its well known School of Management.

Binghamton is located outside Binghamton, New York, a medium-sized, frigid, upstate city. A bit quirky, the layout of the campus is similar to the shape of a human brain. In the past few years, the university has been consistently involved in construction, updating its University Union, building new residence halls, improving its technology center, and unveiling a new soccer and lacrosse stadium. The campus also includes a large nature preserve with wetlands and a pond.

As a large university, one of Binghamton's strength is the diversity of its student body. There is much more to do on campus than off in its rather remote location; but overall, Binghamton features a solid education for an extraordinarily low price.

Academics

Binghamton offers close to 130 majors, with strong programs in accounting and business administration. According to *BusinessWeek* magazine, the School of Management at Binghamton is the 12th best public business school in the country. The level of academic rigor at Binghamton depends on the major you choose and the professors you encounter. "You can coast or you can study nonstop," remarks a student. Expect to find yourself in some very large classes—seven percent of the courses have 100 or more students.

SUNY's general education requirements are extensive and rather convoluted. Students must complete one course in each of the following areas: composition, oral communication, pluralism in the United States (courses that track the experience of at least three different major cultural groups), global interdependencies (courses related to the development of non-western regions and/or how these regions have interacted with the west), laboratory science, social science, mathematics/reasoning, aesthetics, humanities, and physical activity/wellness. Students pursuing degrees other than engineering also have a foreign language requirement.

The Binghamton Scholars Program caters to the most academically talented students. Each year, 40 incoming freshmen get to take advantage of small classes with others in the program that targets "communication skills and leadership." These courses tend to be hands-on and include projects and experiential learning. "In addition to the class work," explains a participant, "we have individual access to professors." Successful students will earn the distinction of "All-University Honors" or "Binghamton Scholars Honors."

Within the Harpur College of Arts and Sciences, students yearning to forge their own disciplinary path can participate in the Individualized Major Program. During their sophomore or junior year, students develop a proposal for an individualized major that will combine coursework in at least three departments. They also select a faculty advisor to guide them through the process.

Binghamton has opportunities galore for students to earn accelerated degrees. These programs are a "true bargain," notes a student: students earn their master's degree in just five years and take master's level courses in their fourth year at the lower price of undergraduate rather than graduate tuition. There are a wide range of programs. For example, students can earn a liberal arts BA and a Management MA, different types of engineering BS and MS, and masters' in teaching in several

The Ultimate
Guide to America's
Best Colleges

sciences, not to mention the long list in the arts and sciences and the many majors that can be combined with a Master's of Public Administration.

The School of Management is the "strongest" of Binghamton's academic offerings, according to one student. Students get real-world experience using top-notch facilities and programs. The university boasts, "the school houses the Zurack Trading Room where top students manage a portfolio of more than $140,000 using the same trading software used by Wall Street professionals ... A new Linux Laboratory allows our Management Information Systems students and their counterparts in the Computer Science program ... to assist local businesses in solving real-world business problems using open source technologies."

Binghamton itself sponsors 25 study-abroad and international exchange sites, in addition to 520 more administered by the SUNY system. Students who still want more can apply to other study-abroad programs as well. There are many options to study abroad for a summer or winter break for those who don't want to spend a whole semester away.

The Career Development Center at SUNY Binghamton has a full schedule of career fairs, workshops, and other events, but little out of the ordinary. Programs linking alumni and current students for career development are practically non-existent, but there is a strong e-recruiting and on-campus recruiting program. "There are resources available, but you need to take the initiative," notes a student.

Student Life

There are more than 300 official organizations on campus. Some of the most popular include ESCAPE, "a student-run bus company that makes weekend trips into New York City," the campus TV station, and the Asian Student Union. For less-structured fun, students also relax at a bowling alley and pool on campus. Greek life enjoys a moderate prominence on campus. There are 27 social frats and 18 social sororities, and about one in 10 students go Greek. "The frat parties are fun, especially when you're a freshman," one student comments, "but most upperclassmen steer clear of them."

Throughout the year, LateNite Binghamton sponsors a variety of events in the University Union South on Friday and Saturday nights. The vast majority of weekends feature movie screenings, but other events like trivia, games, or crafts are also common. Spring-Fling at Binghamton is almost a psychological necessity to help students get through the winter, as evidenced by the "Stepping on the Coat" ceremony in which students trample their winter attire. Students also step out to host a free Picnic in the Park for the whole Binghamton community, step right up to join in carnival games, and step to the beats of famous musical performers. A somewhat less-comprehensible tradition is the Passing of the Vegetables, popular with students in the natural sciences. To welcome the winter, students (including pre-kindergarten students from the campus's own school) stand in a circle and, as the name suggests, pass around vegetables from the fall harvest.

Binghamton fields 19 Division I teams. Basketball remains the most popular and has a loyal fan base. There is no football team. "We'd have more school spirit if we had a football team," one stu-

SUNY – BINGHAMTON UNIVERSITY

Highlights

Students
Total enrollment: 15,308
Undergrads: 12,356
Freshmen: 2,664
From out-of-state: 13%
From public schools: 89%
Male/Female: 53%/47%
Live on-campus: 61%
In fraternities: 12%
In sororities: 10%
Off-campus employment rating: Excellent
Caucasian: 52%
African American: 5%
Hispanic: 9%
Asian / Pacific Islander: 13%
Native American: 0%
Mixed (2+ ethnicities): 2%
International: 12%

Academics
Calendar: Semester
Student/faculty ratio: 20:1
Class size 9 or fewer: 9%
Class size 10-29: 55%
Class size 30-49: 20%
Class size 50-99: 8%
Class size 100 or more: 8%
Six-year graduation rate: 79%
Graduates who immediately go to graduate school: 41%

Most Popular Majors
Engineering
Biological science
Psychology

Admissions
Applicants: 28,232
Accepted: 12,104
Acceptance rate: 42.9%
Placed on wait list: 1,588
Average GPA: 3.6
ACT range: 27-30
SAT Math range: 630-710
SAT Reading range: 590-675
SAT Writing range: 21-56
Top 10% of class: 55%
Top 25% of class: 88%
Top 50% of class: 99%

613

College Profiles

SUNY – BINGHAMTON UNIVERSITY

Admissions Criteria

Academic criteria:
Grades: ☆ ☆ ☆
Difficulty of class schedule: ☆ ☆ ☆
Class rank: ☆ ☆
Standardized test scores: ☆ ☆ ☆
Teacher recommendations: ☆ ☆
Personal statement: ☆ ☆
Non-academic criteria considered:
Extracurricular activities
Special talents, interests, abilities
Character/personal qualities
Volunteer work
Work experience
Geographical location
Minority affiliation
Alumni relationship

Deadlines

Early Action: November 15
Early Decision: No
Regular Action: January 15 (priority)
Rolling (final)
Common Application: Accepted

Financial Aid

In-state tuition: $5,570
Out-of-state tuition: $14,720
Room: $8,054
Board: $4,392
Books: $1,000
Freshmen receiving need-based aid: 46%
Undergrads rec. need-based aid: 48%
Avg. % of need met by financial aid: 74%
Avg. aid package (freshmen): $10,590
Avg. aid package (undergrads): $11,783
Avg. debt upon graduation: $23,710

School Spirit

Mascot: Baxter the Bearcat
Colors: Green and white
Song: *In the Rolling Hills of Binghamton*

dent laments. For students who want to keep fit without getting involved in athletics, the well-appointed gym offers 45 fitness classes every week. Students who love the outdoors will be pleased that the campus has its own nature preserve. In addition to being a popular destination for runners, snow-shoe pedestrians, and cross-country skiers, the preserve hosts many outdoor gym classes and is a rich research resource for ecology and biology students.

Although there is a lot to keep students busy on campus, the limited off-campus offerings are a major drawback. Students can take a taxi or drive to downtown Binghamton, but there is little to do in the quiet, post-industrial town. "We could use some more nightlife," says a student. In the sake of fairness, it should be noted that Binghamton is home to a professional opera company, symphony orchestra, and the Binghamton Mets.

Housing at Binghamton is organized into six residential communities that each include multiple buildings. Offerings include two apartment communities for upperclassmen and non-traditionally-aged freshmen, one of which, Susquehanna, is a "24-hour quiet community." Several communities are "living-learning communities" with faculty fellows, special courses, and community service opportunities. Binghamton recently built new, environmentally-friendly dorms known as East Campus Housing.

Student Body

"No matter what your interests, you'll find a niche," says a student because of the size of the student body. In addition, because the university is so affordable, "there are students from every economic background." Ethnic diversity is high, but geographic diversity is low, which is not surprising given the break in tuition for in-state students.

You May Not Know

- Founded in 1946, the University of Binghamton is a mere child in the grand scheme of U.S. university history.
- Binghamton is among the 18 most environmentally-friendly campuses in the U.S., according to the Princeton Review.
- Laundry is free for on-campus residents, so there's no need to wait for breaks to lug home your dirty clothes.

Distinguished Alumni

Jeffery Gaspin, President of NBC; Tony Kornheiser, ESPN commentator; Ingrid Michaelson, singer/songwriter.

Admissions and Financial Aid

The admissions office describes Binghamton students as "highly intelligent and curious," "adventurous," and "active." The admissions website includes a blog with advice from current students and admissions reps.

Binghamton appears on *Forbes'* magazine's list of "America's Best College Buys." The university offers a low-cost, quality education even for out-of-state students. Although merit scholarships are offered, most include a need-based component. There are more than 275 university-wide scholarship programs. Most do not require a separate application.

STATE UNIVERSITY OF NEW YORK GENESEO

Overview

At first glance, one might mistake the 220-acre campus of State University of New York (SUNY) Geneseo as a private college, with its 46 ivy-covered buildings, legendary sunsets, and gorgeous location in the Finger Lakes region of upstate New York. This medium-sized college in the small town of Geneseo—where 70 percent of the approximately 8,000 fulltime residents work or are affiliated with the college—is actually a public college with corresponding low-cost tuition. New Yorkers refer to the school as the "Ivy of the SUNYs" or "Harvard on the Hill," monikers merited by the fact that the school is the most difficult in the SUNY system to gain admittance.

Besides beautiful views and a rigorous core curriculum, SUNY Geneseo also boasts award-winning leadership programs as well as model programs in residentially-based learning. No classes are taught by teaching assistants (TAs), and students interested in science will appreciate a 105,000-square-foot Integrated Science Facility, a $32 million building that even has a nuclear accelerator. Of course, students looking for the vibrancy of New York City won't find it in this locale, and students from out of state or out of country are a rare bunch.

Prospective students will want to be prepared for an academically engaged environment—more than 50 percent of students move on to graduate school immediately after graduation, and according to the college, more than 96 percent of students "were satisfied with Geneseo's intellectual challenge." The college's survey of 2011 graduates found that 89 percent would choose SUNY again, which means that, defying the stereotype of mean or grumpy New Yorkers, there are some happy campers somewhere in the Empire State.

Academics

There are 47 undergraduate programs and 21 interdisciplinary minors at SUNY Geneseo. All students complete the General Education curriculum, a common core of courses in natural science, social science, fine arts, humanities, and critical reasoning. These include two survey courses in western humanities, competency in a foreign language, a course in non-Western traditions, and more. Strong programs include biology and majors in the School of the Arts.

The Edgar Fellows Program invites about 30 incoming students and 10 current first-year students each year for an intensive honors experience that includes seminar courses, research opportunities, and co-curricular activities. Fellows are required to complete a Capstone project. Up to fifteen $2,000 scholarships are available for Edgar Fellows each year.

The Adirondack Adventure is a four-day academic program designed to help freshmen transition into college life while still earning college credit. This is no ordinary wilderness adventure—there are selected readings from Thoreau, Emerson, and Muir, ropes courses and other team-building activities, journaling, and a final paper. "It's a combination of recreation and reading some of the greatest literature," says a student.

Geneseo Opportunities for Leadership Development (GOLD) offers 250 workshops during the academic year. There are 70 volunteer instructors, and hundreds of students participate in the program. "The workshops give hands-on strategies that you can use not only in college but afterward as well," reports a participant. "They cover everything from time management to business skills." The acclaimed program has won several national awards—graduating seniors are even asked in job interviews whether they participated in the GOLD program.

SUNY sponsors more than 600 international study programs, and more than 25 percent of students participate. Students may opt for Geneseo programs in 20 countries, SUNY programs in 65 countries, or non-SUNY programs.

SUNY GENESEO

Four-year public
Founded: 1871
Geneseo, NY
Small town
Pop. 8,019

Address:
1 College Circle
Geneseo, NY
14454-1401

Admissions:
866-245-5211

Financial Aid:
585-245-5731

admissions@geneseo.edu

www.geneseo.edu

SUNY GENESEO

Students

Total enrollment: 5,557
Undergrads: 5,388
Freshmen: 997
Part-time students: 2%
From out-of-state: 2%
From public schools: 82%
Male/Female: 42%/58%
Live on-campus: 54%
Off-campus employment rating: Poor
Caucasian: 75%
African American: 2%
Hispanic: 6%
Asian / Pacific Islander: 7%
Native American: 0%
Mixed (2+ ethnicities): 2%
International: 3%

Academics

Calendar: Semester
Student/faculty ratio: 19:1
Class size 9 or fewer: 9%
Class size 10-29: 58%
Class size 30-49: 26%
Class size 50-99: 5%
Class size 100 or more: 2%
Returning freshmen: 90%
Six-year graduation rate: 79%
Graduates who immediately enter career
 related to major: 28%

Most Popular Majors

Psychology
Biology
Business administration

Admissions

Applicants: 9,164
Accepted: 4,184
Acceptance rate: 45.7%
Placed on wait list: 1,350
Enrolled from wait list: 47
Average GPA: 3.6
ACT range: 27-29
SAT Math range: 600-700
SAT Reading range: 580-690
SAT Writing range: Not reported
Top 10% of class: 54%
Top 25% of class: 85%
Top 50% of class: 98%

More than 50 percent of students—twice the national average, according to the college—attend graduate school fulltime immediately following graduation. The school also boasts a 92 percent medical school acceptance rate.

Student Life

There are more than 200 recognized student organizations at SUNY Geneseo. These include the student newspaper *The Lamron*, a Federal Reserve Challenge team, and the popular Musical Theatre Club. Students hang out at the on-campus club Knight Spot and at the College Union. The Union supports a number of programs, such as Geneseo Lake Knight (GLK), which ensures late-night entertainment from 10 p.m. to 2 a.m. every Friday and Saturday. "It's a good alternative if you aren't into the party scene," notes a student.

"Weeks of Welcome" offers more than four weeks of programming for entering students to acclimate to campus with opportunities for involvement, learning, and action. Events in the first week include a President's Welcome Picnic, a New Student Convocation, and Volunteer Fair. Students looking for a less academic good time will enjoy MidKnight Madness in mid-October, the highly attended pep rally which kicks off the NCAA Winter Sports season. The Halloween Monster Mash Bash gives students a chance to party in their best costumes. "There are some crazy costumes, many of them handmade," says an observer. Spring Fest is another eagerly anticipated outdoor all-campus event.

There are 12 fraternities and 15 sororities on campus, and Greek history goes back 170 years at SUNY Geneseo. The "Greek tree" on campus is part of a tradition where Greek groups paint a specific tree at night, which continues to grow and produce leaves in spite of being covered in countless layers of paint.

Of SUNY Geneseo's twenty Division III varsity teams, basketball and hockey games garner the most student fans. The most recent title is the 2005 national championship for the women's cross-country team. The school also won conference titles for women's tennis and men's lacrosse in recent years. There are 13 club sports, including ice hockey, rugby, and Ultimate Frisbee.

SUNY Geneseo's campus is 10 minutes from Letchworth State Park, known as the "Grand Canyon of the East" with three major waterfalls, lush forests, and miles of hiking trails, plus plenty of other outdoor adventures such as whitewater rafting, kayaking, and even hot air ballooning. Conesus Lake is nearby and offers camping opportunities. The closest major city is Rochester, 30 minutes away.

Housing is guaranteed for all four years, and on-campus residence is required for freshman and sophomores. There are 17 residence halls, including townhouses and special interest halls such as Eco House, Writer's House, and Dante House, a global service and citizenship-themed residence and the only college house run exclusively for first-year students.

Student Body

SUNY Geneseo's undergrads represent "the range from underprivileged to very wealthy" since tuition prices (just over $5,800!) are accessible for many. There is moderate ethnic diversity, with 17 percent multicultural students, as well as a small international student population of about three percent. There is very low geographic diversity. It's not surprising that hardly any student hails from outside New York since SUNY is, after all, a state school. Students describe themselves as "academically minded" but able to "have a good time."

You May Not Know

- SUNY Geneseo was founded as the Wadsworth Normal and Training School in 1871 and became a state liberal arts college in 1948.
- Among the Geneseo lexicon is Cardiac Hill, a steep hill that some students must climb to reach campus; the Bear, a statue of the animal; and GFR, which stands for either the Geneseo First Response emergency team or the Geneseo Family Restaurant.
- SUNY Geneseo is home to the "Seuss Spruce," a tree that resembles a Dr. Seuss illustration because of its crooked and slightly spiral shape.

Distinguished Alumni

My Hang Huynh, chemist; Chelsea Noble, film and TV actress; William Sadler, actor in *The Shawshank Redemption*; Jenna Wolfe, anchor of NBC's *Weekend Today*.

Admissions and Financial Aid

According to SUNY Geneseo, admissions decisions are based primarily on high school academic record and the results of college entrance exams. Rigor of high school programs matter—honors-level courses and AP or IB courses are preferred. However, grades and test scores aren't the whole picture. Since the review process is holistic, the admissions teams also closely reviews the personal essay, co-curricular resume, and letter(s) of recommendation. According to the college, the combination of information about one's academic and extracurricular achievements "enables us to most accurately determine who to make offers to out of a very competitive applicant pool."

The Geneseo Foundation supports a variety of merit scholarships for incoming freshmen and undergrads. These scholarships are funded by annual and endowed contributions from alumni, emeriti, faculty, staff, students, businesses, and corporations, so there's quite a wide range. For example, the Key Bank Annual Scholarship helps freshmen who demonstrate financial need; the Presidential Merit Annual Scholarship gives four $3,000 renewable scholarships to outstanding entering students selected by admissions; and the James and Julia Lockhart Endowed Scholarship offers a $4,150 freshman-year scholarship to an outstanding entering student. While scholarship amounts don't seem high, it's important to remember that they cover a large fraction of the low cost of tuition at SUNY Geneseo.

SUNY GENESEO

Highlights

Admissions Criteria
Academic criteria:
Grades: ☆ ☆ ☆
Difficulty of class schedule: ☆ ☆ ☆
Class rank: ☆ ☆
Standardized test scores: ☆ ☆ ☆
Teacher recommendations: ☆ ☆
Personal statement: ☆ ☆
Non-academic criteria considered:
Extracurricular activities
Special talents, interests, abilities
Character/personal qualities
Volunteer work
Work experience
State of residency
Minority affiliation
Alumni relationship

Deadlines
Early Action: No
Early Decision: November 15
Regular Action: January 1 (final)
Notification of admission by: March 1
Common Application: Accepted

Financial Aid
In-state tuition: $5,870
Out-of-state tuition: $15,320
Room: $7,090
Board: $4,152
Books: $1,000
Freshmen receiving need-based aid: 38%
Undergrads rec. need-based aid: 39%
Avg. % of need met by financial aid: 68%
Avg. aid package (freshmen): $6,006
Avg. aid package (undergrads): $9,144
Avg. debt upon graduation: $21,000

School Spirit
Mascot: Knights
Colors: Blue and white

Four-year public
Founded: 1967
Purchase, NY
Large town
Pop. 23,000

Address:
735 Anderson Hill
Road
Purchase, NY
10577

Admissions:
914-251-6300

Financial Aid:
914-251-6350

admissions@pur-
chase.edu

www.purchase.edu

STATE UNIVERSITY OF NEW YORK – PURCHASE COLLEGE

Overview

Entering the SUNY Purchase College campus, you will see Henry Moore's distinctive *Two Large Forms*, just one of many other permanent outdoor sculptures scattered across the 500+ acre suburban campus. The sculptures hint at the visual and performing arts focus of this medium-sized college, an emphasis that becomes obvious upon seeing the Performing Arts Center and internationally renowned Neuberger Museum of Art.

Designed as "a city within the country," SUNY Purchase doesn't really have much of a college-town atmosphere. There are no fraternities or sororities, and with nearly four out of 10 students enrolled in the School of Arts, art is available everywhere you turn. New York City is about half an hour away, for those who want to swap the country environment for more cosmopolitan horizons.

Liberal, artsy students will find themselves in good company. Not everyone will like the intensity of school where some conservatory students are in class or rehearsal 15 hours a day—but for those who thrive on this creative energy and rigor, SUNY Purchase will be an excellent (and inspiring!) choice.

Academics

Sixty-five percent of students are in the School of Liberal Arts and Sciences, and 33 percent of students in the School of the Arts. There are more than 50 undergraduate majors and minors—the newest is theater and performance, first offered in fall 2011. Besides the arts, strong programs are in journalism; media, society, and the arts; and women's studies.

All undergraduates are required to complete the common core curriculum, which satisfies the general education requirements at all SUNY campuses. Students must take 30 credits across the seven areas of math, natural science, social sciences, the arts, humanities, languages and cultures, and health and wellness. Freshmen take a course in basic communication/college writing. Students who pursue BA and BS degrees undertake a two-semester senior project. BFA and MusB students conduct a final exhibition, film, or recital.

The conservatories are intensive, as one student says, "at other schools the sciences are the hardest majors. Here the conservatories are the most challenging." The Conservatory of Theatre Arts offers demanding conservatory training in the master-apprentice tradition for a limited number of highly gifted students. The acting program enrolls just 70 students, and a typical week involves 27 to 40 hours of work directly with faculty, with a comparable amount of time in preparation for class, meaning that a typical day can begin with classes at 8 a.m. and end with the last rehearsal at 11 p.m. The Conservatory of Dance also offers conservatory-style training in the master-apprentice tradition, enrolling 140 students from 31 states and 17 countries. In the Conservatory of Music, which has about 400 students, classes are small, training is personal, and all students perform. The Music Building is a four-story building with music studios open for practice until 2 a.m.

The Neuberger Museum of Art is a focal point for art classes, with its more than 7,000 art pieces from 20th-century American and European art, traditional and contemporary African art, and a growing international art collection. "As an art student, it's phenomenal to have one of the nation's top museums right in our backyard," notes a student.

Options for study abroad include Purchase summer programs, Purchase exchange programs, and SUNY programs. In the international exchange programs, students attend classes at a host institution while remaining students at Purchase.

SUNY Purchase offers a large number of on-campus internships, and students say that the proximity to New York offers "incredible opportunities." The Career

The Ultimate
Guide to America's
Best Colleges

Development Center has won awards for excellence in programming and advancing diversity.

Student Life

Even though almost 70 percent of students live on campus, many still go home on the weekends, so campus is not as lively as it could be. Students hang out at the on-campus Pub and at the Student Center, affectionately called "The Stood." This student-operated facility offers billiards, ping pong, a videogame arcade, two concert venues, and a student art gallery. The student-run Co-op offers vegan, vegetarian, and organic food at wholesale prices, concerts, plus coffee and tea all day for just 25 cents a cup. "I've met more vegans here than I have in my entire lifetime," laughs a student.

Other student groups include the college's own TV station and an online newspaper. Cultural—and counter-cultural—activities can be found throughout campus, from the more than 300 public annual events at the Performing Arts Center to a student-run women's health clinic where all students can access educational materials, condoms, and, once a semester, attend the "Women Out Loud" event featuring music, poetry, food, and sex tool raffles. "You have to be open to pretty much anything to fit in here," one student comments.

The annual Culture Shock festival in mid-April turns SUNY Purchase into a county fair for two days, with carnival rides, food vendors, and musical artists. Culture Shock began in the 1990s as a showcase of Purchase College bands but has quickly grown to its current trend-setter status. Also in the spring is Purchase Wide Open, which showcases the creative work of students. The event coincides with Homecoming and Family Day, drawing large audiences. Earlier in the fall, Zombie Prom draws students-dressed-as-Zombies for an evening of fun in the Student Center.

There are no Greek organizations—students seem more than capable of imaginatively finding other ways to entertain themselves. "If we did have fraternities and sororities, we'd all make fun of the few who joined," says a student.

SUNY's 15 Division III teams include the men's swim team, just added in 2010. A six-lane pool, state-of-the-art fitness center, 14 tennis courts, and a cross-country trail make up some of the excellent athletic facilities available to students. There is a recreation and intramurals program—think Zumba classes, Ultimate Frisbee, and kick ball—plus an aquatics program that takes advantage of the pool. And, of course, New York City is about a half hour train ride away, a veritable cultural and arts haven for SUNY Purchase's students.

All freshmen are assigned to the residence halls housing the First Year Experience. After freshman year, housing isn't guaranteed, and room selection is based on GPA and credit hours. The college recently added two residence halls and an apartment complex. The newest, Fort Awesome, has residential, classroom, and retail space.

Student Body

Given SUNY Purchase's focus on arts, it's not surprising that students say they are "very artsy creative"—though the ways in which they express this creativity *may* be surprising. Students also tend to be liberal, perhaps again fitting expectations for a school where the artistic pulse is so vibrant. "If you were the Prom Queen

SUNY – PURCHASE COLLEGE

SUNY – PURCHASE COLLEGE

Admissions Criteria

Academic criteria:
Grades: ☆
Difficulty of class schedule: ☆
Class rank: ☆
Standardized test scores: ☆ ☆
Teacher recommendations: ☆
Personal statement: ☆ ☆ ☆
Non-academic criteria considered:
Interview
Extracurricular activities
Special talents, interests, abilities
Character/personal qualities
State of residency

Deadlines

Early Action: November 15
Early Decision: No
Regular Action: Rolling admissions
Common Application: Accepted

Financial Aid

In-state tuition: $5,570
Out-of-state tuition: $14,820
Room: $7,378
Board: $4,188
Books: $1,168
Freshmen receiving need-based aid: 64%
Undergrads rec. need-based aid: 62%
Avg. % of need met by financial aid: 53%
Avg. aid package (freshmen): $9,124
Avg. aid package (undergrads): $10,079
Avg. debt upon graduation: $26,684

School Spirit

Mascot: Panther
Colors: Royal blue and white

or football captain in high school, you probably won't fit in here," one student says.

There is high ethnic diversity, with 24 percent minority students. There is low geographic diversity—about one in five students is from outside of New York—though higher than at some other SUNY schools. Students hail from 35 countries.

You May Not Know

- SUNY Purchase's traditional school colors are heliotrope and puce. An alumna who came to Purchase the first year it was open recalls that many of the students who had just lived through the psychedelic '60s had chosen these "outrageous colors" for graduation, not realizing they'd also be school colors!
- The land for Purchase was originally a 500-acre working farm.
- The Performing Arts Center is a frequent location for major motion picture shoots. It also hosts about 150 days of classical music recording each year.

Distinguished Alumni

Nasreem Huq, Bangladeshi women's rights activist; Gayle Madeira, dancer, choreographer, and painter; Moby, American songwriter and musician; Carl Safina, named among "100 Notable Conservationists of the 20th Century" by *Audubon Magazine*.

Admissions and Financial Aid

According to the college admissions office, the school seeks "highly motivated, hard-working, and academically strong students with a consistent record of achievement in a challenging high school curriculum." The minimal coursework requirements are four years of English, three years of math, lab science, and social studies, and two years of a foreign language. All students are encouraged to take a rigorous college prep curriculum. There are additional requirements for the conservatories such as an audition for dance, music, and acting and a portfolio review for art and design. Admissions decisions are rolling and are mailed out beginning in January.

Institutional scholarships are offered by the Purchase College Foundation and are contingent upon the completion of each semester that is awarded. These scholarships require a donor thank you letter, 3.5 GPA, and community service component.

STATE UNIVERSITY OF NEW YORK – STONY BROOK UNIVERSITY

SUNY – STONY BROOK UNIVERSITY

Four-year public
Founded: 1957
Stony Brook, NY
Large town
Pop. 13,740

Address:
118 Administration
Stony Brook, NY
11794

Admissions:
800-USB-SUNY

Financial Aid:
631-632-6840

enroll@stonybrook.edu

www.stonybrook.edu

Overview

Located in a large town on the North Shore of Long Island, SUNY Stony Brook is one of the State University of New York system's four University Centers. Like many very large public universities, Stony Brook claims to give its students a small-college feel and liberal arts education, while offering all the resources of a large research institution. As such, SB certainly delivers: the Carnegie Foundation rated the university as having "very high research activity." SB's many accolades attest to the quality of its research and undergraduate programs. The *London Times* Higher Education World University Rankings places SB in the top one percent of universities worldwide, and the National Science Foundation recognizes SB for its combination of research with undergraduate education.

But while it delivers on quality, SB may not quite deliver on the small-college feel when it comes to academics: with the exception of students in select, limited-enrollment programs, most students have a hard time getting face time with professors or even getting into some classes. However, SB *does* deliver its promise of a small-college feel in its campus life. This is particularly evident in the Undergraduate College system, in which students are grouped according to similar academic interests.

College life is engaging, and the campus itself offers plenty to do in terms of recreation facilities and events: the grounds cover 1,100 acres of wooded land, including a park preserve, and the school is encircled by a six-mile bike and jogging path. Overall, especially for students in engineering and the sciences, SB offers excellent academic and research preparation—and the extra effort you'll have to put into getting to know professors may even give your interpersonal and networking skills a boost.

Academics

SB provides 66 undergraduate majors, the strongest among them being any of its engineering or natural science majors. SB also offers a unique program in Sustainability Studies: in conjunction with the College of Business, students may earn a BS in business management with a specialization in sustainable business or choose a joint BS-MBA program. All of these programs offer ample opportunity for travel, internships, and research.

Students must complete the Diversified Education Curriculum (DEC), which consists of one to three classes in mathematics, basic composition and critical thinking competency, as well as foreign language studies. Additional areas include information management, natural sciences, social science, American history, western civilization, other world civilizations, humanities, and the arts.

It's not surprising that at such a large, research-based school, professors are sometimes not as accessible as students would like. One student explains that they must "reach out to professors in order to get individual attention." Classes can be large, especially introductory lectures, and "it can be a challenge to get the classes we want as freshmen," notes an underclassman.

SB works to mitigate these issues with a number of programs. All freshmen are assigned to one of six Undergraduate Colleges, which are organized around academic interests (Arts, Culture, and Humanities; Global Studies; Human Development; Information and Technology Studies; Leadership and Service; and Science and Society). Freshmen in the same College are housed in the same quadrangle, and the College provides specialized advising and event programming. "You can really get into your interests when you study, eat, and socialize exclusively with people from your College," says a student.

As part of the Undergraduate College experience, students are required to complete small, College-specific, Freshmen Seminars 101 and 102. The 101 seminar introduces students to college, covering topics ranging from academic advising and

621

College Profiles

SUNY – STONY BROOK UNIVERSITY

Students

Total enrollment: 24,149
Undergrads: 16,003
Freshmen: 2,676
Part-time students: 8%
From out-of-state: 14%
From public schools: 85%
Male/Female: 53%/47%
Live on-campus: 61%
In fraternities: 2%
In sororities: 3%
Off-campus employment rating: Good
Caucasian: 37%
African American: 6%
Hispanic: 10%
Asian / Pacific Islander: 24%
Native American: 0%
Mixed (2+ ethnicities): 2%
International: 10%

Academics

Calendar: Semester
Student/faculty ratio: 18:1
Class size 9 or fewer: 13%
Class size 10-29: 52%
Class size 30-49: 15%
Class size 50-99: 12%
Class size 100 or more: 9%
Returning freshmen: 90%
Six-year graduation rate: 70%

Most Popular Majors

Psychology
Health science
Biology

Admissions

Applicants: 27,513
Accepted: 11,023
Acceptance rate: 40.1%
Placed on wait list: 2,884
Enrolled from wait list: 169
Average GPA: 3.7
ACT range: 25-29
SAT Math range: 600-700
SAT Reading range: 530-640
SAT Writing range: 10-36
Top 10% of class: 42%
Top 25% of class: 75%
Top 50% of class: 95%

study skills to health and financial literacy. Tenured faculty teach 102 seminars, working with fewer than 20 students on a topic of their particular expertise.

Honors College is another option for students looking to get to know professors and take advantage of SB's academic resources. About 60 students per year are accepted: these students complete a special Honors curriculum consisting of five seminars (which replaces most of the DEC) and take four elective courses outside their major. They must also complete four one-credit "mini-courses" on a wide variety of topics in addition to a faculty-supervised senior project in the major. All Honors students receive merit scholarships and are eligible for housing in the Honors College residence, early registration, and special advising.

Premed students who have been accepted to Honors College or the Women in Science and Engineering (WISE) program may also apply to the Scholars in Medicine Program. This eight-year program guarantees admission to the SB School of Medicine, thus allowing students more time to broaden their intellectual horizons and participate in research rather than stressing about med school admissions.

Any student in any field can get involved in the NSF-recognized Undergraduate Research and Creative Activities (URECA) program, which funds faculty-supervised research and research-related travel. URECA runs several 10-week residential summer research courses of study, among which are the URECA Summer Program for students in all disciplines, and the CESAME Summer Undergraduate Stem Cell Research program. Students in the latter conduct research in faculty members' labs and the Howard Hughes Medical Institute. All students participating in these programs receive stipends from URECA.

Both international exchange and SB faculty-led programs are available in a number of countries, during summer/winter sessions as well as during semesters. SB faculty lead semester programs in Kenya and Madagascar, and intersession programs in Russia, the UK, Italy, Japan, Tanzania, and Jamaica.

The SB Career Center offers a week-long job and internship fair accompanied by alumni advising. Those wanting to attend grad school should know that the *Wall Street Journal* has ranked SB eighth in national public universities for graduates going on to elite grad programs.

Student Life

More than half of SB students live on campus, which makes for an "always active" campus social life. SB has more than 300 student organizations, including the Red Hot Marching Band and several environmental organizations that collaborate to put on SB's week-long Earth Day celebration, Earthstock. No classes are scheduled on Wednesdays between 12:40 and 2:10 pm; instead, there's Campus Life Time, which gives students an opportunity to kick back with carnival games, concerts, free food, speakers, and plenty of "time to just relax with friends."

Other big events include April's Roth Pond Regatta, in which student clubs and administrative offices form teams that build watercraft out of cardboard, duct tape, and paint and then race them over Roth Pond; predictably, everybody ends up in the water. Every spring also brings Strawberry Fest, which features student performances, music, and most importantly, yummy treats made with strawberries.

While the number of fraternities and sororities (16 and 18, respectively) is high, participation is extremely low—which is because the school lifted its ban on Greek organizations only in 2009. "The Greeks haven't gained any traction," says a student.

SB's nine men's and nine women's Division I varsity sports teams get a good deal of support, particularly when the football team plays its rival Hofstra. In addition to football, women's cross country, men's soccer, men's basketball, and men's lacrosse have all won recent conference championships. SB offers three major fitness facilities (a fitness center, a wellness center, and sports complex) in addition to a fitness center in every residence quadrangle. Intramural sports are plentiful and range from the usual suspects (tennis, basketball) to the less anticipated (bowling, rifle).

Students who want to hit up New York City can do so with ease: it's about a 90-minute train ride, but the train station is right on campus. "The city isn't an every weekend kind of trek, but it's nice to be close to the greatest city in the world," one student notes. Otherwise, the beaches of Southhampton are also easily accessible.

Freshmen are guaranteed on-campus housing in residential quadrangles that consist either of dorm- or suite-style residences. For upperclassmen, on-campus apartments are available.

Student Body

Eighty-six percent of SB students come from New York, and reflect the high ethnic diversity of the state. "You'll meet every kind of person imaginable here," says a student, adding, "No matter what you like to do, you will find others who like it too. My roommate plays underwater hockey and shockingly found others who do too."

You May Not Know

- The boulders scattered on campus (used to post flyers on) are 20,000 year-old remnants from Ice Age glaciers.
- SUNY Stony Brook was once known as "Mudville" due to the ubiquitous muddy sludge that construction of the campus dredged up.
- In 1969, the link between smoking and emphysema was discovered by researchers at SB.

Distinguished Alumni

Patricia S. Cowings, first American woman astronaut; Scott Higham, Pulitzer-Prize winning journalist for The Washington Post; Sandy Pearlman, Music Producer and Manager, Blue Oyster Cult; Jef Raskin, initiator of Macintosh project for Apple Computer.

Admissions and Financial Aid

It's worth noting that SB may not be able to cover a student's full financial need. A number of merit scholarships are available that range from $2,000 to the full cost of tuition: scholarships are awarded to National Merit or INTEL Science Talent Search Finalists or Semifinalists, valedictorians or salutatorians, and Honors College Students. Presidential and Provost's Out-Of-State Scholarships are available to highly qualified non-New Yorkers as well.

SUNY – STONY BROOK UNIVERSITY

Highlights

Admissions Criteria
Academic criteria:
Grades: ☆ ☆ ☆
Difficulty of class schedule: ☆ ☆ ☆
Class rank: ☆
Standardized test scores: ☆ ☆ ☆
Teacher recommendations: ☆ ☆
Personal statement: ☆
Non-academic criteria considered:
Interview
Extracurricular activities
Special talents, interests, abilities
Character/personal qualities
Volunteer work
Work experience
Geographical location
Alumni relationship

Deadlines
Early Action: No
Early Decision: No
Regular Action: December 1 (priority)
January 15 (final)
Notification of admission by: April 1
Common Application: Accepted

Financial Aid
In-state tuition: $5,870
Out-of-state tuition: $17,810
Room: $7,246
Board: $4,124
Books: $900
Freshmen receiving need-based aid: 59%
Undergrads rec. need-based aid: 60%
Avg. % of need met by financial aid: 72%
Avg. aid package (freshmen): $11,578
Avg. aid package (undergrads): $12,704
Avg. debt upon graduation: $21,170

School Spirit
Mascot: Seawolves
Colors: Red, blue, and white

Four-year public
Founded: 1844
Albany, NY
Medium city
Pop. 97,660

Address:
1400 Washington
Avenue
Albany, NY
12222

Admissions:
518-442-5435

Financial Aid:
518-442-3202

ugadmissions@albany.
edu

www.albany.edu

STATE UNIVERSITY OF NEW YORK – UNIVERSITY AT ALBANY

Overview

One of the State University of New York system's branches, the University at Albany (UAlbany for short) is a large public university. Located in the mid-sized state capital city of Albany, the campus is in fact divided into three sub-campuses: Uptown Campus, the main campus; Downtown Campus, which includes the Rockefeller College of Public Affairs and Policy and School of Criminal Justice; and East Campus, mostly dedicated to science lab facilities. The Uptown Campus displays extremely unique architecture that can really only be described as "spacey." The focal point is the large pool at the center of the Academic Podium, which features an impressive fountain array and Space-age-looking Carillon tower.

UAlbany may be known more as a party school than for its academics: in 2008, it dropped off the Princeton Review's Party School list, which it topped in 2004; but UAlbany partiers were consoled by their 2009 appearance on the *Playboy* top party school list, even if it was last out of 25 schools. But while the partying may be the most visible aspect of UAlbany, the school also boasts a selection of strong programs, including its College of Nanoscale Sciences and Engineering, which ranks first in the world. Its graduate programs in criminal justice, information technology, and public administration are ranked in the top 10 nationally, which is relevant to undergraduate education, since UAlbany offers dozens of combined bachelor's-master's degrees.

Internships and public service opportunities abound at the nearby state capitol. In these programs, and with the help of a few special academic opportunities and the resources of the broader SUNY system, self-motivated students can succeed.

Academics

UAlbany offers 57 undergraduate majors and over 50 combined degree programs, ranging from programs in business to optometry to law. In addition to its aforementioned flagship schools and graduate programs, the majors in business administration, psychology, and political science are strong as well.

The General Education Program that all UAlbany students must complete is not too burdensome for most students. It requires students to take classes in three areas: "Disciplinary Perspectives" (one class each in arts and humanities, two each in natural and social sciences); "Cultural and Historical Perspectives" (a total of five courses ranging from U.S. history to global and cross-cultural studies); and "Communication and Reasoning Competencies" (five courses in information literacy, oral discourse, and writing). Students must also complete two semesters of a foreign language and a semester of math and statistics. "There are so many classes offered that you can usually find one that both interests you and fulfills a requirement," says a student.

UAlbany's size makes it hard to get access to advisors and professors: students who don't need much hands-on academic supervision and have a clear idea of their future academic and career plans will fare best. "It can take weeks to get an advising appointment," one student notes. "Usually by the time the appointment comes around, you've figured it out on your own."

All first-year students at UAlbany can enroll in Project Renaissance, a year-long, residential integrated interdisciplinary curriculum that offers several different curricular tracks, including prehealth, prelaw, psychology/sociology, as well as a general track, all of which satisfy most General Education requirements. Classes are small and taught by faculty.

For a slightly more selective experience, students can apply to the "top-notch" Honors College, which combines coursework and hands-on research experience. Students in Honors College complete six Honors courses (with 25 students or fewer, all of whom are in Honors) over their first two years; then in their final two years, they complete a senior project or thesis in their major with faculty supervision. Since faculty from across the university offer Honors courses, a wide selection is available and students can also participate in various receptions, speaker series, performances, outings, and even road trips sponsored by the Honors College. Students may live in the Honors community in Melville and Steinmetz Halls on State Quad; rooms are suite-style.

UAlbany is also home to the New York State Writers' Institute, which promotes literature in all forms. Aspiring writers can take advantage of its Visiting Writers speaker series as well as regular Community Writers Workshops. The Institute also runs two- to four-week summer creative writing programs at nearby Skidmore for which students can receive college credit.

Students at UAlbany reap the benefits of SUNY's size when it comes to study abroad. Students can participate in UAlbany's summer or wintersession faculty-led travel courses, language-intensive classes, internships, or volunteer-abroad programs in Tanzania, Ethiopia, Senegal, Italy, the UK, France, Belarus, Russia, India, China, Mexico, Chile, and the Dominican Republic. UAlbany also offers semester-long programs in Spain, France, Chile and internships in Russia. If these programs don't quite fit the bill, students can take advantage of the hundreds of other programs and exchange agreements the SUNY system offers. "The options are pretty much limitless," remarks a student.

Over 150,000 UAlbany alumni nationally are available for career-related networking, and there are plenty of internship opportunities at the state capitol for students interested in politics. "If you're into politics, this is one of the best locations because you can get hands-on experience," notes one student.

Student Life

More than 160 student organizations are active on campus, including the all-male a cappella group the EarthTones, who have performed at major functions at the state capitol. While only a small percentage of students (one percent of men and two percent of women) belong to UAlbany's 18 fraternities and 20 sororities, Greek organizations are the impetus behind most partying at UAlbany.

Drinking plays a very visible role in life at UAlbany, despite some fairly stringent alcohol policies. "Enforcement is pretty strong on campus, but there isn't really enforcement off campus," explains a student. *Albany Times Union* titled one of UAlbany's event an "early morning binge drinking tradition." The St. Patrick's Day celebration—"Kegs and Eggs"—begins with a shuttle to local bars, which open at 7 a.m., and the preferred distribution method for beer is spraying it over the crowds. "This is the kind of thing you only do in college so it's fun to partake," says a student.

But if the party scene isn't your thing, UAlbany offers other less "beery" events too. "While we have a reputation as a party school and that element certainly exists, there are still tons of activities if you're a non-drinker," one student comments. Fountain Day, the college unity day, celebrates the arrival of spring and the end of the school year with plenty of free food, splashing in the fountain at the Academic Podium with thousands of beach balls and rubber ducks, games, and performances. Cookie Day falls every semester

SUNY – UNIVERSITY AT ALBANY

Highlights

Students
Total enrollment: 17,067
Undergrads: 12,875
From out-of-state: 8%
Male/Female: 52%/48%
Live on-campus: 58%
In fraternities: 1%
In sororities: 2%
Off-campus employment rating: Good
Caucasian: 57%
African American: 13%
Hispanic: 12%
Asian / Pacific Islander: 7%
Native American: 0%
Mixed (2+ ethnicities): 2%
International: 4%

Academics
Calendar: Semester
Student/faculty ratio: 19:1
Class size 9 or fewer: 6%
Class size 10-29: 43%
Class size 30-49: 31%
Class size 50-99: 8%
Class size 100 or more: 12%
Returning freshmen: 83%
Six-year graduation rate: 63%
Graduates who immediately go to graduate school: 41%
Graduates who immediately enter career related to major: 57%

Most Popular Majors
Psychology
English
Business administration

Admissions
Applicants: 21,178
Accepted: 11,744
Acceptance rate: 55.5%
Average GPA: 3.5
ACT range: 22-26
SAT Math range: 520-610
SAT Reading range: 490-580
SAT Writing range: Not reported
Top 10% of class: 19%
Top 25% of class: 53%
Top 50% of class: 88%

625

College Profiles

SUNY – UNIVERSITY AT ALBANY

Highlights

Admissions Criteria
Academic criteria:
Grades: ☆ ☆ ☆
Difficulty of class schedule: ☆ ☆ ☆
Class rank: ☆ ☆ ☆
Standardized test scores: ☆ ☆ ☆
Teacher recommendations: ☆ ☆ ☆
Personal statement: ☆ ☆
Non-academic criteria considered:
Extracurricular activities
Special talents, interests, abilities
Character/personal qualities
Volunteer work
Work experience
State of residency
Geographical location
Minority affiliation
Alumni relationship

Deadlines
Early Action: November 15
Early Decision: No
Regular Action: Rolling admissions
Common Application: Accepted

Financial Aid
In-state tuition: $5,870
Out-of-state tuition: $16,190
Room: $7,184
Board: $4,450
Books: $1,200
Freshmen receiving need-based aid: 62%
Undergrads rec. need-based aid: 61%
Avg. % of need met by financial aid: 63%
Avg. aid package (freshmen): $9,925
Avg. aid package (undergrads): $9,723
Avg. debt upon graduation: $24,126

School Spirit
Mascot: Great Danes
Colors: Purple and gold

just before finals: the Spirit Committee and Spirit Street Teams hand out cookies to students for a yummy study break.

Athletics of all types have enthusiastic followings at UAlbany. Sporting events range from intramurals, which draw thousands of participants, to any of UAlbany's eight men's and 11 women's NCAA Division I teams, including its recent conference champion football team. And don't forget to add to the mix the New York Giants Training Camp that happens annually in Albany.

Those looking to get off campus can escape to Dippikill, the university's wilderness retreat 70 miles north in the Adirondack Mountains. At "UAlbany's own little Walden," students and alumni can rent cabins, where they'll need to chop firewood, pump water, and use gas lamps to get by. Those less woodsy can take advantage of urban entertainment options like restaurants, shopping, and bars that can be found in the city of Albany.

Freshmen and sophomores must live in the dorms. Freshmen live in the traditional residence "quads," while upperclassmen can branch out to the highly desirable on-campus apartments or Empire Commons. Living-Learning Communities themed around specific academic or language interests are also available.

Student Body

Most students at UAlbany are from within the state. "Almost everyone can answer the question—upstate or downstate?" remarks a student. As such, the student body tends to be highly ethnically diverse. "The most common element we share is being involved," notes another student.

You May Not Know

- UAlbany has been the site of both the world's largest game of musical chairs in 1985 (5,060 participants) and, in 2005, the largest pillow fight.
- The university's first mascot was Pedwin, a scholarly looking penguin.
- UAlbany's signature statue of Minerva was purchased in 1888, supposedly by using money from a collection of $1 student fines for make-up exams.

Distinguished Alumni

Marc Kramer, CEO, *NY Daily News*; Patrick O'Dea, President and CEO Peet's Coffee; Anthony Vinciquerra, CEO of Fox Networks Group.

Admissions and Financial Aid

The university accepts the Common Application and SUNY application and requires a personal essay and one letter of recommendation. UAlbany's merit scholarships—including Presidential Scholar Awards, Frederick Douglass Scholar Awards, and Achievement Awards—are available and range from $1,000 to $6,000 per year. There is also the Transfer Presidential Scholar Award for transfer students.

STATE UNIVERSITY OF NEW YORK – UNIVERSITY AT BUFFALO

Overview

The University at Buffalo, a large public university, is the biggest of the 64 State University of New York campuses. It is a well-respected research school. The high number of students facilitates a wide variety of activities, academic programs, and social groups, but also makes for a rather impersonal environment with very large classes.

UB is the major source of economic activity in post-industrial Buffalo. It is made up of three different campuses: North, South, and Downtown. North Campus, located in suburban Amherst, is the heart of university life. It is home to many academic buildings and most student housing. Three miles away, South Campus is a reminder of the university's history, with old-fashioned, ivy-covered buildings. South holds the schools of Architecture and Planning, Medicine and Biomedical Sciences, Dental Medicine, Public Health and Health Professions, and Nursing. The still-growing Downtown Campus is currently made up of six university buildings, mostly related to post-graduate studies.

UB provides good quality at a low cost, especially for in-state students and those who qualify for the Honors Program. Students must be able to put up with brutal winters and feel comfortable at a big school to enjoy UB. Those who are seeking a lot of personal contact with professors and a tight-knit social scene may be happier elsewhere; however, those who enjoy the challenge of the "big pond" should consider this large state school and all that it has to offer.

Academics

UB has a whopping 74 undergraduate majors. Some of the strongest programs are in architecture, business administration, computer science, engineering, and nursing. UB is also a good choice for premeds, although there is no specific premed major. In general, the major academic challenge at UB is getting attention from professors and learning effectively in introductory classes that often have several hundred students. "You do sometimes feel like a number in the crowd," one student laments.

The university's general education requirements are extensive and do not offer much flexibility in the choice of courses. Students must take one or two mandatory, introductory writing courses (depending on their placement), one mathematical science course, World Civilizations I and II, a two-course sequence in natural sciences with one semester of laboratory, an American Pluralism course, one social and behavioral science course, one arts course, one humanities course, and two introductory-level language courses (if they do not test out of this requirement).

Students must also complete the online "Library Workbook" which helps orient them to the school library resources. In addition, students must satisfy the Depth Requirement through one of the following options: third-semester language proficiency, an additional mathematical sciences course, one of two Great Discoveries in Science courses, a natural sciences course at or above the 200-level, or any one of a list of other approved depth requirement courses. "There are a lot of requirements to keep track of," a student comments.

As a major research university, UB offers many opportunities for undergraduates. The university is home to a Center for Undergraduate Research and Creative Activities, which offers assistance to students in navigating the overwhelming number of faculty mentor and research project options. In addition, the center administers undergraduate research awards and sponsors a "Celebration of Academic Excellence" research fair each year for students to present their work.

Over 1,000 talented students take part in the University Honors College. The Honors College makes UB feel a little smaller by placing freshmen in a 25-student service-learning "Honors Colloquium" and by offering all honors students small

SUNY – UNIVERSITY AT BUFFALO

Four-year public
Founded: 1846
Buffalo, NY
Medium city
Pop. 261,025

Address:
3435 Main Street
Buffalo, NY
14214

Admissions:
888-822-3648

Financial Aid:
716-645-2450

ub-admissions@buffalo.edu

www.buffalo.edu

SUNY – UNIVERSITY AT BUFFALO

Students

Total enrollment: 28,952
Undergrads: 19,505
Freshmen: 3,650
Part-time students: 8%
From out-of-state: 5%
Male/Female: 54%/46%
Live on-campus: 35%
In fraternities: 2%
In sororities: 2%
Off-campus employment rating: Excellent
Caucasian: 51%
African American: 7%
Hispanic: 7%
Asian / Pacific Islander: 12%
Native American: 0%
Mixed (2+ ethnicities): 2%
International: 16%

Academics

Calendar: Semester
Student/faculty ratio: 14:1
Class size 9 or fewer: 15%
Class size 10-29: 48%
Class size 30-49: 16%
Class size 50-99: 13%
Class size 100 or more: 8%
Returning freshmen: 87%
Six-year graduation rate: 70%

Most Popular Majors

Business administration
Social sciences
Biological sciences

Admissions

Applicants: 22,009
Accepted: 12,525
Acceptance rate: 56.9%
Placed on wait list: 55
Enrolled from wait list: 25
Average GPA: 3.2
ACT range: 23-28
SAT Math range: 550-650
SAT Reading range: 500-600
SAT Writing range: Not reported
Top 10% of class: 30%
Top 25% of class: 63%
Top 50% of class: 94%

"Honors Seminars" that bring them into close contact with professors. Further benefits include priority registration for classes, honors housing, specialized advising from Honors College staff, study abroad, thesis work, and the opportunity to apply for scholarships that support research and creative activities. "It's like a college in a college," one student explains.

Students who know they are headed to professional school can take advantage of UB's Early Assurance Programs and breathe a little easier. The medical, dental, and pharmacy schools at UB offer formal acceptance as early as sophomore year to students who maintain high GPAs. The law school also offers guaranteed admission.

UB offers 65 study-abroad opportunities in 24 countries, including programs that take place during summer and winter breaks. UB and Buffalo State sponsor a summer program at the University of Salamanca in Spain that provides intensive language and culture study.

The Career Services Office offers a three-credit class in career-planning and self-assessment that is especially useful for undecided students. For such a large school, the alumni Mentor Network is relatively small—just 600 but strong.

Student Life

Only one third of students live on campus at UB, but one third of the huge student body is more than enough to keep the campus hopping. There are 24 social fraternities and 16 social sororities on campus. UB supports over 200 official clubs and organizations. The Undergraduate Student Organization, which organizes major annual events like Fall and Spring Fest, is especially influential on campus. Schussmeister's Ski Club is also immensely popular.

When it comes to annual events, UB gives you a lot of bang for your buck. While most universities have one concert a year with one big-name performer, UB has free concerts in the fall *and* in the spring that each include three or four famous acts. Recent Fall Fest and Spring Fest guests include Jason Mraz, Lupe Fiasco, and Nas. "The concerts create a lot of excitement," one student says. During the rest of the year, students don't lack for activities. They celebrate Halloween with the Haunted Union, two days of activities that include a haunted house and a pumpkin-carving contest. A much-loved farewell tradition is the Senior Brunch. Seniors get to relish made-to-order omelets served up by professors—quite the role reversal.

UB boasts 20 Division I teams. Students still turn out for football games, although the team has not had much success recently—they won just four games in the 2012 season. "It's a building time," one student remarks. Students can also watch professional football and hockey games in Buffalo. Students who aren't afraid to get down and dirty can form teams to participate in Oozefest, a huge annual mud volleyball tournament.

Off campus, students enjoy the bars and clubs of downtown Buffalo and spectacular views of Niagara Falls are just half an hour away. Students also escape to Canada, which may have something to do with the fact that the legal drinking age there is 18. "Everyone crosses the border at some point," says a student.

There are 13 residence halls and five apartment buildings at UB, and all but two of them are located on North Campus. The residence halls include designated areas for first-year students who want to live with others that share a common study such as health, architecture, engineering, fine arts, etc. About half of the residence halls offer single rooms.

Student Body

Students say that a wide range of interests is represented on campus, so everyone can find a niche. More students than not are "liberal," but every viewpoint is represented. With 28 percent of students identifying as minorities, ethnic diversity at UB is high. Geographic diversity is very low, with just five percent of students hailing from outside New York.

You May Not Know

- Notoriously un-notorious United States President Millard Fillmore was a co-founder of UB and its first Chancellor.
- UB has over 213,000 alumni in 130 countries.
- Although the university may want to forget this fact, in 2003 it was the site of the first season of an MTV reality show called "Fraternity Life," which documented a frat pledge process.

Distinguished Alumni

Wolf I. Blitzer, CNN Senior Anchor and Host; Brad Grey, CEO of Paramount Pictures Corporation; Robin Li, billionaire and Co-Founder/Chairman/CEO of Baidu.com.

Admissions and Financial Aid

UB gives prospective students the benefit of the doubt in every possible way when it comes to standardized test scores. If you take both the ACT and the SAT, admissions considers the higher one. They also combine SAT reading and math scores from different dates to give you the highest total score.

One aspect of the admissions process that differs from many other schools has to do with declaring majors. Students with the appropriate math background (at least pre-calculus) can be directly admitted to the accounting and business management program, but space is limited. Other departments—architecture, business administration, engineering, exercise science, nuclear medicine technology, and occupational therapy—also directly admit freshmen to a major. Students apply for majors in other departments in their sophomore year. Dance, music, music theatre, and theatre require auditions.

The best merit-based scholarships are the Presidential Scholarships, which give 25 top-scoring freshman applicants a full ride for four years. Students must apply specifically for these. Provost Scholarships are smaller awards starting at $2,500 and are available for academic high-achievers. No extra application is required. There are also scholarships for performing and creative arts, first-generation college students, and students who have graduated from Buffalo Public Schools.

SUNY – UNIVERSITY AT BUFFALO

Highlights

Admissions Criteria
Academic criteria:
Grades: ☆ ☆ ☆
Difficulty of class schedule: ☆ ☆ ☆
Class rank: ☆ ☆
Standardized test scores: ☆ ☆ ☆
Teacher recommendations: ☆ ☆
Personal statement: ☆
Non-academic criteria considered:
Interview
Extracurricular activities
Special talents, interests, abilities
Character/personal qualities
Volunteer work
Work experience
State of residency
Geographical location
Minority affiliation

Deadlines
Early Action: No
Early Decision: November 1
Regular Action: Rolling admissions
Common Application: Accepted

Financial Aid
In-state tuition: $5,870
Out-of-state tuition: $17,810
Room: $6,867
Board: $4,990
Books: $1,164
Freshmen receiving need-based aid: 62%
Undergrads rec. need-based aid: 63%
Avg. % of need met by financial aid: 65%
Avg. aid package (freshmen): $9,505
Avg. aid package (undergrads): $9,410
Avg. debt upon graduation: $16,025

School Spirit
Mascot: Victor E. Bull
Colors: Royal blue and white
Song: *Buffalo Alma Mater*

STEVENS INSTITUTE OF TECHNOLOGY

STEVENS INSTITUTE OF TECHNOLOGY

Four-year private
Founded: 1870
Hoboken, NJ
Medium city
Pop. 50,545

Address:
Castle Point on Hudson
Hoboken, NJ
07030

Admissions:
800-STEVENS

Financial Aid:
201-216-5555

admissions@stevens.edu

www.stevens.edu

Overview

If you were a science or math camp enthusiast growing up, but you're also interested in having a life beyond vectors, fractals, and algorithms when you get to college, Stevens Institute of Technology is a noteworthy choice. With a small enrollment of almost 2,600 undergrads, this 55-acre campus is located in Hoboken, New Jersey, overlooking the Hudson River and the Manhattan skyline.

The campus features a wide range of architecture, from brick to ivy-covered to modern. A highlight on campus is the recently opened Lawrence T. Babbio, Jr. Center for Technology Management, which houses 95,000 square feet in six modern stories. And more importantly, Hoboken—the closely situated downtown New York—and a number of student groups offer plenty of activities for when you're not stuck in the lab.

Academics

The university has 84 majors available—each with its own requirements—but most require math (calculus), science (chemistry, physics), humanities, and physical education. The work load can get pretty intense as students choose their majors at the start of freshman year and follow a track set out for them. "You're expected to hit the ground running," a student explains. Students must take 19-21 credit hours per semester. Strong programs include business, civil engineering, computer science, and mechanical engineering.

In the Scholars Program at Stevens, students apply innovative design to research as undergrads. Under faculty advisement, qualified students work on a project—usually researching, designing, or developing an original device or system, and present their work at professional seminars or engineering and scientific societies. Recent projects have included Neural Tissue Engineering, Indoor Geolocation Technology, and Exploration of Early Photographic Techniques. "The projects are not your run-of-the-mill science fair projects but intensive research projects with real-world applications," says a student.

Some lucky undergrads also have the opportunity to work in the Environmental Entrepreneurship (E2-Lab) Lab, a unique program that integrates market intelligence into the invention process of environmental innovations. Their nickname is Academic Inventureship, and their focus is cutting-edge creation and design. In fact, you might need to be an engineer already to really decipher what it is they actually do!

Stevens also offers a set of pre-professional programs: premed, predentistry, and prelaw. There are required and recommended courses for the premed and predentistry programs but none for prelaw. Advising is available for all of the programs. Students may also pursue accelerated combined degree programs that allow students to take three years of courses at Stevens and then transfer to medical, dental, or law school, receiving their bachelor's degree after completing their first year of graduate school. "This program saves time and money as long as you know that you want to attend one of the professional schools," one student comments.

There are study-abroad opportunities that the university coordinates with a number of institutions in Australia, China, Spain, Switzerland, and the United Kingdom. Those who study through exchange programs at the University of Dundee in Scotland or University College London or through consortium agreements at seven other universities maintain their Stevens financial aid packages.

The Office of Career Development offers career-planning workshops, corporate site visits, and a network of alumni clubs across the country to help put its students into competitive positions. About one-quarter of students attend graduate school within one year of graduating.

Student Life

The university has around 120 official student organizations. Some—like the Yacht Club, Five Elements (the hip-hop appreciation club), and intramural sports—are to get students away from their laborious schoolwork. Others are meant to enhance career training; these include Engineers without Borders, Society of Women Engineers, the American Society of Engineering Management, or the Fashion and Technology Club. "Professional clubs are more popular here than elsewhere because everyone is focused on their future careers," notes a student.

Two of the biggest student events on campus are Techfest and Boken. Techfest is an annual conglomeration of events, shows, and trips that usually occurs as a part of Parents Weekend. Boken is a four-day event each year with a different theme. Activities include fairs, concerts, and shows.

Greek life on campus draws about one fifth of students to brother- or sisterhood. There is a strong council of Greek presidents that keeps the organizations highly involved in student life and offers a number of entertainment opportunities to the entire student body. "It's good to know someone who's a member so you can stay in the loop," says a student.

There are 26 varsity sports at Stevens that compete in Division III. Both men's and women's lacrosse are national powerhouses, but soccer, equestrian, men's tennis, and men's volleyball are also notably successful. With 125 years of history, the lacrosse team at Stevens is the longest continuous program of its kind in the country. Intramural sports include the usual roundup of tennis, flag football, basketball, floor hockey, and indoor soccer.

Being situated in Hoboken gives you the beautiful view of the NYC skyline without the irksome hustle-and-bustle/get-out-of-my-way-you're-walking-too-slow attitude that comes with actually living in the city itself. "New Jersey gets a bad rep, but I think we have the ideal location," one student remarks. It's a very short train ride into the Big Apple when you're in the mood for eating, shopping, and entertainment, but Hoboken offers a charming assortment of things to keep you entertained as well. And when the season is right, you can pile into your roommate's SUV with a bunch of friends and head to Six Flags Great Adventure, roller-coaster capitol of the east coast.

Housing is guaranteed for all four/five years of students' stay at the school, and provides an affordable option, considering it can be expensive to live in Hoboken or NYC. Possibilities include residential halls with quads for singles and apartment-style housing. Some options such as Davis Hall and Riva Pointed have a view of New York City. The Lore-El Center is a Victorian-style home that is a "living and learning experience" for women. Most desirable is the new River Terrace Suites, which has five- to seven-person suites for upperclassmen.

Student Body

Students at Stevens tend to be very academically focused. There are "cliques which tend to congregate" that include "the Greeks, the nerds, and the athletes," say students, "although everyone finds their group."

STEVENS INSTITUTE OF TECHNOLOGY

Highlights

Students
Total enrollment: 5,649
Undergrads: 2,575
From out-of-state: 40%
Male/Female: 73%/27%
Live on-campus: 85%
In fraternities: 19%
In sororities: 20%
Off-campus employment rating: Excellent
Caucasian: 59%
African American: 0%
Hispanic: 0%
Asian / Pacific Islander: 13%
Native American: 9%
Mixed (2+ ethnicities): 0%
International: 4%

Academics
Calendar: Semester
Student/faculty ratio: 9:1
Class size 9 or fewer: 17%
Class size 10-29: 57%
Class size 30-49: 18%
Class size 50-99: 5%
Class size 100 or more: 3%
Graduates who immediately go to graduate school: 24%
Graduates who immediately enter career related to major: 95%

Most Popular Majors
Mechanical engineering
Civil engineering
Business

Admissions
Average GPA: Not reported
ACT range: Not reported
SAT Math range: 640-720
SAT Reading range: 570-670
SAT Writing range: Not reported

STEVENS INSTITUTE OF TECHNOLOGY

Admissions Criteria
Academic criteria:
Grades: ☆ ☆ ☆
Difficulty of class schedule: ☆ ☆ ☆
Class rank: ☆
Standardized test scores: ☆ ☆ ☆
Teacher recommendations: ☆ ☆ ☆
Personal statement: ☆ ☆ ☆
Non-academic criteria considered:
Interview
Extracurricular activities
Special talents, interests, abilities
Character/personal qualities
Volunteer work
Work experience
State of residency
Alumni relationship

Deadlines
Early Action: No
Early Decision: November 15
Regular Action: November 15 or January 15 (priority)
February 1 (final)
Notification of admission by: April 1
Common Application: Accepted

Financial Aid
In-state tuition: $42,920
Out-of-state tuition: $42,920
Room: $6,780
Board: $3,720
Books: $900
Avg. aid package (freshmen): $25,506 for grants or scholarship aid, $11,257 for student loans
Avg. aid package (undergrads): $21,133 for grants or scholarship aid, $6,793 for federal student loans

School Spirit
Mascot: Ducks
Colors: Red and gray

The Ultimate
Guide to America's
Best Colleges

Ethnic diversity is high at 22 percent minority. Geographic diversity is moderate with about 40 percent of students traveling from out of state to attend. Stevens has almost three men for every woman. "The women always lament the dating scene and the quality of men," laughs a student.

You May Not Know

- In the 1960s some students had the chance to live on the S.S. Stevens, a former attack transport turned floating dormitory stationed on the banks of the Hudson.
- The campus may be haunted and boasts the ghost story of Jan of Rotterdam, a Hoboken resident whose spirit roams Castle Point looking for his missing scalp.
- The first American-built steam locomotive ran on a circular track on the Stevens' estate in 1825.

Distinguished Alumni

Lawrence Babbio, Vice Chairman and President of Verizon Communications; Leon Febres Cordero, ME, former President of Ecuador; Mark Crispin, inventor of IMAP; Nate Davis, COO and President of XM Satellite Radio; Eugene McDermott, founder of Texas Instruments.

Admissions and Financial Aid

Success in specific high school courses is often necessary, depending on the area of study in which applicants wish to focus—whether it's the humanities, sciences, or the accelerated premed/dentistry programs. In general, potential students are expected to excel in math and science. Interviews are required for Stevens' hopefuls.

Students who know their way around the stage can apply for the Debaun Performing Arts Scholarship, ($1,000-$5,000 per year). The FIRST Scholarship awards $6,000 to students who have participated in a FIRST team (high school robotics and technology competitions) during junior or senior year. The Science and Technology Center Volunteer Scholarship provides up to $5,000 to students who have experience in volunteering in a science or technology center or museum.

SUSQUEHANNA UNIVERSITY

Overview

Located in the small town of Sellinsgrove on the Susquehanna River, Susquehanna University is one hour from Harrisburg and three hours from NYC, Philadelphia, Baltimore, and DC. The university is affiliated with the Lutheran church, though students claim that religion definitely does not dominate the campus experience.

Susquehanna is a very small, private university with a community feel. A generally homogenous student body, Susquehanna is not a place for students who are seeking diversity. However, students are known to be generally open-minded and the school's study-abroad requirement helps to open students' minds to other cultures.

Though it is a beautiful, tranquil, and green campus, many students struggle with the small and rather isolated setting of Susquehanna. Aside from Market Street—filled with quaint shops and restaurants, a local Walmart, and a movie theater—the area immediately surrounding the college is mostly residential. The only dance club in the area is located on campus. And although Greek life dominates the social scene, many students find the strict administration policies restrictive.

Academics

Susquehanna offers 43 majors, with standout programs in business, biology, music, and theatre. Classes are small with the most common size ranging from 10 to 19 students. Students generally report that the professors are friendly and "accessible," and classes are not known for being "overly" academically demanding.

Students are required to complete a Central Curriculum, which consists of six different sections, each section having its own specific requirements and number of semester hours. Section topics are as follows: Richness of Thought (analytical thought, literary and artistic expression), Natural World (sciences), Human Interactions (social interactions, historical perspectives, ethics), Intellectual Skills (writing, oral, team), Connections (diversity), and a Capstone. "The Central Curriculum courses are a mixed bag. It depends on the professors and the topic," says a student. Courses taken to fulfill Central Curriculum mandates may also be counted towards major and minor requirements.

Special academic opportunities at Susquehanna include the Honors Program, Writers Institute, and Adams Center for Law and Society. The Honors Program accepts 10 percent of the student body to participate in an intensive and individualized program for academically talented students. The Writers Institute—a nationally recognized program—produces four student literary magazines, organizes student readings, and brings acclaimed authors to campus to give readings and to interact with students. The Adams Center for Law and Society's activities and materials "expose students to the theory and practice of law through internships and field experiences, networking, professional seminars, independent study, research projects, and enhanced library resources."

All students at Susquehanna are required to participate in a cross-cultural program designed to broaden their perspective and expose them to different parts of the world. The GO (Global Opportunities) program allows students to study in various educational settings that can encompass short periods of time or even semester-long blocks. Long programs include travel to the University of Gambia, University of Macau, Washington Internship Semester, or Sigmund Weis School of Business in London. Short programs are available in Africa, Asia, Australia, Central and South America, Europe, or the United States/North America. "I chose to study at the Sigmund Weis School of Business in London because I wanted to see the business workings in another country," recalls a student.

Students generally speak highly of the Center for Career Services, which lists available interests and is very useful in assisting students who express interest in finding

SUSQUEHANNA UNIVERSITY

internships. They help students look for jobs after graduation and schedule interviews with employers or graduate schools. Among the companies that frequently hire graduates of Susquehanna are Morgan Stanley, JP Morgan Chase, Geisinger Medical Center, MT&T Bank, Waddell & Reed, and UPS.

Student Life

Susquehanna has 138 official student organizations ranging in interests from religion, music, and theater to service clubs. The school's student-run newspaper, *The Crusader*, covers campus events, activities, and athletics, while its student-run radio station, WQSU, The Pulse, is the third most powerful college station in Pennsylvania. Outdoors clubs are also quite popular. The GeoClub organizes canoe trips across various parts of the country, while the Outdoor Recreation Center facilitates many off-campus excursions including skiing, ice-skating, and fly-fishing.

Susquehanna's on-campus, student-run night club, Trax, is a popular gathering spot for students who want to listen to live bands, comedians, and other performers. The club offers a dance floor, bar, pool tables, and an outside patio and DJ booth. Charlie's coffeehouse, another student-run venue, is a non-alcoholic alternative for students where they can gather to enjoy such entertainment as open mic night, karaoke, and football games. Charlie's is open every night of the week and there is no cover charge.

School traditions such as Fall Frenzy and Spring Weekend are also very popular among students. Both these weekends offer a host of activities on campus such as obstacle courses, concerts, carnival attractions, and alcoholic beverages. "It's nice to let loose as a whole student body," notes a student.

Sixteen percent of men and 14 percent of women join the six fraternities and five sororities on campus. "The Greek organizations don't have a huge effect on most people's lives except members," says a student.

There are 22 Division III sports teams at Susquehanna: 10 men's and 12 women's teams. Football is popular at the university. The Goal Post Trophy (a section of the goal post that was torn down after a football game in 1952) is awarded to the winner of the annual game with rival Juniata College. Track and field is also quite competitive. Intramural sports include aerobic dance, basketball, dodgeball, flag football, indoor soccer, and wiffle ball.

Students say there is not an abundance of things to do off campus, but travel to nearby restaurants for dinner is popular. Options also include visits to Penn State (an hour away) or weekend trips to NYC or DC. "Selinsgrove is a sleepy, little town," one student remarks.

Students are required to live on campus their freshman year, and students who live off campus must get permission to do so through a lottery system. Freshmen are generally placed in double—or sometimes triple—rooms. Each dorm is known to have its own unique personality; for example, some are rowdy and others are full of humanities majors. Students may choose from traditional housing, suites, townhouses, or apartment-style buildings.

Student Body

With a moderate ethnic diversity—only 11 percent minority students—Susquehanna's student body is generally known to be from the upper-middle class, somewhat preppy, but also generally approachable. One student admits, "If you're a bit different in your interests or appearance, it can take a little time to find your group." Geographic diversity is moderate with about half of students hailing from out of state.

While some students claim diversity is generally accepted on campus, others complain that relatively little is ever done to promote it.

You May Not Know

- With a strong reputation for civic engagement, Susquehanna logs an annual average of 20,000 hours of service in the community.
- Each year the university selects a different theme to use in curricular and extracurricular activities.
- The school's intramural flag football and basketball teams advance to national tournaments nearly every season.

Distinguished Alumni

Jay Feaster, former General Manager of the Tampa Bay Lightning; James Jordan, writer and conductor; Bob Mosher, television and radio script writer; John Strangfeld, CEO of Prudential Global Asset Management.

Admissions and Financial Aid

Students applying to Susquehanna who do not believe that their SAT or ACT scores accurately reflect their academic potential have the option to submit two academic writing samples. This "Write Option" allows students to hand in analytical or critical papers— written during their junior or senior year—that better demonstrate their ability to communicate complex ideas, theories, and opinions. Students are also encouraged, when appropriate, to submit creative work. Although Susquehanna has rolling admissions, the preferred deadline for arrival of materials is March 1.

Susquehanna has a number of merit scholarships for those students hoping for financial aid. The Founder's Scholarships, for example, are full-tuition packages awarded to exceptional candidates who demonstrate both a passion for learning and superior academic achievement. Students are required to have a 3.5 cumulative high school GPA as well as a composite ACT score of 30 or a combined 1350 on the Critical Reading and Math sections of the SAT. Students must also complete an interview with a member of the university. Similar to the Founder's Scholarship, University Assistantships are awarded to students who want to engage in professional work experience with a member of the faculty or administration.

Other scholarship awards include the Valedictorian/Salutatorian Award for students who rank first or second in their class, academic scholarships for students with impressive GPAs in challenging courses, and the Janet Weis Writer's Institute Scholarship ($15,000) for students particularly talented in creative writing. Music scholarships ranging in value from $1,000 to $12,000 a year are also available, as are scholarships for legacy, transfer, and international students.

SUSQUEHANNA UNIVERSITY

Highlights

Admissions Criteria
Academic criteria:
Grades: ☆ ☆ ☆
Difficulty of class schedule: ☆ ☆ ☆
Class rank: ☆ ☆
Standardized test scores: ☆ ☆
Teacher recommendations: ☆ ☆
Personal statement: ☆ ☆
Non-academic criteria considered:
Interview
Extracurricular activities
Special talents, interests, abilities
Character/personal qualities
Volunteer work
Work experience
Geographical location
Minority affiliation
Alumni relationship

Deadlines
Early Action: No
Early Decision: December 1
Regular Action: Rolling admissions
Common Application: Accepted

Financial Aid
In-state tuition: $38,280
Out-of-state tuition: $38,280
Room: $5,450
Board: $4,940
Books: $1,800
Freshmen receiving need-based aid: 75%
Undergrads rec. need-based aid: 70%
Avg. % of need met by financial aid: 80%
Avg. aid package (freshmen): $28,548
Avg. aid package (undergrads): $27,226
Avg. debt upon graduation: $32,952

School Spirit
Mascot: Crusaders
Colors: Maroon and orange

SWARTHMORE COLLEGE

Four-year private
Founded: 1864
Swarthmore, PA
Small town
Pop. 6,197

Address:
500 College Avenue
Swarthmore, PA
19081

Admissions:
800-667-3110

Financial Aid:
610-328-8358

admissions@swarth-
more.edu

www.swarthmore.edu

SWARTHMORE COLLEGE

Overview

Swarthmore College is a small, private college recognized as one of the top liberal arts institutions in the country. The quirky students, nicknamed "Swatties," share a love of learning that extends beyond the classroom. The academic environment, while highly rigorous and demanding, lacks any trace of the cut-throat competition found at rival schools.

The physical environment of the college will suit even the most outdoorsy types, while its proximity to downtown Philadelphia and the King of Prussia mall will please everyone else. The campus is a nationally-registered arboretum studded with stone buildings and criss-crossed by hiking trails. As isolated as the campus may feel, downtown Philadelphia is just a half-hour train ride away.

Socially, Swarthmore's nearly non-existent Greek scene, high percentage of students living on campus, and small classes foster deep interpersonal connections and a strong sense of community. Activism and multicultural engagement are a big part of campus life.

Straight-laced students who can't see themselves enjoying events entitled "Screw Your Roommate" and "Pterodactyl Hunt" should probably look elsewhere, but academically-committed freethinkers should pay serious attention to what Swarthmore has to offer.

Academics

Swarthmore's academic environment is intense but more collaborative than competitive. "You're really only competing with yourself," remarks a student. There are 43 majors, with especially strong programs in biology, economics, and political science. Beyond Swarthmore's own offerings, students have access to courses at Haverford, Bryn Mawr, and even the University of Pennsylvania through a consortium arrangement.

One unusual requirement is the natural sciences and engineering practicum, which mandates that students take one course with 18 hours of lab time. Other than that, the requirements are pretty standard: 20 credits outside the major, three courses in each division of the college, and three writing courses or seminars. All first-semester freshmen take their courses pass/fail, in order to ease into high-level academic work without worrying about grades.

Swarthmore offers several special academic programs. First-year seminars, capped at 12 students, allow students to jump into a variety of subjects, from Japanese drama to linear algebra. For upperclassmen, the demanding honors program is modeled after Oxford, with small groups of students working with professors and taking the initiative to both teach and learn. Outside scholars examine the progress of honors students at the end of two years of honors study. "The honors program is really challenging, but it's worth the extra work for what you gain in learning not only your subject matter but about yourself," says a student. Any students interested in putting theory into practice and working with local communities may choose to take Community Based Learning courses.

Study-abroad programs through Swarthmore are limited to just seven countries: Argentina, Costa Rica, France, Germany, Italy, New Zealand, and Turkey. However, students can study abroad through many other approved programs not associated with the college.

Swarthmore's career services office administers an externship program that places Swarthmore students with alumni in their desired career field. There are also five $3,750 grants available for unpaid summer internships.

Student Life

Socializing at Swarthmore is augmented by the fact that 93 percent of students live on campus. Among 100 student organizations, chamber music ensembles, a cappella groups, and the chess club are some of the most popular.

Swarthmore's yearly traditions reflect its quirky flair. Perhaps the oddest event of all is the Pterodactyl Hunt. Students heavily involved in live action role-playing dress up as pterodactyls (and other evil creatures) and attack the school, while others take it upon themselves to defend campus, their beloved bastion of nerdiness. Screw Your Roommate is another event associated with Swarthmore tradition. Students set up roommates on blind dates. The catch? Your roommate gives you a ridiculous costume to wear, and you must find your date, who will be wearing a corresponding one. The awkwardly-costumed, beaming pairs have ranged from Romeo and Juliet to a supply curve and a demand curve. Once they've protected their campus from the onslaught of monsters and found love, students can let off steam with the McCabe Mile Run—a race around the library's basement. "You wouldn't have the full Swarthmore experience without the traditions," says a student.

Not surprising for a somewhat countercultural school, the Greek presence at Swarthmore is minimal. There are only two social fraternities and one sorority on campus, and a small number join.

Swarthmore's 22 varsity sports (10 men's, 12 women's) compete in Division III. The most successful sports are women's swimming, softball, lacrosse, and tennis. Intramural offerings change each year based on student interest and are student-run and managed.

Off campus, the thriving art, music, and social scene of Philadelphia is a short train ride away. For die-hard suburbanites, the King of Prussia mall—the largest mall on the East Coast—is close by. Despite these attractions, the campus itself is rather isolated, with little to do within walking distance. "It's a perfect location to be in the suburbs but still accessible to Philly," comments a student.

Housing is guaranteed for all four years. Residences range from a house for just eight students to a dorm housing 200. Although the vast majority of students live on campus, upperclassmen tend to move off campus. Cross your fingers that you don't end up in Mary Lyon, which is a 15-20 minute walk from campus, unless of course, you see it an opportunity for healthy exercise. Swarthmore's "Dorm Profile" page offers surprisingly frank appraisals of the dorms, including notes on how drafty and poorly-lit some are.

Student Body

"Swatties" tend to be very liberal and focused on academics: they don't study just for a grade, but extend their enthusiasm for learning outside the classroom. Students who consider themselves activists will feel right at home, as will those interested in cross-cultural exchange. The student body is highly ethnically and geographically diverse. "Conservatives are welcome on campus but there are certainly fewer of them," says a student.

SWARTHMORE COLLEGE

Highlights

Students
Total enrollment: 1,552
Undergrads: 1,552
Freshmen: 378
Part-time students: 1%
From out-of-state: 89%
From public schools: 51%
Male/Female: 49%/51%
Live on-campus: 93%
In fraternities: 14%
Off-campus employment rating: Good
Caucasian: 43%
African American: 6%
Hispanic: 13%
Asian / Pacific Islander: 14%
Native American: 0%
Mixed (2+ ethnicities): 8%
International: 8%

Academics
Calendar: Semester
Student/faculty ratio: 8:1
Class size 9 or fewer: 36%
Class size 10-29: 52%
Class size 30-49: 10%
Class size 50-99: 2%
Class size 100 or more: -
Returning freshmen: 97%
Six-year graduation rate: 92%
Graduates who immediately go to graduate school: 21%

Most Popular Majors
Economics
Biology
Political science

Admissions
Applicants: 6,589
Accepted: 935
Acceptance rate: 14.2%
Average GPA: Not reported
ACT range: 30-33
SAT Math range: 670-770
SAT Reading range: 680-780
SAT Writing range: 71-25
Top 10% of class: 92%
Top 25% of class: 98%
Top 50% of class: 100%

637

SWARTHMORE COLLEGE

Highlights

Admissions Criteria
Academic criteria:
Grades: ☆ ☆ ☆
Difficulty of class schedule: ☆ ☆ ☆
Class rank: ☆ ☆ ☆
Standardized test scores: ☆ ☆
Teacher recommendations: ☆ ☆ ☆
Personal statement: ☆ ☆ ☆
Non-academic criteria considered:
Interview
Extracurricular activities
Special talents, interests, abilities
Character/personal qualities
Volunteer work
Work experience
Geographical location
Religious affiliation/commitment
Minority affiliation
Alumni relationship

Deadlines
Early Action: No
Early Decision: November 15
Regular Action: January 1 (final)
Notification of admission by: April 1
Common Application: Accepted

Financial Aid
In-state tuition: $44,368
Out-of-state tuition: $44,368
Room: $6,748
Board: $6,404
Books: $1,210
Freshmen receiving need-based aid: 49%
Undergrads rec. need-based aid: 51%
Avg. % of need met by financial aid: 100%
Avg. aid package (freshmen): $39,427
Avg. aid package (undergrads): $39,255
Avg. debt upon graduation: $20,020

School Spirit
Mascot: Phoenix
Colors: Garnet, gray, and white

You May Not Know

- Lucretia Mott, famous 19th century abolitionist and women's rights advocate, was one of the college's founders.
- The science center on campus was the first undergraduate science facility to receive the U.S. Green Building Council's Leadership in Energy and Environmental Design certification.
- Swarthmore provides free printing—a considerable plus for busy college students reluctant to spend money.

Distinguished Alumni

Jonathan Franzer, author of *The Corrections* and winner of the National Book Award; John Mather, NASA senior scientist and Nobel Laureate; Robert Zoellick, President of the World Bank.

Admissions and Financial Aid

Swarthmore considers students' highest section scores across all SAT dates submitted, so there's no need to stress out if your math score peaks the same day your reading score plummets. In keeping with the personalized ethos of the school, interviews are highly encouraged.

Swarthmore grants about $24 million in scholarships each year. The Philips Evans Scholars Program covers financial need and also provides $1,500 to purchase a computer, annual grants for learning outside the classroom, and access to special mentorship connections, on-campus programming, and trips.

SWEET BRIAR COLLEGE

Overview

The benefits of women-only education might not be apparent to all, but Sweet Briar College offers an attractive package. This very small private liberal arts and sciences school in rural Virginia fosters a high-level and competitive academic environment while tailoring its programs specifically to women and offering plenty of individual attention and self-designed study. All of this takes place among historic red-brick buildings—most of the campus is designated as a National Historic Area and named by the Princeton Review as Sweet Briar America's Most Beautiful Campus—against the stunning natural backdrop of the Blue Ridge Mountains, forests, and small lakes.

Sweet Briar attributes the strength of its academic programs, opportunities, and community to its women-only mission. If you are in the market for focused academics, plenty of contact and opportunities to work with professors, programs designed to give women a competitive edge in the workforce and academia, a community of smart women with a host of bond-building traditions, and an environment where designing your own education is encouraged, you can't lose with Sweet Briar.

At the same time, the preppy atmosphere and adherence to college tradition at Sweet Briar can be off-putting. "Singing is a way of life" at Sweet Briar, the college website declares, and so if you'd rather your college education didn't resemble the next episode of *Glee*, the quirky traditions and singing occasions that permeate life at Sweet Briar may not be your niche. If you aren't planning on bringing a horse to college (your horse will need his own separate application) or shelling out a fair amount of cash to participate in the college's very prominent equestrian programs, and if the idea of the positively Victorian "Ring Game" tradition, in which women announce their engagements to their class, makes your skin crawl, then you might consider looking elsewhere.

Sweet Briar College is an undeniably strong academic environment that offers opportunities that would be unavailable at co-ed, larger, public universities. To be sure, it's a quirky atmosphere steeped with traditions, but a welcoming one, and if that excites you, then Sweet Briar College should merit a closer look.

Academics

According to the college, "we provide leadership opportunities and strong academic programs—in the sciences, math, pre-medicine, pre-veterinary medicine, and government for example—that typically cater to men at other schools." The quality of Sweet Briar's programs designed to give women the one-up in traditionally male fields is evident: some of the strongest of Sweet Briar's 39 offered majors are biology, business, and government. And academics are competitive. "It's acceptable, almost expected, that you be interested in traditionally male dominated fields here," says a student. Sweet Briar also allows students to customize their own majors, combining classes from multiple majors and working with a team of faculty advisors. Getting to know faculty is easy in such a close environment.

Sweet Briar's General Education Program requires four components: first-year writing courses; written and oral communication and quantitative reasoning "Skill" classes; physical activity; and a certain number of courses in "Knowledge" areas that range from foreign language to art to science.

Students who are particularly driven will appreciate the Honors Program and Student Leadership Program. Admission to the Honors Program is offered to merit scholarship holders and select other applicants. The Honors Program encompasses a series of seminars designed to examine certain themes such as "Emerging Ethics" across all disciplines. Honors students also can apply for travel grants for research or conferences and can apply to Honors Summer Research Program, an eight-week period in which students conduct one-on-one research projects with faculty.

SWEET BRIAR COLLEGE

Four-year private women's college
Founded: 1901
Sweet Briar, VA
Rural
Pop. 2,218

Address:
134 Chapel Road
Sweet Briar, VA
24595

Admissions:
800-381-6142

Financial Aid:
800-381-6156

admissions@sbc.edu

www.sbc.edu

SWEET BRIAR COLLEGE

The Student Leadership Program offers certification in leadership skills—including time management, communication, ethical decision-making, and working in groups—by combining academics with hands-on experience. It requires participation in weekly meetings, on-campus activities, conferences, certain approved classes, and community service. "I've truly grown as a leader," admits a student. The program is open to all Sweet Briar students.

Sweet Briar's two major study-abroad programs are the Junior Year in Spain and Junior Year in France. These semester- or year-long programs are offered for high intermediate or advanced speakers, who live with host families in Seville, Paris, or Nice, and can enroll in classes at local universities in addition to program classes. Internships and summer programs are offered as well. Sweet Briar also has exchange agreements with universities in Germany, France, Italy, the UK, and China.

About 97 percent of Sweet Briar graduates are accepted to graduate school or take jobs immediately—well above the average. The Alumnae Association and Career Services manage a program called Alumnae in Residence, in which alumnae visit for a few days throughout the year to share professional experience and expertise and give advice to students.

Student Life

More than 50 student groups and organizations are active at Sweet Briar, including the Sweet Tones, Sweet Briar's a cappella group, and the *Sweet Briar Voice*, the college newspaper. Student groups sponsor a number of events, including the Winter Mixer, a large themed dance event, usually with another school. Late Night Vixens offer events and activities, ranging from band performances and discos to movie nights, on weekend nights in the college pub, the Vixen Den.

But by far the most highly anticipated events of the year are Sweet Briar's traditional events, which include Junior Week, during which juniors must wear goofy outfits given to them by an unknown senior. Junior Week culminates in Junior Banquet, where juniors each have a friend compose and recite an ode to them and seniors pass on their robes to the juniors—these robes are handed down from year to year and decorated by freshmen. Homecoming Week features a Spirit Week Competition between the classes and the Cardboard Boat Regatta, in which engineering students construct and pilot their creations. Lantern Bearing is the final traditional event graduating seniors participate in: each senior asks an underclasswoman to make a lantern for her, and the students proceed through the quad before the underclasswomen sing to the seniors. "Sweet Briar is all about traditions," says a student.

Many of the student groups behind these events and traditions are called "Tap Clubs," social and service oriented groups which take the place of sororities on campus. The 11 Tap Clubs on campus have names like "Aints 'n' Asses" and "Bum Chums," and have their own stereotyped character traits that are used to explain their group. Examples are "Falls on Nose," members "enjoy dancing" but apparently "don't necessarily have any rhythm," etc.

Sweet Briar's seven varsity sports teams compete at Division III level as part of the Old Dominion Athletic Conference—swim and dive and lacrosse are particularly strong. The Fitness and Athletics Center offers 53,000 square feet encompassing racquetball and squash courts, a spinning room, and a field house. Sweet Briar's Riding Program is a major part of students' lives, and many bring their own horses.

The area surrounding the campus offers great outdoor distractions. The Sweet Briar Outdoor Program (SWEBOP) offers outdoor activities, including rock climbing and hiking, designed to foster appreciation of the environment and leadership skills. As part of New Student Orientation, first-year students all participate in the Learning on the Land program, in which students become acquainted with the campus' 3,250 acres and the land's value to the college as a natural and academic resource. It's also possible to get off campus to visit nearby schools, including University of Virginia, or even to roadtrip up to Washington, DC, for a more urban getaway.

Students must either live on campus or commute: most housing options are dorm-style residences, although apartments are available. Freshmen are assigned housing based on their "male visitation" preferences.

Student Body

Students at Sweet Briar are generally focused and competitive, academically oriented, and preppy outside of class. "There are plenty of pearl necklaces and headbands," says a student. About half the students come from outside of Virginia, and ethnic diversity is high.

You May Not Know

- Sweet Briar College campus was a working plantation in the 18th and 19th centuries.
- Every year, the freshman and sophomore classes compete to cover each other's landmarks—the hitching post and sophomore rock, respectively—in paint.
- One decorated "Senior Robe" has been passed down from student to student for 40 years.

Distinguished Alumnae

Elizabeth Harvey FitzGerald, Alpha Laboratories; Sherri L. Manson, Equity Investors, Ltd.

Admissions and Financial Aid

Sweet Briar recommends but does not require interviews, which may assist students in demonstrating the "strength of character" that the admissions office seeks in applicants. Acceptances are mailed between February and April 1.

Sweet Briar offers merit scholarships up to $15,000 per year, renewable annually, based on GPA and SAT/ACT scores, with no separate application needed. Additionally, Create Learn Innovate Manage Build (CLIMB) Scholarships of $10,000 per year, also renewable annually, are offered to students interested in science and engineering; and FIRST Scholarships of $1,000 are available to students who have participated in FIRST Robotics or Tech Challenges. Both require a separate application.

SWEET BRIAR COLLEGE

Highlights

Admissions Criteria
Academic criteria:
Grades: ☆ ☆ ☆
Difficulty of class schedule: ☆ ☆ ☆
Class rank: ☆
Standardized test scores: ☆ ☆
Teacher recommendations: ☆ ☆
Personal statement: ☆ ☆
Non-academic criteria considered:
Interview
Extracurricular activities
Special talents, interests, abilities
Character/personal qualities
Volunteer work
Work experience
State of residency
Minority affiliation
Alumni relationship

Deadlines
Early Action: No
Early Decision: No
Regular Action: February 1 (final)
Common Application: Accepted

Financial Aid
In-state tuition: $33,130
Out-of-state tuition: $33,130
Room: Varies
Board: Varies
Books: $1,200
Freshmen receiving need-based aid: 82%
Undergrads rec. need-based aid: 71%
Avg. % of need met by financial aid: 78%
Avg. aid package (freshmen): $26,448
Avg. aid package (undergrads): $25,289
Avg. debt upon graduation: $23,596

School Spirit
Mascot: Vixen
Colors: Forest green and pink
Song: *Sweet Briar, Sweet Briar, Flower Fair*

641

SYRACUSE UNIVERSITY

Overview

Sports fans will know Syracuse University—a large private university in upstate New York—for its nationally competitive sports programs. The school has 26 national team championships in various sports under its belt. But SU also offers a strong focus on research and a huge number of academic options, 200+ majors in nine different schools. The students, like the academic programs, are a diverse group, and even the campus architecture is a mix of different styles, from nineteenth-century Romanesque structures to contemporary buildings.

But there is one place where there is no diversity: the color orange became the university's official color in 1890, when Syracuse became the first college to adopt only one official color. At such a spirited school—especially when it comes to football and basketball games—this explains the omnipresence of orange, whether as a clothing color or student organization name or even the school mascot.

Situated on University Hill, campus is covered in grass and trees and flanked by residential neighborhoods. *U.S. News & World Report* ranked Syracuse number 62 among undergraduate national universities. You may want to consider your ability to weather brutal winters though: the *Farmer's Almanac* declared Syracuse the "worst winter city." But for those who aren't deterred by the infamous cold and would like to be a part of a school with strong fields of study and a competitive sports program, applying to the SU applicant pool may be just the thing to do.

Academics

Syracuse offers more than 200 undergraduate majors spread across nine individual colleges, with the option to double major or complete a minor (of which there are 90 to choose from). Strong programs include architecture, information management and technology, and psychology. Requirements vary by major, but all students are required to take writing courses. For liberal arts degrees, students must take courses in language or quantitative skills, natural sciences and mathematics, humanities, social sciences, and critical reflections on ethical and social issues. "We have a lot of flexibility to choose classes outside the core curriculum," remarks a student.

Students say they are "competitive but not cutthroat," which isn't surprising given the competitive nature of the application process. However, course loads are manageable, and professors make themselves readily available. "My professors have always been willing to take the time to explain the material," says a student.

The Renée Crown University Honors Program has a separate, rigorous curriculum that includes four honors courses, an honors seminar, demonstrated civic engagement, and a Capstone Project. The Capstone Project begins in the fall of junior year, and more than a dozen awards ranging up to $5,000 support capstone research.

iLEARN, a program of the College of Arts and Sciences, aims to complement traditional classroom and laboratory work with "enhanced out-of-classroom learning experiences." Projects include the Ruth Meyer Scholars program for nominated undergraduate researchers in the College of Arts and Sciences and the university's successful Mock Trial team.

The Mary Ann Shaw Center for Public and Community Service (CPCS) provides a central hub for volunteering, service learning, and leadership on campus. The center is located in the Schine Student center, a 192,000+ square-foot facility that is always bustling with student activity.

Syracuse has offered multiple study-abroad programs since 1911. The SU Abroad currently shares joint programs with universities in more than 40 countries, and the university provides eight international centers with structured programs in several academic disciplines.

SU has more than 230,000 living alumni. Syracuse University Career Services offers practice interviews, guidance on grad school applications, access to an alumni mentor network, career fairs, and more.

Student Life

There are nearly 300 student organizations on campus, showcased each year at the Student Involvement Fair on the University Quad in mid-September. Students with interests in journalism might like to know that CitrusTV is the entirely student-run television studio, and that there is also an independent student newspaper *The Daily Orange* that is more than 100 years old. Every year, the Pulse Performing Arts Series brings performing and visual arts programs to campus, while the University Lectures series brings notable speakers from around the word (previous speakers have included Al Gore, Muhammad Yunus, and Robert Kennedy Jr.).

The student-operated University Union hosts events such as University Block Party, the largest event on campus. This annual spring concert is held in the Carrier Dome on the last weekend of the school year—the sold-out show recently drew in more than 10,000 people. Recent performers included Kid Cudi, Nas, and Damian Marley. "It sells out because of the big-name performers," says a student. Homecoming is another major annual event: the week of festivities is known as Orange Central, with perennial student favorites that include a football fun zone on the Quad and campus decorating contest. National Orange Day puts the focus on service instead of football with service-oriented activities that are fun as well as beneficial to the community.

Greek life plays a major role on campus. There are more than 50 fraternities and sororities on campus. "Rushing can be a little intense," recalls a student, "and it can be a distraction from school-work."

Syracuse University's athletic teams, known as the Orange, compete in 20 Division I varsity sports (eight men's, 12 women's). Football and men's basketball are national competitors, while men's lacrosse and women's field hockey are also competitive. "Basketball games are frenzied," says a student about the team that made the Elite Eight in 2012 and Final Four in 2013. There's a range of intramural sports offered, including the expected basketball and tennis, but there are also the less common ones such as summer sand volleyball and broomball.

Students frequent downtown Syracuse for arts, entertainment, and food, although "it's possible to pretty much stay on campus and find everything you need," notes a student. More ambitious outings include road trips to Ithaca, Niagara Falls, and Montreal.

Freshmen and sophomores are required to live in dorms, and upperclassmen tend to move off campus. "The dorms are okay, but it can be a trek to get to class," one student states.

Student Body

The SU student body is diverse, with a notable population of "hipsters" and city folk, in addition to "outdoorsy" types. Students hail from all 50 states and more than 115 countries. About eight percent of students are from outside the U.S. There is moderate geographic

SYRACUSE UNIVERSITY

Highlights

Students
Total enrollment: 21,029
Undergrads: 14,798
Freshmen: 3,459
From out-of-state: 61%
From public schools: 68%
Male/Female: 44%/56%
Live on-campus: 75%
In fraternities: 21%
In sororities: 26%
Off-campus employment rating: Excellent
Caucasian: 56%
African American: 9%
Hispanic: 10%
Asian / Pacific Islander: 8%
Native American: 1%
Mixed (2+ ethnicities): 2%
International: 8%

Academics
Calendar: Semester
Student/faculty ratio: 16:1
Class size 9 or fewer: 26%
Class size 10-29: 54%
Class size 30-49: 12%
Class size 50-99: 6%
Class size 100 or more: 3%
Six-year graduation rate: 82%
Graduates who immediately enter career related to major: 90%

Most Popular Majors
Psychology
Information management/technology
Architecture

Admissions
Applicants: 25,790
Accepted: 13,240
Acceptance rate: 51.3%
Placed on wait list: 3,661
Enrolled from wait list: 319
Average GPA: 3.6
ACT range: 23-28
SAT Math range: 540-650
SAT Reading range: 510-620
SAT Writing range: 7-33
Top 10% of class: 38%
Top 25% of class: 72%
Top 50% of class: 95%

643

College Profiles

SYRACUSE UNIVERSITY

Admissions Criteria

Academic criteria:
Grades: ☆
Difficulty of class schedule: ☆
Class rank: ☆
Standardized test scores: ☆
Teacher recommendations: ☆
Personal statement: ☆

Non-academic criteria considered:
Interview
Extracurricular activities
Special talents, interests, abilities
Character/personal qualities
Volunteer work
Work experience
State of residency
Geographical location
Minority affiliation
Alumni relationship

Deadlines

Early Action: No
Early Decision: November 15
Regular Action: Rolling admissions
Common Application: Accepted

Financial Aid

In-state tuition: $38,970
Out-of-state tuition: $38,970
Room: $7,430
Board: $6,624
Books: $1,360
Freshmen receiving need-based aid: 58%
Undergrads rec. need-based aid: 59%
Avg. % of need met by financial aid: 93%
Avg. aid package (freshmen): $35,120
Avg. aid package (undergrads): $34,000
Avg. debt upon graduation: $33,504

School Spirit

Mascot: Otto the Orange
Colors: Orange
Song: *Down, Down the Field*

diversity, with 39 percent of students hailing from New York State, while there is high ethnic diversity, with minority students representing 30 percent of the student body.

You May Not Know

- The university has a memorial wall dedicated to the 35 SU students killed in the terrorist bombing on Pam Am Flight 103 in 1988; the university holds Remembrance Week every fall semester.
- SU is affiliated with the United Methodist Church, though the university has been identified as nonsectarian since 1920.
- When Morton J. Savada donated the entire inventory of his Manhattan record store (200,000 records), the university came to have the second largest record collection. Only the Library of Congress holds more.

Distinguished Alumni

Eileen Collins, first female commander of a space shuttle; Robert Jarvik, inventor of the first artificial heart; Joyce Carol Oates, novelist; Arthur Rock, cofounder of Intel.

Admissions and Financial Aid

Syracuse's admissions office offers detailed information to applicants in their "What We Look For" material. Topping off the list is academic performance, "especially senior year accomplishments." Interviews are recommended but not required, as the university likes to get a feel for an applicant's personality through the personal essay and a face-to-face interview if possible. Due to the competitive nature of admissions, the committee emphasizes that "decisions are not always a statement of your ability, but a matter of competition."

All applications are automatically evaluated for merit-based scholarships. The Founders', Chancellor, and Dean's merit scholarship for entering freshman pay up to $12,000 of tuition costs, and are renewable each year. Students applying for The College of Arts and Sciences are considered for the Coronat Scholarship, which is a full scholarship. The university awards more than $178 million in Syracuse University grants and scholarships.

TEXAS A&M UNIVERSITY

Overview

A very large public university located in College Station, Texas, Texas A&M epitomizes the football-crazed, southwestern college experience, rich in Texas tradition. The huge campus, ranging from historic brick to modern architecture, dominates the East Central part of College Station, a small town with a population of just 97,000.

Known for their unwavering loyalty to Texas A&M athletics, "Aggie" students—predominantly Caucasian and conservative—ooze school spirit. With strengths in the natural sciences, agriculture, engineering, and business, along with a loyal and enthusiastic alumni network, Texas A&M beckons to students who are seeking a solid educational, social, and athletically-based college experience.

Academics

Texas A&M offers 129 majors. Specific classes to fulfill the core curriculum vary by major, but all students are required to take English 104, Political Science 206 and 207, and one American history class. Overall, students must take courses in communication, math, natural sciences, humanities, visual and performing arts, social and behavioral sciences, U.S. history and political science, international and cultural diversity, and kinesiology.

Classes at Texas A&M are fairly big, with the most common course size ranging between 20 and 29 students. Students say freshman core classes tend to be "up to several hundred students" and "can be challenging to get into." First Year Seminar (FYS) courses were designed to combat this problem by providing students with the opportunity to take discussion-based classes in more intimate learning environments with 20 or fewer students. "The smaller setting really allows for in-depth discussions," notes a student. Additionally, an advantage of a large school is its ability to offer students courses tailored to their unique interests.

The Honors Program at Texas A&M provides accelerated and challenging courses for academically talented students. Honors students select a combination of courses (Honors and non-Honors) that meet their interests; they also have the option to customize their programs with independent study, graduate-level course work, or upper-division courses. In addition, honors students can participate in the Undergraduate Research Fellows program: a two-semester research experience, conducted with an accomplished Texas A&M faculty member. Undergrad Research Fellows also complete a published Honors thesis, participate in regular scholarly workshops, manage and plan a research budget of at least $300 and have the opportunity to apply for additional funding up to $3,000.

Texas A&M has University Abroad Centers in Costa Rica, Mexico City, and Tuscany. Students can meet with Study Abroad advisors who will help them work to design a program in any country that matches a student's particular interests.

The majority of students report that the school's career center is generally helpful in finding jobs and internships; however, almost all students seem to think that one of the greatest advantages of the resources at Texas A&M is the very strong and involved alumni who engage in campus recruiting. "Networking can help you get an internship or a full-time job," one student comments.

Student Life

With over 700 student organizations on campus, Texas A&M students tend to be very involved in extracurricular activities that span a gamut of interests. The Singing Cadets—founded in 1893 and therefore one of the oldest student organizations on campus—is an all-male choral group that travels nationally and internationally for competitions. The school newspaper, *The Battalion*, and the student-run film society are also popular.

**TEXAS A&M
UNIVERSITY**

Four-year public
Founded: 1876
College Station, TX
Medium city
Pop. 97,543

Address:
P.O. Box 30014
College Station, TX
77842

Admissions:
979-845-3741

Financial Aid:
979-845-3236

admissions@tamu.edu

www.tamu.edu

TEXAS A&M UNIVERSITY

Students

Total enrollment: 50,227
Undergrads: 40,103
Freshmen: 8,139
Part-time students: 10%
From out-of-state: 4%
Male/Female: 52%/48%
Live on-campus: 22%
In fraternities: 5%
In sororities: 12%
Off-campus employment rating: Excellent
Caucasian: 69%
African American: 3%
Hispanic: 18%
Asian / Pacific Islander: 5%
Native American: 0%
Mixed (2+ ethnicities): 2%
International: 2%

Academics

Calendar: Semester
Student/faculty ratio: 21:1
Class size 9 or fewer: 2%
Class size 10-29: 47%
Class size 30-49: 25%
Class size 50-99: 15%
Class size 100 or more: 11%
Returning freshmen: 92%
Six-year graduation rate: 80%

Most Popular Majors

Interdisciplinary studies
Finance
Biomedical sciences

Admissions

Applicants: 27,798
Accepted: 18,663
Acceptance rate: 67.1%
Average GPA: Not reported
ACT range: 24-30
SAT Math range: 570-626
SAT Reading range: 553-602
SAT Writing range: 7-28
Top 10% of class: 60%
Top 25% of class: 91%
Top 50% of class: 99%

As one of the defining characteristics of the university, traditions run deep at Texas A&M. The Elephant Walk, for example, takes place the week before the last regularly scheduled football game. Seniors know it is the last time that they will stand as part of the A&M team (Aggie football fans are called the 12th man—alluding to their undying support to the 11 players on the field and willingness to step on to the field if they were needed to) and they walk around campus reminiscing about the times they've had at the university. Another event is the Aggie bonfire, a 90-year-old tradition in which students build and burn a massive bonfire. Unfortunately, in 1999, 12 people were killed when the bonfire collapsed. This led Texas A&M officials to declare a hiatus on an official Bonfire (however, a student-sponsored coalition still constructs an annual off-campus bonfire). The Big Event was founded by Aggie students and is the largest one-day student-run service project in America, bringing students together to assist local residents.

Though not the dominant social scene on campus, Greek life is certainly visible with five percent of men joining one of the 31 fraternities, and 12 percent of women joining one of the 25 sororities. While the percentage of students involved is not high, this represents more than 3,000 members when you consider how large the student body is. "The fraternity and sorority members tend to be their own clique," notes a student.

Spearheaded by the powerhouse football team, sports are extremely popular at Texas A&M. With 18 Division I sports teams (eight men's and 10 women's), the university bleeds school spirit. "Football games are an all-day, must-attend event," one student declares. Men's basketball and baseball teams are also national competitors.

The small and conservative city of College Station pretty much revolves around Texas A&M. Northgate, a popular night-time hangout, is almost always populated with college students, as is University Drive since it is full of bars and restaurants. Situated 90 minutes away from Houston and Austin, and three hours from Dallas, Texas A&M students are also relatively close to some of the most exciting cities in the Southwest.

Campus housing is divided into two sections: Northside, located close to Northgate and other popular hangout spots; and Southside, the newer and quieter dorms farther away from the heartbeat of campus. Typically students live on campus for freshman year and choose to move off campus afterward. "It's good to live on campus at least one year because you'll make the most friends that way," one student comments.

Student Body

A conservative school, the southwestern-based Texas A&M has a "fairly right-wing" student body. A considerable portion of students are Corps and Cadets attending the military academy within the university.

With 28 percent minority students, Texas A&M is highly ethnically diverse. The same cannot be said, however, about its geographic diversity with just four percent of students coming from outside Texas.

While students claim that those from different ethnic backgrounds tend to stick together, the school is reputed to have a generally accepting attitude towards every race, ethnicity, and religion.

You May Not Know

- When founded, the original mission of the university was to educate white males in farming and military techniques; the letters "A&M" originally stood as an abbreviation for "Agriculture and Mechanical" but now don't stand for anything.
- The five stars on the Aggie Ring (received at the end of students' academic careers) represent intellect, body, spiritual attainment, emotional poise, and integrity of character. Many students "dunk" their ring into a pitcher of beer and chug it as quickly as possible, "earning" it in a different way than intended by the university.
- Texas A&M scientists created a cat named CC, one of the first cloned animals.

Distinguished Alumni

John David Crow, Heisman Trophy winner; Lyle Lovett, musician; Rick Perry, Governor of Texas; Will Wynn, former Mayor of Austin, Texas.

Admissions and Financial Aid

Texas A&M looks for students who have completed the most rigorous educational paths during their high school careers. The university also recommends demonstrating interest and commitment to the school by making campus visits, attending college night programs, meeting with Texas A&M admissions counselors, visiting prospective student centers, or attending Texas A&M University application workshops. Students have the opportunity to indicate whether they have participated in any of the aforementioned "academic association" activities on their application.

Texas A&M offers 12 scholarships for incoming freshmen, awarded on the basis of academic achievement, extracurricular activities, volunteer work, employment, and (less frequently) financial need. Among one of the six academic scholarships available, the Academic Achievement Scholarship is a merit-based scholarship that is awarded to freshmen who have excelled in academics and standardized tests, as well as leadership, community service, and special talents. The scholarship is valued between $10,000-12,000 a year. Out-of-state recipients earn a non-resident tuition waiver for the duration of the scholarships.

Other scholarship programs at Texas A&M include the Century Scholars Program, a partnership between the university and participating high schools throughout Texas. The program's mission is to increase the number of Texas A&M students from underrepresented high schools. Century Scholars are awarded $20,000 over four years, as well as a $1,000 stipend for study abroad.

TEXAS A&M UNIVERSITY

Highlights

Admissions Criteria
Academic criteria:
Grades: ☆ ☆ ☆
Difficulty of class schedule: ☆ ☆ ☆
Class rank: ☆ ☆ ☆
Standardized test scores: ☆ ☆ ☆
Teacher recommendations: ☆
Personal statement: ☆ ☆
Non-academic criteria considered:
Extracurricular activities
Special talents, interests, abilities
Character/personal qualities
Volunteer work
Work experience
Geographical location

Deadlines
Early Action: No
Early Decision: No
Regular Action: Rolling admissions
Common Application: Not accepted

Financial Aid
In-state tuition: $5,297
Out-of-state tuition: $21,917
Room: Varies
Board: Varies
Books: $1,246
Freshmen receiving need-based aid: 49%
Undergrads rec. need-based aid: 41%
Avg. % of need met by financial aid: 70%
Avg. aid package (freshmen): $16,478
Avg. aid package (undergrads): $14,938
Avg. debt upon graduation: $22,716

School Spirit
Mascot: Aggies
Colors: Maroon and white
Song: *The Aggie War Hymn* and *Spirit of Aggieland*

647

TEXAS CHRISTIAN UNIVERSITY

Overview

Texas Christian University is a relatively small, private liberal arts university affiliated with—although not governed by—the Disciples of Christ. The focus at TCU is on its undergraduates, comprising roughly 87 percent of the student body. TCU is known for its business and nursing programs, as well as a wide variety of campus traditions that reflect the culture and history of the university since its founding in 1873.

The TCU campus occupies 272 acres located just a quick drive from downtown Fort Worth. Despite this proximity to a rather large city, the university has taken measures to make sure that students don't feel they are surrounded by urban concrete. Tree-lined University Drive divides TCU's campus into residential (west side) and academic (east side) sections. The campus itself is green—all of its surrounding streets are lined by live oaks—and has a variety of architecture in its academic buildings and residence halls, from Georgian to contemporary.

Many of the buildings are constructed of yellow brick, similar to older buildings in the Fort Worth area, and many feature arches and red tile roofs. Starting roughly a decade ago, much of the campus has been under constant construction in efforts to renovate and modernize certain facilities. Built in 2010, Scharbauer Hall encompasses many of AddRan College's offices and classrooms. Despite this, the university retains a lot of its old charm, perhaps even a staunch "academic" feel.

Academics

The university offers more than 100 undergraduate majors. Regardless of a student's major at TCU, the foundation for all study is the core curriculum. There are three components to the TCU core: essential competencies; human experiences and endeavors; and heritage, mission, vision, and values.

The essential competencies component is just what it sounds like—classes that cover general knowledge requirements for university students. These include mathematical reasoning, oral communication, writing emphasis, and written communication. The human experiences and endeavors component covers "soft" subjects like humanities, social sciences, natural sciences, and fine arts. The third component, heritage, mission, vision, and values, reflects the "heart" portion of the education. These courses focus on promoting good values and citizenship and include classes focused on religious traditions, historical traditions, literary traditions, cultural awareness, global awareness, and social values.

At TCU undergraduates receive attention and nurturing. Students describe the professors as "incredibly helpful" and "going out of their way to be friendly." There are 506 full-time and 305 part-time faculty members; all tend to be accessible and are open to having undergraduates assist them in research. Technical majors at TCU, such as engineering and nursing, tend to have more rigorous curriculums. Programs that the school is generally recognized for include business information systems, engineering, nursing, and art history.

The TCU Honors College is a special program generally aimed at the top eight percent of matriculating students. The Honors College admissions process is separate from normal university admission, and invitations are extended based on a variety of factors ranging from SAT and ACT scores, to class rank and involvement in extracurricular activities.

One interesting program not offered at many other colleges and universities is the Ranch Management Program—instruction in the business of ranching. It requires about one academic year to complete, and students are provided with classroom instruction on basic management principles, as well as ample field experience.

Women's studies is a highly regarded emphasis at TCU. It goes without saying that TCU goals include the promotion of the potential and ideas of women in every facet of life. A concentration in women's studies can include an undergraduate minor, as well as a graduate certificate program. Students may participate in international study, a senior seminar, and an internship through the department.

TCU's global perspective is reflected in its numerous study-abroad programs. These are available both in summer programs and in full semester-long programs that usually will count toward your major or minor. Additionally you can use scholarships and financial aid money that you receive toward study-abroad expenses. Semester-long programs are available in London, Seville, and Florence, while summer programs are a bit more expansive and global and are offered in 11 countries. TCU also has affiliations in an additional 17 countries.

Graduates are generally successful, and there are ample opportunities for post-graduate guidance. TCU's center for career services leads students through the process of crafting a resume, obtaining internships, and securing post-graduation employment. TCU also hosts many career fairs and invites employers to interview on-campus.

Student Life

TCU officials are quick to point out to new students that a very small portion of their time will actually be spent in class. Students are encouraged to get involved in student organizations, of which there are over 200 on campus. Notable groups include the MBA Association for business majors, Habitat for Humanity, and *The Daily Skiff*, TCU's student-run newspaper. There are plenty of other organizations also available for students to take advantage of during their down time.

Traditions are a big part of life at TCU, particularly the varsity athletics programs, and especially football. Tailgating has become a time-tested tradition, "serious business," as one student put it. The football team is highly touted and usually seeded in the single digits. Other sports include baseball, horse riding, and rifle competitions, though these are not as popular. TCU has eight Division I men's sports (with football being Division I-A), and 10 Division I women's sports.

There are other traditions that have become popular through the years, including an annual Casino Night, which used to be held in downtown Fort Worth but has since moved back to campus. Hosted by the Phi Gamma Psi fraternity, this evening of fun attracts many guests. The annual Christmas tree lighting is a popular holiday event that takes place outside the student union. Students enjoy the ceremony as well as the refreshments that are provided. Greek life sponsors many events, many of these based on traditions established since their inception at TCU in 1955. Thirty sororities and fraternities now thrive on campus.

In terms of off-campus activities, the Fort Worth Zoo and the Fort Worth Botanical Gardens offer nearby entertainment options. The Fort Worth Cultural District attracts more than two million visitors a year to its museums and galleries. Downtown Fort Worth and the Sundance Square are also popular destinations.

About half of students reside on campus in one of the residence halls or Greek houses. Students say there's "inexpensive" and "convenient" off-campus housing also available.

TEXAS CHRISTIAN UNIVERSITY

Highlights

Students
Total enrollment: 9,727
Undergrads: 8,456
Freshmen: 1,853
From out-of-state: 49%
From public schools: 62%
Male/Female: 41%/59%
Live on-campus: 47%
In fraternities: 42%
In sororities: 51%
Off-campus employment rating: Excellent
Caucasian: 74%
African American: 5%
Hispanic: 10%
Asian / Pacific Islander: 2%
Native American: 1%
Mixed (2+ ethnicities): 1%
International: 5%

Academics
Calendar: Semester
Student/faculty ratio: 13:1
Class size 9 or fewer: 17%
Class size 10-29: 51%
Class size 30-49: 25%
Class size 50-99: 5%
Class size 100 or more: 2%
Six-year graduation rate: 75%

Most Popular Majors
Strategic communications
Nursing
Finance

Admissions
Applicants: 19,335
Accepted: 7,901
Acceptance rate: 40.9%
Placed on wait list: 2,666
Enrolled from wait list: 269
Average GPA: Not reported
ACT range: 25-30
SAT Math range: 550-650
SAT Reading range: 530-630
SAT Writing range: Not reported
Top 10% of class: 43%
Top 25% of class: 75%
Top 50% of class: 96%

649

TEXAS CHRISTIAN UNIVERSITY

Admissions Criteria

Academic criteria:

Grades: ☆ ☆ ☆
Difficulty of class schedule: ☆ ☆ ☆
Class rank: ☆ ☆ ☆
Standardized test scores: ☆ ☆ ☆
Teacher recommendations: ☆ ☆ ☆
Personal statement: ☆ ☆ ☆

Non-academic criteria considered:

Interview
Extracurricular activities
Special talents, interests, abilities
Character/personal qualities
Volunteer work
Work experience
State of residency
Geographical location
Religious affiliation/commitment
Minority affiliation
Alumni relationship

Deadlines

Early Action: November 1
Early Decision: No
Regular Action: February 15 (final)
Notification of admission by: April 1
Common Application: Accepted

Financial Aid

In-state tuition: $36,500
Out-of-state tuition: $36,500
Room: $6,700
Board: $4,280
Books: $1,050
Freshmen receiving need-based aid: 40%
Undergrads rec. need-based aid: 43%
Avg. % of need met by financial aid: 62%
Avg. aid package (freshmen): $21,669
Avg. aid package (undergrads): $21,185
Avg. debt upon graduation: $38,516

School Spirit

Mascot: Horned Frog
Colors: Purple and white

Student Body

The student body at TCU isn't particularly diverse. Three out of four students are Caucasian, and the student body tends to be conservative, with a strong religious leaning that might be the result of the university's Christian focus. Minorities account for a high percentage of the student body.

The student body enjoys the presence of a strong Greek life, with more than 40 percent of students joining a fraternity or sorority. "There's a range of fraternities and sororities so even if you aren't into the party scene, you can find one that works for you," notes a student.

You May Not Know

- There are more than 40 species of trees on the TCU campus.
- The record attendance for a TCU football game is over 50,000 people.
- The Davey O'Brien award, given to the best NCAA quarterback, was created in honor of a TCU alum.

Distinguished Alumni

Kenneth Barr, Mayor of Fort Worth; Dan Boren, U.S. House of Representatives; Betty Buckley, Broadway singer; John Davis, billionaire entrepreneur; Gordon England, former Secretary of the Navy; John Roach, CEO, Tandy Corporation; Bob Schieffer, anchor, CBS Evening News.

Admissions and Financial Aid

There are certain things that TCU admissions officials regard as important. The student's essay is a "significant part of the application as is the high school counselor's evaluation." Also, activities outside of class are evaluated, as well as any college coursework, and special talents, if the applicant chooses to describe them.

Scholarships are available, based upon the applicant's academic performance, as well as financial need. TCU recognizes exceptional students through academic merit scholarships. These awards are competitive and are based on both objective and subjective criteria. Four-year merit scholarships include the Chancellor's Scholarship, Dean's Scholarship, and Founder's Scholarship.

TEXAS TECH UNIVERSITY

Overview

Like everything else in Texas, Texas Tech University is bigger. The Lubbock campus is over 1,800 acres, making it the second largest contiguous campus in the country. With over 26,000 undergraduates, TTU is the largest higher education institution in the western two thirds of Texas; even its most selective program, the Honors College, enrolls over 1,000 students.

It shouldn't be a surprise, then, that it's easy to get lost or just get by at a large school like TTU: academic supervision and advising can be hard to come by, and lecture classes can easily have hundreds of students. But what TTU does well, it does well. The campus is one of the most beautiful campuses in America: full of Spanish Renaissance-style architecture, the campus was described by author James Michener as one of "the most beautiful west of the Mississippi."

Tech's selective programs, including their Honors College, medical and technological research opportunities, and first-generation college student program, stand out. But TTU's real heart is in sports—particularly football and basketball—and all the extensive tailgating, traditions, and celebrations that go with having some of the "winningest" teams in the country.

Academics

Texas Tech offers 280 majors and a moderate amount of choice when it comes to completing the Core Curriculum, which requires two classes each in written and oral communication; mathematics and natural science, plus a lab component; technology and applied science; and one course each in visual and performing arts. Students must also complete five courses in social and behavioral sciences: two courses in U.S. history, two courses in Texas history (in classic Texas fashion, no other kinds of history are required), and one in individual and group behavior. The Colleges of Agriculture and Engineering are strong, as is the economics major. Classes tend to be on the large side: over half of classes have more than 30 students. Advising and access to professors can be "limited," but the crowds thin out in upper-level classes.

TTU offers several programs that will help ease students' transition to college. IS 1000, the Tech Transition Freshman Seminar, introduces students to the resources available at TTU as well as offering primers in skills like money management. "It gives you some practical but valuable information," says a student. A special and more extensive program, PEGASUS, is offered for first-generation college (FGC) students. PEGASUS pairs freshmen and sophomore first-generation students with an advisor and upperclass FGC student mentor. Regular workshops familiarize students with university resources and skills for success, including financial literacy. The program also requires all students to engage in community service. Special community-building social events are held frequently. Students earn points for participating in all of these events, and points can translate into cash prizes and scholarships.

Tech students can also plug into smaller communities within the university through Freshmen Interest Groups. Students in FIGs live together in Learning Communities or special residence hall floors organized around specific academic interests or majors (ranging from pre-engineering to the visual and performing arts; there is also a PEGASUS FIG) and also enroll together in a pre-bundled academic program of at least two classes, including a FIG-exclusive small seminar. "It creates a smaller environment in the huge environment" of the university, says a student.

Students may apply to the Honors College, which requires students to complete a special introductory First Year Experience class and eight Honors courses in addition to their major. Honors classes are small—no more than 25 students—and discussion-based. Students who complete an Honors thesis will be granted "highest honors." Honors students are additionally entitled to specialized advising, early regis-

TEXAS TECH UNIVERSITY

Four-year public
Founded: 1923
Lubbock, TX
Medium city
Pop. 233,740

Address:
Box 45005
Lubbock, TX
79409

Admissions:
806-742-1480

Financial Aid:
806-742-3681

admissions@ttu.edu

www.ttu.edu

TEXAS TECH UNIVERSITY

Students

Total enrollment: 32,467
Undergrads: 26,481
Part-time students: 11%
From out-of-state: 6%
Male/Female: 55%/45%
Live on-campus: 25%
Caucasian: 66%
African American: 6%
Hispanic: 19%
Asian / Pacific Islander: 3%
Native American: 0%
Mixed (2+ ethnicities): 3%
International: 3%

Academics

Calendar: Semester
Student/faculty ratio: 24:1
Class size 9 or fewer: 3%
Class size 10-29: 45%
Class size 30-49: 27%
Class size 50-99: 16%
Class size 100 or more: 9%
Returning freshmen: 81%
Six-year graduation rate: 62%
Graduates who immediately go to graduate school: 33%
Graduates who immediately enter career related to major: 91%

Most Popular Majors

Business/marketing
Engineering
Family/consumer sciences

Admissions

Applicants: 18,027
Accepted: 11,593
Acceptance rate: 64.3%
Placed on wait list: 734
Enrolled from wait list: 444
Average GPA: Not reported
ACT range: 22-27
SAT Math range: 520-620
SAT Reading range: 500-590
SAT Writing range: 1-14
Top 10% of class: 20%
Top 25% of class: 52%
Top 50% of class: 86%

tration, space in the Honors dorms, special study-abroad programs and scholarships, and funding for students conducting research in collaboration with faculty. Prelaw and premed students can also gain early admission to the law and medical schools at TTU. International Baccalaureate students are assured admission to the Honors College.

All students can get engaged in research (although not necessarily funded) through the Center for Undergraduate Research. The Center offers support and direction for students looking for research opportunities or faculty mentors, as well as workshops on research, grant-writing, and presentation of research. A student-run group, the Undergraduate Research Organization, is an additional resource. Various departments and colleges offer research opportunities, as does the Center for Integration of Science Education (CISER) and Research in the Howard Hughes Medical Institute (TTUHHMI). Through CISER, students with some prior lab research experience can apply to become Undergraduate Research Scholars for biological and medical science, or Undergraduate Technology Scholars in technology and bioinformatics.

Tech has two special study-abroad centers in Seville, Spain, and Quedlinburg, Germany. Semester, summer, or intersession study-abroad trips are also led by faculty to almost two dozen countries. Affiliated and exchange programs are available as well.

Career Services at TTU offers career exploration, job fairs, and interview preparation and a Raider Mentor Network.

Student Life

Over 450 student organizations are active at TTU. The groups in the news most often are the spirit organizations: the Saddle Tramps, High Riders, and the 1998 Sudler Trophy winner for the nation's top marching band, the Goin' Band from Raiderland, all of whom are charged with organizing many of the traditional events that accompany TTU football, including covering campus with red crepe paper before games and ringing Bangin' Bertha and the Victory Bells. On-campus events revolve around football, including the week-long Homecoming celebrations, which include a parade, bonfire, and homecoming court. Tailgating is also a major part of Texas Tech life: over 10,000 students turn out for RaiderGate, the official student tailgate. "This is Texas, so yes, football is a religion," says a student. During the holidays, the buildings on Memorial Circle are lit with more than 25,000 lights, and choral groups perform in the Science Quadrangle to the accompaniment of Baird Memorial Carillon.

For relaxation, students can kick back at the Student Union, which features diverse dining options (what goes better with barbeque than gelato? Right?). Frat parties are popular on campus as well—nearly a fifth of students are members of TTU's 28 fraternities and 17 sororities. Off-campus partying is popular as well, although until 2010 Lubbock was a dry city and, while bars can serve alcoholic drinks, students had to drive 15 minutes out of town to the Strip to buy alcohol.

Texans are fond of football, and that distinction holds true at this campus: football is everybody's favorite sport. The team has had a winning season for 16 consecutive years until 2011 and makes regular bowl appearances. But of TTU's seven men's and eight women's Division I varsity teams, men's and women's basketball have been most successful. Former players on the women's team include Sheryl Swoopes and Krista Kirkland-Gerlich. Bob Knight, the "winningest" coach in NCAA Division I history, coached the men's team to four tournament appearances. "Bobby Knight's name is spoken with reverence," says a student. A standard selection of team and individual intramural sports is offered, including not-so-common mini-golf and sand volleyball. The Robert H. Ewalt Student Recreation Center houses extensive indoor playing courts, a fitness and cardio center, and weight rooms.

Freshmen are required to live on campus. Residence halls are mostly traditional dorm-style buildings, although some suite living is available. Learning Communities organized around a special academic interest are also offered. Off-campus housing is cheap and easy to find, however, so nearly everyone moves off campus after freshman year.

Student Body

Students at Tech are largely from in state, and as such "the conservative students are more outspoken and seem to be the majority," notes a student. Most religious groups on campus are Christian, although ethnic diversity is high. "People tend to group together by ethnic group, but there are diverse groups too," remarks a student.

You May Not Know

- Supposedly TTU engineering students on a field trip discovered a piece of the original "Blarney Stone," which is on display in from of the Electrical Engineering Building.
- One of campus' best-loved landmarks is the statue of Will Rogers and Soapsuds, his horse. The original plan was to face the statue so the two could be riding off into the sunset, but this would have faced Soapsuds' posterior end towards downtown, and so plans were changed. Soapsud's back end now faces TTU rival Texas A&M.
- You'll see plenty of students on campus pointing finger-guns at games and as greetings to one another. This is the "Guns Up" hand signal created in 1972 by a Texas Tech alum.

Distinguished Alumni

Angela Braly, CEO, Wellpoint; Scott Dadich, Creative Director, *Wired Magazine*; Sally Davis, NASA Mission Control; Pat Green, country music entertainer; Rick Husband, Commander, Space Shuttle Columbia.

Admissions and Financial Aid

SAT scores and class rank are all that is required for admission; letters of recommendation, essays, and even transcripts are optional.

TTU offers the Red Raider Guarantee, under which Texas residents whose families earn less than $40,000 are guaranteed the cost of tuition and fees. President's merit scholarships are available, ranging from $2,500 (Silver) to $6,000 (Platinum) per year. These awards are based on standardized test scores and class rank. Up to $12,000 is available annually for National Merit Finalists.

TEXAS TECH UNIVERSITY

Highlights

Admissions Criteria
Academic criteria:
Grades: ☆ ☆ ☆
Difficulty of class schedule: ☆ ☆ ☆
Class rank: ☆ ☆ ☆
Standardized test scores: ☆ ☆ ☆
Teacher recommendations: ☆
Personal statement: ☆ ☆
Non-academic criteria considered:
Extracurricular activities
Special talents, interests, abilities
Character/personal qualities
Volunteer work
Work experience
State of residency
Minority affiliation
Alumni relationship

Deadlines
Early Action: No
Early Decision: No
Regular Action: Rolling admissions
Common Application: Not accepted

Financial Aid
In-state tuition: $8,942
Out-of-state tuition: $19,472
Room: $4,380
Board: $2,945
Books: $1,200
Freshmen receiving need-based aid: 56%
Undergrads rec. need-based aid: 58%
Avg. % of need met by financial aid: 44%
Avg. aid package (freshmen): $9,907
Avg. aid package (undergrads): $10,031
Avg. debt upon graduation: $18,358

School Spirit
Mascot: Raider Red
Colors: Scarlet and black
Song: *Matador Song*

TRINITY COLLEGE

Four-year private
Founded: 1823
Hartford, CT
Major city
Pop. 124,867

Address:
300 Summit Street
Hartford, CT
06106

Admissions:
860-297-2180

Financial Aid:
860-297-2046

admissions.office@
trincoll.edu

www.trincoll.edu

TRINITY COLLEGE

Overview

Trinity College, founded in 1823, is located in Hartford, Connecticut. Two hours from New York City and Boston, the 100-acre campus is made up of Gothic-style buildings that include the Long Walk buildings, the "oldest example of Collegiate Gothic architecture in America," according to the college. Students take advantage of the location in the state's capital for internships and community involvement.

The small liberal arts college is unusual for its size in that it offers an ABET-accredited engineering program. It also offers the first Center for Urban and Global Studies at a liberal arts college.

Academics

Trinity's general requirements consist of foundation writing and math courses, as well as one course each in the arts, humanities, natural sciences, numerical and symbolic reasoning, and the social sciences—a somewhat more flexible array than many other schools. Trinity offers 40 majors and the option for students to design their own. Though the school encourages academic rigor, students are cooperative. "People would look at you funny if you were overly competitive," says a student. Because of the school's small size, research with professors is common. The college is particularly well known for its programs in the humanities, economics, and engineering.

Freshmen at Trinity can take part in the First-Year Program, which allows students to focus on a given topic with 14-15 other students as well as to learn and build student and faculty relationships. At the end of the program, the students' seminar leaders become their advisors, meaning that students are assigned to someone they know personally.

Trinity officials note that it was the first liberal arts college in the country to have a Center for Urban and Global Studies. Through the center's Cities Programs, students learn about urban issues through research projects and internships in Hartford and other cities. The center's Community Learning Initiative pairs almost half of all students with more than 80 community organizations. "We're not isolated from Hartford," explains a student. "Almost every one of us works or volunteers there."

Through the Guided Studies Program, students who have an interest in studying the history of Western thought can do so by enrolling in interdisciplinary classes; students are encouraged to make connections between the individual classes for greater understanding. The program is open to students in any major, but enrollment is limited to about 25 students per class.

Arts-oriented students can take part in the Urban Arts Semester in New York City, where students are fully immersed in the New York arts communities while taking classes, practicing their art, and interning. Trinity brings in guest speakers that focus on a different theme each week; the semester culminates with an exhibition of student-produced works.

Nationally, Trinity ranks fifth among undergraduate colleges in the number of students studying abroad; in fact, more than 40 percent of each graduating class studies abroad. There are 42 programs available for students, including a program in the Himalayas. "I chose to study in Paris because I wanted to improve my French as well as see the great artistic masterpieces in person," recalls a student.

After graduation, 18 percent of students go immediately to grad school. The Career Services office provides individual career counseling as well as an online website with summer and full-time job listings, on-campus interviews, and networking events. There's heavy counseling support for students, starting in freshman year, and 92 percent of freshmen return for their sophomore year.

Student Life

With the vast majority of students living on site, on-campus clubs are a huge part of life at Trinity—there are 104 official organizations. Some of the more popular groups include Encouraging Respect of Sexualities and Students to Unite Science and Humanitarian Interests.

Activities abound on campus. Spring Weekend is a much anticipated event where students pay $20 to revel in music. "We always have great music like Snoop Dogg," recalls one student. The first weekend after classes start, the college holds Do It Day, during which 700 students and faculty take part in service projects throughout Hartford. "I've gardened in a local park and painted a shelter," recalls a participant. "It's inspiring to do so much in just one day." The past few years have seen the rise of the Trinity Hip Hop Festival (held, of course, at the Trinity College Temple of Hip Hop), which attracts international acts. Past musicians have included The Reminders, Eekwol, Emicida, and Amkoullel.

Students say there is an "active but not dominating" Greek life on campus, with seven fraternities and seven sororities on campus (though not all of the groups have houses). Unlike some larger schools, the Greek scene doesn't consume social life at the school— students are just as likely to join the school paper or a sports team.

Trinity competes in Division III sports, with 14 men's teams and 13 women's teams. The squash teams are nationally-recognized, and the baseball, football, and crew teams are well-regarded. Intramurals include flag football, soccer, and Ultimate Frisbee. The Ferris Athletic Center houses a squash center, a 2,100-seat gymnasium, natatorium, indoor rowing facility, 5,400-square- foot fitness center, and field house.

When students venture off campus, they tend to head toward Boston, New York City, or Montreal. Students say that Hartford itself is not a terribly welcoming town, though they do venture into it for service projects and mentoring. "There's a big separation between the city and the college," notes a student.

All students are guaranteed on-campus housing, with older students getting priority based on the annual housing lottery. First-year students are assigned to their hall with other students in their first-year seminar. One of the most desirable options for upperclass students is the Summit Suites, which are recently built and have single bedrooms.

Student Body

Students describe themselves as "liberal leaning" and "primarily preppy." As one student comments, "There is no Trinity type, but we're all pretty outgoing and friendly."

More than four-fifths of students come from out of state, although many are from the Northeast and surrounding areas. Connecticut, Massachusetts, New York, New Jersey, and California are the most represented states. The school is ethnically diverse, with 21 percent of students identifying as minority.

You May Not Know

- Trinity is regarded as one of the "Little Ivies."
- Trinity has made a conscious effort to enroll more minority students since 1968 through financial aid; students

TRINITY COLLEGE

Highlights

Students
Total enrollment: 2,387
Undergrads: 2,301
Freshmen: 593
From out-of-state: 83%
From public schools: 43%
Male/Female: 52%/48%
Live on-campus: 90%
In fraternities: 20%
In sororities: 16%
Off-campus employment rating: Fair
Caucasian: 65%
African American: 7%
Hispanic: 7%
Asian / Pacific Islander: 4%
Native American: 0%
Mixed (2+ ethnicities): 3%
International: 8%

Academics
Calendar: Semester
Student/faculty ratio: 10:1
Class size 9 or fewer: 19%
Class size 10-29: 63%
Class size 30-49: 15%
Class size 50-99: 2%
Class size 100 or more: -
Six-year graduation rate: 83%
Graduates who immediately go to graduate school: 18%

Most Popular Majors
Economics
Political science
English

Admissions
Applicants: 7,720
Accepted: 2,605
Acceptance rate: 33.7%
Placed on wait list: 1,885
Enrolled from wait list: 33
Average GPA: Not reported
ACT range: 24-29
SAT Math range: 600-700
SAT Reading range: 590-690
SAT Writing range: 25-54
Top 10% of class: 69%
Top 25% of class: 90%
Top 50% of class: 100%

655

College Profiles

TRINITY COLLEGE

Admissions Criteria
Academic criteria:
Grades: ☆ ☆ ☆
Difficulty of class schedule: ☆ ☆ ☆
Class rank: ☆ ☆
Standardized test scores: ☆ ☆
Teacher recommendations: ☆ ☆
Personal statement: ☆ ☆
Non-academic criteria considered:
Interview
Extracurricular activities
Special talents, interests, abilities
Character/personal qualities
Volunteer work
Work experience
State of residency
Geographical location
Minority affiliation
Alumni relationship

Deadlines
Early Action: No
Early Decision: November 15
Regular Action: January 1 (final)
Notification of admission by: April 1
Common Application: Accepted

Financial Aid
In-state tuition: $45,300
Out-of-state tuition: $45,300
Room: $8,000
Board: $4,300
Books: $1,000
Freshmen receiving need-based aid: 39%
Undergrads rec. need-based aid: 41%
Avg. % of need met by financial aid: 100%
Avg. aid package (freshmen): $41,912
Avg. aid package (undergrads): $41,862
Avg. debt upon graduation: $18,868

School Spirit
Mascot: Bantams
Colors: Blue and gold

locked college administrators into a meeting space until they agreed to the change.

- The Long Walk is the only part of the college's original plan that was ever actually completed.

Distinguished Alumni

Edward Franklin Albee, playwright; Tom Chappell, founder of Tom's of Maine; Patricia Fargnoli, poet.

Admissions and Financial Aid

During admissions, Trinity focuses on a student's character. The committee looks for students who can demonstrate a desire to improve the community at large, and students who are committed to pluralism and tolerance will fit in well at Trinity. When submitting recommendations, the college prefers that at least one comes from an English or history teacher. Trinity is flexible about test scores, allowing students to submit SAT, any two SAT Subject Tests, or the ACT. If students submit multiple scores, the school will look at the highest ones.

The college meets the full demonstrated financial need of students. Scholarship options are flexible, with a portion of the school's money set aside specifically for scholarships.

TRINITY UNIVERSITY

Overview

Trinity University is a small, private, liberal arts university with a diverse array of programs and one of the nation's largest endowments for a school its size. Perched on a hill overlooking downtown San Antonio, the green campus is studded with red brick buildings and babbling fountains. The vast majority of students live on campus, although downtown San Antonio keeps students entertained.

Trinity's major asset is its small size. Students can get to know their professors and enjoy small classes. The large endowment and small student body translate into generous merit scholarship offerings as well as cushy dorms.

Trinity's Languages Across the Curriculum offers courses to help students improve their language skills by enrolling in upper-level courses in a variety of departments taught in a foreign language. It's an excellent opportunity for students to push their foreign language skills beyond traditional language courses and to learn more specialized vocabularies as they prepare for graduate studies or professions involving foreign language. On the negative side, the study-abroad and career services programs are not as strong.

The heavily-Christian, rather "square" student body is not for everyone—the most popular organization on campus is the student council. Still, in contrast to more study-intensive small liberal arts schools, students do strike a good balance between academic work and socializing.

Academics

Trinity offers 35 majors, with especially strong programs in communication, education, and business administration. All students must fulfill the Common Curriculum requirements, as follows: one writing course, one first-year seminar, proficiency in foreign language, math, and computer skills (can be fulfilled by high school course work and passing a computer exam), fitness education (waived if you played a sport in high school), and a senior experience (a thesis, major capstone course, project, or interdisciplinary seminar). In addition, students must take courses in the "Five Fundamental Understandings." These include cultural heritage, arts and literature, human social interaction, quantitative reasoning, and natural science and technology. "As far as requirements go, these aren't too burdensome," says a student.

Professors are highly accessible at Trinity. Freshmen are assigned advising groups of 10-15, a tradition that is appreciated, given that it facilitates introduction to a faculty advisor as well as a group of other new students. "It's as easy to talk to my professors as it is to my friends," a student comments. "They're very down to earth."

Students who can't get enough of Trinity during the year can spend their summer taking a short, in-depth course that incorporates tours and service learning in what is called an "Intensive Learning Experience." Trinity is also home to just under 30 academic honor societies, most of them major-specific.

Trinity's study-abroad office notes, "Trinity does not try to fit every student into a few pre-selected sites." Their options are indeed limited, but they do have exchange programs with five universities in Mexico, Hong Kong, Taiwan, and South Korea and affiliations with several more study-abroad providers.

The alumni career network at Trinity involves 500 alums, and the university job shadow program shepherds students through the process of setting up one-day externships. However, the program does not provide connections with potential externship mentors, making it a step behind most similar university programs. "It would be nice to have more support from alumni, but those who are involved are really committed," says a student.

TRINITY UNIVERSITY

Four-year private
Founded: 1869
San Antonio, TX
Major city
Pop. 1,359,758

Address:
1 Trinity Place
San Antonio, TX
78212-7200

Admissions:
800-TRINITY

Financial Aid:
210-999-8315

admissions@trinity.edu

www.trinity.edu

TRINITY UNIVERSITY

Students
Total enrollment: 2,525
Undergrads: 2,353
Freshmen: 621
Part-time students: 2%
From out-of-state: 25%
From public schools: 62%
Male/Female: 46%/54%
Live on-campus: 75%
In fraternities: 13%
In sororities: 12%
Off-campus employment rating: Fair
Caucasian: 60%
African American: 4%
Hispanic: 15%
Asian / Pacific Islander: 7%
Native American: 0%
Mixed (2+ ethnicities): 2%
International: 7%

Academics
Calendar: Semester
Student/faculty ratio: 9:1
Class size 9 or fewer: 19%
Class size 10-29: 69%
Class size 30-49: 11%
Class size 50-99: 1%
Class size 100 or more: -
Returning freshmen: 89%
Six-year graduation rate: 80%
Graduates who immediately go to graduate school: 25%
Graduates who immediately enter career related to major: 59%

Admissions
Applicants: 4,402
Accepted: 2,831
Acceptance rate: 64.3%
Placed on wait list: 269
Enrolled from wait list: 20
Average GPA: 3.7
ACT range: 26-31
SAT Math range: 580-670
SAT Reading range: 570-680
SAT Writing range: 15-41
Top 10% of class: 47%
Top 25% of class: 81%
Top 50% of class: 98%

Student Life

There are 130 official student organizations at Trinity. The list of the most popular options includes the Association of Student Representatives, the Greek Council, TIGER (Trinity Intra-Campus Guidance for Event Resources) Council, Trinity Multicultural Network, etc. "You won't find anything too extreme here," one student comments.

Tigerfest brings students together at the beginning of the fall semester for a week of school spirit events, including a formal gala. Christmastime heralds a heart-warming tradition: after the university's Christmas Vespers service, faculty invite students to their homes to literally eat, drink, and be merry. Trinity students also enjoy San Antonio's annual celebration of Fiesta in March. "The whole city gets involved in Fiesta," one student explains. Besides a parade, the 10 days of celebrations feature a flower show, street festivals, a beauty pageant, art showcases, and more. Recently added is a huge Trinity Tiger balloon a la Macy's Thanksgiving Day Parade.

Greek life is prominent on campus, with 12 percent of women joining five sororities and 13 percent of men joining five fraternities. "We have more than social activities," notes a student. "We also volunteer in the community quite a bit."

Eighteen Trinity sports (nine men's, nine women's) compete in Division III. Men's and women's tennis are traditionally strong, and track and swimming are also competitive. Intramurals are offered in basketball, outdoor soccer, volleyball, sand volleyball, dodgeball, wrestling, table tennis, and softball. The Outdoor Recreation office also supports numerous activities. In a recent semester students surfed the Gulf of Mexico, caved under Alamo Heights, hang glided, and backpacked in the Guadalupe Mountains.

There's plenty to do off campus. Downtown San Antonio offers an array of entertainment, dining, and shopping options. Those looking for a more "hip" town can make the 90-mile road trip to Austin. When the Tex-Mex dining in San Antonio makes you long for the real thing, you can hop across the border to Mexico. "At some point you should also visit the Alamo, and the Riverwalk is always fun for eating and just walking alongside it," one student comments.

Students are required to live on campus for three years; in fact, living on campus is integral to the Trinity experience. Freshman dorms are clustered together to foster a sense of camaraderie. Some are grouped according to studies; for example, freshmen in the "Readings from Western Culture" course can live in a residence hall with their classmates. After freshman year, students may live in learning communities centered on such interests as foreign languages and substance-free living. Dorms come equipped with cable TV, refrigerator, and microwave included, and students generally rate the facilities highly.

Student Body

Trinity students find a good balance between academics and social life. Your classmates won't be the top achievers from high school—average high school GPA is a 3.7—but they won't be slackers, either. "I've met a range of people from those who are brilliant to those who barely go to class," one student comments. Most students are Christian; however, Trinity is highly ethnically diverse. There is a very small Jewish population at the school, making up just three percent of the student body, and Muslim students may note that they are recorded on the Trinity website's demographic pie-chart as "one percent Islamic." Geographic diversity is low.

You May Not Know

- It's a tradition to throw students into Miller Fountain on their birthdays.
- When Trinity held its first classes on Sept. 23, 1869, there were five professors and seven students—talk about a good student-faculty ratio!
- San Antonio claims to be the birthplace of chili, so it's no wonder chili cook-offs are so popular on campus and off.

Distinguished Alumni

John Cornyn, Texas Senator; Kathryn Miller Haines, mystery novelist; Bob West, voice of Barney from the popular children's show.

Admissions and Financial Aid

Whether you're courting colleges or crushes, there's nothing more flattering than showing sincere interest. Trinity keeps track of students' contacts with the university through visits or emails or calls, so take advantage of these avenues. Make sure you're prepared to impress the university representative who comes to your high school; he or she might just be the one reading your application.

Trinity has deep pockets, so the school can offer a plethora of academic scholarships based on criteria from debate participation to Presbyterian Church membership to first-generation college student status. Thirty-nine percent of students receive merit-based scholarships. In addition, the school offers general merit scholarships of up to $18,000 a year. These awards are for students who have "distinguished scholastic records" and are based on factors including high school grades, classes taken, class rank, test scores, application essay, writing skills, extracurricular activities, and recommendation letters. The Distinguished Scholar Award provides full-tuition awards and a $5,000 research stipend. For this award, students must complete a Distinguished Scholar application form by December 1.

TRINITY UNIVERSITY

Highlights

Admissions Criteria
Academic criteria:
Grades: ☆ ☆ ☆
Difficulty of class schedule: ☆ ☆ ☆
Class rank: ☆ ☆ ☆
Standardized test scores: ☆ ☆
Teacher recommendations: ☆
Personal statement: ☆ ☆
Non-academic criteria considered:
Interview
Extracurricular activities
Special talents, interests, abilities
Character/personal qualities
Volunteer work
Work experience
State of residency
Geographical location
Minority affiliation
Alumni relationship

Deadlines
Early Action: January 1
Early Decision: November 1
Regular Action: February 1 (final)
Notification of admission by: April 1
Common Application: Accepted

Financial Aid
In-state tuition: $34,152
Out-of-state tuition: $34,152
Room: $6,868
Board: $4,100
Books: $1,000
Freshmen receiving need-based aid: 57%
Undergrads rec. need-based aid: 48%
Avg. % of need met by financial aid: 87%
Avg. aid package (freshmen): $29,216
Avg. aid package (undergrads): $28,521
Avg. debt upon graduation: $42,987

School Spirit
Mascot: Tigers
Colors: Maroon and white

659

College Profiles

TRUMAN STATE UNIVERSITY

Overview

Truman State University, a medium-sized public university, describes itself as Missouri's "only highly selective public university"—notwithstanding the 74 percent acceptance rate. In 2014, the *U.S. News & World Report* ranked the university 10th in the Midwest among regional universities. The college offers strong undergraduate research, internships in business and government, and a Liberal Studies Program with a detailed curriculum.

Truman State is located in Kirksville, Missouri, a community of 17,000 that boasts an eight-screen movie theater and various eateries (though not much else to do). Campus is two blocks south of town square, and most activities revolve around the slightly wooded Quad. Students can enjoy all four seasons of the year—the temperature averages of 75° in July and 25° in January—which makes for varied campus landscapes of blooming flowers in spring and an icy quad in winter.

Students who find the Midwest too insular may shy away from being located in northeastern Missouri, a long drive from any major city: it's 180 miles to Kansas City, 215 to St. Louis, and 390 to Chicago. Luckily, the college is 100 percent wireless, making it possible to connect to the Internet anywhere on campus. Students are also encouraged to study abroad, so there are roads to more culturally diverse settings.

Academics

Truman offers 48 undergraduate and nine graduate programs. All students are required to complete a capstone experience and take a comprehensive exam in their major during their senior year. Students are also required to maintain a portfolio with work that is representative of their in- and out-of-class experiences.

The Liberal Studies Program is based on a curriculum established in 1998 that incorporated Phi Beta Kappa standards. Students are required to take courses that develop the "essential skills" of writing, speech, computer literacy, and even "personal well-being." Modes of Inquiry courses offer disciplinary breadth.

Standout programs include accounting and business administration, for which the university is accredited by the Association to Advance Collegiate Schools of Business (AACSB) International. Truman is in the top 25 in the country for graduates certified by the American Chemical Society and is also strong in mathematics.

Four percent of courses taught at Truman have an enrollment of 50 students or more, so students enjoy small class sizes with more individual attention. "All of my professors know my name," says one student, "and one even gave out his cell phone number."

Truman Week is designed to help incoming students adjust to life at the university. First-years take part-time classes, go on campus and community tours, and participate in social events. "It's the time to start making friends," notes a student.

Students looking for a more challenging courseload can join the Honors Scholar program in the Arts and Sciences. Students are required to take in-depth courses across five areas and have first pick in more rigorous classes on specific topics.

Truman's McNair Program enhances diversity at the school for those interested in pursuing graduate degrees. McNair scholars are matched with faculty mentors who guide them throughout college. Students participate in pre-research internships during their sophomore year, summer research internships during their junior year, and focus on graduate placement in their senior year. There are, in fact, a number of resources for research at Truman, which 1,200 undergrads participate in every year. Truman holds an annual Student Research Conference, and students can also present papers at local conferences and publish in national journals.

According to the university, Truman ranks 13th in the country for the number of students who are able to study abroad. The university offers around 200 summer, semester, and year-long programs. Students may also participate in faculty-led programs such as "Conservation and Management of African Mammals," "Bethsaida Archaeological Dig and Mideast Study Tour," and "Globalization and Poverty in South Asia."

According to students, Truman has "great opportunities for internships." The Harry S. Truman Presidential Museum and Library Internship Program offers first-hand experience in archives, public relations, marketing, educational programming, and visitor services. These opportunities help students develop relevant skills for working in a museum or library. The Missouri Government Internship Program assists juniors and seniors with internships with a Missouri legislator, public official or state agency; and the Career Center offers the typical plethora of career, internship, and graduate school assistance including Career Week, Grad School Prep Week, and a Professional Development Institute.

Student Life

There are more than 200 student organizations at Truman State. Alpha Phi Omega (a co-ed service organization), The American Medical Student Association, and Campus Christian Fellowship are among the largest.

The student union building has two free arcade machines and LCDs for student organizations to advertise. The building is open until midnight as a central gathering place. "It's the best place for people watching," says a student.

According to the University, Truman State is a dry campus, which means alcohol is not allowed anywhere on campus—not even empty bottles in residence halls. "If you're low-key about it, you can find alcohol on campus, but it's easier to get off campus," notes a student.

The opening celebration of the school year is Dawg Fest, which ends the "dawg" days of summer with a campus-wide celebration featuring games, contests, local vendors, and music. Homecoming is always a major event at Truman State. A recent theme was iTruman, which featured a few weeks of activities, from iSTart, the kickoff festivities with food and performances; to iFrost, a cake decorating and eating contest; to iCheer, which was, of course, the pep rally. Final Blowout is Truman's big end-of-the-year event. The daylong celebration brings free food, fun, and a carnival atmosphere to campus as a way to blow off steam and relax before finals.

There are 18 fraternities and 11 sororities. According to the university, a fifth of students belong to these Greek organizations. "The Greek scene is very active, and it helps to know someone who's a member," says a student.

Truman State has 21 Division II teams. The Bulldogs are strong in women's volleyball, men's and women's soccer, and women's swim, which has won seven national titles. There are a number of intramurals, from team sports to tournaments to special events (even Texas Hold 'em!).

There isn't a great number of things to do in Kirksville, though hundreds of students do show up for Big Event. This community service day for the residents of Kirksville is an expression of appreciation for the community's support.

First-year students under the age of 21 are required to live on campus. There are seven residence halls, five of which have been

TRUMAN STATE UNIVERSITY

Students
Total enrollment: 6,237
Undergrads: 5,872
From out-of-state: 20%
Male/Female: 41%/59%
Live on-campus: 45%
In fraternities: 25%
In sororities: 17%
Off-campus employment rating: Good
Caucasian: 81%
African American: 4%
Hispanic: 3%
Asian / Pacific Islander: 2%
Native American: 0%
Mixed (2+ ethnicities): 2%
International: 6%

Academics
Calendar: Semester
Student/faculty ratio: 17:1
Class size 9 or fewer: 16%
Class size 10-29: 52%
Class size 30-49: 28%
Class size 50-99: 3%
Class size 100 or more: 1%
Six-year graduation rate: 69%
Graduates who immediately go to graduate school: 51%
Graduates who immediately enter career related to major: 41%

Most Popular Majors
Biology
Business administration
Psychology

Admissions
Applicants: 4,445
Accepted: 3,275
Acceptance rate: 73.7%
Average GPA: 3.8
ACT range: 24-29
SAT Math range: 550-650
SAT Reading range: 550-710
SAT Writing range: Not reported
Top 10% of class: 46%
Top 25% of class: 79%
Top 50% of class: 97%

661

College Profiles

TRUMAN STATE UNIVERSITY

Admissions Criteria

Academic criteria:

Grades: ☆ ☆ ☆

Difficulty of class schedule: ☆ ☆ ☆

Class rank: ☆ ☆ ☆

Standardized test scores: ☆ ☆ ☆

Teacher recommendations: ☆

Personal statement: ☆ ☆

Non-academic criteria considered:

Extracurricular activities

Special talents, interests, abilities

Character/personal qualities

Volunteer work

Work experience

Geographical location

Minority affiliation

Alumni relationship

Deadlines

Early Action: No

Early Decision: No

Regular Action: Rolling admissions

Common Application: Accepted

Financial Aid

In-state tuition: $7,096

Out-of-state tuition: $12,968

Room: Varies

Board: Varies

Books: $1,000

Freshmen receiving need-based aid: 54%

Undergrads rec. need-based aid: 51%

Avg. % of need met by financial aid: 85%

Avg. aid package (freshmen): $10,818

Avg. aid package (undergrads): $10,906

Avg. debt upon graduation: $20,777

School Spirit

Mascot: Bulldogs

Colors: Purple and white

Song: *Keep the Dreams Alive*

recently renovated. They range in size from 68 students to the nearly 700 students who occupy Centennial Hall. There are also three furnished apartment complexes. About half of students live on campus. "There's been a lot of renovating in the dorms so some are pretty nice," explains a student.

Student Body

One student describes the student body as "overall pretty motivated both academically and in activities." Another says, "There's never really a dull moment because everyone's busy doing something." As might be expected for a public university, there's always something going on. However, only about 20 percent of those busy students hail from out of state, which gives Truman low geographic diversity. Ethnic diversity is also low, with minority students making up only 11 percent of the student population.

You May Not Know

- Truman State University is named after President Harry Truman, the only President born in Missouri.
- Truman is one of only two Missouri public universities with a Phi Beta Kappa chapter.
- Truman was founded in 1867 by Joseph Baldwin; at the time, its name was the First Missouri Normal School and Commercial College.

Distinguished Alumni

John Cauthorn, Missouri senator; Jenna Fischer, actress; Mary Rhodes Russell, Missouri Supreme Court Judge; Gregg Williams, football coach for the New Orleans Saints and former head coach of the Buffalo Bills.

Admissions and Financial Aid

There is no application fee to apply to Truman, and the application for admission also serves as the application for merit-based scholarships. The admission decision is based on high school curriculum and performance, standardized test scores, special talents, and an essay. Nursing students must be accepted into the program as well as the university and go through an individual evaluation. Students who apply by December 1 get priority selection of housing and full consideration for scholarships.

Students receive notification for any of Truman State's "automatic scholarships" in the admissions letter. These awards range from $2,000 to $3,000 and are based on a Combined Ability score that is calculated based on high school rank percent or GPA percent and national percentile on the ACT or SAT. Competitive scholarships, which also do not require separate applications, include the General John J. Pershing Scholarship for full tuition, room and board, plus a $4,000 stipend. There are also talent-based awards in athletics and fine arts.

TUFTS UNIVERSITY

Overview

Sitting atop a hill in Medford/Somerville, Massachusetts, Tufts University's main campus offers a picturesque view of the surrounding city of Boston. The distinctive broccoli-like shapes of elm trees defines Uphill campus, while the large copper beech in the middle of the President's Lawn has long been a favorite spot for students to study and climb. It's not just the trees that make Tufts unique, but also the students, who are a bright and high-achieving group.

The caliber of students is reflected in the fact that this large private university is ranked 28th among national universities by the *U.S. News & World Report*. With strong offerings in both liberal arts and engineering, Tufts is especially renowned for its internationalism, with a very popular program in International Relations, strong study-abroad options, and a large international student population.

For students who appreciate excellence and diversity in course offerings, student life, and location, Tufts will be ideal. Perhaps the biggest drawback is how competitive the college is—the most recent year saw more than 16,000 applications for just 3,500 students accepted.

Academics

There are more than 70 undergraduate degree programs and thousands of courses. About 90 percent of students are in the School of Arts and Sciences and 10 percent in the School of Engineering. Besides international relations, strong programs include engineering, history, and premed. Tufts students can cross-register at a number of Boston area colleges, including Boston College, Boston University, and Brandeis University.

Those in the School of Arts and Sciences are expected to complete University, Foundation, and Distribution requirements. These include two semesters of college writing typically taken in the first year; a foreign language requirement; and a course in World—i.e. non-Western—civilizations. "The writing classes can be a necessary evil for those of us who aren't really writers," says a student.

Undergraduate research is encouraged through the Undergraduate Research Fund, annual spring Undergraduate Research and Scholarship Symposium, and even a Summer Scholars Program where students in any major can do a research apprenticeship with a faculty/clinical mentor.

Among the most highly regarded programs at Tufts is international relations (IR), which more than 600 students declare as a major. The multidisciplinary program draws from 18 departments and eight related programs and is highly diverse, with 15 percent international students. "I've learned about the Chinese economy, Egyptian uprising, and poverty in Bangladesh, all without leaving campus," notes a student. There is a demanding eight-semester language requirement, and more than 80 percent of students study abroad. Over half of IR majors received academic honors and nearly 60 percent complete a double major.

Students looking for unique classes can take nontraditional and multidisciplinary courses at Experimental College (ExCollege), which offers more than 20 new courses—often taught by professionals in the Boston area—to Tufts students each semester. Classes can include "Harry Potter and Christian Thought," "Martial Arts: History, Philosophy, and Life," and "The Objective Analysis of Baseball."

Tufts offers 10 university programs for juniors and seniors to study abroad, including the countries of Chile, China, France, and Germany. Students can also choose from hundreds of approved programs run by non-Tufts providers. Students interested in American government will appreciate the Tufts-in-Washington program, which involves studying at American University through one of three tracks and two days a week of work at an internship, plus an independent research project.

TUFTS UNIVERSITY

Four-year private
Founded: 1852
Medford, MA
Large town
Pop. 56,738

Address:
2 The Green
Medford, MA
02155

Admissions:
617-627-3170

Financial Aid:
617-627-2000

admissions.inquiry@ase.tufts.edu

www.tufts.edu

TUFTS UNIVERSITY

Students
Total enrollment: 10,837
Undergrads: 5,255
Freshmen: 1,309
Part-time students: 2%
From out-of-state: 78%
From public schools: 57%
Male/Female: 49%/51%
Live on-campus: 64%
In fraternities: 19%
In sororities: 11%
Off-campus employment rating: Excellent
Caucasian: 57%
African American: 4%
Hispanic: 7%
Asian / Pacific Islander: 10%
Native American: 0%
Mixed (2+ ethnicities): 4%
International: 7%

Academics
Calendar: Semester
Student/faculty ratio: 9:1
Class size 9 or fewer: 23%
Class size 10-29: 61%
Class size 30-49: 10%
Class size 50-99: 4%
Class size 100 or more: 2%
Returning freshmen: 97%
Six-year graduation rate: 92%

Most Popular Majors
International relations
Economics
Psychology

Admissions
Applicants: 16,378
Accepted: 3,504
Acceptance rate: 21.4%
Average GPA: Not reported
ACT range: 30-33
SAT Math range: 680-760
SAT Reading range: 670-760
SAT Writing range: 64-32
Top 10% of class: 90%
Top 25% of class: 99%
Top 50% of class: 100%

Not surprisingly for high-caliber students, Tufts boasts many prominent alumni. The university is tied with Harvard for having the most number of Fulbright scholars among Massachusetts institutions and its alumni include the founder of eBay, JPMorgan Chase CEO, Dupont CEO, and Pfizer CEO. Career Services offers plenty for students and alumni on their way to success, including individual appointments for career coaching and mock interviews.

Student Life

There are more than 150 student organizations, including a dozen a cappella groups. The largest student group on campus is the Leonard Carmichael Society, the collective group of all service organizations. It helps over 1,000 undergrads connect with the local community each year and has a staff of 85. The replica Cannon serves as a coveted location for groups and individuals to paint announcements.

Other quirky traditions include Pumpkining, a 75-year-old ritual that results in the placement of pumpkins in out-of-the way locations such as on top of statues throughout the campus. The famous (or infamous!) Naked Quad Run involves hundreds of students who strip and run a circuit around the Rez Quad (named after the reservoir that used to be there)—a fun and de-stressing event often fueled by some inhibition-lowering libations. Some students wear costumes or plastic wrap. "It's the ultimate way to get ready for finals," says a student. Before spring finals, students are typically fully clothed as they enjoy Spring Fling, a concert on the President's lawn that has brought Busta Rhymes, the Decemberists, and other music artists to campus.

Greek life is a "vital" part of campus, with 15 percent of undergraduates participating and strong traditions going back more than 150 years. There are 16 fraternities and sororities, including nine fraternities, three sororities, one co-ed independent fraternity, and three culturally-based citywide Greek organizations.

Tufts has 27 Division III teams and two Division I sports—squash and sailing—the sailing team has won more championships than any other team, while men's squash is also highly ranked. Tufts' first national title was in 2010 for men's lacrosse. Intramural sports include badminton, wiffleball, lacrosse, and many more. There's even a Quidditch team named The Tufflepuffs.

The bars and clubs in Medford and Boston—especially the relatively close-to-campus Lansdowne Street—are popular off-campus jaunts for students. Boston, of course, offers professional athletics, museums and cultural events, and access to many other colleges. Students can also spend weekends at the Loj, a retreat center in Woodstock, New Hampshire that offers beautiful hiking, canoeing, skiing, and more. "You should visit the Loj at least once," notes a student.

Students are required to live on campus for the first two years. First-years choose from a dozen residence halls, including four designated exclusively for freshman; sophomores have more choices, and two halls are "seniors only." There are many single-sex housing opportunities for women, and several arts and culture special-interest houses. But perhaps the most important distinction in housing is whether one lives "uphill" or "downhill," a physical and metaphorical separation with roots that go back to the late 19th century.

Student Body

Tufts students describe themselves as liberal, and say this is "not surprising given [their] location." To match the focus on international relations, there is a sizable international population of seven percent. There is plenty of diversity both ethnic and geographically, with 25 percent minority students and 78 percent of students hailing from out of state. There are a large number of diversity initiatives at Tufts, including the Group of Six, which includes The Africana, Asian American, International, Latino, LGBT, and Women's Centers.

You May Not Know

- The Fletcher School of Law and Diplomacy at Tufts is the oldest graduate school of international relations in the country.
- Charles Tufts, a Boston businessman, donated 20 acres of land which was worth $20,000 in the 1840s to start the university.
- Tufts' singular athletic mascot, Jumbo the elephant, hails back to 1885, when P.T. Barnum, the circus showman who was an early trustee and benefactor of Tufts, donated the stuffed hide of Jumbo to the university after he was killed by an oncoming train in Ontario, Canada.

Distinguished Alumni

Ellen Kullman, CEO of DuPont; Pierre Omidyar, eBay founder; William Richardson, Governor of New Mexico and former U.S. Ambassador to the United Nations; Meredith Vieira, *Today Show* co-host.

Admissions and Financial Aid

For the class of 2018, Tufts received a near-record number of applications—16,378 applications. According to Dean Lee Coffin, "we assess 'match' and look for students who genuinely want to make a difference." Dean Coffin recommends that applicants use their authentic, unique voice in applying and speak to why Tufts is an ideal fit for them. Standardized testing score requirements vary depending on the school students apply to—for example, the School of Engineering requires two SAT Subject Tests, one in math and one in science.

Tufts meets 100 percent of the full demonstrated need of all admitted students. There is no merit aid, except for National Merit Scholarship Corporation awards and ROTC program scholarships. Students receive more than $90 million in need- and merit-based aid, with an average of $35,033 per student.

TUFTS UNIVERSITY

Highlights

Admissions Criteria
Academic criteria:
Grades: ☆ ☆ ☆
Difficulty of class schedule: ☆ ☆ ☆
Class rank: ☆ ☆ ☆
Standardized test scores: ☆ ☆
Teacher recommendations: ☆ ☆ ☆
Personal statement: ☆ ☆ ☆
Non-academic criteria considered:
Interview
Extracurricular activities
Special talents, interests, abilities
Character/personal qualities
Volunteer work
Work experience
State of residency
Geographical location
Minority affiliation
Alumni relationship

Deadlines
Early Action: No
Early Decision: November 1 and January 1
Regular Action: January 1 (final)
Notification of admission by: April 1
Common Application: Accepted

Financial Aid
In-state tuition: $45,590
Out-of-state tuition: $45,590
Room: $6,630
Board: $5,550
Books: $800
Freshmen receiving need-based aid: 40%
Undergrads rec. need-based aid: 40%
Avg. % of need met by financial aid: 100%
Avg. aid package (freshmen): $35,033
Avg. aid package (undergrads): $34,802
Avg. debt upon graduation: $23,068

School Spirit
Mascot: Jumbos
Colors: Brown and blue

TULANE
UNIVERSITY

Four-year private
Founded: 1834
New Orleans, LA
Major city
Pop. 360,740

Address:
6823 St. Charles Av-
enue, 210 Gibson Hall
New Orleans, LA
70118

Admissions:
800-873-9283

Financial Aid:
800-335-3210

undergrad.admission@
tulane.edu

www.tulane.edu

TULANE UNIVERSITY

Overview

Tulane University is an internationally acclaimed private university located only four miles from downtown New Orleans. This means many things for students: not only are Jazz fest and Mardi Gras at your doorstep, but the university emphasizes public service and research applied creatively and compassionately to the problems of the city and the surrounding community.

Along with rigorous academics, Tulane offers extensive internship, study abroad, and independent research opportunities. Students fill their free time with sports, Greek life, public service clubs, and the energetic art scene of the city.

Academics

Foundational studies at Tulane University are based on the Newcomb-Tulane Core curriculum, which emphasizes public service and applicable, integrated learning. The program begins freshman year with the Tulane Interdisciplinary Experience Seminar (TIDES), and ends with the senior Capstone Experience, which requires students to undertake a significant applied project relating to their major. Along the way, Tulane students must take a foreign language, a cultural knowledge class, scientific inquiry, and writing.

Beyond the basics, Tulane University offers 169 majors with notably strong programs in business, Latin American studies, and health sciences for pre-meds.

With most class sizes generally under 30, Tulane is both challenging and supportive; it is easy to get to know professors, and professors in turn expect a lot from their students. "Professors certainly make the extra effort," says a student. Exceptional admits are enrolled in the even more rigorous Honors Program, which includes special honors classes, seminars, colloquia, advising, and research opportunities. Women have the unique opportunity to join the Newcomb Scholars program, which is a collaborative learning experience with four years of research, seminars, mentorship, and experiential learning opportunities.

Integrating the community service focus of Tulane into its coursework, students are encouraged to undertake a CPS Independent Study or Honors Thesis. By designing their own courses with a faculty sponsor and collaborating with the community in a service project, students can fulfill their second tier graduation requirement. The project must "apply academic knowledge and critical thinking skills to meet genuine community needs."

Even those who do not opt to write a thesis or pursue independent work are encouraged to get involved with the countless research centers on campus. As just one example, the Center for Bioenvironmental Research studies the aftermath of Hurricane Katrina in the Gulf Coast and New Orleans. "We still feel the effects of Hurricane Katrina," explains a student.

Tulane has an extensive study-abroad program that arranges both semester-long and year-long trips to collaborating universities. These span a broad path from the liberal arts or development studies track at the University of Ghana, to the National Academy of Film and Television in Prague, to OTS/Duke Field Semester in Global Health and Tropical Medicine in San José.

To help students prepare for life after Tulane, exploratory career services and pre-professional advising are coordinated through the Career Center, which arranges internships and almost constant academic advising workshops. According to the university, acceptance rates into law schools and medical schools are higher than the national average.

Student Life

Not surprisingly, New Orleans is an integral part of Tulane student life, with its lively dining, entertainment, music, and arts scenes. "We have the best food in the country here," boasts one student. "Even the sandwiches are amazing." The university community always joins in the fun of Mardi Gras and Jazzfest. Further afield, Tularians take road trips to the Gulf Coast, Houston, Atlanta, and Memphis. That is not to say, however, that on-campus life is any less rewarding. Tulane University has 250 official student organizations, with the most popular being Amnesty International, Business and Law Society, and the Community Action Council. Forty percent of women and 26 percent of men join a sorority or fraternity, making Greek life an integral part of campus activity. "Bars and Greek events are the best party scenes," comments a student.

The Tulane school year is bookended by two raucous events, beginning with Homecoming and ending with the Wave Goodbye Party. Homecoming is a full week of festivities, concerts, and parties leading up to the well-attended football game. At the end of the year, the university presidents host a party for the graduates in Tulane's main quad, complete with New Orleans food, music, and dancing.

Thirteen sports (six men's, seven women's) compete in Division I, with football being competitive, but baseball and women's volleyball gaining national attention. There are 37 competitive club sports such as fencing, soccer, and horse riding, with intramural sports like badminton and volleyball for additional fun. Those students who are athletic but not inclined toward competition may want to check out the well equipped Reily Recreation center, which has an Olympic sized pool. Outdoor Programs organizes at least five trips per quarter to areas near the Gulf Coast.

When it is time to relax and (maybe) get a good night's sleep, all freshman head to their on-campus dorms. More than 50 percent of students live off campus in New Orleans. Those that stay on Tulane grounds enter a housing lottery.

Student Body

Tulane students are a diverse bunch united by an interest in scholarship and public service. In addition to 23 percent of students that identify as minorities (including six percent Hispanic and 10 percent African American), there are also large Jewish and Catholic populations. More than half of students come from public schools. This racial diversity is matched by high geographic diversity with only 13 percent of the student body hailing from Louisiana. Just a glance at the events of the Office of Multicultural Affairs shows how supportive the community is, with cultural shows, religious services of all shapes and sizes, and safe zone training camps.

You May Not Know

- Tulane was forced to close during the Fall of 2005 due to Hurricane Katrina; but after a proactive rebuilding plan and a renewed devotion to the city of New Orleans, over 93 percent of students returned.
- Tulane is a member of the Association of American Universities, a prestigious group of 63 universities with "pre-

TULANE UNIVERSITY

Highlights

Students
Total enrollment: 13,486
Undergrads: 8,423
Part-time students: 24%
From out-of-state: 87%
Male/Female: 42%/58%
Live on-campus: 44%
In fraternities: 26%
In sororities: 40%
Off-campus employment rating: Good
Caucasian: 70%
African American: 10%
Hispanic: 6%
Asian / Pacific Islander: 4%
Native American: 0%
Mixed (2+ ethnicities): 3%
International: 3%

Academics
Calendar: Semester
Student/faculty ratio: 9:1
Class size 9 or fewer: 27%
Class size 10-29: 56%
Class size 30-49: 12%
Class size 50-99: 4%
Class size 100 or more: 1%
Returning freshmen: 89%

Most Popular Majors
Business/marketing
Social science
Biological/life sciences

Admissions
Applicants: 30,080
Accepted: 8,203
Acceptance rate: 27.3%
Placed on wait list: 3,483
Enrolled from wait list: Not reported
Average GPA: 3.5
ACT range: 29-32
SAT Math range: 620-710
SAT Reading range: 630-720
SAT Writing range: 39-50
Top 10% of class: 52%
Top 25% of class: 83%
Top 50% of class: 97%

667

College Profiles

TULANE UNIVERSITY

Admissions Criteria

Academic criteria:
Grades: ☆ ☆ ☆
Difficulty of class schedule: ☆ ☆ ☆
Class rank: ☆ ☆ ☆
Standardized test scores: ☆ ☆ ☆
Teacher recommendations: ☆ ☆
Personal statement: ☆ ☆
Non-academic criteria considered:
Interview
Extracurricular activities
Special talents, interests, abilities
Character/personal qualities
Volunteer work
Work experience
State of residency
Alumni relationship

Deadlines

Early Action: November 15
Early Decision: No
Regular Action: January 15 (final)
Notification of admission by: April 1
Common Application: Not accepted

Financial Aid

In-state tuition: $46,930
Out-of-state tuition: $46,930
Room: $6,862
Board: $5,150
Books: $1,200
Freshmen receiving need-based aid: 40%
Undergrads rec. need-based aid: 40%
Avg. % of need met by financial aid: 91%
Avg. aid package (freshmen): $31,130
Avg. aid package (undergrads): $32,387
Avg. debt upon graduation: $35,100

School Spirit

Mascot: Green Wave
Colors: Olive green and sky blue
Song: *Tulane Fight Song*

eminent programs of graduate and professional education and scholarly research."

- In 2000, the Tulane Center for Gene Therapy became the first American institute to focus on adult stem cell research.

Distinguished Alumni

David Filo, co-founder of Yahoo!; Shirley Ann Grau, Pulitzer-Prize winning author; Lisa P. Jackson, United States Environmental Protection Agency (EPA) Administrator; Luther Terry, former U.S. Surgeon General.

Admissions and Financial Aid

In 2013 Tulane University received 30,000 applications and accepted only 27 percent of them, according to the university. Class rank is especially important, as are school counselor recommendations and standardized test scores. Additional teacher recommendations are only optional, though highly recommended.

Tulane meets approximately 91 percent of demonstrated need. Unlike many private universities of its caliber, a full third of students also receive merit-based aid. Tulane awards scholarships from $7,500 per year to the full-tuition Dean's Honors Scholarship. Most are awarded upon admission (though application is necessary for the Community Service and Dean's Scholarships), and special scholarships are available for Louisiana Residents.

UNION COLLEGE

Overview

Academically, Union College has much to offer. A small private college, Union balances strong liberal arts with rigorous engineering programs. The academic calendar is based on trimesters, which gives students the chance to take three-week mini term courses off campus (mainly abroad), during winter and summer break. For those interested in continuing their education beyond college, Union has several accelerated programs that combine undergraduate and graduate degrees, including programs for medical school and law school.

Union College's location is in downtown Schenectady, a declining city in upstate New York (150 miles north of New York City). There's not much for students to do off campus; however, the campus itself is a lovely mixture of woodlands, formal gardens, and old-fashioned brownstone and red brick buildings.

Union's recently-instated Minerva House system creates a sense of campus cohesion through several residences that bring together the upperclassmen who live there with faculty and underclassmen who attend events there. The Minervas each have their own house budget to be spent at the student residents' discretion on social and academic events. On a more materialistic level, the Minervas are newly-revamped buildings that offer cushy living spaces. In general, housing at Union is high-quality. The Inn is a unique dorm in that it was at one time a hotel.

Although Union is a rather secluded, uneventful place to spend four years, the college attracts students with its accelerated programs, innovative Minerva House system, small classes, and academic excellence.

Academics

Union follows a trimester system, so classes begin later than most schools in the fall, and winter break lasts six weeks. Three-week mini term courses offered during winter and summer breaks whisk students to exotic locations to earn credit with Union professors. Students say one "downside" to the trimester is that their class schedule doesn't mesh well with other friends from high school who attend semester-based colleges.

Union offers 32 majors, with especially strong programs in mechanical engineering, political science, and psychology. All Union students have to complete challenging core and distribution requirements, but they are "not insurmountable," says a student. Freshmen must take a First-Year Preceptorial, which is a year-long, interdisciplinary with activities outside of class (lectures, trips, and other related activities). The second phase of the core is the Sophomore Research Seminar, in which students develop a topic that culminates in a 12-18 page research paper. In addition to these, students must take five courses from at least two different divisions that qualify to fulfill the Writing Across the Curriculum requirement and complete a senior writing experience, for example, a senior thesis. Distribution requirements entail courses in social sciences, humanities, linguistic and cultural competency, quantitative and mathematical reasoning, and science and technology. The Cluster Requirement compels students to take three courses in at least two departments organized around a particular theme.

The annual Steinmetz Symposium underscores Union's commitment to undergraduate research and achievement. Classes are cancelled for a full day so that students can participate in and attend presentations, exhibits, and performances by their peers.

Alum Michael S. Rapaport funds the Ethics Across the Curriculum Initiative, a resource for professors in any department seeking to incorporate an ethical dimension in their courses. Options include infusion of ethics in everyday lessons, special events, or invitations to relevant speakers who can come to campus.

If you like one-stop shopping, Union has several programs that allow you to combine an accelerated professional degree with your undergraduate work. In cooperation with Albany Medical College and Albany Law School, Union offers accelerated medi-

UNION COLLEGE

Four-year private
Founded: 1795
Schenectady, NY
Medium city
Pop. 66,273

Address:
807 Union Street
Schenectady, NY
12308

Admissions:
888-843-6688

Financial Aid:
518-388-6123

admissions@union.
edu

www.union.edu

UNION COLLEGE

Students
Total enrollment: 2,241
Undergrads: 2,241
Freshmen: 600
Part-time students: 1%
From out-of-state: 63%
From public schools: 64%
Male/Female: 54%/46%
Live on-campus: 89%
In fraternities: 38%
In sororities: 38%
Off-campus employment rating: Good
Caucasian: 75%
African American: 4%
Hispanic: 7%
Asian / Pacific Islander: 6%
Native American: 0%
Mixed (2+ ethnicities): 2%
International: 6%

Academics
Calendar: Trimester
Student/faculty ratio: 10:1
Class size 9 or fewer: 21%
Class size 10-29: 67%
Class size 30-49: 12%
Class size 50-99: -
Class size 100 or more: -
Returning freshmen: 94%
Six-year graduation rate: 83%
Graduates who immediately go to graduate school: 30%
Graduates who immediately enter career related to major: 60%

Most Popular Majors
Biology
Psychology
Political science

Admissions
Applicants: 5,565
Accepted: 2,127
Acceptance rate: 38.2%
Placed on wait list: 851
Enrolled from wait list: 14
Average GPA: 3.5
ACT range: 28-32
SAT Math range: 620-700
SAT Reading range: 590-680
SAT Writing range: 20-54
Top 10% of class: 58%
Top 25% of class: 79%
Top 50% of class: 97%

cal and legal degrees. These are named "Leadership in Medicine" and "Law and Public Policy," respectively. The college also offers five-year programs for master's of arts in teaching, MBAs, MBAs in healthcare management, and master's of arts in Latin American studies in conjunction with Georgetown.

Union has impressive study-abroad offerings, with programs in 27 countries. Pre-meds will be intrigued by the National Health Systems term abroad, which examines healthcare in the United States, Canada, Britain, and Denmark.

Union College belongs to the Liberal Arts Career Network, which allows access to internship listings from 31 top liberal arts colleges. The career center also offers eRecruiting, an online database of job and internship opportunities specifically for Union students.

Student Life

The vast majority of Union students live on campus, making the social life lively. There are 115 official student organizations. The most popular groups include the American Society of Mechanical Engineers, Colleges Against Cancer, and the outing club.

Early in the spring, Springfest brings well known musicians to campus for a free outdoor concert, and in May, students don their formal wear to turn peaceful Jackson's Garden into the site of a bustling "Party in the Garden." A somewhat more low-key annual tradition is the Relay for Life, an all-night event which raises money to fight cancer.

With 13 social frats, eight frat houses, six social sororities, and three sorority houses on campus, Greek life is fairly prominent. "The big party scene is at the frats," says a student.

Of Union's 25 varsity sports, only ice hockey competes in Division I. The rest are Division III. Men's and women's ice hockey are the most popular competitive sports on campus. Union also has a range of intramural sports, including quirky options like curling, fencing, and broomball.

Off-campus dining is 5-10 minutes away by car; walking is not a viable option. The town of Schenectady is quaint and quiet. For those who make time to venture off campus, good ski locations abound in the area and Montreal and NYC make manageable road trip destinations.

The Minerva House system, inaugurated in 2004, is a unique aspect of life at Union. The seven Minerva houses are residences for upperclassmen, but they are also meeting spaces for students and faculty alike. Beyond living spaces, the houses have classrooms and lounges. The Minervas host academic and social events open to the whole community and students living there administer their own house budgets. Freshmen live in separate housing. Overall, dorms are spacious and comfortable—especially the newly-renovated Minervas.

Student Body

Students comment that there are many "preppies" on campus who hail mainly from the Northeast. Others don't notice home state alliances as much as just concentrating on their studies. But, there are those students who are focused on "partying hard." Much of the student body is dedicated to athletics, either as participants or as committed fans.

Ethnic diversity with 19 percent minorities is high, and geographic diversity with 63 percent from out of state is moderate.

You May Not Know

- In 1830, Union was counted along with Harvard, Princeton, and Yale as one of the "Big Four."
- According to Union, Jackson's Garden "is the oldest continuously cultivated garden on a college or university campus in the U.S."
- It's a tradition for students to paint a 15th century Chinese stone lion given to the campus as a gift in 1875.

Distinguished Alumni

Baruch Blumberg, Nobel Prize-winning physiologist; Richard K. Templeton, President and CEO of Texas Instruments; Kate White, editor-in-chief of *Cosmopolitan*.

Admissions and Financial Aid

According to the admissions office, the college officials look for students who have high grades and who challenge themselves with Honors and AP courses. The college also seeks students who "can participate enthusiastically and constructively in the life of the college." The admissions office "strongly" advises students to visit the campus.

Merit scholarship offerings are limited. They range from $5,000 to $10,000 a year and do not require a separate application.

UNION COLLEGE

Highlights

Admissions Criteria
Academic criteria:
Grades: ☆ ☆ ☆
Difficulty of class schedule: ☆ ☆ ☆
Class rank: ☆ ☆ ☆
Standardized test scores: ☆ ☆
Teacher recommendations: ☆ ☆
Personal statement: ☆ ☆
Non-academic criteria considered:
Interview
Extracurricular activities
Special talents, interests, abilities
Character/personal qualities
Volunteer work
Work experience
Geographical location
Minority affiliation
Alumni relationship

Deadlines
Early Action: No
Early Decision: November 15
Regular Action: January 15 (final)
Notification of admission by: April 1
Common Application: Accepted

Financial Aid
In-state tuition: $46,314
Out-of-state tuition: $46,314
Room: $6,285
Board: $5,178
Books: $1,500
Freshmen receiving need-based aid: 50%
Undergrads rec. need-based aid: 48%
Avg. % of need met by financial aid: 98%
Avg. aid package (freshmen): $36,912
Avg. aid package (undergrads): $36,295
Avg. debt upon graduation: $27,336

School Spirit
Mascot: Dutchmen/Dutchwomen
Colors: Garnet and grey

Four-year public
Founded: 1954
USAF Academy, CO
Major city
Pop. 426,388

Address:
HQ USAFA/A9A, 2304
Cadet Drive, Suite
3800
USAF Academy, CO
80840

Admissions:
800-443-9266

rr_webmail@usafa.edu

www.usafa.edu

UNITED STATES AIR FORCE ACADEMY

Overview

On the eastern side of the Rampart Range in the Rockies, the 18,000-acre United States Air Force Academy campus sits just eight miles north of Colorado Springs. The Cadet Area, which is arranged around the "Terrazzo" square pavilion, features totally unique, modern architecture—buildings are intended to resemble air- or spacecraft.

The mid-sized USAFA is a completely unique university as well, given its special purpose as the training center for U.S. Air Force cadets. An education at the USAFA offers tremendous benefits but demands huge commitments from its students, academically, physically, professionally, and in terms of sheer years. In exchange for free tuition, extensive character development and leadership training, and the financial support of the Armed Forces until well past retirement, cadets will embark on a highly-regimented four-year program of grueling physical and military training and high-level academics.

All areas of life in the Cadet Wing (as the student body is called) are governed by the "four-class" system, which places first year cadets as "fourth class" cadets (second year cadets are "third class," and so on until the final "first class" or "firsties" year). Each class of cadets must adhere strictly to a rigid set of guidelines dictating behavior. According to the academy, cadets are required "to display prompt obedience, proper conduct, unfailing courtesy, and unqualified honor," and keep "personal appearance, uniforms, room, and equipment neat at all times." During the difficult and most restrictive "fourth class" year, students will sacrifice all comfort and choice and nearly all freedoms. Everything, from classes and training to meals ("breakfast formation"), mandatory study time ("academic call to quarters"), and lights out, is rigidly scheduled. And then cadets will serve at least five years after graduating.

Academics

Education at the USAFA covers four areas: academics, professional military education, character development, and physical education. The program begins with five weeks of Basic Cadet Training (BCT) prior to the beginning of the first year: BCT begins the transition from civilian to military life and puts cadets through military orientation, extensive physical and mental conditioning, weapon skills, and field training. BCT is probably the most demanding period of time at the academy, followed by the "fourth class" year (fourth class cadets are called "doolies," although the USAFA claims cadets don't use that term). This year is the most difficult, not only because cadets are still adapting to military life but also because cadets' behavior, schedules, and even walking routes are most strictly governed. "If you can survive the fourth class year, you really can survive anything," says a student.

Cadets' first two years are largely spent in military training, both in the classroom and outside. They must complete the four-year weekly Cadet Professional Military Education (CPME) course, and the extensive core curriculum courses in science, engineering, social sciences, and the humanities (which accounts for about 60 percent of the academic courseload). The final two years are dedicated to higher-level military training, CPME, and completing one of the academy's 32 broad divisional, disciplinary, or multidisciplinary majors. Summers are spent in two three-week training programs, ranging from combat survival to parachute training, and focusing on leadership training in the final years. All cadets receive a Bachelor of Science degree and are commissioned as second lieutenants in the Air Force.

Academics at the USAFA are demanding and competitive. In 2007, 28 students were accused of cheating. "It's not an excuse, but the pressure to perform is very high," one student explains. Classes tend to be in seminar format, averaging 10 to 19 students, and courses with pre-professional training are offered. The strongest majors include management and various engineering programs (aeronautical, astronautical, electrical, civil, and mechanical). Students are evaluated based on both their academic and military training performance.

As part of the Academy Scholars Program, the most highly academically qualified cadets in each class can participate in a unique curriculum and learning community: small groups of students are enrolled together in special, interactive classes that replace the core curriculum. "It's the best possible experience to have that much individual attention," notes a student.

The Cadet Semester Exchange Abroad Program (CSEAP) allows second-class cadets to spend fall semester at the air force academies of Canada, Chile, France, Germany, Spain, and Japan, while the Cadet Semester Study Abroad Program (CSSAP) provides for a semester of foreign language study at civilian universities in China, Morocco, or Russia.

All cadets will serve at least five years in the Air Force after graduating; about 60 percent will enter flight careers as pilots or navigators, while others will work in space and missile operations and space engineering. "It's a plus to know exactly what you're going to be doing after graduating," one student comments.

Graduate study is permitted in areas the Air Force deems necessary. Some graduates receive scholarships to continue on to civilian grad schools immediately after school; the top 15 percent of each class is eligible for master's degree programs after three years of active duty. About four percent of graduates may continue directly to medical, dental, or nursing school; a similarly small number are permitted to attend law school.

Student Life

Social life, athletics, and extracurriculars are governed by the same rigorous protocol that directs study and military training. Students may participate in about 75 extracurricular activities, which include the Cadet Ski Club, Chorale, Drum and Bugle Corps, or Falconry—training and caring for the live falcons featured at football games. Popular events on campus include Parents' Weekend (one of the few times lowerclass cadets can have visitors), intercollegiate athletic events, and the co-ed dances organized by the Cadet Wing social committees. It probably goes without saying that the USAFA has no Greek system.

In addition to the physical education classes they are required to take, all cadets must participate in athletics, whether on one of the Falcons' 10 women's and 17 men's varsity NCAA Division I teams or in intramural sports. Of the intercollegiate teams, boxing, rugby, men's basketball, and men's ice hockey are the strongest; the Air Force's rivalries with Navy and Army draw plenty of attention. In intramurals, squads compete against one another in standard sports like flag football and basketball or the Air Force's own sport, flickerball. "Because everyone is so fit, even intramurals can get pretty competitive," says a student.

Travel off campus is restricted and requires permission. Fourth-class cadets don't leave campus unless it is for athletic events or scheduled Cadet Wing activities; instead, they spend their little spare time at Arnold Hall for games, dancing, and entertainment. "We just bide our time until we have more privileges," notes a student. Upperclass cadets' off-campus time is subject to individual and squad performance. "Firsties" can enjoy restaurants, theaters,

UNITED STATES AIR FORCE ACADEMY

Students
Total enrollment: 4,120
Undergrads: 4,120
Freshmen: 981
From out-of-state: 91%
Male/Female: 78%/22%
Live on-campus: 100%
Caucasian: 65%
African American: 7%
Hispanic: 9%
Asian / Pacific Islander: 9%
Native American: 1%
Mixed (2+ ethnicities): 7%
International: 1%

Academics
Calendar: Semester
Student/faculty ratio: 8:1
Class size 9 or fewer: 10%
Class size 10-29: 88%
Class size 30-49: 2%
Class size 50-99: -
Class size 100 or more: -
Returning freshmen: 93%
Six-year graduation rate: 80%
Graduates who immediately enter career related to major: 100%

Most Popular Majors
Engineering
Behavioral sciences
Management

Admissions
Applicants: 12,274
Accepted: 1,214
Acceptance rate: 9.9%
Average GPA: 3.9
ACT range: 28-32
SAT Math range: 620-710
SAT Reading range: 590-680
SAT Writing range: Not reported
Top 10% of class: 62%
Top 25% of class: 88%
Top 50% of class: 97%

673

UNITED STATES AIR FORCE ACADEMY

Admissions Criteria

Academic criteria:
Grades: ☆ ☆ ☆
Difficulty of class schedule: ☆ ☆ ☆
Class rank: ☆ ☆ ☆
Standardized test scores: ☆ ☆ ☆
Teacher recommendations: ☆ ☆ ☆
Personal statement: ☆ ☆ ☆
Non-academic criteria considered:
Interview
Extracurricular activities
Special talents, interests, abilities
Character/personal qualities
Volunteer work
Work experience
State of residency
Geographical location
Minority affiliation
Alumni relationship

Deadlines

Early Action: No
Early Decision: No
Regular Action: Rolling admissions
Common Application: Not accepted

Financial Aid

Tuition-free school
Room: Varies
Board: Varies
Books: Varies
Avg. aid package (freshmen): N/A
Avg. aid package (undergrads): N/A

School Spirit

Mascot: Falcons
Colors: Blue and silver
Song: *Air Force Song*

and nightlife in Colorado Springs; and if somehow their need for physical activity isn't satiated, Colorado and the Rockies offer lots of opportunities for skiing, mountain biking, and whitewater rafting.

Cadets are housed in standard double rooms in Vandenberg and Sijan Halls. Note that according to the academy "there is a proper location for everything you're allowed to have in your room and you'll be expected to keep your room in perfect order." Cadets are divided into four groups, each consisting of ten squadrons. Cadets take meals with their squadrons.

Student Body

Ethnic diversity at the USAFA is fairly high, and nearly all cadets are from out of state. Cadets describe themselves as "patriotic," and tend to be "conservative." Campus is overtly Christian, but that has toned down following allegations of anti-Semitism and lack of accommodation for other religions.

Campus is also predominantly male, and sexual harassment and misogynistic attitudes "are still pervasive;" the atmosphere, while not impossible, is "not entirely welcoming for women." A Sexual Assault Response Coordinator is on duty 24/7.

You May Not Know

- The Air Force Drum and Bugle Corps has won 20 of the 30 Inter-Service Academy Drum and Bugle Corps Competitions since their reassignment to the Academy in 1972.
- The first live falcon at USAFA was named "Mach 1." The official mascot is also named "Mach 1."
- The word "doolie" comes from the Greek word for "slave" or "servant."

Distinguished Alumni

Frederick D. Gregory, first African-American to pilot a space vehicle; Shawna Rochelle Kimbrell, first African-American woman to fly in combat; Charles E. Phillips, Jr., President of Oracle Corporation; Gregg Popovich, head coach, San Antonio Spurs; Richard T. Schlosberg, former CEO of the *Los Angeles Times*; Chesley Sullenberger, US Airways pilot who safely landed in the Hudson River.

Admissions and Financial Aid

Appointments to the USAFA are made to applicants who demonstrate high academic achievement, leadership, involvement in athletics, and "good moral character." Only unmarried U.S. citizens are eligible.

Cadets do not pay tuition, and instead receive a very small monthly salary sufficient to cover books, supplies, uniforms, and food.

UNITED STATES COAST GUARD ACADEMY

UNITED STATES COAST GUARD ACADEMY

Four-year public
Founded: 1876
New London, CT
Large town
Pop. 27,569

Address:
15 Mohegan Avenue
New London, CT
06320

Admissions:
800-883-8724

admissions@uscga.
edu

www.cga.edu

Overview

As one of five U.S. Armed Forces training academies, the U.S. Coast Guard Academy is undoubtedly a military organization. Cadets receive rigorous academic, military, and physical training that is largely geared toward their future careers as officers in the Coast Guard. Discipline and obedience are key words: cadets' schedules are strictly regimented, even down to breakfast, lights out, and study time.

Coast Guard cadets are organized into a four class system, with first-class cadets (equivalent to seniors) top-ranked. Fourth-class cadets (equivalent to freshmen) must defer to their third-class mentors and upperclass leaders. It's a major commitment: military rigor extends to academics, and so cadets must work very hard in class; military training taxes cadets, both physically and psychologically; and after Commencement, graduates will serve at least five years in the Coast Guard. But the USCGA is also the smallest of the five U.S. military academies, and as such, it can offer its students a freer, friendlier, more personal environment—what the Academy itself calls "holistic education." Classes are small, and courses of study are easily customized according to interests or skills.

Life at the USCGA is governed as much by tradition and history as by military rulebooks, and so cadets get regular breaks from military austerity. Cadets can even spend limited time off base on weekends and can take advantage of New London, the historic Connecticut waterfront town adjacent to the 110-acre green campus on the Thames River. Ultimately, an education in the USCGA prepares cadets for a demanding but rewarding career in the Coast Guard: 85 percent of graduates elect to serve for longer than their required four years.

Academics

Education at the USCGA is a mix of academic preparation and military training. A cadet's education will begin the summer before his or her fourth-class year with the Coast Guard equivalent of boot camp—Swab Summer. This seven week "military indoctrination" orients cadets to military life and physical conditioning and introduces them to concepts of seamanship; the summer includes a week on the U.S. Coast Guard *Cutter Eagle*, or *USCGC Eagle*. This sail-training tall ship (meaning a traditionally-rigged vessel) serves as the Coast Guard's "seagoing classroom," allowing cadets hands-on experience manning and navigating a ship. "No matter how fit you are, you will feel pain during Swab Summer," says a student.

After Swab Summer, cadets begin their fourth-class year. As fourth-class cadets, they are officially designated "followers," and are assigned a third-class mentor. Fourth- and third-class cadets spend most of their time in military training, completing the core academic and physical requirements and preparing for and applying to one of the USCGA's eight majors (the strongest of which are civil engineering and government). The academic core courses are extensive; they entail two courses each in engineering, writing, American government/history, calculus, physics, chemistry, and a course each in criminal justice, maritime law enforcement, philosophy, statistics, marine science, macroeconomic principles, and leadership and organizational behavior. "It would be nice to have a little more freedom to select classes," notes a student.

Cadets must also complete the Health and Physical Education Program core, which includes classes ranging from lifetime fitness, personal defense, swimming, and "professional rescuer." Cadets will spend the summer before their third-class year at sea on a Coast Guard cutter.

In their final two years, cadets transition from "followers" to "leaders," and as such, spend the summer before their second-class year in various leadership programs, potentially training incoming cadets at Swab Summer, and providing special training in

UNITED STATES COAST GUARD ACADEMY

Students

Total enrollment: 967
Undergrads: 967
Freshmen: 248
From out-of-state: 97%
From public schools: 79%
Male/Female: 68%/32%
Live on-campus: 100%
Caucasian: 71%
African American: 3%
Hispanic: 12%
Asian / Pacific Islander: 5%
Native American: 1%
Mixed (2+ ethnicities): 5%
International: 2%

Academics

Calendar: Semester
Student/faculty ratio: 8:1
Class size 9 or fewer: 9%
Class size 10-29: 90%
Class size 30-49: 1%
Class size 50-99: -
Class size 100 or more: -
Returning freshmen: 93%
Six-year graduation rate: 84%
Graduates who immediately enter career
　related to major: 100%

Most Popular Majors

Marine/environmental sciences
Government
Management

Admissions

Applicants: 1,982
Accepted: 315
Acceptance rate: 15.9%
Placed on wait list: 96
Enrolled from wait list: 26
Average GPA: 3.8
ACT range: 25-30
SAT Math range: 610-680
SAT Reading range: 550-640
SAT Writing range: 7-40
Top 10% of class: 45%
Top 25% of class: 83%
Top 50% of class: 98%

areas like "Weapons Familiarization," "Damage Control and Fire-Fighting," or aviation training. Students complete their majors in their final two years, and serve as overseers, company commanders, and division officers for the third- and fourth- classes of the Cadet Regiment. Students spend their final summer at sea or in various internships. "By the last year, you're 100 percent prepared for a military career," one cadet comments.

All of this is done on a highly regimented schedule: cadets will rise at 0600 for reveille, and complete military training periods, classes, and athletic periods before mandatory evening study time at 2000 and lights out at 2200. Cadets are expected to do well in classes, and academics are fairly rigorous. The Honors Program offers cadets higher-level core courses in their fourth- and third-class years; second- and first-year cadets selected to the Honors Colloquia are eligible for special academic opportunities, like fellowship preparation, international summer internships, and academic conference travel. Study abroad is not offered, although students will get experience traveling abroad during their summer voyages; additionally, second-class cadets may spend their first semester studying at one of the four other U.S. military academies.

All cadets earn Bachelor of Science degrees. Graduates from the USCGA spend five years in service, mostly at sea. About 80 percent of grads continue to grad school under Advanced Degree Programs, funded by the Coast Guard, after two years. Flight school is another option. The Coast Guard will provide lifelong benefits and financial support.

Student Life

Life at the USCGA is not as regimented as at the bigger military academies—cadets have time to participate in over 60 clubs or organizations. The biggest of these is Genesis, the multicultural club; Model UN and Windjammers Drum and Bugle Corps are popular as well. Cadets have some time on weekends after military training to get off campus.

Some traditional events offer cadets excitement, like Reporting-In Day, the first day of Swab Summer, to which parents are invited to see their cadets off, or Commencement formal, the last dance of the year. At other events the Cadets can relax and goof off, like 100th Day, a day 100 days away from Commencement, when class orders reverse and the fourth-class cadets are "kings for a day." One student says, "that's a day we look forward to all year long."

At the same time, it is the military, and there is no drinking or Greek system on campus. "You can't come here expecting to have a traditional college experience," explains a student. All cadets must participate in either intercollegiate sports, on one of the USCGA's 20 Division III or three Division I teams, or in intercompany sports, like baseball, flag football, and basketball.

When cadets do leave campus, they can visit New London's quaint and artsy shops, restaurants, and galleries; a waterfront park, Ocean Beach Park, recently opened and offers space for outdoor activities like sand volleyball. New London is well-connected by rail to the rest of New England; Mystic and Hartford are nearby and, for longer breaks, New York and Boston are within road-tripping distance.

All cadets are housed in the very standard, very Spartan barracks in Chase Hall, where they must live for all four years. "You get used to the living conditions," notes a student.

Student Body

The USCGA is host to high levels of ethnic diversity and makes sincere efforts to celebrate and foster that diversity. It also has the highest percentage of female students of all the U.S. service academies, and was the first of the academies to voluntarily admit women. "The environment is more accepting of women," says a student. Nearly all students are from out of state. Students describe themselves as "more conservative" with "many who are religious" and "very patriotic."

You May Not Know

- When students who were struggling academically became members of the Square Root Club (called so because members' GPAs had to be so low that, when square-rooted, they got larger) they had to pay a midnight visit to the tomb of Hopley Yeaton, the first officer commissioned into the precursor of the Coast Guard. There, according to alternate versions, they either had to sleep on the tomb or light a candle, smoke a pipe, and sharpen their dividers in the hopes that Yeaton's spirit would boost their grades.
- The USCGA's mascot is named Cadet Objee, after the Academy's live bear mascot. Cadet Objee lived with the Corps of Cadets for over 50 years, where he was often left to roam freely through the cadet barracks. He showered in the cadet showers, and he was allowed to eat with the cadets. Eventually he was deemed an "objectionable presence" (hence the name Objee) and removed from the Academy.
- USCGA instruction took place entirely aboard a ship until 1890.

Distinguished Alumni

Erroll M. Brown, first African-American Coast Guard admiral; James Loy, former Commandant of the Coast Guard, former administrator of the Transportation Security Administration, and Deputy Secretary of the Department of Homeland Security; Bruce E. Melnick, NASA astronaut.

Admissions and Financial Aid

Appointment to the USCGA does not require a congressional nomination. In addition to the standard application materials, applicants must pass a three-part physical fitness exam (push-ups, sit-ups, and a mile-and-a-half run) and submit an evaluation from a coach or PE instructor.

Room, board, and tuition are free of charge. Cadets are also paid, amounting to $12,000 annually.

UNITED STATES COAST GUARD ACADEMY

Highlights

Admissions Criteria
Academic criteria:
Grades: ☆ ☆ ☆
Difficulty of class schedule: ☆ ☆ ☆
Class rank: ☆ ☆ ☆
Standardized test scores: ☆ ☆ ☆
Teacher recommendations: ☆ ☆
Personal statement: ☆ ☆
Non-academic criteria considered:
Interview
Extracurricular activities
Special talents, interests, abilities
Character/personal qualities
Volunteer work
Work experience
State of residency
Geographical location
Religious affiliation/commitment
Minority affiliation
Alumni relationship

Deadlines
Early Action: November 15
Early Decision: No
Regular Action: Rolling admissions
Common Application: Not accepted

Financial Aid
Tuition-free school
Room: Varies
Board: Varies
Books: Varies
Avg. aid package (freshmen): N/A
Avg. aid package (undergrads): N/A

School Spirit
Mascot: Objee the Bear
Colors: White, CG blue, and CG red

677

UNITED STATES MILITARY ACADEMY

Overview

Overlooking New York's scenic but somewhat remote Hudson River Valley, the United States Military Academy, more commonly known as West Point, is primarily purposed to train officers for the U.S. Army. With seven weeks of Cadet Basic Training, four years of military classroom instruction, hands-on experience, physical and athletic training, and a strict rank and discipline system within the Corps of Cadets, students will learn to sleep with a rifle in their hands, throw grenades, and drive tanks. By the time they've completed this taxing regimen, cadets will be ready to serve in the Army as second lieutenants—for five years of active service and three years in the reserve.

West Point is also one of the top academic institutions in the country: *U.S. News & World Report* ranks it as 17th in its listing of top liberal arts schools. West Point offers small, discussion-based classes, respected faculty, some research opportunities, and a $65-million library in Jefferson Hall.

West Point cadets even manage to squeeze extracurricular activities into their schedules, alongside mandatory athletics participation. An education at West Point isn't for everyone, but for students who are looking for solid, technically-oriented academics and highly-structured and disciplined leadership training and experience, it can be a rewarding investment.

Academics

Education at West Point is divided into three major areas: academics, military training, and physical education and athletics. All of this is crammed into 47 months and makes for a busy schedule: cadets are "released from quarters" (i.e., wake up) at 0600, attend classes, military training, athletics, and extracurriculars morning and afternoon. Mandatory study time runs from 2030 to 2330, and lights out is at 00 (midnight).

Underpinning all of this is the Cadet Leader Development System, which "prescribes the relationship" between "plebes," as first-year, fourth-class cadets are known, and their upperclass cadet superiors (third-class cadets are called "yearlings;" second-class, "cows;" and first-class, "firsties"). Plebes are "followers," and must behave with the utmost respect and obedience toward upperclass cadets who are given progressively greater leadership roles each year. Third-class cadets will serve as leaders for teams of two or three plebes, while first-class cadets serve as cadet officers. "What keeps us going as plebes is knowing that life will get better," says a student.

All incoming cadets begin their West Point experience with Cadet Basic Training. More commonly called "Beast," it is seven weeks of boot camp, weapons, and tactical training, described by students as "the equivalent of running a marathon every single day." Upon completing Beast, first-year cadets will begin their courses of study at West Point as "plebes." A cadet's first two years are spent completing the hefty core academic curriculum: 26 courses in chemistry, computer science, economics, English, history, international relations, law, leadership, literature, mathematics, military history, philosophy, physical geography, physics, political science, and terrain analysis, along with an engineering sequence. Cadets simultaneously participate in military training, both inside and outside the classroom.

West Point cadets choose one of 42 majors at the end of their second year (management and mechanical engineering are its top programs), and spend their final two years completing that major plus military training. Summers and intersession periods are also spent in military training: third-class cadets participate in eight weeks of field training, while second- and first-class cadets serve in units worldwide, gain leadership experience while training fourth- and third-class cadets, and participate in advanced military training. Cadets graduate with a Bachelor of Science.

Academics are serious and well-respected. Classes are small—almost no classes have over 30 students—and operate on the "Thayer method," instituted by Sylvanus Thayer, West Point's first superintendent. The method emphasizes "West Point's long tradition of daily discussion and frequent grading." One student comments, "like everything else at West Point, the classes are rigorous."

Particularly academically-oriented cadets can get involved with West Point's "Centers of Excellence," which support cadets academically and offer research opportunities. Centers range from the Photonics Research Center to the Office of Artificial Intelligence Analysis and Evaluation.

West Point is expanding its study-abroad options, with an emphasis on increasing foreign language proficiency. Currently, about 500 cadets a year participate in the Foreign Academy Exchange Program, in which groups of cadets third-class and above visit a foreign military academy over spring break. Over 30 countries are available and cadets must have some knowledge of the language. About 150 cadets participate in the Semester Abroad Program at partner universities.

After graduating, cadets enter the arms, support, or service support branches of the army. A limited number of cadets may go on immediately to medical school; others may enter med or law school later in their service careers.

Student Life

More than 100 student clubs exist, including service clubs like Big Brothers and Big Sisters, sports clubs, and even a DJ club. On campus, cadets can spend their little free time at the Cadet Restaurant. Firsties hang out at the predictably named "Firstie Club." Underage drinking and drug use are not permitted and can be punished by loss of privileges or expulsion. "There's too much at stake to risk drinking irresponsibly," explains a student. "You get more than a slap on the wrist." There are no Greek fraternities or sororities.

Each class has its own special event, in addition to the activities and "hops" (dances) put on by the Directorate of Cadet Activities. Parents of fourth-class cadets visit for Plebe Parent Weekend; Yearling Winter Weekend features winter sports and outdoor activities; second-class cadets celebrate the 500th Night until graduation; and 100th Night, for first-class cadets, features a cadet-written and performed musical comedy.

"Every cadet an athlete" is a major tenet of life at West Point; all cadets must participate in physical education classes as well as intercollegiate, club, or intramural sports every semester. West Point fields 15 men's and nine women's Division I varsity teams, and offers a wide variety of intramurals.

Cadets may only go off campus for scheduled training or athletic activities, or with passes. Fourth-class cadets will only have a few weekend leaves per year, while first-class cadets will get about twice the number of leaves second-class cadets do. For cadets who have leave, New York City is only 50 miles south of the campus. "The limits on being able to go off campus make the times we are able to go that much sweeter," notes a student.

Cadets sleep in barracks, two or three to a room. Daily inspections ensure that everything is in order.

UNITED STATES MILITARY ACADEMY

Highlights

Students
Total enrollment: 4,592
Undergrads: 4,592
Freshmen: 1,164
From out-of-state: 94%
From public schools: 74%
Male/Female: 84%/16%
Live on-campus: 100%
Off-campus employment rating: Poor
Caucasian: 71%
African American: 7%
Hispanic: 9%
Asian / Pacific Islander: 6%
Native American: 1%
Mixed (2+ ethnicities): 4%
International: 1%

Academics
Calendar: Semester
Student/faculty ratio: 7:1
Class size 9 or fewer: 10%
Class size 10-29: 89%
Class size 30-49: 2%
Class size 50-99: -
Class size 100 or more: -
Returning freshmen: 94%
Six-year graduation rate: 83%
Graduates who immediately go to graduate school: 2%
Graduates who immediately enter career related to major: 100%

Most Popular Majors
Mechanical engineering
Engineering management
Human geography

Admissions
Applicants: 15,171
Accepted: 1,358
Acceptance rate: 9.0%
Average GPA: Not reported
ACT range: 25-30
SAT Math range: 590-690
SAT Reading range: 560-680
SAT Writing range: 13-40
Top 10% of class: 50%
Top 25% of class: 76%
Top 50% of class: 95%

679

UNITED STATES MILITARY ACADEMY

Admissions Criteria

Academic criteria:
Grades: ☆ ☆ ☆
Difficulty of class schedule: ☆ ☆ ☆
Class rank: ☆ ☆ ☆
Standardized test scores: ☆ ☆ ☆
Teacher recommendations: ☆ ☆
Personal statement: ☆ ☆
Non-academic criteria considered:
Interview
Extracurricular activities
Special talents, interests, abilities
Character/personal qualities
Volunteer work
Work experience
State of residency
Minority affiliation

Deadlines

Early Action: No
Early Decision: No
Regular Action: February 28 (final)
Common Application: Not accepted

Financial Aid

Tuition-free school
Room: Varies
Board: Varies
Books: Varies
Avg. aid package (freshmen): N/A
Avg. aid package (undergrads): N/A

School Spirit

Mascot: Black Knights
Colors: Black, gold, and gray
Song: *Alma Mater*

Student Body

Ethnic diversity is high, and the Congressional nomination system facilitates geographic diversity too. West Point has a reputation for being highly conservative and was ranked by *MSN Encarta* as one of the "Top 10 Socially Conservative Schools" in the nation. "I was a little surprised at just how conservative, religious, and patriotic some are, but I think the atmosphere is moderately accepting," says a student.

This conservatism extends to the academy's attitude toward women, whose presence at the academy is still "limited" and even resented by some. Allegations of sexual harassment and assault of women have surfaced in recent years. Nevertheless, according to an article in *The New York Times*, some female cadets claim that being a woman at the academy is "probably less of a challenge than being a plebe."

You May Not Know

- During the Revolutionary War, the infamous traitor Benedict Arnold offered to turn West Point, of which he held command, over to the British, which would have allowed the British army to divide the colonies in two.
- Some cadets who are failing a class put on their full-dress parade uniform and spin the spurs on the statue memorializing Union general John Sedgwick at midnight, then flee to the barracks as quickly as possible. Legend holds that if Sedgwick's ghost catches the perpetrator, that cadet will fail; if not, the cadet will pass.
- The oldest annual international sporting event in the world (since 1923) is West Point Weekend, a hockey game between West Point and the Royal Military College of Canada.

Distinguished Alumni

Edwin E. "Buzz" Aldrin, NASA astronaut, first manned lunar landing; Kristin Baker, first woman Brigade Commander, U.S. Corps of Cadets; Ulysses S. Grant, General in Chief, Armies of the United States, President of the United States; Robert E. Lee, General in Chief, Confederate Armies; Douglas MacArthur, Supreme Commander of the Pacific, 1941-5.

Admissions and Financial Aid

Applicants must be nominated to West Point by a Congressman. Applicants must also open a candidate file with West Point, preferably in the spring of junior year of high school by filing a Pre-Candidate Questionnaire. The admissions office then determines competitive applicants and will issue further application forms at that point. Candidates must also complete the Candidate Fitness Assessment, which consists of a basketball throw, pull-ups or flexed-arm hang, shuttle run, modified sit-ups, push-ups, and a one-mile run.

No tuition is charged to cadets; instead, they are issued a small monthly salary that increases with each year.

UNITED STATES NAVAL ACADEMY

Overview

The United States Naval Academy at Annapolis is the stuff of legends: boot camp, drills, rigorous discipline, and constant shouting and saluting. It's difficult to imagine this training facility for officers in the U.S. Navy and Marine Corps as a college, and in many ways it is not. Instead of entering as freshmen, first-years enter as fourth-class midshipmen, or "plebes," whose lives are governed by strict regulations and unquestioning deference to rank, grueling military and physical training, and the harshest penalties for breaches of discipline of all the U.S. service academies. There's little time allowed away from the Yard (as the Academy's 338-acre campus is known); summers are spent mostly in military training, and graduates will put in at least five years of active service in the Navy or Marines.

But alongside military training and physical conditioning, midshipmen must also complete USNA's four-year academic program, ranked 12th among national liberal arts schools by *U.S. News & World Report*. Quality opportunities for academic advancement are available, particularly in areas of high importance to the Armed Forces such as nuclear power and Middle East studies. An education at USNA is not a light undertaking, but the potential USNA offers for academic success and leadership development can make an education there rewarding.

Academics

The educational program at USNA entails more than academics. In fact, perhaps the most important component of the educational program is the set of strict regulations that govern the student body (known as the Brigade of Midshipmen). The brigade is structured according to hierarchy of rank, and fourth-class midshipmen ("plebes") fall at the bottom—beneath second-year students (third-class midshipmen, or "youngsters"), third-years or second-class, and first-class or "firsties."

A plebe begins at the USNA with Plebe Summer, an exhausting seven-week indoctrination that amounts to rigorous physical and military training. USNA guarantees that you will end the day "wondering how you will make it through the next day." It's arguable whether the plebe academic year is any easier. Plebes rise at 0500 or 0530 to memorize the day's newspaper articles and meal menus, which they'll have to shout out flawlessly on command; the day is filled with military training, classes, and physical activities; taps or lights-out is at 2300, and bed-checks take place daily. Even the manner in which plebes eat lunch is prescribed: plebes serve upperclassmen, speak only when spoken to, keep their "eyes in the boat" at all times, and eat "only one bite at a time." One student says, "If you can survive being a plebe, you can survive anything."

A plebe's academic courses are dictated by the core curriculum: two classes each in chemistry, calculus, and English, and a class each in U.S. government, leadership, naval science, naval heritage, and navigation. Plebes choose one of USNA's 23 majors at the end of the year. Any of the eight engineering programs—particularly mechanical engineering—and economics are strong. The next three school years are spent finishing the major while summers are filled with summer military training, either at sea, in submarines, or flying naval aircraft.

Academics at USNA are competitive. Fortunately, virtually no class has more than 30 students, so there's plenty of opportunity to "get attention from professors," as one student explains. Midshipmen can also take advantage of USNA's special academic programs. Second-class midshipmen interested in the nuclear Navy can compete for appointments as Bowman Scholars. Bowman Scholars conduct a customized summer research internship; they may also be offered the opportunity to complete a one-year graduate degree immediately following graduation. Qualified second-class midshipmen interested in conducting independent research may submit proposals

UNITED STATES NAVAL ACADEMY

Four-year public
Founded: 1845
Annapolis, MD
Large town
Pop. 38,880

Address:
52 King George Street
Annapolis, MD
21402

Admissions:
888-249-7707

webmail@usna.edu

www.usna.edu

UNITED STATES NAVAL ACADEMY

to the Trident Scholars Program, which allows modification of midshipmen's courses of study.

Studying abroad is not easy, given the demands on midshipmen but it is feasible. Summer and Semester Study Abroad Programs are available for all language programs at USNA. Reflective of the Armed Forces' new focus on the Middle East, USNA's Center for Middle East and Islamic Studies (CMEIS) operates opportunities for academic- and research-related travel. About three dozen midshipmen annually study abroad at foreign universities through the International Programs Office. Exchanges with foreign navies and service academies are also possible.

According to USNA, the range of career options available to its graduates is the broadest of any offered by the U.S. service academies—options include naval aviation, the submarine service, Special Operations, or Special Warfare. A small number of graduates are allowed to go on to medical school or may become commissioned officers in the Marine Corps.

Student Life

Midshipmen can participate in a variety of extracurriculars, including the Drum and Bugle Corps, glee clubs, and religious interest groups. A midshipman's life is focused on campus activities since midshipmen—and plebes especially—don't get much time away from the Yard; close bonds are usually formed within the 140-person companies into which the brigade is divided. "For four years, your company is your family," notes a student.

A few formal "hops" or dances take place throughout the year, like the Ring Dance, for second-class cadets. Perhaps the best-known of USNA's events is the Herndon Monument Climb, in which upperclassmen coat the 21-foot-high obelisk with 100 pounds of lard and tape a "dixie cup" (hat worn by plebes during Plebe Summer) to the top. Plebes work together to climb to the top and replace the cup with a midshipman's cover ("hat"). Army Week, which consists of "covert action" pranks, anticipates the major football game against rival USMA. If Navy beats Army, "carry on" (reduction of restrictions on plebes) is granted until Christmas leave.

USNA is unequivocal about its restrictions on underage drinking and drug use, and will enforce them strictly with random breathalyzer and drug tests. "It's not worth the risk to drink or use drugs," one student remarks. It goes without saying that there are no Greek organizations.

Participation in athletics—either USNA's 21 men's and nine women's varsity Division I teams or intramural or club sports—is mandatory. Men's rowing and rifle team have made strong showings, but by far the most popular sport is football.

With Washington, DC and Baltimore close by, and USNA arranging tickets and transport to cultural events in these cities, the issue isn't finding something to do with free time. Rather, it's getting liberty to do it. Academically successful plebes will get one weekend liberty during the year; youngsters get three weekends per semester; second-class, five; and first class, eight. "We make the most of the limited amount of time we have free," one student says.

All midshipmen are housed in Mother B—Bancroft Hall, the largest college dormitory in the world. Accommodations are Spartan and must be kept in perfect order; inspections occur daily, with more rigorous white-glove/black-sock inspections twice per semester.

Student Body

The nomination system for appointment to USNA ensures geographic diversity in the Brigade of Midshipmen; ethnic diversity is high as well. The overwhelming type at USNA is athletic and "conservative," says a student.

Although women are accepted into the service academies, their presence is often "not welcome," according to some. Not only is the number of incidents of harassment or assault reported at USNA "higher than should be tolerated," (and it has been estimated that this represents only 10 percent of all incidents), but the USNA's "less than desirable" manner of dealing internally with perpetrators rather than in criminal court fosters an atmosphere "that is not friendly to women," says a student; adding, "still we balance this with the amazing educational opportunity and just learn to put up with it."

You May Not Know

- Bill the Goat, the Navy mascot, supposedly originated from a macabre incident when officers trying to preserve the skin of a beloved pet goat decided to provide some half-time entertainment at a Navy football game by wearing the skin.
- John Paul Jones, the Revolutionary War naval hero famous for his words "I have not yet begun to fight," is interred beneath the Cathedral of the Navy.
- The statue of "Tecumseh" on campus was originally the figurehead of the ship "Delaware," wrecked during the Civil War. Midshipmen salute Tecumseh with their left hands and toss pennies at the statue, known as the "God of 2.0" (the minimum passing GPA), for luck.

Distinguished Alumni

Jimmy Carter, 39th President of the United States; Alan Hale, astronomer and discoverer of Hale-Bopp Comet; Alfred Thayer Mahan, naval warfare theorist; Chester W. Nimitz, Commander-in-Chief, U.S. Pacific Fleet, during World War II; Alan Shepard, NASA astronaut.

Admissions and Financial Aid

A nomination from a member of Congress or the Vice President is required for appointment to USNA; students must apply separately to the nomination, and members of Congress set their own dates and procedures. Students must then apply for admission to USNA and pass the Physical Aptitude Exam.

The Navy will pay for tuition and all fees; midshipmen receive a small monthly salary from which most expenses are deducted. Actual cash pay pans out to $100 a month for plebes and rises incrementally to $400 a month for firsties.

UNITED STATES NAVAL ACADEMY

Highlights

Admissions Criteria
Academic criteria:
Grades: ☆ ☆ ☆
Difficulty of class schedule: ☆ ☆ ☆
Class rank: ☆ ☆ ☆
Standardized test scores: ☆ ☆
Teacher recommendations: ☆ ☆ ☆
Personal statement: ☆ ☆ ☆
Non-academic criteria considered:
Interview
Extracurricular activities
Special talents, interests, abilities
Character/personal qualities
Volunteer work
Work experience
State of residency
Geographical location
Minority affiliation
Alumni relationship

Deadlines
Early Action: No
Early Decision: No
Regular Action: Rolling admissions
Common Application: Not accepted

Financial Aid
Tuition-free school
Room: Varies
Board: Varies
Books: $0
Avg. aid package (freshmen): N/A
Avg. aid package (undergrads): N/A

School Spirit
Mascot: Bill the Goat
Colors: Blue and gold
Song: *Anchors Aweigh*

UNIVERSITY OF ALABAMA

Four-year public
Founded: 1831
Tuscaloosa, AL
Medium city
Pop. 91,605

Address:
Box 870100
Tuscaloosa, AL
35487-0100

Admissions:
800-933-BAMA

Financial Aid:
855-469-2262

admissions@ua.edu

www.ua.edu

UNIVERSITY OF ALABAMA

Overview

When you think of the University of Alabama, you probably think football. And for many Saturdays in the fall, you wouldn't be far off. But even for the die-hard athletic fans, Bama is about more than football.

Founded in 1831, UA is the state's first university, a 1,000-acre campus filled with trees, state of the art facilities, and even historic pre-Civil War buildings. It is at the center of Tuscaloosa, a 90,000-person quintessential college town. With a very vibrant Honors College and accessible professors, there's a definite focus on academics. Student life may revolve around football games in the fall but it also includes varied organizations, parties, and entertainment in Tuscaloosa.

Academics

The offerings at UA are rich, with more than 80 majors and 200 fields of study. Strong programs include business administration, communication studies, English, history, music, psychology, and theatre. In addition, the prelaw, predental, and premed programs are standouts. Students may also design their own programs or their own majors and minors through the New College.

The university's core curriculum requires six semester hours of written composition, six hours of writing, six hours in computer-related courses or two semesters in a foreign language, 12 hours in the humanities and fine arts, 12 hours in history and social and behavioral sciences, and 11 hours in the natural sciences and math. "The required classes vary in their quality and relevance to what you want to study," notes a student.

One in five students participates in the Honors College, which offers 15-student seminars and other courses exclusive to those in the college. The Honors College has three divisions: International Honors; which, as might be expected, focuses on interaction with international students and faculty as well as study abroad; Computer-Based Honors which includes a technological research project; and University Fellows, which includes mentorships with professors and internships. "Being a part of the Honors College gives me access to academic opportunities I wouldn't have otherwise," explains a student.

First-year students may also participate in a Freshman Learning Community (FLC), in which 10 to 20 students are matched with a faculty member for the purpose of researching a topic area. During their first semester, the students take several classes together that are related to the study and then meet with the faculty member on a weekly basis to discuss the topic in a one-credit-hour course. "In addition to learning and getting adjusted to college life with other freshmen," comments one student, "I met my very best friends through my FLC."

Students report that the professors have impressive credentials and are accessible but that not all of them are the best teachers. "A grad student assistant can be a godsend, especially in the largest classes," says a student.

The university's Capstone International Academic Programs include faculty-led groups during the interim and summer; exchange programs for a semester or school year; affiliate programs for the summer, semester, or school year; and direct-enroll programs for the summer, semester, or school year. In most cases, students may apply their financial aid from the university to studying abroad. There are also scholarships offered through Capstone International Academic Programs specifically set aside for studying abroad.

In addition to the main Career Center, there are offices dedicated to engineering and to commerce and business administration. Services include mock interviews, walk-in hours, resume and cover letter critiques, and graduate school planning.

Student Life

There is no shortage of activities on campus since 400 student organizations span areas such as the arts, recreation, professions, religion, and politics. Student activity centers on the Ferguson Center, the student union that houses restaurants, student organization offices, the career center, a theatre, and an art gallery. It's one of the popular student hangouts. Sports provide lots of opportunities for students; at the intramural level, there are more than 35 sports and events each year.

Homecoming is one of the largest events on campus. Besides a football game, the weekend offers a parade, pep rally, and bonfire for students, family, and alumni. For a more cultural flair, the university hosts the Realizing the Dream Concert, a performance by the Alabama Symphony Orchestra. Previous concerts have included James Earl Jones, Sidney Poitier, Harry Belafonte, and Della Reese. The university also recently celebrated the 25th anniversary of its Sakura Festival, which features a haiku contest, cherry blossom pictures, art contest, and cultural performances.

The Greek system is strong, with 23 percent of men pledging the 32 fraternities and 33 percent of women pledging the 23 sororities. There are three Greek councils: The Interfraternity Council that oversees fraternities, the Alabama Pan-Hellenic Association that oversees sororities, and the National Pan-Hellenic Council that primarily encompasses minority fraternities and sororities. "If you don't want to feel left out, you should probably pledge," advises a student. "Not everyone does it, but everyone who wants to have all their social options open does."

In the fall, weekends revolve around football games. More than 90,000 fans pour into the Bryant-Denny Stadium—named for football coach Paul "Bear" Bryant and former university President George H. Denny—to watch the games played by the 12-time national championship team. Across campus, tailgating abounds, bringing together students and alumni. Highlights of the season are Homecoming and the Iron Bowl, which matches Bama against rival Auburn. "Even for students who are not that into football, the football games are a big deal. If nothing else, they're an excuse to have a campus-wide party," laughs a student. At the intramural level, there are more than 35 sports and events each year.

Many students go to house and Greek parties and head off campus to the Strip in Tuscaloosa for bars, restaurants and shopping. "You haven't experienced UA if you haven't experienced the Strip," says a student. Tuscaloosa is a true college town with students not only from UA but from nearby community colleges as well. Birmingham is a short one-hour drive away.

Freshmen are required to live on campus, and most students like this policy. "You really get to know the campus and make friends by living on campus," says a student. Students generally describe the housing as "average." One student says, "It's pretty much what you'd expect—not outstanding but not terrible either." The majority of sophomores and above elect to live off campus even though it can be a trek from off-campus housing to class.

Student Body

Some students note the limited diversity among the student body. Alabama is well-represented with 49 percent of students from in

UNIVERSITY OF ALABAMA

Highlights

Students
Total enrollment: 33,503
Undergrads: 28,026
Freshmen: 8,585
Part-time students: 9%
From out-of-state: 51%
Male/Female: 46%/54%
Live on-campus: 28%
In fraternities: 23%
In sororities: 33%
Off-campus employment rating: Good
Caucasian: 79%
African American: 12%
Hispanic: 3%
Asian / Pacific Islander: 1%
Native American: 0%
Mixed (2+ ethnicities): 2%
International: 3%

Academics
Calendar: Semester
Student/faculty ratio: 20:1
Class size 9 or fewer: 13%
Class size 10-29: 51%
Class size 30-49: 19%
Class size 50-99: 11%
Class size 100 or more: 7%
Returning freshmen: 85%
Six-year graduation rate: 67%

Most Popular Majors
Finance
Marketing
Management

Admissions
Applicants: 26,409
Accepted: 14,019
Acceptance rate: 53.1%
Average GPA: 3.6
ACT range: 22-30
SAT Math range: 500-640
SAT Reading range: 500-620
SAT Writing range: 9-19
Top 10% of class: 43%
Top 25% of class: 60%
Top 50% of class: 82%

685

UNIVERSITY OF ALABAMA

Admissions Criteria
Academic criteria:
Grades: ☆ ☆ ☆
Difficulty of class schedule: ☆ ☆ ☆
Class rank: ☆ ☆
Standardized test scores: ☆ ☆ ☆
Teacher recommendations: ☆
Personal statement: ☆
Non-academic criteria considered:
Interview
Extracurricular activities
Special talents, interests, abilities
Character/personal qualities
Volunteer work
Work experience
State of residency
Alumni relationship

Deadlines
Early Action: No
Early Decision: No
Regular Action: Rolling admissions
Common Application: Not accepted

Financial Aid
In-state tuition: $9,200
Out-of-state tuition: $22,950
Room: $5,600
Board: $3,050
Books: $1,200
Freshmen receiving need-based aid: 43%
Undergrads rec. need-based aid: 42%
Avg. % of need met by financial aid: 52%
Avg. aid package (freshmen): $11,479
Avg. aid package (undergrads): $10,485
Avg. debt upon graduation: $27,639

School Spirit
Mascot: Elephant – Big Al
Colors: Crimson and white
Song: *Yea Alabama*

state. African-American students are the largest minority at about 12 percent. Religious groups are predominantly Christian, and students say that many on campus have a conservative slant.

Since this campus was the site of Alabama Governor George Wallace's attempts to prevent desegregation in the 1960s, race relations is of historical significance to the school. "Students tend to keep to their own racial groups," says a student. "Still, there aren't really any signs of discrimination, and it's not like *every* student is white and conservative." Most minority students report that discrimination—and even race itself—is not an issue among today's students.

You May Not Know

- There are four buildings on campus that survived the Civil War and are still in use.
- Only two teams defeated "Bear" at Bryan-Denny Stadium during his 25 years as football coach (Florida in 1963 and Southern Miss in 1982).
- When the university opened in 1831, it had seven buildings and 52 students.

Distinguished Alumni

Hugo Black, U.S. Supreme Court Justice; Timothy Leary, psychologist and writer; Harper Lee, author of *To Kill a Mockingbird*; Joe Namath, Ozzie Newsome and Bart Star, NFL Hall of Fame inductees; Sela Ward, actress.

Admissions and Financial Aid

Admission to the university is based on test scores, GPA, and rigor of high school courses. Instead of sending an admissions essay, students must submit a score from the writing section of the ACT or SAT. Recommendation letters, extracurricular activities, and other achievements are not taken into account.

A separate scholarship application is required to be considered for a number of merit-based scholarships, including the National Merit and National Achievement Finalist Scholarships, Coca-Cola First Generation Scholarship Program, and First Scholars Program. The Academic Elite Scholarship is awarded to up to 10 students and provides the value of tuition for four years, $8,500 in additional funds per year for four years, four years of discounted on-campus housing, and a laptop computer. The National Alumni Association Crimson Scholarships provide the value of tuition for four years, $1,500 in additional funds per year for four years, $300 per year book grant, four years of discounted housing, and a laptop computer. In addition, there are in-state and out-of-state scholarships.

UNIVERSITY OF ARIZONA

Overview

The University of Arizona (UA)—not to be confused with its athletic rival Arizona State University—is located in the heart of Tucson. Its 353-acre campus is home to nearly 200 buildings with red brick facades that shine under the hot Arizona sun against a backdrop of mountains and Sonora desert. Much of main campus is a designated arboretum; visitors can even enjoy a self-guided plant walk. The weather is sunny more than 300 days of the year, which fits the southwestern look of the campus. Most of the 40,000 students love the weather, but it means you have to be able to take the heat.

The University of Arizona Wildcats definitely know how to put the heat on in athletics. Students' attitudes towards academics, however, tend to be cooler and far less competitive; many students prefer parties and football games to studying on the weekends. Luckily, at such a large school, you'll find every type of student under the sun (literally), so bookworms needn't fret. Indeed, UA is distinguished by its membership in the Association of American Universities, an organization of universities with strong research and academic programs. Additionally, UA boasts the third lowest tuition of all the public universities in this group.

Students looking for a quaint and intimate environment should look elsewhere: even UA's $60 million student union is huge, with four levels, 14 restaurants, a video arcade, and more, making it the nation's largest student union not affiliated with a hotel. However, first-years feeling a bit lost or overwhelmed can utilize the $200 million Integrated Learning Center as a home base.

Academics

Students report that academics at University of Arizona generally are "not super competitive," though specific majors and classes can be, especially in the sciences. As a large public university, many of the lower level classes are predictably large and "you can get lost in the crowd."

UA offers more than 100 undergraduate majors, with strong programs in anthropology, astronomy, creative writing, dance, English, and nursing. About 10 percent of UA students are enrolled in the Honors College—many are National Merit and Hispanic Scholars. The interdisciplinary university-wide honors program began in 1962 to offer advising, honors colloquia, and independent study; the program highlights "academics and camaraderie" as well as other "hallmarks."

All students must complete the General Education Curriculum, which consists of Foundations (English composition, math, and second language); Tier One (traditions and cultures, individuals and societies, natural sciences); Tier Two (humanities, individuals and societies, natural sciences, arts); and Diversity Emphasis (one class in gender, race, class, ethnicity, sexual orientation, or non-Western area studies).

Students interested in science research have a special opportunity with BRAVO! The acronym stands for "Biomedical Research Abroad: Vistas Open," a program affiliated with the biology research program that enables undergrads to work in laboratories in other countries. Since its inception in 1992, more than 220 students have worked in 34 industrialized and developing countries.

UA offers study-abroad opportunities in more than 50 countries. The university sends 1,200 students to study abroad and for student exchange programs each year. "I chose to study at the University of Hong Kong because I wanted to learn about the Asian financial industry," notes a student.

The UA Alumni office, in collaboration with Career Services, offers opportunities for current and former students in keeping with the motto, "Wildcat for Life." More than 225,000 former students in 50 states and over 150 countries make up the UA Alumni Club Network, which provides business, career, and social networking opportunities.

UNIVERSITY OF ARIZONA

Four-year public
Founded: 1885
Tucson, AZ
Major city
Pop. 525,796

Address:
P.O. Box 210066
Tucson, AZ
85721-0066

Admissions:
520-621-3237

Financial Aid:
520-621-1858

admissions@arizona.edu

www.arizona.edu

UNIVERSITY OF ARIZONA

Students
Total enrollment: 40,223
Undergrads: 31,565
Part-time students: 11%
From out-of-state: 35%
From public schools: 90%
Male/Female: 48%/52%
Live on-campus: 21%
In fraternities: 10%
In sororities: 11%
Off-campus employment rating: Excellent
Caucasian: 56%
African American: 3%
Hispanic: 23%
Asian / Pacific Islander: 6%
Native American: 1%
Mixed (2+ ethnicities): 4%
International: 5%

Academics
Calendar: Semester
Student/faculty ratio: 22:1
Class size 9 or fewer: 13%
Class size 10-29: 54%
Class size 30-49: 16%
Class size 50-99: 9%
Class size 100 or more: 8%
Returning freshmen: 80%
Six-year graduation rate: 61%

Most Popular Majors
Business
Social sciences
Biological/life sciences

Admissions
Applicants: 26,329
Accepted: 20,251
Acceptance rate: 76.9%
Average GPA: 3.4
ACT range: 21-27
SAT Math range: 500-630
SAT Reading range: 483-600
SAT Writing range: 4-21
Top 10% of class: 32%
Top 25% of class: 63%
Top 50% of class: 90%

Student Life

Even though many students live off campus, a great deal of social activity occurs both on and off campus. As befits such a large and diverse university, there are around 500 student organizations. The marching band, named "The Pride of the Arizona," played at the first Super Bowl and was recently named one of the top five marching bands in the nation. The Arizona Blue Chip Program is a four-year program that offers students leadership-based academic courses, training, and excursions. The annual Spring Fling also lays claims of biggest and best: it is the largest student-run carnival in the United States, with over 3,000 UA students volunteering to put on the four-day event. "It is a massive undertaking and one of the highlights of the year," says a student.

Another tradition is even older than Spring Fling, which began in 1965: each year, freshmen repaint the "A" on Sentinel Peak, aka "A" mountain. The "A" is currently painted red, white, and blue in support of the troops deployed from the September 11 attacks.

Toward the end of the school year, many students use Dead Day to unwind before finals. The student newspaper *Daily Wildcat* called Dead Day a "day of endless possibilities," noting that many chose to take advantage of Dead Day specials at nearby bars. Of course, not everyone drinks: some study, or just use the day to kick back and relax.

About 10 percent of students participate in 50 fraternities and sororities on campus, making Greek life a strong part of the campus scene. "The parties are especially popular among freshmen," explains a student.

The university's 19 Division I sports have collectively won 18 national team championships and 37 Pac-10 conference team championships over the years. UA is best known for basketball, football and baseball—the men's basketball team has made it in to the NCAA tournament 25 consecutive years from 1985 to 2009 and made it to the Sweet Sixteen in 2013. All this winning gives students plenty of opportunities to shout the UA cheer: "Bear Down!" The most dedicated Wildcat fans join ZonaZoo, "one of the biggest, loudest and craziest student fan bases in the country" according to the college, which implores students to "join over 12,000 fellow Wildcats that are part of the madness!" For students who aren't varsity athletes but still want to participate in sports, there are 18 intramural sports on offer, each with competitive, intermediate, and recreational levels.

Off campus, there are a plethora of bars and clubs on 4th Avenue. Some students venture to Nogales, Mexico, where there's no minimum drinking age. For those seeking sober fun, there are plenty of outdoor sports, including hiking and biking in the desert. Surprisingly, there's sometimes even snow on Mt. Lemmon, providing skiing opportunities!

Most students live off campus; but on-campus "living-learning" and theme communities are potential perks for being part of various programs—Honors College, Blue Chip Leadership, women in science, engineering, math, and technology—and there are theme floors for fine arts, health professions, multicultural experience, and ROTC.

Student Body

Keeping in step with the sunny weather, the campus atmosphere is generally "laid back"—except, of course, when the occasion calls for avid sports fans to stand up and cheer! With so many students, there is no University of Arizona "type." In fact, one student says, "You will find every type of person here." The student body is racially diverse, and more than half the 37 percent of students of colors identify as Hispanic. A large number of students hail from Arizona and California, though all 50 states and more than 100 countries are represented within the student body.

You May Not Know

- The University of Arizona was founded in 1885, 27 years before Arizona became a state, making it the first university in the state.
- In 1914, an *L.A. Times* article on football noted that "the Arizona men showed the fight of wildcats," giving birth to UA's mascot.
- The university wildcat mascot Wilbur married fellow mascot Wilma in 1986.

Distinguished Alumni

Richard Carmona, U.S. Surgeon General; Joan Ganz Cooney, creator of *Sesame Street*; Richard Russo, Pulitzer Prize winner.

Admissions and Financial Aid

Residents of Arizona who attend regionally accredited high schools, rank in the top 25 percent of their graduating class, and have no coursework deficiencies are guaranteed admission to UA under their "Assured Admission" policy. All other students go through the "Comprehensive Review" process, which includes looking at competency requirements as determined by coursework or SAT/ACT scores in a number of areas, including second language and fine arts.

The university offers merit-based scholarships for incoming students and transfer students. The Arizona Excellence Award provides up to $14,000 a year for non-Arizona resident students while the Regents High Honors Endorsement Award provides four years of tuition for residents. There are awards for National Merit Semifinalists and Finalists, African-American National Achievement Scholars, and National Hispanic Scholars.

UNIVERSITY OF ARIZONA

Highlights

Admissions Criteria
Academic criteria:
Grades: ☆ ☆ ☆
Difficulty of class schedule: ☆ ☆ ☆
Class rank: ☆
Standardized test scores: ☆ ☆ ☆
Teacher recommendations: ☆
Personal statement: ☆ ☆ ☆
Non-academic criteria considered:
Extracurricular activities
Special talents, interests, abilities
Character/personal qualities
Volunteer work
Work experience
State of residency
Geographical location

Deadlines
Early Action: No
Early Decision: No
Regular Action: Rolling admissions
Common Application: Not accepted

Financial Aid
In-state tuition: $9,114
Out-of-state tuition: $25,310
Room: Varies
Board: Varies
Books: $1,000
Freshmen receiving need-based aid: 53%
Undergrads rec. need-based aid: 51%
Avg. % of need met by financial aid: 61%
Avg. aid package (freshmen): $12,180
Avg. aid package (undergrads): $12,059
Avg. debt upon graduation: $22,269

School Spirit
Mascot: Wildcats
Colors: Cardinal red and navy blue
Song: *Bear Down Fight Song*

689

UNIVERSITY OF ARKANSAS FAYETTEVILLE

Overview

The University of Arkansas (often abbreviated U of A or UA) boasts more than 130 buildings spread across 345 hilly acres in Fayetteville, a hip college town nestled in the Ozark Mountains. The location lacks the glamour of big cities, though Little Rock and Tulsa aren't too far away.

As the state's flagship university, Arkansas has been expanding in recent years, adding 40 new buildings and increasing enrollment with the aim of developing the diversity of its students and the caliber of its research. With a total student population of about 24,000, U of A is smaller than other public universities, which can create a more accessible feel. Students don't just attend for the academics though: most are rabid sports fans, whether they play or watch, and many are proudly from Arkansas and the South.

Academics

The University of Arkansas has nearly 200 undergraduate and graduate degree programs. Students say classes are "difficult but manageable," especially introductory classes that can be attended by a few hundred students and are often taught by teaching assistants. These large classes are not the norm, though. More than 80 percent of classes have fewer than 50 students.

For a bachelor's of arts degree, students must complete a minimum of 54 hours of general education courses in English (two composition courses), history, fine arts, foreign language, philosophy, math, natural sciences with laboratory, social sciences, communications, and world literature. Strong programs include those in the Dale Bumpers College of Agricultural, Food and Life Sciences as well as computer science, engineering, English, and general business. "Our agriculture college is nationally recognized," one student comments.

The Honors College serves all undergraduate majors and offers "small classes, priority registration, special housing, increased interaction with faculty, and enhanced opportunities for hands-on research." Other perks include special study-abroad opportunities. The college is supported by a gift from the family of Walmart founder Sam Walton. The Walton Family Charitable Support Foundation also established the Sam M. Walton College of Business Administration.

To help ease the transition to college, students may sign up for the First Year Experience program, becoming part of the Perspectives course which pairs up to 20 students in the class with a faculty or staff mentor. Participants get priority registration for the spring semester. "Arkansas can be overwhelming without this kind of support," confides one student.

Premed students receive specialized support through the Liebolt Premedical Program. This can include health-profession work, volunteer opportunities, and workshops on medical school application personal statements and interviews.

More than one quarter of U of A students study abroad, with programs ranging from two weeks to one year and spanning Latin America, Africa, Western and Eastern Europe, the Middle East, Asia, Australia, and New Zealand. Students may participate in 16 programs sponsored by the university or numerous others that are recommended. The UA reciprocal exchange program enables students to study abroad for the same cost as a full-time courseload at UA.

The Arkansas Alumni Association and the Career Development Center help students and alumni with job, internship, and grad school searches. Recent Career Development Center events include an All Majors Career Fair, Engineering EXPO, Design Fair, a visit from the State Department Diplomat in Residence, and FBI Careers Workshop.

Student Life

There are plenty of activities to keep AU students busy. There are more than 300 student organizations, including over 50 pluralistic student cultural and religious organizations, clubs connected to different colleges (e.g. agriculture business club, Society of Women Engineers), and other professional, service, and special interest organizations (amateur radio, anime, vegetarianism). And if your favorite club doesn't exist, you can start your own!

The university hosts a number of events throughout the year. Even before school starts, first-year students may participate in Razorback Outreach for Community and Knowledge (ROCK) Camp. During ROCK, students camp and stay in cabins as part of a trip to Buffalo River. Razorbash supplies students with free food and prizes as well as an introduction to more than 100 student organizations. During Make a Difference Day, more than 800 volunteers work on projects such as improving parks, painting nonprofit organization facilities, and collecting food donations.

Twenty-three percent of men and 36 percent of women participate in the 28 Greek organizations on campus. Greek parties are a main part of the social scene and generally open to those who aren't members too. "The parties can get pretty crazy," one student laughs.

The Arkansas Union provides a hub for students to socialize, and the HPER recreational complex houses an impressive 10 racquetball courts, four basketball gyms, indoor track, Olympic size pool, climbing wall, and more. Intramural sports are one of the most popular activities on campus: students participate in over 40 activities, from bowling to dodgeball to Xbox tournaments and more.

UA students are not just avid intramural participants, but huge sports fans as well—especially when it comes to football. The cardinal red Hogs/Razorbacks mascot can be seen throughout campus, especially during the big games of Homecoming and Bama. Home games are played at The Donald W. Reynolds Razorback Stadium, which is often packed with 72,000 cheering fans. "There's no bigger ruckus than when we score a touchdown at a home game," one student comments. Head coach Bobby Petrino was fired in 2012 for having an extramarital affair with a former AU volleyball player, paying her $20,000, and helping her obtain a job in the athletic department.

Off campus, students frequent the bars and restaurants on Dickson Street. Ozark National Forest and the Buffalo National River provide recreational opportunities such as canoeing, hiking, and camping.

Twenty-seven percent of students live in the 17 resident halls and apartments, with more housing slots allotted to freshmen and sophomores than upperclass students. Parking can be a challenge for students living off campus, though a recently opened parking structure with more than 500 spaces has helped to alleviate some of the problem. Students in the honors program may live in an Academic Honors Area, and students in the architecture and engineering schools may choose to live in areas designated for their particular majors.

Freshmen are required to live on campus. Dorm life—as well as the First-Year Experience—helps freshmen adapt to the college academically and socially. Nine major initiatives in the First-Year

UNIVERSITY OF ARKANSAS

Highlights

Students
Total enrollment: 24,537
Undergrads: 20,350
Part-time students: 13%
From out-of-state: 46%
Male/Female: 50%/50%
Live on-campus: 27%
In fraternities: 23%
In sororities: 36%
Off-campus employment rating: Excellent
Caucasian: 79%
African American: 5%
Hispanic: 6%
Asian / Pacific Islander: 3%
Native American: 1%
Mixed (2+ ethnicities): 3%
International: 3%

Academics
Calendar: Semester
Student/faculty ratio: 19:1
Class size 9 or fewer: 12%
Class size 10-29: 49%
Class size 30-49: 21%
Class size 50-99: 11%
Class size 100 or more: 6%
Returning freshmen: 81%
Six-year graduation rate: 60%
Graduates who immediately go to graduate school: 26%
Graduates who immediately enter career related to major: 58%

Most Popular Majors
Marketing
Finance

Admissions
Applicants: 16,749
Accepted: 10,630
Acceptance rate: 63.5%
Average GPA: 3.6
ACT range: 23-28
SAT Math range: 520-630
SAT Reading range: 500-610
SAT Writing range: Not reported
Top 10% of class: 27%
Top 25% of class: 57%
Top 50% of class: 88%

691

College Profiles

UNIVERSITY OF ARKANSAS

Admissions Criteria
Academic criteria:
Grades: ☆ ☆ ☆
Difficulty of class schedule: ☆ ☆ ☆
Class rank: ☆ ☆ ☆
Standardized test scores: ☆ ☆ ☆
Teacher recommendations: ☆
Personal statement: ☆
Non-academic criteria considered:
Extracurricular activities
Special talents, interests, abilities
Character/personal qualities
Volunteer work
Work experience
Geographical location
Minority affiliation

Deadlines
Early Action: November 1
Early Decision: No
Regular Action: Rolling admissions
Common Application: Accepted

Financial Aid
In-state tuition: $6,354
Out-of-state tuition: $17,610
Room: $5,728
Board: $3,314
Books: $1,380
Freshmen receiving need-based aid: 48%
Undergrads rec. need-based aid: 46%
Avg. % of need met by financial aid: 60%
Avg. aid package (freshmen): $10,004
Avg. aid package (undergrads): $9,699
Avg. debt upon graduation: $24,647

School Spirit
Mascot: Razorback
Colors: Red and white

Experience include residence halls, seminar courses, and ROCK Camp.

Student Body

Fifty-four percent of the university's 20,000 undergraduates hail from Arkansas, and there is strong representation of students from the South. "If you don't already say 'ma'am' and 'sir,' you will by the time you graduate," one student says.

According to the student body, they are "religious" and "many are conservative." Eighteen percent of students are from minority backgrounds. The Multicultural Center provides a place to promote cross-cultural change and is one example of how the university strives to create greater diversity among the student body.

You May Not Know

- U of A's one-of-a-kind Senior Walk has more than 125,000 graduates' names inscribed into more than two miles of campus walkways, starting with the graduating class of 1876.
- U of A alumnus Robert D. Maurer was a co-inventor of fiber optic cable and facilitated other major contributions to improving technology and communications.
- Tusk, a 400-pound Russian hog, is UA's live mascot and attends all home Razorback football games.

Distinguished Alumni

J. William Fulbright, former U.S. Senator, creator of the Fulbright Program for International Education Exchange; Mary L. Good, former President of the American Association for the Advancement of Science; S. Robson Walton, Walmart Stores Chairman; Lucinda Williams, Grammy Award-winning country singer.

Admissions and Financial Aid

Arkansas has a set of criteria that, if met, guarantees automatic admission for new freshmen. However, students who do not meet the specific criteria on GPA, ACT or SAT scores, and high school coursework are still encouraged to apply.

Students who apply early admission have priority for housing, orientation, and scholarships. Regular admissions for the fall quarter is on space-available basis. The admissions office also notes its commitment "to the recruitment and graduation of veterans of the United States armed forces."

The university awards 5,000+ scholarships worth more than $18 million each year. Among these are four prestigious merit-based programs for incoming students: the Bodenhammer Fellowship for National Merit or National Achievement finalists, the Boyer Fellowship for students who major in the Sam M. Walton College of Business, the Honors College Fellowship based on academic performance, and the Sturgis Fellowship for students in the J. William Fulbright College of Arts and Sciences. All four of the awards provide $12,500 per year and all but the Boyer Fellowship provide an out-of-state differential.

UNIVERSITY OF CALIFORNIA - BERKELEY

Overview

The mention of UC Berkeley (Cal) usually conjures images from the 1960s of student activists pushing for free speech or protesting the Vietnam War. More recently, Berkeley has been the site of activists living in trees to prevent their removal along with protests against tuition hikes and employee layoffs. But while student activism has always played a role in the university's history—and will continue to do so—there is much more to the university's rich offerings.

Located in the college town of Berkeley in the lively San Francisco Bay Area, Cal is the flagship public university of California and some argue, of the country. Spread across 1,232 acres, the university is home to a large student body focused on academic achievement, a national award-winning faculty, and a plethora of activities both on and off campus. Add to that the gift of California weather (the average temperature throughout the year ranges from the mid-50s to the 70s), and you can see why the University of California–Berkeley is so high on most students' lists.

Academics

With 130 academic departments and 350 degree programs, the university is an academic powerhouse that regularly presides near or at the top of nearly every college ranking of the best public universities in the country. Among its faculty are eight Nobel Prize winners, four Pulitzer Prize winners and more than 350 Guggenheim Fellows. Standouts among its programs are art history, biochemistry and molecular biology, chemistry, computer science, engineering (biomedical, chemical, civil, electrical, industrial, and mechanical and materials science), English, history, math, music, political science, and sociology, all of which ranked in the top five in their fields by the National Research Council.

With such academic strength, it is no wonder that the university draws top students from across the country. This results in a rigorous academic environment in which students regularly spend weekends studying in cafes or the libraries and must apply to enter capped majors such as economics, psychology, and media studies.

There are more than 25,000 undergraduates, and that means some of the introductory classes can number into the hundreds. For example, Chemistry 1A typically has 500 students but smaller discussion sections. "The sections make even the largest classes more personal," says one student. A common complaint among students is the lack of advising. "You have to be the kind of student who takes initiative, or you're not going to make it," remarks a student.

Still, most students say that they are happy with their decision to attend Cal, citing the level of quality of the professors and research opportunities. Many say that the level of competition compels them to strive even harder. "I've met the most intelligent people I've ever known here," states a student.

The university has a series of academic benchmarks, including an entry level writing requirement either by test score or by taking the UC Entry Level Writing Requirement Course at a community college or College Writing R1A at Berkeley. Students must satisfy the American History and Institutes Requirement through high school coursework or standardized exam or by taking an approved course at Berkeley. All students must take an American Cultures course offered in more than 40 departments. "There are a lot of options for the American Cultures course so you'll find something that fits your interests," one student comments. College of Letters and Science students must also take courses in reading and composition, quantitative reasoning, foreign language, and seven-course breadth (arts and literature, biological science, historical studies, international studies, philosophy and values, physical science, and social and behavioral sciences).

Through the Undergraduate Research Apprentice Program (URAP), students work with faculty on "ground-breaking research." Recent projects have included

UNIVERSITY OF CALIFORNIA – BERKELEY

Four-year public
Founded: 1868
Berkeley, CA
Major city
Pop. 113,905

Address:
2200 University Drive
Berkeley, CA
94720

Admissions:
510-642-3175

Financial Aid:
510-642-6442

www.berkeley.edu

UNIVERSITY OF CALIFORNIA – BERKELEY

Students

Total enrollment: 35,899
Undergrads: 25,774
Freshmen: 4,173
Part-time students: 3%
From out-of-state: 19%
Male/Female: 48%/52%
Live on-campus: 26%
In fraternities: 10%
In sororities: 10%
Caucasian: 30%
African American: 2%
Hispanic: 13%
Asian / Pacific Islander: 36%
Native American: 0%
Mixed (2+ ethnicities): 4%
International: 11%

Academics

Calendar: Semester
Student/faculty ratio: 17:1
Class size 9 or fewer: 36%
Class size 10-29: 41%
Class size 30-49: 8%
Class size 50-99: 7%
Class size 100 or more: 7%
Returning freshmen: 96%
Six-year graduation rate: 91%

Admissions

Applicants: 61,731
Accepted: 11,130
Acceptance rate: 18.0%
Placed on wait list: 161
Enrolled from wait list: 107
Average GPA: 3.8
ACT range: 27-33
SAT Math range: 630-770
SAT Reading range: 590-720
SAT Writing range: 46-34
Top 10% of class: 98%
Top 25% of class: 100%

"Narrative Problems in the New Social History of Slavery," "Generating Images that Simulate Vision," and "Was Swine Flu a Media Creation?"

The university offers a plethora of study-abroad opportunities in programs affiliated with the UC system and the university, as well as other exchange and independent programs. The University of California Education Abroad Program encompasses 200 programs in 35 countries that meet UC degree requirements. Through the Global Summer Program, students may study at one of 10 member universities such as ETH Zurich, Peking University, or the University of Cambridge.

Extensive support and events are offered by the Career Center. There are fairs and forums that encompass investment banking, consulting, master's and PhD careers, law school, graduate school, civil and environmental engineering, nonprofit careers, and diversity.

Student Life

There are more than 350 student organizations covering every cause, art and culture, profession, religion, service, and sport imaginable. "If there's something that you like, there's a club for it at Berkeley," says a student.

Throughout the year the university hosts many events that are of interest to students. A definite highlight is Calapalooza, when student organizations welcome classmates back to school and try to recruit new members. E-week in March is a seven-day palette of activities that keeps engineering students busy with trivia night, a poker tournament, and Engineering Olympics. In April, students gather for art, music, and storytelling for Take Back the Night, a resounding call to "shatter the silence surrounding sexual violence, domestic violence, rape, and hate crimes."

About 10 percent of students go Greek and there are more than 60 fraternities and sororities on campus. Students report that parties at the fraternities and co-ops are well-attended. "There's always something going on," notes a student.

Athletics play a major role in campus life. Cal has 27 Division I sports teams and has won more than 70 national championships. Watching athletic events—especially football and basketball games—is a Berkeley tradition. The main athletic event of the year is called the Big Game, the football game against Stanford, Berkeley's rival across the bay. "You don't want to be caught dead on campus wearing red (Stanford's color) on the day of the Big Game," one student comments.

On campus and off, there is never a lack of things to do at Berkeley. For those who want to compete at the intramural level, there are organized intramural teams in basketball, dodgeball, flag football, indoor soccer, speed soccer, softball, tennis ladder, Ultimate Frisbee, and volleyball. And for the non-athletic types, the ever-alive city of Berkeley offers a myriad of restaurants, shopping, and cafes and is a true college town. "You'll never be bored at Berkeley. If anything, you'll be overwhelmed," states a sophomore. But just in case you do want more, you should know that a 30-minute BART ride can sweep you away to San Francisco. Students report that they venture into the city for bars and clubs, shopping, and cultural performances.

On-campus housing is guaranteed for the first two years, and many students recommend that incoming students take advantage of living on campus at least for the first year to establish friendships.

Most upperclass students live off campus and can get assistance finding housing through the college's Cal Rentals. Through the Berkeley Student Cooperative, more than 1,250 students live in 20 housing co-ops, where they contribute work hours to keep housing costs affordable at $3,318 per semester.

Student Body

Berkeley attracts students from across the country and internationally, and its student body reflects this. There are students representing every ethnic, religious, socioeconomic, and even political background. "My roommates are an Upper East Side Manhattanite, a middle-class Midwesterner and a Texan who describes herself as disadvantaged," says a senior. However, students do observe that there is a larger representation of Californians; in fact, 81 percent of students are California residents. In addition, there is a significant Asian-American population (36 percent).

The majority of Berkeley students "range from liberal to *very* liberal," says a student. More than 51 percent of first-year students defined themselves as such in a recent survey by the Office of Student Research. But more than 36 percent of freshmen defined themselves as "middle of the road."

While there is such diversity represented, a unifying factor among pretty much all of the students is a commitment to academics. One student says that she is "constantly amazed by the brilliance of the other students." With Cal's pick among high school high achievers, this is no surprise.

You May Not Know

- The Valley Life Sciences building houses skeletons of a Tyrannosaurus Rex and a Pteranodon.
- Every time the Cal football team scores, the 750-pound cannon is fired.
- Berkeley researchers discovered four elements on the periodic table of elements—lawrencium, californium, berkelium, and seaborgium.

Distinguished Alumni

Scott Adams, creator of Dilbert comic strip; Beverly Cleary, author of books including *Ramona the Pest*; Natalie Coughlin, Olympic gold medalist swimmer; Gregory Peck, actor; Eric Schmidt, CEO of Google; Alice Waters, chef; Earl Warren, U.S. Supreme Court Chief Justice.

Admissions and Financial Aid

The university employs a holistic review of applications, and there are no grade or test score formulas used to determine admission. "We look at the whole person. Achievement can be found in different areas of your life," says an admissions representative. More than 100 readers review applications.

The university awards numerous merit-based scholarships. The Regents' and Chancellor's Scholarship is by invitation only and the most prestigious. A select 200 incoming students receive this award that provides support for up to four years. Cal Opportunity Scholarships are aimed at "high-achieving students who have overcome challenging socio-economic circumstances."

UNIVERSITY OF CALIFORNIA – BERKELEY

Highlights

Admissions Criteria
Academic criteria:
Grades: ☆ ☆ ☆
Difficulty of class schedule: ☆ ☆ ☆
Class rank: N/A
Standardized test scores: ☆ ☆
Teacher recommendations: N/A
Personal statement: ☆ ☆ ☆
Non-academic criteria considered:
Extracurricular activities
Special talents, interests, abilities
Character/personal qualities
Volunteer work
Work experience

Deadlines
Early Action: No
Early Decision: No
Regular Action: November 30 (final)
Notification of admission by: April 1
Common Application: Not accepted

Financial Aid
In-state tuition: $12,864
Out-of-state tuition: $35,742
Room: Varies
Board: Varies
Books: $1,226
Freshmen receiving need-based aid: 65%
Undergrads rec. need-based aid: 57%
Avg. % of need met by financial aid: 81%
Avg. aid package (freshmen): $21,767
Avg. aid package (undergrads): $20,242
Avg. debt upon graduation: $17,964

School Spirit
Mascot: Golden Bears (Oski)
Colors: Blue and gold
Song: *Big C*

695

UNIVERSITY OF
CALIFORNIA –
DAVIS

Four-year public
Founded: 1908
Davis, CA
Large town
Pop. 66,016

Address:
One Shields Avenue
Davis, CA
95616

Admissions:
530-752-2971

Financial Aid:
530-752-2390

undergraduateadmis-
sions@ucdavis.edu

www.ucdavis.edu

UNIVERSITY OF CALIFORNIA – DAVIS

Overview

With 5,200 leafy acres, the University of California at Davis is the largest campus in the UC system, which explains the number of students biking between classes. It is a large public university situated in a medium-sized college town, where students work hard despite the laid-back atmosphere. Davis is consistently rated as one of the top public schools and is ranked #39 among all national universities by *U.S. News & World Report*. If you're interested in agriculture or the pre-healthcare fields, this is definitely the place for you.

The city of Davis, located in California's central valley, is known for its low-key, earthy vibe, and is often referred to as "cow-town" since the surrounding area is rural. It has everything you'd expect from a college town and, in fact, is known for good "town-gown" relations. The campus is lovely, with lots of green spaces. The architecture features buildings varying from traditional dairy barn to modern concrete. Davis is also known for its sustainability efforts.

While Davis is generally regarded as the third or fourth most prestigious UC, there are certainly students who transfer from UCLA or UC Berkeley to Davis, based on the feel of the campus or a particularly strong major that interests them.

Academics

Students enter one of four undergraduate colleges: the College of Letters and Science, the College of Engineering, the College of Biological Sciences, or the College of Agriculture and Environmental Sciences. UC Davis runs on the quarter system, with three 10-week terms and a summer session.

Over 100 academic majors are offered at UC Davis. Biological sciences, agricultural and environmental education, and animal science and management are particularly strong programs. There are no pre-professional majors, such as pre-med, pre-law, or pre-vet, but there are majors that offer preparation for graduate school in these fields, as well as counseling to prepare for graduate school. Students can also double-major or create their own individual major.

There are three components to the general education requirements: topical breadth, which is subdivided into the arts and humanities, science and engineering, and social sciences; social-cultural diversity; and writing experience.

UC Davis is academically rigorous, but some majors are notoriously more difficult than others, and the honors program courses are viewed as being some of the most challenging. Class sizes vary by major, but 63 percent of classes have fewer than 30 students. Davis professors are expected to teach and to do research. Students describe their instructors in a variety of ways, ranging from "very hands-on" to "hardly interested in undergrads." But the bottom line is this: the research facet of a professor's life gives students plenty of opportunities to find professors accessible as well as to participate in groundbreaking research.

Unique academic opportunities at UC Davis abound. The Freshman Seminar Program gives first-year students an opportunity to work more closely with faculty. More than 200 seminars, capped at 19 participants, are offered every year. Freshman seminars foster a greater intellectual engagement with professors and fellow students, and are often interdisciplinary in nature. Seminar offerings are as varied as "Druids: Religion, Wisdom, and Violence," "Animated Film," and "Rocket Science." Undergrads can literally get their feet wet while learning in a "classroom without walls" at the Bodega Marine Laboratory, 100 miles west of Davis, near Bodega Bay. BML is an academic marine laboratory for coastal and environmental research and training and provides valuable research opportunities for faculty and undergraduates alike. Advanced students can take a quarter of intensive classes in the spring or summer.

Incoming freshmen may apply to the prestigious Davis Honors Challenge, which is a four-year honors program for "highly motivated students who want more challenging course work, closer contacts with faculty, and dynamic interactions with similarly motivated peers." Part of the program includes taking honors-only research seminars and courses, culminating in a year-long independent research project. Benefits include an optional living-learning community and priority registration.

UC Davis strongly encourages studying abroad for a quarter, a summer, or a year. There are over 300 programs available in 31 countries. Counseling is available at the Internship and Career Center, which annually matches 5,000 students with paid and unpaid internships. The center works with students on perfecting their resumes and looking for job and internship opportunities, as well as preparing for graduate school.

Student Life

Students find ample choices for club membership among the 452 official student groups. Some of the most popular include the AIDS education project, the wildlife society, ballroom dance, the marching band, and the anime club. The campus newspaper, *California Aggie*, has a staff of over 125 students, and there is also a popular radio station, KDVS.

Some of the most popular events include Picnic Day, an annual open house on campus with live entertainment that is the largest student organized event in the country; the Causeway Classic, a longstanding football rivalry with CSU Sacramento that brings out tons of school spirit and body paint; and the Whole Earth Festival, a three day festival of education, live music, and art events.

All freshmen are guaranteed on-campus housing. More than 90 percent of freshman students live on campus, but many move off campus after the first year, either living in UC Davis apartments or the city of Davis.

While there is significant Greek life on campus, it doesn't dominate the social scene. There are 44 fraternities and sororities, with 10 percent of students participating. Many of the groups also have a cultural or ethnic component.

Students spend free time on campus or relaxing in downtown Davis at coffee shops, the Davis Farmers Market, and arts and live music events. They also manage to get in a few road trips on the weekends, going to Sacramento or San Francisco for a greater variety of activities, and plenty of students can be found on the slopes in Tahoe in the winter for skiing and snowboarding.

UC Davis has excellent sports and recreational facilities, which isn't surprising considering that they have one of the largest club sports programs in the nation, with 1,400 students participating in 35 different club sports, and 14,500 students in 51 different intramural sports. UC Davis is a member of NCAA Division I and has 500 student athletes in 23 varsity sports. The football and wrestling programs are the most competitive. Those who don't want to play a sport but enjoy watching can join the Aggie Pack, a popular student spirit organization.

UNIVERSITY OF CALIFORNIA – DAVIS

Highlights

Students
Total enrollment: 32,354
Undergrads: 25,759
Freshmen: 5,480
Part-time students: 1%
From out-of-state: 8%
Male/Female: 45%/55%
Live on-campus: 25%
Off-campus employment rating: Good
Caucasian: 32%
African American: 2%
Hispanic: 16%
Asian / Pacific Islander: 37%
Native American: 0%
Mixed (2+ ethnicities): 4%
International: 4%

Academics
Calendar: Quarter
Student/faculty ratio: 17:1
Class size 9 or fewer: 12%
Class size 10-29: 51%
Class size 30-49: 13%
Class size 50-99: 12%
Class size 100 or more: 11%
Returning freshmen: 92%
Six-year graduation rate: 81%
Graduates who immediately enter career related to major: 39%

Most Popular Majors
Psychology
Economics
Biological sciences

Admissions
Applicants: 49,333
Accepted: 22,521
Acceptance rate: 45.7%
Placed on wait list: 6,911
Enrolled from wait list: 12
Average GPA: 4.0
ACT range: 24-30
SAT Math range: 570-690
SAT Reading range: 520-640
SAT Writing range: 15-39

697

UNIVERSITY OF CALIFORNIA – DAVIS

Admissions Criteria
Academic criteria:
Grades: ☆ ☆ ☆
Difficulty of class schedule: ☆ ☆ ☆
Class rank: N/A
Standardized test scores: ☆ ☆ ☆
Teacher recommendations: ☆ ☆ ☆
Personal statement: ☆ ☆ ☆
Non-academic criteria considered:
Extracurricular activities
Special talents, interests, abilities
Character/personal qualities
Volunteer work
Work experience

Deadlines
Early Action: No
Early Decision: No
Regular Action: November 30 (final)
Notification of admission by: March 31
Common Application: Not accepted

Financial Aid
In-state tuition: $13,902
Out-of-state tuition: $36,780
Room: Varies
Board: Varies
Books: $1,620
Freshmen receiving need-based aid: 64%
Undergrads rec. need-based aid: 65%
Avg. % of need met by financial aid: 80%
Avg. aid package (freshmen): $21,420
Avg. aid package (undergrads): $19,658
Avg. debt upon graduation: $19,285

School Spirit
Mascot: Gunrock (Mustang)
Colors: Blue and gold
Song: *Aggie Fight*

Student Body

UC Davis students describe themselves as "friendly" and "open." There is a greater sense of community at Davis than the other UCs. Students are hard-working, but the campus still feels laid back. There is high ethnic diversity, with 59 percent of students identifying as minority, the great majority of these (37 percent) identifying as Asian or Pacific Islander. The geographic diversity is low however, with only eight percent of students from out of state.

You May Not Know

- According to the college, the Aggie Pack is the "largest organized student spirit group in the country."
- The City of Davis has more bicycles per capita than any other city in the U.S.
- UC Davis ranked eighth among U.S. universities based on their contributions to society, according to *Washington Monthly*.

Distinguished Alumni

Timothy Mondavi, President and CEO Continuum Wines; Steve Robinson, astronaut; Ann Veneman, executive director of UNICEF and former U.S. Secretary of Agriculture.

Admissions and Financial Aid

The UC system uses its own specific application. Students must meet UC Eligibility, which is done in one of three ways: Eligibility in the Statewide Context, Eligibility in the Local Context (ELC), or by Examination alone. The Statewide Context has three components: subject requirement, scholarship requirement, and examination requirement. To qualify for ELC, students must graduate in the top four percent of their high schools at participating California schools and meet the subject and examination requirements. The subject requirement consists of 15 units of high school classes in certain subjects.

According to the university, 80 percent of the decision is based on academic criteria and 20 percent is based on non-academic. The strength of the high school record is the most important part of the application. Standardized test scores and other criteria, including leadership, talents and initiative are also considered; however, students are asked *not* to send letters of recommendation with the application.

Because there are many qualified candidates, the personal statement is a crucial piece of the application. The admissions office specifies that they want you to write about recent experiences, anything that happened during or after high school, and that if you are writing about an accomplishment, you provide specific examples and details.

Freshmen don't have to apply separately for scholarships, but use their admissions application to apply. The most prestigious of the merit awards is the Regent's Scholarship, which meets a student's demonstrated financial need up to the cost of attendance for in-state students. Students who don't demonstrate financial need receive a $7,500 honorarium. Recipients are generally in the top four percent of their high school class.

UNIVERSITY OF CALIFORNIA – IRVINE

Overview

UC Irvine may be one of the youngest branches in the UC system family, but it is also one of the fastest-growing. Since its opening in 1965, UCI has risen in rankings, coming in 14th among public universities, according to *U.S. News & World Report*. UCI offers its students a wealth of undergraduate faculty-supervised research opportunities in all disciplines—it is home to the UC Humanities Research Institute—but its particular strengths lie in science and math. UCI is a major player in stem cell, breast cancer, and environmental research, and features Nobel-prize winning faculty.

UC Irvine occupies a prime location that borders Newport Beach. With sand and shoreline, Disneyland, and all the delights of LA within easy reach, it's impossible to be bored. What other school offers a link to the local surf report on its homepage? UCI's 1,470-acre campus is arranged in a circle around a botanical garden, Daniel Aldrich Park. It features a life-sized architectural gallery, highlighting modernist buildings designed by renowned architects Frank Gehry and Maya Lin.

The school's academic emphasis is placed on math and the sciences, offering excellent academic and research programs. Many other areas of study are available to students as well. In reality, with a wealth of entertainment options in sunny Southern California, the biggest challenge UCI students will face will be balancing work with play.

Academics

UCI makes clear some benefits of attending a large institution: for starters, there are 163 majors offered. The College of Biological Sciences and Donald Bren School of Information and Computer Sciences are well-respected, as are UCI's mathematics major and pre-med program. UCI's size also offers flexibility to students in completing the fairly extensive General Education Requirements, which break down into three courses each in writing, science and technology, social and behavioral sciences, arts and humanities, and quantitative, symbolic, and computational reasoning. The curriculum also requires students to complete one course each in a foreign language, multicultural studies, and international/global issues, as well as a class with a lab or performance component.

On the other hand, UCI's size means that some of its classes, particularly introductory science and math courses, will be large. Getting on professors' radars may be a challenge for students who aren't aggressive about networking with faculty or pursuing research. Classes at UCI are on the quarter system, so the courses go by quickly. Students who aren't diligent about seeking help from professors when they need it may find themselves struggling without much time to turn things around. "The burden is on you to reach out to your professors. No one will hold your hand," says a student.

Fortunately, UCI offers several programs that try to alleviate these issues. The Campuswide Honors Program offers access to faculty beginning in freshmen year: for their first three years, students will complete a three-quarter core sequence each year in humanities, social sciences, and science (for non-science majors), respectively. The sequences are small, interdisciplinary seminars team-taught by well-respected faculty. In their final year, students engage in a research or creative project. Additionally, Honors students have the advantages of priority registration and Honors housing. Additionally, the Peer Academic Advising Program trains upperclassmen Peer Advisors, who hold office hours for consultations on nearly any subject, ranging from transitioning to college and choosing a major to which classes to take and how best to prepare for grad school. "It's very non-threatening to get help from a peer versus from a professor," remarks one student.

UCI's flagship program is its College of Biological Sciences, which has been recognized as a leader in the western U.S. In addition to outstanding faculty, including

UNIVERSITY OF CALIFORNIA – IRVINE

Students

Total enrollment: 27,479
Undergrads: 22,216
Freshmen: 5,077
Part-time students: 2%
From out-of-state: 3%
From public schools: 78%
Male/Female: 46%/54%
Live on-campus: 38%
In fraternities: 9%
In sororities: 10%
Off-campus employment rating: Good
Caucasian: 19%
African American: 2%
Hispanic: 20%
Asian / Pacific Islander: 47%
Native American: 0%
Mixed (2+ ethnicities): 4%
International: 6%

Academics

Calendar: Quarter
Student/faculty ratio: 19:1
Class size 9 or fewer: 26%
Class size 10-29: 45%
Class size 30-49: 8%
Class size 50-99: 8%
Class size 100 or more: 13%
Returning freshmen: 93%
Six-year graduation rate: 86%
Graduates who immediately go to graduate school: 18%

Most Popular Majors

Biological sciences
Business economics
Psychology/social behavior

Admissions

Applicants: 56,508
Accepted: 23,956
Acceptance rate: 42.4%
Placed on wait list: 3,732
Enrolled from wait list: 1621
Average GPA: 3.9
ACT range: Not reported
SAT Math range: 540-670
SAT Reading range: 470-610
SAT Writing range: 6-27
Top 10% of class: 96%
Top 25% of class: 100%

700

three Nobel-Prize winners, the biological science major offers opportunities for faculty-supervised research. Students in Bio 199 earn course credit for working under faculty as apprentice researchers in any of the 250 biological or medical laboratories.

Of all the University of California schools, many of which are research powerhouses, UCI ranks first in number of undergrads participating in research. This is made possible by the Undergraduate Research Opportunities Program, which helps students in all fields find research opportunities as well as funds. The Program also assists with research proposals, projects, and presentations. UCI funds grants and stipends for participants in any of its several special eight- to ten-week summer research programs, which are designated by tongue-in-cheek acronyms: SURP for all fields, IM-SURE for integrated nano/microtechnology, SURFIT for information technology, and Chem-SURF for chemistry, and so forth.

UCI offers a limited selection of summer Travel-Study programs in the UK, Cyprus, Italy, Argentina, Chile, Costa Rica, Japan, Poland, and Switzerland. UCI also administers "Engaging Globally" courses, in which students take a course on service learning before embarking on a service trip. UCI students may also participate in the UC system's Education Abroad Programs, offering programs at hundreds of institutions in 35 countries. The Global Leadership Certificate Program offers students experience with intercultural groups on campus and leadership training; students must study abroad and complete a three-quarter capstone project.

In addition to offering interview practice, job and internship listings, and career consultations, the UCI Career Center operates Career Connections, a database of local professionals available for networking and advising.

Student Life

UCI has over 450 student groups. The most popular tend to be cultural-interest clubs, including the Chinese Association, Konnect Korean Cultural Awareness Group, and Vietnamese Student Association—reflective of the school's very high Asian population. Cultural-awareness events like Asian Heritage Week, Cinco de Mayo, and Rainbow Festival, which celebrates UCI's diversity, are popular. Wayzgoose is perhaps the highlight of annual on-campus events, featuring carnival rides and games, a Medieval Faire in Aldrich Park, and a beer garden for Anteaters over 21. About one-tenth of students belong to one of UCI's 21 fraternities or 26 sororities.

UCI's nine men's and nine women's Division I varsity teams are enthusiastically supported by the CIA (Completely Insane Anteaters); men's water polo, basketball, and baseball are the strongest teams. A large number of standard intramural sports are available in league or tournament play at five levels for the not-quite-varsity athletes; and for solo fitness buffs, facilities include a well-equipped fitness center as well as outdoor roller rink, sport courts, climbing wall, and test kitchen that features healthy cooking classes. Swimmers and sun-worshippers alike will enjoy the 80-degree outdoor pool on campus.

Off-campus recreational activities are many and varied: Laguna Beach is just 12 miles away, and ski slopes are within a two hour's drive. Disneyland, LA, San Diego, and even Mexico are manageable drives. For entertainment that's closer to home, University Center offers shops and restaurants, as do Fashion Island and South Coast

Plaza malls. One student comments, "If you have a car, you really can do anything—club, sunbathe, ski, anything."

Students are guaranteed housing for their first two years. Freshmen can live in suites in residence halls in either the Middle Earth or Mesa Court communities, while upperclassmen may live in the academic theme or Greek houses that make up Arroyo Vista. Apartments in Campus Village are also an option. Many students move off campus after freshman year. "Apartments are plentiful," says a student.

Student Body

At UCI, Caucasians are in the minority, while ethnic minorities, particularly Asian-Americans, make up a large part of the student body; very few students are from out of state. UCI has a reputation for being on the conservative side, politically, probably due to its location in conservative stronghold Orange County. "I wouldn't say that we're a conservative school," comments a student, "but compared to the other UCs like Berkeley and Santa Cruz, we are."

You Might Not Know

- The atmospheric studies of F. Sherwood Rowland on the formation and decomposition of ozone, which led to the ban on CFCs in aerosols and for which Rowland was awarded a Nobel Prize, were conducted at UCI.
- UCI's "celebrity mascot" is Peter the Anteater, a weirdly buff, 6-foot-9 anteater who has visited the White House and was the first anteater to go to space on the Space Shuttle Endeavor. You can send him fan mail at his website. The ubiquitous campus "battle cry," "Zot!" is allegedly the noise that an anteater makes when it seizes its prey with its two-foot long tongue.
- Irvine has been called the "safest city in America" for five years running.

Distinguished Alumni

Michael Chabon, author; Roy Fielding; co-founder of Apache Foundation; Jon Lovitz, actor and comedian; Alice Sebold, novelist; Shane West, actor.

Admissions and Financial Aid

As one of the fastest-growing UC schools, UCI has recently experienced record numbers of applications, making admission to UCI more competitive than it has ever been. The university doesn't use a formula for admitting students, but looks for excellent academic achievement (the average high school GPA for those accepted is 3.9).

UC Irvine offers merit scholarships of varying amounts. Most prestigious is the Regents' Scholarship, which also provides recipients with priority registration and special library privileges. The Henry Samueli Endowed Scholarship is awarded to students in the School of Engineering. Neither requires an extra application; students must apply by November 30 to be considered for the Regents' Scholarship.

UNIVERSITY OF CALIFORNIA – IRVINE

Highlights

Admissions Criteria
Academic criteria:
Grades: ☆ ☆ ☆
Difficulty of class schedule: ☆ ☆ ☆
Class rank: ☆ ☆
Standardized test scores: ☆ ☆ ☆
Teacher recommendations: N/A
Personal statement: ☆ ☆ ☆
Non-academic criteria considered:
Extracurricular activities
Special talents, interests, abilities
Character/personal qualities
Volunteer work
Work experience
Geographical location

Deadlines
Early Action: No
Early Decision: No
Regular Action: November 30 (final)
Notification of admission by: March 31
Common Application: Not accepted

Financial Aid
In-state tuition: $11,220
Out-of-state tuition: $34,098
Room: Varies
Board: Varies
Books: $1,583
Freshmen receiving need-based aid: 69%
Undergrads rec. need-based aid: 66%
Avg. % of need met by financial aid: 84%
Avg. aid package (freshmen): $22,665
Avg. aid package (undergrads): $20,510
Avg. debt upon graduation: $19,828

School Spirit
Mascot: Anteaters
Colors: Blue and gold
Song: *UCI Fight Song*

Four-year public
Founded: 1919
Los Angeles, CA
Major city
Pop. 3,819,702

Address:
405 Hilgard Avenue
Los Angeles, CA
90095

Admissions:
310-825-3101

Financial Aid:
310-206-0400

ugadm@saonet.ucla.
edu

www.ucla.edu

UNIVERSITY OF CALIFORNIA - LOS ANGELES

Overview

Located in west Los Angeles, just minutes from Beverly Hills and Hollywood and a mere five miles from the Pacific Ocean and the beach, UCLA occupies a 419-acre campus with buildings that run the architectural gamut from Romanesque to sleek modern biotechnology facilities. UCLA is not only the second-ranked public university in the country according to *U.S. News & World Report*, but it is also the 23rd ranked school overall. UCLA's programs and professional schools combine with its high-caliber and readily-available research opportunities, its prime location and weather, and its seriously dominant athletic programs to make UCLA one of the most competitive and selective universities in the nation.

For some, UCLA's size—almost 28,000 undergraduates—can be a drawback. But UCLA claims that "UCLA's strength is its size." The breadth and quality of UCLA's academic and research opportunities are nearly unparalleled. Students simply must be organized and motivated enough to take advantage of them.

It's not easy to get into UCLA, and even students who worked hard in high school won't be able to sit back and rest on their laurels. UCLA students have to step up their game to make the most of all UCLA offers and to stand out among thousands of students. If you're willing to kick your academics into high gear in college, and you can find the golden mean between serious work and serious play, and you want to cheer on Bruins basketball with several thousand of your closest friends, then look no further than UCLA.

Academics

UCLA's college and 12 professional schools offer a total of 129 undergraduate majors. The university as a whole requires all students to complete courses in Entry-Level Writing and American History and Institutions. Each college or school has its own further general education requirements, which can include foreign language, composition courses, or core curriculum specific to the school's field of study. Standout programs include chemistry, drama, economics, engineering, and premed.

Academics are extremely serious, and students work hard to stay on top of classes. UCLA is a large school, but more than half of its classes have fewer than 20 students, and as students enter more advanced or specialized courses, faculty becomes even more accessible. "You can get a little lost in classes, especially freshman year, but conditions improve," says a student.

UCLA's special academic programs are numerous, and many of them help freshmen get in on the ground floor of their chosen fields of study; but they can be overwhelming to students who aren't quite organized enough to plan ahead or who aren't yet sure what their majors will be. "You have to take the initiative," one student notes.

Students with high GPAs, test scores, and class rank can apply to the Honors program in the College of Letters and Science. The Honors Program does not require any particular core curriculum but allows students to choose from a range of Honors-designated courses and Fiat Lux Seminars that are freshmen-only, limited-enrollment classes taught by UCLA's most eminent faculty. "It's nice to have more flexibility to choose classes of interest," one student comments. Honors students are privy to certain perks, including extended borrowing at the libraries, specialized advising, summer research funding, and scholarships. Very organized and highly-qualified students can also apply to the Department Scholars Program, which allows them to simultaneously earn their bachelor's and master's degrees.

By taking General Education Clusters, freshmen can begin to build bonds with faculty and classmates. These groups of classes take place throughout freshman year and are designed to examine a pre-selected theme through different disciplinary lenses. They are taught by either faculty or distinguished grad students.

Students at UCLA may also take advantage of its excellent research facilities—the Student Research Program allows students to work one-on-one with faculty in all areas of research, while summer research opportunities are slightly more science- and technology-oriented. Under SPUR, the Summer Program for Undergraduate Research, students can spend 8-10 weeks of summer working in faculty labs. Additionally, freshmen in life sciences, chemistry, or biochemistry can participate in the Biomedical Sciences Summer Enrichment Program (BISEP), which offers lab experience, workshops on journal-article writing and giving academic presentations, and seminars on applying to grad school.

UCLA students somehow find the time to go abroad: UCLA ranks fifth in the nation in students studying abroad. UCLA's own Travel Study summer programs are diverse and plentiful, offering some domestic trips as well as travel in China, Hong Kong, the UK, France, Germany, Austria, Brazil, South Africa, Morocco, South Korea, Egypt, Belgium, the Netherlands, Spain, Mexico, Switzerland, Greece, and Italy. UCLA also offers a single Quarter Abroad program in Classics in Greece, and students can also participate in the UC-Sponsored Education Abroad Program, which offers 140 exchange agreements in 30 countries. Departments and schools also have their own exchange agreements.

UCLA's size is advantageous to students when it comes to helping UCLA graduates find jobs after graduation. In addition to having the UC system's flagship Career Center, UCLA also has an Alumni Association of 84,000, which often sponsors career- and networking-related events.

Student Life

UCLA offers a whopping 1,000 student organizations on campus, including the *Daily Bruin*, the student newspaper, and the Den, UCLA's official fan group. As a major destination for the arts, UCLA also features a number of arts and dance and musical performance groups, and the annual Spring Sing, a musical performance competition, which draws a huge crowd from UCLA and the surrounding community alike.

There is relatively high participation in Greek life on campus, so it comes as no surprise that Greek Week—which pits UCLA's 32 fraternities and 33 sororities against each other in events like the "Olympics," Family Feud-style games, and a very muddy tug-of-war—is a popular event. Dance Marathon, a 26-hour dance-a-thon designed to raise money and awareness of HIV/AIDS, also gets a high turnout. "It's an exhausting but fun all-night party," recalls a student.

UCLA's powerhouse athletics, whose 22 Division I teams have won more NCAA championships than any other college, dominate the campus scene. Blue and Gold Week, the week leading up to the UCLA-USC football game, features a "Beat SC" parade, car smash, and a Homecoming bonfire. But it is by far the men's basketball team—the most prestigious program in the nation—that generates the most excitement. "Whether our team is winning or losing, we come out to support it," says a student. Almost 8,000 students participate in intramural sports every year as well.

Within minutes of campus, students can take advantage of sunny Southern California weather on the beach. They can also head

UNIVERSITY OF CALIFORNIA – LOS ANGELES

Highlights

Students
Total enrollment: 41,341
Undergrads: 27,941
Freshmen: 5,825
From out-of-state: 1%
From public schools: 70%
Male/Female: 45%/55%
Live on-campus: 36%
In fraternities: 13%
In sororities: 13%
Off-campus employment rating: Good
Caucasian: 30%
African American: 3%
Hispanic: 18%
Asian / Pacific Islander: 33%
Native American: 0%
Mixed (2+ ethnicities): 4%
International: 10%

Academics
Calendar: Quarter
Student/faculty ratio: 16:1
Class size 9 or fewer: 23%
Class size 10-29: 44%
Class size 30-49: 11%
Class size 50-99: 11%
Class size 100 or more: 11%
Returning freshmen: 96%
Six-year graduation rate: 92%

Most Popular Majors
Political science
Psychology
History

Admissions
Applicants: 72,697
Accepted: 15,982
Acceptance rate: 22.0%
Average GPA: 4.2
ACT range: 24-31
SAT Math range: 610-760
SAT Reading range: 570-690
SAT Writing range: 38-40
Top 10% of class: 97%
Top 25% of class: 100%
Top 50% of class: 100%

UNIVERSITY OF CALIFORNIA – LOS ANGELES

Admissions Criteria
Academic criteria:
Grades: ☆ ☆ ☆
Difficulty of class schedule: ☆ ☆ ☆
Class rank: N/A
Standardized test scores: ☆ ☆ ☆
Teacher recommendations: N/A
Personal statement: ☆ ☆ ☆
Non-academic criteria considered:
Extracurricular activities
Special talents, interests, abilities
Character/personal qualities
Volunteer work
Work experience
State of residency
Geographical location

Deadlines
Early Action: No
Early Decision: No
Regular Action: November 30 (final)
Notification of admission by: March 31
Common Application: Not accepted

Financial Aid
In-state tuition: $12,692
Out-of-state tuition: $35,570
Room: Varies
Board: Varies
Books: $1,536
Freshmen receiving need-based aid: 54%
Undergrads rec. need-based aid: 56%
Avg. % of need met by financial aid: 84%
Avg. aid package (freshmen): $21,754
Avg. aid package (undergrads): $20,362
Avg. debt upon graduation: $18,814

School Spirit
Mascot: Bruin
Colors: Blue and gold
Song: *Sons of Westwood*

downtown or to Santa Monica and Beverly Hills for shopping and nightlife. "We are in the most desirable city in the most desirable state in the country," boasts a student.

UCLA guarantees two years of on-campus housing, after which students move off campus. On-campus housing is connected to main campus by Bruin Walk and mostly consists of standard dorm-style rooms and suites. Campus dining is among the best options in the country.

Student Body

To get into UCLA, students need to be well-rounded, and the student body reflects that. Students are an "academically-high achieving" group that knows how and when to have fun. As with most UC schools, nearly everyone is from California; consequently, it's a diverse and "more liberal" student body of which less than a third is Caucasian.

You May Not Know

- UCLA initially used live bears as mascots.
- After the theft of UCLA's Victory Bell by USC students in 1941, the Bell was finally returned in fall of 1942 after UCLA students threatened to kidnap the USC student body president. It is now a permanent USC-UCLA game trophy.
- The first open-heart surgery in the western United States was performed at UCLA's medical center.

Distinguished Alumni

Kareem Abdul-Jabbar, NBA player; Jack Black, actor and musician; Francis Ford Coppola, screenwriter and director; Jackie Joyner-Kersee, track and field athlete; George C. Pimental, inventor of the chemical laser; Jackie Robinson, former Major League Baseball player.

Admissions and Financial Aid

Admission to UCLA is extremely competitive, and academic performance is only one factor out of many when it comes to getting in. Students must demonstrate strength of character as well as their ability to make a contribution to the academic and cultural environment on campus—the admissions office notes that "these qualities may not be reflected in traditional measures of academic achievement." It's worth noticing that the standardized test scores appear lower on the list than character.

Applicants with demonstrated financial need and a record of academic achievement may be eligible for UCLA's merit-based scholarships. These awards range from $500 to $3,000 but are not automatically renewable. UCLA also participates in the UC Regents Scholarship program, which covers the extent of financial need plus a $2,000 honorarium for students demonstrating academic excellence, leadership, and "exceptional promise." Qualified applicants to UCLA are invited to apply for the Regents Scholarship; about 100 are awarded each year.

UNIVERSITY OF CALIFORNIA – RIVERSIDE

Overview

Go one direction at UCR and you'll find yourself in the mountains ready to hit the slopes. Go another and you'll find yourself on the beach taking in some rays. Pass the weekly concert underneath the bell tower and you might find yourself on your way to class.

Located 60 miles outside of LA, University of California Riverside is a large public university with a diverse offering of academic concentrations and an assortment of modern architecture. It's often regarded as the more accessible UC school, desirable to students in that the area offers many things to do.

Academics

Students choose from courses in 155 different majors across different colleges of the Riverside campus: The College of Humanities, Arts, and Social Sciences, the College of Natural and Agricultural Sciences, the Marian and Rosemary Bourns College of Engineering, and the School of Business Administration. Though each of the colleges has its own set of "breadth requirements," they tend to be pretty similar. Usually students are obligated to pursue courses in humanities, social sciences, ethnicity, natural sciences, and mathematics. Stronger programs at the university include biology, business, and psychology.

The work ethic is a friendly one at UCR, where students work together as opposed to against each other. Students say there is "very little" and "practically no competition" at the college. This laid-back atmosphere leaves students plenty of time to make it to the ski lifts on Bear Mountain or catch some waves at Huntington Beach.

If jumping headfirst into academia seems a little daunting, you can always choose components of the CHASS program at UCR to ease your way into it. CHASS Gateway lectures are for freshmen only and provide Peer Educators to help students through the material as they fulfill a college breadth requirement. Or, if it's a bigger lecture you want to explore but you feel intimidated by all the learned upperclassmen, CHASS First-Year Learning Communities gives you a seat in coveted large lecture courses, but you work in smaller freshmen-only discussion groups.

The University Honors Program brings together professors and groups of highly motivated students for research, focused courses, or independent projects. Students in the program take honors courses, typically volunteer 10 hours a quarter, and have required advising meetings. They may reside together in the honors residence halls. "I'm probably learning more from living with other honors students than I do in some of my classes," says a student.

"Do you want to see the world?" belts the introductory music to Worldfest, an annual showcase of the immense study-abroad opportunities for students. If your answer is yes, be sure to check out over 200 opportunities to get out of California and study almost anywhere else on the planet.

The university's career center has online job and internship listings and provides workshops on career and graduate school planning. There are several career fairs throughout the school year including fairs for graduate and professional schools, government jobs, health professions, and last chance jobs.

Student Life

While other schools may reward students after a hard semester's worth of all-night cram sessions with a big concert, UCR only goes a couple of weeks before throwing their annual Block Party, bringing in huge national acts, all the entertainment of a street fair, student performances, and food. Don't worry, they do it all over again with Spring Splash during second semester. The live music doesn't stop at the big events

UNIVERSITY OF CALIFORNIA – RIVERSIDE

Four-year public
Founded: 1954
Riverside, CA
Medium city
Pop. 310,651

Address:
900 University Avenue
Riverside, CA
92521

Admissions:
951-827-3411

Financial Aid:
951-827-3878

admissions@ucr.edu

www.ucr.edu

UNIVERSITY OF CALIFORNIA – RIVERSIDE

Students

Total enrollment: 20,947
Undergrads: 18,539
Freshmen: 4,034
From out-of-state: 3%
From public schools: 90%
Male/Female: 48%/52%
Live on-campus: 31%
In fraternities: 2%
In sororities: 2%
Off-campus employment rating: Excellent
Caucasian: 15%
African American: 6%
Hispanic: 35%
Asian / Pacific Islander: 37%
Native American: 0%
Mixed (2+ ethnicities): 3%
International: 2%

Academics

Calendar: Quarter
Student/faculty ratio: 19:1
Class size 9 or fewer: 14%
Class size 10-29: 49%
Class size 30-49: 9%
Class size 50-99: 16%
Class size 100 or more: 12%
Returning freshmen: 88%
Six-year graduation rate: 66%
Graduates who immediately go to graduate school: 30%

Most Popular Majors

Social sciences
Business/management/marketing/related support services
Biological/biomedical sciences

Admissions

Applicants: 30,395
Accepted: 19,062
Acceptance rate: 62.7%
Placed on wait list: 3,694
Average GPA: 3.6
ACT range: 20-25
SAT Math range: 500-630
SAT Reading range: 470-580
SAT Writing range: 2-20
Top 10% of class: 94%
Top 25% of class: 100%
Top 50% of class: 100%

either. There are concert series that bring local and national acts to campus every week, whether it's to rock the whole night or just between afternoon classes. Students also tend to trek off campus to enjoy the surrounding mountains, which offer great camping, snowboarding and skiing locations, or go to nearby beaches to perfect their perpetual tans. "It's a trek and a lot of traffic, but you can get to the beach on the weekends," comments a student.

There are more than 350 student organizations that range from the expected serious standards like Model UN and student newspapers to paintballing groups, bag-pipe clubs, or the All-Wheel Addicts. When the campus is this diverse, the assortment of student clubs is bound to be just as varied. And although Greek participation isn't as strong as at some other schools (around two percent), there are 40 fraternities and sororities on UCR campus to choose from. Additionally, those who want to embrace their cultural heritage may want to check out organizations specifically for certain minority groups. There are also a number of honor societies; and if you can't get in enough volunteering between classes, you can join those Greek organizations that are specifically service-oriented.

Athletes at Riverside recently switched to competing at the Division I level. Some—such as women's basketball and men's baseball—have hit the ground running, making it to NCAA championships. Other competitive teams include men's golf and women's soccer. School spirit is pretty high, so students should plan to get psyched and give Scotty the Bear, the school's mascot, a high five at the next game.

Freshmen are guaranteed housing, which is easy to find but varies in quality. More than three-quarters of freshmen live in the residence halls, which include doubles, triples, and suites. Roommate assignments are based on a roommate compatibility questionnaire. "The housing office does a pretty good job of matching roommates," confides a student, and adds, "mine is my best friend."

Student Body

University officials say life at the school can be very calm, and the school's atmosphere in general, very quiet. So although the student body is big with 18,000 undergraduates, they tend to be pretty laid back and a rather friendly bunch. Students describe themselves as "relaxed" and "motivated but not over the top." That is not to say that students don't strive for success, but they do so in a low-key manner. Many of undergrads describe themselves as "average college students."

Although the geographic diversity on campus is low with most students coming from within the state, UCR boasts the most ethnically diverse student body in the UC system.

You May Not Know

- Every Wednesday is declared R'Day. Students are encouraged to dawn their best UCR gear, sport their blue and gold and bully anyone who isn't (not really... just don't test them).
- Citrus overload! The city of Riverside hosts the annual Orange Blossom Festival where every food is packed with some creative splash of citrus. Sure the parade part is

cool, but what's better than having orange in everything from BBQ sauce to chocolate cake?

- Every Friday the chancellor writes a letter to the UCR community. It's like a quirky combination of a blog, a written care package, and a university-wide sounding board that is put together by the head of the school.

Distinguished Alumni

Billy Collins, U.S. Poet laureate; Elizabeth George, international bestselling author; Stefani Schaeffer, defense attorney and winner of Donald Trump reality show, *The Apprentice*; Richard R. Schrock, Nobel Laureate in chemistry; Tim White, paleoanthropologist and professor of integrative biology, 2010 *Time Magazine* 100 Most Influential People.

Admissions and Financial Aid

If you hail from within the boundaries of the great state of California, there are a few fast tracks into UC Riverside enrollment. The top four percent of each participating California high school is designated UC eligible. Or, if you've got the numbers, you can obtain admission eligibility with just exam scores (SAT + SAT Subject Tests or ACT + Writing). Luckily out-of-state students can test in as well (but they must score a 425 on the UC index as opposed to the 410 for residents).

Don't let the big test scores intimidate you. There is also a conditional admissions path for students who have not completed the SAT and/or TOEFL requirements prior to graduation. The UCR Admission Preparation Program focuses on instruction in university study skills and gets students ready for the challenges of academic work in a college setting.

There are a number of merit-based scholarships, but they can get competitive considering the requirements or how few are rewarded. If you're willing to have your application scrutinized by the Committee on Scholarships and Honors, there are the Regent's Scholarship, the Chancellor's Scholarship and a handful of scholarships from the alumni association, like the George Beattie Memorial Scholarship ($1,800 awarded annually to a Californian resident) to try for.

UNIVERSITY OF CALIFORNIA – RIVERSIDE

Highlights

Admissions Criteria
Academic criteria:
Grades: ☆ ☆ ☆
Difficulty of class schedule: ☆ ☆ ☆
Class rank: N/A
Standardized test scores: ☆ ☆ ☆
Teacher recommendations: N/A
Personal statement: ☆ ☆ ☆
Non-academic criteria considered:
State of residency

Deadlines
Early Action: No
Early Decision: No
Regular Action: Rolling admissions
Common Application: Not accepted

Financial Aid
In-state tuition: $11,220
Out-of-state tuition: $34,098
Room: Varies
Board: Varies
Books: $1,800
Freshmen receiving need-based aid: 78%
Undergrads rec. need-based aid: 78%
Avg. % of need met by financial aid: 85%
Avg. aid package (freshmen): $23,705
Avg. aid package (undergrads): $20,954
Avg. debt upon graduation: $21,373

School Spirit
Mascot: Highlanders
Colors: Blue and gold
Song: *Brave Scots/Sons of California*

UNIVERSITY OF CALIFORNIA – SAN DIEGO

Four-year public
Founded: 1960
La Jolla, CA
Major city
Pop. 1,326,179

Address:
9500 Gilman Drive
La Jolla, CA
92093

Admissions:
858-534-4831

Financial Aid:
858-534-4480

admissionsinfo@ucsd.
edu

www.ucsd.edu

Overview

One of the youngest members of the UC family, UCSD has skyrocketed to the top of nearly every ranking, coming in ninth on *U.S. News & World Report's* Best Public Universities and 39th of all ranked colleges nationwide. UCSD ranks top five in the nation in terms of research expenditures and first in the UC system, and according to *Newsweek* it is the "hottest" place in the country to study science. UCSD combines powerhouse undergraduate academics—particularly science, medicine, and technology—with a standout location in San Diego's northern beach neighborhood of La Jolla. Many of the 1,200-acre campus' eco-friendly, contemporary-style buildings and residences offer stunning ocean views.

UCSD is a very large university, and its most popular majors are its most competitive: it can be easy to get lost in a hundred-person biology lecture. But UCSD seeks to mitigate that problem with a selection of special academic programs designed to help undergraduates interact with small groups of peers and faculty. Additionally, its unique six-college system creates a "liberal arts" college feel within a large research institution. For competitive science, premed, or engineering students, UCSD is the place to be, combining high-level, high-powered academics with a healthy dose of SoCal lifestyle.

Academics

UCSD offers 186 undergraduate majors, but a hefty chunk of its student body clusters in the division of biological sciences or any of its six engineering programs, including bioengineering and computer science and engineering. Other strong programs include drama, political science, and the Scripps Institution of Oceanography.

Undergraduates are grouped into six residential colleges: Revelle, Eleanor Roosevelt, Earl Warren, Thurgood Marshall, John Muir, and Sixth. Since each college manages its own core curriculum, general education requirements vary according to college: nearly all of them require classes in humanities, social sciences, math, and natural science. Most require a foreign language and others require fine arts. Some colleges have a core class, usually in conjunction with the writing requirement, with a specialized academic focus, for example, Thurgood Marshall College's three-quarter sequence "Dimensions of Culture: Diversity, Justice, Imagination" or Eleanor Roosevelt's "Making of the Modern World." Students take their major and elective courses with classmates from the university at large. "It's a unique system, but it really helps us form connections with our colleges," says a student.

UCSD students take their studies and GPAs very seriously, and the academic environment is intense; in fact, students will frequently stay on extra quarters to boost their GPAs. "There isn't open competition among students, but we all want to do well," one student explains. Classes are on the smaller side—over half have fewer than 30 students—but that varies by major, and introductory classes and popular majors have large lecture classes.

Freshman Seminars are limited-enrollment classes that allow students to explore a topic in depth; since they are only offered pass-fail, these courses are excellent opportunities for freshmen to try something new and different. For hardcore engineering students, the Jacobs School of Engineering offers a number of professional development opportunities, including Teams in Engineering Service (TIES), in which engineering students design and develop technological solutions for local nonprofit organizations. There are also Team Internship Programs, which set up student engineering teams with full-time, paid summer internships. UCSD engineering students form teams to compete against other schools in challenges such as building functional concrete canoes. "You don't have to hide your passion," a student remarks, "even if it's for something nerdy."

UCSD offers all its students the opportunity to participate in internships via the Academic Internship Program. Students in Academic Internship earn academic credit in a field related to their majors; they also complete a research project supervised by a faculty advisor.

A quarter of UCSD students gain experience by studying abroad, making UCSD the seventh-ranked school in students traveling abroad. Most of UCSD's programs are faculty-led summer Global Seminars, which offer credit for two courses over five weeks. The UC-sponsored Education Abroad Program has 200 exchange agreements with universities in 35 countries. Students can also find internships, work, and volunteer opportunities abroad.

Prospects for UCSD grads are promising with 65 percent of graduates planning to enter the workforce and find work in a field related to their major within six months of graduation. UCSD alums rank fifth nationally in salary earnings among graduates from public universities. One third of UCSD graduates enter some kind of postgraduate program within one year of graduation.

Student Life

A quick stroll on Library Walk—the main pedestrian drag connecting Geisel Library to the Medical School—will take students past tables of flyers designed for UCSD's 400+ student organizations. Pre-professional organizations such as Pre-Dental Society and HI-Med (Holistic and Integrative Medicine Interest Group) are big, as are performance and musical groups, including the Tritones, which Taylor Swift picked to perform her back-up vocals at the Academy of Country Music Awards. "We have every type of organization imaginable," remarks a student.

UCSD's extensive campus is chock-full of entertaining distractions: for starters, Library Walk hosts a popular weekly farmer's market. The Price Center's shops and restaurants are a major hub of student life, and the Center also shows current movies at discounted prices and hosts events such as the drag show Bitchy Bingo and regular De-stress Fests that feature free massages, therapy puppies, and cupcakes. The Price Center also houses a restaurant-lounge-nightclub space called the Loft, which puts on rock and hip hop concerts, comedy club nights, and film festivals. On-campus eateries such as the alternative Che Café and Porter's Pub are also popular student gathering spots. Theatre performances regularly make their West Coast or national premieres at UCSD's Tony-Award winning La Jolla Playhouse.

Slightly less culturally edifying is the traditional Watermelon Drop, which celebrates the end of spring quarter finals: supposedly derived from an exam question about the velocity of falling objects, Watermelon Drop features a student elected "Watermelon Queen" dropping a watermelon off the multi-story Urey Hall. UCSD's Welcome Week also features the All-College UnOlympics, which pits colleges against each other in events such as dizzy bat and dance competitions, and features an obstacle course. About a sixth of students belong to UCSD's 19 fraternities and 14 sororities, which also form a prominent part of social life on campus.

Outside of UnOlympics, students can get their physical activity in by visiting any of UCSD's three gym facilities or participating in intramural sports, including bowling. The Outback Adventures

UNIVERSITY OF CALIFORNIA – SAN DIEGO

Highlights

Students
Total enrollment: 28,294
Undergrads: 22,676
From out-of-state: 3%
Male/Female: 51%/49%
Live on-campus: 36%
In fraternities: 14%
In sororities: 14%
Off-campus employment rating: Excellent
Caucasian: 24%
African American: 1%
Hispanic: 16%
Asian / Pacific Islander: 42%
Native American: 0%
Mixed (2+ ethnicities): 4%
International: 9%

Academics
Calendar: Quarter
Student/faculty ratio: 19:1
Class size 9 or fewer: 10%
Class size 10-29: 45%
Class size 30-49: 11%
Class size 50-99: 12%
Class size 100 or more: 22%
Graduates who immediately go to graduate school: 33%
Graduates who immediately enter career related to major: 65%

Most Popular Majors
Biology
Economics
Psychology

Admissions
Average GPA: Not reported
ACT range: 23-30
SAT Math range: 590-710
SAT Reading range: 520-650
SAT Writing range: 550-670

College Profiles

UNIVERSITY OF CALIFORNIA – SAN DIEGO

Admissions Criteria

Academic criteria:
Grades: ☆ ☆ ☆
Difficulty of class schedule: ☆ ☆ ☆
Class rank: N/A
Standardized test scores: ☆ ☆ ☆
Teacher recommendations: N/A
Personal statement: ☆ ☆ ☆
Non-academic criteria considered:
Extracurricular activities
Special talents, interests, abilities
Character/personal qualities
Volunteer work
Work experience
Geographical location

Deadlines

Early Action: No
Early Decision: No
Regular Action: Rolling admissions
Common Application: Not accepted

Financial Aid

In-state tuition: $13,302
Out-of-state tuition: $22,878
Room: Varies
Board: Varies
Books: $1,489
Avg. aid package (freshmen): $21,333
Avg. aid package (undergrads): $21,389

School Spirit

Mascot: Tritons
Colors: Blue and gold

program offers students local hiking and rock climbing outings, challenge courses, and wilderness orientations. UCSD's 23 Division II sports teams draw big crowds, particularly for their competitive soccer games and women's volleyball, tennis, and water polo matches.

If on-campus events and activities don't entice students, restaurants, shopping, and nightlife in La Jolla and San Diego are easily accessible, as both the campus shuttle and city bus system are free for students with IDs. Students can visit Shamu at nearby SeaWorld or visit the world class San Diego Zoo. "You should make it to the touristy spots at least once," one student comments.

Students are guaranteed housing on campus for two years; each college has its own residences. "There's a huge range of dorms, and they're all pretty small," one student explains. Upperclass students tend to move off campus.

Student Body

UCSD students are characterized first and foremost by their intense level of academic focus. "All my classmates seem to have graduated from the top of their high school class," one student notes. UCSD's student body, which is nearly entirely drawn from within the state, reflects California's high social and ethnic diversity: Caucasians are in the minority at UCSD.

You May Not Know

- USCD was ranked #1 campus for surfing by *Surfline*.
- UCSD's Theodor Geisel Library is named after the children's author Dr. Seuss; every year the Library hosts a birthday party in his honor.
- According to campus legend, the space-looking Geisel Library has made appearances as a spaceship in *Close Encounters of the Third Kind* and *Star Trek*.

Distinguished Alumni

Khaled Hosseini, physician and novelist; K. Megan McArthur, NASA astronaut; Guy Tribble, principal architect of the original MacIntosh; Craig Venter, gene scientist, Celera Genomics.

Admissions and Financial Aid

UCSD's competitive admissions evaluation process puts heavy emphasis on academic achievement. While UCSD's admissions office says that the process also notes non-academic talents and achievement, these are not sufficient for admission if not backed by substantial academic merit.

UCSD offers freshmen two merit scholarships. The UC-sponsored Regents Scholarship pays a $2,000 annual honorarium for four years and covers any demonstrated financial need, while the Ellen and Roger Revelle Scholarship pays $10,000, awarded over the course of four years. UCSD no longer sponsors a National Merit Scholarship. To qualify for these awards, students must file their UC Applications for Admission and Scholarships early and complete the FAFSA.

UNIVERSITY OF CALIFORNIA – SANTA BARBARA

Overview

For sun-and-surf gods and goddesses, the 1,000+ acres of UCSB campus on the California coast provides a beautiful location for study and play. While the vast majority of students are beach-loving Californians, students don't just spend all day at the beach: UCSB is a large public university recognized as one of the top public schools in the country. In fact, *U.S. News & World Report* ranks UCSB 11th among U.S. public universities and one of the top 50 universities overall in the nation. Palm trees, 1950s Southern California architecture, and the distinctive Storke Tower (bell and clock tower), the tallest building in Santa Barbara County, give the university an unmistakably Southern California feel.

The university's diversity—more than half of students are minority students—also reflects the demographics of California. At such a large university, there's certainly an opportunity for every taste and mood, though students may need to make an extra effort to carve out a niche for themselves. UCSB is also known for its party scene, reputedly the most festive of the UC system, for better or worse. Students who shy away from huge party scenes might not feel too comfortable at UCSB, but those looking for strong academics alongside opportunities to play in the sun will appreciate University of California-Santa Barbara.

Academics

More than 200 majors, degrees, and credentials are offered at UCSB through its five undergraduate and graduate schools. All UCSB undergrads must complete requirements in Entry Level Writing and American History and Institutions, along with general requirements outlined by each school. These general requirements include foreign language and subject area requirements, differing among the College of Letters and Science, College of Engineering, and College of Creative Studies.

Courses are challenging but not competitive. Students say there are some professors who seem more interested in their research than teaching. "I've had excellent professors who are really dedicated to their students and others who seem to be bothered showing up for class," says a student. There are over 1,000 faculty members, including five Nobel Prize winners. Strong programs include accounting, economics, and the ecology, evolution, and marine biology department, made up of approximately 35 faculty research groups.

Students in the College of Letters and Science can be part of the Honors Program, which confers special library access privileges, advising services, opportunities for publication of work, and eligibility for honors research awards. Students have three different windows of opportunity to apply for honors.

The Educational Opportunity Program (EOP) offers mentorship, academic programs, individual counseling/advising, and other services to all students with a special focus on low-income and first-generation undergraduates. Freshmen Seminars also help guide students through the college transition. These small group seminars of no more than 20 students are taught by volunteer faculty and are designed to cultivate student-faculty relationships.

The Education Abroad Program (EAP) offers 200 programs in 35 countries, from Argentina to Vietnam. Courses satisfy UC degree requirements, and students are able to be part of a membership of 70,000 UC EAP graduates.

Career services at UCSB provide library and online resources, programs, and counseling to assist students and recent graduates with career development, internships, job-seeking, and graduate school.

UNIVERSITY OF CALIFORNIA – SANTA BARBARA

Four-year public
Founded: 1909
Santa Barbara, CA
Large town
Pop. 89,045

Address:
552 University Road
Santa Barbara, CA
93106

Admissions:
805-893-2881

Financial Aid:
805-893-2432

admissions@sa.ucsb.edu

www.ucsb.edu

UNIVERSITY OF CALIFORNIA – SANTA BARBARA

Highlights

Students
Total enrollment: 21,927
Undergrads: 18,977
Freshmen: 4,983
From out-of-state: 4%
From public schools: 86%
Male/Female: 47%/53%
Live on-campus: 37%
In fraternities: 8%
In sororities: 12%
Off-campus employment rating: Excellent
Caucasian: 42%
African American: 2%
Hispanic: 24%
Asian / Pacific Islander: 17%
Native American: 0%
Mixed (2+ ethnicities): 8%
International: 3%

Academics
Calendar: Quarter
Student/faculty ratio: 17:1
Class size 9 or fewer: 28%
Class size 10-29: 45%
Class size 30-49: 9%
Class size 50-99: 10%
Class size 100 or more: 8%
Returning freshmen: 91%
Six-year graduation rate: 80%
Graduates who immediately go to graduate school: 34%

Most Popular Majors
Psychology
Economics
Communications

Admissions
Applicants: 54,830
Accepted: 24,131
Acceptance rate: 44.0%
Placed on wait list: 3,262
Enrolled from wait list: 330
Average GPA: 3.9
ACT range: 24-29
SAT Math range: 570-690
SAT Reading range: 540-660
SAT Writing range: 17-44
Top 10% of class: 96%
Top 25% of class: 98%
Top 50% of class: 100%

Student Life

There are over 400 student organizations at UCSB that cover an extensive gamut of interests. The campus has a reputation for being politically active; the Voter Registration Volunteer Coalition tabled to register voters for three months, and UCSB held the most number of registered voters among colleges in the country according to a representative of the Campus Democrats. The UCSB Multicultural Center sponsors activities that promote awareness of diversity issues on campus through more than 100 events every year: discussions, film screenings, music performances, and more.

Popular annual events include Extravaganza, a free music festival in the spring that attracts over 8,000 people and that has featured Nas, Sublime, Run-D.M.C., Jack Johnson, and other well known performers. State Street, a major avenue in downtown Santa Barbara, is lined with bars and clubs and home of the State Street Crawl—making for fun nights out. Halloween at UCSB and surrounding Isla Vista is a far cry from a night of trick-or-treating: celebrations last for a week and are big and rowdy enough that precautions are taken to keep it safe. Ten percent of undergrads are part of the Greek system, which consists of 39 sororities and fraternities. "The fraternities and sororities definitely have a presence, but it's kind of segregated," says a student.

The UCSB Gauchos compete in 20 sports (10 men's, 10 women's) at the Division I level. Basketball, men's soccer, and water polo are the most competitive. The Sport Club Program boasts over 200 teams with 800 student-athletes and multiple National Champions. Intramurals are even more popular, with 17 sports and over 18,000 participants a year.

Downtown Santa Barbara is popular for its nightlife and dining. For outdoors enthusiasts, there's Los Padres National Forest; and for those who want to connect with a bigger city and can bear the traffic, Los Angeles is a two-hour drive away.

Campus housing is comprised of eight university-run residence halls and two private residence halls. Many freshmen opt to live in one of eight residence halls, and new freshmen are guaranteed housing for their first year if they submit their Statement of Intent to Register by the May 1 deadline. Among the entire student body, over half choose to live in the private apartments in neighboring Isla Vista and surrounding neighborhoods, and about 10 percent commute from home.

Student Body

Though UCSB has a reputation for being a party school, students also know when to focus on their academics. The average GPA for incoming freshmen is 3.9, so students obviously don't ignore their studies.

There is low geographic diversity, with 96 percent of the student body hailing from California—not surprising given the lower tuition rate for in-state students. International students compose just three percent, though with such large numbers of students, that still translates into more than 75 countries. "Most everyone is from California, but within California there's so much diversity that you won't ever have a problem finding your crowd," says a student.

Reflecting the diversity of California as a state, there is high ethnic diversity on campus as well, with particularly large representation of Latino and Asian students. Indeed, 51 percent of students identify as an ethnicity other than Caucasian.

You May Not Know

- UCSB was first founded as an independent teachers' college and joined the University of California system in 1944.
- Through the UCSB library system, more than 74,000 questions are answered per year.
- UCSB marine scientists assisted in developing Ocean in Google Earth, which allows users to take a virtual plunge into oceans worldwide.

Distinguished Alumni

Robert Ballard, oceanographer who discovered the Titanic wreck; Carol Greider, Nobel Prize winner for physiology or medicine; Jack Johnson, singer-songwriter; Barry Zito, major league baseball pitcher for the San Francisco Giants.

Admissions and Financial Aid

UCSB requires, like all UCs, that students meet a subject requirement, examination requirement (SAT or ACT), and scholarship requirement (a minimum GPA of 3.0 for California residents and 3.4 for non-California residents) in order to be eligible for admission. GPA calculations provide extra points for honors and AP classes. Application tips include taking a challenging courseload, completing all standardized tests by December of senior year, and sharing achievements and values in the personal essays.

Outstanding freshmen are considered for the Regents Scholarships, UCSB's most prestigious scholarship award. Over 200 UCSB Regents Scholars receive $6,000 per year for four years along with other benefits, including enrollment in the honors program, guaranteed housing for all four years and priority registration, and opportunities through the Regents and Chancellor's Scholars Association. Scholarships are also available through the Colleges of Creative Studies, Engineering, Letters and Sciences, and the music department.

UNIVERSITY OF CALIFORNIA – SANTA BARBARA

Highlights

Admissions Criteria

Academic criteria:
Grades: ☆ ☆ ☆
Difficulty of class schedule: ☆ ☆ ☆
Class rank: ☆ ☆ ☆
Standardized test scores: ☆ ☆ ☆
Teacher recommendations: N/A
Personal statement: ☆ ☆ ☆
Non-academic criteria considered:
Extracurricular activities
Special talents, interests, abilities
Character/personal qualities
Volunteer work
Work experience

Deadlines

Early Action: No
Early Decision: No
Regular Action: November 30 (final)
Notification of admission by: March 15
Common Application: Not accepted

Financial Aid

In-state tuition: $12,192
Out-of-state tuition: $35,070
Room: Varies
Board: Varies
Books: $1,444
Freshmen receiving need-based aid: 62%
Undergrads rec. need-based aid: 59%
Avg. % of need met by financial aid: 85%
Avg. aid package (freshmen): $23,996
Avg. aid package (undergrads): $21,738
Avg. debt upon graduation: $19,325

School Spirit

Mascot: Gauchos
Colors: Blue and gold

Four-year public
Founded: 1965
Santa Cruz, CA
Large town
Pop. 56,810

Address:
1156 High Street
Santa Cruz, CA
95064

Admissions:
831-459-4008

Financial Aid:
800-944-6050 (March
1-May 1)

admissions@ucsc.edu

www.ucsc.edu

UNIVERSITY OF CALIFORNIA – SANTA CRUZ

Overview

Attending a very liberal and hippie Northern California school, students at University of California-Santa Cruz (UCSC) seek a balance between work and play, with a frequent break for political protests. Although one of the more accessible University of California schools, UCSC is still a top public university and therefore the admissions process is selective, especially for those applying from out of state.

A large public university, the 2,000+ acres of campus is given more of a community feel thanks to the school's residential college system, dividing the campus into 10 separate college communities throughout the grounds. Surrounded by national and state parks with views of Monterey Bay, Santa Cruz is one of the most beautiful campuses in the country, covered with redwood trees and sprawling meadows and architecture ranging from farm-style buildings to more modern ones.

Academics

Santa Cruz offers 91 majors. The strongest programs at the university include biological sciences, art, and economics. The university enacted a general education requirement, mandating that students complete a specific amount of credits in each of the 10 following disciplines: cross-cultural analysis, ethnicity and race, interpreting arts and media, mathematical and formal reasoning, scientific inquiry, statistical reasoning, textual analysis, perspectives (environmental awareness, human behavior, or technology and society), practice (collaborative endeavor, creative process, or service learning), composition, and disciplinary communication. In addition, the school has American History and Institutions and Entry Level Writing requirements, which determine that all students either complete a college-level course in the subject or receive SAT scores of 550 or 680, respectively, in each of the subjects or an AP score of three or above.

Students report classes at Santa Cruz to be challenging, though they can pursue an eclectic variety of interests. Professors are generally "available outside of class to answer questions" if a student is willing to put in the effort—which is important, considering that, in addition to providing letter grades, professors give written evaluations to each student in their class.

Special academic opportunities at UCSC include the school's Departmental and Division Honors program, offering intensive majors and intensive tracks in a variety of departments ranging from anthropology to engineering. Students looking to add more breadth to their academic experience can pursue a combined a double major, fusing topics such as Earth Sciences and Anthropology. The university's Science, Technology, Engineering, and Mathematics (STEM) introduces students to exciting science and engineering opportunities, supporting them in their studies and career preparation with faculty and associated staff. Lastly, through the Field Studies and Internships program, students can receive course credit while they are simultaneously exposed to a variety of field and exchange programs that help to refine practical skills for various organizations and businesses.

UCSC educational offerings are extended to an international scope with the Education Abroad Program. Students may select opportunities based on a variety of factors; for example, whether the experience is with English-speaking hosts or if the student would benefit from knowledge of a foreign language. Other determiners are time related, such as whether students wish to travel during the summer or during a school year term.

On-campus career and networking resources, such as the career center and student-hiring information sessions, are available to students on campus but students report having to invest a significant effort to make these services worthwhile.

Student Life

UCSC has 145 official student organizations including the Buddhist Society and student Film Art Coalition. Although there are seven social fraternities and 13 social sororities on campus, only about one percent of students at UCSC choose to join Greek life. The school was featured in MTV's reality TV show "Fraternity Life" in 2003, but in general students' social and extracurricular lives do not revolve around the Greek scene. "We're just not the joining type," comments a student.

Traditions at UCSC tend to be the more unofficial kind. The "First Rain" occurs once a year when students from all over campus participate in a nude run at sundown after the first rain of the year; in fact, some students can be seen running at any point of the day after it starts raining. Other "unofficial" traditions include climbing Tree Nine, a 100-ft tree with evenly spaced branches behind College Nine, and participating in campus "smoke-offs" for the students' infamous celebration of marijuana on April 20. Among more traditional and mainstream traditions is the school's annual Harvest Festival, run by the Center for Agro-ecology and Sustainable Systems, featuring food, an apple pie back-off, garden talks, and hayrides.

UCSC doesn't revolve around sports as some colleges do. The school doesn't have a football team and some students even complain about a lack of school spirit. There are 11 Division III teams in total (five men's, six women's) and the most competitive teams are tennis, soccer, men's volleyball, and swimming. Although varsity sports are not a big draw, there is still a fervent interest in recreation on the university's beautiful campus, and about a quarter of the student population chooses to participate in intramural athletics. The strongest and most competitive teams include Ultimate Frisbee, rugby, cycling, baseball, men's soccer, and the equestrian team.

Given the beautiful Northern California location of UCSC, students' favorite activities revolve around the outdoors with trips to the nearby beach, forest, and mountains. "You can sunbathe or ski here," one student laughs. Downtown Santa Cruz is quaint but very student-friendly and features popular bars. One club, Catalyst, often brings in famous musicians for concerts. Road trips to San Jose and San Francisco, about two hours away, are also popular for students seeking more of a city vibe.

Freshmen and transfer students are guaranteed housing for their first two years. The extensive residential college housing system features dorms set up around 10 different residential colleges. Each college has its own personality and though they vary in quality, each has its positive and negative attributes.

Student Body

The UCSC student body is predominantly Caucasian and Asian; but with 47 percent minority students, it is highly ethnically diverse. However, only two percent of students hail from out of state.

As a very liberal school, the word most commonly associated with UCSC students is "hippie" and the only students who are reputed to have a hard time fitting in are the conservative ones. "I met one self-proclaimed conservative my freshman year," one student recalls.

UNIVERSITY OF CALIFORNIA – SANTA CRUZ

Highlights

Students
Total enrollment: 17,175
Undergrads: 15,668
From out-of-state: 2%
From public schools: 84%
Male/Female: 47%/53%
Live on-campus: 48%
In fraternities: 1%
In sororities: 1%
Off-campus employment rating: Good
Caucasian: 45%
African American: 3%
Hispanic: 20%
Asian / Pacific Islander: 23%
Native American: 1%
International: 0%

Academics
Calendar: Quarter
Student/faculty ratio: 18:1
Class size 9 or fewer: 12%
Class size 10-29: 56%
Class size 30-49: 9%
Class size 50-99: 9%
Class size 100 or more: 14%
Returning freshmen: 89%
Six-year graduation rate: 73%

Most Popular Majors
Psychology
Business management economics
Literature

Admissions
Applicants: 27,658
Accepted: 17,843
Acceptance rate: 64.5%
Placed on wait list: 1,181
Enrolled from wait list: Not reported
Average GPA: 3.6
ACT range: 22-27
SAT Math range: 520-640
SAT Reading range: 500-630
SAT Writing range: 6-32
Top 10% of class: 96%
Top 25% of class: 100%
Top 50% of class: 100%

715

College Profiles

UNIVERSITY OF CALIFORNIA – SANTA CRUZ

Admissions Criteria
Academic criteria:
Grades: ☆ ☆ ☆
Difficulty of class schedule: ☆ ☆ ☆
Class rank: ☆ ☆
Standardized test scores: ☆ ☆ ☆
Teacher recommendations: N/A
Personal statement: ☆ ☆ ☆
Non-academic criteria considered:
Extracurricular activities
Special talents, interests, abilities
Character/personal qualities
Volunteer work
Work experience
Geographical location

Deadlines
Early Action: No
Early Decision: No
Regular Action: Rolling admissions
Common Application: Not accepted

Financial Aid
In-state tuition: $13,398
Out-of-state tuition: $22,878
Room: Varies
Board: Varies
Books: $1,419
Freshmen receiving need-based aid: 58%
Undergrads rec. need-based aid: 53%
Avg. % of need met by financial aid: 89%
Avg. aid package (freshmen): $16,626
Avg. aid package (undergrads): $16,254
Avg. debt upon graduation: $16,024

School Spirit
Mascot: Banana Slug
Colors: Navy blue and gold

You May Not Know

- UCSC students voted via referendum for the school's current mascot, the banana slug, to replace the older one, the sea lions.
- The university's McHenry Library is home to the Grateful Dead archive.
- Bringing in thousands of visitors, the annual celebration of marijuana on April 20 is nicknamed the University of Casual Sex and Cannibus.

Distinguished Alumni

Richard Harris, NPR reporter; Ron Gonzales, Mayor of San Jose; Deborah Madison, cookbook author/founder of Greens Restaurant; Dana Priest, *Washington Post* reporter/Pulitzer Prize winner; Austin E. Quigley, Dean of Colombia College; Maya Rudolph, SNL actress.

Admissions and Financial Aid

Students can qualify for UCSC admission in three ways: the "state-wide" context (achieving a minimum GPA of 3.0 for California residents or 3.4 for non-California residents), "qualifying in the local context" (being in the top four percent of their class in participating high schools in California), or by having very high test scores that may qualify a student based on merit alone.

UCSC conducts a comprehensive admissions process for each of its perspective students, examining 14 faculty-approved criteria: GPA, test scores, courses completed/planned, honors courses, eligibility in the local context, quality of senior-year program of study, academic opportunities in California high schools, performance in academic subject areas, achievement in special projects, improvement in academic performance, special talents, achievements and awards, participation in educational preparation programs, academic accomplishment within life experiences, and geographic location.

All UCSC students entering or continuing at the university will automatically be considered for scholarships based on their applications and academic record. Some of the scholarships given at UCSC include the Regents Scholarships, awarded to incoming freshmen, which totals a value of $20,000 over a four-year period. Campus Merit Scholarships are given to those students with outstanding academic achievement as well as financial need—the value of this scholarship varies from $500 to $1,500 and is renewable for four-years. Restricted Scholarships recognize students with special attributes like county of residence, academic major, family background, or special interests. A limited number of special scholarships are also available for transfer students.

UNIVERSITY OF CHICAGO

Overview

As the name suggests, the nationally renowned University of Chicago boasts an enviable location. The 203-acre campus is situated in Hyde Park, a neighborhood in Chicago's South Side just 15 minutes from the city center. The older buildings of the Collegiate Gothic style give parts of campus an ambiance similar to the University of Oxford, and the campus' designation as a botanical garden makes for beautiful walks across campus. Students have easy access to broader Chicago, and Hyde Park itself is teeming with restaurants, coffee shops, and bookstores to create a student's paradise, though the area is not immune from crime.

UChicago can also brag about its distinguished academics: more than 80 Nobel Prize winners have been students, researchers, or faculty, and *U.S. News & World Report* ranks the college (UChicago's undergraduate school) fifth nationwide. The 5,000 undergrads and 7,000 graduate students are all highly accomplished academically, making for a rigorous student environment that students sometimes are tempted to grumble about, though most just buckle down and study.

If students are intense in their studies, they also know how to intensely have fun, as epitomized by the four-day Scavenger Hunt in May—the world's biggest, and undoubtedly quirkiest. Indeed, the social traditions at UChicago are far more creative than just your standard frat party, perhaps reflecting the strong arts culture of the school: you might find yourself running naked across campus during the winter festival Kuviasungnerk!

Of course, it's not easy to get into to UChicago, whose admissions process also characterizes the school for combining impressive credentials with creativity. If you jump at the chance to answer admissions essay questions such as "What would you do with a foot-and-a-half tall jar of mustard?" and are ready to work hard and play hard in a vibrant city environment, UChicago may be the right place for you.

Academics

The college at the University of Chicago is the sole undergraduate institution—though there are also four divisions of graduate research and six professional schools—which is divided into five collegiate divisions: biological sciences, physical sciences, social sciences, humanities, and new (for interdisciplinary majors and studies). Undergrads receive BA and BS degrees in 49 majors; 24 minors are also available. Strong areas of study include biological sciences (carbon 14 dating was developed at the university) and economics (the economics department is the home of Steven Levitt, famed author of *Freakonomics*). Prelaw and premed are also notable programs. The country's first living donor liver transplant was performed at the university.

All students are required to satisfy UChicago's core requirement, the Common Core. Many students dislike these classes since they are forced to take difficult classes outside their major area. "I thought we were done taking classes we hated when we graduated from high school," one student complains. The Common Core requirements are quite extensive, including 15 courses to meet the distribution requirement, tested proficiency in a foreign language, passing a swim test, and up to three physical education courses.

Students get plenty of individualized attention, with the most common class size being two to nine students. Classes are extremely rigorous, and many students who were at the top of their class in high school must adjust to being in the middle of the pack at UChicago. "It can be a brutal awakening," one student laments. UChicago's quarter system enables students to take a wider variety of classes than a semester system does, though classes can go by quickly.

Special academic opportunities include joint degree programs, such as the highly competitive Accelerated Medical Scholars Program at the University of Chicago

UNIVERSITY OF CHICAGO

Four-year private
Founded: 1890
Chicago, IL
Major city
Pop. 2,707,120

Address:
5801 South Ellis
Avenue
Chicago, IL
60637

Admissions:
773-702-8650

Financial Aid:
773-702-8655

collegeadmissions@
uchicago.edu

www.uchicago.edu

UNIVERSITY OF CHICAGO

Students

Total enrollment: 12,508
Undergrads: 5,590
Part-time students: 1%
From out-of-state: 86%
From public schools: 61%
Male/Female: 53%/47%
Live on-campus: 55%
Off-campus employment rating: Good
Caucasian: 46%
African American: 5%
Hispanic: 8%
Asian / Pacific Islander: 18%
Native American: 0%
Mixed (2+ ethnicities): 3%
International: 9%

Academics

Calendar: Quarter
Student/faculty ratio: 6:1
Class size 9 or fewer: 38%
Class size 10-29: 50%
Class size 30-49: 7%
Class size 50-99: 4%
Class size 100 or more: 1%
Returning freshmen: 99%
Six-year graduation rate: 92%
Graduates who immediately go to graduate school: 20%

Most Popular Majors

Economics
Biological sciences
Political science

Admissions

Applicants: 25,273
Accepted: 3,345
Acceptance rate: 13.2%
Average GPA: 4.0
ACT range: 31-34
SAT Math range: 710-790
SAT Reading range: 710-780
SAT Writing range: 78-21
Top 10% of class: 97%
Top 25% of class: 99%
Top 50% of class: 100%

Pritzker School of Medicine, which enables students to begin working toward their medical degree as a senior. Aspiring educators will appreciate the Urban Education Institute and the Neighboring Schools Program.

Study-abroad programs at UChicago range in length from a quarter or summer to an academic year. Students can choose from programs in Berlin, Cape Town, Kyoto, Paris, and more to study at a local university. Each year, about 100 Summer International Travel Grants are slated to fund intensive language study or research abroad.

UChicago has over 130,000 living alumni, which provides plenty of opportunity for making connections. "Networking is especially helpful if you stay in the Chicago area," says a student. According to the university, 20 percent of students enter graduate school within a year of graduation.

Student Life

There are more than 400 registered student groups on campus, and if in this plethora of groups you can't find the one you're looking for, you can start your own with seven members and an advisor. Music, theatre, and debate are popular on campus: the Chicago Debate Society has won numerous national championships, and the impressive University Theater is one of the select student-run theater organizations in the country that produces 30-35 shows a year.

UChicago proclaims that while "Greek life isn't as prevalent at Chicago as it may be at other campuses," nearly one in ten students are part of the 14 fraternities and eight sororities. "I think there's just so much else going on that most people don't have time for a fraternity or sorority," one student comments.

More fun and far less conventional than any frat party is UChicago's annual Scavenger Hunt, a four-day event that is the largest scavenger hunt in the world. The tradition has been held in May since 1987, and in the words of the organizers: "ScavHunt is a BFD." A recent list of over 250 items included "the longest possible unbroken strip of orange peel, [0.5 points per inch over 48 inches]" and "That train is looking pretty grimy. Do me a favor and ride it through a drive-through train wash, [12 points]." Freshmen can learn about this tradition and many more at their orientation, the nine-day O-Week.

Other notable UChicago traditions include One-Dollar Shake Day, where milkshakes can be had for a buck every Wednesday at the Reynolds Club, a public square and popular gathering place; Polar Bear Run, the culminating event of Kuviasungnerk, a week-long winter festival on campus involving running across campus, preferably naked or semi-naked; and Festival of the Arts, a weeklong spring festival and art extravaganza. "You'll never be so cold or exhilarated in your life," one student notes.

The 19 Division III athletic teams at University of Chicago are not a major influence on campus. Rather, students stay in shape by participating in over 20 intramural sports and frequenting Ratner Athletics Center, an air-conditioned, 150,000-square-foot facility with a swimming pool and 1,658-seat gymnasium. The most prominent form of exercise is just as quirky as many of UChicago's traditions: students bundled up in winter clothes practicing calisthenics on the snowy ground at the winter festival Kuvaisungnerk.

From shopping to dining to culture to professional athletics, Chicago has it all, and students take advantage of this bounty of opportunities. Michigan Avenue, museums such as the Field Museum, and Navy Pier are just some of the many sights the city has to offer, and the El makes the city very accessible. "It's typical to go out every weekend," one student remarks.

Freshmen live on campus in on-campus housing that is guaranteed for four years, though a good number of upperclassmen take advantage of the opportunity to live off campus in apartments. The University House System consists of 36 Houses in 10 residence halls with an average of 70 students per house. Houses are designed to help with students' social and academic adjustment to the College: for instance, "House Tables" at the residential dining commons provide a "home base" for students to deepen friendships and continue academic discussions. The newest facility, built in fall 2009, is the modern-looking South Campus Residence Hall and Dining Commons.

Student Body

There is high ethnic diversity among University of Chicago's undergraduate body, with 34 percent identifying as minority students. More than 85 percent of students hail from out of state, making for high geographic diversity as well.

Due to the university's selective admissions process—99 percent of students having graduated in the top 25 percent of their high school classes—students are "highly" intelligent and focused on their academics. Many students say that it's not unusual to have debates about history, philosophy, and politics outside the classroom simply because students are truly interested in learning. "No one is here just to earn a grade," one student comments. Students lean liberal on the political spectrum.

Students describe themselves as "quirky," which is possibly self-selecting when you consider the uncommon admissions questions on the application. This quirkiness does not preclude overall diversity: as a top tier college, the University of Chicago has the ability to bring in students with talents and interests in every possible arena.

You May Not Know

- UChicago was founded by oil magnate John D. Rockefeller and on land donated by department store owner Marshall Field in 1890.
- Physics research at the University of Chicago led to the "first man-made, self-sustaining nuclear reaction."
- UChicago houses the largest university press in the country.

Distinguished Alumni

Carol Moseley Braun, first African-American woman elected to U.S. Senate; Jerome Friedman, Nobel Laureate in Physics; Susan Sontag, critic and author; John Paul Stevens, U.S. Supreme Court Justice; Studs Terkel, oral historian, radio host and Pulitzer Prize winner.

UNIVERSITY OF CHICAGO

Highlights

Admissions Criteria
Academic criteria:
Grades: ☆ ☆ ☆
Difficulty of class schedule: ☆ ☆ ☆
Class rank: ☆ ☆
Standardized test scores: ☆
Teacher recommendations: ☆ ☆ ☆
Personal statement: ☆ ☆ ☆
Non-academic criteria considered:
Interview
Extracurricular activities
Special talents, interests, abilities
Character/personal qualities
Volunteer work
Work experience
State of residency
Minority affiliation
Alumni relationship

Deadlines
Early Action: November 1
Early Decision: No
Regular Action: January 2 (final)
Notification of admission by: April 1
Common Application: Accepted

Financial Aid
In-state tuition: $45,324
Out-of-state tuition: $45,324
Room: Varies
Board: Varies
Books: $1,378
Freshmen receiving need-based aid: 45%
Undergrads rec. need-based aid: 45%
Avg. % of need met by financial aid: 100%
Avg. aid package (freshmen): $42,128
Avg. aid package (undergrads): $41,116
Avg. debt upon graduation: $23,930

School Spirit
Colors: Maroon

719

College Profiles

Admissions and Financial Aid

The University of Chicago requires the Common Application. However, there is nothing "common" about the University's famously unorthodox essay questions in the supplement. The university encourages students to "play, analyze (don't agonize), create, and compose" as they tackle questions such as "How did you get caught? (or not caught, as the case may be)" and "How do you feel about Wednesday?" Interviews are encouraged but not required, and alumni interviews around the world are given equal consideration as those held on campus. All students may submit a short creative writing sample or scientific research report.

Admission to UChicago is need-blind. UChicago's need-based financial aid policy meets 100 percent of all students' demonstrated financial need. Financial aid packages for students from families with incomes less than $60,000 do not contain loan components. The Odyssey Scholarship program supports all students whose families make $75,000 or less each year with awards up to $5,225, thus helping students to eliminate the need for loans; most Odyssey Scholars have work-study jobs and summer employment.

UChicago has its own financial aid application in addition to the standard FAFSA and CSS PROFILE. According to the admissions office, full and partial merit scholarships are awarded without consideration of financial need. They are instead based on "outstanding academic and extracurricular achievement, demonstrated leadership, and commitment to their communities." These College Honor and University Scholarships are guaranteed for four years of undergraduate study.

UNIVERSITY OF CINCINNATI

Overview

A public research university with more than 33,000 total students, University of Cincinnati is among the 100 largest universities in the United States. Nicknamed UC, the university's students—especially athletics fans—are known as the Bearcats. Campus is very close to downtown Cincinnati, Ohio, which offers a range of off-campus activities but isn't something all students are thrilled about: some say crime near campus is off-putting. For the small percentage of students living on campus, 24-hour security helps ease their concerns.

UC's campus has a west and east portion bridged by the Campus Green. Recent initiatives have brought some stand-out buildings to campus: The Campus Recreation Center that opened in 2006 was designed by prize-winning architect Thom Mayne while the Vontz Center for Molecular Studies on the medical campus was designed by the famous Frank Gehry. The Tangeman University Center is a distinctive gathering place with an open air, elevated terrace for admiring campus, and a two-level bookstore for purchasing all things Bearcat.

Some students may feel overwhelmed by such a large university—there are 12 colleges and hundreds of degree programs available—and those from out of state will be the distinct minority. Though overall student life will feel lacking compared to campuses where most students (instead of a scant 19. percent) live on campus, there's a strong international student scene that adds cultural vibrancy to campus.

Academics

University of Cincinnati is actually comprised of 12 colleges. Not surprising for such a large university, there are more than 250 undergraduate degree programs. Academic rigor at UC largely depends upon the major and the professor and can vary quite a bit. There is, however, a General Education Core competencies requirement that aims to develop certain skills for all majors. For undergrads, this means a First Year Experience that includes seminars and Learning Communities, methodology and writing courses, and a senior capstone.

The UC's College of Design, Architecture, Art, and Planning (DAAP), the College of Business, and College of Engineering offer strong degree programs. The College Conservatory of Music is ranked sixth in the nation by *U.S. News & World Report*. "Our graduates perform in professional groups across the nation," says a student. The BS degree in nursing—as well as the pre-pharmacy track and psychology in the College of Arts and Sciences—are also strong.

UC was the founder of cooperative education, a model that alternates periods of full-time classes with periods of full-time work. By participating in co-op, students gain a year of hands-on work experience while still undergraduates. "Co-op can lead to a full-time job offer," one student comments. This concept, invented in 1906 by UC's then Dean of the College of Engineering, is today the largest co-op program in the country with 5,000 students involved.

UC's education-abroad programs are quite varied, with options ranging from an exchange program with Korea University to summer trips. Studies can be quarter, semester, or year programs. According to the university, students have studied in over 80 countries in the past five years.

There are more than 222,000 alumni, with about half living the greater Cincinnati area. The Career Development Center helps connect hundreds of employers with thousands of students each year. In addition to traditional career fairs, the center hosts e-Fairs online, part time job fairs, education career fairs, and diversity career fairs.

UNIVERSITY OF CINCINNATI

Four-year public
Founded: 1819
Cincinnati, OH
Major city
Pop. 296,223

Address:
P.O. Box 210063
Cincinnati, OH
45221-0063

Admissions:
800-827-8728

Financial Aid:
513-556-1000

admissions@uc.edu

www.uc.edu

UNIVERSITY OF CINCINNATI

Students

Total enrollment: 33,347
Undergrads: 23,096
Freshmen: 4,160
Part-time students: 15%
From out-of-state: 12%
Male/Female: 49%/51%
Live on-campus: 19%
Off-campus employment rating: Good
Caucasian: 78%
African American: 8%
Hispanic: 3%
Asian / Pacific Islander: 3%
Native American: 0%
Mixed (2+ ethnicities): 2%
International: 3%

Academics

Calendar: Semester
Student/faculty ratio: 18:1
Class size 9 or fewer: 16%
Class size 10-29: 57%
Class size 30-49: 18%
Class size 50-99: 7%
Class size 100 or more: 2%
Returning freshmen: 86%
Six-year graduation rate: 62%

Most Popular Majors

Marketing
Nursing
Communications

Admissions

Applicants: 17,104
Accepted: 11,469
Acceptance rate: 67.1%
Average GPA: 3.5
ACT range: 22-27
SAT Math range: 520-640
SAT Reading range: 510-620
SAT Writing range: 6-23
Top 10% of class: 20%
Top 25% of class: 51%
Top 50% of class: 82%

Student Life

The fact that only one fifth of UC students live on campus affects the social scene quite dramatically. Students are still involved in activities and the campus nightlife, but not to the extent of students at colleges where more of the student body takes advantage of on-campus housing. Frats serve as the main party scene and Greek life is quite prominent, with 22 fraternities and 11 sororities and a history that goes back to 1840. "The parties can get large and loud," one student notes. The Greek scene isn't just social, but service-oriented as well. The annual Greek Week fundraises to support a charity: students aim to raise $55,000 for the Make-a-Wish Foundation. Each year, Greeks at UC contribute more than 20,000 hours of service.

There are about 250 official registered student organizations covering all aspects of student life: academics, athletics, arts, culture, governance, honor societies, politics, professional life, religion, service, and more. There's even a group called Coaster Cats for those interested in the design and manufacturing processes of amusement park rides.

Friday Night Live has been a growing UC tradition since 1999. The program provides Friday night entertainment that's alcohol free—the organizers note, "Don't let that deter you—FNL is always fun." The weeklong Worldfest in late April and early May offers a celebration of "fun, fashion, fellowship, food and food for thought", and the Taste of India is a perennially popular event in the "food" category. The event is always vibrant with input from the many international students and faculty at UC. Previous speakers have included poet Maya Angelou and Nobel laureate Elie Wiesel. Another eagerly anticipated spring event is the Spring Concert, when students get a chance to rock out to a popular performing artist, whose identity is often kept secret for some time—a recent artist was Ludacris.

The UC Bearcats compete in 18 intercollegiate sports at the Division I level. The Dance Team has won four national championships since 2004, but it is the basketball team—with two NCAA national championships under its belt—that draws the biggest crowds. Students have been known to camp out for basketball tickets. There are also intramural and club sports available. In fact, a new category of Club Varsity sports emerged after 2004 Olympian Kelly Salchow emerged from the club team.

Off campus, nearby downtown Cincinnati offers bars, restaurants, clubs, museums, and shopping. Newport on the Levee across the river in Kentucky is also popular for its restaurants and bars. "It overlooks the water and is the best spot for dates," says a student.

There are eight undergraduate residence halls, two of which are university-affiliated but not university-managed options. All rooms come with AC, high-speed Internet, a micro-unit fridge, and cable TV. All halls feature a study lounge and 24-hour security, and no smoking or alcohol is permitted. The Campus Recreation Center is the newest residence hall, and is part of a complex with over 200,000 square feet of recreation facilities and an award winning dining center. "If you're into exercising, this is the place to live," one student comments.

Student Body

It's notable that only a sparse 12 percent of UC students are from out of state, but with a student population as large as UC's you'll find every type of person imaginable on campus. "There is the range from the partying frat guys to the nerds to the artists," one student admits. The international student body is also large and diverse—700 students hailing from more than 100 countries—though most are grad students.

You May Not Know

- According to the Cincinnati Regional Chamber of Commerce, the University of Cincinnati is the second largest employer in Greater Cincinnati with more than 15,000 employees.
- Joseph Strauss, who graduated from the university in 1892, designed the Golden Gate Bridge.
- UC has had a number of firsts: the first antihistamine (Benadryl), first bachelor's degree program in nursing, and first degree program via satellite.

Distinguished Alumni

Michael Graves, architect; Beverly Malone, President of the American Nurses Association; William Howard Taft, U.S. President; Mary Wineberg, 2008 Olympic Gold relay medalist.

Admissions and Financial Aid

UC admissions requires coursework as outlined in the Ohio Articulation Requirements and other fairly straightforward components such as SAT/ACT scores and a personal essay. More specific admissions requirements vary by program. The College-Conservatory of Music only accepts online applications, while other programs allow paper applications. UC strongly encourages a campus visit; daily tours are available throughout the year.

University of Cincinnati awards more than $22 million in merit-based scholarships each year, with the most prestigious programs rewarding community service and leadership in addition to academic performance. Finalists in the National Merit scholarship competition are eligible for the UC121 (sic) Scholarship, which covers in-state tuition and housing and includes admissions to the honors program. International undergrads can apply for the UC Global Scholarship, a renewable $1,000 to $12,000 annual award.

UNIVERSITY OF CINCINNATI

Highlights

Admissions Criteria
Academic criteria:
Grades: ☆ ☆ ☆
Difficulty of class schedule: ☆ ☆ ☆
Class rank: ☆ ☆ ☆
Standardized test scores: ☆ ☆ ☆
Teacher recommendations: N/A
Personal statement: ☆ ☆
Non-academic criteria considered:
Extracurricular activities
Special talents, interests, abilities
State of residency

Deadlines
Early Action: No
Early Decision: No
Regular Action: Rolling admissions
Common Application: Accepted

Financial Aid
In-state tuition: $10,784
Out-of-state tuition: $25,816
Room: Varies
Board: Varies
Books: $1,540
Freshmen receiving need-based aid: 65%
Undergrads rec. need-based aid: 59%
Avg. % of need met by financial aid: 66%
Avg. aid package (freshmen): $8,358
Avg. aid package (undergrads): $8,354
Avg. debt upon graduation: $27,593

School Spirit
Mascot: Bearcat
Colors: Red and black
Song: *Fight Cincinnati*

UNIVERSITY OF
COLORADO –
BOULDER

Four-year public
Founded: 1876
Boulder, CO
Medium city
Pop. 98,889

Address:
Regent Administration
Center, Room 125,
552 UCB
Boulder, CO
80309-0552

Admissions:
303-492-6301

Financial Aid:
303-492-5091

apply@colorado.edu

www.colorado.edu

UNIVERSITY OF COLORADO - BOULDER

Overview

Located in the small and vibrant city of Boulder, Colorado, the CU-Boulder campus is instantly recognizable due to the Italian-style, glowing sandstone buildings topped in red tile. The nearly 800-acre public university boasts a total student population of over 31,000. Considered a Tier 1 research school, CU-Boulder ranks 13th in the nation in sponsored research funding; the university received more than $380 million in research awards.

Named the smartest city in America by *Forbes* magazine, Boulder has many cafes, restaurants, shops, and boutiques that can be reached on foot from campus. An overload of natural beauty is the backdrop, with the Flatiron Mountains rising abruptly and strikingly over a thousand feet at the edge of campus and town. This outdoor setting is important to the local culture. There's unlimited recreation that includes hiking, biking, mountain climbing, skiing, and more.

The excellent quality of living found here comes with a mind-boggling amount of courses and programs to choose from at CU. Students have to be proactive in charting their courses of study. Larger classes aren't uncommon, especially for introductory courses.

Academics

Eighty-five majors are available at CU-Boulder. The largest college is the College of Arts and Sciences. Areas of interest include astrophysical and planetary sciences, dance, drama, English, geography, integrative physiology, physics, and psychology. Strong programs in other colleges are biochemistry, biology, business entrepreneurship, chemistry, engineering, law, and music. The most competitive college is Engineering and Applied Sciences.

In the College of Arts and Sciences, students must fulfill core requirements. These differ somewhat among the majors but broadly require coursework in foreign language, quantitative reasoning and mathematical skills, written communication, historical context, human diversity, United States context, literature and the arts, natural science, contemporary societies, and ideals and values.

All in all, CU-Boulder has excellent resources available, from the faculty—there are four Nobel Prize winners and seven MacArthur "genius grant" fellows—to special academic opportunities like the Honors program. "We have superstar professors," one student comments.

Students must face the reality that even with the many learning choices CU-Boulder offers, they must be actively involved in their own education. Opportunities abound—including 90 research centers, institutes, and laboratories—and students say that some of their professors are literally "geniuses," but as one student confides, "You can get lost in the system." Fifty percent of classes are less than 20 students, but that means 50 percent are more than 20 students.

For high achievers, the Honors program offers over 40 honors classes each semester where classes are capped at 15 students. It's possible to graduate with honors, high honors, and highest honors depending on the quality of a written thesis and defense.

If that's not enough academic choice, study abroad is possible in 70 countries. This is a popular option that over 1,000 students take advantage of each year. "I chose to study in Spain to develop my language skills and become immersed in the culture," one student notes.

After the degree is in hand, the relationship with CU-Boulder doesn't have to end. Alumni can network and find out about internships and career preparation through the career center. The fall career fairs on campus draw local and national companies particularly interested in hiring CU students.

Student Life

Students involve themselves in 600 school clubs and groups such as 180-11, which is shorthand for 180 degree shift at the 11th hour, a club "dedicated to changing the course of humanity before it is too late." Other groups include the Neuroscience club and the immensely popular Freeride club. The latter is the largest campus student group. Freeride sponsors day and overnight trips to nearby resorts for skiing and snowboarding and camping.

When the weather is good, students can be found studying, hanging out, and sun bathing on Farrand Field or lounging on Norlin Quad. When the weather's bad, it's still good because most of Colorado's 26 ski and snowboard resorts are within three hours of campus. One can take a quick snowshoe in Chautauqua Park too, just up the hill from campus.

Certain events students come to know fondly include the Colorado Shakespeare Festival and 4/20. The Shakespeare festival is one of the most nationally lauded and is the seventh in the world to have performed all of Shakespeare's work. The infamous 4/20 weed smoking event draws an estimated 8,000 to campus. It's not a sanctioned event, but pot smokers gather on Farrand Field for a 30-minute community smoke-out and then disperse.

While CU often makes appearances in rankings of top party schools, students say "you don't have to be a part of the party scene." The small to modest Greek scene on the Hill section of campus consists of 21 fraternities and 15 sororities. Since only 11 percent of men and 16 percent of women rush, their major role in the social scene is indeed putting on parties.

CU has 14 Division I teams. There's a lot of love for the football team, affectionately called the Buffs, and incoming students not already diehard fans will be swayed by the masses, or at least by the masses of parties. "Games are an all-day, all-school affair," one student notes. Intramural and club sports are popular too and range from fly fishing and Ultimate Frisbee to water polo and ice hockey.

Boulder has excellent restaurants and bars to cure the munchies and thirst. Ethiopian, Indian, Japanese, Mexican, Nepalese, and Thai food can be found along with pizza, pub fare, and upscale dining for when the parents are in town and paying.

Since freshmen are required to live on campus for two semesters, dorms play a large role in helping to make or break the beginning college experience. Most dorms hold between 200-400 students, and close friendships are usually made in the dorms. Most agree that Williams Village dorm is less desirable because it's a bus ride, albeit not too far, from campus.

Residential Academic Programs (RAPs) give students the chance to live among others with common interests such as the creative and performing arts community, the American west and culture community, honors program, and multicultural leadership student community. There are also Living and Learning communities including those for business, ethnic and racial diversity, and alcohol and drug free living.

Student Body

The student body comes from all over the U.S. and over 100 countries, with a high 19 percent of ethnic diversity.

UNIVERSITY OF COLORADO – BOULDER

Highlights

Students
Total enrollment: 31,725
Undergrads: 25,805
Part-time students: 9%
From out-of-state: 44%
From public schools: 90%
Male/Female: 54%/46%
Live on-campus: 28%
In fraternities: 11%
In sororities: 16%
Off-campus employment rating: Excellent
Caucasian: 75%
African American: 2%
Hispanic: 9%
Asian / Pacific Islander: 5%
Native American: 0%
Mixed (2+ ethnicities): 3%
International: 3%

Academics
Calendar: Semester
Student/faculty ratio: 19:1
Class size 9 or fewer: 10%
Class size 10-29: 57%
Class size 30-49: 17%
Class size 50-99: 9%
Class size 100 or more: 7%
Returning freshmen: 84%
Six-year graduation rate: 68%

Most Popular Majors
Psychology
Integrative physiology
English

Admissions
Applicants: 21,767
Accepted: 18,188
Acceptance rate: 83.6%
Placed on wait list: 841
Enrolled from wait list: 131
Average GPA: 3.6
ACT range: 24-29
SAT Math range: 540-650
SAT Reading range: 530-630
SAT Writing range: Not reported
Top 10% of class: 25%
Top 25% of class: 56%
Top 50% of class: 88%

725

College Profiles

UNIVERSITY OF COLORADO – BOULDER

Admissions Criteria

Academic criteria:
Grades: ☆ ☆ ☆
Difficulty of class schedule: ☆ ☆ ☆
Class rank: ☆ ☆ ☆
Standardized test scores: ☆ ☆ ☆
Teacher recommendations: ☆
Personal statement: ☆ ☆
Non-academic criteria considered:
Extracurricular activities
Special talents, interests, abilities
Character/personal qualities
Volunteer work
Work experience
Geographical location
Minority affiliation
Alumni relationship

Deadlines

Early Action: December 1
Early Decision: No
Regular Action: Rolling admissions
Common Application: Accepted

Financial Aid

In-state tuition: $8,760
Out-of-state tuition: $30,528
Room: Varies
Board: Varies
Books: $1,800
Freshmen receiving need-based aid: 44%
Undergrads rec. need-based aid: 38%
Avg. % of need met by financial aid: 87%
Avg. aid package (freshmen): $12,944
Avg. aid package (undergrads): $13,912
Avg. debt upon graduation: $23,413

School Spirit

Mascot: Ralphie (live buffalo)
Colors: Silver, gold, and black
Song: *Glory Colorado*

There are more than enough "hippies" sporting dreadlocks to go around on campus, but don't forget the "rich contingency" with SUVs and Chanel handbags or the students who seem to dress only in Patagonia and Marmot outdoor clothing, and there are plenty of "hipsters." Like the residents of Boulder, students are "liberal or very liberal," and they "live for the outdoors." They are elated when the weather provides fresh powder days for skiing at the nearby resorts, and conscientious (or, some might say snobby) about what they put into their bodies from microbrews to organic veggies.

You May Not Know

- The University of Colorado at Boulder has produced the fourth highest number of astronauts among U.S. universities; that's 18 astronauts making over 40 flights.
- Ralphie, the CU Mascot, is a real live American bison, appearing at every football game.
- The Conference on World Affairs began at CU-Boulder in 1948. Each year, lots of smart, eccentric, and creative people share ideas at the conference. Topics include global interests, medicine and technology, the environment, activism, and religion. Eleanor Roosevelt, Buckminster Fuller, and Roger Ebert have participated.

Distinguished Alumni

Lynne Cheney, married to former U.S. Vice President Dick Cheney; Trey Parker and Matt Stone, creators of television show *South Park*; Robert Redford, Academy Award-winning actor and director; Byron White, U.S. Supreme Court Justice.

Admissions and Financial Aid

CU has a holistic admissions process with the "primary factor in admissions decisions" being academic achievement. Admission is guaranteed for Colorado high school students meeting the university resident and academic requirements.

Twenty-six percent of incoming freshmen receive some kind of merit-based award. Two well known scholarship programs available to undergraduates are the Presidents Leadership Class (PLC) and the Norlin Scholarships. PLC scholarships are awarded to 50 entering freshmen each year who are civic-minded and show great leadership potential; these students receive up to $12,000 and real-world experience and instruction in leadership and community arenas. Norlin Scholars number 125 and demonstrate creative or academic excellence; they receive $3,000 per academic year.

UNIVERSITY OF CONNECTICUT

Overview

The University of Connecticut, founded in 1881 by brothers Charles and Augustus Storrs, sprawls across one main and five regional campuses, over 4,000 total acres. If you're looking for that East Coast academia feel, you'll find it at this university. The campuses showcase old gothic-style buildings and turn-of-the-century brick, combined with modernized, state-of-the-art classrooms and lecture halls. The university is currently investing $2.8 billion into a building program to further update and transform the high-tech aspects of the campus.

When it comes to public universities, UConn is just about as good as you can get; it's one of the best you can get in New England, according to the *U.S. News & World Report*. Combining solid academics, excellent athletics, and opportunities to try your hand at just about anything, UConn definitely provides quite a bit of bang for your buck.

All freshmen live on Storrs Campus, located about 30 miles east of Hartford, the state capital. Though UConn's home, the rural town of Storrs, doesn't offer much except a picturesque setting, Boston, Providence, and New York are all less than three hours away. Hartford too provides students myriad opportunities to attend musical and artistic performances, sporting events, and downtown clubs and restaurants. But with an undergraduate population of over 17,000 on the main campus, you might find just as much to keep you busy on campus.

Academics

With size, there are options: the University of Connecticut offers 101 majors across 14 distinct schools and colleges. The possibilities are seemingly endless, with strong and established programs in business, economics, education, kinesiology, music, pharmacy studies, premed, and psychology.

Along with requirements for their major, students must complete the university's General Education requirements. This includes finishing a series of courses in the arts and humanities, social science, science and technology, and diversity and multiculturalism. Students must also fulfill requirements in writing, computer technology, information literacy, and a second language.

Special programs and opportunities exist across different schools and departments. The School of Business sponsors the Student Managed Investment Fund, an outreach program that allows undergraduate and graduate finance students to manage a $2 million fund, applying classroom concepts to real life experience. High-achieving premed students can apply to the Special Program in Medicine and Dental Medicine—when accepted as a freshman, a student can plan to complete four years of a prescribed undergraduate curriculum and then is guaranteed admission to either the UConn School of Medicine or the UConn School of Dental Medicine. Only about a dozen students are admitted to this highly competitive program each year.

The academic rigor varies among the university's fields of study—students in engineering and science fields report their classes as the "most intense." Because it is such a large university, students can expect entry-level classes that have up to 300 students; but as students move into upper level classes, the most common class size is 10-19 students. In the same vein, professors are generally very willing to meet with their students, even outside office hours, but "you need to take the initiative," says a student.

UConn offers over 200 study-abroad programs in 65 different countries, across six continents. More than 18 percent of students opt to study abroad. Students can design their own experience, taking courses at foreign universities, doing research and field studies, or participating in internships. UConn works hard to match prospec-

UNIVERSITY OF CONNECTICUT

Four-year public
Founded: 1881
Storrs, CT
Rural
Pop. 15,344

Address:
2131 Hillside Road,
Unit 3088
Storrs, CT
06269-3088

Admissions:
860-486-3137

Financial Aid:
860-486-2819

beahusky@uconn.edu

www.uconn.edu

UNIVERSITY OF CONNECTICUT

728

tive study-abroad students with scholarship opportunities, and the university itself provides many of these.

Overall, 94 percent of recent graduates from UConn schools are either employed or attending graduate or professional school. "Everyone is pretty focused on the future," one student notes.

Student Life

Student organizations are varied with more than 500 available. The official school newspaper is *The Daily Campus* and offers journalistic types the opportunity for hands-on experience. There are intramural athletic teams in many different sports, and over 30 honor societies.

According to the editor of the student newspaper, there is "never a dull moment at UConn." Whether you prefer to make your own party or join an official one, you'll be able to do it. The annual Spring Weekend Concert attracts big names and over 10,000 attendees; in recent years, artists such as 50 Cent, O.A.R., Nas, Jack's Mannequin, and KiD CuDi performed. It's a "let loose" few days say students, cautioning that UConn police recently made 34 arrests throughout the weekend. Other popular events include Winter Weekend, featuring One Ton Sundae (fill your bucket with as much ice cream as you want for only $1!), Homecoming and the annual Lip Sync Competition, and the once-a-year, campus-wide, mud pit volleyball game known as Oozeball. "Wear old clothes," advises a student.

There are 16 fraternities as well as 16 sororities with about one in 10 students joining. Participation in the Greek scene is varied and you can "be completely immersed or barely aware that the fraternities and sororities exist," says a student. UConn is reputed to be a party school, and students have plenty of places to drink on campus, such as at the Celeron Square Apartments. If you want to stray off campus to party, there are a handful of student-friendly bars. "Despite our reputation, there isn't pressure to drink," one student comments.

A member of the Big East Conference, the UConn Division I athletics department is serious business. If you're an avid (or rabid) basketball fan, you'll spend a happy four years here—the university is the second ever to win the men's and women's NCAA National Championship in the same year. Soccer is strong as well, with two national titles under the men's team's belt. And at such a large school, there is a wealth of intramural teams in sports such as sand volleyball, cross-country, ice hockey, inner-tube water polo, and over a dozen more.

All incoming students are guaranteed housing on the main Storrs campus (97 percent of freshmen opt to take it). Freshmen live in either North or Northwest. "You should pick Northwest because it's newer," one student says. Many older students stay on campus—at 72 percent, UConn has the highest percentage of students living on campus of any public university in the country.

Student Body

The student body is fairly diverse, with a high 24 percent minority population but 73 percent of students coming from Connecticut. However, with the immense size of the university, students of "all backgrounds" are represented. With fairly affordable in-state tuition, financial aid, and merit-based scholarships offered, students from "all economic backgrounds" are also represented.

The university is so big, there isn't a cohesive vibe or "type" among all the students on campus—undergraduates are generally students who "study but not too much" and are "actively involved" in extracurricular interests.

You May Not Know

- "The Rock" is a UConn tradition dating back to the 1940s. It is a massive rock on campus, which students and student organizations use as the university's most popular advertising billboard. With virtually daily re-paintings, The Rock has accumulated over 1,200 layers of paint.
- If you think there's no way that kid sitting next to you in class is legal, you're right. Colin Carlson, a child prodigy, began attending the University of Connecticut at age 12.
- One of the first buildings given to the State of Connecticut for the founding of the University was an orphanage used during the Civil War.

Distinguished Alumni

Dr. Tansu Çiller, first female Prime Minister of Turkey; Richard Mastacchio, astronaut; Moby, musician; Joseph W. Polis, President of The Juilliard School.

Admissions and Financial Aid

Admissions counselors judge students based on a holistic view. Important factors are rigor of academic curricula, extracurricular activities, and community involvement. However, with such a large applicant pool, a high GPA and standardized tests scores can help set you apart or distinguish you further.

Applications for special programs, such as the Special Program in Medicine and Dental Medicine and the Special Program in Law, require separate applications. Admission into the University's Honors Program is by invitation only, and based on class rank, secondary school record, and SAT or ACT scores.

UConn offers a series of renewable merit-based scholarships for high school seniors who have demonstrated high levels of academic achievement and leadership. All incoming freshmen are automatically considered for most merit scholarships based on their application; the UConn Nutmeg Scholarship and the Day of Pride Scholarship are both full scholarships, and both require separate applications. These two scholarships are offered to Connecticut residents only, though a couple of the other opportunities are available to out-of-state residents.

UNIVERSITY OF CONNECTICUT

Highlights

Admissions Criteria
Academic criteria:
Grades: ☆ ☆ ☆
Difficulty of class schedule: ☆ ☆ ☆
Class rank: ☆ ☆ ☆
Standardized test scores: ☆ ☆ ☆
Teacher recommendations: ☆ ☆
Personal statement: ☆ ☆
Non-academic criteria considered:
Extracurricular activities
Special talents, interests, abilities
Character/personal qualities
Volunteer work
Work experience
Geographical location
Minority affiliation
Alumni relationship

Deadlines
Early Action: No
Early Decision: No
Regular Action: Rolling admissions
Notification of admission by: March 1
Common Application: Accepted

Financial Aid
In-state tuition: $9,256
Out-of-state tuition: $28,204
Room: $6,278
Board: $5,444
Books: $850
Freshmen receiving need-based aid: 53%
Undergrads rec. need-based aid: 55%
Avg. % of need met by financial aid: 64%
Avg. aid package (freshmen): $12,086
Avg. aid package (undergrads): $12,870
Avg. debt upon graduation: $24,373

School Spirit
Mascot: Husky
Colors: Blue and white
Song: *UConn Husky*

Four-year private
Founded: 1956
Irving, TX
Medium city
Pop. 220,702

Address:
1845 East Northgate
Drive
Irving, TX
75062-4736

Admissions:
800-628-6999

Financial Aid:
800-628-6999

ugadmis@udallas.edu

www.udallas.edu

UNIVERSITY OF DALLAS

Overview

UD was founded in 1956 and is a four-year private institution affiliated with the Roman Catholic Church. Located in Irving, on the northwest side of Dallas, the university is known for its liberal arts-based core curriculum and its commitment to the "study and development of the western tradition of liberal education and the Catholic intellectual tradition."

Irving is a town of 220,000 residents, a short 15-minute drive from downtown Dallas and 40 minutes from Fort Worth. While Irving doesn't offer much as a college town, bars, restaurants, and shopping await the adventurous student willing to take the short drive to downtown Dallas. The Dallas/Fort Worth area is a metropolis with more than 35 museums, major league sports teams, Fortune 500 companies, and a variety of performing arts venues.

The Office of Campus Ministry is an active part of the campus community, offering a variety of activities for students looking to get involved or learn more about the Catholic faith. Lecture series, Bible Study, and volunteer opportunities are just a few of the activities coordinated by the Office of Campus Ministry. All students have the opportunity to explore Rome and the Western tradition through the university's Rome Program.

The University of Dallas calls itself a place where students can grow and develop spiritually, intellectually, and socially. Relatively small, and definitely on the conservative side, but with a strong liberal arts program to back it up, the university is able to offer a competitive private-school education that prepares students for life after graduation.

Academics

UD offers 41 majors. Undergraduate degree programs are available through the Constantin College of Liberal Arts and the College of Business. The college has strong programs in classics, economics, English, history, prelaw, and premed. There is a general core requirement, which exposes students to courses in the humanities, natural sciences, social sciences, foreign languages, mathematics, and the fine arts. The university also has a religion requirement.

With more than 85 percent of classes with fewer than 30 students, students have the opportunity to get to know their professors well. UD offers self-designed majors, independent study, and accelerated study programs. So can freshmen expect to burn the midnight oil? Transitioning from a high school to a university workload always takes some adjustment. One student said, "It's rigorous here, and I usually study for at least a couple of hours every school night." The university places a lot of focus on studying primary sources (rather than relying on textbooks) and describes itself as a place for students who want to think, write, and talk.

One of the unique educational elements of the university is its Rome Program. The Rome Program, part of the university's study-abroad programming for 40 years, immerses students in a rich learning environment that provides context to the university's core curriculum, which includes reading the works of Homer, Plato, Aristotle, Aquinas, and Dante. Students travel to Florence, Venice, Assisi, and Greece, coming face to face with the art and architecture that they read about. "The Rome Program brought all our studies to life," recalls a participant. "It was one of the most memorable experiences I've ever had." The Due Santi (Two Saints) campus in Rome serves as home away from home for students. More than 80 percent of students participate in the Rome Semester as sophomores. Students may alternatively choose from several summer programs in lieu of the typical semester abroad.

The Office of Career Services offers students many services to find success while in school and beyond. The QUAD Program prepares students for interviews for jobs and internships. Personalized career coaching and workshops are also available to students. A respectable percentage of students (30 percent) pursue a graduate degree immediately after graduation. Of those graduating students who go directly into the workforce, about 16 percent enter a field related to their major.

Student Life

UD is not a big party school. University administration is very strict with cracking down on underage drinking, and most campus parties happen in upperclassmen apartments. "You don't see a lot of drinking on campus," says a student. There are only 40 official student organizations, the most popular of which are Sailing Club, Pre-Health Society, Art Club, Lady American Sewing Circle and Talking Society, and Dance Club. There are no fraternities or sororities at the university.

It may not be a party school, but UD does have a fun personality. Groundhog is the longest standing tradition on campus. The event consists of a 5k run, sports, live bands, bonfires, and food. The entire event is planned by students. The university has an observatory, an arts village, and a theater for students.

Recreation and sports facilities for active students include baseball, softball, lacrosse, and soccer fields, basketball, tennis, and volleyball courts, a fitness facility, and an outdoor swimming pool. Students who like to stay active can choose from a variety of intramural sports in which to participate.

In addition to the university's intramural teams, there is also the opportunity to participate in one of 13 Division II intercollegiate sports. Athletic scholarships are not offered by the university. Going against the grain of Texas colleges, there is no football team at the university. "There are plenty of other football teams in Texas to root for," one student comments.

Unlike some schools, UD allows freshmen to have cars on campus. But for those students who do not own a car or do not want to deal with parking permit fees, the Dart bus system has stops on campus and makes it convenient and easy to get around town. "A car isn't a necessity, but a friend with one is," one student laughs.

Incoming freshmen can take advantage of a program called Dallas Year, which provides students with the opportunity to explore off campus. Outings include cultural venues such as zoos, operas, symphonies, museums, and theater productions.

Students under the age of 21 or who have fewer than 90 earned credits are required to live on campus. Many qualifying upperclassmen move to the Old Mill apartments. The university has seven resident halls available for undergraduate students. All freshmen are placed in double occupancy rooms with other freshmen roommates. Students looking for a bit of a social scene should look into the Gregory dorm, which has a reputation for being louder and more interactive.

Student Body

Even though the university is affiliated with the Catholic Church, there are a "moderate" number of students of different religious backgrounds. That being said, students in general do tend to "be politically conservative," including in their views of abortion and same-sex marriage.

UNIVERSITY OF DALLAS

Highlights

Students
Total enrollment: 2,576
Undergrads: 1,356
Part-time students: 2%
From out-of-state: 51%
From public schools: 45%
Male/Female: 48%/52%
Live on-campus: 65%
Off-campus employment rating: Fair
Caucasian: 69%
African American: 1%
Hispanic: 17%
Asian / Pacific Islander: 4%
Native American: 0%
Mixed (2+ ethnicities): 3%
International: 3%

Academics
Calendar: Semester
Student/faculty ratio: 10:1
Class size 9 or fewer: 22%
Class size 10-29: 66%
Class size 30-49: 8%
Class size 50-99: 3%
Class size 100 or more: 1%
Returning freshmen: 80%
Six-year graduation rate: 69%
Graduates who immediately go to graduate school: 30%
Graduates who immediately enter career related to major: 16%

Most Popular Majors
English
Biology
Business leadership

Admissions
Applicants: 1,178
Accepted: 1,032
Acceptance rate: 87.6%
Average GPA: 3.7
ACT range: 23-29
SAT Math range: 530-640
SAT Reading range: 560-670
SAT Writing range: 17-30
Top 10% of class: 53%
Top 25% of class: 72%
Top 50% of class: 85%

731

College Profiles

UNIVERSITY OF DALLAS

Admissions Criteria
Academic criteria:
Grades: ☆ ☆ ☆
Difficulty of class schedule: ☆ ☆ ☆
Class rank: ☆ ☆
Standardized test scores: ☆ ☆ ☆
Teacher recommendations: ☆ ☆ ☆
Personal statement: ☆ ☆ ☆
Non-academic criteria considered:
Interview
Extracurricular activities
Special talents, interests, abilities
Character/personal qualities
Volunteer work
Work experience
State of residency
Alumni relationship

Deadlines
Early Action: December 1
Early Decision: No
Regular Action: Rolling admissions
Common Application: Accepted

Financial Aid
In-state tuition: $30,850
Out-of-state tuition: $30,850
Room: $6,100
Board: $4,400
Books: $1,200
Freshmen receiving need-based aid: 68%
Undergrads rec. need-based aid: 61%
Avg. % of need met by financial aid: 72%
Avg. aid package (freshmen): $26,613
Avg. aid package (undergrads): $25,041
Avg. debt upon graduation: $31,466

School Spirit
Mascot: Crusader
Colors: Navy and white

Breaking down the demographics, minorities make up about one quarter of students, with the largest group being Hispanics at 17 percent. More than half of students come from out of state.

The university places a lot of emphasis on character development and provides many programs to encourage students to make good choices. Some examples of university programming include substance education, heritage awareness programming, new student orientation, health and wellness, and stress management.

You May Not Know

- The Center for Thomas More Studies promotes the study of Thomas More through publication of educational resources, an annual conference at UD, and research grants for scholars.
- Charity Week is a campus tradition that is coordinated by the junior class and raises $15,000 to $20,000 annually for local and national charities.
- UD offers a unique rental program through their university bookstore, allowing students to rent textbooks for a semester.

Distinguished Alumni

Bishop Daniel Flores, youngest Catholic bishop in the country; Peter MacNicol, actor.

Admissions and Financial Aid

UD requires that all prospective students complete an online application, as well as submit a personal statement. Students who visit the university campus between September 1 and December 1, and submit a completed admissions application within 15 days of their visit, can have the application fees waived.

Every student who shows an interest in applying to UD is assigned an admissions counselor. A prospective student's assigned admissions counselor is available by email to help answer questions and provide guidance through the application and college selection process.

Several merit-based scholarships are available to prospective students. The Academic Achievement and National Merit Finalist scholarships provide up to full tuition for qualifying students. Scholarships are also available to students who excel in art, chemistry, classics, drama, French, German, Spanish, physics, and math. The Aspiring Scholars scholarship is available to high school juniors, and the Phi Theta Kappa scholarship is available specifically to transfer students.

UNIVERSITY OF DAYTON

UNIVERSITY OF DAYTON

Four-year private
Founded: 1850
Dayton, OH
Large town
Pop. 142,148

Address:
300 College Park
Dayton, OH
45469

Admissions:
800-837-7433

Financial Aid:
937-229-4411

admission@udayton.edu

www.udayton.edu

Overview

The University of Dayton (UD) is a medium-sized private Roman Catholic university located in Dayton, Ohio. It is the largest private university in Ohio and one of the largest Catholic universities in the nation. Main campus is compact—crossed in less than 10 minutes—with a mix of historic buildings and newer architecture. Student neighborhoods like "The Ghetto" provide a unified sense of community and give their 8,000 undergrads a reason to stick around.

As one might expect of a university in the Midwest, there's a friendly, neighborly atmosphere. Religious faith is a major influence at UD, which has a very active campus ministry program. Students will want to be comfortable with a campus where faith is a priority for many, as would be expected for a Catholic school. There is low ethnic diversity and only moderate geographic diversity, so students looking for a diverse urban environment might want to look elsewhere.

This is not to say that UD is a staid place to study and live. Quite the contrary: students attend sold-out basketball games where a spirit team forms a sea of red; more than 2,000 students convene in Daytona, Florida for a school-sponsored weeklong trip; and 70 percent of students participate in intramurals. Entrepreneurial spirit is also a major force at UD, known for its business programs. Indeed, students who want to become UD Flyers may recall that they are in a town with a history of important entrepreneurs: the Wright Brothers were born in and invented their famous airplane in Dayton.

Academics

The university offers more than 70 majors, including a notable entrepreneurship program. The general education program requires all students to take 11 courses in arts, history, philosophy, religious studies, social science, and physical and life sciences. These courses are spread across a Humanities Base, Thematic Clusters (from cross-disciplinary learning), and Competencies in writing, reasoning, and other fundamental skills. Electronic/computing skills are one of the competencies, which may explain why all students are required to have a notebook computer. Strong programs include business administration and engineering.

The University Honors program offers a more rigorous curriculum through advanced courses. Honors students also have the opportunity to apply for subsidized international study and can conduct individualized research opportunities that culminate in the Honors thesis project.

Students who are not sure about their majors will appreciate the Discover Programs in Arts, Business, Engineering, Engineering Technology, Sciences, and Teacher Education. "Being undecided, it helps to take courses that are applicable to my future major," notes a student. These programs enable first-year students to participate in seminars and courses to discern if the program is a good fit for their interests and skills.

The Davis Center Team in the School of Business Administration oversees the management of $9 million of the university's endowment and is "a financial learning village" for all students. Students gain hands-on experience as portfolio managers, and the program also lays a foundation for careers in the industry. "This program is not for the hobbyist investor but for people who want a career in the financial industry," one student comments. Another way to gain industry experience is through the School of Engineering Cooperative Education program. Students alternate between semesters of full-time study and semesters of full-time, paid work.

Students at UD can study at either of the two other Marianist universities in the U.S. Chaminade University of Honolulu provides exposure to a majority Asian-American culture while St. Mary's University in San Antonio offers a predominantly

UNIVERSITY OF DAYTON

Students
Total enrollment: 11,159
Undergrads: 8,042
Freshmen: 2,191
Part-time students: 7%
From out-of-state: 50%
From public schools: 45%
Male/Female: 51%/49%
Live on-campus: 74%
In fraternities: 9%
In sororities: 15%
Off-campus employment rating: Good
Caucasian: 82%
African American: 3%
Hispanic: 2%
Asian / Pacific Islander: 1%
Native American: 0%
Mixed (2+ ethnicities): 1%
International: 7%

Academics
Calendar: Semester
Student/faculty ratio: 16:1
Class size 9 or fewer: 9%
Class size 10-29: 55%
Class size 30-49: 31%
Class size 50-99: 3%
Class size 100 or more: 1%
Returning freshmen: 88%
Six-year graduation rate: 78%
Graduates who immediately go to graduate school: 53%
Graduates who immediately enter career related to major: 62%

Most Popular Majors
Business/marketing
Engineering
Education

Admissions
Applicants: 15,101
Accepted: 8,336
Acceptance rate: 55.2%
Average GPA: 3.6
ACT range: 24-29
SAT Math range: 503-640
SAT Reading range: 510-620
SAT Writing range: 10-31
Top 10% of class: 26%
Top 25% of class: 57%
Top 50% of class: 88%

Latino-American culture. There are also numerous study-abroad opportunities for a summer, semester, or year, from China to Finland to Morocco.

University of Dayton Career Services has five career advisors, each specializing in different majors. It also offers on-campus recruiting and interviews, career workshops, and the Student Contract Program, where students work off campus for local companies while being paid by the university. "It's a good opportunity to get real-world work experience," one student says.

Student Life

There are more than 180 clubs and organizations, offering opportunities to volunteer for Habit for Humanity, become the broadcast news anchor for Flyer TV, build and race a concrete canoe, or march with the Pride of Dayton marching band. Flyer Enterprises (FE) is one of the largest student-run corporations in the nation. FE offers business training through its eight divisions, employing more than 170 students and earning annual revenues of more than $1.4 million.

The spirit of service is captured at UD during Christmas on Campus, an event that brings 900 school children to a fully decked-out campus to celebrate the winter holiday. It's been a tradition since 1963. "It really makes you think about the true meaning of Christmas," recalls a student.

There are 12 fraternities and nine sororities on campus, with 12 percent of students participating. A number of activities are associated with the Greek organizations, including philanthropy and service events, Greek Week, and National Hazing Prevention Week.

The UD Flyers have 16 Division I teams, with the football team in the Football Championship Subdivision. Men's basketball games are very popular and have high attendance rates; in fact, they are often sold out. Women's basketball is also strong. One student comments, "At other schools, football is the main sport; but here it's basketball." Red Scare—the student group that cheers on the varsity sports teams—has 1,300 undergrad members. An astonishing 70 percent of students participate in intramurals, so it's safe to say that students are active as both fans and athletes.

Top day trips include Cincinnati (an hour away), Indianapolis, (1.5 hours away), and Louisville (2.5 hours away). Then there's the not-to-miss Dayton to Daytona Trip, a tradition for over 30 years that gathers 2,500 UD students for "a week of pool parties, concerts, club events, and all-out madness in the Daytona sun."

About three quarters of students live on campus and in the student neighborhood. ArtStreet is a unique living/learning arts complex for juniors and seniors of all majors. ArtStreet offers multipurpose studio facilities open to the entire community, including the ArtStreet Café, Studio D Gallery, and Thursday Night Live performances.

The Ghetto, students' nickname for the South Student Neighborhood, is the surrounding area of campus where many students live. The area is popular for parties, and for people-watching from the homes' porches. "You can spend literally a whole day on your porch having friends drop by," says a student.

Student Body

Since UD is a Catholic school, religion plays a prominent part in campus activities. It also influences students' shared commitment to service. "Not everyone is Catholic," a student explains, "but you'll probably feel a little like an outsider if you're not religious at all." With so many students living on campus or in the student neighborhoods, there's a tight-knit sense of community that's enhanced by the friendly Midwestern feel. "You say hi to people even if you don't know them," notes a student.

There is low ethnic minority, with about seven percent minority students. There is moderate geographic diversity, with about half of students coming from out of state.

You May Not Know

- The University of Dayton began as a school with 14 students in 1850.
- UD offered the first undergraduate minor in human rights in 1999.
- The athletic mascot is Rudy Flyer, who dresses in a pilot costume to "celebrate Dayton's aviation history" according to the university.

Distinguished Alumni

Erma Bombeck, columnist and humor writer; Kristina Keneally, first female Premier of New South Wales; Chuck Noll, former coach of the Pittsburgh Steelers; Dan Patrick, former ESPN anchor; Charles Pederson, winner of the Nobel Prize in Chemistry.

Admissions and Financial Aid

There is no application fee for electronically submitted applications. Students are strongly encouraged to visit campus to get answers to questions "and discover if this is where [they] belong." According to the admissions office, the university has seen an increase in the number and academic quality of applicants in recent years. The admissions committee may admit students to academic programs different from the ones they applied for, depending on the overall quality of applicants and requirements for a particular major or division.

More than half of students receive need-based financial aid, and 38 percent of students receive merit-based aid. All students are automatically considered for a number of merit scholarships that have minimum GPA and test score requirements. These include the Trustees' Merit scholarship, worth $50,000 or more over four years; the President's Merit scholarship ($36,000 to $60,000), and Dean's Merit ($30,000 to $45,000). There are also music and visual arts and athletic scholarships.

UNIVERSITY OF DAYTON

Highlights

Admissions Criteria
Academic criteria:
Grades: ☆ ☆ ☆
Difficulty of class schedule: ☆ ☆ ☆
Class rank: ☆
Standardized test scores: ☆ ☆ ☆
Teacher recommendations: ☆ ☆
Personal statement: ☆ ☆ ☆
Non-academic criteria considered:
Interview
Extracurricular activities
Special talents, interests, abilities
Character/personal qualities
Volunteer work
Work experience
State of residency
Minority affiliation
Alumni relationship

Deadlines
Early Action: December 15
Early Decision: No
Regular Action: Rolling admissions
Common Application: Accepted

Financial Aid
In-state tuition: $35,800
Out-of-state tuition: $35,800
Room: $6,450
Board: $3,900
Books: $1,000
Freshmen receiving need-based aid: 59%
Undergrads rec. need-based aid: 54%
Avg. % of need met by financial aid: 78%
Avg. aid package (freshmen): $22,850
Avg. aid package (undergrads): $23,137
Avg. debt upon graduation: $40,628

School Spirit
Mascot: Rudy Flyer
Colors: Red and blue
Song: *Dayton Victory March*

UNIVERSITY OF DELAWARE

Overview

Founded as a small private institution in 1743, UD is rooted in antiquity, but definitely not trapped there. The state's flagship university, Delaware (fondly known as UDel) is a research institution with intense levels of activity. UD is a land-grant, sea-grant, and space-grant institution, which means that the federal government provides the college with financial support, strengthening the research potential, especially in the agricultural development field. Now a state-assisted university with a private charter, Delaware provides small classes, a billion-dollar endowment, a gorgeous campus, and a wide variety of academic experiences.

Indeed, walking across campus is a treat for the eyes. With expansive green lawns, brick buildings, and white columns, the UDel campus has the charming mix of southern Georgian-inspired architecture and old-world East Coast academic tradition. UD has been working on a series of campus construction projects; for example, brand new residence halls were built in 2006. Campus is centralized across 2,000 acres in Newark, with satellite locations in Wilmington, Dover, Georgetown, and Lewes. Newark doesn't have much to brag about, but in such a small state, the university's proximity to other areas is significant. Once called a "jewel" of the states by Thomas Jefferson, Delaware sits at a fairly convenient midpoint between New York City and Washington, DC (if you have a car and the patience to make the over-two-hour trip).

With an undergraduate population of 17,000, Delaware is a large but not gigantic university. It has gained a reputation for having a party scene that is especially strong off campus.

Academics

UD offers 125 majors and 75 minors, with the strongest programs including agriculture and natural resources, engineering, and international relations. Some of the most rigorous areas of study are the hard sciences and engineering. UD is focused on "an enriched undergraduate education from start to finish." This includes participating in LIFE, the Learning Integrated Freshman Experience, which clusters students based on majors of study and allows them to participate in discussion groups, tutoring, field trips, lectures, and social activities. Throughout their four years at UDel, all students will participate in a Discovery Learning Experience: this can take the form of studying abroad, doing undergraduate research or independent study, or participating in service-learning or an internship. "Having a hands-on experience is very valuable," one student says.

The University Honors Program, which students must apply for in their initial admission application, is a four-year program that allows students the opportunity to take smaller, Honors-designated courses, live in an Honors residence hall, and receive comprehensive advising. These students also have "a lot of one-on-one time with professors," notes a student. Another opportunity for academically talented students is The Medical Scholars Program, which allows students to earn a bachelors from UD and MD from Jefferson Medical College. The Undergraduate Research Program supports students to work as research assistants and write senior theses about their work. However, an unfortunately common complaint is that "you may get more face time with the teaching assistants (TAs) than your professors."

UDel was the first American university to begin a study-abroad program, when a professor took a small group of students to Paris for the fall semester of 1923. Clearly, the idea caught on. The overseas program is still a huge part of the academic experience at UDel, with offerings in over 35 countries and 1,400 students studying abroad each year.

There are 140,000 living alums from UD, and students can reach out to many of them through the Alumni Mentor Network. The Career Services Center helps students and graduates with career preparation, and job and internship matching.

Student Life

Student groups are prolific on campus, with 300 official student organizations, the most popular of which are theatre, music, political, service groups, and the 26 honor societies. There are 18 fraternities and 11 sororities; about 15 percent of men and 17 percent of women go Greek. Though not overwhelming, the party scene at UDel is infamous (or famous, depending on what you're looking for in a college). According to a University Risk Behaviors Study, 83 percent of students say they drink often, and two-thirds of that percentage report themselves as binge drinkers. "Drinking is a way of life for some," says a student. The parties on campus have been slightly curbed lately, since the institution of the "three-strike policy," which suspends drinkers on the third strike. This didn't have an effect off campus however—significant because more than half of students live off campus.

The arts have a very vibrant support system and an avid student following on campus. Popular events include the singing competition Blue Hen Idol; the Performing Arts Series throughout the year; the Coffeehouse series of Tuesday night performances; and an Amateur Comedian Night. Other popular events include the annual Spring Fling and a Nintendo Wii Tournament.

The Delaware athletic teams are known as the Fightin' Blue Hens—the "Fightin" must be an attempt to dignify YoUDee the mascot, which is in fact a pretty non-threatening blue chicken. There are 23 Division I sports, football being the most popular. Recent titles have been in football (2010), men's ice hockey (2012), and women's basketball (2012). The football team has won six Football Championship Subdivision titles, and "games are definitely a social event," one student notes. Those who want to stay active may choose to join intramural teams and participate in club sports.

Most socializing (other than the popular football tailgates) occurs off campus. Newark has lots of restaurants, shopping, and date spots, including a bowling alley and a movie theatre on Main Street. Students frequently drive the 30 miles to Philadelphia for their bars and clubs. "We have easy access to big city entertainment," one student comments.

In addition to traditional dorms, students may opt for having adjacent apartments with friends; special interest housing such as for the performing arts, leadership, or global awareness; or honors housing. "Expect to live with two roommates as a freshman," one student comments.

Student Body

The student body population is 57 percent female, which equates to "a less-than-desirable dating situation," says a female student. Rates of ethnic diversity are moderate, currently about 17 percent, but there has been a marked annual increase since 2005. Sixty-four percent of students are from out of state; though this is a high number, most students are from the surrounding states of Maryland, New Jersey, New York, and Pennsylvania.

UNIVERSITY OF DELAWARE

Highlights

Students
Total enrollment: 21,081
Undergrads: 17,427
Part-time students: 9%
From out-of-state: 64%
Male/Female: 43%/57%
Live on-campus: 46%
In fraternities: 15%
In sororities: 17%
Off-campus employment rating: Good
Caucasian: 77%
African American: 5%
Hispanic: 6%
Asian / Pacific Islander: 4%
Native American: 0%
Mixed (2+ ethnicities): 2%
International: 4%

Academics
Calendar: 4-1-4 system
Student/faculty ratio: 13:1
Class size 9 or fewer: 14%
Class size 10-29: 47%
Class size 30-49: 23%
Class size 50-99: 11%
Class size 100 or more: 5%
Returning freshmen: 92%
Six-year graduation rate: 80%

Most Popular Majors
Accounting
Nursing
Finance

Admissions
Applicants: 26,225
Accepted: 14,829
Acceptance rate: 56.5%
Placed on wait list: 2,502
Enrolled from wait list: 189
Average GPA: 3.8
ACT range: 24-28
SAT Math range: 560-660
SAT Reading range: 540-650
SAT Writing range: 540-640
Top 10% of class: 40%
Top 25% of class: 76%
Top 50% of class: 97%

737

UNIVERSITY OF DELAWARE

Admissions Criteria
Academic criteria:
Grades: ☆ ☆ ☆
Difficulty of class schedule: ☆ ☆ ☆
Class rank: ☆
Standardized test scores: ☆ ☆
Teacher recommendations: ☆ ☆
Personal statement: ☆ ☆
Non-academic criteria considered:
Interview
Extracurricular activities
Special talents, interests, abilities
Character/personal qualities
Volunteer work
Work experience
Geographical location
Minority affiliation
Alumni relationship

Deadlines
Early Action: No
Early Decision: No
Regular Action: December 1 (priority)
January 15 (final)
Notification of admission by: Mid-March
Common Application: Accepted

Financial Aid
In-state tuition: $10,580
Out-of-state tuition: $28,400
Room: $6,810
Board: $4,390
Books: $800
Freshmen receiving need-based aid: 56%
Undergrads rec. need-based aid: 49%
Avg. % of need met by financial aid: 73%
Avg. aid package (freshmen): $14,427
Avg. aid package (undergrads): $14,442
Avg. debt upon graduation: $34,649

School Spirit
Mascot: YoUDee
Colors: Royal blue and gold
Song: *All Hail to Delaware*

Students have a "wide range of interests," but state that one commonality is partying. "A lot of people party and drink pretty heavily," explains a student, "but if you don't, you'll find your clique too."

You May Not Know

- The first graduating class of UD included three signers of the Declaration of Independence and one signer of the United States Constitution.
- The UD Figure Skating Club has placed in the top three of the U.S. National Championships for the past 10 years.
- The University Gallery has over 10,000 objects, artworks, and artifacts, including one of the largest amber collections in the world and the famous Paul R. Jones Collection of African-American Art.

Distinguished Alumni

Joe Biden, Vice President of the United States; Maureen Johnson, young adult fiction author; Steve Mosko, President of Sony Pictures and Entertainment; Susan Stroman, Tony Award winner, director and choreographer of *The Producers*; George Thorogood, blues rock singer and guitarist.

Admissions and Financial Aid

Important factors for admission to UDel include the rigor of courses taken throughout high school, as well as trends in grades from freshman to senior year. The admissions department shows favoritism to in-state students; and the university advertises a Commitment to Delawareans, which, as they describe it, is "as close to a 'guarantee' as we can make" without actually offering admission. It is an academic roadmap for middle and high school students from Delaware, which outlines the courses that students should take and how well they need to perform in them. If Delawarean students follow the stipulations, they can feel confident of admission to UDel.

Delaware offers more than $100 million in financial aid each year. Just as with admission, favoritism is shown to students from Delaware. Starting in 2009, the university started a pledge to meet the demonstrated financial need of all Delawarean admits. UDel also does work to ensure that no student will graduate with loans in excess of 25 percent of the cost of a four-year education.

Along with need-based financial aid, scholarships are offered to students who excel in art, music, and athletics. Students are judged on the basis of athletic performance, art portfolios, and music auditions for these opportunities. The university offers "an unusually large number of academic scholarships" to roughly one-quarter of the students who are admitted each year. Amounts range from $1,000 annually to full scholarships. All students who apply are automatically considered for these awards. Additional scholarships are offered through ROTC, the College of Agriculture and Natural Resources, and through other majors and programs.

UNIVERSITY OF DENVER

Overview

If your idea of the good life is studying on a picturesque 125-acre campus at the foot of the Rocky Mountains, biking to class through open space, and spending free time skiing, snowboarding, hiking, and camping, then University of Denver is definitely the place for you. Founded in 1864, DU is the oldest private, independent university in the Rocky Mountain region, with roughly 11,700 undergraduate and graduate students. Located just seven miles south of downtown Denver, this urban campus is renowned for its scenic and lush greenery.

DU is also well regarded for its innovative and rigorous undergraduate, graduate, and professional programs in international studies, business, and political science. Further, the university features a strong alumni network with prominent individuals across various fields. As DU describes itself, the university is "a rare balance between cosmopolitan opportunities and the rugged outdoors... something for everyone."

Academics

At DU, you can take advantage of over 100 undergraduate programs, including traditional majors and dual-degree programs across a range of disciplines. Undergraduates are required to participate in regular academic advising, while first-year students in particular are assigned a mentor prior to registration. Students must also review quarterly progress reports with advisors. Students may integrate independent studies, directed studies, internship credit, and ROTC credit throughout their academic program.

The general education curriculum requires students to take a first-year seminar focused on critical reading and writing, two sources in writing and rhetoric, three language courses, one course in math or computer science, two courses in arts and humanities, three courses in math, two courses in social sciences, and a writing-intensive advanced seminar. "The requirements are fewer than before which allows us more flexibility," says a student.

The academic calendar is based on a quarter system, which students describe as "good because you learn a lot of material in a short amount of time, but challenging because you're expected to learn the material so quickly." Strong programs include international studies and political science, and it should be noted that former Secretary of State Condoleezza Rice earned her bachelor's in political science and her doctorate in international studies at this university. Rice also took an international politics class from Dr. Josef Korbel, father of Madeleine Albright who was Secretary of State under President Bill Clinton. Other standout academic programs are also offered through the Daniels College of Business, University College, Faculties of Arts and Humanities, Natural Sciences, Mathematics, Engineering, and Social Sciences, and the Graduate School of International Studies.

Special academic opportunities abound. For instance, students can enroll in interterm courses such as an international travel course on a cruise through the Mediterranean, or "An Organized Walk Down Wall Street" in New York City, or even "Natural Hazards in Hawaii" in the Aloha state. The Pioneer Leadership Program is an academic minor—as well as a living and learning community—that facilitates classes, internships, and community service aimed at providing students with "hands-on experience in leadership."

Through the Cherrington Global Scholars Program, students can spend one quarter abroad—with no additional tuition, room, and board costs—while still meeting degree requirements. There are over 150 programs in over 56 countries, ranging from Argentina to Ireland, and from South Africa to Thailand, and 70 percent of students tend to participate.

UNIVERSITY OF DENVER

Four-year private
Founded: 1864
Denver, CO
Major city
Pop. 619,968

Address:
2199 South University
Boulevard
Denver, CO
80208

Admissions:
800-525-9495

Financial Aid:
303-871-4020

admission@du.edu

www.du.edu

UNIVERSITY OF DENVER

Highlights

Students
Total enrollment: 11,656
Undergrads: 5,394
Freshmen: 1,213
Part-time students: 8%
From out-of-state: 58%
Male/Female: 44%/56%
Live on-campus: 42%
In fraternities: 25%
In sororities: 25%
Off-campus employment rating: Excellent
Caucasian: 68%
African American: 3%
Hispanic: 8%
Asian / Pacific Islander: 4%
Native American: 1%
Mixed (2+ ethnicities): 3%
International: 9%

Academics
Calendar: Quarter
Student/faculty ratio: 11:1
Class size 9 or fewer: 16%
Class size 10-29: 63%
Class size 30-49: 15%
Class size 50-99: 6%
Class size 100 or more: -
Returning freshmen: 86%
Six-year graduation rate: 76%
Graduates who immediately go to graduate school: 23%
Graduates who immediately enter career related to major: 93%

Most Popular Majors
Finance
International business
International studies

Admissions
Applicants: 11,448
Accepted: 7,740
Acceptance rate: 67.6%
Placed on wait list: 926
Enrolled from wait list: 103
Average GPA: 3.7
ACT range: 25-30
SAT Math range: 560-660
SAT Reading range: 550-640
SAT Writing range: 9-36
Top 10% of class: 44%
Top 25% of class: 78%
Top 50% of class: 97%

740

"We have a lot of internship opportunities," ones student notes. Almost 70 percent of students complete an internship while studying at DU. For instance, there are chances to connect with companies such as Frontier Airlines, MillerCoors, and Qwest with headquarters or large operations based in Denver. Graduates can also make use of a vibrant alumni network and alumni association that provides career support long after you have left campus. The career center reports that more than 90 percent of students find a position within six months of graduating.

Student Life

With access to over 100 student clubs and organizations, including 17 academic honor societies, life at University of Denver is quite active. Through the campus Hillel, you can "observe traditional Jewish rituals and year-round events, whether or not you're Jewish." Students can also join members of DU's Alpine Club, which organizes 20-25 outdoor trips annually in a range of sports including backpacking, rock climbing, mountain biking, and ice climbing, or find a grilling society, book club, and a business association among other clubs.

Since 1889, Greek life has been popular. There are nine national fraternities and five national sororities joined by one quarter of student. "We do a lot of community service, including getting the whole school involved on DU Volunteer Day," says a student.

Numerous events take place on campus, many of which are traditions and some of which are new. The Diversity Summit held through the Center for Multicultural Excellence features keynote speakers and workshops on topics such as maintaining a culturally diverse campus. The DU Programs Board sponsors a weekly movie series every Thursday, which showcases three popular-release films often with a huge attendance. Members of the DU community gather once a year to commemorate the university's founding through a ceremony that celebrates achievements and contributions from across the university at a special dinner in downtown Denver.

For the sports-minded, there are 13 intramural sports including broomball and flag football, along with 29 club sports ranging from kayaking to Ultimate Frisbee. Many students tend to ski and snowboard, and groups often go every weekend during the winter. "Hitting the slopes is a way of life," one student explains. The university boasts 17 Division I sports teams. In fact, DU has become renowned as a major force in winter sports; the men's hockey program has played since 1949, becoming one of the most successful programs in college hockey history.

While first- and second-year undergraduates are required to live on campus, some upperclassmen enjoy living close to downtown Denver. "There's more to do," one student says. Students are within driving distance of Boulder, which is very student friendly and close to lots of restaurants, bars, and clubs.

University housing includes Living and Learning Communities, the Pioneer Leadership Program, and Honors Program housing, and each hall offers high-speed and wireless Internet connections, cable and phone service, and laundry facilities.

Student Body

The University of Denver features a student body with high ethnic diversity, as 19 percent is of minority background. There is moderate geographic diversity as well, with 58 percent coming from out of state. With almost 500 students from 88 countries, DU is also fairly international.

Many students love outdoor activities. "It's not unusual to see skis and snowboards strapped on top of cars and students heading to the mountains every day of the week," says a student. "This really is an outdoor paradise," another student adds. Students also say that many are from upper-middle class and upperclass backgrounds. However, merit-based scholarships aim to create a more socio-economically diverse student body so that admittance is not limited to just those who can afford the best snowboards and skis.

You May Not Know

- DU is committed to environmental conservation and sustainability efforts and has pledged to become carbon neutral by 2050.
- The university was founded in 1864 as the Colorado Seminary by John Evans, the former Governor of Colorado Territory, who had been appointed by President Abraham Lincoln.
- Ringing the Victory Bell is a DU custom that goes back decades. In a University Hall spire, a bell would toll to signal class changes and celebrate sporting victories. The bell now hangs in Buchtel Tower for use during Commencement.

Distinguished Alumni

Michelle Kwan, figure-skating champion and American public diplomacy envoy; Paul Laxalt, former Nevada Governor and Senator; Gale Norton, former Secretary of the Interior; Condoleezza Rice, former Secretary of State; Susan Waltz, chair, International Executive Committee, Amnesty International.

Admissions and Financial Aid

The university employs a holistic review and the admissions office states, "We look at more than just your grades." Applicants are "strongly" encouraged to participate in an interview on campus—or in one of 30 cities across the country—called a Hyde interview. According to DU admissions, this allows the admissions officers to learn about the "personal qualities and experiences that aren't necessarily reflected in test scores, GPAs, and essays."

Thirty-two percent of students receive merit-based scholarships. First-year awards range from the Crimson and Gold Scholarship of $10,000 per year to the Chancellor Scholarship of $19,000 per year. Transfer scholarships range from the Long's Peak Scholarship of $3,000 per year to the Pike's Peak Scholarship of $9,000 per year. There are also talent scholarships in athletics, music, art and theater.

UNIVERSITY OF DENVER

Highlights

Admissions Criteria
Academic criteria:
Grades: ☆ ☆ ☆
Difficulty of class schedule: ☆ ☆ ☆
Class rank: N/A
Standardized test scores: ☆ ☆ ☆
Teacher recommendations: ☆ ☆
Personal statement: ☆ ☆
Non-academic criteria considered:
Interview
Extracurricular activities
Special talents, interests, abilities
Character/personal qualities
Volunteer work
Work experience
State of residency
Geographical location
Minority affiliation
Alumni relationship

Deadlines
Early Action: November 1
Early Decision: No
Regular Action: January 15 (final)
Notification of admission by: March 15
Common Application: Accepted

Financial Aid
In-state tuition: $39,744
Out-of-state tuition: $39,744
Room: Varies
Board: Varies
Books: $1,800
Freshmen receiving need-based aid: 49%
Undergrads rec. need-based aid: 44%
Avg. % of need met by financial aid: 83%
Avg. aid package (freshmen): $30,905
Avg. aid package (undergrads): $31,160
Avg. debt upon graduation: $30,268

School Spirit
Mascot: Pioneers
Colors: Crimson and gold
Song: *Fairest of Colleges*

741

Overview

Located in the heart of the Sunshine State, the lush campus of UF provides the ideal setting in which to study hard and play hard while basking under year-round balmy skies. The 2,000-acre campus, located in the suburban environment of Gainesville, is home to more than 900 buildings. The northeast part of the campus is a Historic District in the National Register of Historic Places. True to its everglade roots, the campus is dotted with numerous ponds and parks, including the centrally located Lake Alice and the university golf course.

The fourth largest university in the country and a public school, UF boasts some of the nation's strongest academics, recently ranking 14th on *U.S. News & World Report's* list of public universities. Although a student body of 46,000 (nearly 33,000 undergraduates) can seem overwhelming at times and students must actively pursue their interests and niches, the university provides endless academic and research opportunities. UF isn't your ordinary oversized academic melting pot, though: the incoming class of 2017 had an average GPA of 4.0 and included 1,375 International Baccalaureate students—more than any other university in the country.

University of Florida provides the perfect break from studies by maintaining its status as an athletic powerhouse. In 2006, the Gators became the first university ever to win national championships in football and men's basketball within the same year. More than 90,000 fans consistently turn out to cheer on the football team in "the Swamp" because bearing the orange and blue of "Gator Nation" is a true source of pride.

Academics

With 165 majors—many of which are also pursued as minors—as well as combined degrees and certificate programs, undergraduate academics provide a plethora of options. Particularly strong programs include astronomy, business administration, journalism and communications, engineering, pre-health advising, and zoology. Students must complete general education requirements consisting of three composition sources, nine humanities courses, six math courses, nine physical and biological science courses, and nine social and behavioral science courses. UF is big, and that affects class size; 17 percent of classes have 50 students or more, and some classes are taught by graduate students. "You can get a little lost, especially during freshman year," admits one student.

The university offers an honors program, and students are invited to join upon acceptance to UF. The honors program offers stronger academics in a smaller community and the option of honors housing—a chance to carry on academic conversations beyond the classroom—as well as special extracurricular activities and research internships.

UF also has a University Scholars Program. The opportunity of taking classes from the Tutorials program at Oxford University offers undergraduates a unique chance to work one-on-one with a professor on a research project, giving them a chance to learn research methods and gain experience in a topic outside the conventional classroom setting.

UF is a renowned research university and has $750 million in recently completed or under-construction facilities. "While a lot of research opportunities are for graduate students, there are lots for undergrads too," one student comments. Fitting for the state famous for NASA and the Kennedy Space Center, the university funds one of the top research programs in astronomy; other research institutes include the Moffitt Cancer Center, the McKnight Brain Institute, and the Institute on Aging, which is currently studying whether physical activity can prolong elderly mobility.

If you are looking to study abroad during college, UF has a wide and flexible range of options. The university sponsors exchange programs with schools around the world as well as independent study-abroad programs. UF also offers "sponsored programs," which are usually subject-specific programs that have been designed and taught by a professor. Most of these programs are offered during the summer and provide an excellent opportunity to study one subject in-depth and under the direct guidance of a professor in the field while earning credit.

Even after students leave UF, they still have numerous options available to them, thanks to the UF Alumni Association, which is ranked as one of the top 15 in the world. The association has Gator Clubs and even global branches of the alumni network. Additionally, it sponsors activities and athletic events to maintain connections and allow recent graduates the chance to network and reach out for jobs. "There are alums to connect to in every possible field," notes a student.

Student Life

A student body of more than 46,000 guarantees a diversity of interests, demonstrated by 665 official student organizations. These include student government, the Gator Amateur Radio Club, the Tower Yearbook, Falling Gators Parachute Club, and a host of others.

True to its diverse and accepting roots, the university has several annual traditions designed to integrate all members of the Gator community. People Awareness Week, held every January, promotes the acceptance of, education about, and respect for other ethnicities, religions, and sexual orientations. Homecoming, the annual October football game where alumni return to join current students in rallying the football team, is a must-attend event. It is preceded the night before by Gator Growl, the largest student-run pep rally in the world. "It's a once-in-a-lifetime experience," one student says. Gator Growl is a night of skits, cheers, and comedians and is a sure way to fire everyone up for the Homecoming game. Past guests have included the famed Robin Williams, Bill Cosby, and Jerry Seinfeld.

Although 76 percent of students choose to live off campus, 34 fraternities and 26 sororities ensure that a party is never too hard to find. Only 19 percent of students join fraternities and sororities, but Greek life is certainly a prevalent part of the social network at UF.

Varsity athletics are obviously huge at UF (17 Division I teams), and almost everyone turns out to cheer on the teams; but the university also offers a plethora (over 60!) of club and intramural sports for those looking for a more relaxed way to stay active. Club sports include anything from archery to weightlifting, and intramural sports range from the traditional basketball, soccer, and tennis to a street hockey tournament, a sports trivia competition, and—yes— a rock-paper-scissors tournament in the spring. Students can find ways to stay active inside at one of the three fitness centers, or hit the great outdoors and spend time in the Florida sun. "You can be outdoors almost every day of the year," one student comments.

Local restaurants and bars are student-friendly. Most students have cars, which makes trips to nearby coffee shops and beaches—as

UNIVERSITY OF FLORIDA

Highlights

Students
Total enrollment: 46,118
Undergrads: 32,776
Part-time students: 8%
From out-of-state: 4%
Male/Female: 45%/55%
Live on-campus: 24%
In fraternities: 19%
In sororities: 19%
Off-campus employment rating: Good
Caucasian: 58%
African American: 8%
Hispanic: 18%
Asian / Pacific Islander: 8%
Native American: 0%
Mixed (2+ ethnicities): 3%
International: 1%

Academics
Calendar: Semester
Student/faculty ratio: 21:1
Class size 9 or fewer: 19%
Class size 10-29: 48%
Class size 30-49: 15%
Class size 50-99: 10%
Class size 100 or more: 7%
Returning freshmen: 96%
Six-year graduation rate: 85%

Most Popular Majors
Psychology
Biology
Mechanical engineering

Admissions
Applicants: 27,419
Accepted: 12,092
Acceptance rate: 44.1%
Average GPA: 4.0
ACT range: 26-31
SAT Math range: 590-690
SAT Reading range: 580-670
SAT Writing range: 17-48
Top 10% of class: 77%
Top 25% of class: 98%
Top 50% of class: 100%

743

UNIVERSITY OF FLORIDA

well as longer expeditions to Miami, Jacksonville, and, of course, Disney World and Palm Beach—attractive. There's almost always a way to get off campus and find a change of scenery.

Student Body

University of Florida is aptly named in terms of student origins, with 96 percent of the student body coming from within the state. Eighty-one percent of students live on campus their freshman year. This creates a definite feeling of community as newcomers transition into their first year of college. "Everyone is friendly," a student remarks.

Though most students come from Florida, they represent an array of ethnic backgrounds, with more than one third of students identifying as minorities.

Students love UF, represented by a 96 percent return rate, one of the highest in the country. With more than 330,000 living alumni around the world, the Gator Nation continues to support its members even after they leave campus.

You May Not Know

- Gatorade—the original sugary sports drink—didn't get its name from nowhere: Robert Cade, the director of the UF College of Medicine's renal and electrolyte division, worked closely with the UF football team to develop the drink in 1965.
- UF houses one of the world's largest collections of Lepidoptera (butterflies and moths, in laymen's terms), with over nine million specimens.
- The economic impact of the university on the state is more than $5.8 billion.

Distinguished Alumni

John Atanasoff, inventor of the digital computer; Michael Connelly, best-selling mystery novelist; Faye Dunaway, actress; Bob Graham, former U.S. Senator and Florida Governor; Forrest Sawyer, national broadcast journalist.

Admissions and Financial Aid

Admission to UF is not a guarantee—high academic standards make it a selective and competitive school. Although most students choose to matriculate at the beginning of fall semester, (at the end of August,) the university also offers the Summer B Plan that allows some students to start school in June. Students are encouraged to apply during the preferred application period, between July 1 and November 1. Admission and housing priority will be given to applications received during this time.

UF offers numerous scholarships to alleviate the costs of tuition. Athletic scholarships are an option for those demonstrating excellence in varsity sports, and the university also offers up to twenty $1,000 scholarships to athletes transferring from community colleges. Students may also receive one of many merit scholarships, including the Bright Future Scholarship and the Lombardi Scholars Program, which cover college tuition for some Florida students, as well as major-specific scholarships and out-of-state tuition waivers.

UNIVERSITY OF GEORGIA

Overview

One of the nation's oldest schools, the University of Georgia has recently risen to 20th in *U.S. News & World Report's* ranking of national public universities. This is largely due to Georgia's implementation of the HOPE Scholarship, which covers the cost of tuition. Not surprising, this has helped the school attract the majority of top students in the state.

UGA is a very large school with tens of thousands of undergraduates and an oak-tree-studded 615-acre campus mostly comprised of neoclassical and antebellum-style historic buildings. The students who come to UGA for the parties and football are balanced by the students who come to study and take advantage of special academic programs. Granted, football is the main focus of campus events, and one of the South's longest-established and most active Greek systems exists there. And it's true that UGA has more than a little of Southern sorority girl and old boys' club about it. But students are bound to find like-minded peers, and the widely-touted city of Athens, adjacent to North Campus and 80 miles west of Atlanta, has frequently been called one of the top college towns in the country.

Academics

UGA students can choose from 330 majors across 13 of its schools and colleges. In addition to its highly respected Colleges of Business and Journalism and Mass Communication, it offers strong programs in its Odum School of Ecology, (the first of its kind in the world), College of Veterinary Medicine and Schools of Social Work and Education. Standout majors are accounting, computer science, landscape architecture, psychology, public management, and speech communication. The College of Journalism oversees the highly prestigious Peabody Awards for excellence in electronic media, and as such, houses the extensive Peabody Archives, which contain the top radio and TV shows produced in the last 60 years. "My professors have worked at the Associated Press, *The New York Times*, and NBC News," one student remarks. "Their real-world experience makes class lectures invaluable."

UGA's General Education Core Curriculum requires Foundational Courses: two courses in English and one in math. Distribution requirements include one course each in physical and life sciences with a lab component, quantitative reasoning, humanities and the arts, and three courses each in world languages and cultures and social sciences, including Georgia and U.S. history. Introductory lectures and popular classes tend to be quite large; in fact, 10 percent of classes have over 50 students.

Given that many of the students accepted to UGA were high achievers in high school, academics have the potential to be serious here; but there's also a significant population that attend this state school to party and watch football. So if you're looking for challenging academics, your best bet is to stick with UGA's special programs, as the gamut definitely extends in both directions. "There is a mix of those who are focused on studying and those who'd rather have a beer," one student notes.

Open to students in all fields, the Honors Program offers its own faculty-taught seminars as well as Honors sections of regular lectures. Most class sizes average less than 20 students. Nine Honors courses satisfy the core curriculum requirements. Students must also complete a capstone thesis or project to graduate with High or Highest Honors. Combined degree options include taking graduate courses or even completing a master's as well as bachelor's degree in four years.

The perks that come with participation in Honors are stupendous: not only do Honors students receive priority registration and special housing in Myers Hall, but they are also eligible for a number of special scholarship opportunities. The most basic of these, the Ramsey Honors Scholarship, covers the full cost of tuition plus a stipend and $3,000 for travel-study. The Foundation Fellowship covers the cost of attendance

UNIVERSITY OF GEORGIA

Four-year public
Founded: 1785
Athens, GA
Medium city
Pop. 116,084

Address:
Hodgson Oil Building
Athens, GA
30602

Admissions:
706-542-8776

Financial Aid:
706-542-6147

admproc@uga.edu

www.uga.edu

745

College Profiles

UNIVERSITY OF GEORGIA

Highlights

Students
Total enrollment: 34,519
Undergrads: 26,259
Freshmen: 4,936
Part-time students: 7%
From out-of-state: 11%
From public schools: 81%
Male/Female: 43%/57%
Live on-campus: 27%
In fraternities: 21%
In sororities: 28%
Off-campus employment rating: Fair
Caucasian: 74%
African American: 7%
Hispanic: 5%
Asian / Pacific Islander: 8%
Native American: 0%
Mixed (2+ ethnicities): 2%
International: 1%

Academics
Calendar: Semester
Student/faculty ratio: 18:1
Class size 9 or fewer: 6%
Class size 10-29: 62%
Class size 30-49: 21%
Class size 50-99: 5%
Class size 100 or more: 5%
Returning freshmen: 94%
Six-year graduation rate: 83%
Graduates who immediately go to graduate school: 22%

Most Popular Majors
Psychology
Biology
Finance

Admissions
Applicants: 18,458
Accepted: 10,352
Acceptance rate: 56.1%
Placed on wait list: 1,131
Enrolled from wait list: 158
Average GPA: 3.8
ACT range: 26-30
SAT Math range: 580-670
SAT Reading range: 560-660
SAT Writing range: 14-47
Top 10% of class: 48%
Top 25% of class: 90%
Top 50% of class: 99%

The Ultimate
Guide to America's
Best Colleges

at UGA plus participation in a Maymester study abroad trip, pairs students with a faculty mentor, and even funds yearly travel-study.

Honors students may also participate in research in the first two years of college through the Center for Undergraduate Research Opportunities (CURO) Apprentice Program. "The Honors program has highly motivated and intelligent students," one student remarks. Qualified non-Honors students may also participate in undergraduate research. CURO helps to place students with research projects and mentors. It also administers funded research opportunities like the CURO Apprenticeships or Summer Research Fellowships.

UGA offers its own semester-long study-abroad programs to locations such as Antarctica, Costa Rica, Italy, France, Spain, Argentina, Australia, and New Zealand. Other options include spring and summer break programs in the UK, Italy, Peru, Spain, Costa Rica, France, Fiji, Ecuador, Ghana, Japan, South Korea, South Africa, Brazil, Australia, and Mexico. Though the bulk of its own programs are administered through Maymester courses, students may also participate in exchanges and third-party programs.

UGA's Career Center runs 10 career fairs a year, and colleges and schools offer specialized career advising. Among the top 25 employers of UGA graduates are Google and Deloitte, and Chick-fil-A is also on that list.

Student Life

Students can participate in UGA's more than 600 clubs and organizations, the bulk of these categorized as religious, service-oriented, or Greek. UGA students collectively volunteer about seven million hours a year, while UGA's Redcoat Band was the first in its conference to win the Sudler Trophy for the top college marching band. About a quarter of students are involved in UGA's 27 sororities and 35 fraternities. "Greek life is everything to those who are a part of it," explains a student, "and those who are not still enjoy the parties."

Events like Day of Service are popular on campus, as are most all the charitable activities. The International Street Festival is hosted by UGA's international student organizations and features cultural displays, music and dance performances, and prizes. Locals join students to participate. But by far the most major event on campus is recent national championship Bulldog football, particularly against its rival University of Florida. Alumni swarm campus days before games, and a very large number of students skip class the Friday before a game in order to start tailgating. "Football truly is a religion," one student notes. The very strong women's gymnastics team is also gaining a following. For those sports enthusiasts who are not part of UGA's official teams but still relish the thrill of the game, UGA has extensive intramural fields and facilities, and some teams can be extremely competitive.

Students looking for a break from frat party entertainment have a welcome alternative in Athens. Named the "Number One College Music Scene in America" by *Rolling Stone Magazine*, Athens has been a major player in the rock, country, and bluegrass music scenes, giving birth to bands like the B-52s, Indigo Girls, REM, and Of Montreal. Athens offers plenty of quality bars, so students can choose from a variety of options. "There's always something to do," one student comments.

Freshmen are required to live on campus and are concentrated in Brumby, Russell, and Creswell high-rises. Upperclassmen have the option to live in the other residence halls on West Campus, but more often opt to move off campus.

Student Body

Most UGA students are from Georgia, though the school boasts a high level of ethnic diversity. Campus is largely white, Southern, old school, and Republican, which some believe can make an uncomfortable environment for minorities. Individuals and particularly frats have been known to fly Confederate flags. "There are some divisions along racial lines," one student remarks, "but the less tolerant people are by far a minority."

You Might Not Know

- The UGA Redcoat Band was the first American college band to perform in China in 2006; the band has also been featured on Band of Horses' single "Georgia."
- It is rumored that students who walk under the college's emblematic arch will not graduate on time, or at all, or may even become sterile.
- In addition to UGA's costumed mascot, Hairy Dawg, a live bulldog called Uga makes an appearance at all home football games. Uga is issued a student ID card, wears a tailored jersey made from the same fabric as the players' jerseys, and travels in an air-conditioned dog house.

Distinguished Alumni

Dan Amos, CEO of AFLAC; Brooke Anderson, news anchor, CNN; Kim Basinger, actress; Alton Brown, celebrity chef; John Huey, Editor-in-chief, Time Inc.; Charlayne Hunter-Gault, international journalist; Sonny Perdue, former Governor of Georgia.

Admissions and Financial Aid

Nearly all (97 percent) of in-state freshmen earned the merit-based, Georgia-administered HOPE Scholarship, which covers tuition and fees and even awards a book allowance to qualified Georgia high school students. Other highly qualified students from Georgia or out of state can apply by November 15 to the Foundation Fellowships or Ramsey Honors Scholarships.

Smaller Presidential Scholarships of $3,000 are also awarded, usually in conjunction with a HOPE Scholarship for in-state students or tuition waiver for out-of-state students. Other smaller awards are available to students who enroll in Honors. A FAFSA and submission of UGA application by December 15 is necessary to be considered for all awards.

UNIVERSITY OF GEORGIA

Highlights

Admissions Criteria
Academic criteria:
Grades: ☆ ☆ ☆
Difficulty of class schedule: ☆ ☆ ☆
Class rank: N/A
Standardized test scores: ☆ ☆
Teacher recommendations: ☆
Personal statement: ☆
Non-academic criteria considered:
Extracurricular activities
Special talents, interests, abilities
Character/personal qualities
Volunteer work
Work experience
State of residency

Deadlines
Early Action: October 15
Early Decision: No
Regular Action: October 15 (priority)
January 15 (final)
Common Application: Not accepted

Financial Aid
In-state tuition: $8,028
Out-of-state tuition: $26,238
Room: $5,290
Board: $3,956
Books: $916
Freshmen receiving need-based aid: 38%
Undergrads rec. need-based aid: 39%
Avg. % of need met by financial aid: 66%
Avg. aid package (freshmen): $12,058
Avg. aid package (undergrads): $10,797
Avg. debt upon graduation: $18,438

School Spirit
Mascot: Bulldogs
Colors: Red and black
Song: *Glory!*

Four-year public
Founded: 1907
Honolulu, HI
Major city
Pop. 374,658

Address:
2500 Campus Road
Honolulu, HI
96822

Admissions:
800-823-9771

Financial Aid:
808-956-7251

ar-info@hawaii.edu

www.manoa.hawaii.
edu

UNIVERSITY OF HAWAII AT MANOA

Overview

The flagship of Hawaii's public university system, The University of Hawaii at Manoa, features a 320-acre urban campus just outside the city of Honolulu with uniquely Hawaiian and Asian-Pacific architecture. Plant lovers will delight in UH Manoa's palm tree collection, botanical garden, Japanese Garden, and Native Plants Garden.

The university is known for its educational offerings unique to Hawaii, as well as Asian Studies and travel industry management. There is very strong multiethnic diversity—about one-fifth of students are not Caucasian—and a sense of pride in Hawaiian heritage. The university has a laid-back atmosphere, as one might expect with the gorgeous weather and easy access to beaches, though most students aren't just attending the university to laze around or to take on the role of tourists who visit the islands.

The relaxed environment does mean that students tend to shape the level of rigor of their academics. Research is quite strong at the university—The National Science Foundation ranks UH Manoa in the top 30 public universities in federal research funding for engineering and science—and UH Manoa is the only UH campus with schools of Law, Medicine, Engineering, Nursing and Dental Hygiene, and Social Work, making it a popular choice for in-state residents interested in studying in these fields. The opportunity to bask in the sun, surf, and island-hop is always a perk, but students who can take advantage of UH Manoa's strong offerings in Hawaiian, Pacific, and Asian studies will find themselves leveraged to get a strong education alongside a beautiful tan.

Academics

UH Manoa offers 87 fields of study at the bachelor's level. The school houses the nation's only School of Hawaiian Knowledge. General Education requirements cover four areas: Foundations (three courses), Diversification (breadth requirement), Focus (four courses), and Hawaiian or second-language competence. These include courses on writing and oral communication.

The degree of difficulty of a student's academic program depends on what the individual makes of it. While there are certainly challenging courses offered, students find their academic course loads manageable. "You'd really have to try hard to *not* get a passing grade," says a student. Strong programs include Asian studies, travel industry management, marine biology, and majors in the Shidler College of Business. Students looking for a more rigorous academic experience can apply to the Honors Program, which gives them access to small seminar-style classes and a number of honors courses and seminars. There is also Honors Student housing.

The Access to College Excellence (ACE) learning communities give freshmen a chance to take three general education courses and a small-group seminar with an upperclassman peer mentor. This provides new students a unique way in which to form friendships early on, as these freshman seminars are held in intimate settings. Student sentiment may be split regarding the program, as one student explains, "some people love their seminars, and some think they're just okay."

Summer, semester, and year-long study abroad programs are offered. Only a small number of students go overseas: recently only 400 students participated (out of nearly 14,000 undergrads). There are study-abroad internships available in Florence, London, and Sydney.

With 161,000 alumni living in 50 states and more than 100 countries, UH Manoa graduates have a strong network to tap into. The new Career Development and Student Employment office helps students plan their career lives. Services include on-campus employer recruitment, graduate and law school fairs, and an online database of jobs.

Student Life

There are over 150 student organizations at UH Manoa. *Ka Leo O Hawai'i*, the student newspaper, was founded in 1922 and has a circulation of 7,000. Many clubs seem to fit perfectly with the island-state's culture and environment, such as Hawaii Lion Dance Association and Surf Club.

Students enjoy concerts, ethnic performances, and celebrations year-round. Homecoming Weekend is always festive, with thousands gathering to celebrate the Homecoming Fair, volleyball and football games, class reunions, and special exhibits and lectures. Aloha Stadium holds up to 50,000 fans—a good thing, since football draws big crowds, especially for the last game of the season. Though not held on campus, the annual Kaimuki Kanikapila is a popular craft fair and street festival featuring local handmade arts and crafts, life local entertainment, and free prizes.

Greek life doesn't seem to be a major part of the campus scene. There are six fraternities and sororities on campus, but only one percent of students are involved. "What Greek organizations?" asks a student.

About 450 students are on 20 varsity teams that compete in Division I. Football is the most competitive, while basketball and swimming are also popular. "Football games can get pretty crazy intense," says a student. Intramurals offer a less competitive environment in which to play basketball, volleyball, badminton, or tennis; run on the track; or make laps in the Olympic-sized pool.

Downtown Honolulu is popular for shopping and eating out. The famous volcanic tuff cone Diamond Head and nearby beaches provide endless opportunities for students to appreciate the outdoors. Students also have the chance to go island-hopping, at a much lower expense than tourists from the mainland.

On-campus housing availability is limited, and off-campus housing can get expensive. "A lot of people just live at home and commute," remarks a student. The residence halls lie in two complexes and are all co-ed. There are also Residential Learning Programs that students can apply for in a number of areas: service learning and social justice, outdoor recreation, and of course Hawaiian language and culture.

Student Body

While there are certainly students who come to Hawaii to enjoy paradise (and not necessarily academics), there are plenty of students who are focused on their studies. Given the location, there is special attention paid to environmental issues and the rights of native Hawaiians. As one student explains, "it's pretty much a given that you're concerned about the environment."

There is very high ethnic diversity; Caucasian students make up about one fifth of the student population. Japanese and Hawaiian students make up another quarter, and there are also sizeable populations of students who identify as Filipino, Chinese, and mixed. As a combined group, Asians make up about two-thirds of the student body. There is moderate geographic diversity, with about 30 percent of students coming from out of state, including an international student population of around three percent.

UNIVERSITY OF HAWAII AT MANOA

Highlights

Students
Total enrollment: 20,426
Undergrads: 14,655
From out-of-state: 30%
From public schools: 66%
Male/Female: 46%/54%
Live on-campus: 15%
In fraternities: 1%
In sororities: 1%
Off-campus employment rating: Excellent
Caucasian: 21%
African American: 2%
Hispanic: 2%
Asian / Pacific Islander: 58%
Native American: 0%
Mixed (2+ ethnicities): 14%
International: 3%

Academics
Calendar: Semester
Student/faculty ratio: 14:1
Class size 9 or fewer: 27%
Class size 10-29: 51%
Class size 30-49: 13%
Class size 50-99: 6%
Class size 100 or more: 4%
Returning freshmen: 79%
Six-year graduation rate: 55%
Graduates who immediately go to graduate school: 10%

Most Popular Majors
Psychology
Finance
Interdisciplinary studies

Admissions
Applicants: 6,810
Accepted: 5,528
Acceptance rate: 81.2%
Average GPA: 3.5
ACT range: 21-27
SAT Math range: 500-610
SAT Reading range: 480-580
SAT Writing range: 2-16
Top 10% of class: 27%
Top 25% of class: 59%
Top 50% of class: 91%

749

College Profiles

UNIVERSITY OF HAWAII AT MANOA

Admissions Criteria
Academic criteria:
Grades: ☆ ☆ ☆
Difficulty of class schedule: ☆ ☆ ☆
Class rank: ☆ ☆
Standardized test scores: ☆ ☆ ☆
Teacher recommendations: ☆
Personal statement: ☆
Non-academic criteria considered:
Interview
Extracurricular activities
Special talents, interests, abilities
Geographical location

Deadlines
Early Action: No
Early Decision: No
Regular Action: Rolling admissions
Common Application: Not accepted

Financial Aid
In-state tuition: $9,144
Out-of-state tuition: $26,712
Room: $6,820
Board: $3,209
Books: $1,212
Freshmen receiving need-based aid: 53%
Undergrads rec. need-based aid: 53%
Avg. % of need met by financial aid: 67%
Avg. aid package (freshmen): $11,987
Avg. aid package (undergrads): $11,428
Avg. debt upon graduation: $20,655

School Spirit
Mascot: Warriors, Rainbow Warriors, Rainbow Wahine, Rainbows
Colors: Green, white, black, and silver

You May Not Know
- According to the University, the Lyon Arboretum and Botanical Garden is the "only university botanical garden located in a tropical rainforest in the United States."
- UH Manoa houses Hawaii's only law and medical schools.
- The university is one of only 32 institutions nationwide to be a land-, sea-, and space-grant research institution.

Distinguished Alumni
Patsy Mink, former U.S. Congresswoman; Barack Obama Sr., father of President Barack Obama; Chery Petti, CNN Radio network anchor; Jay H. Shidler, entrepreneur and philanthropist.

Admissions and Financial Aid
Admission requirements at UH Manoa include coursework, minimum test scores and GPAs, and high school ranking. However, UH admissions officials will review applicants who don't meet minimum requirements based on letters of recommendation and an optional letter written by the student. Admissions decisions are made on a rolling basis, typically four to six weeks after an application has been received. Students are encouraged to apply for priority consideration, which increases the chance of receiving financial aid and student housing.

The Centennial Scholarship of $1,000 per year for Hawaii residents and $3,000 for non-residents, and Chancellor's Scholarships of $2,000 per year (residents) and $6,000 per year (nonresidents) are awarded to high-achieving students. The university typically awards about $15 million in scholarships and grants.

UNIVERSITY OF IDAHO

Overview

Many large public universities claim to offer a small-town, small-college feeling despite their size, but University of Idaho actually does it. Located in the small town of Moscow, Idaho, in the scenic woodsy Palouse hills of Idaho, the campus was largely designed by the same firm that designed Central Park in New York, giving it a sleepy New England look and feel that meshes surprisingly well with the fresh air and vast wooded expanses of the Pacific Northwest. And UI has also been recognized by the Carnegie Foundation for its "high research activity" and is particularly strong in engineering: UI maintains ties to the Idaho National Laboratory and receives nearly $100 million in research funding annually—but has a smaller student body than most big research schools.

UI's campus offers more than educational and research facilities. In addition to its library, which is the largest in Idaho, the university farm, a 65-acre arboretum and botanical garden, UI offers a 150-acre golf course, walking trails, and a student recreation center with two gyms and the tallest freestanding climbing wall at any college in the United States. Opportunities for outdoor recreation abound, making balancing work and play for some students a difficult task. The other challenges at UI are likely to come from the social scene. UI is known as a party school, to the objections of portions of the student body—which points to the division of social life at UI into cliques. If you feel at ease navigating a cliquey social scene, have strong interests in research, and relax by hitting whitewater rapids or mountain biking, then zip up your North Face fleece—UI could be the place for you.

Academics

There are 236 majors at the University of Idaho, of which psychology and programs in the Colleges of Engineering and Education are particularly strong. All students must complete the not-overly-burdensome Core Curriculum, which consists of General Core Studies (first-year Core Discovery Course and a humanities, social sciences, international, and capstone course each) as well as two required courses in communications, natural and applied sciences, and a course in mathematical, computer and statistical sciences. The Core Curriculum is "what you'd expect and not too demanding," says a student.

The rigor of an education at UI depends both on the student and the program: engineering is particularly rigorous, while other programs may place fewer demands on students, which can lead to some animosity between engineering students and students in programs perceived as less work. "Basically the engineering students think they're the only ones with a brain," remarks one student. Professors are accessible and supportive, and the most common class size at UI is two to nine students—almost unheard of for such a large research institution.

UI makes its engineering courses widely available to the UI community at large. Students on campus, as well as distance learners, can take advantage of the UI Engineering Outreach program, which offers access to classes and lectures via the internet. Students can earn either a certificate or a master's degree in a number of engineering fields or simply prepare for jobs or graduate school work. A similar program is available in the College of Education.

Research plays a major role in many students' academic careers at UI: funding is available to encourage students in all fields to undertake projects. Through the Student Grant Project, students can apply for funding up to $5,000 to work on scholarly research or creative projects under the supervision of a faculty mentor. SGP also offers Dissemination Funding, to help students publish or present their work. "If you make the effort, you can find research opportunities and maybe even some funding," says a student.

UNIVERSITY OF IDAHO

Four-year public
Founded: 1889
Moscow, ID
Small town
Pop. 24,080

Address:
875 Perimeter Drive
MS 2282
Moscow, ID
83844-2282

Admissions:
888-884-3246

Financial Aid:
888-884-3246

admissions@uidaho.
edu

www.uidaho.edu

UNIVERSITY OF IDAHO

Students

Total enrollment: 12,420
Undergrads: 9,928
Freshmen: 1,938
Part-time students: 18%
From out-of-state: 26%
From public schools: 95%
Male/Female: 53%/47%
Live on-campus: 39%
In fraternities: 17%
In sororities: 18%
Off-campus employment rating: Excellent
Caucasian: 81%
African American: 1%
Hispanic: 8%
Asian / Pacific Islander: 2%
Native American: 1%
Mixed (2+ ethnicities): 3%
International: 3%

Academics

Calendar: Semester
Student/faculty ratio: 18:1
Class size 9 or fewer: 24%
Class size 10-29: 52%
Class size 30-49: 14%
Class size 50-99: 8%
Class size 100 or more: 3%
Returning freshmen: 77%
Six-year graduation rate: 56%

Most Popular Majors

Business
Psychology/communication studies
Curriculum/instruction

Admissions

Applicants: 7,467
Accepted: 4,903
Acceptance rate: 65.7%
Average GPA: 3.4
ACT range: 20-26
SAT Math range: 490-610
SAT Reading range: 480-590
SAT Writing range: 3-14
Top 10% of class: 18%
Top 25% of class: 44%
Top 50% of class: 77%

UI's nationally recognized University Honors Program offers students yet another way in which they may take advantage of the small-college environment at UI. The Honors program provides its own core curriculum and electives (many of which fulfill the university's core requirements) in small discussion-based classes taught by select faculty. Additionally, other special academic opportunities range from "Food for Thought" lunches and "Fireside Chats" with faculty. Other special opportunities include priority registration, access to special scholarships, and preference in the Honors "Living Learning Communities." Applicants with qualifying test scores and high school GPAs submit a written application for admission to the program. Students describe the Honors Program as a "huge advantage for choosing classes" and as a "grouping together of the brightest" students.

UI does not have a large selection of its own study-abroad programs to choose from. It does offer faculty-led trips over spring or summer breaks; these are all program-specific and include architecture studies in Rome and London and international trips to Ghana. Semester- and year-long programs are available through UI-approved third-party programs and include 30 institutions worldwide.

UI's Career Center offers career assessments, interview preparation, job databases, and opportunities to network with alumni. Of UI graduates who enter the workforce, an impressive 87 percent find work in areas related to their majors within six months of graduating; and 93 percent, within one year.

Student Life

UI has a reputation as a party school where Greek life plays a major role—one sixth of students belong to one of UI's 18 fraternities or 14 sororities. "Greek life is THE life," says a student. But UI offers a host of other distractions as well. The university has 128 student organizations, many of which are pre-professional or arts-oriented, such as the theatre group *6th Street Productions*. Other groups appeal to more esoteric interests, including the Student Bagpipers and the UI Bigfoot Research Society.

Many events around UI campus—particularly arts events—draw or include the local Moscow community, including the Tutxinmepu Pow Wow; the highly-acclaimed Lionel Hampton Jazz Festival, which draws the world's premier jazz musicians; and Dancers, Drummers, and Dreamers, a collaborative show between the UI Dance Department and the Lionel Hampton School of Music, featuring student-choreographed work and live music. As one student sums it up, "almost every night of the week there's a performance."

If the arts don't tickle your fancy, then there are plenty of recreational and athletic opportunities to be found, both on campus and off. In true Pacific Northwest fashion, the hills and woods around campus offer year-round activities, ranging from biking and rafting to skiing and snowboarding. Intramurals suit various desired levels of exertion, including flag football, roller and floor hockey, foosball, and even horseshoes. For those more interested in watching sports than participating, UI has eight women's and six men's Division I varsity sports teams, of which football and men's basketball draw the most crowds.

Moscow offers mellow dining and shopping opportunities. More entertainment options are likely to be found in Spokane, Washington, about 80 miles away, or, even better, in Seattle, which is a hefty five-hour drive over the mountains, probably not to be undertaken during snowy weather.

Housing options on campus include traditional dorms, both co-ed and single sex, Greek houses, and, for upperclassmen, apartment-style Living Learning Communities. While many of the communities are open to students in all majors, some are specially focused for students in the College of Natural Resources, Engineering, or the Honors Program, to name a few. A women-only co-op house is also available: in Steel House, residents live and cook together—and even sleep communally on an unheated sleeping porch.

Student Body

UI students tend to stick to their cliques, which break down particularly along Greek/non-Greek or athlete/non-athlete lines. "If you're in a fraternity or sorority or if you're on a team, those are pretty much the only people you hang out with," explains a student. "For the rest of us, people tend to hang out by ethnic group." UI has a moderate number of out-of-state students and moderate ethnic diversity, although many cultural groups are active on campus.

You May Not Know

- When UI opened in 1892, it had one professor.
- Moscow, Idaho, has been named one of the five best college towns to live in by *Men's Journal*.
- The UI campus has 46.5 acres of roof. More interesting is why the UI website lists this.

Distinguished Alumni

Jeffrey Ashby, astronaut; Dirk Kempthorne, Secretary of the Interior and former U.S. Senator and Governor of Idaho.

Admissions and Financial Aid

Applicants who have completed the core distribution requirements in high school and meet the GPA and standardized test requirements of UI are assured admission. However, if a student's GPA or test scores aren't quite what they need to be, an application may be made to the admissions committee.

A number of Idaho-centric merit scholarships are available. For Idaho residents, Go Idaho scholarships of a minimum of $1,000 annually are available, and for non-residents, Discover Idaho scholarships award up to $5,000. No separate application is needed. Twenty-five National Merit Scholarships covering the full cost of attendance are available to those who apply to UI by February 15.

UNIVERSITY OF IDAHO

Highlights

Admissions Criteria
Academic criteria:
Grades: ☆ ☆ ☆
Difficulty of class schedule: N/A
Class rank: N/A
Standardized test scores: ☆ ☆ ☆
Teacher recommendations: N/A
Personal statement: Required for some applicants
Non-academic criteria considered:
State of residency

Deadlines
Early Action: No
Early Decision: No
Regular Action: Rolling admissions
Common Application: Accepted

Financial Aid
In-state tuition: $4,534
Out-of-state tuition: $17,610
Room: Varies
Board: Varies
Books: $1,474
Freshmen receiving need-based aid: 69%
Undergrads rec. need-based aid: 66%
Avg. % of need met by financial aid: 74%
Avg. aid package (freshmen): $13,554
Avg. aid package (undergrads): $13,347
Avg. debt upon graduation: $26,809

School Spirit
Mascot: Joe Vandal
Colors: Silver and gold
Song: *Here We Have Idaho* (alma mater)

College Profiles

Four-year public
Founded: 1867
Champaign, IL
Medium city
Pop. 81,291

Address:
601 East John Street
Champaign, IL
61820-5711

Admissions:
217-333-0302

Financial Aid:
217-333-0100

ugradadmissions@
illinois.edu

www.illinois.edu

UNIVERSITY OF ILLINOIS – URBANA-CHAMPAIGN

Overview

If it's cows and sleepy stretches of suburban life you're looking for, then the University of Illinois Urbana-Champaign is likely not the place for you. Set on the border between the twin cities of Urbana and Champaign just 140 miles south of Chicago, the university is home to a bustling crowd of more than 44,000 students. Greenery is abundant on campus at this classic land grant institution, and buildings on campus historically date back to the 1800s. Many of the university's most prominent buildings, dotting the main campus' 1,468 acres, boast different architectural styles, ranging from Georgian Revival (the Armory was originally built as a military drill hall and athletic facility during WWI) to the Beaux Arts Classical style (the domed roof of the Foellinger Auditorium is made entirely of copper). Brick and grandiose white pillars and window frames make this campus idyllic in its appearance.

The Krannert Center for the Performing Arts, a two-block complex, hosts five theatres and more than 300 events ranging from students to guest performers to community-based artists. The Great Hall is said to be one of the most acoustically perfect halls in the world. A Japan House and arboretum also provide fantastic spaces for student respite, in addition to the university's extensive public library, which averages 24 million items in rotation through its $21 million state-of-the-art facility.

Students at Illinois work hard and play hard too—the university is ranked 11th among public universities by *U.S. News & World Report* and boasts 10 men's and 11 women's Big Ten sports teams. The campus houses an ice arena, tennis courts, wrestling halls, and a newly constructed golf course, and annual events like the freshman convocation ceremony and I-Celebrate Taste of Nevada Street help to round out the student life on campus.

Academics

Though the university boasts 17 separate colleges, with more than 150 undergraduate and more than 100 graduate and professional programs, the standout majors of choice (among the 590 offered and not including self-designed majors) for incoming undergraduates are business and engineering. For business, programs emphasizing accounting, insurance, management, and real estate all rank in the nation's top 10 according to *U.S. News & World Report*. In engineering, aerospace/aeronautical/astronomical, agricultural, chemical, civil, computer, electrical/electronic/communications, environmental health, materials, mechanical, and science/physics all promise ranks in the top 10 as well.

The campus is also, incidentally, home to the National Center for Supercomputing Applications (NCSA), one of the nation's largest and most powerful collections of supercomputers. Researchers from around the world use the facilities to fight AIDS, simulate how galaxies collide and merge, and study how tornadoes and hurricanes form, among other things. The Krannert Center for performing arts, additionally, helps to promote a robust theatre and performing arts program—alumni of the department of theatre have been nominated for both Tony and Emmy awards.

Regardless of major, all students are required to take the university's extensive general education core classes, which include composition, cultural studies, humanities and the arts, natural sciences, quantitative reasoning, social and behavioral sciences, and a foreign language requirement. Most class sizes within majors have 20 to 29 students, but required courses like the GEs can be held in lecture halls of up to 700 or 800 students. "There are some points at which you do feel like a number," remarks a student.

For those freshmen who wish to really challenge themselves, Illinois offers two undergraduate honors programs—one that is college-specific and the other that is campus-wide. In an honors program, students are given the chance to interact with distinguished faculty and explore their respective majors through innovative research, projects, and challenges, and to find community with other ambitious students.

Studying abroad is also a popular undertaking for students, with over 350 top-ranked programs in approximately 60 countries, including Argentina, Belgium, China, the Dominican Republic, Greece, Italy, and South Africa, among other locations. "Studying abroad was a seamless experience," one student says.

After college, the path is pretty well-paved for Fighting Illini grads. Just under half of all students enter graduate school within a year of graduation, and of those who choose not to, approximately 76 percent enter a field related to their major within six months of graduation. The Career Center hosts résumé and cover letter critiques and holds appointments for mock interviews in addition to its extensive internship database. "Many companies recruit right on campus," one student notes.

Student Life

The university is rich in athletic, artistic, and recreational activities, and the 1,000 student organizations provide a vast catalog of ways to get involved. Creative clubs such as Art Fusion @ UIUC bring together artists from different cultural and ethnic backgrounds to create unprecedented forms of art, and recreational organizations like the Falling Illini Skydiving Club promote plenty of exploring in the wild blue yonder.

The campus student union is expansive and includes a courtyard cafe, bowling alley, art gallery, and computer lab in addition to various food vendors. "It's a central meeting spot," one student confirms. Annual events like the Overlooked Film Festival, which honors deserving-but-overlooked films selected by alumnus Roger Ebert, and Big Ten basketball games (always a huge draw and campus event), help bring out the best of school spirit in bright shades of orange and blue.

Add to that 60 social fraternities and 36 social sororities (Greek life comprises 21 percent of students), and it's no wonder the Fighting Illini have a reputation for playing hard in addition to working hard. "Some of the parties are very *Animal House*-like," laughs a student.

Sports are a big part of university life. The Division I athletics department is best known for its men's basketball and football teams, but Illinois has also recently placed in national and conference championships in other sports such as gymnastics, tennis, and wrestling. The newly constructed golf course on campus helps to amp up the athletic diversity as well. The Orange Krush Foundation, an almost entirely student-run group that raises funds for local charities and athletic scholarships such as the Matthew Heldman Memorial Scholarship for future Illini basketball players, continues strong.

Intramural sports also include miniature golf, badminton, flag football, and Ultimate Frisbee, which is especially inviting to incoming freshmen—all of whom are required to live on campus. "I liked living on campus because I met the most people," one student says. There are 23 undergraduate residence halls and special communities, including ones for health care majors and entrepreneurship.

UNIVERSITY OF ILLINOIS AT URBANA-CHAMPAIGN

Highlights

Students
Total enrollment: 44,520
Undergrads: 32,281
Freshmen: 7,932
From out-of-state: 13%
Male/Female: 56%/44%
Live on-campus: 50%
In fraternities: 21%
In sororities: 21%
Off-campus employment rating: Excellent
Caucasian: 56%
African American: 5%
Hispanic: 7%
Asian / Pacific Islander: 14%
Native American: 0%
Mixed (2+ ethnicities): 2%
International: 14%

Academics
Calendar: Semester
Student/faculty ratio: 19:1
Class size 9 or fewer: 12%
Class size 10-29: 52%
Class size 30-49: 16%
Class size 50-99: 10%
Class size 100 or more: 10%
Six-year graduation rate: 84%
Graduates who immediately go to graduate school: 33%

Most Popular Majors
Finance
Engineering
Social sciences/history

Admissions
Applicants: 31,454
Accepted: 19,924
Acceptance rate: 63.3%
Placed on wait list: 2,138
Enrolled from wait list: 437
Average GPA: Not reported
ACT range: 26-31
SAT Math range: 680-790
SAT Reading range: 550-680
SAT Writing range: 17-49
Top 10% of class: 54%
Top 25% of class: 88%
Top 50% of class: 99%

755

UNIVERSITY OF ILLINOIS AT URBANA-CHAMPAIGN

Admissions Criteria
Academic criteria:
Grades: ☆ ☆ ☆
Difficulty of class schedule: ☆ ☆ ☆
Class rank: ☆ ☆
Standardized test scores: ☆ ☆
Teacher recommendations: N/A
Personal statement: ☆ ☆
Non-academic criteria considered:
Extracurricular activities
Special talents, interests, abilities
Character/personal qualities
Volunteer work
Work experience
Geographical location
Minority affiliation

Deadlines
Early Action: November 10
Early Decision: No
Regular Action: November 1 (priority)
January 2 (final)
Common Application: Not accepted

Financial Aid
In-state tuition: $11,834
Out-of-state tuition: $26,216
Room: Varies
Board: Varies
Books: $1,200
Freshmen receiving need-based aid: 49%
Undergrads rec. need-based aid: 46%
Avg. % of need met by financial aid: 63%
Avg. aid package (freshmen): $14,647
Avg. aid package (undergrads): $13,533
Avg. debt upon graduation: $24,657

School Spirit
Colors: Orange and blue
Song: *Illinois Loyalty*

The Ultimate
Guide to America's
Best Colleges

Student Body

Illinois is, not surprisingly, very much skewed toward the in-state crowd, with 87 percent of the student body made up of locals from within the area. There are representative students from each of the 50 states, however, and the population is actually very ethnically diverse. About a quarter of the campus is made of ethnic minorities, and 14 percent of the total population is comprised of international students.

There are more than 32,000 undergraduates at the university, and of these, more than half were ranked in the top 10 percent of their graduating high school classes. Students say they are "focused on their studies but also on getting involved in activities."

You May Not Know

- An "echo plaque" in Foellinger Auditorium is a unique spot on campus—one can stand on the dedication plaque and yell out to the quad and be the only one who can hear the echo.
- Illinois claims to have had the first Homecoming in 1910.
- Illinois became the eleventh institution in the world to ever have two Nobel Prizes (in different fields) awarded to members of its faculty in the same year.

Distinguished Alumni

Rafael Correa, current President of The Republic of Ecuador; Roger Ebert, film critic and first-ever Pulitzer Prize winner in Criticism; Suze Orman, financial advisor, writer, TV personality.

Admissions and Financial Aid

Gaining admissions into Illinois is a pretty standard procedure. The two required essays address the applicant's academic and professional goals and his or her extracurricular activities. Don't be fooled by these questions, thinking that they are common and thereby require "common" answers though. Admissions officers look for passion and cultural insight as they read the essays, which is a lot of character to pack into word limits. Personal characteristics such as socioeconomic background, languages, and special talents are all heavily weighted in the decision-making process as well.

All students are required to apply directly to a major, and any student not admitted to the program of their choice is immediately considered for other programs at the university.

University of Illinois Urbana-Champaign supplies more than 1,500 merit-based scholarships based on academic achievement, talent, leadership, geographic location, and major. One of the most prestigious is the Provost Scholarship, which provides full tuition awards. Some also take into account financial need. For many scholarships, you only need to complete the admissions application to be considered.

UNIVERSITY OF IOWA

Overview

Ranked by *U.S. News & World Report* as among the nation's top 30 public universities, the University of Iowa boasts reputable academics, beautiful scenery, and Big 10 athletics. Prospective students in the creative writing and health fields can expect especially strong courses and top-notch teaching, including exposure to the renowned Iowa Writers' Workshop.

Students work and play (oftentimes emphasizing the latter) against the urban backdrop of Iowa City whilst enjoying the serene murmur of the Iowa River, which runs directly through the heart of campus. Impressive pillared buildings surrounded by the comfortable coffeehouses, urban shops, and endless bars of Iowa City's pedestrian mall provide much to be enjoyed. On the rare occasion that Iowa City fails to offer enough excitement, students only must remember that University of Iowa is situated just 20 miles outside of Cedar Rapids. Yet campus life seldom disappoints, given Iowa's unwavering school spirit.

As part of the Big 10, Hawkeye pride never falters as students cheer on their UI teams in football, wrestling, and basketball. Tailgating festivities begin as soon as the sun rises at the second best party school in the country according to the Princeton Review. So if you're looking for swelling stadiums, vibrant urban life, and a "big pond" campus, look no farther than the University of Iowa.

Academics

Most first-year students are admitted to either the College of Liberal Arts and Sciences or the College of Engineering. Others receive admission to the Tippie College of Business, the College of Medicine, the College of Nursing, or the College of Pharmacy. Each college has different General Education requirements that all students must fulfill prior to graduation, including courses in the social sciences, natural sciences, humanities, and foreign languages.

Iowa offers 276 major and minor options, from accounting to physical therapy to classical languages. The University of Iowa boasts an excellent student/faculty ratio of 16:1, one of the best among large public universities; only three percent of UI's classes have more than 100 students. "With a little effort, you really can get to know your professors," says a student. The strongest and most popular academic programs at Iowa include English (with an emphasis on creative writing), nursing, business, psychology, communication studies, and preparatory medicine. The school is also home to an impressive, nationally recognized teaching hospital that provides med students with amazing learning opportunities.

Iowa offers several outstanding academic opportunities, including the Iowa Writers' Workshop. Founded in 1936, the Writer's Workshop offers talented and emerging writers a two-year haven to imagine, create, and earn a master's of fine arts degree. The workshop has produced 17 Pulitzer Prize winners and three U.S. Poet Laureates. Undergrads can also take courses on creative writing, fiction, and poetry. "I chose Iowa because of the nationally-known Writers' Workshop," one student comments.

Other academic opportunities include an eight-week Summer Research Opportunity Program (SROP) and the university's Honors Program. In SROP, students work with doctorate-level faculty in challenging hands-on research projects that boost them toward graduate and doctorate success. The Honors Program, according to the college, strives to "enhance skills, enrich experiences, and make learning a thrill throughout." Honors College students work and study almost exclusively with Honors College faculty and other Honors College students. Finally, Iowa has recently established its Four-Year Graduation Plan, in which entering students sign a contract agreeing to map out a four-year plan with the help of their advisor, complete with checkpoints that allow them to graduate in four successful years. In turn, the university

UNIVERSITY OF IOWA

Four-year public
Founded: 1847
Iowa City, IA
Medium city
Pop. 68,947

Address:
107 Calvin Hall
Iowa City, IA
52242-1396

Admissions:
319-335-3847

Financial Aid:
319-335-1450

admissions@uiowa.edu

www.uiowa.edu

UNIVERSITY OF IOWA

Students
Total enrollment: 30,119
Undergrads: 21,999
Freshmen: 4,470
Part-time students: 11%
From out-of-state: 48%
From public schools: 92%
Male/Female: 48%/52%
Live on-campus: 31%
In fraternities: 11%
In sororities: 15%
Off-campus employment rating: Excellent
Caucasian: 74%
African American: 3%
Hispanic: 5%
Asian / Pacific Islander: 3%
Native American: 0%
Mixed (2+ ethnicities): 2%
International: 9%

Academics
Calendar: Semester
Student/faculty ratio: 16:1
Class size 9 or fewer: 10%
Class size 10-29: 69%
Class size 30-49: 13%
Class size 50-99: 5%
Class size 100 or more: 3%
Returning freshmen: 86%
Six-year graduation rate: 70%
Graduates who immediately enter career
   related to major: 92%

Most Popular Majors
Business
Inter-departmental studies
Psychology

Admissions
Applicants: 19,430
Accepted: 15,240
Acceptance rate: 78.4%
Average GPA: 3.6
ACT range: 22-28
SAT Math range: 550-690
SAT Reading range: 470-630
SAT Writing range: Not reported
Top 10% of class: 24%
Top 25% of class: 55%
Top 50% of class: 91%

promises to make available certain specified classes. While this is not a mandatory program, more that 70 percent of Iowa's student body volunteer to participate. "My parents appreciate that I won't have to spend a fifth year in college," one student notes.

Another popular academic experience at the University of Iowa is the study-abroad program. Students can choose to spend a semester abroad in one of over 60 different locations worldwide. While these programs typically cost more than Iowa tuition, the university offers $500,000 a year in merit- and need-based scholarships for study abroad.

Iowa's career center offers internships primarily through three programs. The Experience Iowa Internship Program provides students with insight into nonprofit organizations, while the Des Moines Center Internship Program places students at the state capital. A similar plan, the Washington Center Program, offers internships at the nation's capital. "We're in a prime location to get political experience," one student says. Several job and internship fairs are held throughout the year by the career center as well.

Student Life

Iowa offers upwards of 450 different student groups and organizations, from the Student Commission on Programming Entertainment to the *Daily Iowan* and the American Association of Petroleum Geologists. And if there isn't currently a student group that sparks your interest, you can always start your own with the help of a faculty advisor.

In addition to organizations, Iowa promises hundreds of other activities in which to get involved. Riverfest is a weeklong festival with local music, art shows, a Zombie Prom, and food. "I'm looking forward to the Java Jog where we drink coffee and listen to music at various coffee shops," one student comments. Dance Marathon is a 24-hour party that raises money to fight cancer. Volunteers in past marathons have danced their way to raising more than $9 million for patients at the University of Iowa Children's Hospital.

Greek life also plays an important role in the social scene on campus, with 23 sororities and 21 fraternities available for pledging. Iowa's reputation as a party school isn't totally unfounded, although Greek members tend to head out to bars downtown (rather than drink on campus) because of crackdowns on underage drinking by the university. "There's a pretty big division between members and non-members," one student says.

Fanaticism abounds for Big 10 football. Game days are obvious, as all of campus and Iowa City turns black and gold. Up to 71,000 fans crowd into Kinnick Stadium to cheer on their Hawkeyes, who have played in seven national bowl games in the last 10 years. In addition to football, the Hawkeyes can boast their status as a historical powerhouse for wrestling and basketball.

There are plenty of facilities and opportunities for non-varsity athletes including 30 intramural sports, a climbing wall, and outdoor rental center. Students even have access to the Macbride Nature Recreation Area, a 485-acre spot with hiking and cross-country skiing areas. "I love being able to hike or bike after classes," one student comments.

Housing options include residence halls, living-learning communities, Greek houses, and university apartments. Most first-year students live in the residence halls, making it easy to meet other students as well as being centrally located on campus. Living-learning communities include concentrations on writing, science, and the honors program.

Student Body

Iowa's student body has moderate ethnic and geographic diversity, with 13 percent of students identifying as a minority and around half of students coming from out of state. "There's a good mix of people who are conservative and liberal," says a student. Another adds, "There do tend to be cliques of Greek members, athletes, nerds, etc."

Students say that "athletics unite campus and provide a high level of school spirit." Others comment that Iowa students "can party pretty heavy, but there are also plenty of people who would rather be holed up in the library."

You May Not Know

- Iowa's campus is home to 10 libraries, accessible to all students, faculty, and staff.
- The University of Iowa was the first public university to admit men and women on an equal basis.
- *The Daily Iowan*, Iowa's student newspaper, is repeatedly recognized as one of the nation's finest.

Distinguished Alumni

Albert Bandura, father of modern psychology; Tom Brokaw, former NBC News anchor and political analyst; Ashton Kutcher, actor; Ward B. Strang, President and CEO of FedEx SmartPost; Tennessee Williams, Pulitzer Prize winning writer.

Admissions and Financial Aid

The University of Iowa does not accept the Common Application. However, their online application is relatively pain-free and straightforward.

Iowa requires submission of SAT test scores, an official high school transcript, and recommends submission of ACT scores as well. Students with an RAI (Regent Admission Index, based on ACT/SAT scores, high school GPA, and number of high school core courses) of 245 or higher for Iowa residents and 255 or higher for non-residents, who meet the minimum high school course requirements (four years English/language arts, two years single foreign language, three years science, two years algebra, one year geometry) are automatically admitted.

The university offers a number of merit scholarships. The most prestigious is the Presidential Scholarship, a $13,000-a-year award given to 20 students. There are also scholarships available for students in the College of Liberal Arts and Sciences, National Merit Scholarship Program finalists, National Hispanic Scholars finalists, National Achievement finalists, legacy students, underrepresented students, and specific majors.

UNIVERSITY OF IOWA

Highlights

Admissions Criteria
Academic criteria:
Grades: ☆ ☆ ☆
Difficulty of class schedule: ☆ ☆ ☆
Class rank: ☆ ☆ ☆
Standardized test scores: ☆ ☆ ☆
Teacher recommendations: ☆
Personal statement: N/A
Non-academic criteria considered:
Special talents, interests, abilities
Character/personal qualities

Deadlines
Early Action: No
Early Decision: No
Regular Action: Rolling admissions
Common Application: Not accepted

Financial Aid
In-state tuition: $6,678
Out-of-state tuition: $25,548
Room: Varies
Board: Varies
Books: $1,040
Freshmen receiving need-based aid: 46%
Undergrads rec. need-based aid: 46%
Avg. % of need met by financial aid: 63%
Avg. aid package (freshmen): $12,603
Avg. aid package (undergrads): $11,836
Avg. debt upon graduation: $28,554

School Spirit
Mascot: Herky the Hawk
Colors: Black and old gold
Song: *On Iowa*

UNIVERSITY OF
KANSAS

Four-year public
Founded: 1866
Lawrence, KS
Medium city
Pop. 88,727

Address:
1502 Iowa Street
Lawrence, KS
66045-7576

Admissions:
785-864-3911

Financial Aid:
785-864-4700

adm@ku.edu

www.ku.edu

UNIVERSITY OF KANSAS

Overview

A large university has its pros and cons, but the University of Kansas makes it work for them and for it students: in fact, KU's size is probably one of its major assets, translating into plenty of academic benefits that garner its ranking in the top 50 public universities by *U.S. News & World Report*. Additionally, KU is ranked 47th among national public research universities in federal funding for science and engineering research. Its special programs like Honors and study abroad further lend to its notoriety, and its graduate programs are ranked in the top 40. KU's size also makes for incredible diversity of social opportunities, and the sense of school spirit, especially when cheering on Jayhawks football or basketball, is quite simply unbeatable—making the undergrad student body of 19,000 feel just that much more like family.

Located on the wooded hill of Mount Oread, the campus features many beautiful historic buildings dating from the beginning of the last century. In contrast, some modern buildings range from the nondescript to what students call "simply unattractive." Still, the 1,000-acre main campus in Lawrence, Kansas is highly praised for its beauty overall, and the town of Lawrence has frequently been called one of America's best college towns, with high-quality and student-friendly music and sports scenes.

A large school definitely isn't for everyone, and it can be easy to feel like just another face in the crowd if students aren't participating in smaller, more selective special programs. Nevertheless, for students willing to give it a try, KU is one of the more welcoming prominent universities. Its mix of several solid academic programs with a high energy and friendly campus environment makes it one of the country's 10 "cool" schools, according to Mother Jones.

Academics

KU offers nearly 200 majors, of which biology, chemistry, earth and space science, English, history, mathematics, political science, and psychology majors are particularly strong. Also of merit are the Schools of Music and Education and the theatre department. All BA candidates must complete the College of Liberal Arts and Sciences General Education Requirements, consisting of courses in English, "Argument and Reason," math, western civilization, and non-western culture. Distribution mandates—humanities, natural science with a lab component, and social science—and foreign language complete the list. Requirements for BS candidates vary by major. Most general ed and distribution classes are large. "You can get lost in those classes," says a student.

The University Honors Program offers its own courses to first- and second-year students to fulfill general education requirements, and small, 15 to 25-student, faculty-taught Honors seminars for juniors and seniors. Students must also complete a study abroad, departmental honors, research, internship, or community service experience. Honors students receive priority registration and specialized honors advising. First-year Honors students interested in research can apply to the Honors Research Development Program (HRDP), a three-week intensive workshop in basic research methods. HRDP students will be paired with faculty mentors. Students should apply after admission to KU.

Highly qualified first-year students can participate in the Mount Oread Scholars program, which offers specialized advising on classes from professional or faculty advisors during New Student Orientation and before spring semester. Mount Oread scholars can take Honors classes and may be recommended to the Honors Program after freshman year; regular classes are sometimes a part of Mount Oread sections as well.

Students in all disciplines can find funding for independent, faculty-sponsored research or creative projects through Undergraduate Research Awards (UGRA).

Grants are available for up to $2,500. Funded projects in the past have ranged from writing and producing short films to designing a better dental chair.

KU ranks 11th among national universities in students going abroad; almost a third of students participate. Most semester study-abroad options are exchange programs, although KU does run its own Humanities and Western Civilization program in Paris and Florence. KU provides a number of course-specific summer programs, and winter and spring break trips are also offered. "I chose to follow my ancestral ties to Italy," one student remarks.

In addition to the University Career Center, KU has specialized Business, Journalism, Engineering, and Music Career Services Centers. The University Career Center offers resume and cover letter help, interview preparation, career fairs, major advising, financial literacy workshops, and even a professional clothing closet, where students can borrow business clothes at no cost.

Student Life

Thanks to KU's size, students can choose to participate in any one of over 600 student organizations. The intense Marching Jayhawks marching band is a standout, having been around for over 100 years. It was named a top 10 college marching band by *Sports Illustrated*. Community service is a major part of campus activities: students have logged 15,000 volunteer hours through the Center for Community Outreach since 2005.

Life at KU is governed by two major forces: tradition, and Jayhawk athletics. "There are people whose parents and grandparents attended this school," a student explains, "and we still do some of the same traditions." Hawk Week, the welcome event for freshmen, features carnivals, concerts, barbecues, block parties, and an evening dedicated to learning the many Jayhawk traditions, songs, and cheers. Commencement's traditional procession down Mount Oread into Memorial Stadium is also a fondly-remembered event.

But by far the most important events are associated with athletics. Three-time NCAA champion Jayhawk basketball is the major sport of choice here—KU's first basketball coach, James Naismith, literally invented the sport—and KU students pack Allen Fieldhouse, which *ESPN The Magazine* has called the "loudest" sports arena in the country. Probably the only college students to be excited to sing their alma mater (or even know the words), KU students make a big deal out of upholding the many game-day traditions, whether that's "waving the wheat," singing the alma mater, and cheering along with the Rock Chalk Chant. Of KU's other 10 women's and five men's NCAA Division I sports, football is strongest. Recreational athletes can take advantage of the Ambler Student Recreation Fitness Center and its climbing wall or KU's intramural facilities, while the mostly sedentary athletes can still compete in intramural video gaming and sports trivia.

Partying on campus mostly takes place at Greek houses; in fact, KU's 26 fraternities and 16 sororities are the focus of most on-campus socializing, and while they're well represented, they're not exclusive. "Greek life is the center for members and less important for non-members," one student notes. Others will find plenty of entertainment in the city of Lawrence. Bars are plentiful on Massachusetts Street, and Lawrence is known for student-friendly music

UNIVERSITY OF KANSAS

Highlights

Students
Total enrollment: 27,135
Undergrads: 19,169
Freshmen: 4,929
Part-time students: 11%
From out-of-state: 28%
Male/Female: 50%/50%
Live on-campus: 20%
In fraternities: 14%
In sororities: 20%
Off-campus employment rating: Good
Caucasian: 75%
African American: 4%
Hispanic: 6%
Asian / Pacific Islander: 4%
Native American: 1%
Mixed (2+ ethnicities): 4%
International: 6%

Academics
Calendar: Semester
Student/faculty ratio: 18:1
Class size 9 or fewer: 17%
Class size 10-29: 56%
Class size 30-49: 15%
Class size 50-99: 7%
Class size 100 or more: 5%
Returning freshmen: 79%
Six-year graduation rate: 64%

Most Popular Majors
Journalism
Psychology
Communication studies

Admissions
Applicants: 12,389
Accepted: 11,433
Acceptance rate: 92.3%
Average GPA: 3.5
ACT range: 22-28
SAT Math range: Not reported
SAT Reading range: Not reported
SAT Writing range: Not reported
Top 10% of class: 26%
Top 25% of class: 57%
Top 50% of class: 88%

761

UNIVERSITY OF KANSAS

Admissions Criteria
Academic criteria:
Grades: ☆ ☆ ☆
Difficulty of class schedule: ☆ ☆ ☆
Class rank: ☆ ☆ ☆
Standardized test scores: ☆ ☆ ☆
Teacher recommendations: N/A
Personal statement: N/A
Non-academic criteria considered:
State of residency

Deadlines
Early Action: No
Early Decision: No
Regular Action: Rolling admissions
Common Application: Not accepted

Financial Aid
In-state tuition: $9,225
Out-of-state tuition: $23,991
Room: Varies
Board: Varies
Books: $900
Freshmen receiving need-based aid: 48%
Undergrads rec. need-based aid: 46%
Avg. % of need met by financial aid: 55%
Avg. aid package (freshmen): $8,933
Avg. aid package (undergrads): $8,844
Avg. debt upon graduation: $23,468

School Spirit
Mascot: Jayhawk
Colors: Crimson and blue
Song: *I'm a Jayhawk*

venues and its enthusiasm for sports. The American Institute for Economic Research ranks it as one of the top 10 college towns in the U.S., and KU students can ride the T city bus for free. "Lawrence doesn't have the name recognition of Boston, but it really is a true college town," one student says.

Freshmen and some sophomores live on campus. Residence halls with either traditional dorm-style floor plans or suites are the most common. Cooperative living in reduced-rate scholarship halls in which the students are responsible for cooking and cleaning, and apartments are also an option.

Student Body

KU boasts a high level of ethnic diversity, and *Winds of Change* has called KU one of seven U.S. universities that "inspire and encourage" Native American Students. On the whole, students lean left. "You'll find more liberals than conservatives," one student notes.

You May Not Know

- The famed Rock Chalk Chant was originally written in 1886 as a cheer for a science club; Teddy Roosevelt thought it was the greatest college chant he'd ever heard.
- In 1971, a second Jayhawk costumed mascot, Baby Jay, "hatched" on the 50-yard-line during Homecoming; Baby Jay now accompanies the original mascot, Big Jay.
- KU claims to have taught the first class in sociology in 1890; and admittedly, the sociology department at KU is among the first in the country.

Distinguished Alumni

Philip Anschutz, founder of Qwest; Sheila C. Bair, Chairman of the FDIC; Etta Moten Barnett, actress and singer; Steve Doocy, Fox News anchor; Steve Hawley, NASA Director; Paul Rudd, actor; Kathleen Sebelius, U.S. Secretary of Health and Human Services and former Governor of Kansas.

Admissions and Financial Aid

KU requires that its applicants meet one of its admission requirements—either qualifying standardized test scores, ranking in the top third of their high school class, or a 2.0 GPA.

Frequently called a "Best Value" college, KU lives up to that name by offering the Freshman Four-Year Tuition Compact where students will pay a fixed rate throughout all four years. One in four freshmen receives an academic merit scholarship: based on GPA and standardized test scores, the award can range from $1,000 to the full cost of attendance. Interested students must submit separate applications with an essay, along with their application for admission, by December 1.

UNIVERSITY OF KENTUCKY

Overview

Well integrated with the small city of Lexington—called the "Horse Capital of the World"—University of Kentucky is a large public university with a 685-acre campus full of historic red-brick buildings. Attractive newer facilities include the massive, elegant William T. Young Library, with a materials endowment larger than any other public university's, 300 miles of books, and extensive study space, plus a video editing room currently under construction, and the $15.3 million dollar Bernard M. Johnson Athletic Center.

As UK's website coyly states, the school is "pretty good at basketball." They're referring to the Wildcat men's basketball team, which is the "winningest" in the history of college basketball. UK Wildcats take their school spirit very seriously, and on game days (any game day) campus will look like an explosion of blue and white.

But, in addition to its eminent sports record, UK is making an effort to throw down academically as well. In 1997 the university revealed a business plan designed to make UK one of the top 20 public research universities in the nation, and they only gave themselves till 2020 to do it. Under the Top 20 Business Plan, UK aims to increase enrollment, graduation rates, and quality of undergraduate education, hire more faculty, and nearly double its expenditures on research—making UK an up-and-coming and increasingly competitive institution.

Academics

University of Kentucky students can pick from 186 majors and must complete the University Studies Program; the general education requirements, which require students to take courses in math, foreign language, inference-logic, written communication, oral communication, natural sciences, social sciences, humanities; and cross-cultural studies. One of UK's major draws is its College of Agriculture, featuring the Gluck Equine Research Center, one of the largest facilities of its kind in the world, where, according to the college, "four out of five of the major equine vaccinations were developed." Other prominent programs include the College of Communications and Information Studies, the College of Engineering, the Patterson School of Diplomacy and International Commerce, the Gatton School of Business and Economics, the geography and psychology major, and the premed program.

As at most large public universities, classes, especially introductory classes, can be quite large. This may pose a problem for students seeking individualized attention and help, opportunity for discussion, and interaction with professors; but if they can hold on, it gets better. Upper-level courses, depending on the major, will generally thin out—the most common class size is 20-29 students—which gives students a chance to get to know professors. Professors are also available and willing to work with students during office hours. "I've always been able to get in touch with my professors," says a student.

Students can gain access to smaller classes taught by faculty in a few ways. The Discovery Seminar Program offers a number of small freshman seminars taught by well known, influential faculty—these also satisfy area requirements in the University Studies Program. The Honors Program, which requires a separate application, requires that students complete a core curriculum, taking one Honors seminar per semester, and then work on an independent project in their major. Students in the Honors Program get priority class registration, specialized advising, classes limited to 17-20 students, and the opportunity to live in the Honors residence halls, part of the Living Learning Communities.

Students interested in getting off campus for a bit have a number of study-abroad options: UK-sponsored programs are mostly organized by departments or colleges as summer trips. They include destinations in Italy, France, Spain, Ukraine, Germany,

UNIVERSITY OF KENTUCKY

Four-year public
Founded: 1865
Lexington, KY
Medium city
Pop. 301,569

Address:
101 Main Building
Lexington, KY
40506

Admissions:
866-900-4685

Financial Aid:
859-257-3172

admissions@uky.edu

www.uky.edu

UNIVERSITY OF KENTUCKY

Students
Total enrollment: 28,034
Undergrads: 20,827
Part-time students: 8%
From out-of-state: 30%
Male/Female: 50%/50%
Live on-campus: 26%
In fraternities: 16%
In sororities: 25%
Off-campus employment rating: Excellent
Caucasian: 79%
African American: 7%
Hispanic: 3%
Asian / Pacific Islander: 2%
Native American: 0%
Mixed (2+ ethnicities): 2%
International: 3%

Academics
Calendar: Semester
Student/faculty ratio: 18:1
Class size 9 or fewer: 9%
Class size 10-29: 55%
Class size 30-49: 20%
Class size 50-99: 10%
Class size 100 or more: 6%
Returning freshmen: 81%
Six-year graduation rate: 59%

Most Popular Majors
Accounting
Biology
Marketing

Admissions
Applicants: 18,802
Accepted: 12,655
Acceptance rate: 67.3%
Average GPA: 3.5
ACT range: 23-28
SAT Math range: 510-630
SAT Reading range: 500-620
SAT Writing range: 6-24
Top 10% of class: 32%
Top 25% of class: 61%
Top 50% of class: 88%

the UK, Mexico, Ecuador, Guatemala, Costa Rica, the Caribbean, China, Japan, Vietnam, and Ghana. Exchange programs are also available in all of these countries. The Gatton School of Business and Economics has further special exchange agreements with universities in Austria, England, France, Germany, Latvia, Poland, Spain, Switzerland, and South Korea.

The nationally-ranked Stuckert Career Center can help UK students or graduates find internships and jobs. They offer career fairs, individual consultations, interview prep, and job search tools.

Student Life

More than 400 student organizations operate on campus, including the *Kentucky Kernel*, the student newspaper; various singing groups, including gospel choirs; and the UK Dance Ensemble. The Student Activities Board hosts on-campus events for students, including tailgate parties before football games and Campus Ruckus, a welcome party at the beginning of the year that features live music, fireworks, an artificial skating rink, and free food. Homecoming hustles in a week of events, including a parade and concerts with artists that have included O.A.R., Jason Mraz, Red Hot Chili Peppers, Pearl Jam, REM, and Lil Wayne. Student organizations literally paint the town blue to get Lexington and UK into the spirit of Homecoming.

On weekends, Cheap Seats shows sneak previews of soon-to-be-released or still-in-theaters movies for free. In spring, the Little Kentucky Derby celebrates the arrival of the Kentucky Derby with several days of carnivals, concerts, games, cookouts, and races which draw the local community as well as students. Begun as a bicycle race in the 1950s, the Little Kentucky Derby now features a hot-air balloon race, as well as campus-wide scavenger hunts and the very popular ping-pong ball drop, in which thousands of ping-pong balls, some with prize-winning markings, are dropped from Patterson Office Tower.

About three-quarters of UK students live off campus, which does impact the on-campus social scene. UK's strict policy on alcohol, particularly underage consumption, means that most parties take place at off-campus locations. "If you want the real parties, you go off campus," says a student. Lexington, sometimes called the "biggest small town in America," offers not only bars, cafes, and restaurants but also a lively art and cultural scene, including a number of art galleries. The nearby Keeneland thoroughbred race track hosts popular "College Days," where students get free entry to the races and can enter to win $1,000 scholarships. Much of the on-campus social scene is dominated by the Greek system: 23 fraternities and 19 sororities operate on campus, and rushing (which happens at the beginning of the school year) is seen as a major component of making friends at UK. "The fraternities and sororities are especially popular among underclassmen," a student explains.

Possibly more dominant than any other events on campus are UK sports: school spirit is fierce and ubiquitous. Twenty-one varsity teams compete in Division I. Football draws a large crowd, but basketball is the real star at UK: the Wildcats men's team has won eight Division I national championships. "Basketball is more than a religion here," says a fan. Students can also visit the Athletic Center, which features a climbing wall and cardio theater, or play on intramural teams, which range from standard flag football to less-standard "turkey trot" and tug-of-war.

UK's on-campus housing options include three neighborhoods: North, South, and Central. North places students within a few blocks of downtown Lexington, while South and Central locates students close to the library and classrooms, respectively. Residence halls are either standard dorm rooms or suites and offer various special interest themes including Wellness, German, Arts, Civic Engagement, Global Village, New Economy, and Honors Living Learning Communities.

Student Body

Students at UK are mostly from within the state, and so it follows that the student body preserves a distinctly Southern feel: ethnic diversity is moderate and most students are Caucasian and conservative. "Southern hospitality" is the name of the game on campus: students will generally treat each other politely, and most students will at least say hello. "Students are beyond friendly," remarks a student.

You May Not Know

- The longest game in NCAA football history was played at UK's Commonwealth Stadium.
- Weirdly, Young Library has been voted the "Number One Place to Get a Date on Campus."
- UK students once kidnapped a horse that belonged to James Kennedy Patterson, the first president of UK; they painted it with green stripes and left it in the chapel.

Distinguished Alumni

Ashley Judd, actress; Mitch McConnell, current Senate Minority Leader; John Wall, basketball player, Washington Wizards, and 1st pick of the 2010 NBA Draft.

Admissions and Financial Aid

UK has a relatively high acceptance rate, admitting almost 70 percent of applicants. Decisions are based mostly on academic factors such as grades and test scores, but special talents and abilities may also play a part. Required essays are very short—two essays of 150 words or fewer—and may focus on personal topics such as diversity and challenges that you've faced.

University of Kentucky offers a number of merit-based scholarships for in- and out-of-state applicants. These range from $1,500 to $4,500 a year for four years, and do not require separate applications; some require that the UK application be submitted early. Additionally, UK offers First Scholarships of $5,000 per year for first-generation college students; a FAFSA is required.

UNIVERSITY OF KENTUCKY

Highlights

Admissions Criteria
Academic criteria:
Grades: ☆ ☆ ☆
Difficulty of class schedule: ☆ ☆ ☆
Class rank: ☆
Standardized test scores: ☆ ☆ ☆
Teacher recommendations: ☆
Personal statement: ☆
Non-academic criteria considered:
Interview
Extracurricular activities
Special talents, interests, abilities
Character/personal qualities
Volunteer work
State of residency
Geographical location
Minority affiliation
Alumni relationship

Deadlines
Early Action: No
Early Decision: No
Regular Action: Rolling admissions
Common Application: Accepted

Financial Aid
In-state tuition: $9,966
Out-of-state tuition: $21,052
Room: Varies
Board: Varies
Books: Varies
Avg. aid package (freshmen): $12,828
Avg. aid package (undergrads): $12,973

School Spirit
Mascot: Wildcats
Colors: Blue and white
Song: *On, On U of K*

UNIVERSITY OF
MAINE

Four-year public
Founded: 1862
Orono, ME
Rural
Pop. 9,112

Address:
168 College Avenue
Orono, ME
04469

Admissions:
877-486-2364

Financial Aid:
207-581-1324

um-admit@maine.edu

www.umaine.edu

UNIVERSITY OF MAINE

Overview

A large public school set in a beautiful, sprawling, green campus with access to mountain and lakes, the University of Maine seems to attract students who are perhaps just as interested in the outdoors as passionately pursuing their academic careers.

With an average temperature of eight degrees in January—dropping below zero with the wind chill—and a location in a small town with not much excitement or entertainment, it's no wonder UMaine draws 75 percent of its students from local towns accustomed to these living conditions. Regardless, the university has tried hard in recent years to shed its reputation as a party school, and in addition to its serene campus, the university is home to many unique programs and traditions. The Raymond H. Fogler Library, the largest library in the state of Maine, serves as an intellectual hub, attracting scholars, professors, and researchers from around the state and contributing to the college's community of diverse educational, political, and religious interests.

Academics

Through its five unique colleges, the University of Maine offers students their choice in over 176 majors. As part of their general education requirement, students must take classes in six broad categories which include science, human values and social context, mathematics, writing competency, and ethics. In addition to this extensive list of courses, students are also required to complete a capstone experience, which typically takes place toward the end of senior year. This culminates the conclusion of academic experience for each student by drawing together the various threads of his or her undergraduate program and applying them to prospective professional disciplines.

The most common course size at the University of Maine is between 10 and 19 students. However, approximately 12 percent of classes have 50 or more enrolled, and students must make a strong effort to get to know their professors on a personal level. "Intro classes can be large and kind of daunting," admits one student.

Among the university's strongest programs is engineering, which includes extensive research facilities such as the Advanced Manufacturing Center and the Laboratory for Surface Science and Technology. The college of engineering boasts an impressive list of accomplishments, such as creating bulletproof shields made partially of wood from Maine's forests. The students put forth this public announcement asking, "Why stop with Earth? UMaine's College of Engineering is shooting for the moon—literally—by testing materials that could be used to build lunar habitat someday." Located near the Gulf of Maine and the "cradle of North American marine sciences" the college's marine science and natural sciences, forestry, and agriculture programs are also strong.

Students interested in health can choose to pursue the college's pre-professional program, which offers a Health Professions Committee dedicated to advising students on getting into medical school. They may also opt for a Clinical Laboratory curriculum or an accelerated degree program designed for those students who want to attend medical school at the University of New England College of Osteopathic Medicine.

The University of Maine's Honors College attracts some 750 undergraduate students interested in exploring a more profound, interdisciplinary education. The university prides itself on an Honors College that is rich in community value and facilitates both in- and out-of-classroom learning. The university sums it up succinctly when they state, "Small classes, diverse readings, and lively discussions challenge and engage students, while a senior thesis allows them to delve more deeply into issues related to their major."

The University of Maine offers study-abroad opportunities in Western and Eastern Europe, Central and South America, Canada, Australia, New Zealand, Africa, and

Asia. Students also commonly participate in exchange programs with other foreign cultures. "Spending time abroad was one of the most rewarding experiences I've ever had," recalls a student.

UMaine's Explorations program is a great opportunity for students who are unsure what professional or academic path to pursue. Through a first-year seminar and close contact with advisors, students participating in Explorations are guided in their potential major or careers through a series of structured activities. Programs such as these, in addition to personal, psychological, and career guidance plans, help contribute to the success of many graduating students.

Student Life

With 234 official student organizations at UMaine, there is plenty to get involved with on campus. Groups range from the Women's Glee Club to Maine Bound, an outdoor adventures program. Annual events on campus include the Bumstock Festival, a popular outdoor music festival put on by students; Maine Day, a day in which students are given a reprieve from classes to come together with faculty and administration to help "spring-clean" the campus and enjoy barbeques; and Greek Week, when students compete in various activities to win one of the most sought-after Greek titles on campus.

A 600-acre university—complete with 15 miles of hiking, biking, and cross-country skiing trails as well as the Stillwater River—the University of Maine is an obvious attraction for students who love nature. It has easy access to kayaking, canoeing, and plenty of outdoor beauty.

About nine percent of students participate in the school's Greek life, consisting of five fraternities and seven sororities. The frats, in particular, constitute a large part of the social scene on campus. "Even if you aren't a big partier, you should go to at least one frat party just for the experience," says a student.

As members of NCAA Division I, Maine's athletic events are well attended. The men's ice hockey team, winner of two national championships, is especially popular. Club sports are also well received, in particular the alpine skiing and lacrosse teams. There are more than 30 intramural sports, including a bench press meet, free throw contest, mountain bike race, and table tennis. "Ironperson" consists of a medball throw, agility run, 20-yard sled push, and one lap run around the steam plant field. "It's our version of the Ironman," one student notes.

Parties in locations other than campus are increasingly popular—especially due to the fact that the university has made a recent effort to crackdown on parties occurring in on-campus housing. More than half of students live off campus, though they say there isn't too much to do in Orono. Many travel to Bangor, eight miles away, for a wider selection of bars and restaurants.

First-year students live together in a cluster of residence halls, which "helps you get to know your classmates," one student reports. Besides traditional residence halls, the university also offers living learning communities for outdoor adventure, community engagement, quiet study, science, wellness/substance free, honors students, and innovations.

UNIVERSITY OF MAINE

Highlights

Students
Total enrollment: 10,901
Undergrads: 8,778
Freshmen: 1,997
Part-time students: 14%
From out-of-state: 25%
Male/Female: 52%/48%
Live on-campus: 31%
Off-campus employment rating: Fair
Caucasian: 80%
African American: 2%
Hispanic: 2%
Asian / Pacific Islander: 1%
Native American: 1%
Mixed (2+ ethnicities): 2%
International: 3%

Academics
Calendar: Semester
Student/faculty ratio: 15:1
Class size 9 or fewer: 23%
Class size 10-29: 53%
Class size 30-49: 13%
Class size 50-99: 8%
Class size 100 or more: 4%
Returning freshmen: 76%
Six-year graduation rate: 60%

Most Popular Majors
Psychology
Social work
Nursing

Admissions
Applicants: 8,306
Accepted: 6,733
Acceptance rate: 81.1%
Average GPA: 3.4
ACT range: 21-26
SAT Math range: 490-610
SAT Reading range: 480-590
SAT Writing range: 2-16
Top 10% of class: 20%
Top 25% of class: 49%
Top 50% of class: 82%

767

UNIVERSITY OF MAINE

Admissions Criteria
Academic criteria:
Grades: ☆ ☆ ☆
Difficulty of class schedule: ☆ ☆ ☆
Class rank: ☆ ☆ ☆
Standardized test scores: ☆ ☆ ☆
Teacher recommendations: ☆ ☆
Personal statement: ☆ ☆
Non-academic criteria considered:
Extracurricular activities
Special talents, interests, abilities
Character/personal qualities
Volunteer work
Work experience
Geographical location

Deadlines
Early Action: December 15
Early Decision: No
Regular Action: Rolling admissions,
    February 1 (preferred deadline for
    financial aid and housing options)
Common Application: Accepted

Financial Aid
In-state tuition: $10,600
Out-of-state tuition: $27,970
Room: $4,762
Board: $4,350
Books: $1,000
Freshmen receiving need-based aid: 75%
Undergrads rec. need-based aid: 71%
Avg. % of need met by financial aid: 80%
Avg. aid package (freshmen): $15,867
Avg. aid package (undergrads): $14,973
Avg. debt upon graduation: $32,438

School Spirit
Mascot: Black Bears
Colors: Maine blue, navy blue, and white
Song: *Stein Song*

Student Body

The University of Maine does not boast a large amount of geographic or ethnic diversity, though it does have "diversity in interests. You'll see jocks, nerds, rich kids, and hippies," remarks a student. One passion, however, does seem to run fluently throughout the student body in particular: a fond love of the outdoors. "We're outdoors year round even when it's negative 20," one student comments.

You May Not Know

- UMaine's official fight song, the *Stein Song*, is the only college song in history to make the top 10 charts.
- The University of Maine launched the first pulp and paper engineering program in the U.S. in 1913.
- Campus facilities, Corbett and Dunn Halls, were originally built for Olympic athletes.

Distinguished Alumni

Manette Ansay, novelist; Colby Chandler, CEO of Kodak; Doug Hall, Founder/CEO of Eureka! Ranch; Stephen King, author.

Admissions and Financial Aid

UMaine hosts a number of open houses for prospective students that include tours and presentations of specific academic departments, admissions interviews, meetings, and tours. The admissions office states, "Advanced, honors, or AP coursework is encouraged."

All students accepted through early action are eligible for merit scholarships, varying from $500 to $10,000. In addition, the school has selective scholarships reserved for students from particular towns, highs schools, and University of Maine alumni.

UNIVERSITY OF MARY WASHINGTON

Overview

At a university named after George Washington's mother, you would expect a strong sense of American tradition, a historical flavor that is indeed palpable as soon as you step onto the campus of University of Mary Washington (UMW), formerly Mary Washington College. The university features Jeffersonian architecture on 176 neatly landscaped acres. Located in historic Fredericksburg, Virginia, the campus sits atop a steep hill that is in and of itself a historical landmark, having played an important role in the Battle of Fredericksburg.

A medium-sized public university, UMW is one of the oldest universities in northern Virginia, with a school heritage that dates back to the early 1900s. Begun as a women's college, the student body is still predominantly female, a gender imbalance that isn't always preferred by the female students today. Those who aren't as history-obsessed as the student members in the Historic Preservation Club or those majors in the Department of Historical Preservation may be glad to find that there are several new buildings on campus, including a new residence, Eagle Village, and the William M. Anderson Center for convocation and athletic events.

As a public state university, it's not surprising that geographic diversity at UMW is relatively low. Most students are from within the state, and those from outside Virginia tend to come from the east coast. A focus on multiculturalism enlivens campus life. Students wanting to extend their horizons beyond Fredericksburg can drive an hour to Washington, DC or Richmond, Virginia, or study abroad for a real change in cultural awareness.

Academics

UMW offers 38 majors and programs of study, and students can double major or design their own independent major. Students must complete the general education requirements by taking courses in six areas of study. These include a natural science class with a laboratory component and courses in quantitative reasoning, art, global inquiry, and more. Strong areas of study are business administration and education, programs in which undergraduates may obtain teaching licensure.

The university awards Bachelors degrees in art, science, liberal studies, and professional studies. The Bachelor of Liberal Studies is for adults who want to major in one of the traditional arts and sciences disciplines. However, those students who wish to complete a bachelor's degree through evening classes while learning skills that apply to the organizations they lead will most likely pursue the Bachelor of Professional Studies. More than 85 percent of classes have fewer than 30 students, which allows for a lot of interaction between students and professors. "You can't just hide out in class," explains a student. "You're expected to participate."

The First Year Experience (FYE) Community offers freshmen a chance to live and learn together in a program designed to ease the transition into college. Students in FYE enjoy social events and leadership opportunities outside the classroom. According to the university, "while participation in FYE is voluntary, it is highly recommended and offers incoming students an excellent way to get their feet on the ground and make the most of their first year at The University of Mary Washington." One student notes, "I'm glad I participated because it's a built-in social network."

UMW houses a unique Department of Historic Preservation, which offers its own major. It is affiliated with the Center for Historic Preservation, a research and public outreach organization. The Historic Preservation Club, which is a student group, supplements the department with education trips, tours, conferences, and meetings. The club features a long list of events, including a Ghost Walk (haunted tours of Downtown Fredericksburg) and Victoria Ball (an early spring gala with traditional costume and dance).

UNIVERSITY OF MARY WASHINGTON

Four-year public
Founded: 1908
Fredericksburg, VA
Large town
Pop. 25,691

Address:
1301 College Avenue
Fredericksburg, VA
22401

Admissions:
800-468-5614

Financial Aid:
540-654-2468

admit@umw.edu

www.umw.edu

UNIVERSITY OF MARY WASHINGTON

Students

Total enrollment: 5,093
Undergrads: 4,515
Freshmen: 955
Part-time students: 14%
From out-of-state: 13%
From public schools: 87%
Male/Female: 35%/65%
Live on-campus: 61%
Off-campus employment rating: Good
Caucasian: 64%
African American: 6%
Hispanic: 6%
Asian / Pacific Islander: 5%
Native American: 0%
Mixed (2+ ethnicities): 4%
International: 1%

Academics

Calendar: Semester
Student/faculty ratio: 14:1
Class size 9 or fewer: 18%
Class size 10-29: 68%
Class size 30-49: 11%
Class size 50-99: 3%
Class size 100 or more: -
Returning freshmen: 83%
Six-year graduation rate: 76%
Graduates who immediately go to graduate school: 38%
Graduates who immediately enter career related to major: 70%

Most Popular Majors

Business administration
Psychology
English language/literature

Admissions

Applicants: 4,847
Accepted: 3,724
Acceptance rate: 76.8%
Placed on wait list: 352
Enrolled from wait list: 73
Average GPA: 3.5
ACT range: 22-27
SAT Math range: 510-600
SAT Reading range: 520-630
SAT Writing range: 5-29
Top 10% of class: 23%
Top 25% of class: 58%
Top 50% of class: 94%

UMW offers more than 100 exchange- or direct-enrollment opportunities with universities abroad; and there are also 14 UMW faculty-led summer programs. Nearly 300 students study abroad on year-long, semester, or summer programs each year.

The Career Services office hosts an annual Career Day in the fall and Employer Fair in the spring, as well as Wednesday walk-in hours. UMW is on the Peace Corps' list of "Top Producing Colleges and Universities," ranking #1 among small colleges and universities with less than 5,000 undergraduates. Currently, 32 alumni are Peace Corps volunteers.

Student Life

There are approximately 120 student organizations on campus. The nonprofit organization Students Helping Honduras established its first collegiate chapter at UMW (the co-founder is a UMW alum). Cheap Seats Cinema brings film to the university through programming on Channel 27 and movie showings every weekend. *The Bullet*, the university's student newspaper, has been publishing since 1922.

A tradition that's nearly as old as the newspaper is Devil-Goat day, an annual competition among students whose graduating classes fall on even years ("goats") and odd years ("devils"). Large crowds of students turn out for the fun—inflatable obstacle courses, rock walls, airbrush tattoos—and carnival food. Junior Ring Week, another school tradition, celebrates students who achieve junior status. It's a fun event that involves the Junior Ring Dance, a scavenger hunt, and the opportunity for other classes to play innocent pranks on the juniors.

The annual Multicultural Affair draws 3,000 to 4,000 people a year every April. This colorful day features entertainment, international food, ethnic craft vendors, and children's activities for not only students but also the broader Fredericksburg community.

There are no official fraternities or sororities on campus, although Psi Upsilon is the "underground" fraternity. "You won't have scenes from *Animal House* here, but we know how to have a good time," one student remarks.

UMW's 23 varsity teams compete in Division III. The Eagles are strong in swim, men's tennis, and women's basketball, and have won the Capital Athletic Conference All-Sports Award (for overall best athletic program) 11 times. There are also 17 club sports. Intramurals include basketball, badminton, bowling, beach volleyball, and even a bean bag toss contest.

Fredericksburg has a lot of historical offerings: visitors can walk in the footsteps of Civil War generals and visit the home of George Washington. These sites tend to be frequented more by tourists than students. "You should see each of the sites once, but that's probably enough," a student comments. Students can drive to Virginia's Blue Ridge Mountains and to the beaches at Chesapeake Bay and the Atlantic Ocean.

Sixty-one percent of students live on campus in one of 17 residence halls or campus apartments. Juniors and seniors can live in the newly constructed Eagle Village, a residence facility that houses more than 600 students in two-bedroom apartments.

Student Body

Thanks to its roots as an all-women's college, UMW's student body is two-thirds female. "It would be nice to have more guys," says a female student, "but at the same time, I feel very comfortable in this environment." Another student adds, "There really is no stereotypical student here. And there's a range of interests represented."

The university aims to enroll a culturally and ethnically diverse student body and has succeeded in recent years. Overall, about 21 percent of students are minorities.

You May Not Know

- Several buildings on campus are named for notable women from American history. For example, Martha Jefferson Randolph, Thomas Jefferson's daughter, is acknowledged by Randolph Hall.
- UMW is named in honor of Mary Washington, famed Fredericksburg resident and mother of George Washington.
- Most of UMW's Fredericksburg campus is located on Marye's Heights, a steep hill that played an important role in the 1862 Battle of Fredericksburg.

Distinguished Alumni

Marion C. Blakey, President and CEO of Aerospace Industries Association; Frances Cook, retired ambassador; Daniel R. Wolfe, Executive Vice President of Worldwide Creative Operations for Universal Pictures; Desiree Velez, actress.

Admissions and Financial Aid

UMW offers an Honors Admission Option that gives students a non-binding, early notification opportunity. According to the admissions office, "UMW does not admit students by any rigid formula and we seek to enroll a diverse and well-rounded student body." The admissions committee places strong emphasis on the quality of the high school curriculum as evidence of preparation for study in the liberal arts and sciences.

The college emphasizes its affordability; in fact, it was named by *Kiplinger's Personal Finances* in the "100 Best Values in Public Colleges" list in 2014. Students compete for nearly 200 endowed scholarships, including a four-year full-ride Washington Scholarship that honors Virginia high school seniors with exceptional academic credentials. The Alvey Scholars Program is a full-ride scholarship for out-of-state students. Semifinalists for these awards are invited to campus for a banquet, Honors Admission showcase, and individual interview.

UNIVERSITY OF MARY WASHINGTON

Highlights

Admissions Criteria
Academic criteria:
Grades: ☆ ☆ ☆
Difficulty of class schedule: ☆ ☆ ☆
Class rank: ☆ ☆
Standardized test scores: ☆ ☆
Teacher recommendations: ☆ ☆
Personal statement: ☆ ☆
Non-academic criteria considered:
Extracurricular activities
Special talents, interests, abilities
Character/personal qualities
Volunteer work
Work experience
Geographical location
Minority affiliation
Alumni relationship

Deadlines
Early Action: November 15
Early Decision: No
Regular Action: November 15 (priority)
February 1 (final)
Notification of admission by: April 1
Common Application: Accepted

Financial Aid
In-state tuition: $6,758
Out-of-state tuition: $19,628
Room: $5,056
Board: $1,942
Books: $1,100
Freshmen receiving need-based aid: 39%
Undergrads rec. need-based aid: 37%
Avg. % of need met by financial aid: 50%
Avg. aid package (freshmen): $7,700
Avg. aid package (undergrads): $8,129
Avg. debt upon graduation: $23,300

School Spirit
Mascot: Eagles
Colors: Navy, gray, and white

771

Four-year public
Founded: 1963
Baltimore, MD
Large town
Pop. 41,567

Address:
1000 Hilltop Circle
Baltimore, MD
21250

Admissions:
800-UMBC-4U2

Financial Aid:
410-455-2387

admissions@umbc.
edu

www.umbc.edu

UNIVERSITY OF MARYLAND - BALTIMORE COUNTY

Overview

Ranked #1 among up-and-coming universities for the fifth year in a row by *U.S. News & World Report*, the University of Maryland-Baltimore County certainly merits perusal by the serious-minded student. The university boasts a deep commitment to undergraduate education in addition to excelling as a thorough and prestigious research institution, offering exclusive research opportunities to its students amidst an intimate liberal arts education. Maryland also top the lists, among other such institutions as Harvard, Princeton, and Brown, in employing professors unusually committed to undergraduate teaching.

Located just 10 minutes south of Baltimore, Maryland, this honors school offers more than just outstanding academics. The university partners with the Baltimore Collegetown Network to provide college students at 16 different institutions in the Baltimore area with information and deals on restaurants, nightlife, sports, and other municipal attractions. With its modern architecture and bustling nighttime amendments, Baltimore shines as a metropolitan area.

For the outdoors adventurer, the university is also adjacent to some of the finest bike trails on the East Coast, an hour from the mountains, and two hours from the eastern shore and beaches.

Despite having more than 10,000 undergraduate students, UMBC offers a private feel to its students with its plethora of resources and internship opportunities. Its science-oriented focus provides unique opportunities for research-related career paths, as well as countless other connections with leaders in all academic fields.

Academics

General education requirements at UMBC include courses in four broad categories: arts and humanities, social sciences, mathematics and science, and language and culture. These requirements are intended to equip students with lifelong skills such as quantitative reasoning, the ability to communicate effectively in writing and speech, and critical analysis and reasoning, as well as technological literacy.

The academic environment at UMBC can be challenging as well as competitive, but the school provides plentiful resources to aid students in their chosen academic paths, helping each individual student find the tools he or she needs to succeed in a given field. More than 40 majors and more than 40 minors are offered, in all areas of liberal arts study. Strong programs include computer science, political science, and psychology.

Special academic programs at the university include the Honors College, a program that offers talented students an intense learning curriculum through smaller classes and close work with exceptional faculty; the Meyerhoff Scholars Program, which seeks to increase diversity among future leaders in academic fields; and First-Year Academic Seminars, where classes are limited to 20 students. These and other programs provide the opportunity for connection with a faculty member as well as a rigorous academic environment. "We have so many programs that aren't offered at regular public colleges and that set us apart," comments a student.

First-year students are provided special opportunities such as the Collegiate Summer Institute and the New Student Book Experience. Living Learning Communities offers a residential experience that allows students with common intellectual interests to connect. "All new students read the same book over the summer, and then we discuss it," explains one student. "It's a conversation topic that we all share."

Study abroad at UMBC is very popular, with several hundred students taking part every year. Programs are available in over 45 countries across five continents, with three different program options: exchange programs, during which students pay tuition and fees to UMBC; Affiliate Programs, in which UMBC partners with U.S.-based study-abroad programs; and Direct Programs, in which students may enroll directly in the international university of their choosing.

Internships and networking are made easy at UMBC with the Career Services Center, where advisors help students with internships and co-ops, on-campus jobs, and undergraduate research opportunities. Recruitment for full-time jobs can also be done through the UMBCworks career database. "There's lots of help with finding an internship," explains a student. "Being so close to Baltimore makes it pretty easy to find opportunities." Extensive alumni involvement at the university also aids students in easing the stress of the job search.

Student Life

With over 200 student clubs and organizations, including the Interdisciplinary Film Association, Astronomy Club, and the Dance Council of Majors, UMBC provides activities for students with all types of interests. What's more, if students don't find an organization of their particular interest, they may become a Leadership Consultant in the Office of Student Life and spur changes in the student organization system.

The university also provides multiple recreational events throughout the year to keep students' social calendars busy. Quad Mania is a community music festival held on campus in the spring which features live music, food, and games all day long; Band of Brothers and Macklemore and Ryan Lewis have performed! Stress Free Zone, an event put on during finals week, provides students with free snacks, music, games, and giveaways to ease the tenseness associated with exams. Finally, the Leadershape program is a service opportunity for students, including a week-long training session and programming throughout the year aimed at developing and applying service skills to the city of Baltimore.

Greek life on the UMBC campus isn't prominent, In fact, less than five percent of students join the 21 fraternities and sororities on campus. "Greek life is not at the top of many people's lists," remarks a student.

Athletes at UMBC compete in the America East Division I Conference. Of the eight men's and nine women's teams that play in the conference, men's lacrosse, basketball, and swimming and diving are the most competitive. For those non-varsity athletes, intramural teams such as basketball, dodgeball, homerun derby, and Wiffle ball are available and popular on campus.

When UMBC students decide to venture off campus, downtown Baltimore and Washington, DC provide ample entertainment opportunities. A popular destination in Baltimore is Fells Point, best known for its eclectic art galleries, shops, and active nightlife. For the more adventurous, Boston, Philadelphia, and New York City are just road trips away. "Baltimore sometimes gets a bad rap, but our location near so many big cities is amazing," a student comments.

Almost two-thirds of students live off campus. However, on-campus housing is available and varies from dorms to Living/Learning Communities, which incorporate academics into the housing situation.

UNIVERSITY OF MARYLAND – BALTIMORE COUNTY

Highlights

Students
Total enrollment: 13,637
Undergrads: 10,953
Freshmen: 2,126
From out-of-state: 12%
Male/Female: 55%/45%
Live on-campus: 34%
In fraternities: 4%
In sororities: 5%
Off-campus employment rating: Good
Caucasian: 47%
African American: 16%
Hispanic: 5%
Asian / Pacific Islander: 20%
Native American: 0%
Mixed (2+ ethnicities): 3%
International: 4%

Academics
Calendar: 4-1-4 system
Student/faculty ratio: 20:1
Class size 9 or fewer: 15%
Class size 10-29: 49%
Class size 30-49: 24%
Class size 50-99: 8%
Class size 100 or more: 4%
Returning freshmen: 85%
Six-year graduation rate: 57%

Most Popular Majors
Psychology
Computer science
Biological sciences

Admissions
Applicants: 8,672
Accepted: 5,296
Acceptance rate: 61.1%
Placed on wait list: 393
Enrolled from wait list: 160
Average GPA: 3.7
ACT range: 24-29
SAT Math range: 580-670
SAT Reading range: 550-650
SAT Writing range: 9-38
Top 10% of class: 29%
Top 25% of class: 56%
Top 50% of class: 85%

773

College Profiles

UNIVERSITY OF MARYLAND – BALTIMORE COUNTY

Admissions Criteria

Academic criteria:

Grades: ☆ ☆ ☆

Difficulty of class schedule: ☆ ☆ ☆

Class rank: ☆

Standardized test scores: ☆ ☆ ☆

Teacher recommendations: ☆

Personal statement: ☆ ☆

Non-academic criteria considered:

Extracurricular activities

Special talents, interests, abilities

Character/personal qualities

Volunteer work

Work experience

State of residency

Deadlines

Early Action: November 1

Early Decision: No

Regular Action: November 1 (priority)

February 1 (final)

Notification of admission by: February 1

Common Application: Accepted

Financial Aid

In-state tuition: $7,298

Out-of-state tuition: $18,872

Room: $6,126

Board: $3,238

Books: $1,200

Freshmen receiving need-based aid: 45%

Undergrads rec. need-based aid: 49%

Avg. % of need met by financial aid: 56%

Avg. aid package (freshmen): $10,657

Avg. aid package (undergrads): $10,312

Avg. debt upon graduation: $22,600

School Spirit

Mascot: Retrievers

Colors: Black and gold

Song: *UMBC Fight Song*

Student Body

As a public research institution, UMBC does not have a "typical" student profile. Students of all personalities and interests come to study at the university. "There's a true range of people from hip to nerdy, partiers to those who hole up in the library," says one student.

Ethnic diversity at UMBC is very high, with almost half of the student body of minority status. Geographic diversity, on the other hand, is low, with only 12 percent of students hailing from out of state. "If you're looking to meet people from across the country, this probably isn't the place for you," says a student.

You May Not Know

- Catonsville, Maryland, the community outside of Baltimore in which UMBC is located, was rated 49th in the top 100 Best Places to Live by CNNMoney.com.
- UMBC researchers are the leaders in a $7.5 million initiative grant from the U.S. Department of Defense.
- In 2009, the *Daily Beast* named Baltimore the 10th smartest town, due in part to the University of Maryland Baltimore County.

Distinguished Alumni

Mehdi Addadi, Olympic swimmer at the 2000 Summer Olympics; Brian Dannelly, director of *Weeds*, *Pushing Daisies*, and other TV programs; Tony Harris, CNN news anchor; Richard D. Kemp, Elie Wiesel Prize in Ethics.

Admissions and Financial Aid

The admissions committee considers a number of factors in the admissions process. GPA and SAT scores are heartily considered, with a unique focus on the writing portion of the SAT, as the committee believes that writing is an essential skill that should be gleaned from a high school education. In addition, strength of the curriculum, class rank, and other achievements, including the application essay, are considered.

The application fee is waived if you are a National Merit Scholar, National Achievement Scholar, Maryland Distinguished Scholar or a National Hispanic Scholar.

Merit-based scholarships for incoming freshmen include the UMBC Premier Award, for which in-state students receive $15,000 per year and out-of-state students, $22,000, both for four years. Maryland recipients of the UMBC Heritage Award receive $10,000 and out-of-state recipients enjoy $15,000 for four years. If admitted to Honors College, students are also considered for the Honors College Fellows award, which provides $15,000 per year for in-state students and $22,000 for out-of-state students for four years; and the Honors College Award, which awards $1,000 per year for four years.

UNIVERSITY OF MARYLAND – COLLEGE PARK

Overview

What started as a School of Agriculture in 1856 has evolved into a 1,250-acre campus located in College Park with an enrollment of 26,000 undergraduates. Today, University of Maryland College Park is a public institution—co-educational since 1912—that offers many strong academic programs. Designated as an arboretum and botanical garden, there are more than 6,600 trees on campus.

A large university, UMD is conveniently located nine miles from Washington, DC. The Library of Congress, the Smithsonian Institution, the National Archives, and the National Institutes of Health are all a metro stop away. Although the surrounding area isn't the safest neighborhood, the campus itself is relatively safe and the on-campus atmosphere is always abuzz with activity. There are 100 law enforcement members in the university's police department who offer 24-hour escort service to students. UMD has been recently ranked 21st nationally for public universities by *U.S. News & World Report*.

Academics

There are 264 majors offered in 12 different schools: The Clark School of Engineering, College of Agricultural and Natural Resources, College of Arts and Humanities, College of Behavior and Social Sciences, College of Chemical and Life Sciences, College of Computer, Mathematical, and Physical Sciences, College of Education, Merrill College of Journalism, Smith School of Business, School of Architecture, Planning, and Preservation, and School of Public Health. All majors in every degree plan must satisfy general requirements for undergraduates that make up the CORE Liberal Arts and Sciences Studies Program. Students are required to take classes from distributive studies such as the humanities, the arts, sciences, history, and other divisions.

Not surprising for a public university of this size, introductory classes can be composed of several hundred students. In fact, 17 percent of classes have 50 or more students. "Class sizes improve as you move up," says a student. Some of UMD's stronger programs are in architecture, business, engineering, entrepreneurship, finance, international business, journalism, management, management information services, marketing, quantitative analysis, and supply chain management. There are several special academic opportunities students can take part in such as College Park Scholars. This program is by invitation only for freshmen and sophomores and provides the "interpersonal benefits of a small college paired with the intellectual advantages of a major research university." About 75 students a year are selected for this academic and residential community.

Students in the honors college have the opportunity to be part of Gemstone or the Honors Humanities Program. Gemstone participants enjoy four years of multidisciplinary research, while students who "are seeking challenging exposure to the humanities and arts at the university level" find that the Honors Humanities Program emphasizes undergraduate research as well. Both of these programs are very selective but students who are admitted to the Honors College are invited to apply. "You'll meet the most intelligent people," one student notes.

Studying abroad is a unique experience students have the option to pursue. There are nine programs sponsored or administered by Maryland's academic departments. In addition to these, UMD partners with programs that enable students to travel and study in many other countries such as Russia, Australia, and Holland. Besides studying abroad, students can also intern, volunteer, or work abroad. More than 1,900 students at UMD choose to study abroad during the academic school year.

Most students enter the work force after graduating, but approximately 23 percent pursue a graduate degree immediately after graduation. The University Career Cen-

UNIVERSITY OF MARYLAND – COLLEGE PARK

Four-year public
Founded: 1856
College Park, MD
Large town
Pop. 30,587

Address:
College Park, MD
20742-5025

Admissions:
800-422-5867

Financial Aid:
888-313-2404

um-admit@umd.edu

www.umd.edu

UNIVERSITY OF MARYLAND – COLLEGE PARK

Students

Total enrollment: 37,197
Undergrads: 26,487
Freshmen: 4,468
Part-time students: 8%
From out-of-state: 29%
Male/Female: 53%/47%
Live on-campus: 44%
In fraternities: 10%
In sororities: 15%
Off-campus employment rating: Good
Caucasian: 55%
African American: 12%
Hispanic: 8%
Asian / Pacific Islander: 15%
Native American: 0%
Mixed (2+ ethnicities): 3%
International: 3%

Academics

Calendar: Semester
Student/faculty ratio: 18:1
Class size 9 or fewer: 9%
Class size 10-29: 54%
Class size 30-49: 19%
Class size 50-99: 11%
Class size 100 or more: 6%
Returning freshmen: 94%
Six-year graduation rate: 82%

Most Popular Majors

Criminology/criminal justice
Economics
Psychology

Admissions

Applicants: 25,255
Accepted: 11,825
Acceptance rate: 46.8%
Placed on wait list: 969
Enrolled from wait list: Not reported
Average GPA: 4.1 (weighted)
ACT range: Not reported
SAT Math range: 610-720
SAT Reading range: 580-690
SAT Writing range: Not reported
Top 10% of class: 71%
Top 25% of class: 87%
Top 50% of class: 98%

776

ter sponsors career and internship fairs that attract more than 400 employers to the campus. "If you take the initiative to find it, there's a lot of help for finding a job after graduating," one student states.

Student Life

With such a large student population and 540 official student organizations, there is always something to do on campus. The Stamp Student Union offers a bowling alley, a billiards center, a video game arcade, and a movie theater that seats 550. "Drinking is not a prerequisite to having fun," one student notes. College Park is a big college town and the university sponsors activities for students on the weekends.

There are many notable events that happen on campus throughout the year. Many are hosted by the school's student organizations, including Greek Week, Cultural Explosion, Hip Hop Conference, Union All Niter, and Pride Days. Art Attack is an annual outdoor music and art festival that culminates in a concert at Maryland's Byrd stadium. Midnight Madness is described as "a highly anticipated, highly charged, annual event, often featuring fireworks and even a laser light show" to celebrate the first official day of practice for the men's basketball team. "It's another excuse to have a party really," says a student. Carifest, hosted by the Caribbean Student Association, is an annual festival celebrating Caribbean culture with food, music, dancing, and fashion.

Greek life is prominent with 12 percent of students involved in the 36 social fraternities and 27 social sororities, even though only 22 fraternities and 12 sororities have houses on campus. "Members tend to socialize among themselves," one student comments.

UMD is a member of the Atlantic East Coast Conference, with Division I in athletics and Football I-A. The Terrapins have won 37 NCAA national titles, 11 of them in football and one in basketball. The basketball team recently played in 11 straight NCAA championships, and the men's soccer team and women's field hockey team won national titles as well. There are many popular intramurals on campus including flag football, soccer, 3-on-3 basketball, tennis, and badminton.

There are many off-campus activities that students engage in, such as frequenting the Thirsty Turtle, Cornerstone Grill, and the Santa Fe Café. The university's proximity to Washington, DC gives students easy access to bars, restaurants, shopping, cultural events, and the museums of Washington, DC via the Metro. "Everything is pretty easy to get to," one student comments.

Housing at UMD is guaranteed to students for the first year, but many move to off-campus housing for subsequent years or decide to stay at home. Students say that those who opt to stay on campus generally "live in high-rise and low-rise residence halls and in apartment-style units, some with their own kitchens."

Student Body

The student population is composed of 38 percent minorities and is high in ethnic diversity. There is moderate geographic diversity, with 29 percent of students from out of state. Although 93 percent of students live on campus their first year, there are a substantial number of student commuters as well. The social scene on campus is definitely affected by the fact that 56 percent of students live off campus; but even those who commute often stay on campus after classes to hang out.

You May Not Know

- In 2004, UMD celebrated 80 years of making their own ice cream.
- The university has the only accredited Fire Protection Engineering Program in the United States.
- *The Diamondback*, which is the student run newspaper, is published every day from Monday to Friday.

Distinguished Alumni

Sergey Brin, co-founder, Google; Kiran Chetry, co-anchor, CNN's morning show, "American Morning;" Kevin Plank, founder of UnderArmour.

Admissions and Financial Aid

University of Maryland College Park does not accept the Common Application. Not always typical for such a large public university, UMD does a holistic review of each student, looking at 25 factors, including the "essay, extracurricular involvement, recommendations, residency, racial diversity, geographic diversity, high school achievement, special talents, and skills."

There are nine merit scholarships available for entering freshmen. The Banneker/Key Scholarship is the most prestigious and covers full cost of attendance. Other awards include the Creative and Performing Arts Scholarship, which awards entering freshmen who demonstrate extraordinary talent in art, dance, music, or theatre. There are also Departmental Scholarships that are awarded to promising students in specific departments.

UNIVERSITY OF MARYLAND – COLLEGE PARK

Highlights

Admissions Criteria
Academic criteria:
Grades: ☆ ☆ ☆
Difficulty of class schedule: ☆ ☆ ☆
Class rank: ☆ ☆
Standardized test scores: ☆ ☆ ☆
Teacher recommendations: ☆ ☆
Personal statement: ☆ ☆
Non-academic criteria considered:
Extracurricular activities
Special talents, interests, abilities
Character/personal qualities
Volunteer work
Work experience
Geographical location
Minority affiliation
Alumni relationship

Deadlines
Early Action: November 1
Early Decision: No
Regular Action: November 1 (priority)
January 20 (final)
Common Application: Not accepted

Financial Aid
In-state tuition: $9,162
Out-of-state tuition: $28,348
Room: $6,153
Board: $4,127
Books: $1,130
Freshmen receiving need-based aid: 44%
Undergrads rec. need-based aid: 43%
Avg. % of need met by financial aid: 63%
Avg. aid package (freshmen): $11,370
Avg. aid package (undergrads): $11,026
Avg. debt upon graduation: $25,276

School Spirit
Mascot: Terrapin (Testudo)
Colors: Red, white, black, and gold
Song: *Fight Varsity*

777

UNIVERSITY OF
MASSACHU-
SETTS –
AMHERST

Four-year public
Founded: 1863
Amherst, MA
Large town
Pop. 34,874

Address:
37 Mather Drive
Amherst, MA
01003-9313

Admissions:
413-545-0222

Financial Aid:
413-545-0801

mail@admissions.
umass.edu

www.umass.edu

UNIVERSITY OF MASSACHUSETTS - AMHERST

Overview

Ninety miles from Boston in the scenic Pioneer Valley, students at the University of Massachusetts Amherst enjoy what is said to be the #1 college town in America. The quaint New England setting, residential education programs, and relatively small class sizes give every student the opportunity to personalize their education while still taking advantage of world-class research and outstanding faculty.

Students can join the premier honors college in the northeast, create their own major, or take classes at the other four colleges in the Five College consortium: Mt. Holyoke, Smith, Hampshire, and Amherst. With almost 22,000 students at UMass Amherst alone, 338 student groups, 19 NCAA Division I athletic teams, and a lively arts and culture scene, there is never a shortage of things to do.

Academics

Amherst offers 217 majors, and all students must complete the general education requirements, which include classes in writing, math, analytic reasoning, biological and physical world, social world, and cultural diversity. Many students take advantage of the Bachelor's Degree with Individual Concentration (BDIC), which allows them to create their own majors with the help of faculty sponsors.

Like any large university, UMass Amherst has classes of considerable size; one quarter of all classes have over 40 students. That said, 35 percent have under 20! Class size varies dramatically based on major, as do challenge and quality of teaching. Students say that the professors are "totally committed for the most part, although there are a handful you want to avoid." Especially strong programs are in computer science, economics, engineering, management, and sports management.

UMass Amherst is also a member of the unique Five College Consortium, meaning students can enroll in classes at Smith, Mount Holyoke, Amherst, or Hampshire at no extra cost. And they can take the free bus the short distances from campus to campus, or as transportation to social and cultural events. "The Consortium makes the possibilities pretty much limitless," says a student.

For a more rigorous education, exceptional students can join the Commonwealth College—the honors college offering small seminars, close interaction with faculty, research opportunities, and community service. "The seminars create a tight-knit academic environment where you can really delve into the material," notes a student. To support capstone experience projects, the school awards over $67,000 to honors student research.

Students who are not in the honors program also have ample research and career experience opportunities. Noteworthy for studies in management is the Center for Student Business, which gives students hands-on business experience by working as consultants for the many student-run nonprofit businesses on campus.

During the summertime, UMass Amherst hosts Research Experiences for Undergraduates in a wide variety of disciplines, funded by institutions such as the National Science Foundation and the Howard Hughes Medical Foundation. If you discover something remarkable, you can present your results at the Massachusetts Undergraduate Research Conference.

UMass Amherst sponsors more than 300 study-abroad programs in over 50 countries, including Tunisia, Botswana, Italy, Madagascar, Mali, Cyprus, and Sweden. The international programs office even suggests getting a "Green Passport" and carbon offsetting your travels if within your budget!

The Career Services Office connects alumni, students, and employers through networking events, mentorship, and counseling. The somewhat unique "co-op" program allows students to stay enrolled at UMass Amherst without paying tuition, while working for three to nine months at a job related to their major. Co-ops appear on the college transcript and are a great alternative to the classic internship that potential employers note when looking over job applications after graduation. "Because of our location, we have so many internship and co-op opportunities right in our own backyard," one student comments.

Student Life

With such a big community, the Campus Pulse website does well to corral organizations, events, and news and to keep everyone aware of how many fun things there are to do on and off campus. Some of the most popular events are the Spring Concert, at which U2 has performed, and the First Week of classes, where seven days of activities and concerts get students pumped about the school year. "We get some big-name acts on campus," recalls a student. Another interesting and lively event is the Haitian Student Association (HASA) and Casa Dominican (CASA) Cultural Night, which highlights the food and dance of the island of Hispanola and seeks to educate, entertain, and inspire. More low-key events include the "Something Every Friday" movie night and the Magic Triangle Jazz series produced by WMUA, 91.1FM and the Fine Arts Center.

Six percent of men and women are members of the 21 fraternities and 15 sororities. So while there is a Greek scene for those who seek it out, there is much more activity within the 338 student groups, including countless cultural organizations, student government, improv theater groups, newspapers and magazines, and even student run businesses such as the Earthfoods Café and the Bike Co-op. One unique group is Soul TV, which began airing its own broadcast in 1996 to enhance the minority media culture.

As for athletics, UMass Amherst is a member of the Atlantic 10 Conference and the ECAC, Division I, Football Championship Subdivision, and the Hockey East Association Division I. "We currently don't have the strongest teams in the big sports," says a student, "but there are still a good number of fans who show up for games." Intramurals are very popular, including ice hockey, Ultimate Frisbee, and basketball, as are club sports, such as alpine ski racing and lacrosse. Outdoor activities such as kayaking, mountain climbing, and skiing are organized by the Outing Club and are also favorites among students.

According to the college, "time has not tarnished the city's small town connectedness, and the downtown itself is still centered on a traditional New England town common, with shops, cafés, and restaurants lining the streets around it." The university's Mullins Center hosts athletic events and concerts while the Fine Arts Center houses performing arts concerts and an art gallery.

Almost all freshmen live on campus, where students choose dorms based on theme and can participate in Residential Academic Programs, which include in-house classes and are offered in areas as diverse as "Exploring Society through Literature" to "Sustainability." Talent Advancement Programs are another way to get a fast, personal start at UMass Amherst by joining a selective group of students from a single major, enrolling in seminars, and then working closely with faculty and peers. After freshman year, 61 percent of students live on campus, and the housing and residence life office helps by running workshops and renting fairs.

UNIVERSITY OF MASSACHUSETTS – AMHERST

Highlights

Students
Total enrollment: 28,236
Undergrads: 21,928
Freshmen: 4,772
From out-of-state: 27%
Male/Female: 51%/49%
Live on-campus: 61%
In fraternities: 6%
In sororities: 6%
Off-campus employment rating: **Excellent**
Caucasian: 68%
African American: 4%
Hispanic: 5%
Asian / Pacific Islander: 8%
Native American: 0%
Mixed (2+ ethnicities): 2%
International: 2%

Academics
Calendar: Semester
Student/faculty ratio: 18:1
Class size 9 or fewer: 14%
Class size 10-29: 53%
Class size 30-49: 15%
Class size 50-99: 8%
Class size 100 or more: 10%
Returning freshmen: 88%
Six-year graduation rate: 70%

Most Popular Majors
Psychology
Management
Biology

Admissions
Applicants: 34,326
Accepted: 21,470
Acceptance rate: 62.5%
Placed on wait list: 3,808
Enrolled from wait list: 566
Average GPA: 3.7
ACT range: 24-28
SAT Math range: 560-660
SAT Reading range: 530-630
SAT Writing range: Not reported
Top 10% of class: 27%
Top 25% of class: 66%
Top 50% of class: 95%

779

College Profiles

UNIVERSITY OF MASSACHUSETTS – AMHERST

Admissions Criteria
Academic criteria:
Grades: ☆ ☆ ☆
Difficulty of class schedule: ☆ ☆ ☆
Class rank: ☆ ☆
Standardized test scores: ☆ ☆ ☆
Teacher recommendations: ☆ ☆
Personal statement: ☆ ☆
Non-academic criteria considered:
Extracurricular activities
Special talents, interests, abilities
Character/personal qualities
Volunteer work
Work experience
Geographical location
Minority affiliation

Deadlines
Early Action: November 1
Early Decision: No
Regular Action: November 5 (priority)
January 15 (final)
Common Application: Accepted

Financial Aid
In-state tuition: $13,258
Out-of-state tuition: $27,974
Room: Varies
Board: Varies
Books: $1,000
Freshmen receiving need-based aid: 60%
Undergrads rec. need-based aid: 60%
Avg. % of need met by financial aid: 85%
Avg. aid package (freshmen): $13,920
Avg. aid package (undergrads): $15,039
Avg. debt upon graduation: $27,945

School Spirit
Mascot: Minutemen, Minutewomen
Colors: Maroon and white
Song: *Fight UMass*

Student Body

With over 21,000 undergraduates, it's hard to make any blanket statements about the student body. "Overall I'd say we are pretty academically passionate but don't take things too seriously and know how to take advantage of being in the best college town in the country," says a student. There is a niche for everyone, but only 27 percent of students are from out of state. On the other hand, there is high ethnic diversity with 19 percent minority students. As would be expected in a state that has legalized gay marriage, UMass Amherst is full of pretty liberal, tolerant folk.

You May Not Know

- Founded in 1863 as the result of an agricultural land grant, UMass remains committed to the land through environmental sustainability efforts. The university installed its first Interactive Photovoltaic system on top of the Knowles Engineering building, with twenty-five 300 watt-modules, all made in Massachusetts.
- UMass Amherst attracts over $140 million in external research funding every year.
- The mascot for UMass Amherst used to be Chief Matawampe and the team name was "The Redmen," until a controversy prompted students to choose the "Minutemen" as the new official mascot in 1972.

Distinguished Alumni

Catherine 'Cady' Coleman, astronaut; Jeff Corwin, Animal Planet's *The Jeff Corwin Experience*; Julius Erving, Hall of Fame professional basketball player; Kenneth Feinberg, current Obama Administration "Compensation Czar" and former Special Master of the U.S. Government's September 11th Victim Compensation Fund; Peter Laird, co-creator *Teenage Mutant Ninja Turtles*; Jeffrey C. Taylor, founder of Monster.com; Natasha Trethewey, Pulitzer Prize winning poet.

Admissions and Financial Aid

Upon applying, students are asked to identify a first-choice and a second-choice major, though they can select undeclared as well. Competitive majors include communications, computer science, economics, engineering, journalism, management, and sports management. High school record—as well as grade trends, GPA, and difficulty of courses—is generally more important than test scores, but only slightly more important, as the admissions committee also wants to see creativity and engagement in extracurricular activities.

About 60 percent of students receive need-based aid while only 7 percent of students receive merit aid. One example of merit aid is the TEACH grant, which gives $4,000 in annual grants to future teachers who pledge to teach in high-need public schools for four years after they graduate college. The university also awards Chancellor's, Director's and Dean's Scholarships based on grades and test scores. Students coming from the northeast who cannot find a desired major at their state's public college can qualify for reduced tuition through the New England Regional Student Program.

UNIVERSITY OF MIAMI

Overview

Picture palm trees, stunning beaches, and endless sunshine; combine it with engaging academia, artistic community, and vibrant diversity and you have a taste of the colorful lifestyle the University of Miami has to offer. A private university with more than 10,000 undergraduate students, UM is ranked in the top 50 national universities by *U.S. News & World Report* and reigns supreme as the top university in Florida. With President Donna Shalala, former Secretary of Health and Human Services under President Clinton, as well as a $326 million research budget and impressive research facilities, the University of Miami shines as a prestigiously reputable institution with bountiful and versatile opportunities for its students.

The 260-acre main campus of the University sits in Coral Gables, Florida, a suburb just four miles south of bustling downtown Miami. For those with the itch to explore, destination areas South Beach and Coconut Grove are a short drive away, with endless restaurants, shops, and nightclubs that provide both day and nighttime entertainment. In addition, the downtown Miami experience, with tropical attractions, amusement parks, and natural wonders, awaits the arrival of eager students.

Extremely diverse in student body, UM also offers diversity in its on-campus student activities. Athletics and all-day tailgating are very popular on campus. Arts and culture have a substantial presence as well; the acclaimed Department of Theatre Arts has its own theatre right on campus, and the interactive center Casa Bacardi provides opportunities to learn about Cuban culture. New facilities include the Sheldon and Myrna Palley Pavilion for Contemporary Glass and Studio Arts, the BankUnited Center, and the Martha and Austin Weeks Music Library and Technology Center. Also newly added is University Village, the first housing project at UM in over 35 years.

Academics

The University of Miami offers 180 majors. General education requirements include taking courses in mathematics, writing compositions in English, and acquiring knowledge about the world society through studying people, the humanities, and art. The university offers a student-to-faculty ratio of 11:1, with more than 75 percent of classes numbering less than 50 students. Strong academic programs include education, engineering, marine science, biology, finance, and psychology. A particularly engaging program at UM is the marine science program: approximately 300 undergraduate students are provided year-round access to marine environments, with lectures, laboratories, field trips, and independent research opportunities, as well as advising from world-renowned faculty members. "Our location makes this the perfect place to study marine science," says a student.

Among several special academic programs at UM is the General Honors Program, a four-year curriculum that provides challenging courses of study. In order to qualify, incoming freshmen must have SAT or ACT scores higher than 1360 or 31 respectively and must be in the top five percent of their graduating high school classes.

As one of the leading research institutions in the country, UM provides many ways for students to become involved, from a light commitment as a research volunteer, to a weightier, credit-driven commitment as a student researcher. Students must apply to be a researcher to the Office of Undergraduate Research and Community Outreach.

For those more interested in off-campus options, UM also offers study-abroad programs in 32 countries around the world, including such exotic destinations such as Singapore, Trinidad and Tobago, and the Dominican Republic. The university offers study-abroad programs tailored to different majors. "Where better to study marine biology than the Galapagos Islands?" asks a student.

Culminating the UM academic experience, the university provides ample resources for career networking and internships. As incoming freshmen, students have the op-

UNIVERSITY OF MIAMI

Four-year private
Founded: 1925
Coral Gables, FL
Large town
Pop. 47,783

Address:
P.O. Box 248025
Coral Gables, FL
33124

Admissions:
305-284-4323

Financial Aid:
305-284-5212

admission@miami.edu

www.miami.edu

UNIVERSITY OF MIAMI

Students

Total enrollment: 16,172
Undergrads: 10,590
Freshmen: 2,292
Part-time students: 6%
From out-of-state: 58%
From public schools: 62%
Male/Female: 49%/51%
Live on-campus: 39%
In fraternities: 21%
In sororities: 22%
Off-campus employment rating: Excellent
Caucasian: 43%
African American: 7%
Hispanic: 23%
Asian / Pacific Islander: 5%
Native American: 0%
Mixed (2+ ethnicities): 2%
International: 13%

Academics

Calendar: Semester
Student/faculty ratio: 11:1
Class size 9 or fewer: 17%
Class size 10-29: 57%
Class size 30-49: 20%
Class size 50-99: 5%
Class size 100 or more: 2%
Returning freshmen: 91%
Six-year graduation rate: 81%
Graduates who immediately go to graduate school: 28%
Graduates who immediately enter career related to major: 57%

Most Popular Majors

Business/marketing
Biological/life sciences
Social sciences

Admissions

Applicants: 27,757
Accepted: 11,020
Acceptance rate: 39.7%
Average GPA: 4.2 (weighted)
ACT range: 28-32
SAT Math range: 630-720
SAT Reading range: 600-700
SAT Writing range: 23-50
Top 10% of class: 69%
Top 25% of class: 90%
Top 50% of class: 96%

782

tion to apply for Miami Commitment, a program specializing in gaining a head start on possible careers. "I've met with my mentor each month for career guidance," one student remarks. For any student, numerous internship opportunities are available due to the university's proximity to the professional bustle of the city of Miami.

Student Life

In addition to preparing for life after UM, students at Miami have seemingly infinite ways to enjoy the here and now, whether it is through student groups, athletics, or the arts. With over 270 student groups, there exists a group to spark everyone's interests, from Minority Women in Medicine, to Hip-Hop Club, to the group entitled Random Acts of Kindness. Common hang-out spots are the University Center and the Rathskeller (or "the Rat"), with many lounge areas, club meeting areas, and even celebrity sightings, such as Bo Burnham after his UM spring performance.

In addition to celebrity concerts, Miami hosts many events throughout the year. SportsFest is a three-day competition where players from the different residential colleges compete in 28 different athletic events. International Week is a week dedicated to exploring arts and culture through a display of music, food, and traditions from around the world. Philanthropy at UM shines through on Fun Day, when mentally-challenged citizens from the greater Miami area come to the university for a day of activities run by UM students. One of the biggest service days on campus is Ghandi Day, when 1,200 students volunteer at local service centers.

Philanthropy can also be pursued at UM through joining Greek life. About 21 percent of students at Miami choose to be part of the 21 fraternities and 15 sororities, which offer scholarships, leadership positions, and extensive social networks.

Greek and non-Greek students alike come together for athletic events at UM, due to the outstanding success of its 18 Division I varsity sports teams, the Hurricanes. The 'Canes have won five national titles in football, and the UM baseball team follows close behind with four. "School spirit reaches an ultimate high during football games," says a student. Tailgating for these events can be an all-day affair and a highly anticipated social gathering for UM student fans. Support continues even though more than 70 football players have been investigated since 2011 for allegedly receiving money and other gifts from a booster.

Any student can participate in athletics at UM through the intramurals program, which includes sports such as basketball, soccer, tennis, and even fantasy football. For those who simply wish to get into shape, the newly renovated Herbert Wellness Center offers top-of-the-line fitness equipment.

The excitement of student life at UM continues with the copious number of ventures available outside campus. The bars and clubs of Coconut Grove attract hoards of students in pursuit of lively nightlife, of which Miami has no deficit. By day, students head over to South Beach to enjoy the sun, partake in water sports, and grab lunch in charming beachside restaurants. "We have the best beaches in the country," brags a student.

After busy nights and days, some UM students return to dormitories, others to apartments, and still others to Greek houses.

The dormitories are in the form of residential colleges, Oxford and Cambridge style, each college fostering its own unique community. Colleges have live-in faculty and student staff, as well as dorm barbeques, faculty dinners, and guest speakers.

Student Body

The University of Miami holds an impeccable reputation for pro-social interaction among its student body. The university is known for diversity in student population, with high ethnic diversity (37 percent minority and 13 percent international), and moderate geographic diversity, with 58 percent of students hailing from out of state. Such an assortment in cultures and backgrounds results in no strong political or religious leanings, and instead appeals to global acceptance. "The atmosphere is laid back, and everyone is very friendly," says a student.

You May Not Know

- The Lowe Art Museum on campus houses the largest and most varied art collection in South Florida.
- During finals, the office of the president hangs hammocks and puts up large air-conditioned tents around campus so students have non-conventional places to study.
- Manatees lounge in the lakes and canals on campus.

Distinguished Alumni

Ralph Alvarez, President and COO of the McDonald's Corporation; Joseph A. Boyd, Jr., former Chief Justice of the Florida Supreme Court; Gloria Estefan, singer, songwriter, and five-time Grammy Award winner; Porfirio Lobo Sosa, current President of Honduras.

Admissions and Financial Aid

According to the university, "a competitive freshman student for admission has a strong A-/B+ average, around a 1320 SAT and/or around a 30 ACT test score, and ranks in the top 10 percent of the graduating class." The university requires the Common Application and has an early option.

Merit-based scholarships are offered regardless of need and are given out typically to 50 percent of the incoming freshman class. The Isaac Bashevis Singer Scholarship is a full tuition scholarship given to students with a top one percent class rank, an A+ average and a 34 ACT or 1500 SAT. The second largest scholarship is the University Scholarship which grants $24,000 annually for students in the top five percent class rank, with an A average and a 32 ACT or 1400 SAT. The Florida Bright Futures Scholarship, available to Florida residents, will not cover the full tuition at UM due to the university's private status.

UNIVERSITY OF MIAMI

Highlights

Admissions Criteria
Academic criteria:
Grades: ☆ ☆ ☆
Difficulty of class schedule: ☆ ☆ ☆
Class rank: ☆ ☆ ☆
Standardized test scores: ☆ ☆ ☆
Teacher recommendations: ☆ ☆ ☆
Personal statement: ☆ ☆ ☆
Non-academic criteria considered:
Extracurricular activities
Special talents, interests, abilities
Character/personal qualities
Volunteer work
Work experience
State of residency
Geographical location
Minority affiliation
Alumni relationship

Deadlines
Early Action: November 1
Early Decision: November 1
Regular Action: January 1 (final)
Notification of admission by: April 15
Common Application: Accepted

Financial Aid
In-state tuition: $41,580
Out-of-state tuition: $41,580
Room: $7,122
Board: $5,192
Books: $910
Freshmen receiving need-based aid: 48%
Undergrads rec. need-based aid: 47%
Avg. % of need met by financial aid: 80%
Avg. aid package (freshmen): $34,845
Avg. aid package (undergrads): $33,932
Avg. debt upon graduation: $26,786

School Spirit
Mascot: Sebastian the Ibis
Colors: Orange, green, and white
Song: *Alma Mater*

Four-year public
Founded: 1817
Ann Arbor, MI
Medium city
Pop. 114,925

Address:
515 East Jefferson
Street
Ann Arbor, MI
48109

Admissions:
734-764-7433

Financial Aid:
734-763-6600

www.umich.edu

The Ultimate
Guide to America's
Best Colleges

UNIVERSITY OF MICHIGAN

Overview

The University of Michigan isn't stretching the truth when it promises to have "something for everyone." It ranks fourth among public universities according to *U.S. News & World Report*. The school also has a vibrant, enthusiastic football culture—serious-minded students transform into screaming, chanting fans in the nearly 110,000-seat stadium. If you're intimidated by studying with almost 28,000 undergrads, rest assured that the average class size is just 10 to 19. In addition, unique living-learning communities like the Residential Colleges help foster close relationships between students and faculty similar to the stats of much smaller universities. While the academic life is challenging, there is a thriving social scene and lots to do in lively Ann Arbor. Over 1,350 organizations provide activities on campus for a highly diverse student body.

UM's sprawling campus has a mix of architectural styles, from modern to classical to gothic. The campus sits in Ann Arbor, an exemplary college town with a wide variety of food and entertainment options catering to students—especially those who like frozen yogurt and bubble tea. True to its name, Ann Arbor is unusually full of trees; students craving the attractions of a city but dreading the concrete jungle will feel comfortable because they literally get the best of both.

The major drawback of the university is that, while it has something for everyone, it does not have a reasonable price tag for out-of-state students. Merit-based and need-based financial aid packages are both available, though, and many merit scholarships are worth $20,000 a year. A relatively low percentage of students live on campus. This helps with finances, but social life, while quite healthy, isn't as dorm-based as at some schools.

UM is a well-rounded university that stretches students' minds without too much stressful competition, fosters diversity and inclusion, has a range of activities wide enough to please the pickiest student, and, to top it all off, plays a pretty good game of football.

Academics

UM is academically rigorous. "The atmosphere isn't cut-throat competitive, but students do challenge themselves," says a student. The university offers 60 concentrations (the equivalent of majors). The biology, engineering, and political science programs are especially respected. Preparation for premed and prelaw is also strong.

Students pursuing a Bachelor of Arts (called an AB at Michigan) must demonstrate fourth-semester foreign language proficiency, take one or two quantitative reasoning courses, and earn 30 credits spread across five categories outside their field. In addition, UM has two unusual, yet sensible, course requirements: an upper-level writing course and a class related to race and ethnicity. The writing course brings students up to speed on the specific kinds of writing needed in their own discipline. In the college's words, the race and ethnicity requirement "is to prepare students to live and work in a multi-ethnic, multi-racial environment."

First Year Seminars are optional courses limited to 20 students in a class. These studies allow freshmen to get to know their classmates, as well as a professor, in a comfortable environment. While there are about 60 seminars offered, spaces are highly coveted and can be difficult to attain. "The seminars are a more personalized experience," one student notes. Titles of FYS courses could be "Say It Loud: Black Culture in America," "Jane Austen and Economics," or "An Introduction to Cryptology."

The Honors Program at UM offers access to advanced courses, special lectures and programming, and the opportunity to live in honors housing. Students in these courses get more interaction with professors. Honors classes give students the best of both worlds—the resources of a large research university with the community and individualized attention of a smaller school. "Being in the program makes you work harder because you're surrounded by such talented people," one student remarks.

The Residential College (RC) is a living-learning community for liberal arts students. There are five concentrations specifically for RC students, but students who live in the RC can choose other areas of study as well. The hallmark of the RC is its small, interdisciplinary, highly-participatory bounty of courses.

The Undergraduate Research Opportunity Program, which has won several national awards, matches around 1,000 students with 600 faculty members and research scientists to engage in research, beginning in their first year. UROP funds the research, including a smaller number of Summer Research Fellowships Programs.

UM students can study abroad in 42 countries. Beyond traditional study-abroad programs, UM also offers the Global Intercultural Experience for Undergraduates, which sends students out for a three- to four-week summer service project followed by a year of additional intercultural coursework. Students in this program also participate in paid internships.

The Public Service Intern Program through the Career Center connects students with internships in Washington, DC with alumni mentors. The university has more living alumni than any other university—400,000 of them—so there are ample networking opportunities. "The alumni network is especially strong in Michigan and the areas nearby," one student notes.

Student Life

Students congregate at the "Diag," a quad in the center of campus. And for structured activities, there are a truly impressive 1,350 organizations to choose from, many of them multicultural. Other popular options include the Ballroom Dance Club, the Muslim Student Association, the Entrepreneur and Venture Club (145 members), and Habitat for Humanity.

Football is indeed a big deal at UM, and students pack the stands at home games. The stadium holds almost 110,000 fans eager to break into Michigan's rousing fight song, "The Victors." One student remarks, "Football is like a religion, and the players are like demigods."

Of course, there's much more going on than just football. At the Dance Marathon, hundreds continue dancing (or at least standing) for 30 hours to raise money for children's therapy at local hospitals. Powwow is another student-run event that is held off campus. It features competitions in American Indian dance, singing, and drumming.

Greek life is fairly prominent, with about one in six men and one fifth of women joining the 41 fraternities and 25 sororities. Greeks here are an unusually exclusive bunch—parties are open only to members. "There's a divide between members and non-members," one student comments.

As mentioned, UM is serious about its football—and with good reason. The Wolverines are Division I with 42 Big Ten championships and 11 national championships under their belts. The men's hockey team boasts nine national titles, and the men's basketball team has also won a national title. As you'd expect from UM's "something for everyone" reputation, the range of intramural sports is unbeatable.

Ann Arbor is a dynamic college town with plenty to do. Student-friendly stores, restaurants, and bars line Main Street. You might

UNIVERSITY OF MICHIGAN

Highlights

Students
Total enrollment: 43,426
Undergrads: 27,979
Freshmen: 6,351
Part-time students: 3%
From out-of-state: 40%
Male/Female: 51%/49%
Live on-campus: 34%
In fraternities: 16%
In sororities: 21%
Off-campus employment rating: Excellent
Caucasian: 65%
African American: 4%
Hispanic: 4%
Asian / Pacific Islander: 12%
Native American: 0%
Mixed (2+ ethnicities): 3%
International: 6%

Academics
Calendar: Trimester
Student/faculty ratio: 16:1
Class size 9 or fewer: 14%
Class size 10-29: 57%
Class size 30-49: 11%
Class size 50-99: 10%
Class size 100 or more: 7%
Returning freshmen: 97%
Six-year graduation rate: 90%

Most Popular Majors
Psychology
Business administration
Mechanical engineering

Admissions
Applicants: 42,544
Accepted: 15,551
Acceptance rate: 36.6%
Placed on wait list: 13,615
Enrolled from wait list: 74
Average GPA: 3.8
ACT range: 28-32
SAT Math range: 650-760
SAT Reading range: 610-700
SAT Writing range: 38-47

UNIVERSITY OF MICHIGAN

run into friends sipping bubble tea at one of several popular cafe hangouts or meet at the historic Michigan State Theater to catch a silent movie with live organ accompaniment. The Nichols Arboretum ("the Arb") is a picturesque location for a picnic date. "It's a great college town," says a student.

Housing is guaranteed for the first year, but only about 34 percent of the undergrad population lives on campus, making it somewhat of a residential ghost town compared to many schools. As a result, the social scene on campus is not bustling. The most coveted dorms are Mosher-Jordan Hall (aka "MoJo," making it a definite winner in the nickname department) and Baits I and II. Baits II is reserved for lucky freshmen.

Student Body

UM is so big that you can find an entire gamut of opinions on just about anything, but the majority of students are "politically liberal." There's more consensus when it comes to academic focus. UM is home to serious students, 84 percent of whom graduated in the top 10 percent of their high school classes. "Demonstrated intelligence is a prerequisite for coming here," says a student.

The university takes pride in its extremely high diversity, with a 23 percent minority student body. Geographic diversity is only moderate, probably because UM is such a great deal for in-state students.

You May Not Know

- Famous American composer John Philip Sousa called "The Victors," Michigan's fight song, "the best college march ever written."
- In 1866, the University of Michigan had the highest enrollment in the U.S.
- Ann Arbor is both the #1 college sports town according to *Forbes* magazine and the #4 town for families according to *Parenting* magazine.

Distinguished Alumni

Tom Brady, New England Patriots quarterback; Madonna, pop sensation; Arthur Miller, author of *Death of a Salesman*; Charles Walgreen, founder of Walgreen's drugstores.

Admissions and Financial Aid

Admissions follows a modified rolling schedule with decisions starting in the late fall until the spring. Apply in the early fall for the best chance of acceptance.

UM is hard on the checkbook for out-of-state students—even more so than some private colleges. There is some hope, though, through scholarships. Most awards are administered by specific colleges or schools and do not require separate applications. Around 150 College of Literature, Science, and the Arts freshmen receive scholarships of up to $20,000. Also, the need-based M-PACT program replaces loans with grants for in-state students whose Expected Family Contribution is $6,000 or less, removing the obstacle of crushing after-college debt for around 1,800 students.

UNIVERSITY OF MINNESOTA – TWIN CITIES

Overview

To enjoy the University of Minnesota Twin Cities (nicknamed "the U"), you should not be intimidated by crowds, sports, and harsh winters. Undergrads number a whopping 34,000, making for a wide variety of people to meet and things to do. The Golden Gophers are an athletic powerhouse in football, basketball, and ice hockey. To help students embrace the frigid winters, "Snow Week" tempts them with winter sports, hot chocolate, and movies.

Twin Cities has two campuses. The greener St. Paul campus hosts the food, agricultural, natural resource sciences and biological sciences colleges. The Minneapolis campus is the center for colleges, dorms, and Greek houses. This campus is itself divided between the East and West Bank of the Mississippi River. Campus is well-integrated with fun and hip Minneapolis neighborhoods. Students will never lack night and weekend outings. Overall, Minneapolis is more "happening" than you thought the Midwest ever could be.

Academically, research is the school's strongpoint. The Undergraduate Research Program even recruits incoming freshmen for guaranteed research positions. While the school's academics are generally rigorous—especially in engineering and business-related majors—classes are large and students must make an effort to stand out and to gain access to professors.

Academics

Academic requirements for liberal arts include typical distribution requirements (courses across a variety of fields) plus four writing-intensive courses after the freshman writing course. There are also classes in five "designated themes" relevant to 21st century life, such as "Diversity and Social Justice in the United States" and "Technology and Society."

Expect to be a face in the crowd in your classes. In 19 percent of courses, you'll be one of 50 or more students and you'll be lucky if your professor even knows you by sight (although you might get to know your TA very well). "It can be intimidating, but even in the largest classes you can go during office hours to meet with your professor," says a student.

There are 195 majors offered, and business-related majors and engineering are the U's strongest programs. If you're an academic achiever, you might rank among the 10 percent of students with access to the special programs, courses, advising, and residences available through the Honors Program.

In terms of special opportunities, the U has a few. Freshman seminars are an opportunity to be in a small class and interact directly with professors—they're capped at 20 students. The Four-Year Graduation Program offers a guarantee that, if you plan your course of study and pass your classes, the university will make sure that you can get into all the classes you need to graduate in four years. Failing that, you'll get approval for a substitute course or free tuition for the course you need if you have to stay longer than four years. While this sounds like a nice perk, the program also highlights that at such a big school "it can be a challenge to get the courses that you need," as noted by a student.

Research represents perhaps the best way to take advantage of the resources of a large school. The Undergraduate Research Office singles out students for guaranteed research positions based on their freshman application.

The U has a cornucopia of study-abroad opportunities—nearly 300 programs in over 60 countries. You can even study at a college somewhere else in the U.S. or Canada through the National Student Exchange. The U clearly recognizes that students need as many options as possible to get a break from Minnesota winters.

UNIVERSITY OF MINNESOTA – TWIN CITIES

Four-year public
Founded: 1851
Minneapolis, MN
Major city
Pop. 387,753

Address:
100 Church Street, SE
Minneapolis, MN
55455-0213

Admissions:
800-752-1000

Financial Aid:
800-400-8636

www.umn.edu

UNIVERSITY OF MINNESOTA – TWIN CITIES

Students

Total enrollment: 51,853
Undergrads: 34,469
Freshmen: 6,257
Part-time students: 16%
From out-of-state: 31%
Male/Female: 49%/51%
Live on-campus: 21%
Off-campus employment rating: Excellent
Caucasian: 70%
African American: 4%
Hispanic: 3%
Asian / Pacific Islander: 8%
Native American: 0%
Mixed (2+ ethnicities): 3%
International: 9%

Academics

Calendar: Semester
Student/faculty ratio: 21:1
Class size 9 or fewer: 14%
Class size 10-29: 51%
Class size 30-49: 15%
Class size 50-99: 11%
Class size 100 or more: 8%
Returning freshmen: 91%
Six-year graduation rate: 73%

Most Popular Majors

Psychology
Journalism
Political science

Admissions

Applicants: 38,174
Accepted: 18,900
Acceptance rate: 49.5%
Average GPA: Not reported
ACT range: 25-30
SAT Math range: 620-740
SAT Reading range: 540-690
SAT Writing range: 15-43
Top 10% of class: 44%
Top 25% of class: 80%
Top 50% of class: 99%

The U stands out for its great career opportunities on campus and off. The U of M job and internship fair fills the Minneapolis Convention Center with 250 employers, open exclusively to U of M students. There's also a unique program guaranteeing a job to the first 500 incoming freshmen who sign up. "The resources are there for you to take advantage of," one student comments.

Student Life

On campus, the Coffman Memorial Union is the place to be. The colossal building is home to a ton of study spaces (including a room with a view of the Mississippi); "Goldy's Game Room" with bowling, pool, and arcade games; the "Whole Music Club," a concert venue; in-house Starbucks and Jamba Juice; and student services like the post office and bookstore. "You can hang out all day there," says a student.

Snow Week is a fun and quirky week in February full of a number of winter events that range from dog sledding to ice skating to snow-related movie screenings and comedy shows. Spring Jam is the opposite of Snow Week—a week of events celebrating the April thaw with a student band competition, "ballyhoo" (a dance competition), and a campus block party. The quaintly-named Gophers After Dark events series is a great source of free late-night entertainment, from laser tag to murder mystery theater.

There are 29 social fraternities and 15 social sororities on campus with a low percentage of undergrads getting involved; however, those wishing to go Greek will find about 1,800 compatriots. One student explains, "Unless you walk through frat row, you won't really see much presence from the fraternities and sororities."

The Golden Gophers are one of only 13 colleges in the country with NCAA Division I and I-A football, men's and women's basketball, and ice hockey teams. The Gophers have an intense football rivalry with the University of Wisconsin-Madison Badgers, spurred by their equally unimposing, woodland mammal mascots. The football team has brought home six national titles, men's basketball has snagged two, and the hockey team—composed almost entirely of ice-adapted Minnesota natives—boasts three. The women's basketball team is nothing to sneeze at either, having played in six NCAA tournaments.

The U's campus is well-integrated with the city of Minneapolis, and there is convenient bus transportation to hip downtown areas. Minneapolis is a bustling metropolis, whose artistic, hip vibe gives life to the Midwest's stuffy image. For students, it has another plus: it's walkable and much more affordable than comparable destinations on the coasts. Besides a smorgasbord of nightlife, entertainment, and gallery options, the city boasts 17 farmers' markets, an annual Fringe Festival, 22 nearby lakes for all the water sports your heart desires, and shopping at the Mall of America. "There's always something to do or see," one student remarks.

Only 21 percent of students live on campus, so the social scene is not as campus-centered as at other schools. Housing options include dorms in the "Superblock," four halls on neighboring blocks. These halls, especially Centennial Hall, bear an unfortunate resemblance to poorly-designed housing projects. Still, Centennial has many single rooms and decent amenities. Two Superblock buildings are for freshmen only. The university also has apartment-style housing options, and there are 20 living learning communities based on interests and/or foreign language study, including special options for honors students.

Student Body

For the most part, students are fairly academically-focused, with 80 percent coming from the top quarter of their high school classes. "There is no U of M 'type,'" a student explains, "because our campus is so diverse." However, another student remarks that much of the student body is "involved in more than one activity and follows the sport teams."

The student body is moderately ethnically diverse (18 percent minority) and moderately geographically diverse (31 percent from out of state).

You May Not Know

- The U was founded in 1851, seven years before Minnesota officially became a state.
- University of Minnesota Twin Cities is the only public, Big 10 school in a major city.
- In the summer you can catch a vaudeville-style act courtesy of the U of M Showboat Players aboard the *Minnesota Centennial Showboat*.

Distinguished Alumni

Norman Borlaug, author and Nobel Peace Prize winner; Bob Dylan, singer and songwriter; Garrison Keillor, creator and host of *Prairie Home Companion*.

Admissions and Financial Aid

The admissions process at the U is more cut-and-dried than holistic. At least that means no pesky essay to write! The most important factors are your grades, rank, and standardized test scores. To be competitive, you should complete the core subject requirements or, even better, go beyond them.

Students from the Dakotas, Wisconsin, and Manitoba enjoy tuition reciprocity, which means their tuition will be lower than for most out-of-state residents.

University-wide and college-specific academic merit scholarships are available in amounts from $1,000 to $48,000, though most are closer to $1,000. The largest is the Maroon and Gold Leadership Award ($12,000 per year for four years) for Minnesota residents in the top three percent of their graduating classes. Athletic scholarships are available at the discretion of coaches and may be full or partial.

UNIVERSITY OF MINNESOTA – TWIN CITIES

Highlights

Admissions Criteria
Academic criteria:
Grades: ☆ ☆ ☆
Difficulty of class schedule: ☆ ☆ ☆
Class rank: ☆ ☆ ☆
Standardized test scores: ☆ ☆ ☆
Teacher recommendations: N/A
Personal statement: N/A
Non-academic criteria considered:
Extracurricular activities
Special talents, interests, abilities
Character/personal qualities
Volunteer work
Work experience
State of residency
Geographical location
Minority affiliation
Alumni relationship

Deadlines
Early Action: No
Early Decision: No
Regular Action: Rolling admissions
Common Application: Not accepted

Financial Aid
In-state tuition: $12,060
Out-of-state tuition: $18,310
Room: $4,730
Board: $3,802
Books: $1,000
Freshmen receiving need-based aid: 53%
Undergrads rec. need-based aid: 52%
Avg. % of need met by financial aid: 70%
Avg. aid package (freshmen): $12,910
Avg. aid package (undergrads): $12,756
Avg. debt upon graduation: $29,702

School Spirit
Mascot: Golden Gophers
Colors: Maroon and gold

UNIVERSITY OF
MISSISSIPPI

Four-year public
Founded: 1844
University, MS
Small town
Pop. 19,393

Address:
P.O. Box 1848
University, MS
38677-1848

Admissions:
800-OLEMISS (in-
state)

Financial Aid:
800-OLEMISS (in-
state)

admissions@olemiss.
edu

www.olemiss.edu

THE UNIVERSITY OF MISSISSIPPI

Overview

The University of Mississippi is a product of another time. The iconic image of the school is its Lyceum building, completed in 1848, with its stately white columns. The campus is nestled in a slow-paced yet surprisingly hip southern town once home to literary great William Faulkner—and not-so-literary yet still somewhat-great John Grisham. Students' idea of a good time on the weekend is donning preppy attire in the school colors and tailgating all day long. The school hosts a "Miss University" pageant while sororities and fraternities are a huge presence on campus. The university has a definite state school feel, with 62 percent in-state students and barely any international students.

Despite its strong connections to the past, "Ole Miss" is moving forward. In 2012, the university commemorated the 50th anniversary of the enrollment of James Meredith, the first African American student ever to attend the university. Meredith had to fight all the way to the Supreme Court and receive protection from U.S. Marshals and Army troops against rioting students and segregationists to walk through the doors of the university, despite his ample qualifications. Today, 17 percent of the student body is African American.

Academically, the school has some strong programs, especially in accounting, but it is not as academically well-known as some other state schools across the nation. Admission is not particularly competitive. Still, in-state tuition and an array of merit scholarships may make it a financially savvy choice for highly motivated students, especially if they can make it into the more academically rigorous environment of the Honors College.

Academics

The University of Mississippi requires all students to complete the requirements of its core curriculum in addition to those of their majors and minors. All freshmen must complete the 30-hours of required core curriculum courses: six hours of English composition; three hours of college algebra or quantitative reasoning or statistics; six hours of laboratory science; and 15 hours of humanities, social/behavioral sciences, and fine arts.

The university offers several special academic programs and is home to the well-regarded Sally McDonnell Barksdale Honors College (SMBHC). Honors students get priority course enrollment throughout their college career and can take advantage of special experiential learning opportunities, including Freshman Venture, a chance to travel anywhere in America to interview regular old Americans and learn what makes us tick. Honors students are also offered fellowships for study abroad and funding for unpaid internships. "There are a lot of perks of being an honors student, and we tend to hang out together," notes a student.

Academically gifted incoming freshmen may be invited to become Provost Scholars. Provost Scholars have access to enrichment programs outside class that allow them to schmooze with professors and the Provost as well as special courses and reserved sections of courses.

Students who are eager to begin their Ole Miss experience a little early and earn some credits can participate in the JumpStart program, which allows them to take courses the summer before their freshman year. For those who want another way to get adjusted to college life, The Ole Miss Experience (EDHE 105) is a freshman crash course on the university as well as life skills and study techniques. It is wildly popular with students, with up to 70 percent of freshmen enrolled.

The most popular academic programs at University of Mississippi are elementary education, marketing, and finance. The accounting program is very strong; UM boasts that their accountancy school is consistently ranked among the top 10 in the U.S. The school also hosts several unique research centers, including the Center for the Study of Southern Culture, Center for Intelligence and Security Studies, and National Food Management Service Institute.

Students who wish to study abroad may do so through the university's 80 exchange programs and affiliated programs. There are also short-term study abroad programs over summer and winter sessions, which could consist of international internships, language-intensive programs, or courses led by UM professors or faculty from partner universities.

In addition to opportunities outside the United States, the university offers several methods of gaining work or academic experience within the U.S. Through the Study USA program, students can travel across the U.S. to take unique field courses with UM professors during school breaks. Examples of recent courses include "Carson Mounds Archaeology Field School," "Exotic in Miami: Biology of Invasive Species," and "Las Vegas Resort Course."

Setting it apart from other universities with a less hands-on approach, UM does an especially good job of providing a support system for students who want to intern in Washington, D.C. The Washington Internship Experience is a semester combining an internship and academic coursework.

Student Life

Greek life is a major presence on campus at Ole Miss. There are 16 fraternities and 12 sororities on campus, which draw 31 percent of men and 36 percent of women. Recruitment can be quite competitive, especially for sororities. It's a tradition for women who have just received their sorority bids to run to their sorority house, where they will be greeted with gifts, food, and drink. It's also a tradition for the men of UM to sit on lawn chairs to get a prime view of the newly-minted sorority girls' run. "Our traditions may seem old-fashioned, but we just see them as having a good time," says a sorority member. Of course, like any large university, UM offers plenty of extracurriculars to keep students busy outside the Greek world—over 250 of them, in fact.

Whether the team is strong or not, to say the least, football games draw huge crowds and are the main focus of social life during the season. "Everybody, and I mean everybody goes to the football games," notes a student. Tailgating is extremely popular, to the extent that the game itself can feel like an afterthought. Preppy outfits in the school's signature crimson and navy are the order of the day.

Football isn't the only game in town, even if it feels like it. The university also has a decent men's baseball team. For those less inspired by a mainstream sports environment, intramural sports offerings include ultimate frisbee, volleyball, table tennis, and more.

Oxford, Mississippi is a charming town that mixes a progressive, bike-friendly vibe with a proud history and small town environment. There are regular events like "Sunday Shop and Dine" and the "Oxford Art Crawl" for town and gown alike to enjoy. There are several historic sites and museums to visit in town, the most famous of which is William Faulkner's old home, Rowan Oak.

Thirty percent of students live in on-campus housing at UM. Most freshmen live in "traditional halls," which is a euphemism for "average old dorms." Those who are in living learning communities or freshman-interest groups get an upgrade to more comfortable "contemporary halls," which have en suite bathrooms, study rooms and TV lounges. The university also offers residential colleges

UNIVERSITY OF MISSISSIPPI

Highlights

Students
Total enrollment: 18,794
Undergrads: 16,060
Freshmen: 5,052
Part-time students: 7%
From out-of-state: 51%
Male/Female: 45%/55%
Live on-campus: 30%
In fraternities: 31%
In sororities: 36%
Caucasian: 75%
African American: 17%
Hispanic: 3%
Asian / Pacific Islander: 2%
Native American: 0%
Mixed (2+ ethnicities): 2%
International: 2%

Academics
Calendar: Semester
Student/faculty ratio: 19:1
Class size 9 or fewer: 19%
Class size 10-29: 52%
Class size 30-49: 14%
Class size 50-99: 11%
Class size 100 or more: 3%
Returning freshmen: 81%
Six-year graduation rate: 58%

Most Popular Majors
Elementary education
Marketing
Finance

Admissions
Applicants: 13,934
Accepted: 8,507
Acceptance rate: 61.1%
Average GPA: 3.4
ACT range: 21-27
SAT Math range: 480-600
SAT Reading range: 480-600
SAT Writing range: Not reported
Top 10% of class: 17%
Top 25% of class: 47%
Top 50% of class: 77%

College Profiles

UNIVERSITY OF MISSISSIPPI

Admissions Criteria
Academic criteria:
Grades: ☆ ☆ ☆
Difficulty of class schedule: ☆ ☆ ☆
Class rank: ☆ ☆
Standardized test scores: ☆ ☆
Teacher recommendations: N/A
Personal statement: N/A
Non-academic criteria considered:
Special talents, interests, abilities
Character/personal qualities
State of residency

Deadlines
Early Action: No
Early Decision: No
Regular Action: Rolling admissions
Common Application: Not accepted

Financial Aid
In-state tuition: $6,660
Out-of-state tuition: $17,628
Room: Varies
Board: Varies
Books: $1,200
Freshmen receiving need-based aid: 49%
Undergrads rec. need-based aid: 52%
Avg. % of need met by financial aid: 74%
Avg. aid package (freshmen): $9,347
Avg. aid package (undergrads): $7,583
Avg. debt upon graduation: $23,986

School Spirit
Mascot: Ole Miss Rebels
Colors: Cardinal red and navy

"on the Oxford model," made up of students and professors living together in a community.

Student Body

Currently, the student body is 17 percent African American, two percent Asian, and three percent Latino. Fifty-one percent of enrolled students are from Mississippi, and international students make up only about two percent of the student body. Despite the relatively high percentage of students of color attending today and the university's efforts to increase diversity, campus culture is still dominated by preppy, conservative, white southerners who enjoy playing "Dixie" at football games, say some students. Recently, the university has gotten some bad press over a rally after Obama's election in which some yelled racial slurs and homophobic heckling at a performance of *The Laramie Project*. The university's bias investigation team took both events seriously and attempted to promote productive dialogue in their wake. "There are a minority of students who give our college a bad name. There are many more of us who don't share these views," states one student. In recent years, minority enrollment has been rising, as has the average GPA of admitted students.

You May Not Know

- Ole Miss's school colors, crimson and navy blue, are an homage to the colors of Harvard and Yale, respectively.
- The UM Medical Center in Jackson was the site of the world's first human lung and heart transplants, in 1963 and 1964, respectively.
- Each year, the school hosts a Miss University pageant for its female students. Winners go on to compete in the Miss Mississippi pageant. Two Miss University winners have won the Miss America crown.

Distinguished Alumni

Reuben Anderson, first African American Mississippi Supreme Court Justice; Harold Burson, founder of international PR firm Burson-Marsteller; William Faulkner, Nobel-prize winning author; John Grisham, best-selling author of legal novels; Michael Oher, Baltimore Ravens left tackle and inspiration for the film *The Blindside*; Eli Manning, New York Giants quarterback and two-time Super Bowl champion.

Admissions and Financial Aid

UM offers admission to students who meet minimum GPAs on the Mississippi College Preparatory Curriculum or minimum SAT or ACT scores. For example, Mississippi residents who have completed the CPC with a GPA of 3.2 are admitted. If you don't make the grade, rest assured that you can still be considered through a "comprehensive screening process (counseling and testing)." Students who do not pass the screening may be offered a chance to brush up on essential pre-college skills at a Summer Developmental Program at UM after their senior year of high school. At the other end of the spectrum, high-achieving students can be offered early admission at the end of their junior year. The university offers many merit scholarships.

UNIVERSITY OF MISSOURI - COLUMBIA

Overview

University of Missouri – Columbia, also known as MU or "Mizzou," is a very large public school in the Midwest: large not only in terms of student population (nearly 35,000) and campus size (1,372 acres and 372 buildings), but also in school spirit. With a powerhouse football team and the honor of beginning the tradition of Homecoming, Mizzou's Tigers are known to balance academics with a robust social life.

MU is about 120 miles from both Kansas City and St. Louis. The campus has a designated botanic garden with 18 buildings on the National Register of Historic Places that range in architecture from red brick to limestone. Visitors admire the distinctive MU Columns; Jesse Hall with its 105-foot dome that stands taller than the base of the building; and the Memorial Union archway, which people traditionally pass under while showing respect to the MU alumni who lost their lives in service to their country.

The largest of the University of Missouri schools, MU's library collection is the largest in the state. The college grants 25 percent of the state's bachelor's degrees from a public university, and 64 percent of the doctoral degrees. Some students could find such a large school overwhelming, but first-year programming and other opportunities can create a more intimate environment. Students happy to be immersed in the Midwest culture at a slightly conservative school, where sports and Greek life are a major part of the social scene, will find Mizzou to be a good fit.

Academics

Mizzou offers more than 280 degree programs through 19 schools and colleges. There are 92 bachelor's degrees and the option to design your own degree. To graduate, all students must satisfy requirements in math, English, writing, and American History/Government, and must complete a capstone course/experience. Strong programs include agriculture, journalism, health sciences, and degrees in the school of engineering.

Academic rigor varies from major to major, but for the most part students say they can handle their academic loads. "Sure we study but definitely not 24/7," says a student. While the student body is large, the school offers special programming for first-year students to adjust to the environment.

The MU Honors College is open to the top 15 percent of undergrads. Honors College is a self-proclaimed "University within a University" where students can enjoy small seminar-style courses, live in honors housing, and conduct independent research.

Aspiring leaders can participate in The Civic Leaders Internship Program (CLIP), which allows students to intern in publicly-funded offices. Students get academic credit, orientation, and ongoing support for internships.

The McNair Scholars Program prepares undergrads for graduate study. Students from low-income and underrepresented backgrounds have a chance to participate in a number of enrichment opportunities, including receiving a stipend to conduct research with faculty mentors. Student may also receive guidance through the grad school application process and can even prepare to be a teaching assistant.

With a semester of careful prior planning, MU students can study abroad through MU International Center, departmental, partner, and non-MU programs. Exchange programs enable transferrable tuition, and there are also internship and faculty-led programs.

Mizzou has more than 258,000 living alumni worldwide, nearly half of whom reside in the Missouri area, largely centered around St. Louis and Kansas City. "If you stay in the area, the alumni network is really powerful," remarks a student. The Career Center provides over 100 hours of training to student Career Specialists, who offer valuable support and advice.

UNIVERSITY OF MISSOURI – COLUMBIA

Students

Total enrollment: 34,748
Undergrads: 26,996
Freshmen: 7,467
Part-time students: 7%
From out-of-state: 35%
Male/Female: 48%/52%
Live on-campus: 26%
In fraternities: 22%
In sororities: 28%
Off-campus employment rating: Excellent
Caucasian: 80%
African American: 8%
Hispanic: 3%
Asian / Pacific Islander: 2%
Native American: 0%
Mixed (2+ ethnicities): 2%
International: 3%

Academics

Calendar: Semester
Student/faculty ratio: 20:1
Class size 9 or fewer: 19%
Class size 10-29: 51%
Class size 30-49: 15%
Class size 50-99: 8%
Class size 100 or more: 7%
Returning freshmen: 84%
Six-year graduation rate: 71%
Graduates who immediately go to graduate school: 30%
Graduates who immediately enter career related to major: 85%

Most Popular Majors

Business/marketing
Communications/journalism
Health professions/related sciences

Admissions

Applicants: 20,564
Accepted: 16,752
Acceptance rate: 81.5%
Average GPA: Not reported
ACT range: 23-29
SAT Math range: 530-650
SAT Reading range: 510-640
SAT Writing range: Not reported
Top 10% of class: 26%
Top 25% of class: 56%
Top 50% of class: 86%

794

Student Life

There are over 700 registered student organizations at Mizzou, with academic and service organizations among the most popular. Special interest clubs represent a gamut of interests, from ballroom dance to Collegiate Cattlewomen to Tigers for Tigers (tiger conservation). The student newspaper, the *Maneater*, comes out every Tuesday and Friday and has been published since 1955.

Mizzou boasts the largest student-run Homecoming in the nation—perhaps not surprising, given that the university began the Homecoming tradition for the nation in 1911. The annual parade and spirit rally draw thousands to campus, and there is an emphasis on community service, campus decorations, the talent competition, and other activities. MU holds the world's record for largest peacetime blood drive on a college campus during Homecoming. "Homecoming is what everyone looks forward to," explains a student.

The nickname "Tigers" has accompanied Mizzou's athletic teams since the Civil War period. The current mascot, Truman the Tiger, was named after President Truman, who was from Independence, Missouri. Before classes begin in August, the freshman class takes the Tiger Walk from Mizzou's Columns to Jesse Hall to symbolize their entrance into MU. Seniors take the Tiger Prowl upon graduation.

In the spring, exceptional student leaders are recognized during the annual Tap Day ceremony. Members of six honorary societies "tap" their new inductees into their societies—inductees whose identities have been kept secret until the day of the ceremony.

Mizzou has one of the largest Greek systems in the country, with 50 fraternities and sororities. About one quarter of the undergrad population (approximated at 6,000+ students) go Greek. Greek Town lies to the north of Memorial Stadium while Greek Row (a.k.a. Frat Row) lies in East Campus. Some of the Greek organizations even reside in historical residences worth millions of dollars. "You need to join or know someone who's a member to have the best social options," remarks a student.

Mizzou's 18 athletic teams (eight men's, 10 women's) compete in Division I. Football is by far the most popular sport, which befits a team known to be a national powerhouse. "Football games are pretty crazy," laughs a student. Mizzou is also strong in men's basketball and baseball. There are more than 40 clubs and recreational sports.

Columbia is a great college town for dining, shopping, and low-key entertainment. "If you look hard enough, there's something to do every night," says a student. St. Louis and Kansas City are each a couple hours drive away for bigger city activities.

Freshmen that are younger than 20 must live on campus. Students describe the dorms as "standard" and "what you'd expect." Freshmen have the option of living with housemates in one of over 100 Freshmen Interest Groups (FIGs). This amounts to living in the same housing and taking three classes with a group of 15-20 students. Other options include more than 20 Learning Communities, themed around academic majors and common interests.

Student Body

Mizzou's student body leans politically conservative. Many students are religiously devout and hail from the Midwest. For the most part,

Mizzou students are motivated academically. "I haven't met many slackers," comments a student.

There is moderate student diversity, with about 15 percent minority students. The school notes that in fall 2011, black student enrollment rose 10 percent and Latino student enrollment rose 12.8 percent. There is fairly low geographic diversity, with only about 35 percent of students hailing from out of state. Three percent of the student body are international students from more than 100 countries.

You May Not Know

- Walter Williams started the world's first school of journalism in 1908. On the first day of the school, the students and faculty published the *University Missourian*.
- MU held the nation's first Homecoming in 1911, when football coach C.L. Brewer encouraged "old grads" to "come back home" for the game against the University of Kansas.
- As part of their educations, students may operate a bed and breakfast, manage a floral shop, or work in the "country's only university-owned TV network affiliate."

Distinguished Alumni

Emily Newell Blair, co-founder of the League of Women Voters; Chuck Roberts, anchor, *CNN Headline News*; Elizabeth Vargas, co-anchor of *20/20*; Samuel Walton, founder of Wal-Mart.

Admissions and Financial Aid

Besides required coursework, Mizzou also has a formula based on class rank and test scores that determines whether a student qualifies for admission. Students with lower test scores can compensate with higher class rank, and vice versa. Students from non-ranking high schools are evaluated based on academic achievement and test scores.

In a recent year, MU students received $65 million in internal and external scholarship aid. Criteria for scholarships include merit (academics, athletics, community service), need, and special characteristics such as ethnicity, residence, intended major, and so forth. Students are automatically considered for some scholarships, while others require filling out the MU Annual Scholarship Application. Scholarships of $10,000 per year include the Dr. Donald Suggs Scholarship (for residents and non-residents) and the Mizzou Scholars Award (for Missouri residents only). According to MU, the college provides more than $244 million in financial aid each year.

UNIVERSITY OF MISSOURI – COLUMBIA

Highlights

Admissions Criteria
Academic criteria:
Grades: ☆ ☆
Difficulty of class schedule: ☆ ☆
Class rank: ☆ ☆ ☆
Standardized test scores: ☆ ☆ ☆
Teacher recommendations: ☆
Personal statement: ☆
Non-academic criteria considered:
Special talents, interests, abilities
Volunteer work
Work experience
State of residency
Minority affiliation

Deadlines
Early Action: No
Early Decision: No
Regular Action: Rolling admissions
Common Application: Not accepted

Financial Aid
In-state tuition: $9,272
Out-of-state tuition: $22,440
Room: Varies
Board: Varies
Books: $930
Freshmen receiving need-based aid: 53%
Undergrads rec. need-based aid: 50%
Avg. % of need met by financial aid: 79%
Avg. aid package (freshmen): $14,150
Avg. aid package (undergrads): $13,342
Avg. debt upon graduation: $23,588

School Spirit
Mascot: Tigers
Colors: Black and gold

UNIVERSITY OF MONTANA

Four-year public
Founded: 1893
Missoula, MT
Medium city
Pop. 67,290

Address:
32 Campus Drive
Missoula, MT
59812

Admissions:
800-462-8636

Financial Aid:
406-243-5373

admiss@umontana.
edu

www.umt.edu

Overview

The University of Montana at Missoula is a large public school—the largest of the University of Montana system—and offers a dynamic range of academic fields. The studies-focused student will find that the academic programs can be hit or miss, but the combination of the honors college and available merit scholarships can significantly sweeten the deal. UM is a scenic paradise for outdoorsy types, and the student body knows how to have fun.

UM is located in Missoula, MT, the second largest city in the state with a population of around 67,000. The campus is literally minutes away from the wilderness and features architecture ranging from redbrick to modern. If the outdoors makes you sneeze and the thought of a logging-themed dance makes you shudder, UM is not for you. But if you are looking for a large school and are already wondering how best to pack your fishing rod for college, UM is a great fit.

Academics

University of Montana offers a whopping 114 majors, and the strongest programs are wildlife biology, anthropology, and forestry. One student sums it up this way, "if you take one look at our campus, you'll understand why we're nationally recognized for wildlife biology and forestry." All students must complete coursework in each of 11 "groups," earning between 28 and 49 credits to fulfill general education requirements. The groups are as follows: English Writing Skills, Mathematics, Modern and Classical Languages or Symbolic Systems, Expressive Arts, Literary and Artistic Studies, Historical and Cultural Studies, Social Sciences, Ethics and Human Values, American and European Perspectives, Indigenous and Global Perspectives, and Natural Sciences. The level of academic rigor varies greatly between majors, but the extensive general education requirements help students scope out the difficulty level of different fields and find the one of greatest interest. Additionally, students say that professors tend to be helpful and accessible.

Freshmen participate in the First-Year Reading Experience, a study series centered on a single book. Events include workshops and panels on related topics as well as appearances by the author. In addition to this program, University of Montana's First-Year Interest Groups provide a comprehensive way to help students get to know other freshmen. While most school's first-year programs include a single first-year seminar, UM's FIG program is set up to have 15 to 20 students register for the same block of four to five classes related to a common interest. They also share a one-credit seminar led by a senior that acquaints them with campus life and activities. "I met some of my best friends through FIG. It's the best introduction you can have to the university and to other people," says a student.

Davidson Honors College is a great opportunity for 700 students to enjoy the perks of a smaller school within a larger university setting. Honors students take challenging courses capped at 20 students each. They also work closely with faculty, completing undergraduate research that culminates in a senior honors research project.

One drawback of the large student body is that it can sometimes be difficult to get into the courses that you want. To deal with this problem, the university has created the "Four Bear (Four Year) Graduation Plan" to give enrollment priority to full-time students committed to graduating after four consecutive years. If students have met all the program's requirements but still cannot graduate on time, the university will cover fees incurred after the planned graduation date. "My family appreciates that we won't have to pay for a fifth year of tuition, something that a lot of my friends at other public schools have faced," confides a student.

UM students can study abroad in 39 different countries through exchanges with partner universities, the International Student Exchange Program, or faculty-directed programs. In faculty-directed study, UM students travel abroad and earn credits for a course led by a UM professor. Most of these courses last a few weeks or span a winter-session.

The Office of Career Services administers the Ask-an-Alum Networking Program, which matches students with alumni for informational interviews, career mentoring, and job-shadowing. They also sponsor themed lunches bringing alums from different fields to campus for panel discussions.

Student Life

Like any large university, UM has a large number and a wide range of student activities, including 150 official student organizations. Marching and pep bands are among the most popular activities as are theater and service groups. Greek life is not a huge presence on campus, as there are only six social fraternities and four social sororities on campus with five frat houses and four sorority houses. One student explains, "there's so much to do outdoors that we aren't wrapped up in fraternities and sororities."

Beyond year-round activities, there are a few special events each year at UM, such as the Foresters' Ball, described as "an old logging town themed dance." If you can figure out what that means without scratching your head even a little bit, apply to UM immediately. Apparently, it has something to do with the old west, saloons, chili, a live band, a pretend jail, and a pretend wedding chapel. "There's no other dance in the country like the Foresters' Ball," laughs a student. "It's so fitting for our forested surroundings." Students who put in over 80 hours of work setting up for the dance receive the dances' profits in the form of scholarship money.

Slightly more conventional events include the homecoming celebration and Maggotfest. Homecoming is done in grand fashion with a big parade, an art fair, a 5K race, and of course a football game. "The lighting of the M" has been a homecoming tradition since 1919. Students put lights on a huge concrete M on the side of a hill to show their UM pride. Finally, Maggotfest is a popular weekend rugby tournament hosted by the Maggots, University of Montana's team. In the truly fun-loving spirit of the sport, teams play in costume, present humorous skits, and party all weekend long.

UM's 14 sports teams (six men's, eight women's) compete in Division I. Football is the most popular sport, and both basketball teams are also competitive. UM does not offer a huge variety of intramural sports, although inner tube water polo, always a college favorite, is among the choices. "We have so many options for outdoor sports that there's not much of a need for organized intramural sports," says a student.

Off-campus life at UM is mostly off the beaten path. There is an endless list of outdoor activities to take advantage of in the area: fly-fishing, camping, backpacking, rafting, and skiing, to name just a few. UM's outdoor program provides equipment rentals, organized trips, and a bike and ski maintenance shop where you can fix up your equipment. Students also frequent downtown Missoula to enjoy low-key entertainment, an off-beat atmosphere, and a quirky music scene. "It's not the big city, but there's plenty to do in Missoula," one student comments.

Most students at UM live off campus, so campus social life is not as bustling as at many other schools. However, freshmen must

UNIVERSITY OF MONTANA

Highlights

Students
Total enrollment: 15,669
Undergrads: 13,370
Part-time students: 20%
From out-of-state: 39%
Male/Female: 47%/53%
Live on-campus: 27%
In fraternities: 6%
In sororities: 6%
Off-campus employment rating: Fair
Caucasian: 85%
African American: 1%
Hispanic: 3%
Asian / Pacific Islander: 1%
Native American: 3%
Mixed (2+ ethnicities): 3%
International: 3%

Academics
Calendar: Semester
Student/faculty ratio: 20:1
Class size 9 or fewer: 16%
Class size 10-29: 62%
Class size 30-49: 12%
Class size 50-99: 5%
Class size 100 or more: 5%
Returning freshmen: 72%
Six-year graduation rate: 47%
Graduates who immediately go to graduate school: 21%

Most Popular Majors
Business administration
English
Education

Admissions
Applicants: 5,634
Accepted: 2,866
Acceptance rate: 50.9%
Average GPA: 3.3
ACT range: 21-26
SAT Math range: 490-590
SAT Reading range: 490-600
SAT Writing range: 3-16
Top 10% of class: 18%
Top 25% of class: 41%
Top 50% of class: 74%

797

College Profiles

UNIVERSITY OF MONTANA

Admissions Criteria

Academic criteria:
Grades: ☆ ☆ ☆
Difficulty of class schedule: ☆ ☆ ☆
Class rank: ☆ ☆ ☆
Standardized test scores: ☆ ☆ ☆
Teacher recommendations: ☆
Personal statement: ☆
Non-academic criteria considered:
Extracurricular activities
Special talents, interests, abilities
State of residency

Deadlines

Early Action: No
Early Decision: No
Regular Action: Rolling admissions
Common Application: Accepted

Financial Aid

In-state tuition: $6,071
Out-of-state tuition: $20,896
Room: Varies
Board: Varies
Books: $950
Freshmen receiving need-based aid: 63%
Undergrads rec. need-based aid: 62%
Avg. % of need met by financial aid: 59%
Avg. aid package (freshmen): $7,599
Avg. aid package (undergrads): $7,393
Avg. debt upon graduation: $20,532

School Spirit

Mascot: Grizzlies
Colors: Copper, silver, and gold
Song: *Up with Montana*

live on campus, and they are interspersed throughout campus housing rather than concentrated into designated freshman buildings or areas of campus. There are a couple of single sex dorms. Elrod Hall is one of the most popular residence halls because it has single rooms with personal sinks.

Student Body

The majority of the student body at UM is outdoorsy and environmentally conscious. Campus is an enclave for left-leaning students within the more conservative community surrounding the university. "Town-gown relations are fine, but we know that most of us differ politically from the people who live here," says as student. Ethnic diversity and geographic diversity are moderate.

You May Not Know

- It is rumored that Jeanette Rankin, the first woman in the U.S. Congress, haunts the campus building named after her.
- UM was named America's most scenic campus by *Rolling Stone* magazine.
- The campus library houses the oldest authorized edition of Lewis and Clark's journals.

Distinguished Alumni

A.B. Guthrie, Jr., novelist and winner of the Pulitzer Prize; George Montgomery, actor; Jeanette Rankin, first female member of the U.S. Congress.

Admissions and Financial Aid

Criteria for UM admissions include class requirements as well as admissions requirements that are based on standardized test scores and/or GPA. Students who do not meet these requirements may be admitted on a conditional basis and required to take preparatory courses.

Perhaps the most prestigious scholarship at UM is the Davidson Honors College Presidential Leadership Scholarship for incoming freshmen applying to the honors college. No separate application is required. In addition, students from Western states who have strong high school GPAs and high standardized test scores may be eligible for the Western Undergraduate Exchange Scholarship, which covers 150 percent of the price of in-state tuition. Also check with the academic department you are entering, as many administer their own merit scholarships.

UNIVERSITY OF NEBRASKA – LINCOLN

Overview

Ranked in the top 50 public universities by *U.S. News & World Report*, the University of Nebraska-Lincoln (UNL) stands strong academically. The university has notoriously earned this eminent standing, considering that the development of the first undergraduate psychology laboratory, the first awarding of a doctoral degree west of the Mississippi, and the birth of the discipline of ecology all occurred within UNL walls. A leader in research in both the sciences and humanities, UNL promises an invaluable education.

With more than 19,000 undergraduate students, this large public university boasts a formidable reputation in more than just academics. Students at UNL have over 500 student organizations available to join, and, of course, the University is famous for its athletics. The Huskers football team enjoys one of the best championship traditions in college football history.

Students who attend UNL will reside in the vibrant, bustling city of Lincoln, Nebraska. With a flourishing business community, a lively culture and entertainment scene, and the most parkland per capita in the nation, Lincoln was rated as the #1 U.S. city in quality of life by a 2004 State University of New York study. The university and the city of Lincoln are tightly intertwined, with the populace of the city enjoying cultural performances and exhibitions from the university's School of Music, Johnny Carson School of Theatre, and the Sheldon Museum of Art.

Currently in development is the Nebraska Innovation Campus plan, a sustainable research project. The 249-acre addition to campus will allow for private sectors as well as motivated students to become intimate partners of the university and its research efforts, encouraging economic growth for the state of Nebraska.

Academics

UNL emphasizes hearty academic development for its students by offering 150 majors. The general academic program at UNL is entitled Achievement-Centered Education and requires that courses in communication, math, science, history, social science, ethics, and global awareness be satisfied.

As can be expected from a large public university, the classes are also large, with 15 percent numbering over 50 students and introductory lecture courses often having several hundred. "You have to take the initiative to get help from professors or TAs," one student comments. Strong academic programs at UNL include agriculture, business, and communications. For those who enter freshman year without knowing their major, UNL's Division of General Studies works individually with students to help them explore a variety of fields.

A particularly strong aspect of the UNL education is the assortment of special academic programs offered. The Honors Program gives high-achieving students the opportunity to immerse themselves in research and to grow through the process of discovery in their field of work. The Raikes School of Computer Science and Management provides another venue for academic excellence, giving selected students the chance to become involved in expanding information technology and globalization of business. Students are chosen for this program based on academic excellence, leadership, and interest in the fields of computer science and business. Yet another enriched course is the Undergraduate Creative Activities and Research Experiences Program (UCARE) in which students pursue projects in a variety of fields, anywhere from "Effects of DES in Rats of Different Congenic Lines" in the animal science department, to "Prefabrication of the House in the Mid-Twentieth Century" in the architecture department.

UNIVERSITY OF NEBRASKA – LINCOLN

Four-year public
Founded: 1869
Lincoln, NE
Medium city
Pop. 262,341

Address:
14th and R Streets
Lincoln, NE
68588-0419

Admissions:
800-742-8800

Financial Aid:
800-742-8800, extension 2030

admissions@unl.edu

www.unl.edu

UNIVERSITY OF NEBRASKA – LINCOLN

Countless potential research projects are available to students through other venues, such as the Cedar Point Biological Station, the Summer Research Program, and the McNair Scholars Program for graduate students.

The university offers study-abroad programs it administers, exchange programs, affiliate programs, and independently approved programs. Students may opt to study abroad for a school year, semester, or during winter or spring break. "What they say is true: studying abroad will change your life," says one student.

The career services office offers a fall and spring career fair as well as an online virtual career fair, education recruitment day, mock interviews, and alumni of color career forum among other events. "There's help available," a student notes. "You just have to seek it out." The alumni association offers networking opportunities through its 60 chapters.

Student Life

Perhaps the most outstanding aspect of UNL is its 500 student organizations. They range from community volunteer groups, to nightlife activity committees such as Homecoming Committee, to Men's Bowling Club or the Master Bakers Association.

When their goal is simply to relax, students at UNL hang at the Student Union, a building offering a computer lab, study lounge, and art gallery, as well as a warm relief between classes during harsh Nebraska winters. Students particularly enjoy the art gallery, which houses art from around the world. "Admiring artwork gives perspective to a busy day," one student comments.

The allures of countless social events keep UNL students entertained. Jumpstarting the year is Big Red Welcome, a three-day festival of activities in August with free food, prizes, and entertainment. A long-standing tradition at UNL is Ivy Day, a day in November that is set aside to celebrate the success of university scholars by planting ivy on the grounds along University Hall. January ushers in a new year on the calendar as well as another anticipated event—Chinese New Year—a night filled with various parties, performances, and cultural celebrations. In addition, the university hosts more common events such as Homecoming celebrations, an end of year bash, and Greek Week. "We find something to celebrate throughout the year," one student laughs.

Greek organizations are a prominent part of student life at UNL, with 17 percent of men and 21 percent of women pledging the 29 fraternities and 19 sororities. Greek life offers not only social networking but also the chance for leadership positions, philanthropy projects, and a supportive, four-year academic community. In fact, students in the Greek programs at UNL exceed other students in average GPA. "It's not all about parties," one student comments.

The 23 varsity athletics teams at UNL participate in the Division I, Big 12 Conference, and collectively have won a total of 23 national titles. The football team alone has won five NCAA national titles and boasts three winners of Heisman trophies. The team plays in Memorial Stadium, housing 81,000 ecstatic fans and drawing in 300 consecutive sellout home football games. The fighting Huskers have won many titles in the female arena—in gymnastics, volleyball, and bowling, among others. For the non-varsity athlete, intramurals abound on campus, from track and field and sand volleyball to riflery and foosball.

For those students who crave off-campus entertainment, the city of Lincoln offers plenty of student-friendly bars and restaurants, as well as the acclaimed Haymarket shopping area. UNL students enjoy downtown Lincoln with its ideal college atmosphere, exploring shops and art galleries by day and taking advantage of over 100 nightclubs for evening entertainment.

Freshmen are required to live on campus and are given the choice of 17 difference residence halls, all of which provide central air conditioning, cable TV, and direct internet connection. The university also provides apartment-style halls, family housing, and academically-oriented housing options.

Student Body

UNL provides through sheer size a student body with diversity of interests. Ethnically and geographically, however, the university lacks diversity, with 10 percent minorities and only 20 percent of students hailing from out of state. "Where we lack in ethnic diversity, we make up for in diversity of interests," a student explains. "You'll find every kind of person here." Through its Diversity Recruitment Initiatives, the university strives to recruit low-income, multicultural students.

You May Not Know

- In 2009, $84 million of UNL's research funding came from federal funding such as the National Science Foundation, the Department of Energy, and the National Endowment for the Humanities.
- In 2007, the magazine *The Scientist* rated UNL eighth in its "Best Places to Work in Academia."
- The university houses the International Quilt Study Center and Museum, attracting visitors from around the world to view the world's largest collection of quilts.

Distinguished Alumni

Gene Budig, former commissioner of Major League Baseball's American League and current President of West Virginia University; Johnny Carson, former host of the *Tonight Show*; Ted Kooser, winner of 2005 Pulitzer Prize for Poetry.

Admissions and Financial Aid

A typical student seeking admission to UNL must either be ranked in the top half of his or her high school class or have received an ACT or SAT score of 20 or 950 respectively. Some colleges at the university have additional requirements. A personal statement (250 words or less) is not necessary for admission but is considered for certain merit-based scholarships that require high school class rank and ACT/SAT scores as well. One such scholarship, the David Distinguished Scholarship, is given to outstanding incoming freshmen and awards $1,000 a year for up to four years. The Regents Scholarship is awarded to outstanding Nebraska high school graduates and provides full tuition for up to four years.

UNIVERSITY OF NEBRASKA – LINCOLN

Highlights

Admissions Criteria
Academic criteria:
Grades: ☆ ☆
Difficulty of class schedule: ☆ ☆
Class rank: ☆ ☆ ☆
Standardized test scores: ☆ ☆ ☆
Teacher recommendations: ☆
Personal statement: N/A
Non-academic criteria considered:
Special talents, interests, abilities
State of residency

Deadlines
Early Action: No
Early Decision: No
Regular Action: Rolling admissions
Common Application: Not accepted

Financial Aid
In-state tuition: $6,480
Out-of-state tuition: $19,807
Room: Varies
Board: Varies
Books: $1,050
Freshmen receiving need-based aid: 53%
Undergrads rec. need-based aid: 46%
Avg. % of need met by financial aid: 78%
Avg. aid package (freshmen): $12,466
Avg. aid package (undergrads): $12,087
Avg. debt upon graduation: $23,280

School Spirit
Mascot: Herbie Husker
Colors: Scarlet and cream
Song: *There is No Place Like Nebraska*

College Profiles

Overview

Blue, the official color of the University of New Hampshire, speaks to the spirit of the campus—calm, collected, and scholarly. Founded in initial association with Dartmouth in 1866, the university was first located in Hanover before relocating to Durham in 1891. The college took on its current moniker in 1923.

Billing itself as a "land, sea, and space grant university," UNH offers its students exposure to life and learning in all three dimensions while they stroll and study on a campus embellished with the round arches and stone belt courses typical of its Romanesque Revival architecture. Yet the spirit of New England remains firmly lodged in the campus' buildings and lawns. And its host city Hanover boasts of its "rolling hills and riverbeds" and colorful founding during the American Revolution.

Students and faculty alike take advantage of the hour-long commute to Boston, and ski buffs can slalom to their hearts' content amid the nearby slopes. But UNH is more than just a warm lodge for winter athletes; the large public university sports manifold departments and research centers of which students may easily avail themselves.

Academics

More than 50 academic courses of study are on offer to students of the University of New Hampshire. The strongest include majors in environmental horticulture, biology, engineering, and history. Students are required to take one course each in writing skills, quantitative reasoning, historical perspectives, foreign culture (or study abroad), fine arts, social science, and works of philosophy, literature, and ideas. They must also complete three courses in biological science, physical science, or technology. "The requirements aren't too overwhelming," one student remarks.

The university offers a number of programs to promote undergraduate research. One student comments, "Research isn't limited to graduate students like at some schools." The Undergraduate Research Opportunities Program awards students grants and fellowships in order to fund research and creative projects, going so far as to even support traveling and registration fees associated with a student's endeavor. Similarly generous funding can be found overseas via the International Research Opportunities Program. "Highly motivated, first-year students" can reap hefty rewards through the Research Experience and Apprenticeship Program (REAP), which brings together students and appropriate mentors during the summer.

UNH also sponsors an Honors Program; smaller course sizes and international travel can be counted among the bonuses of Honors acceptance. In addition, students may live in an Honors residential hall, attend Honors courses, and receive individual advising. Students are invited to the program when they are accepted to the college. Those "typically" admitted "rank in the top 10 percent of their class with combined SAT scores of 1970 or higher or an ACT score of 29 or higher, and will have excelled in all areas of their secondary school's most challenging academic curriculum," according to the university.

Those itching to engage America's neighbors to the North can join the National Student Exchange Program and study at one of 180 U.S. or Canadian campuses for up to a full year. UNH has quite the resources needed for a quality study-abroad or exchange-abroad program. Highlights include summers at Cambridge, a junior year to be spent in Dijon, and an offering in New Zealand.

The University Advising and Career Center describes the scale of its resources with a modest phrase: "quite a lot!" A large database of job and internship leads are available as is daily walk-in advising. Students may connect with alumni through the Pathways Mentoring Program, which includes monthly mentoring meetings and three on-campus meetings.

Student Life

Out of the seemingly innumerable organizations on campus (there are around 200), a few emerge as highlights: the Hepcats Swing Club and Shotokan Karate Club are raves, and the Oyster Restoration Project has also attracted some newfound buzz. The New Hampshire Outing Club features many popular outdoorsy outings and owns two cabins in the White Mountains that can be rented for $5 per person per night. Trips include hiking Mt. Hancock and South Hancock, rock climbing at Patuckaway State Park, and camping at the Peak of Cadillac Mountain where campers can be "the first people in the U.S. to see the sun rise" according to the club. "We have access to hiking, rock climbing, canoeing, and skiing," one student boasts.

But nothing at UNH earns more clamor than its campus events. The most spectacular of such fests include the International Fiesta at Smith Hall, with international meals and entertainment taking place outside on the lawn of the eponymous residential house. Hockey and football own a huge presence on campus and perennially tout a large wave of campus-wide support. The Winter Carnival is a weekend of ski, sled, and snowshoe competitions, and student groups also pit themselves against one another in building snow sculptures. The annual JukeBox is held to introduce students to the many campus organizations, (although not in a staid way); past JukeBoxes have included bands, swing dance, and free hugs.

Nine percent of the student body participates in Greek life, joining one of the seven sororities or 11 fraternities sponsored by UNH. "Members and non-members still socialize together," one student remarks.

Athletically, UNH offers 18 Division I teams. The men's hockey team has appeared at the NCAA tournaments eight times consecutively, and the women's team for four. You may also want to keep abreast of any airborne perch—throwing a fish on the ice upon the team's first goal of a match is now a tradition. Students can also live it up over games of broomball. Intramurals include floor hockey, soccer, and softball.

At the nearby Dairy Bar, it's common to see students nursing tasty sundaes during study breaks, and volunteering activities also attract student attention. The 2,600 acres of forest, field, and farmland offer a plethora of opportunities right on campus for outdoor activities.

Housing is categorized into one of three types: exclusively freshmen, mixed-year, and upperclassmen-only. Students are first assigned their housing situation randomly. When given the choice, upperclassmen not unexpectedly opt to live in apartment-style residences.

Student Body

The best way to describe UNH's diversity would be "almost non-existent;" or below 10 percent. The university loses out on minority students to New England's better known institutions.

According to the students themselves, they are mostly "liberal politically" and rank academic focus as a high priority. More than half of students hail from New Hampshire.

UNIVERSITY OF NEW HAMPSHIRE

Highlights

Students
Total enrollment: 15,301
Undergrads: 12,811
Freshmen: 3,190
From out-of-state: 44%
From public schools: 75%
Male/Female: 46%/54%
Live on-campus: 57%
In fraternities: 8%
In sororities: 10%
Off-campus employment rating: Excellent
Caucasian: 82%
African American: 1%
Hispanic: 2%
Asian / Pacific Islander: 2%
Native American: 0%
Mixed (2+ ethnicities): 2%
International: 1%

Academics
Calendar: 4-1-4 system
Student/faculty ratio: 20:1
Class size 9 or fewer: 16%
Class size 10-29: 50%
Class size 30-49: 17%
Class size 50-99: 10%
Class size 100 or more: 6%
Returning freshmen: 86%
Six-year graduation rate: 77%
Graduates who immediately go to graduate school: 28%

Most Popular Majors
Business administration
Psychology
English

Admissions
Applicants: 17,234
Accepted: 13,433
Acceptance rate: 77.9%
Average GPA: Not reported
ACT range: 22-27
SAT Math range: 500-610
SAT Reading range: 490-590
SAT Writing range: 2-20
Top 10% of class: 18%
Top 25% of class: 50%
Top 50% of class: 90%

803

College Profiles

UNIVERSITY OF NEW HAMPSHIRE

Admissions Criteria
Academic criteria:
Grades: ☆ ☆ ☆
Difficulty of class schedule: ☆ ☆ ☆
Class rank: ☆ ☆ ☆
Standardized test scores: ☆
Teacher recommendations: ☆ ☆
Personal statement: ☆
Non-academic criteria considered:
Extracurricular activities
Special talents, interests, abilities
Character/personal qualities
Volunteer work
Work experience
Geographical location
Minority affiliation
Alumni relationship

Deadlines
Early Action: November 15
Early Decision: No
Regular Action: Rolling admissions
Common Application: Accepted

Financial Aid
In-state tuition: $13,670
Out-of-state tuition: $26,130
Room: $5,016
Board: $3,784
Books: $1,200
Freshmen receiving need-based aid: 69%
Undergrads rec. need-based aid: 67%
Avg. % of need met by financial aid: 78%
Avg. aid package (freshmen): $21,088
Avg. aid package (undergrads): $20,939
Avg. debt upon graduation: $35,168

School Spirit
Mascot: Wildcat
Colors: Blue and white
Song: *Fight for the Blue*

You May Not Know

- The first women were admitted as students in 1890.
- The University earned top marks in an evaluation of the campus' environmental sustainability, with a "grade" of A-.
- The awesome ASUM Club lets the beat roll on; students of any major can jam on an instrument of their choice with the organization.

Distinguished Alumni

Tricia Dinn-Luoma, Olympic Gold medalist; John Irving, novelist and screenwriter; Richard H. Linnehan, astronaut; Mike O'Malley, actor; Harl Pease Jr., Captain, World War II.

Admissions

What will get you in to the University of New Hampshire? Your academic record and the rigor of your program of study. These stand out as key indicators of admissions success; most students have earned averages of B+ or higher in their high school classes. Pay close heed as well to your standing and rank in your class, as the majority of those selected by UNH will have earned a rank in the top 25th percentile.

The excellence of your course of study can do more than get you accepted; it can serve as a marker of greater success. "That senior who has developed the highest ideals of good citizenship during his or her course of study" can earn the Class of 1899 Prize given to students at UNH.

Entering students are eligible for merit scholarships, including Governor's Success Scholarship for residents of $10,000 per year, the Presidential Scholarship for up to $10,000 per year, and the Dean's Scholarship for up to $6,000 per year. International students are eligible for out-of-state student scholarships.

UNIVERSITY OF NEW MEXICO

Overview

The University of New Mexico is the state's flagship research university and its largest post-secondary institution based on total enrollment. UNM's primary campus is located on 600 acres in the heights of Albuquerque, just one mile to the east of downtown. The central campus houses the main academic facilities, while the north campus is home to UNM's Schools of Law and Medicine. The south campus serves as the location for most of the university's athletic facilities.

UNM's Albuquerque campus is known for its unique "Pueblo Revival" architectural style, which was inspired by the New Mexican pueblos and Spanish missions. Popular outdoor spaces like the nationally renowned Campus Arboretum and the Duck Pond give students a taste of New Mexico's natural beauty and botanical diversity. In addition to its main campus, UNM also has branch campuses in Gallup, Los Alamos, Taos, Valencia, and a new campus, UNM West in Rio Rancho.

With such a large undergraduate population, most students at UNM live off campus in one of several surrounding neighborhoods in Albuquerque, a diverse city of over 500,000. Still, student life on campus remains fairly vibrant with the Student Union Building (SUB) serving as a center of activity. Overall the university is an excellent Southwestern option and one of the region's leading institutions.

Academics

UNM offers more than 215 degree and certificate options and 201 undergraduate majors. UNM also has nationally recognized programs in Latin American Studies, anthropology and photography. Other strong programs include electrical engineering, computer science, and environmental studies. All undergraduates must complete the university's Core Curriculum, roughly 37 credit hours of courses spanning writing and speaking, mathematics, physical and natural sciences, social and behavioral sciences, humanities, foreign language, and fine arts.

Freshmen entering UNM will find a number of academic programs designed to help first-year students make a smooth transition into college. Among these programs are Freshmen Learning Communities, or FLCs, which are small classes taught by distinguished faculty in a wide range of subjects. Freshmen Interest Groups, or FIGs, are available during students' first semester at UNM and are designed to place students with similar interests in small advising groups for two-class blocks. Similarly, during their first semester, freshmen can enroll in College Success Seminars (CSS), which, according to the college, are designed to "enhance each student's transition to University life." Students can also access the University Advisement Center for academic counseling, including dedicated advising for premed students.

In addition to providing strong undergraduate programs, UNM is also a growing research institution. It is currently ranked among the top five universities in funding received from National Institutes of Health (NIH), spending nearly $300 million annually for research. The university is home to expansive laboratory, computing, and information systems facilities, and it maintains collaborative ties with Sandia National Laboratories and Los Alamos National Laboratory. As part of its emphasis on research, UNM holds an annual Undergraduate Research and Creativity Conference, Ronald McNair Scholar Program, Profound, and WISE (Women in Science and Engineering). Freshmen are invited to participate in the new Research Quest Day, designed specifically to highlight work done by first-year students and others who are involved in Research Service Learning Programs. "If you want to research, this is the place to be," says one student.

Since some students wish to spread their wings overseas, UNM offers a variety of study-abroad options. Those who are involved in the Rome Program take classes focusing on Italian language, art, and culture. UNM also offers exchange programs

UNIVERSITY OF
NEW MEXICO

Four-year public
Founded: 1889
Albuquerque, NM
Major city
Pop. 552,804

Address:
1 University of New
Mexico
Albuquerque, NM
87131-0001

Admissions:
505-277-8900

Financial Aid:
505-277-8900

apply@unm.edu

www.unm.edu

UNIVERSITY OF NEW MEXICO

Students

Total enrollment: 29,033
From out-of-state: 11%
Male/Female: 44%/56%
Live-on campus: Not reported
Off-campus employment rating: Good
Caucasian: 39%
African American: 3%
Hispanic: 42%
Asian / Pacific Islander: 3%
Native American: 0%
Mixed (2+ ethnicities): 3%
International: 2%

Academics

Calendar: Semester
Student/faculty ratio: 26:1
Class size 9 or fewer: 18%
Class size 10-29: 55%
Class size 30-49: 14%
Class size 50-99: 10%
Class size 100 or more: 4%
Returning freshmen: 77%
Six-year graduation rate: 45%

Most Popular Majors

Business
Psychology
Elementary education

Admissions

Applicants: 11,467
Accepted: 7,405
Acceptance rate: 64.6%
Average GPA: 3.2
ACT range: 19-25
SAT Math range: 470-600
SAT Reading range: 470-610
SAT Writing range: Not reported

that allow students to study at a foreign university in one of 26 countries while earning credits toward their degree. For students who may not be able to spend an entire semester abroad, short-term programs are available during the summer.

During their time at UNM, students can prepare for post-graduation employment with the aid of the Office of Career Services. The OCS helps students connect to jobs and internships through on-campus recruiting, career fairs, and the Lobo Career Connection job and internship database.

Student Life

The Student Union Building, or SUB, houses a food court and a movie theater in addition to offices for student government and other organizations. Students are encouraged to get involved in the 400 student-run groups on campus, and of course if they cannot find an activity to suite their interests, they are welcome to start a new club. UNM's Recreational Services sponsors a variety of intramural sports, fitness classes, and even Getaway Trips where students can try rock climbing, whitewater kayaking, or scuba diving.

Popular traditions at the university include the Hanging of the Greens, a holiday celebration held in December when the campus is decorated with "farolitos" (small lanterns) and carolers make their way to the University House for hot cocoa and bizcochitos (a traditional cookie). The Red Rally is a large bonfire and pep rally held before the annual football game with rival New Mexico State.

For students interested in sorority or fraternity membership, there are 24 Greek chapters at UNM, several of which are housed. Still, the Greek community remains small, with a population of only about 500 students.

UNM boasts 16 NCAA Division I athletic teams. The Lobos basketball teams play at "the Pit," the university arena that is known for its ferocious atmosphere, which came in 13th in *Sports Illustrated's* rankings of the top 20 sports venues of the century. The women's basketball team is also successful and has reached the NCAA tournament for the past six years, winning the conference title in four of the last five seasons. Lobos football also continues to impress, having played in four recent NCAA bowl games.

With many adult and part-time students—as well as a large majority of undergraduates—living off campus, much student activity takes place outside the campus proper. Albuquerque is a rapidly growing city with a population estimated to reach one million within the next two decades. As such, it provides plenty of entertainment for students with a variety of bars and restaurants, nightclubs, and a diverse range of museums, theaters, dance companies, and festivals occurring throughout the year. Famous events include the Albuquerque International Balloon Fiesta, which fills the desert skies with hot air balloons, and the Gathering of Nations PowWow, which draws dancers, singers, and drummers from over 500 tribes. For the outdoor enthusiasts at UNM, hiking and biking trails abound in the surrounding Sandia and Manzano foothills. Skiing is also only a short drive away in the winter, as Albuquerque is literally one of the nation's highest major cities, with an elevation ranging from 4,900 to 6,700 feet above sea level.

Living on campus is another way for students to get involved with life at the university. UNM provides dormitory, apartment, and suite-style housing. Residence halls have free internet access, cable television, and much needed air conditioning to combat the hot climate. The university's 1,975 housing units are filled on a first-come, first-served basis.

Student Body

One factor that makes University of New Mexico's student body unique is the large number of non-traditional students. The university enrolls approximately 11,500 evening and weekend adult students, and 25 percent of undergraduates are part-time students. "There's not a lot of time shared between traditional and adult students because part-time students are usually working while we're in class," explains one student.

Ethnic diversity among the student body at UNM is high, with 51 percent of students coming from minority backgrounds and 42 percent noted as Hispanic. With a student population that spans not only racial frontiers but age frontiers as well, UNM maintains a diverse political and social climate, and there are opportunities for activism regardless of one's ideological orientation.

You May Not Know

- UNM's KUNM-FM radio station is one of two National Public Radio stations in Albuquerque. In 2008 it won the Associated Press award for Station of the Year.
- UNM's Model United Nations team ranks as one of the best in the nation, having won awards at the Harvard World Model United Competition.
- The UNM Fiestas is a popular end-of-the-year festival held every spring that includes Spring Storm, a community service event, as well as a large concert.

Distinguished Alumni

Shirley Hufstedler, first United States Secretary of Education; Bruce King, former three term Governor of New Mexico; Brian Urlacher, Chicago Bears linebacker.

Admissions and Financial Aid

The most important factors for admission to UNM are the applicant's secondary school record and standardized test scores. The university also reviews and takes into account its applicants' personal statements and extracurricular involvement, but teacher recommendations are not required. Decisions for admission are made on a rolling basis, so potential students are encouraged to apply early.

Those students that have been high achievers in high school are eligible to compete for a number of UNM's merit-based scholarships. The university offers scholarships available for both New Mexico residents and out-of-state students, with some scholarships, such as the Regents' and National Scholars awards, totaling up to $13,875 per academic year and renewable for four years.

UNIVERSITY OF NEW MEXICO

Highlights

Admissions Criteria
Academic criteria:
Grades: ☆ ☆ ☆
Difficulty of class schedule: ☆ ☆ ☆
Class rank: N/A
Standardized test scores: ☆ ☆
Teacher recommendations: N/A
Personal statement: N/A
Non-academic criteria considered:
State of residency

Deadlines
Early Action: No
Early Decision: No
Regular Action: Rolling admissions
Common Application: Not accepted

Financial Aid
In-state tuition: $6,447
Out-of-state tuition: $20,688
Room: Varies
Board: Varies
Books: Varies
Avg. aid package (freshmen): $5,430 for grants or scholarship aid, $5,278 for student loans
Avg. aid package (undergrads): $9,905 for grants or scholarship aid, $7,165 for federal student loans

School Spirit
Mascot: Lobos
Colors: Cherry and silver
Song: *Hail to Thee New Mexico*

UNIVERSITY OF NORTH CAROLINA – ASHEVILLE

Overview

As one of the smallest schools of the 16-school University of North Carolina system, the midsized UNC Asheville can offer students the feeling and community of a small liberal arts school while at the same time drawing on the resources of the extensive UNC system. Recognized as a leading public liberal arts school, UNC Asheville offers an in-depth core curriculum, and large lecture classes are rare. The community feeling on the school's 265-acre campus in the Blue Ridge Mountains extends to the city of Asheville just one mile south, a lively and eclectic center for arts, culture, food, and a healthy dose of political protest.

Academics at UNC Asheville are what you make of them: classes are not necessarily demanding, but students who are motivated enough to take advantage of the special programs UNC Asheville offers will find plenty of equally academically-focused peers, access to faculty, research opportunities, and a commitment to undergraduate education not always found at its bigger counterparts. UNC Asheville's funky vibe may not appeal to everyone, but if the drum-circle coffee-shop scene isn't your thing, then maybe the region's bountiful outdoor recreation opportunities are: UNC Asheville sits at the intersection of the Swannanoa and French Broad Rivers, prime territory for white-water rafting, hiking, and mountain biking. Options and flexibility uncharacteristic of institutions its size are UNC Asheville's main draws, along with a feeling of community and plenty of activities.

Academics

UNC Asheville offers 35 majors. Students must complete the extensive Integrative Liberal Studies general education curriculum. The curriculum begins with an introductory liberal studies colloquium. In addition to that, students must also complete an array of classes organized under "Learning Foundations" (academic writing, foreign language proficiency, math, lab science, and health and wellness) and "Intensives" (information literacy, quantitative reasoning, diversity, and three writing courses) as well as humanities and arts requirements and a "Topical Cluster," a set of a natural science, social science, and elective courses organized around a broad theme. Finally, students must participate in a capstone senior colloquium.

UNC Asheville's students who are interested in challenging themselves academically have a range of special programs to choose from. "You can choose to challenge yourself or you can choose to take it easy depending on your major and how much else you get involved in," says a student. Some of the introductory colloquia at UNC Asheville are designated as Freshman Living Learning Intensive Program (FLLIP) classes; freshmen who choose one of these classes are housed together in Founders Hall, where the faculty teaching FLLIP classes and special FLLIP residential education staff coordinate class-related co-curricular activities.

Students in the Honors Program take Honors sections of the Integrative Liberal Studies requirements, special topics courses, and an Honors Liberal Studies Senior Colloquium with a required service-learning component. All Honors classes have fewer than 15 students, and students are eligible for special travel opportunities, including the Honors Semester in London.

UNC Asheville places a strong emphasis on service-learning. Every year in September, the freshman class takes part in Active Citizens Together (ACT) during Asheville Day, a community-wide service function. A number of classes are also designated as Service Learning Courses, which are facilitated by a service-learning adjunct; some of these courses can include service trips, such as one that was taken to Bolivia. "The service work I did was so rewarding that I would have done it even without earning college credit," says a student.

UNIVERSITY OF NORTH CAROLINA – ASHEVILLE

Four-year public
Founded: 1927
Asheville, NC
Medium city
Pop. 84,458

Address:
1 University Heights
Asheville, NC
28804

Admissions:
800-531-9842

Financial Aid:
828-251-6535

admissions@unca.edu

www.unca.edu

808

The Ultimate Guide to America's Best Colleges

Several programs are aimed at students with specific academic interests. UNC Asheville accommodates engineering students with two programs offered in conjunction with North Carolina State University. Students in the Two-Plus-Two Engineering Program spend their first two years at UNC Asheville and then transfer to NCSU to complete their majors; they can also take advantage of NCSU's co-op education program.

A Joint UNC Asheville-NCSU Bachelor of Science in Engineering degree with a concentration in Mechatronics allows students to remain on the UNC Asheville campus for all four years, completing an engineering-themed liberal arts core while studying "Mechatronics," combining mechanical, electrical, and computer engineering.

Highly qualified North Carolina residents who plan on a career in teaching can apply to the Teaching Fellows Program, which awards students a four-year scholarship of $26,000 and covers tuition, books, fees, and some summer programs. Students complete a bachelor's while also earning their teaching licenses and can participate in summer programs at Cambridge and the Winter Adventure Trip to schools throughout the country. Following completion of the program, students must teach for four years in state public schools.

Students interested in environmental sciences have access to research opportunities at the National Environmental Modeling and Analysis Center, a multi-disciplinary research institution that not only conducts research in forest sustainability and flood mitigation but also specializes in "science communication," working to improve the public sector's "climate literacy" and to help develop decision-making tools for policy-makers and planners.

Students in all fields can conduct their own research with funding from the Undergraduate Research Program. Students may work with faculty mentors for at least one term or summer to complete a scholarly or creative work that is to be either published or presented. Students are eligible for travel grants as well as research funding; in summer, students can also earn a stipend.

UNC Asheville offers its own study-abroad programs, led by faculty and held over spring break (Costa Rica, Bolivia) or summer (the UK, Greece and Turkey, Italy, Ghana, Spain). The university has a small number of direct exchange agreements with institutions in the UK, France, Japan, South Korea, and Hong Kong. Students can also participate in the UNC system's exchange programs, which include schools in more than 40 countries.

The Career Center, in addition to offering help in choosing majors and careers, cover letter and resume critiques, mock interviews, and job and internship fairs, also runs the alumni Mentor Network Program. Within 10 years of graduating, 43 percent of graduates earn a graduate degree.

Student Life

Almost 50 student organizations are active at UNC Asheville, including the *Blue Banner*, the weekly student newspaper; ASHE Student Environmental Action Coalition, the largest student-run environmental organization in the country; and the Bulldog Stompers, the "clogging" (as in the shoes) club. With only two sororities and two fraternities, Greek life is peripheral.

A number of all-campus celebratory events are held throughout the school year, beginning with Block Party, a carnival featuring

UNIVERSITY OF NORTH CAROLINA – ASHEVILLE

Highlights

Students
Total enrollment: 3,751
Undergrads: 3,693
Freshmen: 717
Part-time students: 17%
From out-of-state: 17%
Male/Female: 42%/58%
Live on-campus: 38%
In fraternities: 3%
In sororities: 3%
Off-campus employment rating: Good
Caucasian: 85%
African American: 3%
Hispanic: 4%
Asian / Pacific Islander: 1%
Native American: 0%
Mixed (2+ ethnicities): 3%
International: 1%

Academics
Calendar: Semester
Student/faculty ratio: 14:1
Class size 9 or fewer: 13%
Class size 10-29: 76%
Class size 30-49: 9%
Class size 50-99: 1%
Class size 100 or more: -
Returning freshmen: 78%
Six-year graduation rate: 55%

Most Popular Majors
Psychology
Health/wellness promotion
Literature

Admissions
Applicants: 3,018
Accepted: 1,926
Acceptance rate: 63.8%
Average GPA: 4.1 (weighted)
ACT range: 23-27
SAT Math range: 550-640
SAT Reading range: 550-650
SAT Writing range: 6-31
Top 10% of class: 22%
Top 25% of class: 62%
Top 50% of class: 96%

UNIVERSITY OF NORTH CAROLINA – ASHEVILLE

Highlights

Admissions Criteria
Academic criteria:
Grades: ☆ ☆ ☆
Difficulty of class schedule: ☆ ☆ ☆
Class rank: ☆ ☆
Standardized test scores: ☆ ☆ ☆
Teacher recommendations: ☆ ☆
Personal statement: ☆ ☆
Non-academic criteria considered:
Interview
Extracurricular activities
Special talents, interests, abilities
Volunteer work
Work experience
Geographical location
Minority affiliation
Alumni relationship

Deadlines
Early Action: November 15
Early Decision: No
Regular Action: Rolling admissions
Common Application: Accepted

Financial Aid
In-state tuition: $6,242
Out-of-state tuition: $20,064
Room: $4,522
Board: $3,334
Books: Varies
Freshmen receiving need-based aid: 53%
Undergrads rec. need-based aid: 57%
Avg. % of need met by financial aid: 77%
Avg. aid package (freshmen): $10,699
Avg. aid package (undergrads): $11,852
Avg. debt upon graduation: $17,696

School Spirit
Mascot: Bulldogs
Colors: Royal blue and white

food, games, and rides. Just before finals in spring, the Lawn Party offers carnival rides, games, and food as well as comedians and concerts to help students unwind; faculty also cook a midnight breakfast for students during exam weeks. Of UNC Asheville's 11 Division I athletic teams, men's basketball is by far the most popular, and basketball games are major events. "There is no more excitement than at a home game," remarks a student. The season kicks off with Jammin' at the Justice, which features music and every college student's favorite, "lots of free stuff."

Students who aren't varsity athletes can take advantage of the Health and Fitness Center's facilities, which include a dance studio and multipurpose courts, or they may choose to play one of six intramural sports. UNC Outdoors offers kayaking, white-water rafting, rock-climbing, and spelunking trips in the nearby national and state parks and forests. "If you don't do outdoor activities, you're missing out on half of the college experience here," says a student.

Students can catch the free city bus to Asheville, a pedestrian-friendly downtown that offers plenty of artsy and eclectic shopping and dining, as well as the Orange Peel, ranked by *Rolling Stone* as one of the country's top five entertainment venues. Asheville is home to a large population of hippies, aging hippies, and hippies-turned-yuppie, which makes for a quirky and politically active atmosphere.

Freshmen are required to live on campus; upperclassmen may opt to do so but more frequently move off campus. Residence halls are suite-style.

Student Body

A good portion of the student body is academically focused. "We get the work done that needs to get done," notes a student. Given Asheville's status as a hippie town, the campus tends to lean to the left. "Some of the hippie vibe rubs off on us," laughs a student. Most students are from in state, making ethnic diversity low.

You Might Not Know

- Students pat the head of the statue of Rocky, the school mascot. It is located in front of the Justice Athletics Center and the tradition is that a pat will bring good luck. The Bulldog mascot has previously been named Puck, Chug-A-Lug, and Winston.
- During the Great Depression, UNC Asheville accepted vegetables, eggs, and milk as tuition payments.
- The nearby Biltmore Estate is the largest private residence in the country.

Distinguished Alumni

Kenny George, tallest player in NCAA basketball history; Wilma Dykeman Stokely, writer; Ty Wigginton, professional baseball player.

Admissions and Financial Aid

UNC Asheville does not stipulate minimum GPAs or test scores, but students must fulfill the state's high school graduation requirements.

Merit scholarships are available, ranging from $1,000 to the full cost of tuition. To be considered for these, students must submit their applications and supplemental materials by November 15.

UNIVERSITY OF NORTH CAROLINA – CHAPEL HILL

UNIVERSITY OF NORTH CAROLINA – CHAPEL HILL

Four-year public
Founded: 1789
Chapel Hill, NC
Large town
Pop. 58,011

Address:
South Building, CB #9100
Chapel Hill, NC 27599-9100

Admissions:
919-966-3621

Financial Aid:
919-962-8396

unchelp@admissions.unc.edu

www.unc.edu

Overview

A public university with over 18,000 undergraduate students, the University of North Carolina at Chapel Hill stands out in more ways than one. The school has a long history—it opened in 1789 as the nation's first public university—and it is often called a "public ivy," a tribute to its strong blend of academics and athletics. Located eight miles south of Durham, the beautiful Chapel Hill campus boasts 729 acres, as well as an art museum, planetarium, and numerous botany-related locales, including an arboretum, garden classrooms, and a botanical garden.

Contrary to the belief that greater size means sacrificing quality and individual success, UNC-Chapel Hill provides first-rate academics and is ranked the fifth best public university by *U.S. News & World Report*. Although some classes have over a hundred students, the school offers several programs which create smaller communities.

UNC sports—especially men's basketball—are big, and most students turn out to support them. More than 500 student organizations and numerous annual traditions represent the spirit of the "Tar Heels" and keep this "first public university" at the top of the charts.

Academics

Academics at UNC-Chapel Hill represent the university's endless resources—the school offers 223 majors. Strong undergraduate programs include journalism and business. In order to graduate, students must complete three "approaches" and four "foundation" courses. The "foundation" core consists of a two-part sequence in written and oral communication, a foreign language, quantitative reasoning, and "lifetime fitness." The "approaches" courses include two classes in physical and life sciences, three in social and behavioral sciences, and two in humanities and fine arts. Students who enroll in the College of Arts and Sciences must complete an additional nine hours.

Classes at UNC come in a range of sizes: most introductory classes have over 50 students, and some lectures have several hundred. Upper level classes are often fewer than 20 students and provide a more intimate setting and direct interactions with professors. "The only advantage to the very large class size is that you can hide at the back of class," laughs a student.

One alternative to large undergraduate lectures is First Year Seminars, classes of no more than 24 students that range in content from building a robot to writing a play, or studying geology in a natural setting instead of using textbooks. Students relish the opportunity to interact in a close-knit environment and thrive on the excitement that their professors bring to teaching interesting subjects through hands-on methods.

UNC has an Honors College that is quite selective, offering early admission to 200 high school students, with a few later opportunities for applications as well. Classes are fewer than 24 students, and the college matches students with advisors based on study interests. The Honors College is the "best way to take advantage of everything the college has to offer," notes a participant.

UNC provides ample study-abroad opportunities, with over 300 programs in 70 countries. Undergrads receive 12-18 hours of credit for each semester abroad and can study for a summer or a whole year. Students can also explore the world through school-funded research and may apply for up to $750 for small research grants, or $3,000 for research (such as a summer-long program) through the Office of Undergraduate Research. Any student can participate in or design a project and can work in nearby Research Triangle Park, the largest research park in the nation. Students may also apply to the Carolina Research Scholar Program, earning the title of "Carolina Research Scholar" on their transcript. To be eligible, students must complete one multi-disciplinary course and two research-intensive courses, as well as make a pre-

UNIVERSITY OF NORTH CAROLINA – CHAPEL HILL

Students
Total enrollment: 29,278
Undergrads: 18,503
Freshmen: 4,298
From out-of-state: 16%
From public schools: 79%
Male/Female: 42%/58%
Live on-campus: 46%
In fraternities: 17%
In sororities: 17%
Off-campus employment rating: Excellent
Caucasian: 66%
African American: 9%
Hispanic: 8%
Asian / Pacific Islander: 8%
Native American: 1%
Mixed (2+ ethnicities): 3%
International: 3%

Academics
Calendar: Semester
Student/faculty ratio: 14:1
Class size 9 or fewer: 7%
Class size 10-29: 59%
Class size 30-49: 21%
Class size 50-99: 6%
Class size 100 or more: 7%
Six-year graduation rate: 89%
Graduates who immediately go to graduate school: 28%
Graduates who immediately enter career related to major: 53%

Most Popular Majors
Psychology
Biology
Journalism/mass communication

Admissions
Applicants: 28,437
Accepted: 7,847
Acceptance rate: 27.6%
Placed on wait list: 2,986
Enrolled from wait list: 194
Average GPA: 4.5
ACT range: 27-32
SAT Math range: 610-710
SAT Reading range: 590-690
SAT Writing range: 24-47
Top 10% of class: 79%
Top 25% of class: 97%
Top 50% of class: 99%

sentation of research. The university provides funding for students to conduct internships including stipends for non-profit, arts, and summer internships. There are several career fairs offered during the school year. Of those who work after graduating, 53 percent work in a field related to their major within one year of graduating.

Student Life

Although over half the student body lives off campus, UNC is active with 543 student-run clubs and groups. These range from sports and wellness, such as the meditation club, to civil rights clubs and hobby groups, such as the Honduran Health Alliance and the Kiteboarding Club. Groups include 32 fraternities and 23 sororities, which engage approximately 17 percent of the student body.

UNC has strong varsity sports that participate in Division I athletics (Division I-A for football) in the Atlantic Coast Conference. The school has won 37 NCAA national titles. Men's basketball is also popular, having won six national titles, and these games attract nearly 22,000 fans to watch rivals such as Duke and North Carolina State University. "Football is the big sport at other colleges, but here it's basketball," one fan notes.

Club and intramural sports offer several options to students, ranging from Aussie Rules Football to Texas Hold 'Em teams. The Outdoor Education Center boasts facilities that include 11 tennis courts, three sand volleyball courts, an 18-hole golf course, a climbing wall, and a 20-acre wooded space.

Fallfest, the first school-wide celebration of the year, welcomes students back with a giant celebration. That sets the tone for future events such as Midnight Madness, the annual first night of the basketball season, where the UNC men's and women's teams show off their talents—a win during basketball season guarantees that everyone will celebrate on nearby Franklin Street. "It is a huge all-night, all-campus party," one student remarks. The university also hosts outdoor movie nights, picnics for residence halls, and music events in Memorial Hall.

Off campus, students enjoy the vibrant college town of Chapel Hill. There are plenty of restaurants and bars catering to students, and Duke and North Carolina State are close by. "We don't lack things to do," one student comments.

For students living on campus, the university provides single-sex and co-ed dorms, fraternity and sorority houses, and apartments. Over 80 percent of freshmen choose to live on campus, most in South Campus, which creates a smaller community feeling. Students can also choose Living-Learning Community housing, in which students with similar interests, such as foreign languages or community service, can live together. "Living in the dorms is the best opportunity to make close friends," one student explains.

Student Body

True to its geographic roots, UNC has an air of southern hospitality, along with somewhat more conservative political leanings. "People will hold the door open for you, and everyone is overly friendly," says a student. More than 65 percent of the student population is Caucasian, and three-fifths are women. Due to North Carolina state law—at least 82 percent of students must be from within state—geographic diversity is low, and many attendees are local. Over 90 percent of students attend full time, though, and students do come from every state and more than 100 countries, so the school retains a feeling of diversity.

Despite their conservative bent, students certainly have a diversity of views about politics, religion, and every issue imaginable. Numerous clubs support various religious and ethnic interests.

You May Not Know

- The school's official mascot—a ram—was chosen in 1924 by a cheerleader because Jack Merritt, a popular member of the football team, was nicknamed the "Battering Ram."
- The school has produced more Rhodes Scholars in the past five years than any other public university.
- UNC-Chapel Hill was chartered the same year that George Washington was inaugurated as the first President of the United States.

Distinguished Alumni

Erskine Bowles, former White House Communications Director, President of the University of North Carolina System; John Edwards, former U.S. Senator and presidential candidate; James K. Polk, former U.S. President.

Admissions and Financial Aid

UNC has strong academics, and looks for students who will contribute to that environment. The school does not accept the Common Application. Admission for out-of-state students is particularly difficult, as they compete for only 16 percent of spots within the incoming class. All applications are read at least two times, though—often three—to guarantee that the school selects the best class that it can.

UNC offers many merit- and need-based scholarships. The Morehead-Cain Scholarship, billed as the oldest merit scholarship in the nation, funds students for four years and four summers at UNC. Starting the summer before freshman year, students pursue work in outdoor leadership, public service, international relations, and private enterprise. The Robertson Scholars Program, available to approximately 18 students each from UNC and Duke, is another full-coverage merit-based award that allows students to take advantage of the faculty and programs from both universities.

The Carolina Covenant guarantees that qualified students who need financial aid will be able to attend UNC and can graduate debt-free if they work 10-12 hours a week in a federal work-study job. Covenant Scholars also receive academic support to help them thrive in college.

UNIVERSITY OF NORTH CAROLINA – CHAPEL HILL

Highlights

Admissions Criteria

Academic criteria:
Grades: ☆ ☆ ☆
Difficulty of class schedule: ☆ ☆ ☆
Class rank: ☆ ☆ ☆
Standardized test scores: ☆ ☆ ☆
Teacher recommendations: ☆ ☆ ☆
Personal statement: ☆ ☆ ☆
Non-academic criteria considered:
Extracurricular activities
Special talents, interests, abilities
Character/personal qualities
Volunteer work
Work experience
Minority affiliation
Alumni relationship

Deadlines

Early Action: October 15
Early Decision: No
Regular Action: November 3 (priority)
January 7 (final)
Common Application: Accepted

Financial Aid

In-state tuition: $8,340
Out-of-state tuition: $30,122
Room: $5,756
Board: $4,252
Books: $1,328
Freshmen receiving need-based aid: 43%
Undergrads rec. need-based aid: 43%
Avg. % of need met by financial aid: 100%
Avg. aid package (freshmen): $15,939
Avg. aid package (undergrads): $15,983
Avg. debt upon graduation: $16,983

School Spirit

Mascot: Rameses the Ram
Colors: Light blue and white
Song: *Hark the Sound*

UNIVERSITY OF NORTH CAROLINA - GREENSBORO

Four-year public
Founded: 1891
Greensboro, NC
Medium city
Pop. 273,425

Address:
P.O. Box 26170
Greensboro, NC
27402

Admissions:
336-334-5243

Financial Aid:
336-334-5702

admissions@uncg.edu

www.uncg.edu

Overview

The University of North Carolina - Greensboro is a large public university with strengths in the liberal arts and sciences, as well as a strong reputation in lesser known programs like kinesiology, human development, and family studies. While the school's academic intensity depends upon one's chosen major, students praise their professors' dedication across the board. High achievers can take advantage of the university's honors programs, including an international honors program showcasing the university's commitment to global education. When it comes to social life, students say the scene can be cliquish, although the heavily-female student body is highly ethnically diverse.

UNCG is close to downtown Greensboro, about 80 miles northwest of Raleigh, and 100 miles northeast of Charlotte. The campus features architecture ranging from red brick colonial to modern. The amenities of Greensboro and the proximity of other schools ensure that students find plenty to do off campus.

UNCG's low tuition makes it a steal for in-state students. The university has further committed itself to a unique all-expenses-paid scholarship and support program called the "UNCG Guarantee" for students living at the poverty level.

Academics

UNCG offers 85 undergraduate majors, including strong programs in nursing and education. The school's general education requirements are extensive, mandating courses in each of the following categories: humanities and fine arts, historical perspectives, natural sciences, mathematics, reasoning and discourse, and social and behavioral science. In addition, students must take four Global Perspectives courses (which may include up to two language courses), two writing intensive courses (one within the major), and two speaking intensive courses (one within the major). The level of academic rigor varies from major to major, but students enjoy the overall high quality of instruction and the accessibility of professors. "All of my professors really care about teaching and go above and beyond," says a student.

Thanks to a $6 billion donation, UNCG has just begun the "UNCG Guarantee" program. The Guarantee offers full scholarships—including room and board, textbooks, and other related expenses—to students whose families live at or below the poverty line. In addition to the scholarship, Guarantee Scholars attend special programs and workshops. They are also matched with alumni mentors who promise to devote at least five hours each month to mentoring.

Highly dedicated professors teach freshmen seminars, which focus on developing critical reading and writing skills. "We had really deep discussions in the literature seminar," relates one student. Another opportunity not to be missed is the chance to go on an Alternative Spring Break trip. Each year, a small group of students and faculty travels to spend the spring break on service-learning rather than sun-tanning.

UNCG has two different honors programs. The International Honors Program is for incoming freshmen and transfers, and it includes small classes (usually fewer than 25 students) with an international focus, study abroad, and language classes. IHP students also participate in regular lunch discussions and can present papers at the Undergraduate Honors Symposium. The Disciplinary Honors Program is for students who are already at UNCG and have earned a 3.3 GPA. Students get the chance to collaborate with professors to create individualized courses in their major. The program culminates in a senior Honors research or creative project.

UNCG has extensive study-abroad offerings, including partnerships with over 90 programs in 20 countries. In most cases, the cost of studying abroad for a semester is comparable to the cost of a semester at UNCG. International Honors students each receive a $1,300 grant for a semester or year abroad and $450 for a summer abroad.

The Career Services Center runs highly useful events with a fun flair to prepare students for the working world. Highlights include Schmooza Palooza, a crash course in networking followed by a chance to put those skills to work with alumni and local professionals. Additionally, students can apply for $1,000 in funding for internships, participate in on-campus recruiting, and connect with alumni through a mentoring network.

Student Life

There are over 200 official student organizations at UNCG. Some of the most popular and influential are groups like the student newspaper, the *Carolinian*; and the student-run radio station. Students also flock to *Coraddi*, a fine arts magazine, and *Kaleidoscope*, a video magazine. Greek life plays a fairly important role on the campus, which is home to 10 social fraternities and 10 social sororities. However, as one student explains, "Greek parties are not the only thing happening on campus."

Students celebrate their university's birthday on Founder's Day, Oct. 5, by adorning a statue of the university's first president, Charles Duncan McIver, with a wreath. They also attend commemorative events like a session led by the university archivist and enjoy a reception. Spring Fling has less history but perhaps is more fun. During an April weekend, the university brings famous musical performers and comedians to entertain students. Other Fling events run by students include a fashion show and a step performance. At the annual International Festival, students can wander among booths representing over 30 countries, sampling traditional foods and learning more about a variety of cultures. There are also a number of international music and dance performances to enjoy.

UNCG boasts 16 varsity teams (eight men's, eight women's) that compete in Division I. Men's and women's soccer and men's basketball are the most competitive. There are intramurals as well, including standard offerings like soccer and volleyball.

Downtown Greensboro is a destination for dining, shopping, and entertainment. Students hang out at the Spring Garden Bar and Grill or grab a slice at New York Pizza. Several nearby colleges provide a chance to meet people outside of UNCG. "Because there are so few guys here, it's a huge plus to be able to meet them from other colleges," explains a student. For the adventurous, the great outdoors beckons with beaches and mountains just a few hours away from campus.

Students are not required to live on campus, and many do not. "The high rises and Quad are not great, and that's where most freshmen are placed," says a student. Students may choose to live in Special Interest Communities, which bring students closer to faculty members affiliated with their living community and provide built-in social circles. Some SICs include an academic component, bringing students together in the classroom as well as the residence hall.

Student Body

There is a heavy female skew in the student population at UNCG. The school is highly ethnically diverse, but students describe the social scene as "often segregated by ethnic group, fraternity or

UNIVERSITY OF NORTH CAROLINA – GREENSBORO

Highlights

Students
Total enrollment: 18,172
Undergrads: 14,674
Freshmen: 3,618
Part-time students: 12%
From out-of-state: 8%
From public schools: 95%
Male/Female: 34%/66%
Live on-campus: 30%
In fraternities: 4%
In sororities: 4%
Off-campus employment rating: Good
Caucasian: 59%
African American: 25%
Hispanic: 6%
Asian / Pacific Islander: 4%
Native American: 0%
Mixed (2+ ethnicities): 4%
International: 1%

Academics
Calendar: Semester
Student/faculty ratio: 17:1
Class size 9 or fewer: 20%
Class size 10-29: 51%
Class size 30-49: 16%
Class size 50-99: 10%
Class size 100 or more: 3%
Returning freshmen: 76%
Six-year graduation rate: 54%

Most Popular Majors
Psychology
Elementary education (K-6)
Business administration

Admissions
Applicants: 10,108
Accepted: 6,065
Acceptance rate: 60.0%
Average GPA: 3.5
ACT range: Not reported
SAT Math range: 470-560
SAT Reading range: 460-560
SAT Writing range: 1-9
Top 10% of class: 23%
Top 25% of class: 48%
Top 50% of class: 80%

815

College Profiles

UNIVERSITY OF NORTH CAROLINA – GREENSBORO

Admissions Criteria
Academic criteria:
Grades: ☆ ☆ ☆
Difficulty of class schedule: ☆ ☆ ☆
Class rank: ☆
Standardized test scores: ☆ ☆ ☆
Teacher recommendations: ☆
Personal statement: ☆ ☆
Non-academic criteria considered:
State of residency

Deadlines
Early Action: January 15
Early Decision: No
Regular Action: Rolling admissions
Common Application: Accepted

Financial Aid
In-state tuition: $3,932
Out-of-state tuition: $17,730
Room: $5,950
Board: $2,998
Books: $1,300
Freshmen receiving need-based aid: 81%
Undergrads rec. need-based aid: 81%
Avg. % of need met by financial aid: 54%
Avg. aid package (freshmen): $9,665
Avg. aid package (undergrads): $9,827
Avg. debt upon graduation: $24,199

School Spirit
Mascot: Spiro the Spartan
Colors: Blue and gold
Song: *The University Song*

---

sorority, or athletic team." Geographic diversity is very low. As one student put it, "if you aren't from North Carolina, you may not feel very at home."

You May Not Know

- It's not surprising that the student population is overwhelmingly female, since men were not admitted until 1964.
- UNCG is home to an award-winning opera theater.
- In 2005, the university built a new clock tower with chimes that mimic Big Ben.

Distinguished Alumni

Claudia Emerson, Pulitzer Prize-winning author; Emmylou Harris, Grammy-winning singer/songwriter; Beth Leavel, Tony-winning Broadway actress.

Admissions and Financial Aid

UNC-system schools require a weighted GPA of at least 2.3, a threshold that students must meet in order to be considered for admission. The university encourages students to apply during the fall to receive a decision by mid-December, although students may apply as late as March 1.

There are 30 scholarships awarded each year to incoming freshmen through the Merit Awards Program. Scholarship amounts range from $2,500 to full tuition and can also cover fees, room and board. Winners typically have a minimum SAT score of 1250 or ACT score of 27 and a minimum GPA of 3.5. A separate Merit Awards Program application is required.

UNIVERSITY OF NOTRE DAME

Overview

Notre Dame is a medium-sized private university that is at the forefront of Catholic higher education in the United States. The university is highly selective and has strong academic programs, including a renowned theology department and an optional "Great Books" curriculum for liberal arts students.

Faith plays a central role in life at Notre Dame. The vast majority of students are Catholic, but the school tries to foster a sense of inclusion. The university even promises to help students of other faiths find transportation to and from their own services. All students must take two theology courses, but they do not have to be related to Catholicism. Despite the university's commitment to welcome students who are not Catholic, the Catholic ethos pervades life at Notre Dame, especially when it comes to dormitories. Students can attend masses in each dorm. All dorms are single-sex, and students of the opposite gender are not allowed in private rooms after certain hours.

Besides Catholicism, the most important religion at Notre Dame is football. Students burst with pride for the "Fighting Irish," and football games are highly popular events.

There is not much to do in South Bend, Indiana, although Notre Dame's campus—with its abundance of greenery, lakes, and the striking Golden Dome—is a tourist attraction in and of itself. With construction of the "Eddy Street Commons" completed, Notre Dame has a more traditional college town area nearby.

Notre Dame is a perfect fit for cream-of-the-crop devoutly Catholic students. Other students should consider that academics are taught in a highly religious atmosphere, and that there is minimal social life. The lackluster Midwestern location may also make it less attractive, despite the sterling academics.

Academics

Students can choose from 121 majors at Notre Dame. Programs in English, history, engineering, and, of course, theology are the stand-outs. Students applaud professors for being highly "involved" and for demonstrating an intense "passion for teaching." The general academic requirements are strikingly simple when compared to the intricate dictates of other schools: one course in composition, two in math, two in science, one in history, one in social science, two in theology, two in philosophy, one in fine arts or literature, and two in physical education. In addition to these requirements, different colleges have their own supplementary requirements.

When students arrive on campus, they will find themselves safely ensconced in the First Year of Studies program, regardless of college or major. All first years follow the standard First Year Curriculum, with much hand-holding from full-time advisors who want to ease student adjustment to college and help newcomers select courses. "The extra attention helps," says a student. In April, students enter upper-level programs in their chosen departments.

After the first year, students may choose to enter the three-year Program of Liberal Studies. Centered on "Great Books" courses, the school prides itself on this program's interdisciplinary characteristics and intellectual depth. Take note: the program publicizes that it offers "seminars and tutorials anchored in the Western and Catholic traditions," so avant-garde it is *not*. Square as it may seem to some though, it is an opportunity to take "intimate classes" with "dedicated professors" and to meet one-on-one with a professor and develop a senior essay.

The Department of Theology, one of the most highly-regarded departments at the university, is a unique asset. It is at the forefront on topics like liberation theology and the Dead Sea Scrolls. Besides its intellectual firepower, the Department of Theology offers small classes, helps students develop spiritually, and encourages

UNIVERSITY OF NOTRE DAME

Four-year private
Founded: 1842
Notre Dame, IN
Medium city
Pop. 5,973

Address:
220 Main Building
Notre Dame, IN
46556

Admissions:
574-631-7505

Financial Aid:
574-631-6436

admissions@nd.edu

www.nd.edu

817

UNIVERSITY OF NOTRE DAME

Students
Total enrollment: 12,126
Undergrads: 8,475
Freshmen: 2,014
From out-of-state: 92%
From public schools: 42%
Male/Female: 53%/47%
Live on-campus: 80%
Off-campus employment rating: Fair
Caucasian: 72%
African American: 3%
Hispanic: 10%
Asian / Pacific Islander: 7%
Native American: 0%
Mixed (2+ ethnicities): 3%
International: 4%

Academics
Calendar: Semester
Student/faculty ratio: 11:1
Class size 9 or fewer: 15%
Class size 10-29: 54%
Class size 30-49: 21%
Class size 50-99: 8%
Class size 100 or more: 3%
Returning freshmen: 97%
Six-year graduation rate: 97%

Most Popular Majors
Finance/business economics
Government/international studies
Accountancy

Admissions
Applicants: 16,957
Accepted: 3,947
Acceptance rate: 23.3%
Placed on wait list: 2,461
Enrolled from wait list: 86
Average GPA: Not reported
ACT range: 31-34
SAT Math range: 680-770
SAT Reading range: 660-750
SAT Writing range: 54-38
Top 10% of class: 89%
Top 25% of class: 97%
Top 50% of class: 100%

community service. The department boasts, "students at Notre Dame cite the vibrant spiritual life on campus as a special reason they enjoy living and studying here."

At Notre Dame, more than half of the student body studies abroad. There are 40 programs affiliated with the university in 20 countries. In addition to traditional study-abroad programs, there are special intern-abroad options as well. For instance, premeds may be tempted by medical internships in Puebla, Mexico or in London.

The Career Office at Notre Dame has the usual smorgasbord of offerings, including many off-campus career fairs. There is also a Wall Street Externship Program that lasts three days to three weeks during the summer, but participation is limited to around 20 students. Formal programs fostering connections between alumni and current students for networking are "not very prominent," says a student. Thirty-seven percent of students attend graduate school within one year of graduating.

Student Life

There are 350 official student organizations at Notre Dame, with the most popular activities related to music, theater, politics, and service. There are no Greek organizations on campus, but service plays a big part of life at Notre Dame, with over 80 percent of students participating in such activities.

If you like to break it down, you won't lack opportunities at Notre Dame. Every two weeks, residence halls host dances for students, including formals. Additionally, the university also hosts a week-long spring festival called An Tostal with games, food, carnival rides, and performances. At the start of the fun, the swim team hosts "Pig Tostal," a pig roast.

The Notre Dame Literary Festival (formerly the Sophomore Literary Festival) is held every spring and brings well known authors to campus to give presentations and host workshops. Past guests have included such greats as Kurt Vonnegut, Arthur Miller, and Tennessee Williams. Students have the chance to read their own work at this student-run literary extravaganza.

Notre Dame has a storied football legacy. Games are an all-weekend affair with pep rallies on Friday nights, tailgating before Saturday games, and, of course, the games themselves. Frank Leahy, a former football head coach at Notre Dame, summed up the importance of the game by saying, "lads, you're not to miss practice unless your parents died or you died." The program made national news when the death of the girlfriend of its star linebacker Manti Te'o was discovered to be a hoax in 2013. "We were the butt of many jokes," notes a student.

"To say that football is a religion would be an understatement," says a student. But while "Fighting Irish" football is the most prominent sport in the public eye, basketball is also popular among students; and the school can boast another success in that the women's swimming and diving team has won 14 conference championships.

South Bend—where Notre Dame is located—is anything *but* a cultural capital. Still, it is not bereft of activity. You can catch a show at the Morris Performing Arts Center or, if you can't get enough football on campus, check out the College Football Hall of Fame. Fiddler's Hearth, an old-fashioned public house (translation:

pub), hosts live Irish music. Of course, you'll always have the great outdoors, with a nearby botanical garden and a famous open-air farmer's market.

Notre Dame is home to 29 single-sex dorms. To help keep student morals sparkling clean, Notre Dame generously supervises gender mixing by enforcing "parietals," hours during which members of the opposite sex are permitted in individual dorm rooms. Students describe parietals as "restrictive" and the "absolute worst thing about Notre Dame." However, every residence hall has a lounge where co-ed mingling is allowed 24 hours a day.

The university has recently built two new dorms, Duncan Hall for men and Ryan Hall for women, but the rest of the dorms are relatively old. Each hall has a chapel and holds mass every week. Every hall also has a rector—a member of a religious order, a priest, or a lay person. These persons act as "teachers, counselors, disciplinarians, and friends" to dorm residents.

Student Body

Due to the presence of so many religious students, the student body tends to lean to the right. More than 80 percent of students are Catholic. "You won't be excluded if you're not Catholic, but you will feel more included if you are," notes a student. Ethnic and geographic diversity are high.

You May Not Know

- The official name of the university is Notre Dame du Lac, "Our Lady of the Lake."
- The large mural depicting Christ—visible from the football field—is affectionately known as "Touchdown Jesus."
- Notre Dame's $5.5 billion endowment ranks among the top 20 highest endowments of U.S. colleges and universities.

Distinguished Alumni

Alan Page, Minnesota Supreme Court Justice; Condoleezza Rice, 66th United States Secretary of State; Hannah Storm, ESPN SportsCenter anchor.

Admissions and Financial Aid

It is not easy to get into Notre Dame. To have a fighting chance to become one of the Fighting Irish you should be near the top of your high school class and earn between a 1390 and 1490 on the SAT or between 32 and 34 on the ACT. Your extracurricular experiences should show leadership. Work hard to write a good application essay. Notre Dame notes that good applicants don't just "tell us facts about themselves...but show us their uniqueness in a variety of different ways."

All students are considered for scholarships and grants upon application. Among those who apply early, 25 students will be named Hesburgh-Yusko Scholars and earn $25,000 a year for up to four years, plus four fully-funded summer enrichment experiences.

UNIVERSITY OF NOTRE DAME

Highlights

Admissions Criteria

Academic criteria:
Grades: ☆ ☆ ☆
Difficulty of class schedule: ☆ ☆ ☆
Class rank: ☆ ☆
Standardized test scores: ☆ ☆
Teacher recommendations: ☆ ☆
Personal statement: ☆ ☆
Non-academic criteria considered:
Extracurricular activities
Special talents, interests, abilities
Character/personal qualities
Volunteer work
Work experience
State of residency
Religious affiliation/commitment
Minority affiliation
Alumni relationship

Deadlines

Early Action: November 1
Early Decision: No
Regular Action: December 31 (final)
Notification of admission by: April 10
Common Application: Accepted

Financial Aid

In-state tuition: $44,605
Out-of-state tuition: $44,605
Room: Varies
Board: Varies
Books: $950
Freshmen receiving need-based aid: 51%
Undergrads rec. need-based aid: 50%
Avg. % of need met by financial aid: 100%
Avg. aid package (freshmen): $38,664
Avg. aid package (undergrads): $38,818
Avg. debt upon graduation: $29,480

School Spirit

Mascot: Leprechaun
Colors: Blue and gold
Song: *Notre Dame Victory March*

819

UNIVERSITY OF OKLAHOMA

UNIVERSITY OF OKLAHOMA

Four-year public
Founded: 1890
Norman, OK
Medium city
Pop. 113,273

Address:
660 Parrington Oval
Norman, OK
73019-0390

Admissions:
405-325-2252

Financial Aid:
405-325-4521

admrec@ou.edu

www.ou.edu

Overview

The University of Oklahoma—or as true loyalists refer to it, OU—seems to put respectable effort into giving students some of the perks of a smaller college. But don't let this fool you, it still offers the size (and of course the fabled football team) of a very large public university with almost 22,000 undergraduates strong.

The 3,200-acre campus is located just a half hour from downtown Oklahoma City, in Norman, the state's third largest city. It is filled with restaurants, shopping, Southern charm, and of course loads of alumni who couldn't get enough of what the city has to offer and never moved away. The university continues to develop facilities, putting some $1.5 billion into renovation and construction projects over the course of the past fifteen years. A large number of high achieving students continue to choose OU, and yes, the football team continues to bring home the victories. As a public institution with top rankings in the number of Rhodes Scholars it produces, National Merit Scholars enrolled, and students enjoying the low costs of education, the Sooners here have trouble finding things to complain about.

Academics

The general education curriculum at OU includes a 40-hour commitment to courses in these core areas: symbolic and oral communication, composition, mathematics, foreign language, natural sciences (including one course with a lab component), social sciences and humanities, and one course as part of the Senior Capstone Experience. The college offers 344 majors with strong programs in business administration, communication, dance, theater, elementary and secondary education, international and area studies, and meteorology. The School of Meteorology is the largest in the country and ranked seventh in the country for atmospheric science. In addition, according to the university, more Native American languages are taught for college credit at OU than at any other university in the world.

The school boasts a number of notable academic achievements while also paying close attention to incoming freshmen. For example, the class size of first-year English composition courses is capped at 19 students to provide a more intimate learning environment. The Honors College at OU is one of the largest when it comes to public universities, giving students expert advising and placing them in classrooms with fewer than 20 students. Another plus for Honors students is the privilege of living in the Honors House. "All high achievers should apply for the Honors College," says a student. Another favorite is the Undergraduate Research Opportunities Program that funds ambitious and hands-on student research projects with grants of up to $500. The college's Oklahoma Scholar-Leadership Enrichment Program allows small groups of students to study more rigorously and develop relationships with visiting scholars.

OU has a wide range of study-abroad opportunities—174 student-exchange agreements with universities in 66 different countries. Students may participate in faculty-led trips, direct enrollment programs, and foreign language immersion. Students who are able to take classes in Italian may be interested in the university's flagship Arezzo program, placing them in the Italian city located between Rome and France.

The career services program has a HIREsooner service with a number of large profile corporate partners. A huge database of employers hire directly from OU graduates.

Student Life

There are around 400 active student organizations on campus, including everything from the Campus Activities Council that organizes some of the college's large scale events to Sooner Off-Road, a group that designs and builds a small baja vehicle for competition. Then there's the Spirit of Grace Liturgical Dancers who perform at churches throughout Oklahoma, foreign language groups, and a host of others. A word to the wise: if you're thinking of joining the debate team, start practicing. These students won the national championship for the third time in four years.

The university is all about getting students psyched for what comes next. Howdy Week welcomes incoming freshmen and gets them excited for their first semester with snow cones, BBQ, and live music. Big Red Rally pumps up OU fans for another season of Sooner Football with tons of memorabilia to give away, the expected spirit squads, local bands, and celebrities. Service is also a big event that students get behind during... well, The Big Event. This is an official day of service where 5,000 students, faculty, and staff volunteers give their time to the central Oklahoma area.

With about one fifth of male students in fraternities and one quarter of women in sororities, the Greek scene on campus is pretty dominant, but not overwhelming. "The Greeks think you have to join to have a social life, but that really isn't true," says a student. The university itself describes the Greek life on campus as "thriving" with over 50 national chapters of fraternities and sororities.

To put it lightly, football is a pretty big deal at OU—big enough for former president George Lyny Cross to have said, "I want a university the football team can be proud of." Over 82,000 fans pour into the stadium on game day screaming "Boomer Sooner," and the results usually determine students' moods for the rest of the week. This is especially true when it comes to the Red Rivalry with University of Texas. Football isn't the only sport on campus though. With nine men's and nine women's teams competing in the Big 12 Conference of NCAA Division I, there are a lot of athletics to be proud of.

Campus Corner is the main spot to hang out when you're not in the student union or tailgating a big game. This area in town is filled with restaurants and shops that cater mainly to the university community.

Almost all freshmen are required to live in university housing, usually one of the large towers on the main campus. Faculty members and their families are also placed in residence halls to foster intergenerational interactions and build relationships outside the classroom. The OU Cousins program hosts facilities that are made up of half international students. In addition, the university owns a number of apartment complexes around campus, and the fraternity and sorority houses are some of the largest in the nation.

Student Body

Ethnic diversity on the main campus in Norman is high with minorities making up 28 percent of the student body. Geographic diversity is moderate as only 37 percent of students hail from beyond the borders of Oklahoma. The campus is predominantly Christian with a moderately conservative political leaning.

The average GPA of incoming freshmen is 3.6, and the school has the highest percentage of National Merit Scholars enrolled among the public universities in the country. Students at OU are not limited by the school's large size, and students here are high achieving.

UNIVERSITY OF OKLAHOMA

Highlights

Students
Total enrollment: 31,086
Undergrads: 21,982
Freshmen: 4,869
Part-time students: 14%
From out-of-state: 37%
Male/Female: 49%/51%
Live on-campus: 30%
In fraternities: 22%
In sororities: 26%
Off-campus employment rating: Excellent
Caucasian: 63%
African American: 5%
Hispanic: 7%
Asian / Pacific Islander: 6%
Native American: 5%
Mixed (2+ ethnicities): 5%
International: 4%

Academics
Calendar: Semester
Student/faculty ratio: 18:1
Class size 9 or fewer: 13%
Class size 10-29: 56%
Class size 30-49: 20%
Class size 50-99: 7%
Class size 100 or more: 4%
Returning freshmen: 84%
Six-year graduation rate: 66%

Most Popular Majors
Nursing
Petroleum engineering
Psychology

Admissions
Applicants: 11,650
Accepted: 9,220
Acceptance rate: 79.1%
Placed on wait list: 2,878
Enrolled from wait list: 2093
Average GPA: 3.6
ACT range: 23-29
SAT Math range: 540-660
SAT Reading range: 510-640
SAT Writing range: Not reported
Top 10% of class: 33%
Top 25% of class: 66%
Top 50% of class: 93%

821

College Profiles

UNIVERSITY OF OKLAHOMA

Admissions Criteria
Academic criteria:
Grades: ☆ ☆ ☆
Difficulty of class schedule: ☆ ☆ ☆
Class rank: ☆ ☆ ☆
Standardized test scores: ☆ ☆ ☆
Teacher recommendations: ☆
Personal statement: ☆ ☆ ☆
Non-academic criteria considered:
Interview
Extracurricular activities
Special talents, interests, abilities
Volunteer work
Work experience
Alumni relationship

Deadlines
Early Action: No
Early Decision: No
Regular Action: Rolling admissions
Common Application: Accepted

Financial Aid
In-state tuition: $3,957
Out-of-state tuition: $16,146
Room: $4,772
Board: $3,946
Books: $848
Freshmen receiving need-based aid: 50%
Undergrads rec. need-based aid: 51%
Avg. % of need met by financial aid: 82%
Avg. aid package (freshmen): $11,837
Avg. aid package (undergrads): $11,948
Avg. debt upon graduation: $26,574

School Spirit
Mascot: Sooners
Colors: Crimson and cream
Song: *Boomer Sooner*

You May Not Know

- These looks don't fade! The gardens, fountains, sculptures, and benches beautifying the campus have their own endowment of $3 million.
- The Sam Noble Oklahoma Museum of Natural History is the second largest university-affiliated natural history museum. Seven million artifacts are displayed on 40 acres of land.
- The Bizzell Memorial Library on campus has a huge history of science collection and offers the opportunity to hold a book with Galileo's handwriting in the palm of your hands!

Distinguished Alumni

Pat Bowlen, Denver Broncos owner; Stacey Dales, former WNBA player; Fred Haise, Apollo 13 astronaut; Ed Harris, actor; Brad Henry, current Oklahoma Governor; James Garner, actor; Dennis Weaver, actor.

Admissions and Financial Aid

OU's automatic admissions program is available to students with an un-weighted GPA of 3.0 (or 3.5 for out of staters) who rank in the top 25 percent of their high school graduating class. Students with exemplary ACT and SAT scores may also fast-track the application process.

Acceptance to the Honors College is competitive, and students must have a composite ACT score of 30 or higher or SAT score of 1330 or higher and be the top 10 percent of their high school class or have a minimum 3.75 GPA. A strong emphasis is placed on a 400 to 500-word essay.

The university is proud to offer a lot of bang for your buck and is consistently rated by Institutional Research and Evaluation as one of the best buys when it comes to a bachelor's degree in the United States. Undergraduates receive merit aid from the wide array of scholarships offered through financial aid services and can apply to most College of Arts and Sciences scholarships in one fell swoop with their OUFAN forms. There are dozens of merit-based scholarships offered by the university, including a guaranteed scholarship for National Merit Scholars that provides up to $45,500 for residents and $89,500 for non-residents.

UNIVERSITY OF OREGON

Overview

The University of Oregon, set in a lush 265-acre campus in Eugene, Oregon, is an oasis of research in the midst of the wilderness. The campus is home to more than 500 varieties of trees and is close to the Willamette River, Pacific Ocean, and the Cascade Mountains. Reflecting the nature around it, recent campus developments have been aimed at creating sustainable architecture, and the Lillis Business Complex, completed in 2003, utilizes one of the "largest photovoltaic arrays in the Northwest" and has the first green, planted roof at a university.

While it is a large public university with over 20,000 undergraduates enrolled, the school creates many opportunities that create an environment similar to that of a small private liberal arts college. There are special interest halls, small freshman seminars, and freshman interest groups.

The city is certainly rainy, as one would expect in that geographic region; but what with over 250 student groups and a multitude of events happening at any given time on campus, student life is vibrant.

Academics

Students at University of Oregon are spoiled for choice, with 76 majors offered. Education requirements include general-education classes and major requirements. General-ed classes fall into arts and letters, social science, and science.

Besides the standard undergraduate options, the university has a number of focused programs. These include the College of Education, the School of Architecture and Allied Arts, the Lundquist College of Business, and the School of Journalism. These specialized schools offer unique opportunities to their students and specialized majors, such as metalsmithing and jewelry, or communication disorders and sciences. The business program prides itself on its sports business curriculum, and its annual business plan competition, the New Venture Championship. The Princeton Review placed the Lundquist Center for Entrepreneurship at number 20 out of 2,300 business programs. The School of Journalism students produce *Mosaic*, an award-wining newspaper, and *Flux*, an eclectic print magazine of photography and feature articles.

Freshmen get special attention with Freshman Interest Groups and Freshman Seminars. The Interest Groups involve 25 first-year students who take two general education courses together in the fall term. These revolve around a topic of common interest such as Hip Hop and Politics of Race, and Religious Objects as Icons. Freshman seminars emphasize the experience of a discussion-based small class and include topics such as African history expressed through dance and the history and structure of encryption technology. Freshman seminars are also focused on writing, communication, and critical analysis. "While the freshman seminars can be a mixed bag, they are still worth it for you to be able to meet other freshmen and to be a part of a small class," says a student.

For the academically inclined, the Robert D. Clark Honors College is a chance to gain the small liberal arts experience within the large university. The Honors College has approximately 700 students, which offers exclusive classes at a low faculty-to-student ratio (25:1 maximum). Honors College students are required to complete a senior thesis in their major area.

UO boasts over 140 study-abroad programs in over 90 countries. Closer to home, the university offers students the opportunity to participate in programs associated with its Institute of Marine Biology on the southern Oregon coast.

Graduates are offered a wide range of services. The Alumni Association has a membership of 18,000 and hosts an online Career Center where alumni may connect with each other or with current students.

UNIVERSITY OF OREGON

Four-year public
Founded: 1876
Eugene, OR
Medium city
Pop. 156,929

Address:
1226 University of Oregon
Eugene, OR
97403-1226

Admissions:
800-232-3825

Financial Aid:
800-760-6953

uoadmit@uoregon.edu

www.uoregon.edu

UNIVERSITY OF OREGON

Students

Total enrollment: 24,518
Undergrads: 20,809
Freshmen: 5,131
Part-time students: 9%
From out-of-state: 45%
Male/Female: 48%/52%
Live on-campus: 20%
In fraternities: 10%
In sororities: 15%
Off-campus employment rating: Fair
Caucasian: 67%
African American: 2%
Hispanic: 7%
Asian / Pacific Islander: 6%
Native American: 1%
Mixed (2+ ethnicities): 5%
International: 11%

Academics

Calendar: Quarter
Student/faculty ratio: 19:1
Class size 9 or fewer: 14%
Class size 10-29: 53%
Class size 30-49: 17%
Class size 50-99: 9%
Class size 100 or more: 7%
Returning freshmen: 85%
Six-year graduation rate: 68%

Most Popular Majors

Business administration
Psychology
Sociology

Admissions

Applicants: 21,263
Accepted: 15,770
Acceptance rate: 74.2%
Placed on wait list: 1,714
Enrolled from wait list: 479
Average GPA: 3.6
ACT range: Not reported
SAT Math range: 502-616
SAT Reading range: 489-608
SAT Writing range: Not reported
Top 10% of class: 28%
Top 25% of class: 63%
Top 50% of class: 94%

824

Student Life

There are over 250 student groups on campus, with a gamut of interests that spans everything from film fanatics to ballroom dance to sustainability. The UO Outdoor program is particularly popular, with 150-200 student-initiated outings launched each year. The program also hosts presentations, films, natural history classes, and skill clinics, such as kayak pool sessions. The Erb Memorial Union is the center of student social life, home to the student governing body ASUO and a place where students can hang out, eat meals, and play pool or ping pong.

There are a variety of annual campus-wide events that tempt students to jump in and participate. For example, the school year kicks off with InterMingle, a welcome event that is part activities fair, part carnival. The annual spring Willamette Valley Folk Festival draws local and international musicians to campus. In June and July, the university hosts the Oregon Bach Festival, an international festival of choral and orchestral music that attracts more than 30,000 attendees. In fact, Eugene was included in *Rolling Stone's* list of "America's Top 10 Campus Music Scenes that Rock."

Besides the cultural activities, athletics are also a big part of campus life. The university competes in 15 Division I sports and offers club sports including rugby, water polo, and rowing. The football rivalry between University of Oregon and Oregon State University is heated, so much so that it is commonly referred to as the "Civil War." The cross-country and track and field program is particular strong, with 12 NCAA titles under their belt, explaining Eugene's nickname, "Track Town."

All students are guaranteed four years of housing, but many upperclass students move off campus. Fewer than 10 percent of sophomores, juniors, and seniors stay on campus. Housing choices include eight residential halls, as well as those that are themed according to special interests. These include the Civic Engagement/Leadership Hall, the Creative Arts Hall, the Multicultural Hall, and the Wellness and Substance Free Dorm. Uniquely, there is also a Gender Equity Hall, in which students may live in co-ed rooms. Besides the various halls, there are 15 fraternities and 15 sororities on campus, with over 2,500 students involved in Greek life. "You feel the presence of the fraternities and sororities, but they aren't the dominant scene," remarks a student.

Finally, students who wish to get off campus often participate in outdoor activities such as surfing, skiing, river rafting, and rock climbing, as the Pacific Ocean and the Cascade Mountains are both within an hour of Eugene.

Student Body

The university has a high number of minority students (21 percent), and international students hail from such diverse places as Hong Kong, Kuwait, Saudi Arabia, Qatar, and Vietnam. The student body is generally liberal and there is a strong focus on sustainability and environmental awareness. The students' concern is reflected by the university—for example, the Green Chemistry Laboratory on campus is the first of its kind to use only nontoxic materials.

You May Not Know

- Parts of the film *National Lampoon's Animal House* were filmed at the university including the Omega House.
- Oregon is the only college to have a duck as a mascot. Donald Duck is an honorary graduate of the university.
- Eugene was ranked one of the top 10 college towns in the country by Livability.com.

Distinguished Alumni

Steve Dykes, Pulitzer Prize winner; Ken Kesey, author of *One Flew over the Cuckoo's Nest*; William Murphy, Nobel Laureate; Jeff Whitty, Tony Award winner for the musical *Avenue Q*; Gary Zimmerman, Pro Football Hall of Fame member.

Admissions and Financial Aid

There is no early decision process for the University of Oregon, but there is Early Action, and regular applications are taken on a rolling basis. While there is no interview requirement, prospective students are welcome to make appointments with admissions counselors to discuss questions or issues about the application process.

On their website, the university provides some guidelines for what it considers baselines for applying, and chances for admission. For "automatic admission," it suggests a GPA of at least 3.4, though any student with a GPA over 3.0 still stands a good chance of admission.

The university provides many different merit-based scholarships. The General University Scholarship, which is a one-year award between $1,000 and $3,000, is available to all eligible freshmen; in fact, all incoming freshman are automatically considered for the award. The Presidential Scholarship is offered to incoming freshmen from Oregon who have stellar academic records and a "significant history of leadership and volunteer service activities." These scholars receive $8,000 per year, renewable up to four years of study. The Diversity Excellence Scholarship (DES) offers scholarships from partial to full tuition and fee waivers, eligible to any student who is U.S. citizen, though preference is still given to Oregon students. This award aims to "recognize students who enhance the educational experience of all students by sharing diverse cultural experience." Financial need and background are taken into account for this award.

UNIVERSITY OF OREGON

Highlights

Admissions Criteria
Academic criteria:
Grades: ☆ ☆ ☆
Difficulty of class schedule: ☆ ☆ ☆
Class rank: ☆
Standardized test scores: ☆ ☆
Teacher recommendations: ☆
Personal statement: ☆
Non-academic criteria considered:
Extracurricular activities
Special talents, interests, abilities
Volunteer work
Work experience
Geographical location
Minority affiliation

Deadlines
Early Action: November 1
Early Decision: No
Regular Action: Rolling admissions
Common Application: Not accepted

Financial Aid
In-state tuition: $8,280
Out-of-state tuition: $28,305
Room: Varies
Board: Varies
Books: $1,050
Freshmen receiving need-based aid: 43%
Undergrads rec. need-based aid: 44%
Avg. % of need met by financial aid: 47%
Avg. aid package (freshmen): $9,763
Avg. aid package (undergrads): $9,848
Avg. debt upon graduation: $24,528

School Spirit
Mascot: Ducks
Colors: Green and yellow
Song: *Mighty Oregon*

UNIVERSITY OF THE PACIFIC

Overview

Nestled not far from the Bay Area is University of the Pacific (UOP), a medium-size private university affiliated with the United Methodist Church. Pacific has a reputation for being highly focused on its students. It has a variety of offerings and was cited by *U.S. News & World Report* as "a great school at a great price." The school also has a healthy social environment and proximity to many exciting places in California.

Pacific is located in Stockton, California—a medium-sized city in between Sacramento and the Bay Area. It features red brick buildings, some with historical columns, and the Calaveras River runs through the center of campus. The university has more than 60 laboratories, a 56,000 square foot biology building, gallery space, and two theatres. Overall the college has a lot to offer in a location that makes it very attractive.

Academics

There isn't a specified core curriculum at UOP, but there are general requirements. All students must complete general education mandates, including Pacific Seminars, the Breadth Program, and the Fundamental Skills program. The Seminars cover a wide variety of topics, from self-reflection, to society, to critical thinking. "I took the seminar on what a good society is," relates one student. "We had some mind-blowing discussions." For the Breadth Program, students are required to take one course in six to nine areas. The program is "broad" as its name suggests and is a good venue for gaining insight into future study interests. The Fundamental Skills program covers reading skills, writing skills, and quantitative analysis.

Academic rigor varies by major, but the school shows a unique level of dedication to its students by guaranteeing graduation in four years. If the four year timeline isn't fulfilled, the school pays the difference on additional time at school. This is not commonly offered by most colleges and/or universities, and students should take note of it as a selling point. Strong programs at Pacific include business, pre-pharmacy, biology, international studies, sports sciences, and engineering.

Pacific has an Honors Program that "encourages students to take leadership and service roles." Freshmen Honors students have the option of living in the Honors Residence halls. Participation in the Honors Program is by invitation; each student who is accepted to the university is considered based on grades, test scores, and motivation. Pacific also offers accelerated degree programs in certain fields, such as business, dental hygiene and dentistry, education, pharmacy, speech-language pathology, legal scholars-honors law program, physical therapy, and international studies.

Because Pacific is home to a large number of foreign students, it seems natural that it would offer overseas study opportunities in 50 different countries. Students who study abroad and international students at Pacific, take a course called Cross-Cultural Training I. The course covers "American values and assumptions, cross-cultural communication, cross-cultural adjustment, and research on the host country." "The preparation is immense," says a student.

UOP has a comprehensive Career Center offering services and programs designed to meet the needs of students, alumni, and employers. Tiger Jobs is the online portal for students, and the center is also connected to Facebook and LinkedIn, maintaining an alumni network. Pacific's career center is on the cutting edge and helps students find jobs through many networks.

Student Life

Student life is active at Pacific with more than 100 clubs of all types. Popular organizations include the Conservatory Composer's Club, where students compose and perform new music; the Association of Engineering Students; and the K-PAC Student Radio, which is popular both on campus and in the neighborhood.

Pacific has over 150 years of traditions. One of the newer events is Tiger Roar. Started in 2003, Tiger Roar is part of New Student Convocation. Held during Welcome Weekend, the UOP community gathers outside of the Concert Hall to surprise new students with a ROAR. "You'd be shocked how loud it can be," laughs one student. Painting the rocks is a longstanding student competition—another tradition—to show school pride. Also popular is the annual All Campus Party and Senior Celebration, which includes free food, music, a dunk tank, volleyball, and prizes.

Twenty percent of men and 19 percent of women are members of a fraternity or sorority. There are eight fraternities, seven sororities, and 15 professional fraternities at Pacific. It's apparent by these numbers that Pacific is social, but by no means a party school; many of the students join professional fraternities to get a leg up in their future careers. "We know how to have a good time, but we're also responsible enough to wake up the next day and do service or study," remarks a student.

University of the Pacific competes in Division I athletics and is the only private school in the Big West Conference. There are 16 intercollegiate sports, seven men's and nine women's. The most competitive of these are men's basketball and women's volleyball. The men's basketball team has competed in the NCAA tournament from 2004 to 2006 and in 2013.

Off-campus activities are related somewhat to Pacific's location in the central valley, affording students close proximity to quite a few exciting places in California. Road trips to San Francisco are not uncommon for big city entertainment. Beaches in Santa Cruz and Monterey are also only a few hours away. "There aren't many schools where the beaches and skiing are both only a couple of hours away," says a student.

Pacific encourages on-campus living. It requires all freshmen and sophomore students who are under the age of 23 to live on campus. There are 14 residence halls, six apartment communities, as well as fraternity/sorority housing. Almost half of the entire student body lives in campus housing, and the on-campus residential system receives good ratings from UOP students. "The dorms are okay for freshmen—you might have to share a bathroom with the whole hall—but your options get better when you become a junior," comments an upperclassman.

Student Body

The student body is diverse in terms of personality and interests. Some are very academically and career focused, while others have a more laid-back approach to their studies and even their extracurricular activities. "You'll meet every type of person here," says a student. Many students at Pacific share a common interest in community service and are heavily involved in extracurricular activities, which is to say they're a fairly well-rounded group.

There is high ethnic diversity with more than 50 percent of students identifying as minority. Asian Americans make up almost one third of the student body. About eight percent of students hail from out of state.

UNIVERSITY OF THE PACIFIC

Highlights

Students
Total enrollment: 6,652
Undergrads: 3,867
Part-time students: 3%
From out-of-state: 8%
Male/Female: 47%/53%
Live on-campus: 46%
In fraternities: 20%
In sororities: 19%
Caucasian: 34%
African American: 3%
Hispanic: 19%
Asian / Pacific Islander: 32%
Native American: 1%
Mixed (2+ ethnicities): 3%
International: 5%

Academics
Calendar: Semester
Student/faculty ratio: 14:1
Class size 9 or fewer: 29%
Class size 10-29: 53%
Class size 30-49: 15%
Class size 50-99: 4%
Class size 100 or more: -
Returning freshmen: 83%
Six-year graduation rate: 63%

Admissions
Applicants: 22,972
Accepted: 8,678
Acceptance rate: 37.8%
Placed on wait list: 1,840
Enrolled from wait list: 45
Average GPA: 3.5
ACT range: 23-29
SAT Math range: 550-690
SAT Reading range: 520-650
SAT Writing range: 14-31
Top 10% of class: 44%
Top 25% of class: 75%
Top 50% of class: 93%

827

UNIVERSITY OF THE PACIFIC

Admissions Criteria
Academic criteria:
Grades: ☆ ☆ ☆
Difficulty of class schedule: ☆ ☆ ☆
Class rank: ☆
Standardized test scores: ☆ ☆
Teacher recommendations: ☆ ☆
Personal statement: ☆ ☆
Non-academic criteria considered:
Extracurricular activities
Special talents, interests, abilities
Character/personal qualities
Volunteer work
Work experience
State of residency
Geographical location
Alumni relationship

Deadlines
Early Action: November 15
Early Decision: No
Regular Action: Rolling admissions
Common Application: Accepted

Financial Aid
In-state tuition: $39,290
Out-of-state tuition: $39,290
Room: Varies
Board: Varies
Books: $1,665
Freshmen receiving need-based aid: 70%
Undergrads rec. need-based aid: 73%
Avg. aid package (freshmen): $26,896
Avg. aid package (undergrads): $29,279

School Spirit
Mascot: Tigers
Colors: Orange and black
Song: *Tiger Fight Song*

You May Not Know

- Movies including *Raiders of the Lost Ark*, *Glory Days*, and *All the Kings Men* were filmed at Pacific.
- University of the Pacific's women's volleyball team has brought the university its two national championships.
- Stockton hosts an annual Asparagus Festival, featuring fried asparagus; and Italian Street Painting Festival, when neighborhood sidewalks are decorated in chalk.

Distinguished Alumni

Pete Carroll, NFL head coach, former USC head coach; Jamie Lee Curtis, actress; Arthur A. Dugoni, President, American Dental Association; Chris Isaak, actor and musician; Bill Lockyer, California Attorney General.

Admissions and Financial Aid

Admissions at Pacific is selective, and the application itself is unique as many of the elements are optional. For example, recommendations and the personal statement are not required but add depth. Necessary documents include the online application, high school transcripts, and SAT or ACT scores. SAT Subject Test scores, like recommendations and the personal statement, are also optional.

Pacific offers a variety of scholarships. Admitted students are automatically considered for some awards, with priority given to freshmen and transfer students. Freshman applicants are given automatic consideration for both the Regents and Presidents scholarships, which are annual awards of $10,000 and $6,500, respectively. Additional applications are required for the Powell Scholarship ($15,000 annually), MESA Scholarships (for math and science), athletic scholarships, and other talent-based scholarships. The Powell Scholarship is the most prestigious at the university and is awarded to students with the most raw academic and leadership potential.

UNIVERSITY OF PENNSYLVANIA

Overview

Tradition permeates the look and feel of UPenn, the oldest *university* in the nation (Harvard is the oldest *college* in the nation). The Gothic architecture on campus is reminiscent of universities in the UK, and the campus encompasses a national historic district. Brick and ivy surrounded by manicured green lawns separate University City from the rest of Philadelphia. Over the next decade, the university plans to expand across the Schuylkill River.

Strong liberal arts and strong pre-professional education meet at this large private Ivy League institution. Penn is perhaps the most social and spirited member of the Ivy Leagues. You'll hear "The Red and Blue" sung by sports fans clad in Penn colors; and after the third quarter of every football game, fans throw toast onto Franklin Field (since toasting with alcohol was banned in the 1970s)—sometimes 30,000 pieces of toast in a single game!

Of course, at such a competitive institution, life isn't all fun and games. Academics are intense and students can get competitive as they strive for academic excellence and set themselves up for powerful careers after graduation. Students who feel they can thrive in this high-achieving environment will want to try hard—and cross their fingers—to get into this highly selective university.

Academics

UPenn's four undergraduate schools offer more than 85 majors, and students can also pursue individualized majors. While the College of Arts and Sciences, School of Engineering and Applied Science, School of Nursing, and The Wharton School each has its own set of required courses, they all share a common writing requirement. There are also 12 graduate and professional schools, and through Penn's "One University" policy, undergrads may take classes at any of them except for the graduate medical, veterinary, and dental schools. Students may also study at nearby Bryn Mawr, Haverford, and Swarthmore.

Academics at UPenn are "intense because pretty much everyone is an overachiever," says a student. The College of Arts and Sciences offers the most academic freedom and flexibility, but each school is sure to challenge students' intellects. There is also a tangible level of competition among students. "Outward competition isn't as prevalent as an overwhelming feeling of competition," one student explains. Strong programs include business, economics, international studies, and nursing.

Students who are up to the challenge may apply to become Benjamin Franklin Scholars. If chosen, they will participate in Benjamin Franklin Seminars and pursue research projects of their own creation with the help of an advising team. The program also has summer research grants, and many students become authors or co-authors of published papers. Another option for motivated students is the University Scholars program, which enables students to do in-depth research and to get an early start on their graduate and professional courses while still undergrads. University Scholars have access to a special fund and meet weekly for lunches to discuss their research.

All incoming students may participate in Freshman Seminars, meant to give each first-year individual contact with a faculty member in a small class focused on a specific topic. Students can also take preceptorials, short non-credit seminars generated by students and led by faculty, grad students, external educators, and exceptional undergraduates. There are no grades and tests and these popular courses emphasize hands-on learning.

According to the university, Penn ranks first among Ivy League schools in number of students studying abroad, with more than 1,700 students traveling to nearly 50 countries around the world. Students can study at Cambridge University, Edinburgh

UNIVERSITY OF PENNSYLVANIA

Four-year private
Founded: 1740
Philadelphia, PA
Major city
Pop. 1,536,471

Address:
34th & Spruce Streets
Philadelphia, PA
19104

Admissions:
215-898-7507

Financial Aid:
215-898-1988

info@admissions.
upenn.edu

www.upenn.edu

UNIVERSITY OF PENNSYLVANIA

Students
Total enrollment: 21,339
Undergrads: 9,682
Part-time students: 3%
From out-of-state: 81%
Male/Female: 50%/50%
Live on-campus: 56%
In fraternities: 30%
In sororities: 27%
Off-campus employment rating: Excellent
Caucasian: 45%
African American: 7%
Hispanic: 9%
Asian / Pacific Islander: 19%
Native American: 0%
Mixed (2+ ethnicities): 3%
International: 12%

Academics
Calendar: Semester
Student/faculty ratio: 6:1
Class size 9 or fewer: 27%
Class size 10-29: 56%
Class size 30-49: 8%
Class size 50-99: 7%
Class size 100 or more: 2%
Returning freshmen: 98%
Six-year graduation rate: 96%
Graduates who immediately go to graduate school: 20%
Graduates who immediately enter career related to major: 61%

Most Popular Majors
Finance
Economics
Nursing

Admissions
Applicants: 31,218
Accepted: 3,935
Acceptance rate: 12.6%
Placed on wait list: 2,017
Enrolled from wait list: 87
Average GPA: 3.9
ACT range: 30-34
SAT Math range: 690-780
SAT Reading range: 660-760
SAT Writing range: 68-28
Top 10% of class: 94%
Top 25% of class: 99%
Top 50% of class: 100%

830

University, University of Hong Kong, and other well known institutions around the world.

There are more than 260,000 living alumni of Penn. "The alumni network is a powerful asset for us," says a student. The Career Services Office and library offer guidance in career planning, job searching, and graduate study.

Student Life

UPenn has more than 350 student organizations, many with deep historical roots like the university itself. The Philomathean Society, founded in 1813, is the "oldest continually existing collegiate literary society in the United States" according to the organization. Founded in 1888, the Mask and Wig Club is an all-male musical theatrical group whose music has been covered by Frank Sinatra, Tommy Dorsey, and Benny Goodman.

Greek life at Penn goes back 160 years and is a vibrant part of undergraduate life, with more than a quarter of all undergraduates participating in 46 fraternity and sorority chapters. The Fraternity Sorority System provides a living/learning environment that many students appreciate, and also gives back to the community through thousands of community service hours and philanthropic dollars each year. "There's more to Greek life than the parties," comments a student.

Campus-wide events at UPenn continue the theme of traditions, though they certainly aren't staid. Hey Day, begun in 1916 as a "Moving-Up" celebration to mark the advancement of each class, now signals the official graduation from junior to senior year. The event features a parade of students donning red T-shirts, canes, and straw hats. Harkening back to 1895 are the Penn Relays, the oldest relay competition in the country. The April event lasts for three days at Franklin Field and brings in athletes from high schools and colleges worldwide—even Olympic athletes—drawing more than 100,000 spectators. Spring is also the time for Spring Fling, a chance for 10,000 students to revel in the sun before final exams. Food, inflatables, live performances, and more fill the Quad. "We cherish the days when we can be outside in the sun," one student notes.

Penn's athletic teams, the Quakers, are no pacifists in competition: they have won their league football championship six times since 2000, and in basketball 23 times from 1970 to 2007. "We are the Ivy League athletic powerhouse," one student remarks. From the first days of a single cricket team, there are now 31 teams (16 men's, 15 women's) that compete in Division I sports. Football is the most competitive and most popular, while basketball, field hockey, and lacrosse are also competitive.

Students frequently go off campus to downtown Philadelphia for dining, entertainment, pro sports events, and shopping. "There are plenty of options in Philly," says a student. Road trips to New York City and Washington, DC are also common outings.

Most freshmen live on campus. Students live in one of nearly 40 themed College Houses (from world cinema to science and technology) or co-ed dorms. Upperclassmen tend to move to high-rise apartment-style housing off campus.

Student Body

According to Penn students, they are "very focused" on academics and bent on progressing their careers, not surprising, given their high-achieving records in high school. Thirty-eight percent of students identify as African-American, Hispanic, Asian, or Native American and another 12 percent are international, giving the university high ethnic diversity. Geographic diversity within the United States is also well represented, with 81 percent of students hailing from outside Pennsylvania.

You May Not Know

- Penn is one of the first academic institutions to follow a multidisciplinary model pioneered in Europe where multiple "faculties" such as theology, classics, and medicine are combined into one institution.
- The American Medical Association was founded at Penn.
- UPenn owns the official arboretum in the state of Pennsylvania, Morris Arboretum, located in northwestern Philadelphia.

Distinguished Alumni

Warren Buffett, investor and philanthropist; John Legend, musician/vocalist/songwriter and six-time Grammy Award-Winner; Andrea Mitchell, NBC News; Arlen Specter, Senior U.S. Senator for Pennsylvania.

Admissions and Financial Aid

Penn's admissions office notes that most successful applicants rank in the top five percent of their high school classes, though they look beyond just class rank to "pay close attention to the types and levels of courses taken." Notably, the university stresses the importance of recommendations and requires two of them. They also request a student's entire standardized testing history. Children of alumni should apply early decision to receive preference.

Penn does not offer merit scholarships, but it does offer extensive financial aid. Since 2009, students who qualify for need-based aid no longer have loans as part of their financial aid package, enabling them to graduate debt-free.

UNIVERSITY OF PENNSYLVANIA

Highlights

Admissions Criteria
Academic criteria:
Grades: ☆ ☆ ☆
Difficulty of class schedule: ☆ ☆ ☆
Class rank: ☆ ☆
Standardized test scores: ☆ ☆ ☆
Teacher recommendations: ☆ ☆ ☆
Personal statement: ☆ ☆ ☆
Non-academic criteria considered:
Interview
Extracurricular activities
Special talents, interests, abilities
Character/personal qualities
Volunteer work
Work experience
Geographical location
Minority affiliation
Alumni relationship

Deadlines
Early Action: No
Early Decision: November 1
Regular Action: January 1 (final)
Common Application: Accepted

Financial Aid
In-state tuition: $40,594
Out-of-state tuition: $40,594
Room: $8,330
Board: $4,592
Books: $1,190
Freshmen receiving need-based aid: 47%
Undergrads rec. need-based aid: 45%
Avg. % of need met by financial aid: 100%
Avg. aid package (freshmen): $40,582
Avg. aid package (undergrads): $39,011
Avg. debt upon graduation: $21,190

School Spirit
Mascot: Quakers
Colors: Red and blue
Song: *The Red and the Blue*

UNIVERSITY OF PITTSBURGH

UNIVERSITY OF PITTSBURGH

Four-year public
Founded: 1787
Pittsburgh, PA
Major city
Pop. 307,484

Address:
4200 Fifth Avenue
Pittsburgh, PA
15260

Admissions:
412-624-7488

Financial Aid:
412-624-7488

oafa@pitt.edu

www.pitt.edu

Overview

A nationally recognized institution of research, the University of Pittsburgh carries with it a reputation of excellence. This large public university is among the oldest in the nation, offering outstanding academic programs in the arts and sciences as well as professional fields. From a strong business program, to the dental medicine program, to the Swanson School of Engineering, Pitt provides endless opportunities for academic success.

Located in the Pittsburgh suburb of Oakland, right next to Carnegie Mellon, the University of Pittsburgh balances its strong academic commitment with offerings of an exciting social life. A survey recently ranked Pittsburgh as "second-most attractive college town" of U.S. cities its size. With Pitt Arts, museums, and sports, the city lives up to its ranking.

Architecture in Pittsburgh is mainly modern, with the city having a vibrant industrial past. Students often boast of the convenience of having the city as their campus, reaping the benefits of a wide variety of leisure activities available at their fingertips. A new facility at Pittsburgh is Ruskin Hall, the University's apartment-style housing accommodation that houses 416 students.

Academics

Students at Pitt have the option of attaining over 100 undergraduate degrees from any of 12 schools in the university, each with its own degree requirements. In the School of Arts and Sciences, students must complete courses in writing and quantitative reasoning, along with classes within the humanities, social sciences, natural sciences, and the arts. Supplemental courses applicable to one's chosen major are also required.

Students at Pitt are academically competitive. Despite the large size of the school, professors are readily available to aid students' in their studies. "I've had a few professors who haven't been very responsive," confides a student, "but most are easy to get in touch with." Strong undergraduate programs include philosophy, economics, and psychology.

The Honors College is a specially tailored program for those who are "exceptionally curious and self-motivated." Students who are a part of the Honors College are privy to opportunities such as reading groups, an academic quiz team competition, and a film and lecture series.

For those students who are interested in on-the-job training—or by necessity, must work—during their college years, the University of Pittsburgh offers Cooperative Programs, which allow students to rotate in four-month shifts between school and the workplace. They are administered by the Swanson School of Engineering for computer science, chemistry, and engineering majors.

The University Center for International Studies is a multidisciplinary program that works with 19 affiliated institutions worldwide. A part of the federal government National Resource Centers Program, the University Center for International Studies participates in East Asian, Latin American, Russian and East European, and European Studies. "There is no better place to study international education," says a student. The University Center for International Studies provides a thorough study-abroad program for Pitt students, with countless sites available all over the globe. Students are highly encouraged to go abroad, and no language requirement exists as all classes are offered in English.

The Career Development office provides counseling on choosing majors, resumes and cover letters, interviewing, and graduate school planning. Events include career fairs, creative careers events, non-profit career fairs, and federal career days. Networking at Pitt is facilitated by the Pitt Career Network, providing bountiful opportunities for communication with professionals in whichever careers may be of interest to students.

Student Life

The University of Pittsburgh offers more than 400 student organizations from which to choose. These span a gamut of interests from the American Institute of Architecture Students, to the Obscure Movie Group, to Four-Square Club. New organizations are always arising, with a quick and easy process available for forming new groups. With 22 fraternities and 16 sororities on campus, Greek life has a prominent presence at Pitt; however, only about 10 percent of students participate. "There's a lot more to do than join a fraternity or sorority," says a student.

Social events abound on campus. Family Weekend is a relaxing time filled with family activities and discounted football tickets. The Holiday Cantata is a jazzy musical entertainment event just before the holidays, and there are countless concerts, commencements, and sporting events taking place at the Petersen Events Center. Perhaps the longest standing tradition at Pitt is Lantern Night, a ceremony dedicated to celebrating freshman women entering Pitt.

The university participates in the Division I Big East Conference, with eight men's and nine women's varsity teams. The Pitt Panthers have won national titles in football, as well as conference titles and national rankings in many sports, for example, men's basketball, wrestling, gymnastics, and swimming. "Football games are a true event," says a student. Pitt home games typically count an attendance of 50-60,000 fans. Intramurals such as badminton, basketball, and handball are also popular on campus.

For off-campus diversion, Pitt students visit friends at nearby Carnegie Mellon or head to downtown Pittsburgh for shopping, great restaurants, and bustling nightlife. "Most people don't think much of Pittsburgh," comments a student, "but there's more to do here than you'd think." Scenic parks and mountains are also nearby for those craving outdoor activities.

The majority of students live on campus their first year in apartment-style dorm housing. According to students, dorm quality ranges from nice to poor, depending on the age of the building. Though housing is guaranteed for three years, the majority of students choose to venture off campus in their later years at Pitt. "You should get off campus as soon as you can," advises a student.

Student Body

Due to the university's large size, a "typical" Pitt student really doesn't exist. In general, Pitt students are focused on academics and are able to find their individual niche among the immensity of the 18,000 undergraduate students at the university. "No matter what your interests, you'll find your group," says a student.

Ethnic diversity is moderate, with a 17 percent minority population. Geographic diversity is also moderate, with 31 percent of students hailing from out of state. The student body is balanced between men and women.

UNIVERSITY OF PITTSBURGH

Highlights

Students
Total enrollment: 28,769
Undergrads: 18,429
Freshmen: 3,678
Part-time students: 6%
From out-of-state: 31%
Male/Female: 50%/50%
Live on-campus: 44%
In fraternities: 11%
In sororities: 9%
Off-campus employment rating: Excellent
Caucasian: 76%
African American: 6%
Hispanic: 2%
Asian / Pacific Islander: 6%
Native American: 0%
Mixed (2+ ethnicities): 3%
International: 3%

Academics
Calendar: Semester
Student/faculty ratio: 14:1
Class size 9 or fewer: 6%
Class size 10-29: 52%
Class size 30-49: 21%
Class size 50-99: 14%
Class size 100 or more: 6%
Returning freshmen: 93%
Six-year graduation rate: 79%

Most Popular Majors
Psychology
History
Communication

Admissions
Applicants: 24,871
Accepted: 13,959
Acceptance rate: 56.1%
Placed on wait list: 1,119
Enrolled from wait list: 31
Average GPA: 3.9
ACT range: 26-30
SAT Math range: 600-680
SAT Reading range: 570-660
SAT Writing range: 12-45
Top 10% of class: 52%
Top 25% of class: 86%
Top 50% of class: 99%

833

College Profiles

UNIVERSITY OF PITTSBURGH

Admissions Criteria
Academic criteria:
Grades: ☆ ☆ ☆
Difficulty of class schedule: ☆ ☆ ☆
Class rank: ☆
Standardized test scores: ☆ ☆ ☆
Teacher recommendations: ☆
Personal statement: ☆ ☆
Non-academic criteria considered:
Extracurricular activities
Special talents, interests, abilities
Character/personal qualities
Volunteer work
Work experience
Geographical location
Minority affiliation

Deadlines
Early Action: No
Early Decision: No
Regular Action: Rolling admissions
Common Application: Not accepted

Financial Aid
In-state tuition: $16,240
Out-of-state tuition: $26,246
Room: $5,700
Board: $3,730
Books: $1,132
Freshmen receiving need-based aid: 55%
Undergrads rec. need-based aid: 55%
Avg. % of need met by financial aid: 56%
Avg. aid package (freshmen): $15,810
Avg. aid package (undergrads): $12,338
Avg. debt upon graduation: $33,662

School Spirit
Mascot: Panthers
Colors: Blue and gold
Song: *Hail to Pitt*

You May Not Know

- Pitt installed its first campus-wide energy management system in 1975—being "green" is nothing new at this school!
- The University of Pittsburgh ranks nationally as a top university as far as annual research support from the National Institutes of Health.
- Pitt was ranked in the top 100 "best college values" among universities in the nation by *Money* magazine.

Distinguished Alumni

Michael Chabon, Pulitzer Prize Winner; Orrin Hatch, U.S. Senator; Gene Kelly, Academy Award Winner; Roger Kingdom, two-time Olympic gold medalist in track and field; Wangari Maathai, 2004 Nobel Peace Prize Winner; Fred Rogers, Host of *Mister Rogers' Neighborhood*; August Wilson, 1987 Pulitzer Prize-winning playwright.

Admissions and Financial Aid

Pitt operates on rolling admissions. Students are encouraged to apply early, as spots in smaller schools and programs—such as the School of Pharmacy, for example—fill up quickly. Admission is based on high school transcripts and SAT/ACT scores. Although essays and letters of recommendation are not required, students are strongly encouraged to include them in their applications.

Students who complete the full admissions application, along with all necessary documents, will automatically be considered for merit-based scholarships. GPA and test scores are weighed, along with the difficulty of the curriculum taken in high school. These scholarships are entirely merit-based and are awarded without taking into account the student's FAFSA.

UNIVERSITY OF PUGET SOUND

Overview

The University of Puget Sound is a private, liberal arts college founded in 1888. While it may be less known on the East Coast, its reputation has been steadily growing in the Pacific Northwest thanks to a revamped curriculum and renewed focus on strong academics, and a commitment to undergraduate education. The school has also been recognized as a university committed to sustainability.

The 97-acre campus is located in a residential neighborhood of Tacoma, about 35 miles south of Seattle, close to shopping, downtown, and the waterfront. The campus is beautifully situated in the stunning natural environment of the Pacific Northwest, surrounded by the Cascade and Olympic mountain ranges. The architecture on campus is mostly brick buildings in the Tudor-Gothic style, arranged around main quads. A new Science Center and modern crystalline gazebo café demonstrate the university's emphasis on offering great facilities, which also include a sculpture building, a natural history museum, theatres, labs, an observatory, concert hall, and an arboretum. The mix of modern architecture and red brick buildings is reminiscent of historic East Coast campuses, and the natural setting is unbeatable.

Academics

Students describe the academics as challenging but not unmanageable. There are more than 1,200 courses offered annually, and 50 majors, minors, and programs to choose from, as well as interesting interdisciplinary programs like International Political Economy and Science, Technology, and Society. Additionally, the School of Music has a conservatory-quality program. "There are some incredibly talented musicians," notes a student. Some of the strongest majors include business administration and management, English, and sociology.

With 91 percent of classes having 29 or fewer students, the opportunity to take small, discussion-based classes is "a real plus," says a student. Class sizes tend to be small enough that genuine relationships with professors are easy to come by.

The Core Curriculum is seen as the foundation of the liberal arts education, introducing students to a range of intellectual approaches for understanding culture, society, and the physical world. The Core Curriculum includes two first-year seminars—Scholarly and Creative Inquiry and Writing and Rhetoric—that allow for intellectual exploration of a focused area of interest. Students also take classes in five "Approaches to Knowing" categories: fine arts, humanities, mathematics, natural science, and social science. Finally, students take an upper-level, integrative course in "Connections," an exploration of interdisciplinary thinking.

The Honors Program is a four-year study plan within the Core Curriculum. Students are selected based on their academic performance. An intensive three-year sequence allows students to study the major classics from the Western tradition and undertake a comparative study of Near Eastern, South Asian, and East Asian civilizations. Honor students use these courses as a foundation for the honors senior thesis.

Another special program is the Business Leadership Program. Each year within the School of Business and Leadership, 25 freshmen are admitted to this interdisciplinary program with classes, seminars, field trips, a required internship, and a business mentorship. The program allows students to combine a business education in a liberal arts environment, leading to success for those who want to attend graduate school or find positions at respected non-profits and corporate employers. "We get hands-on experience in business as well as make connections with current business leaders," comments a student.

There is also an option to do a Special Interdisciplinary Major, where you can craft your own academic course by creating a major between two or more departments, schools, or programs.

UNIVERSITY OF PUGET SOUND

Four-year private
Founded: 1888
Tacoma, WA
Medium city
Pop. 200,678

Address:
1500 North Warner Street
Tacoma, WA 98416

Admissions:
800-396-7191

Financial Aid:
800-396-7192

admission@puget-sound.edu

www.pugetsound.edu

UNIVERSITY OF PUGET SOUND

Highlights

Students
Total enrollment: 2,857
Undergrads: 2,578
Freshmen: 661
Part-time students: 1%
From out-of-state: 78%
From public schools: 74%
Male/Female: 43%/57%
Live on-campus: 57%
In fraternities: 21%
In sororities: 30%
Off-campus employment rating: Excellent
Caucasian: 74%
African American: 2%
Hispanic: 7%
Asian / Pacific Islander: 7%
Native American: 1%
Mixed (2+ ethnicities): 7%
International: 1%

Academics
Calendar: Semester
Student/faculty ratio: 12:1
Class size 9 or fewer: 10%
Class size 10-29: 81%
Class size 30-49: 8%
Class size 50-99: 1%
Class size 100 or more: -
Returning freshmen: 86%
Six-year graduation rate: 77%

Most Popular Majors
Business administration
Politics/government
Psychology

Admissions
Applicants: 4,472
Accepted: 3,698
Acceptance rate: 82.7%
Placed on wait list: 367
Enrolled from wait list: 80
Average GPA: Not reported
ACT range: 26-30
SAT Math range: 580-660
SAT Reading range: 570-688
SAT Writing range: 14-46
Top 10% of class: 36%
Top 25% of class: 67%
Top 50% of class: 93%

Study abroad has become a central part of the Puget Sound experience, with 40 percent of students studying abroad before they graduate. Programs are offered all over the world, including Argentina, Australia, Botswana, China, Czech Republic, Egypt, El Salvador, Germany, Ghana, Morocco, Namibia, South Africa, and many more.

Puget Sound encourages civic engagement and taking advantage of internship opportunities. Every summer approximately 60 research grants are awarded to undergraduates. Career counseling and graduate school counseling is available, and Puget Sound post-baccalaureates have found a high acceptance rate as applicants to health profession graduate programs. Many students enter the workforce, while 24 percent pursue a graduate degree within one year.

Student Life

Students at the University of Puget Sound manage to make time for more than just academics and outdoor recreation; there are 75 official student organizations, and about 75 percent of students are involved in service activities in Tacoma and the broader community. Popular groups on campus include music ensembles, Puget Sound Outdoors, Students for a Democratic Society, Students for a Sustainable Campus, and *The Trail* student newspaper.

Puget Sound is also a school with many honored traditions, including LogJam!, a popular campus-wide celebration that comes at the end of the first week of fall classes. Conversely, Midnight Breakfast celebrates the end of the year in the Student Union Building on the last day of classes. If you want to be involved in film, you can take part in Foolish Pleasures, an annual festival of digital films written, directed, acted, and produced by students.

Greek life is relatively popular, with almost one quarter of students joining the three fraternities and four sororities. But there are ample opportunities for fun outside the toga genre as well. "You don't have to join [a sorority or fraternity] in order to find things to do," one student comments.

University of Puget Sound has 23 Division III athletic teams (11 men's, 12 women's). The men's basketball team has been particularly successful, and both crew teams are also quite competitive. Women's soccer has taken nine consecutive Northwest Conference titles, and women's swimming won a record-breaking 11 Northwest Conference titles in a row. The athletic facilities are both for varsity athletes and the many students who participate in intramural sports, including basketball, dodgeball, football, sailing, soccer, Ultimate Frisbee, and volleyball.

Like any decent college town, you won't want for independent bookstores and coffeehouses, but it's the recreational opportunities offered by the location of the university that make it so unique. Some of the most popular hang-out spots off campus include Point Defiance Park, the Mandolin Café, the Grand Cinema, and Metropolitan Market. There are numerous outings offered through clubs on campus for hiking, skiing, backpacking, camping, snowshoeing, or kayaking. Part of the allure of the Pacific Northwest is also the proximity to cities like Seattle, Portland, Oregon, and Vancouver, British Columbia.

Puget Sound is a residential college, but with varied housing options. Freshmen are guaranteed housing, and 57 percent of students live on campus, but nearly all students living off campus are within walking distance. Students can live in a fraternity or sorority house, choose to live in one of 21 theme houses, or opt for suite-style living or college-owned houses. Campus life is highly rated, with students enjoying the campus dining options and the "overall nice" dorms.

Student Body

As one might expect in the Pacific Northwest, students are known for being "passionate about outdoor recreation" and are "left-leaning politically." One student notes, "It's not unusual to spend every weekend hiking or camping or to see protests for sustainability."

Puget Sound has a high level of ethnic diversity (24 percent minority) and a high amount of geographic diversity. More than three-quarters of students hail from out of state, with representation from 50 states and 11 countries.

You May Not Know

- The student radio station, KUPS "The Sound," received the mtvU Radio Woodie award for Best College Radio Station.
- PETA recognized Puget Sound as one of the nation's most vegetarian-friendly campuses.
- The Hatchet is the official symbol for the sports teams.

Distinguished Alumni

Deanna Oppenheimer, Chief Executive of UK Retail Banking, Barclays; William Canfield, President, Genzyme Glycobiology Research Institute; Richard M. Brooks, CEO/Director of Zumiez Inc.

Admissions and Financial Aid

In addition to the typical factors considered for admission (such as high school courses and grades), the admissions office takes into account a recommended interview. According to the admissions office, "We take great care to match an applicant's academic and personal accomplishments with our goal of enrolling an academically talented and diverse student body." Early decision is an option in applying; early decision allows students advance notification about scholarships and preference for placement in housing and advising.

There are a number of merit scholarships available. All incoming freshman are considered for Alumni, Faculty, Dean's, President's, and Trustee scholarships, which range from $4,000 to $17,000, based on the admission application, academic performance, and standardized test scores. Other merit scholarships include the National Merit Scholarships for National Merit Finalists who list the University of Puget Sound as their first choice college; the Lillis Family Foundation Scholarship, which provides full tuition and room and board to two freshmen; and the All-Washington Academic Team Scholarship for top academic achievers at the community college level. Additionally there are scholarships for the arts, forensics, music, or theatre.

UNIVERSITY OF PUGET SOUND

Highlights

Admissions Criteria
Academic criteria:
Grades: ☆ ☆ ☆
Difficulty of class schedule: ☆ ☆ ☆
Class rank: ☆
Standardized test scores: ☆ ☆
Teacher recommendations: ☆ ☆
Personal statement: ☆ ☆ ☆
Non-academic criteria considered:
Interview
Extracurricular activities
Special talents, interests, abilities
Character/personal qualities
Volunteer work
Work experience
State of residency
Minority affiliation
Alumni relationship

Deadlines
Early Action: No
Early Decision: November 15
Regular Action: January 15 (final)
Notification of admission by: April 1
Common Application: Accepted

Financial Aid
In-state tuition: $41,640
Out-of-state tuition: $41,640
Room: $5,940
Board: $4,840
Books: $1,000
Freshmen receiving need-based aid: 61%
Undergrads rec. need-based aid: 64%
Avg. % of need met by financial aid: 78%
Avg. aid package (freshmen): $28,062
Avg. aid package (undergrads): $30,235
Avg. debt upon graduation: $28,923

School Spirit
Mascot: Loggers
Colors: Maroon and white

Four-year private
Founded: 1907
Redlands, CA
Large town
Pop. 69,752

Address:
P.O. Box 3080
Redlands, CA
92373

Admissions:
800-455-5064

Financial Aid:
909-748-8047

admissions@redlands.
edu

www.redlands.edu

UNIVERSITY OF REDLANDS

Overview

The only California university rated as both an A+ school and Best Value by *U.S. News & World Report*, the University of Redlands certainly has much to offer. The private, independent university provides a personalized education, freeing its students to create and pursue their own academic interests. Small classes at Redlands provide a rich atmosphere with dedicated professors and individualized attention, giving students the tools they need to attain academic success.

Redlands lies a mere 65 miles east of Los Angeles, in a 140-acre campus covered with old oak trees, lush green lawns and a palm-tree lined front entrance. The university is made up of a range of architecture from historical, elegant columned buildings to more modern, state-of-the-art facilities. Redlands boasts of the exceptional beauty of its campus through an extensive campus tour group made up of thoroughly trained Redlands students, both exceptionally knowledgeable and positively thrilled about their school.

Life at Redlands is more than classes and naturalistic beauty—students enjoy exciting social calendars. Specialty clubs at Redlands include such eccentric groups as "Magic: The Gathering," a group solely organized for students who enjoy indulging in magic tricks.

Providing an overall experience of academic, environmental, and social richness, the University of Redlands proves a strong contender among liberal arts institutions.

Academics

The university follows a liberal arts philosophy, offering over 30 majors in the College of Arts and Sciences. Freshmen must take First-Year Seminars, in which faculty mentors advise students on planning their majors, summers, internships, and short-term travel courses. As part of the college's Liberal Arts Foundation, all students must take courses in areas including cross-cultural studies, foreign language, human behavior, humanities, math, state and economy, and writing. Students describe the Liberal Arts Foundation as "extensive" and "a lot to manage." Strong majors to pursue at Redlands include English, music, and business.

Redlands offers pre-orientation programs, or "First Year Journeys," in seven different locations, providing students the option to form supportive relationships with peers even before they arrive on campus. Once there, students may choose from several academic programs, for example, Johnson Center for Integrative Studies, a unique academic program in which students have no set distribution requirements. Though the course load is challenging, students enjoy the independence of the Johnston program and the opportunity to chart their own curriculums.

The Whitehead Leadership Society is another special academic program in which students are nominated to be leaders. Part of the students' training includes providing active service and support to the university community and promoting an honorable academic climate. Also unique is the Proudian Interdisciplinary Honors Study program, in which 12 students from each grade are chosen to participate in three special seminars on interdisciplinary topics.

The university also offers a May Term, an intensive four-week semester in which students focus on one class or go to a travel class offered in various countries. "The May Term is the highlight of the year," comments a student, adding, "when else do you have the opportunity to travel for four weeks in the name of education?" Similarly, students may study abroad at Redlands, with over dozens of worldwide programs offered, including a specialized program in Salzburg, Austria.

Redlands offers endless opportunities for networking, with its highly-ranked business school and mentor program, matching hundreds of students each year with successful careers or continuing studies.

Student Life

With over 120 student groups on campus, including Mock Trial, Improv Company, and "Doing Activities with Great Spirit," the University of Redlands offers recreation to students with a variety of interests. Social calendars are always full with the many events put on by groups on campus.

One such event, the Feast of Lights, is a service of worship that serves as an introduction to the Christmas season for Redlands students, and includes scripture, poetry, music, and drama. Another event, the Multicultural Festival, celebrates diversity with music, food, arts and crafts, activities, and performances by various cultural groups; and yet another event is Sister's Day Dinner, a dinner put on by Rangi Ya Giza, a non-Greek, diversity-based brotherhood that organizes many multicultural events on campus as a way to raise awareness of national and global issues.

There are 12 Greek organizations on campus; about 13 percent of the male student body joins a fraternity and 20 percent of the female student body joins a sorority. Students say the Greek organizations are "low key" and "relatively open" to non-members.

The University of Redlands has 21 teams (10 men's and 11 women's) that compete in Division III. Of all the fighting Bulldogs, women's water polo is most competitive in its division, while football, soccer, men's basketball, and softball are also contenders in the division. "It's not that we don't care about sports," remarks a student, "but it's not the center of our universe."

For those who seek off-campus diversion, road trips to Los Angeles for chic dining, endless shopping, and other nighttime entertainment are very popular among students. Both the beaches and mountains are also nearby for outdoor recreation.

Students are guaranteed housing every year, and 53 percent of students live on campus in the nine residence halls and two apartment complexes. Each hall has its own personality and provides students with places to study and socialize. Freshmen are encouraged to look into Merriam Hall, a theme-based living learning community based on green and sustainable living and environmental activism.

Student Body

Students at the University of Redlands are academically focused; students in the College of Arts and Sciences tend to be more traditional in their political and religious leanings while students in the Johnston Center tend to be more liberal and free-spirited. "The freedom of the Johnson Center attracts the more independent types," says a student.

Of its undergraduate student body of 3,000 students, ethnic diversity is high (39 percent of students are of minority status), while geographic diversity is moderate—27 percent of students hail from out of state.

You May Not Know

- For the last 15+ years, Redlands graduates have ranked in the top 30 liberal arts college graduates for starting and mid-career salaries, according to Payscale.com.
- *U.S. News & World Report* ranks University of Redlands in the Top 15 Western Regional Universities, with one of the lowest student-to-faculty ratios.

UNIVERSITY OF REDLANDS

Highlights

Students
Total enrollment: 4,956
Undergrads: 3,360
Freshmen: 724
Part-time students: 22%
From out-of-state: 27%
Male/Female: 44%/56%
Live on-campus: 53%
In fraternities: 13%
In sororities: 20%
Off-campus employment rating: Fair
Caucasian: 49%
African American: 5%
Hispanic: 25%
Asian / Pacific Islander: 5%
Native American: 1%
Mixed (2+ ethnicities): 3%
International: 1%

Academics
Calendar: 4-4-1 system
Student/faculty ratio: 15:1
Class size 9 or fewer: 19%
Class size 10-29: 70%
Class size 30-49: 10%
Class size 50-99: 1%
Class size 100 or more: -
Returning freshmen: 87%
Six-year graduation rate: 63%
Graduates who immediately go to graduate school: 31%

Most Popular Majors
Business administration
Liberal studies
Psychology

Admissions
Applicants: 4,501
Accepted: 3,099
Acceptance rate: 68.9%
Average GPA: 3.6
ACT range: 22-26
SAT Math range: 530-620
SAT Reading range: 520-620
SAT Writing range: 4-27
Top 10% of class: 28%
Top 25% of class: 64%
Top 50% of class: 91%

839

College Profiles

UNIVERSITY OF REDLANDS

Highlights

Admissions Criteria
Academic criteria:
Grades: ☆ ☆ ☆
Difficulty of class schedule: ☆ ☆ ☆
Class rank: N/A
Standardized test scores: ☆ ☆
Teacher recommendations: ☆ ☆ ☆
Personal statement: ☆ ☆
Non-academic criteria considered:
Interview
Extracurricular activities
Special talents, interests, abilities
Character/personal qualities
Volunteer work
Work experience
State of residency
Geographical location
Minority affiliation
Alumni relationship

Deadlines
Early Action: November 1
Early Decision: No
Regular Action: Rolling admissions
Common Application: Accepted

Financial Aid
In-state tuition: $40,990
Out-of-state tuition: $40,990
Room: Varies
Board: Varies
Books: $1,710
Freshmen receiving need-based aid: 82%
Undergrads rec. need-based aid: 84%
Avg. % of need met by financial aid: 87%
Avg. aid package (freshmen): $33,263
Avg. aid package (undergrads): $32,719
Avg. debt upon graduation: $32,035

School Spirit
Mascot: Bulldogs
Colors: Maroon and gray
Song: *Och Tamale*

- The Redlands Och Tamale Chant is a cheer with silly verses including, "wing wang trickey trackey poo foo; Joozy woozy skizzle wazzle."

Distinguished Alumni

Gerald A. Albright, American jazz saxophonist; Gale Brandeis, award-winning author and poet; Glen and Les Charles, co-creators and producers of "Cheers" and writers for "The Mary Tyler Moore Show"; Susan Essex, Senior Vice President at Warner Bros. Pictures; Rashid Ghazi, partner at Paragon Marketing Group; Stephen Olson, CEO, The Olson Company.

Admissions and Financial Aid

The University of Redlands uses a rolling admissions process; however, the traditional admissions period is September 1 to March 1 of each year. The university considers only those teacher evaluations that come from academic instructors rather than club sponsors or athletic coaches. SAT or ACT scores and information gleaned from the Common Application also add weight to the decision-making process.

Merit-based scholarships include the Presidential Scholarships, which are GPA-based and award up to $2,500 a year, Achievement Awards based on academic excellence and extracurricular involvement that grant up to $3,500 a year, as well as Creative Writing, Theatre, Music, and Debate Awards that grant anywhere from $500 to $8,000 a year.

UNIVERSITY OF RHODE ISLAND

Overview

University of Rhode Island (URI), the only land-grant, sea-grant, and urban grant university in the state, is home to some 13,000 undergrads and 3,000 grad students. The main campus is located in the small town of Kingston, 19 miles from Newport and 30 miles from Providence. A large public university formerly known for its party school reputation, URI is rising in academic strength, particularly in nursing and the sciences.

Surrounded by farmland, campus is only a few miles from the coast and features a mixture of architecture, from old New England to modern. The Center for Biotechnology and Life Sciences attests to URI's growing emphasis on environmental and life sciences. Students will have to overcome the dark winters of Rhode Island in the small dorms at the university, and those seeking high ethnic and geographic diversity may be better off looking elsewhere. However, those looking for a solid undergraduate education that doesn't skimp on fun—whether through sports or Greek life or an annual mud volleyball fundraiser—may find URI's land, sea, and urban opportunities appealing.

Academics

URI offers more than 100 majors within seven colleges. The General Education Program includes courses in English, math, fine arts, foreign language, letters, natural science, and social science, covering an extensive breadth of areas. The difficulty of classes varies by major. Students enroll in the University College, which offers guidance in helping students figure out their majors. "The science majors say that they have the toughest classes," comments a student.

In spite of its large size, URI has a student-to-faculty ratio of 16:1, and more than two-thirds of classes have less than 30 attendees. Students say that professors are helpful and accessible. "If you make the effort, you can get a lot of time with your professors," one student notes. Strong programs include those in the College of Nursing, College of Engineering, and College of Environmental and Life Sciences.

The International Engineering Program is a five-year, dual-degree interdisciplinary program that gives students the chance to study engineering and a language of their choice (French, Spanish, German, or Chinese). One of the five years is spent abroad, including a semester of study and a six-month internship.

In 2009, URI opened the Center for Biotechnology and Life Sciences, with 140,000 square feet for teaching laboratories, a two-story 300-seat auditorium, and research facilities for the growing environmental biotechnology, life, and health sciences programs. "The labs are cutting edge," one student explains.

The University Honors Program gives academically talented students access to small classes and faculty mentors, apartment-style housing, and an honors colloquium. The program is open to all students with a 3.0 GPA or higher, and students must complete a number of honors requirements, including a Senior Honors Project.

First-year students are privy to Grand Challenge Courses, small classes focused on pressing issues in Arts and Literature, Letters, Natural Sciences, and Social Sciences. Courses are taught by full-time faculty engaged in research. For students interested in taking their work outside the classroom, Outreach is a teaching, research, and service program that links students with communities beyond the university.

The Office of International Education offers more than 200 affiliated study programs in more than 40 countries. Programs include the National Student Exchange, which enables students to study for up to one year at one of nearly 200 NSE member colleges and universities.

The Career Services office provides both online and offline support, including walk-in career advising. In addition, they host fairs that highlight international ca-

UNIVERSITY OF RHODE ISLAND

Four-year public
Founded: 1892
Kingston, RI
Small town
Pop. 6,974

Address:
Nemand Hall
14 Upper College Road
Kingston, RI
02881-0806

Admissions:
401-874-7100

Financial Aid:
401-874-5526

admission@uri.edu

www.uri.edu

UNIVERSITY OF RHODE ISLAND

Students

Total enrollment: 16,451
Undergrads: 13,398
Part-time students: 11%
From out-of-state: 52%
Male/Female: 46%/54%
Live on-campus: 44%
In fraternities: 12%
In sororities: 13%
Off-campus employment rating: Good
Caucasian: 70%
African American: 5%
Hispanic: 8%
Asian / Pacific Islander: 3%
Native American: 0%
Mixed (2+ ethnicities): 2%
International: 1%

Academics

Calendar: Semester
Student/faculty ratio: 16:1
Class size 9 or fewer: 10%
Class size 10-29: 59%
Class size 30-49: 21%
Class size 50-99: 5%
Class size 100 or more: 5%
Returning freshmen: 81%
Six-year graduation rate: 63%

Most Popular Majors

Nursing
Psychology
Communication studies

Admissions

Applicants: 20,637
Accepted: 15,875
Acceptance rate: 76.9%
Placed on wait list: 1,559
Enrolled from wait list: 108
Average GPA: 3.3
ACT range: 21-26
SAT Math range: 500-600
SAT Reading range: 490-580
SAT Writing range: 1-18
Top 10% of class: 17%
Top 25% of class: 48%
Top 50% of class: 83%

reers, graduate school, nursing, engineering, and technology. URI's 21,000-square-foot Alumni Center provides a welcoming space for returning alumni. Along with Career Services, the Alumni Association provides career guidance. There's also an Alumni Mentoring Program, Alumni of Color Network, and other special programs. "I feel like we'll always have support from the university long after graduating," one student notes.

Student Life

URI has more than 100 student organizations funded by the URI Student Senate. These include the Student Entertainment Committee (SEC) that organizes concerts and other campus-wide entertainment, and the Student Alumni Association that also promotes popular events, such as those associated with the Rhody the Ram mascot program. Students who enjoy dance may enroll in intermediate classes for dues of only $10 a semester. The studious may join any of 40 different honors societies, and the journalistic may want to check out *The Good 5¢ Cigar*, URI's daily, student-run newspaper that has a circulation of about 5,000.

URI's annual Spring Festival is held at URI's East Farm and features plant sales, workshops, and displays. The event was started in 2002 by a group of URI Master Gardeners who volunteered at the farm. Today, it attracts nearly 3,000 visitors to the 70-acre research facility. Also in spring is the annual oozeball tournament, which draws 80-100 teams of six to participate in a crazy volleyball game played in several inches of thick mud. It's a "dirty" day, but worth it since it is a fundraiser for other campus events such as the Homecoming bonfire and Midnight Madness, which kick off the basketball season in the fall. "I'd recommend being a spectator rather than a participant," one student laughs.

The Greek community is made up of 23 organizations—13 fraternities and 10 sororities. There are more than 1,600 active members, or about 12 percent of the men and 13 percent of the women in the student body, making it a significant part of campus life for many. "The scene can be a little high school at times," one student remarks.

The Rams compete in 16 sports (seven men's, nine women's) at the Division I level. Men's basketball and football are popular, and sailing is also very competitive. "There's a lot of school spirit surrounding our teams," one student says. Club sports include over 600 student-athletes in 17 sports, and Intramurals also offer an extensive menu of activities, from regular leagues to informal tournaments and one-day events.

Newport, 19 miles away from campus, is popular for the beach, eateries, and shopping venues. Students sometimes take weekend trips to Boston (75 miles away), Providence (30 miles away), or New York City (160 miles away).

Most freshmen live on campus in dorms that are known to be very small. These corridor-style residence halls make up the "Freshman Village," and there is typically one Resident Advisor for every 25 students. Students in Living and Learning Communities also have Resident Academic Mentors (RAMs, a convenient pun on the school's mascot). These LLCs are themed, typically with an academic focus for freshmen and various themes for upperclassmen, including the Rainbow Diversity House, an Honors Cluster, and Women in Leadership House.

Student Body

Many of URI's undergraduates go for the social aspect of the university, so you're likely to encounter more social butterflies than bookworms. "I wouldn't say we're a party school, but we know how to let loose," one student comments. The student body "leans left" politically. There is moderate geographic diversity, with 52 percent of students from out of state; 41 nations and nearly all 50 states are represented. There is moderate ethnic diversity. According to the university, many minority students are low-income students from Rhode Island's core urban cities.

You May Not Know

- Rhody the Ram, URI's official mascot, was at one time a real ram that lived at a nearby dairy.
- URI was first chartered as an agricultural school in 1888, and the original site of the school was Oliver Watson Farm. The original farmhouse is still on campus today, serving as a small museum.
- The film *Hard Luck* was shot at the W. Alton Jones Campus of URI.

Distinguished Alumni

Lincoln Almond, former Rhode Island Governor; Christiane Amanpour, CNN chief international correspondent; Elizabeth Craig, biochemistry professor; Dana Quigley, professional golfer.

Admissions and Financial Aid

URI expects applicants to have completed a minimum of 18 units of college preparatory coursework, with additional requirements for those interested in engineering, businesses, chemistry, computer science, physics, nursing, and pharmacy. Freshmen with advanced standing—those who meet the minimum requirements—are considered for admission based on grades and the types of courses they've taken. Students' high school records (coursework, grades) are given the most weight, followed by standardized tests.

No separate application is required for URI's merit-based scholarships, known as Centennial Scholarships, though students wanting to be considered must apply by the December 1 Early Action Deadline. Students who have taken a challenging curriculum, have a GPA of at least 3.4 and a class rank in the top 25 percent, and who have shown leadership or service involvement, are more likely to receive these awards. There are also Transfer Merit Awards and Phi Theta Kappa Transfer Scholarships. The University provides grants to several hundred students with demonstrated financial need.

UNIVERSITY OF RHODE ISLAND

Highlights

Admissions Criteria
Academic criteria:
Grades: ☆ ☆ ☆
Difficulty of class schedule: ☆ ☆ ☆
Class rank: ☆ ☆
Standardized test scores: ☆ ☆
Teacher recommendations: ☆
Personal statement: ☆ ☆
Non-academic criteria considered:
Extracurricular activities
Special talents, interests, abilities
Character/personal qualities
Volunteer work
Work experience
State of residency
Geographical location
Minority affiliation
Alumni relationship

Deadlines
Early Action: December 1
Early Decision: No
Regular Action: Rolling admissions
Common Application: Accepted

Financial Aid
In-state tuition: $10,878
Out-of-state tuition: $26,444
Room: $7,150
Board: $4,180
Books: $1,200
Freshmen receiving need-based aid: 62%
Undergrads rec. need-based aid: 67%
Avg. % of need met by financial aid: 58%
Avg. aid package (freshmen): $15,701
Avg. aid package (undergrads): $14,901
Avg. debt upon graduation: $30,387

School Spirit
Mascot: Rams
Colors: Light blue and white
Song: *Rhode Island Bowm*

Overview

University of Richmond (UR), located six miles from downtown Richmond, Virginia and 90 miles from the nation's capital, is a picturesque, suburban campus covered with greenery that surrounds Gothic architecture. The campus is rapidly changing, with renovations that include an expansion of the stadium, a 57,000-square-foot International Center, and an addition to the School of Business.

This small private liberal arts university in the Old South has unique offerings through the Jepson School of Leadership. The student body divides men and women into separate student governments and traditions via a "coordinate system" that consists of two complementary colleges: Richmond College for men and Westhampton College for women. Both colleges provide separate residential communities, though the challenging classes and varied student organizations are all co-ed. Students looking for a strong academic program with accessible professors and a vibrant Greek scene outside of class may enjoy UR—as long as they're happy living in the South and don't mind some degree of gender segregation in their residential lives.

Academics

UR offers more than 100 majors and minors, plus master's and law degrees, through five schools: the School of Arts and Sciences, Robins School of Business, Jepson School of Leadership Studies, University of Richmond School of Law, and the School of Continuing Studies.

UR's general education curriculum is a liberal arts core made up of four components: First-Year Seminars, Communication Skills, Field of Study, and Wellness. Two First-Year Seminars link students with distinguished faculty and offer more than 30 study topics to choose from. The Communication Skills requirement entails demonstrating competency in oral communication and proficiency in a foreign language. Field of Study is the breadth requirement in six areas; and finally, Wellness includes a short alcohol awareness program and two elective mini-workshops.

Students say that classes are small but challenging. It is easy to get to know professors outside the classroom, not surprising, given the 9:1 student-faculty ratio and the fact that all classes are taught by professors rather than teaching assistants. "All my professors have gone above and beyond in their efforts," one student says. Strong programs include business administration, political science, and biology.

There is no university-wide honors program, though 11 departments offer honors courses and each outlines different requirements. Generally there is a minimum GPA and honors thesis requirement.

Students interested in business will appreciate the career guidance/mentoring program offered by The Robins School of Business Executive Advisory Council (EAC), a group of about 50 senior executives with a variety of business backgrounds. Students connect one-on-one with these business professionals throughout the academic year. "To meet an executive and see what he or she does on a day-to-day basis helps me understand what I want—and don't want—in my future career," one student notes.

The Jepson School of Leadership offers a BA in leadership studies. Interested students must apply for admission during the fall semester of their second year. The program includes an honors option and encourages study abroad.

In the past decade, UR has strengthened its international offerings, as evidenced by the $20.5 million Carole Weinstein International Center, which opened in 2010. About half of undergraduates participate in study-abroad programs. "We have a real focus on learning about the global society," one student says. There's also a residential program on campus called Global House that has brought together American students and international students from Afghanistan to Zimbabwe.

There are about 45,000 alumni living in all 50 states, Washington, DC, and more than 60 countries, and 35 UR alumni chapters across the United States. A survey of the class of 2011 graduates (of which there was a 50 percent response rate) showed 96 percent employment after one year, primarily in business/industry but also in government, education, and health/medical services. Of those surveyed, 26 percent had enrolled in or completed a graduate program.

Student Life

Richmond's 240+ student organizations include 27 honorary societies, 17 religious groups, a student newspaper, and a radio station. "Pretty much everyone is involved in something," one student comments. There is an emphasis on service, with the Bonner Center for Civic Engagement coordinating volunteer and community-based coursework. Spanning the northeast end of Westhampton Lake, the 65,000-square-foot Tyler Haynes Commons is a central hub for social gatherings and student activities, including the Bookstore, a game room, and the Cellar, a campus pub and restaurant.

The $22.5 million, 165,000-square-foot Modlin Center for the Arts is home to the art and art history, music and theater, and dance departments on campus, and offers the annual Modlin Great Performance Series plus the Department of Music's annual free concert series.

UR traditions include Investiture and Proclamation Night; these are ceremonies for first-year men and women, respectively, to contemplate their college futures. In February, Ring Dance honors the academic achievements of junior women in high style: men wear tuxedoes and women wear gowns for the blockbuster Saturday night party at the posh Jefferson Hotel. Spring brings Pig Roast, a large annual event for students and alumni at fraternity lodges. Dancing, pulled pork sandwiches, and plenty of beer make the event festive for everyone involved.

More than 20 percent of students participate in the 15 fraternities and sororities on campus, making for a very active Greek scene on campus. "Joining gives you the most opportunities to make close friends," one member says.

The UR Spiders compete in 19 varsity sports at the Division I level. Football, which competes in FCS (formerly Division I-AA) and men's and women's basketball are the most competitive—in 2008, UR became NCAA Division I National Football Champions. "Game days are a big deal," one student says. In addition, there are 25 club sports that more than 600 students participate in, as well as intramural options.

The popular Spider Shuttle offers students round-trip rides to local malls and other locations, including the airport and Amtrak station during certain breaks. Students with cars can road trip to Williamsburg or Washington, DC. The close proximity of the Blue Ridge Mountains offers students a wealth of opportunities for outdoor activities as well.

Almost 90 percent of students live on campus. "There's a cohesive school community with pretty much everyone on campus," one student notes. In addition to traditional dorms, students can elect to live in unique first-year communities; these same-sex living-learning communities include Women in Math and Science and Spinning your Web, a leadership program for men.

UNIVERSITY OF RICHMOND

Highlights

Students
Total enrollment: 3,626
Undergrads: 3,074
Freshmen: 781
Part-time students: 1%
From out-of-state: 84%
From public schools: 56%
Male/Female: 45%/55%
Live on-campus: 89%
In fraternities: 19%
In sororities: 24%
Off-campus employment rating: Excellent
Caucasian: 56%
African American: 7%
Hispanic: 6%
Asian / Pacific Islander: 6%
Native American: 0%
Mixed (2+ ethnicities): 2%
International: 11%

Academics
Calendar: Semester
Student/faculty ratio: 9:1
Class size 9 or fewer: 16%
Class size 10-29: 81%
Class size 30-49: 3%
Class size 50-99: -
Class size 100 or more: -

Most Popular Majors
Business administration
International education
Leadership studies

Admissions
Applicants: 10,232
Accepted: 3,101
Acceptance rate: 30.3%
Placed on wait list: 3,939
Enrolled from wait list: 13
Average GPA: Not reported
ACT range: 28-32
SAT Math range: 620-720
SAT Reading range: 580-700
SAT Writing range: 24-49
Top 10% of class: 59%
Top 25% of class: 89%
Top 50% of class: 99%

845

UNIVERSITY OF RICHMOND

Admissions Criteria
Academic criteria:
Grades: ☆ ☆ ☆
Difficulty of class schedule: ☆ ☆ ☆
Class rank: ☆ ☆
Standardized test scores: ☆ ☆
Teacher recommendations: ☆
Personal statement: ☆ ☆
Non-academic criteria considered:
Interview
Extracurricular activities
Special talents, interests, abilities
Character/personal qualities
Volunteer work
Work experience
Geographical location
Minority affiliation
Alumni relationship

Deadlines
Early Action: No
Early Decision: November 15
Regular Action: January 15 (final)
Notification of admission by: April 1
Common Application: Accepted

Financial Aid
In-state tuition: $45,320
Out-of-state tuition: $45,320
Room: $4,650
Board: $5,620
Books: $1,050
Freshmen receiving need-based aid: 40%
Undergrads rec. need-based aid: 43%
Avg. % of need met by financial aid: 100%
Avg. aid package (freshmen): $41,347
Avg. aid package (undergrads): $41,836
Avg. debt upon graduation: $21,825

School Spirit
Mascot: Spider
Colors: Red and blue
Song: *Spider Born and Spider Bred*

Student Body

UR's student body certainly has its share of preppy northeasterners, but overall people are "pretty chill" and "super-friendly," says a student. There is high ethnic diversity, with 21 percent students of color and 11 percent international students from more than 60 countries. A fifth of students are first-generation college students, and more than half attended public schools. There is high geographic diversity, with 84 percent of students from outside Virginia.

UR's Common Ground program aims for diversity and inclusion on campus.

You May Not Know

- The university was founded in 1830 originally as a seminary for men to learn literature and theology.
- In the early 1900s, freshmen were called "rats" and had strict rules including that they couldn't smoke cigars until after Christmas, were forced to wear a red and blue hat at all times, and needed to assist upperclass students with carrying their books.
- In October 1992 at the university, George H.W. Bush, Bill Clinton, and Ross Perot participated in the first presidential three-way debate.

Distinguished Alumni

Bruce Hornsby, singer; Saul Krugman, medical researcher who discovered a vaccine against hepatitis B; Charles Stanley, senior pastor of the First Baptist Church in Atlanta; Mary Sue Terry, former Attorney General of Virginia.

Admissions and Financial Aid

The admissions office states, "At Richmond, there is no typical candidate." While the school does take a holistic view of factors outside academic success—including service, special talents, and life experience—there are some minimum requirements, including 16 units of secondary school coursework in certain areas. Competitive candidates will typically have exceeded this minimum requirement, with three to four units in science, history, and foreign language at the highest levels available at their schools.

Richmond has need-blind admission and meets 100 percent of demonstrated need. The university spent $65.5 million in financial aid for the 2012-13 school year, with 67 percent of students receiving grants or scholarships. One in 13 students receives a merit scholarship, with a total of $8 million awarded annually. Merit-based scholarships include The Richmond Scholars Program, which covers full tuition with some room and board, and the Presidential and Trustee Scholarships, which awards amounts up to $15,000. Virginians with family income under $40,000 receive full scholarships.

UNIVERSITY OF ROCHESTER

Overview

The University of Rochester's main campus is called "River Campus," as it is situated along the Genesee River just outside downtown Rochester. The main landmark on campus is the dome of the Rush Rees Library, where the Hopeman Memorial Carillon's 50 bells chime every 15 minutes. The school's location in the city of Rochester is ideal for students who enjoy the thriving cultural life of a large city with an offbeat, alternative vibe.

The University of Rochester is selective and academically rigorous. That combined with its chilly, snowy climate means you have to be okay with spending a significant amount of your time warm and cozy in the library or the lab. The "Rochester Curriculum" allows students a great degree of freedom in choosing their coursework. That freedom and academic rigor comes at a price; the university charges very high tuition, offset by the average of almost $37,000 in annual financial aid per student.

One way to make the high cost of tuition worthwhile is to take advantage of one of Rochester's unique fifth-year programs. The competitive Kauffman Entrepreneurial Year and Take-Five programs both allow students to take on a fifth year of study completely tuition-free.

Famous for its Eastman School of Music, Rochester is also gaining a reputation as a great school for a cappella. If you love early peppy singing with the mysterious absence of instrumentation, then by golly you'll love Rochester.

Academics

The hallmark of Rochester's academic program is the "Rochester Curriculum." The whole point of the Rochester Curriculum is that it is not a curriculum at all. Students choose a major within one of the three categories of humanities, social sciences, and natural sciences and engineering. To gain breadth beyond the major, students also complete "clusters" of courses in the other two major categories. Each cluster is a group of related classes that total at least 12 credits. To give a few examples, you could complete a humanities cluster called "Visual and Literary Arts of the Diaspora," a social sciences cluster called "Theoretical Economics," or a natural sciences and engineering cluster called "Biology and Behavior." If you minor in a different division than your major, you don't have to complete a cluster in that division. The upshot is that you never have to take a specific course to fulfill a requirement. This leeway makes it relatively easy for students to double or triple major and to rack up minors. The only other requirement is the completion of an introductory writing course. "I love the freedom we have to choose what we study," remarks a student.

Rochester has two truly unique special academic programs that allow students to spend a fifth-year studying tuition-free. The entrepreneurially-minded will be thrilled to discover that Rochester's Kauffman Entrepreneurial Year (KEY) Program funds students to spend up to an entire year on "internships, special projects, relevant coursework, business plan development, and research into various facets of entrepreneurship." In addition, the Take-Five Program lets students spend a free fifth year studying a subject outside their major that has caught their fancy. "We are the only school where parents are happy it takes us five years to graduate," one student notes.

Students who enter the university with particularly strong academic records and a clear idea of their interests can apply for several unique combined bachelor's and advanced degree programs at Rochester called Combined-Admissions Programs (CAPS). Rochester Early Medical Scholars (REMS) get automatic acceptance to the university's medical school after graduation. Other programs allow students to earn an undergraduate and MBA degree in six years or an undergraduate degree and master's in engineering or education in five years.

UNIVERSITY OF ROCHESTER

Students

Total enrollment: 10,510
Undergrads: 5,785
Part-time students: 5%
From out-of-state: 64%
From public schools: 75%
Male/Female: 48%/52%
Live on-campus: 83%
In fraternities: 6%
In sororities: 6%
Off-campus employment rating: Fair
Caucasian: 56%
African American: 5%
Hispanic: 6%
Asian / Pacific Islander: 11%
Native American: 0%
Mixed (2+ ethnicities): 3%
International: 13%

Academics

Calendar: Semester
Student/faculty ratio: 10:1
Class size 9 or fewer: 35%
Class size 10-29: 44%
Class size 30-49: 8%
Class size 50-99: 9%
Class size 100 or more: 3%
Six-year graduation rate: 85%
Graduates who immediately go to graduate school: 31%
Graduates who immediately enter career related to major: 62%

Most Popular Majors

Psychology
Political science
Financial economics

Admissions

Applicants: 14,987
Accepted: 5,370
Acceptance rate: 35.8%
Placed on wait list: 2,029
Enrolled from wait list: 56
Average GPA: 3.8
ACT range: 28-32
SAT Math range: 640-740
SAT Reading range: 600-700
SAT Writing range: 27-51
Top 10% of class: 75%
Top 25% of class: 97%
Top 50% of class: 100%

848

Rochester has the array of study-abroad opportunities that one would expect from a university of its caliber, and the school reports that around one-third of students take advantage of them. Rochester sponsors semester-long study/intern programs in London, Berlin, Bonn, Cologne, Brussels, Edinburgh, and Madrid.

The university's career office puts on several annual networking events to connect students with alumni, in addition to providing career advising services and maintaining a jobs database. Students who wish to pursue internships but need financial support can apply for Reach Funding of up to $3,000.

Student Life

The University of Rochester is home to over 200 student organizations. While the school has a range of activities for everyone, it is worth noting that students interested in music will have a huge buffet of activity choices thanks to the Eastman School of Music's many clubs and ensembles. A capella is especially popular at Rochester. In 2011, a particularly successful a capella group called "The Yellowjackets" was featured on the NBC show *The Sing-Off*.

The special events at Rochester range from the typical to the odd and adorable. Like many schools, Rochester has a big celebration to mark the end of classes in the spring, complete with a big-name musical act. The bash is called Dandelion Day or D-Day. Unlike most other schools—except Oxford, which originated the idea—Rochester has a big, cozy medieval-style "Boar's Head Dinner" just before winter break. Students and faculty alike attend in costume. To help students survive the bleak midwinter, the school also hosts a Winter Carnival that features an all-nighter, post-all-nighter breakfast feast, and ice sculptures.

Greek life claims the allegiance of a large number of students. Six percent of students are members of the 16 fraternities and 15 sororities on-campus. The atmosphere is not that of a major party school, though—everyone is working too hard for that.

Rochester plays in Division III for the most part, though their men's squash team is in the top five in Division I. Rochester is not a sports-crazy school by any means, so don't expect a rah-rah culture of mandatory attendance at football or basketball games. That said, there's plenty of opportunity to get involved in a quirky club sport like Quidditch. The array of intramural sports options is relatively small compared to schools of comparable size. The city's snowy climate makes for plenty of skiing and snowboarding options. "It seems like it's a prerequisite that you know how to ski or snowboard to come here," comments one student.

Rochester is a hip city. It will appeal to you if you don't mind cold weather and prefer the vibe of a funky, rejuvenated Rust Belt city to the center-of-everything feel you might get elsewhere on the East Coast (read: New York City). Rochester has a lot going for it culturally, from tons of large- and small-scale live music venues to the International Museum of Photography to eclectic restaurants and cafes. It features a popular music store with vinyl records and many used bookstores, two amenities required before any city can earn its hipster cred. What's more, Rochester hosts not just one but two international film festivals each year. Those seeking nightlife can check out the offerings on the East End. "There's always something to do in Rochester," one student comments.

The university reports that 83 percent of undergrads live on campus, with all freshmen required to live in freshman halls. Affinity and special interest housing, either designated by floor or taking up an entire house, is available, with themes from "quiet-study" to anime to community service. Upperclassman have several apartment-style housing options. The best pick may well be the newly-built Riverview Apartments. The majority of off-campus living options are shared houses rather than apartments, and rent tends to be affordable compared to other East Coast cities.

Student Body

The student body at Rochester is pretty white—56 percent of undergrads are Caucasian, in fact. International students make up a notable 13 percent of the student body. The majority of students (64 percent) come from out of state. The mindset on campus tends to be very academically-focused, without the wild party scene you would find at other large schools. "We know how to have fun, but it's not a crazy party scene," describes a student, adding, "Most of us are pretty focused on academics. Our social lives are secondary."

You May Not Know

- If your quest is to find the only full-size antique Italian organ currently in North America—and, really, who isn't wondering where that might be—look no farther than the university's Memorial Art Gallery.
- The National Institutes of Health designated the University of Rochester as a Center for AIDS Research in 2013, a sign of the university's status at the forefront of research on the disease.
- The university's renowned Eastman School of Music is named after George Eastman, founder of Eastman Kodak (headquartered in Rochester) and a generous donor to the university.

Distinguished Alumni

Francis Bellamy, author of the first *Pledge of Allegiance*; Renee Fleming, opera star; Michael Kanfer, Academy Award-winning visual effects artist behind *Harry Potter and the Sorcerer's Stone*; Andy Thomas, CEO of Heineken USA.

Admissions and Financial Aid

Admission to Rochester is very competitive, with a 36 percent acceptance rate. The school offers both Early Decision and Priority Review options in addition to its regular admissions cycle. Priority Review is perfect for the type-A commitment-phobe. It allows students to apply early without making any binding commitment. Do note that Early Decision applicants can indicate a preference for a residence hall, unlike other applicants. The university bills itself as "test-flexible," meaning that it accepts a wide variety of standardized tests for admission review, including AP and IB scores. Students may submit multiple test scores, and Rochester will consider their best performance.

UNIVERSITY OF ROCHESTER

Highlights

Admissions Criteria
Academic criteria:
Grades: ☆ ☆ ☆
Difficulty of class schedule: ☆ ☆ ☆
Class rank: ☆
Standardized test scores: ☆ ☆
Teacher recommendations: ☆ ☆ ☆
Personal statement: ☆ ☆
Non-academic criteria considered:
Interview
Extracurricular activities
Special talents, interests, abilities
Character/personal qualities
Volunteer work
Work experience
State of residency
Geographical location
Minority affiliation
Alumni relationship

Deadlines
Early Action: No
Early Decision: November 1
Regular Action: December 1 (priority)
January 1 (final)
Notification of admission by: April 1
Common Application: Accepted

Financial Aid
In-state tuition: $44,580
Out-of-state tuition: $44,580
Room: $8,020
Board: $5,108
Books: $1,290
Freshmen receiving need-based aid: 56%
Undergrads rec. need-based aid: 55%
Avg. % of need met by financial aid: 89%
Avg. aid package (freshmen): $37,988
Avg. aid package (undergrads): $36,815
Avg. debt upon graduation: $27,601

School Spirit
Mascot: Yellowjacket
Colors: Blue and yellow
Song: *The Genesee*

849

UNIVERSITY OF
SAN DIEGO

Four-year private
Founded: 1949
San Diego, CA
Major city
Pop. 1,326,179

Address:
5998 Alcala Park
San Diego, CA
92110-2492

Admissions:
800-248-4873

Financial Aid:
800-248-4873

admissions@sandi-
ego.edu

www.sandiego.edu

UNIVERSITY OF SAN DIEGO

Overview

The University of San Diego is a moderately competitive Catholic university whose architecture and location make it a stunner. The campus stands out from more staid peers thanks to its graceful Spanish Renaissance architecture, which recalls the Universidad de Alcalá (no ivy-covered castles here), and its ocean views. Located just outside San Diego, USD offers students—known as "Toreros," or bullfighters—access to natural and urban activities alike.

USD is not for students looking for a wild party scene. It caters to a more serious crowd, especially those interested in a deep engagement with the Catholic tradition and those committed to community service. That said, there is plenty of fun to be had, from participating in successful Division I teams to trying out wakeboarding at the unparalleled Mission Bay Aquatic Center to cooing at the critters at the San Diego Zoo.

It doesn't have the name recognition of, say, Stanford, but USD is a good option for motivated students thanks to its small classes and opportunities to get to know professors starting from day one. The school also has high participation rates in its study abroad programs—though why so many students ever want to leave its lovely campus is a mystery.

Academics

The University of San Diego has an extensive core curriculum, making up 40-50 percent of the credits needed to graduate, which most students complete by sophomore year. The core courses are in three general areas: Indispensable Competencies (writing, math, foreign language), Traditions (theology and religious studies and philosophy), and Horizons (natural sciences, diversity of human experience, humanities and fine arts, and social sciences). The Traditions requirements set the USD core apart from most other core curricula, which lack a theology component. Students fulfill major requirements in addition to the core, with the most popular majors being finance, business administration, and communication studies. Toreros in the honors program can enjoy team-taught interdisciplinary courses, more challenging versions of core courses, and eligibility for special research grants for honors theses.

Students in their first year at USD participate in the preceptorial program, which entails taking an 18-student course with a professor who serves as their preceptor—that is, an academic advisor who focuses on helping them acclimate to intellectual life at the university level. The preceptorial experience is made that much more meaningful because all freshman live in Living Learning Communities with their preceptorial classmates (see Student Life). "The preceptorial program really helped me acclimate to college and gave me built-in friends and a built-in study group," describes a student.

The University of San Diego stands out in the realm of study abroad opportunities, and has been ranked in the top three study abroad universities by *U.S. News & World Report* based on a nearly 69 percent study abroad participation rate among undergrads. USD has a unique Second Year Experience program that allows freshmen to apply for an immersive study abroad experience in their sophomore year and to take a global awareness course before heading off. "SYE was the highlight of my college experience. I was completely immersed in another culture," says a student. The university offers study abroad opportunities in more than 30 countries and administers its own program in Madrid.

The career office at USD offers the standard career development opportunities including an online job and internship database, on-campus interviewing, and counseling for graduate school and careers. There are many opportunities for students to do research with professors, and the university holds an annual undergraduate research conference called "Creative Collaborations" for students to present their work.

Student Life

USD is a good place for students with a conscience and has been recognized by the Carnegie Foundation as a "Community Engagement" university. Students can take a variety of service learning courses—including one that involves renovating a house for a family in need in time for Thanksgiving each year. "Service is almost expected of you as a student here," states a student. The University Ministry at USD is also highly active, providing a Resident Minister for each living area, organizing spiritual retreats and workshops, and bringing students on service-focused day trips to Tijuana called "Breaking Ground."

USD's teams compete in Division I—and compete well. The school has won the West Coast Conference Commissioner's Cup, awarded to the school with the most successful overall athletic program in the conference, for five years straight. Although its teams are winners, they don't draw a crowd of students or inspire a lot of school spirit. Club sports are popular, with about 400 students participating. Ten intramural sports are also on offer, including inner tube water polo. Outdoor Adventure programs get students off campus and into the wild for activities like snorkeling with leopard sharks and desert yoga. In addition to competitive sports and rugged outdoor activities, students can pursue their interests through over 160 student organizations.

There are six fraternities and eight fraternities at the university. The school emphasizes academic achievement and requires students to complete 12 units of coursework with a minimum 2.5 GPA in order to participate in Greek recruitment. About 25 percent of the student body goes Greek.

Off campus, outdoorsy students have access to the glories of the San Diego area, from beaches to deserts to ski slopes. The Mission Bay Aquatic Center, the largest waterfront recreation facility in the world, is the stuff of any landlocked high school student's daydreams, with instruction available in myriad aquatic activities like surfing, sailing, and waterskiing. "If you aren't into water sports before you come here, you will be after," says a student. The more indoorsy will enjoy the city's art galleries and museums.

Many universities offer First-Year Experience housing programs, but USD goes above-and-beyond by offering a Second-Year Experience housing option as well. Freshmen are required to live on campus if they are neither married nor living with their parents. All freshmen live in Living-Learning Communities connected to their preceptorial classes and focused on concepts such as Change, Faith and Reason, and Sustainability. The LLCs organize theme-related activities and outings. Upperclassmen can live in apartment-style housing or off-campus. In total, 45 percent of all undergraduates live on campus.

Student Body

USD has high ethnic diversity, with the strongest presence from Latinos at 18 percent of the student body. International students make up a sizable six percent of undergrads. Just over half of USD students are from California. As you might expect, nearly half—48 percent—of all students are Roman Catholic. "There is a strong Catholic presence, but you never feel excluded if you're not Catho-

UNIVERSITY OF SAN DIEGO

Highlights

Students
Total enrollment: 8,105
Undergrads: 5,457
Freshmen: 1,074
From out-of-state: 42%
From public schools: 58%
Male/Female: 45%/55%
Live on-campus: 45%
In fraternities: 20%
In sororities: 32%
Off-campus employment rating: Excellent
Caucasian: 57%
African American: 3%
Hispanic: 18%
Asian / Pacific Islander: 6%
Native American: 0%
Mixed (2+ ethnicities): 5%
International: 6%

Academics
Calendar: 4-1-4 system
Student/faculty ratio: 15:1
Class size 9 or fewer: 14%
Class size 10-29: 55%
Class size 30-49: 30%
Class size 50-99: -
Class size 100 or more: -
Graduates who immediately enter career related to major: 88%

Most Popular Majors
Business administration
Communications studies
Accountancy

Admissions
Applicants: 16,578
Accepted: 7,060
Acceptance rate: 42.6%
Placed on wait list: 2,382
Enrolled from wait list: 457
Average GPA: 3.9
ACT range: 25-30
SAT Math range: 570-670
SAT Reading range: 550-650
SAT Writing range: 10-49
Top 10% of class: 46%
Top 25% of class: 77%
Top 50% of class: 95%

851

College Profiles

UNIVERSITY OF SAN DIEGO

Admissions Criteria
Academic criteria:
Grades: ☆ ☆ ☆
Difficulty of class schedule: ☆ ☆ ☆
Class rank: ☆ ☆
Standardized test scores: ☆ ☆ ☆
Teacher recommendations: ☆ ☆
Personal statement: ☆ ☆
Non-academic criteria considered:
Interview
Extracurricular activities
Special talents, interests, abilities
Character/personal qualities
Volunteer work
Work experience
State of residency
Geographical location
Religious affiliation/commitment
Minority affiliation
Alumni relationship

Deadlines
Early Action: No
Early Decision: No
Regular Action: Rolling admissions
Common Application: Accepted

Financial Aid
In-state tuition: $40,900
Out-of-state tuition: $40,900
Room: Varies
Board: Varies
Books: $1,710
Freshmen receiving need-based aid: 56%
Undergrads rec. need-based aid: 53%
Avg. % of need met by financial aid: 71%
Avg. aid package (freshmen): $29,600
Avg. aid package (undergrads): $29,830
Avg. debt upon graduation: $29,874

School Spirit
Mascot: Toreros
Colors: Blue and white
Song: *USD Alma Mater*

lic," notes a student. Women slightly outnumber men 55 percent to 45 percent.

You May Not Know

- Eight players from USD's 2012-2013 men's baseball team have gone pro.
- The university was founded in 1949 by Bishop Charles Francis Buddy and Mother Rosalie Clifton Hill. Mother Hill claimed that "beauty, truth, and goodness" were important parts of any education, and aimed to create a beautiful campus to entice students to find truth and goodness there.
- In the 1970s and 1980s, it was popular for students to hold Friday keggers in the canyon just off campus. Perhaps one of you reading this can revive that dear, oh-so-classy tradition.

Distinguished Alumni

Mike Brown, former LA Lakers Head Coach; Carlos Bustamante, mayor of Tijuana; The Most Reverend Salvatore J. Cordileone, Archbishop of San Francisco; Lowell McAdam, President and CEO of Verizon Communications; Jim Parsons, actor, famous for his role as Sheldon Cooper on *The Big Bang Theory*.

Admissions and Financial Aid

USD is unique in that it has a Late Consideration option and no Early Decision option. Late Consideration applicants who submit an application by Feb. 1 will be considered only after all regular decision applicants have been notified of a decision. USD accepts the Common Application with two supplementary questions: "How does USD stand out among all the colleges to which you are applying?" and "Please briefly elaborate on one of your activities or work experiences that is most meaningful to you."

There is no separate application for merit scholarships, which are awarded only to freshman applicants and may be continued each year based on GPA requirements. Merit awards range from $10,000 to $25,000 per year. Special scholarships are available for student musicians and singers. The Changemaker Scholarship is also awarded to students who "take action and create positive social change in the world around them."

UNIVERSITY OF SAN FRANCISCO

Overview

San Francisco's oldest university, the mid-size Jesuit University of San Francisco, occupies a 50-acre campus nestled on a hilltop near the "Panhandle" of Golden Gate Park. The two towers of the campus' Italian Renaissance-style St. Ignatius Church are among the city skyline's most recognizable landmarks, indicative of both the school's traditional Jesuit liberal arts roots and its adaptations to more modern, urban, liberal surroundings—including strong pre-professional programs and a willingness to be flexible with the Church's intransigent stances on certain social issues.

USF advertises itself with the tagline "academic excellence in the service of humankind." While this sounds like a summary of an upcoming *Spiderman* movie, USF strives to realize this motto in accordance with Jesuit educational tradition: a firm foundation in the liberal arts coupled with strong commitment to social justice, starting with meeting the needs of the city of San Francisco. In return, San Francisco, one of the entertainment, shopping, and food capitals of the West Coast, won't fail students who need a break: the real difficulty will be managing to fit all of the sight-seeing, eating, and entertainment into four short but busy years.

Academics

USF's liberal arts core curriculum requires students to complete one to three classes in each of six areas: foundations of communication; math and the sciences; humanities; philosophy, theology, religious studies, and ethics; social sciences; and visual and performing arts. Additionally, USF requires a course each in service-learning, with a mandatory 25-hour service activity, and cultural diversity. "Everyone wants to give back, and we'd probably all be involved in service even without the requirement," says one student. Arts majors must complete four semesters of a foreign language; science majors, two. Academics at USF are serious on the whole, although majors vary in rigor. Of the 46 majors that USF offers, its pre-professional programs—particularly the Schools of Business and Professional Studies and Nursing—stand out as competitive and demanding, as does its communications studies major.

USF offers two programs that allow students in all majors to complete their liberal arts core with smaller, higher-level seminars: the Honors Program in the Humanities, and the Saint Ignatius Institute, which more closely resembles Honors programs at other schools. Students in the Honors Program take a curriculum of five Honors seminars, which replaces a portion of the core curriculum. Juniors and seniors can conduct independent, faculty-mentored research. Students can apply to Honors during their freshmen or sophomore year. The Saint Ignatius Institute (SII) similarly replaces the core curriculum with heavy-duty liberal arts courses that are half the size of regular classes and places an emphasis on reading primary sources in philosophy, theology, art, and literature; SII additionally combines academics with co-curricular activities, including spring break service trips, a fall retreat, and the SII-only study-abroad program at Oxford. SII students have the option to live with their classmates in an SII-only wing of Phelan Hall.

Students who are interested in service-learning also have the option of community-based living and learning. Sophomores and juniors from all majors can apply to the Erasmus Community, a year-long academic and co-curricular program focused on ethics, service, and social justice that fulfills a portion of students' core curriculum and their service-learning requirement. The program culminates in a two-week service trip to an underdeveloped region. "The trip is life-changing," shares one student.

Students who have demonstrated an interest in a career in teaching (through academic experiences, community service, and working with children or youths) can apply to the five-year Dual Degree in Teacher Preparation (DDTP) program. Participants earn both a bachelor's and master's over the course of four years, and spend the fifth

UNIVERSITY OF SAN FRANCISCO

Four-year private
Founded: 1855
San Francisco, CA
Major city
Pop. 812,826

Address:
2130 Fulton Street
San Francisco, CA
94117-1080

Admissions:
800-CALL-USF

Financial Aid:
415-422-2620

admission@usfca.edu

www.usfca.edu

UNIVERSITY OF SAN FRANCISCO

Students

Total enrollment: 10,017
Undergrads: 6,344
Part-time students: 4%
From out-of-state: 26%
From public schools: 46%
Male/Female: 37%/63%
Live on-campus: 38%
In fraternities: 1%
In sororities: 1%
Off-campus employment rating: Excellent
Caucasian: 34%
African American: 3%
Hispanic: 19%
Asian / Pacific Islander: 19%
Native American: 0%
Mixed (2+ ethnicities): 7%
International: 16%

Academics

Calendar: 4-1-4 system
Student/faculty ratio: 15:1
Class size 9 or fewer: 11%
Class size 10-29: 61%
Class size 30-49: 25%
Class size 50-99: 3%
Class size 100 or more: -
Returning freshmen: 88%
Six-year graduation rate: 67%
Graduates who immediately go to graduate school: 30%

Most Popular Majors

Registered nursing/registered nurse
Business administration/management
Psychology

Admissions

Applicants: 11,223
Accepted: 7,762
Acceptance rate: 69.2%
Placed on wait list: 618
Enrolled from wait list: 4
Average GPA: 3.6
ACT range: 22-27
SAT Math range: 530-630
SAT Reading range: 510-620
SAT Writing range: 7-31
Top 10% of class: 26%
Top 25% of class: 59%
Top 50% of class: 91%

854

year completing two fieldwork experiences student teaching at local schools and earning a preliminary California teaching credential.

Given its Catholic connections, USF can offer its students a number of study-abroad options either through direct programs hosted at foreign institutions or through partnerships with other universities. More than 500 students study abroad each year, and there are some scholarships available for doing so.

The Career Services Center offers the usual smorgasbord of career counseling, interview practice, and résumé critiques, but it also offers an online alumni mentorship program called EdgeOnCollege.

Student Life

Almost 100 student groups operate on the USF campus. While the majority of them are service- or academic-oriented, a healthy smattering of art and performance clubs exist as well, including the College Players, which the college notes is the "oldest student-run theater group west of the Mississippi." Cultural groups put on a number of very popular events throughout the year, including the Hui O'Hawaii Club's Luau, featuring traditional dance, music, and food; and Culturescape, a dance and music showcase featuring all of USF's cultural clubs. Other popular events are centered on Homecoming, including a concert that has featured artists like Lupe Fiasco, a carnival, and Family Weekend. A Greek system exists, but USF's one fraternity and one sorority don't draw a large portion of the student body. "There's too much to do off campus to be tied to a fraternity or sorority," remarks one student.

Soccer is the major sport on campus; both USF's men's and women's teams are highly competitive. Of the rest of USF's 14 Division I varsity sports, basketball, baseball, and women's volleyball are also popular. Koret Health and Recreation Center also offers a variety of facilities for the non-varsity athlete, including an Olympic-sized pool, various sport courts, the "Combatives Room" for martial arts, and a lounge with a sundeck. The Intramural Residence Hall Challenge encourages some healthy rivalries, allowing teams to challenge other floors within their residence.

San Francisco offers a healthy balance of fresh air and city life: students can explore the trails and gardens in Golden Gate Park, while the Haight next door offers a mix of history, hippies, and hipsters amidst Victorian homes. San Francisco neighborhoods at large offer endlessly diverse eating, drinking, shopping, and entertainment options accessible by underground Bay Area Rapid Transit (BART) trains or Muni buses. "San Francisco is the best college city in the country," says a student.

Freshmen and sophomores are guaranteed housing on campus, in co-ed or all-female dorms. Some suite-style options are also available. Upperclassmen have the option to live in residence halls but frequently rent apartments near campus. "You should live on campus for at least a couple years to be able to form friendships," advises one student.

Student Body

The USF student body is predictably liberal and ethnically diverse, given its location and the fact that most students come from within California. The gender ratio is heavy on the side of the women.

"We're not full of hippies, but we're a laid-back, friendly group," one student comments.

You Might Not Know

- The Koret Health and Recreation Center was recognized as having the "Best Gym and Pool" by the *SF Weekly*.
- Solar paneling on the Gleeson Library and Koret Center, among other buildings, provide up to 16 percent of the campus' energy needs.
- Three members of the 1951 USF football team were eventually inducted into the NFL Hall of Fame, the most members from any one college football team. The 1951 team was also invited to the Orange Bowl, but the Southern Conference refused to allow the team's two African-American players participate. The team refused to play without them—resulting in the termination of the school's football program due to lack of funding.

Distinguished Alumni

Gordon Bowker, co-founder of Starbucks; Michael Franti, musician; Ollie Matson, NFL Hall-of-Famer; Paul Otellini, CEO of Intel; Joe Rosenthal, photographer, winner of Pulitzer Prize for his photo *Raising the Flag on Iwo Jima*; Pierre Salinger, U.S. Senator and Press Secretary for President John F. Kennedy.

Admissions and Financial Aid

The high school coursework that USF recommends to applicants varies for science majors and those applying to the School of Nursing—otherwise they are fairly standard. USF does not require SAT Subject Test scores. While students are not required to be Catholic in order to attend USF—and many students who apply and are accepted are not Catholic—applicants should demonstrate the Jesuit value of making significant commitment to community improvement.

USF distributes two types of merit scholarships. Most highly qualified students are eligible for the University Scholars Program, a renewable award that defrays the cost of tuition significantly. Students with high levels of academic achievement who did not qualify for the University Scholars Program are eligible for USF Academic Merit Awards, ranging from $5,000 to $9,000. Students must apply by November 15 to be considered.

UNIVERSITY OF SAN FRANCISCO

Highlights

Admissions Criteria
Academic criteria:
Grades: ☆ ☆ ☆
Difficulty of class schedule: ☆ ☆ ☆
Class rank: ☆
Standardized test scores: ☆ ☆ ☆
Teacher recommendations: ☆ ☆ ☆
Personal statement: ☆ ☆
Non-academic criteria considered:
Extracurricular activities
Special talents, interests, abilities
Character/personal qualities
Volunteer work
Work experience
State of residency
Minority affiliation
Alumni relationship

Deadlines
Early Action: November 15
Early Decision: No
Regular Action: Rolling admissions
Common Application: Accepted

Financial Aid
In-state tuition: $39,840
Out-of-state tuition: $39,840
Room: $8,730
Board: $4,260
Books: $1,500
Avg. aid package (freshmen): $22,805 for grants or scholarship aid, $7,954 for student loans
Avg. aid package (undergrads): $22,575 for grants or scholarship aid, $7,633 for federal student loans

School Spirit
Mascot: Dons
Colors: Green, gold, and white

Four-year public
Founded: 1801
Columbia, SC
Major city
Pop. 130,591

Address:
Office of Undergradu-
ate Admissions
902 Sumter Street
Access
Lieber College
Columbia, SC
29208

Admissions:
800-868-5872

Financial Aid:
803-777-8134

admissions-ugrad@
sc.edu

www.sc.edu

UNIVERSITY OF SOUTH CAROLINA – COLUMBIA

Overview

In the heart of the "Bible Belt" the University of South Carolina is located in the capital city of Columbia. A very large public school, the campus features historical buildings, sprawling greens, and architecture ranging from 19th century to modern.

Despite its obvious location in what is usually thought to be a conservative part of the country, the USC campus is moderate in its views. With a particularly spirited student body, most USC students are involved with political issues as well as social and extracurricular activities when they are not busy rooting for the school's sports teams.

Academics

The University of South Carolina offers 246 majors, with general education require-ments that augment department studies and "allow students to become well-rounded, well-educated citizens." General education requirements include six English credits, six numerical and analytical reasoning credits, 12 liberal arts credits (three of which must be in history, three in fine arts, and three in social or behavioral sciences), seven credits in natural sciences (at least one course with a laboratory requirement), and a demonstrated ability to comprehend the topic and main ideas written and spoken in one foreign language. Students describe the general education requirements as "pretty typical."

According to students, classes at USC are challenging, but difficulty varies from department to department. Professors are generally accessible and there are ample opportunities for students to take classes in intimate settings, despite the large size of the student body. With so many programs available, academic freedom is a strong suit of the university. Among the most prominent programs are business, political science, and biology.

The South Carolina Honors College provides students the chance for an indi-vidualized educational experience complete with one-on-one advising, an extensive four-year curriculum covering all majors, small classes (around 14 students), and special housing opportunities. The college aims to ensure that each student has the chance to really get to know faculty members. "If you have the grades, it's worth it to get into the Honors College because of the extra attention you'll get," says a student.

The Emerging Leaders Circle is another special academic opportunity at USC in which undergraduate business students—selected for campus-wide and community leadership—are invited to participate in various personal and professional develop-ment activities. Those interested in service-learning opportunities can benefit from USC's program which assigns students challenging community tasks, teaching them how to assess a community's needs, strengths, and resources, and fosters reciprocal learning and critical engagement.

The University of South Carolina offers study-abroad programs in France, Ger-many, Italy, Russia, Spain, and Costa Rica. Students with strong academic records can also apply for the school's EuroScholars program which gives the students the unique opportunity to spend a junior semester at a top European research institution.

The majority of students report the school's career center and rather strong alumni network to be helpful in finding jobs and internships during and after college.

Student Life

With 300 official student organizations, students may choose from a plethora of on-campus activities at USC, including music, theater, politics, service, and special-interest groups. Some popular clubs are the Mountaineering and Whitewater Club, the Dance Company, and the The Lion Quizbowl Society.

Popular events and traditions also abound. First Night Carolina is an event focused on freshmen, who are transported by shuttle bus to a secret location featuring free food, music, and the chance to mingle with their future classmates. Tiger Burn occurs the week before the annual rival football game with Clemson. Excitement is heightened by the Tiger Burn pep rally where students are challenged to get excited about the prospect of beating the Tigers. Shopping Day occurs at the end of every semester, when freshmen and sophomores (who usually have the most difficulty getting into full classes) are able to camp out for an opening in a class that becomes available after the Honors College registration deadline. "It might seem crazy to camp out for a class, but it's also a social event," explains a student.

Greek life is a definite part of the USC scene, with about 20 percent of students choosing to join one of 22 fraternities and 16 sororities. However, Greek life is visible but not prominent. Students who are not interested in joining the community can still have an active social life.

Athletics and school pride comprise a huge focus for the average USC student. The university competes in Division I athletics with eight men's and 10 women's teams. Baseball—USC won the 2010 national championship—and basketball are national contenders, but the main athletic attraction is the football team. Even if they aren't winning the games, tailgating and attending football games at USC is almost a quintessential component of the student experience. "The whole campus pretty much tailgates," says a student. For those interested in recreational sports, intramural teams such as flag football, indoor soccer, sand volleyball, Ultimate Frisbee, and bowling are also very popular.

When looking for things to do off campus, most students travel into downtown Columbia for dining and entertainment. The nightlife revolves around the two areas, Five Points and the Visa, filled with bars and clubs frequented by USC students. Some will also take road trips to Myrtle Beach or nearby mountain ranges for outdoor fun.

All freshmen are required to live on campus in either co-ed or single-sex freshman dorms with hall or suite-style bathrooms. Because most students rate their dorm experience and facilities as nothing above average, most upperclassmen prefer to move off campus as soon as they have the chance.

Student Body

University of South Carolina students tend to lean towards conservative political beliefs. However, with such a large student population there is a spectrum of personalities ranging from the academically focused to socialites. Ethnic diversity is high with 21 percent minority students. Geographic diversity is moderate, with 31 percent of students hailing from out of state, mainly the South. USC guys are described as more "chivalrous and charming" than most college males, and many women are indeed "southern belles."

You May Not Know

- The University of South Carolina contributes $4 billion a year to the state's economy.

UNIVERSITY OF SOUTH CAROLINA – COLUMBIA

Highlights

Students
Total enrollment: 31,288
Undergrads: 23,363
Freshmen: 6,109
Part-time students: 7%
From out-of-state: 31%
Male/Female: 46%/54%
Live on-campus: 36%
In fraternities: 13%
In sororities: 28%
Off-campus employment rating: Good
Caucasian: 77%
African American: 11%
Hispanic: 4%
Asian / Pacific Islander: 3%
Native American: 0%
Mixed (2+ ethnicities): 3%
International: 2%

Academics
Calendar: Semester
Student/faculty ratio: 17:1
Class size 9 or fewer: 15%
Class size 10-29: 56%
Class size 30-49: 19%
Class size 50-99: 7%
Class size 100 or more: 3%
Returning freshmen: 87%
Six-year graduation rate: 72%

Most Popular Majors
Biological sciences
Nursing
General experimental psychology

Admissions
Applicants: 23,429
Accepted: 14,199
Acceptance rate: 60.6%
Average GPA: 4.0
ACT range: 24-29
SAT Math range: 560-650
SAT Reading range: 540-640
SAT Writing range: Not reported
Top 10% of class: 30%
Top 25% of class: 67%
Top 50% of class: 94%

857

UNIVERSITY OF SOUTH CAROLINA – COLUMBIA

Admissions Criteria

Academic criteria:
Grades: ☆ ☆ ☆
Difficulty of class schedule: ☆ ☆ ☆
Class rank: ☆
Standardized test scores: ☆ ☆ ☆
Teacher recommendations: ☆
Personal statement: ☆
Non-academic criteria considered:
Extracurricular activities
Special talents, interests, abilities
Character/personal qualities
Volunteer work
Work experience
Minority affiliation
Alumni relationship

Deadlines

Early Action: October 1
Early Decision: No
Regular Action: December 1 (final)
Notification of admission by: March 15
Common Application: Not accepted

Financial Aid

In-state tuition: $10,391
Out-of-state tuition: $28,061
Room: $5,988
Board: $2,921
Books: $994
Freshmen receiving need-based aid: 51%
Undergrads rec. need-based aid: 52%
Avg. % of need met by financial aid: 74%
Avg. aid package (freshmen): $12,340
Avg. aid package (undergrads): $13,012
Avg. debt upon graduation: $25,022

School Spirit

Mascot: Cocky
Colors: Garnet and black
Song: *We Hail Thee Carolina*

- The sociology department now offers a course solely focusing on the pop singer and phenomenon, Lady Gaga.
- Many of the buildings on campus, including upperclassmen apartments, faculty office buildings, and classrooms, pre-date the Civil War.

Distinguished Alumni

Alex English, NBA Hall of Famer; Larry Kellner, CEO of Continental Airlines; Andrew Markham, NFL player; Darius Rucker, musician and lead singer of the band Hootie and the Blowfish.

Admissions and Financial Aid

University of South Carolina's admissions officials primarily base their admission decisions on students' high school transcripts and SAT/ACT scores. On average, around three-quarters of students admitted score 1120 or higher on the SAT, 24 or higher on the ACT, and have a 3.5 GPA on a 4.0 scale.

The majority of USC's scholarship opportunities are based on exceptional standardized test scores and GPAs, in combination with factors such as leadership and/or community involvement. For example, the $10,000 Carolina Scholars Award is given to 20 students with strong academic records who were also leaders in their high school communities. The University also awards up to $10,000 to students who were National Merit Finalists, National Achievement Finalists, or National Hispanic Recognition Program Scholars, and automatically awards $3,000 to students who were ranked first in their class at the end of their junior year or later.

In addition to departmental scholarships, a variety of in-state scholarships ranging from $2,000 to $6,700, as well as out-of-state scholarships for as much as $15,000, are available.

UNIVERSITY OF SOUTHERN CALIFORNIA

Overview

Not so long ago, the University of Southern California (USC) was known primarily as a party school for rich Southern California students. But this fairly large, private university has revamped its image and literally re-created itself. USC experienced a huge influx of money and research funding and is becoming increasingly selective; now a nationally recognized institution, it came in 23rd in *U.S. News & World Report's* ranking of top national universities. The university's 229-acre University Park campus is right next to downtown Los Angeles in the city's Arts and Education Corridor. This location gives students plenty of access to opportunities, networking, and even internships with LA's world-class art, performance, and media scenes, complementing USC's strong Schools of Music, Theatre, and Journalism.

USC's campus is attractive, filled with palm trees, parks and plazas, and Italian Romanesque-style buildings. On-campus fun—particularly football games and tailgating—is popular, and the rest of LA has plenty of nightlife, shopping, food, and beaches to offer. Aside from getting around in not-so-pedestrian-friendly Los Angeles, the real challenge is deciding what to do and how students at the "transformed" USC will fit it all into four busy years of class, research, extracurriculars, and SoCal-style fun.

Academics

USC's size is both an asset and a drawback. It allows unparalleled choice: students can choose from 436 majors across the College of Letters, Arts, and Sciences and 17 professional schools. The strongest of these are the Schools of Theatre and Music, the Viterbi School of Engineering, the Marshall School of Business, and the Annenberg School of Communication and Journalism. It also allows students flexibility in fulfilling the General Education Requirements (which consist of "Foundations" and "Case Studies"), Writing Program, and the Diversity Requirement. For the latter, students must choose one course each in "Western Culture and Traditions," "Global Culture and Traditions," "Scientific Inquiry," "Science and Its Significance," "Arts and Letters," and "Social Issues," as well as complete the two-course writing requirement and a course with a multicultural component.

But USC's size also means that classes, especially introductory ones, can have hundreds of people in them; 14 percent of classes have more than 50 students. "Almost all my professors are really committed to teaching," explains one student, "so even in my larger classes it's easy to get help." Fortunately, USC offers several programs that allow students to work with faculty and smaller groups of peers starting as early as freshman year.

Freshmen Seminars are two-hour, weekly seminars taught on a topic of "personal interest" to the seminar teacher; enrollment is limited to 18 to encourage discussion, and graded on a low-pressure credit/no credit basis. Seminars have included classes like "Seinfeld is Life." First-Year Investigations (FYIs) are similar, in that they are faculty-taught seminars in which students undertake some kind of academic or creative project to complement the course material. "Understanding Los Angeles" and "Behavioral Science in Action" are two examples.

USC offers two Honors programs: the science-based Freshman Science Honors (FSH) and the general-education Thematic Option. Freshman Science Honors offers an advanced freshman natural science course sequence; classes are small, taught by stand-out faculty and graduate assistants, and feature "enriched" lab sections that allow students to work with advanced technology and methods. Special social events, lectures, and field trips facilitate the forming of community and bonding with professors. Premed students might also consider the eight-year Baccalaureate/MD Program, which guarantees students admission to USC's Keck School of Medicine.

UNIVERSITY OF SOUTHERN CALIFORNIA

Four-year private
Founded: 1880
Los Angeles, CA
Major city
Pop. 3,819,702

Address:
University Park
Los Angeles, CA
90089

Admissions:
213-740-1111

Financial Aid:
213-740-1111

admitusc@usc.edu

www.usc.edu

UNIVERSITY OF SOUTHERN CALIFORNIA

Students
Total enrollment: 39,958
Undergrads: 18,316
Freshmen: 3,715
Part-time students: 4%
From out-of-state: 49%
From public schools: 56%
Male/Female: 49%/51%
Live on-campus: 38%
In fraternities: 25%
In sororities: 21%
Off-campus employment rating: Excellent
Caucasian: 39%
African American: 4%
Hispanic: 14%
Asian / Pacific Islander: 23%
Native American: 0%
Mixed (2+ ethnicities): 4%
International: 12%

Academics
Calendar: Semester
Student/faculty ratio: 9:1
Class size 9 or fewer: 14%
Class size 10-29: 55%
Class size 30-49: 17%
Class size 50-99: 9%
Class size 100 or more: 5%
Returning freshmen: 97%
Six-year graduation rate: 90%

Most Popular Majors
Business
Communication
Psychology

Admissions
Applicants: 46,104
Accepted: 9,187
Acceptance rate: 19.9%
Average GPA: 3.7
ACT range: 29-33
SAT Math range: 650-760
SAT Reading range: 620-720
SAT Writing range: 50-39

Thematic Option (TO) replaces the General Education Requirements and Writing Program with its own curriculum of interdisciplinary classes. TO faculty participate in outside social and educational events, as well, which include films, dinners, speakers, and field trips. Applicants with a high school GPA of around 4.0 and qualifying test scores may be invited to apply. "If you're academically inclined, USC has a lot of opportunities to enhance your experience," one student notes.

With more than $560 million in research funding, USC can support student research. Students in any major may work as research assistants for faculty or conduct independent, faculty-supervised research. They can apply for funding through Student Opportunities for Academic Research (SOAR) or Summer Undergraduate Research Fund (SURF).

Problems without Passports programs emphasize "inquiry learning." Classes explore issues such as global health, environmental science, and conflict resolution in international destinations like Belize, Brazil, Cambodia, Egypt, Kazakhstan, the UK, or domestic ones like Washington, DC, and USC's Wrigley Marine Science Center on Catalina Island. USC runs its own four-week "Maymester" study-abroad program immediately following Spring Semester; otherwise, departments or schools hold their own programs in Belgium, China, France, Italy, Japan, South Korea, Spain, Switzerland, and the UK. USC only runs one semester-abroad program at its Marine Science Center; otherwise, students may participate in approved third-party programs.

USC students can take advantage of the resume and cover letter critiques, career fairs, and internship workshops held by the Career Planning and Placement Center. Members of the "Trojan Family" of 233,000 alumni can opt to participate in the Trojan Network, which offers networking opportunities to current students. "You really can get an interview or even a job through the alumni connections," one student says.

Student Life

With more than 750 student organizations on campus, students can get involved in just about anything. The Spirit of Troy marching band is one of USC's best known groups, having performed at the Academy Awards and Rose Parade, as are the USC Song Girls (i.e., cheerleaders). Football is a "monstrous" deal at USC, even if the team was sanctioned by the NCAA in 2010. Football-related events like Conquest! and Homecoming are consequently very popular as well. A week of school spirit events, concerts, and bonfires lead up to the Homecoming and cross-town rival UCLA games, respectively.

USC still retains some of its party-school heritage (a fifth of students are Greeks, and the school has a whopping 37 fraternities and 25 sororities), so massive day-long tailgates are high priority, as are Greek parties. "We don't like the party school reputation," one student comments, "but there are plenty of parties to be had if that's your scene."

Students looking for more cultural stimulation can attend one of the film festivals or speaker series put on by USC's Arts and Humanities Initiative, Visions and Voices.

Of USC's nine men's and nine women's NCAA Division I sports teams, football—with its 11 national championship wins—is clearly the stand-out program. Game days, especially against rivals UCLA and Notre Dame, are practically holidays; campus is decked out in cardinal and gold. "There's no better natural high than screaming amongst 90,000 people," says a student. An extensive but standard array of intramurals is on offer as well.

Off campus, you'll need a car to get pretty much anywhere; but if you have a car or a friend who does, you're in luck. While LA is known for its shopping, clubs, restaurants, and, of course, the beach, it's also not far from prime skiing and hiking territory.

Freshmen are guaranteed housing on campus, which mostly consists of either traditional or suite-style dorms located close to the main parts of campus. Upperclassmen may live in residence halls or in on-campus apartments, but many also live off campus. Campus security (which employs over 200 people) extends for several blocks beyond campus, and Campus Cruiser provides vehicle or walking escorts between 5 p.m. and 3 a.m. "If you use common sense, you won't have a problem," one student comments.

Student Body

USC students have in the past been stereotyped as "spoiled" and "rich," but that's an increasingly obsolete type, thanks to USC's commitment to recruiting first-generation, disadvantaged, and diverse students. "There are still people who fit the old stereotype, but most of us don't," notes a student. Ethnic diversity at USC is high, and USC is a leader in the country in international student enrollment.

You May Not Know

- USC has sent more athletes to the Olympics (more than 400) than any other university.
- USC's Spirit of Troy marching band can be heard on the title track of Fleetwood Mac's platinum album "Tusk."
- USC is the oldest private research university in the West; when it first opened in 1880, Los Angeles had no paved streets, electricity, or telephones.

Distinguished Alumni

Judd Apatow, film director; Neil Armstrong, first man on the Moon; Warren Christopher, former United States Secretary of State; Frank Gehry, architect; Suzanne Nora Johnson, Vice Chairman, Goldman Sachs; George Lucas, film director; Kyra Sedgwick, actress; OJ Simpson, NFL Hall of Famer.

Admissions and Financial Aid

When assessing applicants, USC's admissions office gives special consideration to applicants who have taken rigorous courses of study or who have demonstrated "steady and substantial" improvement throughout high school. Interviews are optional and offered on a first-come, first-served basis: if USC is your top choice, you'd better sign up ASAP. Some programs, like theatre, may require extra materials.

Qualified applicants (with standardized test scores in the top one to two percent) who submit their materials by December 1 may be eligible for one of 100 full-tuition Trustee Scholarships or one of 200 half-tuition Presidential Scholarships.

UNIVERSITY OF SOUTHERN CALIFORNIA

Highlights

Admissions Criteria
Academic criteria:
Grades: ☆ ☆ ☆
Difficulty of class schedule: ☆ ☆ ☆
Class rank: ☆
Standardized test scores: ☆ ☆ ☆
Teacher recommendations: ☆ ☆ ☆
Personal statement: ☆ ☆ ☆
Non-academic criteria considered:
Interview
Extracurricular activities
Special talents, interests, abilities
Character/personal qualities
Volunteer work
Work experience
State of residency
Minority affiliation
Alumni relationship

Deadlines
Early Action: No
Early Decision: No
Regular Action: December 1 (priority)
January 10 (final)
Notification of admission by: April 1
Common Application: Accepted

Financial Aid
In-state tuition: $45,602
Out-of-state tuition: $45,602
Room: $7,702
Board: $5,200
Books: $1,500
Freshmen receiving need-based aid: 38%
Undergrads rec. need-based aid: 42%
Avg. % of need met by financial aid: 100%
Avg. aid package (freshmen): $41,752
Avg. aid package (undergrads): $41,017
Avg. debt upon graduation: $28,575

School Spirit
Mascot: Traveler
Colors: Cardinal and gold
Song: *Fight On*

861

Four-year public
Founded: 1794
Knoxville, TN
Medium city
Pop. 180,761

Address:
320 Student Services
Building
Knoxville, TN
37996

Admissions:
865-974-2184

Financial Aid:
865-974-3131

admissions@utk.edu

www.utk.edu

UNIVERSITY OF TENNESSEE AT KNOXVILLE

Overview

The University of Tennessee at Knoxville is a big school, no doubt, but it is also known for its big-hearted faculty and student body. The 21,000 undergraduate students may seem daunting to anyone considering UT, but the school does its best to keep student-to-faculty ratios moderate (17:1) and provides many options for students to get individual attention, especially within the honors program. UT is also an athlete's school, with powerhouse teams in football and both men and women's volleyball. The popularity of sports on campus creates a vibrant atmosphere of school spirit, evidenced by the well-attended football games.

UT is located near the Great Smoky Mountains in the city of Knoxville, giving students the choice of escaping into nature or diving into city life. The campus, meanwhile, is undergoing a complete overhaul of design, ranging from road-removal to refurbishing old buildings. The plan, which is scheduled for completion in 2026, aims to create more areas of green open space.

Academics

Between UT's 11 colleges, it offers more than 300 degree programs, among which the strongest are business, engineering, and psychology. Other schools include Agricultural Sciences and Natural Resources; Architecture and Design; Arts and Sciences; Communication and Information; Education, Health, and Human Sciences; Law; Nursing; Social Work; the Space Institute; and Veterinary Medicine.

Undergraduates have a comprehensive but flexible set of requirements, which include three courses in communicating through writing, one course in oral communication, and two courses in quantitative reasoning. Subject area requirements cover natural sciences, arts and humanities, social sciences, and cultures and civilizations. Students say that the requirements "allow flexibility" and that there's a "huge range of classes to select from."

All freshmen participate in a one-unit pass/no-credit Freshman Seminar Program. Seminar topics are varied and can include such studies as The Natural History of Love, American Sign Language, Science of Basketball Shooting, and Discovering Your Personality.

Within such a large university, the level of academic rigor can vary. However, for students who wish to challenge themselves, there are various Honors programs, ranging from departmental level to more exclusive programs. The Chancellor's Honors Program is a university-wide program with a membership of approximately 5-10 percent of the undergraduate population. Honors theses are encouraged but not required for this program, but there is a special curriculum. "Writing a thesis was very challenging, but when I was done, it was inspiring to hold it in my hands and see what I had accomplished," says a student.

More competitive is the Baker Scholars Program, which is for students interested in "the public life of the nation and its role in the global community." Students in this program—usually juniors and seniors— conduct a year-long research project to address public policy. Baker Scholars are paired with faculty mentors.

Finally, the most exclusive program is the Haslam Scholars, a four-year intensive curriculum for 15 incoming first-year students each year. Students are given a laptop, the equivalent of $4,000 in support of a joint study-abroad experience, and $5,000 in support of individual thesis research. The Haslam Scholar's Program focuses on leadership and service qualities, beginning with a summer program for freshmen and ending with a senior seminar.

For those who would like to study abroad, UT provides many options, which they categorize as exchanges—direct, faculty-led, third-party, and academic internships. Faculty-led programs are usually held during the summer and spring break, and allow students to work closely with a member of the UT faculty, while internships are a good way for students to gain practical work experience and academic credit. Students may intern during the summer or combine a part-time internship with a traditional year abroad program. UT collaborates with many third-party programs, providing study-abroad opportunities in such diverse places as Cyprus, Finland, Ghana, Vietnam, and Wales.

UT alumni number in the hundreds of thousands and thus make up an extensive career network. According to the university, the Tennessee Apprentice Program, started in 2009, is a "job-shadowing opportunity that connects alumni with students who wish to learn more about a specific career field." "I know several people who got jobs because they were hired by UT alums," says a student.

Student Life

Student life at UT is packed with activities. There are 370 registered student organizations to pick from, covering every possible student interest. The university operates two radio stations and a student newspaper *The Daily Beacon*, which has a staff of over one hundred students. UT also has thriving religious organizations, all located along "Church Row," which include the UT Christian Student Fellowship and student centers for Protestants, Methodists, and Catholics.

Central hang-out locations include the Pedestrian Mall and its adjoining Amphitheater, where students are often seen playing Frisbee and lounging in the sun. T-RECS, the Tennessee Recreational Center for Students, is an athletic complex for all students and faculty. Though it serves the non-athlete population, it houses an Olympic-sized swimming pool and a generous array of exercise and training equipment. One student describes the facilities as "amazing."

In terms of athletics, UT has 18 sports that compete in Division I. The football and both men's and women's basketball teams are national powerhouses, but football is king in terms of popularity. The Volunteers have won multiple National Championship victories. Super Bowl champion Peyton Manning and NFL Hall of Fame player Reggie White both started their careers at UT. Football games are among the most well attended events on campus, with games attracting an average attendance that is par with the top three universities in the country. "Games are like a party with 100,000 of your closest friends," says a student.

Other major campus events include twice yearly Vol Night Long substance abuse-awareness events, hosted by the Campus Entertainment Board. In the spring, the campus rocks out to Volapalooza, a campus-wide music event that has hosted Cake, Dashboard Confessional, and Ben Folds in past years. Off campus, students can hike and camp in the Great Smoky Mountains or go into nearby Dollywood or Gatlinburg for some culture and entertainment.

UT has 26 fraternities and 19 sororities, making Greek life a significant part of campus, with about one in six students joining. The fraternities boast 5,000 man-hours devoted to community service last year. Students say the Greek organizations have a "strong presence" on campus and that the "parties are particularly popular among underclassmen."

UNIVERSITY OF TENNESSEE – KNOXVILLE

Highlights

Students
Total enrollment: 29,833
Undergrads: 20,916
Part-time students: 6%
From out-of-state: 10%
Male/Female: 51%/49%
Live on-campus: 37%
In fraternities: 13%
In sororities: 21%
Off-campus employment rating: Good
Caucasian: 81%
African American: 7%
Hispanic: 3%
Asian / Pacific Islander: 3%
Native American: 0%
Mixed (2+ ethnicities): 3%
International: 2%

Academics
Calendar: Semester
Student/faculty ratio: 17:1
Class size 9 or fewer: 15%
Class size 10-29: 59%
Class size 30-49: 19%
Class size 50-99: 4%
Class size 100 or more: 3%
Six-year graduation rate: 66%
Graduates who immediately enter career
    related to major: 86%

Most Popular Majors
Psychology
Logistic/transportation
Political science

Admissions
Applicants: 14,398
Accepted: 9,693
Acceptance rate: 67.3%
Placed on wait list: 2,051
Enrolled from wait list: 19
Average GPA: 3.9
ACT range: 24-29
SAT Math range: 530-650
SAT Reading range: 530-640
SAT Writing range: Not reported
Top 10% of class: 50%
Top 25% of class: 90%
Top 50% of class: 100%

863

UNIVERSITY OF TENNESSEE – KNOXVILLE

Admissions Criteria

Academic criteria:
Grades: ☆ ☆ ☆
Difficulty of class schedule: ☆ ☆ ☆
Class rank: ☆
Standardized test scores: ☆ ☆ ☆
Teacher recommendations: ☆
Personal statement: ☆
Non-academic criteria considered:
Extracurricular activities
Special talents, interests, abilities
Character/personal qualities
Volunteer work
Work experience
Geographical location
Minority affiliation
Alumni relationship

Deadlines

Early Action: No
Early Decision: No
Regular Action: November 1 (priority)
December 1 (final)
Notification of admission by: March 31
Common Application: Accepted

Financial Aid

In-state tuition: $9,780
Out-of-state tuition: $27,970
Room: Varies
Board: Varies
Books: $1,536
Freshmen receiving need-based aid: 61%
Undergrads rec. need-based aid: 59%
Avg. % of need met by financial aid: 62%
Avg. aid package (freshmen): $12,866
Avg. aid package (undergrads): $11,410
Avg. debt upon graduation: $22,860

School Spirit

Mascot: Smokey, Blue-Tic Coon Hound
Colors: Orange and white
Song: *Rocky Top*

Freshmen live in dorms, of which there are 12 on campus, housing a total of 7,500 students. Most of the halls are suite-style, with two double-occupancy rooms sharing a bathroom. However, many of these dorms are quite old; so while freshmen are required to live on campus, many upperclassmen move off campus.

Student Body

UT is striking in its lack of geographic diversity, with only 10 percent hailing from out of state. The university has moderate ethnic diversity with 16 percent minority students. The International House and the Black Cultural Center are two places that host cultural events and provide tutoring.

You May Not Know

- In 1953 the college had a contest to select a live mascot. The Rev. William C. Brooks won with his Bluetick Coonhound "Smokey."
- Tennessee is known as the "Volunteer State" for the large number of Tennesseans who volunteered for military service since the Revolutionary War.
- UT holds papers from the three U.S. Presidents from the state—Andrew Jackson, James K. Polk, and Andrew Johnson.

Distinguished Alumni

Lamar Alexander, U.S. Senator; Yeda Crusius, Governor of Rio Grande do Sul, Brazil; Todd Helton, MLB player; Peyton Manning, NFL quarterback; Margaret Seddon, U.S. Astronaut.

Admissions and Financial Aid

UT admissions officials seek students who can "reflect its mission" and who represent the diversity of the state of Tennessee. The admissions office stresses that applicants' GPAs will be weighted to reflect honors, AP, and IB courses. Applicants are also allowed to combine ACT or SAT scores and only submit their best scores. Recommendation letters from teachers are optional but encouraged.

In terms of scholarships, there are many opportunities available for incoming freshmen, including merit-based scholarships. The prestigious four-year Chancellor's scholarships are usually given to students with an average high school GPA of 3.96 or higher.

UNIVERSITY OF TEXAS AT AUSTIN

Overview

Consistently rated as one of the top 20 public schools in the nation, the University of Texas at Austin lives up to its ranking. The university is located in the college town of Austin, Texas, a destination spot for artistic creativity, music, and nighttime enjoyment amidst a backdrop of historic limestone and contemporary Southwestern architecture. The university expresses the artistic dedication of its city by putting on an extensive arts calendar of performances each year.

Not only does UT excel in the arts, but in academics as well. The great size of the research-based university, with its total student population of 52,000 students, allows for extensive educational variety: the institution offers over 300 nationally ranked degree programs in 15 colleges. Needless to say, students at Texas never feel restricted in their choice of studies since they enjoy an extensive spectrum of educational opportunities.

The truly praiseworthy aspect of the University of Texas is its undying devotion to cultivating the entire person, with academics, athletics, and social life included. The Texas Longhorns ranked fifth among Division I schools in 2008 by the National Association of Collegiate Directors of Athletics, and the large student population is known to be a hotbed of social opportunities. Students at Texas enjoy on-campus performances by Kanye West and Keith Urban, as well as unique events such as the annual student organizations fair "Party on the Plaza." For a student looking for stimulating academics, elite athletics, and abundant fun, UT is a university to explore.

Academics

At UT, academic requirements are taken seriously: all students, regardless of major, must complete a 42-hour core curriculum including English, mathematics, American history, American and Texas government, behavioral sciences, and natural sciences. The academic environment is competitive, with extremely large class sizes. Because the university is research-based, many professors pursue their own research in addition to teaching. "There are solid and less-than-solid professors, but most of mine have been outstanding," one student says.

With over 135 academic programs from which to choose at Texas, strong academic programs include business, liberal arts, and engineering. Students may elect to pursue any one of the 10 undergraduate business majors offered, participate in the Business Honors Program and take accelerated classes that are designed after MBA courses, or participate in the Business Foundations Program for non-business majors. According to the college, engineering students are recruited by companies including Dell, IBM, and National Instruments. All of the undergraduate engineering programs are ranked in the top 20 by *U.S. News & World Report*, and many are ranked in the top 10. "Our engineering graduates are sought after," boasts a student.

A special academic opportunity is the Honors Program, in which admitted students enjoy smaller classes, individual contact with faculty, and take part in honors intramural sports as well as enjoy special honors dinners together. Another special program is Signature Courses, in which freshmen have their interests matched to those of faculty, resulting in student schedules that are specially created, often with an emphasis on writing and speaking courses that can be applied to any major. In First-Year Interest Groups, students are placed into 25-person groups and share two to four classes together. They also attend a weekly seminar facilitated by a staff member. In this way, the FIG blends academics with social interactions, creating a valuable experience for students.

For those with the itch to travel, the University of Texas at Austin boasts one of the largest study-abroad programs in the U.S., with programs in over 50 different

UNIVERSITY OF TEXAS – AUSTIN

Four-year public
Founded: 1883
Austin, TX
Major city
Pop. 820,611

Address:
110 Inner Campus
Drive Stop G1100
Austin, TX
78712-1702

Admissions:
512-475-7399

Financial Aid:
512-475-6282

www.utexas.edu

UNIVERSITY OF TEXAS – AUSTIN

Students

Total enrollment: 52,186
Undergrads: 39,955
Freshmen: 8,559
Part-time students: 7%
From out-of-state: 7%
Male/Female: 49%/51%
Live on-campus: 19%
In fraternities: 3%
In sororities: 4%
Off-campus employment rating: Fair
Caucasian: 49%
African American: 4%
Hispanic: 21%
Asian / Pacific Islander: 18%
Native American: 0%
Mixed (2+ ethnicities): 2%
International: 5%

Academics

Calendar: Semester
Student/faculty ratio: 18:1
Class size 9 or fewer: 6%
Class size 10-29: 53%
Class size 30-49: 15%
Class size 50-99: 15%
Class size 100 or more: 11%
Returning freshmen: 93%
Six-year graduation rate: 79%

Most Popular Majors

Biological sciences
Liberal arts
Business administration

Admissions

Applicants: 35,431
Accepted: 16,563
Acceptance rate: 46.7%
Placed on wait list: 321
Enrolled from wait list: 34
Average GPA: Not reported
ACT range: 25-31
SAT Math range: 580-710
SAT Reading range: 550-670
SAT Writing range: 18-38
Top 10% of class: 72%
Top 25% of class: 91%
Top 50% of class: 98%

countries. Many of the programs have internship opportunities or options that lead to graduate studies.

UT equips its students with the intellectual tools to succeed and also provides an extensive recruiting network: "HireTexas: Access-UT" connects Texas students with employers from different fields around the globe. Many of the schools have their own career services offices, offering specialized services for students in their majors.

Student Life

UT offers 900 official student organizations, with new ones being added each year. Popular organizations include religious groups, minority and international student groups, and musical groups, as well as the Urban Sustainability Collective and the Broccoli Club, a group dedicated to performing droll and interesting plays.

A prominent event on campus is Texas Revue, a night in April where thousands of students enjoy the talented dancers, singers, and musicians at the university as they put on one-act plays and performances. Other events include the 40 Acres Fest, a huge annual concert that brings in famous artists such as Big Boi, Suite 709 and Sleigh Bells; and Party on the Plaza, the enormous, highly anticipated student organization fair with sponsored lunch, charity dunk tanks, and a mini-putt golf challenge. "Almost every weekend there's a fair or festival going on," says a student.

Greek life is active on campus, with three percent of the male population participating in a fraternity and four percent of the female population in a sorority. "It's a big Greek scene because everything here is big," one student states, "but you don't have to be part of a fraternity or sorority to have fun."

When it comes to athletics, UT's nine men's and women's 11 varsity teams that compete in the Division I Big 12 Conference dominate the scene. Sports are a huge focus of student life, with the university having one of the top overall athletics programs in the country and perennial championship contenders in eight different teams. With this level of elite athletics, students at UT cannot help but feel that Longhorn pride. For those who are interested in athletics at the non-competitive level, there are more than 25 intramural team sports, tournaments, and special events including the usual such as basketball, Ultimate Frisbee, and flag football and the less usual such as a sports trivia bowl, billiards, and March Bracket Madness.

For those who prefer off-campus activities (and 81 percent of students do live off campus), there is the city of Austin to check out. From outdoors activities, to musical entertainment, endless dining and shopping, and weekend trips to Texas Hill Country, there are bountiful opportunities for off-campus explorations while studying at UT. "This is one of the top college towns in the country," explains a student. "The music and bars are amazing."

The large percentage of students living off campus is due to the immense size of the student body—there is not enough room on campus to house all students. For those who must live off campus, the university provides shuttles to and from their residences.

Student Body

With a student body of more than 50,000, everyone can find his or her niche at UT. "Whether you're a nerd or hipster or somewhere in between, you'll fit in," says a student. Students describe themselves as "friendly," "polite," and "very active." Ethnic diversity is high, with a 45 percent minority presence. Geographic diversity, however, is low, with only seven percent of students hailing from out of state.

You May Not Know

- UT was named one of the original eight Public Ivy institutions, named as such because they provide an Ivy League education at a public school price.
- The Texas Revue at UT is the largest student talent show in the state of Texas.
- The Harry Ransom Center, a place of cultural archives, contains the world's first photograph, among other worldly treasures.

Distinguished Alumni

Wes Anderson, writer/director; Laura Bush, former first lady; Walter Cronkite, former news anchor; Janis Joplin, singer; Gary C. Kelly, CEO of Southwest Airlines; Matthew McConaughey, actor.

Admissions and Financial Aid

The UT admissions committee considers both academic achievements—including class rank, SAT/ACT test scores, and high school coursework—and personal achievements such as extracurricular activities, written essays, and teacher recommendations. SAT Subject Tests are not required but are considered. There is also an automatic admissions process based on class rank that changes every year; these students do not receive holistic review.

Students may apply for merit-based scholarships through the ApplyTexas Application. There are many scholarships available, ranging from $400 a year (Glenn Maloney Memorial Scholarship) to full tuition. The President's Achievement Scholarship awards up to $5,000 a year, and the First Generation Scholarship provides $2,500 a year for four years. All awards are detailed at www.texas-scholarships.org. There are both public university scholarships and privately funded scholarships; all merit-based scholarships take grades and test scores into consideration.

UNIVERSITY OF TEXAS – AUSTIN

Highlights

Admissions Criteria
Academic criteria:
Grades: ☆ ☆ ☆
Difficulty of class schedule: ☆ ☆ ☆
Class rank: ☆ ☆ ☆
Standardized test scores: ☆ ☆
Teacher recommendations: ☆
Personal statement: ☆ ☆
Non-academic criteria considered:
Extracurricular activities
Special talents, interests, abilities
Character/personal qualities
Volunteer work
Work experience
Minority affiliation

Deadlines
Early Action: No
Early Decision: No
Regular Action: Rolling admissions
Common Application: Accepted

Financial Aid
In-state tuition: $9,790
Out-of-state tuition: $33,824
Room: Varies
Board: Varies
Books: $750
Freshmen receiving need-based aid: 48%
Undergrads rec. need-based aid: 45%
Avg. % of need met by financial aid: 66%
Avg. aid package (freshmen): $13,669
Avg. aid package (undergrads): $12,333
Avg. debt upon graduation: $26,097

School Spirit
Mascot: Bevo (Longhorn Steer)
Colors: Burnt orange and white
Song: *Eyes of Texas*

Overview

The University of Toronto has a lot—of students, campuses, colleges, and things to do in the city of Toronto. This is a large public university, sprawled across three campuses: St. George (downtown), Mississauga (west), and Scarborough (east). Each of the three U of T campuses offers a different student life experience. The St. George campus is the largest campus and is located in the center of downtown Toronto. The Mississauga campus offers 225 acres of green space but is still within reach of downtown. The Scarborough campus is described by the college as the "greenest" with 300 acres of parkland. It is a "particularly strong" artistic community.

The university offers students the chance to study in the campus environment that suits them best, providing a spectrum of academic fields, including strong research, social sciences, life sciences, and engineering programs across its different locations. U of T works to build smaller community settings for students through its seven colleges on the St. George campus and the smaller Mississauga and Scarborough facilities. Throughout the university as a whole, there is a diverse group of students, a variety of architecture from modern to gothic, and endless entertainment in one of Canada's hippest cities.

Academics

The university offers 224 majors. Some of the stronger academic programs include engineering sciences, computer sciences, life sciences, and humanities. However, the classes can be a bit overwhelming when it comes to size. "Con Hall," a lecture facility with around a 1,700-person seating capacity, can overflow with students. Fortunately, that usually happens with just first-year introductory courses. "It's normal to feel a little lost during your first year," explains a student, "but you find your way after that."

In order to navigate these expansive academic seas, the university divides students into FLCs (First Year Learning Communities called "flicks"), groups of 24 to 30 first-years in the same area of study. Besides heading to some of the same core courses, these students meet regularly outside class to get familiarized with some of the resources the school offers, as well as to have fun. FLCs include life science, computer science, commerce, economics, philosophy, and international relations. Students describe the FLCs as "essential" and "a great way to make friends."

First-years also can enroll in one of nearly 200 seminars open only to newly admitted Faculty of Arts and Science students. Sign up if you're looking for a discussion of course material in a small group setting, as well as a chance to hone your writing and presentation skills—or if you ever want a professor to recognize you.

The Professional Experience Year Program (PEY) provides students with 12-16 month paid internships that aim to help participants gain industry experience. The co-op program also gives students hands-on work experience, placing 1,500 students in paid 12- to 16-week jobs. Typical pay ranges from $9.25 to $21 per hour.

Students may participate in international and Canadian exchanges for a term or a full year through the International Student Exchange Office. There are also study-abroad programs in areas including Australia, Central Europe, China, Japan, Jordan, Kenya, and Mexico.

The career services centre provides access to job listings, workshops, and special events designed to help graduating students find employment, even for students as far as two years out of school. There are a number of career fairs including a Recent Graduates Job Fair.

Student Life

The university has more than 1,100 official student organizations, the most popular of which are a wide array of music groups. There are a number of others that are quite distinctive and as whacky as the Society for Creative Anachronism, international folk dance club, or the student newspaper. "The Society for Creative Anachronism recreates Medieval and Renaissance times," one student explains.

Annual events include Envirofest, a four-day event with sustainability speeches, movie screenings, and teach-ins. "There's even Earth Bingo Night, which is more fun than it sounds," laughs a student. Winterfest is a six-day festival including skating, a pub crawl, battle of the bands, and campus-wide capture-the-flag competition. "It's a fun way to escape the cold, or at least celebrate it," says a student. The Follies is a campus community theatre group that has recently performed musicals including *The Rocky Horror Show*, *Urinetown*, and *Assassins*.

Fraternities at University of Toronto are some of the oldest in all of Canada. They aren't the biggest today, but they do offer the typical social gatherings. "There's so much else to do that not a lot of people get involved in Greek organizations," says a student.

The university has 47 teams competing in the Ontario University Athletics and Canadian Interuniversity Sport conferences. Men's and women's hockey are undoubtedly the school's powerhouses, while football is popular, and rowing and Nordic skiing continue to grow. The intramural program is quite large with more than 10,000 participants. Besides regular intramural sports, students may try out and participate in the more competitive Tri-Campus program that involves students from all three campuses.

Going to school in Toronto gives students access to culture and entertainment. The Toronto International Film Festival, one of the most prestigious in the world, draws a quarter million in attendance to view some of the best that cinema has to offer. Nuit Blanche is a free all-night arts festival (or "contemporary art thing" as Toronto's Executive Director of Culture puts it). With more than 600 pieces from over 2,000 artists, the event has become one of the country's most anticipated cultural affairs, even if only for a few hours each year. But if these seem too artsy, don't fret. The city celebrates Caribbean heritage and things "get wild" in traditional Carnival-like fashion. "There's always a party to go to in Toronto," says a student.

And when it comes to living in Toronto, you might really have to. Not all first-year students are guaranteed housing. There is housing available on all three campuses but many students live off campus or commute. University housing includes dorms, apartment-style, townhouse-style, and living-and-learning communities. Those who live off campus utilize the Student Housing Service office, which provides listings of thousands of rentals.

Student Body

It's hard to put a finger on what the typical U of T undergrad is like, but in general, students describe themselves as "friendly," "outgoing," "politically and socially active." With so many students, colleges, campuses, and city attractions, everyone can find a niche. Ethnic diversity is high (42 percent minority) while geographic diversity tends to be rather low.

UNIVERSITY OF TORONTO

Highlights

Students
Total enrollment: 82,041
Undergrads: 66,398
Freshmen: 18,485
Part-time students: 10%
From out-of-state: 13%
Male/Female: 44%/56%
Live on-campus: 16%

Academics
Calendar: Trimester
Student/faculty ratio: 24:1
Class size 9 or fewer: 34%
Class size 10-29: 50%
Class size 30-49: 12%
Class size 50-99: 4%
Class size 100 or more: -
Returning freshmen: 91%
Six-year graduation rate: 82%

Admissions
Applicants: 70,920
Accepted: 47,800
Acceptance rate: 67.4%
Average GPA: Not reported
ACT range: Not reported
SAT Math range: Not reported
SAT Reading range: Not reported
SAT Writing range: Not reported

UNIVERSITY OF TORONTO

Admissions Criteria
Academic criteria:
Grades: ☆ ☆ ☆
Difficulty of class schedule: ☆ ☆ ☆
Class rank: N/A
Standardized test scores: ☆ ☆ ☆
Teacher recommendations: N/A
Personal statement: N/A
Non-academic criteria considered:
State of residency

Deadlines
Early Action: No
Early Decision: No
Regular Action: March 1 (final)
Notification of admission by: April 30
Common Application: Not accepted

Financial Aid
In-state tuition: $5,865
Out-of-state tuition: $33,679
Room: Varies
Board: Varies
Books: $1,500
Avg. aid package (freshmen): Not reported
Avg. aid package (undergrads): Not reported

School Spirit
Mascot: True Blue
Colors: Blue and white

You May Not Know

- Sometimes when students talk about the "The Varsity Blues" they mean it. The U of T football team holds the record for longest losing streak with 49 games.
- The university has its own farmers' market, offering products such as cheeses of Canada, natural bee products, and food from ecological and sustainable growers.
- The Royal Ontario Museum, Pollution Probe, Canadian Opera Company, and the Toronto Symphony are all products of the university.

Distinguished Alumni

Rosalie Abella, judge on the Supreme Court of Canada; David Cronenberg, film director; Malcolm Gladwell, writer for *The New Yorker*; Lorne Michaels, producer of *Saturday Night Live*; John Stackhouse, Editor-in-chief of the *Globe and Mail*.

Admissions and Financial Aid

For applicants from the U.S., the university requires two SAT Subject Tests. The school sets the achievement bar very high for its neighbors to the south, and admissions officers expect scores above 600 across SAT components and at least 26 on the ACT. Some programs require even higher numbers.

The university awards 1,900 general scholarships and over 4,000 departmental scholarships every year. Canadian students with high admissions averages and A's in required courses are eligible for the President's Entrance Scholarship of at least $2,000.

UNIVERSITY OF TULSA

Overview

The University of Tulsa, or TU, as the mid-sized, private university likes to be called, offers a solid combination of good value, small class size, and select stand-out programs. *Kiplinger* calls TU one of America's "Best Value Colleges," given its reasonable price tag and its quality special programs—most notably, the unique and exciting Cyber Corps Program, a cross between the *X-Files*, *CSI*, and spy school—and facilities, including the Gilcrease Museum, which houses the world's largest collection of artifacts, art, and documents pertaining to the American West, and the state-of-the-art Lorton Performance Center, which opened in 2011.

TU's 200-acre campus consists of English Gothic-style stone buildings and spreads around the open grassy space called "the U." Campus neighbors downtown Tulsa. However dubious Tulsa's distinction as the cultural capital of Oklahoma might seem, Tulsa's many art and historic museums, as well as its lively music scene, offer students as much intellectual stimulation as they do entertainment possibilities. For students with particular interests, TU offers cutting-edge programs with opportunities for hands-on experience complemented by a small but diverse urban setting.

Academics

Before embarking on any of TU's 103 majors, students usually spend their first two years knocking out the Tulsa Curriculum, which consists of a core and general course requirements. The core curriculum covers fundamental skills, including two courses in writing, one or more math classes, and one to two years of foreign language. To complete the general curriculum, students must take courses across three blocks: "Aesthetic Inquiry and Creative Experience," "Historical and Social Interpretation," and "Scientific Investigation," which includes a lab course. All students must complete a senior project.

A three-year Honors program is also available, in which students take one honors course per semester, satisfying requirements from the general curriculum. All Honors students receive a scholarship and can elect to live in the Honors House Residence Hall; applicants must submit a separate application to be considered for the program.

TU's strongest majors are computer science, any of its engineering majors, geology, history, and music. While academic rigor varies according to program, students can expect a high standard from nearly all of their classes: not only does TU boast an advantageous student-faculty ratio, but hardly any of its classes have more than 50 students (over half of classes have fewer than 19 students).

But where the University of Tulsa truly shines is through its specialized programs. TU's flagship program is its much-touted Cyber Corps Program, a two-year program of study in information security, recognized by the NSA as a Center of Academic Excellence in Information Assurance Education. Claiming to produce graduates with skill sets like the well known tv star MacGyver—over 90 percent of whom go on to work in cyber-security or intelligence for the CIA, FBI, or NSA—the Cyber Corps Program gives students practical training not only in computer science, security, and hacking, but in lock-picking and dumpster diving. Students are even given the assignment to stalk each other online and in person and can work with secret service agents and in crime labs solving homicides. "Where else can you learn how to hack a major site as a class assignment?" asks one participant in the program. And as if stalking and dumpster-diving aren't enough of a draw, the Cyber Corps Program also offers its students scholarships that cover tuition and books, as well as hefty stipends and room and board allowances. A paid summer internship is also provided.

For students in business-related majors, the International Business and Entrepreneurship Institute (IBEI) offers practical experience, including internships, workshops, seminars, competitions, and networking opportunities. The Institute is partnered with local corporations as well as the Oklahoma Department of Commerce. The

UNIVERSITY OF TULSA

Four-year private
Founded: 1894
Tulsa, OK
Major city
Pop. 396,466

Address:
800 South Tucker
Drive
Tulsa, OK
74104-3189

Admissions:
800-331-3050

Financial Aid:
918-631-2526

admission@utulsa.edu

www.utulsa.edu

UNIVERSITY OF TULSA

Students

Total enrollment: 4,326
Undergrads: 3,160
Freshmen: 1,079
Part-time students: 5%
From out-of-state: 47%
From public schools: 70%
Male/Female: 57%/43%
Live on-campus: 74%
In fraternities: 21%
In sororities: 23%
Off-campus employment rating: Fair
Caucasian: 58%
African American: 5%
Hispanic: 4%
Asian / Pacific Islander: 3%
Native American: 4%
Mixed (2+ ethnicities): 2%
International: 22%

Academics

Calendar: Semester
Student/faculty ratio: 11:1
Class size 9 or fewer: 31%
Class size 10-29: 48%
Class size 30-49: 18%
Class size 50-99: 2%
Class size 100 or more: -
Six-year graduation rate: 66%
Graduates who immediately go to graduate school: 33%
Graduates who immediately enter career related to major: 82%

Most Popular Majors

Petroleum engineering
Management
Energy management

Admissions

Applicants: 6,948
Accepted: 2,844
Acceptance rate: 40.9%
Placed on wait list: 320
Enrolled from wait list: 83
Average GPA: 3.8
ACT range: 25-31
SAT Math range: 590-700
SAT Reading range: 570-710
SAT Writing range: Not reported
Top 10% of class: 72%
Top 25% of class: 86%
Top 50% of class: 98%

872

IBEI is also a major hub for TU's burgeoning entrepreneurship and Bachelor of Science in International Business and Language (BSIBL) programs.

Undergraduate research is also well-provided-for at TU: the College of Engineering and Natural Sciences offers specialized summer research programs in chemistry, geosciences, and physics. A special agreement with Los Alamos National Laboratory (of Manhattan Project fame) allows students to complete summer internships under the mentorship of a Los Alamos scientist or engineer. The Tulsa Undergraduate Research Challenge funds student research in all disciplines. Students are encouraged to present their findings at academic conferences, to publish articles, and/or to present meaningful works of art to the community. Students are supervised by a faculty mentor, and must engage in some kind of community service project as well. "If you want to research as an undergrad, the opportunities are here," says a student.

TU offers its own, program-specific study-abroad courses or internships abroad for fall, spring, and summer semesters. Programs include locations in Costa Rica, the UK, France, Turkey, Argentina, Australia, New Zealand, Italy, Russia, Germany, Vietnam, China, and Mexico. It also holds exchange partnerships with universities in Austria, the UK, Finland, France, Germany, Singapore, Spain, Switzerland, Australia, and New Zealand.

More than 80 percent of TU graduates entering the workforce find work in fields related to their majors within six months of graduation. A third go on to graduate study within a year of graduating; the pre-med program has a 78 percent record of acceptance into medical school.

Student Life

With many students living on campus, TU has a thriving on-campus social scene—particularly its seven fraternities and nine sororities, to which more than one fifth of the student body belongs. In addition, TU has 169 student organizations, many of which are professionally- or academically-oriented (including TU Women's Robotics and the intriguingly-named Association of Unmanned Vehicular Systems). Students can also audition for the marching band Sound of the Golden Hurricane or join service organizations.

Popular events on campus include a variety of "fests," such as Oozefest, a muddy volleyball tournament; and Springfest, an outdoor concert held on the U that draws popular acts. Homecoming brings together nearly the entire campus, particularly for the annual Bonfire on the U.

Of TU's 18 varsity Golden Hurricanes sports teams, football is the most popular, although women's golf and men's basketball have won national championships. Intramurals are a big part of social life on campus; nearly 80 percent of students participate. Offerings can range from time-honored sports to some less traditional such as putt putt golf, bowling, and pool. Students who prefer to get their recreation solo can take advantage of TU's sports and athletics facilities, nearly all of which were constructed or renovated within the last 10 years. The Collins Fitness Center features indoor tracks, gyms, sport courts, a lounge with big-screen TV, and even a Starbucks; the Mabee Gym houses squash and racquetball courts.

Tulsa might surprise students with its variety of entertainment options. Students are most likely to take advantage of Utica Square's shops and restaurants, or bars across the street from campus; but for more exciting day trips, students can visit nearby museums, take a drive down historic Route 66, or climb sand dunes and spot camels at Little Sahara State Park. Tulsa is also host to a number of music, food, and cultural festivals. "Tulsa may not be the first city to come to mind when you think of college towns," remarks a student, "but it's got a lot going on."

Freshmen and sophomores are required to live on campus in traditional dorm-style residences or in suites or apartments on campus. "The good thing about the dorms is that you really get to know people," explains a student. "There's always someone awake to talk to, even at 2 in the morning." All-male and all-female housing options are available.

Student Body

The academic qualifications of students at TU might be intimidating—one in 10 was a National Merit Finalist; the 2013 freshman class had a mean GPA of 3.8; and almost three-quarters graduated in the top 10 percent of their high school classes. But TU students have a reputation for being overwhelmingly welcoming and "so friendly you feel like you've known them your whole life."

Ethnic diversity is on the moderate side, and nearly half of students come from outside Oklahoma. These demographics make TU a place open to diversity.

You Might Not Know

- Traditionally, when graduating seniors finish their final exam, they get to ring the Cupola bell; some come back for seconds on Commencement Day.
- John Mabee Hall, the all-male dorm known as "the John," hosts an annual flag-football "Toilet Bowl." Its all-female counterpart, Lottie Jane Mabee Hall is called "the Jane." The Honors House is often called "Gyro House," because it is sandwiched between two Greek fraternities.
- TU grew out of the Presbyterian School for Indian Girls, founded in 1882 in Muskogee.

Distinguished Alumni

S.E. Hinton, author; Nancy Lopez, professional golfer; Gordon Matthews, creator of voicemail technology; Mary Kay Place, actress and singer.

Admissions and Financial Aid

Although TU does not strictly require an essay or personal interview, they are "strongly" recommended. Students wishing to be considered for scholarships must give an interview; these are held in major cities throughout the South.

TU offers merit scholarships, most notably the National Merit/Presidential Scholars award, which covers at the very least base tuition for eight semesters. University, Supplemental, and Provost Scholarships are also available, as are $3,000 International Baccalaureate awards.

UNIVERSITY OF TULSA

Highlights

Admissions Criteria
Academic criteria:
Grades: ☆ ☆ ☆
Difficulty of class schedule: ☆ ☆ ☆
Class rank: ☆ ☆ ☆
Standardized test scores: ☆ ☆ ☆
Teacher recommendations: ☆ ☆
Personal statement: ☆ ☆
Non-academic criteria considered:
Interview
Extracurricular activities
Special talents, interests, abilities
Character/personal qualities
Volunteer work
Work experience
State of residency
Minority affiliation
Alumni relationship

Deadlines
Early Action: November 1
Early Decision: No
Regular Action: Rolling admissions
Common Application: Accepted

Financial Aid
In-state tuition: $34,030
Out-of-state tuition: $34,030
Room: $5,800
Board: $4,626
Books: $1,200
Freshmen receiving need-based aid: 51%
Undergrads rec. need-based aid: 43%
Avg. % of need met by financial aid: 80%
Avg. aid package (freshmen): $28,906
Avg. aid package (undergrads): $27,670
Avg. debt upon graduation: $33,768

School Spirit
Mascot: Captain `Cane
Colors: Gold, blue, and crimson
Song: *Hurricane Fight Song*

UNIVERSITY OF UTAH

UNIVERSITY OF UTAH

Four-year public
Founded: 1850
Salt Lake City, UT
Major city
Pop. 189,899

Address:
201 Presidents Circle
Salt Lake City, UT
84112

Admissions:
800-444-8638

Financial Aid:
800-444-8638

admissions@utah.edu

www.utah.edu

Overview

Nationally known as a stronghold in technology research and business startups, the University of Utah is the education destination for the aspiring young professional. This very large public school combines high academic standards with stellar research and professional opportunities. Add to that a leading academic healthcare program and Office of Diversity, and the result is a stimulating learning environment.

The truly unique aspect of the University of Utah experience is the setting: situated in Salt Lake City among the foothills and snowcaps of the Wasatch Mountains, the U offers picturesque views and natural beauty rare to a university. Architecture ranges from 19th-century style buildings to more modern athletic facilities, providing a mix of charm and functionality.

In this lavish setting, U students can enjoy an abundance of activities. From an expansive Health, Physical Education, and Recreation Complex, which houses four gymnasiums and three pools, to the Crimson Commons which offers bowling, billiards, and a video arcade, students are never short of on-campus entertainment. The U also offers a thorough outdoors program that includes adventure trip packages and how-to clinics for mountainous sports such as skiing, rock climbing, and sea kayaking.

Brand new to the campus in 2010 is the Student Involvement Center, where all student activities are conveniently organized and accessible, emphasizing the university's devotion to a holistic educational experience.

Academics

This devotion continues with the U's general academic requirements in diverse fields of study. Students are required to take classes in American Institutions, Lower Division Writing, Quantitative Reasoning, and Intellectual Explorations. Intellectual Explorations requirements differ depending on the student's major, of which 72 are offered at the U, but contain courses in the fine arts, humanities, social sciences, and physical, life, and applied sciences.

Students collaborate academically at the U rather than compete. "We share information about which classes are the best and help each other out with assignments," says a student. Relatively small class sizes, with more than two-thirds having fewer than 29 students, encourage this behavior and create a small-community feel within the large institution. "If you ask for help, it's available from professors," one student notes. Strong academic programs at the U include business and biology.

Among many special academic programs at Utah is Honors College, where qualified students can earn Honors Degrees and Certificates in smaller class settings. Benefits of participation include living in the Honors Living Learning Communities, being advised by Honors professors, and taking part in mentorship programs. Entering freshmen are admitted based on their GPA and the university's admissions index. "The Honors students are incredibly talented academically," notes a student.

Learning Engagement Achievement Progress (LEAP) is an offering of smaller seminar classes that can be used to fulfill General Education requirements. Generally, about one third of students elect to join this program. Participants are matched with faculty and peer advisors. "I recommend LEAP to all entering freshmen because you get more attention," one student explains. "You'll be able to meet people through the program too."

Another special academic program at the U is offered through the Center for Teaching and Learning Excellence. This program allows students pursuing careers in teaching to work with faculty on pedagogical research projects or to address department issues on campus.

True to its reputation, technology and research-based opportunities are prevalent on campus. Students can apply for Assistantships to aid faculty members with their research, or they can become part of the Technology Commercialization Office, which works on developing products from new technologies and promoting economic growth. Particularly engaging is the Utah Entrepreneur Challenge, a student-run competition in which students submit business ideas and receive generous prizes if named winner or runner-up.

Other programs at the U include study abroad, with choices in over 40 countries spread over four continents. Offerings sport intriguing titles such as "Occupational Therapy in Ukraine" and "Living with Nature in Norway," emphasizing the study of foreign culture as it relates to career networking opportunities.

The U has a strong focus on helping students find careers, with an accommodating "UCareerLink" online database and frequent career fairs. The university also holds fairs with information on graduate schools and offers several programs of test preparation for the GRE, MCAT, LSAT, or GMAT. The Career Services office conducts an online survey of graduates so that students can see the specific companies and job titles held by recent graduates by major.

Student Life

At such a large institution, U students are bombarded by student activity options, with over 150 student organizations to choose from. One such group, OneLove Ski and Snowboarding Club, seeks to satisfy the thrill-seekers by providing an affordable, convenient, and fun way to hit the slopes. For those seeking service opportunities, the Franklin Elementary group helps underprivileged children in the community who need extra academic attention.

In addition to student groups, the U holds campus-wide events that are sure to keep students' social calendars busy. Crimson Nights are student-run events held on Fridays that include bowling, free food, inflatable obstacle courses, and all-night dancing, and are free to all U students. PlazaFest is an activities fair in January that provides information about student clubs amidst a slew of games, music, and prizes. Once a year, the university holds Friday Night Live, a student-written comedy sketch show performed in front of a live audience.

The Greek system offers eight fraternities and six sororities on campus, although only three percent of men and four percent of women participate. "You don't really hear too much from the Greek organizations," says a student.

For those with competitive drive, athletics at the U thrive with seven men's and 11 women's varsity Division I teams. Strong sports include football, men's basketball, and women's gymnastics, all with competitive NCAA standings. Intramurals are also popular on campus, such as basketball, dodgeball, table tennis, and Ultimate Frisbee.

Off-campus recreation is very prominent at the U since 86 percent of students actually do live off campus. Destination spots include the Port-O-Call Social Club, the Gateway in downtown Salt Lake City, and the nearby ski slopes. "Skiing and snowboarding are the unofficial pastime of our student body," one student says.

Students may apply to live in University Student Apartments, which offers one bedroom to three bedroom floor plans. "The apartments allow more privacy and space between you and the other people who live in the building," one student states. Also available, though less popular, is suite-style Residence Hall housing.

UNIVERSITY OF UTAH

Highlights

Students
Total enrollment: 32,388
Undergrads: 24,840
Freshmen: 4,277
Part-time students: 29%
From out-of-state: 18%
From public schools: 95%
Male/Female: 56%/44%
Live on-campus: 14%
In fraternities: 3%
In sororities: 4%
Off-campus employment rating: Excellent
Caucasian: 72%
African American: 1%
Hispanic: 8%
Asian / Pacific Islander: 5%
Native American: 1%
Mixed (2+ ethnicities): 3%
International: 6%

Academics
Calendar: Semester
Student/faculty ratio: 13:1
Class size 9 or fewer: 19%
Class size 10-29: 49%
Class size 30-49: 16%
Class size 50-99: 10%
Class size 100 or more: 5%
Returning freshmen: 88%
Six-year graduation rate: 59%
Graduates who immediately go to graduate school: 18%

Most Popular Majors
Psychology
Human development/family studies
Economics

Admissions
Applicants: 11,118
Accepted: 9,187
Acceptance rate: 82.6%
Average GPA: 3.6
ACT range: 21-27
SAT Math range: 510-650
SAT Reading range: 510-620
SAT Writing range: 5-26
Top 10% of class: 24%
Top 25% of class: 48%
Top 50% of class: 82%

875

College Profiles

UNIVERSITY OF UTAH

Admissions Criteria

Academic criteria:
Grades: ☆ ☆ ☆
Difficulty of class schedule: ☆ ☆ ☆
Class rank: ☆
Standardized test scores: ☆ ☆ ☆
Teacher recommendations: ☆
Personal statement: ☆
Non-academic criteria considered:
Interview
Extracurricular activities
Special talents, interests, abilities
Character/personal qualities
State of residency
Minority affiliation

Deadlines

Early Action: No
Early Decision: No
Regular Action: Rolling admissions
Common Application: Not accepted

Financial Aid

In-state tuition: $6,588
Out-of-state tuition: $23,072
Room: $3,334
Board: $1,440
Books: $1,000
Freshmen receiving need-based aid: 42%
Undergrads rec. need-based aid: 46%
Avg. % of need met by financial aid: 61%
Avg. aid package (freshmen): $14,194
Avg. aid package (undergrads): $15,437
Avg. debt upon graduation: $20,796

School Spirit

Mascot: Swoop (red-tailed hawk)
Colors: Crimson and white
Song: *Utah Man*

Student Body

The student body has a large Mormon contingent, not surprising, since the Church of Latter-Day Saints is headquartered in Salt Lake City. "If you're not Mormon you may feel a little left out at times because so many students are religious," one student comments.

While the students are noted for being religious, there are "no overwhelming political leanings." The academic focus of the student body is predominantly oriented towards technology and the sciences. Most students are from in state (82 percent); while ethnic diversity is moderate (18 percent are minority students).

You May Not Know

- The University of Utah is top-ranking in the country at creating new startups, along with MIT and Johns Hopkins.
- *Forbes* ranked the university 15th in commercialization dollars generated per research dollar.
- The university offers over 200 fully online, and very popular, credit courses.

Distinguished Alumni

Orson Scott Card, author; Ed Catmull, co-founder of Pixar; Jim Clark, founder of Silicon Graphics; Gordon B. Hinckley, LDS Church president; David Neeleman, founder of JetBlue; Chris Shelton, baseball player; John Warnock, co-founder of Adobe Systems.

Admissions and Financial Aid

Freshmen applicants are encouraged to apply as early as possible within the priority filing application period (November 1-December 1) since early applicants have an advantage when space is limited. High school transcripts are carefully reviewed, and though SAT scores are accepted, ACT scores are preferred. Students should have a cumulative GPA of 2.6 and ACT or SAT scores of 18 or 860 respectively.

Merit-based scholarships include the President's Scholarship, which awards 50 students up to $27,000 a semester; the Honors at Entrance Scholarship, which awards academically outstanding Utah residents with full tuition coverage; and the Top Ten Scholarship, offering $1,000 the first year, among others.

UNIVERSITY OF VERMONT

Overview

Sure, 11,000 enrolled undergrads, a few competitive Division I sports teams, and a campus nestled in your typically charming college town might make University of Vermont sound like any other state school at first. But as the fifth oldest university in New England, UVM, as it's referred to, actually has a lot of aspects that give it the feel of a liberal arts college.

The school is situated in Burlington, a small city that tends to really woo its visitors. The setting is gorgeous along the shore of Lake Champlain and it is surrounded by mountains. University Row is littered with historic buildings, yet the city center is hopping with lively attractions from nightclubs and international cuisine to art galleries and theaters.

Academics

There are 179 majors offered at UVM, and each undergraduate college determines its own required courses. However, the university places strong emphasis on diversity, enough so that it makes it a mandatory aspect of the curriculum. Every student has to take either two 3-credit courses in Race and Racism in the U.S., or one from this category and another in Human and Societal Diversity.

All courses are taught by professors (not something you'll find at every school) while teaching assistants stick to leading discussion sections. Classes start out on the large side freshman year; but as studies progress, classes tend to have fewer students. "I have two classes with five or less students in them," says a student. The strongest programs include business, environmental studies, and the ALANA (African-American, Latino, Asian, and Native American) U.S. Ethnic Studies program.

Each year 100 students are admitted to the honors college where they have the opportunity to participate in special courses and seminars, museum visits, and faculty dinners and graduate as Honors College Scholars. In addition to this honors college, students may apply to the School of Environment and Natural Resources to be Lola Aiken Scholars. Those accepted will participate in case studies of significant environmental issues, interact with guest speakers, go on field trips, and have a chance to live with other students in Aiken Scholar housing.

The Office of Undergraduate Research offers mini-grants to students pursuing unique research projects under the mentorship of faculty in both fall and spring semesters, as well as other competitive awards throughout the year.

The university has a diverse set of study-abroad opportunities from exchange programs with universities in 33 countries, to the Buckham Program for English students to study in Canterbury, England. The Oaxaca Program offers field-study excursions and overnight visits to indigenous villages in Mexico, and the Belize Program focuses on sustainable development.

UVM's career services department offers a number of services. The most prominent is the Career Connection, a network of alumni, parents, and friends available to advise students about careers, internships, job searches, and graduate school.

Student Life

The first few weeks of school are packed with gathering staples for college life and settling in, but some of the campus activities add a bit of a hippy twist to these tasks. There is a convocation that ends in a procession to a candlelight induction ceremony (don't forget to do the summer reading). And the fall activities fest shows students that there are ways of enjoying the outdoors they didn't think would exist at college—like fly fishing or playing Quidditch. Some students might realize they're not as good at pool as they thought in the stunning Dudley H. Davis Center, but learn not to take it too seriously since everyone is going rock climbing the next day anyway. Incoming

UNIVERSITY OF VERMONT

Four-year public
Founded: 1791
Burlington, VT
Large town
Pop. 42,645

Address:
South Prospect Street
Burlington, VT
05405-0160

Admissions:
802-656-3370

Financial Aid:
802-656-5700

admissions@uvm.edu

www.uvm.edu

UNIVERSITY OF VERMONT

Students
Total enrollment: 13,097
Undergrads: 11,211
Freshmen: 2,655
Part-time students: 11%
From out-of-state: 78%
From public schools: 70%
Male/Female: 44%/56%
Live on-campus: 50%
In fraternities: 7%
In sororities: 6%
Off-campus employment rating: Good
Caucasian: 84%
African American: 1%
Hispanic: 4%
Asian / Pacific Islander: 2%
Native American: 0%
Mixed (2+ ethnicities): 3%
International: 2%

Academics
Calendar: Semester
Student/faculty ratio: 17:1
Class size 9 or fewer: 19%
Class size 10-29: 51%
Class size 30-49: 16%
Class size 50-99: 8%
Class size 100 or more: 5%
Returning freshmen: 85%
Six-year graduation rate: 76%
Graduates who immediately enter career
    related to major: 61%

Most Popular Majors
Business administration
Psychology
English

Admissions
Applicants: 21,808
Accepted: 16,716
Acceptance rate: 76.7%
Placed on wait list: 2,471
Enrolled from wait list: 60
Average GPA: Not reported
ACT range: 24-29
SAT Math range: 550-650
SAT Reading range: 540-640
SAT Writing range: 8-42
Top 10% of class: 34%
Top 25% of class: 71%
Top 50% of class: 96%

878

students also have the option to be led through the woods for a week by upperclassmen doing the standard kumbaya community building and self-discovery thing that one would expect from a university that gave the world members of the band Phish.

There are more than 140 student organizations at UVM. Perhaps the most notable club on campus is The Outing Club (did we mention students enjoy nature?). Having a university so close to such an expansive outdoor setting makes it easy for this group to organize weekend excursions including hiking, white water rafting, and even snowshoeing—it's all a part of UVM life. "If you're not into the outdoors, you will be by the time you leave here," laughs a student.

There are eight fraternities and six sororities that draw seven percent of the men and six percent of the women at the university into their ranks. This means the opportunity is there for students attracted to brotherhood or sisterhood, but these groups don't overpower the social scene on campus by any means.

The University has 18 teams that compete at the NCAA Division I level. Men's hockey is a national powerhouse and the ski team dominates, proudly boasting six national championships. Men's and women's basketball and men's soccer are also popular, and attendance at games shows student body support.

Freshmen and sophomores are required to live on campus, but many of them migrate off campus for junior and senior year. Besides traditional residence halls, there are residential learning and special-interest communities such as GreenHouse, honors, music, a quiet lifestyle, and the outdoor experience program.

Off campus you'll find plenty of attractions to enjoy. There are clusters of shops, restaurants, clubs, and gatherings on Church Street Marketplace that sprawl into a collection of bike paths, skate parks, and waterfront attractions. Many students also take advantage of the nearby ski resorts by spending plenty of time on the slopes around Stowe and Sugarbush. If you're ever at a lack of things to do, just check the /Bored site, the university's cool collection of events and entertainment to always make sure you have ways to ignore coursework.

Student Body

The student body is rather left-leaning and has the diverse set of characters you'd expect its beautiful location in Burlington to attract, including hippies, "New England types" and "snow bums." There's high geographic diversity with 78 percent of students coming from out of state, but ethnic diversity tends to be low to moderate.

You May Not Know

- University of Vermont was the first university to admit women and African-American students into the honor society, Phi Beta Kappa.
- The cornerstone of the Old Mill standing on University Row was laid by Marquis de Lafayette, an important French general in the American Revolution.
- The University of the Green Mountain takes going "green" seriously. All copy paper on campus is 100

percent recycled and chlorine-free, there is a Guide to Green Living at UVM published regularly, and sustainability courses are offered each semester.

Distinguished Alumni

Jon Kilik, film producer of such projects as *Malcolm X*, *Do the Right Thing*, *Dead Man Walking*, and *Babel*; E. Annie Proulx, author of *Brokeback Mountain* and Pulitzer Prize winner; Henry Jarvis Raymond, co-founder of *The New York Times*; Tim "The Tank" Thomas, pro-hockey goal tender; Jody Williams, Nobel Laureate of Peace.

Admissions and Financial Aid

UVM is pretty standard in terms of what the admissions office asks for. The university accepts the Common Application plus a short supplement and considers factors that include academic rigor, standing in the graduating class, standardized test scores, trends in academic performance, and the "competitive nature of the student's prior academic environment." There are some school- and college-specific requirements, which are listed on the university's website.

UVM offers a gamut of merit-based scholarships for both in- and out-of-state applicants. The Presidential Scholarship provides four-year awards of up to $6,000 for out-of-state students. Vermont residents who are selected to be Green and Gold Scholars receive a full-tuition, four-year scholarship. A student is automatically considered for these scholarships as a first-time, first-year prospect simply by submitting the application for admissions (well, that was easy). Keep your grades and test scores up and you might even qualify for multiple scholarships.

UNIVERSITY OF VERMONT

Highlights

Admissions Criteria
Academic criteria:
Grades: ☆ ☆ ☆
Difficulty of class schedule: ☆ ☆ ☆
Class rank: ☆ ☆
Standardized test scores: ☆ ☆
Teacher recommendations: ☆
Personal statement: ☆ ☆
Non-academic criteria considered:
Extracurricular activities
Special talents, interests, abilities
Character/personal qualities
Volunteer work
Work experience
Geographical location
Minority affiliation
Alumni relationship

Deadlines
Early Action: November 1
Early Decision: No
Regular Action: January 15 (final)
Notification of admission by: March 31
Common Application: Accepted

Financial Aid
In-state tuition: $13,728
Out-of-state tuition: $34,656
Room: Varies
Board: Varies
Books: $1,200
Freshmen receiving need-based aid: 59%
Undergrads rec. need-based aid: 58%
Avg. % of need met by financial aid: 65%
Avg. aid package (freshmen): $21,925
Avg. aid package (undergrads): $21,696
Avg. debt upon graduation: $28,256

School Spirit
Mascot: Rally Catamount
Colors: Green and gold
Song: *Champlain*

Four-year public
Founded: 1819
Charlottesville, VA
Medium city
Pop. 43,511

Address:
P.O. Box 400160
Charlottesville, VA
22903

Admissions:
434-982-3200

Financial Aid:
434-982-6000

undergradadmission@
virginia.edu

www.virginia.edu

UNIVERSITY OF VIRGINIA

Overview

When Thomas Jefferson founded the University of Virginia in 1819, he wanted to establish a "publicly-supported school…[with] a national character and stature," according to the university. Jefferson's vision undoubtedly has been fulfilled. Today, UVA encompasses 12 schools with almost 24,000 students and is ranked as second among public universities by *U.S. News & World Report*.

Architectural highlights on the 1,167-acre campus include the Rotunda and Academical Village, both designed by Thomas Jefferson. The Academical Village is a collection of 10 classic-styled pavilions with a shared lawn. Surrounding the Academical Village are gardens so grand that they have been designated as a World Heritage Site by UNESCO along with the Taj Mahal and Great Wall of China.

Academics

UVA is academically challenging but not to the extent that it's unmanageable. The school places a great deal of importance on academics, as its reputation suggests, but it also provides resources to help out along the way. "As I expected, the work is tough, but my classmates offer a lot of support," says a student.

While some of the school's 195 majors—like English, history, and commerce—have received national attention for the strength of their curriculum, overall, all programs have strong faculty. "We have Pulitzer Prize winners, Guggenheim fellows, and superstar professors," boasts a student.

UVA takes its commitment to the undergraduate learning experience seriously, as evidenced by the Echols Scholars program. All students who apply to the College of Arts and Sciences, known at the university as "the College," are considered for the program; there's no special application process. It's upon admittance to the program that things start getting special: the ability to create a unique interdisciplinary major (past examples include "aesthetics" through the study of Classics and Latin), priority registration, an actively involved faculty advisor, and exemption from the university's Area Requirements. "I've met the most intelligent, hard-working people through the Echols program," one student notes. Science Scholars offers a similar degree of exemptions and priorities, though specialized within the science majors, and a 3.4 from the program guarantees admission to the master's program.

Undergraduates in all 51 degree-programs are required to take six credits (most courses are three credits each) in both social sciences and humanities, three credits in both historical studies and Non-Western perspectives, and 12 credits in mathematics and natural sciences. Social sciences, humanities, and mathematics and natural sciences all require that the credits be dispersed among two or more departments.

The School of Engineering and Applied Sciences has a more specialized spread of mandatory classes dependent on the major. SEAS, one of the most renowned programs at the university, also has its own scholar's program: Rodman Scholars—a parallel to the Echols Scholars program of the College (they even share specialty housing). As part of this community, Rodman Scholars also get exclusive access to engineering seminars.

Students from any discipline are eligible to complete an accelerated Bachelor/Master's of Public Policy program that requires 24 credits of graduate-level coursework but allows the condensing of what would normally be six years into five. Additional parts of the program are pre-fall-semester Public Service Retreats and a required post-fourth-year summer internship in a non-profit, private sector corporation or consulting firm, or in any level of government agency either within the U.S. or abroad.

Students can get involved academically through research. The Harrison Undergraduate Research Awards program funds undergraduate research projects, and the school offers an Undergraduate Research Network for students to connect with each other. The Center for Undergraduate Excellence has an annual awards ceremony.

There's a whole range of study-abroad programs for students to choose from, including architecture programs in Spain, Denmark, Germany, England, Jamaica, China, and Italy; business programs in China, Denmark, England, France, Ireland, Italy, New Zealand, Spain, and Singapore; and hundreds of other opportunities through the university in general. Other opportunities include exchange programs and credit transfers from a number of other universities' programs.

The University Career Services office is easy to find and easy to get in touch with at UVA—they even have a Twitter account. The office provides specialized forums and expos for careers in economics, education, and health professions. "You can drop in and get advice or make an appointment for in-depth help," one student says. The alumni network is strong and past grads participate in campus activities such as events and fairs.

Student Life

UVA has over 700 clubs and organizations. Even for a school with over 15,000 undergraduates, that's a huge number, allowing for clubs like the Aerosol Art Club (dedicated to the history and techniques of the medium), the Mahogany Dance Troupe, an African and African-American inspired dance group, and the 'Hoos (derived from the cheer, "Cavaliers Wa-hoo-wa!") for Watching Good Movies.

Among the clubs are 16 sorority houses and 27 fraternity houses. Greek life makes up about 22 percent of the undergraduate population. It's huge: obviously not completely unavoidable, but pervasive. "You'll make the most friends and have the most social activities if you join," one member says.

But some of the most popular events are Greek-influence-free: the Lighting of Lawn, the night before fall exam period when lights are strung up on the Lawn and a cappella groups perform in the Rotunda; the first football game of the year, and Homecoming, for instance.

Football is arguably the most popular of the 23 (11 men's, 12 women's) Division I varsity programs that are part of the Atlantic Coast Conference, though the basketball team has had notable success at the national level as well. "We haven't had much to celebrate recently, but the hard core fans still turn out," one student remarks. Both the men's and women's lacrosse teams are nationally ranked, as are the women's cross-country team and the men's soccer team. The school also has popular intramural teams—inter-tube water polo among them.

While campus has much to offer, there are entertainment choices for students outside UVA's grounds as well. Charlottesville has, in the past, been rated the best place to live, thanks to its rich history, great food, and no lack of things to do. "The Corner" is home to a handful of student bars with atmospheres that can end up feeling like frat parties, and the Downtown Mall has a few less college-dominated options.

Freshmen are required to live on campus (in one of six dorms), and though there are suite-style, apartment-style, and the historic

UNIVERSITY OF VIRGINIA

Highlights

Students
Total enrollment: 23,907
Undergrads: 15,822
Freshmen: 3,396
Part-time students: 6%
From out-of-state: 26%
From public schools: 72%
Male/Female: 45%/55%
Live on-campus: 41%
In fraternities: 21%
In sororities: 22%
Off-campus employment rating: Fair
Caucasian: 60%
African American: 6%
Hispanic: 5%
Asian / Pacific Islander: 11%
Native American: 0%
Mixed (2+ ethnicities): 4%
International: 6%

Academics
Calendar: Semester
Student/faculty ratio: 16:1
Class size 9 or fewer: 18%
Class size 10-29: 51%
Class size 30-49: 16%
Class size 50-99: 9%
Class size 100 or more: 7%
Returning freshmen: 97%
Six-year graduation rate: 93%

Most Popular Majors
Economics
Psychology
Commerce

Admissions
Applicants: 27,193
Accepted: 8,046
Acceptance rate: 29.6%
Placed on wait list: 4,393
Enrolled from wait list: 284
Average GPA: 4.2 (weighted)
ACT range: 28-32
SAT Math range: 640-740
SAT Reading range: 620-720
SAT Writing range: 42-43
Top 10% of class: 93%
Top 25% of class: 98%
Top 50% of class: 99%

881

College Profiles

UNIVERSITY OF VIRGINIA

Admissions Criteria
Academic criteria:
Grades: ☆ ☆ ☆
Difficulty of class schedule: ☆ ☆ ☆
Class rank: ☆ ☆ ☆
Standardized test scores: ☆ ☆
Teacher recommendations: ☆ ☆ ☆
Personal statement: ☆ ☆
Non-academic criteria considered:
Extracurricular activities
Special talents, interests, abilities
Character/personal qualities
Volunteer work
Work experience
Geographical location
Minority affiliation
Alumni relationship

Deadlines
Early Action: November 1
Early Decision: No
Regular Action: January 1 (final)
Notification of admission by: April 1
Common Application: Accepted

Financial Aid
In-state tuition: $10,016
Out-of-state tuition: $36,720
Room: $5,337
Board: $4,380
Books: $1,240
Freshmen receiving need-based aid: 32%
Undergrads rec. need-based aid: 32%
Avg. % of need met by financial aid: 98%
Avg. aid package (freshmen): $22,824
Avg. aid package (undergrads): $23,008
Avg. debt upon graduation: $21,591

School Spirit
Mascot: Cavalier
Colors: Orange and blue
Song: *The Good Old Song*

Lawn residences (for seniors only) available to returning undergraduates, most upperclassmen move off campus. "There are a lot of options nearby," remarks one student.

Student Body

The population at UVA is largely made up of "white, preppy" Virginia natives, but at a public school with a big Greek life, that's somewhat to be expected. It ranks high in ethnic diversity (25 percent minorities), with moderate geographic diversity (26 percent from out of state).

Charlottesville is a very left-leaning area, though campus itself leans right. "All political viewpoints are represented, but we have more conservatives than you'd expect," explains a student.

You May Not Know

- The Rotunda, the school's original library, was modeled after the Pantheon in Rome.
- In 1895, an electrical fire started in the annex, and engineering professor William H. Echols tried to save the Rotunda by dynamiting the connecting bridge. The salvation attempt failed and actually sent the fire spreading more rapidly. The marble statue of the founder that is still in the Rotunda today survived the fire.
- The UVA campus is a UNESCO World Heritage Site.

Distinguished Alumni

Tiki Barber, former running back for the New York Giants; Edward M. Kennedy; former U.S. Senator for Massachusetts; Timothy Koogle, former President and CEO of Yahoo; Bill Nelson, U.S. senator and one of the astronauts on the Columbia space shuttle team in 1988; Charles T. Pepper, namesake of "Dr. Pepper;" John Snow, U.S. Secretary of the Treasury.

Admissions and Financial Aid

UVA uses the Common Application with its own supplement. Beyond the normal testing, high school transcript, and recommendations, UVA requires certain high school unit minimums in various areas of study: four in English, four in college-prep-level mathematics, two in a foreign language, two in science (biology, chemistry, or physics), and three for engineering, one of which must be physics.

Merit scholarships are available through individual departments, and UVA also offers around 30 Jefferson Scholars merit scholarships intended to cover the entire cost of attendance for four years. In order to be eligible for the scholarship, students need to be nominated by their schools. Finalists are invited to campus for a weekend—the end of which concludes the selection process—packed full of seminars, exams, and personal interviews. Applications for the scholarship are technically due by January 1, though December 1 is the recommended date.

UNIVERSITY OF WASHINGTON

Overview

The University of Washington, or "U-Dub," is a huge public university located in the heart of Seattle. Its campus is almost one square mile large. Mountains are visible to the East and West, and the Sound is not too far off. Many green spaces and trees temper the university's gothic architecture with the lushness of nature.

In general, UW offers strong academics and vast resources—especially in the sciences—and a hoppin' social life. Despite challenging courses, students manage to maintain a laid-back, west coast attitude. While faced with boundless opportunities, first-years might be a bit daunted at first, as they have to find their own way through school and rely less on advising and mentoring services than perhaps at smaller institutions. However, UW is surprisingly personable and student-focused for its size, and—if you are sick of it all—you have the singular ability to run away to the mountains for the weekend!

Academics

The university's general education requirements are centered on English Composition and three other subject areas that are entitled "Visual, Learning, and Performing Arts" (VLPA), "Individuals and Societies" (I&S), and "The Natural World." Together with a foreign language requirement that extends into the third quarter, the function of the general education core is to provide students with a broad liberal arts foundation. On the whole, the course work at UW is challenging and there is minimal "hand-holding," as would be expected from a school so large. UW offers 272 majors and prides itself especially in its biology, business, engineering, and architecture programs.

UW has many academic opportunities, many of which are available to students immediately upon matriculation. As freshmen, students may arrive on campus a month early and engage in any one of a number of Discovery Seminars taught by leading faculty on a wide range of topics. These seminars provide an exciting intellectual introduction into UW life.

Once school has begun, freshmen can participate in Freshman Interest Groups (FIGs). A FIG consists of a group of 20-25 freshmen who share a common interest, and thus take a block of four or five classes together. This facilitates group discussions, the sharing of thoughts, and ultimately making friends. "FIGs are the best introduction to UW," says a student.

Students may also choose to enroll in Honors as freshmen. This program fosters intellectual excellence and strives to give students a broad background with a deep fundamental understanding of one academic discipline. Students in the Honors Program receive faculty and peer advising, invitations to fellowships and research, and access to privileged campus facilities (for example, Honors Computer Lab).

For students interested in undergraduate research, UW offers a bounty of resources. The Undergraduate Research Program helps students set up projects, identify faculty mentors, and find funding. At the end of every term there is a Research Symposium, where students present their work to others in the community.

Should these opportunities not completely satisfy your thirst for new experiences, (and you want to escape the Seattle rain), you are in luck! The study-abroad program is vast, offering a choice of 70 university exchanges, as well as about 30 UW programs spread across the year. UW students who choose to participate do pay extra for the privilege of taking a course from faculty abroad.

While the networking opportunities afforded by a large, public school like UW may not rival those of an elite private school, they are nonetheless plentiful. The Career Center offers nearly daily workshops, fairs, and other programs with topics centered on jobs, internships, and graduate school. The Husky Career Network connects more than 5,000 alumni to mentor students.

UNIVERSITY OF WASHINGTON

Four-year public
Founded: 1861
Seattle, WA
Major city
Pop. 620,778

Address:
1410 NE Campus
Parkway
Box 355852
Seattle, WA
98195

Admissions:
206-543-9686

Financial Aid:
206-543-6101

www.washington.edu

UNIVERSITY OF WASHINGTON

Students

Total enrollment: 42,568
Undergrads: 28,933
Part-time students: 10%
From out-of-state: 17%
Male/Female: 48%/52%
Live on-campus: 13%
In fraternities: 6%
In sororities: 5%
Off-campus employment rating: Excellent
Caucasian: 45%
African American: 3%
Hispanic: 6%
Asian / Pacific Islander: 25%
Native American: 1%
Mixed (2+ ethnicities): 4%
International: 12%

Academics

Calendar: Quarter
Student/faculty ratio: 12:1
Class size 9 or fewer: 13%
Class size 10-29: 50%
Class size 30-49: 18%
Class size 50-99: 11%
Class size 100 or more: 8%
Returning freshmen: 93%
Six-year graduation rate: 80%

Most Popular Majors

Art/sciences
Business administration
Engineering

Admissions

Applicants: 26,138
Accepted: 15,460
Acceptance rate: 59.1%
Placed on wait list: 2,350
Enrolled from wait list: 588
Average GPA: 3.8
ACT range: 24-30
SAT Math range: 580-700
SAT Reading range: 520-650
SAT Writing range: 9-35
Top 10% of class: 92%
Top 25% of class: 98%
Top 50% of class: 100%

Student Life

The University of Washington has a myriad of student groups and organization (370 in all!). In fact, to accommodate them all, they are currently finishing construction on a new Husky Union Building (the "HUB"), which will serve as a center for student groups and communities. The university also has a full schedule of events during the year that often include the greater Seattle community. At the Winterfest, UW hosts a day of fun and games, including horse-drawn carriage rides, a storybook village, and performances by many student groups. In the spring, students run the largest event on campus—the Powwow—a celebration of Native American heritage that draws on average 8,000 visitors.

University of Washington has a small Greek community with a big presence. While only about five percent of the student body is officially part of a fraternity or sorority, there are Greek parties and fundraisers all year round. "We embody school spirit," says a member.

The UW Huskies athletic program consists of 19 sports (nine men's, 10 women's) that compete in Division I of the Pac-10. Football, men's basketball, and women's volleyball are among national competitors and are cheered on by high school spirit; a sea of purple turns out at most every game. UW is an active campus and offers every intramural sport imaginable, as well as more competitive club teams. The Intramurals Activities center houses a climbing wall, pool, indoor courts, gym, and track, and you can head to the waterfront activities center to rent canoes and rowboats or join the Yacht, rowing, or kayak club and explore Lake Washington. "Everyone participates in some kind of outdoor activity," one student explains.

The University District of Seattle offers everything a college student could want, from quiet alleyway cafes serving authentic Seattle coffee to Boba tea shops, sports bars, and late night Mexican restaurants. Nearby downtown Seattle lures students to a fantastic live music scene, nightlife, museums, and fine dining. Seattle Mariners (Major League Baseball) and Seahawks (National Football League) play nearby. "If you aren't a Mariners fan when you start here, you will be by the time you finish," one student claims. And don't forget to take advantage of the Northwest's incredible wilderness areas, with the Cascades, Mt. Rainier, and Olympic National forest so nearby there is no shortage of backpacking, skiing, and climbing opportunities.

Most students live on campus for freshman year, while three-quarters of students move off campus afterward. There are honors and other specific themed housing, with Residential Freshman Interest Groups that give a more small-college feel to the first quarter of life at a large university. Students take classes together, and sometimes go on field trips. Other housing options include the Sustainability Community, Arts Community, Business Community, and International Community.

Student Body

UW is not a geographically diverse campus, with 83 percent of students hailing from Washington State. Less than 10 percent of the student population is African-American or Hispanic, while 25 percent are Asian or Pacific Islander. Social circles can sometimes be distinct among Greek, dorm, and commuter groups. "People tend to stick with those whom they are most similar to," one student says.

On the whole, University of Washington students are known for being outdoorsy and social, though in a school so large there are any number of different social and academic spectrums. The student body is generally "more liberal."

You May Not Know

- The University of Washington was the first public university on the West Coast (founded in 1861).
- Today the school attracts the largest amount of federal research money than any public or private university save Johns Hopkins.
- The 1936 Washington Varsity Crew won the Olympic gold medal at the Berlin Olympic Games. They had met for the first time at the Olympic trials!

Distinguished Alumni

Michael P. Anderson, NASA astronaut on the *Columbia*; Jeffrey Brotman, founder and President of Costco; Dale Chihuly, glass artist and a founder of the Pilchuck Glass School; Rita R. Colwell, Director of the United States National Science Foundation; Thomas Foley, former Speaker of the U.S. House of Representatives; Bill and Melinda Gates, Microsoft CEO and founders of the Bill and Melinda Gates Foundation; Donald Petersen, CEO of Ford Motor Co.; Marilynne Robinson, Pulitzer Prize for Fiction.

Admissions and Financial Aid

While the admissions board does look carefully at GPA and SAT/ACT scores, there is no "minimum" score assuring acceptance and no SAT subject tests are required. Instead, the university takes into account factors such as public service, life experiences, demonstrated academic commitment, and diversity of viewpoints. UW does *not* take the Common Application.

While more than a third of students receive need-based aid, only three percent of undergraduates receive merit aid, though merit scholarships are available through departments, the Honors Program, and the Washington NASA Space Grant. The Mary Gates Scholarship Fund is a prestigious award covering a Washington resident's full tuition and books for all four years.

UNIVERSITY OF WASHINGTON

Highlights

Admissions Criteria
Academic criteria:
Grades: ☆ ☆ ☆
Difficulty of class schedule: ☆ ☆ ☆
Class rank: N/A
Standardized test scores: ☆ ☆ ☆
Teacher recommendations: N/A
Personal statement: ☆ ☆ ☆
Non-academic criteria considered:
Extracurricular activities
Special talents, interests, abilities
Character/personal qualities
Volunteer work
Work experience

Deadlines
Early Action: No
Early Decision: No
Regular Action: December 1 (final)
Notification of admission by: March 31
Common Application: Not accepted

Financial Aid
In-state tuition: $11,902
Out-of-state tuition: $31,476
Room: Varies
Board: Varies
Books: $1,206
Freshmen receiving need-based aid: 38%
Undergrads rec. need-based aid: 43%
Avg. % of need met by financial aid: 82%
Avg. aid package (freshmen): $17,000
Avg. aid package (undergrads): $18,600
Avg. debt upon graduation: $20,800

School Spirit
Mascot: Husky
Colors: Purple and gold
Song: *Bow Down to Washington*

UNIVERSITY OF WISCONSIN - MADISON

Four-year public
Founded: 1848
Madison, WI
Medium city
Pop. 236,901

Address:
500 Lincoln Drive
Madison, WI
53706

Admissions:
608-262-3961

Financial Aid:
608-262-3060

onwisconsin@admis-
sions.wisc.edu

www.wisc.edu

Overview

When it comes to public universities, few shine brighter than the University of Wisconsin-Madison. The institution is among the largest and most-respected in the nation, consistently recognized as a leader in both academics and public service. The size may be intimidating for some—there are more than 42,000 undergraduates and graduate students—but this makes for a spirited student body that is enthusiastic about athletics and scholarship. The university clearly takes research seriously: it shelled out $1 billion on research expenditures in 2010, making it the third highest spender in science and engineering in the nation.

About a mile from the state capitol, UW-Madison sits on a piece of land between Lake Mendota and Lake Monona. The architecture is historic, but with a modern touch, and the hub of campus life is the Memorial Union—known locally as "the Union." Madison, Wisconsin tops many "best" lists—best place to live and work, best college sports town, one of America's safest cities, and a top green city. UW is also located within a few hours of several other major cities, including Milwaukee, Chicago, and Minneapolis. UW-Madison also has a police force, food service site, hospital, recreational facilities, botanical gardens, and an on-campus dairy.

In 2008, the Student Services Tower opened in the middle of campus. The building houses the Student Activity Center with more than 800 student organizations and has panoramic views of campus and plush study rooms.

Academics

UW-Madison academics are top notch and the school places a large emphasis on scholarship. The university offers 136 undergraduate majors, 155 masters, 109 doctoral, and six professional degree programs.

The school's general education requirements are fairly comprehensive, so it goes without saying that the curriculum isn't completely flexible, and might even be a bit rigid for some. All UW-Madison students must complete "breadth" coursework, including natural science, humanities, and social studies. They must also complete "communication" coursework—courses dedicated to reading, listening, and better public speaking—as well as an ethnic studies course and "quantitative reasoning" courses specially designed to apply mathematical logic to a variety of situations.

Majors generally vary in academic rigor. Engineering or business, for example, can be "very intensive," according to one student, but there are also majors that won't involve as much workload. Introductory classes will generally be very large, but as students begin to specialize, classes naturally shrink. "Be prepared for some classes with a couple hundred students at the beginning," one student states. Some well known programs include business, economics, political science, psychology, and biology.

UW-Madison offers Honors and Scholars Programs designed to challenge students. "We get more personal interaction with professors than those who aren't in the Honors program," says a participant. Admission to the program is competitive, and students may apply as entering freshmen as well as while they are in college if they have a minimum 3.3 GPA.

UW-Madison provides over 50 service-learning courses each year for those students who are community-minded. Examples of previous course titles include "Engage Children in Science-Led Computer Sci Clubs," "Homelessness," and "Adults with Disabilities." Students not only learn during class time but participate in hands-on projects. "You gain a new perspective that goes beyond simply volunteering because you study the social science behind the issue before tackling it," explains a student.

There are nine different types of research fellowships available at UW-Madison. Options include the Community Scholars Program, Undergraduate Research Scholars, and Undergraduate Research Opportunities in Biology.

UW-Madison is ranked in the top 10 for number of students who go abroad. Would-be travelers have more than 180 programs to choose from in over 70 countries around the world. Students may apply for awards that provide stipends to assist with costs. Graduation abroad is also an option, and some seniors choose to study abroad during senior year.

For those concerned about career opportunities after graduation, UW-Madison has a career services office complete with resume advice, counselors, internship opportunities, and on-campus recruiting by employers including Google, D.E. Shaw, and others. The office assists students for one year after they graduate.

Student Life

The large student body and the spirited support for athletics make student life at UW-Madison unique. UW-Madison was ranked eighth among party schools by the Princeton Review in 2014. However, it's one of those rare places where the excitement for partying is matched by a desire to learn and change things. It was also ranked 10th among "Party Schools that Pay" by PayScale for its starting and career salary levels. Thus there are 819 student organizations to satisfy even the most obscure interest. They range from environment-based, (such as Big Red Go Green), to professional, (like the Aspiring Nurses Organization and the Finance and Investment Society).

Events within Madison are popular among the student body. Just as the university itself is big, the activities tend to be equally large-scale. The State Street Halloween party, an annual event held in Madison, has become known as a gathering place for thousands of partygoers. The Mifflin Street Block Party, also an annual celebration in Madison, is a large-scale block party that attracts 20,000 participants. "We go all out for our parties," one student says. Football games are popular. Students and alums fill Camp Randall Stadium—which seats approximately 80,000 people—to cheer on the Badgers.

For over 150 years, UW-Madison has embraced Greek life as a way to foster friendship and leadership on campus. There are 26 fraternities and 11 sororities, and UW-Madison makes it clear that Greek life is important—they advertise the fact that over 70 percent of Fortune 500 CEOs and U.S. Senators were part of a fraternity or sorority while in college. "Being a member is about more than attending parties," explains a student. "We do several community service projects a year."

UW Madison is part of the Big Ten athletic conference and an NCAA Division I school. There are 23 different varsity sports (11 for men, and 12 for women). UW-Madison's football team is all the rage, routinely ranked among the top football teams in the nation with games often broadcast on national television. "School spirit comes out in force on game days," one student remarks.

With its proximity to the center of Madison, students have access to a rapidly growing city that has been voted one of the best places to live. During the winter months, sports enthusiasts enjoy ice-skating, fishing, skiing, and playing hockey. Recreational choices for the rest of the year include sailing, bicycling, and hiking. Downtown Madison also offers a plethora of shopping, dining, and entertainment options for the adventurous to explore.

UNIVERSITY OF WISCONSIN – MADISON

Highlights

Students
Total enrollment: 42,820
Undergrads: 30,863
Part-time students: 9%
From out-of-state: 38%
Male/Female: 48%/52%
Live on-campus: 25%
In fraternities: 9%
In sororities: 8%
Off-campus employment rating: Excellent
Caucasian: 77%
African American: 2%
Hispanic: 4%
Asian / Pacific Islander: 6%
Native American: 0%
Mixed (2+ ethnicities): 2%
International: 7%

Academics
Calendar: Semester
Student/faculty ratio: 17:1
Class size 9 or fewer: 12%
Class size 10-29: 56%
Class size 30-49: 12%
Class size 50-99: 10%
Class size 100 or more: 9%
Returning freshmen: 95%
Six-year graduation rate: 83%

Most Popular Majors
Economics
Political science
Biology

Admissions
Applicants: 29,034
Accepted: 15,841
Acceptance rate: 54.6%
Average GPA: 3.8
ACT range: 26-30
SAT Math range: 630-750
SAT Reading range: 530-650
SAT Writing range: 15-54
Top 10% of class: 58%
Top 25% of class: 94%
Top 50% of class: 100%

887

College Profiles

UNIVERSITY OF WISCONSIN – MADISON

Admissions Criteria

Academic criteria:
Grades: ☆ ☆ ☆
Difficulty of class schedule: ☆ ☆ ☆
Class rank: ☆ ☆ ☆
Standardized test scores: ☆ ☆
Teacher recommendations: ☆
Personal statement: ☆ ☆
Non-academic criteria considered:
Extracurricular activities
Special talents, interests, abilities
Character/personal qualities
Volunteer work
Work experience
Minority affiliation
Alumni relationship

Deadlines

Early Action: No
Early Decision: No
Regular Action: Rolling admissions
Common Application: Not accepted

Financial Aid

In-state tuition: $10,403
Out-of-state tuition: $26,653
Room: Varies
Board: Varies
Books: $1,200
Freshmen receiving need-based aid: 39%
Undergrads rec. need-based aid: 39%
Avg. % of need met by financial aid: 73%
Avg. aid package (freshmen): $12,279
Avg. aid package (undergrads): $12,862
Avg. debt upon graduation: $24,700

School Spirit

Mascot: Bucky Badger
Colors: Cardinal and white
Song: *On, Wisconsin*

The majority of students at UW-Madison live off campus, but on-campus housing is available and ranges from dorms (both co-ed and single sex) to apartments and houses. Since the university is located in the middle of a large city, there are safety issues from time to time, but the university provides escort services to transport and protect students at night.

Student Body

The student body is regionally diverse, but possibly not as ethnically diverse as some other large schools. Roughly 77 percent of the student body is Caucasian and skewed toward Midwesterners and locals. Minorities make up a moderate portion of students (14 percent) and seven percent of students hail from other countries. The gender ratio is roughly even, but there tends to be a rivalry between Midwesterners and those from the East or West coast. "Those from the coasts tend to think they're a little more worldly," remarks a student. "Still," says another, "you will find your clique no matter what your interests are."

You May Not Know

- Men's basketball has won 17 Big Ten titles (the last in 2008) and Men's Football has won 14 Big Ten titles (the last in 2012).
- Third-year law students throw white canes over the goalpost at Homecoming. According to superstition, if they catch the canes, the graduating students will win their first case.
- Seventeen Nobel Prizes and 30 Pulitzer Prizes have been awarded to faculty or alumni of UW.

Distinguished Alumni

Carol Bartz, President and CEO, Yahoo; Laurel Clark, NASA astronaut on Columbia; William S. Harley, co-founder of Harley-Davidson; Devin Harris, basketball player, Utah Jazz; Phil Hellmuth, professional poker player; Charles Lindbergh, first pilot to fly nonstop across the Atlantic Ocean; Frederick Jackson Turner, historian; Frank Lloyd Wright, architect.

Admissions and Financial Aid

Admissions at UW-Madison is definitely competitive. Admissions counselors review each application individually and are looking for students who display talent, leadership, community involvement, and a desire to make a difference. Successful applicants are usually those who have challenged themselves in high school with honors and AP courses, and are ranked in the 85th-96th percentile in their graduating class.

Merit-based scholarships are available from individual colleges and departments within the university. The College of Letters and Science recently awarded 30 scholarships but typically receives about 1,200 applications. According to the college, students should show strengths in at least two of these areas: "academic achievement, force of character, creative accomplishment, leadership, community service, financial need, and diversity."

UNIVERSITY OF WYOMING

Overview

Nestled between two mountain ranges in southeastern Wyoming, the University of Wyoming (UW) is certainly more remote than many colleges. Nonetheless, this large public university draws almost 13,000 students from all 50 states and 75 countries. As the only university in Wyoming, UW infuses energy and diversity to the town of Laramie (population 31,000 without the students). The school welcomes future students to a "modest and warm community."

While the people may be friendly, the weather can certainly get frigid and windy—not surprising since the campus lies on the high Laramie Plains at an elevation of 7,200 feet. The cold certainly doesn't keep students holed up though: the UW community is known as an outdoors-loving group and an environmentally aware one. There's a "Bike Library" where students can rent bicycles for a semester and a popular Outdoor Program. Fittingly, the School of Agriculture and Natural Resources stands out from UW's other academic offerings.

As at many larger public universities, getting the most out of UW requires seeking out academic opportunities and the best professors. Not all students will be content at a school where the center of campus is called Prexy's Pasture; indeed, this large grassy area at the center of campus was formerly used for livestock grazing. Those seeking the exhilaration of a bigger city, and a more ethnically diverse location, probably won't settle on Laramie. But for many students, both from Wyoming and outside the Cowboy State, UW is a great place to study and roam during their undergraduate years.

Academics

UW offers 80 bachelor's and 95 graduate degree programs across seven colleges. Students pursuing a BA or BS are required to complete the General Education Curriculum, which includes courses in sciences, foreign language, upper division courses outside of the major, and a course on non-Western perspectives. "There are about 30 non-Western courses to choose among—including anthropology, history, music, and religion—so it's not a difficult requirement to fulfill," says a student. For those in professional degree programs, the requirements are slightly mitigated.

Academic rigor varies by major at UW. Class sizes tend to be larger for introductory courses but get smaller as students progress to more advanced classes. Students say that the quality of teaching is varied "entirely based on the individual professor," as does their availability to help outside of class. The College of Agriculture and Natural Resources is particularly strong at UW, offering scholarships for majors as well as a speaker series. In addition, the College of Business and College of Engineering and Applied Science are stand-outs.

The accomplished and ambitious undergraduates in the University Honors program complete a five-course curriculum: the two-course freshman colloquium and one course in each year thereafter, including a senior seminar. Students enjoy access to award-winning faculty, independent research, special scholarships, and early pre-registration for classes.

Each year at the end of April, Undergraduate Research Day celebrates the accomplishments of student researchers across a diverse array of disciplines. Each student gives a 15-minute oral presentation followed by a five-minute Q&A session. "It's nerve-racking to do but a huge accomplishment," says a student. Undergraduate research fellowships offer students in science and engineering the opportunity to receive stipends throughout the fall and spring semesters and during summer in order to pursue research with a faculty mentor. For intensive research experiences, the Summer Research Apprentice Program offers minorities, first-generation college

UNIVERSITY OF WYOMING

Four-year public
Founded: 1886
Laramie, WY
Large town
Pop. 31,312

Address:
1000 East University
Avenue
Laramie, WY
82071

Admissions:
800-342-5996

Financial Aid:
307-766-2116

admissions@uwyo.edu

www.uwyo.edu

UNIVERSITY OF WYOMING

Highlights

Students
Total enrollment: 12,903
Undergrads: 10,194
Freshmen: 2,230
Part-time students: 18%
From out-of-state: 46%
Male/Female: 48%/52%
Live on-campus: 23%
In fraternities: 5%
In sororities: 4%
Off-campus employment rating: Good
Caucasian: 81%
African American: 1%
Hispanic: 5%
Asian / Pacific Islander: 1%
Native American: 1%
Mixed (2+ ethnicities): 2%
International: 4%

Academics
Calendar: Semester
Student/faculty ratio: 14:1
Class size 9 or fewer: 14%
Class size 10-29: 57%
Class size 30-49: 19%
Class size 50-99: 6%
Class size 100 or more: 4%
Returning freshmen: 76%
Six-year graduation rate: 53%
Graduates who immediately go to graduate school: 19%
Graduates who immediately enter career related to major: 55%

Most Popular Majors
Nursing
Elementary education
Psychology

Admissions
Applicants: 4,181
Accepted: 4,001
Acceptance rate: 95.7%
Average GPA: 3.5
ACT range: 22-27
SAT Math range: 500-630
SAT Reading range: 480-610
SAT Writing range: Not reported
Top 10% of class: 22%
Top 25% of class: 52%
Top 50% of class: 83%

students, and female students paid research opportunities with a UW professor in science, math, or engineering.

Students can spend a full academic year, a semester, or a summer abroad while earning UW credit through exchange programs, UW affiliated programs, and faculty-led programs. There are a number of scholarships to support study abroad.

The Center for Advising and Career Services (CACS) helps students and alumni with career development and job search needs. UW alumni have free, unlimited access to Experience, an exclusive network of alumni and employers.

Student Life

The Wyoming Union is both geographically and metaphorically the center of student life on campus—UW's campus "living room" since 1939. The building offers more than 19,000 square feet of meeting space, the bookstore, and a number of dining options. "You'll always run into someone you know at the Union," notes a student. The Campus Activities Center, home to more than 200+ student organizations, is also housed in the Union.

UW serves as a hub for cultural events in Laramie, with a variety of performing arts events such as rock concerts in the Arena Auditorium and classical concerts and performances at the Fine Arts Center. Friday Night Fever offers free and alcohol-free late-night entertainment, with unique offerings ranging from comedians and hypnotists to salsa dancing and even inflatable games. Students who like to have alcohol with their fun can be sure to get home safely: since 2000, SafeRide has offered a service to prevent drinking and driving—it has transported more than 160,000 passengers so far. "You can drink or not drink and you'll find something to do," one student remarks.

The Greek community at UW is a small but tight-knit group, proud of having more than 100 years of tradition on campus (since 1903). "For the most part, fraternity and sorority members stick to themselves," one student comments. The Greek Community emphasizes the famous Wyoming and American leaders who participated in Greek life, including two former Wyoming senators.

UW has seven men's and eight women's Division I teams; the athletic program competes annually for conference and national championships. Basketball and football games are typically well-attended; football is in the Football Bowl Subdivision.

The prominent Outdoor Program offers plenty of opportunities for outdoor adventure, whether in the university's very own indoor climbing wall or at seasonal outings off campus. Dry as Wyoming may seem, there's even a SCUBA course. There are 18 different club sports and an Intramural Sports Program of more than 45 sports that claims to be "one of the largest and most diverse programs in the Rocky Mountain Region." Many events are held in the Half Acre Gymnasium, which has recently undergone a $27 million renovation.

Off campus, outdoor activities like rock climbing, hiking, skiing, fishing, and hunting are popular. Laramie is a fairly small town with limited offerings in the form of shopping, bars, and restaurants. "It's about what you'd expect from a town of 30,000 people," notes a student.

All students are required to live in one of six residence halls freshman year unless they are married or have families. Many students move off campus after freshman year, though Crane Hall is reserved for upperclassmen and has mostly single occupancy rooms. The 12-story-tall McIntyre hall is Wyoming's tallest building!

Student Body

Not everybody is a cowboy or cowgirl, but you will find some students wearing boots and large buckles on University of Wyoming's campus. A commonality among students is a "passion for outdoor recreation" and a "laid-back" approach to school and social life.

There is moderate ethnic diversity, though resources exist for the approximately 10 percent of the student body who are minority students, such as the Multicultural Resource Center.

There is a moderate amount of geographic diversity, with nearly half of students coming from outside of Wyoming. Perhaps surprising for a state school, there are students from all 50 states and more than 75 countries represented. Multicultural Affairs within the Dean of Students' Office offers programs and services for minority students.

You May Not Know

- UW was founded in September 1886, before the territory was admitted as the 44th state.
- The University of Wyoming is unusual in that its location within the state is provided by the Constitution of the State of Wyoming.
- UW's American Heritage Center is one of the largest non-governmental archives west of the Mississippi.

Distinguished Alumni

Dick Cheney, former Vice President of the United States; Cynthia Lummis, attorney and former State Treasurer and legislator; Ardis J. Meier, Chief Pharmacy Consultant to USAF Surgeon; Alan K. Simpson, former U.S. Senator.

Admissions and Financial Aid

Admissions decisions are made on a rolling basis, and there are "Assured Admission" and "Conditional Admission" options. Graduates of a Wyoming high school with a GPA above 2.75 who turn in their ACT or SAT test scores are guaranteed admission; for non-Wyoming graduates, the minimum GPA is 3.0 and there are standardized test score prerequisites. All applicants must meet requirements for completion of 13 high school units, including four units of English and three each of math, science, and broadly defined "cultural context" courses. Conditional admission makes it possible for some students who don't meet Assured Admission requirements to get in.

UW offers general scholarships awarded at the time of admission and competitive scholarships. The Trustees' Scholars Award, UW's top academic scholarship, covers tuition, fees, room, and board for four years to 75 freshmen. For out-of-state students, the Rocky Mountain Scholars Award provides up to $5,000 in annual scholarship support.

UNIVERSITY OF WYOMING

Highlights

Admissions Criteria
Academic criteria:
Grades: ☆ ☆ ☆
Difficulty of class schedule: ☆ ☆ ☆
Class rank: N/A
Standardized test scores: ☆ ☆ ☆
Teacher recommendations: ☆
Personal statement: ☆
Non-academic criteria considered:
Interview
Extracurricular activities
Special talents, interests, abilities
Character/personal qualities

Deadlines
Early Action: No
Early Decision: No
Regular Action: Rolling admissions
Common Application: Not accepted

Financial Aid
In-state tuition: $3,240
Out-of-state tuition: $12,960
Room: $4,027
Board: $5,424
Books: $1,200
Freshmen receiving need-based aid: 49%
Undergrads rec. need-based aid: 47%
Avg. % of need met by financial aid: 62%
Avg. aid package (freshmen): $9,259
Avg. aid package (undergrads): $9,117
Avg. debt upon graduation: $21,241

School Spirit
Mascot: Cowboy Joe
Colors: Brown and gold
Song: *Ragtime Cowboy Joe*

891

URSINUS COLLEGE

Four-year private
Founded: 1869
Collegeville, PA
Large town
Pop. 8,050

Address:
Box 1000, 601 Main St.
Collegeville, PA 19426

Admissions:
610-409-3200

Financial Aid:
610-409-3600

admissions@ursinus.edu

www.ursinus.edu

Overview

Ursinus College combines strong liberal arts and premed programs with a suburban liberal arts college experience—all within 30 minutes of Philadelphia. Students rave about their close relationships with instructors, who are often their neighbors as a result of school-sanctioned housing in nearby homes as well as dorms. Faculty members return the favor by encouraging student involvement in their research.

The 170-acre campus features a plaza and outdoor sculpture collection. The Berman Museum of Art offers more than 4,000 objects to more than 30,000 annual visitors. Though the historical buildings and brick walkways give the college a traditional feel, the school is still tech-savvy: all students are issued laptop computers as part of their Ursinus experience.

Academics

Ursinus offers 27 majors and 52 minors. Students are required to fulfill coursework in their major and in the liberal studies core. The core requires two classes in the Common Intellectual Experience, two units of a foreign language, a math course, a lab science, a social science, a humanities course, and an arts class. It also requires something unique to Ursinus—two classes emphasizing diversity: one focused on the U.S. and one focused outside the U.S. and Western Europe. "I appreciated the classes because they gave us a deeper understanding of race and ethnicity both domestically and abroad," says a student. Students are also required to fulfill an Independent Learning Experience, during which they may do research, student teach, study abroad, complete an internship, or take engineering courses, among other things.

The overall small size of Ursinus College makes it possible to have classes with fewer students than is the case in many schools; in fact, courses are often taught as two-to-nine-person seminars. The Common Intellectual Experience classes in the core curriculum are presented as small discussion seminars in which freshmen get one-on-one time with faculty and classmates. Common readings include the words of Plato, Michelangelo, Leonardo, Galileo, and Descartes. In addition to studying as a group, first-years also live together to facilitate academic discussions outside the classroom.

The sciences are popular at Ursinus, especially biology, psychology, and chemistry. Students can take part in the Pre-Medical program, which provides advisors who can help with essays, interviews, recommendation letters for medical school, and more. "It's nice to have on-going support for applying to medical school so I know I'm taking the right classes and knowledgeable about research opportunities," remarks a student.

Sophomores and juniors at Ursinus are eligible to participate in the Summer Fellows program, in which students conduct an independent research project with a faculty mentor. Students receive access to the school's resources, a $2,500 stipend, and summer campus housing. Ursinus also takes part in Project Pericles and organizes events to encourage political engagement among students.

Those with their eyes turned towards foreign issues can earn the International Studies Certificate, which requires 28 hours of coursework on understanding international societies and issues. Students must also have an "independent learning experience that is international in scope."

Ursinus promotes study abroad on every continent except Antarctica either through school-sponsored programs or the more than 50 additional opportunities offered by other schools and open to Ursinus College students. Options include faculty-led and non-Ursinus programs, international internships and service learning, and field work. Faculty-led programs are available in Beijing, Florence, Madrid, Tubingen, and the Yucatan. "Even though our college doesn't have many programs of its own, we still have a lot of options open to us," says a student.

Career Services assists students with jobs, internships, and graduate school. Students have recently interned at organizations including Ridley State Park, *Runners World* magazine, Mt. Gretna Playhouse, and Abington Memorial Hospital. The office sponsors an annual job, internship, and networking fair as well as the online UC CareerNet for postings throughout the year.

After graduation, 24 percent of students head to grad school within the next year. Of those who enter the workplace, 35 percent are employed in a field related to their major within six months and 60 percent are employed in a related career within a year. Many students enter the educational field, whether as public and private school teachers or as participants in Teach For America.

Student Life

Because Ursinus is so heavily residential, student clubs are a huge part of student life. The school has 80 official organizations, including seven fraternities and five sororities that attract 10 percent of the men and 15 percent of the women—an unusual presence in a small liberal arts college. "I think the fraternities and sororities add a much needed social option," says a member. "Plus, we aren't exclusive."

Organizations span the gamut for almost every interest. Notable groups are the on-campus newspaper, *The Grizzly*; the Dance Dance Revolution club; and a Jazz Society. Popular student events include Airband, an annual fundraiser that goes beyond just air guitar. Besides a lip synching contest, students participate in date auctions, raffles, and coin drops. "We have some pretty talented lip synch performers," laughs a student.

Relay for Life is an annual all-night fundraiser for cancer research in which team members take turns walking or running around a track for contributions. More than 40 teams typically participate to raise funds for the American Cancer Society.

An entire day is set aside for the Celebration of Student Achievement (CoSA). Students present research they have taken part in or give performances in the arts. Students apply to be part of the program.

Ursinus boasts 24 Division III sports programs—with strong field hockey and women's rugby teams. There are eight intramurals and seven sports clubs, including wiffle ball, scuba diving, and paintball.

Off campus, students gather at local shops such as the Java Trench to mingle with classmates. The nearby Collegeville neighborhood offers options for dinner. Philadelphia is a 30-minute drive away and has all the attractions of a decent-sized city. "For big concerts and events we make the drive to Philly," says a student.

Most students live on campus. Housing is a mix of old Victorian-era homes (holding 5-30 students apiece) and traditional dorms. Placement is decided by a lottery system, with upperclassmen getting preference. The Victorian houses are the most coveted of the living quarters, as one might imagine. "The Victorian houses define the Ursinus experience," says a student.

Student Body

Though Ursinus has a strong focus on international studies, the student body itself is fairly homogenous. Students say that the school pulls heavily from "pretty wealthy" families in the northeast

URSINUS COLLEGE

Highlights

Students
Total enrollment: 1,680
Undergrads: 1,680
Part-time students: 2%
From out-of-state: 50%
Male/Female: 49%/51%
Live on-campus: 95%
In fraternities: 10%
In sororities: 15%
Off-campus employment rating: Excellent
Caucasian: 77%
African American: 6%
Hispanic: 5%
Asian / Pacific Islander: 5%
Native American: 0%
Mixed (2+ ethnicities): 2%
International: 1%

Academics
Calendar: Semester
Student/faculty ratio: 11:1
Class size 9 or fewer: 47%
Class size 10-29: 50%
Class size 30-49: 2%
Class size 50-99: 1%
Class size 100 or more: -
Graduates who immediately go to graduate school: 24%
Graduates who immediately enter career related to major: 35%

Most Popular Majors
Biology
Economics
Psychology

Admissions
Applicants: 3,518
Accepted: 2,455
Acceptance rate: 69.8%
Placed on wait list: 142
Enrolled from wait list: 38
Average GPA: Not reported
ACT range: 24-29
SAT Math range: 540-660
SAT Reading range: 540-650
SAT Writing range: Not reported
Top 10% of class: 33%
Top 25% of class: 70%
Top 50% of class: 94%

893

College Profiles

URSINUS COLLEGE

Admissions Criteria

Academic criteria:
Grades: ☆ ☆ ☆
Difficulty of class schedule: ☆ ☆ ☆
Class rank: ☆ ☆
Standardized test scores: ☆
Teacher recommendations: ☆ ☆
Personal statement: ☆ ☆
Non-academic criteria considered:
Interview
Extracurricular activities
Special talents, interests, abilities
Character/personal qualities
Volunteer work
Work experience
State of residency
Minority affiliation
Alumni relationship

Deadlines

Early Action: December 1
Early Decision: February 1
Regular Action: December 1 (priority)
February 15 (final)
Common Application: Accepted

Financial Aid

In-state tuition: $44,350
Out-of-state tuition: $44,350
Room: Varies
Board: Varies
Books: $1,000
Freshmen receiving need-based aid: 70%
Undergrads rec. need-based aid: 74%
Avg. % of need met by financial aid: 78%
Avg. aid package (freshmen): $32,368
Avg. aid package (undergrads): $32,363
Avg. debt upon graduation: $26,776

School Spirit

Mascot: Bears
Colors: Red, old gold, and black

although the university cites that it had the second-highest increase in the country in the percentage of Pell Grant students between 2000 and 2008. There is moderate ethnic diversity (18 percent of students identify as non-white) and about half the school's students come from out of state. About one percent are international students.

You May Not Know

- The reclusive J.D. Salinger attended Ursinus briefly. He wrote a school paper column entitled "The Skipped Diploma."
- The school's original buildings were a Mennonite prep school that had gone out of business.
- The school's first female student, Minerva Weinberger, was valedictorian of the class of 1884.

Distinguished Alumni

Joseph DeSimone, professor at the University of North Carolina; Spencer Foreman, MD, retired President of Montefiore Medical Center in New York City; J.D. Salinger, novelist.

Admissions and Financial Aid

Standardized test scores are optional for most applicants, and those who choose not to submit their scores are not penalized. The college strongly recommends that students interview as part of their application process. Though not required, it helps the school get a feel for how a student would fit in at Ursinus.

Students can apply for the Creative Writing Award, the winner of which receives a $30,000 scholarship and the chance to live in J.D. Salinger's old dorm room. Other awards include the Steinbright and Zacharias National Scholarships, which are worth $30,000 and are renewable for four years. African American and Latino/a students who are active in advocacy work can apply for the Tower Scholarship, an offering of up to $30,000 a year for four years. Funding is available for student research, and because students aren't competing with graduate students, it's more readily available.

VANDERBILT UNIVERSITY

Overview

Vanderbilt University has long been acclaimed one of the top universities of the South. A medium-sized private research university, Vanderbilt consists of four schools: College of Arts and Science, School of Engineering, Blair School of Music, and Peabody College of Education and Human Development. Located in the heart of Music City, Nashville, Tennessee, Vanderbilt boasts a campus covered in green with buildings dating back to 1873 and architecture ranging in style from Gothic to modern.

Known for dressing up simply to attend football games, students at Vanderbilt are notorious for their preppy style and conservative views. Criticized in the past for a lack of ethnic, geographic, or socioeconomic diversity—and largely dominated by the wealthy, Caucasian, Greek scene—the administration in recent years has made a strong effort to diversify its student body, recruiting students with a wide range of backgrounds and interests. While some see this effort to transform the student body as a positive change, others claim it leads to further segregation among students. Nevertheless, all Vandy students seem to share a strong, unmistakable drive toward academic achievement and extracurricular involvement.

Academics

A school with a reputation that largely revolves around its academics, Vanderbilt's courses are challenging and intense; however, professors are readily available and happy to help students with any questions or concerns. "I almost always get responses from my professors by email within 24 hours," says a student. The majority of classes are taught as seminars and are usually small in size. Among the school's strongest programs are engineering, social sciences, music, education and human development, as well as premed.

In addition to pursuing one of Vanderbilt's 222 majors, students are expected to complete three other areas of general education: the first year common experience, the writing requirement, and the liberal arts requirement. The First Year Common Experience is composed solely of one writing seminar, while the Writing Requirement consists of one introductory writing course as well as one introductory (100 or 200-level) oral communication course. A series of 13 mandated courses ranging in subjects from mathematics and natural sciences to humanities and creative arts comprises the Liberal Arts requirement. In addition, students who choose to pick majors outside the College of Arts and Science must fulfill the requirements of their respective schools.

There are a number of special academic opportunities available at Vanderbilt. For example, the Honors Program invites a select number of freshmen with outstanding academic performance to participate in special seminars, courses, and independent-study projects. The Four Plus One Program allows students to work with their advisors in creating five-year programs of study in which they can obtain both their Bachelor of Arts degree in addition to their Master's degree. There are also ample opportunities for research. Through the school's summer undergraduate research program, students can conduct research with a full-time faculty member over a 10-week period and receive a $4,000 stipend. Other research opportunities can be pursued through the school's Medical Center or through one of the school's four initiatives in Energy and Environment, Health Care, Defense and National Security, and Information Technology.

Vanderbilt's academic opportunities are extended to an international scope through the school's Global Education Office, which boasts more than 100 study-abroad programs. A standout is the Vanderbilt Initiative for Scholarship and Global Engagement (VISAGE), a year-long program in which students take a course at the university and then study or serve abroad.

VANDERBILT UNIVERSITY

Four-year private
Founded: 1873
Nashville, TN
Major city
Pop. 609,644

Address:
2305 West End Avenue
Nashville, TN
37203

Admissions:
800-288-0432

Financial Aid:
800-288-0204

admissions@vanderbilt.edu

www.vanderbilt.edu

VANDERBILT UNIVERSITY

Students

Total enrollment: 12,710
Undergrads: 6,796
Freshmen: 1,608
Part-time students: 1%
From out-of-state: 90%
From public schools: 64%
Male/Female: 50%/50%
Live on-campus: 83%
Off-campus employment rating: Excellent
Caucasian: 62%
African American: 8%
Hispanic: 8%
Asian / Pacific Islander: 8%
Native American: 0%
Mixed (2+ ethnicities): 5%
International: 6%

Academics

Calendar: Semester
Student/faculty ratio: 8:1
Class size 9 or fewer: 28%
Class size 10-29: 51%
Class size 30-49: 13%
Class size 50-99: 6%
Class size 100 or more: 3%
Returning freshmen: 96%
Six-year graduation rate: 92%

Most Popular Majors

Social sciences
Engineering
Psychology

Admissions

Applicants: 28,348
Accepted: 4,034
Acceptance rate: 14.2%
Placed on wait list: 5,653
Enrolled from wait list: 253
Average GPA: 3.8
ACT range: 32-34
SAT Math range: 710-790
SAT Reading range: 690-770
SAT Writing range: 64-30
Top 10% of class: 90%
Top 25% of class: 98%
Top 50% of class: 99%

896

The college's Career Center encourages students to complete a questionnaire that is designed to create an Individualized Coaching Action Plan (ICAP) for them. Advisors use the information to pinpoint students' needs and serve them most effectively. In addition, students can pursue one of the many networking/internship resources available to them through the school's databases, utilizing programs such as Internships-USA or CareerLink. "You have to do some legwork on your own, but there's help if you ask," explains a student.

Student Life

Vanderbilt students pride themselves in their ability to balance their social and academic commitments. And there certainly is no shortage of student activities. Vanderbilt's 350 official student organizations range from the school newspaper, *The Hustler*, to the Sailing club, and even the snowmobile club.

Greek life constitutes a large part of social offerings on campus, with 35 percent of the male student body joining one of the school's 18 fraternities and 50 percent of the female student body belonging to one of 16 sororities. "The Greek scene is dominant," says a student.

The biggest annual event at Vanderbilt is the school's spring outdoors music festival, Rites of Spring, that features some of today's most popular musicians in various genres. The weekend, which includes games, events, and outdoor festivities, is intended to give Vandy students a chance to relax before their final period of classes and exams. The Honor Code Signing Ceremony takes place at the beginning of a student's freshman year and marks the signing of a pledge in which students commit to maintaining academic integrity. Aside from graduation, it is the only time the entire class is assembled at the same place at the same time. Football tailgates are also very popular events among students and feature a host of guys clad in khaki shorts, polo shirts, ties and Ray-Bans, while the women don sundresses and sandals.

Vanderbilt boasts a very competitive sports program that competes in Division I in the SEC. There are six men's and nine women's sports teams, and the men's football, baseball, and basketball are among the nation's top contenders. There are plenty of intramural sports to become involved with as well, from badminton and billiards to water polo and Ultimate Frisbee.

When not busy studying, attending sporting events, or participating in other student activities, Vanderbilt students can entertain a plethora of options for things to do off campus. There is no lack of nightlife, food, or the arts. The city of Nashville is bursting with Southern charm and undeniable love for country music. Those who are not interested in attending live music events can follow Nashville's NFL, NHL, or minor league baseball teams.

Typically, most students at Vanderbilt choose to live on campus for all four years, either in dorms or fraternity/sorority houses. The Commons draws all freshmen students together in 10 houses located in a specified living area on campus. "It's the best situation because you really get to know the other freshmen," explains a student.

Student Body

Located in the Bible Belt of America, it's not surprising that Vanderbilt's student body has a reputation for being politically conservative, in addition to overwhelmingly rich and Caucasian. Students are stereotyped as generally good-looking and "overly concerned" with their appearance. For some, this heavy emphasis on physical image is "superficial" and "frustrating," giving rise to a claim that the campus is a self-segregating community, divided by socio-economic status. However, in recent years, the university has made an effort to diversify its campus, recruiting students from the North and further transforming the school's religious and political leanings. "Things are better than you'd think from our stereotype," says a student.

Today, Vanderbilt is a geographically diverse campus, with 90 percent of its students hailing from out of state. It is also ethnically diverse with 29 percent minority students.

You May Not Know

- Vanderbilt was founded by Commodore Cornelius Vanderbilt, the wealthiest man in America.
- Every naturally grown tree in Tennessee is represented on Vanderbilt's campus.
- Vanderbilt was the first college in the South to recruit an African-American athlete, Perry Wallace, in 1960.

Distinguished Alumni

Bill Bain, founder of Bain & Company; Dierks Bentley, country singer; Doug Parker, Chairman/CEO/President US Airways; James Patterson, bestselling author of contemporary thrillers; Robert Penn Warren, Pulitzer Prize winner.

Admissions and Financial Aid

The admissions office describes its process as holistic and comprehensive, considering all parts of a student's application. The school states they do not "employ cutoffs for standardized testing or grade-point averages. Instead, they look for students who have demonstrated strong academic skills and a depth of intellectual curiosity, who have actively contributed to their community." Vanderbilt looks for students who have taken rigorous course loads, contributed meaningfully to their schools or communities, and those who show a "diversity of thought" and the ability to empathize with others and see from different perspectives in life.

Through a very competitive selection process, Vanderbilt awards two percent (250 recipients total) of incoming freshmen one of three signature merit scholarships that provide full tuitions for four years, plus summer stipends for study abroad, research, or service projects. These selections include the Ingram Scholars, for students who want to combine a professional or business career with a commitment to community service; the Cornelius Vanderbilt Scholars, for students with strong academic and leadership achievements; and Chancellor Scholars, for students who have worked to bridge gaps in economically, socially, and racially diverse groups.

VANDERBILT UNIVERSITY

Highlights

Admissions Criteria
Academic criteria:
Grades: ☆ ☆ ☆
Difficulty of class schedule: ☆ ☆ ☆
Class rank: ☆ ☆ ☆
Standardized test scores: ☆ ☆ ☆
Teacher recommendations: ☆ ☆
Personal statement: ☆ ☆ ☆
Non-academic criteria considered:
Interview
Extracurricular activities
Special talents, interests, abilities
Character/personal qualities
Volunteer work
Work experience
Geographical location
Minority affiliation
Alumni relationship

Deadlines
Early Action: No
Early Decision: November 1
Regular Action: January 3 (final)
Notification of admission by: April 1
Common Application: Accepted

Financial Aid
In-state tuition: $41,928
Out-of-state tuition: $41,928
Room: $9,208
Board: $4,886
Books: $1,370
Freshmen receiving need-based aid: 51%
Undergrads rec. need-based aid: 48%
Avg. % of need met by financial aid: 100%
Avg. aid package (freshmen): $44,416
Avg. aid package (undergrads): $43,794
Avg. debt upon graduation: $17,349

School Spirit
Mascot: Commodore
Colors: Black and gold
Song: *Dynamite*

VASSAR COLLEGE

VASSAR COLLEGE

Four-year private
Founded: 1861
Poughkeepsie, NY
Large town
Pop. 32,790

Address:
124 Raymond Avenue
Poughkeepsie, NY
12604

Admissions:
800-827-7270

Financial Aid:
845-437-5320

admissions@vassar.
edu

www.vassar.edu

Overview

Sprawling across 1,000 acres of the Hudson River Valley, Vassar College is undeniably one of the most picturesque college campuses in the country. Vassar sits on the outskirts of the small but scenic city of Poughkeepsie, New York, just 75 miles from the Big Apple. Collegiate Gothic architecture, formal gardens, and expansive parks and trails can make a stroll across Vassar's campus feel like a scene from a Jane Austen novel, but more modern buildings, including a Bauhaus-style residence, keep it from feeling dated. Two rivers, a lake, a wetlands trail—all on campus—and the Catskill Mountains and Appalachian Trail within a short distance make Vassar a haven for hikers and "outdoorsy" types.

Vassar's appearance reflects the character of this liberal arts school, originally founded as a women's college but made co-ed in 1969. English is one of the most popular majors, as are those in the visual and performing arts and social sciences. With nearly 70 percent of students heading to graduate school or professional school within five years of completing their degrees, Vassar maintains a strongly intellectual tradition: *U.S. News & World Report* lists Vassar as the 13th-ranked liberal arts college in the nation.

Students value individualism just as much outside classes as in them. The arts are generously highlighted at Vassar, which boasts extensive facilities. In addition to designing their own majors, Vassar students design their own parties and social functions—the absence of the Greek system allows student groups and residences to put on events that are more creative than the average frat party.

Vassar students pride themselves on thinking independently in all areas of life. If you prefer to march to the beat of your own drum, then Vassar may be the place for you.

Academics

Vassar is a college, rather than a university, which means that the entire institution is dedicated to undergraduate education. There are 29 departments that offer 51 majors. Students may also take a "correlate sequence"—meaning that they choose a minor—in most programs. Vassar is particularly strong in English, psychology, political science, and drama.

Vassar's general education requirements are few, which encourages students to pursue interdisciplinary or self-designed concentrations. All students must take a small-group First-Year Writing Seminar and a course with a strongly quantitative element; they must also be proficient in a foreign language. Beyond that, students are free to major in programs offered by various departments or they can opt for interdepartmental or multidisciplinary programs such as biochemistry and geography/anthropology; urban studies; American culture; science, technology, and society; or an individually designed concentration.

The benefits of attending a college with no graduate students become clear when it comes to class size and individual attention from professors: 89 percent of classes have fewer than 30 students, and since there are no grad students, all classes are taught by professors. "I love having personal contact with my professors," says a student.

In addition, Vassar offers undergraduates a host of science and engineering options that would not be so readily available at other institutions. Students may spend the summer working on projects in several areas of the sciences when they attend the Undergraduate Research Summer Institute. Ford Scholarships allow students, particularly minority participants, to take part in research in the humanities and social sciences. Off-campus opportunities include the Vassar-Dartmouth Dual Degree Program in Engineering, which enables students to spend junior year at Dartmouth's Thayer School of Engineering.

Vassar offers an array of study-abroad programs in France, Germany, Ireland, Italy, Spain, and Russia, and students can also participate in selected external programs throughout the world. Vassar's arrangements with other institutions in the U.S. as well as participation in the Twelve College Exchange Program provides additional opportunities. Almost half of Vassar students spend either a semester or a year abroad. "I think studying abroad should be mandatory," says a student.

While almost three-quarters of Vassar graduates go on to post-graduate study within five years of graduation, those who enter the workforce are generally successful: 57 percent of Vassar graduates who enter the workforce are able to find jobs in their field of study within six months of graduating. Vassar's Career Development Office offers a database of 3,000 alumni available for networking and career advice.

Student Life

Over 100 student groups are active on campus, with the performing arts figuring prominently in students' extracurricular activities. Among a number of acting groups at Vassar, Philatheis is a completely student-run theater group. The college offers an abundance of performance spaces, including the Powerhouse Theatre, the black-box theatre, and the state-of-the-art proscenium theater and scene and costume shops at the Vogelstein Center for Drama and Film. The Vassar Night Owls are the country's oldest all-female a cappella group and have been featured on Comedy Central.

These and other student groups are responsible for facilitating most of the campus' 1,600 annual activities and events. Highlights include Founder's Day, a festival in the spring featuring carnival rides, performing bands, and beer. In addition, student groups regularly sponsor parties—usually themed—called Mug Nights, at the on-campus pub, Matthew's Mug (hence, the name of the event). Student residences also put on their fair share of entertainment: Raymond House's yearly Halloween haunted house draws faculty as well as students, while Josselyn House puts on an annual "Heaven and Hell" themed party. Vassar has no Greek system, so a large part of the party scene is centered on student groups and residences. "We really don't miss fraternities or sororities," says a student.

Despite recent successes from the women's volleyball and tennis teams, Vassar's Division III sports teams draw little enthusiasm. Fitness and recreation, on the other hand, are major parts of Vassar students' lives: the scenic campus and its surroundings are conducive to outdoor activities, while the relatively new Athletics and Fitness Center draws almost as many visitors as the library does.

Although Poughkeepsie is a fairly high crime area, it does offer some bars that attract students. The Hudson River Valley area at large, including Mohonk State Park, is a hiker's and outdoors enthusiast's dream, while neighboring towns feature historic mansions and sites such as the Franklin Delano Roosevelt Library and Estate. Foodies will appreciate that the Culinary Institute of America is nearby and operates several restaurants. "The Apple Pie Bakery Café has the very best cakes," claims a student.

Most students, however, stay close to Vassar—it can be hard to get off campus, and there are safety issues in Poughkeepsie, so most live on campus. Vassar offers nine traditional dorms that house a

VASSAR COLLEGE

Highlights

Students
Total enrollment: 2,406
Undergrads: 2,406
Freshmen: 660
Part-time students: 1%
From out-of-state: 72%
From public schools: 66%
Male/Female: 44%/56%
Live on-campus: 95%
Off-campus employment rating: Fair
Caucasian: 62%
African American: 6%
Hispanic: 11%
Asian / Pacific Islander: 9%
Mixed (2+ ethnicities): 5%
International: 7%

Academics
Calendar: Semester
Student/faculty ratio: 8:1
Class size 9 or fewer: 22%
Class size 10-29: 67%
Class size 30-49: 10%
Class size 50-99: 1%
Class size 100 or more: -
Six-year graduation rate: 91%
Graduates who immediately go to graduate school: 23%
Graduates who immediately enter career related to major: 57%

Most Popular Majors
English
Political science
Economics

Admissions
Applicants: 7,908
Accepted: 1,806
Acceptance rate: 22.8%
Placed on wait list: 1,340
Enrolled from wait list: 29
Average GPA: 3.8
ACT range: 29-32
SAT Math range: 650-740
SAT Reading range: 660-750
SAT Writing range: 54-39
Top 10% of class: 70%
Top 25% of class: 95%
Top 50% of class: 100%

899

College Profiles

VASSAR COLLEGE

Admissions Criteria
Academic criteria:
Grades: ☆ ☆ ☆
Difficulty of class schedule: ☆ ☆ ☆
Class rank: ☆ ☆
Standardized test scores: ☆ ☆
Teacher recommendations: ☆ ☆
Personal statement: ☆ ☆
Non-academic criteria considered:
Interview
Extracurricular activities
Special talents, interests, abilities
Character/personal qualities
Volunteer work
Work experience
State of residency
Geographical location
Minority affiliation
Alumni relationship

Deadlines
Early Action: No
Early Decision: November 15
Regular Action: January 1 (final)
Notification of admission by: April 1
Common Application: Accepted

Financial Aid
In-state tuition: $47,180
Out-of-state tuition: $47,180
Room: $6,070
Board: $5,110
Books: $900
Freshmen receiving need-based aid: 59%
Undergrads rec. need-based aid: 60%
Avg. % of need met by financial aid: 100%
Avg. aid package (freshmen): $45,236
Avg. aid package (undergrads): $44,768
Avg. debt upon graduation: $17,234

School Spirit
Mascot: Brewers
Colors: Rose and grey

few hundred freshmen, sophomores, and juniors; one of these is all-female. Upperclassmen may choose from alternate housing options, which include a student-run cooperative house and apartments.

Student Body

Vassar's constant encouragement to its students to "think independently" attracts a student body that values uniqueness. To use the word "hipster" might be going too far, but only just. "You'll fit in if you're not afraid to be yourself," says a student. Vassar students tend toward an artsy-intellectual type—many students list philosophy or gender studies courses as "must-take" classes—and lean left politically. But this atmosphere of liberal arts intellectualism does not preclude a heavy involvement with sciences or technology and medical school is a common post-graduation goal.

Vassar's gender distribution favors women slightly, perhaps reflecting its origins as a women's college. Thirty-one percent of Vassar's students are minorities; almost three-quarters of the student population come from out of state.

You May Not Know

- Maria Mitchell, famed 19th-century American astronomer and the first female member of the American Academy of Arts and Sciences, became the first faculty member at Vassar in 1865.
- Two of Vassar's buildings, Main Building and the Maria Mitchell Observatory, are National Historic Landmarks.
- Vassar College has its very own Quidditch team, the Butterbeer Brewers, who took second place at the 2008 U.S. College Quidditch Cup.

Distinguished Alumni

Caterina Fake, founder of Flickr; Bernadine Healy, first woman director of the National Institutes of Health; Lisa Kudrow, actress; Vera Cooper Rubin, discoverer of "dark matter;" Meryl Streep, actress.

Admissions and Financial Aid

Vassar uses the Common Application with a supplement. Students interested in art, music, or dance may submit a supplemental sample of their work along with their application. Vassar does not require interviews, but it does offer "informational interviews" with Vassar alumni throughout the world as a "way to learn about Vassar from a different perspective." These interviews are "non-evaluative," and the lack of an interview does not affect application status.

Admission to Vassar is need-blind. While Vassar does not award athletic or academic merit scholarships, it does meet 100 percent of demonstrated need of all its students—international or domestic—for all four years. Vassar partners with QuestBridge, a program that works to open up opportunities in higher education for academically talented low-income or underserved youth: QuestBridge packages, which offer grants that cover the cost of tuition without loans, typically include federal work-study and student summer jobs.

VILLANOVA UNIVERSITY

Overview

Medium-sized Villanova University occupies an attractive, wooded 254-acre suburban campus—just 12 miles west of Philadelphia—offering an oasis of green park spaces, ivy-covered Gothic revival buildings, and the elegant tall spires of St. Thomas of Villanova Church, all within easy access of the East Coast's second-largest city. Villanova is probably better known for its championship basketball teams than anything else; but in addition to being a great basketball school, Villanova offers a well-respected liberal arts core and some of the most highly-ranked pre-professional and undergraduate engineering programs in the country. Villanova's School of Business and undergraduate engineering programs have been ranked in the top 10 by *Bloomberg BusinessWeek* and *U.S. News & World Report*, respectively, and its College of Nursing has been named a Center of Excellence in Nursing Education by the National League for Nursing.

Villanova is a Roman Catholic school, and although Villanova's Catholicism isn't its only defining feature, it certainly plays a major role in academics as well as extracurriculars. In fact, the Catholic emphasis of the school is most apparent in the school's overwhelming commitment to charity and service: more than three-quarters of students participate in some kind of service activity. Villanova students are also known for their very active social lives, both on campus and off. And should that get boring, Philadelphia is well-connected to campus by train, and strategically located between New York City and Washington, DC; the famed Jersey Shore, Pocono Mountains, and Chesapeake Bay are all within 100 miles.

A Catholic education isn't for everyone—theology classes are required, and the demographic that the school attracts is a pretty homogenous pool of wealthier East Coast preppy types—but Villanova, with its powerhouse athletics and fan base, liberal arts core, pre-professional programs, and commitment to service, offers more dimensions than just a Catholic education.

Academics

Villanova provides 94 majors across four schools and colleges. While Villanova is broadly known for well-rounded academics, its Colleges of Engineering and Nursing and School of Business stand out, particularly the latter's finance and marketing majors. Each school has its own different core requirements, but some elements are the same throughout: all students must take the two-semester "Augustine and Culture Seminars," one or two theology courses, and at least one course each in philosophy and/or ethics, math, English, and natural and/or social sciences. All schools except for nursing require some combination of arts, history, humanities, or diversity classes; modern language requirements are variable. Science requirements are more extensive in the Colleges of Nursing and Engineering.

Students looking to participate in Honors classes will be pleased to find a flexible program, which allows them to major in Honors by taking 10 or 12 Honors courses (students may also complete an additional major), or to earn Honors in Liberal Studies, by taking eight Honors courses and completing a different major. All classes in the Honors Program are small, discussion- and research-based seminars that fulfill core requirements in every discipline except for natural science and engineering. "Honors classes are not ones where you can sit back and not participate," says a student. A senior Honors thesis is required. Honors students have access to specialized peer advising and faculty mentoring, can enroll in classes at nearby Bryn Mawr, can participate in university-sponsored field trips, and are eligible to apply for one of 20 Connelly-Delouvrier International Scholarships to fund an academic semester abroad.

The College of Engineering also offers well-respected five-year combined bachelor's and master's degree programs in chemical, civil and environmental, electrical and computer, and mechanical engineering. Interested students can apply to the

VILLANOVA UNIVERSITY

Four-year private
Founded: 1842
Villanova, PA
Small town
Pop. 9,189

Address:
800 Lancaster Avenue
Villanova, PA
19085

Admissions:
610-519-4000

Financial Aid:
610-519-4010

gotovu@villanova.edu

www.villanova.edu

VILLANOVA UNIVERSITY

Students
Total enrollment: 9,959
Undergrads: 7,100
Part-time students: 7%
From out-of-state: 83%
From public schools: 55%
Male/Female: 49%/51%
Live on-campus: 70%
In fraternities: 18%
In sororities: 39%
Off-campus employment rating: Excellent
Caucasian: 74%
African American: 5%
Hispanic: 7%
Asian / Pacific Islander: 6%
Native American: 0%
Mixed (2+ ethnicities): 2%
International: 3%

Academics
Calendar: Semester
Student/faculty ratio: 11:1
Class size 9 or fewer: 9%
Class size 10-29: 66%
Class size 30-49: 23%
Class size 50-99: 2%
Class size 100 or more: 1%
Returning freshmen: 94%
Six-year graduation rate: 88%
Graduates who immediately go to graduate school: 16%
Graduates who immediately enter career related to major: 73%

Most Popular Majors
Nursing
Finance
Communication

Admissions
Applicants: 14,901
Accepted: 6,798
Acceptance rate: 45.6%
Placed on wait list: 5,063
Enrolled from wait list: 199
Average GPA: 3.9
ACT range: 28-31
SAT Math range: 610-710
SAT Reading range: 590-680
SAT Writing range: 25-49
Top 10% of class: 58%
Top 25% of class: 87%
Top 50% of class: 97%

902

program during their junior year. "Engineering graduates are CEOs, professors, and NASA astronauts," notes a student.

Villanova—under the Villanova Undergraduate Research Fellows (VURF) Program—can provide funding for faculty-supervised student research and research-related travel and supplies. Through the Summer Housing Program, room and board are provided to students working in labs or conducting research on campus.

Villanova also offers a wide selection of study-abroad options, in which most students participate. Semester programs are available in the UK, Italy, Australia, and Spain. Villanova also runs its own summer programs in business, art and culture, literature and language, and field research. Additionally it operates the Learning Communities Abroad (LCA) Program, which combines a Citizenship and Globalization course with six- to seven-week work placement programs in London or Madrid. Students can find funding for their time abroad through the Connelly-Delovrier International Scholars Program, which provides funding for select students taking Honors courses and to Presidential Scholarship recipients.

Of Villanova graduates, 16 percent attend graduate school within one year, and 73 percent are employed in fields related to their major within six months; the median starting salary is $51,000. Villanova is also particularly strong in internship placements—nearly 60 percent of graduates held internships during their college careers.

Student Life

While they're dedicated academically, that is only a part of Villanova student life. They are also extremely active both in terms of student activities and socializing: Villanova boasts 230 student groups. Overwhelmingly the most popular of these are service organizations like Habitat for Humanity, but the five-division Villanova Band is itself the largest group on campus.

Service is also a major component of campus' annual events. Literally thousands of students volunteer for the Special Olympics Pennsylvania Fall Festival held at Villanova; it is the largest student-run Special Olympics event in the world. Students provide training and support for athletes and organize 260 events in 23 sports. "Almost everyone volunteers in some form," one student remarks.

Other activities on campus include the standard college-type events and the very traditional. From their first day, new arrivals are welcomed to campus with the St. Thomas of Villanova Day parade in full academic regalia. Another favorite is NovaFest—a week-long event featuring dance parties, free food, and musical performances—which has recently been consolidated into a Spring Concert in an effort to bring better musical acts, like the Fray, All-American Rejects, and Goo Goo Dolls to campus. Students will also find plenty to do at Connelly Center, which includes a food court, movie theatre and rental shop, and hosts concerts and other performances as part of the Late Night entertainment series. None of Villanova's 13 fraternities or 14 sororities are housed on campus; sororities, to which 39 percent of campus women belong, are much more popular than fraternities.

When it comes to athletics, Villanova fosters an enthusiastic fan base for its 10 men's and 12 women's Division I varsity teams. The campus favorite, Villanova's men's basketball team, is a regular at the NCAA championships, and the cross country and track and field teams are strong as well. "Basketball games are filled with loud, rowdy fans," says a student. More than 40 club and intramural sports are available for the more casual athlete; and Villanova participates in the City 6, which organizes tournaments with teams from other Division I schools in the Philly area.

Philadelphia is a very easy train ride away, and students can sample its art scene, restaurants, nightlife, and sights; the rest of the mid-Atlantic is easily accessible for bigger ventures. Also nearby is the King of Prussia Mall, the largest mall in the country.

Freshmen are housed in dorms on South Campus, while sophomores live on the Quad, which is made up of Sheehan and Sullivan Halls. Upperclassmen can move into apartments on West Campus or to locations off campus.

Student Body

Villanova students are known for being committed academically as well as being highly social. Villanova boasts high levels of geographic and ethnic diversity, but about 80 percent of students are Catholic. Given the Catholic Church's stance on homosexuality, Villanova, like most Catholic schools, struggles with that aspect of diversity. According to an article in the school newspaper, Villanova is a "not entirely homophobic" and "mostly tolerant" school.

You May Not Know

- Villanova plans to be environmentally neutral by 2050.
- A popular meeting place on campus, a statue called *The Awakening*, is generally known as "the Oreo" based on its appearance.
- Villanova houses the Liberty Bell's "Sister Bell." This replacement bell was ordered after the original cracked in 1753.

Distinguished Alumni

Maria Bello, actress; Steve Chen, principal architect of the Cray X-MP Supercomputer; Bradley Cooper, actor; Jim Croce, musician; Edward Guinan, discoverer of Neptune's rings; John Joseph O'Connor, Cardinal and Archbishop of the Archdiocese of New York.

Admissions and Financial Aid

Villanova's largest and most prestigious merit scholarship award is the Presidential Scholarship, which covers the full cost of tuition, fees, and books for academically qualified students of "diverse intellectual, social, racial, and economic backgrounds." About 30 of these are awarded annually, and students must be nominated by their schools.

Villanova also offers Villanova Scholarship awards of variable amounts to qualified students demonstrating academic need; all application materials must be submitted by January 7.

VILLANOVA UNIVERSITY

Highlights

Admissions Criteria
Academic criteria:
Grades: ☆ ☆ ☆
Difficulty of class schedule: ☆ ☆ ☆
Class rank: ☆ ☆ ☆
Standardized test scores: ☆ ☆ ☆
Teacher recommendations: ☆ ☆
Personal statement: ☆ ☆
Non-academic criteria considered:
Extracurricular activities
Special talents, interests, abilities
Character/personal qualities
Volunteer work
Work experience
Geographical location
Minority affiliation
Alumni relationship

Deadlines
Early Action: November 1
Early Decision: No
Regular Action: January 15 (final)
Notification of admission by: April 1
Common Application: Accepted

Financial Aid
In-state tuition: $43,840
Out-of-state tuition: $43,840
Room: $6,286
Board: $5,570
Books: $988
Freshmen receiving need-based aid: 51%
Undergrads rec. need-based aid: 48%
Avg. % of need met by financial aid: 80%
Avg. aid package (freshmen): $33,169
Avg. aid package (undergrads): $31,592
Avg. debt upon graduation: $35,297

School Spirit
Mascot: Wildcat
Colors: Blue and white
Song: *V for Villanova*

VIRGINIA TECH

Four-year public
Founded: 1872
Blacksburg, VA
Large town
Pop. 42,600

Address:
201 Burruss Hall
Blacksburg, VA
24061

Admissions:
540-231-6267

Financial Aid:
540-231-5179

vtadmiss@vt.edu

www.vt.edu

VIRGINIA POLYTECHNIC INSTITUTE AND STATE UNIVERSITY (VIRGINIA TECH)

Overview

On a plateau near the Appalachian Mountains, Virginia Tech—more commonly known by students as VT—is a very large public university renowned for its technical majors. While the fact that students are required to have a laptop or tablet computer may make the university seem particularly "techie," there's also a liberal arts curriculum required for all undergrads.

Located in Blacksburg, a dream town for outdoor enthusiasts, the university has the distinction of being ranked 25th among public universities by *U.S. News & World Report*. VT also has the painful legacy of being the location of the 2007 shooting in which 33 people were killed. As a testament to students' strong sense of community and spirit (VT students proudly call themselves "The Hokies"), the Hokie Spirit Memorial Fund (HSMF) was set up within a day of the shooting. The fund has distributed $8 million to help remember and honor the victims.

These days, students show Hokie pride at far less tragic events; football games are especially popular. Most of the buildings are even made of "Hokie Stone," a grayish limestone with hues of brown and pink. As with many large public universities, students will need to navigate large classes that aren't always taught by professors, and in-state students are disproportionately represented. Nonetheless, students looking for a strong sense of community school spirit together with strong academics will find it worthwhile to check out VT's offerings.

Academics

Virginia Tech offers more than 70 undergraduate majors and minors. The university has eight colleges and two schools, making for a wide range of academic opportunities. The Curriculum for Liberal Education, which is required for all undergraduates, includes a dozen classes across seven different areas, from Writing and Discourse to Quantitative and Symbolic Reasoning to Critical Issues in a Global Context.

Some of the introductory classes—especially in the sciences—can be very large, with teaching assistants (TAs) doing a lot of the heavy lifting in regard to classroom instruction, but this is less likely as students enter classes associated with their majors. "Mostly during freshman year you'll probably be stuck in some very large classes," says a student. Strong programs include architecture (ranked with highest distinction by DesignIntelligence from the Design Futures Council), courses in the Pamplin College of Business (ranked 10th among public institutions by the Association to Advance Collegiate Schools of Business International), and engineering (ranked 13th by the *Wall Street Journal* for top colleges favored by employers).

Students undecided about what to major in—or those who are exploring several different options—are designated University Studies majors and assigned a professional academic advisor. Students can remain University Studies majors until the end of their sophomore year. "My advisor helped me decide on a major after looking at possible future career paths with the two majors I was considering," notes a student.

Admission to the University Honors program is by invitation only. Perks include the opportunity to live in one of two Honors Residential Communities, scholarships for Honors students, an intimate small college environment, and greater contact with faculty and advisors.

SEED, the Student Endowment for Educational Development, is another organization to which students must apply in order to participate. Most who join are business students, since SEED manages $4 million for the Virginia Tech Foundation. "It's not for the casual participant," comments a student.

Virginia Tech's Education Abroad program sends approximately 1,200 students overseas every year to 48 countries. Education Abroad is part of the Office of International Research, Education, and Development (OIRED), which has projects throughout Asia, Africa, Latin America, the Caribbean, and Europe.

Much to the delight of students looking for real-world job experience, VT has an extensive Cooperative Education/Internship Program. Co-ops usually consist of three full-time work terms alternated with school terms that involve a single employer, resulting in a five-year degree program. Internships are often held in summer and may be full- or part-time, paid or unpaid.

Student Life

There are more than 700 student organizations. The university itself states, "whether you're looking for Greek life or robot wars, there's a club for you." It only takes three people to start a club, and it's easy to add on to that number. The Squires Student Center offers an enormous space—more than 230,000 square feet and five floors—for eating, lounging, meeting, and more. Alcohol is prohibited in the dorms, so more parties are held off campus than on.

For more than 100 years, the Ring Tradition has been a long-standing symbol of Virginia Tech. Each graduating class designs a unique ring collection, and the major annual Ring Dance honors this unique celebration. The Dance represents the transition from junior to senior year, with a ritualized ring exchange among couples, fine dining, and a culminating display of fireworks on the Drillfield. "The Ring Dance is very romantic with a special Ring Dance song and balloons falling from the ceiling," recalls a student.

Freshmen are introduced to the spirited traditions of VT at Hokie Hi, a welcome event that includes a high-energy picnic and Gobblerfest, a street fair that recently drew 18,000 people and continued with late night activities in the Squires Student Center. Another major event is VT's American Cancer Society's Relay for Life, which earned the university an award for top net income two years in a row. The university strives to live up to its motto "Ut Prosim, That I May Serve."

Greek life is a major presence on campus, with—count 'em—65 nationally affiliated fraternities and sororities. Greek parties are open to non-members. "Since we can go to the parties anyway, I didn't really see the point in joining a fraternity," says one student.

Virginia Tech boasts a strong athletics program of 21 Division I varsity teams. Football is especially cherished, and the Hokies have had seven straight seasons of winning at least 10 games. Students and alums tailgate all day long for games. "Tailgating is one of the most popular extracurricular activities," one student comments. Baseball, men's soccer, softball, and men's and women's basketball are also strong. All of the teams are called the Hokies, except for the creatively-named variant H2Okies for the swim team.

Students often enjoy Virginia's natural beauty by hiking, fishing, and camping in the Appalachian Mountains. Blacksburg has a college town feel, with students hanging out at downtown bars and local restaurants, visiting Lane Stadium for major football games, and watching movies at the historic Lyric Theater.

Students are required to live on campus for the first year, and more than 9,000 undergrads live in a wide variety of housing arrangements. The 18 buildings of Oak Lane Community are located behind the golf course, and house the fraternities and sororities.

VIRGINIA TECH

Highlights

Students
Total enrollment: 31,087
Undergrads: 23,859
Freshmen: 5,970
Part-time students: 2%
From out-of-state: 26%
Male/Female: 59%/41%
Live on-campus: 38%
In fraternities: 13%
In sororities: 24%
Caucasian: 73%
African American: 3%
Hispanic: 5%
Asian / Pacific Islander: 8%
Native American: 0%
Mixed (2+ ethnicities): 4%
International: 3%

Academics
Calendar: Semester
Student/faculty ratio: 16:1
Class size 9 or fewer: 8%
Class size 10-29: 44%
Class size 30-49: 27%
Class size 50-99: 13%
Class size 100 or more: 8%
Returning freshmen: 93%
Six-year graduation rate: 83%

Most Popular Majors
Biological sciences
Psychology
Mechanical engineering

Admissions
Applicants: 20,191
Accepted: 14,210
Acceptance rate: 70.4%
Placed on wait list: 2,217
Enrolled from wait list: 110
Average GPA: 3.9
ACT range: Not reported
SAT Math range: 570-680
SAT Reading range: 540-640
SAT Writing range: 3-22
Top 10% of class: 44%
Top 25% of class: 84%
Top 50% of class: 99%

College Profiles

VIRGINIA TECH

These feature recreational fields plus volleyball and basketball courts. Living Learning Communities include Academic Major Learning Communities (primarily for freshmen) and themed dormatories such as substance-free housing. VT offers residential honors communities in which students live and take classes together.

Student Body

According to students, the main thing that unites the student body is "massive amounts" of school spirit, which runs high especially for the football team. You'll find students festooned in Chicago Maroon and burnt orange, sporting VT memorabilia and proudly declaring themselves part of the Hokie family. Men outnumber women by more than 4,200, though the overall percentage—59 percent vs. 41 percent—is fairly balanced compared to other schools with technical focuses.

Defying expectations for a school in the South, there is high ethnic diversity at VT, with about 20 percent of the undergraduate population identifying as minority students. Multicultural Programs and Services promotes awareness, education, retention, leadership development, and community building among the diverse constituent groups.

There is moderate geographic diversity, with about 26 percent of students coming from outside the Commonwealth of Virginia. Only about three percent of students are international.

You May Not Know

- VT is one of the few universities in the United States that maintains a corps of cadets.
- The university mascot, the Hokie, was not originally a turkey. The word was created by O.M. Stull (class of 1896), who used it in a cheer he wrote for a competition. The turkey came about in 1913.
- In 2003, VT created a supercomputer that ranked as the third fastest in the world.

Distinguished Alumni

Bridget Berman, CEO of Giogrio Armani Corporation; Jim Buckmaster, CEO of craigslist.org; Chet Culver, Governor of Iowa; Molly Line, reporter for Fox News.

Admissions and Financial Aid

According to Virginia Tech, the academic directors place greatest emphasis on the strength of the high school curriculum, GPA, and standardized test scores when choosing the almost 6,000 entering freshmen from an applicant pool of more than 20,000. Other factors in the holistic review include ethnicity, first-generation (to attend college), leadership, service, intended major, and the personal statement.

VT offers General Scholarships between $1,500 and $3,000, Presidential Campus Enrichment Awards to increase diversity, University Honors Scholarships, athletic scholarships, and other categories of funding. There are also scholarships specific to certain colleges and departments. Forty-three percent of students receive need-based aid, and 12 percent of students receive merit-based aid.

WABASH COLLEGE

Overview

Wabash is a very small, private, all-male liberal arts college with a respected academic reputation. The student body is governed by one rule—the Gentleman's Rule—which states that students are to conduct themselves at all times as gentlemen and responsible citizens. As the Gentleman's Rule attests, the Wabash ethos is full of reversions to a bygone age of elite, all-male education. The student body tends to be conservative, the pastimes full of old-timey school spirit, and the social life frat-drenched.

Wabash College is situated in Crawfordsville, Indiana, a small town of around 16,000, located approximately 45 miles northwest of Indianapolis. The campus is home to Georgian-style buildings and many trees, which form part of the Fuller Arboretum.

In many ways, Wabash is an anachronism, a vibrantly alive bunch of young men steeped in traditions of times long gone. If you think of yourself as a "gentleman" and you don't mind living in the "middle of nowhere" with precious few other students, you can be sure to get a high quality education at this strong academic institution.

Academics

Wabash offers just 22 majors, so students must be sure that the program they want exists at the college. The strongest programs are in biology and political science, and the school offers a good foundation for prebusiness and premed students. The academic environment is challenging and "can be competitive at times," says a student. The vast majority of classes are small—mostly under 19 students.

Wabash has some unusually old-fashioned course requirements. In addition to a written senior exam, all students must pass a senior oral examination, presumably administered by a Socrates-like figure in academic robes. "Everyone dreads the oral exam," notes a student. Students must also take an "Enduring Questions" course in their sophomore year to explore "fundamental questions of humanity." More run-of-the-mill requirements include a small, discussion-based freshman tutorial, a Cultures and Traditions sophomore course, a composition course for those who do not test out of the requirement, and proficiency in a foreign language. Finally, distribution requirements demand one course in language studies, three in literature and fine arts, three in behavioral science, three in natural sciences and mathematics, one in quantitative skills, and two course credits in history, philosophy, or religion. Most students must complete a minor or concentration within their major department.

Students can take advantage of "Immersion Learning" courses, mainly offered during spring break. These courses provide experiential learning in a variety of sites across the U.S. and abroad. The best part is that, unlike at most colleges, "Immersion Learning" courses are free of charge. Topics range from "Invertebrate Biology" in Belize to "St. Francis of Assisi" in Italy. In addition to these special programs, Wabash students can study abroad in over 140 countries.

On a more practical, career-focused note, Wabash offers five pre-professional programs: business, health and allied sciences, law, secondary teaching, and engineering. Prebusiness is perhaps the most structured and extensive, as it includes a series of courses called the "Business Sequence" and a special notation on the student's transcript. Prelaw and prehealth programs consist of advising and assistance with the professional school application process. Prelaw preparation also includes Moot Court (with real, live lawyers as judges) and field trips to law schools in Indiana. The Secondary Teaching Preparation Program allows students to obtain their license during senior year. Engineering is a "3-2" program in conjunction with Columbia and Washington University—three years of Wabash liberal arts and two years of Columbia or Wash U engineering culminating in both a BA and a BS.

WABASH COLLEGE

Four-year private men's college
Founded: 1832
Crawfordsville, IN
Small town
Pop. 16,042

Address:
P.O. Box 352
Crawfordsville, IN 47933

Admissions:
800-345-5385

Financial Aid:
800-718-9746

admissions@wabash.edu

www.wabash.edu

WABASH COLLEGE

Highlights

Students
Total enrollment: 906
Undergrads: 906
Freshmen: 252
From out-of-state: 28%
From public schools: 86%
Male/Female: 100%/ 0%
Live on-campus: 93%
In fraternities: 51%
Off-campus employment rating: Fair
Caucasian: 76%
African American: 6%
Hispanic: 5%
Asian / Pacific Islander: 2%
Native American: 1%
Mixed (2+ ethnicities): 3%
International: 7%

Academics
Calendar: Semester
Student/faculty ratio: 10:1
Class size 9 or fewer: 35%
Class size 10-29: 54%
Class size 30-49: 9%
Class size 50-99: 2%
Class size 100 or more: -
Returning freshmen: 86%
Six-year graduation rate: 73%
Graduates who immediately go to graduate school: 24%

Most Popular Majors
Biology
English
History

Admissions
Applicants: 1,331
Accepted: 892
Acceptance rate: 67.0%
Placed on wait list: 93
Enrolled from wait list: 1
Average GPA: 3.6
ACT range: 22-28
SAT Math range: 530-655
SAT Reading range: 510-620
SAT Writing range: 6-19
Top 10% of class: 37%
Top 25% of class: 70%
Top 50% of class: 94%

Wabash offers funding for students to pursue research and internships. Students submit grant proposals for collaborative research with faculty, independent investigation, conference attendance, and summer internships.

The career services office at Wabash has deep pockets when it comes to funding summer internships. There are several different programs, mostly with a business focus, that include stipends of close to $3,000. "The stipend opens up the possibilities when you don't have to worry about finding a paid internship," says a student. Wabash also offers a structured summer experience called "Business Immersion" that combines class work, guest lectures, and the opportunity to present the results of hands-on projects to a panel of business experts.

Student Life

Among on-campus activities, the Sphinx Club is one of the most respected groups. The club, a "spirit and leadership organization," is composed of juniors and seniors who hold leadership positions on campus. The Sphinx Club sponsors events like pre-football cookouts and weekly TGIF parties for students and professors. "A lot of guys aspire to be members," notes a student. Working on the school newspaper, the *Bachelor*, is another popular activity.

Besides Sphinx Club men and journalists, the other big men on campus are football players and frat brothers. A whopping 51 percent of the student body joins a fraternity, and the frat scene is the "epicenter of social life," says a student. There are nine fraternities, each with its own frat house on campus.

The traditions at Wabash are, well, very traditional. Each year, the Chapel Sing kicks off homecoming weekend. Freshmen line up outside the chapel to belt out the school song, while members of the Sphinx Club weave among them to see which freshmen know all the words. Those who don't pass the test receive a shameful, spray-painted scarlet W on their T-shirts. Homecoming also includes performances and concerts in addition to the inevitable football game.

The annual rugby match against rivals DePauw University, known as the Monon Bell, is another highlight of the year: teams compete to win the "Monon Keg" trophy. The week before the event is called "Bell Week," and freshman take turns guarding the campus from (mostly hypothetical) invasions of DePauw vandals.

Finally, Pan-Hellenic Week is a bonanza of parties and inter-frat competitions that include a huge block party (minus the block) complete with bed races. For those who have never heard of bed races, they entail one lucky fellow sitting on a mattress inside a shopping cart while his compatriots push and pull him along.

Aside from its illustrious contingent of all-star bed racers, Wabash fields 10 varsity sports teams that compete in Division III. The most popular among fans are football and swimming. The cross country team is respectable as well.

When it comes to off-campus life, Crawfordsville is far from a hot spot. Students often travel to Indianapolis (an hour away by car) or Lafayette, home of Purdue University. The Cactus Bar in Lafayette is a popular late night attraction for Wabash men, with a packed dance floor and a resident "piano man." One student notes,

"We have to create our own fun because we don't have much to work with in Crawfordsville."

Students are required to live on campus for the first two years (unless they commute from home) in one of five residence halls. Freshmen don't have too much of a chance of scoring a single; but, on the other hand, a total of 68 upperclassmen can live in singles in Morris or Wolcott. There is only one dining hall for dorm residents. More than half of the student body live in frat houses.

Student Body

Most students are academically-oriented, but they also party hard. "We're balanced between being serious and letting loose," one student states. Politically, the student body has a "conservative slant." Geographic diversity is moderate; around 72 percent of Wabash men hail from Indiana. Ethnic diversity is also moderate.

You May Not Know

- Wabash has one of the highest per-student endowments in the nation.
- In 1832, when Wabash was founded, Crawfordsville, Indiana was a frontier town.
- Wabash's rather bellicose English motto is "Wabash Always Fights."

Distinguished Alumni

Bob Charles, inventor of the Happy Meal; Gary Croghan, Mayo Clinic oncologist and Father of the PSA Test; Thomas Riley Marshall, Vice President to Woodrow Wilson.

Admissions and Financial Aid

The alumni have a huge part in reaching out to potential students. Recently, alumni referred 340 students who applied, and 107 of them attend the college.

Wabash offers relatively generous merit-scholarship opportunities, several of which require a special visit to campus. For instance, to win a Top Ten Scholarship for $60,000 over four years, students ranked in the top ten percent of their high school class must attend the Top Ten visit day. Those in the top five percent can win an additional $10,000 through the same program.

Candidates for a Fine Arts Scholarship in creative writing, music, theater, or visual arts (up to $50,000 over four years) must come to campus to audition or display their work. The most coveted scholarship available, the Lilly Award, also requires a campus visit. This scholarship, which includes tuition, fees, and room and board for four years, is awarded based on the criteria of "character, creativity, and academic accomplishment."

WABASH COLLEGE

Highlights

Admissions Criteria
Academic criteria:
Grades: ☆ ☆ ☆
Difficulty of class schedule: ☆ ☆ ☆
Class rank: ☆ ☆ ☆
Standardized test scores: ☆ ☆
Teacher recommendations: ☆
Personal statement: ☆
Non-academic criteria considered:
Interview
Extracurricular activities
Special talents, interests, abilities
Character/personal qualities
Volunteer work
Work experience
State of residency
Geographical location
Minority affiliation
Alumni relationship

Deadlines
Early Action: December 1
Early Decision: November 15
Regular Action: Rolling admissions
Common Application: Accepted

Financial Aid
In-state tuition: $35,000
Out-of-state tuition: $35,000
Room: $4,310
Board: $4,200
Books: $1,500
Freshmen receiving need-based aid: 83%
Undergrads rec. need-based aid: 81%
Avg. % of need met by financial aid: 97%
Avg. aid package (freshmen): $31,769
Avg. aid package (undergrads): $29,423
Avg. debt upon graduation: $28,919

School Spirit
Mascot: Wally Wabash
Colors: Scarlet
Song: *Old Wabash*

WAKE FOREST UNIVERSITY

Four-year private
Founded: 1834
Winston Salem, NC
Medium city
Pop. 232,385

Address:
P.O. Box 7373, Reyn-
olds Station
Winston Salem, NC
27109

Admissions:
336-758-5201

Financial Aid:
336-758-5154

admissions@wfu.edu

www.wfu.edu

Overview

Wake Forest is a medium-sized, private, liberal arts university that combines the resources of a large university with the community feel of a smaller school. Challenging academics are balanced by a vibrant social life. Although there's not much to do off campus, there are strong athletics programs, many student organizations, and an active Greek scene to keep students occupied on campus. Undergraduate research is well supported and there are myriad study-abroad options.

Located in the Piedmont region of North Carolina in the city of Winston-Salem, the state's fourth largest city, Wake Forest boasts a pleasantly green campus dotted with Georgian buildings. The university's Reynolda Gardens provide a scenic place to hike or picnic among the blooms. The campus sits in a low-key residential neighborhood.

Sure, the nightlife is nonexistent, the workload can be intimidating, and conservative Southern "preppiness" is the order of the day. Still, Wake Forest is perfect for students who want to make the most of their academics, experience a tight-knit community of students and faculty, and get involved with meaningful research all while enjoying a mild climate and a healthy social scene. And the university is especially tough to pass up if you manage to land one of its many generous merit scholarships.

Academics

Don't expect an easy ride at the university students have nicknamed "Work Forest." The university's demanding classes require an impressive work ethic to succeed, but there is help available: the school's size and impressive student/faculty ratio create a close community of highly-invested teachers and learners. "The professors are very helpful, but they won't hold your hand," explains a student. "You have to invest yourself in the work."

Wake Forest has five required basic courses: a First Year seminar, a writing seminar, foreign language (everyone must work up to taking a literature course in a foreign language), and health science. On top of that, students must take courses in five divisions as well as courses fulfilling Quantitative Reasoning and Cultural Diversity requirements.

There are 71 majors at Wake Forest. Besides the undergraduate Wake Forest College, a liberal arts school, the university has four other graduate divisions: the Graduate School of Arts and Sciences, the Schools of Business, the School of Divinity, the School of Law, and the School of Medicine.

Academic programs in business and enterprise management and psychology and the offerings for pre-health students are particularly strong. There is a required Business and Enterprise Management internship which requires students to work at least 200 hours and a minimum of five weeks, giving them what students say is "invaluable hands-on experience." Psychology students are housed in the new Greene Hall, which has research labs, classrooms, and study areas. Pre-health students have access to advisors who help them with class selection and grad school selection and applications. There are also programs throughout the school year to help students with self-assessments, interviewing, and essay writing.

The school also has an array of special opportunities. There are several programs to help ensure that summers are productive. "There's no such thing as kicking back at the beach during the summer," one student says. The Summer Management Program gives non-business majors the opportunity to get intensive instruction and hands-on experience in business fundamentals—and for credit. The Summer Research Program, offered through the graduate school, provides four different programs in the biomedical field that give undergrads the chance to do laboratory research.

Those who want a more cosmopolitan summer can participate in an internship and an academic course (both for credit) through the WAKE Washington DC program.

Wake Forest values undergraduate research and puts its money where its mouth is. The Undergraduate Research and Creative Activities Center (URECA) is devoted to promoting links between undergraduates and faculty and making sure that undergraduates can make the most of research opportunities. Beyond Summer Research Fellowships, there are several more specifically targeted programs. The Richter Scholars Program gives undergrads $6,000 for independent study off campus (including abroad). There is also funding for undergrads to travel to present research at conferences (Starr Program) and up to $5,000 for individual or team creative projects with faculty mentors (through Atlantic Coast Conference Inter-institutional Academic Collaborative).

Wake Forest has over 400 study-abroad programs in over 70 countries, and over 60 percent of students participate in them. The university offers 11 scholarship programs to assist students with the costs of studying abroad, including the Richter Scholarship and Global Citizens Scholarship which award up to $5,000 each.

Career Services administers the Alumni Career Assistance Program, a network 2,000 strong to help students carve out their after-college paths. These alums provide informational interviews and networking opportunities. "It's amazing how helpful the alumni are and how readily they'll answer questions or tell you what it's like to work where they work," says a student.

Student Life

Among 176 student organizations, the most popular include social justice groups like Amnesty International, the Disabilities Awareness Coalition, and the Student Environmental Action Coalition. Other stand-outs are the Handbell Choir and the Anthony Aston Players theater group.

Activities promote camaraderie among students and spice up campus social life. Springfest is a free party with games, music, movie screenings, and plenty of free swag that lasts several days, highlighted by "Shag on the Mag," where students dance to live music on the Magnolia Quad. "It's fun," remarks a student. "It's warm and everyone's having a good time." Homecoming features the typical college tailgating experience along with big-name musical performances. In between special events like these, students can get their fill of facts (and prizes) at the Student Union's popular Tuesday Trivia.

With 52 percent of women and 38 percent of men pledging, the Greek scene is a big part of campus social life. "The parties can get pretty large and on the crazy side," laughs a student. There are 14 social frats and 10 social sororities on campus.

Wake Forest is home to 16 Division I varsity sports (eight men's and eight women's). Football and men's basketball are historically competitive, as is women's field hockey. "We are going through some building years in football," notes a student. A good range of intramurals are offered, including flag football, tennis, inner tube water polo, and bowling.

Off-campus life is a bit lackluster, since Winston-Salem is rather sprawling and the campus is in a residential area. Glamour,

WAKE FOREST UNIVERSITY

Highlights

Students
Total enrollment: 7,432
Undergrads: 4,815
Part-time students: 1%
From out-of-state: 80%
Male/Female: 48%/52%
Live on-campus: 68%
In fraternities: 38%
In sororities: 52%
Off-campus employment rating: Excellent
Caucasian: 76%
African American: 7%
Hispanic: 5%
Asian / Pacific Islander: 5%
Native American: 0%
Mixed (2+ ethnicities): 2%
International: 3%

Academics
Calendar: Semester
Student/faculty ratio: 11:1
Class size 9 or fewer: 13%
Class size 10-29: 66%
Class size 30-49: 19%
Class size 50-99: 2%
Class size 100 or more: -
Returning freshmen: 94%
Six-year graduation rate: 88%

Admissions
Applicants: 11,407
Accepted: 3,875
Acceptance rate: 34.0%
Average GPA: Not reported
ACT range: 29-31
SAT Math range: 630-710
SAT Reading range: 620-700
SAT Writing range: Not reported
Top 10% of class: 79%
Top 25% of class: 94%
Top 50% of class: 99%

WAKE FOREST UNIVERSITY

Admissions Criteria

Academic criteria:
Grades: ☆ ☆ ☆
Difficulty of class schedule: ☆ ☆ ☆
Class rank: ☆ ☆ ☆
Standardized test scores: ☆
Teacher recommendations: ☆ ☆
Personal statement: ☆ ☆ ☆
Non-academic criteria considered:
Interview
Extracurricular activities
Special talents, interests, abilities
Character/personal qualities
Volunteer work
Geographical location
Religious affiliation/commitment
Minority affiliation
Alumni relationship

Deadlines

Early Action: No
Early Decision: January 1
Regular Action: January 1 (final)
Notification of admission by: April 1
Common Application: Accepted

Financial Aid

In-state tuition: $44,200
Out-of-state tuition: $44,200
Room: $8,000
Board: $4,000
Books: $1,100
Freshmen receiving need-based aid: 39%
Undergrads rec. need-based aid: 41%
Avg. % of need met by financial aid: 99%
Avg. aid package (freshmen): $34,647
Avg. aid package (undergrads): $32,015
Avg. debt upon graduation: $33,262

School Spirit

Mascot: Demon Deacon
Colors: Old gold and black
Song: *O Here's to Wake Forest*

excitement, and clubs of any sort are hard to find, but there are low-key places to eat, hang out, and listen to a band play. Putter's is a popular destination off campus for students who want a good steak or some bar food before a football game. For outdoor fun, students go swimming at Belews Creek Lake, about half an hour's drive away. "Most of our fun consists of hanging out with friends so it doesn't really matter that we don't have the best nightlife," says a student.

Wake Forest guarantees housing for all four years. Both freshmen and sophomores are required to live on campus. One freshman residence hall is designated as substance-free housing. Theme houses are each home to around 15 students who share interests like theater, crew, radio, service, etc.

Student Body

The student body tends to be "a little on the conservative side" and somewhat "preppy," says one student. While the academics are rigorous, students balance their work with active social lives. Since there's not much to do off campus, especially for those under 21, frat parties are the weekend mainstay. Ethnic diversity (19 percent minority) and geographic diversity (80 percent from out of state) are high.

You May Not Know

- Wake Forest was one of the first top 30 national universities to make standardized test scores optional in its application.
- Graduates received sheepskin diplomas at graduation until 1981.
- Wake Forest's original location was near Raleigh. It relocated in 1956 after receiving a large endowment.

Distinguished Alumni

Richard Burr, U.S. Senator; Al Hunt, journalist; Arnold Palmer, professional golfer.

Admissions and Financial Aid

The admissions director advises applicants to make sure to put a lot of effort into crafting well-written essays and short answers and to make sure that their own voices, (not suggestions from their English teachers), shine through.

Wake Forest's merit aid resources are considerable. For 23 high academic achievers—SAT scores above 1500, top one percent of their class—named scholarships provide tuition, room, and board, $1,500 for personal expenses, $500 for study-abroad costs, and the chance to apply for $3,000 in summer funding each year. Twenty students with talent in art, debate, dance, music, and theater will snag $12,500 in renewable scholarships.

WARREN WILSON COLLEGE

Overview

At Warren Wilson College—a very small private college in the valley of the Blue Ridge Mountains near Asheville, North Carolina—undergrads enjoy a gorgeous, rural 1,100-acre campus for study, work, and play. The college is an outdoor-lover's Mecca, with a 300-acre student-run farm and market garden of mixed crops and livestock, 600 acres of maintained forest, and 25 miles of hiking trails, all shared by less than 1,000 students. Forty-five buildings sit on the 40 acres of main campus, and the Swannanoa River snakes picturesquely right through the middle of campus.

The college maintains a Presbyterian affiliation and emphasizes a strong work ethic. Indeed, this philosophy is all but enshrined in "the Triad," WWC's unique curriculum of work, academics, and service that requires every student to work an on-campus job and complete 100 hours of community service. Sustainability at Warren Wilson is not just a buzzword but a way of life. The college has won numerous awards for its efforts in creating an institutional culture of earth awareness, including a Campus Sustainability Award.

One look at what students are focusing their efforts on—majoring in Outdoor Leadership, designing majors such as Environmental Spirituality and Art, removing invasive plants on the annual Work Day—makes it obvious that a love for the environment drives students. The college motto sums up WWC perfectly: "We're not for everyone... but then again, maybe you're not everyone."

Living on a remote campus without Greek life or varsity sports, devoting a large amount of time and energy working outdoors, and taking classes with a tight-knit, collaborative community of folks isn't everyone's cup of tea—but if it's yours, then you'll certainly want to consider Warren Wilson College.

Academics

WWC offers 48 majors and special advising areas and 28 minors, with a curriculum that is driven by the "Triad Education Program." Required courses include classes in academics, work, and services. Freshmen take a first-year seminar and writing course, and all students must complete at least one class within each of the school's eight liberal arts areas, providing a base from which to pursue numerous concentrations.

Students are not competitive with each other, instead going above and beyond to cooperate. "It's a collaborative atmosphere," one student notes. Professors are very helpful; in fact, small classes help students cultivate close relationships with faculty. Standout programs are in creative writing, English, environmental studies, and prelaw advising.

Unique to the college is the major in outdoor leadership, a program that includes technical and interpersonal skills, along with broad learning in administrative issues. Future outdoor leaders take 17 core courses—among them Backcountry Skills and Techniques, Group Process, and Wilderness First Responder—plus a number of electives. "There aren't many places where your major requires you to go kayaking and rock climbing," a student comments.

All freshmen are required to take First-Year Seminars, which are designed to hone academic skills and help students connect with faculty, peers, and staff. Recent topics included "Conservation Psychology: Humans and the Rest of Nature," "Changing the World: International Social Service," and, for those who want to learn more about where their college is located, "A History of the Southern Highlands." This explains the school's global studies concentration, as well as its minor, in Appalachian Studies. Classes include an introduction to the regional field of study, history courses, and even courses on mandolin, banjo, fiddle, and ballad singing. "We have a very unique location and want to study it," one student says.

WARREN WILSON COLLEGE

Four-year private
Founded: 1894
Asheville, NC
Small town
Pop. 83,393

Address:
P.O. Box 9000
Asheville, NC
28815

Admissions:
800-934-3536

Financial Aid:
828-771-2082

admit@warren-wilson.edu

www.warren-wilson.edu

WARREN WILSON COLLEGE

Students
Total enrollment: 924
Undergrads: 852
Freshmen: 264
Part-time students: 1%
From out-of-state: 79%
From public schools: 84%
Male/Female: 38%/62%
Live on-campus: 90%
Off-campus employment rating: Excellent
Caucasian: 85%
African American: 4%
Hispanic: 3%
Asian / Pacific Islander: 2%
Native American: 0%
Mixed (2+ ethnicities): 3%
International: 3%

Academics
Calendar: Semester
Student/faculty ratio: 12:1
Class size 9 or fewer: 27%
Class size 10-29: 72%
Class size 30-49: 1%
Class size 50-99: -
Class size 100 or more: -
Returning freshmen: 69%
Six-year graduation rate: 57%
Graduates who immediately go to graduate school: 13%
Graduates who immediately enter career related to major: 75%

Most Popular Majors
Environmental studies
Global studies
Biology

Admissions
Applicants: 951
Accepted: 685
Acceptance rate: 72.0%
Average GPA: 3.5
ACT range: 23-28
SAT Math range: 480-590
SAT Reading range: 510-660
SAT Writing range: 7-32
Top 10% of class: 21%
Top 25% of class: 42%
Top 50% of class: 83%

914

WWC's honors programs emphasize scholarly research and provide incentives and recognition for talented students. Honors are offered through the biology, chemistry, English, and environmental studies departments. The Three-two Cooperative Program is an accelerated plan by which students can earn a BA from Warren Wilson in three years and a professional degree in forestry or environmental management from Duke University in two years.

Though international study is not required, 65 to 75 percent of WWC students study abroad through the college's International Program. The school provides funding for the excursions, which include semester exchanges in universities of a dozen countries, from China to Ecuador to Spain. Short-term courses involve on-campus study plus group travel during summer or winter break.

According to the college, 65 percent of Warren Wilson students go on to grad school—13 percent within a year of graduation. Three-quarters of students report full-time employment within six months of graduation.

Student Life

There are more than 20 student organizations. Every student is a member of the Student Caucus, which meets Sundays at 6 p.m. to discuss campus issues. Other groups include the Activities Crew, which plans weekly programs, from dances to lectures to bands. The Gladfelter Student Center houses the cafeteria, Cow Pie café, post office, and bookstore. The Spiritual Life Committee overseas religious life on campus, including Jewish and Christian groups and even a student-designed and constructed meditation hut. Moonshine and Mayhem—WWC's Ultimate Frisbee tournament—not only offers great competition but also a pulled pork BBQ dinner and some of North Carolina's finest (whiskey, that is).

Homecoming, held during the first full weekend in October, is a celebratory time at the university. The festivities are kicked off with a BBQ on the fields of the farm. Add to that live bluegrass music, hay rides, dancing, and a bonfire. "There's an agricultural bent to Homecoming," a student explains.

Warren Wilson's annual rite of spring is called Work Day, when the school's focus on caring for the earth takes center stage right at home. One the deans described it as "celebrating community with sweat equity"—and sweat students do. No classes are scheduled, and the entire campus community fans out across the 1,100-acre campus to work on outdoor projects, from cleaning the river to pulling out invasive plants to maintaining the cemetery.

Unlike many colleges, varsity athletics do not provide the centerpiece for activities and events. WWC has seven USCAA Division II teams, including mountain biking. "We have some unusual bragging rights," a student comments. "The mountain biking team usually places or wins its division." The college is strong in women's swimming and mountain biking as well. In addition to club and intramural sports, Outdoor Programs offers backpacking, day hiking, caving, canoeing, and much more. The weekend programs and weekly activities are usually free to students.

A 10-minute drive—or free city bus ride for WWC students—Asheville is an art community and college town. The largest city in North Carolina offers music, dining, food co-ops, independent bookstores, organic markets, and more. Luckily for eco-loving

WWC students, the area surrounding the college is an outdoor Mecca. Blue Ridge Parkway is a five-minute drive from campus, and the Appalachian Trail is less than an hour away.

Ninety percent of Warren Wilson College students live in one of the fifteen campus residence halls. These housing facilities are small, typically ranging from 17 to 125 students. The distinctive 36-bed EcoDorm is a green building with solar panels on the awning and an "edible landscape" that is grown using permaculture techniques.

Student Body

Considering the mission of the college, it's not surprising that WWC students are "passionate about the environment." Many students are focused on learning, rather than motivated solely by grades. The great majority of students are "liberal or very liberal."

The WWC student body is moderate in ethnic diversity, with about 12 percent of students identifying as minority students. "I would like to see more diversity on campus," says a student. There is high geographic diversity, with 79 percent of students hailing from out of state. For such a small student body, an impressive 45 states and 20 countries are represented.

You May Not Know

- The college's history traces back to 1894, when the Asheville Farm School started with 25 boys. The school offered only the first three years of elementary education.
- The ruins of a 1910 dam built to power the school's electricity can still be reached by hiking on the college's trails.
- Alma Shippy was the first African-American to attend WWC and one of the first to attend a segregated college by invitation and not by court order.

Distinguished Alumni

Sara Benincasa, comedian; Tony Earley, writer; James Franco, Academy Award–nominated actor; David Wilcox, folk musician.

Admissions and Financial Aid

According to the school, admissions officers look at the academic qualifications and potential of each prospective student. All available information is considered, ranging from academic records to extracurricular activities to test scores and references. The college seeks "a balanced student with high standards of scholarship, personal integrity, and a desire to support the mission of the College." There is no fee to apply.

Warren Wilson's merit awards include the Valedictorian/Salutatorian scholarships, National Merit Scholars Finalist awards, and NC Residential Scholarships, all of $4,000 per year. There are also work, service, and sustainability scholarships of $2,000 and Honors Scholarships of up to $8,000 per year.

WARREN WILSON COLLEGE

Highlights

Admissions Criteria
Academic criteria:
Grades: ☆ ☆ ☆
Difficulty of class schedule: ☆ ☆ ☆
Class rank: ☆ ☆ ☆
Standardized test scores: ☆ ☆
Teacher recommendations: ☆ ☆
Personal statement: ☆ ☆ ☆
Non-academic criteria considered:
Interview
Extracurricular activities
Special talents, interests, abilities
Character/personal qualities
Volunteer work
Work experience
State of residency

Deadlines
Early Action: No
Early Decision: November 15
Regular Action: January 31 (final)
Notification of admission by: February 28
Common Application: Accepted

Financial Aid
In-state tuition: $29,150
Out-of-state tuition: $29,150
Room: Varies
Board: Varies
Books: $820
Freshmen receiving need-based aid: 67%
Undergrads rec. need-based aid: 66%
Avg. % of need met by financial aid: 71%
Avg. aid package (freshmen): $26,074
Avg. aid package (undergrads): $23,653
Avg. debt upon graduation: $23,239

School Spirit
Mascot: Fighting Owls
Colors: Green, blue, and gold

915

WASHINGTON
& JEFFERSON
COLLEGE

Four-year private
Founded: 1781
Washington, PA
Small town
Pop. 13,691

Address:
60 South Lincoln
Street
Washington, PA
15301

Admissions:
724-223-6025

Financial Aid:
724-223-6019

admission@washjeff.
edu

www.washjeff.edu

Overview

Washington and Jefferson College, or W&J, as it is called, isn't the highest profile liberal arts school in the country, nor is it the highest-ranked, coming in as "Tier One," according to *U.S. News & World Report*. But this small school in Washington, Pennsylvania, 30 miles southwest of Pittsburgh, is one of the oldest colleges in America, and it fiercely insists that *U.S. News & World Report's* rankings don't do it justice. Rankings and numbers aside, W&J, as an undergraduates-only college, can offer unparalleled attention to its students, particularly in its highly respected and successful pre-professional and science programs, although its size may limit students' options in terms of courses, majors, study abroad, and even entertainment and recreation.

While the sleepy small town of Washington hasn't got much to offer and has had rocky relations with the college, the 60-acre campus itself features attractive historic buildings and newer construction built to match. Campus also boasts a 54-acre biological field station and the $33 million Swanson Science Center, completed in 2010, which provides multidisciplinary and high-tech labs geared for science and non-science majors alike. For science majors and pre-professional students, W&J offers a nurturing environment with a record of success that can more than compensate for its small size and lack of options and diversity.

Academics

Students at W&J have 31 majors to choose from, of which the strongest are education and child development and business administration. An overall theme permeates its extensive pre-professional programs, education, health professions, and prelaw program—*strong* preparation. In fact, of W&J graduates applying to law or health professional schools, 90 percent are accepted, and that's an impressive record.

Workloads are especially demanding, bordering on unmanageable, particularly because almost no class has more than 30 students. This means that everyone has to show up to class ready to actively participate. "There's no hiding out," explains a student. "You have to do the work."

All students at W&J follow a "4-1-4" academic calendar, taking four classes during fall and spring semester and one during the Intersession in January. They must complete the College-Wide Requirements, beginning with a First-Year Seminar, which is a small-group class that studies a subject in-depth and emphasizes writing and presentation skills. Students must also take skills courses—three writing-intensive courses, oral communication, quantitative reasoning, foreign language, information technology, and physical education—and meet distribution requirements in the arts, humanities, social sciences, natural science or math, and cultural diversity.

Students may elect to participate in special academic programs. For example, an "integrated semester" is occasionally offered, which consists of a set of courses centered on a single theme and culminating in an interdisciplinary project. Students who complete two of these courses (and the project) will receive special designations on their diplomas. Juniors and seniors with qualifying GPAs can complete a faculty-supervised Honors project that entails significant research and writing. Successful completion of the project enables students to graduate with Honors.

Students also have plenty of opportunity to pursue their own interests under the Magellan Project, which supports and funds students "in crafting and in telling compelling stories of curiosity and achievement," which most other schools might call "research and creative projects." Magellan Project Coordinators are available to mentor students in designing projects, composing proposals, and finding funding, and the Project itself funds summer research and even internships, many of which are offered through W&J departments to the tune of $1,000 to $3,000. One student comments, "Having someone help you through the process makes research seem more accessible."

Much of independent study and research takes place during Intersession, perhaps the most exciting time of the year for W&J students. Intersession allows students to take a single course, either on campus or abroad, or to pursue off-campus internships or independent research or study. On-campus courses are usually more exciting and alternative than regular-semester classes—offerings have included classes on printmaking, Hitchcock movies, children's theatre, and hacking, while abroad programs visit the UK, Japan, and New Zealand. "Traveling is great during Intersession, but even if that's not in the cards, then being on campus is fun too. There's a more laid-back and fun vibe," says a student.

Other than its Intersession trips, W&J's study-abroad program makes apparent the shortcomings of a university of its size. A single semester program in the Gambia is offered; otherwise, students can participate in outside programs and exchanges in Egypt, South Africa, China, Hong Kong, Japan, South Korea, Australia, Austria, Denmark, France, Germany, the UK, Norway, Netherlands, Spain, Russia, Chile, Costa Rica, Ecuador, Mexico, and Washington, DC.

W&J's Office of Career Services helps place about three-quarters of graduates in grad school or jobs in their field within six months of graduation; an active and tight-knit alumni network, the Career Resource Networks, aids considerably in this effort. The Franklin Internship Award helps financially support students who intern.

Student Life

Given that the town of Washington is a bit of a drag and that students are required to live on campus for all four years, campus is the major focus of social life. Students hang out at the Hub, the Commons, or Rossin Campus Center, and participate in over 70 student organizations. Academic and pre-professional clubs, like the Denominators math club, are popular, and the student newspaper *Red & Black* has existed for over 100 years. "You can go for days at a time without leaving campus," one student says.

The Spring and Fall concerts—which have featured Girl Talk, Saves the Day, Third Eye Blind, and the Clarks in past performances—draw big crowds. Other annual events include the festivities surrounding the lighting of the Christmas tree on Barista Terrace for Holiday Light-Up Night. Holiday-themed food, a gingerbread-house decorating contest, and music are all part of the entertainment. The Street Fair held on South Lincoln features free food, prizes, games, inflatable obstacle courses, movies, and musical performances.

The most popular groups and activities are W&J's six fraternities and four sororities and intramural or club sports; more than 40 percent of students are Greek participants, and almost half of students are involved in a sport of some kind. In fact, fitness and athletics are a major part of campus culture—*Men's Fitness* has ranked W&J as the "14th Fittest College in America"—and its intramurals range from flag football and volleyball to ping pong and Texas hold-em. "You can be as competitive as you want, although most people don't take intramurals too seriously," says a student.

WASHINGTON & JEFFERSON COLLEGE

Highlights

Students
Total enrollment: 1,429
Undergrads: 1,429
Freshmen: 376
From out-of-state: 28%
From public schools: 83%
Male/Female: 49%/51%
Live on-campus: 91%
In fraternities: 37%
In sororities: 43%
Off-campus employment rating: Good
Caucasian: 81%
African American: 3%
Hispanic: 3%
Asian / Pacific Islander: 2%
Native American: 1%
Mixed (2+ ethnicities): 2%
International: 3%

Academics
Calendar: 4-1-4 system
Student/faculty ratio: 11:1
Class size 9 or fewer: 25%
Class size 10-29: 71%
Class size 30-49: 4%
Class size 50-99: -
Class size 100 or more: -
Graduates who immediately go to graduate school: 36%

Most Popular Majors
Business/accounting
Psychology
English

Admissions
Applicants: 6,504
Accepted: 2,651
Acceptance rate: 40.8%
Placed on wait list: 46
Enrolled from wait list: 6
Average GPA: 3.3
ACT range: 23-28
SAT Math range: 520-620
SAT Reading range: 520-610
SAT Writing range: Not reported
Top 10% of class: 32%
Top 25% of class: 57%
Top 50% of class: 91%

917

WASHINGTON & JEFFERSON COLLEGE

Admissions Criteria

Academic criteria:
Grades: ☆ ☆ ☆
Difficulty of class schedule: ☆ ☆ ☆
Class rank: ☆ ☆ ☆
Standardized test scores: ☆ ☆
Teacher recommendations: ☆ ☆ ☆
Personal statement: ☆ ☆ ☆
Non-academic criteria considered:
Interview
Extracurricular activities
Special talents, interests, abilities
Character/personal qualities
Volunteer work
Work experience
Geographical location
Minority affiliation
Alumni relationship

Deadlines

Early Action: January 15
Early Decision: December 1
Regular Action: Rolling admissions
Common Application: Accepted

Financial Aid

In-state tuition: $39,250
Out-of-state tuition: $39,250
Room: $5,970
Board: $3,990
Books: $800
Freshmen receiving need-based aid: 79%
Undergrads rec. need-based aid: 77%
Avg. % of need met by financial aid: 76%
Avg. aid package (freshmen): $28,300
Avg. aid package (undergrads): $27,800

School Spirit

Mascot: Presidents
Colors: Red and black

In addition to its sports clubs and intramurals, W&J has 23 NCAA Division III varsity teams who carry on a tradition of athletic excellence. Overall, W&J has won over 100 conference titles. The football team has won 18 of the past 21 conference championships.

Washington is limited in terms of distractions, but Pittsburgh is only half an hour away and offers plenty of dining, shopping, and drinking options, particularly in the Strip district. Students who are into cultural entities and major league sporting events will find the city worthy of their interest. "Weeknight trips to the city are very common," one student notes.

Students live mostly in dorm-style residences, but suite-style housing and "Theme Community Living" organized around a common academic or cultural interest are available as well. "Personally, I like that we live on campus all four years because we form the strongest friendships and build the most school spirit," one student says.

Student Body

Students at W&J are known for being hard-core studiers during the week, but they relax and play hard on the weekends. "We know how to have a balance," a student explains. Most W&J students are from Pennsylvania, although the mostly white student body doesn't reflect much of the state's larger cities' diversity.

You May Not Know

- Originally the college was housed in three log cabin Presbyterian colleges.
- The college's fight song is sung to the tune of "99 Bottles of Beer" and mocks W&J's rival colleges, the University of Pittsburgh and Washington Female Seminary.
- One of W&J's "Theme Community Living" houses is a Pet House, which allows students to bring cats, small dogs, birds, rodents, and fish to campus.

Distinguished Alumni

John Astin, actor; Richard Clark, President and CEO of Merck & Co.; Stephen Foster, 19th-century American songwriter; John S. Reed, former Chairmen of Citigroup and the New York Stock Exchange; Tom Rooney, U.S. Congressman from Florida.

Admissions and Financial Aid

No essays or letters of recommendation are required for admissions, but recommendations will be considered if submitted. Students may also apply "Score Optional" and participate in a personal interview instead of submitting SAT/ACT scores.

Applicants are automatically considered for one of W&J's merit scholarships—the Challenge Grant, Dean's Award, Scholar's Award, and Howard J. Burnett Presidential Scholarship. Offers of merit scholarships can also be made later in a student's career.

WASHINGTON AND LEE UNIVERSITY

Overview

Washington and Lee is a small, private university ranked 14th among liberal arts colleges by *U.S. News & World Report*. The university stands out for the small size of its classes, strong service programs, distinctive Spring Term courses, and extensive merit scholarships. Perhaps the most unique feature of the university is its Honor System. Students can choose when and where to take exams, may enter most university buildings 24 hours a day, and should expect that their unattended belongings will always be safe. Beyond these examples, the Honor System creates an ethos of trust which encourages honest and honorable behavior. "It sounds so idealistic, but we truly abide by the Honor System," says a student.

The university is located in the cozy town of Lexington, Virginia. Outdoor activities abound nearby. The campus's architecture includes antebellum buildings as well as more recent, up-to-date additions. The most historic part of campus, the Liberty Hall Ruins, dates back to 1793. The ruins are a popular place to spend time and enjoy breathtaking views of the mountains.

Washington and Lee undoubtedly provides a challenging and intensive education, with many special academic opportunities and generous funding. Its location is a pleasant choice for those who like to spend time enjoying nature. Nevertheless, students whose interests lean toward the "alternative" and/or whose backgrounds are more humble than upper crust may feel out of place. But if an old South school with a small-town atmosphere is your cup of tea, Washington and Lee is worth checking out.

Academics

Washington and Lee offers 37 majors. The strongest programs include business administration, foreign languages, and English. Many students also choose to minor in creative writing. Regardless of the academic program, students can't hide from professors just because they haven't done homework: 98 percent of classes have fewer than 30 students. All that face time with professors makes for a collegial atmosphere between faculty and students and encourages high academic expectations. "Classes aren't so much lectures as interactive discussions," one student notes.

W&L's core curriculum is flexible, something that can be attributed to "Foundation and Distribution Requirements" rather than a set list of core courses. The "Foundation" consists of one writing class, a foreign language course "at the literature level," one math or computer science course, and a PE requirement, which includes a swim test. To satisfy the "Distribution" requirements, students must take four courses in the Arts and Humanities and four courses in the Sciences and Social Sciences.

Each spring, students can enjoy intensive, four-week Spring Term courses. There are more than 200 to choose from, both in the U.S. and abroad. According to the school, these courses are based on professors' ideas of "dream classes"—that is, they are the kind of classes that professors dream about teaching. A small sampling of the spicy class titles makes this clear: "Drawing Italy," "The Science of Cooking," and "Psychology Mythbusters." As one student explains, "These are some of the best, most intriguing classes."

The Robert E. Lee Undergraduate Research Program offers invaluable support to students who wish to pursue investigative studies during the summer. Nominated by professors, recipients of the awards work either on their own personal research projects or as research assistants to professors.

Students with a commitment to service will find many outlets. In addition to a minor in Poverty and Human Capability Studies, the university administers many service opportunities. The Bonner Scholars Program provides a way for students to receive 1,800 hours of leadership training, earn work-study wages for service in the Lexington community, and go on group service trips. "It's a huge commitment but the most rewarding experience," one student states. Beyond the service-learning

WASHINGTON AND LEE UNIVERSITY

Four-year private
Founded: 1749
Lexington, VA
Small town
Pop. 6,995

Address:
204 West Washington
Street
Lexington, VA
24450-2116

Admissions:
540-463-8710

Financial Aid:
540-458-8717

admissions@wlu.edu

www.wlu.edu

WASHINGTON AND LEE UNIVERSITY

Students

Total enrollment: 2,302
Undergrads: 1,838
Freshmen: 479
From out-of-state: 87%
From public schools: 55%
Male/Female: 51%/49%
Live on-campus: 59%
In fraternities: 81%
In sororities: 82%
Off-campus employment rating: Good
Caucasian: 83%
African American: 3%
Hispanic: 3%
Asian / Pacific Islander: 3%
Native American: 0%
Mixed (2+ ethnicities): 2%
International: 4%

Academics

Calendar: 4-4-1 system
Student/faculty ratio: 8:1
Class size 9 or fewer: 22%
Class size 10-29: 76%
Class size 30-49: 2%
Class size 50-99: -
Class size 100 or more: -
Six-year graduation rate: 90%
Graduates who immediately go to graduate school: 32%
Graduates who immediately enter career related to major: 83%

Most Popular Majors

Business administration
Economics
Politics

Admissions

Applicants: 5,972
Accepted: 1,163
Acceptance rate: 19.5%
Placed on wait list: 2,002
Enrolled from wait list: 89
Average GPA: Not reported
ACT range: 29-32
SAT Math range: 650-740
SAT Reading range: 650-740
SAT Writing range: 46-44
Top 10% of class: 80%
Top 25% of class: 98%
Top 50% of class: 100%

920

courses, the Shepherd Alliance Summer Internship Program allows W&L students to work alongside interns from other colleges with organizations that support impoverished communities. The program supplies funds for students to live with other interns (board included).

Washington and Lee's study-abroad office offers program recommendations for students in different academic departments with possibilities that include 21 countries. One slightly non-traditional option is a July through December cultural immersion program in Brazil. Students focus on studying Portuguese and conducting research regarding energy and the environment.

To help students prepare for their futures, W&L's career services office administers the "Colonnade Connections" database, which allows students to search for alumni in their intended career field. Most colleges offer on-campus interviews, but W&L goes a step beyond by offering off-campus interviewing in Washington, DC, Chicago, New York, and Boston. Thirty-two percent of students attend graduate school within one year of graduating.

Student Life

There are more than 100 official student organizations at Washington and Lee. Some of the most popular include vocal groups and service clubs. A stand-out is the Outing Club, which charges just $40 for a four-year membership that includes access to equipment and day trips for any adventurous outdoor activity from backpacking to scuba certification to climbing.

One of the most well known W&L traditions is the Mock Convention. Every four years, the campus comes together to predict whom the political party currently out of office will choose as its presidential candidate. Led by the Mock Convention Executive Committee, students simulate a real political party convention, complete with state chairs, national news coverage, and extensive research on the part of the principal participants. "The Mock Convention really got me interested in the real election," comments a student. "I followed every detail." A cherished ritual since 1908, the convention is renowned for its accuracy, as it boasts a record of 18 for 24.

Students have a no less exciting (but perhaps more relaxed) time each year at the much anticipated Fancy Dress Ball. Since 1907, the school has hosted a black-tie ball with themes that have ranged from "Colonial American Costumes" (1907) to "King Arthur's Court" (1950) to "Lost Cities of Gold" (2014). Although it takes place in the gym, there's no danger of feeling like you're back at the prom— word on the street has it that the ball's budget is $80,000. "It truly is a spectacular night," comments a student. At the opposite end of the spectrum is the Buffalo Creek Music Festival, a weekend of outdoor concerts, camping, partying, and bonfires that takes place on a farm near Lexington.

Greek life is extremely prominent at W&L. Eighty-one percent of men and 82 percent of women join the 17 fraternities and seven sororities on campus. "There's a lot of pressure to join, but there is enough variety among the Greek groups that you can find the best fit," says a student.

W&L fields 23 Division III teams that compete in the imposingly-named Old Dominion Athletic Conference. The school has snagged the ODAC "Commissioner's Cup" for athletic excellence

13 out of the past 15 years. Women's basketball and soccer have both recently won coveted titles.

Off campus, students can wander around small, quaint Lexington and enjoy local restaurants, although nightlife is not the area's strong suit. "We have to be creative about entertaining ourselves," one student notes. The small and friendly Blue Sky Bakery in Lexington is a popular hang-out and Jordan's Point Park is a well loved destination for outdoorsy students. Mother Nature also beckons from the nearby Blue Ridge Mountains.

Freshmen and sophomores must live on campus at W&L. The dining hall serves up dishes fresh from local farms and the school's own garden. First year halls are tiny communities of just 15 students each, and 40 percent of the rooms are singles. Dorms do not have air-conditioning, so students expect to suffer a bit during the hotter months. Juniors and seniors who choose to stay on campus can live in suite-style dorms and apartments.

Student Body

W&L students have a reputation of hailing from upper crust backgrounds. "There are some people whom I'm afraid to approach, but there are also down-to-earth, normal people," says a student. Perhaps to cut through the hoity-toitiness, the school maintains a "speaking tradition" which encourages students to greet one another on campus. This practice creates a friendly atmosphere. With 11 percent minority students, ethnic diversity is moderate. Geographic diversity is high.

You May Not Know

- The W&L campus is home to an authentic Japanese Tea House.
- It's traditional to streak down the university's historic Colonnade.
- The school is named after George Washington, whose large donation in 1796 saved the school from fiscal disaster, and Robert E. Lee, who put the university on the map while serving as its president.

Distinguished Alumni

Roger Mudd, former journalist for the Washington bureau of CBS News; Cy Twombly, contemporary artist; Tom Wolfe, author of books including *The Right Stuff*.

Admissions and Financial Aid

Students can apply using either the Common Application or the special W&L application; the school claims not to have a preference between the two. In their "holistic rather than formulaic" admissions review process, admissions officers look for students who take demanding courses, including "academic" electives.

A full ten percent of the freshman class—40 students—receive the merit-based Johnson Scholarship, which allows students with "academic and personal promise" to go to W&L for free. The process is intense and includes an extra essay and on-campus competition for 200 finalists.

WASHINGTON AND LEE UNIVERSITY

Admissions Criteria
Academic criteria:
Grades: ☆ ☆ ☆
Difficulty of class schedule: ☆ ☆ ☆
Class rank: ☆ ☆ ☆
Standardized test scores: ☆ ☆ ☆
Teacher recommendations: ☆ ☆
Personal statement: ☆ ☆
Non-academic criteria considered:
Interview
Extracurricular activities
Special talents, interests, abilities
Character/personal qualities
Volunteer work
Work experience
Geographical location
Minority affiliation
Alumni relationship

Deadlines
Early Action: No
Early Decision: November 1
Regular Action: January 1 (final)
Notification of admission by: April 1
Common Application: Accepted

Financial Aid
In-state tuition: $43,570
Out-of-state tuition: $43,570
Room: $4,500
Board: $5,750
Books: $1,800
Freshmen receiving need-based aid: 45%
Undergrads rec. need-based aid: 41%
Avg. % of need met by financial aid: 100%
Avg. aid package (freshmen): $44,349
Avg. aid package (undergrads): $44,800
Avg. debt upon graduation: $23,409

School Spirit
Mascot: Generals
Colors: Royal blue and white
Song: *W&L Swing*

WASHINGTON
STATE
UNIVERSITY

Four-year public
Founded: 1890
Pullman, WA
Large town
Pop. 29,913

Address:
P.O. Box 645910
Pullman, WA
99164-5910

Admissions:
888-468-6978

Financial Aid:
509-335-9711

admiss2@wsu.edu

www.wsu.edu

WASHINGTON STATE UNIVERSITY

Overview

Washington State University (Wazzu) is frequently overshadowed by its urban rival, the University of Washington, but that's mostly a product of its rather remote location. WSU's 620-acre campus—with its mostly red-brick buildings—is located in the small town of Pullman, on the border of eastern Washington and Idaho. With over 23,000 undergraduates, it's a large school that takes on a more intimate feeling given its small-town surroundings. However remote, though, WSU also gets a bad rep as a party school, having made a number of appearances on *Playboy* magazine's list of top party schools (coming in 16th in 2009.) The school notes though that this ranking is based on student nominations, not a scientific method.

But WSU's size means that students will always be able to find social circles that don't focus on partying, and WSU offers plenty of reasons to be a part of their student body. WSU can boast of several stand-out programs, including a broadcast news program ranked in the nation's top four. The small-town, slightly backwoods location lends itself to a folksy, quirky atmosphere (WSU's website enthusiastically gushes that "We turn the middle of nowhere into the center of everything!"), and offers plenty of entertainment options if the great outdoors and athletics are your cup of tea.

Academics

WSU students spend about a third of their college careers completing the General Education Curriculum, which is divided into three tiers. Tier I includes courses in world civilizations, communications, and math; Tier II, arts, humanities, social sciences, intercultural studies, American diversity, biology, and physics, which includes a lab; and Tier III, a capstone research course in a discipline outside the student's major.

At a large school like WSU, classes, particularly introductory lecture courses, can get quite large, but the university caps writing courses at 26 students. The intensity of WSU's 95 majors varies, so academics are as challenging or as lax as students make them. However, a handful of WSU's programs are rock-solid and rigorous, offering thorough academics and hands-on experience. These include the Edward R. Murrow College of Communications' broadcast news and broadcast production majors, the Colleges of Business and Veterinary Medicine, and the interior design and zoology majors.

The Edward R. Murrow College of Communications is WSU's flagship program, named for its famous alumnus. The most comprehensive in the state of Washington, only WSU's program offers sequences in all six fields of communication (advertising, broadcasting, communication, communication studies, journalism, and public relations). The college's digital, computer-based labs, studios, and editing suites give students experience working with the newest technologies. The college places a particular emphasis on hands-on experience: its students produce a daily TV newscast, and internships are readily available. "You get experience from classes that you can immediately apply to a real-world job," explains a student.

Students in WSU's top 10-ranked zoology and veterinary medicine programs can also take advantage of top-notch facilities. Partially as a result of its remote location, WSU can offer students access not only to excellent laboratories, but also to a 58-acre wildlife preserve, forest plantations, various ecosystem study-sites, and a Bear Center that houses live adult grizzly bears. "You don't just study animals from a book, but you interact with them hands-on," says a student.

WSU offers a unique Honors College program, which places a particular emphasis on global issues, in addition to research programs, discussion-based liberal arts seminars, an Honors faculty advisor, and a required Honors thesis. The Honors College curriculum replaces the General Education Curriculum. Students also may participate in Honors College faculty-led summer-abroad trips to Europe and South America. Honors comes with certain perks such as living in the Honors Hall and eligibility for special scholarships.

Students who want to explore topics further or simply need some help on class assignments will find what they're looking for at the Center for Undergraduate Education (CUE). Many students visit the CUE to take advantage of its computer lab, high-tech classrooms, and walk-in tutoring. "I probably would've failed my class if it weren't for the tutoring help," one student confides.

WSU's own study-abroad programs are generally program specific: its faculty-led trips allow students to visit China, Switzerland, Italy, Morocco, Greece, Thailand, Ecuador, Peru, Spain, Portugal, and France. Semester- or year-long exchange programs are available with institutions in Australia, Costa Rica, Denmark, France, Germany, Japan, Mexico, the UK, Singapore, and Switzerland.

Largely as a result of WSU's emphasis on practical experience, the *Wall Street Journal* has called WSU one of the nation's 25 best schools from which to hire.

Student Life

Of WSU's more than 300 student groups, many are pre-professional or sports-related (4-H and equestrian sports are especially popular), but if those don't tickle your fancy, perhaps one of WSU's more esoteric clubs—like the 2nd Amendment Gun Club, Dairy Club, or Pyromaniacs Clay Club—will. A fifth of the student population belongs to one of WSU's 29 fraternities or 19 sororities. Students can get acquainted with the student groups at Cougfest in August or Springfest, while also enjoying carnival rides, free food, inflatable jousting, and a beer garden.

Popular locations on campus include the Compton Union Building (CUB), which offers a number of restaurants and shops. Up All Night, an alternative to the party scene, is also held in the CUB, enticing students with free food (always a perk), performances, and games. Students can frequent the award-winning Student Recreation Center, home to the country's largest cardio and free-weight area and the largest intramural program west of the Mississippi. It ranks in the top 20 in the nation and offers 75 team or individual sports. Beasley Coliseum has hosted performers including Taylor Swift, Elton John, ZZ Top, Jeff Dunham, and Jay Leno.

Students looking to party should probably head off campus, as the university administration enforces strict alcohol policies on campus to combat their image as a party school. "Some people say the partying is tapering off. You can choose to party as much or as little as you'd like," says a student. Off-campus partiers will be happy to know that WSU is the safest major research campus in the country.

Another focal point of campus activities is athletics: WSU football—particularly its annual clash with its rival, the University of Washington, in the Apple Cup—attracts plenty of tailgaters and sports fans alike. WSU's nine women's and six men's varsity Division I sports teams also draw a big following from the locals in Pullman, contributing to WSU's small-town feel.

WASHINGTON STATE UNIVERSITY

Highlights

Students
Total enrollment: 27,679
Undergrads: 23,135
Part-time students: 13%
From out-of-state: 12%
Male/Female: 50%/50%
Live on-campus: 26%
In fraternities: 19%
In sororities: 18%
Off-campus employment rating: Good
Caucasian: 68%
African American: 3%
Hispanic: 9%
Asian / Pacific Islander: 5%
Native American: 1%
Mixed (2+ ethnicities): 6%
International: 4%

Academics
Calendar: Semester
Student/faculty ratio: 15:1
Class size 9 or fewer: 12%
Class size 10-29: 46%
Class size 30-49: 19%
Class size 50-99: 14%
Class size 100 or more: 10%
Returning freshmen: 84%
Six-year graduation rate: 67%

Most Popular Majors
Business, management, marketing/related support services
Social sciences
Health professions/related clinical sciences

Admissions
Applicants: 14,825
Accepted: 11,268
Acceptance rate: 76.0%
Average GPA: 3.3
ACT range: 20-26
SAT Math range: 470-600
SAT Reading range: 460-570
SAT Writing range: 1-11
Top 10% of class: 26%
Top 25% of class: 46%
Top 50% of class: 78%

923

WASHINGTON STATE UNIVERSITY

Admissions Criteria

Academic criteria:
Grades: ☆ ☆
Difficulty of class schedule: ☆ ☆
Class rank: ☆ ☆
Standardized test scores: ☆ ☆ ☆
Teacher recommendations: ☆
Personal statement: ☆ ☆
Non-academic criteria considered:
Extracurricular activities
Special talents, interests, abilities
Character/personal qualities
Volunteer work
Work experience
State of residency

Deadlines

Early Action: No
Early Decision: No
Regular Action: Rolling admissions
Common Application: Not accepted

Financial Aid

In-state tuition: $11,396
Out-of-state tuition: $24,478
Room: $6,930
Board: $3,938
Books: $936
Freshmen receiving need-based aid: 56%
Undergrads rec. need-based aid: 56%
Avg. % of need met by financial aid: 92%
Avg. aid package (freshmen): $16,949
Avg. aid package (undergrads): $16,861
Avg. debt upon graduation: $23,433

School Spirit

Mascot: Cougar
Colors: Crimson and gray
Song: *Cougar Fight Song*

Pullman itself doesn't have a whole lot to offer, aside from a smattering of bars and restaurants, like the Daily Grind or Ferdinand's Creamery. But outdoor recreation enthusiasts will find no end of opportunities for rock-climbing, hiking, and winter sports, particularly on nearby Idaho's powdery slopes. The Outdoor Recreation Center can facilitate student rentals and it hosts a ski-swap; it also organizes trips to places like Utah and the Oregon Coast. "This is heaven for outdoor enthusiasts," comments a student.

WSU requires its students to live on campus for their freshmen year. Students who live on campus are housed in monolithic high-rise buildings that aren't particularly exceptional; suite-style and traditional dorm rooms are also available. "Housing for freshmen is so-so," says a student.

Student Body

The "party school" reputation doesn't speak to WSU's entire student population. WSU students are partiers and non-partiers alike; what's more likely to bring them together is a pervasive interest in outdoor sports, recreation, and sustainability, given that most of them are native Washingtonians. One student explains, "if you don't care about the environment, you'll be looked down on."

WSU has a high level of ethnic diversity. According to one student, people from eastern Washington tend to be more conservative in general than those from urban centers like Seattle.

You May Not Know

- Various buildings on the WSU campus are reputed to be haunted; the ghosts include a man named Railroad Sam and a woman supposedly (but not actually) murdered by Ted Bundy.
- Butch the Cougar, the WSU mascot, was named the Capital One Mascot of the Year.
- The ear and tail of Piccolo, the only horse to beat Seabiscuit twice, are buried on campus.

Distinguished Alumni

Sherman J. Alexie, Jr., poet, author, and film director; Paul Allen, co-founder of Microsoft; Gary Larson, syndicated cartoonist of *Far Side*; Patty L. Murray, U.S. Senator; Edward R. Murrow, broadcast journalist.

Admissions and Financial Aid

WSU does not require a personal statement for admission, but does recommend it. Students who have above a 3.5 high school GPA or are in the top 10 percent of their class are automatically admitted under the Assured Admission program.

Washington residents with qualifying academic records are eligible for University Achievement Awards of between $2,000 to $4,000. Washington students from low- and middle-income families are eligible for the Cougar Commitment award, which covers full tuition and fees. For out-of-state students, Cougar Academic awards of between $4,000 and $9,000 are available.

WASHINGTON UNIVERSITY IN ST. LOUIS

Overview

Students looking for an Ivy League-caliber school, outside of the actual Ivies themselves, will find it in St. Louis's Washington University. In fact, it's pretty much as good as it gets, if you can foot the bill. Ranked 14th in the country by *U.S. News & World Report*, Wash U offers dozens of top-ranked programs and research funding comparable to the Ivy-league schools and Stanford. Moreover, the personalized attention and the staggering array of specialized undergraduate programs just might make Wash U a more nurturing environment for undergrads than other prestigious schools that focus more on their graduate students. And while Wash U students certainly work hard to earn their school's stellar academic reputation, they also play hard and know how to relax: "We're not as uptight as Ivy League students," states a student.

Wash U's location is fairly ideal: located in the suburbs of St. Louis, the 169-acre campus is just west of Forest Park, one of the nation's largest urban parks (500 acres larger than Central Park), and the site of the 1904 World's Fair. Campus mostly consists of historic Collegiate Gothic buildings.

Washington University is host to a vibrant campus culture. Wash U students even have their own "lingo," so you may hear students mentioning the WGE (pronounced "wiggy"), HIGE ("higgy"), or the WUPD ("woopty"). And while campus is the hub of social life, students can also visit Forest Park to take advantage of its walking and biking trails, museum, and theatre. The best zoo in the country is also nearby.

Academics

Wash U offers 134 majors. Strong programs exist in nearly every discipline—in particular, biology, English literature, computer science, and political science. The premed and prelaw programs are also top-notch. Nearly all of Wash U's classes are challenging—easy classes exist, but Wash U students aren't likely to let themselves slack off. Access to and communication with professors is very easy: the most common class size is a staggeringly low two to nine students.

Wash U requires an extensive general studies core called the "Discovery Curriculum." It requires classes in "Core Skills" (writing and quantitative analysis), "Social and Cultural Perspectives" (social differentiation and cultural diversity), and Coherent Course Work. Students must complete at least three classes in each of four areas: natural sciences and mathematics, social sciences, language and the arts, and textual and historical studies. At least two classes in each area must be in a "cluster" of related courses. "One downside of Wash U is how tedious the required classes can be to fulfill," notes a student. A capstone experience in the major is encouraged.

Wash U's multitude of first-year programs is its real point of pride: freshmen can either register or apply for seven specialized study plans tailored to meet nearly every academic interest. "These programs set our school apart from the Ivies," remarks a student.

For those who are already certain that they're headed to med school, the Medicine and Society program is a first-year-long seminar of arts and science courses, with an emphasis on medical anthropology. It is specifically designed to complement premed studies. A four-year program follows, in which students take a pre-determined curriculum, complete an internship, and, in their final year, write a thesis. The highly-selective University Scholars in Medicine program allows students to be admitted simultaneously to Wash U as an undergrad and to Wash U's medical school as a med student. University Scholars receive special med school mentoring, attend special educational events at the med school, and can conduct their own research and shadow med students.

Other select studies are Mind, Brain, and Behavior; Texts and Traditions; China in the Global Context; and International Leadership. Similar to the Medicine and

WASHINGTON UNIVERSITY IN ST. LOUIS

Four-year private
Founded: 1853
St. Louis, MO
Major city
Pop. 318,069

Address:
Campus Box 1089, 1
Brookings Drive
St. Louis, MO
63130-4899

Admissions:
800-638-0700

Financial Aid:
888-547-6670

admissions@wustl.edu

www.wustl.edu

925

WASHINGTON UNIVERSITY IN ST. LOUIS

Highlights

Students

Total enrollment: 13,952
Undergrads: 7,259
Part-time students: 11%
From out-of-state: 93%
From public schools: 57%
Male/Female: 48%/52%
Live on-campus: 79%
In fraternities: 25%
In sororities: 25%
Off-campus employment rating: Excellent
Caucasian: 56%
African American: 6%
Hispanic: 5%
Asian / Pacific Islander: 16%
Native American: 0%
Mixed (2+ ethnicities): 3%
International: 8%

Academics

Calendar: Semester
Student/faculty ratio: 7:1
Class size 9 or fewer: 27%
Class size 10-29: 50%
Class size 30-49: 11%
Class size 50-99: 8%
Class size 100 or more: 3%
Returning freshmen: 96%
Six-year graduation rate: 94%
Graduates who immediately go to graduate school: 33%

Most Popular Majors

Psychology
Bioengineering/biomedical engineering
Anthropology

Admissions

Applicants: 27,265
Accepted: 5,876
Acceptance rate: 21.6%
Average GPA: Not reported
ACT range: 32-34
SAT Math range: 720-790
SAT Reading range: 700-770
SAT Writing range: 73-26
Top 10% of class: 96%
Top 25% of class: 100%
Top 50% of class: 100%

Society program, the two-year Mind, Brain, and Behavior program allows students hands-on experience in medical research. Texts and Traditions is a two-year, five-seminar sequence on foundational texts in Western thought and literature, while China in the Global Context and International Leadership are international programs that augment seminars with speaker series and specialized advising on study abroad and international careers. For students who aren't ready to commit to a multi-year program, small, faculty-led freshmen seminars or FOCUS seminars are great options.

Two freshmen summer programs allow those students to get oriented at Wash U and register for classes before the semester starts. One student says that the summer programs "help you make friends before the first day of class" and are "a huge social advantage." The ArtSci Summer Weekend program introduces students to university resources and offers advising for fall classes. The Freshmen Summer Academic Program is also an orientation program, but this five-week residential course includes an introductory writing course plus one other class to satisfy its requirements.

More than a third of Wash U students study abroad, either through one of Wash U's own programs or a pre-approved third-party program. Washington University is unique in that each of its departments has its own study-abroad advisor. Wash U offers summer programs, usually with intensive language courses, in China, Ecuador, France, Germany, Italy, Kenya, Mexico, and Spain. Other possible destinations include Chile, India, Kazakhstan, Morocco, Senegal, and the UK. It also offers its own semester programs in China, France, Germany, Spain, and Chile.

The Career Center at Wash U offers a number of preparatory programs, ranging from etiquette dinners to career fairs.

Student Life

On-campus culture is a large part of life at Wash U. Over 300 student groups work to produce major events on campus: Ashoka, the South Asian Student Association, puts on a show featuring student talent to celebrate Diwali in fall; and Team 31 Productions is responsible for free WILD (Walk In Lay Down) concerts that are held each semester in Brookings Quad and feature major musical acts. In the past, these have included Major Lazer, OK Go, Black Eyed Peas, Outkast, and Busta Rhymes. Wash U also is home to the oldest student-run carnival in the country, Thurtene, a charity fundraiser.

Students may find out about these and other events from the announcements that appear as graffiti on the Underpass in South 40, where residence halls are concentrated to the south of campus. The Swamp, South 40's main open field (named appropriately since it is prone to flooding), hosts outdoor movies and First Friday events with free food and games on the first Friday of class. "It seems like every week there's a festival or a campus-wide party," comments a student. "Simply put, we know how to have fun." A quarter of students belong to Wash U's 11 fraternities and seven sororities, so Greek events are popular as well.

Sporty types can choose from 25 intramural sports (including arm-wrestling) or can turn out to support any of Wash U's eight men's and nine women's Division III varsity sports teams. Both men's and women's basketball teams have made it to the Final

Four twice in the last four years, and men's tennis and women's volleyball have won several division championships. Students can get their fitness fix in Forest Park or they can head off campus to see St. Louis' professional sports teams play.

Campus is connected to St. Louis via the MetroLink, or students can walk to the University City Loop, which is full of student-friendly restaurants and bars—St. Louis has been called one of "Forbes' Best Places for Singles."

Students are housed in the South 40 in residence halls that feature dorm-style and suite-style living. "The dorms are not hotel quality but pretty nice nonetheless," says a student. First-year students are guaranteed housing, and three-quarters of students live on campus. Wash U also operates some apartments near campus.

Student Body

A high-profile university like Wash U draws students from nearly every background, making ethnic and geographic diversity quite high.

Students as a whole can be characterized as academically-focused, but not as competitive or intense as Ivy Leaguers. "We work hard and we play hard," remarks a student.

You May Not Know

- Campus buildings are full of "gargoyles" that include traditional gargoyle figures as well as beer-drinking students, owls reading books, and even dinosaurs.
- Current university regulations prohibit buildings from being taller than the roof of Brookings Hall, which is 585.77 feet above sea level.
- KWUR, the student-run radio station, was named Best Radio Station in St. Louis, although its signal only extends a few blocks beyond campus.

Distinguished Alumni

Kristin Bauer, actress; Jon Feltheimer, CEO of Lionsgate Films; Donald Livingston, Constitutional scholar; David Rubinstein, activist and founder of Save Darfur Coalition.

Admissions and Financial Aid

Most importantly, admissions at Wash U are not need-blind, meaning that if the admissions office is on the fence about your application, your ability to pay may become a factor in whether they accept you or not.

That being said, students can apply for many merit scholarships: university-wide scholarships range from eight $3,000 Entrepreneurial Scholars Awards to John B. Ervin or Annika Rodriguez Scholars full-tuition awards. Students must apply separately for these scholarships by November 15 for early decision or January 15 for regular. School-specific scholarships from $1,000 to full tuition are available as well; students must apply separately by January 15.

WASHINGTON UNIVERSITY IN ST. LOUIS

Highlights

Admissions Criteria
Academic criteria:
Grades: ☆ ☆ ☆
Difficulty of class schedule: ☆ ☆ ☆
Class rank: ☆ ☆ ☆
Standardized test scores: ☆ ☆ ☆
Teacher recommendations: ☆ ☆ ☆
Personal statement: ☆ ☆ ☆
Non-academic criteria considered:
Interview
Extracurricular activities
Special talents, interests, abilities
Character/personal qualities
Volunteer work
Work experience
State of residency
Minority affiliation
Alumni relationship

Deadlines
Early Action: No
Early Decision: November 15
Regular Action: January 15 (final)
Notification of admission by: April 1
Common Application: Accepted

Financial Aid
In-state tuition: $44,100
Out-of-state tuition: $44,100
Room: $9,437
Board: $4,540
Books: $940
Freshmen receiving need-based aid: 41%
Undergrads rec. need-based aid: 40%
Avg. % of need met by financial aid: 100%
Avg. aid package (freshmen): $35,508
Avg. aid package (undergrads): $34,558

School Spirit
Mascot: Bears
Colors: Red and green

927

WELLESLEY COLLEGE

WELLESLEY COLLEGE

Four-year private women's college
Founded: 1870
Wellesley, MA
Large town
Pop. 26,613

Address:
106 Central Street
Wellesley, MA
02481-8203

Admissions:
781-283-2270

Financial Aid:
781-283-2360

admission@wellesley.edu

www.wellesley.edu

Overview

Wellesley College—a strictly undergraduate institution—is a small, private liberal arts school widely regarded as the nation's best women's college. The distinctly beautiful campus 12 miles west of Boston is admired by tourists and students alike. Architecture ranging from Gothic styles to modern science facilities is integrated into evergreen and deciduous woodlands, open meadows, two botanical gardens, and tranquil Lake Waban, where you might find students training for intramural crew regattas or floating in a college canoe. Class Trees, planted by each graduating class during their sophomore year, can be found throughout the campus.

While tourists might have the luxury to stroll about campus, Wellesley students are more likely to be found engaged in rigorous academics, summer internships, study abroad, and volunteer/research opportunities. With cross-registration at MIT and Brandeis, collaborations with Babson and Olin, and exchange programs with over a dozen schools, there is no shortage of classes to choose from.

Of course, a college comprised of all women isn't for everyone, though nearby Boston is teeming with 250,000 college students—including men. Admissions is highly selective. Women who were already stellar in academics and strongly engaged in high school should look to be surrounded by a diverse group of similarly high-achieving women. They will most likely find Wellesley to be a good fit.

Academics

Wellesley offers 56 departmental and interdepartmental majors. Interdisciplinary fields like international relations and American studies made up over one third of majors. Strong programs include economics, English, psychology, and political sciences.

To graduate, all Wellesley students must take 32 units of coursework, nine of which must meet the distribution mandates in a number of academic areas. There are also foreign language, quantitative reasoning, multicultural, and physical education requirements. The "Grade III" requirement translates to a minimum of four units taken at the 300-level.

Academics at Wellesley are "engaging but challenging," says a student. In fact, students are known for being very driven and committed to their studies, and "almost every weekday night the libraries are filled with people studying." Students aren't limited to Wellesley campus in their studies; cross-registration with MIT and Brandeis is possible, while the Three-College Alliance with Babson and Olin promotes interdisciplinary collaboration as well. There are also exchange programs with the Twelve Colleges (Amherst, Bowdoin, Connecticut College, Dartmouth, Mount Holyoke, Smith, Trinity, Vassar, Wesleyan, and Wheaton), Spelman, Mills, and others.

Wellesley's network of academic centers provides ample opportunity for research and service work. The Child Study Center is one of the first laboratory preschools in the United States, and students may volunteer, apply for work study, or pursue independent study. Wellesley's Centers for Women, one of the world's largest organizational network dedicated to gender-focused research/action, is home to over 45 projects, 1,000 staff, and 40 Wellesley student employees.

Three-quarters of students participate in internships in more than 50 summer programs. Of these students, 20 percent intern abroad in over 30 countries. "Internships are a way of life here," says a student. Each year, 300 participants receive internship stipends of $3,000 from the Center for Work and Service. Other avenues for study abroad are available through the Office of International Studies. Over 50 percent of juniors study abroad through these programs, with options that range from a semester to a full year. Additionally, there are Wintersession programs in January led by faculty.

Wellesley's outside-the-classroom educational opportunities are celebrated each year at Tanner Conference in the fall, which showcases internships and research projects. The Ruhlman Conference gives students an additional chance to present research projects.

There are over 36,000 living alumnae of Wellesley. The Alumnae Association's programs, clubs, mentoring, and volunteer leadership help forge strong bonds between Wellesley's graduates. According to the college, 80 percent of Wellesley graduates attend graduate or professional schools within 10 years of receiving their diplomas, and acceptance rates to law schools and medical schools have been 84 percent and 70 percent, respectively, in recent years. "If you ask an alumnus for help, she'll give it," says a student.

Student Life

There are over 150 student organizations on campus, from à la Mode, the school's only fashion and design organization, to Zeta Alpha, a literary society that sponsors a campus-wide short story and poetry contest each year.

Instead of sororities, Wellesley has social and academic clubs, including the Shakespeare Society and Tau Zeta Epsilon Arts and Music Society. Several of these societies are similar to sororities in that they have a "rushing"-like process they call "tea-ing," and in hosting parties on campus. "The clubs are far from the *Animal House* scene, though" explains a student.

One of the most popular parties every year is Dyke Ball, a sold-out event in April of more than 1,000 creatively dressed people dancing the night away in Tishman Commons. As one student comments, "This is the must-not-miss party of the year."

Other Wellesley traditions have a quaint feel, perhaps because some date as far back as the late 1800s. Several traditions center on Lake Waban. At the start of freshman year, all incoming women throw pennies into Lake Waban, while at the end of the year, upperclass women race with wooden hoops to win a number of prizes. One lucky winner is deemed to have the first success as a graduate, receives flowers from the college president, and then gets tossed into Lake Waban. Lake Day, an event that isn't announced until the night before, is an autumn event DJ'd by the college radio station, replete with fried-doughnuts and moonwalks.

The women of Wellesley compete at the Division III level in 13 varsity sports. Lacrosse, swimming, and softball are among the strongest. There are also eight club sports (including equestrian, synchronized swimming, and rugby) and over a dozen intramurals (including, notably, inner-tube water polo and mini-marathon).

Boston's dining, arts, recreation, and nightlife are less than a half hour away from Wellesley. Multiple professional sports teams and their games are also part of the city's draw. On Marathon Monday, "the city" comes to Wellesley, which marks the halfway point of the Boston Marathon. Wellesley students cheer runners on in what has come to be known as the "Wellesley Scream Tunnel."

Virtually every student lives on campus in one of 21 very well-maintained residence halls, none of which are exclusive for freshmen. Residence halls vary in size from 140-285 students, and upperclassmen tend to get singles. Each hall has a distinct history and character: in Casa Cervantes, students only speak Spanish; in

WELLESLEY COLLEGE

Highlights

Students
Total enrollment: 2,481
Undergrads: 2,481
Freshmen: 586
Part-time students: 5%
From out-of-state: 87%
From public schools: 59%
Male/Female: 2%/98%
Live on-campus: 93%
Off-campus employment rating: Good
Caucasian: 43%
African American: 6%
Hispanic: 9%
Asian / Pacific Islander: 20%
Native American: 0%
Mixed (2+ ethnicities): 5%
International: 12%

Academics
Calendar: Semester
Student/faculty ratio: 7:1
Class size 9 or fewer: 24%
Class size 10-29: 68%
Class size 30-49: 7%
Class size 50-99: -
Class size 100 or more: -
Returning freshmen: 97%
Six-year graduation rate: 92%

Most Popular Majors
Economics
Political science
English

Admissions
Applicants: 4,478
Accepted: 1,349
Acceptance rate: 30.1%
Average GPA: Not reported
ACT range: 29-32
SAT Math range: 640-740
SAT Reading range: 650-740
SAT Writing range: 56-36
Top 10% of class: 78%

929

WELLESLEY COLLEGE

Admissions Criteria

Academic criteria:
Grades: ☆ ☆ ☆
Difficulty of class schedule: ☆ ☆ ☆
Class rank: ☆ ☆
Standardized test scores: ☆ ☆ ☆
Teacher recommendations: ☆ ☆ ☆
Personal statement: ☆ ☆ ☆
Non-academic criteria considered:
Interview
Extracurricular activities
Special talents, interests, abilities
Character/personal qualities
Volunteer work
Work experience
Geographical location
Minority affiliation
Alumni relationship

Deadlines

Early Action: No
Early Decision: November 1
Regular Action: January 15 (final)
Notification of admission by: April 1
Common Application: Accepted

Financial Aid

In-state tuition: $43,288
Out-of-state tuition: $43,288
Room: $6,846
Board: $6,642
Books: $800
Freshmen receiving need-based aid: 61%
Undergrads rec. need-based aid: 60%
Avg. % of need met by financial aid:
    100%
Avg. aid package (freshmen): $39,937
Avg. aid package (undergrads): $40,236
Avg. debt upon graduation: $14,189

School Spirit

Mascot: Wellesley Blue
Colors: Blue

the newest hall, McAffee, rooms have a medieval flair with a 15th-century French fireplace and a Gothic ceiling from Austria.

Student Body

Wellesley's student body is extremely diverse, hailing from all 50 states and over 80 countries. The student body is known to be liberal leaning. There is high geographic and ethnic diversity, with 12 percent international students and 40 percent students of color.

The all-women environment is not for everyone, but most students praise having a single-sex student body. "Even those of us who are straight don't miss the men," says a student. "We can easily find them in nearby campuses, and they come in droves to our campus too."

You May Not Know

- *Mona Lisa Smile* was filmed on campus; the film's plot focused on a female professor who taught at the college in the 1950s.
- Green Hall is named after Hetty Green, famous for being a multimillionaire miser.
- Two out of three female U.S. Secretaries of State have been Wellesley grads.

Distinguished Alumnae

Madeleine Albright, former U.S. Secretary of State; Madame Chiang Kai-shek, former first lady of the Republic of China; Hillary Clinton, Secretary of State; Pamela Melroy, Commander of NASA space shuttle.

Admissions and Financial Aid

According to the college, admissions decisions are based on a number of factors, including "academic achievement, motivation, and creativity" as demonstrated by high school classes, extracurricular and leadership activities, standardized test scores, letters of recommendation, and more. Interviews are recommended but not required. Accepted students can defer enrollment for one year.

Admissions to Wellesley is need-blind. Though the college does not offer merit scholarships for incoming freshmen, they do have a very extensive need-based financial aid program. As the website plainly states, "Wellesley is committed to meeting 100 percent of the demonstrated financial need of every admitted student." This equates to more than $53 million in grants and scholarships, and an average annual aid award of more than $40,000. The College eliminated student loans for students from families with incomes under $60,000.

WELLS COLLEGE

Overview

With about 500 students, many people have simply never heard of Wells, a very small private liberal arts college, 40 miles southwest of Syracuse. Not originally a co-educational university, Wells first opened its doors to men in 2005, and today it is a rather female-dominated campus with a lopsided student body ratio of 69 percent female and 31 percent males. As a result, Wells offers a unique, personalized college experience for those seeking an open-minded student body and lots of individual attention and guidance.

Five hours from NYC, in the central part of New York State overlooking Cayuga Lake, Wells' 365-acre campus boasts large, old, ivy-covered buildings and rolling lawns. With a student-faculty ratio of 10:1, students get the chance to really know their professors, participating in seminar-style—rarely lecture—classes. Those who might be frustrated by Wells' lack of class choices or resources can benefit from the school's exchange program with Cornell University.

"At Wells, there are limitations to being at such a small school," says a student, "but the upside is you know everyone well, including your professors."

Academics

Wells College students can choose from one of the school's 25 majors, though the university's strongest programs include biology, psychology, and English. Students describe most classes as challenging, but due to the very small size of the school, professors are readily available for help outside class. "All my professors not only know my name but know my siblings' names too," laughs a student.

In order to ensure a well rounded education for their students, Wells has a series of distribution requirements: two courses in a single foreign language, one course in formal reasoning, three courses in the arts and humanities, three courses in the natural/laboratory and social sciences, four classes in physical education (including wellness and swimming), and two experiential learning opportunities (such as internships, study abroad, off-campus student in the U.S., or student teaching). Additionally, the school requests that students take one first-year writing seminar, which includes content-driven, discussion, and writing assignments. "I could see my writing improve dramatically from so much practice in the seminar," remarks a student. These small classes aim to prepare students for upper-level courses by developing essential college skills and a global comprehension of issues.

Among other special academic opportunities, the Wells College-Cornell University Exchange program provides students with the ability to enhance the depth of their educational experience by taking classes offered at Cornell, located nearby to Wells. Additionally, the school's 4+1, 3/2, and 3/4 programs allow students to earn two degrees in five or seven years. These programs require either three or four years of study in the liberal arts at Wells, followed by one, two, or four years, respectively, at an affiliated institution.

Ample undergraduate research opportunities are available at Wells, as students work side by side with professors on original research projects. Aside from giving students an edge in graduate school and career tracks, these opportunities often lead to students becoming co-authors in papers published in scholarly journals. Many students participate in research as part of their senior thesis: a required essay or project during final year that requires a profound analysis of a topic that is relevant and important to the student.

Wells programs are offered in Sevilla (for advanced Spanish), Paris (arts), Belize (sustainable community development), Dakar, and Florence. "You don't even have to speak Italian to study in Florence, although it's certainly helpful," says a student. According to the study abroad office, the college provides students with services such

WELLS COLLEGE

Four-year private
Founded: 1868
Aurora, NY
Rural
Pop. 722

Address:
170 Main Street
Aurora, NY
13026

Admissions:
800-952-9355

Financial Aid:
315-364-3289

admissions@wells.edu

www.wells.edu

931

WELLS COLLEGE

Students
Total enrollment: 507
Undergrads: 507
Freshmen: 137
Part-time students: 2%
From out-of-state: 25%
From public schools: 85%
Male/Female: 31%/69%
Live on-campus: 88%
Off-campus employment rating: Fair
Caucasian: 64%
African American: 11%
Hispanic: 7%
Asian / Pacific Islander: 3%
Native American: 0%
Mixed (2+ ethnicities): 3%
International: 1%

Academics
Calendar: Semester
Student/faculty ratio: 10:1
Class size 9 or fewer: 39%
Class size 10-29: 60%
Class size 30-49: 1%
Class size 50-99: -
Class size 100 or more: -
Returning freshmen: 76%
Six-year graduation rate: 57%
Graduates who immediately go to graduate school: 25%

Most Popular Majors
Psychology
Sociology/anthropology
English

Admissions
Applicants: 1,610
Accepted: 1,264
Acceptance rate: 78.5%
Average GPA: 3.5
ACT range: 21-27
SAT Math range: 470-580
SAT Reading range: 480-600
SAT Writing range: 2-18
Top 10% of class: 21%
Top 25% of class: 61%
Top 50% of class: 80%

as assistance with travel arrangements, helping with student visas, and an in-country orientation program.

Since Wells encourages its student to combine traditional and real-world experiences, it is not surprising that the Wells Office of Career Development Services regularly coordinates internships across the country. Students typically intern at more than 200 locations in a school year. Besides its own graduate school fair, students are invited to attend job fairs at Cornell University, Ithaca College, and in Rochester. The office also helps put students in touch with alumni for networking and career advice.

Student Life

Wells prides itself on the fact that, due to its small size, "even a first-year student can obtain an upper-level position in student government, serve as an editor on a student publication, have a top role in a theatre/dance event, or play on an athletic team." The American Red Cross Club, Bookworms, Ninja v. Pirates Club, Japanese Club, and the Whirligigs are just a few of the 48 popular, official student organizations. Student involvement in organizations such as these help compensate for the lack of Greek life at Wells. "I wouldn't say we have the best social life, but we do *have* a social life," says a student.

Wells is also brimming with special events and school traditions. For example, the school's annual "Weihnachten" festival celebrates the holiday spirit by organizing a night featuring skits, student and teacher elves, singing groups, cookies, and hot chocolate. Students also enjoy getting the chance to mingle with professors every weekday afternoon in Macmillian Hall's Art Exhibit room at the school's teatime. And student traditions like "20 Days" —an ongoing event in which freshmen choose 20 embarrassing things for seniors to wear, do, and say in the last 20 days before they graduate—helps to foster an undeniable camaraderie and playfulness amongst the student body.

Wells College participates in 14 different Division III varsity sports, with five men's, eight women's, and one mixed team. The women's soccer and field hockey are among the strongest sports while intramural teams such as basketball, canoeing, indoor soccer, and cross-country skiing are also quite popular. Outdoor activities include fishing, sailing, skiing, windsurfing, and hiking trips to the Catskills and Adirondacks.

Wells students often travel to nearby Cornell or Ithaca College (30 minutes away) to augment their social lives. Some adventurous types select New York City or Montreal for longer trips.

Housing is guaranteed on campus at Wells in one of the college's five female or co-ed residence halls, and only seniors are permitted to move off campus. However, the food is notoriously reputed to be bad throughout campus. "I actually lost weight because of the food here," says a student.

Student Body

As a previously all-women school, the Wells student body is 69 percent female. It is a generally "progressive" and "liberal leaning" student body. "Our school is small and everyone knows everyone else, which also means that everyone is friendly and open," says a student. With 24 percent minority students, Wells is highly ethnically diverse; and with 25 percent of students hailing from out of state, it is moderately geographically diverse as well.

You May Not Know

- The Wells motto is "Habere et Dispertire": To Have and To Share.
- *U.S. News & World Report* recently ranked Wells College as #24 on the "Great Schools, Great Price" list.
- Wells often frequents lists of the most haunted campuses in the nation.

Distinguished Alumni

Helen Barolini, Italian-American author of novels and essays; Frances Cleveland, First Lady and wife of President Grover Cleveland; Edit Kinney Gaylord, founder of Inasmuch Foundation and Ethics and Excellence in Journalism Foundation; Pleasant Rowland, creator of American Girl brand dolls.

Admissions and Financial Aid

The school states that a Wells student is "expected to possess the intellectual curiosity, motivation, and maturity to profit from the experience Wells offers." Students who apply to Wells must have completed four years of English, three or more years of math, three of more years of social science, two or more years of laboratory science, and two or more years of a foreign language. An interview with a member of the admissions staff or a Wells alumna is also strongly recommended.

The university has a number of merit scholarships available for students seeking financial assistance. For example, the Scholarships for Leaders Program awards qualifying students between $8,000 and $12,000 each year. Additionally a student may qualify to receive a Henry Wells Scholars and Scholarships for Leaders award at the time of his or her acceptance. The Henry Wells Scholars Program, a $15,000 scholarship each year, includes a guaranteed first-year internship during Winter break and $3,000 to spend on an internship or related academic experience.

WELLS COLLEGE

Highlights

Admissions Criteria
Academic criteria:
Grades: ☆ ☆ ☆
Difficulty of class schedule: ☆ ☆ ☆
Class rank: ☆
Standardized test scores: ☆ ☆ ☆
Teacher recommendations: ☆ ☆ ☆
Personal statement: ☆ ☆
Non-academic criteria considered:
Interview
Extracurricular activities
Special talents, interests, abilities
Character/personal qualities
Volunteer work
Work experience
State of residency
Alumni relationship

Deadlines
Early Action: December 15
Early Decision: December 15
Regular Action: December 15 (priority)
March 1 (final)
Notification of admission by: April 1
Common Application: Accepted

Financial Aid
In-state tuition: $34,400
Out-of-state tuition: $34,400
Room: Varies
Board: Varies
Books: $800
Freshmen receiving need-based aid: 88%
Undergrads rec. need-based aid: 89%
Avg. % of need met by financial aid: 81%
Avg. aid package (freshmen): $31,987
Avg. aid package (undergrads): $28,027
Avg. debt upon graduation: $26,062

School Spirit
Mascot: Express
Colors: Red and white

933

WESLEYAN
UNIVERSITY

Four-year private
Founded: 1831
Middletown, CT
Medium city
Pop. 47,749

Address:
70 Wyllys Avenue
Middletown, CT
06459

Admissions:
860-685-3000

Financial Aid:
860-685-2800

admissions@wes-
leyan.edu

www.wesleyan.edu

WESLEYAN UNIVERSITY

Overview

Everything you need to know about Wesleyan University can probably be found in the small private university's three major rankings: ranked 17th among liberal arts schools by *U.S. News & World Report*, Wesleyan also makes an appearance on Huffington Post's Top 10 Hipster Schools list and narrowly beat out Sarah Lawrence (on an "annoying technicality") to be named "America's Most Annoying Liberal Arts College" by the online blog Gawker, a title that students variously applaud, dismiss, or attack. And while all of these labels probably fit, they don't quite do justice to the one-of-a-kind academic and cultural milieu at Wesleyan. The central Connecticut school offers the standard perks of a small liberal arts school, plus some. Small classes, plenty of contact with faculty, customized tutorials and majors, and an attractive New England campus full of historic red-brick and brownstone buildings once described by Charles Dickens as the "handsomest street in America" are but a few of the reasons to check out this well-respected school just a hop and a skip from the quaint and artsy community of Middletown, Connecticut.

Like many other universities, Wesleyan claims that in-class learning permeates every aspect of student life and that classroom discussions expand outside of class—and *unlike* many schools, at Wesleyan, it's true. Students take their learning seriously and strive to apply it, discuss it, and experiment with it in every part of their lives, whether in one of Wesleyan's "alterna-frats," at political protests, or in creative work. When taken to extremes, it translates to insufferable obscurity, political-correctness, and pedantry (fans of *How I Met Your Mother* will recall Wesleyan alum Ted's most pretentious moments), but Wesleyan students' enthusiasm for lively intellectual inquiry is genuine—hence the recent 30 percent surge in applications. And while the counter-culture pedantic artsy hipster stereotype associated with Wesleyan students certainly has some truthful roots, Wesleyan has produced scientists, artists, and businesspeople, both mainstream and alternative—the only traits they really have in common is their creativity, eclecticism, enthusiastic curiosity, and love of learning.

Academics

Wesleyan has General Education "Expectations," not requirements—but while they're not strictly mandated on their own, most of Wesleyan's 59 undergraduate majors and programs will *require* that you complete the "expectations." Stage 1 of the General Education Expectations is that students will take two credits in each of three areas—natural sciences and mathematics (NSM), social and behavioral sciences (SBS), and the humanities and the arts (HA)—over their first two years. In Stage 2, students will take an additional course in each area during their final two years.

The highly academic atmosphere is further reinforced by the fact that students work directly with faculty, and that hardly any classes have more than 49 students. Especially strong programs are the majors in English, government, history, and music. Film studies, as well, has turned out a number of prolific alums ranging from *Mad Men* creator Matthew Weiner, Joss Whedon, behind the cult classics *Buffy the Vampire Slayer* and *Firefly*, and even Michael Bay of *Transformers* fame. The film studies program has a "national reputation," says a student.

Highly independent students (and at Wesleyan, who isn't?) are encouraged to pursue special major options. Pre-designed interdepartmental majors are offered, including African-American Studies and Science in Society. Students can also custom design a "University major" under supervision of faculty from two or more departments. Students apply to a major mid-sophomore year.

Wesleyan also offers two Colleges—Letters and Social Sciences—which are programs with broadly interdisciplinary majors that cover European literature, history, philosophy and economics, history, and government, respectively. Both colleges offer structured three-year curricula of seminars, colloquia, and tutorials; all students take comprehensive exams and complete a senior thesis or essay. The College of Letters additionally requires a semester abroad and proficiency in a foreign language. "Through the colleges, we have our own informal intellectual clique," explains a student. "It's hard not to get wrapped up in the material."

Students who don't want to commit themselves to a three-year program can look to the limited-enrollment, in-depth First Year Initiative Seminars or Living Learning Seminars, in which all students in an intensive freshman seminar are housed together. "Discussions continue long after class ends," one student comments.

Wesleyan's own study-abroad offerings are limited: it offers semester programs in Israel, Italy, Spain, France, and Germany. However, students may also participate in a number of pre-approved outside programs.

The Career Resource Center at Wesleyan offers the usual buffet of services as well as special fairs focused on careers in public service or urban public education and networking with alumni, as well as WesCAN, a database of alumni mentors.

Student Life

According to Wesleyan, students there "do about seven things at once," ranging from participating in one (or seven!) of the campus' 230 student organizations—which include such groups as the theatre group, Second Stage, or the fire-spinning club, Prometheus—or lounging around with friends at Foss Hill. Much of student life revolves around political activism or the artsy scene. "It's like we all have a picketing sign at the ready," laughs one student. Wesleyan students have a long history of political protesting, including sit-ins for need-blind admissions and staff labor unions. Wesleyan celebrates its history of political activism at Buttstock, where students "stick it to the man" in a watered-down free food, rock concert, and bounce house kind of way by signing petitions. Other popular events include the Asian-American performance showcase Mabuhay and the Wesleyan's Long Lane Farm's Pumpkin Festival, which raises awareness about local farming.

The five fraternities include national organizations as well as Wesleyan's unique local fraternities or "literary societies," perhaps best described by *Gawker* as "alterna-frats." These societies attract literary and artsy hipsters—they're as likely to be holding an all-night poetry reading as they are to be throwing the reputedly "best" parties on campus. One alterna-frat, the Eclectic Society, claims to be the oldest local fraternity in the country: the creator of Blue Man Group and members of the band MGMT were members. While they may be the best-known feature of Wesleyan, only a very small percentage of the student body participates. "Most of us look down on the people who join because we're not about the group mentality," says a student.

Wesleyan offers recreational athletes the standard intramurals as well as broomball, dodgeball, and squash. The Freeman Athletic Center features a 7,500-square-foot fitness center, Olympic-sized pool, and skating rink. In addition, nearby state parks serve up outdoor opportunities.

Wesleyan's 29 varsity athletic teams play in Division III; men's lacrosse and water polo have been strong in recent years, but the

WESLEYAN UNIVERSITY

Students
Total enrollment: 3,262
Undergrads: 2,940
Freshmen: 756
From out-of-state: 93%
From public schools: 49%
Male/Female: 48%/52%
Live on-campus: 98%
In fraternities: 4%
Off-campus employment rating: Good
Caucasian: 52%
African American: 7%
Hispanic: 10%
Asian / Pacific Islander: 9%
Native American: 0%
Mixed (2+ ethnicities): 6%
International: 8%

Academics
Calendar: Semester
Student/faculty ratio: 9:1
Class size 9 or fewer: 18%
Class size 10-29: 65%
Class size 30-49: 12%
Class size 50-99: 3%
Class size 100 or more: 2%
Graduates who immediately go to graduate school: 17%
Graduates who immediately enter career related to major: 43%

Most Popular Majors
Government
Psychology
Economics

Admissions
Applicants: 10,046
Accepted: 2,102
Acceptance rate: 20.9%
Placed on wait list: 2,234
Enrolled from wait list: 48
Average GPA: 3.7
ACT range: 29-33
SAT Math range: 660-740
SAT Reading range: 640-740
SAT Writing range: 53-37
Top 10% of class: 69%
Top 25% of class: 92%
Top 50% of class: 98%

935

College Profiles

WESLEYAN UNIVERSITY

Admissions Criteria

Academic criteria:
Grades: ☆ ☆ ☆
Difficulty of class schedule: ☆ ☆ ☆
Class rank: ☆ ☆
Standardized test scores: ☆ ☆
Teacher recommendations: ☆ ☆
Personal statement: ☆ ☆
Non-academic criteria considered:
Interview
Extracurricular activities
Special talents, interests, abilities
Character/personal qualities
Volunteer work
Work experience
State of residency
Geographical location
Minority affiliation
Alumni relationship

Deadlines

Early Action: No
Early Decision: November 15
Regular Action: January 1 (final)
Notification of admission by: April 1
Common Application: Accepted

Financial Aid

In-state tuition: $46,674
Out-of-state tuition: $46,674
Room: Varies
Board: Varies
Books: $2,665
Freshmen receiving need-based aid: 47%
Undergrads rec. need-based aid: 49%
Avg. % of need met by financial aid: 100%
Avg. aid package (freshmen): $42,088
Avg. aid package (undergrads): $42,653
Avg. debt upon graduation: $20,966

School Spirit

Mascot: Cardinals
Colors: Cardinal red and black
Song: *Wesleyan Fight Song*

level of enthusiasm about sporting events is generally underwhelming.

Middletown is well-suited to Wesleyan: it's a small, artsy community full of shops, art galleries, restaurants, and bookstores. One student comments, "My weekends are spent in the town's coffee shops." Students can also partake of Yale's cultural scene in New Haven, just half an hour away.

Students are guaranteed housing on campus for four years and nearly all take advantage of it. Freshman-only housing and themed program residences are available. Freshmen mostly live in dorm-style double rooms, while singles, suites, apartment-style housing, and even wood-frame houses are available to upperclassmen.

Student Body

The *Huffington Post* "Top Ten Hipster Schools" ranking more or less sums up the typical Wesleyan student. Students are independent, intellectual, creative, and politically active. They're dedicated to learning for the sake of learning, yet liberal in their approach. Pot use is pretty common on campus. "People don't even hide their bongs," says a student.

Wesleyan's student body is quite diverse, and as such, the college is committed to promoting awareness and tolerance—nearly all students are from out of state and ethnic diversity is high.

You May Not Know

- Wesleyan claims that one of its students threw the first forward pass completed in a college football game in 1906 in a game against Yale.
- Wesleyan's original school color was lavender.
- In the 19th century, "Cannon Scrap" was an event held on Washington's Birthday, in which freshmen tried to fire the Douglas Cannon and sophomores attempted to stop them. Once that event died out, stealing the cannon became a tradition. The cannon has been presented to the Russian Mission at the UN, been presented to the White House as a protest against the Vietnam War, and baked into a birthday cake. The current location of the Douglas Cannon is unknown.

Distinguished Alumni

Taft Armandroff, Director, W. M. Keck Observatory; Ruth Behar, anthropologist and filmmaker; Ambrose Burfoot, Editor, *Runner's World Magazine*; Daniel Handler, children's author under pseudonym Lemony Snicket; Lin-Manuel Miranda, composer and lyricist of *In the Heights*; Bradley Whitford, actor.

Admissions and Financial Aid

Students can get a special glimpse into Wesleyan's admissions process in Jacques Steinberg's book *The Gatekeepers*, although requirements and recommended curricula don't differ much from that of most schools.

Wesleyan does not give merit scholarships but meets the full financial need of all students. Full tuition merit-based scholarships are available for one outstanding applicant from each of the 11 Asian countries under the Freeman Asian Scholars Program.

WEST VIRGINIA UNIVERSITY

Overview

Some college mascots seem incongruous, but not West Virginia University's Mountaineers. If this public university's setting in the rugged, scenic hills of West Virginia doesn't make it clear, then outdoorsy, active, and friendly WVU students seal the deal as they embrace the "Mountaineer" *ethos* wholeheartedly.

As if the natural surroundings were not striking enough, the university's two sprawling campuses—one in small but bustling downtown Morgantown and one in Evansdale—are covered in ivy and feature a number of historic buildings. The Personal Rapid Transit (PRT) system, a network of computer-driven pods, connects the campuses and downtown locations.

Friendly Mountaineers and lively social life abound at WVU; students like their parties and generally are not excessively academically-focused. What's more likely to be a problem is getting individual attention from professors: it is easy to get lost in an undergraduate student body of almost 23,000. Fortunately, WVU has a number of programs that offer perks to motivated and talented students. So if hiking, whitewater rafting, and unwinding in a downtown bar or café is your idea of relaxing, and if you don't mind being one of 50 students in a lecture or if you have the drive to pursue Honors, WVU offers it all in a friendly and scenic environmental package.

Academics

WVU's 13 schools offer 185 programs. The College of Engineering and Mineral Resources; the Robert C. Byrd Health Sciences Center, which encompasses the Schools of Dentistry, Medicine, Nursing, and Pharmacy; and the Perley Isaac Reed School of Journalism are particularly strong.

WVU's General Education Curriculum (GEC) is demanding. The first component is University 101, a transitions course for freshmen. The GEC lists nine further requirements, which hash out to 12 or 13 courses that include English, math, science, "Issues in Contemporary Society," artistic expression, and non-western culture, among many others. On top of all this, the writing requirement and the mandate for a "capstone" course with significant amounts of independent research, writing, and oral presentation rounds out the curriculum.

The real challenge at WVU comes from its size: over two-thirds of its classes have 20 or more students, sometimes up to 100. Access to professors can be difficult, which means that students may be hard pressed to get help, or may not be able to get letters of recommendations for jobs, internships, and grad school unless they are particularly tenacious. "You have to make a real effort to get individual attention," says a student.

WVU has a few programs that help students stand out: qualified students may apply to WVU Honors College, which offers independent study and research opportunities, priority registration, and classes that are limited to 20 students or fewer and are taught by "premiere faculty." Honors College students also have the opportunity to live in Honors Hall.

For premed Honors students, Honors College and the WVU School of Medicine offer a program called MedBound, which provides a specialized curriculum taught by med school professors, med school faculty mentors, research opportunities at the Health Sciences Center, and guaranteed admissions to WVU's med school. But it's not easy. MedBound demands that its students complete a major in science or math as well as a minor in humanities or social studies, write an Honors thesis, participate in research, take four semesters of a foreign language, do community service, and score highly on the MCAT. "You have to be pretty certain this is the path you want to take," says a student. Others interested in the sciences can participate in Summer Undergraduate Research Experience (SURE), a program in which students participate in lab research with professors for eight weeks of summer.

WEST VIRGINIA UNIVERSITY

Four-year public
Founded: 1867
Morgantown, WV
Large town
Pop. 30,293

Address:
P.O. Box 6201
Morgantown, WV
26506-6201

Admissions:
800-344-WVU1

Financial Aid:
800-344-WVU1

go2wvu@mail.wvu.edu

www.wvu.edu

WEST VIRGINIA UNIVERSITY

Students

Total enrollment: 29,707
Undergrads: 22,827
Freshmen: 6,420
Part-time students: 7%
From out-of-state: 56%
Male/Female: 54%/46%
Live on-campus: 25%
In fraternities: 8%
In sororities: 9%
Off-campus employment rating: Good
Caucasian: 85%
African American: 4%
Hispanic: 3%
Asian / Pacific Islander: 2%
Native American: 0%
Mixed (2+ ethnicities): 3%
International: 3%

Academics

Calendar: Semester
Student/faculty ratio: 23:1
Class size 9 or fewer: 16%
Class size 10-29: 47%
Class size 30-49: 19%
Class size 50-99: 10%
Class size 100 or more: 8%
Returning freshmen: 77%
Six-year graduation rate: 56%

Most Popular Majors

Business
Engineering
Nursing

Admissions

Applicants: 16,521
Accepted: 14,060
Acceptance rate: 85.1%
Average GPA: 3.4
ACT range: 21-26
SAT Math range: 470-580
SAT Reading range: 460-560
SAT Writing range: Not reported
Top 10% of class: 17%
Top 25% of class: 41%
Top 50% of class: 75%

WVU also has programs that promote travel and outdoor excursions. The Mountaineer Adventure Program (MAP) is an orientation experience for incoming freshmen or transfer students where they are led on small-group multi-day camping, hiking, and white-water rafting trips in the wilderness of West Virginia. MAP also runs international trips to South America and New Zealand that focus on the study of sustainability. In addition to MAP, WVU offers a number of study-abroad programs: faculty-led programs over breaks, semester Mountaineer Programs Abroad, and WVU exchange programs with foreign universities in Australia, Austria, Brazil, Canada, Denmark, Estonia, France, Germany, Hong Kong, Hungary, Ireland, Italy, Japan, Mexico, Morocco, South Africa, South Korea, Spain, Sweden, Taiwan, Trinidad and Tobago, Turkey, and the United Kingdom.

WVU provides support to graduating students seeking jobs. The Alumni Association and Career Services Center offer comprehensive but basic "Life 101" workshops that cover post-graduation tasks such as interviewing or planning a budget. About half of WVU graduates find work in a field related to their major within six months of graduation.

Student Life

More than 350 student groups and organizations are active on campus, including WWVU-FM College Radio and the student-run newspaper, the *Daily Athenaeum*, which was named the region's Best All-Around Daily Student Newspaper by the Society of Professional Journalists.

A number of activities and events draw crowds to campus. The all-night concert FallFest has recently featured artists including Akon, Daughtry, Third Eye Blind, and Girl Talk. Popular WVUp All Night serves as an alternative to the downtown bar scene: Thursday through Saturday nights, the Mountainlair Student Union offers activities such as pool, bowling, movie nights, and the ultimate draw: free food. WVU also brings eminent thinkers, authors, and public figures to campus for its free speaker series, Festival of Ideas.

Given that most students move off campus after freshman year, Greek life is not as prevalent at WVU as one would think. WVU has 16 fraternities, 13 of which are housed on campus; and eight of WVU's eight sororities are also housed on campus. "The parties are more popular with underclassmen," comments a student.

All students rally around WVU's 16 Division I sports programs. The men's basketball and football teams regularly appear in national competitions, and the rifle team has been ranked first in the nation. Intramurals include bowling, in the Mountainlair's own bowling alley.

Appropriate to their "Mountaineer" name, WVU students are avid fans of the outdoors and can enjoy hiking, biking, skiing, and white-water rafting near campus. "We have some of the most beautiful places for hiking," says a student. Morgantown has been called America's "Number One Small City" and offers a great variety of bars, coffee shops, boutiques, and restaurants. If you're into a more urban setting, Pittsburgh, Washington, DC, and Columbus are within reasonable driving distance as well.

WVU offers traditional residence halls, dorms that have emphases on certain majors or activities (such as Braxton Tower, an engineering and science hall), and residential colleges with programs that facilitate student and faculty interaction. Halls on the newer Evansdale campus tend to be nicer, according to students. Although all freshmen are required to live on campus, most students move off campus after their first year.

Student Body

WVU students have a reputation for being friendly partiers—which might be why the average freshman GPA is an underwhelming 2.5. "To be honest, most students aren't the most focused on academics, but many are decent students," says a student. Almost half of the students hail from in state and ethnic diversity is moderate with 12 percent minority students.

You May Not Know

- WVU tuition in 1867, the year the university opened, was $8.00.
- In 1984, WVU student Georgeann Wells became the first woman to slam dunk a basketball in a game. She was inducted into the dunking fraternity, Phi Slama Jama.
- Mountaineer Week, a week-long school spirit event, features the self-explanatory PRT Cram. The record is 97 people crammed into a PRT car that is designed to fit only 16 people.

Distinguished Alumni

John Chambers, CEO of Cisco Systems; Don Knotts, actor; Jerry West, President of Basketball Operation, Memphis Grizzlies.

Admissions and Financial Aid

WVU makes applying a snap, since it does not require an essay or letters of recommendation. If you wish to apply directly to a certain school or program—Honors College, engineering, nursing, or journalism, among others—the required SAT/ACT scores and GPAs may be higher.

All applicants are automatically considered for merit scholarships. These range from $1,000 to $3,000 annually, either for the first year or for all four. For larger scholarships, which can include the entire cost of all four years plus stipends, all application materials must be submitted by designated early deadlines. West Virginia residents who meet the eligibility requirements can additionally apply for PROMISE scholarships, which cover the entire cost of tuition for all four years. They must file the FAFSA.

WEST VIRGINIA UNIVERSITY

Highlights

Admissions Criteria
Academic criteria:
Grades: ☆ ☆
Difficulty of class schedule: ☆ ☆
Class rank: N/A
Standardized test scores: ☆ ☆ ☆
Teacher recommendations: ☆
Personal statement: N/A
Non-academic criteria considered:
Extracurricular activities
Special talents, interests, abilities
Work experience

Deadlines
Early Action: No
Early Decision: No
Regular Action: Rolling admissions
Common Application: Accepted

Financial Aid
In-state tuition: $6,456
Out-of-state tuition: $19,632
Room: Varies
Board: Varies
Books: $1,100
Freshmen receiving need-based aid: 78%
Undergrads rec. need-based aid: 61%
Avg. % of need met by financial aid: 75%
Avg. aid package (freshmen): $5,361
Avg. aid package (undergrads): $6,270
Avg. debt upon graduation: $27,511

School Spirit
Mascot: Mountaineer
Colors: Old gold and blue
Song: *Hail West Virginia*

WHEATON COLLEGE (ILLINOIS)

Overview

Wheaton is a small, private liberal arts college located in an older upscale suburb of Chicago. The school has a strong Christian focus and is peppered with a number of interesting traditions. While Wheaton is nondenominational in that it is not affiliated with a particular church, students do pledge to lead Christian lives.

Wheaton's 80-acre campus features fountains and walkways that cross one of its main quads. Blanchard Hall, a limestone building modeled after those found at Oxford University, anchors the campus. New additions include the Todd M. Beamer Student Center that was named after an alumnus who died on United Flight 93; it was completed in 2004. The 128,000-square-foot Science Center, completed in 2010, has eight teaching labs, an observatory, and a green house.

Although the campus is always filled with students, it is completely dry (of alcohol, but not a sense of community). It is an attractive option for those seeking an education in a spiritual environment, especially those pursuing the sciences or music.

Academics

While conservatory students have slightly different General Ed requirements, all other undergrads must take Biblical content, foreign language, quantitative skills, oral communication, writing, and applied health science (for first year students, think gym class for big kids). The college offers 51 majors as well as a self-designed major program.

At Wheaton the class sizes are small, the course work challenging, and the material taught from a Christian world view. "It's helpful to have a religious foundation because religion comes up in class discussions even in those that are not religion classes," says a student. Strong programs include psychology, business/economics, music, English, and applied health science. The well known music conservatory makes six bachelor of music degrees available and offers opportunities for performing in Chicago.

Interested students can enroll in the college's Dual Degree program. The first three years are spent on campus getting the thorough Christian liberal arts education Wheaton offers. Once that is complete, students may transfer to an ABET accredited engineering school to study engineering for two years.

The HNGR (Human Needs and Global Resources) program combines a formal classroom education with field-based service-learning internships around the world. Students tackle programs such as poverty, hunger, and health issues in a number of underdeveloped areas, all while working toward their degree.

Wheaton offers remote and study-abroad opportunities in a wide array of countries. Remote programs include a "Christian camp" at HoneyRock, an 800-acre forested campus that is 360 miles north of the main campus; biology, geology, and environmental science courses during the summer at the Science Station in Black Hills, SD; Wheaton-in-Washington, a summer program in Washington, DC; and the Engineering Cooperative Program, a five-year program with the Illinois Institute of Technology. "You will have a new perspective on life after studying at HoneyRock," says a participant. Abroad, students may participate in Wheaton programs in London, Israel, Argentina, East Africa, England, France, Germany, or Spain. The Holy Lands program takes students to Egypt, Greece, Italy, Jordan, Syria, and Israel for Biblical and archaeological studies.

The career services department at Wheaton gives students access to a network of alumni, message boards, and services. Walk-in and scheduled appointments are available. Recent internship opportunities have included environmental public outreach, corporate relations at Allstate, and corporate and diplomatic work at the Chicago Council on Global Affairs. "Our location opens up a lot of possibilities for getting hands-on experience through internships," one student notes.

Student Life

Most students take part in campus life at Wheaton, which is understandable, given that 90 percent of the student body resides on campus. There are 87 official student groups, including Pep Band, Hawai'i Club, and Knights of Thunder (the campus chess group). You'll find plenty of students hanging out at the Stupe Café, part of the Todd M. Beamer Center. There is also an ongoing concert series on campus that aims to encourage students—as well as community members—to explore artistic expression and to take time to enjoy life. All these acts, however, pale in comparison to the annual Talent Show, the most anticipated tradition of the academic year, and a major part of parent weekends since it features such a wide variety of acts.

There's no Greek life at Wheaton. The campus is dry and despite the whole water-into-wine thing, raging hard at your frat's Friday Late-Nite isn't exactly what most people would consider model Christian behavior. However, the volunteer and community aspects that the Greek scene offers are available in countless other ways on campus.

The college has 21 different men's and women's sports teams that play in NCAA Division III, with soccer being the most competitive and bearing the Thunder name. The football team has recently sent a few players pro, and the annual homecoming game brings back plenty of alumni as one of the biggest events on the school's calendar.

Campus isn't too far from downtown Chicago, and while freshmen aren't allowed to have cars, upperclassmen venture into the city as they so please. "We can hit the clubs, attend a baseball game, or shop in Chicago," says a student. The campus has its own cultural attractions too, such as the Billy Graham Center, a museum and library with a focus on evangelical pursuits.

All undergraduates are required to live on campus for the first three years. And although dorms are co-ed, floors are separated by sex. Freshmen live in either Fischer Hall, the livelier option, or Smith-Traber Hall, for the more studious.

Student Body

All students must pledge to lead a Christian Life, an oath which comes with a number of responsibilities that the school is pretty serious about. Students say that the student body leans towards the "middle socioeconomically." Many of the students on campus fall into types. One of those is the group of conservatory students, those who worship the Western musical canon almost as much as scripture and might be caught discussing the music selection after Sunday Mass rather than the sermon. Another type on campus is the homeschooling group, making up about 10 percent of each class.

Ethnic diversity on campus is moderate at 17 percent minority, and geographic diversity is high with 79 percent of students from out of state.

You May Not Know

- Fraternities were never a part of the original campus, but around the turn of the 20th century 95 percent of students were part of the "Lits," literary societies that provided a social outlet each with its own unique personality.

WHEATON COLLEGE

Highlights

Students
Total enrollment: 3,034
Undergrads: 2,508
Freshmen: 636
Part-time students: 3%
From out-of-state: 79%
From public schools: 53%
Male/Female: 49%/51%
Live on-campus: 90%
Off-campus employment rating: Good
Caucasian: 80%
African American: 2%
Hispanic: 4%
Asian / Pacific Islander: 8%
Native American: 0%
Mixed (2+ ethnicities): 3%
International: 2%

Academics
Calendar: Semester
Student/faculty ratio: 12:1
Class size 9 or fewer: 18%
Class size 10-29: 59%
Class size 30-49: 17%
Class size 50-99: 5%
Class size 100 or more: 1%
Returning freshmen: 95%
Six-year graduation rate: 90%
Graduates who immediately go to graduate school: 27%

Most Popular Majors
English
Business/economics
Communication

Admissions
Applicants: 1,959
Accepted: 1,346
Acceptance rate: 68.7%
Placed on wait list: 428
Enrolled from wait list: 35
Average GPA: 3.7
ACT range: 27-32
SAT Math range: 610-700
SAT Reading range: 600-720
SAT Writing range: 28-49
Top 10% of class: 58%
Top 25% of class: 84%
Top 50% of class: 97%

College Profiles

WHEATON COLLEGE

Admissions Criteria
Academic criteria:
Grades: ☆ ☆ ☆
Difficulty of class schedule: ☆ ☆ ☆
Class rank: ☆
Standardized test scores: ☆ ☆ ☆
Teacher recommendations: ☆ ☆ ☆
Personal statement: ☆ ☆ ☆
Non-academic criteria considered:
Interview
Extracurricular activities
Special talents, interests, abilities
Character/personal qualities
Volunteer work
Work experience
Geographical location
Religious affiliation/commitment
Minority affiliation
Alumni relationship

Deadlines
Early Action: November 1
Early Decision: No
Regular Action: January 10 (final)
Notification of admission by: April 1
Common Application: Not accepted

Financial Aid
In-state tuition: $30,880
Out-of-state tuition: $30,880
Room: $5,150
Board: $3,620
Books: $840
Freshmen receiving need-based aid: 56%
Undergrads rec. need-based aid: 53%
Avg. % of need met by financial aid: 88%
Avg. aid package (freshmen): $22,466
Avg. aid package (undergrads): $22,384
Avg. debt upon graduation: $24,067

School Spirit
Mascot: Thunder
Colors: Orange and blue

- At Wheaton the juniors take the cake, or at least they used to. There was a long-standing tradition where the senior class buried a fruitcake during the first day of classes that the juniors had the academic year to find it. Too many fake cakes later, stricter rules were enforced on the ritual.
- Former professor Mark Noll was named by *Time Magazine* as one of the 25 most influential Evangelicals in America.

Distinguished Alumni

Wes Craven, film writer and director / horror film mega-mogul; Michael Gerson, former chief speechwriter for President George W. Bush; Richard C. Halverson, former Chaplain of the U.S. Senate; Bonnie Pruett Wurzbacher, Senior Vice-president of Coca-Cola.

Admissions and Financial Aid

In its own words, the first thing the school looks for in a potential student is "evidence of a vital Christian experience." In addition to this, Wheaton hopes to admit students who seek a liberal arts education and have followed a challenging course load based on a college preparatory curriculum. Interviews are an optional part of the application process and are scheduled upon request. Phone interviews are also available to potential students.

There are a number of merit scholarships. The President's Award provides $3,500 per year to incoming freshmen, and the National Merit Scholarship provides $5,000 per year for National Merit finalists who list the college as their first choice. Additional awards include the James E. Burr Scholarship ($1,000-$4,000) for students of underrepresented minority groups, Dorothy Dixon Scholarship in Education ($2,000 minimum per recipient) for students enrolled in the education program, and the Special Achievement Award in Music ($1,000-$5,000) for students enrolled in the conservatory.

WHEATON COLLEGE (MASSACHUSETTS)

Overview

Students looking for an intimate college experience may find Wheaton a good fit. A small, private liberal arts school, Wheaton encourages students to pursue both the humanities and interdisciplinary studies. The college values traditions, such as the Head of the Peacock regatta—where students build and race homemade boats on the college's heated duck pond—or an unwritten rule stating that only seniors can use the main chapel door.

Wheaton College is located in Norton, 35 miles from Boston, 20 miles from Providence, and a train ride away from New York City. The campus has many collegiate-looking, red-brick buildings, a heated duck pond, and Twisted Sisters, a sculpture of branches created by Patrick Dougherty and 40 Wheaton students. A new building—the LEED-certified Mars Center for Science and Technology—opened in 2011.

Academics

Wheaton offers 47 majors, and it also gives students the option to create their own. Students are required to fulfill four core areas of study to graduate: Foundations, Connections, major coursework, and electives. Foundations coursework consists of a first-year seminar; a writing class (unless exempted based on AP scores); foreign language; a math or computer science class; a "Beyond the West" class emphasizing some aspect of a non-Western society; and an "Infusions" class that addresses race issues as they relate to gender, class, sexuality, religion, and technology both in the U.S. and abroad. Connections courses are cross-listed between departments to encourage students to link information from multiple disciplines.

Classes are challenging, but students insist that they "aren't competitive with each other," and because of the broad-ranging curriculum, students are likely to find some things come more easily to them than others. Students are encouraged to make connections among disciplines by studying a single topic through classes from multiple departments. "I feel like you view the material through multiple lenses," one student explains.

The school has especially strong psychology, economics, and English programs. The psychology department offers experiential opportunities through research projects, experiential courses, and internships. The psychology labs offer students research opportunities that may include studying children's social behavior at the Amen Nursery School or adult visual perception. Economics course offerings include the expected as well as specialized courses such as "Sweatshops in the World Economy" and "Women in the United States Economy." According to the English department, students not only learn about traditional British and American literature but also peruse film, romance, fantasy, and other less-traditional literature.

Students are able to propose their own ways to fulfill the Connections requirement through the Student-Initiated Connections program—this provides a certain amount of freedom within the general requirements structure. In addition, motivated students can participate in dual degree programs, in which they may pursue either a graduate degree or a second bachelor's degree. After completing work at Wheaton, students move on to the partner school that will award them a master's degree—the program offers students the chance to pursue a BS in Engineering, an MA in Integrated Marketing Communication, a BFA, an MA in Religion, a Doctor of Optometry, or an MBA.

Students are encouraged to pursue Research Partnerships with faculty members. Because there are no graduate students, undergrads don't have to compete with them for research positions. Students who qualify can even be paid for their research assistance.

WHEATON COLLEGE

Four-year private
Founded: 1834
Norton, MA
Large town
Pop. 18,036

Address:
26 East Main Street
Norton, MA
02766

Admissions:
800-394-6003

Financial Aid:
800-541-3639

admission@wheaton-college.edu

www.wheatoncollege.edu

WHEATON COLLEGE

Highlights

Students
Total enrollment: 1,616
Undergrads: 1,616
Freshmen: 475
From out-of-state: 70%
From public schools: 64%
Male/Female: 36%/64%
Live on-campus: 95%
Off-campus employment rating: Fair
Caucasian: 73%
African American: 5%
Hispanic: 7%
Asian / Pacific Islander: 3%
Native American: 0%
Mixed (2+ ethnicities): 3%
International: 8%

Academics
Calendar: Semester
Student/faculty ratio: 11:1
Class size 9 or fewer: 16%
Class size 10-29: 68%
Class size 30-49: 14%
Class size 50-99: 2%
Class size 100 or more: -
Returning freshmen: 86%
Six-year graduation rate: 82%
Graduates who immediately go to graduate school: 14%
Graduates who immediately enter career related to major: 36%

Most Popular Majors
Psychology
English
Economics

Admissions
Applicants: 4,046
Accepted: 2,603
Acceptance rate: 64.3%
Placed on wait list: 377
Enrolled from wait list: 16
Average GPA: 3.5
ACT range: 25-30
SAT Math range: 560-650
SAT Reading range: 560-670
SAT Writing range: Not reported
Top 10% of class: 38%
Top 25% of class: 78%
Top 50% of class: 99%

Students have more options than a traditional semester abroad at Wheaton—they may participate in any of 50 programs and travel to over 40 countries. There are several choices of program types, to include internships, volunteer opportunities, and faculty-led trips. When conducting an internship abroad, students also attend classes. "It's invaluable to not only live in another country but to work there as well," says a student. "You get a real sense of everyday life."

The college offers funding for students to pursue summer internships, and recent recipients have worked at sites such as Univision Television, Sandia National Laboratories, and several hospitals. After Wheaton, 14 percent of students head to graduate school within a year. Within six months of graduation, 36 percent of students are in careers related to their majors. Many graduates go into programs such as Teach for America.

Student Life

Almost all students live on campus, making the school club scene at Wheaton quite vibrant. There are 90 official student organizations. With so many clubs, students can find their niche—from student theater, to the Anthropology Club, to the Dimple Divers improv club. The somewhat unfortunately named Loser Concert Series (named for a late alumna) brings a huge variety of classical instrumental and vocal music to Wheaton, many of them free of charge. Through the Haas Visiting Artists Program, artists of all genres come to the school to work with students through master classes, lectures, and collaboration with community members. Each year, the school hosts the Boston Bash, a semi-formal dance that encourages the college community to come celebrate the seniors and have fun in Boston. The campus doesn't have a Greek system. "We don't need it because we're like one big fraternity anyway," says a student.

Wheaton competes with 21 sports in Division III, and is known for a particularly strong women's track and field team. The school has a variety of traditional intramural teams (basketball, soccer, tennis, etc.) and some more unusual ones—such as a Wii Sports league and the Head of the Peacock regatta. "The regatta probably seems weird to outsiders," a student comments, "but to us, it's an event that everyone participates in."

Norton can be pretty "quiet," and students refer to life at Wheaton as being in the "whubble." On weekends, some may head to Providence and Boston, both accessible by train. "We don't go to Boston every weekend, but we make the trek because we need more than what Norton has to offer," one student explains.

Students in their first three years share traditional dorm-style housing (in doubles, triples, or quads)—seniors get things a little better, and have the choice of singles or doubles. The school offers an exceptional number of themed houses for interested students that tend to focus on green living, the arts, social justice, and minority groups. Each house has its own student president and faculty/staff advisor.

Student Body

Wheaton, which started as an all-women's school and only became co-ed in 1988, still skews female (about 64 percent). "There are limited options for dating not only because there aren't many men but also because we're such a small school to begin with," says a female student. Students say it has a little bit of a crunchy-granola feel and students tend to be "more liberal"—though there is a College Republicans club.

In general, students wear a stereotype (which some students embrace) of being "excessively wealthy." The school's student body is moderate in diversity, however, with 18 percent of students identifying as members of ethnic minorities. "I'd like to see more students from different backgrounds not only ethnically and racially but also socio-economically," comments a student. Geographic diversity is moderate: 70 percent of students are from out of state.

You May Not Know

- The school has its own apple orchard.
- The school pond is known as Peacock Pond because of the peacock-shaped weather vane on the Chapel, which its waters often reflect. Each student must swim in the pond before they graduate.
- Sitting on the library steps is a strictly senior privilege— and the steps are designed so students can perform Greek tragedies on them.

Distinguished Alumni

Catherine Keener, actress; Lesley Stahl, co-editor of 60 Minutes; Christine Todd Whitman, former administrator of the EPA and member of President Bush's cabinet.

Admissions and Financial Aid

Besides typical criteria such as grades, difficulty of courses, and extracurricular activities, the college also considers writing ability. The admissions office implores, "Show us who you really are. What makes you special, and what drives you?" Submitting test scores and writing samples is optional—the school does require transcripts and teacher evaluations, however. The application fee is waived for students who apply online.

Wheaton offers merit aid through three levels of scholarship. The Community and Regional Scholarships award $10,000, the Trustee Scholarships award $12,500, and the Balfour Scholarships award $17,500. Students are automatically considered for the scholarships with their admission applications, and the rewards are renewable.

WHEATON COLLEGE

Highlights

Admissions Criteria
Academic criteria:
Grades: ☆ ☆ ☆
Difficulty of class schedule: ☆ ☆ ☆
Class rank: ☆ ☆
Standardized test scores: N/A
Teacher recommendations: ☆ ☆
Personal statement: ☆ ☆ ☆
Non-academic criteria considered:
Interview
Extracurricular activities
Special talents, interests, abilities
Character/personal qualities
Volunteer work
Work experience
Geographical location
Minority affiliation
Alumni relationship

Deadlines
Early Action: November 15
Early Decision: November 15
Regular Action: January 15 (final)
Notification of admission by: April 1
Common Application: Accepted

Financial Aid
In-state tuition: $44,780
Out-of-state tuition: $44,780
Room: $6,140
Board: $5,360
Books: $940
Freshmen receiving need-based aid: 69%
Undergrads rec. need-based aid: 65%
Avg. % of need met by financial aid: 94%
Avg. aid package (freshmen): $33,378
Avg. aid package (undergrads): $34,888
Avg. debt upon graduation: $27,520

School Spirit
Mascot: Lyons
Colors: Blue and white

WHITMAN COLLEGE

WHITMAN COLLEGE

Four-year private
Founded: 1882
Walla Walla, WA
Large town
Pop. 32,148

Address:
345 Boyer Avenue
Walla Walla, WA
99362-2083

Admissions:
877-462-9448

Financial Aid:
509-527-5178

admission@whitman.
edu

www.whitman.edu

Overview

Whitman College, a small, private liberal arts college, is located in Walla Walla, Washington. The rural town is about four hours from Portland and five hours from Seattle. Colonial buildings are nestled among streams, trees, and numerous outdoor sculptures on campus and surrounded by the scenic mountains, rivers, and forests of the Pacific Northwest, providing plenty of natural splendor to behold as well as a plethora of outdoor opportunities.

Despite challenging academics—particularly for combined programs in fields such as engineering and computer science, law, and forestry and environmental management—Whitman has a laidback atmosphere. Sports and Greek life make up much of the social and recreational scene on campus among the more than 1,500 undergrads. Not surprising for students who walk past College Creek and ponds full of ducks and the occasional pair of white geese on their way to classes, the outdoors are much celebrated at Whitman.

Admittedly, southeast Washington state isn't exactly the most exciting location in the U.S., but Whitman attracts nature-lovers who enjoy being surrounded by smart—but not overly-stressed out—people. The student community may not be huge, but international and multicultural students add diverse perspectives that keep campus life vibrant and appealing.

Academics

Whitman offers 46 majors and 31 minors. The General Studies Program requires a First-Year Experience (called Encounters) and distribution requirements that include courses in "critical voices," social sciences, humanities, science, fine arts, cultural pluralism, and quantitative analysis. A recent Critical Voices reading list included the books *Orientalism, Brown: The Last Discovery of America*, and *Bastard out of Carolina*. The First year Experience (named Encounters) is a two-semester introduction to liberal arts. "Be prepared for everything from *The Odyssey* to Shakespeare to Toni Morrison," says a student.

Academics at Whitman are challenging but not competitive. "We cooperate with each other on homework and studying," says a student. "You can always count on a classmate." Seniors must pass written and oral assessments in their majors. Strong programs include politics, history, and biology.

Whitman offers Combined Programs such as a 3-2 engineering and computer science sequence where students follow three years of liberal arts education at Whitman with two years at CalTech, Columbia, Duke, University of Washington, or Washington University. There's also a special 3-3 law program with Columbia University and a forestry and environmental management program in partnership with Duke University.

The annual Whitman Undergraduate Conference is one of only two such conferences in the nation. Classes are canceled for the day so that the entire community can admire Whitman undergraduates' research projects and creative endeavors.

Whitman offers semester- and year-long study-abroad opportunities that 50 percent of juniors take advantage of. There are 42 Partner Programs in 23 countries in addition to urban-based programs in Chicago, Philadelphia, and Washington, DC. Additionally, there are faculty-led summer programs; a recent trip was to China and Ecuador. Semester in the West is a unique interdisciplinary field program in environmental studies that gives a select group of 21 students the chance to have field meetings with upwards of 60 leaders in conservation, ecology, environmental writing, and social justice.

Whitman's student engagement center offers career and internship resources. The college also proudly notes that nearly half of alumni regularly give to or volunteer

The Ultimate
Guide to America's
Best Colleges

for Whitman, and that the school is in the top 20 of all colleges in the U.S. for alumni giving. "We're tight-knit while we're students and also when we're alums," says a recent graduate.

Student Life

The Reid Campus Center serves as a gathering place for all of Whitman, faculty and students alike. It's especially popular when Whitman President George Bridges holds office hours in the coffeehouse. Students can also rent sports equipment and sign up for community service there. Ankeny Field is home to students playing Ultimate Frisbee and pick-up soccer, studying, or simply sunbathing and hanging out.

Greek life is a major part of the social scene on campus, with 51 percent of men and 37 percent of women joining one of the eight fraternities or sororities. There are seven Greek houses on campus. More than 100 student groups also represent a wide range of interests—from Action for Animals, which promotes veganism and other animal rights, to Youth Adventure Program, which enables Whitman students to lead outdoor and environmental education programs for youth. The student-owned and operated radio station KWCW is affectionately known as "K-Dub," while the student-staffed art and literary magazine *blue moon* showcases art, prose, and poetry.

Every year, Whitman's Coalition Against Homophobia plans the Day of Drag—which encourage students to wear gender-non-conforming clothes all day—and Dragfest, a themed dance party, all meant to challenge gender constructs (though students might be more concerned about who has the best outfit). Duckfest, also in the spring, invites the entire campus to create duck art to place around campus as a fun, creative event and a tribute to the large number of ducks running around the school. There are always plenty of duck puns incorporated in the art, from "Duck Tape" to "Snakes on a Duck." One student notes, "We do have a silly side." Onionfest is not, as some might suspect, a tribute to Walla Walla's famous sweet onions, but a three-day Ultimate Frisbee festival that brings about 500 players to campus from all over the Pacific Northwest. "This is verification that Ultimate can be a serious sport," one student says.

About 20 percent of Whitman men and women compete in 14 varsity sports at the Division III level, among which tennis and basketball are most competitive. The cycling team has also been quite successful. Though considered a club sport, Whitman cycling is extremely competitive. Intramurals are popular at Whitman, with more than 70 percent of students involved. As one student sees it, "Intramurals are more fun than competitive." Off-campus activities like hiking, biking, and backpacking continue the athletic theme, and adventurous types will want to take advantage of weekends to drive to rock climbing or whitewater rafting.

Freshmen and sophomores are required to live on campus, and 66 percent of students choose to live in school housing. Students don't complain, since dorms are comfortable and spacious. There are 11 special interest houses that provide an intimate living environment for four to 10 students and a larger Interest House Community that meets every Sunday morning for brunch.

WHITMAN COLLEGE

Highlights

Students
Total enrollment: 1,539
Undergrads: 1,539
Freshmen: 382
Part-time students: 2%
From out-of-state: 65%
From public schools: 67%
Male/Female: 43%/57%
Live on-campus: 66%
In fraternities: 51%
In sororities: 37%
Off-campus employment rating: Fair
Caucasian: 72%
African American: 1%
Hispanic: 6%
Asian / Pacific Islander: 8%
Native American: 1%
Mixed (2+ ethnicities): 3%
International: 3%

Academics
Calendar: Semester
Student/faculty ratio: 9:1
Class size 9 or fewer: 17%
Class size 10-29: 69%
Class size 30-49: 13%
Class size 50-99: -
Class size 100 or more: -
Returning freshmen: 94%
Six-year graduation rate: 88%

Most Popular Majors
Biology
Economics
Psychology

Admissions
Applicants: 2,854
Accepted: 1,388
Acceptance rate: 48.6%
Placed on wait list: 671
Enrolled from wait list: 10
Average GPA: 3.8
ACT range: 27-31
SAT Math range: 610-700
SAT Reading range: 610-740
SAT Writing range: 33-51
Top 10% of class: 62%
Top 25% of class: 89%
Top 50% of class: 100%

WHITMAN COLLEGE

Admissions Criteria
Academic criteria:
Grades: ☆ ☆ ☆
Difficulty of class schedule: ☆ ☆ ☆
Class rank: ☆
Standardized test scores: ☆ ☆
Teacher recommendations: ☆ ☆
Personal statement: ☆ ☆ ☆
Non-academic criteria considered:
Interview
Extracurricular activities
Special talents, interests, abilities
Character/personal qualities
Volunteer work
Work experience
Geographical location
Minority affiliation
Alumni relationship

Deadlines
Early Action: No
Early Decision: November 15
Regular Action: November 15 (priority)
January 15 (final)
Notification of admission by: April 1
Common Application: Accepted

Financial Aid
In-state tuition: $43,150
Out-of-state tuition: $43,150
Room: $5,040
Board: $5,860
Books: $1,400
Freshmen receiving need-based aid: 43%
Undergrads rec. need-based aid: 47%
Avg. % of need met by financial aid: 97%
Avg. aid package (freshmen): $31,278
Avg. aid package (undergrads): $32,267
Avg. debt upon graduation: $15,042

School Spirit
Mascot: Missionaries
Colors: Navy and maize

Student Body

Whitman students are known for being "very friendly" and "outdoorsy." By their own assessment, students say they are a "down-to-earth and friendly bunch." In general, students are liberal.

There is moderate geographic diversity, with 65 percent of students hailing from out of state. A large multicultural community represents nearly all 50 states and more than 30 countries, and minorities make up 19 percent of the student body.

You May Not Know

- Whitman was the first school in the U.S. to require comprehensive exams for graduation and the first Northwest college to facilitate a Phi Beta Kappa chapter.

- Whitman was originally founded as a seminary in 1859 by territorial legislative charter as a memorial to Marcus and Narcissa Whitman, missionaries who died in the Whitman Massacre.

- Started by students in the 1970s, Whitman's Interest House program was the first program of its kind in the Pacific Northwest.

Distinguished Alumni

John Markoff, *New York Times* journalist; Kathryn Shaw, Canadian director, actor, and writer; Pat Thibaudeau, former Washington State senator; Adam West, actor who portrayed *Batman*.

Admissions and Financial Aid

According to the Dean of Admission, the college primarily looks at academic preparation when they are evaluating applications. Extracurricular activities are also considered as an indicator of a student's potential contribution to the Whitman community.

All students who apply for Whitman are automatically considered for a number of merit-based scholarships. Achievement scholarships range from $8,000 to $12,000 and are renewable over four years. The Eells Scholarship assists students with financial need by providing tuition and fees for four years and includes a research grant. The Lomen-Douglas scholarship runs the gamut all the way to $47,000 and goes to students who can increase the "socioeconomic and multicultural diversity awareness" at Whitman. Separate applications are required for a few music and arts scholarships. Whitman's Office of Financial Aid Services administers more than $24 million in financial aid each year.

WHITTIER COLLEGE

Overview

Nestled conveniently between bustling Los Angeles and sunny Orange County, Whittier College boasts an outstanding setting in which to gain a liberal arts education. The college provides the charm of Spanish architecture, green lawns, and palm trees characteristic of the Golden State. A small, individualized environment pushes students to question and explore their surroundings and develop critical thinking skills.

Whittier College was established in the Quaker tradition; according to the college, it "aims to foster … an appreciation for the complexities of the modern world and workplace while never losing sight of the importance of social responsibility." Tolerance is cherished at Whittier: the college prides itself on cultural diversity, with 59 percent of its student body of minority descent and a federal designation as a Hispanic-Serving Institution.

Whittier boasts high percentages of students studying abroad and enjoys a specialized partnership with DIS-Copenhagen, a boon for students pursuing research opportunities and going on to graduate school. The college also prides itself on its 21 NCAA Division III sports teams and recurring championships in lacrosse and water polo. Additionally, Whittier provides an active Center for the Performing Arts, and the Campus Center houses an outdoor amphitheatre, dining facilities, and meeting spaces.

Academics

True to its dedication to individualized education, Whittier tends to have small classes (43 percent have 10-19 students), which are discussion-based and "really allow you to get to know your professors," as one student explains. The Freshman Year Experience strives to build relationships between student and faculty and includes the First Year Mentoring Program, Freshman Orientation, Living Learning Communities, Freshman Writing Seminar, and Poet to Poet Seminar—units focused on class discussion and critical writing skills, culminating in a substantial final research paper. Students are also required to take nine credits in communication; 12 credits in cultural perspectives; and 10 credits in connections, courses that are team-taught and that integrate "scientific and mathematical methods and ideas with analysis of cultural or societal issues."

Whittier offers 30 majors and 30 minors and has strong programs in biology, business, and psychology. Special academic programs include the Whittier Scholars Program, in which students design their own educational plan with the help of faculty advisors and the Broadoaks Children's School of Whittier College, a demonstration school providing a "learning laboratory" for college students who are studying psychology and child advocacy. Students may also take part in the Peer Mentor Program by tutoring other Whittier students; the College and Community Program where students work with local non-profit organizations; and the Leadership, Experience, and Programs office, where students are trained in leadership skills. Also unique to Whittier is the mini-semester in January, where students can take the whole month to pursue an individual academic project.

Many Whittier students choose to study abroad, with choices that include Mexico, Chile, Paris, Rome, India, China, Egypt, and South Africa, and the most popular stemming from a 50-year partnership with DIC-Copenhagen. Students also use relationships fostered during these experiences, as well as extensive opportunities through research and other intimate faculty collaboration on campus, as networking for careers or continuing education after college.

Due to the college's proximity to Los Angeles, internship opportunities abound, from Merrill Lynch and First Heritage Bank to Sony Pictures and the J. Paul Getty Museum. "We're in such an ideal location for internships," one student says. The

WHITTIER COLLEGE

Four-year private
Founded: 1887
Whittier, CA
Large town
Pop. 85,943

Address:
13406 East Philadelphia Street
Whittier, CA 90608

Admissions:
888-200-0369

Financial Aid:
562-907-4285

admission@whittier.edu

www.whittier.edu

WHITTIER COLLEGE

Highlights

Students

Total enrollment: 2,448
Undergrads: 1,670
Freshmen: 418
Part-time students: 2%
From out-of-state: 40%
Male/Female: 47%/53%
Live on-campus: 49%
In fraternities: 10%
In sororities: 13%
Off-campus employment rating: Fair
Caucasian: 34%
African American: 5%
Hispanic: 41%
Asian / Pacific Islander: 9%
Native American: 0%
Mixed (2+ ethnicities): 4%
International: 3%

Academics

Calendar: 4-1-4 system
Student/faculty ratio: 13:1
Class size 9 or fewer: 15%
Class size 10-29: 74%
Class size 30-49: 10%
Class size 50-99: -
Class size 100 or more: -
Returning freshmen: 78%
Six-year graduation rate: 67%
Graduates who immediately go to graduate school: 20%
Graduates who immediately enter career related to major: 66%

Most Popular Majors

Business administration
Political science
English

Admissions

Applicants: 4,123
Accepted: 2,622
Acceptance rate: 63.6%
Average GPA: 3.4
ACT range: 20-25
SAT Math range: 480-590
SAT Reading range: 460-580
SAT Writing range: 3-17
Top 10% of class: 28%
Top 25% of class: 44%
Top 50% of class: 92%

Office of Career Planning and the Office of Alumni Relations facilitate the Backpack-to-Briefcase Program in which students learn about careers and network with alumni. The session on sports and sports management had alumni working as the running backs coach of the Tennessee Titans, an attorney and sports agent, and a senior manager of service for the LA Galaxy soccer team.

Student Life

With 70 student organizations offered on campus, Whittier provides plenty of material with which students can fill their social calendars. Notable organizations include an active Psychology Club, the Black Arts and Cultural Dance Club, Equestrian Club, as well as an active and diverse Culture Center.

Many annual events held on campus attract the interest of students and alums alike. SportsFest is a highly anticipated intramural sports competition—a loose take-off on the Olympics—with unique themes such as "Quest for the Booty" or "Johnny Poet and the Sorcerer's Stone," inspired by the school mascot, the Poets. "It's all in good fun," laughs a student. "No one really cares who wins."

Another event, Tardeada, is a cultural fest of music, food, and performances dating back over three decades. The Hawai`ian Islanders Club Lu`au and Lancer Society Mona Kai is a themed all-campus party transforming a parking lot into a Hawaiian beach scene with the aid of more than 40 tons of sand. "Everyone wears Hawaiian print shirts and leis, and you dance in the sand at the 'beach,'" one student explains.

The Greek scene on campus is relatively prominent, with 10 percent of men and 13 percent of women joining the three fraternities and five sororities. The organizations are local and include the first fraternity, the Franklin Society, which was founded on the "virtues espoused by Benjamin Franklin."

As far as athletics, the 21 NCAA Division III teams at Whittier often boast a successful lacrosse season, and are also formidable in football and soccer. Intramurals are widespread on campus, with basketball and baseball as well as break-dancing and "wickets and balls."

For those with an off-campus craving, Los Angeles and Orange County are a short drive away for dining, lively nightlife, shopping, hiking, beaching, and Disneyland. "We have the ideal location—an incredible nightlife, the mountains, and the beach all within driving distance," says a student. "You either need a car or a friend with a car."

Although a good number of students live off campus and take ample advantage of these amenities, the 49 percent who do live on campus enjoy the tight-knit community. There are seven residence halls that accommodate between 20 and 210 students. Some, like Harris Hall and Turner Hall, have views of Los Angeles.

Student Body

Whittier College boasts one of the most diverse student bodies of any liberal arts school, with 59 percent minority students. Hispanic students make up the largest minority group at 41 percent. The college also has moderate geographic diversity, with 40 percent of students hailing from out of state. Many students at Whittier are first generation college students and thus are "particularly committed to academics," says a student. There are also those, however, who are more focused on "parties and having fun than their studies;" the contrast between the groups adds to the college's diversity.

You May Not Know

- Thirty-five percent of Whittier professors are from outside the United States.
- Students have painted messages on "the Rock" (a large rock on campus for which societies and other groups schedule rock-painting throughout the year) on a daily basis since the 1920s. The President of the college even gets involved.
- From the highest point on campus, one can see the lights of Los Angeles and the Pacific Ocean.

Distinguished Alumni

Jim Colborn, former Major League Baseball pitcher; Florence-Marie Cooper, former United States federal judge; Robert D. Durham, justice, Oregon Supreme Court; Richard Nixon, U.S. President; Arthur Allan Seidelman, Emmy-winning director; Jessamyn West, author.

Admissions and Financial Aid

The admissions committee looks for appropriate high school preparation in a prospective Whittier student. Four years of English, three years of mathematics, three years of science, and two years in a foreign language are highly recommended. The committee also checks difficulty and diversity in a student's course list.

Applicants must submit either SAT or ACT scores, but the committee knows that some students simply "don't test well." They will also take into consideration the student's extracurricular activities and other ways the students spends his or her time.

Whittier awards several merit-based scholarships to talented students, and private donors award restricted scholarships to particularly gifted students. The John Greenleaf Whittier Academic Merit Scholarship is awarded after an intensive three-day program in which outstanding high school students compete for the scholarship that is worth up to full tuition. Qualifying students must have a minimum GPA of 3.5 and SAT scores of at least 1800. Students are invited to compete for the scholarship based on their admission application.

WHITTIER COLLEGE

Highlights

Admissions Criteria
Academic criteria:
Grades: ☆ ☆ ☆
Difficulty of class schedule: ☆ ☆ ☆
Class rank: ☆
Standardized test scores: ☆ ☆
Teacher recommendations: ☆ ☆
Personal statement: ☆ ☆ ☆
Non-academic criteria considered:
Interview
Extracurricular activities
Special talents, interests, abilities
Character/personal qualities
Volunteer work
Work experience
Geographical location
Minority affiliation
Alumni relationship

Deadlines
Early Action: December 1
Early Decision: No
Regular Action: Rolling admissions
Common Application: Accepted

Financial Aid
In-state tuition: $39,736
Out-of-state tuition: $39,736
Room: Varies
Board: Varies
Books: $650
Freshmen receiving need-based aid: 81%
Undergrads rec. need-based aid: 79%
Avg. % of need met by financial aid: 72%
Avg. aid package (freshmen): $30,802
Avg. aid package (undergrads): $30,737
Avg. debt upon graduation: $25,212

School Spirit
Mascot: Poets
Colors: Purple and gold

Four-year private
Founded: 1842
Salem, OR
Medium city
Pop. 156,244

Address:
900 State Street
Salem, OR
97301

Admissions:
503-370-6303

Financial Aid:
503-370-6273

libarts@willamette.edu

www.willamette.edu

The Ultimate
Guide to America's
Best Colleges

WILLAMETTE UNIVERSITY

Overview

Across the street from the Oregon State Capitol in the city of Salem, Willamette University's red brick buildings, set against trees and ample green space, are home to the academic ambitions of 2,100 undergraduates. This private liberal arts university affiliated with the Methodist church has an intimate feel and offers a low-key but challenging academic atmosphere, apropos of a school in the Pacific Northwest.

Also not surprising for a Pacific Northwest school is the love of the outdoors proclaimed by students and faculty and alike. From the LEED-certified residential commons to a student-tended 3,600-square-foot farm to a huge array of outdoorsy clubs (kayaking, snowboarding, skiing, fishing, and more), opportunities to celebrate and protect nature abound. Students aren't just passionate for the environment but for volunteering more generally: the strong culture of service on campus reflects the university's motto, "Not unto ourselves alone are we born." Willamette was one of only six colleges and universities nationwide to receive the 2009 Higher Education Community Service Honor Roll Presidential Award.

Students looking for a highly dynamic and diverse environment may not find it in a small school where most students hail from white, conservative, middle-class backgrounds (though the open-mindedness of students prevents stereotyping). However, those looking for a solid liberal arts background in the beautiful Pacific Northwest amongst a community of service- and nature-loving peers may want to send an application off to Willamette University right away.

Academics

Willamette's College of Liberal Arts, the university's undergraduate school, offers 34 majors. The General Education requirements include a first-year College Colloquium, a semester-long seminar; three writing courses; two quantitative and analytical reasoning courses; and study in a foreign language. Students must also take courses across six "modes of inquiry" that include "creating in the arts," "thinking historically," and "interpreting texts."

A whopping 48 percent of all classes have 10-19 students, which creates a more intimate learning environment. "One of the best qualities is small class size," says a student. "I know each of my professors on an academic and personal level." Strong programs include biology, economics, politics, and psychology. Students are serious about their studies and even turn to library nights as a way to merge their social and academic worlds.

Joint degree programs take advantage of the three graduate schools (law, management, and education) at Willamette. The combined BA/MBA program takes five years; the BA/JD can be completed in six years, and the BA/MAT can be finished in four years. There are also special BA/BS programs with engineering schools at other universities (Columbia, USC, Washington University) and a forestry program in partnership with Duke University.

The Humanities Senior Seminar offers seniors a chance to focus intensively on a single significant work (e.g. *The Second Sex* by Simone de Beauvoir or James Joyce's *Ulysses*) with the help of a visiting scholar who works with students to develop their theses. Students in any field can apply for The Carson Undergraduate Research Grant, which offers up to $3,000 for student research projects.

It's not uncommon to see seventh graders on campus when the Willamette Academy enrolls student youth from underrepresented communities who want to attend a four-year college; most students are the first in their families to attend college. "It threw me off at first to see such young kids; but once I learned they were the first in their family to attend college, I really admired their efforts," one student shares.

Half of undergraduates study abroad in 40 different countries. The International Student Exchange Program enables students to enroll directly in other universities around the world. But students don't need to venture far to experience Japanese culture, since the Tokyo University of America is co-located with Willamette.

Internships and networking in the political realm are particularly strong at Willamette since the university is located so close to the state capitol and the state Supreme Court. According to the college, students have been the recipients of 126 National Scholarships (Fulbright, Truman, Goldwater, National Science Foundation, etc.) and more than 270 Willamette alumni have joined the Peace Corps since its inception in 1961.

Student Life

Willamette has more than 100 student groups representing a wide range of interests: performing arts, sports, politics, culture, religion, and more. It's easy to start (or revive) a club based on one's interests. The weekly *Willamette Collegian* has been publishing since 1875, and the university's numerous musical ensembles include the Willamette Jazz Collective and Chamber Choir. Willamette's Zena Farm is tended by the Alternative Agriculture Community and Compost Club; the kitchen garden has produced goodies that include garlic, figs, and asparagus.

Volunteerism is particularly strong at Willamette; students dedicate more than 60,000 hours of service a year, and the Office of Community Service Learning makes finding opportunities easy. The "Take a Break" program is quite popular: these spring break service trips have included addressing poverty in Chicago, immigration in Arizona, and homeless youth in Seattle.

All students are welcomed to campus through Opening Days, a student-run, five-day orientation that includes a tour of Salem, a grass volleyball tournament, and plenty of academic programming to get students acquainted with Willamette. Multicultural students have the option of attending "Ohana," which means "family" in Hawaiian, a five-day retreat limited to 25 participants. In April, the annual lu'au offers a taste of Hawaiian culture and a different theme each year for all students. Not long after, Wulapalooza brings guitar licks and much more to campus. According to the college, this "earth, art, and music festival" was founded by students in 1998 as a creative outlet and now attracts nationally recognized musical talent.

There are three sororities and four fraternities on campus, each with its own house. "We are some of the most active students on campus not only for socializing but for community service too," says a member.

The Willamette Bearcats compete in 20 varsity sports (10 men's, 10 women's) in the Division III Northwest Conference. Men's basketball is popular and cross country is also competitive. Willamette's club sports are particularly active, and many of the clubs attest to students' love of the outdoors: backpacking, climbing, cycling, kayak, "rod and reel"—and even scuba divers club. Intramurals include six leagues, two mini-leagues, and plenty of tournaments (paper football, dodgeball, and more).

Nearby downtown Salem provides opportunities for low-key nights out with dining, shopping, and entertainment. The Cascade Mountains and Mount Hood are popular destinations for skiing and snowboarding.

WILLAMETTE UNIVERSITY

Highlights

Students
Total enrollment: 2,933
Undergrads: 2,103
Freshmen: 564
Part-time students: 6%
From out-of-state: 78%
From public schools: 69%
Male/Female: 45%/55%
Live on-campus: 68%
In fraternities: 18%
In sororities: 20%
Off-campus employment rating: Good
Caucasian: 60%
African American: 2%
Hispanic: 8%
Asian / Pacific Islander: 7%
Native American: 1%
Mixed (2+ ethnicities): 7%
International: 7%

Academics
Calendar: Semester
Student/faculty ratio: 10:1
Class size 9 or fewer: 19%
Class size 10-29: 74%
Class size 30-49: 6%
Class size 50-99: -
Class size 100 or more: -
Graduates who immediately go to graduate school: 20%

Most Popular Majors
Biology
Politics
Economics

Admissions
Applicants: 6,462
Accepted: 5,370
Acceptance rate: 83.1%
Placed on wait list: 48
Enrolled from wait list: 8
Average GPA: 3.7
ACT range: 25-30
SAT Math range: 560-660
SAT Reading range: 560-680
SAT Writing range: 13-37
Top 10% of class: 38%
Top 25% of class: 66%
Top 50% of class: 92%

953

College Profiles

WILLAMETTE UNIVERSITY

Admissions Criteria

Academic criteria:
Grades: ☆ ☆ ☆
Difficulty of class schedule: ☆ ☆ ☆
Class rank: ☆ ☆ ☆
Standardized test scores: ☆ ☆ ☆
Teacher recommendations: ☆ ☆
Personal statement: ☆ ☆ ☆
Non-academic criteria considered:
Interview
Extracurricular activities
Special talents, interests, abilities
Character/personal qualities
State of residency
Geographical location
Minority affiliation
Alumni relationship

Deadlines

Early Action: November 1
Early Decision: No
Regular Action: February 1 (priority)
Notification of admission by: March 15
Common Application: Accepted

Financial Aid

In-state tuition: $41,990
Out-of-state tuition: $41,990
Room: Varies
Board: Varies
Books: $950
Freshmen receiving need-based aid: 70%
Undergrads rec. need-based aid: 66%
Avg. % of need met by financial aid: 87%
Avg. aid package (freshmen): $29,552
Avg. aid package (undergrads): $32,296
Avg. debt upon graduation: $26,740

School Spirit

Mascot: Bearcats
Colors: Cardinal and gold

Freshmen and sophomores are required to live on campus. Besides Greek housing, all 11 residences at Willamette are co-ed. Dorms tend to earn reputations as being either more social or more studious. The $17 million LEED Gold certified Kaneko Commons project offers rooms to envy with air-conditioning, private bathrooms, and fully-furnished floors. Programming is designed to provide learning opportunities outside the classroom, and the commons are self-governed with a strong faculty presence.

Student Body

Though many of Willamette's undergrads come from "white" and "less liberal" backgrounds, students are "more liberal than their parents" and "welcome everyone." The general outgoing nature of the campus encourages this receptive attitude. There is high ethnic diversity (25 percent minorities), high geographic diversity with 78 percent of students from out of state, and a good representation of international students (seven percent).

You May Not Know

- Willamette had the first medical school in 1866, and first law school in 1883, in the Pacific Northwest.
- The football team traveled to Hawaii for a football game on December 6, 1941. The day after the game, instead of enjoying the island, some players and fans witnessed the bombing of Pearl Harbor.
- Kicker Liz Heaston was the first female to play and score in a college football game in 1997.

Distinguished Alumni

James Albaugh, CEO of Boeing Integrated Defense Systems; Virginia Linder, Oregon Supreme Court chief justice; Dale Mortensen, winner of 2010 Nobel Peace Prize in Economics; Marie Watt, contemporary artist.

Admissions and Financial Aid

According to Willamette, the admissions officers "focus a great deal of attention on [a student's] academic record." Students benefit from demonstrating a rigorous high school academic program through four years that includes, English, math, history, laboratory science, and foreign language—art, music, and theater classes are also helpful. SAT scores and recommendations are duly considered, and interviews with a member of the admissions committee are optional though recommended.

Admissions to Willamette has become increasingly competitive, with the number of applicants to the College of Liberal arts increasing by more than 80 percent since 2002.

All accepted applicants to Willamette are automatically considered for merit-based scholarships, which award exceptional academic achievement. Talent Scholarships for music, theater, and forensics require auditions and/or special recommendations, while the Mark O. Hatfield Scholarship for an outstanding commitment to public service also requires a separate application.

WILLIAMS COLLEGE

Overview

Williams College is a small, private college that consistently ranks as one of the top liberal arts institutions in the country. The academic environment is challenging, with small, personalized classes and much interaction between students and professors. Tutorials, courses of just two students and one professor, are priceless opportunities for intensive study and independent work. Students at Williams are serious about their academics. They don't even break for the winter. Instead, a month of Winter Study is a chance to take unusual courses, undertake research, or polish up a thesis.

The social life is campus-focused, since there is little to do in the small town of Williamstown and over 90 percent of students live on campus. Social ties among the highly diverse student body tend to be close-knit. Students begin their time at Williams staying in family-type dorms of just 22 freshmen. Greek life is nonexistent, since the university phased out fraternities and sororities in 1962. Athletics are also not as large a part of student life here as at many schools, but students can get involved with 117 official student organizations to keep busy outside academics.

Williams College is tucked away in the northwest corner of Massachusetts. It is approximately 135 miles from Boston and 45 miles from Albany. The peaceful and stunning campus includes the scenic Hopkins Memorial Forest, and the architectural styles of its buildings range from Federal to contemporary.

Students looking for a party-filled, eventful time at college should avoid Williams. Even those who would just like a well-rounded college experience might find the intensity of Williams College suffocating. However, serious students who want to seclude themselves in a highly-engaging academic environment without the distractions of Greek life or a bustling town should jump at the chance to attend Williams.

Academics

Williams offers 35 majors. The art history, studio art, economics, and English programs are particularly strong. Distribution requirements include divisional (two classes in each of these categories: languages and the arts, social studies, and science and mathematics); exploring diversity initiative (one course in broadly-defined areas like comparative study of cultures and societies, empathetic understanding, power and privilege, etc.); quantitative/formal reasoning (one course); and writing (two courses requiring over 20 pages of writing each).

The curriculum at Williams is challenging. Students claim to have a heavier workload than their peers at competing institutions, including the Ivies. Most classes are very small and personal. "The upside is that you get a lot of attention from professors. The downside is that you get a lot of attention from professors. That means we're always studying," says a student.

The academic calendar has four-month fall and spring semesters with a one-month Winter Study in between. Don't expect a restful winter break at home once you're at Williams. Instead, you'll spend the month of January on Winter Study—either in pass/fail courses, research (including research abroad), independent projects, internships, or thesis work. It's a nice chance to take a quirky course without any pressure or to knuckle down and do research without the added demands of the regular semester. "Winter Study is my favorite time of the year—it's time to recharge and think totally differently," says a student.

The two-students/one-professor tutorials are a major draw for highly-engaged students. The program is modeled after one at Oxford. Each week, one student makes a presentation of independent work to be critiqued by the professor and the other student. Tutorials are offered in a variety of subjects, not just the humanities, and over half of Williams students take at least one during their tenure.

WILLIAMS COLLEGE

Four-year private
Founded: 1793
Williamstown, MA
Rural
Pop. 8,424

Address:
880 Main Street
Williamstown, MA
01267

Admissions:
413-597-2211

Financial Aid:
413-597-4181

admission@williams.
edu

www.williams.edu

WILLIAMS COLLEGE

A student whose interests don't fit within existing departments can create his or her own "Contract Major." The college is strict about the criteria for a valid contract major—it must be truly distinct from any department or combination of departments, and students undertaking one cannot double major.

Williams emphasizes undergraduate research. Many departments in the sciences, math, and psychology fields offer paid research-assistant positions for undergrads over the summer. At the end of sophomore year, students from underrepresented minority groups and first-generation college students can apply to be among the 10 Williams College Undergraduate Research Fellows selected each year. Fellows work with faculty members and receive research funding during the summer as well as throughout the academic year.

Williams itself doesn't sponsor many study-abroad programs. Its study-away offerings are limited to the Williams-at-Exeter Programme at Oxford, Williams-in-Africa in Capetown, the Marine Biological Laboratory in Woods Hole, Massachusetts, and the Williams-Mystic Seaport Program in Connecticut. Students may, however, study abroad through any accredited foreign university or through over 250 pre-approved programs across the U.S. and around the world.

The Office of Career Counseling administers the Williams Alumni Sponsored Internship Program, which funds about 60 students for summer public service internships. Students also have access to a database of contact information for over 25,000 alumni.

Student Life

If tough academics aren't enough to keep you busy on campus, there are 117 official student organizations to choose from. A cappella groups, the brass ensemble, and community service groups are particularly popular. "There's a performance almost every night of the week," says a student.

Williams has several fun traditions to spice up the academic year. Just when you think you'll never get through the months of ice and snow, February's Winter Carnival brightens the horizon with fireworks, ski races, movies, snow sculpture contests, and dance competitions—all for free. Each April, the college brings a big-name musical performer to entertain at Spring Fling. During the night on the semester's last day of classes, brains can be heard sizzling from midnight to 8 a.m. as the Williams Trivia Contest is broadcast live on the radio. Tellingly, Williams' students' method for distracting themselves from the stress of finals is to stress out about trivia for hours instead.

There have been no frats or sororities since 1962, so students who don't relish the thought of running into toga-clad Greeks on Friday nights can breathe a sigh of relief. "We don't miss the Greek scene," says a student.

Williams—a member of the New England College Wrestling Association (Division III) and the New England Small Colleges Athletic Conference (Division III)—offers 32 varsity sports (16 men's, 16 women's). The college's traditional rivals are the fiercest schools around (hardly)—Amherst and Wesleyan. Baseball, women's swimming and diving, crew, and tennis are among the most competitive sports.

The most popular off-campus activity is listening to the crickets. Williamstown is small, with few convenient places for students to shop or dine out. "We tend to learn to make do with what we have on campus," says a student. If you're willing to drive 3.5 hours, a weekend trip to New York City can break the monotony.

The housing situation for freshmen at Williams is uncommonly warm and fuzzy. They live in "entries," groups of 22 freshmen and two Junior Advisors. Junior Advisors are uncompensated, and the college's website describes them as "resources—not rule enforcers." The whole idea is to create a supportive, family atmosphere. However, if you were looking forward to going to college and living *away* from a family, you might find the environment a little claustrophobic. Even beyond freshman year, an extremely high percentage of students live on campus.

Student Body

One common thread unites the ethnically and socioeconomically diverse students at Williams: they came to college to work hard. Students tend to focus with laser-sharp intensity on their academic life. This is not surprising, given that 92 percent of students graduated in the top 10 percent of their high school class.

The student body is highly geographically diverse with only 14 percent of students from in state. In addition, Williams is highly ethnically diverse with 35 percent minority students.

You May Not Know

- In 1838, Nathaniel Hawthorne described the Williams grads he observed at commencement as "unpolished bumpkins."
- Each year, the graduating class drops a watch from the top of the chapel. If it breaks, it signifies good luck for the class.
- Williams College was the first school in America to dress its graduates in cap and gown at commencement in order to reduce obvious distinctions in dress between richer and poorer students.

Distinguished Alumni

Walker Evans, photographer; Elia Kazan, director of *A Streetcar Named Desire*; George Steinbrenner, owner of the New York Yankees.

Admissions and Financial Aid

Standardized test scores will be taken "with a grain of salt," according to the Williams admissions office, but they are an important factor to "help distinguish an application." The most important criterion for Williams is the high school transcript, with special attention paid to junior and senior years.

Williams does not offer merit-based scholarships but does have a need-blind admission policy and meets 100 percent of demonstrated need. Williams also offers the Tyng Scholarships, which are need-based and meet a student's demonstrated need for undergraduate and graduate studies.

WILLIAMS COLLEGE

Highlights

Admissions Criteria
Academic criteria:
Grades: ☆ ☆ ☆
Difficulty of class schedule: ☆ ☆ ☆
Class rank: ☆ ☆ ☆
Standardized test scores: ☆ ☆ ☆
Teacher recommendations: ☆ ☆ ☆
Personal statement: ☆ ☆ ☆
Non-academic criteria considered:
Extracurricular activities
Special talents, interests, abilities
Character/personal qualities
Volunteer work
Work experience
State of residency
Geographical location
Minority affiliation
Alumni relationship

Deadlines
Early Action: No
Early Decision: November 10
Regular Action: January 1 (final)
Notification of admission by: April 1
Common Application: Accepted

Financial Aid
In-state tuition: $46,330
Out-of-state tuition: $46,330
Room: $6,060
Board: $6,240
Books: $800
Freshmen receiving need-based aid: 53%
Undergrads rec. need-based aid: 53%
Avg. % of need met by financial aid: 100%
Avg. aid package (freshmen): $44,508
Avg. aid package (undergrads): $43,747
Avg. debt upon graduation: $12,749

School Spirit
Mascot: Ephs

957

College Profiles

WITTENBERG
UNIVERSITY

Four-year private
Founded: 1845
Springfield, OH
Large town
Pop. 60,333

Address:
P.O. Box 720
Springfield, OH
45501

Admissions:
800-677-7558, exten-
sion 6314

Financial Aid:
800-677-7558

admission@witten-
berg.edu

www.wittenberg.edu

Overview

A private liberal arts college in the small city of Springfield, Ohio, Wittenberg University boasts 26 buildings that lie on 114 rolling acres. The university features stately architecture and stone steps covered in bright autumn leaves, lending support to the university's claim that the "campus has been widely acclaimed for its beauty and award-winning architecture."

Though small in size, Wittenberg is a powerhouse in athletics—several teams have had the most championships in conference history. Besides sports, Greek life forms a major part of campus culture, with a third of students participating. The fact that most students live on campus, coupled with the 11:1 ratio of students to student organizations, ensures that there's no shortage of on-campus activities.

A university with fewer than 2,000 students may feel like *too* tight-knit of a community for some. Diversity—both geographic and, especially, ethnic—is fairly low among the student body, though numerous programs work to bring an international flavor and welcoming feel to campus. Students get to know their professors fairly well, so it's fortunate that Wittenberg has more Ohio Professors of the Year than any university in the state.

Academics

Wittenberg offers more than 60 majors, minors, and special programs. General Education requirements and learning goals are divided into three categories: Foundations (writing, mathematics, foreign language competency, speaking, research, and computing), Arts and Sciences, and Co-Curricular Activities. This last category includes a requirement for two semester hours of physical activity courses or the completion of two seasons of intercollegiate athletics, and Community Service 100, which requires direct service and reflection.

More than 90 percent of classes have fewer than 30 students. Because of the attention from professors, students typically don't slack off in class. "Discussions are small, and everyone is expected to participate," says a student. Strong programs include education, English, and political science.

All first-year students are required to participate in Wittenberg Seminars (Witt-Sems), which explore specific topics from a variety of perspectives as an introduction to liberal arts education. Courses often have intriguing names, like "High Brow, Low Brow, and No Brow: *The New Yorker* and the Liberal Arts" and "Why We Believe Weird Things." One student comments, "For one class project, we studied ESP and astrology."

The Wittenberg Honors Program has grown in recent years; winners of the prestigious Smith and Matthies Awards are automatically inducted. Honors students enjoy special seminars during sophomore and junior year and complete a senior honors thesis or project. Honors students have 24-hour access to their own building on campus, the Matthies House.

Future business leaders can take advantage of WittEntrepreneurs, a program that offers academic courses in entrepreneurship, student-run program-owned business ventures, and an incubator program. One example of an on-campus venture is the WittEntrepreneurs and Village Markets of Africa Alliance, which sells artisanal fair trade products to support Kenyan artists.

Students interested in teaching should check out Wittenberg's Institute for Education Innovation, a university-community-school partnership that features research and programs in the areas of Urban Partners, Teaching Innovations, and Community Outreach.

Study-abroad options include semester, full-year, and the popular semester break and summer programs. Recent summer study-abroad programs offered trips to Lesotho, Spain, Russia, and Guatemala. About 20 percent of students have an international experience sometime during their four years. The American International Association is a student organization that cultivates an international community on campus

According to the university, more than 70 percent of all students go on to obtain graduate degrees. There are over 35,000 Wittenberg alumni.

Student Life

More than 120 active student organizations appeal to Wittenberg students who desire activities outside the classroom. The student-run newspaper *The Torch* goes out on campus every Thursday. The American International Association cultivates an international community at the university through a number of events, including an annual fashion show and Formal in the spring. Students hang out at the Student Union, Ringside Bar, and the Hollow, a grassy area for sunbathing and people-watching.

Homecoming brings alumni back to campus during a weekend of festivities, from Greek open houses to the crowning of Homecoming King and Queen to, of course, the main focus: the football game. Traditionally, the AIA also holds Crossroads, an event that features culinary treats from the countries represented by students on campus. Given the major Greek presence on campus, it's not surprising that Greek Week is another popular fall event, with lawn and street games, a lip sync contest, and a community service project to bring together the Greek community. In the spring, music-loving students celebrate Wittefest, which features a wide range of musical offerings, inflatable games, and plenty of food.

More than one quarter of all students join Wittenberg's Greek system (and nearly half of student leaders are part of fraternities/sororities). Luckily, the other three-quarters of students needn't feel left out, as there aren't strong dividing lines between members and non-members and parties tend to be open to everyone. "If you know someone in a fraternity, you're good to go," one student comments.

Wittenberg has 23 Division III teams; the Tigers are especially strong in men's and women's basketball, football, volleyball, and field hockey. According to the college, Wittenberg has the "winningest" small college football team and men's basketball program in the country and an average of four teams per year participate in a national championship. "We're the athletic powerhouse in our division," one student brags.

Springfield, a city of about 60,000 residents, hosts the start of the 80-mile-long Little Miami Scenic Trail that ends near Cincinnati. Students looking for more entertainment can drive 30 minutes to Dayton, an hour to Columbus, and two hours to Indianapolis.

Students are required to live on campus for their first two years in one of seven residence halls, and 83 percent of all students opt to live on campus. The oldest residence, Myers Hall, was the first campus building and a National Historic Site. Polis House brings an international flavor to Ohio with its International Studies students and international residents.

Student Body

Wittenberg's 1,900 students represent more than 39 states and about 30 foreign countries. There is a moderate-sized ethnic mi-

WITTENBERG UNIVERSITY

Highlights

Students
Total enrollment: 1,894
Undergrads: 1,881
Freshmen: 521
Part-time students: 5%
From out-of-state: 30%
From public schools: 80%
Male/Female: 45%/55%
Live on-campus: 83%
In fraternities: 30%
In sororities: 33%
Off-campus employment rating: Fair
Caucasian: 81%
African American: 7%
Hispanic: 3%
Asian / Pacific Islander: 1%
Native American: 0%
Mixed (2+ ethnicities): 3%
International: 2%

Academics
Calendar: Semester
Student/faculty ratio: 11:1
Class size 9 or fewer: 22%
Class size 10-29: 70%
Class size 30-49: 7%
Class size 50-99: -
Class size 100 or more: -
Returning freshmen: 78%
Six-year graduation rate: 65%

Most Popular Majors
Business
Biology
Education

Admissions
Applicants: 4,887
Accepted: 4,455
Acceptance rate: 91.2%
Average GPA: 3.4
ACT range: 23-28
SAT Math range: 500-620
SAT Reading range: 500-620
SAT Writing range: Not reported
Top 10% of class: 23%
Top 25% of class: 48%
Top 50% of class: 79%

959

WITTENBERG UNIVERSITY

Admissions Criteria

Academic criteria:
Grades: ☆ ☆ ☆
Difficulty of class schedule: ☆ ☆ ☆
Class rank: ☆ ☆ ☆
Standardized test scores: ☆
Teacher recommendations: ☆ ☆
Personal statement: ☆ ☆
Non-academic criteria considered:
Interview
Extracurricular activities
Special talents, interests, abilities
Character/personal qualities
Volunteer work
Work experience
State of residency
Alumni relationship

Deadlines

Early Action: December 1
Early Decision: November 15
Regular Action: Rolling admissions
Common Application: Accepted

Financial Aid

In-state tuition: $37,230
Out-of-state tuition: $37,230
Room: $5,056
Board: $4,680
Books: $1,000
Freshmen receiving need-based aid: 83%
Undergrads rec. need-based aid: 79%
Avg. % of need met by financial aid: 80%
Avg. aid package (freshmen): $30,942
Avg. aid package (undergrads): $30,154
Avg. debt upon graduation: $31,712

School Spirit

Mascot: Tiger
Colors: Red and white

nority population, though student groups such as Concerned Black Students offer support. Multicultural Student Programs include the annual Unity March, an event that brings out bands, choirs, and student organizations to promote interracial unity between the University and the city of Springfield. "We could certainly enjoy higher levels of diversity," notes a student.

There are slightly more female students (55 percent) than male students and moderate geographic diversity, with about 30 percent of students hailing from outside the Buckeye state. "You'll find a friendly Midwest vibe here," says a student.

You May Not Know

- A secret society at the university is The Shifters, who are not-so-secret in that it's easy to identify them by the paper clips they wear on their clothing.
- In 1935, the first women's athletic team began in field hockey.
- The first college radio station, WCSO, was started at the university in 1922.

Distinguished Alumni

Al Davis, owner of the Oakland Raiders enterprise; Sara Dukat, Paralympics athlete; John McLaughlin, former CIA Deputy Director.

Admissions and Financial Aid

Since the class of 2012, students have no longer been required to submit an SAT or ACT score. The vice president of enrollment states that this decision was made to find students who not only have impressive academic records, but are also leaders "committed to service and actively engaged in the world around them." Applicants are judged based on academic performance, co-curricular involvement, personal references, and writing ability.

Almost 80 percent of students receive need-based aid, and one-fifth of students receive merit-based aid. The university offers more than $9 million each year in scholarships and grants. All applicants are automatically considered for merit scholarships. The competitive Presidential Scholarship covers full tuition; students are invited to campus to compete for the award. There are other major scholarships for Lutheran students, veterans, and minorities. Smaller special interest awards recognize leadership, service, artistic ability, and the like.

WOFFORD COLLEGE

Overview

Wofford College is a small, tight-knit liberal arts college located in Spartanburg, South Carolina. Though it doesn't have the national name recognition of larger schools, it's consistently ranked as one of the top liberal arts schools in the South. The school is affiliated with the Methodist church but welcomes students of all religious walks.

Wofford shares Spartanburg with five other higher education institutions, giving the small school more of a "college town" feel than it might otherwise have. One of the landmarks of its 170-acre campus is Main Building, originally constructed in 1854 and renovated in 2007.

Seniors may live in the Village—1,200-square-foot apartments completed in 2011 with full kitchens, private bedrooms, living rooms, and porches. For students looking for a small school with a focus on service and a strong academic environment, Wofford is the place to be.

Academics

All students are required to take classes in English, fine arts, a foreign language, a natural science, history, philosophy, religion, cultures and peoples, math, PE, and Humanities 101 along with their major coursework. Students are also required to complete a yearly project during the non-traditional Interim term between fall and spring semesters. Options include studying off campus or abroad, doing an internship or service learning project, or conducting an independent study project. Students get guidance from faculty members, and most projects are graded H (pass with honors), P (pass), or F (fail) versus traditional letter grades. "Interim is the best part of the school year because we have so much flexibility about how we want to learn," says a student.

Because the school is small, professor-student relationships are intense. "There's no skipping class without the professor knowing," says one student. The closeness of the relationships also motivates students to study, because it's "obvious to everyone when you don't do the work." Wofford is known for its strong biology, psychology, and business economics programs. "If you really want to work in business, the business economics major is a great foundation," comments a student.

Students can take part in a variety of unique educational opportunities at Wofford. The Success Initiative (SI) puts participating students together in teams and encourages them to "think like entrepreneurs" while designing and carrying out projects. Unlike some liberal arts schools with curriculums that seem like they'll never apply to the real world, SI projects are intended to be tangible—whether it's making a music video or building a medical clinic in the third world. "While I like my regular classes, through SI I'm able to not just study an issue but do something about it," explains a student.

Students who participate in Wofford's Learning Communities are able to take two seemingly unrelated classes (typically a humanities and a science course) which, when paired, create unusual connections. Past learning communities have focused on theatre physics and science, pseudoscience, and belief.

Unique to Wofford is its summer reading initiative, the culmination of which is an informal book discussion over the Novel Experience meal during orientation week—it immediately gives students and faculty something to talk about while they get to know one another. "It's nice to have something serious to talk about besides what everyone did over the summer," laughs a student.

And finally, for those students interested in research, there's the Community of Scholars. In the Community, 19 students do full-time research for 10 weeks of summer; then the students, along with the 10 Faculty Fellows, come together to discuss their research and build collaborative bonds in a way that hyper-competitive science schools do not. Recent projects through the program have included "Hindu Music in

WOFFORD COLLEGE

Four-year private
Founded: 1854
Spartanburg, SC
Medium city
Pop. 37,334

Address:
429 North Church
Street
Spartanburg, SC
29303-3663

Admissions:
864-597-4130

Financial Aid:
864-597-4160

admission@wofford.
edu

www.wofford.edu

WOFFORD COLLEGE

Highlights

Students

Total enrollment: 1,588
Undergrads: 1,588
Freshmen: 466
Part-time students: 3%
From out-of-state: 52%
From public schools: 65%
Male/Female: 51%/49%
Live on-campus: 93%
In fraternities: 43%
In sororities: 55%
Off-campus employment rating: Good
Caucasian: 81%
African American: 8%
Hispanic: 2%
Asian / Pacific Islander: 3%
Native American: 0%
Mixed (2+ ethnicities): 2%
International: 2%

Academics

Calendar: 4-1-4 system
Student/faculty ratio: 11:1
Class size 9 or fewer: 14%
Class size 10-29: 83%
Class size 30-49: 3%
Class size 50-99: -
Class size 100 or more: -
Graduates who immediately go to graduate school: 46%
Graduates who immediately enter career related to major: 41%

Most Popular Majors

Biology
Finance
Government

Admissions

Applicants: 3,197
Accepted: 2,005
Acceptance rate: 62.7%
Placed on wait list: 78
Enrolled from wait list: 4
Average GPA: 3.6
ACT range: 23-28
SAT Math range: 590-680
SAT Reading range: 570-670
SAT Writing range: 11-41
Top 10% of class: 55%
Top 25% of class: 79%
Top 50% of class: 98%

the Bible Belt," "Economic Development and Pollution in China," and "Examination of Health Care Systems around the World."

Wofford offers more than 200 study-abroad programs in 59 countries. The school keeps a stable of student bloggers who are studying abroad so interested students can get a feel for what it's like. Besides regular financial aid, the college also offers Wofford Travel Grants for summer, fall, interim, and spring travel.

The Career Services office provides Executive Services in which alumni and other leaders work with current students to expose them to different industries. Recent speakers have included the former mayor of Spartanburg, a representative of the office of the public defender, and a radiologist. After Wofford, 46 percent of graduates head straight to grad school. More than 40 percent enter a field related to their major within six months, often at accounting firms and banks.

Student Life

The school newspaper at Wofford is honest—according to these journalists, most of the school's activities are on campus, and Spartanburg's pretty quiet. However, there are 98 student clubs, including the Micah 6 Bonner Leadership Program (in which students work with local churches on social justice issues) and a glee club.

The big event for Greek life is Boys' Bid Day, where the frat and sorority pledges dress up by pledge class and mud wrestle (the last part includes participation by the whole campus). "It's not as easy as you would think to get mud out of your hair," laughs a student. Spring Weekend, organized by the Wofford Activities Council, encompasses festivities that include a departmental golf cart race and a slip and slide. "There's also group tie dying, which is really the only way tie dying should be done," says a student. The musically inclined can go caroling at Christmas.

Unusual for such a small school, there are eight fraternities and four sororities on campus—almost half the school is involved with Greek life. "There can be a division between members and non-members," comments a student.

Wofford has 17 Division I sports teams, including a football team (they're the smallest D-I school with a football team, and the second-smallest D-I school overall). The college has well regarded football, baseball, and men's basketball teams; cheering them on is a big part of Wofford's social scene. "We are the underdogs so we have to show a lot of support for our athletes," explains a student. There are a variety of intramural sports as well, including fly fishing and rock climbing in addition to more traditional offerings.

When students head off campus, they can either go to the other schools in Spartanburg (nearby Converse College is a favorite) or they can head to other towns. "Shopping is limited—we have a mall and a Super Walmart though," says a student. Greenville (about 30 miles away) is the nearest big city, though Charlotte and Atlanta are also close enough for longer weekend trips.

The vast majority of students live on campus. Freshmen live in doubles in Greene Hall (for women) and Marsh Hall (for the men). Rising sophomores and above are assigned housing based on a lottery system. "There's a real strategy to ranking your choices for the housing lottery," says a student.

Student Body

According to Wofford students, they are "committed to both studies and activities" and "slightly more conservative" than some schools. There is a "very large" Southern contingency, although students insist newcomers "never feel out of place because everyone is so friendly."

The school has a moderate level of racial diversity (15 percent of students identify as members of a minority) and moderate geographic diversity (52 percent of students are from out of state, though they're typically from the Southeast).

Distinguished Alumni

Fisher DeBerry, inductee in the College Football Hall of Fame; Wendy Nix, ESPN anchor; Carl Julian Sanders, former American Bishop in the United Methodist Church.

Admissions and Financial Aid

Wofford, like most schools, recommends high school students take four years of English and math, three years of lab science, three years of a foreign language, and two years of social studies. The college says that they're interested in applicants' "courses, level of curriculum, class rank, test scores, grades, extracurricular leadership, and a recommendation from the high school guidance counselor."

All first-year students are considered for merit aid. This includes the Richardson Scholarship (a full ride plus a monthly stipend, a laptop, overseas summer internships, and a January travel experience) and the Wofford Scholars program (with scholarships worth between $8,000 and $160,000 over four years). Bonner Scholars, if they demonstrate need and merit, serve as volunteers and receive a $4,000 stipend for their work; the program is intended to allow students in need of financial aid to volunteer.

WOFFORD COLLEGE

Highlights

Admissions Criteria
Academic criteria:
Grades: ☆ ☆ ☆
Difficulty of class schedule: ☆ ☆ ☆
Class rank: ☆ ☆
Standardized test scores: ☆ ☆
Teacher recommendations: ☆
Personal statement: ☆ ☆
Non-academic criteria considered:
Interview
Extracurricular activities
Special talents, interests, abilities
Character/personal qualities
Volunteer work
Work experience
State of residency
Geographical location
Minority affiliation
Alumni relationship

Deadlines
Early Action: November 15
Early Decision: November 1
Regular Action: February 1 (final)
Notification of admission by: March 15
Common Application: Accepted

Financial Aid
In-state tuition: $35,515
Out-of-state tuition: $35,515
Room: Varies
Board: Varies
Books: $1,200
Freshmen receiving need-based aid: 66%
Undergrads rec. need-based aid: 60%
Avg. % of need met by financial aid: 83%
Avg. aid package (freshmen): $27,554
Avg. aid package (undergrads): $27,803
Avg. debt upon graduation: $22,118

School Spirit
Mascot: Terriers
Colors: Old gold and black

Overview

Worcester, Massachusetts, just an hour's drive from Boston, may not be where you would expect to find 13 colleges. Among the schools is Worcester Polytechnic Institute (WPI)—a small private university with a strong emphasis on science, engineering, and technology—sitting on a hilltop, secluded on 80 acres. The traditional architecture hints at WPI's old roots as one of the nation's oldest technological universities.

While the buildings may look traditional, many of the programs at WPI certainly are not. Two unique projects engage students in small teams to address real-world problems all over the globe; there are no failing grades; and the university has an uncommon focus on green and sustainability issues. Also, rather than semesters or quarters, WPI operates on a seven-week term.

Some students may be turned off by the gender imbalance at Worcester, and while not everyone can be stereotyped as a geek, certain activities and clubs (the weekly gaming night, the Rubik's Cube Club, for example) might convince you otherwise. Not surprisingly, students who aren't turned on to science and technology won't appreciate the wide array of opportunities for research and collaborative projects that WPI has to offer.

Academics

WPI offers over 50 different degree programs. "'Tech' is in our name so it's not surprising that more of us pursue tech-related degrees," comments a student.

WPI's unique seven-week term is even more fast-paced than the academic quarter. Students take three courses per term, and there are four terms total, two in fall and two in the spring. "I have a love/hate relationship with the seven-week term," says a student. "I love that everything is fast-paced but sometimes it's too much so."

Projects count as the equivalent of three courses, and all students are required to complete two projects: the Interactive Qualifying Project (IQP) and the Major Qualifying Project (MQP). IQP groups students into teams of two to four and challenges them to apply science and technology to social issues; about 60 percent of students complete this requirement abroad. The MQP is also team-based and involves research or design within a student's major. Other mandated courses include five classes in the humanities and arts plus a capstone seminar/practicum, two courses in the social sciences, and four PE courses. Most classes are small "seminar" size of two to nine students.

Strong programs include engineering (mechanical, robotics, biomedical, electrical and computer, and more) and computer science. Students can also design their own majors through Individually Designed Programs. Combined Bachelor's Master's Programs offer accelerated five-year plans for BS/MS in Fire Protection Engineering and Mathematics.

The Chemistry and Biochemistry Scholars Program supports chemistry majors through special academic advising, research opportunities as early as freshman year, field trips and industry tours, and even a scholarship ranging from $12,500 to $25,000, renewable over four years. Students in CBSP have the chance to work on research that addresses real-life challenges such as Alzheimer's and crop pests. All students have the opportunity to conduct research through faculty research labs, summer research experiences, and other fellowships. "If you want to do research and put in a little effort, you'll find an opportunity," says a student.

More than half of WPI's students complete at least one academic project off campus thanks to the Global Perspective Program. With 25 national and international project centers, students study in places as diverse as Bangkok, Cape Town, and Copenhagen.

WPI's Career Development Center offers a plethora of services to students, from mock interviews to job shadowing to job listings. The university notes that WPI was recently ranked in the top 10 engineering schools for highest starting median salary.

Student Life

With 200 student organizations, activities, and teams, there are lots of social and special interest groups. The Genius! Entrepreneurship Club discusses technological concepts. Other clubs fall under the "Science/Technology and Gaming" category. Music and theater groups and cultural and religious groups help foster, as WPI puts it, "a sense of community without conformity."

WPI's Campus Center serves as a main social hub with its dining options, a game room, TVs, and more. Students have plenty of weekly events to attend, from Tuesday Socials, when the Social Dance Club takes over Campus Center stage; Coffeehouse, which brings folk artists to campus every Tuesday; Friday Night Gaming, board games that go from dinnertime to as late as two or three in the morning; and Sunday Movies. "Other people might think we're geeky for liking board games, but frankly, we don't care," says a student.

Two of the biggest annual events at WPI draw students and community members at the beginning and end of the school. Gaming Weekend, a biannual three-day event on Labor Day weekend, kicks off the school year with all kinds of games, from role playing games to Duck, Duck, Goose; while Quadfest brings music, movies, and student organization booths to campus on the last week of school in a massive celebration of the year's end. Each year's Quadfest is themed; past names have run the gamut from "Sesame Street" to "Pirates?".

Other annual events include Dragon Night, hosted by WPI's Chinese Student Association. It features Chinese food and lion dancing to celebrate the Chinese New Year. For those inclined to generosity, Penny Wars is a yearly fundraiser where clubs and Greek Organizations compete to raise money for charity.

Greek life is a major facet of WPI: 28 percent of men and 41 percent of women belong. There are 18 Greek organizations in total, though the ratio of fraternities (13) to sororities (five) is predictably skewed given the large male population. Alpha Phi Omega is the co-ed community service fraternity that puts on an annual Service Auction (horseback riding, baking a pie, or building a sandcastle, anyone?) along with other events. "The frats range from pretty geeky to those who like to party," comments a student.

WPI's 20 men's and women's varsity sports teams compete in Division III. Basketball, football, and baseball are the most popular, and student support for WPI's teams is vibrant. Over half of all students are involved in intramurals on campus. "Intramurals are more for fun and stress relief than for showing athletic prowess," one student notes.

Off campus, Worcester's Highland Street is popular for its restaurants and coffee shops, while the DCU Center offers concerts, minor league hockey, and other events. Boston is a one-hour commuter rail ride away.

First-year students are guaranteed on-campus housing, which includes singles, doubles, and triples along with suites for four

WORCESTER POLYTECHNIC INSTITUTE

Highlights

Students
Total enrollment: 5,957
Undergrads: 3,952
Freshmen: 948
From out-of-state: 53%
From public schools: 66%
Male/Female: 68%/32%
Live on-campus: 56%
In fraternities: 28%
In sororities: 41%
Off-campus employment rating: Good
Caucasian: 66%
African American: 2%
Hispanic: 7%
Asian / Pacific Islander: 5%
Native American: 0%
Mixed (2+ ethnicities): 3%
International: 12%

Academics
Calendar: Quarter
Student/faculty ratio: 14:1
Class size 9 or fewer: 56%
Class size 10-29: 22%
Class size 30-49: 12%
Class size 50-99: 8%
Class size 100 or more: 2%
Graduates who immediately go to graduate school: 28%

Most Popular Majors
Mechanical engineering
Electrical/computer engineering
Biology/biotechnology

Admissions
Applicants: 7,585
Accepted: 3,986
Acceptance rate: 52.6%
Placed on wait list: 2,033
Enrolled from wait list: 73
Average GPA: 3.8
ACT range: 27-32
SAT Math range: 640-720
SAT Reading range: 560-670
SAT Writing range: 14-47
Top 10% of class: 66%
Top 25% of class: 92%
Top 50% of class: 99%

965

College Profiles

WORCESTER POLYTECHNIC INSTITUTE

Admissions Criteria

Academic criteria:
Grades: ☆ ☆ ☆
Difficulty of class schedule: ☆ ☆ ☆
Class rank: ☆ ☆
Standardized test scores: ☆ ☆
Teacher recommendations: ☆
Personal statement: ☆
Non-academic criteria considered:
Interview
Extracurricular activities
Special talents, interests, abilities
Character/personal qualities
Volunteer work
Work experience
State of residency
Geographical location
Alumni relationship

Deadlines

Early Action: November 10 and January 1
Early Decision: No
Regular Action: February 1 (final)
Notification of admission by: April 1
Common Application: Accepted

Financial Aid

In-state tuition: $42,178
Out-of-state tuition: $42,178
Room: $7,466
Board: $5,616
Books: $1,000
Freshmen receiving need-based aid: 73%
Undergrads rec. need-based aid: 70%
Avg. % of need met by financial aid: 72%
Avg. aid package (freshmen): $31,426
Avg. aid package (undergrads): $30,954

School Spirit

Mascot: Goat
Colors: Crimson and silver
Song: *Alma Mater*

to six people and apartments for anywhere between two to seven people. Roughly 40 percent of students live off campus in homes, apartments, and Greek houses.

Student Body

"We're not afraid to let our geek flag fly," says a student, adding, "of course not everyone is a geek or at least not *openly* a geek." WPI has moderate ethnic diversity and a heavy gender imbalance with male students making up over 68 percent of the nearly 4,000 undergrads. There is moderate geographic diversity, with about half of students from out of state.

You May Not Know

- WPI was founded in 1865 as the Worcester Free Institute of Industrial Science. It was one of the nation's first engineering and technology schools.
- A WPI superstition says that setting foot on the seal in the center of the WPI quad will prevent a student from graduating in four years; students walk around the seal to get to their seats during graduation but walk over the seal as they leave.
- WPI has one of 35 civilian research nuclear reactors licensed to operate in the U.S., and is the only nuclear reactor in North America housed in a wood-framed building.

Distinguished Alumni

W. Todd Atkin, U.S. Representative from Missouri; Curtis Carlson, President and CEO of SRI International; Robert Goddard, physicist and inventor who built the world's first liquid-fueled rocket; Nancy Pimental, a writer for *South Park*.

Admissions and Financial Aid

In keeping with WPI's emphasis on science and math, academic requirements for all applicants include four years of math, including pre-calculus and two years of lab sciences. Applicants' letters of recommendations must also come from a science or math teacher. WPI's "Flex Path" allows students to who do not feel their SAT and ACT test scores reflect their potential to send in samples of academic work or extracurricular projects in lieu of standardized test scores. Examples include research papers, portfolios, and overviews of leadership experiences. The average student who applies is in the top 11 percent of his or her class.

All admitted applicants are considered for WPI's academic scholarships, which range from $12,500 to $25,000 and are renewable for four years. Valedictorians, salutatorians, and IB diploma graduates with a diploma score of 40 or greater are guaranteed a minimum scholarship of $19,000, as are National Merit, National Achievement and National Hispanic Recognition Finalists. WPI also offers a range of scholarships, including full-tuition, four year awards, for FIRST (For Inspiration and Recognition of Science and Technology) participants.

XAVIER UNIVERSITY OF LOUISIANA

Overview

As Xavier University of Louisiana states, "There are 102 historically Black colleges and 253 Catholic colleges in the United States, yet only one is both Black and Catholic." And while Xavier's status as a historically Black college and its Catholicism are crucial parts of its identity, there's more to the small New Orleans school than even its unique status. Xavier offers several top-notch programs in the sciences, including its premed program, which places the most African-American students into med school of any school in the country. Xavier also offers some of the most funding for research, especially in the sciences, among comparable schools.

Xavier's strict Catholicism makes for a sometimes bland on-campus scene, and safety issues in the neighborhood—known as the Triangle near Carrollton and Washington—and New Orleans' high crime rates (not to mention Xavier's strict rules regarding leaving campus) may make it hard to get away, and some of the more outrageous earthly delights that New Orleans has to offer may not exactly jive with Xavier's Catholic values. With its Catholic mission, especially as it manifests itself in the social scene and conduct code restrictions, Xavier may not be for everyone, but nevertheless welcomes other religious affiliations and races. It's doors are open to students in the sciences, providing a unique environment in one of the most diverse cities of the world.

Academics

Students can choose from 47 majors, but Xavier's most popular and largest major, biology, also happens to be its strongest. Xavier's premed program offers specialized advising, MCAT preparation, and med school application assistance augmented by special honors societies. "If you're African-American and serious about going to medical school, this should be your top-choice college," advises a student.

Xavier ensures that all students receive a solid liberal arts education through its expansive tripartite Core Curriculum. The Fundamental Core requires two courses each in English and a foreign language, and one class each in math and a natural science course with lab component. The Essential Core requires the First-Year Experience course, plus two classes each in philosophy and theology and a course each in African-American studies, communication, fine arts, history, physical education, natural sciences, social sciences, and world literature. The Expansive Core requires students to take a course in two of the four areas of fine arts, humanities, social sciences, and natural sciences outside the major or minor. Around 87 percent of classes have fewer than 30 students, which offers plenty of opportunity for interacting with faculty. "The professors are very hands-on," notes a student.

Xavier offers a number of special programs, although they are nearly all concentrated in the sciences. The Across Curriculum Thinking (ACT) Program offers liberal arts students an interdisciplinary menu of class discussions, film series, and guest speakers, orchestrated by faculty mentors and centered on a certain year-long theme, such as "Social Justice," "Globalization," or "Propaganda," to augment their in-class studies.

Xavier's special science programs include a Dual Degree Engineering program, in which students interested in engineering work for three years at Xavier towards a BA or BS in biology, chemistry, computer science, or physics before transferring to an affiliated engineering school to complete their engineering training. Affiliated schools include Georgia Institute of Technology, Notre Dame University, Tulane, University of Maryland, and University of Wisconsin-Madison.

In addition to its highly respected and successful premed program, Xavier's Premedical Office allows premed or predental students in chemistry or biology the opportunity to forego their senior year at Xavier and substitute courses taken in their

XAVIER UNIVERSITY OF LOUISIANA

Four-year private
Founded: 1915
New Orleans, LA
Major city
Pop. 360,740

Address:
One Drexel Drive
New Orleans, LA
70125

Admissions:
877-XAVIERU

Financial Aid:
504-520-7517

apply@xula.edu

www.xula.edu

XAVIER UNIVERSITY OF LOUISIANA

Students
Total enrollment: 3,178
Undergrads: 2,525
Freshmen: 877
From out-of-state: 49%
From public schools: 24%
Male/Female: 29%/71%
Live on-campus: 47%
In fraternities: 3%
In sororities: 6%
Off-campus employment rating: Fair
Caucasian: 3%
African American: 78%
Hispanic: 2%
Asian / Pacific Islander: 10%
Native American: 0%
Mixed (2+ ethnicities): 3%
International: 2%

Academics
Calendar: Semester
Student/faculty ratio: 13:1
Class size 9 or fewer: 26%
Class size 10-29: 61%
Class size 30-49: 9%
Class size 50-99: 3%
Class size 100 or more: 1%
Six-year graduation rate: 47%
Graduates who immediately go to graduate school: 31%
Graduates who immediately enter career related to major: 28%

Most Popular Majors
Biology
Physical sciences
Psychology

Admissions
Applicants: 3,987
Accepted: 2,532
Acceptance rate: 63.5%
Placed on wait list: 172
Enrolled from wait list: 8
Average GPA: 3.3
ACT range: 19-25
SAT Math range: 440-550
SAT Reading range: 430-560
SAT Writing range: 1-7
Top 10% of class: 33%
Top 25% of class: 60%
Top 50% of class: 83%

968

first year of medical or dental school instead. This accelerated program is "definitely more difficult" than the standard premed route, and students who are interested in it should have high GPAs and test scores.

Xavier also enjoys plenty of research monies, ranking first among Historically Black Colleges and Universities in funding from the NIH per capita. Funding is available to students through the Center for Undergraduate Research, an institution that also aids students in becoming involved in one of the many research opportunities that abound at Xavier. Undergrads can work with the chemistry department, various laboratories and initiatives underwritten by the NSF and NIH in computational and biomedical sciences, and the affiliated Louisiana Cancer Research Consortium, as well as Tulane/Xavier Centers for Bioenvironmental Science or Excellence in Women's Health. The Xavier Research Experience for Undergraduates also provides funding to students, usually rising sophomores, who wish to conduct summer research in biology, chemistry, and physics. Students in environmental biology can participate in the Tulane/Xavier Undergraduate Research Mentoring (URM) Project, which also provides GRE prep.

Xavier does not run its own study-abroad programs, but students with sophomore standing can participate in one of 30 affiliated third-party study-abroad programs worldwide.

The Office of Career Services can help students explore career options, find jobs and internships, and prepare for interviews. "The alumni network is very tight, and you can contact alumni who will help answer questions and even provide leads," says a student.

Student Life

Of Xavier's approximately 75 student organizations, service groups like Habitat for Humanity and pre-professional groups dominate, but there are some performance groups, like the Pom Pom Squad and Da Stoop radio club. On campus, students mostly hang out at the University Center, where the dining hall, bookstore, lounges, coffee ship, and internet café are located. The annual Springfest brings a major musical act to campus, and the festivities usually include a Dorm Step-Off. Particularly reminiscent of high school are the University Ball and Miss Xavier Coronation Ceremony.

Greek life is fairly dominant on campus, although a very small percentage of students belong to the four fraternities (three percent) and four sororities (six percent); Greek Step-Offs are also popular. "We have some real talent," a student remarks.

Xavier imposes strict regulations on some aspects of conduct, which some students may find restrictive: Xavier is a dry campus, and any student "in the presence of alcohol" is in violation of the alcohol policy. Guests in residence halls must be registered and can only visit during certain hours; overnight guests must be approved by the Office of Housing and Residence Life and the Hall Director two weeks in advance, and a fee per night is charged. Students must "sign out" from their residence halls if they are going to spend the night elsewhere, and curfew (at 12:30 a.m. for freshmen on school nights) is enforced. Violation of these policies can result in serious disciplinary action, including expulsion. "I understand that the college wants to keep us safe, but it's very Big Brother," one student comments. As a result, social life at Xavier is quite different that most other colleges.

Xavier doesn't have a football team, so it stands to reason that of its 16 NCAA Division I varsity teams, basketball is the most popular. Xavier's teams have made it to the Elite Eight several times in the last decade. Campus Recreational Sports operates tournaments and activities for all students, including the more standard sports as well as ping-pong, dodgeball, billiards, dominoes, spades, and the "Wacky Olympics."

New Orleans offers plenty of diversions for students, including restaurants, clubs, bars, shopping, sight-seeing, and, of course, Mardi Gras.

Most dorms at Xavier are single sex. For freshmen, residence halls are dorm-style; upperclassmen may live in dorms or suites and on-campus apartments. Given the very strict housing regulations it's unsurprising that most students move off campus. "Brockman is the dorm to avoid," warns a student.

Student Body

Despite Xavier's special purpose as a Black Catholic university, almost three-quarters of the student body are not Catholic, and other ethnic minorities are fairly well represented. About half of students come from out of state. Xavier does have a skewed gender distribution, however, with women accounting for 71 percent of the student body. Students describe themselves as "focused on our future professions" and "very active."

You Might Not Know

- Xavier's campus is sometimes called the Emerald City, which refers to the many buildings on campus with green roofs.
- For whatever reason, opening a window in a residence hall is a punishable offense.
- Xavier originated in 1925 as a coeducational secondary school for Native Americans and African-Americans, founded by Katharine Drexel, who has since been canonized as a saint, and the Sisters of the Blessed Sacrament, who still maintain a presence on campus today.

Distinguished Alumni

Regina Benjamin, U.S. Surgeon General; Alvin J. Boutte, founder and CEO of Indecorp, the largest African-American-owned financial institution in the country; Charles Champion, named one of America's 50 Most Influential Pharmacists; Alexis Herman, first African-American U.S. Secretary of Labor.

Admissions and Financial Aid

First-time applicants to Xavier are automatically considered for full-tuition awards, merit, university, President's, and Board of Trustees Scholarships. These may require personal statements, unless submitted as part of the Common Application. Merit scholarships are also available for students who attended U.S. Catholic high schools or public schools in New Orleans or Jefferson parishes.

XAVIER UNIVERSITY OF LOUISIANA

Highlights

Admissions Criteria
Academic criteria:
Grades: ☆ ☆ ☆
Difficulty of class schedule: ☆ ☆ ☆
Class rank: ☆ ☆
Standardized test scores: ☆ ☆ ☆
Teacher recommendations: ☆ ☆ ☆
Personal statement: ☆ ☆
Non-academic criteria considered:
Interview
Extracurricular activities
Special talents, interests, abilities
Character/personal qualities
Volunteer work
Work experience
State of residency
Alumni relationship

Deadlines
Early Action: January 15
Early Decision: No
Regular Action: Rolling admissions
Common Application: Accepted

Financial Aid
In-state tuition: $18,500
Out-of-state tuition: $18,500
Room: Varies
Board: Varies
Books: $1,200
Freshmen receiving need-based aid: 85%
Undergrads rec. need-based aid: 85%
Avg. % of need met by financial aid: 14%
Avg. aid package (freshmen): $18,622
Avg. aid package (undergrads): $17,797
Avg. debt upon graduation: $33,610

School Spirit
Mascot: Gold Rush
Colors: Gold and white

YALE
UNIVERSITY

Four-year private
Founded: 1701
New Haven, CT
Medium city
Pop. 129,585

Address:
P.O. Box 208234
New Haven, CT
06520

Admissions:
203-432-9300

Financial Aid:
203-432-2700

student.questions@
yale.edu

www.yale.edu

YALE UNIVERSITY

Overview

Whether you're looking up at the collegiate gothic towers, moats, and stained glass, attending a lecture by a world renowned professor, or being astonished by the fact that you're surrounded by so many young people that have already accomplished so much, this medium-sized private college's excitement seems inexhaustible. Its impressiveness has been enough to earn it top ratings time and time again, recently ranking third among national universities by *U.S. News & World Report*.

There are a few features that take a bit of warming up to. The sun disappears for what feels like months of devitalizing rain yet leads to enjoyable springs. The surrounding city suffers a crime rate that students tend to exaggerate, although a security staff of 150 and common sense are enough to make students feel safe. And the campus seems to be endlessly under construction, although this gives students new state-of-the-art facilities.

The undergraduate school is divided into 12 colleges to which all 5,400 students are "selectively and randomly" assigned before their freshman year, thus creating a microcosm in every building. For some, their commitment to this residence is one of life-long pride while others too cool for school spirit move off campus to enjoy their own super hip counter culture.

The workload seems to fit the aspirations of all that attend. The overachievers ravenously gorge on impossible problem sets and abandon sleep altogether to meet assignment deadlines. Meanwhile, students looking to enjoy other aspects the school has to offer surreptitiously pass back and forth selections from the "Gut List," a collection of courses that even the biggest class-skipping, procrastinating, assignment-ignoring student could pass as once revealed on Gawker.com.

The university has so much to take advantage of that upon exiting, every graduate feels guilty about not completing his or her bucket list that might include such items as exploring the two art museums on campus, making it to the anticipated Yale Symphony Orchestra midnight Halloween Show, or attending every one of the myriad of infamously themed parties the administration would never want to admit take place.

Academics

The undergraduate curriculum comes with a handful of requirements generic enough to complete without too much grumbling: two courses in the humanities and arts, two courses in the social sciences, and two courses in science. Students must also fulfill skills mandates by taking two quantitative reasoning courses, two writing courses, and courses that demonstrate and improve their proficiency in foreign languages. With courses in over 75 majors, there are plenty of choices that fulfill these requirements. The college also offers freshman seminars in a multitude of different subjects (Architecture and Utopia, Radiation and the Universe, and Digital Photorealism just to name a few) as well as small-sized seminars sponsored by the residential colleges.

The university boasts a serious commitment to its college students, requiring all tenured professors of arts and science to teach undergraduate students. Details such as this—and the fact the more than 85 percent of classes have fewer than 30 students—have earned the school a top 10 ranking for undergraduate teaching in the country by *U.S. News & World Report*. "The professors are highly committed and with impressive credentials. Most know how to keep us enrapt in the material too," says a student.

Some of the school's strongest programs include biology, economics, English, political science, and theater studies. But there are also a number of unique opportunities to take part in. Directed Studies is a selective freshman program where students take year-long courses in literature, philosophy, and historical and political thought, exploring the entire canon of Western civilization. One student says the program is nicknamed Directed Suicide because the workload is "as painful as tiny little cuts you could inflict on yourself in the name of academia." Perspectives on Science and Engineering is an interdepartmental program offering qualified first-year students an introduction to a diverse collection of science and engineering faculty and their research. A mouthwatering assortment of research such as this is a wonderful way to encourage students to take part in conducting research in any of the more than 800 university laboratories.

The university also prepares its undergrads for their post-graduation life with a career services department that offers counseling, professional school advising, and employment and internship opportunities. This department also boasts more inter-national internships than any other Ivy League according to the director of undergraduate career services. There is a wide array of study-abroad opportunities as well. Notable ones including the joint-undergraduate program with Peking University in China, the Yale-in-London program, and the Summer Session, which sends students to any of a number of locations around the globe.

But what may be the most important part of the academic experience as an undergraduate at Yale is the school's "shopping period"—two weeks at the beginning of each semester during which a student doesn't have to commit to any course. The time is consid-ered an opportunity to explore any subject that looks interesting, evaluate a professor's style, or test drive the trek to a 9 a.m. course on the other side of campus. "It's a try-before-you-buy period, and it has helped me avoid some dreadful choices as well as make some surprisingly great ones," explains a student.

Student Life

Yale builds little families as soon as students step on campus, Old Campus to be specific—a collection of freshman housing where one lives with other members of his or her residential college and a small collection of seniors who act as everything from academic advisors to shoulders to cry on. After the first year, students upgrade to live directly in their residential colleges, each complete with its own dining hall, library, and basements full of printing presses, theatre space, gyms, and butteries.

The Master's Teas provide intimate moments in which students may interact directly with important figures such as Howard Dean and Junot Diaz, Denzel Washington or Kareem Abdul-Jabbar. "You're bombarded with so many opportunities to meet famous people that it helps you get past the star-gazing temptation to hav-ing a real interaction with some very important people," comments a student.

There are more than 400 student groups on campus, including volunteer organizations, senior societies, religious groups, and resi-dential college activity councils. Some even have world recognition such as the Whiffenpoofs, a 14-member a cappella group—the old-est in the world—that has performed for United States Presidents and the Dalai Lama, gracing stages at Carnegie Hall, Lincoln Center, and the Rose Bowl. There are others shrouded in mystery such as the Skull and Bones Society, with enough folklore to inspire a series of films (*The Skulls*) and an alumni group including George Bush Jr. and Sr., John Kerry, and William Howard Taft.

YALE UNIVERSITY

Highlights

Students
Total enrollment: 11,906
Undergrads: 5,405
Freshmen: 1,356
From out-of-state: 94%
From public schools: 57%
Male/Female: 50%/50%
Live on-campus: 87%
Off-campus employment rating: Good
Caucasian: 47%
African American: 7%
Hispanic: 10%
Asian / Pacific Islander: 16%
Native American: 1%
Mixed (2+ ethnicities): 6%
International: 10%

Academics
Calendar: Semester
Student/faculty ratio: 6:1
Class size 9 or fewer: 32%
Class size 10-29: 54%
Class size 30-49: 6%
Class size 50-99: 5%
Class size 100 or more: 3%
Returning freshmen: 99%
Six-year graduation rate: 96%
Graduates who immediately go to gradu-
    ate school: 20%

Most Popular Majors
Political science
Economics
History

Admissions
Applicants: 28,977
Accepted: 2,043
Acceptance rate: 7.1%
Placed on wait list: 1,000
Enrolled from wait list: 70
Average GPA: Not reported
ACT range: 32-35
SAT Math range: 710-790
SAT Reading range: 700-800
SAT Writing range: 81-17
Top 10% of class: 95%
Top 25% of class: 99%
Top 50% of class: 100%

971

YALE UNIVERSITY

Admissions Criteria

Academic criteria:
Grades: ☆ ☆ ☆
Difficulty of class schedule: ☆ ☆ ☆
Class rank: ☆ ☆ ☆
Standardized test scores: ☆ ☆ ☆
Teacher recommendations: ☆ ☆ ☆
Personal statement: ☆ ☆ ☆
Non-academic criteria considered:
Interview
Extracurricular activities
Special talents, interests, abilities
Character/personal qualities
Volunteer work
Work experience
Geographical location
Minority affiliation
Alumni relationship

Deadlines

Early Action: November 1
Early Decision: No
Regular Action: December 31 (final)
Notification of admission by: April 1
Common Application: Accepted

Financial Aid

In-state tuition: $44,000
Out-of-state tuition: $44,000
Room: Varies
Board: Varies
Books: Varies
Freshmen receiving need-based aid: 54%
Undergrads rec. need-based aid: 56%
Avg. % of need met by financial aid: 100%
Avg. aid package (freshmen): $43,571
Avg. aid package (undergrads): $43,116
Avg. debt upon graduation: $8,940

School Spirit

Mascot: Bulldog
Colors: Blue and white
Song: *Down the Field*

The Greek life on campus is existent but not dominant. Most theorize that the small numbers attracted to fraternities and sororities (estimated at about 15 percent of the student body) are due to the vibrant sense of community available in endless forms, including the residential college system, cultural houses, and senior societies. No matter what, the frats will still draw droves of curious freshmen to beaten-up houses. And the less visible sororities offer a support system and motivational engine to women who seek them out.

New Haven has a number of small bars and night clubs for older students to explore, the most popular of which is Toad's Place—inspiring the catchphrase on Wednesday and Saturday nights "all roads lead to Toad's." But most often students are living it up on campus during their down time. The undergrads are surprisingly clever and tenacious in their pursuit to party. The academic year is riddled with an array of quirky get-togethers from Safety Dance, a giant 80s themed party with spandex and slap bracelets galore; The Inferno, a devilish Halloween party; as well as dances hosted by each college where roommates set each other up on blind dates known as Screws. Students blow off steam in all sorts of events, such as a recent occurrence when an unknown group of students resurrected a rowdy tradition still banned by the university, (yet constantly discussed), known as Bladderball, a bedlam at which students try to push a giant ball to their residential college.

When it comes to games, the college is an NCAA Division I member, with 35 varsity sports and a large number of club teams. Athletes, as well as all members of the Yale community, get to train in the second-largest indoor gymnasium in the world, Payne Whitney Gym, which consists of more than 12 acres of indoor space. Students competing in intramural sports for the glory of their residential colleges will often meet there as well to play everything from volleyball and soccer to ping pong and inner tube water polo. Points are closely measured and the most dominant college at the end of the academic year is awarded the coveted Tyng Cup.

The most important athletic event—heck, the ONLY athletic event as far as most are concerned—is the classic Yale-Harvard football game that occurs at the kickoff of the university's week-long Thanksgiving break. The world stops turning, celebrity alumni from both schools gather round at the tailgates, and the winning side storms the field to claim victory as well as overall superiority.

Student Body

The campus is very liberal leaning, even if the smaller groups of conservative students never let you forget their existence. The university strives to create an incredibly tolerant and accepting environment and inspires an open mind to the incredibly diverse backgrounds that attend.

Although many students care about scores in their classes, it is not a cutthroat environment. Many approach their course load not with the mentality of learning just to earn grades, but learning for the love of learning. "It's a given that you help out other students in your class and work together," says a student.

There is high geographic diversity with 94 percent of students hailing from out of state and high ethnic diversity with 40 percent minority students.

You May Not Know

- Freshman counselors live with first-year students, making great efforts NOT to be disciplinary figures but instead to help freshmen make the best decisions during that transition period from high school to college. The next three years students find more freedom, with only the residential college's Dean living among them.

- Yale scientists ruffled some feathers when they changed how people think of dinosaurs. A Yale research team recently uncovered the vibrant colors of species extinct for more than 150 million years.

- Yale and some of the streets of downtown New Haven transformed during filming of the latest Indiana Jones, *The Kingdom of the Crystal Skull* (2008). It's not the fictional Marshall College that the motorcycle chase takes place in, but Yale!

Distinguished Alumni

George Akerlof, Nobel Laureate of economics; Anderson Cooper, journalist and television personality; Paul Giammatti, actor; Sarah Hughes, Olympic gold medalist figure skater; Charles Ives, composer; Edward Norton, actor; Cole Porter, composer; Garry Trudeau, creator and cartoonist of the Doonesbury comic strip.

Admissions and Financial Aid

One of the most frequently asked questions is what Yale is looking for in applicants. According to the university, "Yale is above all an academic institution, and thus academic strength is our first consideration in evaluating any candidate." What also come into heavy consideration are the teacher and counselor recommendations. Interviews are encouraged, if possible, but not required, and can only help, never hurt, an applicant. Admissions officers also look closely at the two personal essays submitted with the application in order to get a sense of who a candidate is as a person.

Students have the option to apply single-choice early action to Yale. Applicants are encouraged to use the online Common Application with the Yale Supplement. There are no merit scholarships offered by Yale. Luckily, with such a hefty price tag on a Yale degree, applying for financial aid does nothing to hurt one's chances of getting in. Yale and other Ivy League schools, most especially Harvard, entered a financial-aid arms race in the late 1900s, which led to huge incentives for students from families that wouldn't normally consider such expensive schools. Families earning $60,000 or less do not have to pay anything for their student's education, and a quick glance over other details of Yale's policy gives evidence that they are committed to bringing any student accepted into their ranks, not letting monetary issues stand in the way.

INDEX OF AMERICA'S BEST COLLEGES

Adelphi University, 45
Garden City, NY

Agnes Scott College, 48
Decatur, GA

Albion College, 51
Albion, MI

Alfred University, 54
Alfred, NY

Allegheny College, 57
Meadville, PA

Alma College, 60
Alma, MI

American University, 63
Washington, DC

Amherst College, 66
Amherst, MA

Arizona State University, 69
Tempe, AZ

Auburn University, 72
Auburn, AL

Austin College, 75
Sherman, TX

Babson College, 78
Babson Park, MA

Bard College, 81
Annandale on Hudson, NY

Barnard College, 84
New York, NY

Bates College, 87
Lewiston, ME

Baylor University, 90
Waco, TX

Beloit College, 93
Beloit, WI

Bennington College, 96
Bennington, VT

Bentley University, 99
Waltham, MA

Birmingham-Southern College, 102
Birmingham, AL

Boston College, 105
Chestnut Hill, MA

Boston University, 108
Boston, MA

Bowdoin College, 111
Brunswick, ME

Brandeis University, 114
Waltham, MA

Brigham Young University - Provo, 117
Provo, UT

Brown University, 120
Providence, RI

Bryn Mawr College, 124
Bryn Mawr, PA

Bucknell University, 127
Lewisburg, PA

California Institute of Technology, 130
Pasadena, CA

Calvin College, 134
Grand Rapids, MI

Carleton College, 137
Northfield, MN

Carnegie Mellon University, 140
Pittsburgh, PA

Case Western Reserve University, 143
Cleveland, OH

Catholic University of America, 146
Washington, DC

Centre College, 149
Danville, KY

Chapman University, 152
Orange, CA

Claremont McKenna College, 158
Claremont, CA

Clark University, 161
Worcester, MA

Clarkson University, 164
Potsdam, NY

Clemson University, 167
Clemson, SC

Colby College, 170
Waterville, ME

Colgate University, 173
Hamilton, NY

College of Charleston, 176
Charleston, SC

College of New Jersey, 179
Ewing, NJ

College of the Atlantic, 182
Bar Harbor, ME

College of the Holy Cross, 185
Worcester, MA

College of William and Mary, 188
Williamsburg, VA

College of Wooster, 191
Wooster, OH

Colorado College, 194
Colorado Springs, CO

Colorado School of Mines, 197
Golden, CO

Colorado State University, 200
Fort Collins, CO

Columbia University, 203
New York, NY

Connecticut College, 207
New London, CT

The Cooper Union for the Advancement of Science and Art, 210
New York, NY

Cornell College, 213
Mount Vernon, IA

Cornell University, 216
Ithaca, NY

Creighton University, 220
Omaha, NE

CUNY - Queens College, 155
Flushing, NY

Dartmouth College, 223
Hanover, NH

Davidson College, 227
  Davidson, NC

Deep Springs College, 230
  Dyer, NV

Denison University, 233
  Granville, OH

DePaul University, 236
  Chicago, IL

DePauw University, 239
  Greencastle, IN

Dickinson College, 242
  Carlisle, PA

Drew University, 245
  Madison, NJ

Drexel University, 248
  Philadelphia, PA

Duke University, 251
  Durham, NC

Earlham College, 255
  Richmond, IN

Eckerd College, 258
  St. Petersburg, FL

Elon University, 261
  Elon, NC

Emerson College, 264
  Boston, MA

Emory University, 267
  Atlanta, GA

Eugene Lang College The New
School for Liberal Arts, 270
  New York, NY

Evergreen State College, 273
  Olympia, WA

Fairfield University, 276
  Fairfield, CT

Florida Institute of Technology,
279
  Melbourne, FL

Florida Southern College, 282
  Lakeland, FL

Florida State University, 285
  Tallahassee, FL

Fordham University, 288
  New York, NY

Franklin & Marshall College, 291
  Lancaster, PA

Furman University, 294
  Greenville, SC

George Mason University, 297
  Fairfax, VA

George Washington University,
300
  Washington, DC

Georgetown University, 303
  Washington, DC

Georgia Institute of Technology,
307
  Atlanta, GA

Gettysburg College, 310
  Gettysburg, PA

Goucher College, 313
  Baltimore, MD

Grinnell College, 316
  Grinnell, IA

Guilford College, 319
  Greensboro, NC

Gustavus Adolphus College, 322
  St. Peter, MN

Hamilton College, 325
  Clinton, NY

Hampden-Sydney College, 328
  Hampden-Sydney, VA

Hampshire College, 331
  Amherst, MA

Harvard University, 334
  Cambridge, MA

Harvey Mudd College, 338
  Claremont, CA

Haverford College, 341
  Haverford, PA

Hendrix College, 344
  Conway, AR

Hiram College, 347
  Hiram, OH

Hobart and William Smith
Colleges, 350
  Geneva, NY

Hofstra University, 353
  Hempstead, NY

Hollins University, 356
  Roanoke, VA

Hope College, 359
  Holland, MI

Howard University, 362
  Washington, DC

Illinois Institute of Technology,
365
  Chicago, IL

Illinois Wesleyan University, 368
  Bloomington, IL

Indiana University Bloomington,
371
  Bloomington, IN

Iowa State University, 374
  Ames, IA

Ithaca College, 377
  Ithaca, NY

James Madison University, 380
  Harrisonburg, VA

Johns Hopkins University, 383
  Baltimore, MD

Juniata College, 387
  Huntingdon, PA

Kalamazoo College, 390
  Kalamazoo, MI

Kansas State University, 393
  Manhattan, KS

Kenyon College, 396
  Gambier, OH

Knox College, 399
  Galesburg, IL

Lafayette College, 402
  Easton, PA

Lake Forest College, 405
  Lake Forest, IL

Lawrence University, 408
  Appleton, WI

Lehigh University, 411
  Bethlehem, PA

Lewis & Clark College, 414
  Portland, OR

Louisiana State University -
Baton Rouge, 417
  Baton Rouge, LA

Loyola Marymount University,
420
  Los Angeles, CA

Loyola University Chicago, 423
  Chicago, IL

Loyola University New Orleans,
426
  New Orleans, LA

Macalester College, 429
  St. Paul, MN

Index

Manhattanville College, 432
Purchase, NY

Marlboro College, 435
Marlboro, VT

Marquette University, 438
Milwaukee, WI

Massachusetts Institute of
Technology, 441
Cambridge, MA

McGill University, 445
Montreal, CN

Miami University - Oxford, 448
Oxford, OH

Michigan State University, 451
East Lansing, MI

Middlebury College, 454
Middlebury, VT

Mills College, 457
Oakland, CA

Millsaps College, 460
Jackson, MS

Montana Tech of the University
of Montana, 463
Butte, MT

Morehouse College, 466
Atlanta, GA

Mount Holyoke College, 469
South Hadley, MA

Muhlenberg College, 472
Allentown, PA

New College of Florida, 475
Sarasota, FL

New Jersey Institute of
Technology, 478
Newark, NJ

New Mexico Institute of Mining
and Technology, 481
Socorro, NM

New York University, 484
New York, NY

North Carolina State University -
Raleigh, 487
Raleigh, NC

Northeastern University, 490
Boston, MA

Northwestern University, 493
Evanston, IL

Oberlin College, 496
Oberlin, OH

Occidental College, 499
Los Angeles, CA

Oglethorpe University, 502
Atlanta, GA

Ohio State University -
Columbus, 505
Columbus, OH

Ohio University, 508
Athens, OH

Ohio Wesleyan University, 511
Delaware, OH

Oregon State University, 514
Corvallis, OR

Pennsylvania State University -
University Park, 517
University Park, PA

Pepperdine University, 520
Malibu, CA

Pitzer College, 523
Claremont, CA

Pomona College, 526
Claremont, CA

Princeton University, 529
Princeton, NJ

Purdue University - West
Lafayette, 533
West Lafayette, IN

Quinnipiac University, 536
Hamden, CT

Randolph College, 539
Lynchburg, VA

Reed College, 542
Portland, OR

Rensselaer Polytechnic Institute,
545
Troy, NY

Rhode Island School of Design,
548
Providence, RI

Rhodes College, 551
Memphis, TN

Rice University, 554
Houston, TX

Ripon College, 557
Ripon, WI

Rochester Institute of
Technology, 560
Rochester, NY

Rollins College, 563
Winter Park, FL

Rose-Hulman Institute of
Technology, 566
Terre Haute, IN

Rutgers, the State University of
New Jersey - New Brunswick,
569
Piscataway, NJ

Santa Clara University, 572
Santa Clara, CA

Sarah Lawrence College, 575
Bronxville, NY

Scripps College, 578
Claremont, CA

Seattle University, 581
Seattle, WA

Sewanee: University of the South,
584
Sewanee, TN

Skidmore College, 587
Saratoga Springs, NY

Smith College, 590
Northampton, MA

Southern Methodist University,
593
Dallas, TX

Spelman College, 596
Atlanta, GA

St. John's College, 599
Annapolis, MD

St. John's College, 599
Santa Fe, NM

St. Lawrence University, 602
Canton, NY

St. Olaf College, 605
Northfield, MN

Stanford University, 608
Stanford, CA

Stevens Institute of Technology,
630
Hoboken, NJ

SUNY - Binghamton University,
612
Binghamton, NY

SUNY - Purchase College, 618
Purchase, NY

SUNY - Stony Brook University, 621
Stony Brook, NY

SUNY - University at Albany, 624
Albany, NY

SUNY - University at Buffalo, 627
Buffalo, NY

SUNY College of Arts and Sciences - Geneseo, 615
Geneseo, NY

Susquehanna University, 633
Selinsgrove, PA

Swarthmore College, 636
Swarthmore, PA

Sweet Briar College, 639
Sweet Briar, VA

Syracuse University, 642
Syracuse, NY

Texas A&M University - College Station, 645
College Station, TX

Texas Christian University, 648
Fort Worth, TX

Texas Tech University, 651
Lubbock, TX

Trinity College, 654
Hartford, CT

Trinity University, 657
San Antonio, TX

Truman State University, 660
Kirksville, MO

Tufts University, 663
Medford, MA

Tulane University, 666
New Orleans, LA

Union College, 669
Schenectady, NY

United States Air Force Academy, 672
USAF Academy, CO

United States Coast Guard Academy, 675
New London, CT

United States Military Academy, 678
West Point, NY

United States Naval Academy, 681
Annapolis, MD

University of Alabama, 684
Tuscaloosa, AL

University of Arizona, 687
Tucson, AZ

University of Arkansas, 690
Fayetteville, AR

University of California - Berkeley, 693
Berkeley, CA

University of California - Davis, 696
Davis, CA

University of California - Irvine, 699
Irvine, CA

University of California - Los Angeles, 702
Los Angeles, CA

University of California - Riverside, 705
Riverside, CA

University of California - San Diego, 708
La Jolla, CA

University of California - Santa Barbara, 711
Santa Barbara, CA

University of California - Santa Cruz, 714
Santa Cruz, CA

University of Chicago, 717
Chicago, IL

University of Cincinnati, 721
Cincinnati, OH

University of Colorado - Boulder, 724
Boulder, CO

University of Connecticut, 727
Storrs, CT

University of Dallas, 730
Irving, TX

University of Dayton, 733
Dayton, OH

University of Delaware, 736
Newark, DE

University of Denver, 739
Denver, CO

University of Florida, 742
Gainesville, FL

University of Georgia, 745
Athens, GA

University of Hawaii - Manoa, 748
Honolulu, HI

University of Idaho, 751
Moscow, ID

University of Illinois at Urbana-Champaign, 754
Champaign, IL

University of Iowa, 757
Iowa City, IA

University of Kansas, 760
Lawrence, KS

University of Kentucky, 763
Lexington, KY

University of Maine, 766
Orono, ME

University of Mary Washington, 769
Fredericksburg, VA

University of Maryland - Baltimore County, 772
Baltimore, MD

University of Maryland - College Park, 775
College Park, MD

University of Massachusetts - Amherst, 778
Amherst, MA

University of Miami, 781
Coral Gables, FL

University of Michigan - Ann Arbor, 784
Ann Arbor, MI

University of Minnesota - Twin Cities, 787
Minneapolis, MN

University of Mississippi, 790
University, MS

University of Missouri-Columbia, 793
Columbia, MO

University of Montana, 796
Missoula, MT

University of Nebraska - Lincoln, 799
Lincoln, NE

University of New Hampshire, 802
Durham, NH

University of New Mexico, 805
Albuquerque, NM

University of North Carolina - Asheville, 808
Asheville, NC

University of North Carolina - Chapel Hill, 811
Chapel Hill, NC

University of North Carolina - Greensboro, 814
Greensboro, NC

University of Notre Dame, 817
Notre Dame, IN

University of Oklahoma, 820
Norman, OK

University of Oregon, 823
Eugene, OR

University of Pennsylvania, 829
Philadelphia, PA

University of Pittsburgh, 832
Pittsburgh, PA

University of Puget Sound, 835
Tacoma, WA

University of Redlands, 838
Redlands, CA

University of Rhode Island, 841
Kingston, RI

University of Richmond, 844
Richmond, VA

University of Rochester, 847
Rochester, NY

University of San Diego, 850
San Diego, CA

University of San Francisco, 853
San Francisco, CA

University of South Carolina - Columbia, 856
Columbia, SC

University of Southern California, 859
Los Angeles, CA

University of Tennessee - Knoxville, 862
Knoxville, TN

University of Texas - Austin, 865
Austin, TX

University of the Pacific, 826
Stockton, CA

University of Toronto, 868
Toronto, Ontario, CN

University of Tulsa, 871
Tulsa, OK

University of Utah, 874
Salt Lake City, UT

University of Vermont, 877
Burlington, VT

University of Virginia, 880
Charlottesville, VA

University of Washington, 883
Seattle, WA

University of Wisconsin - Madison, 886
Madison, WI

University of Wyoming, 889
Laramie, WY

Ursinus College, 892
Collegeville, PA

Vanderbilt University, 895
Nashville, TN

Vassar College, 898
Poughkeepsie, NY

Villanova University, 901
Villanova, PA

Virginia Tech, 904
Blacksburg, VA

Wabash College, 907
Crawfordsville, IN

Wake Forest University, 910
Winston Salem, NC

Warren Wilson College, 913
Asheville, NC

Washington & Jefferson College, 916
Washington, PA

Washington and Lee University, 919
Lexington, VA

Washington State University, 922
Pullman, WA

Washington University in St. Louis, 925
St. Louis, MO

Wellesley College, 928
Wellesley, MA

Wells College, 931
Aurora, NY

Wesleyan University, 934
Middletown, CT

West Virginia University, 937
Morgantown, WV

Wheaton College, 940
Wheaton, IL

Wheaton College, 943
Norton, MA

Whitman College, 946
Walla Walla, WA

Whittier College, 949
Whittier, CA

Willamette University, 952
Salem, OR

Williams College, 955
Williamstown, MA

Wittenberg University, 958
Springfield, OH

Wofford College, 961
Spartanburg, SC

Worcester Polytechnic Institute, 964
Worcester, MA

Xavier University of Louisiana, 967
New Orleans, LA

Yale University, 970
New Haven, CT

INDEX OF COLLEGES BY LOCATION

ALABAMA
Auburn University
Birmingham-Southern College
University of Alabama

ARIZONA
Arizona State University
University of Arizona

ARKANSAS
Hendrix College
University of Arkansas

CALIFORNIA
California Institute of Technology
Chapman University
Claremont McKenna College
Harvey Mudd College
Loyola Marymount University
Mills College
Occidental College
Pepperdine University
Pitzer College
Pomona College
Santa Clara University
Scripps College
Stanford University
University of California - Berkeley
University of California - Davis
University of California - Irvine
University of California - Los Angeles
University of California - Riverside
University of California - San Diego
University of California - Santa Barbara
University of California - Santa Cruz
University of Redlands
University of San Diego
University of San Francisco
University of Southern California
University of the Pacific
Whittier College

COLORADO
Colorado College
Colorado School of Mines
Colorado State University
United States Air Force Academy

University of Colorado - Boulder
University of Denver

CONNECTICUT
Connecticut College
Fairfield University
Quinnipiac University
Trinity College
United States Coast Guard Academy
University of Connecticut
Wesleyan University
Yale University

DELAWARE
University of Delaware

DISTRICT OF COLUMBIA
American University
Catholic University of America
George Washington University
Georgetown University
Howard University

FLORIDA
Eckerd College
Florida Institute of Technology
Florida Southern College
Florida State University
New College of Florida
Rollins College
University of Florida
University of Miami

GEORGIA
Agnes Scott College
Emory University
Georgia Institute of Technology
Morehouse College
Oglethorpe University
Spelman College
University of Georgia

HAWAII
University of Hawaii - Manoa

IDAHO
University of Idaho

ILLINOIS
DePaul University
Illinois Institute of Technology
Illinois Wesleyan University
Knox College

Lake Forest College
Loyola University Chicago
Northwestern University
University of Chicago
University of Illinois at Urbana-Champaign
Wheaton College

INDIANA
DePauw University
Earlham College
Indiana University Bloomington
Purdue University - West Lafayette
Rose-Hulman Institute of Technology
University of Notre Dame
Wabash College

IOWA
Cornell College
Grinnell College
Iowa State University
University of Iowa

KANSAS
Kansas State University
University of Kansas

KENTUCKY
Centre College
University of Kentucky

LOUISIANA
Louisiana State University - Baton Rouge
Loyola University New Orleans
Tulane University
Xavier University of Louisiana

MAINE
Bates College
Bowdoin College
Colby College
College of the Atlantic
University of Maine

MARYLAND
Goucher College
Johns Hopkins University

St. John's College
United States Naval Academy
University of Maryland -
  Baltimore County
University of Maryland - College
  Park

MASSACHUSETTS
Amherst College
Babson College
Bentley University
Boston College
Boston University
Brandeis University
Clark University
College of the Holy Cross
Emerson College
Hampshire College
Harvard University
Massachusetts Institute of
  Technology
Mount Holyoke College
Northeastern University
Smith College
Tufts University
University of Massachusetts -
  Amherst
Wellesley College
Wheaton College
Williams College
Worcester Polytechnic Institute

MICHIGAN
Albion College
Alma College
Calvin College
Hope College
Kalamazoo College
Michigan State University
University of Michigan - Ann
  Arbor

MINNESOTA
Carleton College
Gustavus Adolphus College
Macalester College
St. Olaf College
University of Minnesota - Twin
  Cities

MISSISSIPPI
Millsaps College
University of Mississippi

MISSOURI
Truman State University
University of Missouri-Columbia
Washington University in St.
  Louis

MONTANA
Montana Tech of the University
  of Montana
University of Montana

NEBRASKA
Creighton University
University of Nebraska - Lincoln

NEVADA
Deep Springs College

NEW HAMPSHIRE
Dartmouth College
University of New Hampshire

NEW JERSEY
College of New Jersey
Drew University
New Jersey Institute of
  Technology
Princeton University
Rutgers, the State University of
  New Jersey - New Brunswick
Stevens Institute of Technology

NEW MEXICO
New Mexico Institute of Mining
  and Technology
St. John's College
University of New Mexico

NEW YORK
Adelphi University
Alfred University
Bard College
Barnard College
Clarkson University
Colgate University
Columbia University
The Cooper Union for the
  Advancement of Science and
  Art
Cornell University
CUNY - Queens College
Eugene Lang College The New
  School for Liberal Arts
Fordham University
Hamilton College

Hobart and William Smith
  Colleges
Hofstra University
Ithaca College
Manhattanville College
New York University
Rensselaer Polytechnic Institute
Rochester Institute of Technology
Sarah Lawrence College
Skidmore College
St. Lawrence University
SUNY - Binghamton University
SUNY - Purchase College
SUNY - Stony Brook University
SUNY - University at Albany
SUNY - University at Buffalo
SUNY College of Arts and
  Sciences - Geneseo
Syracuse University
Union College
United States Military Academy
University of Rochester
Vassar College
Wells College

NORTH CAROLINA
Davidson College
Duke University
Elon University
Guilford College
North Carolina State University
  - Raleigh
University of North Carolina -
  Asheville
University of North Carolina -
  Chapel Hill
University of North Carolina -
  Greensboro
Wake Forest University
Warren Wilson College

OHIO
Case Western Reserve University
College of Wooster
Denison University
Hiram College
Kenyon College
Miami University - Oxford
Oberlin College
Ohio State University - Columbus
Ohio University
Ohio Wesleyan University
University of Cincinnati
University of Dayton
Wittenberg University

The Ultimate Guide to
America's Best Colleges

OKLAHOMA
University of Oklahoma
University of Tulsa

OREGON
Lewis & Clark College
Oregon State University
Reed College
University of Oregon
Willamette University

PENNSYLVANIA
Allegheny College
Bryn Mawr College
Bucknell University
Carnegie Mellon University
Dickinson College
Drexel University
Franklin & Marshall College
Gettysburg College
Haverford College
Juniata College
Lafayette College
Lehigh University
Muhlenberg College
Pennsylvania State University - University Park
Susquehanna University
Swarthmore College
University of Pennsylvania
University of Pittsburgh
Ursinus College
Villanova University
Washington & Jefferson College

RHODE ISLAND
Brown University
Rhode Island School of Design
University of Rhode Island

SOUTH CAROLINA
Clemson University
College of Charleston
Furman University
University of South Carolina - Columbia
Wofford College

TENNESSEE
Rhodes College
Sewanee: University of the South
University of Tennessee - Knoxville
Vanderbilt University

TEXAS
Austin College
Baylor University

Rice University
Southern Methodist University
Texas A&M University - College Station
Texas Christian University
Texas Tech University
Trinity University
University of Dallas
University of Texas - Austin

UTAH
Brigham Young University - Provo
University of Utah

VERMONT
Bennington College
Marlboro College
Middlebury College
University of Vermont

VIRGINIA
College of William and Mary
George Mason University
Hampden-Sydney College
Hollins University
James Madison University
Randolph College
Sweet Briar College
University of Mary Washington
University of Richmond
University of Virginia
Virginia Tech
Washington and Lee University

WASHINGTON
Evergreen State College
Seattle University
University of Puget Sound
University of Washington
Washington State University
Whitman College

WEST VIRGINIA
West Virginia University

WISCONSIN
Beloit College
Lawrence University
Marquette University
Ripon College
University of Wisconsin - Madison

WYOMING
University of Wyoming

CANADA
McGill University
University of Toronto

APPENDIX A:
COLLEGE SEARCH WORKSHEET

Make a copy of this worksheet for each college you are considering.

Name of college: _____

Location: _____

Number of undergraduates: _____

Email: _____

Phone: _____

Academics

Faculty/student ratio: _____

Department(s) that I'm most interested in: _____

Requirements (senior project/thesis, required courses, etc.): _____

Classes that I'd like to take: _____
_____
_____

Research or other special academic program opportunities: _____
_____
_____

Study abroad opportunities: _____
_____
_____

Student Life

Clubs or organizations I'd like to join: _____
_____
_____

Role of Greek organizations on campus: _____

Role of athletics on campus: _____

Intercollegiate or intramural athletic prospects: _____

Prevalence of drinking/parties: _____

Fun things to do off campus: _____
_____
_____

Notable things about the dorms, whether students usually live on or off campus,
availability and cost of off-campus housing: _____
_____

Notable things about the quality of the food and meal plans offered: _____
_____

Notable things about campus such as the student center or on-campus pub:
_____

Admissions

For accepted freshmen:_____

SAT Critical Reading range: _____ ❏ Required ❏ Recommended

SAT Math range: _____ ❏ Required ❏ Recommended

SAT Writing range: _____ ❏ Required ❏ Recommended

ACT Composite range: _____ ❏ Required ❏ Recommended

ACT Writing test: _____ ❏ Required ❏ Recommended

SAT Subject tests: _____ ❏ Required ❏ Recommended

Average GPA: _____

Percentage accepted early: _____

Percentage accepted regular decision: _____

❏ Reach college ❏ Good chance of being admitted to
❏ Very likely to be admitted

If early admission is offered, description of: _____

Early admission deadline: _____

Regular admission deadline: _____

Requirements:
❏ Common Application accepted
❏ Supplementary forms required
❏ Online application form accepted
❏ Number of long essays: _____
❏ Number of short essays: _____
❏ Counselor evaluation
❏ Number of teacher evaluations: _____
❏ Interview recommended
❏ Interview required

Financial Aid

Email: _____

Phone: _____

Annual tuition: _____

Room and board: _____

Fees: _____

Average financial aid package: _____
❏ Need-blind admission
❏ Meets all demonstrated financial need
❏ Merit-based aid

Priority financial aid deadline: _____

Regular financial aid deadline: _____

Forms required:
❏ FAFSA
❏ CSS/PROFILE
❏ College's own form

Average student loan debt for graduates: _____

Summary

Notes from campus visits/talking with people from the college: _____
_____

What I like the most about the college: _____
_____

What I like the least about the college: _____
_____

COST OF ATTENDANCE

College					
Tuition and fees					
Room and board/rent and food					
Books and other supplies					
Personal items					
Medical insurance					
Travel					
Total cost of attendance					

FINANCIAL AID WORKSHEET

College					
Financial aid phone number					
Financial aid email					
Total Cost of Attendance (See above)					
Financial Aid Offered					
Scholarships/grants					
Loans					
Work-study					
Total					
Expected Family Contribution (EFC)					
Student contribution					
Parent contribution					
Total					
Unmet Need					

The Ultimate Guide to America's Best Colleges

Cost of Attendance – Financial Aid Offered – Expected Family Contribution = Unmet Need

ABOUT T

Harvard graduat[...] [...]be are the founders of Su[...] [...]ncluding: *The Ultimate Schola*[...] [...]*ul College Admission Essays, Get Free Cash for College, 1001 Ways to Pay for College,* and *How to Write a Winning Scholarship Essay.*

Together, Gen and Kelly were accepted to every school to which they applied, including all the Ivy League colleges and won over $100,000 in merit-based scholarships. They were able to graduate from Harvard debt-free.

Gen and Kelly give workshops across the country and write the nationally syndicated "Ask the SuperCollege Experts" column. They have made hundreds of appearances on television and radio and have served as expert sources for *USA Today*, the *New York Times, U.S. News & World Report, New York Daily News, San Jose Mercury News, Chronicle of Higher Education*, CNN, and *Seventeen.*

Gen grew up in Waialua, Hawaii. A graduate of Waialua High School, he was the first student from his school to be accepted at Harvard, where he graduated magna cum laude with a degree in both History and East Asian Studies.

Kelly attended Whitney High School, a nationally ranked public high school in her hometown of Cerritos, California. She graduated magna cum laude from Harvard with a degree in Sociology.

The Tanabes' approach to college admission is from a practical, hands-on point of view. Drawing on the collective knowledge and experiences of students, they provide real strategies students can use to find, select, get into, and pay for the college of their dreams.

Gen and Kelly live in Belmont, California with their sons Zane and Kane and dog Sushi.